A PICTORIAL HISTORY OF PSYCHOLOGY

A PICTORIAL HISTORY OF PSYCHOLOGY

EDITED BY

WOLFGANG G. BRINGMANN, PH.D.
Professor of Psychology
University of South Alabama
Mobile, Alabama

HELMUT E. LÜCK, DR. PHIL.
Professor of Psychology
Psychological Institute
FernUniversität
Hagen, Germany

RUDOLF MILLER, DR. PHIL. HABIL.
Lecturer
Psychological Institute
FernUniversität
Hagen, Germany

CHARLES E. EARLY, PH.D.
Professor of Psychology
Roanoke College
Salem, Virginia

Quintessence Publishing Co, Inc
Chicago, Berlin, London, Tokyo, São Paulo,
Moscow, Prague, and Warsaw

Expanded from *Illustrierte Geschichte der Psychologie*, published in
German in 1993 by Quintessenz Verlags-GmbH, Munich, Germany.

Library of Congress Cataloging-in-Publication Data

A pictorial history of psychology / edited by Wolfgang G. Bringmann
 . . . [et al.].
 p.   cm.
 Includes translated chapters from: Illustrierte Geschichte der Psychologie,
edited by Helmut E. Lück and Rudolf Miller, published in 1993.
 Includes bibliographical references and index.
 Hardcover: ISBN 0-86715-292-3
 Softcover: ISBN 0-86715-330-X
 1. Psychology—History—Pictorial works. I. Bringmann, Wolfgang G.
II. Lück, Helmut E. Illustrierte Geschichte der Psychologie.
English. Selections.
BF81.P47 1997
150′.9′022—dc20   96-24728
                                                     CIP

quintessence
books

©1997 by Quintessence Publishing Co, Inc

Quintessence Publishing Co, Inc
551 N. Kimberly Drive
Carol Stream, IL 60188-1881

Printed in Canada

Contents

Contributors

Johannes Abresch, Dr. phil., Wuppertal, Germany

Catalina M. Arata, Ph.D., Assistant Professor,
Department of Psychology, University of South Alabama,
Mobile, Alabama

Rudolf Arnheim, Dr. phil., Harvard University Professor Emeritus of
Psychology, Ann Arbor, Michigan

William D. G. Balance, Ph.D., Professor of Psychology,
University of Windsor, Windsor, Ontario

Paul Ballantyne, M.A., Department of Psychology, York University,
Downsview, Ontario

Philip M. Bartle, B.Sc., Mobile, Alabama

Eberhard Bauer, D.P., Institut für Grenzgebiete der Psychologie und
Psychohygiene, Freiburg, Germany

Elisabeth Baumgartner, Dr. phil., Lecturer, Psychological Institute IV,
Universität Würzburg, Würzburg, Germany

Wilhelm Baumgartner, Dr. phil., Professor of Philosophy, Universität
Würzburg, Würzburg, Germany

Günther Bäumler, Dr. rer. nat., Professor of Psychology, Technische
Hochschule München, Munich, Germany

Peter J. Behrens, Ph.D., Assistant Professor of Psychology,
Pennsylvania State University–Allentown, Fogelsville, Pennsylvania

Ludy T. Benjamin, Jr., Ph.D., Professor of Psychology,
Texas A&M University, College Station, Texas

Arthur L. Blumenthal, Ph.D., Harvard Extension School,
Cambridge, Massachusetts

Horst-Peter Brauns, Dr. phil., Institute for General Psychology,
Freie Universität Berlin, Berlin, Germany

Michael W. Bringmann, Ph.D., Mobile, Alabama

Norma J. Bringmann, B.A., Mobile, Alabama

Wolfgang G. Bringmann, Ph.D., Professor of Psychology, University
of South Alabama, Mobile, Alabama

Josef Brožek, Ph.D., Professor Emeritus, Lehigh University,
Bethlehem, Pennsylvania

Klaus Jürgen Bruder, Dr. phil., Professor of Psychology,
Freie Universität Berlin, Berlin, Germany

Almuth Bruder-Bezzel, Dr. phil., Psychoanalyst, Berlin, Germany

William H. M. Bryant, M.A., Department of Psychology,
Texas A&M University, College Station, Texas

Brian R. Burke, M.D., Psychiatrist, Windsor, Ontario

Ronda J. Carpenter, Ph.D., Professor of Psychology, Roanoke
College, Salem, Virginia

Helio Carpintero, Ph.D., Professor of Psychology,
Universidad Complutense, Madrid, Spain

Charles W. Clark, Ph.D., Associate Professor of History, St. Andrews
Presbyterian College, Laurinburg, North Carolina

Steven R. Coleman, Ph.D., Professor of Psychology, Cleveland State
University, Cleveland, Ohio

Jacqueline L. Cunningham, Ph.D., Children's National Medical Center, Washington, DC

Annette Daigger, Dr. phil., Robert Musil Research Center, Universität
des Saarlandes, Saarbrücken, Germany

Kurt Danziger, Dr. phil., Professor Emeritus, Don Mills, Ontario

Nino Dazzi, Ph.D., Dean, Faculty of Psychology, Universita Degli Studi
di Roma, Rome, Italy

Douwe Draaisma, Ph.D., Universiteit Groningen, Groningen,
Netherlands

Peter van Drunen, Universiteit Groningen, Groningen, Netherlands

Charles E. Early, Ph.D., Professor of Psychology, Roanoke College,
Salem, Virginia

Wilfried Echterhoff, Dr. rer. nat., Professor of Psychology,
Bergische Universität, Wuppertal, Germany

Reinhard Fabian, Dr. phil., Research Center for Austrian Philosophy,
Graz, Austria

Raymond E. Fancher, Ph.D., Professor of Psychology, York
University, North York, Ontario

Ernst Federn, Psychoanalyst, Vienna, Austria

L. Dodge Fernald, Ph.D., Senior Lecturer of Psychology,
Harvard University, Cambridge, Massachussetts

Herbert Fitzek, Dr. phil., Psychologisches Institut,
Universität Köln, Cologne, Germany

Joseph F. Fitzpatrick Ph.D., Professor of Biology, University of South
Alabama, Mobile, Alabama

Rainer Funk, Dr. phil., Psychoanalyst, Tübingen, Germany

Ulfried Geuter, Dr. phil. habil., Journalist, Berlin, Germany

Angela Graf-Nold, Dr. phil., Zürich, Switzerland

Horst U. K. Gundlach, Dr. phil. habil., Institute for the History of
Modern Psychology, Universität Passau, Passau, Germany

Hartmut Häcker, Dr. phil., Professor of Psychology, Bergische
Universität, Wuppertal, Germany

Bridget O. Hannahan, Ph.D., Clinical Psychologist, Mobile, Alabama

Horst Heidbrink, Dr. phil., Psychological Institute, FernUniversität,
Hagen, Germany

Pegge Hewett, B.Sc., Mobile, Alabama

Robert R. Hoffman, Ph.D., Associate Professor of Psychology,
Adelphi University, Long Island, New York

Jiři Hoskovec, Dr. phil., Professor of Psychology,
Charles University, Prague, Czech Republic

Nancy K. Innis, Ph.D., Associate Professor of Psychology,
University of Western Ontario, London, Ontario

Maria F. Ippolito, M.A., Department of Psychology, Bowling Green State University, Bowling Green, Ohio

Thomas T. Jackson, Ph.D., Professor of Psychology, Fort Hays State University, Hays, Kansas

Siegfried Jaeger, Dr. phil., Psychological Institute, Freie Universität Berlin, Berlin, Germany

Jürgen Jahnke, Dr. phil., Professor of Psychology, Pädagogische Hochschule Freiburg, Freiburg, Germany

Gustav Jahoda, Ph.D., Professor of Psychology, University of Strathclyde, Glasgow, Scotland

Gerhard Kaminski, Dr. phil., Professor Emeritus of Psychology, Universität Tübingen, Tübingen, Germany

Simon Kemp, Ph.D., Senior Lecturer of Psychology, University of Canterbury, Christchurch, New Zealand

György Kiss, Dr. phil. habil., Professor of Psychology, Budapest Müszaki Egyetem, Pszichologiai Intezet, Budapest, Hungary

Michael J. Kral, Ph.D., Associate Professor of Psychology, University of Windsor, Windsor, Ontario

Elke M. Kurz, M.A., Department of Psychology, Bowling Green State University, Bowling Green, Ohio

Enrique Lafuente, Ph.D., Assistant Professor of Psychology, Universidad Nacional de Educación a Distancia, Madrid, Spain

Hans Jürgen Lander, Dr. rer. nat. habil., Professor Emeritus of Psychology, Universität Leipzig, Leipzig, Germany

Antoon A. Leenaars, Ph.D., Clinical Psychologist, Windsor, Ontario

Ramón León, Ph.D., Professor of Psychology, Lima, Peru

Michael Ley, D.P., Faculty of Education, Friedrich-Wilhelms-Universität Bonn, Bonn, Germany

Elena Liotta, Ph.D., Orvieto, Italy

Helmut E. Lück, Dr. phil., Professor of Psychology, Psychological Institute, FernUniversität, Hagen, Germany

Wolfgang G. Mack, Dr. phil., Professor of Psychology, Psychological Institute, Universität Potsdam, Potsdam, Germany

Marion White McPherson, Ph.D., Associate Director, Archives of the History of American Psychology, Professor of Psychology (retired), University of Akron, Akron, Ohio

Paul McReynolds, Ph.D., Professor Emeritus of Psychology, University of Nevada, Reno, Nevada

Karen L. Marrero, M.A., Archival Assistant, University of Windsor, Windsor, Ontario

Luciano Mecacci , Ph.D., Professor of Psychology, Universita Degli Studi di Firenze, Florence, Italy

Wolfram Meischner, Dr. phil. habil., Professor Emeritus of Psychology, Universität Leipzig, Leipzig, Germany

Anneros Meischner-Metge, Dr. phil., Chief Lecturer, Psychological Institute, Universität Leipzig, Leipzig, Germany

Rudolf Miller, Dr. phil. habil., Lecturer, Psychological Institute, FernUniversität, Hagen, Germany

Henry L. Minton, Ph.D., Professor of Psychology, University of Windsor, Windsor, Ontario

Wesley G. Morgan, Ph.D., Associate Professor of Psychology, University of Tennessee–Knoxville, Knoxville, Tennessee

Robert A. Neimeyer, Ph.D., Professor of Psychology, University of Memphis, Memphis, Tennessee.

Régine Plas, Ph.D., Lecturer, Université René Descartes, Paris, France

John A. Popplestone, Ph.D., Director, Archives of the History of American Psychology, Professor of Psychology, University of Akron, Akron, Ohio

Paul Probst, Dr. phil., Professor of Psychology, Universität Hamburg, Hamburg, Germany

Daniel N. Robinson, Ph.D., Professor of Psychology, Georgetown University, Washington, DC

David K. Robinson, Ph.D., Associate Professor of European History, Northeast Missouri State University, Kirksville, Missouri

Giuseppe Roccatagliata, M.D., Associate Professor of Psychiatry, Clinica Neurologica Università, Genoa, Italy

Brigitte A. Rollett, Dr. phil., Professor of Developmental Psychology, Psychological Institute, Universität Wien, Vienna, Austria

Saul Rosenzweig, Ph.D., Professor, Departments of Psychology and Psychiatry, Washington University, St. Louis, Missouri

Viktor Sarris, Dr. phil., Professor of Psychology, Psychological Institute, Johann-Wolfgang-von-Goethe-Universität, Frankfurt, Germany

Rüdiger Schiferer, Senior Librarian, Österreichischen Nationalbibliothek, Vienna, Austria

Heinz-Dieter Schmalt, Dr. phil. habil., Professor of Psychology, Bergische Universität, Wuppertal, Germany

Wilfred Schmidt, Ph.D., Professor Emeritus of Psychology, University of Alberta, Edmonton, Alberta

Christina Schröder, Dr. phil. habil., Leipzig, Germany

Alvin H. Smith, Ph.D., Professor of Psychology, St. Andrews Presbyterian College, Laurinburg, North Carolina

Siegfried Ludwig Sporer, Ph.D., Professor of Psychology, University of Aberdeen, Old Aberdeen, Scotland

Helga Sprung, Dr. rer. nat., Institute for General Psychology, Freie Universität Berlin, Berlin, Germany

Lothar Sprung, Dr. rer. nat. habil., Professor Emeritus of Psychology, Humboldt Universität Berlin, Berlin, Germany

Pieter J. van Strien, Dr. phil., Professor Emeritus of Psychology, Rijksuniversiteit Groningen, Groningen, Netherlands

Hannes Stubbe, Dr. phil. habil., Professor of Psychology, Mannheim, Germany

Marianne L. Teuber, M.A., Art Historian, Independent Scholar, Arlington, Massachussetts

B. Michael Thorne, Ph.D., Professor of Psychology, Mississippi State University, Mississippi State, Mississippi

Ryan D. Tweney, Ph.D., Professor of Psychology, Bowling Green State University, Bowling Green, Ohio

Gustav A. Ungerer, Editor, Chemical-Technical Library, Heidelberg, Germany

René van der Veer, Ph.D., Assistant Professor, Department of Education, Universiteit Leiden, Leiden, Netherlands

Ursula Voss, Ph.D., Psychological Institute, Johann-Wolfgang-von-Goethe Universität, Frankfurt, Germany

Inge Weber, Dr. rer. nat., Psychologist and Psychoanalyst, Göttingen, Germany

Ursula Welsch, Munich, Germany

Gerd Wiendieck, Dr. rer. pol., Professor of Psychology, Psychological Institute, FernUniversität, Hagen, Germany

Herbert Will, Dr. med., Psychoanalyst, Munich, Germany

Robert H. Wozniak, Ph.D., Professor of Psychology, Bryn Mawr College, Bryn Mawr, Pennsylvania

Vladimir P. Zinchenko, Ph.D, Russian Academy of Education, Moscow, Russia

Foreword

When a new book appears, one warily approaches the promising stranger in a tentative way. To become acquainted with it, one often first looks at the illustrations because pictures are more readily understood than words. Of course, psychology, being a science, deals with concepts, and concepts are abstract. Nevertheless, concepts rely on tangible things that can be handled, listened to, or seen. Visual things especially give life to concepts. Just now, I happen to remember something that takes me back to the distant past when I was a student at the University of Berlin in Germany. Although not exactly conceptual, it is a thoroughly visual memory. At the Psychological Institute, there was a room for the sound archive of the ethnologist Erich Maria von Hornboestel, a specialist of folk music, especially African music. These songs had been recorded on wax cylinders. Kept in velvet-lined boxes, they could be played by means of one of those machines with a tin trumpet we remember from His Master's Voice. Thus, our student days, even as they were devoted to theory, were nevertheless filled with memorable images.

Recalling the thoughts and images of my early days in psychology also triggers memories of the apparatus we had to build to support our experiments and of the many schematic shapes we had drawn on paper to test our subjects. Many examples of such equipment are reproduced in this book. There are also the intimidating portraits of our bearded forebears, to whom we owe the early discoveries of psychology—people like Wilhelm Wundt, William James, and Sigmund Freud.

All of these illustrations confirm what the philosopher Immanuel Kant insisted on, namely that concepts without images are empty. He also said, however, that images without concepts are blind.

Psychology is therefore based on a framework of fundamental principles that guide us beyond the changing periods of time in our learning, teaching, and exploring.

Psychology as a science is little more than a century old, but even in antiquity thinkers like Aristotle and Plato contributed to the sharpening of those basic principles. Closer to our own century, David Hume, René Descartes, Baruch Spinoza, and Friedrich Nietzsche have bequeathed to us observations and ideas of such import that even today no intelligent psychologist could shape his or her basic theories without them.

I myself have been served by psychology for about 70 years, and some of the events and facts described in this book as history live in my mind as a part of my own experience. I remember, for example, how the director of our Institute, the Gestalt psychologist Wolfgang Köhler, recruited me, then a young student, to act as the representative of the student body to address the patriarch psychologist Carl Stumpf at a torchlight parade in his honor. I have forgotten what I said on that occasion, as we gathered in front of the apartment building where Stumpf lived on the third floor; but even though the details of many such experiences have faded with time, I am still guided by the basic insights and principles I received from my teachers during those years. In this book, one finds that those very insights and many other time-honored principles from the past are revived and transmitted to a new generation.

Rudolf Arnheim
Professor Emeritus of the Psychology of Art
Harvard University

Preface

If it is true that human memory is the essence of an individual's sense of personal identity, then it surely follows that history, which is a kind of collective memory, is vital to the sense of integrity that holds together a scientific discipline like psychology. Just as we better know and understand other people when we know the influences at work in their past, so can we only really understand an intellectual enterprise like psychology by learning about the historical currents and personalities that have shaped it. By seeing the forces at work that have created the field, we immediately gain a powerful vantage point for understanding the disparate threads that have been woven together to form modern scientific psychology.

Psychology, of course, conjures up a variety of images in the public eye—but it's probably safe to assume that the most common of these images are those associated with therapy or the control of behavior. Unfortunately, this perception, while important, nevertheless severely limits the true scope of the discipline. In this book, we attempt to enlarge the reader's understanding of psychology by opening up its past in such a way as to make it ever more accessible to both the psychologist and non-psychologist alike. We have done so in two ways: first by drawing together between these covers over 100 articles that were authored or co-authored by approximately the same number of experts, and secondly, by strongly emphasizing the use of illustrations. Many of the pictures in this book are presented here for the first time, and it is likely that never before have so many pictures on so many subjects from psychology's past been assembled in one book.

The preparation and publication of *A Pictorial History of Psychology* was inspired by an earlier German version titled *Illustrierte Geschichte der Psychologie* (The Illustrated History of Psychology) edited by Helmut E. Lück and Rudolf Miller of Fern Universität at Hagen, Germany. This work, which was first published in the fall of 1993, received excellent reviews and has sold so well that a second edition is being contemplated. Even before its publication, plans were discussed for the development of an expanded special edition of the volume for English-speaking readers. That expanded version is the present book, *A Pictorial History of Psychology*, edited by Wolfgang G. Bringmann, Helmut E. Lück, Rudolf Miller, and Charles E. Early. The book is a joint cross-Atlantic venture between German and American psychologists with varied special interests and many years of combined experience in both researching and teaching the history of psychology. It contains 57 translations from the German edition and 50 new English–language essays by historians of psychology from around the world. The volume covers the history of psychology from Greek antiquity to recent developments in American cognitive psychology with a total of 107 articles by 109 authors from 15 different countries. The book is copiously illustrated with more than 650 illustrations and tables on 615 pages of text.

The book is organized into the following seven subsections:

    I. The Beginnings (17 chapters)
    II. From Psychophysics to Behaviorism (24)
    III. Gestalt Psychology (10)
    IV. Human Development and Personality (15)
    V. Psychiatry, Psychoanalysis, and Abnormal Psychology (14)
    VI. Growth of Branches (12)
    VII. International Developments (15)

Comprehensive name and subject indexes, as well as a list of illustration credits and sources, round out the book.

We would like to thank Rudolf Arnheim, for his kind words in support of this project, and Jennifer Duranceau, who actively helped with the demanding tasks of manuscript preparation. We also wish to offer a special thanks to our wives, Norma Bringmann, Barbara Lück, Karin Miller, and Sylvia Early, who provided encouragement as well as valuable comments, suggestions, and assistance on the numerous details that go into editing a book of this scope.

Preface to the German Edition

T ake hold of the true and old!" This adage from the personal bookplate of Jonas Cohen, a German philosopher and student of Wilhelm Wundt, exemplifies the spirit behind this book. However, our plans for a book on the history of psychology— with many previously unpublished illustrations— were less guided by nostalgia than by a desire to help modern psychologists discover more about the origins of their discipline, and what the field actually looked like at the beginning. Specifically, we have tried to make the history of our discipline more visible, to establish connections between past and present, to highlight developmental trends, and thus, to make the past come alive.

We hope to achieve these goals by presenting the development of modern psychology within its social and cultural context, including its relationship to other disciplines such as literature and even music. Our plans for the book, which were influenced by our experience as editors of the newsletter *Geschichte der Psychologie* (History of Psychology) and our journal *Geschichte und Psychologie* (History and Psychology), were realized throught the efforts of the many contributing authors to this edited volume. Whether or not the final product of our labors is a success is, of course, a judgment that rests with the reader.

We are grateful that so many colleagues became actively involved in our project. The contributing authors provided a wealth of information about many interesting and little-known events and relationships in the history of psychology. Indeed, there are many articles in this book that will appeal to the widest range of tastes. Thus the menu of events as described herein is offered as a more engaging alternative to the dry and often dull fare of the more traditional textbooks, monographs, and collections of readings that so often characterize the history of

our field. While our book is not intended to replace the format and presentation found in traditional works, we hope it will serve as a highly useful addition and supplement to the more mainstream histories of psychology. In addition, however, the novel approach found here can provide a solid introduction to the history of psychology for those who are new to the field. We hope that our book will enable the reader to discover how interesting, fascinating, and informative the history of psychology can be when it is presented from a highly visual perspective.

While many of the photographs and illustrations that appear in this book are well known, we are particularly pleased to include many more that are published here for the first time. Foremost credit for these hundreds of historical illustrations must be given to the more than 60 contributors to this work. Additional photographs were obtained through the courtesy of relatives and descendants of eminent psychologists, and from the personal collections of fellow historians of psychology. We also wish to offer a special thanks to Rudolf Arnheim, an expert on the psychology of visual representations and whose contributions to European and American psychology are widely recognized, for agreeing to write a foreword for the book.

Mrs. Ingeborg Schäfer of the Psychology program at FernUniversität prepared a major part of the manuscript for publication. We greatly appreciate her help, as well as the assistance of Mr. Peter Becker, who prepared the illustrations. In addition, we want to thank Mr. Klaus Nuyken, who helped with the planning of the book, and Mr. Horst Dieter Rossaker, who was our text editor.

Helmut E. Lück and Rudolf Miller
Hagen, Spring 1993

Acknowledgments

The publication of this volume was made possible by the generous cooperation of the many individuals and institutions that provided original illustrations. The editors and publisher would like to especially acknowledge the assistance of the individuals and organizations listed below. Readers who wish additional information may contact the editors for complete mailing addresses.

Individuals

Maria Abeille-Ehrenfels, Alexandra Adler, Kurt Adler, Peter J. Behrens, Ludy T. Benjamin Jr., Binet Family Archive, Josef Brožek, Roger Brown, Jerome Bruner, Barry Bunch, Noam Chomsky, C. N. Cofer, Steven R. Coleman, Annette Daigger, Kurt Danziger, Nino Dazzi, Heman Desai, Peter van Drunen, William K. Estes, David Finkelhor, Rainer Funk, Linda Goin-Goodtimes, Horst U. K. Gundlach, Tibor Horváth, Jiří Hoskovec, Toshio Iritani, Jürgen Jahnke, Siegfried Jaeger, Gustav Jahoda, Alexander James, James Jenkins, Franz Jung, Otto Jutzler, Gerhard Kaminski, Karin Kohler-Green, Antoon A. Leenaars, Miriam Lewin, Paul McReynolds, Marion White McPherson, Luciano Mecacci, George Miller, Henry L. Minton, Wesley G. Morgan, Ulric Neisser, Régine Plas, John A. Popplestone, David K. Robinson, Giuseppe Roccatagliata, Marion Sabish, Rüdiger Schiferer, Angela Schorr, G. Siemsen, Herbert Simon, Siegfried Ludwig Sporer, Helga Sprung, Lothar Sprung, Carl-Alfred Stumpf, Ingeborg Stumpf, Thomas Szasz, B. Michael Thorne, Tolman Family Archive, Doris Tucker, Gustav A. Ungerer, Francis Vogtner, Michael Wertheimer, Artur Wirth, Witasek Family, Robert H. Wozniak, Hermann Wundt

Institutions

Akademie der Künste Berlin (Germany); American Association for the Advancement of Science (USA); American Philosophical Society (USA); American Psychological Association (USA); Andreas-Salomé Archive (Germany); Archives of the History of American Psychology (USA); Archiv der Franz Brentano Forschung (Germany); Art Resources (USA); Artists Rights Resources (USA); Berufsverband Deutscher Psychologen (Germany); Bildarchiv Preußischer Kulturbesitz (Germany); Bilderarchiv der österreichischen Nationalbibliothek (Austria); Bibliothek des Institutes für Grenzgebiete der Psychologie (Germany); Bundesarchiv (Germany); Cambridge University Press (England); Chicago Sun–Times (USA); Open Court Publishing Company (USA); Clark University Press (USA); Ernst-Mach-Institut (Germany); Forschungsstelle für österreichische Philosophie (Austria); Fort Hays State University (USA); Georg-Groddeck-Gesellschaft (Germany); Goethe-Museum (Germany); Harper Collins Inc. (USA); Henry Holt Company (USA); Historisches Museum der Stadt Frankfurt (Germany); Houghton Library, Harvard University (USA); Harvard University Archives (USA); Institut für Grenzgebiete der Psychologie und Psychohygiene (Germany), Institut für Geschichte der Neueren Psychologie, Universität Passau (Germany); Institut für Psychologie, J. W. v. Goethe Universität (Germany); Johns Hopkins University Press (USA); Kenneth Spencer Research Library, University of Kansas (USA); Language Research Center, Georgia State University (USA); Humboldt Universitätsarchiv (Germany); Macmillan Company (USA); Milton Erickson Foundation (USA); Museumarchiv Burghölzli (Switzerland); Musil-Archiv (Austria); National Archives, Washington, DC (USA); National Library of Medicine (USA); Niedersächsische Staats- und Universitätsbibliothek (Germany); Sammlung Albertina (Austria); Staatsarchiv des Kantons (Switzerland); Stichting Historische Materialen Psychologie (Netherlands); Stoelting Co. (USA); United States Holocaust Museum (USA); Universitätsarchiv Freiburg (Germany); Universitätsbibliothek Freiburg (Germaný); Universitätsbibliothek Graz (Austria); Universitätsarchiv Heidelberg (Germany); Universitätsarchiv Mannheim (Germany); Universitätsarchiv Marburg (Germany); Universitätsarchiv Leipzig, (Germany); Universiteit Groningen (Netherlands); Universiteitsmuseum, Rijksuniversiteit Groningen (Netherlands); Universiteitsmuseum, Rijksuniversiteit Utrecht (Netherlands); University of Alberta Archives (Canada); University of California at Berkeley, Department of Psychology (USA); University of Chicago Press (USA); University of Illinois Press (USA); University of Nebraska (USA); Wundtnachlaß, Universität Leipzig (Germany); Yale University Library (USA); Zentral Bibliothek Zürich (Switzerland); Zentrum für Fernstudienentwicklung, FernUniversität (Germany)

Introduction

It has only been during the last several decades of the 20th century that the history of psychology has become a broadly recognized empirical subspecialty of modern psychology. It all seems to have begun in 1960 with Robert Watson's article "The History of Psychology: A Neglected Area." Watson sought to call attention to the history of psychology by reporting that in 1958 only about 60 of 15,000 members of the American Psychological Association (APA) included it among their interests. He concluded further that "almost all psychologists simply have not been interested in [the history of psychology] enough to be curious about it, let alone to work and publish in this area" (1960, p. 27). In September of 1960, Watson's reforming efforts included the organization of a "special history of psychology interest group," which in 1965 became Division 26 of the American Psychological Association. It had a charter membership of 211 and now has more than 1,000 fellows and members.

The next major event for the history of psychology as a discipline was the establishment of an unofficial newsletter, which by January 1965 evolved under Watson's editorship into *The Journal for the History of the Behavioral Sciences*. When, in 1967, Watson was appointed to a senior professorship at the University of New Hampshire, he established the first history of psychology PhD program in the world. A special summer school for predoctoral and postdoctoral students in the history of psychology was inaugurated by Watson and Josef Brožek in the summer of 1968 with generous financial support from the American National Science Foundation. One important outcome of these historical workshops was the 1968 establishment of *Cheiron*, the International Organization for the History of the Behavioral and Social Sciences.

International developments in the history of psychology during the more than three decades since Watson's challenge are far too numerous to be mentioned in detail in the present context, but a few of the highlights include: (1) a dramatic increase in the publication of quality historical research around the world; (2) the founding of history of psychology organizations around the world; (3) the organization of special and regular scientific meetings with a historical focus—such as the 1980 meeting of the International Union of Scientific Psychology in honor of William Wundt; and, last but not least, (4) the establishment of archives, museums, and research libraries in the history of psychology in the United States and several other countries.

As Raymond Fancher of York University in Canada, the president of APA's Division 26, recently suggested, the task now is to disseminate the wealth of new information about the history of our field, not only among those with specialized historical interests and expertise, "but also to the much larger number of APA members who have more general interests in their discipline's history. This . . . goal entails making historical research not only accessible but also meaningful and useful to mainstream psychologists"—and, we may add, to the educated public as well.

THE BEGINNINGS

Aristotle and Psychology

Daniel N. Robinson

Aristotle was born in 384 B.C. in the Macedonian village of Stagira, not far from today's Salonika. His father was physician to Amyntas, King of Macedonia and grandfather of Alexander the Great, who was for a time Aristotle's pupil. For some twenty years beginning about 368–367 B.C. and until the time of Plato's death (348 B.C.), Aristotle was a student in the famous Academy in Athens, composing dialogues early in his scholarly life and fully absorbing the spirit and much of the content of Plato's teaching.

Figure 1 Roman portait bust of Aristotle.

After Plato's death Aristotle left Athens for a period that included marriage, the tutoring of Alexander, extensive naturalistic research, and the forging of plans for his own school. The latter was established as the Lyceum in Athens. It was here that Aristotle composed (or dictated) those treatises which spawned the succeeding centuries of "Aristotelianism." Under mounting political pressure in the wake of Alexander's death (323 B.C.), Aristotle left Athens the year before his own death (322 B.C.) leaving, he said, according to one account, lest Athens ". . . sin against Philosophy a second time."

Only a small fraction of Aristotle's total writings has survived the ages, however, and even this fraction has had to wind its way through any number of intermediary reactions and contested translations. The following account is based solely on those works now unarguably regarded as authentic. It should be noted that in these works there are inconsistencies and ambiguities even on matters of central importance. Accordingly, what is offered as Aristotle's psychology should be regarded as but a number of generalizations that must serve chiefly as an invitation to the works themselves.

Sources of Aristotle's Psychology

There has been no writer on psychological subjects as wide-ranging and systematic as Aristotle. His treatises include a comparative psychology in which the different psychological dispositions and traits of many animal types are described; a physiological psychology addressed chiefly to the processes of perception, emotion, memory, and motivation; a developmental psychology concerned principally with early education and the formation of character; a moral psychology designed to illuminate the basis upon which human life may flourish and realize its full potentialities; and a political psychology which establishes the relationship between the citizen and the state (the *polis*) and the conditions of necessary nurturance and teaching that only the *polis* can provide. Although his treatise *On the Soul* is often taken to be his most developed psychological work, it is better regarded as something of an outline or distillation of his thought. His comparative psychology is further developed in both his *History of the Animals* and *Parts of the Animals;* his psychology of human emotion in his *Rhetoric, Nichomachean and Eudemian Ethics;* his psychology of learning and memory in his *On Memory and Reminiscences;* his social and political psychology in his ethical treatises and his *Politics.* In light of the range of works that must be consulted to arrive at a clear understanding of his systematic psychology, it is advisable to consider his position on the various components of this psychology rather than examining each of the works separately.

Aristotelian Explanation

The most direct entrance into Aristotle's psychological theories is by way of his approach to explanation or understanding generally. Something is understood when its causes are known as the maxim claims, "Happy is one who knows the causes of things." In his writings on natural science (e.g., his *Physics*) as well as in his logical treatises (*Posterior Analytics*), Aristotle notes that an understanding of causes calls for a fourfold analysis. An object or event is causally brought about in part because it possesses a certain materiality. Marble can be permanently shaped in a way that water cannot. One of the "causes" of a statue then is just its material composition, and this is its *material cause*. But an entity is only a statue (or vase or house) when it possesses the requisite or identifying form of such things or functions as such things should. Without the requisite form the thing cannot be a statue or vase or house. There is then a *formal cause*. For matter to be formed, it must be worked on and altered. The art of shipbuilding, says Aristotle, is not in the wood; otherwise we would have ships by nature. The various physical manipulations by which raw matter is given an identifiable form constitute the *efficient cause* of the thing. Behind all of these causal modalities, however, are considerations of purpose: *what the thing is for.* That end or goal (*telos*) or pur-

pose which is realized by the thing is what Aristotle calls the *final cause*, because it is temporally the last to be achieved, though it is conceptually prior to all the rest. The ultimate explanation is *teleological* in that it is framed in terms of "that for the sake of which" the material, formal, and efficient causes were invoked.

To explain anything requires an examination of all four causal modalities, though Aristotle explains that often the formal and the final causes are the same. That is, there are instances in which the very form of something discloses its purpose. This applies to the soul (*psyche*) in interesting ways. For Aristotle, the term psyche refers, as he says in *On the Soul*, to "the first principle of living things" (*arche zoon*). The soul is to be regarded as the very form of operation or activity by virtue of which something is animated. An entity that is "ensouled," so to speak, possesses both matter and form; both a materiality and a collection of functions. Thus, if the eye were a body then sight would be its soul. Aristotle's analogy is suggestive here. Vision is at once the form of an eye's proper operation and that for the sake of which eyes have been created or have evolved or have appeared in the animal kingdom. A blind eye would, then, be an eye in name only, like, he says, the physician's hand in a stone statue.

If living things are to be understood, then they, too, must be absorbed into a larger teleological framework within which form and function become part of an intelligible narrative. It is within this framework that Aristotle examines the sensory, motor, motivational, and social aspects of animal life. He carefully describes anatomical nuances and shows how these favor the survival and prosperity of different types of animals. He notes the comparability of organs in human and nonhuman primates; the manner in which types are shaped and adapted to local habitats; the instinctual behavior that serves the interests of herds and flocks and schools. It would not be until the age of Darwin that a more thorough natural history and theoretical explanation of the plant and animal kingdoms would be composed.

Aristotelian Classification

The distinction between plant and animal begins with sensation (*aisthesis*) which, says Aristotle, is part of the very definition of *animal*. In this he is referring not simply to the physical effect a stimulus

Figure 2 Page from a medieval manuscript of Aristotle's *Ethics*.

has on a body, but the awareness animals have of such effects. (Were an eye removed and placed on the road, a light shining on it would not result in *aisthesis*). Though not drawing himself into questions about animal consciousness, Aristotle is essentially a "common sense" psychologist on such matters, taking for granted that intelligent behavior is evidence of an awareness of the external world. Indeed, with a few notable exceptions, the psychological powers granted to human beings are regarded by Aristotle as being broadly represented throughout that part of the animal kingdom visible to the unaided eye. Thus, his theories of perception, memory, motivation, and rudimentary learning are grounded in biological processes found in a wide variety of animal forms and types. Memory is the result of the formation of actual traces or icons such as those a heated stylus makes in soft wax. Learning is often no more than the formation of such associations as a result of repeated exposure or practice, fortified by rewards and punishments. The primary impulses behind behavior are biological drives occasioned by the needs of the body. Even where the anatomies are radically different, the same ends (e.g., nutrition, procreation, locomotion, sensation) are achieved homologously.

With human life a power or faculty occurs which is not evident in other animals. In *On the Soul* this power is not referred to as reason (*nous*) but as the capacity to comprehend universal propositions (*epistemonikon*). This power allows human beings to free their conduct from control by specific stimuli and to behave instead in response to general principles. It is by virtue of this power that human beings are fit for rule by law and can organize themselves in irreducibly political communities. As rational beings, humans are able to articulate goals or ends that go beyond the biological needs of the body. Moreover, the choices they make can be predicated on actual deliberations rather than being compelled by the stronger of two competing motives. To choose on the basis of a principle is to make a deliberated choice (*prohairesis*) and thus to be responsible for it. Thus does rationality yield the power of deliberation and render the actor morally responsible for the choices made.

In Plato's *Republic* Socrates repeats the "convenient fiction" of "men of gold, men of silver, men of brass, men of iron"; a fiction nonetheless fortifying his essentially eugenic approach to the selection and training of the guardians of the *polis*. Aristotle, too, insists that not all human beings possess comparable powers of rationality and (therefore) comparable moral or political worth. The ethical and political treatises promise a certain kind of elevated life only to a certain class of men; those of a chivalric or knightly nature, the *kaloi kagathoi*, who will always be a conspicuous minority within the crowd. Even those having the capacity to achieve so elevated a life require early and constant education within the *polis*. Rationality is not present in the infant or child and generally is only incompletely developed in women. There are, too, defective persons who, though able to conform themselves to the rational dictates of others, are not able to frame a rational course of life for themselves. These are called *natural slaves* by Aristotle and are distinguished from the class of slaves and servants won in battle.

Reason, Passion, and the Rule of Law

The need for early discipline and life-long education, even for the *kalos kagathos*, is that men are not totally rational, only potentially so. Human psychology, owing to the fact that man, too, is an animal, is marked by emotionality and tendencies toward sensual gratification. Anger, love, and other emotional states are entirely natural, with versions of each displayed by nonhuman animals. But if full humanity is to be achieved, the emotions must submit to rational dictates, to the "royal rule" of reason. Through discipline and education the child conforms his behavior as if he were fully rational—though he isn't. In time, however, when rational principles can be comprehended, the young man has already developed habits of reasonable conduct which now can be attached to the principles themselves. Man, says Aristotle, is "the very worst of animals" when separated from the rule of law. Outside the *polis* and the rule of law, one must find only the barbarian whose stateless and lawless existence places him lower on the scale of humanity and makes him a constant threat. Thus, the *Politics* insists that "it is right that Hellenes shall rule barbarians."

In an ostensibly odd passage in the *Politics*, Aristotle argues that, in a sense, the state is prior both to the family and to the individual. But keeping in mind the respect in which the final cause is the last to be realized but the first to be conceived, the passage becomes clearer. Man is by nature a social animal, strongly inclined to live in the company of others. But as a rational creature with the power of deliberated choice, man's social affiliations are not to be at the level of instinctual herding. Rather, the affiliations must serve a higher purpose; the purpose of realizing that which could not be realized in isolation. Social life is a life of practice. It allows the cultivation and expression of those potentialities dubbed the moral virtues—courage, temperance, magnanimity, justice, liberality, and the rest. Each of the virtues is the midpoint on a continuum of dispositions, the extreme points marking off the vices. Courage, on this account, is the mean (the "golden mean") between the vicious extremes of cowardliness and heedlessness. And because these virtuous dispositions are the result of choice and self-control, they are available only to beings with reason (*nous*) and the power of deliberated choice (*prohairesis*). Accordingly, only human beings can have the virtues.

Aristotle is always sensitive to the problem of the infinite regression in developing teleological explanations. To say that legs are for walking is then to raise a question as to what walking is for, etc. The regress must stop somewhere; that is, there must be something that is sought for its own sake and not for the sake of something more fundamental. For Aristotle, that which human beings seek for its own sake and not for the sake of anything else is what he calls in the Greek *eudaimonia*, which has traditionally been rendered as "happiness." The latter, however, has come to be regarded as a species of episodic pleasure or hedonistic joy and therefore no longer fits as the translation of *eudaimonia*. The inveterate pleasure-seeker is the *apolaustikos* who is in fact a slave to his own needs and has thus surrendered reason to passion. Such a person seems to instantiate the being Aristotle describes as "one who would be a slave everywhere." It is better, then, to take *eudaimonia* as referring to a flourishing form of life that is also the right form. Only human beings can know a eudaimonic life, and very few of them, alas.

In this connection, it is important to identify a tension in Aristotle's psychology between the life of practice and the speculative life. The former is featured in the *Eudemian Ethics*, the latter in the *Nichomachean Ethics*. In the former, *eudaimonia* is associated with an active life within the *polis*—the life of the giver of good laws, a symbol of civic virtue. In the latter, *eudaimonia* is achieved only by the *philosophos* given over to a life of contemplation of "first things;" a life whose dominant activity is undertaken for its own sake and not for the sake of anything else. This form of life, says Aristotle, is akin to that lived by those "on the Isle of the Blest," closer to gods themselves.

Needless to say, no one writing in the fourth century B.C. on so exhaustive a subject could possibly avoid error and misapprehension. Even as the Hippocratic physicians were identifying the brain as the organ causally associated with cognition, perception, memory, and emotion, Aristotle would argue that its essential function was one of cooling the blood. His psychophysiological theories were centered on the heart primarily because of the importance he attached to temperature variations as sources of motive energy. In this he reveals a dominant characteristic of ancient Greek analysis: viz., analysis by such contrasts as hot and cold, hard and soft, solid and liquid. This is very much at work in his theory of gender differences, according to which the male is relatively hot, the woman cooler; the fetus in the cooler womb developing less completely into a female, the fetus in the warmer womb developing completely into a male, etc. But even in these cases Aristotle's conclusions were tied to observations, were offered as generalizations admitting of exceptions, and were presented in a way allowing of empirical refutations. That later centuries of committed Aristotelians would seek to elevate his conjectures to the level of dogmatic truths is something he could not foresee.

Bibliography

Barnes, J. (Ed.). (1984). *The complete works of Aristotle.* Princeton: Princeton University Press.

Robinson, D. (1989). *Aristotle's psychology.* New York: Columbia University Press.

Sherman, N. (1988). *Aristotle: The fabric of character.* Oxford: Clarendon Press.

Veatch, H. (1974). *Aristotle: A contemporary approach.* Bloomington: University of Indiana Press.

The Inner Senses: A Medieval Theory of Cognitive Functioning in the Ventricles of the Brain

Simon Kemp

The psychological lore of the Middle Ages is often thought to be an unoriginal summary of ancient theories forced into a straitjacket of religious orthodoxy. This caricature is not altogether groundless. The views of the ancient philosophers, particularly Aristotle, were esteemed in the Middle Ages. And medieval Christians, Jews, and Moslems frequently did try to reconcile religious and psychological questions. On the other hand, medieval scholars came up with theories of psychological functions that were neither completely derived from ancient writers nor determined by theology. One such medieval theory, the focus of this chapter, held that a number of cognitive processes were performed in the ventricles of the brain.

Origin of the Theory

The first written version of the *theory of the inner senses* has not survived. Nor is it certain who first thought of it, although it has been attributed to a third-century A.D. physician named Posidonius (e.g., see Roccatagliata, 1986). However, the idea is stated as fact by the early Christian writers Nemesius and Saint Augustine, so it must have been current at the end of the fourth century A.D. (Augustine, 426/1982; Nemesius, 400/1955).

The theory amalgamated Aristotle's psychology and Galen's physiology. The idea that some cognitive functions—for example, memory and the ability to form visual images—were carried out in some part of the body was stressed by Aristotle in his psychological work *De Anima* (Aristotle, 350 B.C./1931), but the great Greek philosopher did not house these abilities in the brain at all. Claudius

Galenus of Pergamon, the Greek anatomist who was at one time the personal physician of the Roman Emperor Commodus, described the anatomy of the brain and its ventricles but did not assign any cognitive function to any particular part. He thought that the brain itself, rather than its ventricles, was responsible for our ability to remember and think.

The ventricles of the brain are fluid-filled cavities which are nowadays thought to fulfill no psychological function at all. Galen's physical description of them was actually reasonably accurate (for the actual arrangement, see Figure 1), except for one critical detail: He thought that the sensory nerves, which carry information from the eyes and ears and

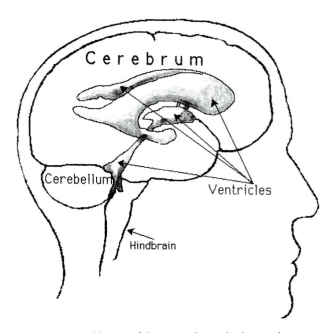

Figure 1 Actual layout of the ventricles in the human brain.

other sensory organs to the brain, fed directly into the front ventricle (Galen, 170/1980).

Avicenna's Theory of the Inner Senses

Although medieval theologians and philosophers often wrote about the theory of the inner senses and sometimes squabbled about its details (Harvey, 1975; Kemp & Fletcher, 1993), it was always thought to be essentially a medical theory. Certainly in the later Middle Ages it was the account of the great Islamic physician Ibn Sina, or Avicenna as he was known in Western Europe, that was most influential and most authoritative.

Avicenna, Abu 'Ali al-Husayn ibn Sina to give him his full name, was born in Bukhara, which at the time of his birth in 980 A.D. formed a part of Persia. (It is at present in Uzbekistan.) He spent the whole of his life in Persia as a physician and administrator. His life seems to have been eventful: He fell into and out of official favor, and until his death in 1037 he retained a keen interest in women and wine. Despite an active public and personal life, he wrote widely on philosophy and medicine, and these writings were generally influential in Christendom as well as in the Islamic lands. In particular, his *Canon of Medicine* was a standard medical text in Europe from the 13th to the 17th centuries.

According to Avicenna, the three ventricles of the brain performed five distinct cognitive processes (Avicenna, 1020/1968). A schematic view of these processes and the way Avicenna distributed them among the ventricles is shown in Figure 2. As Figures 3, 4, and 5 show, the medieval anatomy was a rather simplified version of the actual one.

Incoming sensory information from the different senses was all fed into the *common sense* [Latin: *sensus communis*], which was located at the front of the front ventricle. This, Avicenna explained, is how we put together the information from different

senses to form perceptions of objects. For example, he said, it is why we connect the white face of a performer with the sound of singing, so that we perceive someone singing. If animals did not have this power, he pointed out, they would not be able to associate the smell or appearance of food with its taste. The common sense operates quickly but not instantaneously. This is why when it rains we see slanting lines of rain rather than single droplets (Avicenna, 1020/1968, Vol. 4, pp. 1–3).

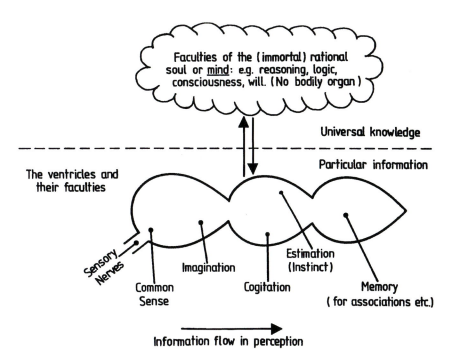

Figure 2 Illustration of Avicenna's account of the inner senses.

The images produced in the common sense are stored in the *imagination* [Latin: *imaginatio* or *formans*] located at the back of the front ventricle. When we recall a scene we have witnessed previously, the image is brought out of storage and displayed again in the common sense. This, according to Avicenna, is how visual images come about.

The front ventricle puts together and stores sensory information without any interpretation of it. The sensory information can be passed through to the middle ventricle via a narrow passage that Avicenna supposed could be opened by raising a small worm-like organ known as the vermis. The two processes of the middle ventricle were responsible for some of the abstraction of meaning from the stored images. The first of these processes, termed *cogitation* [Latin: *cogitans*], puts together or subtracts different images. Thus, to take a later medieval example, we can imagine a golden mountain by putting together images of a mountain and of gold, even though no golden mountain exists and we therefore have no stored image of one (Aquinas, 1273/1964). Similarly, we can imagine a man with no head by subtracting part of the image.

The second process in the middle ventricle is that of *estimation* [Latin: *estimatio*]. This involves the abstraction of the *implications* [Latin: *intentiones*] of the image. These implications are abstracted either instinctively, because they are innate to the person or animal, or as the result of associative learning. So, to use two more of Avicenna's examples, a sheep will instinctively fear a wolf even if it has never encountered one before, since it can recognize the threat to it that is one of the implications of the appearance of the wolf. Also a dog will cringe in terror from a stick with which it has been previously beaten.

Avicenna believed that this kind of process occurred in humans too. A baby, for example, instinctively blinks if you try to clean something out of its eye, and someone might instinctively have an aversion to honey because of its dung-like appearance (Avicenna, 1020/1968, Vol. 4, pp. 37–39).

Finally, the rear ventricle contained the single faculty of *memory* [Latin: *memoria*]. This consisted of the associations and meanings derived by estimation. Note that the inner senses actually contained two memories, one for images located at the rear of the front ventricle and one for their associated meanings or evaluations in the rear ventricle.

In Avicenna's account, the cognitive psychology of animals could be completely explained by the operations in their ventricles. Humans, however, had extra capabilities provided by their rational souls, which enabled them to reason and manipulate abstract concepts. Avicenna—along with virtually every other medieval theorist—believed that the rational soul was immortal and thus not housed in the brain or any part of the body. Moreover, in normally functioning human beings the rational soul was in command of the operations of the inner senses so that imagining or remembering a particular scene could be carried out at will.

The Inner Senses at Work

Reasonable questions to ask of any psychological theory are: What can we do with it? What phenomena can it explain or predict? On this count, Avicenna's theory of the inner senses shapes up well, and he himself discussed a number of psychological phenomena. Two to which he gave special attention are reconstructive memory and dreaming.

The idea that many of the events we recall are not really remembered but rather reconstructed from scraps of information is a common one in present-day psychology (Burt & Kemp, 1991). Avicenna's idea that the inner senses contained two different stores (the imagination in the front ventricle and the memory in the rear ventricle) suggested a ready mechanism for reconstruction.

Consider, for example,

> when you have forgotten the meaning implicit in some image you have seen. Then you consider the action which that image suggested and, when you know the action, you will know what taste and what shape and what colour it ought to have, and you will invoke the corresponding association; and when you do this, you will acquire something similar to the form which is in the imagination and you can restore the corresponding association in memory. (Avicenna, 1020/1968, Vol. 4, p. 10. My translation)

In normal waking life the images that are presented to the common sense either arise from perceiving the world or by someone intentionally imagining something. However, when people are asleep, the control of the rational soul is loosened, and the inner senses operate on their own. In this case the images in the common sense are basically meaningless, the result of purposeless movements in the fluid that fills the front ventricle. These uncon-

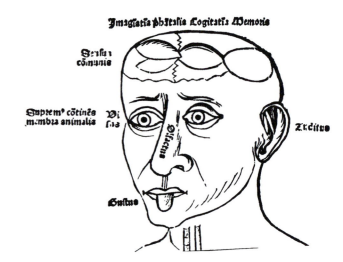

Figure 3 Late medieval depiction of the inner senses.

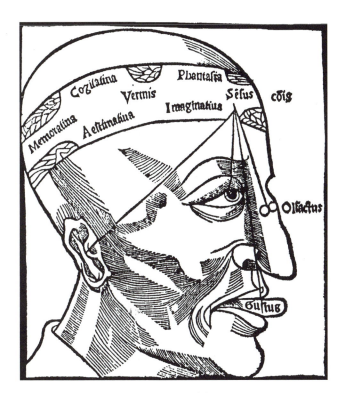

Figure 4 Late medieval depiction of the inner senses.

trolled images are dreams. Normally people experience this type of imagery when they are asleep. However, it is also possible for uncontrolled images to be experienced when awake, particularly in cases of mental disorder.

Later History of the Theory

The theory of the inner senses seems to have attracted near universal belief in Western Europe as well as in the Islamic countries until well into the 16th century. For example, it is discussed in several places in an immensely popular 13th-century encyclopedia compiled by the Franciscan monk Bartholomaeus Anglicus (1260/1975).

Sometimes the different medieval scholars varied the details. For example, Saint Thomas Aquinas (1273/1964), the 13th-century theologian whose writings are still of great importance for the Catholic Church, suggested that there were really only four inner senses. He thought that the work of the cogitative power could be performed by the imagination.

Succeeding scholars also sometimes used the theory to describe new phenomena. For example, different kinds of mental disorder could be predicted and explained by the malfunction of different cerebral ventricles. It was quite common in Western Europe in the later Middle Ages to distinguish the mental disorders of mania, melancholy, and lethargy as resulting from disturbances in the front, middle, and rear ventricles respectively (Bartholomaeus Anglicus, 1260/1975; Clarke, 1975; Kemp, 1990).

In 1486, two Dominican monks, Heinrich Kramer and James Sprenger, wrote a manual for witch-hunters, the infamous *Malleus Maleficarum* (The Hammer of the Witches). In this book the theory of the inner senses was used to explain how devils can bring about madness and hallucinations by insinuating themselves into the cerebral ventricles and literally stirring up the fluid in them. This, Kramer and Sprenger went on to explain, is the basis of how men can be bewitched into believing they have lost their "virile members" (Kramer & Sprenger, 1486/1971).

The advent of printing meant that from the later 15th century, diagrams of the layout and function of the cerebral ventricles appeared frequently in books. Figures 3, 4, and 5 are examples of these late medieval illustrations. (See also Clarke & Dewhurst, 1972.)

If the reasons why the theory of the inner senses came to be believed in the fourth century are obscure, the reason for its demise is not. Although

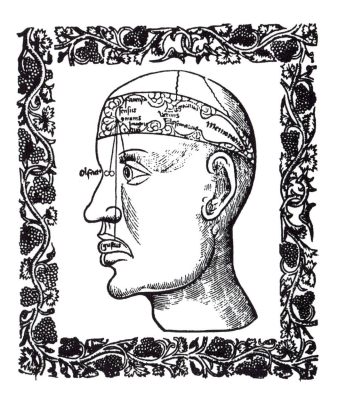

Figure 5 Late medieval depiction of the inner senses.

dissections of the human body (and presumably also of the human brain) were carried out in medieval medical schools (Demaitre, 1975), the dissectors did not apparently learn from their work that anything was amiss with the simplified anatomy reported in the medieval texts. But when the gifted anatomist Andreas Vesalius performed his dissections of the human body and reported the results in his *De Humanis Corporis Fabrica* (The Fabric of the Human Body) in 1543, he pointed out a number of discrepancies between the actual anatomy of the brain and his contemporaries' beliefs about it (Singer, 1952).

In the first place, he pointed out that the actual arrangement of the cerebral ventricles had become grossly oversimplified. Second, he remarked that human beings, although far more intelligent and rational, had a ventricular structure very similar to that of animals. Neither of these findings necessarily contradicted the theory, although Vesalius, who was never slow to find fault with the theories of his predecessors and teachers, argued that they did. But his third result really was fatal. Galen was wrong: The sensory nerves do not connect to any of the ventricles of the brain but rather to the hind brain.

The collapse of the physiological basis of the theory quickly led to its rejection by savants all over Europe. Various attempts were subsequently made to provide a new physiology which would still maintain the rich psychology of the inner senses theory. For example, in the 17th century the English anatomist Thomas Willis suggested that the sensory nerves, which connected to the medulla oblongata, sent projections up to the corpus callosum which functioned as a white screen for receiving images (Willis, 1672/1971). However, neither Willis's nor any other of the theories that were suggested attracted the sort of widespread belief the inner senses theory had previously enjoyed (Kemp & Fletcher, 1993). The medieval theory, which so neatly united physiology and psychology, was discredited, but it was not replaced.

Bibliography

Aquinas, T. (1964). *Summa theologiae* [Compendium of theology] (Various Trans.). London: Blackfriars. (Original work completed about 1273)

Aristotle. (1931). *The works of Aristotle* (W. D. Ross, Ed.; Various Trans.) Oxford: Clarendon. (Original works written about 350 B.C.)

Augustine. (1982). *The literal meaning of Genesis* (J. H. Taylor, Trans.). New York: Newman. (Original work written about 426)

Avicenna. (1968). *Avicenna Latinus. Liber de anima seu sextus de naturalibus IV-V* [Book about the soul or the sixth book on nature] (S. van Riet, Ed.). Leuven, Belgium: Peeters. (Original work written about 1020)

Bartholomaeus Anglicus. (1975). *On the properties of things* (M. C. Seymour, Ed.; J. Trevisa, Trans.). Oxford: Clarendon. (Original work written about 1260)

Burt, C. D. B., & Kemp, S. (1991). Retrospective duration estimation of public events. *Memory & Cognition, 19,* 252–262.

Clarke, B. (1975). *Mental disorder in earlier Britain.* Bangor: University of Wales.

Clarke, E., & Dewhurst, K. (1972). *An illustrated history of brain function.* Oxford: Sandford.

Demaitre, L. (1975). Theory and practice in medical education at the University of Montpelier in the thirteenth and fourteenth centuries. *Journal of the History of Medicine and Allied Sciences, 30,* 103–123.

Galen, C. (1980). *On the doctrines of Hippocrates and Plato* (P. De Lacy, Trans.). Berlin: Akademie. (Original work written about 170)

Harvey, E. R. (1975). *The inward wits: Psychological theory in the Middle Ages and the Renaissance.* London: Warburg Institute.

Kemp, S. (1990). *Medieval psychology.* Westport, CT: Greenwood.

Kemp, S., & Fletcher, G. J. O. (1993). The medieval theory of the inner senses. *American Journal of Psychology, 106,* 559–576.

Kramer, H., & Sprenger, J. (1971). *Malleus Maleficarum* [The hammer of the witches] (M. Summers, Trans.). New York: Arrow. (Original work published 1486)

Nemesius. (1955). A treatise on the nature of man. In W. Telfer (Ed.), *The library of Christian classics: Vol. 4: Cyril of Jerusalem and Nemesius of Emesa* (pp. 203–453). London: SCM Press. (Original work written about 400)

Roccatagliata, G. (1986). *A history of ancient psychiatry.* New York: Greenwood.

Singer, C. (1952). *Vesalius on the human brain.* London: Oxford University Press.

Willis, T. (1971). *Two discourses concerning the soul of brutes, which is that of the vital and sensitive in man* (S. Pordage, Trans.). Gainesville, FL: Scholars Facsimiles and Reprints. (Original work published 1672)

Psichiologia, φυχολογία, Psychology

Gustav A. Ungerer
Wolfgang G. Bringmann

The collection of writings titled *Peri Psyches* was composed by Aristotle (384–322 B.C.) during different periods of his life. They are particularly significant to psychology because it is here that Aristotle laid the foundation for the empirical study of psychology by future generations. From the beginning of the 16th until about the middle of the 17th century, the word *psychology* was created and used in the titles of books and was very likely also used in everyday life. In the account that follows, scholars who used the word *psychology* will be presented in chronological order. All book titles and other pertinent information will be translated into idiomatic English; however, the original texts and terms will be presented in the reference list found at the end of this essay.

Psichiologia

Marco Marulic (1450–1524), the Croatian humanist (Tijan, 1967), was recently identified as the scholar who may have invented and first used the word *psychology* (Kristic, 1964). The son of a noble family, Marulic was born on August 18, 1450, in the harbor city of Split on the Adriatic coast. He received his education in the "classical languages and literature, poetry, rhetoric" and "philosophy" at the University of Padua in Italy (Tijan, 1967). He also was an accomplished painter and sculptor. In 1480, Marulic withdrew from society to live a religious life, even though he didn't belong to a monastic order. He was best known for his books on moral theology, which were published in multiple editions and translations. In Croatia, he is still regarded as a national hero through his epic poem and vernacular libretto expressed in the opera *Judith* (1521).

According to Kruno Kristic (1964), a Yugoslav historian of psychology, Marulic employed a variation of the term *psychology* as early as 1506. He also used the word *psichiologia* in the title of his 1524 book about *The Psychology of Human Thought—Volume 1*. This information is found in an early biography of Marulic by his friend and the executor of his will, Bozicevic Natalis. Natalis did not actually see this book, but remembered its title when he wrote

Figure 1 Roman copy of a Greek portrait bust of Aristotle.

the biography. Marulic's psychology book appears to be lost, and it now appears that there is little chance of recovering a copy in Split or elsewhere in the former Yugoslavia. However, the precise reference to "Volume 1" of Marulic's book suggests that the volume may have indeed existed at one time. Assumptions and conclusions about the contents of Marulic's *Psychiologia* were offered by Diamond (1984). The actual word *psichiologia* is a strange version of a Greco-Latin word formation which may have developed in the relatively isolated region of the Balkans. It is also possible that Marulic may have created the new word somewhat mechanically after reading Giovanni Tortelli's (1406–1466) handbook (1471) containing similar artificial words like *orthographia*, *aethiologia*, and *tropologia*.

Melanchthon

Phillip Melanchthon (1497–1560), the Protestant reformer and philological advisor to Martin Luther (1483–1546), was incorrectly identified as the person "who first used the word 'psychologia' in his lectures" (Roback, 1961; Lapointe, 1970). The extent of Melanchthon's knowledge of Latin, Greek, and Hebrew was truly encyclopedic. His contributions to the German Bible translation are almost indistinguishable from those of Luther himself.

Beginning in 1518, Melanchthon served for 42 years as Professor of Greek at the University of Wittenberg in the German Duchy of Saxony. Apart from instruction in the classical languages, he offered academic courses in theology, philosophy, cosmology, and physics each year to hundreds of freshman students at the then new state university.

Figure 2 Portrait drawing of Melanchthon.

His importance to the history of psychology derives from the publication of his Latin book, *Commentary about the Soul* (1540), which was a handbook of philosophical psychology for the first ten generations of philosophers and theologians in Protestant Europe. According to his published correspondence (Bretschneider, 1834–1860), Melanchthon worked on this book as early as 1535: "I am just writing on the part which deals with the soul, and which will cover human nature in general." Two years later he informed friends in Switzerland that the part of his book on physics, which dealt with the human soul, would appear soon in Wittenberg. Finally, in January of 1540, Melanchthon was able to send a copy of his new book to his Swiss friends with the following comments (Bretschneider, 1834–1860):

> I wanted to present the physical and psychic conditions of man according to the wisdom of the classical authors and our own understanding. . . . I wrote the book for professors and students to assist them in acquiring scientific knowledge in this field. . . . All educated readers of my book are invited to send me their criticisms and suggestions, which may help me add new information in [future editions of the book]. (p. 388)

Between the first edition of 1540 and the time of Melanchthon's death in 1560, *About the Soul* was published in eight editions. The legend that Melanchthon invented the word *psychology* goes back almost 150 years. At that time, Melanchthon's psychology book was included in a collection of reprints of the works of the major Protestant reformers. The chief editor of the ambitious project was Carl Gottlieb Bretschneider (1776–1848), a liberal German theologian. The Latin introduction to Melanchthon's book explicitly mentioned that: "Melanchthon was the first among the German [authors] whom we know, who dealt in this book [with the topic of] psychology" (Bretschneider, 1834–1860, Vol. 13, p. 1).

This straightforward and rather innocuous sentence was apparently misunderstood by later authors (e.g., Lapointe, 1970; Roback, 1961, etc.) who may not have had access to Bretschneider's edition of Melanchthon's book, and who consequently drew the wrong conclusion about Melanchthon's relationship to the word *psychology*. In fact, Melanchthon, like most humanists of this period, was a purist in his use of the Latin and Greek languages. He disdained the combination of these languages and explicitly referred to his psychology book in his correspondence either by its Latin title *De anima* or by the Greek equivalent *Peri psyches*.

Psychologia

The next documented user of the word *psychology* was Johannes Thomas Freigius (1543–1583), a German philosopher and university teacher. Freigius was born in the small university town of Freiburg in the Black Forest region of Germany. After receiving his doctorate in law from Basel University at the age of 24, he studied dialectics, rhetoric, philology, mathematics, and the natural sciences as preparation for professorships he later held at academic institutions in Freiburg, Basel, and Altdorf.

Freigius became an enthusiastic disciple of the famous French theologian, philosopher, university reformer, and eventual Protestant martyr, Petrus Ramus (1515–1572), after meeting him in Basel. Throughout the remainder of his life, Freigius fought tirelessly for academic freedom and against the scholastic traditions of his academic superiors and the authorities of the Catholic Church. His numerous publications applied the didactic principles of Ramism to the different academic fields. Freigius first used the term *psychologia* in his 1575 *Catalogue of Common Places*, which was added to the beginning of his philosophical treatise *Ciceronianus* (1575). Four years later, the word *psychologia* appeared once more in the Latin book *Quaestiones Physicae* (Freigius, 1579), which focused on the human soul. After resigning his last academic position in Altdorf, Freigius died from the plague in 1583, at the age of 40, in Basel along with his three children.

Psichologie

Noel Taillepied (1540–1589) appears to have been the first author to use the word *psichologie* in French, his native language, and not in Latin. A native of Rouen, he completed a doctorate in theology and eventually became a teaching member of the Capuchin order. Intellectually, Taillepied belongs to a group of highly prolific apologists for tradi-

tional Catholicism during the Counter Reformation. A learned but rather gullible monk, Taillepied wrote a book with a long and intriguing title *Psychology. The book about the reality of spirits, knowledge of erring souls, phantoms, miracles and strange happenings, which at times precede the death of important personalities, or announce that affairs of state are falling apart* (1588).

The title of the second edition, and several others before 1616, no longer contains the word *psichologie*. It is possible that Taillepied removed the word when he realized that his word had been used in the heretical writings of the French Ramists. Taillepied must have been familiar with Aristotle's psychological writings because he published a French book on the dialectics, physics, and ethics of Aristotle in 1583.

φυχολογία

According to Francois Lapointe, who wrote an important article (1970) on the origin of the term *psychology:* "The first author who gave a treatise . . . under the title 'Psychology' was Rudolf Goeckel or

Figure 3 Portrait of Goclenius.

Rudolphus Goclenius (1547–1628) of Marburg [University] (1970, p. 640). Actually, Goclenius used the Greek form of *psychology* in the long title of a collection of works by various authors (1596).

During the same year (1590), Goclenius supervised a Latin dissertation by his student, Martin Möller, which had the title *Psychological Problems of Human Understanding*. Since Goclenius wrote the word *psychology* in Greek letters, its relationship to Aristotle's book *On the Soul* becomes more apparent.

Goclenius was an encyclopedic and very productive author who at one time held four different professorships in "Physics, Logic, Mathematics, and Ethics" at Marburg University in the German Landgraviate of Hesse. Altogether, he directed more than 600 master's theses and formal oral examinations! Like Ramus and Freigius, he was a strong advocate of academic freedom from the interference of religious or political authorities.

Max Dessoir (1867–1947), the German historian of psychology, credited Goclenius with the invention of the word *psychologia* but denied that he had made any other contributions to the field (Dessoir, 1894, p. 23). Modern psychologists are likely to be more interested in his writings about the "psychology of tears" and the "physiology and psychology of taste."

After the middle of the 17th century, the word *psychologia* became less popular. For example, a *Dictionary of Philosophy* (1613) by Goclenius does not contain the word. His 1604 essay "Preliminary Thoughts about the Human Soul" deals with psychological subject matters but omits the new term (Lapointe, 1970, 1972).

Psychologica Anthropologica

Otto Casmann (1562–1607), another student of Goclenius, actually used the Latin term *Psychologia* in a book title two years before his teacher: *Psychological Anthropology or the Science and Knowledge of the Soul* (1594). Two years later Casmann published what was apparently the second volume of his psychology book: *Anthropology Part II. Containing the Empirical Study of the Human System* (1596). It is

of special interest that Casmann removed the topic of *somatology*, or physiology proper, from his discussion of psychology. He also referred to psychology as a "doctrina" which can be translated as *knowledge*, *explanation*, or *science*. Finally, E. Neuhaus (1582–1638), one of Casmann's students, published a book that summarized the reasons for studying psychology (1635).

Thus, we have a solid tradition of three academic generations where the word *psychology* was used and books were written about psychological topics at a small provincial university over the difficult years of the Thirty Years War.

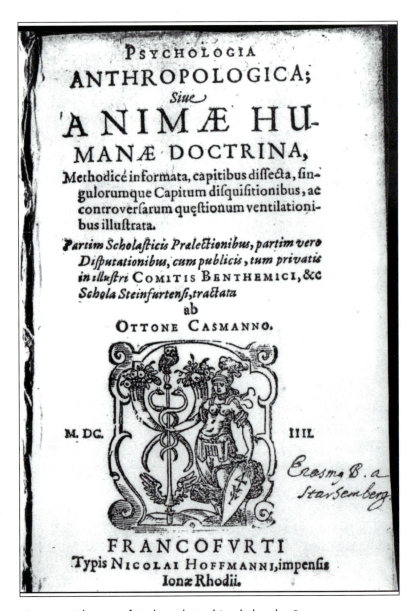

Figure 4 Title page of *Anthropological Psychology* by Casmann.

Figure 5 Portrait of Christian Wolff.

Psichologie and Psychology

After the early use of the term by Taillepied, the word *psichologie* appears to have disappeared from French publications. It resurfaced 166 years later in the book *Essay about Psychology* (1754) by the French scientist and philosopher Charles Bonnet (1720–1793). This work was preceded in France by translations of the philosophical and psychological writings of Christian Wolff (1679–1754), who used the French term *psichologie* in his German writings about psychology (1732, 1734). The French writer and philosopher Denis Diderot (1713–1784) helped make the word popular through a "Psichologie" article in his famous encyclopedia (1751–1781).

In England, the word *psychology* appeared first in Latin works by Gowan (1681) and by Broughton (1703). Generally, however, the word *Pneumatologia* or *pneumatology* was more frequently used to describe psychological events. David Hartley (1705–1757) used the term *psychology* twice in his works (Lapointe, 1972).

After the use of the word *psychology* had become established in England near the end of the 18th century, the first psychology titles appeared in the United States. For example, in 1840, Friedrich August Rauch (1806–1841), a political refugee from Germany and theology professor, published the first American textbook containing the word: *Psychology,*

or a View of the Human Soul; including Anthropology. In 1842, another important psychology book was issued by Samuel Schmucker (1799–1873), a theology professor at the Theological Seminary at Gettysburg. In the United States this work, *Psychology, Elements of a New System of Mental Philosophy on the Basis of Consciousness and Common Sense*, served as a popular college textbook of psychology for the next 30 years (Lapointe, 1970).

In conclusion, our etymological story of the word *psychology* has focused primarily on the origin and early use of the word, and less on its meaning, during the 16th and early 17th centuries. Some of the numerous publications which dealt with psychological subject matter but which used terms like *peri psyches*, *de anima*, or *pneumatologia*, were covered only in passing, but we have attempted to convey enough information about the biographical, scientific, and political context in which the word *psychol-*

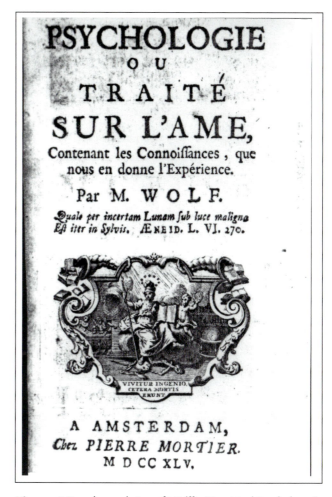

Figure 6 French translation of Wolff's "Empirical Psychology."

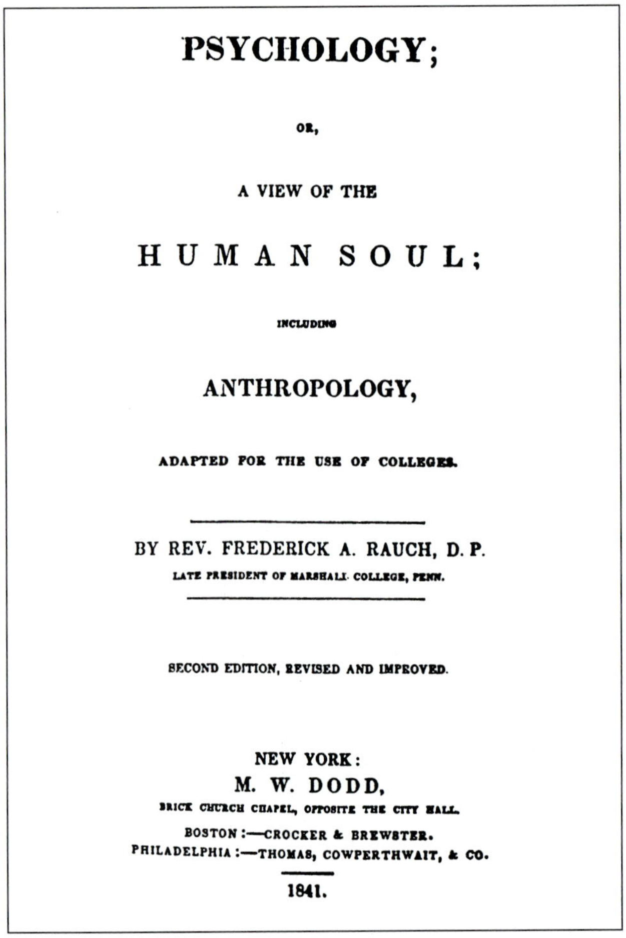

PSYCHOLOGY;

OR,

A VIEW OF THE

H U M A N   S O U L ;

INCLUDING

ANTHROPOLOGY,

ADAPTED FOR THE USE OF COLLEGES.

_____

BY REV. FREDERICK A. RAUCH, D. P.
LATE PRESIDENT OF MARSHALL COLLEGE, PENN.

_____

SECOND EDITION, REVISED AND IMPROVED.

NEW YORK:
M. W. DODD,
BRICK CHURCH CHAPEL, OPPOSITE THE CITY HALL.
BOSTON :—CROCKER & BREWSTER.
PHILADELPHIA :—THOMAS, COWPERTHWAIT, & CO.

1841.

Figure 7 Title page of the first American psychology textbook by Rauch.

ogy was created and used in order to provide some sense of the rich history behind the designation given to our field.

Bibliography

Barnes, J. (Ed.). (1984). *The complete works of Aristotle.* Princeton: Princeton University Press.

Bonnet, C. (1755). *Essai de psychologie.* London.

Bretschneider, C. G. (Ed.). (1834–1860). *Philippi Melanchthoni Opera.* Halle: Schwetschlee.

Broughton, J. (1703). *Psychologia, or an account of the rational soul.* London: Bennett.

Carus, F. G. (1808). *Geschichte der Psychologie.* Leipzig: Barth.

Casmann, O. (1594, 1604). *Psychologia anthropologica, sive animae humanae doctrina.* Hannover: Fischer.

Dessoir, M. (1902). *Geschichte der neueren deutschen psychologie.* Berlin: Duncker.

Diamond, W. (1984). What Marulus meant by "Psycholoigia." *Storia e Critica della Psicologia, 5,* 38–49.

Diderot, D. (1751–1781). *Encyclopedie raisonné, des arts et métier.* Paris: Briasson.

Freigius, J. T. (1575). *Cicernioamus.* Basel: Henripetri.

Freigius, J. T. (1579). *Quaestiones physicae.* Basel: Henripetri.

Goclenius, R. (1596). *De praecipuis materriis psychologicis.* Frankfurt.

Goclenius, R. (1597). *Autores varii de psychologia.* Marburg: Egenolph.

Goclenius, R. (1613). *Lexicon philosophicum Graecum.* Marburg: Hutwelker.

Gowan, T. (1681). *Ars sciendi, sin logica.* London.

Hamilton, W. (1868). *Lectures on metaphysics and logic* (Vols. 1–4). Edinburgh: Blackwell.

Kristic, K. (1964). Marko Marulic. The author of the term "psychology." *Acta Instituti Psychologici Universitatis Zagabriensis, 28,* 7–17, 35–48.

Lapointe, F. H. (1970). Origin and evolution of the term "psychology." *American Psychologist, 25,* 640–646.

Lapointe, F. H. (1972). Who originated the term "psychology?" *Journal of the History of the Behavioral Sciences, 8,* 328–335.

Neuhaus, E. (1635). *Theatrum ingenii humani siue de cognoscenda hominum indole et secretis animi moribus.* Amsterdam: Jansson.

Rauch, F. G. (1840). *Psychology; or a view of the human soul; including anthropology.* New York: Dodd.

Roback, A. A. (1961). *History of psychology and psychiatry.* New York: Philosophical Library.

Schmucker, S. (1842). *Psychology, elements of a new system of mental philosophy on the basis of consciousness and common sense.* New York: Harper.

Taillepied, N. (1588). *Psichologie ou traité de l'apparition des esprits.* Paris: Bichon.

Tijan, P. (1967). Marulik, Marko. *New Catholic Encyclopedia.* New York: McGraw Hill.

Tortelli (1471). *Orthographia.* Venice: Jensen.

Wolff, C. (1732). *Psychologia empirica.* Frankfurt: Renger.

Wolff, C. (1734). *Psychologia rationalis.* Frankfurt: Renger.

Christian Thomasius:
A Man Ahead of His Time

Paul McReynolds

In the course of events it occasionally happens that a solitary genius comes up with an idea that is so far ahead of its time that not only is the idea not accepted, but is hardly even noticed by people of the period. Then decades, or even centuries later, the idea is discovered—or rediscovered—with considerable excitement and acclaim. A classic example of this sequence is found in the third century B.C. when Aristarchos of Samos said that the Earth revolved around the sun, rather than the reverse, as believed by everyone else until Copernicus set the matter straight some 1700 years later. Something of this sort, though on a less dramatic scale, can be said to have occurred in psychology with respect to the thought of Christian Thomasius (1655–1728) in the latter 17th century. Thomasius' thinking may be directly linked to contemporary advances in personology.

The foresightful idea that Thomasius had was that individual differences in personality traits might be represented quantitatively; that is, by numbers on scales (McReynolds & Ludwig, 1984, 1987). Not only did he generate this insight, he also proposed specific rating scales and collected quantitative data on actual individuals. This latter point is important because it is, of course, one thing to have an innovative idea in a nascent sense and quite another to actually implement that idea. So far as can be ascertained, Thomasius was the first person in history to develop—and apply—personality rating scales, and in so doing he was also the first to gather quantitative psychological data on subjects. While it is remotely conceivable that Pythagoras, Galen, or some figure from antiquity may have preceded Thomasius in this empirical approach, no such record survives. And it is clear that prior to Thomasius (and for a long time thereafter) the pri-

mary trend in speculating about human behavior was to develop broad explanatory conceptions, such as the theory of humors, but without attempting to apply such notions by actually measuring psychological variables in real people. It is against

Figure 1 Christian Thomasius.

19

this long prescientific tradition that Thomasius' solitary contribution stands out.

Before examining the psychological contributions of Thomasius in more detail, the following will provide a brief look at the man, his career, and his times (Tonelli, 1967; White, 1919). Thomasius was born on January 1, 1655, in Leipzig, which was in the principality of Saxony, a unit of the Holy Roman Empire. The devastating Thirty Years War was only seven years in the past. Germany was not then a united nation but was made up of numerous, largely autonomous political units, interrelated in an intricate system of interlocking and overlapping authorities. Closely associated with the complex political rivalries was a pattern of intense religious conflicts involving the Lutheran, Calvinist, and Roman Catholic faiths.

The popular culture in which the young Thomasius matured was characterized by widespread superstition and intolerance. The identification and execution of alleged witches was commonplace, and the use of torture in the judicial system was not unusual. The winds of the Enlightenment reached the German states later than the nations to the west, and Thomasius himself was destined to be a leading figure in the evolving German Enlightenment (Beck, 1969).

Thomasius was educated at the University of Leipzig, where his father was a professor, and at Frankfurt on the Oder, in Brandenburg. During this period the general academic orientation was toward the past, and lectures were, by tradition, delivered in Latin. Thomasius concentrated on philosophy and law and began teaching at Leipzig in 1682. As he matured he was deeply influenced by the teachings of Samuel von Pufendorf (1632–1694), who espoused an empirical approach to jurisprudence based on reason rather than revelation. Thomasius thus came to believe that philosophy should be practical and directed toward human needs and that knowledge should be based on direct observation.

Thomasius was a highly vocal leader in the effort to combat the widespread persecution of alleged heretics and witches. Because of his outspoken nature and his defense of unpopular causes such as the right of Lutherans and Calvinists to marry each other, he became increasingly unpopular at Leipzig. This opposition reached a crescendo in 1688 when he announced that he would lecture in German rather than Latin. In 1690 Thomasius was forbidden to publish or lecture, and in order to avoid arrest he fled to Berlin. He later received an appointment by

the Elector Friedrich III to the faculty of the Ritter Academie in Halle. In 1694, when this institution was converted to the University of Halle, Thomasius became its rector, a position he held until his death in 1728.

As a person Thomasius was intellectually brilliant, brash, and strong-willed. Largely devoid of modesty, he believed dogmatically in the rightness of his own opinions. In the highly contentious culture in which he lived, he was a polemicist of no little skill and was said to have certain eccentricities, such as sometimes wearing a sword while he lectured. Thomasius was a prolific author, writing mainly in the areas of jurisprudence, logic, and ethics. Among his more influential books were *Introduction to Logic* (1691) and *Practical Ethics* (1696). His specific works on psychological assessment were not part of his major corpus; however, they reflect the same interest in observation and practical affairs.

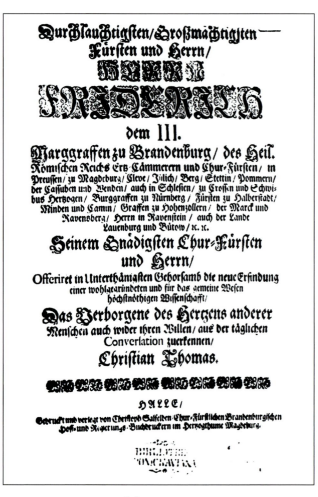

Figure 2 Cover page of Thomasius' *New Discovery* (1691).

On December 31, 1691—the day before his 37th birthday—Thomasius published a short tract, consisting of 11 double-columned pages, with the intriguing title *New Discovery of a Solid Science, Most Necessary for the Community, for Discerning the Secrets of the Heart of Other Men from Daily Conversation, Even Against Their Will* (1691). This paper, which can be referred to as *New Discovery*, was published in the form of a letter to Friedrich III but was distributed among various intellectuals, as was the custom. As implied by the title, Thomasius asserted in the tract that he had developed a scientific technique for determining the nature of persons. Although few details of the technique were revealed, Thomasius did say that he had frequently demonstrated the accuracy of his method.

Thomasius' proposal was severely criticized in the March 1692 issue of Wilhelm Tentzel's monthly journal. Partly in response to this deprecatory review, Thomasius published a book-length account of his assessment system in September of the same year; this was titled *Further Elucidation by Different Examples of the Recent Proposal for a New Science for Discerning the Nature of Other Men's Minds* (1692). Though much of this book is defensive and polemical, it also includes a detailed description of his assessment system, particularly in its fifth chapter.

Thomasius posited four major personality tendencies, or dimensions. These were *rational love, sensuousness, social ambition,* and *acquisitiveness.* All human inclinations arise from these four, or from combinations of them, with one of the four always dominant in a person. Individuals differ with respect to which of the four traits is dominant and also with respect to the characteristic proportions of the other three. Rational love is close to what we now call altruism. The remaining three tendencies refer to different kinds of self-interest: Sensuousness concerns sensory pleasures, including sex and good food; social ambition concerns seeking recognition, the approbation of others; and acquisitiveness is the tendency to obtain and keep valuable things. In a negative sense the latter three inclinations could be thought of as lust, ostentatiousness, and greed.

Thomasius' postulation of four basic traits was not original; indeed, such a quadripartite notion goes back to classical times in the theory of the humors and was commonplace in Thomasius' time. The noteworthy feature of Thomasius' taxonomy was its motivational emphasis—thus, his four traits have the flavor of inclinations or needs, rather than of simple descriptive categories such as sanguine or

Figure 3 Cover page of Thomasius' *Further Elucidations* (1692).

melancholic. The truly unique feature of his system, however, was that he proposed that each of the four traits could be conceived as dimensions, and he assigned numerical values to show their relative strengths in given individuals, so as to facilitate comparisons between different people.

The assessment method devised by Thomasius involved two steps: first, he obtained all the information he could on an individual; secondly, he rated that person on each of the four inclinations. His principal means of gaining personal information was to engage the subject in extended casual conversation, without the person knowing that he was being evaluated. He also utilized all other kinds of data—occupational, educational, and the like—that were available. In making his ratings Thomasius devised and utilized a 60-point scale. Since he typically utilized 5-point intervals, beginning with 5, this amounted, in effect, to a 12-point scale.

Table 1 shows the values assigned to each variable by Thomasius on four persons. Note that the

Table 1 Thomasius' Ratings of Four Subjects

Example 1		Example 2		Example 3		Example 4	
Sensuousness	60	Acquisitiveness	60	Sensuousness	60	Acquisitiveness	60
Acquisitiveness	55	Sensuousness	55	Acquisitiveness	55	Sensuousness	45–50
Social ambition	10	Social ambition	20	Social ambition	20	Social ambition	20–25
Rational love	5	Rational love	5	Rational love	5	Rational love	5

Table 2 Thomasius' Data on Interrater Reliability

	Thomasius	Rater A	Rater B
Sensuousness	60	60 or 55	60
Acquisitiveness	55	55 or 60	40
Social ambition	20	15	20
Rational love	5	5	5

Note: The table presents the independent ratings by Thomasius and two associates of the same individual, known to all three.

dominant trait is placed first, and that Rational Love is lowest in all four. It was Thomasius' custom to assign the dominant dimension a value of 60 degrees, and the weakest dimension a value of 5. For each of the cases reported in *Further Elucidation* Thomasius provided a detailed personality description. He also used the relative values to compare individuals. His stated purpose in developing his quantitative system was to make personality judgments more objective. He taught his students to use his system and cautioned against rater biases. He was also aware of the importance of rater reliability. On one case (Example 3 in Table 1) he asked two associates, who also knew the subject well, to rate him independently. The three sets of ratings are shown in Table 2. It may be noted that they agree quite well.

Thomasius' approach to the scientific understanding of the individual personality was an integral part of his broader interest in making knowledge objective and useful. Among the earlier psychological writers who may have influenced him were Pierre Charron, Marin de La Chambre, Baltasar Gracian, and Juan Huarte. His idea of numerical scales marking off human traits in degrees may have been suggested— though this is conjectural—by an analogy with expansion-type thermometers. Though such instruments had not yet come into general use in Thomasius' time, they did exist. As for his choice of a 60-point scale, this may (again, mere speculation) have been adapted by analogy with measures of time.

Whatever its antecedents, Thomasius' venture into quantitative psychology was a strikingly original and highly prescient achievement. Though

derided by some of his contemporaries, others found it of interest. Thomasius briefly discussed his system further in 1696 in his *Practical Ethics*, and *Further Elucidations* went through at least four editions. Nevertheless, the influence of Thomasius' quantitative system on the development of psychology was extremely minimal, if not entirely absent. The basic reason for this is that the system was so alien to the speculative psychology of the time that it could not be meaningfully assimilated into that psychology. Thus it was that the use of rating scales as a standard method had to await the time of Francis Galton (1880) nearly two centuries later.

Bibliography

Beck, L. W. (1969). *Early German philosophy: Kant and his predecessors.* Cambridge: Harvard University Press.

Galton, F. C. (1880). Statistics of mental imagery. *Mind, 5,* 301–318.

McReynolds, P., & Ludwig, K. (1984). Christian Thomasius and the origin of psychological rating scales. *Isis, 75,* 546–553.

McReynolds, P., & Ludwig, K. (1987). On the history of rating scales. *Personality and Individual Differences, 8,* 281–283.

Thomasius, C. (1691). *Einleitung zu der Vernunfft-Lehre.* Halle: C. Salfeld.

Thomasius, C. (1691). *Die neue Erfindung einer wohlgegründeten und für das gemeine Wesen höchstnöthigen Wissenschaft das Verborgene des Herzens anderer Menschen auch wider ihren Willen aus der täglichen Conversation zu erkennen.* Halle: C. Salfeld.

Thomasius, C. (1692). *Weitere Erleuterung durch unterschiedene Exempel des ohnelängst gethanen Vorschlags wegen der neuen Wissenschaft anderer Menschen Gemüther erkennen zu lernen.* Halle: C. Salfeld.

Thomasius, C. (1696). *Ausübung der Sitten-Lehre.* Halle: C. Salfeld.

Tonelli, G. (1967). Thomasius, Christian. In P. Edwards (Ed.), *The encyclopedia of philosophy* (Vol. 8, pp. 116–118). New York: Macmillan.

White, A. D. (1919). *Seven great statesmen in the warfare of humanity with unreason.* New York: Century.

The Witchcraze in 17th-Century Europe

Charles W. Clark

Between 1450 and 1750 over 200,000 people in Europe were accused of the crime of witchcraft, and at least 100,000 of them were executed. Of those executed, approximately 80% to 85% were women. The middle of the 17th century was when the "witchcraze" reached its peak, especially in the German territories, Switzerland, Scotland, and France. The nature and source of the beliefs that led to the trials and executions, the reasons for the outbreak of the violent persecutions at this particular time, the characteristics of the victims and the accusers, and the motives for the cessation of the trials have all been subject to significant scholarly inquiry and debate since the time of the events themselves. While many details remain to be examined, the broad outlines have become clearer in recent years. In order to understand the nature of witchcraft as it was understood by early modern Europeans and its modern interpreters, a rather typical trial is instructive.

In 1587 Walpurga Häusmannin, a poor widow and midwife ("[a] malefic and miserable woman"), was tried, convicted, and executed for being a witch. "Broadsides," or publications depicting the trials of witches, as seen in Figures 1 and 2, were often published by witchhunters in towns near the ones where the trials took place to warn the inhabitants of the dangers of practicing witchcraft. Walpurga's trial could have been published as a similar warning. During her trial, the evidence was written down by the authorities of the town of Dillingen and she confessed, under torture, to a number of crimes. She confessed that she had seduced a man who, instead of appearing at her home to "indulge in lustful intercourse," was replaced by the Evil One (the Devil) in the disguise of the man in question. For several nights she had intercourse with the Evil One during which times she "surrendered body and soul"

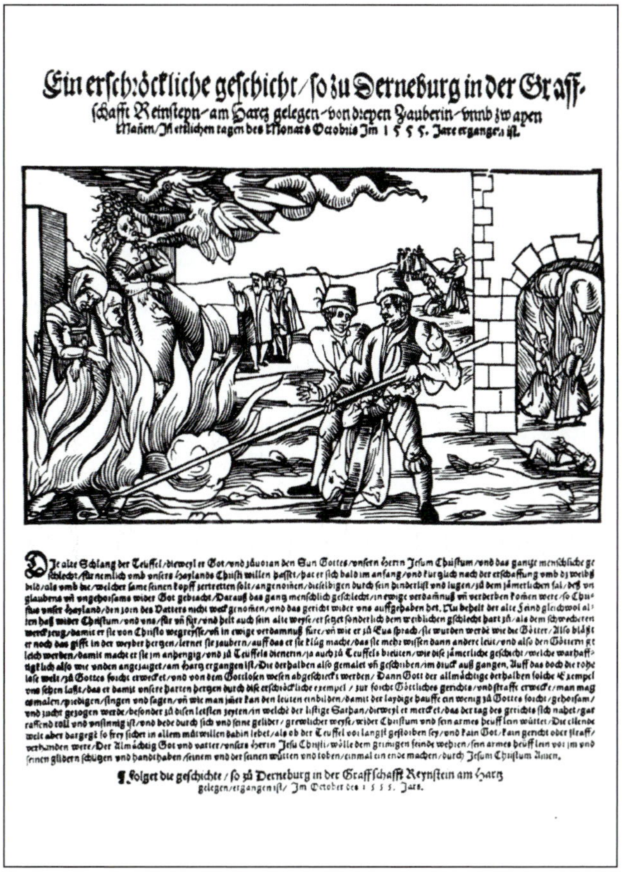

![Figure 1 broadside]

Figure 1 Broadside newsletter about the public burning and execution of three witches (Germany, 1555).

(Figure 3). Finally, after scratching her across the shoulder, he made her sign a paper selling her soul to him (Figure 4).

Later, she said, she traveled on a pitchfork by night to a gathering where she worshipped the Great Devil and renounced her Christian faith (Figures 5 and 6). She was baptized with a new name, Federlin, by the Devil (Figure 7).

Figure 2 Newsletter about the infernal deeds and execution of the witch Anna Eberlehrin (Germany, 1669).

Figure 3 The Devil making love to a witch (Germany, 1489).

At other gatherings, she engaged in sexual intercourse with the Devil, ate a good roast or a baby, and profaned the holy wafers. She testified she was given a salve with which she could harm people, animals, and even crops. She was ordered to kill babies, and she confessed to murdering over 40. A detailed confession of how she killed a number of the children, usually with the salve, followed. She confessed, also, to touching a woman on the arm who, ever since, suffered pain in that area. She said she helped a man with a cart and touched him on his head so that he was near death at the time of the trial. Other confessions followed that she had killed cows and horses, and dug up and eaten babies and used their bones to make hail (Figure 8).

After her confession, the town judge and jury, by the authority of the Bishop of Augsburg, and under the aegis of Emperor Charles V's Common Law and Criminal Code, convicted her and ordered that she be burned at the stake and her ashes thrown into the river. Her goods were to be given over to the "Treasury of the Most High Lord." Before that sen-

tence, however, she was to be torn by red-hot pincers five times, and because she used her right hand in her profession of midwife, it was to be cut off prior to execution.

Walpurga's case illustrates most of the common features of witchcraft trials and raises significant issues for scholars of the period. By examining the details of the case, the major historical explanations concerning witchcraft will become evident. According to one scholar, there are over 40 explanatory models which deserve attention (Quaife, 1987, p. 5).

A number of historians of psychology and psychiatry have studied the mental state of the witch. Among those were the pioneering efforts of G. Zilboorg and others (Zilboorg, 1939; Zilboorg and Henry, 1941). In the case of Walpurga, her bizarre confession appears to be grounds for assuming a pathological state. Zilboorg believed that her case and that of thousands of others really represented an increase in mental illness in the 16th and 17th centuries.

Zilboorg had argued that the *Malleus Malefi-*

carum, the "Hammer of Witches," a textbook written in the 1480s and published in 1486 by two Dominican friars, Johann Sprenger and Heinrich Kramer (Institoris), represented a series of "case studies" of psychopathology. "In brief," he said, "the *Malleus Maleficarum* might with a little editing serve as an excellent modern textbook of descriptive clinical psychiatry of the 15th century, if the word *witch* were substituted by the word *patient*, and the devil eliminated" (Zilboorg, 1939, p. 58). The accused, as discussed in the book, were in fact either hysterics or schizophrenics mistakenly diagnosed as witches because of the prevailing demonological interpretation of abnormal behavior used by theologians and physicians. For Zilboorg, it was Johann Weyer, the author of *De Praestigiis Daemonum* (On the Trickery of Demons) (1583/1991), who was the real founder of "modern psychiatry" because he attacked the demonologists' notion of the causes of witchcraft and sought "natural causes" (usually "melancholy") for the actions of the accused old women (Zilboorg & Henry, 1941, p. 213).

Zilboorg's simplistic notions and those of others seeking exclusive psychiatric or psychopathological explanations have been challenged recently in the works of Rosen (1962), Schoeneman (1977), and Spanos (1978) among others. Schoeneman argues that the studies by Zilboorg, as well as the view found in Alexander and Selesnick's *History of Psychiatry* (1966)—which have been cited in various other histories of psychiatry— seriously distort the realities of witchcraft in the 16th and 17th centuries (Schoeneman, 1977, p. 349). According to Schoeneman, the evidence indicates that most of the alleged witches appeared normal, as did Walpurga prior to her torture. Some of the witches that Weyer said were suffering from "melancholy" were probably undergoing menopause or suffering from senility. In any case, critics argue, the treatment of the mentally ill had a long history before the witch trials and was not altered significantly by the witch trials. Contemporaries had little trouble separating the mentally ill from the witches (Quaife, 1987, p. 205).

While the psychopathological explanations of witchcraft are not sufficient to explain the phenomenon, other avenues of investigation have proven more enlightening. Examination of the accusations against Walpurga reveals a belief structure of the early modern Europeans that leads to a better understanding of the function of a witch in society. The accusations against Walpurga fit into two general categories: performing supernaturally caused evil deeds or *maleficia*, such as killing babies or cattle or causing hail, and signing a "pact" with the Devil to give her the power to do her evil deeds. One or both of these charges were typical of most of the trials—although those where torture was not used, especially in England, seldom raised the issue

Figure 4 Satan applying his claw mark to an apprentice sorcerer (Italy, 1626).

of the Devil's pact. Norman Cohn has shown that the combination of peasant beliefs in magic and elite beliefs in heresy fused in the 14th century to create the stereotype of the witch as a tool used by the Devil to overturn Christian society. He also has described the popular belief that the Devil was becoming more active during these centuries and recruiting minions to use diabolical magic to help his cause (Cohn, 1975, pp. 164–205).

The belief that certain people had the power to perform magic is as old as humanity, and certainly people who claimed to have those powers, ("cunning men or women," "wise women," etc.) appeared

Figure 5 Demons riding to the Sabbath on a pitchfork (Germany, 1489).

Figure 6 Witches concocting an ointment to be used for flying to the Sabbath (Germany, 1514).

in every village in Europe. Studies by Keith Thomas and Alan MacFarlane using anthropological methodology have focused on the functionalism of magical beliefs in early modern English society (Thomas, 1971; MacFarlane, 1970), and Richard Horsley argued that belief in magical powers residing in an old village woman might have actually protected her from more powerful neighbors (Horsley, 1979a, p. 92; Monter, 1976, p. 124). When unexplainable misfortune struck an individual or a community, the magical powers of the witch could easily be blamed, and she served as a scapegoat for the entire population. That may explain the process, but why did the numbers of trials increase when they did? According to Thomas and MacFarlane, what changed the status quo was a combination of religious and economic factors. The pressures of the Protestant Reformation in England removed the local Catholic priest as a source of "counter-magic," and reformers urged passive resistance to maleficium. The Protestant insistence on self-help removed the incentive for charity to neighbors and made the poor special targets of accusation when the guilt of the former giver was

transferred to anger toward the beggar at the door (Thomas, 1971, pp. 477–501). Obviously this explanation does not fit Catholic countries or take into account complex economic situations in many areas.

Walpurga fits many other features of the stereotype of the witches who were tried all over Europe (and in the American colonies as well). She was old, poor, widowed, and a midwife. Most of the accused were over forty, and many over fifty. They were generally poor, not the poorest in society, but often poorer than their accusers (see Monter, 1976, pp. 115–126; Midelfort, 1972, pp. 164–190; Levack, 1987, pp. 123–138). Widows made up over half of all of the accused about whom we have records. Finally, she was a midwife, and while a number of scholars have noted that the profession was an especially vulnerable one because of the large number of infant deaths in this period (often as high as one in six), recent works have challenged the notion of the midwife witch. David Harley (1990) finds that the evidence is based on credulous historians who have taken questionable records as fact. Lyndal Roper (1994) argues it was more likely the "lying-in" nurses who had access to babies for a longer period than did the midwives and who were, therefore, prone to accusations of child murder. Further, she stresses the accusations of women by women as part of a pattern of envy and fear of the postmenopausal infertile woman by the vulnerable new mother who was externalizing her postnatal depression.

Walpurga was a woman as well as a midwife, and gender issues have come to the forefront in many recent studies. Quaife has neatly summarized the most popular arguments in his work although he argues that it was the vulnerability of the woman rather than merely her gender that led to witchcraft accusations (Quaife, 1987, pp. 79–112). Other scholars insist that the increase in trials was a result of the rise of virulent misogyny and that its expression through sexual violence against women was spread in part by Protestant reformers, who viewed single women not under the control of a male as particularly dangerous and as sexual servants of the Devil (Klaits, 1985, pp. 48–59; Hester, 1992, pp. 144–155, 198–201; Muchembled, 1990, p. 151).

Walpurga became a sexual servant of the Devil especially after he convinced her to fly to a "devilish meeting" where she met with other witches to feast, to revel, to worship him, and to desecrate the holy sacraments. While some scholars, such as Zilboorg mentioned above, have seen this as evidence of the witch's deranged mental state, others have concentrated on the features of these meetings, or sabbat(h)s, as they usually are called, and their origins in the folk beliefs of Europeans. Norman Cohn argued that "left to themselves, the peasants would never have created mass witch-hunts—these occurred only where and when authorities had become convinced of the reality of the sabbat and of nocturnal flights to the sabbat" (Cohn, 1975, p. 252). He further notes, as most scholars accept, that no such meetings ever took place and there is no evidence whatsoever for a society of witches that met anywhere (Cohn, 1975, pp. 99–125).

Carlo Ginzburg has studied the folkloric origins of the sabbat throughout Europe, finding its roots in beliefs that have spread from as far away as central Asia. The beliefs in night-flying, shape-shifting, can-

nibalistic feasts, and the like were common among Europeans, and these provided the repertoire upon which the accused, especially under torture, could draw to confess (Ginzburg, 1991). On the other hand, as most scholars agree, the anti-Christian activities attested to at the sabbat were also the product of leading questions supplied by the clerical elite from their manuals. These guides were also used by lay authorities when questioning the suspects. Only someone sufficiently versed in Catholic

Figure 7 Satan rebaptizing a young sorcerer (Italy, 1626).

dogma and practice—probably not an ignorant peasant woman—could have described the desecration in such precise and offensive terms.

The problem of how so many witches could assemble in the anti-Christian conspiracy of the sabbat was solved by the contemporary elite notion of flying by diabolical aid, but the process of flying was still a problem. In Walpurga's case, other than the reference to the pitchfork as a means of conveyance, the mechanism is not discussed. In many other trials, however, the rubbing of ointments on the witch's body or the conveyance (often a broomstick, butter churn, or some kind of animal) has led modern researchers to conclude that atropines or hallucinogenic substances causing visions might be involved (Harner, 1973; Ginzburg, 1991, pp. 303–304).

Research suggests that many substances frequently mentioned in the confessions of accused

Figure 8 Witches brewing up a hailstorm (Germany, 1489).

Infanticide, abortion, illegitimate births, sexual misconduct, adultery, and other crimes attributed to women were singled out for special prosecution as society cracked down on women's behavior. Finally, the introduction of "spectral evidence" or deeds committed by the "spirit" of the accused who need not be physically present at the scene of the crime meant that no one could produce an alibi, even if witnesses saw the defendant elsewhere at the time (Levack, 1987, pp. 63–92; Larner, 1978, pp. 35–67).

The new legal methods led to panics in many parts of Europe as more and more names came out under torture. In some villages, only a few women were left after the trials. After reaching a peak in the middle of the 17th century in most parts of Europe, the numbers of trials and executions began to drop. Why the witchcraze ended has been the subject of as much debate as its beginning. Many scholars point to the new skepticism of the judges and contemporary observers, like the Jesuit confessor Fredrich von Spee (1631). He argued that torture does not reveal truth; the accused confesses to avoid further pain (trans. in Kors and Peters, 1972, pp. 351–357). A skeptical judge of the Spanish Inquisition, Father Alonso Salazar, conducted an experiment in 1611 to test the validity of confessed witches' accounts of the sabbat. He took the witches to the site, one by one, and questioned them on who was there, where the Devil sat, what they ate, and so on. The accounts each gave were contradictory on almost every point. His conclusion was that no proof existed that any witchcraft activity had taken place at all (Klaits, 1985, pp. 168–169).

Legal procedures changed, too, in the late 17th century: Conviction required solid proof of maleficia, torture procedures were restricted, and new governmental statutes restricted prosecutions or hunting for witches. Modern scholars point out also that when the trials became numerous in one area, the stereotype of the witch broke down as younger women were tried as were more men, and even children. Further, the prosecutions moved up the social scale as more prosperous citizens were accused. Even contemporaries noted that if one could not identify a witch with any certainty, then anyone or everyone could be tried (Levack, 1987, pp. 212–217; Klaits, 1985, pp. 163–165).

A number of scholars have traced the end of the witch hunts to a new and more critical attitude among the elite—those who had begun the trials in the first place. Old dogmatic ways of thinking were replaced by general skepticism or doubt as evi-

witches—whether taken orally or absorbed through the skin—might actually cause sensations of flying as well as of sexual pleasure. Real experiences or not, the authorities were sufficiently persuaded of the threat to Christendom to put thousands of old women on trial.

The accused, such as Walpurga, frequently were tried in secular courts, and scholars have found that the changing nature of law and the legal procedures also influenced the increase in the number of trials in the 17th century. Statutes and procedures based on Roman law, with its more abstract notion of crimes against the state rather than an individual, replaced the older laws. Secular courts took over more and more of the cases from Inquisitional courts. Legal procedures changed to allow the use of torture to extract evidence on the grounds that the nature of the crime was especially heinous and the belief that one could not lie with the application of pain. Courts allowed testimony from children and women for the first time. Women themselves began to be held accountable under the law for their deeds; whereas, previously, men often were held responsible for their wives' or daughters' activities.

denced by men such as Descartes and Montaigne. It was the latter who said, "After all, it is putting a very high price on one's conjectures to have a man roasted alive because of them" (quoted in Klaits, 1985, p. 165). Central governments, too, became more concerned about "hot" religious passions and their potential for disorder, so they discouraged more active forms of witch hunting. Among the religious reformers themselves, a re-reading of the New Testament convinced many that Christ's power was so superior to that of the Devil that no one had anything to fear. Less religious folks found skepticism more popular, and it became less fashionable among that group to believe in anything to do with the supernatural. Only the ignorant peasants, they said, could believe in the reality of witches. Besides, the universe, according to the new scientists, operates by fixed laws, leaving no room for the magical or the miraculous (Levack, 1987, pp. 217–227; Klaits, 1985, pp. 170–172). Finally, the attitude toward women was changing, making them less likely candidates for the Devil's purposes. Christian theologians and moralists argued that both men and women had sexual desires and that they were neutral and normal for humans. On the other hand, some believed that women were, in fact, asexual, and were more immune to sexual temptation than were men. By denying women's sexuality, these men made it impossible to believe that any woman would be enticed by the Devil into a diabolical sexual union. Woman as passive, woman as morally superior, woman as the image of the ideal replaced the older notion of the lustful, out-of-control creature who needed a man to keep her in place (Klaits, 1985, pp. 172–173; Merchant, 1980, pp. 149–163).

The majority of trials were over by 1700 in most areas of Europe and the Americas, but witchcraft beliefs continued, especially among the peasant classes, for a long time after the authorities decided not to prosecute. In spite of the changing attitudes of the elite classes, those beliefs have lasted in many places even until today.

Bibliography

Alexander, F. G., & Selesnick, S. T. (1966). *The history of psychiatry.* New York: Harper & Row.

Cohn, N. (1975). *Europe's inner demons.* New York: New American Library.

Ginzburg, C. (1985). *The night battles: Witchcraft and agrarian cults in the sixteenth and seventeenth centuries* (J. Tedeschi & A. Tedeschi, Trans.). New York: Viking Penguin.

Ginzburg, C. (1991). *Ecstasies: Deciphering the witches' sabbath.* (R. Rosenthal, Trans.). New York: Pantheon Books.

Harley, D. (1990). Historians as demonologists: The myth of the midwife-witch. *The Social History of Medicine, 3,* 1–26.

Harner, M. J. (1973). The role of hallucinogenic plants in European witchcraft. In M. J. Harner (Ed.), *Hallucinogens and Shamanism.* New York: Oxford University Press.

Hester, M. (1992). *Lewd women and wicked witches: A study of the dynamics of male domination.* London: Routledge.

Horsley, R. (1979a). Further reflections on witchcraft and European folklore. *History of Religions, 19,* 71–95.

Horsley, R. A. (1979b). Who were the witches? The social roles of the accused in European witch trials. *Journal of Interdisciplinary History, 9,* 689–715.

Kieckhefer, R. (1976). *European witch trials: Their foundations in popular and learned cultures, 1300–1500.* Berkeley: University of California Press.

Klaits, J. (1985). *Servants of satan: The age of the witch hunts.* Bloomington: Indiana University Press.

Kors, A., & Peters, E. (Eds.). (1972). *Witchcraft in Europe, 1100–1700: A documentary history.* Philadelphia: University of Pennsylvania Press.

Larner, C. (1984). *Witchcraft and religion.* Oxford: Basil Blackwell.

Levack, B. P. (1987). *The witch-hunt in early modern Europe.* New York: Longman.

MacFarlane, A. (1970). *Witchcraft in Tudor and Stuart England: A regional and comparative study.* New York: Harper and Row.

Merchant, C. (1980). *The death of nature: Women, ecology, and the scientific revolution.* San Francisco: Harper and Row Publishers.

Midelfort, H. C. E. (1972). *Witch hunting in southwestern Germany, 1562–1684: The social and intellectual foundations.* Stanford: Stanford University Press.

Monter, E. W. (Ed.). (1969). *European witchcraft.* New York: John Wiley and Sons.

Monter, E. W. (1976). *Witchcraft in France and Switzerland.* Ithaca: Cornell University Press.

Muchembled, R. (1990). Satanic myths and cultural reality. In B. Ankarloo & G. Henningsen (Eds.), *Early modern witchcraft: Centres and peripheries.* New York: Oxford University Press.

Quaife, G. R. (1987). *Godly zeal and furious rage: The witch in early modern Europe.* New York: St. Martin's Press.

Roper, L. (1994). *Oedipus and the devil: Witchcraft, sexuality, and religion in early modern Europe.* London: Routledge.

Rosen, G. (1962). Psychopathology in the social process: Dance frenzies, demonic possession, revival movements and similar so-called psychic epidemics; An interpretation. *Bulletin of the History of Medicine, 36,* 13–44.

Schoeneman, T. J. (1977). The role of mental illness in the European witch hunts of the sixteenth and seventeenth centuries: An assessment. *Journal of the History of the Behavioral Sciences, 13,* 337–351.

Spanos, N. P. (1978). Witchcraft in histories of psychiatry: A critical analysis and an alternative conceptualization. *Psychological Bulletin, 85,* 417–439.

Thomas, K. (1971). *Religion and the decline of magic.* New York: Charles Scribner's Sons.

Weyer, J. (1991). *De praestigiis daemonum* (J. Shea, Trans.). In G. Mora & B. Kohl (Eds.), *Witches, devils, and doctors in the Renaissance: Johann Weyer, De praestigiis daemonum* (Vol. 73). Binghamton, NY: Medieval and Renaissance Texts and Studies. (Original work published 1563)

Zilboorg, G. (1939). *The medical man and the witch during the Renaissance.* New York: Cooper Square Publishers.

Zilboorg, G., & Henry, G. W. (1941). *A history of medical psychology.* New York: Norton.

Physiognomy, Phrenology, and Non-Verbal Communication

Jürgen Jahnke

Systematic attempts to explain mental traits, personal characteristics and emotional states from the facial features, body structure, and habitual patterns of posture and movement can be traced back to antiquity. The most important early treatise in the field is the book *Physiognomonica*, which has been traced to the Aristotelian traditions of the fourth century B.C. (Degkwitz, 1988). This work contains detailed descriptions of the basic methodology of physiognomy. For example, it recommends that physiognomic analysis should always begin with the delineation of distinct, external features of the body (i.e., skin, hair, and flesh texture) and then relate these characteristics to specific personality types (i.e., hero, coward, dunce, prude, or scold). The physiognomical diagnosis of the Aristotelian school was very similar to the method of character description and analysis proposed by Theophrastus (372–287 B.C.). For example, the "meek" or "peaceful" character was described in physical terms as an individual "of healthy appearance" who is "tall, fleshy," and "well proportioned." In addition, he has "straight posture" and " a receding hairline" (Degkwitz, 1988, p. 24). Classical physiognomy also used differences in external, physical appearance to make predictions about the behavioral potentials of men and women, of various national and ethnic groups, and even of different animal species.

During the Middle Ages, the principles and methods of physiognomy received further elaboration through the accretion of mystical and astrological theories and speculations. In the Renaissance, the Italian natural philosopher, Giovanni Battista della Porta (1535–1615), strongly influenced early modern physiognomy by his encyclopedic text, *De humana*

physiognomonia (1586). He critically summarized the older works in the field and organized them into a handbook of body morphology. Unfortunately, his striking and much reprinted illustrations of similari-

Figure 1 Title page of della Porta's chief work with physiognomies of humans and animals (1586).

Figure 2 Silhouette portraits of Lavater and his family.

ties between animals and humans attracted far more attention than his methodological contributions to the field.

The search for valid, empirical relationships between the human body and the human mind became reactivated in Europe during the 18th century. In particular, the topic of physiognomy was hotly debated among scholars and the lay public after the publication of the *Essays on Physiognomy Designated to Promote the Knowledge and Love of Mankind* (1775–1778) by the Swiss minister Johann Caspar Lavater (1741–1801).

Figure 2 illustrates facial similarities between parents and children with examples from Lavater's own family:

Father, mother, son and daughter [are shown]. The transition from the tip of the nose to the mouth is indistinct in the father. Not the father's but the mother's odd forehead was transmitted to son and daughter. Both [children] have the mother's blue eyes with a touch of the father's liveliness, like their four deceased siblings. In particular, the mother's weak but highly curved eyebrows were inherited by the children. The children inherited the strong structure of their bones and the fiery spirit from their father and the calm, softness and gentleness from the mother. Both parents transmitted their nervous sensitivity. Since both father and mother have

slightly protruding upper lips, the children have similar protruding upper lips.

According to Lavater (1789):

. . . physiognomy is as capable of becoming as [good] a science as any of the sciences, mathematics, of course, excepted. As capable as experimental philosophy for it is experimental philosophy; as capable as physics, for it is a part of physical art; as capable as theology, for it is theology; as capable as belles lettres, for it appertains to belles lettres. Like all these, it may to a certain extent be reduced to rule, and acquire an appropriate character, by which it may be taught. As in every other science, so in this, much must be left to sensibility and genius. At present [physiognomy] is deficient in determinate signs and rules. (Vol.1, p. 37)

Another example of Lavater's didactic approach to physiognomy is shown in Figure 3. This illustration from the German edition of the *Essays* (1775–1778, Vol.1) shows the profiles of "6 orphan boys," whose "personalities, talents, aptitudes, strength," and "general outlook on life" were known to Lavater from his personal contact with them. Lavater posed 16 questions about the young orphans, which his readers were to answer on the basis of their physiognomic skills, and printed the "correct" answers on the next page in a style reminiscent of a programmed textbook.

Question 1	"Is there a stupid [person] or one with a weak mind among the profiles?" ("All boys are intelligent and have good abilities.")
Question 2	"Who is the most intelligent?" (6 "judging from his nose.")
Question 3	"Who is the most sensitive?" (1 or 3)
Question 4	"Who is the quickest?" (3)
Question 5	"Who is the slowest?" (1 "This is a hard one, even for me.")
Question 6	"Who is the most elegant?" (3)
Question 7	"Who has the most honest face?" (1 and 5 "are in competition.")
Question 8	"Who is the most suited for education?" (3)
Question 9	"Who has the best sense of humor?" (2)
Question 10	"Who is the quietest?" ("1 and 5 are again in competition.")
Question 11	"Who has the strongest character?" (4 and 5)
Question 12	"Who can be influenced most?" (2, 3, and 6)
Question 13	"Who is the wittiest?" (2 and "even more" 3)
Question 14	"Who is most orderly and industrious?" (5)
Question 15	"Who is the most decisive?" (4)
Question 16	"Who is the most talented?" (5)

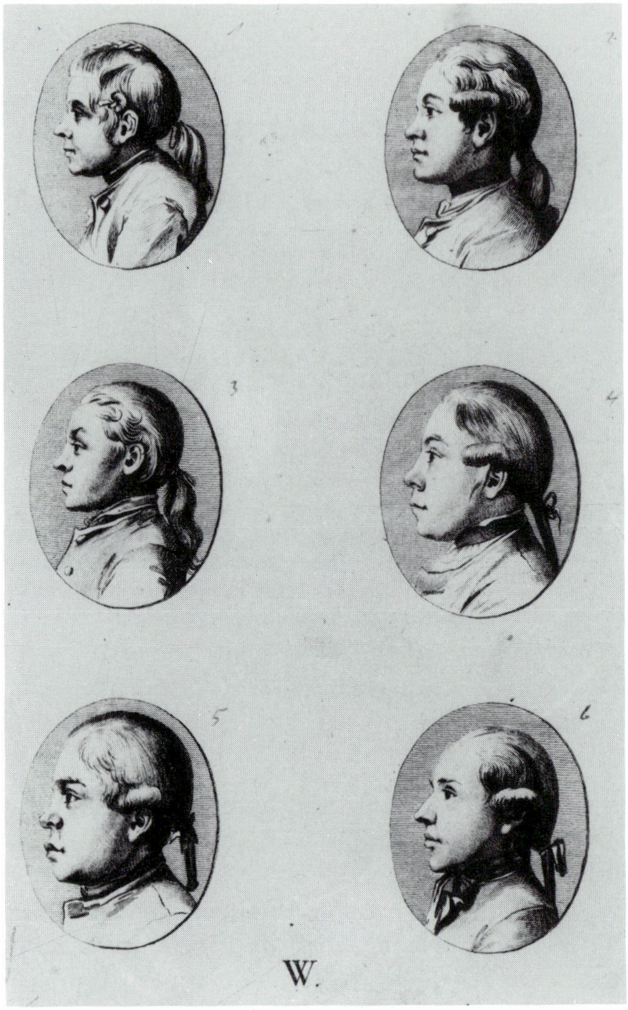

Figure 3 Six orphan boys.

Lavater's enthusiastic but naive claims about the almost universal validity of his physiognomic signs were sharply criticized by Georg Christoph Lichtenberg (1742–1799), the acerbic philosopher and physicist of Göttingen University. The hunchbacked and almost proverbially unattractive Lichtenberg dealt with Lavater's theories in a polemic essay "On Physiognomy against the Physiognomists" (Lichtenberg, 1972, pp. 256–295) Elsewhere, he concluded (Lichtenberg, 1968): "If physiognomy ever becomes what Lavater wants it to be, one will hang the children before they can carry out the deeds which merit the gallows. Thus, a new type of confirmation will have to be carried out each year —a physiognomic autodafe" (p. 532).

The Göttingen misanthrope also published a biting satire of Lavater's assessment of the young orphans under the title "Fragment of Tails," shown in Figure 4. The parody diagnosed the personalities of "6 anonymous and mostly inactive pigs" from the silhouettes of their tails. Like Lavater, Lichtenberg also provided his readers with a set of 16 questions to help them identify the personal characteristics of 8 members of a German duelling fraternity from the outlines of their fashionable cues or "pigtails" (Lichtenberg, 1972, pp. 533–538).

The German anatomist Franz Joseph Gall (1758–1828) moved the basic physiognomic problem beneath the surface of the body by searching for innate psychological dispositions in the "elevations and depressions" of the human skull (Oehler-Klein, 1990). His approach, which variously has been called "cranioscopy" or "phrenology," became immensely popular during the 19th century in Europe and especially in North America. Even crimes were explained in phrenological terminology.

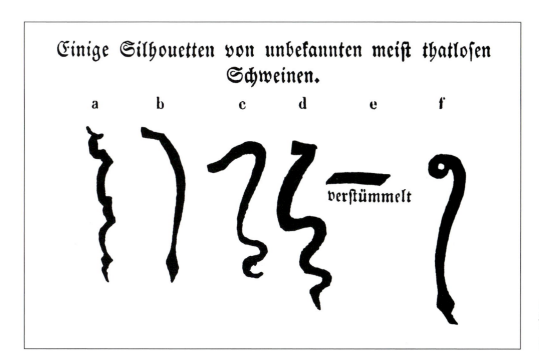

Einige Silhouetten von unbekannten meist thatlosen Schweinen.

a   b   c   d   e   f

verstümmelt

Figure 4 Lichtenberg's Silhouettes of the tails of "anonymous and mostly inactive pigs."

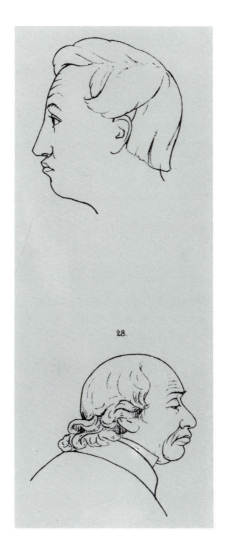

28.

Figure 5 Two illustrations of the facial expression of "critical attention" (top) with a practical illustration of the "wine taster" by Hasenclever.

Figure 6 "Expressive" and "representational" gestures. (Engel, 1785/1786).

able muscles of the face," which "convert transitory mimic movements through frequent repetition into physiognomic features" (p. 148f). Piderit's book, which concentrated on facial expressions alone, was regarded as an "encyclopedia" of mimics and physiognomy by none other than Karl Bühler (1879–1963).

Finally, the meaning of gestures, posture, and other bodily movements were addressed late in the 18th century by Johann Jakob Engel (1741–1802), in his book *Ideas for a Mimic* (1785–1786). This work distinguished between the "expressive" and "representational" behavior of actors. According to Engel (1785–1786): "Pantomime, unlike speech, cannot express mixed feelings. The soft and tender feelings of love (Figure 6, top) cannot be combined with anger (Figure 6, bottom). Language can say the word 'love' in an angry tone, but for gestures and posture this is impossible" (Vol. 2, p. 60f).

Engel's ideas were the "first systematic experiment in the field of pathognomy" (Bühler, 1933, p. 32) and can be directly related to recent research on body language and non-verbal communication (Argyle, 1975).

For example, the shocking poisoning of a husband by his wife was explained as follows (Scheve, 1851): ". . . when the skull [of the murderess] was opened with a saw during the *post mortem*, it showed the exceptional thickness [of bone tissue]. . . . The bone was significantly thinner at the location of the organs of destructiveness and decisiveness" (p. 19).

Since it had become customary to locate the sense of intellectual discrimination or intelligence in the center of the forehead, even the art of portrait painting was influenced by phrenology (Piderit, 1867): "Painters perceived their subjects 'through the glasses of phrenology' and portrayed famous men [routinely] with high and rounded foreheads, just like saints were previously painted with a halo [during the Middle Ages]" (p. 37).

Theodor Piderit (1826–1912), the German physician and explorer, criticized phrenology sharply. He based his *Scientific System of Mimics and Physiognomy* (1867) ". . . primarily on the numerous, mov-

Bibliography

Argyle, M. (1975). *Bodily communication*. London: Methuen.

Bühler, K. (1933). *Ausdruckstheorie*. Jena: Fischer.

Degkwitz, A. (1988). *Die pseudoaristotelischen "Physiognomonica."* Freiburg University: Dissertation.

Engel, J. J. (1785–1786). *Ideen zu einer Mimik*. Berlin: Mylius.

Lavater, J. C. (1775–1778). *Physiognomische Fragmente, zur Beförderung der Menschenkenntnis und Menschenliebe*. Leipzig and Winterthur: Weidmanns Erben and Reich.

Lavater, J. C. (1789). *Essays on physiognomy: for the promotion of the knowledge and the love of mankind* (3 vols). London: J. Robinson.

Lichtenberg, G. C. (1968–1972). *Schriften und Briefe*. W. Promies (Ed.) Vol. 1 (1968): Sudelbücher 1; Vol. 3 (1972): Aufsätze, Entwürfe, Gedichte, Erklärungen der Hogarthischen Kupferstiche. Munich: Hanser.

Oehler-Klein, S. (1990). *Die Schädellehre Franz Joseph Galls in Literatur und Kritik des 19. Jahrhunderts*. Stuttgart: Fischer.

Porta, G. della (1586). *De humana physiognomonia*. libri IV. Vici, Aequensis: J. Cacchius.

Piderit, T. (1867). *Wissenschaftliches System der Mimik und Physiognomik*. Detmold: Klingenberg.

Scheve, G. (1851). *Phrenologische Bilder*. Leipzig: Weber.

Goethe as an Early Behavior Therapist

Wolfgang G. Bringmann
Ursula Voss
William D. G. Balance

Long before the advent of modern behavior therapy, the German author Johann Wolfgang von Goethe (1749–1832) applied surprisingly "modern" methods to successfully treat his many painful neurotic symptoms. The nature of his emotional problems, the specific treatment methods he employed, and the success he achieved are all described in the following account taken from Book IX of his autobiography *Dichtung und Wahrheit* (Poetry and Truth, 1848–1849).

The specific passage deals with his stay at Strassburg University as a 20-year-old law student from April 1770 to August 1771:

> I found myself in a state of health which furthered me sufficiently in all that I would and should undertake; only there was a certain irritability left behind, which did not always let me be in equilibrium. A loud sound was disagreeable to me, diseased objects awakened in me loathing and horror. But I was especially troubled by giddiness which came over me every time that I looked down from a height. All these infirmities I tried to remedy, and indeed, as I wished to lose no time, in a somewhat violent way. In the evening when they beat the tattoo, I went near the multitude of drums, the powerful rolling and beating of which might have made one's heart burst in one's bosom. All alone I ascended to the highest pinnacle of the minster spire, and sat in what is called the neck, under the knob or crown, for a quarter of an hour, before I would venture to step out again in the open square. One sees a boundless prospect before, while the nearest objects and ornaments conceal the church, and everything upon and above which one stands. It is exactly as if one was oneself carried up into the air in a balloon. Such troublesome and painful sensations I repeated until the impressions became quite indifferent to me, and I have since then derived great advantage from this training, in mountain travels and geological

Figure 1 Anonymous silhouette of Goethe (ca. 1770).

> studies, and on great buildings, where I have vied with the carpenters in running over the bare beams and the cornices of the edifice, and even in Rome, where one must run similar risks to obtain a nearer view of important works of art. Anatomy also was of double value to me, as it taught me to tolerate the most repulsive sights, while I satisfied my thirst for knowledge. And thus I attended, also, the clinical course of the elder Doctor Ehrmann, as well as the lectures of his son on obstetrics, with the double view of becoming acquainted with all conditions and of freeing myself from all apprehensions as to repulsive things. And I have actually succeeded so far,

that nothing of this kind could ever put me out of my self-possession. But I sought to steel myself not only against these impressions on the senses, but also against the infections of the imagination. The awful and shuddering impressions of the darkness in churchyards, solitary places, churches and chapels by night, and whatever may be connected with them, I contrived to render likewise indifferent; and in this, also, I went so far that day and night, and every locality were quite the same to me; so that even when, in later times, a desire came over me once more to feel in such scenes the pleasing shudder of youth, I could scarcely force this, in any degree, by the strangest and most fearful images which I called up. (pp. 320–322)

Goethe's use of behavior therapy was not restricted to his Strassburg period (Bringmann, Krichev, & Balance). More than 10 years later, he used in vivo desensitization procedures to overcome his "extreme shyness, timidity and embarrassment in public situations, a serious handicap in his diplomatic activities" (Eissler, 1963). He also seems to have recommended "behavior therapy" to a seriously depressed theology student, who had approached him for help (Eissler, 1963). Finally, he cogently expressed the advantage of action-over-insight–oriented therapies in his educational novel *Wilhelm Meister* (1926): "To heal psychic ailments, that we have contracted through misfortune or fault of our own, the understanding avails nothing, reason little, time much, but resolute action everything" (p. 213).

Figure 2 Copper engraving of Strassburg Cathedral (ca. 1760).

Bibliography

Bringmann, W., Krichev, A., & Balance, W. (1970). Goethe as behavior therapist. *Journal of the History of the Behavioral Sciences, 6,* 151–155.

Eissler, R. (1963). *Goethe: A psychoanalytic study.* Detroit: Wayne State University Press.

Goethe, J. W. v. (1926). *Wilhelm Meister.* London: Dent.

Goethe, J. W. v. (1962). *Dichtung und Wahrheit* (2nd ed., Vol. IX). Zürich: Artemis. (Original work published 1848–1849)

Michel, C. (1982). *Goethe.* Frankfurt: Insel.

An 18th-Century Baby Biography

Wolfgang G. Bringmann
Pegge Hewett
Gustav A. Ungerer

Historians of psychology have traditionally subscribed to the famous adage expressed by Hermann Ebbinghaus (1850–1909) that "psychology has a long past but a short history" (Ebbinghaus, 1911). As far as the history of developmental psychology is concerned, it has been suggested that before Darwin (Diamond, 1974)

> child psychology was limited to occasional bits and snatches such as Aristotle's mention that children do not dream before the age of four (!) or Locke's reminder that supposedly innate truths are not known to children in advance of experience. In the 18th century Smellie recognized the need for the systematic study of child behavior but he could not spare the time. (p. 469)

During our research for the 1983 *International William T. Preyer Symposium* at Jena University in Germany, we discovered a sophisticated study of early child behavior which was conducted and published almost 100 years before Darwin's 1877 publication of the "Biographical Sketch of an Infant Mind."

Prehistory

In 1785, Joachim Heinrich Campe (1746–1818), the German author and educational reformer, issued an invitation to the educated public to collect a "faithful" account

> of the entire physical and moral treatment of the child including the observed effects and consequences; observations of the first expressions of independence, attention, joy and pain; advances in physical and mental development; gradual formation of language and the child's own very simple grammar; the beginnings of individual differences and emotions; basic patterns of future personality, etc. (p. xxvif)

Campe was aware that such a project would not be easy (Campe, 1785): "For one person this task is almost too great. Two equally astute observers would be needed to divide the responsibility among themselves. One would remain with the child, while the other would record his observations" (p. xxv).

Campe's call for baby diaries resulted in the preparation and publication of a number of diaries (Jaeger, 1985). However, we shall focus on a work that was begun four years before Campe announced

Figure 1 Portrait of Campe.

37

NB. 9. Journal eines Vaters über sein Kind, enthaltend: eine treue Darstellung der gesammten physischen und moralischen Behandlung des Kindes, nebst den wahrgenommenen Folgen und Wirkungen derselben; Bemerkung der ersten Aeußerungen von Selbstthätigkeit, Aufmerksamkeit, Freude und Schmerz; Gebrauch des Körpers und seiner einzelnen Glieder, vornehmlich der Sinne; Fortschritte der körperlichen und geistigen Entwickelung; allmähliche Bildung der Sprache und der ganz eigenen sehr simpeln Kindergrammatik; erste Keime der individuellen Neigun-

Figure 2 Announcement of competition for baby biography.

Figure 3 Portrait of Dietrich Tiedemann.

his competition. This was the *Observations on the Development of Mental Abilities in Children* (1787) by the German philosopher Dietrich Tiedemann (1748–1803).

An Eclectic Philosopher

Dietrich Tiedemann, the "eclectic philosopher and historian of philosophy," was born on April 3, 1748, in the small town of Bremervörde in North Germany. His father was the local mayor, who educated Dietrich (his oldest son) at home until the age of 15 by encouraging him to read as much as possible.

During high school, Tiedemann first became acquainted with the writings of the British empiricists and the French encyclopedists (Ufer, 1897). From 1767 to 1769, he studied theology, philology, philosophy, and mathematics at nearby Göttingen University. After serving for five years as the private tutor of a nobleman's children in Russia, Tiedemann returned to Göttingen to complete his studies of ancient languages and philosophy. Next, Tiedemann taught Latin and Greek at the prestigious "Carolinum College" in Kassel from 1776 to 1786. He was promoted to a full professorship in philosophy at Marburg University in 1786. His new responsibilities included the teaching of regular courses in logic, metaphysics, natural law, ethics, history of philosophy, and psychology. According to Ufer, Tiedemann's psychology was strongly influenced by the empiricism of the German philosophers and psy-

chologists, Johann Nicholas Tetens (1736–1807) and Karl Philipp Moritz (1756–1793).

Tiedemann's Developmental Diary

Tiedemann apparently began collecting developmental information about his son between 1781 and 1784 in Kassel before Campe issued his famous invitation for a diary record. The *Observations* were first published in 1787 after the beginning of Tiedemann's Marburg appointment. The article appeared in the second and third volume of the *Hessian Contributions to Scholarship and Art*, which Tiedemann edited together with two friends. It took almost a hundred years before partial French translations (Michelant, 1863; Perez, 1881) were published. In 1890, an English translation (Soldau, 1890) was made from the abridged French version by Perez (1881). Finally, the full German text was republished 116 years after its first appearance (Ufer, 1897).

Figure 4 Silhouette of Dietrich Tiedemann.

Figure 5 Title page of Tiedemann's book on the "Origin of Language" (1773).

Tiedemann's *Observations* were also used in his posthumous *Handbook of Psychology for Lectures and Self-Instructions* (1804, pp. 401–431) to bolster his associationistic views of human development.

Tiedemann's "baby diary" covers the period from August 23, 1781, to February 14, 1784. The entire account is 13,000 words or about 42 pages long. A typical entry consists of three to eight lines of direct observations, which are supplemented by one-half to four pages of comments and interpretations.

His notes for October 2, 1781, give a good flavor of his approach. At that time little Friedrich Tiedemann was about two months old (1787):

> Some sensory experiences [of the child], especially those of taste, can now be distinguished with some confidence. On October 2 (1781), bitter medicine was accepted only after great resistance. The boy now can distinguish between himself and the objects surrounding him. He does this by grabbing things and by stretching his hands and even his entire body toward a desired object. He is not very skilled with his fingers as yet. If he manages to reach something, it is

> often more a matter of chance than of intention. It is astonishing how much practice and trial and error are required for the acquisition of simple movements, which appear easy to adults, as if they were born with them! (p. 318)

After separating Tiedemann's comments from his direct observations, a total of 2,650 words of text remain for each of 41 individual days. Thus, on the average, a single observation of about 43 words was recorded every 22 days during the entire two-and-a-half years.

Friedrich Tiedemann

Altogether, Tiedemann's little son appears to have been a healthy and rather bright child. His developmental milestones are, in fact, a good deal in advance of those reported in more recent observational records and yield a mental age of 47 months at the age of 30 months, and, hence an IQ slightly above 150 (Gesell, 1925). This estimate gains further support from the later life and career of the child, Friedrich Tiedemann (1781–1861), who eventually became an eminent German physiologist at Heidelberg University during the first half of the 19th century.

After studying medicine at Marburg and Würzburg, Tiedemann received his MD at the age of 23 and qualified shortly afterwards as an instructor of medicine. Only one year later, he became Professor of Anatomy and Zoology at Landsburg University in Bavaria. Eleven years later, he received a call to Heidelberg University, where he taught for the next 31 years.

Tiedemann published extensively in German, French, and English about the topics of digestion, nutrition, and neuro-anatomy. His psychological interests are reflected in his regular lectures on Gall's phrenology and his study of racial differences, *On the Brain of the Negro, compared with that of the European and the Orang-Outang* (1836). Although the title may imply a strong racist orientation, Tiedemann's book was a model of objective scholarship. Thus, we read in this copiously illustrated monograph the following summary of his extensive anatomical studies (1836):

> (I) In general, or, on the average, the brain of the Negro is just as big as that of the European or other human races.
>
> (II) The cranial nerves of Negroes are not thicker than those of Europeans.
>
> (III) The spinal cord, the brain stem, the cerebellum and the cortex of the Negro show no significant differences in their external appearance or their structure from those of the European.
>
> (IV) The brain of the Negro does not resemble that of the orang-outang any more than [does] that of the European.

Friedrich Tiedemann resigned his professorship at Heidelberg in 1849 after his son, Gustav Nikolaus Tiedemann (1808-1849) was executed by a Prussian firing squad on August 11, 1849. Tiedemann junior was the last commander of the German Fortress "Rastadt," where the German revolutionaries made their last stand against the overwhelming forces of reactionary Prussia.

Later Developments

After a period of neglect, the diary method of developmental research became popular once again with

Figure 6 Friedrich Tiedemann of Heidelberg University.

the 1876 publication of Hippolyte Taine's (1828–1893) study of language acquisition by his daughter. Darwin recorded his observations of the physical and mental development of his oldest child in 1840 but did not publish them until 1877 after he read Taine's "very interesting account" (Darwin, 1877). Even Wilhelm Wundt (1832–1920), who seriously questioned the scientific status of developmental psychology, collected extensive diary information about the language development of his two oldest children (Wundt, 1900, pp. 284–304). Preyer's classic, *The Mind of the Child* (1882, 1888–1889), may be viewed as the culmination of this research approach. In particular, his detailed "rules" for the preparation of baby biographies are still relevant today.

Modern developmental psychologists are fully aware of the limits of the diary method of child study. Nonetheless, they acknowledge its benefits as a research tool (Kessen, Haith, & Salapatek, 1970):

> Despite their weaknesses, the [baby] biographies are essential in our study of language, emo-

DER GOUVERNEUR TIDEMAN.

Figure 7 Nikolaus Tiedemann.

tional expression, problem solving, representation and imitation in infants and they remain invaluable sources of observation and of leads toward better controlled observation on other matters of interest to the psychologist of infancy, particularly in the period between the newborn hospital stay and the child's entrance into nursery school. (p. 303)

Bibliography

Campe, J. H. (Ed.). (1785–1791). *Allgemeine Revision des gesamten Schul- und Erziehungswesens von einer Gesellschaft praktischer Erzieher* (Vols. 1–16). Hamburg: Bohn.

Darwin, C. (1877). A biographical sketch of an infant. *Mind, 1,* 285–294.

Diamond, S. (Ed.). (1974). *The roots of psychology.* New York: Basic Books.

Ebbinghaus, H. (1911). *Psychology: An elementary textbook.* Boston: Heath.

Gesell, A. (1925). *The mental growth of the pre-school child: A psychological outline of normal development from birth to the sixth year, including a system of developmental diagnosis.* New York: Macmillan.

Jaeger, S. (1985). The diary method in developmental psychology. In G. Eckardt, W. G. Bringmann, & L. Sprung (Eds.), *Contributions to a history of developmental psychology* (pp. 63–74). Berlin: Mouton.

Kessen, W., Haith, M., & Salapatek, P. (1970). Infancy. In P. H. Mussen (Ed.), *Carmichael's manual of child psychology* (3rd ed., p. 303). New York: Wiley.

Michelant, H. (1863). Observations sur le development de facultes d'ame chez les enfants. *Journal General de l'Instruction Publique,* pp. 251–291, 309, 319.

Perez, B. (1881). *Thieri Tiedemann et la Science de l'Enfant.* Paris: Bailliere.

Preyer, W. (1882). *Die Seele des Kindes.* Leipzig: Grieben.

Soldau, F. L. (1890). *Tiedemann's record of an infant.* Syracuse, NY: Bardeen.

Taine, H. (1876). Note sur l'acquisition de langage chez les enfants et dans l'espèce humaine. *Revue Philosophique, 1,* 3-23.

Tiedemann, D. (1787). Beobachtung über die Entwicklung der Seelenfähigkeiten bei Kindern. *Hessische Beiträge zur Gelehrsamkeit und Kunst, 2,* 313–333; *3,* 486–502.

Tiedemann, D. (1804). *Handbuch der Psychologie zum Gebranch der Vorlesungen und zur Selbst bestimmt.* Leipzig: Barth.

Tiedemann, F. (1836). On the brain of the Negro, compared with that of the European and the Orang-Outang. London: Taylor.

Ufer, C. (1897). *Dietrich Tiedemann's Beobachtungen über die Entwicklung der Seelenfähigkeiten bei Kindern.* Altenburg, Germany: Bond.

Wundt, W. (1900). *Die Sprache* (Vol. 1). Leipzig: Engelmann.

Gnothi Sauton: The Journal of Experiential Psychology

Jürgen Jahnke

In the spring of 1782, Karl Philipp Moritz (1756–1793), the respected vice principal of the "Gray Cloisters" Latin School in Berlin, announced his ambitious plans for a new journal to "All Admirers and Promoters of Useful Information and the Sciences" and to "All Observers of the Human Heart" (Moritz, 1782, p. 485). This novel publication was given the catchy Greek title *Gnothi Sauton* (Know Thyself). Its lengthy subtitle characterized the journal further as the *Magazine of Experiential Psychology, a Reader for the Learned and Nonlearned* (Moritz, Pockels, & Maimon, 1783–1793). This publication was Germany's first psychological journal, and Moritz published it for 10 years, from 1783 until his death, with occasional editorial assistance from the philanthropist educator Karl Friedrich Pockels (1757–1814) and the Jewish philosopher Salomon Maimon (1754–1800).

Gnothi Sauton

The chief purpose of the new publication was the collection of *Facta*—factual self-observations and psychological observations of others. No attempt was made to develop a theoretical system from the materials, and the formulation of moral lessons was discouraged. All readers, whether experts or laymen in the field, were encouraged to become authors by submitting pertinent manuscripts to *Gnothi Sauton* (Davis, 1985; Schrimpf, 1980b).

Following the suggestion of the Berlin philosopher Moses Mendelssohn (1729–1786), individual articles were organized under subheadings derived from the medical science and philosophy of the times (e.g., "Mental Pathology," "Natural History of the Mind," "Mental Semiotics," and "Mental Therapeutics").

The content of the journal was dominated by psychopathological case histories (Förstl, Angermeyer, & Howard, 1991), but articles about premonitions, prophecies, dreams, and visions were also quite common. Essays about topics from developmental psychology and the field of linguistics followed on an irregular basis.

The following free translation of the German titles from the first part of Volume III of the journal gives a good illustration of its diverse content (Moritz, 1785, GS III, 1, p. 128):

Figure 1 Karl Philipp Moritz (1756–1793).

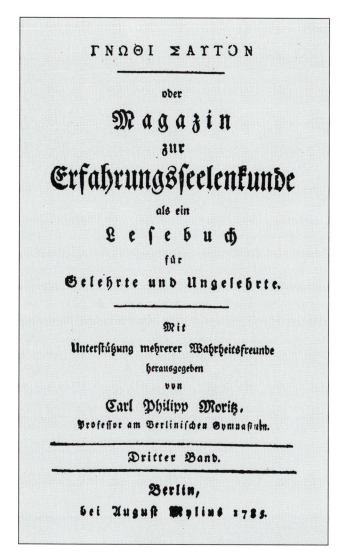

Figures 2 and 3 Title page and table of contents for Vol. III 1 (1785) of *Gnothi Sauton*.

An insane Lenten sermon

A story of moral failure (continuation)

[Story of] a basket maker who preached a revival sermon in a trance

Prediction of disaster

Failure of a prophecy made in a state of melancholia

The beginnings of speech in children

Composing poetry while asleep

Psychological remarks on spontaneous laughter

Comparison of adolescent personality traits

A letter about the treatment of the mind

An unfortunate attachment to the theater

Reflections of a former hypochondriac

The following autobiographical account is a good example of the type of material that was included in the journal on a regular basis (Moritz, GS II, 1, p. 71):

> On the Natural History of the Mind
> I
> Doubts About One's Own Existence
> (From a Letter)
>
> In my thirteenth year I fell by an accident into a pond and got stuck in its bottom until I was close to drowning but I was pulled out by the help of other people.
>
> From this time on, I believed whenever I got to thinking about myself that I had really drowned at that time. Whatever I saw, heard or felt were not real sensations of my body but memories of my former life.
>
> I believed that I possessed no body but remained on earth only in spirit or that I only imagined that I lived on earth.

Figure 4 Title page of *Anton Reiser* (part four, 1790).

> All these ideas I experienced at an age when I had no knowledge of skeptics or idealists. My religious teachings had given me the idea that heaven and earth were merely two spatially separated containers. At that time, these thoughts disagreed with my generally limited ideas about life.
>
> This deception lasted for three years until I changed my residence and came into a completely new situation. Finally, my new experiences convinced me that my sensory experiences were real and not imaginary events. I have never been able to explain this strange condition.

Moritz was fully aware of the complexity and the methodological difficulties of studying these "soft" facts, which many of his contemporaries regarded merely as "empty fantasies" (Moritz, GS VII, 3, p. 4). However, even today, "psychological medicine still has to deal with the issues that were eagerly discussed in the journal" (Förstl, Angermeyer, & Howard, 1991, p. 303). Thus, *Gnothi Sauton* remains a unique social and psycho-historical document due to its explicit and anti-theoretical stance and, in particular, its tolerance for the personal idiosyncrasies of its readers-authors.

Anton Reiser

According to Moritz , anyone "who wants to become a true observer of man must begin with himself [and] trace the history of his own heart, from his earliest childhood on, as faithfully as possible" (Moritz, 1782, p. 492). Consequently, he began to publish an anonymous account of his own childhood under the title "Fragments from Anton Reiser's Life" in the second volume of the journal (Moritz, GS II, 1, p. 76f.). Moritz reconstructed his development as a child in the form of "internal history." However, he did not neglect to recall and describe in painstaking detail the external conditions and circumstances of his life (Schrimpf, 1980a, 1980b).

When *Anton Reiser* was finally published in four slender volumes between 1785 and 1790, Moritz added the subtitle *A Psychological Novel*. He also stressed that his book consisted primarily of "observations from real life." Moritz viewed both his journal and his autobiographical novel as part of his research for an empirical psychology. For him, *Anton Reiser* functioned as a type of "observatorium," which allowed him an almost microscopic analysis of the "small, unimportant, and even trifling circumstances" of his own life (Müller, 1987, p. 172). The work dramatically illustrated how a dysfunctional childhood, filled with poverty, rejection, and religious fanaticism, can still nurture hope for a meaningful and harmonious life. Early experiences with the tortuous and confusing methods of mysti-

Figure 5 Bronze bust of Karl Philipp Moritz (Bronze by T. L. Major, 1793).

cal and pietist self-study enabled Moritz to develop his own secular and objective form of psychological introspection.

Moritz discontinued his work on the journal and his autobiographical novel between 1786 and 1788. He spent these years in Italy on studies of classical mythology and aesthetics. In Rome and Naples, he also developed a close friendship with Johann Wolfgang von Goethe (1749–1832). Returning to Berlin in 1789, Moritz received a prestigious appointment as Professor of Art Theory. His psychological interests decreased, and he devoted his remaining years to the analysis of aesthetic, and especially, linguistic problems. Throughout the 19th century, neither philosophical nor experimental psychologists in Germany showed much interest in the psychological writings of Moritz (Dessoir, 1897–1902). His memory was preserved in German literary history, however, and he has become recognized as a forerunner of psychoanalysis (Bezold, 1984; Bowlby, 1979; Herrmann, 1988; Schrimpf, 1980a).

Bibliography

Bezold, R. (1984). *Popularphilosophie und Erfahrungsseelenkunde im Werk von Karl Philipp Moritz*. Würzburg: Königshausen und Neumann.

Bowlby, M. (1979). *Karl Philipp Moritz: At the Fringe of Genius*. Toronto: University Press.

Davies, M. L. (1985). Karl Philipp Moritz's Erfahrungsseelenkunde: Its social and intellectual origins. *Oxford German Studies, 16*, 13–35.

Dessoir, M. (1897–1902). *Geschichte der neueren deutschen Psychologie*. Berlin: Duncker.

Förstl, H., Angermeyer, M., & Howard, R. (1991). Karl Philipp Moritz's Journal of Empirical Psychology (1783–1793): An analysis of 124 case reports. *Psychological medicine, 21* 299–304.

Herrmann, U. (1988). Karl Philipp Moritz-Die "innere Geschichte" des Menschen. In G. Jüttemann (Ed.), *Wegbereiter der Historischen Psychologie* (pp. 48–55). Munich: Beltz.

Moritz, K. P. (1782). Vorschlag zu einem Magazin einer Erfahrungsseelenkunde. *Deutsches Museum, I.*, 453–503. (Reprint in Moritz et al. 1783–1793, Vol. 1).

Moritz, K. P. (1978). *Anton Reiser*. Westport, CT: Hyperion.

Moritz, K. P. (1987). *Anton Reiser, Ein psychologisher Roman*. Munich: Beck.

Moritz, K. P., Pockels, C. F., & Maimon, S. (1783–1793). *Gnothi sauton oder Magazin zur Erfahrungsseelenkunde als ein Lesebuch für Gelehrte und Ungelehrte* (Vols. 1–10) (Reprint: 1978/1979). Lindau, Germany: Antiqua.

Müller, L. (1987). *Die kranke Seele und das Licht der Erkenntnis: Karl Philipp Moritz 'Anton Reiser.'* Frankfurt: Athenaeum.

Schrimpf, H. J. (1980a). *Karl Philipp Moritz*. Stuttgart: Metzler.

Schrimpf, H. J. (1980b). Das Magazin zur Erfahrungsseelenkunde und sein Herausgeber. *Zeitschrift für deutsche Philologie, 99*, 161–187.

Johannes Müller and the Principle of Sensory Metamorphosis

Herbert Fitzek

Few topics have attracted more attention in psychology than the sensory experience of optical phenomena. This observation is as applicable to modern psychology as it is to psychology's past, but it is the past to which we now turn our attention. A key figure in the development of this field was the German physiologist, morphologist, and sensory psychologist, Johannes Peter Müller (1801–1858), whose contributions to the psychology of perception have often been overlooked.

Johannes Müller was born in the small city of Koblenz on the Rhine in the German Kingdom of Prussia. He began his higher education at the nearby University of Bonn and was at first strongly influenced by the Romantic approach to science that was not uncommon at the time. However, it is apparent in his 1822 medical dissertation that he adopted a significantly more empirical approach to the natural sciences as he developed intellectually.

The beginning of Müller's academic career coincided with efforts to redefine the relationship between physiology and psychology. The Romantic scientists of the period still viewed psychology as the highest and purest of the sciences and gave it precedence over all other scientific disciplines. As a young doctoral candidate, Müller was already aware that psychology would soon reach the limits of its empirical knowledge about organic phenomena and consequently was in dire need of a more solid and extensive physiological grounding. Hence Müller was fully convinced that "Nobody can be a psychologist, unless he first becomes a physiologist" (Haberling, 1924, p. 39). Müller himself did not discover his own way of combining physiological and psychological studies until he became a post-graduate student at Berlin University during the years 1821 to 1824.

Müller described his solution to the physiology-psychology dilemma on the occasion of his formal appointment as a medical instructor at Bonn University. His inaugural lecture, "The Necessity of Physiology for a Philosophical View of Nature," attracted attention far beyond the small Prussian university (Hagner & Wahrig-Schmidt, 1992). He began his presentation by noting that the observation and

Figure 1 Portrait of Johannes Peter Müller (1801–1858) by Lawrence.

description of events occurring in the living organism were the chief tasks of physiology. He ended his lecture with an invitation to his fellow researchers to concentrate their full attention on the immediate sensory characteristics of physiological phenomena. Physiologists no longer had to limit themselves to the in vitro study of dead matter but could now investigate the functions of an organism on an in vivo basis. However, they must always keep in mind that the phenomenon they were studying at a given time was only part of a whole organism (Müller, 1824/1947; Uexküll, 1947).

Johannes Müller's maxims opened the way for a novel understanding of the relationship between physiological and psychological research. His ideas were further elaborated in his books titled *Comparative Physiological Studies about the Visual Sense of Man and Animals and an Experiment on the Movements of the Human Eye and Sight* (1826a) and *Fantastic Visual Phenomena* (1826b). These two works provide a comparison of the physiological basis of visual perception with a psychological analysis of the same phenomena. Müller's discoveries in this area thus constitute a milestone in the development of scientific psychology—a milestone which was not fully recognized until two generations later.

Like physiology, the psychology of Müller's time carried the burden of Romanticism. In opposition, Müller argued against philosophical "speculation [in physiology]" and the "sterile basis of the so-called empirical psychology" (Müller, 1826b, p. v). What then is the specific content of Müller's psychology and his book *Fantastic Visual Phenomena*? When Müller discusses "fantastic" phenomena within the context of his psychology, he is referring to the general sensory character of psychological phenomena and not just to special or spectacular visual effects. Like physiology, psychology must have actual sensory or phenomenological events at the heart of its subject matter.

Ordinarily, we focus our attention on an object; we see a house, a stone, or a flower. The traditional psychology of Müller's day perceived only the basic sensory phenomena and regarded vision as a succession of disparate ideas. Müller called this view "pitiful." Such an approach concentrates only on the obvious and overlooks "the context and the limits of sensory experience" (1826b, p. 95). Müller wanted psychology to move away from the *object* of vision to the understanding of vision as a series of activities which may be described as the "creation, formation [and] transformation" of sensory phenomena in the visual field. By moving from the content to the *process* of vision, psychology would, for the first time, be able to study how the content of vision changes in real life situations (Müller, 1826b).

What evidence did Müller find for his new model? Early in his career he learned to work without the artificial elimination of natural functions. According to Müller, the sensory aspects of visual fixation could be studied by simply minimizing the influence of external reality. Thus Müller studied perceptual phenomena in a darkened room, while falling asleep, as it occurred in daydreams, and in perception with the eyes closed. Working about the same time as Johannes Evangelista Purkinje (1787–1869), Müller carried out the first systematic observations of sensory phenomena "in the dark."

Figure 2 Drawing of image perceived with closed eye ("entropic phenomenon") by Johannes E. Purkinje (1787–1869).

Both Müller and Purkinje discovered that sensory experiences continue even when the eye is closed—that is, the origin and transformation of Gestalt patterns continue. However, even though the visual experiences become more fleeting and somewhat less distinct, they do not appear to be random, but rather seem to follow regular patterns. Müller's own descriptions and examples from the scientific literature clearly document the regularity of the observed phenomena. The study of fantastic visual phenomena indicates that our fantastic life is anything but chaotic. The images of our fantasies are not confused but clear and configurational. Furthermore, they do not differ substantially from person to person but follow a distinctly regular pattern. Far from

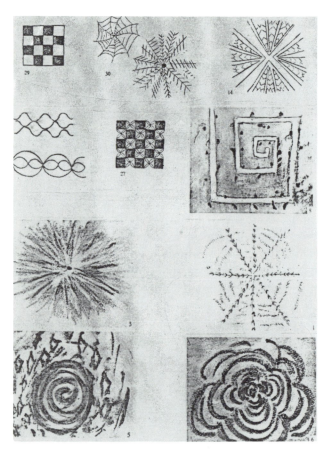

Figure 3 Luminous images of the retina or phosphenes produced by mechanical stimulation (recorded by Smythies).

multi-volume *Handbook of Human Physiology* (1834), which exerted a decisive influence on the development of 19th-century physiology. Müller was able to establish his own school of physiological thought which produced such luminaries in physiology—and particularly sensory physiology—as Ernst Brücke (1819–1892), Hermann Helmholtz (1821–1894), and Wilhelm Wundt (1832–1920).

The rediscovery of the sensory nature of perception and its Gestalt organization began with the students of Müller's own famous students—his intellectual "grandchildren." These included Brücke's student, Sigmund Freud (1856–1939), the early Berlin Gestalt psychologists who as students stud-

Figure 4 Metamorphic Imagination: "First Dream—Crime and Punishment" by J. J. Grandville.

being random, they seem to follow their own logic (Fitzek, 1994).

In clear contrast to the bias of traditional experts in perceptual psychology, Müller formulated his general "principle of metamorphosis," which formed the basis for his explanation of both the expansion and restriction of Gestalt phenomena in all of the sensory modalities. Through the formulation of this empirical principle, Müller was at last able to demonstrate that psychology could make lawful predictions about natural phenomena.

In the long period between Romanticism and the foundation of psychophysics by Gustav Theodor Fechner (1801–1887), Johannes Müller was the lone proponent of an empirical psychology. Unfortunately, visual Gestalt phenomena were merely a temporary interest during his early life. During his professorial years at Berlin University, Müller expanded his work on sensory physiology into his famous,

ied Helmholtz, and Friedrich Sander (1889–1971), who was Wundt's last assistant. In a sense, all of these scholars supported a Gestalt-oriented description and reconstruction of psychological phenomena. Although their theories appear to differ radically at first glance, they all focus on the metamorphoses of meaning—whether it be in dreams, in the organization of perception, or in the development of concrete, day-to-day behavior patterns (Fitzek & Salber, 1996). Today, the discoveries by Müller's "grandchildren" have been expanded into a "Morphology of Mental Events" (Salber, 1986), which makes it possible to better understand how to shape reality by means of an unconscious inference through Gestalt principles.

As an example, the general principle of metamorphosis can be identified in the visual (pictorial) representations used by modern science. Pictures and other visual models help organize the scientist's perception of whatever phenomena is being studied. The same can also be said to a less formal degree for describing how we navigate through the complexity of our everyday existence. Furthermore, the process occurs whether we are aware of it or not. Psychology has only rarely adopted pictorial representations of behavior in a systematic way (Vroon & Draaisma, 1985; Leary, 1990). The natural sciences, however, have long provided better examples of visual models. At the beginning of this century physics discovered the value in a visual representation of its concepts and as a result has greatly increased its understanding of nature (Rascher, 1989). Thus it is no accident that by taking a look at the recent concepts of chaos theory, complexity, and "self-regulating systems," we rediscover Müller's "fantastic visual phenomena." You don't have to accept this on faith, just take another look. . . .

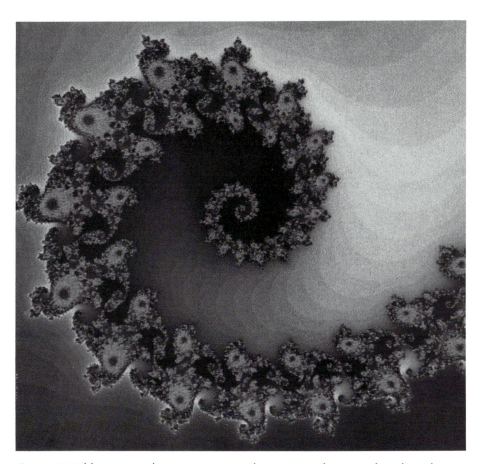

Figure 5 Visible metamorphoses portray natural events according to modern chaos theory.

Bibliography

Fitzek, H. (1994). *Der Fall Morphologie. Biographie einer Wissenschaft.* Bonn: Bouvier.

Fitzek, H., & Salber, W. (1996). *Gestaltpsychologie. Ihre Geschichte und ihr Gebrauch von 1900 bis heute.* Darmstadt: Wissenschaftliche Buchgesellschaft.

Haberling W. (1924). *Johannes Müller. Das Leven des rheinischen Naturforschers.* Leipzig: Akademische Verlagsanstalt.

Hagner, M., & Wahrig-Schmidt, B. (1992). *Johannes Müller und die Philosophie.* Berlin: Akademie Verlag.

Leary, D. (Ed). (1990). *Metaphors in the History of Psychology.* Cambridge: Cambridge University Press.

Müller, J. (1947). Vom dem Bedürfnis der Physiologie nach einer philosophischen Naturbetrachtung. In J. v. Uexküll (Ed.). *Der Sinn des Lebens.* Godesberg: Küpper. (Original work published 1824)

Müller, J. (1826a). *Sur vergleichenden Physiologie des Gesichtssinnes des Menschen und der Thier nebst einem Versuch über die Bewegungen der Augen und über den menschlichen Blick.* Leipzig: Cnobloch.

Müller, J. (1826b). *Über die phantastichen Gesichtserscheinungen. Eine physiologische Untersuchung.* Coblenz: Hölscher.

Purkinje, J. E. (1819). *Beiträge sur Kenntnis des Sehens in subjektiver Hinsicht.* Prague: Fr. Vetterl.

Rascher, R. (1989). *Die Erlebnisdimension in der Physik.* Wiesbaden: Deutscher Universitäts-Verlag.

Salber, W. (1986). *Morphologie des seelischen Geschehens.* Cologne: Tavros, Arbeitskreis Morphologische Psychologie.

Uexküll, J. v. (1947). *Der Sinn des Lebens.* Godesberg: Küpper.

Vroon, P. & Draisma, D. (1985). *De Mens als Metafoor Over verglijkingen van mens en machine in filosofie en psychologie.* Baarn, Netherlands: Ambo.

Charles Darwin and Psychology

Joseph F. Fitzpatrick
Wolfgang G. Bringmann

The theory of evolution by Charles Darwin (1809–1882) had a crucial impact on the development of modern psychology. He directly influenced, among others, the work of such diverse and original early modern psychologists as Gustav Theodor Fechner (1801–1887), William Thierry Preyer (1841–1897), G. Stanley Hall (1884–1924), and James M. Baldwin (1861–1934). Darwin's chief works, *The Origin of Species* (1859) and *The Descent of Man* (1871), presented and supported the basic psychological view that man exists on a continuum with other organisms, and that both man and animals can be studied scientifically. Of special interest to psychologists are Darwin's writings on early child development (1877) and his empirical and theoretical studies of emotions in animals and man (1872).

Child Study

Despite his serious and rational bent, Darwin was an emotional man and an intensely loving—one might even say doting—father, who was deeply moved by the premature death of three of his children. Of particular interest is his developmental diary about his son, William Erasmus Darwin (1839–1914), a portion of which was published in the July 1877 issue of the British philosophical journal *Mind*. Darwin and his wife began to record their observations and mini-experiments "37 years ago," in 1839, when their oldest child was less than a week old:

> During the first seven days various reflex actions, namely sneezing, hiccuping, yawning, stretching, and of course sucking and screaming were well performed by my infant. On the seventh day, I touched the naked sole of his foot with a bit of paper, and he jerked it away, curling at the same time his toes, like a much older child when tickled. (Darwin, 1877, p. 19)

In addition to the straightforward descriptions of the child's behavior, the brief manuscript is replete with questions and reflections about the ontogenesis of the human personality. As William grew up, Darwin was especially interested in distinguishing between learned and hereditary behavior patterns. How much influence the publication of Darwin's diary had on William Preyer's *Die Seele des Kindes*

Figure 1 Darwin and his son William.

51

Figure 2 Pouting child.

Figure 3 Pouting chimpanzee.

(1882) is still undetermined; however, there is no question that Darwinism dominated Preyer's physiological and psychological thought. Preyer's book is generally considered a seminal text in developmental psychology, and Preyer himself one of the founders of the discipline. He engaged in an extended correspondence with Darwin on evolution and behavior until shortly before Darwin's death (Fitzpatrick & Bringmann, 1995).

Emotional Expression

Darwin's book, *The Expression of Emotions in Man and Animals* (1872), continues to hold a special attraction for psychologists. He based this work on data drawn from (a) the earliest behavior and photographs of his son William, (b) the photographs of staged emotions by actors, and (c) samples of emotional behavior by a broad spectrum of domestic and wild animals, including cats, swans, chimpanzees, and even his own big dog named "Bob." The photograph of the little boy and the woodcut of a mature chimp (Figures 2 and 3) were included to illustrate the emotion of "sulkiness: or making a

snout" (Darwin, 1872, pp. 232–233). Darwin's views about the existence of universal emotional expressions between animals and man are still of limited use today. We know now that some emotions appear to be common to all cultures.

Apart from their historical interest, Darwin's contributions to child study and the nature of emotional expressions retain an important place in the field of psychology. He was among the first to ask the important questions; he provided a sound methodology; and finally, his two psychological works are a pleasure to read.

Bibliography

Darwin, C. (1872). *The expression of emotion in man and animals*. London: Murray.

Darwin, C. (1877). Biographical sketch of an infant. *Mind, 2*, 285–294.

Eckardt, G., Bringmann, W. G., & Sprung, L. (Eds.). (1985). *Contributions to a history of developmental psychology*. Berlin: Mouton.

Fitzpatick, J. F., Jr. & Bringmann, W. G. (1995). William Preyer and Charles Darwin. In S. Jaeger, I. Staeuble, L. Sprung, & H.-P. Brauns (Ed.), *Psychologie im sozialkultrellen wandel—Kontinuitäten Discontinuitäten* (pp. 238–244). Frankfurt: Lang.

Preyer, W. (1882). *Die Seele des Kindes*. Leipzig: Grieben.

Galton's Hat and the Invention of Intelligence Tests

Raymond E. Fancher

T he idea for the modern intelligence test was introduced by Francis Galton (1822–1911) in 1865, when he imagined the development of an examination designed to select young men and women of unusual—and presumably hereditary—"natural ability," to be the parents in a new eugenic society (Galton, 1865). When Galton subsequently tried to develop such tests, most notably in the Anthropometric Laboratory he established at London's South Kensington Museum in 1884, he mainly employed physiologically based measures such as reaction time and sensory discrimination tasks. He thought that these would assess individual differences in the efficiency of the brain and nervous system, on which inherited natural ability or intelligence presumably depended. Consistent with his general neurophysiological orientation, Galton firmly believed that large brains must be associated with general mental power. Thus his Anthropometric Laboratory also collected measures of head size, and when Galton solicited questionnaire data from eminent scientists for his *English Men of Science* survey, he did not fail to ask for their "measurement round inside of hat" (Galton, 1874).

Some of Galton's biographers have linked this belief to the supposition that he himself had a large head. According to one account, Prime Minister William Gladstone visited the laboratory to be measured and was "amusingly insistent" about the large size of his head, although it turned out to be "less than Spottiswoode's, Sharpey's and Galton's own" (Pearson, 1914–1930, Vol. 2, p. 379n). Another biographer states that "throughout his life, [Galton] retained a belief in the high intelligence of those, *like himself,* with large heads" (Forrest, 1974, p. 37, emphasis added). In light of Galton's reputation as a genius (the subtitle of Forrest's biography is *The*

Life and Work of a Victorian Genius) and his own distinguished hereditary background (his mother was a Darwin, and his grandmother a Barclay of British banking fame), these assertions imply that Galton's entire theory of hereditary genius represented a not very subtle form of self-congratulation.

Figure 1 Francis Galton with hat.

But in actual fact Galton's head was quite small. Contrary to Pearson, the Galton Papers in the Library at University College London (Folder 82) contain a document entitled "Comparative measurements of F. G. and W. E. Gladstone," in Galton's own handwriting, which gives Gladstone's head length and breadth as 8.1″ and 6.6″ respectively, while his own measures were a puny 7.1″ and 6.15″. And the raw data for the *English Men of Science* study reveal Galton's own hat circumference (21⅛″) as the fifth smallest out of the 99 measurements he obtained (Hilts, 1975, pp. 77–84). Thus Galton obviously held his belief in the connection between head size and intelligence with full knowledge that he himself had a relatively small head.

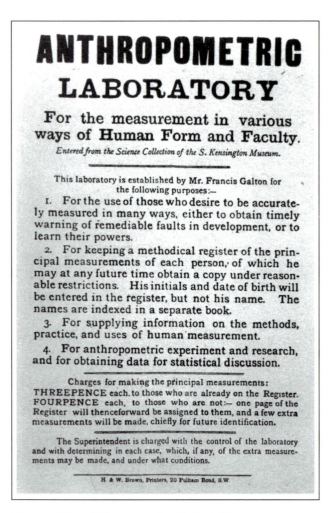

Figure 2 Broadside announcing Galton's laboratory

In truth, Galton's theory of hereditary genius was less a case of self-flattery than an attempt to account for his own perceived intellectual limita-

tions—for he actually held a rather modest opinion of his own relative abilities. In childhood he had been acclaimed by his doting family as a prodigy, and both he and they hoped he would go on to a distinguished university career. But he wound up performing only at a high average level at Cambridge, as his best efforts could not match those of the very top students. His relative failure precipitated an emotional breakdown and withdrawal from honors competition altogether. After several years of desultory drifting, Galton consulted a professional phrenologist who must have consoled him by declaring that his relative failure had not been due to moral weakness, but to a brain naturally unsuited to high levels of academic booklearning (Fancher, 1985, p. 24). Acting on the phrenologist's suggestion that his brain *was* well suited for success in more practical, outdoorsy kinds of pursuits, Galton soon embarked on an exploring expedition to Southwest Africa, which won the Royal Geographical Society's Gold Medal and launched him on his productive career.

Nevertheless, memories of his academic failure lingered. In *Hereditary Genius* (1869/1972) Galton likened intellectual to athletic ability in that training and education in both, no matter how intensive, always arrives at a limit. Just as the highly trained athlete eventually reaches a point where training serves only to maintain and no longer to improve performance, so does the aspiring intellectual reach a limit. In Galton's words, "the eager boy [who at first] fondly believes it to be within his reach to become one of the heroes who have left their mark upon the history of the world" gains experience in the various competitions of school and university, until finally "he learns precisely of what performances he is capable, and what other enterprises lie beyond his compass" (Galton, 1869/1972, pp. 57–58). In short, even the most highly schooled individuals will eventually come up against their own innate limitations.

In accounting for those limitations, Galton must naturally have looked to his own experience. Coming as he did from a highly privileged background, he could not easily blame his failure to achieve his high academic ambitions on a poor environment. But he *could* explain it on the basis of insufficient innate "natural ability," probably the result of a small and inappropriately configured brain. Thus when selecting measures of natural ability for his Anthropometric Laboratory, head size was an obvi-

Figure 3 Galton's Anthropometric Laboratory at the London Health Exhibition in 1884 (Pearson, 1914).

ous choice. Galton continued to believe in the association between head size and intelligence throughout his long life. When his disciple Karl Pearson used newly developed statistical techniques in 1901 and found a correlation of only +0.1 between head size and academic records for 1,000 Cambridge students, Galton wrote: "The non-correlation of ability and size of head continues to puzzle me the more I recall my own measurements and observations of the most eminent men of the day" (Pearson, 1914–1930, Vol. 3a, p. 248).

Soon after, however, it became generally recognized that the whole Galtonian program for testing intelligence was a blind alley, and that the neurophysiologically oriented theory on which it was based may have been plausible but was ultimately incorrect. Intelligence testing of the kind we know today had to await the very different kinds of procedures pioneered by Alfred Binet to diagnose mental retardation (Fancher, 1985). But Galton had firmly established the basic idea and hope for an intelligence test and also introduced the controversial notion that any "intelligence" it measures must be largely determined by heredity. Needless to say, the controversy continues today.

Bibliography

Fancher, R. E. (1985). *The intelligence men: Makers of the IQ controversy.* New York: Norton.

Forrest, D. W. (1974). *Francis Galton: The life and work of a Victorian genius.* London: Elek.

Galton, F. (1865). Hereditary talent and character. *Macmillan's Magazine, 12,* 157–166, 318–327.

Galton, F. (1874). *English men of science: Their nature and nurture.* London: Macmillan.

Galton, F. (1972). *Hereditary genius* (2nd ed.). Gloucester, MA: Peter Smith. (Original work published 1869)

Hilts, V. L. (1975). A guide to Francis Galton's "English men of science." *Transactions of the American Philosophical Society, 65,* Part 5.

Pearson, K. (1914–1930). *The life, letters and labours of Francis Galton* (Vols. 1–3). Cambridge: Cambridge University Press.

Metaphors of Memory:
The Case of Photography

Douwe Draaisma

In the course of its history, psychology has often drawn on mechanical analogies and metaphors to explain mental processes. Philosophers and psychologists alike have used the most advanced technologies of their day and age to offer a comprehensible image of the hidden processes in the human mind. Today computers and holograms are presented as metaphors for brain and mind, the most recent episode in a tradition stretching back to, perhaps, Plato, who likened memory to a wax tablet for registering "impressions" (Leary, 1990). Some of the best parts of the story of psychology can be told in metaphors. In theories of perception and visual memory, these metaphors were often taken from the domain of optical machinery and technologies for storing and retrieving visual information (Draaisma, 1995). A well-known example is Descartes' use of the camera obscura to elucidate the optical processes in the

"O Mister Daguerre! Sure you're not aware
Of half the impressions you're making."

(London, August 1839)

eye. The iris, Descartes explained in his *Dioptrics* (1637), is like the pinhole in the wall of a camera obscura. The crystal liquid is like the lens and the retina serves as a screen, receiving the projection of the visual image (Descartes, 1637). As in a *camera obscura*, the projected image is smaller and inverted, but all other geometric characteristics remain intact.

About a century later the French philosopher and materialist Lamettrie took recourse to another curious piece of optical apparatus, the *laterna magica*, to explain the working of visual memory. Our brain, he argued in *Man a Machine* (1747), functions like a "medullary screen upon which images of the objects painted in the eye are projected as by a magic lantern" (Lamettrie, 1912, p. 107).

The fleeting succession of images projected in a camera obscura, however, could not be retained. This, of course, was the essential difference between the camera obscura and photography. The invention of photography in 1839 introduced the possibility of conserving and reproducing the image projected upon the screen in a camera obscura (Tillmanns, 1981). Capturing the image on a light-sensitive surface, cameras were a happy combination of optics and chemistry. Photography gave the camera obscura a memory.

Soon after its public introduction, photography

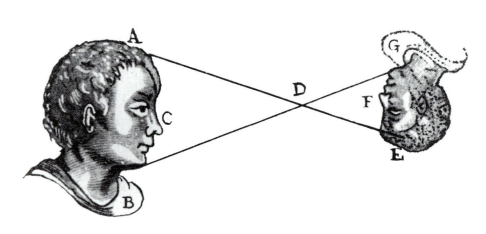

Figure 1 The projected image, both in a camera obscura and in a human eye, is a smaller and inverted copy of the original stimulus, according to Descartes (1637).

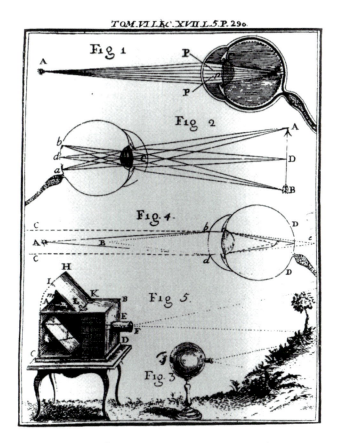

Figure 2 In 18th-century treatises on optics the camera obscura served as a popular analogy for the functional structure of the human eye (Plessen, 1993).

traces stored in a latent form: "just as the invisible impression left upon the sensitive paper of the Photographer is developed into a picture by the application of particular chemical re-agents" (p. 436). Maudsley tells us about an epileptic boy who could repeat a long article word for word after reading it only once. This is the kind of memory, Maudsley explained (1876) "in which the person seems to read a photographic copy of former impressions with his mind's eye" (p. 518). He had even heard of another case of someone who could repeat *backwards* what he had just read. In addition, Ladd (1891) in America, Delboeuf (1880) in Belgium, Kußmaul (1881) in Germany, all used photographic metaphors in the exposition of their theories.

Taken as a class, photographic metaphors stressed the notion of the engram as a static and fixed neuronal trace. Draper (1868), for example, presented human memory as a register of indelible traces: "I believe that a shadow never falls upon a wall without leaving thereupon its permanent trace—a trace which might be made visible by resorting to proper processes. All kinds of photographic drawing are in their degree examples of the kind" (p. 288).

The neuronal substrate of our memories, according to Draper, bears a strong resemblance to the duration, the emergence, and the extinction of impressions on photographic preparations (1878):

> Thus I have seen landscapes and architectural views taken in Mexico, developed, as artists say, months subsequently in New York, the images coming out, after the long voyage, in all their proper forms and in all their proper contrast of light and shade. The photograph had forgotten nothing. (pp. 133–134)

Draper was a prominent physiologist and the author of a much-used handbook in physiology (Draper, 1868). He was also a pioneer of photography. In 1840 he made the first Daguerreotype portrait (Taft, 1942). A few years later he experimented with a new photographic process called *ambrotype,* in which a weakly illuminated negative was placed against a background of black velvet in order to appear as a positive. This type of photography, Draper felt, was particularly apt to illustrate the hidden nature of memory traces. Our minds are

> silent galleries, with silhouettes of whatever we have done upon its walls. These images are too faint to be noticed, except when we are in twilight reveries or are asleep and withdrawn from external influences. Then the mind turns inward and looks over the ambrotypes she has col-

turned up as a psychological metaphor which came to dominate the early theories of visual memory until the invention of the cinematographer made these metaphors seem obsolete and out of place. Books and articles by neurologists and psychologists easily provide a handful of examples. The French neurologist Luys, for instance, referred to the then newly reported research by Niépce de Saint-Victor which proved that a pattern of light rays could be stored on a sensitive plate, kept there in the form of "silent vibrations" or latent vibrations, and could then be reproduced at a later stage (Luys, 1878, p. 106). If inorganic material has this capacity, Luys argued, why not assume it in the organic material of nervous tissue as well? Our brain presents a natural parallel to the artificial processes in photography. Photographic metaphors of this type were especially popular in circles of "mental physiologists." For example, Carpenter (1879) wrote that photography might help to explain how it is possible for memories to *seem* to have disappeared and then, under certain special conditions, be revived again. It was all a matter of

Figure 3 Ambrotype portrait of the American physiologist and photographer John William Draper.

lected—ambrotypes, for they are truly unfading impressions—and, combining them together, as they chance to occur, constructs from them the panorama of a dream. (Draper, 1878, p. 135)

Considering that the image of an ambrotype became visible only against a pitchdark background, this was an elegant metaphor indeed.

Photographic metaphors also served to explain specific memory processes because they displayed a close correspondence between the technical manipulation of optical patterns and the neurological processing of visual images. A good case in point is Francis Galton's theory of "generic images," which was inspired by a photographic procedure of his own invention, a device called *compound photography.*

In 1877, Galton was invited to conduct an inquiry into the relation between "criminal types" and their features. His first attempts, uncoiling measuring tapes around delinquents' heads and holding their skulls between rulers, remained fruitless. The differences were too small to be meaningful. Galton then experimented with an ingenious photographic procedure. He collected a series of portraits and photographed these one by one onto the same plate, dividing the exposure time through the number of portraits. The result was a composite portrait depicting the "average" face of the men on the origi-

nal portraits. Each composite portrait presented a reinforcement of shared features. Since individual peculiarities remained underexposed they disappeared from the final portrait. Galton claimed that his compound photography was a form of "pictorial statistics," presenting at the same time an average and a visualization of variance. Sharper outlines indicated less variance.

Galton was extremely pleased with his invention. He lectured and wrote extensively on his compound photography and published many specimens. Some of the more spectacular applications included his portrait of Alexander the Great, taken from six different medals; the composite portraits of 12 officers and 11 privates; and even the composite portraits of thoroughbreds, used for predicting the probable features of their offspring. A collection of specimens appeared as the frontispiece in Galton's *Inquiries into Human Faculty and Its Development* (1883/1907). In the same memoir, read before the Anthropological Institute in 1878 and which announced his compound photography, Galton hinted on the close analogy between a composite portrait and a generalized visual image (1907): "A composite portrait represents the picture that would rise before the mind's eye of a man who had the gift of pictorial imagination in an exalted degree" (pp. 223–224). In a lecture for the Royal Institution one year later, Galton incorporated compound

Figure 4 Composite portraits of English delinquents, made by superimposing a series of individual portraits.

Galton concluded his lecture by pointing out an additional advantage of his analogy between generic images and composite pictures. The latter, he remarked, may be studied at leisure, and can be subjected to experiments and careful statistical examination. It is to be expected that from these investigations we may draw conclusions on "the nature of certain mental processes which are too mobile and evanescent to be directly dealt with" (Galton, 1907, p. 233). According to Galton, composite portraiture could serve as a *simulation*.

Galton's metaphor was held in great esteem by his contemporaries. Alfred Binet was one of the few to criticize its use. He felt that compound photography was too mechanical to be a plausible analogy for the intricacies of memory. Were the human eye to take the position of the lens in Galton's apparatus, Binet claimed, the resulting image would not resemble a photographic average. Our memories are determined by our tastes and predilections, by attention and emotions, and by innumerable psychological factors absent in compound photography (Binet, 1886, p. 109). Still, Galton's metaphor caught the imagination of his time to an extraordinary degree, as did most photographic metaphors. A short reflection on the mesmerizing force of technical metaphors in 19th-century psychology of memory may well be called for.

It should be remembered that photography was an extremely impressive technology to the 19th-century mind. Specifically, three characteristics contributed to its metaphoric appeal. First, it carried the suggestion of truth. A photograph was seen as a direct registration of a visual scene. In comparison, all other visual arts were said to lack this realistic quality. Second, photography was a semiautomatic process, which allowed reality to reflect itself on a receiving surface. Between the lens and the plate optical information found its own way without any human intervention. And third, photography offered a powerful illustration of information stored in a latent, coded way—a mechanical parallel to a type of neurological processing in which the image-like quality of visual scenes disappears. As Draper (1868) explained, there is no resemblance between our perceptions and their substrate in memory "any more

photography as a metaphor in his theory of memory. Speaking of the physiological basis of memory, Galton explained that our brain functions like the sensitive plate in the apparatus for compound photography, blending specific visual memories into "generic images" (Galton, 1907, p. 229). The term *generic* referred to *genus,* indicating that this type of image was a true generalization. Galton argued that his composite portraiture solved the problem, real enough in an empiricist epistemology, of how it is possible for human memory to contain representations of types when no such things were ever presented to the senses. In fact, Galton's formulations closely resemble current theories on prototype abstraction, suggested in the context of connectionist research, when he specifies that his portraits are the photographic equivalents of representations "that are not copies of any individual, but represent the characteristic features of classes" (Galton, 1907, p. 230).

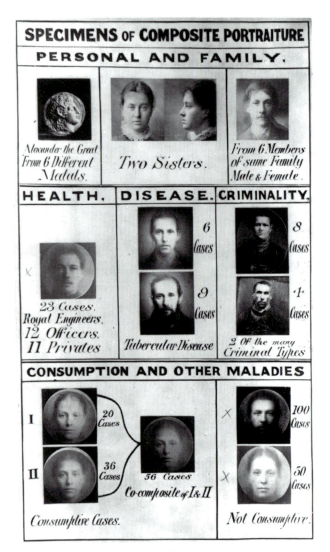

Figure 5 Frontispiece of Galton's *Inquiries into Human Faculty and Its Development* (1883).

This very quality is perhaps the most direct link to the use of metaphors in recent theories of visual memory. Pribram's notion of holographic memory, for instance, serves to outline the physical possibility of distributed memory traces, relatively immune to disruption by local lesions—a quality shared by brains, holograms, and neural networks, called "graceful degradation" (Pribram, 1966). In this particular respect the Pribrams of our days resemble Descartes, Lamettrie, Galton and other theorists of memory, who interpreted human recollection in terms of the latest optical machinery.

Acknowledgment

The author wishes to thank Ruth Benschap for her helpful comments in the preparation of this chapter.

Bibliography

Binet, A. (1886). *La psychologie du raisonnement*. Paris: Alcan.

Carpenter, W. B. (1879). *Principles of mental physiology*. London: Kegan Paul. (Original work published 1874)

Descartes, R. (1637). *Discours de la méthode. La Dioptrique*. Leiden: Jean Maire.

Delboeuf, J. (1880). Le sommeil et les rêves: Leurs rapports avec la théorie de la mémoire. *Revue Philosophique, Vol. IX*, 129–169; 413–417.

Draaisma, D. (1995). *De metaforenmachine. Een geschiedenis van het geheugen*. Groningen: Historische Uitgeverij.

Draper, J. W. (1868). *Human physiology*. New York: Harper & Brothers. (Original work published 1857)

Draper, J. W. (1878). *History of the conflict between religion and science*. London: Kegan Paul.

Galton, F. (1907). *Inquiries into human faculty and its developments*. London: Dent & Sons. (Original work published 1883)

Gernsheim, H. (1968). *L. J. M. Daguerre*. New York: Dover.

Kussmaul, A. (1881). *Die Störungen der Sprache*. Leipzig: Vogel.

Ladd, G. T. (1891). *Physiological psychology*. London: Longmans Green. (Original work published 1887)

Lamettrie, J. O. de. (1912). *Man a machine*. Chicago: The Open Court. (Original work published 1747)

Leary, D. E. (Ed.). (1990). *Metaphors in the history of psychology*. New York: Cambridge University Press.

Luys, J. (1878). *Le cerveau et ses fonctions*. Paris: Germer Baillière. (Original work published 1876)

Maudsley, H. (1876). *The physiology of mind*. London: Macmillan. (Original work published 1868)

Pearson, K. R. (1924). *The life, letters and labours of Francis Galton* (Vol. 2). Cambridge: Cambridge University Press.

Plessen, M.-L. von (Ed.). (1993). *Sehsucht. Das Panorama als Massenunterhaltung des 19. Jahrhunderts*. Bonn: Kunst- und Ausstellungshalle der Bundesrepublik Deutschland.

Pribram, K. R. (1966). Some dimensions of remembering: Steps toward a neuropsychological model of memory. In J. Gaito (Ed.), *Macromolecules and behavior* (pp. 165–187). Amsterdam: North-Holland.

Taft, R. (1942). *Photography and the American scene. A social history, 1839–1889*. New York: Macmillan.

Tillmanns, U. (1981). *Geschichte der Photographie*. Stuttgart: Huber Frauenfeld.

than there is between the letters of a message delivered in a telegraphic office and the signals which the telegraph gives to the distant station" (p. 288).

As one gathers from these examples, it would be unfounded to dismiss photographic metaphors—or indeed any technical metaphor—as purely rhetorical figures. Most metaphors served in the context of professional communication. Their most important function seems to have been the presentation of evidence that hypothetical processes, be they mental or neurological, were physically possible. The physical architecture of photography delineated a domain of material possibilities, offering visible proof that information could be stored away in a material medium and kept there until it was reproduced.

Brentano: Psychology from an Empirical Standpoint

Elisabeth Baumgartner
Wilhelm Baumgartner

Franz Brentano (1838–1917) was among the most eminent pioneers and founders of modern psychology. His work and influence extended not only into psychology, however, but into philosophy as well. As a result of his widespread contributions, Brentano continues to attract the attention of contemporary historians of psychology.

Methodology

Brentano first proposed his revolutionary views about psychology during the 1866 public defense of his second dissertation. His position was also expressed explicitly in the title of his best-known book, *Psychology from an Empirical Standpoint* (1874/1995b). In this book Brentano tells us: "The method of psychology is no other than that of [natural] science, [except] that experience forms its basis" (p. 154). Psychological phenomena or functions can be understood directly on the basis of experience (called *empeiria* by the Greeks).

Psychological functions can be studied by (a) the method of inner perception, which was later developed into the method of introspection or self-perception by the Würzburg School; (b) the logical method, which can describe inner processes in statements and propositions meeting the criteria of linguistic criticism and logic; and (c) the method of experimental research, employed by Brentano in his research on the senses (1907). The latter method required a psychological laboratory, and Brentano requested funding for the establishment of such a facility (a "psychological cabinet," as he referred to it) at the University of Vienna as early as 1874.

In his posthumous book, *Descriptive Psychology* (1982/1995a), Brentano sought to clarify the irreducible elements and interrelated structures of the psyche by the "analytical description" of "psychic acts." In earlier work (1874/1995b, 1911b) he also included a comprehensive "classification of psychic phenomena," which he used to construct and explain "the whole" of mental life from its "parts."

Divisions of Psychology

According to Brentano (1982/1995a):

> [Psychology is] the science of the mental life of man. . . . It tries to identify the elements of human consciousness and to specify how they

Figure 1 Photograph of Brentano as a Catholic priest (Würzburg, 1864).

are interrelated. It further seeks to find out the conditions with which the individual phenomena are related causally. The first of these tasks is to be carried out by psychognosis (descriptive psychology or phenomenology), while the second task belongs to genetic psychology. (p. 1)

Brentano made this distinction on the basis of psychology's methodology. First, there must be *analytic*, or "purely descriptive," psychology, whose aim is to investigate mental phenomena in the same self-evident manner in which they are presented—through "inner perception" or "inner experience." Then there is *genetic* psychology, which permits some causal explanations. However, it was "obvious" for Brentano that "genetic psychology will never fulfill its special task without the inclusion of physio-chemical processes and the identification of anatomical structures" (Brentano, 1982/1995a, p. 1).

In Brentano's words, genetic psychology "totally lacks precision." It operates on a probabilistic basis until it can identify all of the relevant genetic parameters completely and distinctly. On the other hand, descriptive psychology defines the components of mental events as long as these are experienced directly. Thus, descriptive psychology is the foundation of genetic psychology. However, as it becomes more sophisticated, genetic psychology can provide reciprocal services to psychognosis or descriptive psychology.

Intentionality

Brentano regarded *intentionality* as the chief characteristic of mental life (1874/1995b):

> Every mental phenomenon is characterized by what the Scholastics of the Middle Ages called the intentional (or mental) inexistence of an object, and what we might call, though not without ambiguity, reference to a content, direction toward an object (which is not to be understood here as meaning a thing), or immanent objectivity. Every mental phenomenon includes something as object within itself, although they do not all do so in the same way. In presentation something is presented, in judgment something is affirmed or denied, in love, loved, in hate, hated, in desire, desired, and so on. (p. 88)

The above may well be the best-known quotation from Brentano's work. With this core statement, he provided the foundations for not only his own "act psychology," but also the Graz School of Psychology, the Würzburg School, and even attribution theory and cognitive psychology. Brentano has also been called the "grandfather of phenomenology"

(Ryle, 1976). He stressed that psychic functions (ideas, judgments, emotions) are acts, or subjective behaviors (1889/1969, p. 14), which are *intentional*, or directed toward something. Intentional thought or behavior is always directed toward an object and includes a self-reference.

Brentano's Life and Work

Despite his considerable impact on the development of psychology and philosophy, Brentano's work has generally attracted little attention, with the exception of his concept of intentionality. Reasons for the relative neglect of this seminal figure can be found by looking into his life and times.

Brentano's academic studies were centered around philosophy and theology. In 1862, he received his doctorate from Tübingen University with a dissertation titled "On the several senses of being in Aristotle"(1862/1981). Brentano became a Catholic priest two years later, and in 1866 he became qualified to teach at Würzburg University after completing his second dissertation about "The Psychology of Aristotle" (1867/1977). His teaching

Figure 2 Brentano in Vienna (ca. 1890).

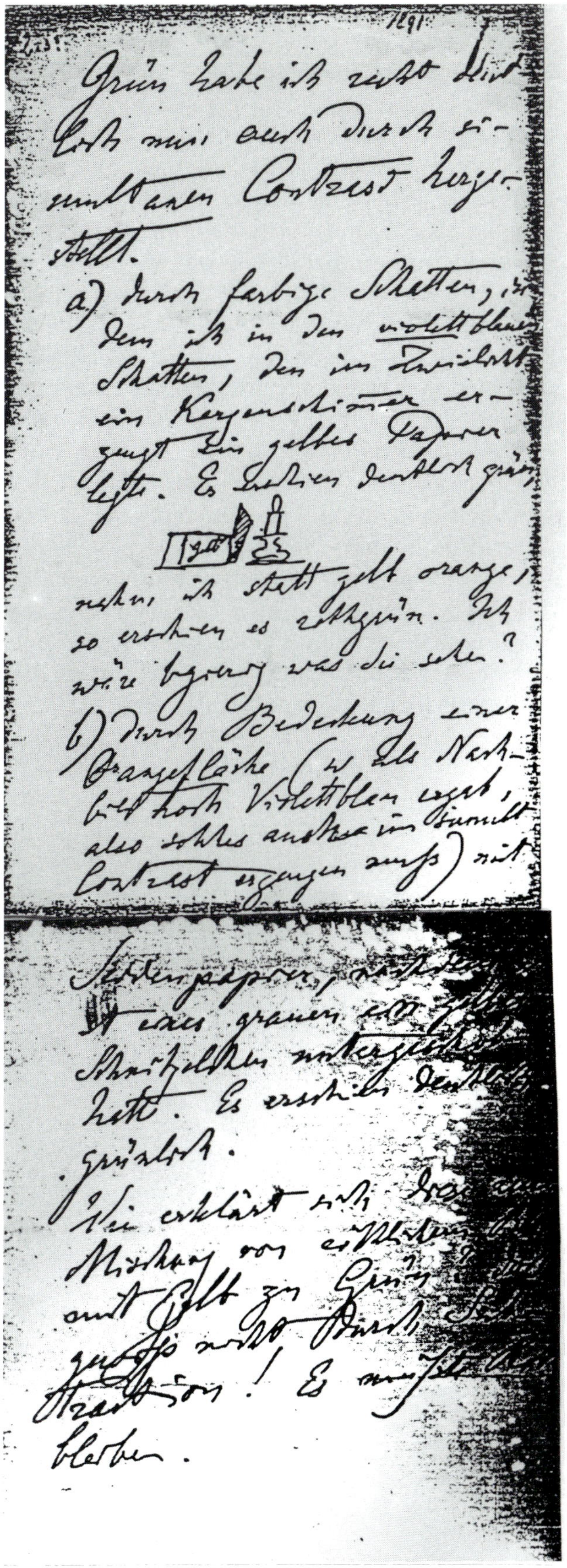

Figure 3 Description of color vision experiment by Brentano during his Vienna period (March 2, 1891).

attracted numerous students (Kraus, 1919), including Carl Stumpf (1848–1936), the founder of the Berlin School of Gestalt Psychology, Anton Marty (1847–1914), a leading member of the Prague School of Linguistics, and Hermann Schell (1850–1906), a controversial Catholic theologian.

During the summer of 1869, the dogma of papal infallibility was hotly debated in Catholic circles around the world. Brentano became directly involved in the controversy when Wilhelm von Ketteler (1811–1877), a German bishop and social reformer, asked him to write a position paper about the dogma for the National Conference of German Bishops. In this document, Brentano stated that infallibility opposed the traditions of the Catholic Church and could not be justified on logical grounds. When the dogma of infallibility was eventually proclaimed in Rome, Brentano's position at Würzburg became untenable, and consequently, he resigned in 1873 from both the priesthood and his professorial appointment.

Shortly afterwards, in January of 1874, Brentano was awarded a prestigious position as a full professor at the University of Vienna. His call to Vienna was justified by his "aptitude for ingenious and productive scholarship"and by his "notorious and impressive success" as an academic teacher (Stremeyer, 1873, 1874). His students at Vienna included Edmund Husserl (1859–1938), the founder of phenomenology; Christian von Ehrenfels (1859–1932), who first formulated the principles of Gestalt psychology; Alexius Meinong (1853–1920), the founder of the Graz School of Psychology and of object theory; Thomas G. Masaryk (1850–1937), the first president of Czechoslovakia; and Sigmund Freud (1856–1939), the founder of psychoanalysis.

The year 1879 brought another radical disruption to Brentano's life. He finally left the Catholic Church and made plans to marry Ida von Lieben (1855–1894). Unfortunately, it was illegal in Austria for former priests to marry and to hold an official position at the same time. Brentano tried to get around the restriction by becoming a citizen of the Kingdom of Saxony beforehand. The couple was married in Leipzig in 1880, but upon his return to Vienna, Brentano was nevertheless forced to give up his chair at the university. Efforts to help him regain his tenured appointment failed, so once again Brentano had to obtain permission to offer lectures and seminars. As an unsalaried and untenurable instructor, he was neither authorized to direct dissertations nor participate in the academic self-gov-

Figure 4 Franz Brentano in Florence (ca. 1900).

ernment. However, he continued his psychological researches in the field of color vision, as indicated in the following excerpt from a letter to his friend, Anton Marty, in Prague (Brentano, 1891):

> I was able to produce a visible green by . . . placing a yellow sheet of paper in the purple-bluish shadow made by the dim light of a candle. . . . When I used orange [paper], the color red-green appeared. . . . I am eager to know what you can see under these conditions. . . . When I covered the orange surface with tissue paper, under which I placed a tiny piece of gray rather than yellow paper, the color green appeared. How can red-blue and yellow become green? Certainly not by subtraction! The Color should remain red. (p. 2)

After his wife died in 1894, Brentano decided to leave Austria. Before his departure, he published an explanation for this decision in four polemic newspaper articles under the title "My Last Wishes for Austria" (Brentano, 1895). He moved to Italy and eventually settled down in Florence into the life of a private scholar. In later years, his eyesight weakened dramatically. He became unable to read and

write and had to depend on the support of his second wife. When Italy entered World War I, Brentano, an avowed pacifist, moved to Zürich, where he died on March 17, 1917.

The circumstances of Brentano's life indicate why his ideas were not widely accepted in the academic world of his time. He did not publish much during his active university career, partly because he was so very critical of his own work. After his retirement, however, five major books were finally published (Brentano; 1889/1969, 1907, 1911a, 1911c/1978). Many of Brentano's ideas were further elaborated by his students, who did not always give him credit for ideas that he originated.

The Franz Brentano Research Center in Würzburg, Germany, has assumed responsibility for documenting Brentano's unique accomplishments. Special projects include the publication of scientific editions of Brentano's published and posthumous works and an edition of his extensive correspondence. In addition, the Würzburg group also publishes a series of book-length *Brentano Studies* (1988–1991) for an international audience.

Bibliography

Baumgartner, E. (1985). *Intentionalität, Begriffsgeschichte und Begriffsanwendung in der Psychologie.* Würzburg: Königshausen & Neumann.

Baumgartner, W., & Burkard, F. P. (1990). Franz Brentano. Eine Skizze seines Lebens und seiner Werke; Franz-Brentano-Bibliographie. In W. L. Gombocz, R. Haller, & N. Henrichs (Eds.), *Internationale Bibliographie zur Österreichischen Philosophie* (pp. 17–53; 54–159). Amsterdam-Atlanta: Rodopi.

Baumgartner, W., Burkard, F. P., & Wiedmann, F. (Eds.). (1988ff). *Brentano Studien,* I–V. Würzburg: Dettelbach: Röll.

Brentano, F. (1866) A*d disputationem qua theses gratiosi philosophorum ordinis consensu et auctoritate pro imenetranda venia docendi in alma universitate julio-maximiliana defendet.* Aschaffenburg: J.W. Schipner.

Brentano, F. (1891, March 2). Letter to Anton Marty (unpublished). Würzburg: Franz Brentano Forschung.

Brentano, F. (1895). *Meine letzen Wünsche für Österreich* [My last wishes for Austria]. Stuttgart: Cotta.

Brentano, F. (1907). *Untersuchungen sur Sinnespsychologie.* Hamburg: Meiner.

Brentano, F. (1911a). *Aristoteles Lehre vom Ursprung des menschlichen Geistes.* Leipzig: Veit & Co.

Brentano, F. (1911b). *Von der Klassifikation der psychischen Phänomene.* Leipzig: Quelle & Meyer.

Brentano, F. (1969) *The origin of our knowledge of right and wrong.* (Rev. ed.) London: Routledge & Kegan Paul. (Original work published 1889: *Vom Ursprung sittlicher Erkenntnis*)

Brentano, F. (1977). *The psychology of Aristotle.* Berkeley: University of California Press. (Original work published 1867: *Die Psychologie des Aristoteles*)

Brentano, F. (1978). *Aristotle and his world view.* Berkeley: University of California Press. (Original work published 1911c: *Aristoteles und seine Weltanschauung*)

Brentano, F. (1981). *On the several senses of being in Aristotle: Aristotle Metaphysics Z. 1.* (2nd ed.) Berkeley: University of California Press. (Original work published 1862: *Von der mannigfachen Bedeutung des Seienden nach Aristoteles*)

Brentano, F. (1995a). *Descriptive psychology.* London: Routledge. (Original work published 1982: *Deskriptive Psychologie*)

Brentano, F. (1995b). *Psychology from an empirical standpoint.* London: Routledge. (Original work published 1874: *Psychologie vom empirischen Standpunkte*)

Chisholm, R. M. (1982). *Brentano and Meinong Studies.* Amsterdam–Atlanta: Rodopi.

Chisholm, R. M., & Haller, R. (Eds.). (1978). *Die Philosophie Franz Brentanos.* Amsterdam: Rodopi.

Kraus, O. (Ed.). (1919). *Franz Brentano. Zur Kenntnis seines Lebens und seiner Lehre.* Munich: Beck.

McAlister, L. L. (Ed.). (1976). *The Philosophy of Brentano.* London: Duckworth.

Ryle, G. (1976). Disgusted grandfather of phenomenology. *Times Higher Education Supplement*, p. 19 (September 10).

Stremeyer, K. V. (1873,1874). *Majestätsvortrag. (12-30-1873).* Vienna: Allgemeines Verwaltungsarchiv.

William James: America's Premier Psychologist

Klaus Jürgen Bruder

The career of William James (1842–1910) is, in many ways, similar to that of other prominent figures in the history of modern psychology. As James himself put it: "I originally studied medicine in order to be a physiologist, but drifted into psychology and philosophy from a sort of fatality" (Menard, 1911, p. 5).

James appears to have been strongly predisposed toward the study of philosophy by the intellectual climate that was characteristic of the James family during his formative years. However, he could not approach his philosophical interests directly, because his father, who himself despised the natural sciences, nevertheless wanted his eldest son to become a scientist. Becoming a psychologist was, therefore, a natural compromise between philosophy and the natural sciences and, more importantly, a genuine act of personal emancipation.

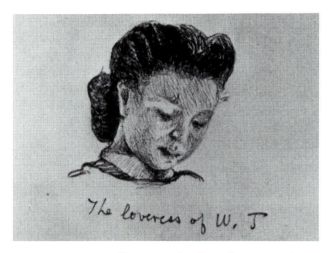

Figure 1 Drawing of his sister Alice by William James (1860 /fMS AM 1092.2). (Figures 1–7 reprinted by permission of the Houghton Library, Harvard University. Shelf marks given with dates.)

William James was born on January 11, 1842, in Manhattan. He was the eldest of the five children of Henry James (1811–1882), a wealthy Swedenborgian philosopher and author, and his wife, Mary James (née Walsh) (1810–1882). The second child born into the family was Henry James (1843–1916), who grew up to become the well-known writer. Two more brothers, Garth Wilkinson James (1845–1883) and Robertson James (1846–1910) followed Henry, and finally, in 1848, the much beloved sister, Alice James (1848–1892), was born.

Henry James, Sr., took on the full responsibility for the education of his children. They accompanied him on his "impulsive journeyings" throughout Europe. The children were instructed by private tutors from 1855 to 1858 in France and England, and from 1859 to 1860 in Germany and Switzerland. As a result, William attended public school in New York for only three years.

In the late fall of 1860 William's father gave him grudging permission to take painting lessons in the studio of William M. Hunt (1824–1879) and John La Farge (1835–1910) in Newport, R.I., where the family had lived after 1858. James, however, gave up the painting lessons after less than a year and enrolled as a student at the Lawrence Scientific School in Boston, which was loosely attached to Harvard University.

Later, after his family moved to Boston in 1864, James became a student at the Harvard Medical School. His medical studies, which normally would have taken years, including a brief internship, were interrupted by William's participation in a scientific expedition to Brazil (1865–1866). During this journey, he became seriously ill. A long period of physical, emotional, and mental recovery was spent in Europe—particularly in Germany. His intensive philosophical, psychological, and aesthetic studies in Dres-

66

The course, which was offered for a second time in 1876, focused on "The Relations between Physiology and Psychology" and included a few simple demonstrations and laboratory experiments. Around this time, James also opened his own small laboratory "in a tiny room under the stairway of the Agassiz Museum . . . [with] a metronome, a device for whirling frogs, a horopter chart and one or two bits of apparatus" (Allen, 1967, p.194) Promotion to the rank of assistant professor of physiology and a 50-percent raise in salary followed in 1876.

James's accomplishments in the new field of psychology were recognized two years later, in 1878, by an invitation to write a comprehensive textbook in introductory psychology for the prestigious publishing firm of Henry Holt and Company of New York. During the same year, the 36-year-old James married Alice Gibbons (1849–1922), who, in a manner of

Figure 2 William James as an art student in Newport, R.I. (ca. 1861/pfMS AM 1092).

den, Berlin, Heidelberg, Geneva, France, and assorted Bohemian spas may well have formed the experiential basis for his later *stream of consciousness* concept.

Upon his return to the United States, James finally completed his medical education at Harvard University in 1869. Between 1869 and 1872 he experienced another serious personal crisis accompanied by severe depression. Like so many of his upper-class countrymen at the time, James was seriously afraid of becoming mentally ill. To protect himself from his "sickening" introspection and his excessive inclination toward brooding about philosophical questions, James forced himself to develop greater intellectual and mental discipline. Specifically, he credited the writings of Charles B. Renouvier (1815–1903), the idealistic French philosopher, for having rescued him from this episode. According to James, Renouvier taught him to believe in personal freedom and, thus, to liberate himself from the doom of determinism.

In the spring of 1872, James was offered a one-year instructorship at Harvard to teach a course in "Comparative Anatomy and Physiology." James viewed this appointment as an opportunity to gain more self-discipline and to begin making a name for himself as a scientist.

In the fall of 1875, James, who had never himself taken a course in psychology, offered the first graduate course in psychology at Harvard University.

Figure 3 William James as the newly appointed Instructor of Anatomy and Physiology (1873/bMS AM 1092.9 [1174]).

Figure 4 Henry and William James (ca. 1902/pfMS AM 1092 box 2).

speaking, had been chosen for him by his father. Alice was a 27-year-old school-teacher who shared his interests in European culture, literary tastes, and a liberal world view. The marriage also seems to have initiated a lengthy period of serious psychosomatic illness in James's only sister Alice, a condition from which she never recovered.

In 1879, William's first son, Henry James (1879–1947), who was named after his paternal grandfather and uncle, was born. It was also during that same year that James began to offer regular courses in philosophy. Less than a year later, in 1880, he received a professorial appointment in philosophy at Harvard. Promotions to full professorship in philosophy and the sub-discipline of psychology followed in 1885 and 1889, respectively. The 1880s also brought many dramatic changes in the family constellation. In 1882 alone, James's mother died from pneumonia; in June his second son, William James (1882–1916), was born; and in December his father died "tranquil and painlessly" at the age of 71. A third son, Herman James, "a beautiful, Jewish-looking, sturdy and lively boy" was born in January of 1884. However, Herman became ill with whooping cough and died from pneumonia in June of the next

Figure 5 The James residence at 95 Irving Street, Cambridge, Massachusetts in winter (pfMS AM 1092).

Varietes of Religious Experience. (James.)

(I) "Paradoxical as it may appear to Thee, O Lord —

from G. K. Chesterton drawn by him.

Figure 6 Caricature by G. K. Chesterton of James presenting the Gifford Lectures on "The Varieties of Religious Experience" (1908/Autograph file [Chesterton]).

The Principles James introduced the *stream of consciousness* metaphor, and the book served both as a handbook of experimental psychology and as a reasoned critique of the field from the perspective of individual psychology. James believed that the work on this "strictly positivistic" magnum opus had at last liberated him from his "monistic superstitions" and the "fetters of determinism" under which he had grown up. He now hoped to be able to deal confidently and victoriously with not merely psychological questions, but finally, with significant philosophical issues as well. Consequently, he felt free to turn over the responsibility for the experimental psychology laboratory at Harvard to Hugo Münsterberg (1863–1916) in 1892. During the same year, his sister Alice died at the age of 44. Her generous bequest enabled James and his entire family to take a leisurely sabbatical in Europe.

The remaining years of James's life were dedicated to the writing and publication of increasingly original works in philosophy, ethics, and religion. These efforts were to reveal gradually the central concepts of his personal philosophy, which were only hinted at in *The Principles*. *The Will to Believe and Other Essays in Popular Philosophy* (1897) illustrated once again his search for intellectual freedom through self-discipline.

During one of his journeys to Europe—this one to help him recover from serious heart disease—James wrote his famous "Gifford Lectures" for presentation at Edinburgh University. In these essays, which were shortly afterwards published under the title *Varieties of Religious Experience* (1902), James passionately described the religious perspective on life and defended it from attacks by the materialistic science of his time.

Shortly before his retirement from the increasing burdens of academic teaching, James published a summation of his philosophical views under the title *Pragmatism: A New Name for Some Old Ways of Thinking* (1907). This collection of writings, which takes a clear stand on behalf of the individual's right and responsibility to think independently, is perhaps James's most original contribution to modern philosophy. His ideas on the subject were continued in the 1909 essays *A Pluralistic Universe* and *The Meaning of Truth*.

William James died from "heart failure" but "without pain or consciousness" around 2:00 AM on August 26, 1910, in Chocorua, shortly after one more trip to all the places he loved in Europe. His final

year. Two more children, daughter Mary Margaret (Porter) (1887–1947) and the youngest child, Alexander Robertson James (1890–1946), were born at three-year intervals.

After 1886, occasional weekends and most summers were spent at the family's vacation retreat, a heavily wooded farm with a "weatherbeaten" house near Chocorua Mountain in nearby New Hampshire. During the same period, James spent lengthy periods of time either alone, or occasionally with his family, in Germany, England, France, Italy, and Switzerland, working on his writings and seeking to recover from his numerous physical and emotional illnesses. At last, in 1889, the James family moved into their newly-built mansion at 95 Irving Street in Cambridge, Massachusetts.

In 1890 James published *The Principles of Psychology* in two heavy volumes. This work was clearly a crowning achievement, despite its long gestation, and it earned James a solid place as one of the most important psychologists of his time. In

Figure 7 James and his daughter Margaret (1892/pfMS AM 1092).

works, *Some Problems of Philosophy* and *Essays in Radical Empiricism*, were published posthumously in 1911 and 1912, respectively.

Bibliography

Allen, G. (1967). *William James*. New York: Viking.

Bruder K. J. (1982). *Psychologie ohne Bewußtsein*. Frankfurt: Suhrkamp.

Bruder, K. J. (1988). William James' "Stream of consciousness"—Ausdruck nicht der Auflösung, sondern der Realität des Ich. Paper read at 7th Annual Cheiron-Europe Conference, Budapest.

Bruder, K. J. (1989a). William James: Das Ich, der gegenwärtige Augenblick im Strom des Bewußtseins. In M. Pfister (Ed.), *Krise and Modernisierung des Ich* (Vol. I., pp. 9–20). Passau: Rothe.

Bruder, K. J. (1989b). Die Selbstfreisetzung des Ich in der Metapher seiner Auflösung. William James' "Strom des Bewußtseins." *Psychologie und Geschichte*, *1*, 4–83.

Bruder, K. J. (1990a). Die kulturellen und biographischen Hintergründe der besonderen Darstellungsform der Psychologie in den "Principles" von William James. Paper presented at 9th Annual Cheiron-Europe Conference, Weimar, Germany.

Bruder, K. J. (1990b). Subjectivity and the Post Modern Discourse. Paper presented at "Principles Congress," Amsterdam.

Bruder, K. J. (1991). Zwischen Kant and Freud: Die Institutionalisierung der Psychologie als selbständige Wissenschaft. In G. Jüttemann, K. Sonntag, & C. Wulf (Eds.), *Die Seele. Ihre Geschichte im Abendland* (pp. 319–339). Weinheim: PVU.

James, W. (1890). *The principles of psychology* (Vols. 1 & 2). New York: Holt.

James, W. (1897). *The will to believe, and other essays in popular philosophy*. New York: Longmans, Green & Company.

James, W. (1902). *The varieties of religious experience*. New York: Longmans, Green & Company.

James, W. (1907). *Pragmatism: A new name for some old ways of thinking*. New York: Longmans, Green & Company.

James, W. (1909a). *A pluralistic universe*. New York: Longmans, Green & Company.

James, W. (1909b). *The meaning of truth*. New York: Longmans, Green & Company.

James W. (1911). *Some problems of philosophy*. New York: Longmans, Green & Company.

James, W. (1912). *Essays in radical empircism*. New York: Longmans, Green & Company.

Menard, A. (1911). *Analyse et critique des principes de la psychologie de W. James*. Paris: Alcan.

Myers, G. (1986). *William James*. New Haven, CT: Yale University Press.

Parapsychology

Eberhard Bauer

The word *parapsychology* was coined in 1889 by Max Dessoir (1867–1947) of Berlin University, the historian of psychology who defined his new creation in the following ponderous paragraph (1889):

> Since the [Greek prefix] 'para' is used to refer to something which occurs beyond or outside the ordinary one can refer to phenomena which exceed or go beyond normal mental life as "parapsychological [events]." Hence the field of study which deals with these issues can be called parapsychology. . . . The word is not beautiful, but, in my opinion it has the advantage of characterizing the still unknown border region between everyday life and [clearly] abnormal and pathological states [of mind]. (p. 341)

Dessoir's definition implies a close association between parapsychological phenomena and the field of psychology. Historically speaking, the definition of parapsychology as a subspecialty of academic psychology remains problematic. The reason for these difficulties is the "occult atmosphere" (Dessoir, 1889) that surrounds the field of parapsychology despite all the efforts of its leaders to become scientifically respectable. The complex and multilayered subject matter of parapsychology, which resists inclusion among the traditional academic specialties, is another obstacle. Finally, it is quite possible that many mainstream psychologists disdain or oppose the study of parapsychology because they are afraid of diminishing psychology's status and reputation as a modern science (Rhine, 1976; Schmeidler, 1989). The first organized effort to attempt to investigate "mental phenomena, which go beyond normal mental life" objectively and systematically occurred seven years before Dessoir named the new field of study. This was, of course, the 1882 foundation of the Society for Psychical Research (SPR) in London, which is still active today. Its founding members included eminent scholars and scientists of the Victorian Establishment like the physicist, Sir William Barrett (1844–1925), the Cambridge philosopher Henry Sidgwick (1838–1901), the classicist Frederick H.

Figure 1 Experimental setting for the 1920 Heymans-Brugmans study of telepathy. The experimental subject's hand was to be guided from a distant room.

Figure 2 Participants at the 1921 Copenhagen Congress.

Myers (1843–1901), and the musicologist Edmund Gurney (1847–1888). The goals of SPR included research questions which can be traced to the heritage of mesmerism and early mid-19th century spiritualism, such as the study of hypnotism, the various forms of mesmeric trance, accompanied by anesthesia, clairvoyance, and related phenomena (cf. Beloff, 1993; Oppenheim, 1985).

Much early research focused on the question of "direct" thought transfer from one person to another, occurring independently of known sensory channels. As early as 1882, such extrasensory communication was named *telepathy* by Myers, who soon afterwards published his famous book, *Phantasms of the Living* (1886) together with Gurney and Frank Podmore (1855–1910), another founder of the SPR (Gurney, Myers, & Podmor, 1886). This collection of reports about spontaneous paranormal experiences included dreams about distant, synchronic events, appearances or phantasms of living or dying persons and so-called "veridical hallucinations." All of these strange experiences reflected real events, and the persons who experienced them could not have learned about them by normal means. Occa-

sionally academic psychologists focused on possible sources of error in telepathic experiments, especially in situations where sender and receiver were in close proximity or even in the same room. Alternative explanations, offered by these psychologists, included unconscious muscular movements, which might serve as unintentional cues during the search for hidden objects, underestimating influence of hyperesthesia, unintentional whispering, chance effects, and, of course, fraud (Hansen & Lehman, 1895; Munsterberg, 1889).

Almost from the beginning, the SPR sought to refute the previously mentioned objections by developing a canon of strict, evidentiary guidelines (Gurney, 1887), which incorporated suggestions for controlling deception during the popular seances with so-called physical mediums of the period. The question of fraud was to be a major problem surrounding the 1877–1878 performances of Henry Slade (1840–1904), the famous American medium and his patron, the astrophysicist Friedrich Zollner (1834–1882) of Leipzig University. Incidentally, both Gustav Theodor Fechner (1801–1887) and Wilhelm Wundt (1832–1920) participated in mediumistic sessions with Slade. Fechner, on the whole, was cautiously impressed with Slade's accomplishments, but Wundt opposed all spiritistic activities as unscientific fraud (Bringmann, Bringmann & Bauer, 1990; Wundt, 1879).

The SPR *Proceedings*, published after 1882, contain rich case histories and clinical examples from the border region between psychical research and abnormal psychology or psychopathology. Specific examples of clinical interest to early parapsychologists include split or multiple personalities, dissociative conditions, sensory and motor automatisms, transmediumistic phenomena, automatic writing, and sensory hallucinations. Occasionally, pioneer studies investigated lucid dreams, out-of-body or near-death experiences, and other similar topics, which today attract attention among some of the more open-minded traditional psychologists. Therefore, it is not surprising that a number of prominent psychologists, psychopathologists, and psychotherapists like Pierre Janet (1859–1947), Hippolyte Bernheim (1840–1919), Sigmund Freud (1856–1939), Carl Gustav Jung (1875–1961), Morton Prince (1854–1929), Theodore Flournoy (1854–1920), and William James (1842–1910) were interested in the SPR, with many actively supporting its work.

An American branch organization of the SPR was established in 1885 at the initiative of James, who served as its president from 1894 to 1895. This organization still exists under the name of the American Society for Psychical Research (ASPR). Its first president was the astronomer Simon Newcomb (1835–1909). The Wundt student, G. Stanley Hall (1844–1924), and the physicians Henry Bowditch (1840–1911) and Charles S. Minot (1852–1914) served as vice presidents. Following the example of the London group, James and his associates conducted studies of hypnotic induction, post-hypnotic suggestion, the therapeutic use of automatic writing, and crystal gazing. James was especially involved in a series of experimental sessions with the American medium Leonora Piper (1859–1950), which convinced him of the reality of paranormal phenomena (i.e., telepathy, clairvoyance). The early research of the ASPR played a role in the development of the American Psychological Association which should not be underestimated. This work also gave impetus to the establishment of the field of experimental psychopathology (cf. Taylor, 1986). Topics from the field of psychical research were included in the first congresses of psychology almost as a matter of course. For example, an international call for a census of veridical hallucinations, which occurred at the same time as the death of friends or acquaintances and suggested the possibility of telepathic contacts, was issued during the first Paris congress. The results of this original survey were reported by Sidgwick during the second congress of psychology in London, which he chaired as president.

After the beginning of the 20th century, some studies of telepathy and clairvoyance began to be conducted at university departments or institutes of experimental psychology. The studies by Leonard Troland (1839–1932) at Harvard University need to be mentioned, as well as the statistical investigations of Coover (1872–1938) at Stanford University about the guessing of playing cards and lotto numbers, which were supported by a special Psychical Research Fellowship until 1937. The most impressive experiments were performed in 1920 by the Dutch psychology professors Brugmans (1885–1961) and Heymans (1857–1930) at the Psychological Institute of Groningen University

Figure 3 Albert von Schrenck-Notzing, pioneer of German parapsychology.

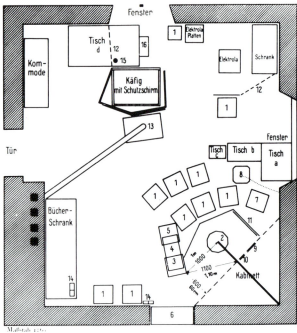

Figure 4 Floor plan of Schrenck-Notzing's laboratory.

Figure 5 Photographs of Rhine's Zener Card experiment.

(Draaisma, 1992). In these experiments, the hand of the experimental subject, who was located in another room, was to be guided telepathically by the experimenters. The overall design of the experiment followed psychophysical principles. The highly significant results were reported in 1921 at the first International Congress for Psychical Research in Copenhagen. These conferences, which were later also held in Warsaw (1923), Paris (1927), Athens (1930), and Oslo (1935), provided an important forum for scientific discussions for somewhat isolated parapsychologists from England, France, and Germany.

Two interesting books about extrasensory phenomena, *Telepathy and Clairvoyance* (1919) and *Introduction to Occultism and Spiritism* (1921) were published in Germany after World War I by Rudolf Tischner (1879–1961), an ophthalmologist. Other studies focused primarily on the study of physical mediumship, which at that time included the movement of distant objects and the highly controversial materialization or bodily appearance of spirits. A major advocate of this area of study was the wealthy German physician and psychotherapist, Albert von Schrenck-Notzing (1862–1929). The economically independent baron established his well-equipped private laboratory in Munich. He also pub-

lished and financed the *Zeitschrift fuer Parapsychologie* (Journal for Parapsychology), the successor of the 1874 journal *Psychische Studien* (Psychic Studies), until 1934. Since most of the materialization research with mediums took place in the dark, Schrenck-Notzing placed great value on objective security and control procedures to minimize the danger of self-deception by the audience and fraud by the experimenters. Nevertheless, he suffered frequent, sharp attacks by experimental psychologists like H. Henning (1925) and H. Schole (1929). Schrenck-Notzing also developed a cooperative relationship with the Berlin engineer Fritz Grunewald (1885–1925) and the self-styled animal psychologist, Karl Krall (1863–1929) of Munich. Krall's invention of an electric medium control was employed at least once during the examination of the Austrian medium Rudi Schneider (1918–1957). Krall also worked in his own paraphysical laboratories, but few details of his specific research are known.

In 1932 the eminent Leipzig biologist Hans Driesch (1867–1941) published the first German handbook of parapsychological methods, *Parapsychology: The Science of Occult Phenomena*. Driesch and the Tubingen philosopher, Traugott Konstantin Oesterreich (1880–1949), argued for the academic integration of parapsychology and the foundation of a German organization for experts in the field.

In the United States, William McDougall (1871–1938) set up a parapsychological laboratory at Duke University in North Carolina. Under the direction of the biologist Joseph B. Rhine (1895–1980), this institute conducted extensive, quantitative experiments exploring telepathy, clairvoyance, and precognition. His first publication, *Extra-Sensory Perception* (1934), gained paradigmatic importance for the establishment of psi research as an academic discipline. The findings of Rhine's laboratory, which were published in the *Journal of Parapsychology* from 1937 on, created quite a stir among American psychologists. The Duke group responded to the numerous, methodological criticisms of its research (i.e., misuse of statistical techniques, reporting of incomplete data, insufficient shuffling of Zener cards, and poor experimental controls) with the book, *Extra-Sensory Perception After Sixty Years* (1940), which was the first review of experimental parapsychology (Pratt, et al., 1940).

In Germany, it was Hans Bender (1907–1991) who performed the first experimental study of clairvoyance at the Institute of Psychology at Bonn University. His results were published in the prestigious *Zeitschrift fuer Psychologie* (1935). Bender represented German parapsychology for almost four decades after World War II until his death. He established his own Institute for Border Areas of Psychology and Mental Hygiene in 1950 in Freiburg. Bender

Figure 6 A 1926 session in Krall's laboratory.

was appointed to an academic chair for Border Areas of Psychology at Freiburg University in 1954. In 1957, the *Zeitschrift fuer Parapsychologie* began publication. It is still the only German scientific publication in the field. Bender was succeeded in 1975 by his student, Johannes Mischo (born 1930) who, after Bender's death in 1991, was elected as the new director of the independent institute.

Rhine's former laboratory continues to function as a private foundation under the name Rhine Research Center together with the Institute for Parapsychology. Robert L. Morris of Edinburgh University, who holds the Koestler Chair of Parapsychology, is the only full professor of parapsychology in Europe since the closing of the Parapsychological Laboratory of Utrecht University in 1988. The Parapsychological Association, an international organization for professional parapsychology, which was founded in 1957 at the suggestion of Rhine, became a member of the American Association for the Advancement of Science in 1969. It now has about 280 members from the natural and social sciences and the humanities.

Bibliography

Bauer, E. (1991). Periods of historical development of parapsychology in Germany—an overview. In D. L. Delanoy (Ed.), *Proceedings of the 34th Annual Convention of the Parapsychological Association, Presented Papers* (pp. 18–34). Parapsychological Association, Inc.

Beloff, J. (1993). *Parapsychology: A concise history*. London: Athlone Press.

Bender. H. (1935). Zum Problem der außersinnlichen Wahrnehmung. *Zeitschrift für Psychologie, 135,* 20–130.

Bringmann, W. B., Bringmann, N. J., & Bauer, E. (1990). Fechner und die Parapsychologie. *Zeitschrift für Parapsychologie und Grenzgebiete der Psychologie, 32,* 19–43.

Dessoir, M. (1889). Die Parapsychologie. *Sphinx, 7,* 341–344.

Draaisma, D. (1992). De witte kraai van Heymans: De Groninger telepathie-experimenten. In D. Draaisma (Ed.), *Eem laboratorium vor de ziel: Gerard Heymans en het begin van de experimentele psychologie* (pp. 80–95). Groningen: Historische Uitgevrij & Universiteitsmuseum.

Driesch, H. (1932). *Parapsychologie, die Wissenschaft von den "okkulten" Erscheinungen*. Munich: Bruckmann.

Gurney, E. (1887). *Telepathie: Eine Erwiderung auf die Kritik des Herrn Prof. W. Preyer*. Leipzig: Friedrich.

Gurney, E., Myers, F. W. H., & Podmor, F. (1886). *Phantasms of the living* (Vols. 1 & 2). London: Trübner.

Hansen, F. C., & Lehman, A. (1895). *Über unwillkürliches Flüstern: eine kritische Untersuchung und experimentelle Untersuchung der sogenannten Gedankenübertragung*. Leipzig: Engelmann.

Henning, H. (1925). *Psychologie der Gegenwart*. Leipzig: Kröner.

Mauskopf, S. H., & McVaugh, M. R. (1980). *The elusive science. Origins of experimental psychical research*. Baltimore: Johns Hopkins University Press.

Munsterberg, H. (1889). *Gedankenübertragung*. Freiburg i. Br.: Mohr.

Oppenheim, J. (1985). *The other world: Spiritualism and psychical research*. 1850–1914. Cambridge: Cambridge University Press.

Pratt, J. G., Rhine, J. B., Smith, B. M., Stuart, C. E., & Greenwood, J. A. (1940). *Extrasensory perception after sixty years: A critical appraisal of the research in extrasensory perception*. New York: Holt.

Rhine. J. (1976). Parapsychology and psychology: The shifting relationship today. *Journal of Parapsychology, 40,* 115–135.

Schmeidler, G. (1989). *Parapsychology and psychology: Matches and mismatches*. London: McFarland.

Schole, H. (1929). *Okkultismus und Wissenschaft: Kritik des okkultistischen Forschens und Denkens*. Göttingen: Vandenhoek & Ruprecht.

Taylor, E. (1986). The American Society for Psychical Research, 1884–1889. In D. H. Weiner & D. I. Radin (Eds.), *Research in Parapsychology 1985* (pp. 187–196). Metuchen, NJ & London: Scarecrow Press.

Tischner, R. (1919). *Über Telepathie und Hellsehen: experimentelltheoretische Untersuchungen*. Wiesbaden: Bergmann.

Tischner. R. (1921). *Einführung in den Okkultismus und Spiritismus*. Munich: Bergmann.

Van Over, R. (Ed.). (1972). *Psychology and extrasensory perceptions*. New York: Mentor Books.

Wundt, W. (1879). *Der Spiritismus*. Leipzig: Engelmann.

Clever Hans: Fact or Fiction?

Wolfgang G. Bringmann
Johannes Abresch

Thinking and speaking animals, the traditional heroes of myths, legends, fables, and fairy tales, continue their adventures in the laboratories of modern comparative and cognitive psychology. According to Schütt (1990), controversies about the existence and nature of animal cognition go back to antiquity. While most philosophers and early psychologists believed that animals experience sensations, have memories, and can learn, it was generally thought that they were incapable of reasoning and of developing and using concepts. There were, of course, a few reluctant exceptions, like the Stoic philosopher Chrysippos of Soloi (280–206 B.C.). He believed that dogs could at least understand basic disjunctive syllogisms. For example, given three possible directions A, B, or C, if a spoor cannot be discerned in direction A or B, a dog may proceed in the only remaining direction, C, without relying on his sense of smell.

In the late summer of 1904, Germany's nascent experimental psychology was challenged to provide a scientific explanation for the miraculous achievements of a famous performing horse (Pfungst, 1907). This black Russian stallion with white fetlocks and a stately bearing and his owner Wilhelm von Osten (1838–1909) gave free, daily performances in the cramped courtyard of an old tenement building in the northern suburbs of Berlin. The horse had learned to answer questions and to communicate the solution of problems posed to him in German, by tapping his hoofs or by moving his head.

The horse's impressive accomplishments reportedly included counting and basic mathematics up to compound fractions. The animal could correctly identify colors, musical tones, and German coins. It could read and spell German by means of a special "letter board" and seemed to carry a calendar in its head. The horse, who had been named Hans by its owner, was given the nickname "Clever Hans," under which it is still known to modern students of animal psychology.

Figure 1 Clever Hans surrounded by his admirers (Berlin 1904).

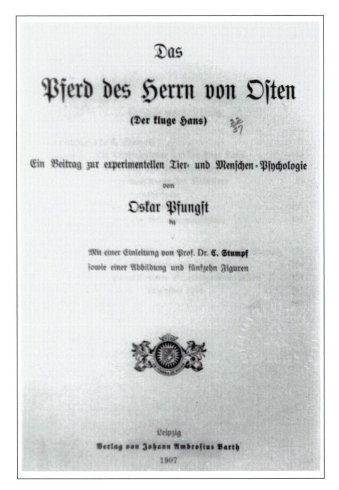

Figure 2 Title page of the original monograph about "Mr. von Osten's Horse, Clever Hans."

also published the final results (1907). In 1904 Pfungst was a 30-year-old doctoral candidate who functioned as an unpaid volunteer assistant to Stumpf. After an initial career in banking, he had studied philosophy, philology, the natural sciences, and medicine in Munich and Berlin.

Pfungst's study of Clever Hans closely followed the standard research paradigm of microbiological investigations at Berlin University (Abresch & Lück, 1994). For six weeks he collected background information about von Osten, Clever Hans, and, especially, the manner in which von Osten had trained Hans. Pfungst was assisted by Dr. Erich von Hornbostel (1877–1935), who served as "recording secretary" for the project.

In early December of 1904, Carl Stumpf, who was the director of the Clever Hans project, summarized the most important findings as follows:

> During the last weeks, I tried to explain the accomplishments of "Clever Hans" experimentally in cooperation with Dr. E. von Hornbostel and the doctoral . . . candidate O. Pfungst . . . . The following results were found: The horse failed when the solution of . . . [the problem used] . . . was unknown to anyone among those present. For example, when a written number of objects to be counted were presented in such a manner that they remained invisible to all present, and in particular, to the questioner [of the horse]. Thus, [it is clear] that [the horse] can neither read nor do arithmetic.

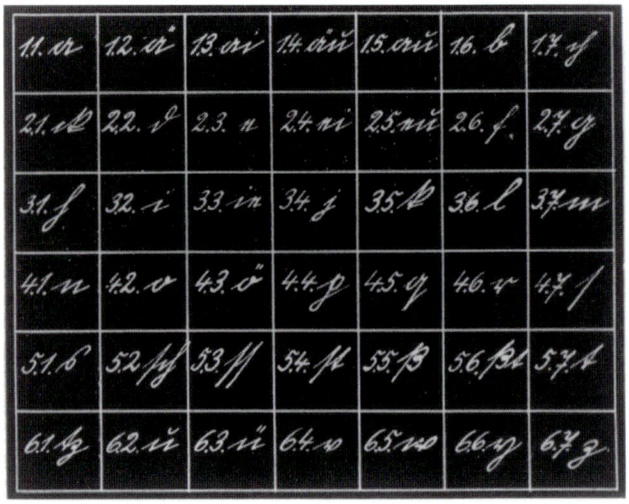

Mr. von Osten was a retired elementary school teacher who believed that his endless toil as a public school teacher qualified him to identify and promote the intellectual potential of rural children and perhaps even farm animals. Specifically, as a follower of the German school reformer Friedrich Adolf Diesterweg (1790–1866), von Osten hoped to show that anyone—even a horse—was capable of learning, provided the teacher was knowledgeable and applied the appropriate didactic methods.

To determine the true nature of the animal's abilities and to exonerate von Osten, who had been accused of fraud and deception, a special investigative committee, the "Hans Commission" (Stumpf, 1907) was established. Its 13 members included educators, veterinarians, horse trainers, physiologists, and Carl Stumpf (1848–1936), the eminent professor of psychology and philosophy at Berlin University. The actual investigation into the matter, however, was carried out by Oskar Pfungst (1874–1933), who

Figure 3 Letter board used to help Clever Hans spell out his answers.

[Clever Hans] failed also when sufficiently large blinders kept him from seeing the people who were familiar with the solution of a task. [The horse] apparently relies on optical cues. . . . These cues do not have to be given intentionally. (Pfungst, 1907, p. 261)

Furthermore, according to Stumpf:

the horse must have learned during its pro-longed instruction in arithmetic . . . to observe the . . . small gestures of his teacher . . . and to use them as signals to stop [counting or moving his head].

The movements, which guided the animal's reactions are so small . . . that even experienced observers have missed them. Mr. Pfungst, whose power of observation has been especially sharp-ened by his laboratory research, succeeded in identifying . . . Mr. von Osten's . . . movements on which the accomplishments of the horse are based. (Pfungst, 1907, p. 262)

Concealed signals of various types were, of course, nothing new since they had been used by animal trainers during the Middle Ages (Pfungst, 1907, p. 164f). In fact, even during the period of the Hans controversy, a Berlin circus displayed a mare named Rosa who had been taught to respond to the head movements of her trainer (Pfungst, 1907, p. 11). The noisy signals and the dramatic gestures of lion trainers were generally known, especially to the members of the Hans Commission, but such obvi-ous signals were not used by von Osten or the other examiners. Clever Hans responded to almost every-one, including the Prussian minister of education, high-ranking politicians, and, of course, to German generals. At one time, even William II (1859–1941), the last German emperor, expressed an interest in meeting and testing the famous horse. The study of Clever Hans was a serious challenge to modern Ger-man psychology, and we can understand why Pro-fessor Stumpf eagerly turned the actual research project over to Oskar Pfungst, his enthusiastic but unpaid assistant.

Pfungst's book and its English translation, *Clever Hans* (1911), include a variety of so-called quantita-tive results, including a number of tables (pp. 30–66). Because Pfungst reported his results in a fragmentary and highly selective manner, it is impossible to re-analyze them today. One thing, however, is very clear from a careful examination of the tabulated results: Pfungst was the only member of Stumpf's team who was able to detect von Osten's microsignals (Pfungst, 1907, p. 43).

After completing his study of Clever Hans,

Figure 4 Signed portrait of "Baron Wilhelm von Osten."

Pfungst continued his laboratory research on sub-liminal perception (Pfungst, 1907, pp. 77–100), which, despite his sensational results, is little known today.

Although Pfungst was admittedly the only per-son who ever observed the microsignal interactions between Hans and von Osten, his findings and explanations of the "Clever Hans Phenomenon" (Pfungst, 1907, pp. 101–172) were fully accepted by the public and experts. Even today, the story of Clever Hans is regarded as a classic example of out-standing psychological research (Fernald, 1984; Rosenthal, 1963; Sebeok & Rosenthal, 1981).

After his spectacular success with Clever Hans, Pfungst exposed several other "thinking and speak-ing" dogs and performing apes as frauds. His later research included longitudinal and sensory isola-tion studies of chimps and the raising of a young

Figure 5 Clever Hans and his second owner Karl Krall.

Krall was a wealthy jeweler and friend of von Osten. In Elberfeld, Krall conducted extensive studies of Hans, and of Muhamed and Zarif, two Arabian stallions, who were especially "gifted" in mathematics. Between 1908 and 1914, Krall's "Animal School" instructed more than 20 different animals, including dogs, horses, donkeys, apes, and even an elephant. In the context of this work, Krall invented various pieces of apparatus and procedures to help him observe and record the behavior of his animals more reliably. Krall's letter board for horses and dogs contains all of the German letters. An animal was

wolf. After completion of such projects, Pfungst would typically send the brains of his animal subjects to his friend, the neuro-anatomist Ludwig Edinger (1855–1918), at Frankfurt University for histological analysis. In 1925, Pfungst, who did not hold an earned Ph.D. or M.D., was given an honorary doctorate by Frankfurt University in recognition of his contributions to the diagnosis and treatment of war-related brain injuries (Abresch & Lück, 1994). Pfungst also made some naive and rather excessive claims about the limitations of animal intelligence which were later refuted by the primate research of his Berlin colleague and friend, Wolfgang Köhler (1887–1967).

Pfungst died in 1932 after an extended illness. Unfortunately, his rich scientific estate, with notes, films, photographs, and sound recordings pertaining to his work, was lost during World War II. Mr. von Osten never accepted the contention that Clever Hans was just an ordinary animal, and he even tried to use a phrenological analysis of Hans's skull to bolster his claims. Late in life, von Osten is said to have cursed Clever Hans, blaming the horse for all his bad luck in life (Krall, 1912, p. 349). Shortly after von Osten's death on June 29, 1909, Hans was moved to a farm in western Germany, and in late July of the same year, was adopted by Karl Krall (1863–1929) of nearby Elberfeld.

Figure 6 Mr. Krall loved horses even as a child.

taught to spell words by tapping the number coordinates of each letter with its hoofs or paws. Krall

ogists and zoologists, Krall's Society for Animal Psychology (SAP) existed from 1913 to 1934. The goal of the SAP was the establishment of a scientific basis for the protection of animals, and soon branches of the group were founded all over Germany and abroad.

Dogs were the favorite subjects of Krall's disciples. Their teachers were often educated, upper-class women with strong personalities who loved animals and had the leisure to train their pets. The best known of these female animal guardians was Henny Jutzler-Kindermann (1891–1979). She was the first German woman to receive a univer-

Figure 7 Krall and his famous Elberfeld horses Zarif and Muhamed.

published his findings in his copiously illustrated book titled *Thinking Animals* (1912). This somewhat disorganized work of more than 500 pages and numerous illustrations and original photographs is still immensely readable. Of particular interest is the detailed chronicle of the entire Clever Hans controversy and the painstaking description of Krall's own work with the famous animal (Krall, 1912, pp. 273–402, 415–455). This book exists also in Swedish and Russian translations.

For a number of years Krall also edited and published his own journal, *The Soul of the Animal*, which included articles such as "The Learned Horses of Elberfeld," "Animal Psychology," and "Questions of Animal Protection." Krall's private research institute attracted many visitors from Germany and abroad. However, his method of animal training also drew the ire of animal protectionists, who suspected him of vivisectionism and accused him of "overstressing" his four-legged students with his demanding academic curriculum. The caricature in Figure 8 shows Krall as the teacher and his three students, Zarif, "Mustafa," and Hans D. The angry woman in the background symbolizes animal protectionists.

Despite continuing attacks by academic psychol-

Figure 8 Caricature of Krall and his school for horses.

Figure 9 Henny Jutzler-Kindermann chatting with her dog Schlump by means of a letter board (ca. 1938).

sity degree in the new field of agricultural science. During World War I, Mrs. Kindermann, who was the manager of a "Princely Estate" in Germany, taught her dog Lola to converse with her by letter board about various topics, including philosophy and religion. An English edition of her charming book was published in 1922 in London. Until the beginning of World War II, about 100 animals were trained by Krall and his followers, with varying success. This work was documented by Mrs. Jutzler-Kindermann in her 1954 publication *Can Animals Think? YES*, which was endorsed warmly by Albert Schweitzer (1875–1965), the famous missionary physician and philosopher. Interestingly, before receiving his first doctorate in Berlin, Schweitzer served as a subject for auditory experiments in Stumpf's laboratory. Thus, it is quite possible that Schweitzer was also familiar with the Clever Hans project.

Even today, attempts to teach animals to speak and think are not uncommon (Savage-Rumbaugh, 1986; Herman, 1980; Thun-Hohenstein, 1983). However, modern psychologists in general are rather skeptical about such efforts and point out that the basic issue was solved long ago by Oskar Pfungst (Rosenthal, 1963; Sebeok & Rosenthal, 1981).

Bibliography

Abresch, J. & Lück, H. E. (1994). *Der Kluge Hans, Oskar Pfungst und die Himrinde*. In H. Gundlach (Ed.): *Arbeiten zur Psychologiegeschichte* (pp. 83–94). Göttingen: Hogrefe.

Emisch, H. (1909). *Ludwig Edinger. Hirnanatomie und Psychologie*. Mainz, Germany: Fischer.

Fernald, D. (1984). *The Hans Legacy*. Hillsdale, NJ: Earlbaum.

Griffin, D. (1992). *Animal Minds*. Chicago: University of Chicago Press.

Herman, L. (Ed.). (1980). *Cetacean Behavior: Mechanism and Function*. New York: Wiley.

Jutzler-Kindermann, H. (1954). *Können Tiere denken? Ja*. Schopfheim, Germany: Selbstverlag.

Kindermann, H. (1922). *Lola. The thought and speech of animals*. London: Methuen.

Köhler, W. (1917). *The Mentality of Apes*. New York: Harcourt.

Krall, K. (1912). *Denkende Tiere*. Leipzig: Engelmann.

Pfungst, O. (1907). *Das Pferd des Herrn von Osten. (Der kluge Hans)*. Leipzig: Barth.

Pfungst, O. (1911). *Clever Hans*. New York: Holt.

Rosenthal, R. (1963). On the social psychology of the psychological effect: The experimenter's hypothesis as unintended determinant of experimental results. *American Scientist, 8,* 183–189.

Savage-Rumbaugh, S. (1986). *Ape Language*. New York: Columbia University Press.

Sebeok, T., & Rosenthal, R. (Eds.). (1981). *The Clever Hans Phenomenon*. New York: Annals of the New York Academy of Science.

Schütt, H. P. (Ed.). (1990). *Die Vernunft der Tiere*. Frankfurt: Keip.

Terrace, H. S. (1979). *Nim: A chimpanzee who learned sign language*. New York: Columbia University Press.

Thun-Hohenstein, E. (1983). *Herr ist dumm*. Vienna: Zsolnay.

FROM PSYCHOPHYSICS TO BEHAVIORISM

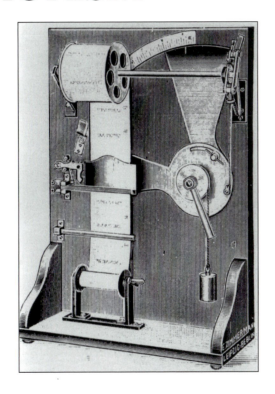

Wilhelm von Humboldt and the German University

David K. Robinson

It must first be noted that there were two famous men with the name Humboldt. In fact they were brothers who each influenced the development of German universities. The elder brother, Wilhelm (1767–1835), restructured the ideology of education in Germany during a short term in the Prussian government; whereas the younger Humboldt, Alexander (1769–1859), had a longer-term, more personal interaction with the development of natural sciences in German universities.

In his own day Wilhelm von Humboldt's fame was probably eclipsed by that of his more flamboyant younger brother, the explorer-scientist Alexander. Alexander von Humboldt's books on earth science and his explorations inspired others, and he personally advised many scientists and some of the university administrators who supported science. In perhaps the most famous example of his influence, Alexander von Humboldt became acquainted with Justus Liebig in Gay-Lussac's laboratory in Paris, then arranged for the young German chemist to begin his professorial career in Giessen, where Liebig's laboratory essentially organized modern organic chemistry. Alexander's name is implied in the term "Humboldtian science" (Cannon, 1978), but Wilhelm is the namesake of the "Humboldtian university" or Humboldtian reforms in education. Accordingly, the balance of this article focuses on Wilhelm's contributions.

On February 28, 1809, Wilhelm von Humboldt, having served six happy years in Rome as Prussia's representative to the Vatican, entered office as privy counselor and Director of the Office for Religion and Education in a newly reorganized Ministry of the Interior. Although he was also nominally in charge of religious affairs in Prussia, it was clear to everyone that King Frederick William III called Humboldt to reform education, and in his place an able undersecretary became the caretaker of church matters. Before he took office, Humboldt was a recognized political liberal who had written on the need for limitations on state power. He was also prominent for his work in classical philology and his writings on a neohumanistic concept of *Bildung* (education, or more literally, self-formation) (Sorkin, 1983). Hum-

Figure 1 Lithographic portrait of Wilhelm von Humboldt by Krüger and Oldermann (1830).

Figure 2 The young Alexander von Humboldt at the Orinoco River in South America, painted by Weitsch (1806).

boldt was given his new position at the insistence of the new reform prime minister, Baron Karl Heinrich vom und zum Stein.

When Humboldt returned from Italy, the Prussian monarch and his inner circle were desperate to change things—in a state often noted for its conservatism—because in 1806 the Prussian army had totally collapsed at the Battle of Jena-Auerstadt and Prussia was effectively occupied by Napoleon's troops. Stein wanted to spearhead a "revolution from above" in Prussia—reform and modernization of the agrarian economy, government administration, the army, and education.

The educational reforms were therefore part of Stein's plan to defeat the French indirectly. The French revolutionaries and Napoleon had set the challenge with their own educational reforms of both lower schools and higher education (especially *les grandes écoles*). Stein's reform program soon had to proceed without him because he was dismissed after only 14 months as prime minister when Napoleon became alarmed at his anti-French poli-

tics. Although Stein was replaced by the more cautious Baron Karl von Hardenberg, the Prussian government remained committed to internal reforms (often called the Stein-Hardenberg reforms) insofar as they were allowed by the French emperor and they fit the overall goal to strengthen and modernize Prussia.

It was a time of great contradictions—in all of Europe really, and certainly in Germany. Although Austria temporarily regained ascendancy in Central Europe after Napoleon's defeat, the modernized Prussian state would eventually unite the German nation. In the early 19th century this European ethnic group, which later became notorious for its nationalism, produced some of the most profoundly cosmopolitan and humanitarian intellectuals: Goethe, Schiller, Heine, Beethoven, etc., and the Humboldt brothers. Germany became a highly prominent land of scholars and scientists in the 19th century, and this was due, at least in part, to Wilhelm von Humboldt's educational reforms.

Wilhelm von Humboldt served as director of Prussian education for only 16 months, but during that short term of office he wrote the plans for the sweeping reforms that helped make German education the world standard well into the 20th century. Oddly enough, Humboldt, this Prussian aristocrat who did so much to reform German education, had never been to school himself. He and his siblings had been tutored at home, and he studied less than two years at two German universities, Frankfurt-an-der-Oder and Göttingen.

Humboldt did not make up his educational system from whole cloth. Prussia already had the distinction of being the first European government to require elementary education for all boys (in 1763, an enlightened measure of Frederick the Great). The elementary schools were usually poor, though, and Humboldt and his assistants worked to reform them as well. Drawing upon the enlightened educational theories of Rousseau, Pestalozzi, and Herbart, Humboldt drafted plans and regulations for primary education and for the normal schools where primary teachers were trained.

Although he was influenced by other reformers in setting standards for elementary schools, Humboldt's own ideas of educational development shaped the humanistic gymnasium (classical school) that prepared boys for the universities. The classical curriculum emphasized Latin, Greek, mathematics, German, and history. Humboldt devised a tough state examination system for the university-educated gymnasium teachers, and he instituted the formal high school graduation examination (*Abitur*) that marked the conclusion of gymnasium studies and also served as the university entrance examination (the exclusive entrance examination in Prussia after 1834). These reforms raised the educational standards and the social status of the teachers in classical schools. Humboldt appears to have ignored the question of education of females altogether, and until the 20th century women would not be admitted as regular students in German-speaking universities (with minor and local exceptions), since they normally did not receive the classical education required for entrance to the university.

Humboldt's most tangible action was probably the founding of Berlin University. It has, in fact, been known as Humboldt University since 1949, when the East German government removed the founding monarch's name (the customary way to name universities in Germany) and replaced it with that of the humanist educational reformer.

German universities had been alternately thriving and declining since the first ones (Prague, Heidelberg) were organized during the late 14th century. When Napoleon began to sweep over Europe, there were about 45 German-speaking universities, but most had been languishing with few students, and soon 22 of them would close due to the upheaval in Europe (Hammerstein, 1987). It was an opportune time to make needed changes.

Humboldt did not originate the idea to open a university in the Prussian capital, but he was instrumental in bringing that idea to reality. Berlin in 1800 was certainly not the European metropolis it would become by the century's close, but since the Prussian Academy of Sciences, the Academy of Arts, the Charité hospital and medical school, and other learned bodies had their home there, certain influential Prussians had been calling for the establishment of a university in Berlin. In reply to this suggestion and shortly after the defeat at Jena, King Frederick William III reportedly said, "The state must replace with intellectual strength what it has lost in material resources" (Fallon, 1980, p. 9).

Prussia already had three universities—at Halle, Königsberg, and Frankfurt-an-der-Oder. The university at Frankfurt-an-der-Oder had long been moribund, and Humboldt knew it because he had been enrolled there briefly. The Prussian university at Halle, on the other hand, had been a showcase of educational progress during the Enlightenment. Humboldt knew about Halle mostly through his friend and fellow classicist, Friedrich August Wolf, who was Professor of Classical Philology there. Wolf's graduate seminar, which helped shape Humboldt's emphasis on university research, became a model for specialized advanced training for all subjects in German universities and, eventually, the world. Halle University, however, was temporarily closed due to the French occupation of the town in 1806.

As Humboldt began his work in educational reform in 1809, the small East Prussian university town of Königsberg hosted the Prussian government for a few months as French troops roamed the streets of Berlin. Königsberg was the home of the philosopher Immanuel Kant, whom Humboldt certainly admired and whose categorical imperative was carefully incorporated into Humboldt's neohumanistic philosophy of education. While in Königsberg, however, Humboldt did not spend time with the philosopher; instead, he was a regular at the makeshift court, in conversation with the royal family and other ministers. A few months later, when the government returned to Berlin, Humboldt had finished his plans for the lower schools and was devoting more attention to plans for the new university and to ideals for university education in general.

The reformed German university, in Humboldt's grand conception, was not to be a school for specialization. Instead it was to be the community where the process of higher education would be further perfected by those who were most able to continue their studies. It was to be the peak of the national education pyramid that had its ultimate foundation in the reformed elementary schools in every village and neighborhood and in the humanistic gymnasia, where young men sharpened their minds and learned to learn.

Humboldt's reforms actually revived and extended many of the traditions of the German university, up to that time a much criticized institution. He strongly emphasized faculty research, for one thing, to elevate the philosophical faculty to at least a level of equality with the three professional faculties (theology, law, and medicine). As the 19th century unfolded, the writers and researchers on the philosophical faculties in German universities gained even more prestige and state support.

In Humboldt's view, university professors should

Figure 3 Main administrative building, Berlin University, in a 19th-century photograph.

theoretically structure their own curricula by choosing courses as they pleased.

Humboldt's political liberalism inclined him to minimize government interference in university operations once they were established. He successfully put an end to legal restrictions on where Prussians could study, thereby encouraging competition for students among all German universities. He also argued that Prussian universities should have financial and administrative independence and even begged the Prussian king to grant Berlin University its own lands and endowment so that it could operate independently of the national budget. In these efforts Humboldt failed, but the king did donate the ample palace of Prince Henry, brother to Frederick the Great, as a home for the university on Unter den Linden. By the time he resigned his position, Humboldt had established the ideals of university self-governance, academic freedom, and the dual commitment to teaching and scholarly research.

Humboldt accepted diplomatic posting to Vienna in 1810, where in 1814–15 he assisted Hardenberg, Prussia's major delegate to the Congress of Vienna, in dealing with the many questions facing Europe's leaders once they had defeated Napoleon. In 1819, as the Carlsbad Decrees of Austria's Prince Metternich gave German governments tighter control over the universities, and as Europe clearly entered a period of conservative reaction, Wilhelm von Humboldt retired from government service altogether and went home to Tegel (near Berlin) and his scholarly research. His own philological writings contributed to the development of modern linguistics; his social approach to language studies developed into *Völkerpsychologie* (folk psychology), a term he coined (Zusne, 1984, p. 199).

Berlin University flourished and served as a model for the German system of higher education. German universities expanded, new ones were founded, and enrollments and international reputa-

devote themselves to both research and teaching, not primarily to one or the other. He thought that something magical happens to researchers who impart their special knowledge to students; the teaching invigorates their research, and research increases their teaching effectiveness, and so on. Although Humboldt was absolutely convinced of his education theory, he himself had been educated almost entirely by tutors and had himself never taught at any level. He was, however, a recognized researcher and writer, and his ideas have had a lasting effect on education in Germany and, to some extent, on education in the rest of the world.

It was in the area of faculty self-governance that Humboldt made his last official contribution to the organization of Berlin University. Shortly before he was called back into diplomatic service, he appointed (and served on) a commission, chaired by the theologian and philosopher Friedrich Schleiermacher, to organize Berlin University for its opening in 1810. This commission reaffirmed many German university traditions; for example, it gave full professors full responsibility for university governance through the four faculties, which elected their deans and rector. In line with Humboldt's neohumanist conception of higher education as well as with German tradition, the commission guaranteed academic freedom both for professors and for students, whose academic freedom meant they could

tion increased. Aspects of the Berlin or Humboldtian model were quickly copied, and other German universities competed with Berlin and each other to build teaching and research throughout the 19th and early 20th centuries. New research led to new specializations, more research seminars, specialized institutes, sometimes even new university disciplines: Liebig in organic chemistry, Helmholtz and Ludwig in physiology, and Wundt in experimental psychology are prominent examples. The German universities were indeed successful, though not always in all the ways Humboldt had planned. Students

Figure 4 Leading politicians at the Congress of Vienna (1814–1815) after a painting by Isabey (1767–1855). Humboldt is behind and just to the right of the French statesman Talleyrand, whose arm is leaning on the table.

were generally more concerned with professional examinations administered by the governments of their home states or countries than with their academic freedom, and the prestige of research had its effect on the faculty. As a prominent historian of education has observed, "the dynamics and success of the seminar methods and the research ethic" moved the universities and their students toward specialization, "taking away much of the vaunted German sense of the 'unity of science,' a cardinal point of university ideology since Humboldt's day, but more and more honored in the breach as the 19th century wore on" (McClelland, 1980, p. 180).

How much of the success of the German university can be attributed to reformers like Humboldt, and how much of it followed naturally from the rapid growth of a previously suppressed national economy and culture, especially once unification was achieved in 1871? "At the worst, Humboldt's ideals remained a benchmark by which later reformers and rebels could judge the illiberal realities of German culture" (Grafton, 1981, p. 378). Academic freedom quickly collapsed in the face of the Nazi takeover. After World War II, scholars from both the German Democratic Republic and the Federal Republic of Germany claimed Humboldt's legacy, though they certainly did not agree on what that

legacy was. Nevertheless, his ideals could still form a basis for dealing with the practical difficulties facing the universities of reunified Germany today. By 1900 the German university had influenced higher learning throughout the world, especially at the graduate level, so we all have shared in Humboldt's legacy and probably still do.

Bibliography

Cannon, S. F. (1978). *Science in culture: The early Victorian period.* New York: Dawson and Science History Publications.

Fallon, D. (1980). *The German university: A heroic idea in conflict with the modern world.* Boulder: Colorado Associated University Press.

Grafton, A. (1981). Wilhelm von Humboldt. *The American Scholar, 50* (3), 371–381.

Hammerstein, N. (1987). History of German universities. *History of European Ideas, 8* (2), 139–145.

Haym, R. (1965). *Wilhelm von Humboldt: Lebensbild und Charakteristik.* Osnabrück, Germany: O. Zeller. (Original work published 1856)

Lenz, M. (1910–1918). *Geschichte der Königlichen Friedrich-Wilhelm-Universität zu Berlin* (Vols. 1–4). Halle: Verlag der Buchhandlung des Waisenhauses.

McClelland, C. E. (1980). *State, society, and university in Germany, 1700–1914.* Cambridge: Cambridge University Press.

Sorkin, D. (1983). Wilhelm von Humboldt: The theory and practice of self-formation (*Bildung*). *Journal of the History of Ideas, 44* (1), 55–73.

Sweet, P. R. (1978). *Wilhelm von Humboldt: A biography.* (Vols. 1 & 2). Columbus: Ohio State University Press.

Zusne, L. (1984). Biographical dictionary of psychology. Westport, CT: Greenwood Press.

Jan Evangelista Purkyně (Purkinje)

Josef Brožek
Jiří Hoskovec

During his long and productive life, Jan Evangelista Purkinje (1787–1869) was involved in an unusually wide range of activities. In his youth he earned his keep as a choir-boy. Later he functioned successively as a high school teacher, private tutor, assistant in anatomy, professor of physiology and pathology at the University of Breslau (today's Wroclaw, in Poland), and professor of physiology in Prague. He was a founder and editor of an early Czech scientific journal (*Živa*, 1853–1863) and served as elected deputy of the Bohemian Provincial Diet (1861–1866). However, first and foremost, Purkinje was an innovative biomedical investigator whose scientific career was initiated by brilliant psychological research on vision (1819, 1823, 1825). The breadth of his scientific interests is indicated by the headings of Kruta's (1969, pp. 114–128) list of secondary references: Physiology, Vision—Subjective phenomena, Examination of the Eye, Posture and equilibrium, Physiological pharmacology, Ciliary motion, Digestion, Phonetics (Physiology of Human Speech), Wakefulness and sleep, Finger prints, Cell theory, Nerve Cells and fibers, Heart, Purkinje fibers, Physiological institutes, and Philosophy. In this article we are interested primarily in Purkinje's contributions to psychology, but first it may be useful to begin with a practical issue concerning his name.

Figure 1 Portrait of J. E. Purkinje.

How to Spell and Pronounce Purkinje's Name

The name consists of three syllables, with the tonal accent placed on the first syllable. In Czech, the name is spelled "Purkyně." The "y" that follows the letter "k" should cause no problem, since in modern Czech "y" and "i" are phonetically identical. But how about the terminal letter, "ě," with its "hook"? In its form, the "hook" looks like an upside down French *accent circonflexe* but its function is totally different: It "softens" the preceding "n." The correct pronunciation would be indicated in French (and in Italian) by "gn," as in cognac. In English, the first "n" in onion, pinion, or better yet, canyon, sound like the Czech "soft n."

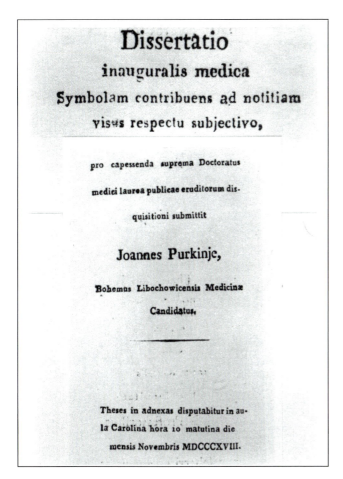

Figure 2 Announcement of the defense of Purkinje's doctoral dissertation "Contributions to the Knowledge of the Psychological Aspects of Vision."

In German the name is spelled "Purkinje"; the combination "nje" yields a sound very similar, though not identical, to the Czech "soft n." Matters become worse—much worse—in English, in which the German form of the name is used. First, the stress is shifted from the first to the second syllable. Secondly, the whole word is pronounced as if it were an English word: P'r-`kin-dzhi. The standard English pronunciation makes the name totally unintelligible to Purkinje's countrymen.

A Bit of Chronology

Purkinje was born in 1787, to Czech parents, in Libochovice, in the North of Bohemia, a region that today constitutes the western part of the Czech Republic. In 1798 he joined a boys' choir in Mikulov, in southern Moravia, and in the years 1801 to 1804, he attended a high school there taught by Piarist Fathers. When he finished high school, Purkinje

joined the Piarist order, which he left in 1807. Following three years of studying philosophy at the University of Prague—during which he earned his living as a tutor in two Prague families—he became a tutor for the family of Baron Hilprandt in Blatná, in Southern Bohemia. In the years 1814 to 1818 Purkinje studied at the medical faculty of the University of Prague and received the degree of Doctor of Medicine in 1818. His thesis, which was listed in the announcement of its defense in Latin, was written in German and dealt with "Contributions to the Knowledge of Vision in its Subjective Aspects." The thesis was published in German, in Prague, in 1819. Kruta (1969, p. 77) lists three contemporary reviews of the thesis which were published in German medical and scientific journals. The thesis was also reprinted in Berlin in 1823 as the first volume of *Observations and Experiments on the Physiology of the Senses*. The second volume (*New Contributions*) was published in 1825. It is this second volume that contains a brief note on the changes of the visibility of spectral

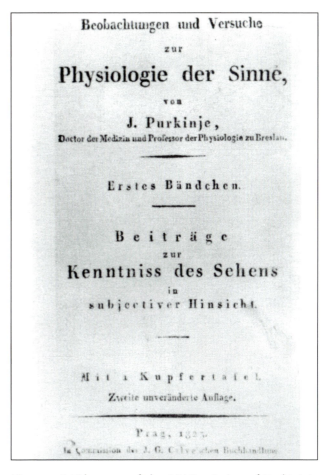

Figure 3 Title page of the 1819 printing of Purkinje's doctoral dissertation.

colors in the course of light adaptation—a phenomenon which later came to be known as the "Purkinje Shift," or "Purkinje Phenomenon" (Figure 4). An extensive and highly appreciative summary of Purkinje's "Essay on the Subjective Phenomena of Vision," based on the 1823 reprint, was prepared by England's Charles Wheatstone and was published anonymously in 1830 (pp. 107–117). Continental historians of science, including such Purkinje specialists as V. Kruta (1969), were apparently unaware of this important document. We owe thanks to Professor N. J. Wade of the University of Dundee, Scotland, for bringing it to wider attention and making it more readily available (Wade, 1983).

In 1823, Purkinje became a professor at the University of Breslau's Medical School. He remained there until 1850, at which time he returned to Prague. Purkinje died in Prague in 1869.

Insert: Description of the "Purkinje phenomenon"
(Purkinje, 1825; repr.1918, p. 118;
transl. Brožek, 1989)

" The intensity of illumination has a marked effect on the brightness of the perceived colors. In order to convince ourselves of this fully, let us place before us [spectral] colors at daybreak, when it just begins to dawn, be it ever so slightly. At the beginning we see only dark and gray. Just the calors that [in daylight] are most vivid, the reds and the greens, appear darkest. One is unable to differentiate between rosy red and yellow. I could first perceive the blue. The shades of red that in daylight are the brightest, namely, crimson, cinnabarine, and orange, appear for a long time very dark...The green appears [at first] bluish and its yellow tinge develops as the day progresses".

Figure 4 English translation of the first description of the Purkinje Phenomenon (1825).

Bibliographies—Primary References

A detailed bibliography of Purkinje's writings, arranged by topics, was prepared by Kruta (1961). It differs from the headings of Kruta's 1969 bibliography, which was noted in the introductory paragraph of this account, so it will be presented here as well. The 1961 bibliography has 11 sections relevant to our interest here: I. Vision, Space perception; II. Vertigo, The nervous system; III. Acoustics, Phonetics; IV. Touch, Senses in general; V. Consciousness, Sleep, Psyche; VI. Physiological pharmacology; X. Varia; and XI. The concept of physiology.

Kruta's 1969 volume (pp. 76–113) contains a chronological list of Purkinje's own publications, and in the Appendix to Volume XIII (1985) of Purkinje's *Opera Omnia* the primary references (254–275), are also arranged chronologically. The bibliography is comprehensive. In both bibliographies the titles are given in the original languages only, with no translations.

The arrangement of primary references to Purkinje's work in Volume I of Watson's bibliographic opus (1974, pp. 343–344) is also chronological. The original titles are given for Purkinje's publications written in German. For those written in Czech, only the translations are provided, in parentheses. In addition to the two collections of Purkinje's works (*Opera Omnia*, 1918–1985; *Opera Selecta*, 1948), some 20 legitimate and correct references are given. Unfortunately, confusion reigns regarding the bibliographical details about Purkinje's *Contributions* (1819 and 1823) and *New Contributions* (1825).

Bibliographies—Secondary References

Kruta's extensive bibliography (1985, pp. 276–299) of the writings about Purkinje's life and work is organized topically, with the first section bearing on Purkinje's family, childhood, and youth. The second section contains references to books that provide photographic documentation. In addition to sections dealing with physiological topics there is a separate section on psychology, with 21 entries. Unfortunately, there are no references to publications that appeared after 1971, the year when the bibliography was completed.

Watson's bibliography of secondary references (1976, pp. 850–853) contains 63 entries. Interestingly, there is minimal overlap with the reference list prepared by Kruta. Watson's bibliography contains 52 non-overlapping references. This documents the significance of Watson's bibliography of secondary references for historians of psychology interested in Purkinje's psychological research.

In addition, Watson (1976, pp. 852–853) lists over 70 "secondary, short-title references" in which Purkinje is one of six or more eminent authors whose work is cited in a given reference.

E. G. Boring on Purkinje

Boring's two treatises (1929/1950; 1942) stand out among historical works inasmuch as substantial attention is devoted to Purkinje. Boring held a high opinion of Purkinje as a scientist (1950, p. 20), and in particular, he stressed Purkinje's contributions to the study of the senses—an area in which Purkinje shared interest with Johannes Müller. Boring also noted (1) Purkinje's excellence as a practitioner of phenomenology (especially its application to the study of vision—see p. 21); (2) the more general role, shared with Johann Wolfgang Goethe, of promoting rigorous descriptive study of psychological phenomena; (3) pioneering studies on vestibular function (p. 79)—a subject explored experimentally in animals by Flourens; (4) description of the changes in our perception of colors when the intensity of illumination increases or decreases (p. 103); (5) changes in the perceived color of the stimulus as it passes from the center of the retina to the periphery, first reported by Thomas Young (pp. 103–104); and (6) Purkinje's support of the theory of the accommodation of the eye by alteration of the convexity of the crystalline lens (p. 106).

Boring also recorded Hermann Helmholtz's high opinion of Purkinje's powers of observation: "It might seem that nothing would be easier than to be conscious of one's sensations; and yet experience shows that for discovery of subjective sensations some special talent is needed such as Purkinje manifests in the highest degree" (p. 314).

Important additional information on Purkinje's contributions is presented in Boring's treatise *Sensation and Perception in the History of Experimental Psychology* (1942). In this work Boring summarized Purkinje's work on vision as follows:

> He described the phenomena that result from 'inadequate' stimulation of the retina by pressure on the eyeball and by electrical currents, thus supplying data for Johannes Müller's doctrine of specific nerve energies. He examined the effect of dazzling light and its results in after-images and the flight of colors, the effects of dark adaptation, the facts about the blind spot, the relation of fixation to the size of the pupil, the phenomenon of single and double vision with the two eyes, and the general facts of after-images. . . . All of this is in his first volume. Although his second volume is somewhat more physiological, it includes phenomenological accounts of the changes in color sensitivity in indirect vision from 0 to 90 degrees from the fovea, of true and

> apparent movement in the visual field and why the moving eye does not produce the perception of movement, and the effect of strong light upon colors. (pp. 117–118)

Boring also referred to the Purkinje Phenomenon and later in the text (pp. 177–178) returned to it in greater detail. Finally, Boring discussed several other aspects of Purkinje's work, including the changes in the shape of the lens of the eye in the course of accommodation (p. 277), vertigo resulting from spinning the observer around (p. 536), and in particular, the apparent movement of stationary objects surrounding the subject when the rotation of the body is stopped (p. 588).

One of the reasons we have offered the above account of Purkinje's accomplishments in such detail is that we hope it will correct the widespread misconception that his work was limited to the

Figure 5 Rotary chair used by Purkinje in the study of eye movements.

Figure 6 Purkinje's photographic studies of physiognomy, in which he served as subject. The facial photographs were to indicate "roguishness, good humor, scorn, anger, rejection, disappointment, and thoughtfulness."

Purkinje Phenomenon. We have the uncomfortable feeling that without Boring's comprehensive coverage of Purkinje's work, Purkinje would not have been accorded the status of an "eminent contributor to psychology." On the basis of the ratings computed by an international panel of historians of psychology in which 27 was the maximal achievable score, Purkinje received a score of 24 (cf. Watson, 1974, p. 343). This is a score that places him in the company of men such as Charles Bell (1774–1842), an English anatomist; Paul Broca (1824–1880), a French neurologist; and P. Flourens (1794–1867), a French physiologist.

New Sources of Information: Purkinje's Breslau Lectures

The texts of Purkinje's lecture notes, written in a not readily decipherable Gothic script, remained locked in the form of manuscripts for some 150 years. As a result, their content was unavailable to historians of psychology. However, during the years 1973 to 1985, the materials were transcribed and published (Brožek & Hoskovec, 1987). The original manuscripts are held in the Literary Archives of the Museum of Czech Literature, in Prague. Both the lectures on empirical psychology and those on physiological psychology are available in two versions.

The lectures on empirical psychology are presented on pages 20–48 and 49–76 of the 1987 transcription, respectively, and the lectures on physiological psychology appear on pages 77–91 and 92–101. The lectures differ in the degree of completeness, but the second version of physiological psychology is particularly fragmentary. Thorough historical analyses remain to be carried out.

It was not until the spring of 1986 that one of us (J. H.) had the opportunity to visit the library and the archives of the University of Wroclaw (known as Breslau in Purkinje's days). On the basis of the lecture catalogues, published both in Latin and in German, it was possible to establish that Purkinje lectured on Empirical Psychology in the summer semesters of 1827 and 1836. The lectures on Physiological Psychology were given during the summer semesters of 1840 and 1842.

Paragraph 4 of version I of (Empirical) Psychology (p. 21) deals with "Sources" of information. The two fundamental sources are specified as (1) the experiences acquired, accidentally, in the course of one's life, and (2) the "new experiences obtained in an artificial way" (*psychische Experimente*). More interesting are the two sentences that follow which are concerned specifically with psychological phenomena such as individual differences in intelligence and emotions (*Erforschung der verschiedenar-*

tigen individuellen Charaktere der Geistes—und Gefuehlsanlagen): "This leads us to the study of history and poetry but also of nature, including the instincts and drives of animals. Consequently, we can differentiate between subjective psychology (*Autognosie*) and objective psychology."

To the disappointment of modern readers, neither in the lecture notes on empirical psychology nor in those on physiological psychology does Purkinje ever cite the results of experiments that others or he himself carried out. Equally disappointing is the absence of references, except for a marginal note, later crossed out, at the end of the paragraph on "Sources" (p. 21) that reads "Lit(eratur) v(ide) Pierers Woerterbuch." Most probably the author is referring to the work of Johann Friedrich Pierer (1767–1832), which was published in Altenberg by Literatur-Comptoir in 8 volumes during the years 1816–1829.

New Source of Information: Prague Fragments

We place Purkinje's "Psychological Fragments," written in Czech, in the 1860s. The manuscript bears no date, and we have no indirect evidence that would make it possible to arrive at a more precise date. The manuscript is limited to a short introductory section, historical in nature, entitled "A Glance at Contemporary Psychology," and the title of the next chapter, "Foundations of Empirical Psychology." We do not know what Purkinje intended to include in this book nor why it came to an abrupt end, but it does document Purkinje's interest in the history of psychology (for an English translation see Brožek & Hoskovec, 1987, pp. 116–118).

Anniversaries: 100 Years After Purkinje's Death

In 1969, V. Kruta published a short account, in English, of Purkinje's contributions to the progress of physiology, with a bibliography of his works. It contains numerous illustrations, a report on Purkinje's Institute of Physiology in Breslau (pp. 47–67), and dates in Purkinje's life. Kruta also organized a centenary symposium, held in Prague on September 8–10, 1969, and edited the proceedings (Kruta, 1971). Of special interest here is the section on "vision and eye." It contains contributions on (1) the shadows

of the retinal blood vessels (the "Purkinje tree"—see Ratliff, 1971), (2) differential visibility of colors in scotopic and photopic vision (the "Purkinje shift"—see Granit, 1971), and (3) neurophysiological evidence concerning afterimages, entoptic light sensation, and visual illusions (Jung, 1971). Brožek (1971) described some of the tasks preparatory to a systematic monograph on Purkinje's contribution to psychology.

Anniversaries: 200 Years After Purkinje's Birth

An international scientific conference on "J. Purkyně in Science and Culture" took place in Prague on August 26–30, 1987. The proceedings were edited by J. Purš, a member of the Czechoslovak Academy of Sciences, and published in English in two large volumes in 1988. Section IV contains, among other things, contributions on Purkinje's work cited in Johannes Müller's famous *Handbuch der Physiologie* 1833–1840 (Lohff, 1988), Purkinje and conditioned reflexes (Dostálek, 1988), and Purkinje's studies of vertigo (Černý, 1988). Particularly relevant is V. Kuthan's (1988) paper on Purkinje's contributions to the physiology of vision, and Vetter's (1988) account of the reception of Purkinje's early work in England.

Several other book-length references on Purkinje should be noted, including a volume registering Purkinje's correspondence (Halas, 1987), a listing of archival documents bearing on Purkinje's life and work (Beran, 1987), as well as reproductions of relevant documents held at the State Central Archives in Prague (Strbková, 1987) and in the Archives of Charles University (Anonymous, 1986). The volume edited by Brožek and Hoskovec (1987) was focused on previously unpublished manuscripts.

Overviews of Purkinje's life and work came from the pen of Kotek and Niklíček (1987), in English, and Kirsche (1989), in German. Prague's Faculty of General Medicine (Anonymous, 1985) prepared a history of the Physiological Institute, which was documented by photographs that also referred to Purkinje and his times. In a volume titled *Science in Purkyně's Time* (Janko and Štrbáňová, 1988, in Czech) a long chapter (pp. 122–145) deals with Purkinje and international science. These publications, stimulated by the 200th anniversary of his birth, have substantially enriched our information about Purkinje's life and work.

*Bibliography**

Anonymous. (1985). [*From the history of the Physiological Institute*]. Prague: Faculty of General Medicine, Charles University.

Anonymous. (1986). [*J. E. Purkyně in documents of the Archives of Charles University*]. Prague: Charles University.

Beran, J. (Comp.). (1987). [*A list of sources bearing on the life and work of J. E. Purkyně, kept in Czechoslovak archives*]. Prague: Czechoslovak Academy of Sciences.

Boring, E. G. (1942). *Sensation and perception in the history of experimental psychology*. New York: Appleton-Century-Crofts.

Boring, E. G. (1950). *A history of experimental psychology*. New York: Appleton-Century-Crofts. (Original work published 1929)

Brožek, J. (1971). Purkyně and psychology in a historical research perspective. In V. Kruta (Ed.), *J. E. Purkyně, 1787–1869: A centenary symposium* (pp. 105–118). Brno: J. E. Purkyně University.

Brožek, J., & Hoskovec, J. (1987). *J. E. Purkyně and psychology with a focus on unpublished manuscripts*. Prague: Academia.

Černý, E. (1988). J. E. Purkyně and his work on vertigo. In J. Purš (Ed.), *Jan Evangelista Purkyně in science and culture* (Vols. 1 & 2, pp. 611–628). Prague: Czechoslovak Academy of Sciences.

Dostálek, C. (1988). J. E. Purkyně and conditioned reflexes. In J. Purš (Ed.), *Jan Evangelista Purkyně in science and culture* (Vols. 1 & 2, pp. 523–529). Prague: Czechoslovak Academy of Sciences.

Granit, P. (1971). Some comment on the Purkinje shift. In V. Kruta (Ed.), *J. E. Purkyně, 1787–1869: A centenary symposium* (pp. 93–99). Brno: J. E. Purkyně University.

Halas, F. X. (1987). [*A register of the correspondence of J. E. Purkyně*]. Prague: Academia.

Janko, J., & Štrbáňová, S. (1988). [*Science in Purkyně's time*]. Prague: Academia.

Jung, R. (1971) Afterimages, visual illusions, and neuronal mechanisms. In V. Kruta (Ed.), *J. E. Purkyně, 1787–1869: A centenary symposium* (pp. 101–103). Brno: J. E. Purkyně University.

Kirsche, W. (1989). *Jan Evangelista Purkyně, 1787–1869*. Berlin: Akademie-Verlag.

Kotek, V., & Niklíček, L. (1987). *Jan Evangelista Purkyně and his place in the history of medicine and natural sciences of the 19th century*. Prague: Academia.

Kruta, V. (1961). Purkyně als Physiologe. In R. Zaunik (Ed.), *Purkyně-Symposium* (pp. 57–76). Leipzig: Barth.

Kruta, V. (1969). *J. E. Purkyně, physiologist*. Prague: Academia.

Kruta, V. (1985). [Bibliography: Works on Purkyně]. In V. Kruta & V. Zapletal (Eds.), *J. E. Purkyně, Opera omnia* (T. XIII, pp. 276–299). Autobiographica Bibliographia. Prague: Academia.

Kruta, V. (Ed.). (1971). *J. E. Purkyně, 1787–1869: A centenary symposium*. Brno: J. E. Purkyně University.

Kuthan, V. (1988). Achievement of J. E. Purkyně in the physiology of vision and ophthalmology. In J. Purš (Ed.), *Jan Evangelista Purkyně in science and culture* (Vols. 1 & 2, pp. 565–592). Prague: Czechoslovak Academy of Sciences.

Lohff, B. (1988). Purkyně's researches included in Johannes Müller's *Handbuch der Physiologie*. In J. Purs (Ed.), *Jan Evangelista Purkyně in science and culture* (Vols. 1 & 2, pp. 511–522). Prague: Czechoslovak Academy of Sciences.

Purkinje, J. E. (1819). *Beitraege zur Kentniss des Sehens in subjectiver Hinsicht*. Prague: Fr. Vetterl.

Purkinje, J. E. (1823). *Beobachtungen und Versuche zur Physiologie der Sinne. Erstes Baendchen. Beitraege zur Kenntniss des Sehens in subjectiver Hinsicht. Zweite unveraenderte Auflage*. Prague: J. G. Calve.

Purkinje, J. E. (1825). *Beobachtungen und Versuche zur Physiologie der Sinne. Zweites Baendchen. Neue Beitraege zur Kenntniss des Sehens in subjectiver Hinsicht*. Berlin: G. Reimer.

Purš, J. (Ed.). (1988). *Jan Evangelista Purkyně in science and culture* (Vols. 1 & 2). Prague: Czechoslovak Academy of Sciences.

Ratliff, F. (1971). On the objective study of subjective phenomena. In V. Kruta (Ed.), *J. E. Purkyně, 1787–1869: A centenary symposium* (pp. 77–92). Brno: J. E. Purkyně University.

Štrbková, M. (Comp.). (1987). [*Reproductions: To the 200th birthday of J.E. Purkyně*]. Prague: State Central Archives.

Vetter, M. (1988). The reception of Purkyně's scientific studies by British scientists during the first half of the nineteenth century. In J. Purš (Ed.), *Jan Evangelista Purkyně in science and culture* (Vols. 1–2, pp. 401–422). Prague: Czechoslovak Academy of Sciences.

Wade, N. J. (Ed.). (1983). *Brewster and Wheatstone on vision*. London: Academic Press.

Watson, R. I. (1974). *Eminent contributors to psychology: Vol. 1. A bibliography of primary references; (1976) Vol. 2. A bibliography of secondary sources*. New York: Springer Publishing Co.

Wheatstone, C. (1938). Contributions to the physiology of vision. *Philosophical Transactions of the Royal Society, 128*, 371–394.

---

*Note: Texts in brackets were translated from Czech.

Ernst Heinrich Weber

Horst-Peter Brauns

Psychophysics, the experimental branch of modern psychology, which first accomplished the measurement of sensations more than a century ago, provided modern psychology with a solid foundation as a quantitative and nomothetic science. Its founder, Ernst Heinrich Weber (1795–1878), the eminent German anatomist and physiologist, was given the accolade "Father of Psychophysics" by none other than his slightly younger student, fellow psychophysicist, and friend Gustav Theodor Fechner (1801–1887).

Ernst Heinrich Weber was born on June 24, 1795, in the small university community of Wittenberg in

Figure 2 Group portrait (left to right) of Eduard F. Weber, Wilhelm E. Weber, and Ernst Heinrich Weber (ca. 1845).

Figure 1 Photograph of Ernst Heinrich Weber as a retired professor.

the German Electorate of Saxony, son of a theology professor and the third of his 13 children. Weber was the descendant and blood relative of a number of eminent 19th-century German scholars and scientists. For example, one of his brothers, Wilhelm Eduard Weber (1804–1891), a colleague and close friend of the German mathematician and astronomer Karl Friedrich Gauss (1777–1855), was appointed to a full professorship of physics at Göttingen University in the German Kingdom of Hannover at the age of 27. The same brother gained universal acclaim, when he resigned his prestigious chair from 1837 to 1849 in sharp protest against the abolishment of the constitutional system of government in Hannover. The youngest brother, Eduard Friedrich Weber (1806–1871) worked as prorector and anatomy professor in the medical faculty of Leipzig University, and Theodor Weber (1829–1914), Ernst's son, held a medical professorship at his father's alma mater for many years.

After gaining an expert knowledge of Latin at the prestigious Prince's Academy in Meißen, Weber studied medicine in Wittenberg. He received his medical degree in 1815 at the age of 20 and qualified two years later as a medical instructor at Leipzig University. He taught at Leipzig from 1821 to 1871 as a full professor of anatomy and physiology. Wilhelm Wundt (1832–1920), who knew him personally, respected E. H. Weber as the "honored senior professor" of Leipzig University and proudly lived for some time in Weber's former university apartment in the old, inner city of Leipzig.

Weber's numerous publications in almost all branches of medicine include research on the comparative anatomy of the central nervous system, the auditory system in animals and man, the anatomy and function of the sex organs, circulation, the blood corpuscles, and the liver. As an academic teacher, Weber not only labored for the improvement of medical education but edited and published two textbooks in anatomy with novel didactic features. He represented Leipzig University in the Royal Saxon Legislature and acted as an active proponent of polytechnical societies, which generally propagated the application of scientific discoveries in industry and commerce.

As early as 1825, Weber and his 21-year-old brother, Wilhelm, copublished a pioneering book *Experimental Wave Theory*, which summarized the empirical studies of the flow and movement of waves in liquids and, especially, elastic tubes. They discovered the basic laws of hydrodynamics and applied these principles to the circulation of the blood. The results of their wave research were based in part on a series of elegant multivariate and quantitative experiments. Weber dedicated their important book to Ernst Florens Friedrich Chladni (1756–1827), a family friend and mentor, who deserves broad recognition in the history of physics as the founder of modern acoustics.

Core elements of modern research in physics and related fields, like the design of multivariate

experimental studies and the precise measurement of results, were also put into practice in Weber's personal studies in sensory physiology and sensory psychology. Many of these experiments, like his study *Sense of Touch and Common Sensibility* (1846), were also summarized in Wagner's famous *Dictionary of Physiology* (1846).

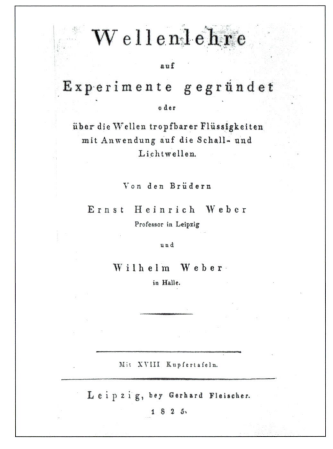

Figure 3 Title page of *Experimental Wave Theory* by E. H. Weber and W. Weber (1825).

As early as 1860, Fechner included Weber's research on weight judgments in his *Elements of Psychophysics* (1860). Specifically, these studies of sensory discrimination involve one of the first two-factorial experimental designs with repeated measurements. The results of the weight studies indicate that just noticeable differences (jnds), increases or decreases in reported weight estimates, are related in a predictable manner to the original (comparison) weight. Weber carried out similar metric experimental research in almost all sense modalities. His consistent results led him to

Figure 4 Title page of *Theory of Touch and Common Sensibility* (1851) by E. H. Weber.

the conclusion ". . . that human beings perceive relative rather than absolute differences when they observe differences between objects" (1851, p. 174). This discovery was later given the eponym "Weber's Law" by Fechner.

Weber's research on touch sensitivity of the skin in different regions of the human body by means of the prongs of a compass-like instrument is even better known than his studies of weight perception. These researches on human touch sensitivity form the beginning of a long tradition of psychological research, which is still active today. More recently, these studies have encouraged follow-up investigations in anatomy and physiology as well as a fascinating critical assessment by philosophy.

It is debatable whether Weber's psychophysical research ". . . did more for the true progress of psychology than . . . Aristotle . . . or Hobbes," as Ebbinghaus (1907, p. 128) suggested. We must, however, acknowledge that he provided an exemplary solution to the basic problems of human sensory perception through his replicable, experimental research. Weber's research in the twin fields of sensory physiology and sensory psychology became paradigmatic for the early work of Fechner, Wundt, and other 19th-century psychologists. Fechner expanded Weber's empirical results into a comprehensive, mathematical law about the functional rela-

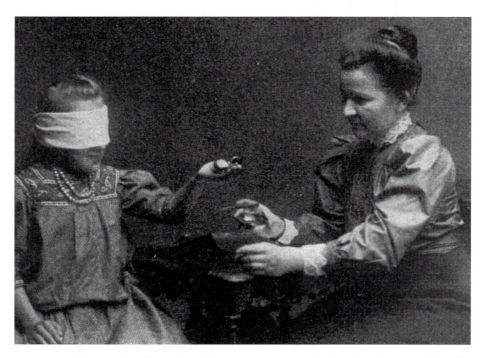

Figure 5 Photograph of weight judging experiment with female subject and female experimenter.

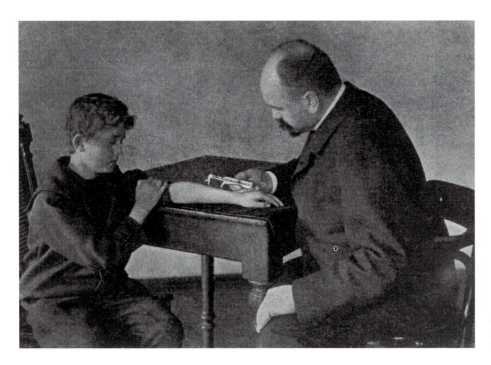

Figure 6 Photograph of touch sensitivity experiment with male subject and male experimenter.

tionships between physical stimuli and psychological perceptions. Wundt, on the other hand, used Weber's compass method to assess the touch sensitivity of female medical patients (Wundt, 1920) during his 1855–1856 internship at Heidelberg University Hospital. More importantly, Weber's use of the scientific methodology of the physics of his time, which he explicitly called to the attention of his psychological contemporaries, played a key role in placing the nascent field of 19th-century experimental psychology on a solid empirical and experimental basis.

Bibliography

Brauns, H. P. (1990). Fechners experimentelle Versuchsplanung in "Elemente der Psychophysik" im Lichte heutiger Methodenlehre des psychologischen Experiments. *Psychologie und Geschichte 1.*, 10–23.

Brauns, H. P. (1994). Zur Lage der Psychologie um das Jahr 1850. In H. Gundlach (Ed.), *Psychologiegeschichtliche Arbeiten*, pp. 207–218. Göttingen: Hogrefe.

Ebbinghaus, H. (1907). Psychologie. In P. Hinneberg (Ed.), *Die Kultur der Gegenwart*, Part I, Section VI, Systematische Philosophie, pp. 173–246. Berlin: Teubner.

Fechner, G. T. (1860). *Elemente der Psychophysik*. Leipzig: Breitkopf & Härtel.

Weber, E. H. (1846). Der Tastsinn und das Gemeingefühl. In R. Wagner (Ed.). *Handwörterbuch der Physiologie*, Vol. 3, Section 2, Leipzig: Koehler.

Weber, E. H. (1851). *Annotationes anatomicae et physiologicae*. Leipzig: Koehler.

Weber, E. H. (1851). *Die Lehre vom Tastsinne und Gemeingefühle*. Braunschweig, Germany: Vieweg.

Weber, E. H., & Weber, W. (1825). *Wellenlehre auf Experimente gegründet*. Leipzig: Fleischer.

Wundt, W. (1920). *Erlebtes und Erkanntes*. Stuttgart: Kröner.

Fechner and Lotze

Anneros Meischner-Metge
Wolfram Meischner

According to Wundt's *Outline of Psychology* (1896/1907), the scientific works of Gustav Theodor Fechner (1801–1887) and Rudolf Hermann Lotze (1817–1881) played a major role in the development of modern experimental psychology. Specifically, Wundt felt that it was Fechner's expert knowledge of physics and mathematics and his inclination to explore the deepest problems of human existence that enabled him to establish the psychological specialty of psychophysics. Lotze, on the other hand, made particularly valuable contributions through his efforts to define psychology in terms of its relationship to philosophy and physiology.

Gustav Theodor Fechner

Gustav Theodor Fechner began his medical studies in 1817 at Leipzig University in the German Kingdom of Saxony by studying physiology under Ernst Heinrich Weber (1795–1878) and algebra with Karl Brandon Mollweide (1774–1825). Although he passed his final medical examinations with ease, Fechner decided not to become a physician because he felt "unsure" about the field and was convinced that he "lacked any practical talent to help people." His skeptical views of medicine are also reflected in his early satirical publications such as "Proof that the Moon Consists of Iodine" (1821) and "In Praise of Modern Medicine and Natural History" (1822). Both of these were published under the pen name "Dr. Mises." During that same period, Fechner became an enthusiastic follower of Lorenz Oken (1779–1851), the German naturalist and speculative philosopher. Fechner received his doctorate in 1823 and, at the same time, qualified for a position as a lecturer with the philosophy faculty at Leipzig University. In 1824, Leipzig University invited him to

Figure 1 Fechner as a young boy.

teach courses in physics as a temporary replacement for his former teacher Ludwig Wilhelm Gilbert (1769–1824). In addition, he supported himself as a "literary day laborer" by translating *A Textbook of Chemistry* (Thénard, 1825–1833) and *A Textbook of Physics* (Biot, 1824–1825) from French into German for the Voss Publishing Company in Leipzig. Fechner's involvement in the publication of these major

Figure 2 Fechner as a professor (ca. 1850).

or preservation of ideas that help to preserve mankind and nature" (p. 7).

In 1860 Fechner published the two volumes of his *Principles of Psychophysics*. This achievement clearly establishes his position as the founder of psychophysics and also guarantees his place in the history of psychology. His basic ideas about psychophysics were first introduced in two earlier books, *Zend Avesta* (1851) and *Psychological Measurement* (1858), and in a lecture on "The Basic Law of Psychophysics," which he presented in 1859 before the Royal Saxon Academy of Sciences. For Fechner, psychophysics was: "an exact theory about the functional relationships between body and soul and between the bodily, mental, somatic and psychological world" (1860, p. 8). Specifically, Fechner distinguished between "external psychophysics" or the relationship between the mental and the external, physical environment, and "inner psychophysics," which deals with the relationship between mental events and the internal environment of the body. The psychophysical "method of

scientific works and his own experimental research on Galvanism, electrochemistry, and electromagnetism in *Textbook of Galvanism* (1829), *Basic Textbook of Electromagnetism* (1831), and *On the Measurement of the Galvanic Chain* (1834) led to his appointment as a tenured professor of physics at his alma mater. In 1840, Fechner had to give up teaching and research in physics as a consequence of a serious eye illness, which affected his entire life. After an extended period of convalescence, he began offering informal courses on a variety of philosophical topics at Leipzig in 1846. In the first course, on " The Highest Good and Human Will," Fechner gave expression to his personal creed (1846): "Man should teach himself and others . . . to gain as much pleasure as possible and to learn as much as possible about everything that can promote happiness in the world" (p. 10). Similarly, in his *Little Book About Life After Death* (1836), Fechner stressed each individual's collective responsibility: "Man's . . . immortality derives from anything he contributes during life to the creation, development,

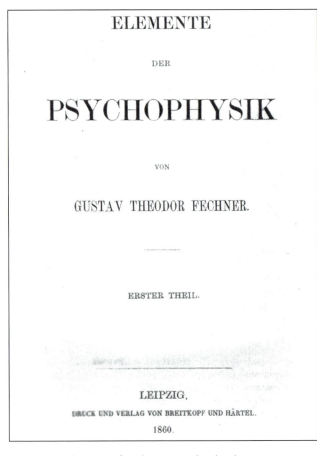

Figure 3 Title page of Fechner's *Psychophysik*.

102

just noticeable differences," which Fechner adapted from Ernst Heinrich Weber, and the "method of right and wrong cases," which can be traced back to Karl Vierordt (1818–1884) and Alfred Wilhelm Volkmann (1800–1877), constitute the core of psychophysics. The method of "mean errors" was a traditional research procedure, which, according to Fechner, has been used for ages by anyone interested in the collection of precise scientific observations.

Fechner's later works, *On the Matter of Psychophysics* (1877) and *Revision of Psychophysics* (1882), contain his replies to the discussions and criticisms of his early psychophysical writings. The following comments are taken from an 1886 letter to Wilhelm Wundt (1832–1920): "It is my general view that too much computation takes place in [modern] psychophysics and too little experimentation. . . . I believe that . . . mathematical thought has been wasted on worthless experiments. It would have been better to collect more and better results" (April 13, 1886).

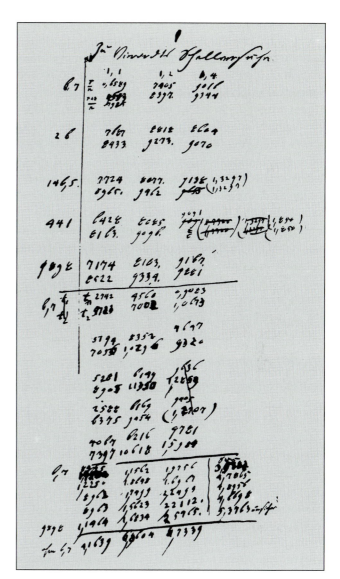

Figure 5 Facsimile of Fechner's record of sound experiments.

In 1888, Fechner's last scientific treatise, "On the Principles of Psychological Measurement and Weber's Law," was published in volume 4 of Wundt's *Philosophical Studies*. This essay was a rejoinder to the claim of the German philosopher Adolf Elsas (1855–1895) that exact measurement was not possible in psychology (Elsas, 1886).

After the publication of his *Psychophysics*, Fechner focused primarily on methodological questions and the development of his ideas about the empirical study of aesthetics. Fechner's writings in this field include experimental investigations of the famous "Golden Section"; articles and an 1871 opinion survey about the authenticity of the "Darmstadt" and "Dresden Madonnas" by Hans Holbein

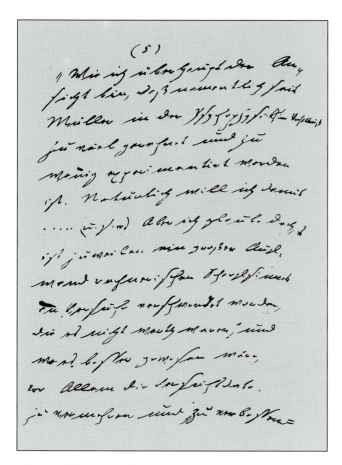

Figure 4 Facsimile of Fechner's letter to Wundt (1886).

the Younger (1497/98–1543) and various applications of his psychophysical methods to the study of artistic preferences. In sharp contrast to mere philosophical discussions of taste, Fechner collected empirical information about what the people of his time actually regarded as beautiful (Fechner, 1872).

Fechner's philosophical writings are generally viewed as being filled with contradictions and mystical speculations. Nonetheless, these works contain many original ideas and deep thoughts about man's unity with nature and the universe. His ideas about movement and nature's tendency toward stability or equilibrium; his thinking about part-whole relationships; and his original, synechological views, all find relevance today in modern systems theory. Fechner's entire work is permeated by his conviction that a supreme law, which he called the "divine principle," works at all times in the world.

Rudolf Hermann Lotze

Rudolf Hermann Lotze, the son of a military physician, was born on May 21, 1817, in Bautzen, a provincial town in the German Kingdom of Saxony. After graduating from a classical high school in nearby Zittau, Lotze began his medical studies in the spring of 1834 at Leipzig University when he was 16 years old. His teachers included Alfred Wilhelm Volkmann, Johannes Christian August Clarus (1774–1854), Gustav Theodor Fechner (1801–1887), Ernst Heinrich Weber (1795–1866), and Christian Hermann Weisse (1801–1878). In 1838, Lotze received doctorates in both medicine and philosophy. One year later, in the fall of 1839, the young physician was appointed to the position of instructor of medicine and philosophy at Leipzig. He was promoted to the rank of untenured professor at Christmas in 1842; and in 1844, at the age of only 27, he was appointed to succeed the eminent philosopher and educator Johann Friedrich Herbart (1776–1841) at Göttingen University. During his 37 years at Göttingen, Lotze's inspiring lectures and many books attracted numerous students, including Carl Stumpf (1848–1931), Georg Elias Müller (1850–1934), and countless Americans. In 1881, Hermann von Helmholtz (1821–1894) and Eduard Zeller (1814–1908) persuaded Lotze to accept the prestigious chair of psychology at Berlin University in Prussia. He accepted but shortly thereafter died from pneumonia on July 1, 1881.

Unlike Fechner, his teacher and long-time friend,

Lotze was no experimental scientist, but he was an outstanding theoretician in medicine, psychology, and philosophy. His successful polemics against vitalism in medicine and his mechanistic explanation of life influenced biological thinking for decades (Hertwig, 1897).

Figure 6 Fechner as an old man.

It was Lotze's famous chapters "Life and the Force of Life," "Instinct," and "Soul and the Life of the Soul" in Wagner's encyclopedic *Dictionary of Physiology* (1842, 1845, 1848) that established his eminent position in the history of modern psychology. His books *Medical Psychology or the Physiology of the Soul* (1852) and *Microcosm—Ideas on Natural History and the History of Mankind* (1856–1864) elaborated his psychological views in detail. According to Lotze, psychology stands as a mediator between

Figure 7 Rudolf Hermann Lotze.

writings. Wundt's idea that sensations and emotions comprise the basic elements of mental life can easily be traced back to Lotze's physiological psychology. The same is true for Wundt's theory of emotions (specifically, the pleasure-displeasure polarity), his theory of perception, and even his anthropological or folk psychology (Woodward, 1982).

Lotze's evolutionary thought was primarily influenced by Georg W. F. Hegel (1770–1831) and Lorenz Oken (1779–1851). For Lotze, it was one of the chief tasks of psychology to provide "an empirical, yet sufficiently speculative, description of mental development from the animal world to human society" (Lotze, 1989, p. 234). Thus, Lotze, like Wundt, became a pioneer of historical psychology who proposed a developmental history of mankind (Wundt, 1912). For Lotze, psychology was a core discipline which has a fundamental importance for clarifying "the future of human souls in the universe" (Lotze, 1989, p. 234).

philosophy and physiology. Before psychology can become an autonomous field of study, it must clarify its relationship with the neighboring fields of physiology and philosophy. Psychology clearly needs a philosophical basis because it will always be confronted with difficult and, at times, almost insoluble theoretical and methodological questions. Psychology's relationship to physiology is less complicated, for unlike physiology, psychology is not a natural science. Psychological-mental events basically possess a qualitative character and differ radically from physical and physiological events, but at the same time, body and soul interact. For example, physiological events provide the sensory and motor antecedents of mental events; hence, a "physiological psychology" is needed to unite both fields.

It is quite obvious that Wilhelm Wundt was influenced by Lotze's theoretical views and that he consequently recognized Lotze's importance as a pioneer of experimental psychology (Wundt, 1922, p. 22). Wundt referred to many of Lotze's ideas in his *Principles of Physiological Psychology* (1874), and his influence can also be discerned in Wundt's other

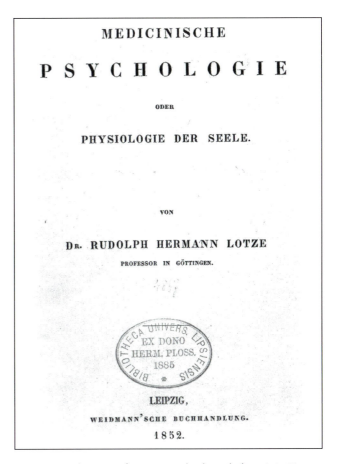

Figure 8 Title page of Lotze's *Medical Psychology* (1852).

Mikrokosmus.

Ideen zur Naturgeschichte und Geschichte
der Menschheit.

Versuch einer Anthropologie

von

Hermann Lotze.

BIBL.
VNIVERS.
LIPS.

Dritter Band.

7. Die Geschichte. 8. Der Fortschritt. 9. Der Zusammenhang
der Dinge.

Leipzig,
Verlag von S. Hirzel.
1864.

Figure 9 Title page of Lotze's *Mikrokosmus* (1856–1864).

In conclusion, Fechner and Lotze are rightly counted among the forerunners of modern psychology. Fechner contributed most to the methodological development of modern experimental psychology, whereas Lotze helped secure a firm physiological basis for general as well as applied studies in psychology.

Bibliography

Altmann, I. (1995). *Bibliographie Gustav Theodor Fechner.* Leipzig: Verlag im Wissenschaftszentrum.

Elsas, A. (1886). *Uber die psychophysik. Physicalische und erkenntniss theoretische Betrachtungen, von Dr. Adolf Elsas.* Marburg: N.G. Elwer.

Fechner, G.T. (1836). *Das Büchlein vom Leben nach dem Tode.* Dresden: Grimmer.

Fechner, G.T. (1846). *Ueber das höchste Gut.* Leipzig: Breitkopt & Härtell.

Fechner, G.T. (1858). Das psychische Maß. In I. H. Fichte, H. Ulrici, & I.W. Wirth (Eds.), *Zeitschrift für Philosophie und philosophische Kritik* (pp.1–2). Halle: Breitkopf & Härtel.

Fechner, G.T. (1860). *Elemente der Psychophysik* (Vols. 1–2). Leipzig: Breitkopt & Härtel.

Fechner, G. T. (1872). *Berichte über das auf der Dresdener Holbein-Ausstellung ausgelegte Album.* Leipzig: Breitkopf & Härtell.

Fechner, G.T. (1876). *Vorschule der Äesthetik.* Leipzig: Breitkopf & Härtel.

Hertwig, O. (1897). *Zeit- Streitfragen der Biologie.* Part II. Jena: Fischer.

Kuntze, J. (1892). *Gustave Theodor Fechner (Dr. Mises).* Leipzig: Breitkopf & Härtel.

Lotze, H. (1842). Leben- und Lebenskraft. In R. Wagner (Ed.), *Handwörterbuch der Physiologie* (Vol 1, pp. *ix–lviii*). Braunschweig, Germany: Vieweg.

Lotze, H. (1845). Instinkt. In R. Wagner (Ed.), *Handwörterbuch der Physiologie* (Vol. 2, pp. 191–209). Braunschweig, Germany: Vieweg.

Lotze, H. (1848). Seele und Seelenleben. In R. Wagner (Ed.), *Handwörterbuch der Physiologie* (Vol. 3, pp. 142–246). Braunschweig, Germany: Vieweg.

Lotze, H. (1852). *Medizinische Psychologie oder Physiologie der Seele.* Leipzig: Hirzel.

Lotze, H. (1856–1864). *Microkosmus* (Vols. 1–3). Leipzig: Hirzel.

Lotze, H. (1989). *Kleine Schriften zur Psychologie.* Berlin: Springer.

Mises, Dr. (1821). *Beweiss, dass der Mond aus Jodine bestehe.* Penig, Germany: Germanien.

Mises, Dr. (1822). *Panegyrikus der jetzigen Medicin und Naturgeschichte.* Leipzig: Hartmann.

Woodward, W. (1982). *From the science of language to Völkerpsychologie: Lotze, Steinthal, Lazarus and Wundt.* Heidelberg: Psychologisches Institüt.

Wundt, W. (1874). *Grundzüge der Physiologischen Physiologie.* Leipzig: Engelmann.

Wundt, W. (1907). *Outlines of Psychology* (7th. ed.; C.H. Judd, Trans.). Leipzig: Engelmann. (Original work published 1896)

Wundt, W. (1912). *Elemente der Völkerpsychologie.* Leipzig: Kröner.

Wundt, W. (1922). *Grundriß der Psychologie* (15th. ed.). Leipzig: Kröner.

Hermann von Helmholtz

Horst-Peter Brauns

Why should Hermann von Helmholtz (1821–1894) be included among major personalities in the history of psychology? After all, he first became famous as a 26-year-old military physician when he published his mathematical formula on the principle of the conservation of energy. Today, this achievement would be honored with the Nobel Prize in Physics! Moreover, he culminated his

Figure 2 Helmholtz Memorial Postage Stamp (Germany, 1971).

long academic career with a prestigious appointment as a full professor of physics, not psychology, at Berlin University. In addition, he served as Director of the Imperial Institute for Physics and Technology in Berlin from 1871 to 1894 after spending 23 years as an eminent teacher of medicine at several major German universities. Again, considering the nature of these appointments and accomplishments, one may wonder what Helmholtz has to do with the development of modern psychology. To answer this question, we begin with a look at his background.

As a weak and rather homely-looking child, the musically and technically gifted Helmholtz discovered many principles of geometry on his own while playing with a set of large building blocks. Somewhat later, as a high school student in the Prussian garrison city of Potsdam, he enjoyed working out optical problems during boring Latin classes. He also performed simple optical experiments during his leisure hours. His father was an impecunious teacher of classics and literature at the Potsdam Grammar School. Helmholtz's mother was a lineal descendant of William Penn (1621–1670), the Quaker

Figure 1 Hermann von Helmholtz at the age of 27 (March 23, 1848).

founder of colonial Pennsylvania, which may help explain the strong interest of the mature Helmholtz for English culture, philosophy, and science. Because of financial problems, Helmholtz received his medical education at the Royal Prussian Surgical Institute in Berlin from 1838 to 1842. Afterwards, he worked for seven years as an army surgeon in Berlin.

In 1848, Helmholtz received his first academic appointment as an instructor of anatomy at the Berlin Academy of Arts through the recommendation of Ernst Wilhelm Brücke (1819–1892), his friend and physiology teacher. Brücke later became Sigmund Freud's mentor at the University of Vienna. In 1849, Helmholtz's medical dissertation in neurophysiology and his early research on the process of digestion and muscular metabolism helped him gain an untenured, junior professorship at Königsberg University in East Prussia. At this provincial institution, Helmholtz, in 1850, successfully measured the velocity of nervous transmission and, consequently, in 1851, he was promoted to a full professorship at Königsberg. Next, Helmholtz accepted prestigious professorships of physiology and anatomy at the Prussian University of Bonn (1851–1857) and a professorship of physiology at the University of Heidelberg (1857–1871) in the German Grand Duchy of Baden (1857–1870). Until his death on September 8, 1894, Helmholtz held the esteemed appointment as professor of physics at the University of Berlin and served as President of the Imperial German Institute for Physical Technology.

Despite his fame, Helmholtz clearly was no professional psychologist. Nonetheless, much of his scientific work directly impacted on psychology and continues to be relevant to the twin fields of physiological and experimental psychology up to the present time.

Wilhelm Wundt (1832–1920), the founder of modern scientific psychology, worked as a teaching assistant for Helmholtz from 1857 to 1865 in the Physiological Institute at Heidelberg University. During this period, Wundt developed and published his initial plans for a new, experimental psychology as described in his *Contributions to a Theory of Sensory Perception* (1862) and his 1863 *Lectures About Animal and Human Souls.*

Somewhat later, in 1874, the 18-year-old medical student, Sigmund Freud, enthusiastically studied Helmholtz's *Popular Scientific Lectures* (1865–1871), vowing that he would be "happy as a child" to spend the winter term of 1874–1875 as one of Helmholtz's students in Berlin. Because of financial problems, however, Freud was unable to realize his plans to study under Helmholtz and couldn't even afford to purchase a used edition of Helmholtz's *Treatise on Physiological Optics* (1856–1866).

Figure 3 Helmholtz at Heidelberg.

In 1880, Helmholtz was asked to evaluate the second dissertation of Hermann Ebbinghaus (1850–1909), *Memory: An Experimental Investigation* (1880/1983). He concluded that this research was "intelligently designed and carefully and patiently carried out." He noted further that Ebbinghaus's research dissertation showed "a good understanding of mathematics." Finally, he concluded that "the results [of Ebbinghaus's research] are not too impressive but one cannot always anticipate this at the beginning of an investigation" (Helmholtz, 1880/1983).

In 1890, shortly before his death, Helmholtz became one of the editors of the new *Journal for the Psychology and Physiology of the Sense Organs* along with Ebbinghaus, Arthur König (1856–1901), Georg E. Müller (1850–1934), William T. Preyer (1841–1897), and Carl. G. Stumpf (1848–1936). Specifically, he contributed the inaugural article in the first issue as well as four additional articles on various topics in the psychology of perception.

Helmholtz exerted a stronger and more direct influence on the nascent field of experimental psychology through the publication of his monumental monographs about the physiology of vision and acoustics. His *Treatise on Physiological Optics* was published in three installments from 1856–1866, and his book *On the Sensation of Tone* (1862/1954) involved, respectively, 10 and 8 years of painstaking research. A good deal of pertinent content from these works was soon afterwards incorporated into major textbooks of experimental psychology like Wundt's famous *Principles of Psychology* (1874).

In addition, Helmholtz was able to contribute his novel, quantitative model of research to the new psychology. For example, Fechner included information from the visual and acoustical experiments conducted by Helmholtz in his *Elements of Psychophysics* (1860, Vol. 2, p. 549). Helmholtz, in turn, followed Fechner's suggestions and recommendations in some of his later studies of sensory physiology and psychology.

More importantly, Helmholtz helped raise the scientific status of psychology by delineating specific areas of sensory physiology, which required a psychological, rather than merely a physiological, analysis. Specifically, Helmholtz stressed that the study of optical and acoustical phenomena required the collaboration of psychologists as well as physicists and physiologists. He acknowledged, however (Helmholtz, 1856–1866) that: "where psychological processes intervene there appears to be much greater room for individual peculiarities than in other regions of physiology" (p. III). Whereas physical optics deals with the "pathway of light in the eye" and physiological optics focuses on the "theory of sensations in the visual apparatus," psychology is concerned with "the theoretical understanding of visual sensations, including the ideas, which are developed about objects in the external world on the basis of visual sensations" (Helmholtz, 1856–1866, p. 30).

It was during his brief association with Königsberg University that Helmholtz first became interested in the study of sensory perception—which required an expert knowledge of "philosophy and science" (Helmholtz, 1855, p. 90). According to Helmholtz, psychology by itself is not very useful in "elucidating the [basic] processes which trans-

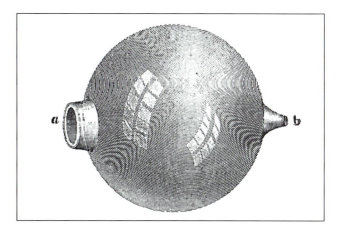

Figure 4 Helmholtz resonance sphere.

form the sensation of light into the perception of the external world" (1855, p. 111). Nonetheless, unconscious (psychological) processes or inferences, which "take place without our understanding and cannot be altered by our will," (1855, p. 110) also play a role in the process of sensation. Helmholtz's perceptual theory was strongly influenced by the views of his teacher and mentor, the eminent German physiologist Johannes Peter Müller (1801–1858).

The research methodology that Helmholtz used rests squarely on the natural sciences, particularly

Figure 5 Helmholtz vibration microscope.

Figure 6 Helmholtz—"Imperial Chancellor of German Physics."

vation. As Helmholtz put it: "A relatively small number of well-designed experiments enables me to determine the causal conditions of an event with greater confidence than many millions of observations for which I could not change the [research] conditions at will" (p. 451).

In conclusion, Hermann von Helmholtz's research in the twin fields of sensory physiology and sensory psychology significantly strengthened and expanded the scientific basis of the nascent field of quantitative, experimental psychology. By delineating and defining the field of psychological research and its relationship to physics and physiology, Helmholtz helped modern experimental psychology gain its legitimate place among the recognized scientific disciplines.

Bibliography

Ebbinghaus, H. (1983). Ueber das Gedächtniß. In W. Traxel (Ed.), *H. Ebbinghaus, Urmanuskript 'Ueber des Gedächtniß,' 1880.* Passau: Passavia. (Original work written in 1880)

Fechner, G. T. (1860). *Elemente der Psychophysik.* Leipzig: Breitkopf & Härtel.

Helmholtz, H. (1852). Über die Natur der menschlichen Sinnesempfindungen. In H. v. Helmholtz (Ed.) (1883), *Wissenschaftliche Abhandlungen,* Vol. 2, pp. 591–609. Leipzig: Barth.

Helmholtz, H. (1855). Über das Sehen des Menschen. In H. v. Helmholtz (Ed.) (1896), *Vorträge und Reden,* Vol.1, pp. 85–138. Braunschweig, Germany: Vieweg.

Helmholtz, H. (1856–1866). *Handbuch der physiologischen Optik.* Hamburg: Voss.

Helmholtz, H. (1862). *Die Lehre von den Tonempfindungen.* Braunschweig, Germany: Vieweg.

Helmholtz, H. (1865–1871). *Populaire wissenschaftliche Vorträge.* Braunschweig, Germany: Vieweg.

Helmholtz, H. (1880). *Gutachten von Hermann von Helmholtz aus dem Jahre 1880 über die Habilitationsschrift von H. Ebbinghaus 'Ueber das Gedächtniß.'* Universitätsarchiv der Humboldt Universität zu Berlin, Philosophische Fakultät, DeKanat, Akte Nr. 1210, Blatt 168.

Helmholtz, H. (1891). Erinnerungen: In H. v. Helmholtz, (Ed.) (1896), *Vorträge und Reden,* Vol.1, pp. 3–21. Braunschweig, Germany: Vieweg.

physics. According to Helmholtz (1891), "my researches were logical applications of the experimental and mathematical methods which were developed in the natural sciences. These were [only] adapted for specific purposes with minor modifications" (p. 13).

Helmholtz applied the same approach to his empirical research in the psychology of perception. He developed his own research equipment, when this was necessary. If no suitable mathematical formulas were available, Helmholtz developed these as well. For him, the experiment was always the method of choice since it provided the researcher with far more convincing results than natural obser-

Time-Measuring Apparatus in Psychology

Horst U. K. Gundlach

Time-measuring devices played a significant role in the development of experimental psychology. Time is one and, as some philosophers claimed, the *only* dimension mental processes can exhibit. This leads to a rather poor comparison with physical processes, which have four dimensions to unfold, three spatial and one temporal. This reasoning led the celebrated Königsberg philosopher Immanuel Kant to pontificate that psychology would never be able to develop into something deserving of the dignified title of "science."

It took more than half a century before scientists recovered from this charge and actually started to explore the potential of *mental chronometry*, the term for time measurement within the realm of mental processes. The advent of new techniques of short time measurement which were unavailable in Kant's time assisted greatly. The stimulus for investigating the temporal characteristics of mental processes came from outside psychology. Two domains were of chief importance: astronomy and the problem of the personal equation; and neurophysiology and research into the velocity of the transmission of nerve impulses.

Some 200 years ago, the Greenwich royal astronomer Nevil Maskelyne (1732–1811) sacked his assistant Kinnebrook on the charge that his observations of stellar transmissions were invariably almost one second later than those of his master. This error was too significant to be tolerated in astronomical observations, but it appeared in other observations as well. The tenacity of the error so intrigued the Königsberg astronomer Friedrich Wilhelm Bessel (1784–1846) that he started an investigation with the uncomfortable result that any astronomer, independent of training and acuity of senses, showed a specific and personal deviation from his colleagues' observational measurements. This became known as the *personal equation.* Astronomers remained puzzled by this curious phenomenon, which lacked a proper explanation, and continued to investigate. They concluded that the cause must be located in the observer and his physiological and psychological makeup.

Physiologists had for a long time assumed that the velocity of nervous transmission was equal to the speed of light and, therefore, given the relative shortness of nerve cells, not measurable. Hermann Helmholtz (1821–1894), while professor at Königsberg, defied this unconfirmed notion and in 1850 published his surprising results—he found nerve transmission much slower than even the transmission of sound in air. The import of this discovery for psychology is obvious. Since mental processes happen in the nervous system, the speed of transmission in this system must be of significance for the temporal structure of mental acts. This discovery opened doorways for the clarification and explanation of the personal equation as well as for the functioning of the mind in general. Psychologists did not hurry to explore this new territory since the methods for time measurement were still cumbersome, but as the technology advanced, psychology embarked on this path of exploration.

Two different ways to do short time chronometry developed and were adapted for psychological research, both of them based on the same physical principle: The oscillation frequency of a vibrating metal bar is constant as long as the temperature stays constant. Departing from this principle, two diverging methods of chronometry developed, usually called *chronography* and *chronoscopy*.

Chronography uses a large metal rod, customarily in the shape of a tuning fork, and produces traces of its oscillations which are then directly inspected and counted. Chronoscopy, on the other hand, uses a fairly small metal piece as the escapement or regulating spring which controls a mechanical clockwork. Chronoscopy, as a rule, is a lot more comfortable to use than chronography. It has, however, the drawback of being susceptible to various influences that may disturb how it functions.

Chronography

The basic equipment for chronography is a metal bar, usually a tuning fork, with a known oscillatory frequency and a revolving drum wrapped with a smoked paper on which the traces of the oscillating metal are drawn. A second and parallel string of markings captures the timing of the process, which has to be determined in its temporal stretch. The duration can be calculated by counting the number of oscillations between the two sets of markings and dividing by the frequency.

Early and still insufficient methods of chronography were devised at the beginning of the 18th century. By the middle of the century, astronomers

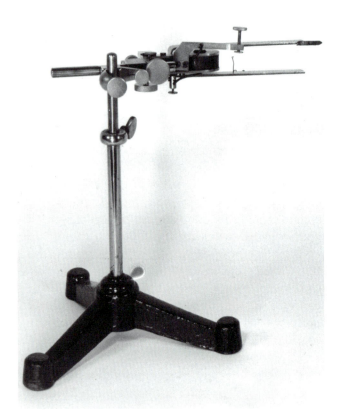

Figure 1 Tuning fork with writing spike.

used an improved version for research in the personal equation. The revolving drum was usually driven by a weight, an invention of Thomas Young (1773–1829). In 1842, Carl Ludwig (1816–1895) improved this construction by having a clockwork move the drum. Under the name of *kymograph*, it became a standard item for many purposes in physiological laboratories and later in psychological laboratories as well. In Figure 1, the electromagnet between the two branches of the fork serves to operate the fork. The tuning fork has to be placed next to a kymograph so that the spike touches the sooted paper on the drum and produces markings when the fork is activated and the drum revolves.

As shown in Figures 2 and 3, the kymograph was driven by a robust clockwork which was not precise enough for exact measurements. Figure 2 shows a kymograph with a descending drum that allows use for longer periods, since the markings do not coincide after the first full turn. Multiple pointers allow the measurement of temporal relations between various variables.

The operation of a chronograph and the evaluation of its measurements was a time-consuming affair. One had to smoke the kymograph paper, a procedure for which special sooting devices working with gas or naphthalene flames were available. After the recording, the paper had to be fixed and coated in a shellac solution. All this was a tedious, dirty, and odiferous task. Evaluation involved the tiresome counting of the oscillations of the curve and comparing them with other markings. If, for example, the tuning fork had a frequency of 880 oscillations per second, the determination of a reaction time of 1 second demanded the exact counting of 880 bumps on the sooty paper.

The chronographic method, which was later also used in psychological laboratories, was considered to be less proficient than measurements with the chronoscope. It was, however, less subject to errors and was also used as a calibrating device for the chronoscope.

The Chronoscope

The term *chronoscope* has become the accepted designation for clocks in which the clockwork or hands are started and stopped through the opening or interrupting of an electrical current operating in an electromagnet. The clockwork itself is regulated by a small metal bar which emits a sound corre-

Figure 2 Kymograph with descending drum.

Figure 3 Kymograph with four pointers.

sponding to its frequency. When the sound changes by an octave, for example, the experimenter is dutifully notified, but, unfortunately, the subject is disturbed by whatever noise the clock emits.

The first instrument properly called a chronoscope was invented by the Englishman Charles Wheatstone (1802–1875). It had, however, a fault that made it unsuitable for the measurement of very short time spans—exactly the ones for which experimental psychology became notorious. The source of the error is due to the fact that the electromagnet operates directly on the clockwork which naturally takes time to go from idleness to working speed. The clock is inaccurate during this interval. The shorter the time span to be measured, the more significant the error.

Matthias Hipp (1813–1893), a watchmaker and inventor from the Swabian region of Germany, invented a clever device that solved this problem. He let the electromagnet operate not on the clockwork itself, but on the clock hands. The clockwork is put into proper action before the onset of the event to be timed, but the hands are still disconnected and it is the magnet which moves the handle into gear. This eliminated the initial error of

Wheatstone's construction. Hipp's invention became known as "Hipp's chronoscope" to generations of psychology students. Figures 4 and 5 show the clockwork—which is completely mechanical—driven by the weight. Starting and stopping is done by pulling the cords below the clockwork. Clock faces allow both one-thousandth and one-tenth of a second readings. The rear view in Figure 5 shows a double pair of magnets, which means this is one of the "new" models—on sale since 1875—since the "old" model had only one pair. Figure 6 shows a modified model of Hipp's chronoscope. It had three clock faces and was designed to measure longer time spans.

It might be remarked in passing that neither Wheatstone nor Hipp intended to help psychologists in search of a proper instrument for their not yet conceived experiments. Wheatstone wanted to build an instrument to be used in military ballistics, or gunnery, as the English call it, to determine the velocity of projections from the mouth of the gun to the target. Hipp's invention was published so as to leave no doubt that this article was perfect for the inquisitive artillerist.

The chronoscope did its duty in ballistics. In

Figure 4 Hipp's chronoscope, the new model (with a double pair of magnets) introduced in 1875.

Figure 5 Hipp's chronoscope (new model), rear view (the double pair of magnets visible on the right).

addition, it served in diverse sciences, such as astronomy, physics, physiology, and, eventually, psychology. It is an obvious case of a spin-off product of military research.

Figure 6 Modified model of Hipp's chronoscope, for measuring longer time spans.

The Prussian astronomer Adolph Hirsch (1830–1901), who worked in Neuchâtel, Switzerland, is credited for being the first to attack the personal equation with a Hipp chronoscope. The very same instrument was borrowed from his good friend Matthias Hipp, who had founded a factory in Neuchâtel and volunteered as a subject.

The first psychologist to embrace the paradigm set by Hirsch's research into the personal equation was none other than Wilhelm Wundt (1832–1920). There can be no doubt that the Hipp chronoscope owes its place in psychology to Wundt, through his example, his research, his writing, and his teaching. The first six editions of Wundt's *Principles of Physiological Psychology* (1874–1911) bear witness to his persistent attempts at improving the apparatus and enabling its use in dealing with new problems.

It must be stated, therefore, that the Hipp chronoscope was an established short-duration chronometer by 1860, that it received a bit more appli-

Figure 7 Wundt's control hammer, small version.

cational comfort in 1875, and that it was still in full swing among psychologists when Wundt retired from his teaching post in 1912.

Numerous additional items are needed in order to use the chronoscope in an experiment. Galvanic elements to produce the electrical current; rheocord and Ohm meter to regulate the current; Pohl counterpoises; and the reaction keys, voice keys, or whatever registers the onset of the subject's reaction. The whole arrangement leaves many potential sources for errors, e.g., the tension of the magnet springs, the varying strength of the current used, magnetization, and demagnetization. The method of calibration was to use something that provided a fixed, unchanging time interval against which the chronoscope could be set.

Hipp himself sold a so-called gravity apparatus where a dropping steel ball would determine a constant time span against which the chronoscope had to be calibrated at regular intervals. Pendulums were also devised for this purpose. Another way was to use a chronograph. The method that became common in psychology was the use of a so-called control hammer—a device invented by Siemens and Pflüger and improved upon by Wundt. The control hammer (Figure 7) is released electromagnetically. While falling, it touches two different contacts. As it progresses at a constant rate of acceleration, the movement between the contacts always involves the same time interval against which the chronoscope can be calibrated.

The incessant need for calibrating, verifying, and adjusting proved to be the sore spot in the use of chronoscopy. At least it was neither dirty nor smelly—unless it was done with chronographical methods. All in all, the chronoscope has to be perceived and assessed in its environment—a menagerie of accessories needed in order to employ the chronoscope in a trustworthy fashion—supposing that accuracy to the millisecond, or at least something in that ballpark, was needed. A carefully calibrated and well-supervised chronoscope could indeed deliver that.

The chronoscope was a rather expensive device, equaled in cost only by the control hammer. The combined expenses of these two instruments were a weighty burden to be paid by a usually underfunded field of research. Typically, students were allowed to touch the chronoscope only after many semesters of menial toil in the laboratory. It was a small wonder then, that inventors and manufacturers were eager to offer cheaper substitutes. The chronoscope of d'Arsonval was one such invention. As seen in Figure 8, it had a reaction key, a pressure stimulator, and a protective case. It was portable, comparatively noiseless, and ran for almost 15 minutes. Stopwatches were also used when the time span to be measured was not extremely small. In the field of applied psychology, in particular, the chronoscope had to give way to the stopwatch. With the advent of relatively inexpensive electrical clocks, chronography and chronoscopy became relegated to history.

Figure 8 Chronoscope of d'Arsonval.

Bibliography

Helmholtz, H. (1850). Vorläufiger Bericht über die Fortpflanzungs-geschwindigkeit der Nervenreizung. *Archiv für Anatomie, Physiologie und wissenschaftliche Medicin 1850*, 71–73.

Helmholtz, H. (1850). Messungen über den zeitlichen Verlauf der Zuckung animalischer Muskeln und die Fortpflanzungs-geschwindigkeit der Reizung in den Nerven. *Archiv für Anatomie, Physiologie und wissenschaftliche Medicin, 1850,* 276–364.

Helmholtz, H. (1850). Ueber die Fortpflanzungsgeschwindigkeit der Nervenreizung. *Annalen der Physik und Chemie, 79,* 329–330.

Hirsch, A. (1862/1864). Expériences chronoscopiques sur la vitesse de différentes sensations et de la transmission nerveuse. *Bulletin de la Société de Sciences Naturelles de Neuchatel 1861 à 1864, 6,* 100–114.

Hirsch, A. (1865a). Chronoskopische Versuche über die Geschwindigkeit der verschiedenen Sinneseindrücke und der Nerven-Leitung. *Untersuchungen zur Naturlehre des Menschen und der Thiere, 9,* 183–199.

Hirsch, A. (1865b). Ueber die persönliche Gleichung und Correction bei chronographischen Durchgangs-Beobachtungen, *Untersuchungen zur Naturlehre des Menschen und der Thiere, 9,* 200–208.

Oelschläger, W. (1849). Das Wheatstonesche Chronoskop, verbessrt durch Uhrmacher Hipp in Reutlingen. *Annalen der Physik und Chemie, 74,* 589–591.

Philippe, J. (1899). *Technique du chronomètre de d'Arsonval pour la mesure des temps psychiques.* Paris: Georges Carré et C. Naud.

Rémond, A. (1888). *Contribution à l'Etude de la Vitesse des courants nerveux et de la durée des actes psychiques les plus simples à l'état normal et à l'état pathologique.* Nancy, France: Paul Sordoillet.

Wundt, W. (1874). *Grundzüge der physiologischen Psychologie.* Leipzig: Engelmann.

Wundt, W. (1880). *Grundzüge der physiologischen Psychologie* (2nd ed., Vols. 1 & 2). (2nd ed.). Leipzig: Engelmann.

Wundt, W. (1887). *Grundzüge der physiologischen Psychologie* (3rd ed., Vols. 1 & 2). Leipzig: Engelmann.

Wundt, W. (1893). *Grundzüge der physiologischen Psychologie* (4th ed., Vols. 1 & 2). Leipzig: Engelmann.

Wundt, W. (1902, 1903). *Grundzüge der physiologischen Psychologie* (5th ed., Vols. 1–3). Leipzig: Engelmann.

Wundt, W. (1908, 1910, 1911). *Grundzüge der physiologischen Psychologie.* (6th ed., Vols. 1–3). Leipzig: Engelmann.

Wilhelm Wundt

Arthur L. Blumenthal

At the beginning of psychology's modern era—the time of the broad movement that emphasized the new scientific psychology, the rise of psychological research centers, journals, and graduate students—stands the formidable instigating presence of Wilhelm Wundt (1832–1920), the strongest initial force behind those beginnings and still the most prolific academic psychologist of all time. According to D. K. Robinson's (1987) archival research, approximately 17,000 students passed

Figure 1 Wundt as "experimental subject" surrounded by his collaborators Dittrich (seated), Wirth, Klemm, and Sander (left to right).

through Wundt's lecture course on general psychology. And as historian E. G. Boring (1929/1950) never let us forget, Wundt published more than any other psychologist, living or dead. If psychology could be compared to archeology, Wundt's own particular contribution, now resting heavily on library shelves, would stand like the ancient pyramids and the sphinx. For all but a few dedicated specialists, it remains just that huge, mysterious, and enigmatic.

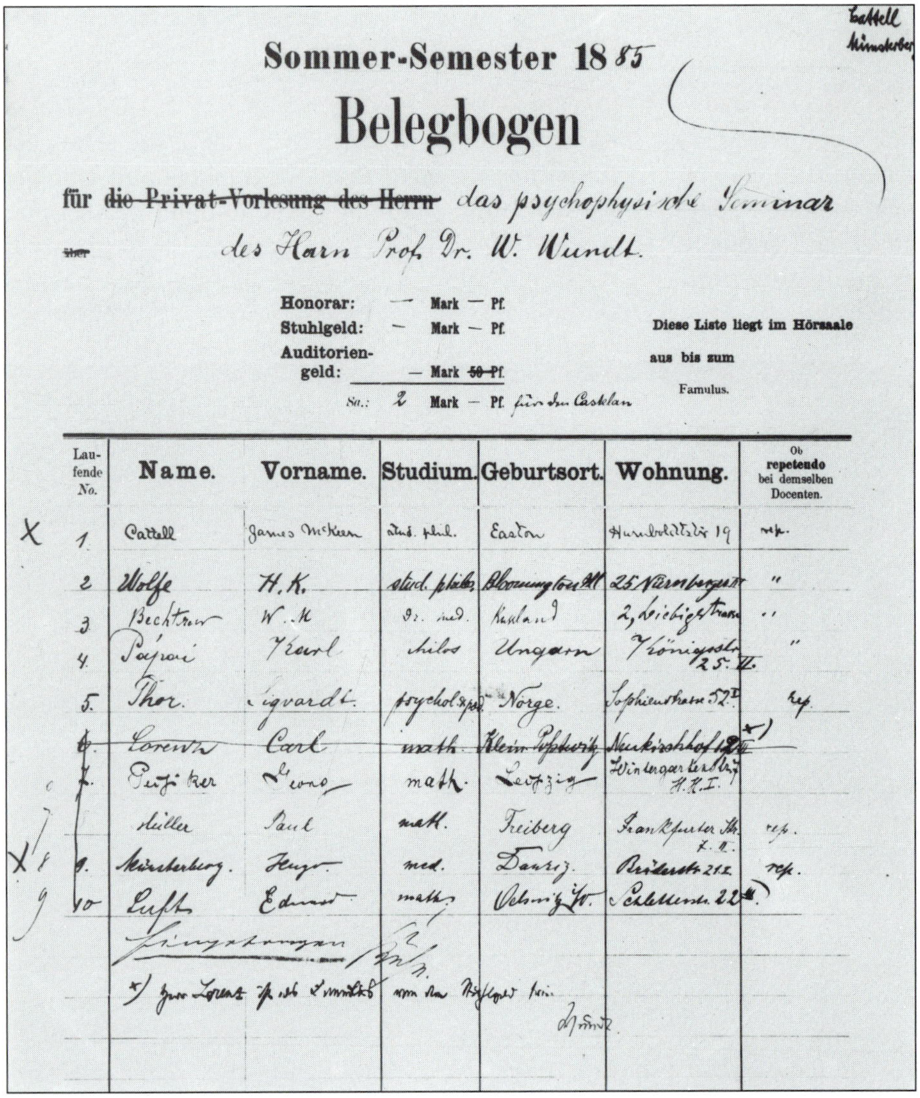

tual traditions which that implies), and the radical changes in *Zeitgeist* (spirit of the times), it is no wonder that Wundt might seem as remote as the pyramids. But what must concern us here is rather more curious and challenging than those easily observed historical barriers. The result of that turbulent history has been the creation of a mythological Wundt—a caricature that served to justify later movements. But it is a caricature that current historians are now working to correct (see, for instance, the volume of Wundt research edited by W. Bringmann and R. Tweney, 1980).

The removal of Wundtian theory and literature from the awareness of most 20th-century psychologists has well served the later schools of behaviorism, Gestalt psychology, psychoanalytic psychology, and perhaps many other 20th-century psychological theorists. Wundt fell into the misfortune of becoming the tribal elder (in Freudian terms) that the young warriors were compelled to slay in their pursuit of the affections of Mother Psychology. And slay they did, as they went on to write polemical histories of modern psychology in the century that followed the Wundtian era.

All of that led to what is not an atypical distortion of intellectual history. Consider an illustrative comparative example: The once thoroughly dominant behaviorism is now under attack from some well-funded new cognitive psychologists who may be creating a trend that could lead to a similar debasing and falsifying of the image of behaviorism in the next century. At the present rate of change in

Figure 2 Class register for Wundt's "Psychophysical Seminar" during the 1885 summer term, with signatures of H. K. Wolfe, V. M. Bekhterev, James McKeen Cattell, and Hugo Münsterberg.

Since Wundt's time, psychology has moved rapidly through radical cyclical changes. With the unspeakable tragedies of the World Wars, the shift of dominance in psychology from German to American universities (with all the differences in intellec-

historical chapters, behaviorism, like Wundtian psychology, could become popularly conceived as a thoroughly misguided movement that foisted nothing but a dark age upon psychology.

began developing apparatus for psychological research and a private laboratory in the 1860s. He was appointed to a professorship at Zurich in 1874 and at Leipzig the following year, where laboratory space was made available in 1879.

Figure 3 Title page of Wundt's autobiography, *My Life and Work* (1920).

Figure 4 Drawing of Wundt portrait after an 1874 photograph.

Background

After a short period as a medical doctor in the 1850s, Wundt emerged as a research physiologist and assistant to the distinguished Helmholtz at Heidelberg. His interests then turned almost immediately to psychology and to cultural studies, the latter interest having occupied his mind since early youth (Bringmann, Bringmann, & Balance, 1980). His voluminous writings on psychological topics began in the 1860s and continued until his death in 1920. His *Physiological Psychology* (1874) was a large compendium of research findings and theories which he revised and expanded continually until the last days of his life. He virtually never stopped writing it. He

Wundt's primary inspiration was the creation of scientific psychology, which for him meant the formulation of general explanatory laws of mental processes. He embarked on this with the aid of experiments, naturalistic observations, logic, historical studies, and more. The anticipations of that effort, both pro and con, were developing in German philosophy throughout the 19th century. Though not an experimentalist, the philosopher Herbart, with his mathematical theories of mental mechanics, gave focus to the movement toward this end earlier in the century. Herbart's system was the leading theoretical model that many early experimental and theoretical psychologists in Germany had to contend with. Not only Wundt, but also Fechner, Freud, and G. E. Müller sprang variously from or reacted to Herbartian theory. Herbart's was essentially a theory of mental elements, a mental chemistry, in which innumerable mental molecules attracted or repelled one another into and out of the field of consciousness by virtue of their individual powers of attraction or repulsion.

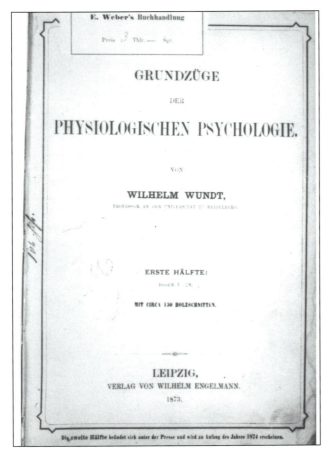

Figure 5 Title page of the first half of Wundt's *Principles of Physiological Psychology* (1873).

It was *opposition* to such a mechanistic and atomistic model that created and sustained Wundtian psychology—which, given Wundt's background, was steeped in the more organismic and holistic forms of German idealist philosophy. Herbart, in Wundt's opinion, was moving close to what became for Wundt the "enemy camp"—the British associationist philosophy that Wundt relentlessly satirized (see Wundt, 1914, and Blumenthal, 1980).

The discussion of mental elements is an obvious feature of Wundt's texts. Yet, it is there because it

was a pressing issue in his time due to the Herbartian background and debates. If one were to be relevant at that time as a psychological theorist in Germany, one had to address Herbart. But read carefully what Wundt says in his mature system—not glancing at isolated phrases out of context—to see Wundt's crusade against this older mental chemistry in both its German (Herbartian) form and its British associationist versions. For Wundt, unlike Herbart, no isolated sensation or bit of memory had meaning independent of some larger psychic configuration or context of which it was a member (this came to be known as Wundt's "law of psychological relativity"). Furthermore, Wundt believed that "mental elements" were only theoretical constructs and could never be observed in isolation. And what the Herbartian and associationist descriptions of mental processes lacked most severely, in Wundt's view, was the inclusion of a predominant central control (or volitional) process (Blumenthal, 1979; Danziger, 1980b).

Fundamental Processes

If the primary principle of Freudian psychology may be identified as repression, and the primary principle of Skinnerian behaviorism identified as reinforcement, then likewise, the primary point of Wundtian psychology is the central mental control process—focal attention. In the old terminology of Wundt's German intellectual tradition, this was known by the now-archaic term *apperception*. The study of attention/apperception, in Wundt's sphere, was not limited to questions of channel capacity, early versus late selectivity, and related questions that came to dominate later 20th-century research on attention. Attention researchers today are concerned chiefly with information flow, in which attention is a bottleneck, or gate, or filter, that restricts the flow. In Wundtian psychology, attention was a creative process, a central action that, under volitional self-control, selected a sample of the chaos of sensations and memories and integrated them, producing emergent phenomena, or new qualities or features, not found in the raw external information input (Wundt's principle of "creative synthesis"). He speculated that this capacity is the primary function of the brain's frontal lobes.

That principle of creative apperception appeared in Wundt's first psychological writing (1862). And it

Figure 6 Title page of Wundt's *Contributions to a Theory of Sense Perception* (1862).

chological basis of cultural differences in languages, customs, value systems, etc.—all as extensions of his central-processor psychological theory. Wundt's voluminous cultural psychology emphasizes his view that mental differences among the peoples of the world are culturally determined. This principle of cultural determination influenced Franz Boas (1858–1942), then a young anthropology student in attendance at Wundt's lectures, who later impressed it so firmly upon anthropology. Such a view was at odds with the opinions held by many intellectuals of the day who saw differences among societies as being racially based (on this point regarding Wundt, see Brock, 1992).

When the key principle of focal self-control, or apperception, was elaborated (by the 1880s), Wundt's psychology developed its foundation in emotional and volitional processes. It was shortly after his move to the professorship at Leipzig, and through the influence of Friedrich Paulsen (1846–1908) who at that time was his contemporary in philosophy at Berlin, that Wundt's psychology became known as the "school of voluntaristic psychology." The emotion theory that supported this study of volition was Wundt's tridimensional, bipolar theory of emotional quality, which has reappeared in a variety of forms in the hands of psychologists later in the 20th century who seemed scarcely aware of Wundt's priority.

Americans in Leipzig

Little of the Wundtian system transferred to the soon-to-be dominant American theater of psychology. As an American student attending courses on the history of psychology, I received a parochial review of the odyssey of those 20-year-old Americans, armed with a college course in German, who ventured to Leipzig in the late 19th century to earn their advanced degrees under Wundt's tutelage. Wundt must have been very generous in accepting them. Our literature on the history of psychology contains descriptions of Wundt's mannerisms, the shape of his beard, the layout of his lecture hall, the clothes he wore, the jokes he told, and much gossip about his personal relations with other people, rather than much of substance about his theoretical system. Naturally, then, we have been led to believe that there was little or no theoretical system. A good deal of effort over the last 20 years by a few

was pointed to in his last writings as the most consistent aspect of his unusually long career as a psychological theorist (Wundt, 1920). The derivative study of the development of self-control as alternations between *controlled* and *automatic* processes received extensive treatment—a theme that is again quite prominent in theoretical psychology today.

As far as Wundt was concerned, creating a scientific psychology meant, in part, finding ways to objectify mental processes to reach public agreement about what they are and how they function. Wundt began in the early 1860s with two powerful and still effective technical advances: (1) Fechnerian psychophysics and (2) reaction-time measurement in milliseconds. To his philosophical critics of that day, such work appeared to deal with the trivial minutiae of mental processes. Wundt, however, soon showed himself to be most unlikely to limit himself to minutiae. From the outset his psychology included cultural psychology—the study of the psy-

driven historians, though, has shown that Wundt, if nothing else, was systematic theory incarnate. It was understandably the very rare, young American with a BA degree from a place like Lafayette College, Williams College, or Wesleyan College in the 1880s, who could understand and absorb much of the theoretical constructs, debates, and analyses—all couched in the superpolysyllabic German words emanating from the halls of Leipzig.

But we Americans could understand the Englishman Titchener, at Cornell, who had spent almost two years in Leipzig, and whose English was of the grandest style, as was his personality. He was an awesome force in the early shaping of American psychology. Titchener's Oxford-grown psychology, stemming from James Mill and John Stuart Mill, and extended by the new positivist thinking of Ernst Mach and Richard Avenarius, became by default, or perhaps by the sheer power of Titchener's personality, our mistaken image of Wundt. This has been shown in a detailed historical analysis by Danziger (1979, 1980a). Titchener named his school of thought "structuralism"—a term that American psychologists immediately attached to Wundt. Wundt, however, was solidly rooted in the German idealist philosophies of his own native background (e.g., Kant, Fichte, Schopenhauer, Leibniz). He would have been the last to abandon them for British empiricism, Austrian positivism, or American behaviorism—all of which he criticized.

It did not take much knowledge of German to understand the laboratory apparatus built first for measuring reaction times in the study of microge-

netic apperceptive processes. The Americans certainly did transfer those devices back to their homeland and held them up as examples of Wundtian psychology, but perhaps not with the best understanding of what Wundt was using them for. Sterile debates were provoked among American historians concerning the precise timing of the founding of the first laboratory of psychology, whether at Leipzig or Harvard, as if that were a significant issue in the history of psychology. This fascination with apparatus is not difficult to understand should you be able to see the quaint and charming display of Wundtian-era apparatus recently assembled at Harvard.

Yet after the turn of the century, and in contrast to the growing development of laboratory apparatus, Wundt became uneasy with regard to the new breed of "apparatus men" who were beginning to dominate psychology and whom he referred to, in despair, as "tinkerers and mere technicians" having a very constricted vision of the greater goals of the science (Robinson, 1987).

In those years, Wundt's *Outlines of Psychology*, translated by C. H. Judd, was the textbook in the hands of readers limited to English. It is a catalogue of research findings and a listing of principles of mental life—a reference book for students. The English translation gave it perhaps an even duller aspect. Alongside Titchener's masterful writings, and particularly alongside the great literary masterworks that came at that same time from William James, Wundt's humble *Outlines* obviously could not sustain the interest of many Anglo-American readers. Yet when Wundt wanted to be a writer, he could demonstrate a lively and humorous literary flair. This we see in some of his never-translated position papers published in the *Philosophical Studies*, his *Essays*, and in his many book reviews and articles in popular magazines. And from what I can determine from eyewitness accounts, Wundt as a lecturer surpassed James and Titchener in sheer style. Near the end of his career the numbers of students in attendance at Leipzig approached 1,000.

Psycholinguistics

When one reads through the 1920s literature that assesses Wundt's work—the more sophisticated assessments, written mostly in German, by those who remained close to him and labored beside him until his last days—one finds frequent references to

Figure 7 Main classroom building of Leipzig University, which contained Wundt's institute (1896).

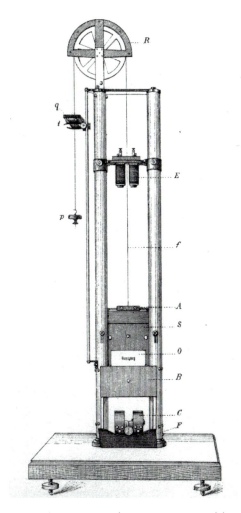

Figure 8 Demonstration tachistoscope invented by J. McK. Cattell.

external *sequentiality*—a string of sounds, hand gestures, or marks on paper. This is the masterful piece of microgenetic skill, a true piece of mental gymnastics, according to Wundt, requiring capabilities perhaps equal to those of a concert pianist, so that it's a wonder there aren't more lapses, stutterings, or other speech errors than normally occur.

The articulate person, according to this theory, focuses his mental image and transforms it effortlessly into well-organized and modulated phrases incorporating artful word selection. To such a person these complex mental manipulations and transformations have become a highly automatized skill. Because of that automatization, the attention of the articulate speaker has more freedom to concentrate on the subject matter, the topic of his speech, rather than on the mechanics of the language.

The inarticulate person, on the other hand, communicates with grunts, false starts, and slow short sentences, and frequently loses his place in his topic, all because his less skillful, nonautomatized, elemental language processes are still under laborious, attention-demanding, voluntary control.

The mental acts of one who listens to or reads language are the inverse of the above and involve similar complex skills that depend on automatization for their best performance. The effective listener or reader must have his or her attention freed from lower-level language mechanics to anticipate and think about the content of what is being communicated.

In his many chapters on language, Wundt is carried into the study of linguistic structures and rules. In doing so, he virtually became a linguist and contributed fundamentally to the discipline of linguistics. Texts on the history of linguistics frequently cite his work. (For a review of Wundtian psycholinguistics, see Blumenthal, 1970.)

Approaching General Explanatory Laws

Many more pages than current space permits would be required to discuss all the facets and developments of Wundt's psychology, let alone the huge amount of research on a large variety of approaches that emanated from Leipzig. (For some elaboration, see Woodworth, 1938, and Blumenthal, 1985.) In addition to the studies of control processes, emotion, volition, language, cultural processes, and the variety of research methodologies that were applied, Wundt left, in the final chapters of his many books, a

Wundt's psycholinguistics as being perhaps his most imposing accomplishment. It is most appropriate to introduce it in any, even brief, review of Wundt. His major writings on language are contained in the first volume (1900/1913) of his multivolume cultural psychology series. Here Wundt argued that the *sentence* is the fundamental unit of language and that it takes its subject-predicate form from the underlying actions of the mental processes of judgment. Those processes are explained as the result of an analytical power in the process of apperception as it segregates and partitions aspects of global memories, images, or perception in order to set them up for transmission through some linguistic code system. Psychologically considered, the fundamentally challenging act of language production is the task of transforming a mental *simultaneity* (an image, thought, or perception) into an

set of explanatory principles, sometimes called laws, that describe, in his system, the more general operating characteristics of attention/apperception. There were three principles of the microgenetic functions of immediate mental processes, and three parallel principles of longer-term processes that were more relevant to developmental and cultural psychology studies.

First is the principle of *creative synthesis,* already introduced above. It identifies the action of the creation of emergent properties in the central focus of attention—qualities that cannot be derived simply from the properties of external stimulation. Contextual, emotional, and motivational schemas determine the course of this process. In modern terms, this is "constructivist" theory.

Second is the principle of *psychological relativity* that describes mental processes as having an identity only as parts of larger configurations or contexts. Whereas the first principle is about the synthesis of qualities, this second principle is about analysis, stating that any item of attention focusing is focused upon within some greater context that gives it meaning. In analyzing the individual words of a sentence, for instance, we find that the mean-ings of those words are determined by their role in the larger sentence.

Third is the principle of *psychological contrasts,* an elaboration of the second principle. Simply stated, antithetical experiences intensify each other. After a period of pain, a slight pleasure is all the more enjoyable. A sweet substance tastes sweeter if eaten after something sour.

The next three principles focus on longer-developing social-cultural processes, yet parallel the three previous ones:

Fourth is what Wundt named the principle of *heterogeneity of ends.* When a purposeful action produces a change or result, that result is often different from the one intended. This discrepancy prompts further action. Wundt considered this process to be a developmental principle of considerable scope, since the changes that occur are often emergent cultural forms or new cultural products that cannot be derived directly from the cultural elements that went into their formation.

Fifth is the principle of *mental growth.* As cultural or mental forms evolve and become progressively differentiated, older and simpler forms evolve into more elaborate forms that must be understood in terms of their relation to their larger configurations or the historical context. The acquisition of language in a child, for instance, begins with global expressions that unfold into evermore differentiated parts of speech which have meaning only in relation to their global parent forms.

Sixth is the principle of *development toward opposites.* The development of cultural forms, ideas, or attitudes have bipolar qualities and fluctuate between opposites. A period of one type of activity or experience builds up pressure to seek some opposite form of experience—such opponent-process effects are studied today in motivational psychology. These tendencies are found, according to Wundt, not only in the life of the individual but also in the cyclical patterns of history, of economics, and of social fads.

The Decline

At the onset of World War I, Wundt's facilities at Leipzig had grown into a multistoried institute with subdivisions for cultural psychology, psychophysics, developmental psychology, psycholin-

Figure 9 Title page of Wundt's *Völkerpsychologie* (Cultural Psychology), Volume 9 concerning the psychology of legal systems. With a dedication to his student and successor, Felix Krueger.

Figure 10 Wundt in old age.

Bibliography

Blumenthal, A. L. (1970). *Language and psychology: Historical aspects of psycholinguistics.* New York: John Wiley.

Blumenthal, A. L. (1979). Wilhelm Wundt: Psychology as the propaedeutic science. In C. Buxton (Ed.), *Points of view in the history of modern psychology* (pp. 19–50). Orlando: Academic Press.

Blumenthal, A. L. (1980). Wilhelm Wundt and early American psychology: A clash of cultures. In R. Rieber (Ed.), *Wilhelm Wundt and the making of a scientific psychology* (pp. 117–135). New York: Plenum.

Blumenthal, A. L. (1985). Wilhelm Wundt: Psychology as the propaedeutic science. In C. E. Buxton (Ed.), *Points of view in the history of modern psychology* (pp. 19–50). New York: Academic Press.

Boring, E. G. (1950). *A history of experimental psychology.* New York: Appleton. (Original work published 1950)

Bringmann, W., Bringmann, N., & Balance, W. (1980). Wilhelm Maximilian Wundt 1832–1874: The formative years. In W. Bringmann & R. Tweney (Eds.), *Wundt Studies* (pp. 13–32). Toronto: Hogrefe.

Brock, A. (1992). Was Wundt a 'Nazi'?: Völkerpsychologie, racism and anti-Semitism. *Theory and Psychology, 2,* 205–223.

Danziger, K. (1979). The positivist repudiation of Wundt. *Journal of the History of the Behavioral Sciences, 15,* 205–230.

Danziger, K. (1980a). The history of introspection reconsidered. *Journal of the History of the Behavioral Sciences, 16,* 241–262.

Danziger, K. (1980b). Wundt's theory of behavior and volition. In R. Rieber (Ed.), *Wilhelm Wundt and the making of a scientific psychology* (pp. 89–115). New York: Plenum.

Robinson, D. K. (1987). *Wilhelm Wundt and the establishment of experimental psychology, 1875–1914: The context of a new field of scientific research.* Doctoral dissertation, University of California, Berkeley.

Woodworth, R. (1938). *Experimental psychology.* New York: Holt.

Wundt, W. (1862). *Beiträge zur Theorie der Sinneswahrnehmung.* Leipzig: Winter.

Wundt, W. (1863). *Vorlesungen ueber die Menschen—und Thierseele* (Vols. 1–2). Leipzig: Voss.

Wundt, W. (1900/1913). *Die Sprache.* Leipzig: Engelmann.

Wundt, W. (1914). *Die Nationen und irhen Philosophien.* Leipzig: Kröner.

Wundt, W. (1920). *Erlebtes und Erkanntes.* Stuttgart: Kröner.

guistics, and more; each under the leadership of a subdirector who reported to Wundt. But at this grandest moment, it was all on the eve of a great decline caused by war, then economic chaos, then Hitler, and then the World War II bombing raids that destroyed it. But still, as suggested to at the beginning of this chapter, its worse fate may have been the treatment received at the hands of American historians of psychology during those same years.

Wundt's Laboratories

Wolfgang G. Bringmann
Ursula Voss
Gustav A. Ungerer

Ever since the first edition of Boring's *A History of Experimental Psychology* (1929), it has become accepted knowledge among psychologists that Wilhelm Wundt (1832–1920) ". . . founded the first psychological laboratory of the world. . . ." at Leipzig University in Germany in 1879 (p. 318). This information has been included as a small but crucial detail—perhaps the psychologists' equivalent of the discovery of America by Columbus—in countless introductory psychology textbooks.

This classical date was challenged by Harper (1949) almost 50 years ago, when he marshalled information in support of the view that ". . . the world's first psychological laboratory . . . had been established by William James (1842–1910) in Lawrence Hall of Harvard University four years

before the foundation of Wundt's institute" (p. 173). One year later Harper (1950), perhaps as a gesture of reconciliation, concluded from his reading of Wundt's brief history of his institute (1909) that: "It appears now that there were actually two first laboratories that were established simultaneously in the United States and in Germany. Wundt's Leipzig laboratory was one of them. William James' laboratory at Harvard was the other" (p. 158).

Thus, the beginnings of Wundt's Leipzig laboratory would be changed to 1875, the time at which Wundt joined the faculty at Leipzig University as full professor of philosophy. Boring quickly accepted the accuracy of Harper's statement (Boring, 1963, 1965). However, the two editions of his history (1929, 1950) still give credit to Wundt for founding

Figure 1 Refectory building of Leipzig University where Wundt established his famous Leipzig Laboratory in 1879.

126

the first laboratory in experimental psychology in 1879 at Leipzig University. Moreover, in 1965 Boring editorialized at length on the pernicious habits of psychologists to rely on data in the history of their field which at best are subjective and arrived at long after the events occurred (1965). Addressing himself specifically to the founding of Wundt's Leipzig laboratory, he made the following comments (Boring, 1965):

> The founding was thus subjective. Wundt, scientific psychology's great entrepreneur, examined the growth of his enterprise and picked 1879 as the best date. It could not have been apparent at the time what significance that date would come to have, but history needs its markers in order to be readily understood and remembered, and the students of history are inconvenienced by dates on which to hang the skein of events that need to be kept in order. In 1879 there was no ceremony at the founding of Leipzig's *Psychological Institute*. Wundt made no special speech, cut no ribbon at the entrance, dedicated no corner-stone for the old refectory building, nor could he even have recognized the significance of what was getting under way. History and progress moved on with their accustomed gradualness, and only later was Wundt able to fix an absolute threshold to the growth curve of his laboratory. (p. 8)

These are undoubtedly impressive words! Their accuracy, however, can be seriously questioned and needs to be re-examined in the light of pertinent archival and documentary evidence.

Wundt and the Laboratory Method before Leipzig

Wundt's own early life experiences with the laboratory method seem to parallel the development of the seminar method of research instruction in Germany at large during the 19th century (Bringmann & Ungerer, 1980). Wundt, the youngest son of a Protestant minister, had little access to scientific information in the small provincial town where he grew up (Bringmann, Balance, & Evans, 1975). During his high school years from 1845 to 1851 at the Heidelberg Lyceum, biology was taught for only two years, including occasional field trips. Mathematics and the other natural sciences covered less than 2% of Wundt's high school curriculum and included no laboratory work whatsoever. During his first year as a medical student at Tübingen University from 1851 to 1852, Wundt became quickly disillusioned with his basic medical courses, which again centered primarily on books and provided no opportunity for experimental work (Wundt, 1920).

Wundt: Kochsalzgehalt des Harns. 355

habe ich den Gehalt des Harns an Kochsalz bei völligem Ausschluss desselben aus der Nahrung zu ermitteln gesucht. Was die Untersuchungsmethode betrifft, so wählte ich theils den Weg der Gewichtsbestimmung durch salpetersaures Silberoxyd, theils die vor Kurzem von Liebig empfohlene Titrirmethode, theils auch beide neben einander.

Da der Gehalt des Harns an Chlornatrium jedenfalls nach der Art der Nahrung, vielleicht aber auch nach den Individualitäten verschieden ist, so war es, als ich die nachfolgenden Versuche an mir selber anzustellen begann, zunächst nothwendig, den Gehalt meines Harns an Kochsalz bei völlig normaler Lebensweise zu bestimmen. Ich theile hierüber die Analysen von folgenden 6 Tagen mit, an denen des Morgens nüchtern, des Mittags vor Tisch und des Abends der Urin gesammelt wurde.

In 10 Cub.-Cent. Harn.

Milligrm. Kochsalz.

	Morgen.	Mittag.	Abend.
I.	73.18	70,64	73.4
II.	37.3	66	79.1
III.	83.2	62.5	62.5
IV.	50	60,98	104.1
V.	77.9	73	99,82
VI.	74,3	102	109

Die Reaction des Harns war immer sauer, das spec. Gew. schwankte zwischen 1,015 und 1,030.

Ich versuchte es nun einige Tage lang ohne allen Kochsalzgenuss und wieder bei sehr regelmässiger Lebensweise zuzubringen. Die Hauptnahrung bestand aus etwa ¼ Kilogrm. Fleisch täglich, etwas Gemüse und ½ Kilogrm. Brod, sämmtliche Speisen ohne Salz zubereitet. Um mit annähernder Genauigkeit die Gesammtmenge des ausgeschiedenen Kochsalzes im Verhältniss zum aufgenommenen berechnen zu können, habe ich aber nicht nur von jedem Urin 10 Cub.-Cent. zur Analyse verwandt, sondern auch die Gesammtmenge desselben gemessen.

Figure 2 Title page of Wundt's first published research on salt deprivation.

Returning from Tübingen to Heidelberg University for the winter term of 1852, Wundt was fortunate to enroll in the chemistry course of Robert Bunsen (1811–1899), who had founded one of the earliest German chemical laboratories at Marburg University in 1840. Under Bunsen's influence, Wundt carried out his first research project (1853) on the effects of salt deprivation on the chemical composition of his own urine. According to Wundt (Figure 2), he existed during this experiment on a daily diet of "... 500 grams of meat, some vegetables, and two pounds of bread. All food was prepared without salt" (1853, p. 355). Wundt enjoyed this humble study immensely because it was published and even quoted in the scientific literature. The young Wundt was deeply impressed by Bunsen and particularly admired "the demonstrations of marvelous perfection" (Wundt, 1920, p. 76) which illustrated the lectures. To his strong disappointment, however, Wundt also discovered that Bunsen (Wundt, 1920): ". . . had little time for beginning students . . . (and) turned them over to his assistants who were still new in their positions" (p. 77). Wundt resigned from Bunsen's institute without delay and entered instead the private chemical laboratory of a young instructor who had impressed him with his interest and devotion to his students and their researches (Bringmann & Ungerer, 1980).

In 1854, Wundt carried out his first independent research (1855). Since Heidelberg University did not have a physiological laboratory at that time, he collected his data at home in his mother's kitchen without elaborate research facilities. Although queasy about vivisectioning, his mother served as his laboratory assistant. Additional published research, which was completed at that time under similarly primitive research conditions, includes Wundt's belated and not quite official dissertation (1856) and his first venture into experimental psychology (1858).

During the summer semester of 1856, Wundt went for one semester to Berlin University to do postgraduate work in physiology in the laboratories of Johannes Müller (1801–1858) and Emil DuBois Reymond (1818–1896). In comparison to even the meager research facilities at Heidelberg University, the conditions under which these eminent scientists had to work appalled Wundt (1920):

> Gustav Magnus kept the physical collection in his home and it was not at all possible for students to work in his laboratory . . . Johannes Müller worked during the Winter in the old anatomy building. In the summer he used a few rooms on the upper floor of the University's main building. One floor above Müller was the so-called laboratory of Du-Bois Reymond. Actually, it consisted only of a hallway in which students were placed and of a room in which he worked himself. (pp. 107–108)

Wundt's next involvement with the laboratory came in the summer of 1857 when he offered his first course in experimental physiology to four students in his mother's apartment (Bringmann & Balance, 1975). However, severe illness prevented Wundt from completing this project.

During his convalescence, Wundt applied for an appointment as laboratory assistant to Hermann von Helmholtz (1821–1894) in the newly established Physiological Institute of Heidelberg University

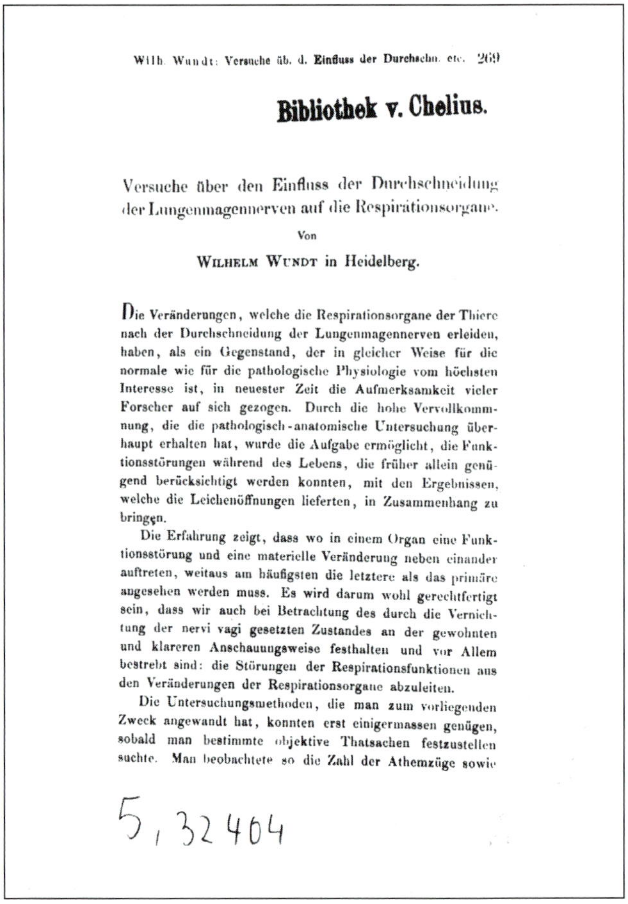

Wilh. Wundt: Versuche üb. d. Einfluss der Durchschn. etc. 269

Bibliothek v. Chelius.

Versuche über den Einfluss der Durchschneidung der Lungenmagennerven auf die Respirationsorgane.

Von

Wilhelm Wundt in Heidelberg.

Die Veränderungen, welche die Respirationsorgane der Thiere nach der Durchschneidung der Lungenmagennerven erleiden, haben, als ein Gegenstand, der in gleicher Weise für die normale wie für die pathologische Physiologie vom höchsten Interesse ist, in neuester Zeit die Aufmerksamkeit vieler Forscher auf sich gezogen. Durch die hohe Vervollkommnung, die die pathologisch-anatomische Untersuchung überhaupt erhalten hat, wurde die Aufgabe ermöglicht, die Funktionsstörungen während des Lebens, die früher allein genügend berücksichtigt werden konnten, mit den Ergebnissen, welche die Leichenöffnungen lieferten, in Zusammenhang zu bringen.

Die Erfahrung zeigt, dass wo in einem Organ eine Funktionsstörung und eine materielle Veränderung neben einander auftreten, weitaus am häufigsten die letztere als das primäre angesehen werden muss. Es wird darum wohl gerechtfertigt sein, dass wir auch bei Betrachtung des durch die Vernichtung der nervi vagi gesetzten Zustandes an der gewohnten und klareren Anschauungsweise festhalten und vor Allem bestrebt sind: die Störungen der Respirationsfunktionen aus den Veränderungen der Respirationsorgane abzuleiten.

Die Untersuchungsmethoden, die man zum vorliegenden Zweck angewandt hat, konnten erst einigermassen genügen, sobald man bestimmte objektive Thatsachen festzustellen suchte. Man beobachtete so die Zahl der Athemzüge sowie

5, 32404

Figure 3 Title page of Wundt's prizewinning research on the effect of cutting the vagus nerve (1855, p. 269).

(Bringmann, Bringmann, & Cottrell, 1976). Helmholtz, much like Bunsen, turned his laboratory instruction over to his young assistant, who provided most of the instruction for beginning medical students. Although Wundt carried out these responsibilities faithfully, he appears to have been bored with such routine duties. Nevertheless, he made good use of the nearly seven years of his association with Helmholtz to perform and publish much of his early experimental research (Bringmann & Ungerer, 1980). When he resigned his appointment in the spring of 1865 (Bringmann, Bringmann, & Cottrell, 1976), he established a laboratory in his own apartment which he maintained for nearly 10 years. Wundt's private physiological institute in Heidelberg must have been a relatively large and well-equipped laboratory, because he was able to use it during the summer of 1871 to teach required courses in experimental physiology (Bringmann, Bringmann, & Cottrell, 1976). At that time, Helmholtz was called to Berlin as a professor of physics.

Figure 4 Earliest existing Wundt photograph (ca. 1865).

In conclusion, Wundt was an experienced, self-taught expert in laboratory research long before he received his call to Leipzig University as a professor of philosophy. He had worked for nearly 23 years in various laboratories as a student, a teaching assistant, and an independent researcher in his own psycho-physiological institute. He was able to maintain a small storage room in which he kept his physiological equipment and teaching aids. Although he often supplemented his formal lectures with demonstrations, he did not regard such activities as research. Real research was a challenging empirical activity for Wundt which required active participation and regular publication of research results in scientific journals.

The Leipzig Institute for Experimental Psychology

Wundt's call to the chair of philosophy at Leipzig University was a remarkable event. Internal disagreements at Leipzig had kept the position vacant for about a decade. It was also a most daring act for such an ancient institution to employ an ". . . experimental physician as philosopher. . . ." (Schlotte, 1955/1956) who had done most of his previous work in physiology. Wundt was in no position to make big demands but was able to negotiate the assignment of a small room for the storage of his research and teaching equipment (Wundt, 1909):

> When the present director [of the Institute for Experimental Psychology] joined the faculty of the University on October 1, 1875, the Royal Ministry with the concurrence of the Academic Senate placed at his disposal a small former lecture hall in the refectory building for the storage of his demonstration equipment for his psychological lectures and his equipment for personal experimental work. (p. 118)

Thus Wundt makes it clear that he had no functional laboratory when he came to Leipzig in the fall of 1875. He was assigned only a storage facility for his various equipment. The view that Wundt did not have an active laboratory at Leipzig before 1879 receives additional support from the fact that Wundt concentrated primarily on the teaching of philosophical subjects during his first four years there. An examination of his publication list from that time shows no major publication in experimental psychology and related fields between 1875 and 1879. The bibliography for these years consists primarily of book reviews in philosophy and psychology.

In the fall of 1874, more than 17 years after first qualifying as an academic teacher, Wundt was at long last given an appointment as Professor of Inductive Philosophy at Zürich University (Bringmann, Balance, & Evans, 1975). At that time, Zürich University, which had only been founded in 1833, was still a very humble institution. It had only 10 classrooms in an old decrepit building and no library of its own. Nevertheless, Wundt was able to obtain a special room "on the third floor of the main university building" (Wundt, 1874a) for the storage of the large collection of "physiological equipment and teaching aids" which he had brought from Heidelberg (Wundt, 1874b). Moreover, evidence exists that Wundt also maintained a small laboratory for his personal research in the farmhouse which he and his wife rented in the Unterstrass suburb of Zürich (Bringmann & Ungerer, 1980).

Although, as Boring (1965) pointed out, there was no ceremony when the laboratory opened, Wundt not only reported on a specific date for the foundation of his laboratory, he provided detailed information about the circumstances under which this laboratory was initiated. It seems that laboratory activities evolved from informal "bull sessions" between Wundt and some of his early students following the formal class meetings of his psychology seminar (Wundt, 1909):

> From the Fall of 1879 on, individual students began to occupy themselves in this room in the refectory building with experimental projects. Thus came about the first study originating from this seminar . . . the investigation of Dr. Max Friedrich . . . on the duration of apperception during simple and complex ideas. . . . This work began in the winter of 1879–80 and was published as a dissertation in 1883 and in Volume 1 of the "Philosophical Studies" . . . In the following semesters several students and younger instructors participated in the practica and research projects which initially were not listed in the catalogue. (pp. 118–119)

From this description it is clear that the actual experimental research seems to have been carried out by Wundt's students. The first completed project was Friedrich's dissertation, which was eventually published in 1881. Only a small number of students and instructors, who were personal acquaintances of Wundt, were involved in this work. The storage room thus became a laboratory when it was utilized for publishable research.

The first written reference to Wundt's laboratory can be found in a letter of recommendation, which Wundt wrote for G. S. Hall on June 18, 1880, and which Hall seems to have used in obtaining his appointment at Johns Hopkins University in 1883 (Bringmann and Bringmann, 1980).

Specifically, Wundt made the following pertinent comments about Hall and his laboratory (Wundt, 1880):

> I have come to know Dr. G. Stanley Hall well through frequent personal contacts during his extended stay in Leipzig as a man of comprehensive, great scientific interest and solid independent judgment. In particular, Mr. Hall has been able to gain a rare knowledge of the German scientific literature not only in psychology but also in the related subjects of sensory- and neurophysiology. He has participated in the work of my Psychophysical Laboratory during the Winter Semester of 1879–80 and the Summer Semester of 1880 with great industry and success. (p. 2)

Additional support for the 1879 date comes from the pen of Dr. Friedrich, who carried out the first experimental research in Wundt's Leipzig laboratory during the winter semester of 1879–1880. Friedrich published a summary of his dissertation in the first issue of Wundt's new journal, *Philosophical Studies* in the late fall of 1881. His research article is very helpful in gaining a picture of Wundt's laboratory. Friedrich, who was by training a mathematician and not a philosopher, acknowledges in his article that his research was carried out ". . . under the direction of Professor Dr. Wundt . . . during the Winter Semester of 1879–80. . . ." (1881, p. 39). Pilot work was begun in early December with Wundt, Hall, and Friedrich being the first participants in the project. The collection of research data was resumed on January 17 and ended on March 5, 1880. Dr. Martin Trautschold, another early collaborator of Wundt's, is the first person to refer to Wundt's "Psychophysical Laboratory" in print (1882, p. 213). His dissertation research was completed during the summer of 1880. Wundt and Hall again served as experimental subjects.

Recognition of a somewhat different type came in the fall of 1882 in the form of a personal visit by William James (1840–1910) who mentioned Wundt's laboratory in a chatty letter to his new friend Carl

Figure 5 Silhouette of Wundt as a lecturer at Leipzig University.

Stumpf (1840–1936) of Prague University. Writing from Paris on November 26, 1882, James made the following comments about Wundt and his laboratory: "Wundt in Leipzig impressed me as very agreeable personally. He has a ready smile and is entirely unaffected and unpretending in his manner. I heard him twice and was twice in his laboratory. . . ."

Still further support for the 1879 date can be found in an 1888 article by Wundt's first assistant, James McKeen Cattell, in the journal *Mind* in 1888. This account of the Leipzig laboratory was submitted to Wundt for approval prior to publication.

Wundt supported his private laboratory out of his own pocket until 1881, but two more years were to pass before the laboratory was officially recognized by being listed in the university catalogue (Fensch, 1977). This recognition came only after Wundt was offered an attractive position at nearby Breslau University (Schlotte, 1955/1956). It was in this first facility that Wundt's earliest and perhaps his most prominent students, G. Stanley Hall (1844–1924), Emil Kraepelin (1856–1926), and James McKeen Cattell (1860–1944), did their work. Soon afterwards, Wundt expanded his laboratory into additional rooms in an adjacent building which had been vacated by the school of pharmacy. In 1892, Wundt's institute was moved once again to the third floor of a nearby classroom building which had previously housed the department of gynecology (Wundt, 1909). The new facility provided a total of 11 work rooms which were all equipped with electrical connections. Finally, in

the fall of 1897, Wundt was able to move his institute to the top floor of two new buildings (Paulinum and Johanneum), which had been designed to his specifications and which served as a model for many similar laboratories in Germany and abroad until their destruction in World War II (Füssler, 1961).

Summary and Discussion

In summary, we have reassessed the claims by Harper (1949, 1950) and Boring (1963, 1965) that Wundt established his laboratory at Leipzig University in 1875 and not in 1879. Available primary sources, which were utilized in the present study, clearly show that Harper and Boring came to their conclusion on the basis of an erroneous translation from the original German. Wundt was assigned only a storage room for his equipment when he came to Leipzig in the fall of 1875. In fact, he did not gain access to this facility until the spring of 1876 (Fensch, 1977). Moreover, his extensive experience in laboratory work over more than two decades before coming to Leipzig would not have permitted him to define a mere storage room as a laboratory. Rather, Wundt seems to have spent the first four years in Leipzig immersing himself in the literature of philosophy and related fields. His actual laboratory evolved during the 1879–1880 academic year when one of his students conducted the first publishable research in the old refectory building.

Although William James seems to have used some sort of laboratory in 1875, a careful reading of Harper's article (1949) indicates that James operated at best a small teaching or demonstration laboratory at Harvard University in experimental physiology "in 1874–75 or 1876" (Perry, 1935). William James, according to his biographer Perry, ". . . not only disliked the psychological laboratory but came to disbelieve in any fruitfulness commensurable with the effort expended" (1935, p. 315). Experimental psychology at Harvard University got its real start only after James wrote to Wundt student Hugo Münsterberg (1863–1916) to come to America in February 1892 to ". . . take charge of the Psychological Laboratory. . . ."

Wundt had established a formal laboratory of this type as early as 1865

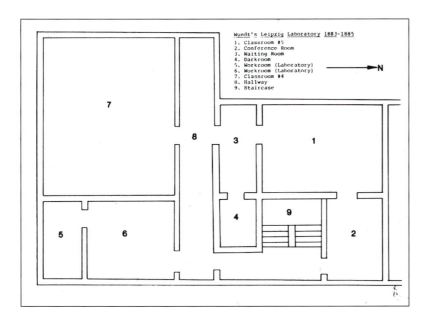

Figure 6 Groundplan of Wundt's early laboratory (ca. 1883).

while he was still at Heidelberg. He supported this private institute, in which he carried out extensive physiological and psychological studies, out of his own pocket until he left Heidelberg for Zürich University in 1874. The building in which Wundt maintained this early laboratory still exists today across the street from the Psychological Institute of Heidelberg University (Bringmann, Balance, & Evans 1975).

Without Wundt's humble but functional laboratory at Leipzig there would have been no dissertation by the mathematician Max Friedrich in 1879–1880. The credit for promoting psychology as an autonomous science thus clearly belongs to Wundt. In contrast to James and Stumpf, who both disliked the tedium of laboratory work and taught only relatively few students, Wundt attracted nearly 200 doctoral students between 1875 and 1919 (Bringmann & Ungerer, 1980). As Benjamin so cogently stated (1979): "Wundt's lab quickly became the stellar attraction for would-be psychologists . . . from Europe and North America. . . . These psychol-

ogists were the founders of many of the early psychological laboratories" (p. 1).

That is the point! Students from all over the world, including America, were inspired to carry out research in Wundt's institute and to publish their results and thus spread scientific psychology all around the world.

Bibliography

Benjamin, L. (1979). A century of science. *APA Monitor, 10*, 1–3.

Boring, E. G. (1929). *A history of experimental psychology*. New York: Appleton.

Boring, E. G. (1950). *A history of experimental psychology*. (2nd ed.). New York: Appleton.

Boring, E. G. (1963). *History, psychology and science*. New York: Wiley.

Boring E. G. (1965). On the subjectivity of important historical dates: Leipzig, 1879. *Journal of the History of the Behavioral Sciences, 1*, 5–9.

Bringmann, W. G., & Balance, W. (1975). Wilhelm Wundt: Part 1. (Lehr und Wanderjahre). *Psychologie Heute, 2*, 12–18, 44–47.

Bringmann, W., Balance, W., & Evans, R. (1975). Wilhelm Wundt 1832–1920: a brief biographical sketch. *Journal of the History of the Behavioral Sciences, 11*, 287–279.

Bringmann, W., Bringmann G., & Cottrell, D. (1976). Helmholtz und Wundt an der Heidelberger Universität. *Heidelberger Jahrbücher, 20*, 79–88.

Bringmann, W., & Bringmann, N. (1980). Wilhelm Wundt and his first American student. In W. G. Bringmann & R. D. Tweney (Eds.), *Wundt studies* (pp. 176–192). Toronto: Hogrefe.

Bringmann, W., & Ungerer, G. (1980). The foundation of the Institute for Experimental Psychology at Leipzig University. *Psychological Research, 42*, 5–18.

Fensch, D. (1977). Zur Rolle Wilhelm Wundt's bei der Institutionalisierung der Psychologie in Leipzig. *Psychologie-Historische Manuskript, 1*, 60–66.

Friedrich, M. (1881). Über die Apperceptionsdauer bei einfachen und zusammengesetzten Vorstellungen. *Philosophische Studien, 1*, 39–77.

Füssler, H. (1961). *Leipziger Universitätsbauten*. Leipzig: VEB Biographisches Institut.

Harper, R. (1949). The laboratory of William James. *Harvard Alumni Bulletin*, 169–173.

Harper, R. (1950). The first psychological laboratory. *Isis, 41*, 158–161.

Perry, R. B. (1935). *The thought and character of William James* (Vols. 1–2). Boston: Little, Brown, & Company.

Ross, D. G. (1972). *G. Stanley Hall*. Chicago: University of Chicago Press.

Schlotte, F. (1955/1956). Beiträge zum Lebensbild Wilhelm Wundts aus seinem Briefwechsel. *Wissenschaftliche Zeitschrift der Karl-Marx-Universität, 5*, 333–349.

Trautscholdt, M. (1882). Experimentelle Untersuchungen Über die Association der Vorstellungen. *Philosophische Studien, 1*, 213–250.

Wundt, W. (1853). Über den Kochsalzgehalt des Harns. *Journal für practische chemie, 59*, 354–363.

Wundt, W. (1855). Versuche über den Einfluss der Durchschneidung des Lungenmagennerven auf die Respirationsorgane. *Johannes Müllers Archiv für Anatomie, Physiologie und wissenschaftliche Medicin*, 269–313.

Wundt, W. (1856). *Untersuchungen über das Verhalten der Nerven in entzündeten und degenerierten Organen*. Heidelberg: Mohr.

Wundt, W. (1858). Über den Gefühlsinn mit besonderer Rücksicht auf dessen räumliche Wahrnehmungen. *Henle und Pfeuffers Zeitschrift für rationelle Medicin, 3*, 229–293.

Wundt, W. (1909). Das Institut für Experimentelle Psychology. In Rektor und Senat (Eds.), *Festschrift zur Feisser des 500-jährigen-Bestehens der Universität Leipzig* (Vol. 4). Leipzig; Hirzel.

Wundt, W. (1920). *Erlebtes und Erkanntes*. Stuttgart: Kröner.

Figure 7 Giant building on Heidelberg's main street where Wundt maintained an early, private laboratory from ca. 1865–1874.

Max Friedrich and the Origins of Experimental Psychology

Peter J. Behrens

In the summer of 1876, a 20-year-old graduate of the Hannover Technical Institute in Germany returned to his home city, Leipzig, to enroll at the university, one of Europe's oldest and most prestigious (Eulenburg, 1909; Hart, 1874). He did so, he

Figure 1 Portrait of Wilhelm Wundt (ca. 1880).

later wrote, "to devote myself wholly to the study of pure science" (Friedrich, 1881). Beginning in the winter semester 1876–1877, Max Friedrich became a matriculated student at Leipzig in Mathematics and natural science. His professors included some of the most important figures of the day, including Neumann in mathematics, Hankel in physics, Zöllner in astronomy, and Wundt in psychology. He even enrolled at the University of Berlin in the winter semester 1878–1879 to study under the great historian Kirchoff, the famous physiologist DuBois-Reymond, and others. At the end of his study, in May 1881, he received a PhD from Leipzig.

This route toward an advanced degree was not unusual in 19th-century Europe. Students like Friedrich who aspired to a professional career often attended more than one university in the process. They enjoyed almost unlimited academic freedom before sitting for a state examination to qualify for a teaching or other professional position (Hart, 1874).

What is known about the life and career of Max Friedrich is limited largely to his own Leipzig vita, written on the occasion of the award of his doctoral degree (Friedrich, 1881). According to his vita, he was born on August 14, 1856, in the suburban area of Reudnitz, near Leipzig. An appreciation for the value of education in general, and science in particular, probably developed early through the influence of his father, Dr. Friedrich Friedrich, a professional writer. The younger Friedrich began his education at a classical high school in Berlin, but when his family moved to Eisenach, he graduated from the local modern high school there. At the Polytechnic Institute at Hannover he studied mathematics, physics, and mechanics. He thus benefited from the larger social, political, and economic development that characterized Germany in the second half of the 19th century through the influence of the Prussian system of state education. This included the academic high school; the community, or burgher schools; and the technical high school. By the 1870s the Prussian system of state education, with its emphasis on uniformity and specialization, was considered by many the most advanced in Europe (Brasch, 1890; Russell, 1910).

At Leipzig, Friedrich completed a total of 31 lecture and seminar courses between the winter semester of 1876–1877 and the winter semester of 1879–1880. His studies included three courses under Wundt, the first in the summer semester of 1878, "History of Modern Philosophy." During the winter semester 1879–1880, when he conducted his research, Friedrich was enrolled in Wundt's "Psychological Society."

In February of 1880 Friedrich successfully passed a formal examination which qualified him as a high school teacher in Saxony. Soon afterwards,

Figure 2 Friedrich's formal application for a PhD. (February 8, 1881).

he obtained a probationary position at the famous St. Thomas School in Leipzig. He held this position through the spring of 1881, when his finished dissertation was presented to his university committee, which included Wundt and six other members of the philosophical faculty (Behrens, 1984). Figure 2 is a reproduction of Friedrich's application for his PhD.

In May of 1881 Friedrich moved to the nearby city of Bautzen as a high school teacher. It is here that the personal story of Max Friedrich ends. There is no further record of his life or accomplishments, save for Wundt's brief mention of Friedrich's work in a letter 30 years later (Boring, 1965).

Friedrich's dissertation was published under the title "On the Duration of Apperception for Simple and Complex Visual Stimuli" in the first volume of Wundt's own journal, *Philosophical Studies* (Friedrich, 1883). It might well have been of only parenthetical interest to historians, except that Max Friedrich was Wilhelm Wundt's first student in the experimental psychology program at Leipzig, and because he was the recipient of the first doctoral degree in experimental psychology (Behrens, 1980; Tinker, 1932).

Friedrich's research was most likely conducted in a regular classroom at Leipzig since Wundt's facilities were not yet available. Wundt, it can be argued, may be the real subject of the historical account, because it was classic Wundtian psychology that defined Friedrich's work and, indeed, that of Wundt's later, more well-known students such as Emil Kraepelin, Hugo Münsterberg, and the Americans, J. M. Cattell and Harry Wolfe (Hall, 1912). By virtue of its acceptance as a fulfillment of the university criteria for the PhD, Friedrich's dissertation gave definition to the "new" psychology at Leipzig, a character that was to continue for two decades, with scores of dissertations to follow (Tinker, 1932) and receive favorable, but fleeting, reception in America (Rieber, 1980; Titchener, 1906).

Wundt's Theory of Experience

Friedrich's study was first and foremost an experimental investigation of Wundt's theory of experience (Sprung & Sprung, 1981). The theory stated that consciousness has two levels: sensations and feelings that lie within a range of consciousness, and the small portion of these sensations and feelings which are brought within the focus of consciousness. The range of consciousness involves

Figure 3 Konvikt or cafeteria building of Leipzig University where Max Friedrich conducted his dissertation research in a regular classroom.

those events that are perceived, but the narrower focus of consciousness involves those events that are recognized, or apperceived. Hence, for Wundt, mental activity was divided into two distinct processes which, along with the act of the will to cause movement, were the significant psychological aspects of experience. Two purely physiological processes, however, Wundt also identified as the process of conduction of the stimulus from the sense organ to the brain and the process of conduction of the motor impulse to the muscles. Altogether, then, five distinct events comprised experience (Friedrich, 1883).

F. C. Donders, the Dutch physiologist, alternatively had proposed 12 elements in experience in an 1868 paper, titled "On the Speed of Mental Processes," a publication to which Friedrich made several references in his paper (Donders, 1969). However, Donders was quick to point out that the individual times for these processes to occur could not be empirically determined. Friedrich, on the other hand, was specifically intent on the measurement of the duration of the apperceptive process, or recognition time, and it was to this that his experimental arrangements were addressed through a standard scientific methodology of the day, the reaction time experiment.

The Reaction Time Methodology

The use of the reaction time (RT) methodology for the study of mental activity had its origins in the laboratories of the European physiologists, such as Helmholtz, Hirsch, and DuBois-Reymond, whose research was directed to the measurement of the speed of nervous conduction in the sensory systems of animals and humans (Boring, 1957). This methodology was adopted for the psychological laboratory in the last quarter of the 19th century and largely defined it as scientific, if not experimental, in the strictest sense of the word. In fact, several investigations before Friedrich's had been conducted in university laboratories around Europe on the timing of mental activity. As early as 1865, for example, J. J. de Jaager and other students of F. C. Donders at the University of Utrecht had conducted experiments on the RT to auditory, tactile, and visual stimuli, including colors. This work resulted in de Jaager's doctor of medicine degree (de Jaager, 1970/1865). Several years later an investigation of color vision was published on the speed of mental events (von Kries & Auerbach, 1877). Thus, Friedrich's study conformed to an existing paradigm for the measurement of mental activity. Then, too, by 1880, advances in the sensitivity and reliability of laboratory apparatus used for the presentation of stimuli and recording of reactions allowed more complex experimental designs for the study of RT and variables related to RT, even though several fundamental problems inherent in the methodology remained, such as practice effects and observer bias. Not until the 1890s, however, did investigators, like Oswald Külpe, begin to seriously challenge the validity of the methodology (Boring, 1957).

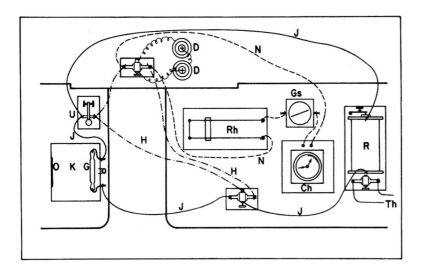

Figure 4 A diagram of Friedrich's apparatus to measure apperception time to colors and numbers.

Friedrich's Experimental Design and Procedure

"There appears only one way to reach the desired objective," wrote Friedrich in relation to the measurement of the apperception time (Friedrich, 1883, p. 41). Two experimental conditions were needed. One condition would contain the processes of conduction, perception, will, and movement, but not apperception. The second would contain all five events. Subtraction of the former RT from the latter would then yield the length of the apperceptive process (Friedrich, 1883, p. 41).

But Friedrich's particular design was not the only one available to him at the time. Another had been introduced by Donders in his 1868 paper. Friedrich made reference to the differences between the measurement techniques of Wundt and Donders, but, of course, deferred to Wundt's as the "proper" one for the study of apperception. He said of Donders's technique: "The objections raised by Professor Wundt have not been refuted by our own experiments" (Friedrich, 1883, p. 42).

Friedrich's study included two conditions containing apperception, one for colors, which he called simple visual images, and one for numbers, which he called complex visual images. He argued that the presentation of colors and numbers satisfied the conditions under which apperception would occur, because the successive appearance of one of two or more stimuli and an ensuing reaction involved recognition. Since Wundt's theory held that apperception time is of increasingly longer duration the more complex the stimulus, the RT to numbers was predicted to be longer than the RT to

colors, and the RT to multiple stimuli (colors or numbers) was predicted to be longer than the RT to only one stimulus (a color or a number). Some experiments were also conducted with simple geometric forms, but results were not reported.

Friedrich, Wundt, and two other students also studying under Wundt at the time served alternately as subjects and experimenters. G. Stanley Hall, the American, had received his doctoral degree from Harvard in 1878, but was studying the "new" psychology at Leipzig (Bringmann & Bringmann, 1980). Ernst Tischer, the third graduate student, like Friedrich, was a student in mathematics and natural science and went on to receive his PhD under Wundt in 1882, also for an experimental study on reaction time (Tischer, 1882).

Figure 4 is a reproduction of the diagram of Friedrich's apparatus. A closed box (K) contained an aperture in one wall (O) to view the stimulus at a distance of 250 mm. In the line of vision between the eye and the stimulus was an illumination device known as a Geissler tube (G). The experimenter illuminated the stimulus and set a chronoscope (CH), or timing device, into motion. By releasing a lever (U) similar to a telegraph key, the subject reacted to the stimulus and stopped the chronoscope. "The position of the pointers on the chronoscope before and after an experiment yielded the time interval between the onset of the stimulus and the ensuing reaction" (Friedrich, 1883, p. 47).

Friedrich's Results

Series of experiments from December 1879 to March 1880 involved simple visual stimuli of black, white,

Table 1 Mean Apperception Times in Hundredths of Seconds for the Two- and Four-Color Experiments

	Experiment	
	Two-Color	**Four-Color**
Wundt	086	147
Tischer	047	068
Friedrich	050	144

and colored circular surfaces 42 mm in diameter and complex visual stimuli of numbers ranging from one to six digits. Apperception times were always calculated by the subtraction method; that is, by subtracting the RT in a condition without the apperceptive process from the RT in a condition which contained the apperceptive process. The former condition was the simple reaction time to a flash of light. Comparing the results of the experiments with colors, Friedrich concluded: "A definite difference between the experiments with two and four colors is apparent" (Friedrich, 1883, p. 56). Table 1 summarizes these results.

Apperception times for the complex visual stimuli, numbers, were obtained similarly by subtracting the simple RT from the mean RTs for each number. Friedrich concluded that "as expected from the beginning, the reaction times increase in general with the number of digits" (Friedrich, 1883, p. 66). Table 2 summarizes his results for this condition.

Friedrich's Conclusions

The results from all of the experiments with colors and numbers were interpreted by Friedrich as support for Wundt's theory of experience; namely, that apperception time increases with an increase in the amount and complexity of visual stimulation. He used several plausible psychological principles to account for these results, including attention, expectancy, and practice—principles not unfamiliar to students of perception today. Friedrich also discussed fatigue, but dismissed it as unimportant,

because of the small number of experiments conducted each day.

Even though, in general, RTs increased with the number of digits, inconsistencies occurred and Friedrich was obliged to offer explanations. For example, some numbers of four digits produced shorter RTs than numbers of fewer digits, and some single-digit numbers produced RTs longer than two- and three-digit numbers. In these cases, Friedrich used practice and expectancy to account for the results. Wundt, in fact, near the end of the experiments, produced RTs as fast to the six-digit numbers as to one-, two-, and three-digit numbers. Because Hall and Tischer did not participate regularly in the experiments, their RTs varied more than those of Friedrich and Wundt.

Friedrich found that the apperception times decreased over the course of experiments, and this occurred more frequently the more complex the stimulus. So, for example, there was a relatively greater decrease in RTs to the numbers than to the colors. He cited two effects of practice. One was called a progressive effect and involved the decrease in RT with increased practice. A second effect was the decrease in RT with training, but dependent upon the nature of the task. Friedrich concluded that the simple RT was influenced very little by practice, but that recognition times for more complex visual stimuli are greatly influenced by practice. He even went so far as to suggest that a psychological law might be involved: "The question arises how far reaction time can be decreased with practice. . . . It is probable that a certain law could emerge here" (Friedrich, 1883, p. 68).

Table 2 Mean Apperception Times in Hundredths of Seconds for Numbers of One to Six Digits

	Number of Digits					
	1	**2**	**3**	**4**	**5**	**6**
Wundt	344	361	354	459	573	817
Hall	379	423	657	900	1,203	1,593
Tischer	290	380	493	709	849	1,197
Friedrich	320	346	344	481	670	1,043

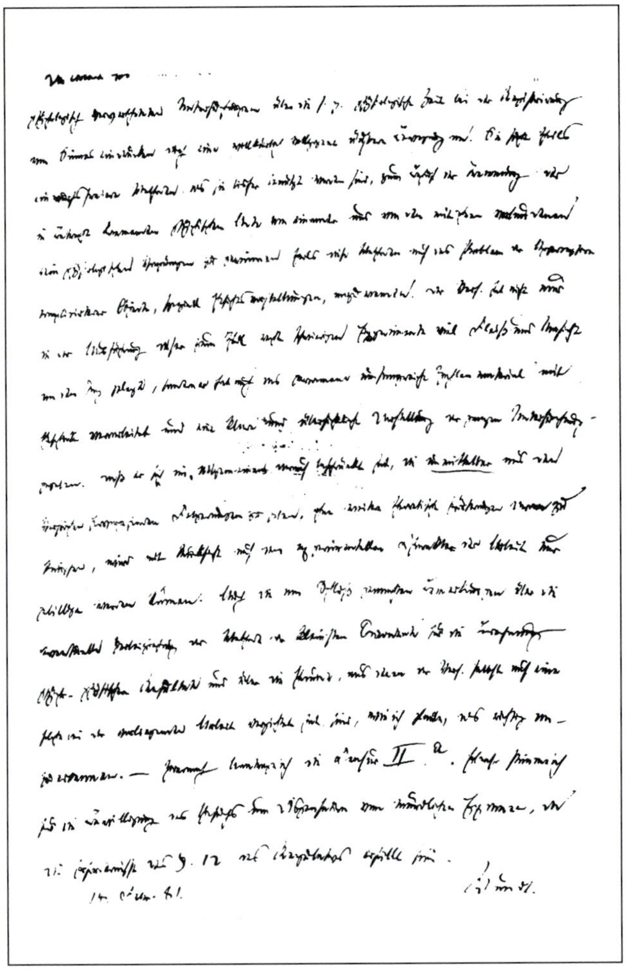

Figure 5 Wundt's handwritten evaluation of Friedrich's dissertation.

Epilogue

Max Friedrich, like his teacher Wilhelm Wundt, stands as a symbol of transition in the history of psychology. In the broad context of history, Friedrich's education represents the "high industrial" phase of 19th-century Europe, characterized by students whose pursuits were technical, scientific, and applied. By 1880, for example, only 35% of Leipzig's students came from the professional classes (Ringer, 1979). Technical training and applied science were, nevertheless, viewed with some suspicion in formal academic circles, with their long traditions of classical and liberal education. The comments by a Leipzig University official on Friedrich's dissertation are indicative of this. He stated that Friedrich's technical education at the Realgymnasium should not "stand in the way" of the doctoral degree and concurred with the committee to grant the degree (Friedrich, 1881).

In the narrower context of the development of experimental psychology, Friedrich appears to represent the type of student Wundt envisioned for the "new" psychology, one whose training was grounded in objective science (Hall, 1912; Sprung & Sprung, 1981). To this end, Friedrich submitted his data to considerable mathematical analysis from probability theory and statistics. In addition, he felt compelled to extend his analysis to the methodology of the experimental investigation of apperception in a subsequent short paper (Friedrich, 1884).

Wundt evaluated Friedrich's work with the following handwritten assessment (February 14, 1881):

1. The study of the doctoral candidate, Friedrich, relates to recent psychological researches about the so-called physiological time during the recording of sensory impressions, which are associated with intentional [physical] movement.

2. His research made the effort to search for better methods than those used in the past in the hope of separating the respective psychic acts from their associated physical events. He also applied his methods for the first time to the perception of complex objects, primarily of a visual nature.

3. The author [of this dissertation] demonstrated much industry and understanding in the performance of these rather difficult experiments. In addition, he analyzed the extensive numerical results with considerable skill.

4. His general adherence to the direct implication of his findings has been approved in the view of the experimental nature of his researches.

5. Similarly, [the author's] comments about the omission of the use of the method of least squares for the analysis of psychophysical results can be judged acceptable.

6. Consequently, I recommend the grade of IIa [praiseworthy for this dissertation].

7. I also concur that the candidate should be freed from the [traditional] oral examination [for the PhD], according to paragraph 12 of the [doctoral] regulations [of Leipzig University].

Wundt
2-14-(18)81

Although this approach did not receive unqualified endorsement, as recorded by Cattell and others (Rieber, 1980; Sokal, 1980), the success of Wundt's Institut was ultimately tied both to the supportive structure of the Prussian state system and Wundt's own dedication to the ideals of the new science of psychology (Danziger, 1980). Ironically, Friedrich's dissertation did more than propel him into a professional career; it became the symbol of the redefinition of psychology on both sides of the Atlantic (Behrens, 1984).

Bibliography

Behrens, P. J. (1980). An edited translation of the first dissertation in experimental psychology by Max Friedrich at Leipzig University in Germany. *Psychological Research, 42*, 19–38.

Behrens, P. J. (1984). The first Ph.D. programs in experimental psychology at Leipzig University, Germany and The Johns Hopkins University, U. S. A. In S. Bem, H. Rappard, & W. van Hoorn (Eds.), *Studies in the History of Psychology and the Social Sciences, 2* (pp. 280–295). Leiden: Rijksuniversiteit Leiden.

Boring, E. G. (1957). *History of experimental psychology* (2nd. ed.). New York: Appleton-Century-Crofts.

Boring, E. G. (1965). On the subjectivity of important historical dates: Leipzig 1879. *Journal of the History of the Behavioral Sciences, 1*, 5–9.

Brasch, M. (1890). *Auf deutschen Hochschulen II: Geschichte der Universität Leipzig*. Leipzig: Academische Monatshefte.

Bringmann, N. J., & Bringmann, W. G. (1980). Wilhelm Wundt and his first American student. In W. G. Bringmann & R. D. Tweney (Eds.), *Wundt studies* (pp. 176–192). Toronto: C. J. Hogrefe.

Danziger, K. (1980). Wundt's psychological experiment in the light of his philosophy of science. *Psychological Research, 42*, 109–122.

de Jaager, J. J. (1970). Reaction time and mental processes. In J. Brozek & M. S. Sibinga (Eds. and Trans.), *Origins of psychometry*. Nieukoop, The Netherlands: de Graf. (Original work published 1865)

Donders, F. C. (1969). On the speed of mental processes. In W. G. Koster (Ed. and Trans.), *Attention and performance: II*. Amsterdam: North-Holland. (Reprinted from *Acta Psychologica, 30*, 412–431)

Eulenberg, F. (1909). *Die Entwicklung der Universität Leipzig*. Leipzig: Hirzel.

Friedrich, M. (1881). *Unpublished vita*. Leipzig University Archives. Leipzig, Germany.

Friedrich, M. (1883). Über die Apperceptionsdauer bei einfachen und zusammengesetzten Vorstellungen. *Philosophische Studien, 1*, 39–77.

Friedrich, M. (1884). Zur Methodik der Apperceptionsversuche. *Philosophische Studien, 2*, 66–72.

Hall, G. S. (1912). *Founders of modern psychology*. New York: Appleton.

Hart, J. M. (1874). *German universities*. New York: Putnam.

von Kries, J., & Auerbach, F. (1877). Die Zeitdauer einfachster psychischer Vorgänge. *Archiv für Anatomie und Physiologie, 15*, 297–378.

Rieber, R. W. (Ed.). (1980). *Wilhelm Wundt and the making of a scientific psychology*. New York: Plenum.

Ringer, F. K. (1979). *Education and society in modern Europe*. Bloomington: Indiana University.

Russell, J. E. (1910). *German higher schools*. London: Longmans, Green.

Sokal, M. (1980). Graduate study with Wundt: Two eyewitness accounts. In W. G. Bringmann & R. D. Tweney (Eds.), *Wundt studies* (pp. 210–225). Toronto: C. J. Hogrefe.

Sprung, L., & Sprung, H. (1981). Wilhelm Maximillian Wundt: Ancestor or model? *Zeitschrift für Psychologie, 3*, 237–246.

Tinker, M. A. (1932). Wundt's doctoral students and their theses. *American Journal of Psychology, 44*, 630–637.

Tischer, E. (1882). *Unpublished vita*. Leipzig University Archives. Leipzig, Germany.

Titchener, E. B. (1906). *Experimental psychology: A manual of laboratory practice* (Vol. 1). New York: MacMillan.

Verzeichnisse der Universität Leipzig Vorlesungen (1876–1880). Leipzig: Edelmann.

Wilhelm Wundt: The American Connection

Ludy T. Benjamin, Jr.

Americans have been studying abroad in Europe since the birth of the United States. And in the latter half of the 19th century the percentage of Americans pursuing degrees in Europe was at its peak. Although there were numerous reasons for this intellectual migration, one broad appeal of such study was exposure to the art, architecture, and history of many centuries. In short, European study afforded a cultural richness that was synonymous with being well educated. With the beginning of the 19th century, Americans migrating to Europe for study increasingly chose German universities.

The prestigious universities at Heidelberg, Leipzig, and Göttingen were several hundred years old when the University of Berlin, founded in 1809, advanced its philosophy of the natural and human sciences, thus changing the face of university education. The philosophy promoted an active epistemology, particularly with regard to all scholarly studies, and a freedom of teaching and inquiry that had not been characteristic of universities. Well-equipped laboratories were established where professors were encouraged to conduct research and to involve their advanced students in that work, teaching them the methods of original inquiry. Professors were given a great deal of freedom to teach what they wished and to research questions of their own choosing. The German concept of academic freedom also extended to the curriculum; students were given considerable freedom in selecting courses toward their degrees (Fallon, 1980; Thwing, 1928).

The University of Leipzig was already 470 years old when Wilhelm Wundt (1832–1920) founded his psychology laboratory there in 1879, a place where the questions of mind were investigated with methodologies borrowed from philosophy, physiol-

ogy, and psychophysics. Americans interested in the new science were among the many who came to Leipzig to work in Wundt's laboratory. Some of them did not earn degrees there, such as Howard C. Warren, and others, for example G. Stanley Hall, visited as postdoctoral students. Yet 33 Americans completed their doctorates with Wundt, with 15 of those beginning their careers as psychologists (Benjamin, Durkin, Link, Vestal, & Acord, 1992).

Less than a decade after Wundt had opened his laboratory, his American students were founding psychology laboratories on their side of the Atlantic. By 1900 there were 42 American psychology laboratories; 13 of those were founded by Wundt's students and another 4 were begun by psychologists who had taken their degrees with one of Wundt's students. As mentor for the early American psychology laboratories, Wundt stands unchallenged; his closest competitor, G. Stanley Hall, can claim only 5 (Hilgard, 1987).

Although trained by Wundt and his assistants, the American students did not replicate the Leipzig model in founding their laboratories. E. B. Titchener, an Englishman and an 1892 Wundt doctorate, established his Cornell laboratory along Wundtian lines (which is not to say that he was a Wundt clone; see Blumenthal, 1975, and Leahey, 1981), emphasizing the method of introspection. But he alone could be construed as Wundtian on American soil. In contrast, the American labs were far more eclectic, and as interest in applied psychology grew and as American psychology sought to distance itself still further from philosophy, these labs abandoned the largely experiential Leipzig methods, an occurrence that Danziger (1990) has described as the repudiation of Wundt.

Wundt's American laboratory founders included

James McKeen Cattell (University of Pennsylvania and Columbia University), Harry Kirke Wolfe (University of Nebraska), Frank Angell (Cornell and Stanford Universities), Edward A. Pace (Catholic University), Edward W. Scripture (Yale University), George M. Stratton (University of California, Berkeley), Charles Judd (Wesleyan and New York Universities), and Walter Dill Scott (Northwestern University). Another of Wundt's American doctorates, Lightner Witmer, took over Cattell's laboratory at Pennsylvania where he founded the first psychology clinic in America in 1896. Several of these and other Wundt students are discussed elsewhere in this volume. This article will focus on the careers in applied psychology of three of these laboratory founders—Cattell, Wolfe, and Scott—each of whom was involved in the mental testing that was to be, perhaps, the defining characteristic of the first half-century of American psychology.

James McKeen Cattell (1860–1944)

Cattell's career as a psychologist spanned nearly 60 years. He began his graduate work in Germany at the universities of Göttingen and Leipzig before returning to the United States for doctoral work at Johns Hopkins University. But he left Hopkins after a year to return to Leipzig where he earned his doctorate with Wundt in 1886 (the first American psychology graduate at Leipzig). During his association with Wundt and Leipzig University, Cattell designed and built a "gravity chronometer" to present a visual stimulus, such as a word, at a specified time interval. After a brief stay on the faculty of the University of Pennsylvania and a visit to Francis Galton's psychology laboratory in England, Cattell moved to Columbia University to head the philosophy department there. Among his early students were Edward L. Thorndike and Robert S. Woodworth, both of whom joined the Columbia faculty after graduation and helped make the Columbia department one of the best psychology programs in America.

As a student at Leipzig, Cattell's views of Wundt seem mixed. He acknowledged the reputation that Wundt had built through his writing but was apparently unimpressed with some of Wundt's work in psychology. In letters to his parents he was often critical of Wundt, noting that he had

discovered errors in his work and lamenting the significance of Wundt's work, especially the studies on reaction time and mental processes (Sokal, 1980a, 1981). Scholars have argued just how much influence Wundt exerted on Cattell, and the arguments are partially fueled by different statements offered by Cattell at different times in his career.

Cattell actually labored only a few years in his laboratories at Pennsylvania and Columbia. Instead, he spent most of his career as an editor and publisher. Arguably Cattell's most significant contribution to American psychology was his 50-year service as editor and publisher of *Science*, a position that allowed the new psychology to have a very visible voice in the broader scientific community. That work has been treated well by Sokal (1980b). However, the focus of this brief treatment is Cattell's work in anthropometric mental testing, research that occupied Cattell and his students for the last decade of the 19th century.

Perhaps Cattell's interest in individual differences began with his studies at Johns Hopkins, work that was continued at Leipzig. But the real impetus for his work in measuring mental differences came from his contact with Galton. Sokal (1982) has written that Galton gave Cattell his scientific goal: "the measurement of the psychological differences between people" (p. 327). Using a combination of methods he had learned at Johns Hopkins,

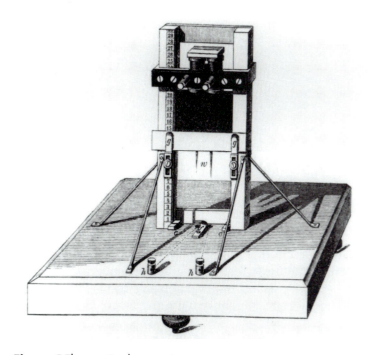

Figure 1 The gravity chronometer.

Leipzig, and London, Cattell explained the rationale of his ambitious program of research in an 1890 article in the journal *Mind*:

> Psychology cannot attain the certainty and exactness of the physical sciences, unless it rests on a foundation of experiment and measurement. A step in this direction could be made by applying a series of mental tests and measurements to a large number of individuals. The results would be of considerable scientific value in discovering the constancy of mental processes, their interdependence, and their variation under different circumstances. (p. 373)

Figure 2 James McKeen Cattell at age 32.

In the remainder of the article Cattell described a series of 10 tests that he had been conducting in the Pennsylvania laboratory: strength of grip, speed of movements, skin sensitivity, pain thresholds, weight judgments, reaction time to sound, speed in color naming, bisection of a line, time judgments, and memory for spoken letters. These tests included motor tests, sensory tests, and what Cattell labeled "mental tests," which marked the coining of that term. Cattell also provided a list of 50 different tests, related to the 10 listed above, that he hoped could be investigated to determine which tests would prove most useful for applications outside the laboratory.

It is not clear that Cattell understood how the tests might be applied; no mention of such appears. However, in an addendum to the Cattell article (1890) Galton calls him to task: "One of the most important objects of measurement is hardly if at all alluded to here . . . the sets of measures should be compared with an independent estimate of the man's powers. We thus may learn which of the measures are most instructive" (p. 380).

After a three-year hiatus caused by his move from Pennsylvania, Cattell began a monumental testing program at Columbia in 1894, administering an exhaustive battery of sensory, motor, and mental tests to all incoming students. Cattell argued that all colleges should adopt a similar testing program, noting that such data could help students correct defects, and that with subsequent testing the course of mental development might be better understood. Galton's words had also been heard. In the conclusion to an article describing the Columbia testing program, Cattell wondered, "How far can we predict one thing from our knowledge of another? What can we learn from the tests of elementary traits regarding the higher intellectual and emotional life?" (Cattell & Farrand, 1896, p. 648). And Galton would soon provide the method for Cattell to answer those questions.

Cattell's pleas for others to follow his testing program went largely unheeded. Some of his critics saw little value in the motor and sensory tests and called for a testing program that focused wholly on tests of higher mental processes. But Cattell persisted in his broad-based program, convinced that he was building a database that would prove significant for psychology. In 1897, Clark Wissler enrolled at Columbia to work with Cattell on his mental testing program. Wissler used the correlational techniques developed by Galton to test the relatedness of the various tests in Cattell's battery and between those tests and other variables such as course grades of the Columbia students. It was an effort to answer the questions that Cattell and Farrand had raised in their 1896 article. To their dismay they discovered an abundance of zero or near-zero correlations. This joint failure of prediction and interrelatedness marked the end of anthropometric mental testing—soon to be replaced in America by Alfred Binet's method—and the end of Cattell's career as an experimental psychologist (Sokal, 1987). It is ironic that the beginning and end of that career came from Galton's hand. Although anthropometric testing was dead, mental testing was not.

Figure 3 The main student work room of H. K. Wolfe's psychology laboratory at the University of Nebraska (ca. 1896).

Harry Kirke Wolfe (1858–1918)

When Cattell began his second year of study at Leipzig in 1884, he was joined by another American student, Harry Kirke Wolfe. Wolfe had come to Germany from Nebraska the previous year, enrolling at the University of Berlin to pursue a doctorate in the classics. At Berlin he encountered a 34-year-old instructor, Hermann Ebbinghaus, who gave Wolfe his first exposure to the new psychology. Wolfe took two classes with Ebbinghaus, who greatly influenced him. However, he left Berlin at the end of his first year to pursue psychology training at Leipzig, apparently because Ebbinghaus's faculty status as a Privatdozent would not allow him to supervise doctoral work.

At Leipzig, Wolfe chose memory as the topic for his dissertation, an unusual choice for one of

Wundt's students and clear evidence of Ebbinghaus' influence. The study (Wolfe, 1886) was on the memory for tones and with the earlier work by Ebbinghaus was the only research William James cited in his treatment of memory in his *Principles of Psychology* (1890).

After a few years working in the public schools in California, Wolfe accepted the chair in philosophy at the University of Nebraska in 1889. There he began a laboratory in psychology for his own research and for the training of undergraduate students. The laboratory, although meager in its instrumentation, closely mirrored Wundt's lab in emphasizing measurements of sensation and reaction time. In Wolfe's career at Nebraska, which lasted, although not uninterrupted, until his death in 1918, the university administration never offered much financial support for the psychology laboratory. So Wolfe was forced to borrow, build, and use his personal funds to keep the lab functioning. It proved to be an important training ground for an inordinately large number of undergraduate students who would go on to prominence in psychology, for example, Walter Pillsbury, Madison Bentley, Edwin Guthrie, Horace English, Carl Warden, and Frederick Kuhlmann (Benjamin, 1991). At Nebraska, Wolfe was heavily involved in the training of school teachers, adding a program in pedagogy to the philosophy and psychology lines of his department. His interests in education were long-standing; his parents had been teachers, and he had been a teacher both before and after his graduate study.

Wolfe would spend his entire career as a soldier in the child study movement, a nation-wide effort of parents, teachers, and psychologists, spearheaded by G. Stanley Hall to learn all there was to know about the child: sensory capabilities, physical characteristics, humor, play, religious ideas, and so forth. With this new knowledge, education would no longer be guesswork but would be a science (Davidson & Benjamin, 1987).

Initially, Hall was not an enthusiastic supporter of mental testing, relying instead on the use of questionnaires. Wolfe, however, as early as 1890, espoused the belief that mental testing was critical if teachers were to be given the tools to do their job. His research on abilities emphasized sensory capabilities in vision and hearing, focusing also on sensory deficits and the ways in which those affected learning. The word *learning* is key; all of Wolfe's work can be linked to understanding how children learn and ways to improve that learning.

In addition to sensory tests, Wolfe developed tests of memory, imagination, attention, reasoning, and moral development. He believed that knowledge from such tests would aid in classifying children, thereby allowing the needs of the individual child to be met. One of Wolfe's greatest hopes for the child study work was that it would lead to the development of a measure of intelligence. He labeled his research program "scientific pedagogy," and in it he sought to bring the methods of the new psychology to bear on the problems of education.

Unlike Hall's reliance on questionnaires, much of Wolfe's child study research used the psychophysical methods he had learned at Leipzig. Characteristic of this work was a study begun in 1893 to investigate the effects of size on judgments of weight. Data were collected over a period of four years in which subjects lifted paper bags, lead and wooden weights, and brass cylinders. The work was suggested by the difficulty in judging the weight of objects of differing densities, recognizing, for example, that a pound of lead was known to be psychologically heavier than a pound of feathers. Wolfe found that despite considerable experience with substances differing in specific gravity, individuals were not very accurate in weight estimation. He noted that perceptual errors increased as the differences between the specific gravities of the two substances increased and that, even with practice, individuals were not likely to decrease the magnitude of their errors. Visual information dominated kinesthetic information with the result that large errors in weight estimation were made by the subjects (Wolfe, 1898).

The pedagogical intent of the research was clear to Wolfe. He speculated that the sense of sight was

Figure 4 H. K. Wolfe (ca. 1895).

growing in dominance to the detriment of the other senses, and if so, schools would need to structure activities to increase the proficiency of the other sensory systems. The results of Wolfe's dissertation on tone memory had convinced him of the possibility of improved performance by training the senses. And drawing from the legacy of the British empiricists, Wolfe argued that psychologists needed to understand the interaction of the senses and the limits of those senses if the process of learning was to be improved.

The child study movement was never successful in fulfilling its grandiose ambitions: Psychologists searched for laws of human behavior, university administrators sought a better means of training teachers, educators desired better quantitative measures of schools' performances, and parents wanted information on child rearing. Too many people from too many diverse perspectives with too many different needs made those ambitions impossible to realize. However, the child study movement was the first effort to study children scientifically and to apply psychology to the practical problems of those who dealt with children. Wolfe never lost faith in the promise of child study. In truth his research had little impact on the nature of education, but his role as mentor to many individuals who would apply psychology to education was considerable.

Walter Dill Scott (1869–1955)

A native of Illinois, Walter D. Scott had planned a career as a missionary after earning a degree from McCormick Theological Seminary in Chicago. But when no missionary post was available, he turned his interests instead to psychology, arriving in Leipzig in 1898. He took his degree with Wundt in 1900, writing a theoretical and historical dissertation on the psychology of impulses. He returned to the United States to accept a lectureship in psychology and pedagogy at Northwestern University, where his brother was a member of the faculty and where he had earned his undergraduate degree in 1895.

With some advice from a visit with E. B. Titchener at Cornell, Scott began development of a small psychology laboratory for student training at Northwestern in 1900; the following year he was named director of that lab. His commitment to the lab is questionable; indeed he had participated minimally, if at all, in the laboratory work at Leipzig. And he published no research done in the Northwestern lab. Instead, very early he turned his interests in psychology to business applications, initially in the field of advertising.

Scott's career in applied psychology began with a lecture he gave at a meeting of advertising executives in Chicago in late 1901. One of those in attendance was John L. Mahin, head of a major Chicago advertising agency. He was intrigued by Scott's remarks and met with him later to discuss the potential contribution of psychology to advertising. Mahin offered to start publication of a magazine on advertising if Scott would write a series of 12 articles on psychology for the publication. Scott agreed, and *Mahin's Magazine* began monthly publication in 1902 with Mahin's promise to his readers to work toward developing advertising as an exact science. Scott's initial contribution was a brief discussion of the laws of association of ideas: habit, recency, and vividness (Scott, 1902).

The article on association was followed by others on suggestion, on the direct command as a form of argumentation, on the psychological value of the return coupon, on perception and apperception, on illusions, and on individual differences in mental imagery (Ferguson, 1962). Only one of those contributions—a study on the legibility of type faces of timetables for the Burlington Railroad—was based on any research by Scott. The majority were grounded in his own armchair theorizing, which seemed to appeal to Mahin and his readers.

Those dozen articles from *Mahin's Magazine* were republished as Scott's first book, *The Theory of Advertising* (1903). Scott's contributions were quite popular, and Mahin convinced him to continue his articles. Scott wrote another 21 articles through the end of 1904, and these were collected in a second book, *The Psychology of Advertising* (1908). Scott's advice was apparently much in demand, and he continued to write for a number of popular and trade outlets including *The Woman's Herald, Atlantic Monthly, Business World*, and *Advertising World*. In fact many of the articles written for one magazine were published in identical form in other magazines.

By 1905 Scott was engaged in some applied research, mostly investigating practical problems supplied to him by businesses that were willing to pay for the research to be done. Yet most of the articles he was writing were not based on any personal research. The content represented quite accurately the current knowledge base in psychology, but the applications to advertising were largely speculative. In engaging in such speculation, Scott was not alone among his psychologist colleagues.

Scott's popularity in the business community derived in part from the common-sense nature of his advice, from his motivational prescriptions, and from his knowledge of public speaking (which he offered in *The Psychology of Public Speaking*, 1906). By 1911 he had published two more books in business psychology: *Increasing Human Efficiency in Business* (1911a) and *Influencing Men in Business* (1911b). If Scott ever felt the stigma often associated with applied work, it seemed to have little if any impact on him; he was a business psychologist, arguably the first American to work in the field that has become known as industrial-organizational psychology, and of which he is often labeled the founder.

The business community continued to demand Scott's services as writer, speaker, and researcher.

Businesses, such as the American Tobacco Company, came to Scott with very real problems, especially those of employee selection and training. Borrowing from the earlier work of Galton and Cattell, Scott constructed a series of mental tests that were intended to assess specific business skills, particularly as related to personnel selection. The tests were individualized to each company, depending on what Scott learned about the company's needs and practices.

Scott's work in employee selection much impressed Walter Van Dyke Bingham, director of the Division of Applied Psychology at the Carnegie Institute of Technology. He hired Scott in 1916 to become director of the newly established Bureau of Salesmanship Research, a research unit supported by funds from 30 Pittsburgh businesses. There Scott developed a series of rating scales that were used in employee selection. That work was interrupted in 1917 when the United States entered World War I, although in a sense it was carried directly into war work. As head of the Committee on the Classification of Personnel in the Army (CCPA), Scott used his "Rating Scale for Selecting Salesmen" with minimal modification as a "Rating Scale for Selecting Captains." Of all the mental testing efforts by psychologists in the war, this program proved to be the most successful, and for his work Scott was awarded the prestigious Distinguished Service Medal of the United States in 1919 (see von Mayrhauser, 1989, for a discussion of Scott's work during the war). Figure 5 shows Walter Dill Scott at the 1919 meeting of the American Psychological Association at Cambridge, Massachusetts. Scott was APA president that year. Standing behind him is Harry L. Hollingworth, who completed his doctorate in psychology with Cattell and whose lifelong research was in applied psychology.

When the war was over, Scott and several members of the CCPA organized themselves into a psychological consulting firm that offered direct services to businesses: The Scott Company, founded in 1919. Scott served as president, and because of his excellent reputation in the business community, he was responsible for procuring most of the contracts. But when Scott assumed the presidency of Northwestern University in 1920, leaving the consulting business in the hands of his colleagues, the viability of the company diminished, and it closed its doors in 1923, having served more than 40 clients in its brief existence. Scott spent the last 19 years of his professional life as one of the most successful administrators in Northwestern's history. His pioneering and successful contacts with the business community and the noted success of his work during the war are clear foundations for the field of applied psychology.

Figure 5 Walter Dill Scott at the 1919 meeting of the American Psychological Association.

Conclusion

This brief article has sketched the careers of three of Wundt's American doctorates, all of whom sought to expand the domain of the new psychology via application, principally in the fields of education and business, and predominantly through the method of mental testing. Wundt's psychology clearly differed from that of his American students. Yet this difference was not a reflection on the adequacy of the new science. In studying the new science with Wundt, the Americans learned research methods and a scientific attitude (see O'Donnell,

1985). The methodological training taught his students how to answer the questions of mind, and they modified that training to answer their own questions, both in and out of the laboratory. However, more important, Wundt imbued his students with a scientific attitude that allowed them to frame those questions in ways that created a science of mind.

Bibliography

Benjamin, L. T., Jr. (1991). *Harry Kirke Wolfe: Pioneer in psychology.* Lincoln: University of Nebraska Press.

Benjamin, L. T., Jr., Durkin, M., Link, M., Vestal, M., & Acord, J. (1992). Wundt's American doctoral students. *American Psychologist, 47,* 123–131.

Blumenthal, A. L. (1975). A reappraisal of Wilhelm Wundt. *American Psychologist, 30,* 1081–1088.

Cattell, J. McK. (1890). Mental tests and measurements. *Mind, 15,* 373–381.

Cattell, J. McK., & Farrand, L. (1896). Physical and mental measurements of the students of Columbia University. *Psychological Review, 3,* 618–648.

Danziger, K. (1990). *Constructing the subject: Historical origins of psychological research.* New York: Cambridge University Press.

Davidson, E. S., & Benjamin, L. T., Jr. (1987). A history of the child study movement in America. In J. A. Glover & R. R. Ronning (Eds.), *Historical foundations of educational psychology* (pp. 41–60). New York: Plenum Press.

Fallon, D. (1980). *The German university: A heroic ideal in conflict with the modern world.* Boulder, CO: Associated Universities Press.

Ferguson, L. (1962). *The heritage of industrial psychology: Walter Dill Scott, first industrial psychologist.* Privately printed.

Hilgard, E. R. (1987). *Psychology in America: A historical survey.* San Diego, CA: Harcourt Brace Jovanovich.

James, W. (1890). *Principles of psychology* (Vols. 1 & 2). New York: Henry Holt.

Leahey, T. H. (1981). The mistaken mirror: On Wundt and Titchener's psychologies. *Journal of the History of the Behavioral Sciences, 17,* 273–282.

von Mayrhauser, R. T. (1989). Making intelligence functional: Walter Dill Scott and applied psychological testing in World War I. *Journal of the History of the Behavioral Sciences, 25,* 60–72.

O'Donnell, J. M. (1985). *The origins of behaviorism: American psychology, 1870–1920.* New York: New York University Press.

Scott, W. D. (1902). Association of ideas. *Mahin's Magazine, 1,* 10–13.

Scott, W. D. (1903). *The theory of advertising.* Boston: Small, Maynard & Co.

Scott, W. D. (1906). *The psychology of public speaking.* New York: Noble and Noble.

Scott, W. D. (1908). *The psychology of advertising.* Boston: Small, Maynard & Co.

Scott, W. D. (1911a). *Increasing human efficiency in business.* New York: Macmillan.

Scott, W. D. (1911b). *Influencing men in business.* New York: Ronald Press.

Sokal, M. M. (1980a). Graduate study with Wundt: Two eyewitness accounts. In W. G. Bringmann & R. D. Tweney (Eds.), *Wundt studies: A centennial collection* (pp. 210–225). Toronto: C. J. Hogrefe.

Sokal, M. M. (1980b). "Science" and James McKeen Cattell, 1894–1945. *Science, 209,* 43–52.

Sokal, M. M. (Ed.) (1981). *An education in psychology: James McKeen Cattell's journal and letters from Germany and England, 1880–1888.* Cambridge: MIT Press.

Sokal, M. M. (1982). James McKeen Cattell and the failure of anthropometric mental testing, 1890–1901. In W. R. Woodward & M. G. Ash (Eds.), *The problematic science: Psychology in nineteenth-century thought* (pp. 322–345). New York: Praeger.

Sokal, M. M. (1987). James McKeen Cattell and mental anthropometry: Nineteenth-century science and reform and the origins of psychological testing. In M. M. Sokal (Ed.), *Psychological testing and American society, 1890–1930.* New Brunswick, NJ: Rutgers University Press.

Thwing, C. (1928). *The Americans and the German university: One hundred years of history.* New York: Macmillan.

Wolfe, H. K. (1886). Untersuchungen über das Tongedächtniss. *Philosophische Studien, 3,* 534–571.

Wolfe, H. K. (1898). Some effects of size on judgments of weight. *Psychological Review, 5,* 25–54.

Wilhelm Wundt's "*Völkerpsychologie*"

Gustav Jahoda

The theme of the relationship between the individual and the community is a perennial one. Plato took the view that the character of a community is at once the product and the maker of the individual's character. The issue was taken up in the writings of Johann Friedrich Herbart (1776–1841) during the early part of the 19th century. Herbart, best known for his attempt to create a mathematical psychology, treated this theme in his textbook of psychology (1816, 1901), arguing that a psychology dealing only with the isolated individual is bound to be inadequate. He put forward the idea of a "psychology of politics" which corresponds roughly to what we now call social psychology, but failed to develop it. Yet, in a subsequent work, *The Science of Psychology* (1824–1828/1968), he insisted that the only real fact was the individual, denying the existence of a superordinate folk soul.

The interest of Herbart's contemporary, Wilhelm von Humboldt (1767–1835), was focused on language, but not in any narrow sense, as the title of his major work indicates: *The Diversity of Human Language Structure and its Influence on the Mental Development of Mankind* (1836). For Humboldt, an individual is not a closed system, but rather, the product of past generations and all the surrounding influences, integrated into the larger unit of the nation; and this relationship is largely mediated by a common language.

Both men powerfully influenced Moritz Lazarus (1824–1903), a man with a background in philosophy and physiology. In 1851, he wrote a seminal article entitled "On the concept and possibility of a '*völkerpsychologie*'" declaring that he had named a novel and as yet unexplored field of study. Lazarus was later joined by the philologist Hajm Steinthal (1823–1899), who followed Humboldt in regarding

Figure 1 Moritz Lazarus.

language as the key to the soul of a people. They collaborated on the project of establishing the discipline of *völkerpsychologie* and founded a journal dedicated to it. Their ideas do not readily lend themselves to a concise summary, being wide-ranging but also rather diffuse. Essentially, they sought to draw parallels between individual and collective

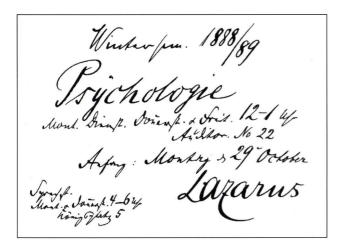

Figure 2 Lecture announcement by Lazarus (1888/1889).

called in another context "a magnificent failure." The journal, intended to stimulate relevant research, remained largely confined to peripheral issues and did little to advance the goal of its founders.

Midway through the 19th century, at the time Lazarus and Steinthal were seeking to found *völkerpsychologie*, Wilhelm Wundt (1832–1920) was just beginning his academic career, and there is no doubt that he was well aware of the new movement. This is reflected in his first book on the theory of perception (1862), in which he already saw the future of psychology moving along two complementary lines, synchronic and diachronic. The former would be based on experiments and statistics, while the latter would be an account of the evolution of the human spirit.

In the second volume of his *Lectures on the Mental Life of Humans and Animals* (1863), Wundt pursued this theme, proposing that individual psychology should be supplemented by *völkerpsychologie*

functioning. To characterize the latter, their central concept is that of the spirit or mentality of a people. For instance, just as the health of the individual depends on the health of the body, so the state of the spirit of the people depends on the health of the "body politic," or the state. Again, the restriction of consciousness of the individual to a particular issue corresponds to the preoccupation of the collective with a particular set of events, such as a war. The unity of the collective is cemented by a common language.

Ultimately, however, and in spite of some vacillations, they came down on the side of Herbart in insisting that only the individual mind is objectively real. It was this view which later came under critical attack by Wundt as the key weakness of their position. In other respects there are many similarities between Wundt's version of *völkerpsychologie* and that of Lazarus and Steinthal. For instance, both distinguished between a general development of the human spirit at large over historical time and ethnic psychology dealing with particular peoples.

But while Lazarus and Steinthal treated both as integral parts of the task of *völkerpsychologie*, Wundt excluded the latter. A common aim was that of arriving at general laws of historical development, but while Lazarus and Steinthal wanted to study the laws governing the growth of that awkward entity—the spirit of the people—Wundt had more concrete objectives, which will be further described below. It should be said that this bare sketch does not do justice to the bold originality of Lazarus and Steinthal and to their many perceptive comments. Nonetheless, their over-elaborate theoretical edifice must be regarded as what Bruner

Figure 3 Title page of *The Life of the Soul* by Lazarus (1856).

Figure 4 Hajm Steinthal in old age.

G. BROKESCH   1886.   LEIPZIG.

Figure 5 Wilhelm Wundt (1886).

and comparative psychology. Ethnology, concerned with primitive people, would provide useful materials. He also discussed the methods of folk psychology and introduced for the first time a notion that became central to his thought, namely the key importance of customs and morals. These are not invented and are in a certain sense "natural," emerging from social interaction, yet also influenced by external factors, such as climate. Wundt went on to characterize various "primitive" peoples in derogatory terms he was later to regret. Another topic discussed was that of religion, which, together with customs and morals, he regarded as essential in tracing the mental development of humanity.

In his *Principles of Physiological Psychology* (1874), Wundt sought to redefine the scope of psychology, which he claimed was fundamental for all the human and social sciences. For him, at that stage, individual and physiological psychology together constituted an explanatory natural science, while *völkerpsychologie* was essentially

descriptive and secondary. This did not mean, however, that it had ceased to fascinate him—quite the opposite. He began to lecture on it in 1875, first in Zurich and then at Leipzig, where he had been newly appointed.

In the second volume of his *Logic* (1883), known as *Methodology*, two sections deal extensively with comparative and so-called "historico-psychological" methods. The standard of comparison was the "normal human mind," implicitly that of adult Europeans, to be compared with animals, children, the mentally ill, and people of other races and nationalities. The latter was, for Wundt, the task of ethnic psychology, as distinct from *völkerpsychologie,* though it could provide relevant data. The reason for this exclusion is that ethnic psychology is concerned with singularities, while *völkerpsychologie* aims at general laws of human development on a historical scale. The tool for this purpose, according to Wundt, was the historico-psychological approach, focusing on three main domains: language, myth and/or customs, and morals. The last of this trinity figured very largely in his *Ethics* (1880), which is probably the reason why the 10 volumes of Wundt's *Völkerpsychologie* (1900–1920) contain far more on language and myth.

Around this time, a distinguished philologist, Hermann Paul (1880), launched a critical onslaught on Wundt's *völkerpsychologie*. His central argument, put crudely, was that mental processes exist only inside individual persons, and therefore *völkerpsychologie* is a meaningless abstraction. Wundt's defense does not lend itself to brief summary, since it turns on a terminological distinction in German between spirit or mind and soul, that is virtually untranslatable. At any rate, Wundt maintained that the shared contents of the soul of the people were of the same order of reality as those of the individual soul. In this he was on rather shaky ground, though similar notions were not uncommon at the time, e.g., Durkheim's (1898) conception of individual versus collective representations.

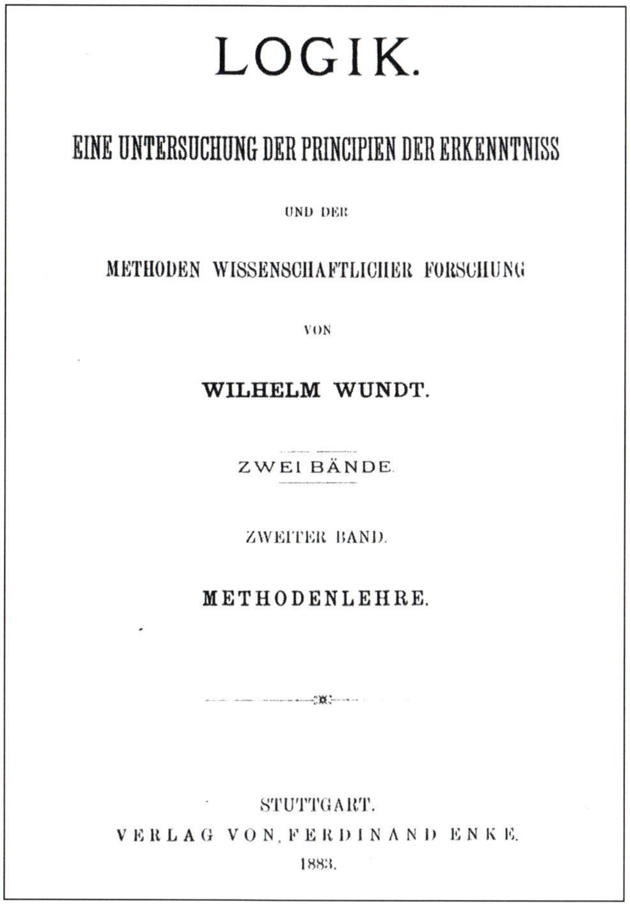

LOGIK.

EINE UNTERSUCHUNG DER PRINCIPIEN DER ERKENNTNISS

UND DER

METHODEN WISSENSCHAFTLICHER FORSCHUNG

VON

WILHELM WUNDT.

ZWEI BÄNDE.

ZWEITER BAND.

METHODENLEHRE.

⁂

STUTTGART.
VERLAG VON FERDINAND ENKE.
1883.

Figure 6 Title page of *Logic* (1883) by Wundt.

By the time of the fourth edition of the *Principles* (1893), Wundt had elevated the status of *völkerpsychologie* to a level of equality with experimental psychology. Although having different tasks, he declared, they belong together as two main parts of scientific psychology. The third edition of the *Logic*, which appeared in the same year, expanded the argument. At the outset Wundt insisted that it is on principle not possible for psychology to confine itself to individuals. This is because individual development is determined by the mental environment, and this in turn is the outcome of multiple interactions throughout history. This mental environment, roughly equivalent to what is nowadays known as culture, consists of his usual array of language, customs, religion, and myth. At any particular period there exists a milieu which influences individuals, and without it no person could reach what he called "mental individuality"; or, as we would say, humans as we know them are inconceivable in the absence of culture.

Wundt then went on to discuss in greater depth the relationship between individual psychology and *völkerpsychologie*. His arguments are highly convoluted and cannot be pursued here (for details cf. Jahoda, 1993). What it boils down to is that he sought to demonstrate two propositions that seem incompatible: first, that individual psychology and *völkerpsychologie* are equally important parts of a whole; second, that in the last analysis individual psychology is nevertheless more fundamental. The fact that he wrestled with these issues indicates his increasing preoccupation with *völkerpsychologie* and its relation not merely to individual psychology but also to other auxiliary disciplines. For instance, he explained that *völkerpsychologie* takes its raw material from both philology and history; but the information provided by these specialties is merely the means whereby folk psychology strives to arrive at general psychological laws.

So far nothing has been said about the 10 volumes of the *Völkerpsychologie,* which began to appear in 1900. The reason is that, contrary to what is often assumed, these volumes contain little about the theory as such. Except for part of the volume on language, which is still a classic and has been translated, they consist of a massive collection of often outdated accounts of myths, rituals, religion, customs, and so on. It requires dogged persistence to plow through even a single volume, let alone the whole set. There is little in it that one would now regard as psychology, but Wundt, from his standpoint, identified all the myths, etc., as "mental products," therefore relevant to his concerns.

Wundt also wrote a book translated as *Elements of Folk Psychology* (1912), which is readable and often read under the illusion that it is a summary of the 10 volumes. Rather, it is a history of social evolution, of the type popular around the turn of the century, which Wundt regarded as a kind of supplement to the *Völkerpsychologie* proper.

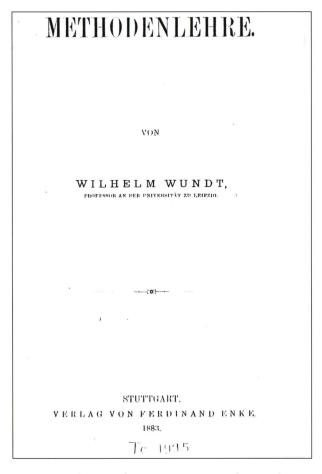

Figure 7 Title page of *Methodology* (1883) by Wundt.

The later fate of Wundt's concept of *völkerpsychologie* is probably at least partly due to the fact that he never produced a single concise presentation of his basic ideas. The 10 volumes are not only practically unreadable for the most part; their theoretical rationale also has to be pieced together from scattered writings. Another consequence was that, with very few exceptions, the writings were not translated. Accordingly, after Wundt's death, interest was maintained only in Germany, and even there for little more than a decade. Moreover, some of the

reactions were negative; for instance, Thurnwald (1929) was highly critical, and rightly so, of Wundt's use of ethnographic reports. In any case, by the 1920s the center of gravity in psychology had begun to shift to America. There, Wundt's main English-speaking disciple and spokesman, Titchener, was totally unsympathetic to *völkerpsychologie*, misrepresenting Wundt's ideas on this topic even in the obituary he wrote (Titchener, 1921).

It has only been during the last two decades or so, when increasing attention has come to be focused on social factors in psychological functioning, that there has been a revival of interest and a re-evaluation of Wundt's contribution in this sphere (e.g., Danziger, 1983; Schneider, 1990; Oelze, 1991; Brock, 1992). In particular, one of his central ideas, namely the key role played by social interactions in shaping the mind, has come to be recognized as a profound truth.

Bibliography

Brock, A. (1992). Was Wundt a 'Nazi'? *Theory and Psychology, 2*, 205–223.

Danziger, K. (1983). Origins and basic principles of Wundt's Völkerpsychologie. *British Journal of Psychology, 22*, 303–313.

Durkheim, E. (1898). Representations individuelles et representations collectives. *Revue de Métaphysique et de Morale, VI*, 273–302.

Herbart, J. F. (1816). *Lehrbuch zur Psychologie*. Königsburg: Unzer.

Herbart, J. F. (1968). *Psychologie als Wissenchaft, neu gegründet auf Erfahrung, Metaphysik und Mathematik* (Vols. 1 & 2). Amsterdam: Bonset. (Original work published 1824–1828)

Humboldt, W. (1836). *Über die Verschiedenheit des menschlichen Sprachbaus und ihren Einfluß auf die geistige Entwicklung des Menschengeschlechts*. Berlin: Akademie der Wissenchaften.

Jahoda, G. (1993). *Crossroads between culture and mind*. Cambridge, MA: Harvard University Press.

Oelze, B. (1991). *Wilhelm Wundt. Die Konzeption der Völkerpsychologie*. Münster, Germany: Waxmann.

Paul, Hermann. (1880). *Principien der Sprachgeschichte*. Halle: Niemeyer.

Schneider, C. M. (1990). *Wilhelm Wundt's Völkerpsychologie*. Bonn: Bouvier.

Titchener, E. B. (1921). Wilhelm Wundt. *American Journal of Psychology, 32*, 161–177.

Thurnwald, R. (1929). Grundprobleme der vergleichenden Völkerpsychologie. *Zeitschrift für die gesamte Staatswissenschaft, 87*, 240–296.

Wundt, W. (1862). *Beiträge zur Theorie der Sinneswahrnehmung*. Leipzig & Heidelberg: C. F. Winter.

Wundt, W (1863). *Vorlesungen über die Menschen- und Thierseele*. Leipzig: Leopold Voss.

Wundt, W. (1874). *Grundzüge der physiologischen Psychologie*. Leipzig: Engelmann.

Wundt, W. (1880). *Ethik*. Stuttgart: Ehnke.

Wundt, W. (1883). *Logik*. Stuttgart: Ehnke.

Wundt, W. (1888). Über Ziele und Wege der Völkerpsychologie. *Philosophische Studien, IV*, 1–27.

Wundt, W. (1893). *Grundzüge der physiologischen Psychologie* (4th ed.). Leipzig: Engelmann.

Wundt, W. (1900–1920) *Völkerpsychologie* (Vols. 1–10). Leipzig: Engelmann.

Wundt, W. (1912). *Elemente der Völkerpsychologie*. Leipzig: Kröner.

Edward Bradford Titchener (1867–1927)

Ryan D. Tweney

ortunate visitors to Cornell's Psychology Department during the first quarter of the 20th century might find themselves invited to Edward Bradford Titchener's study (Figure 1). Titchener, the reigning head of the system of psychology known as structuralism, was a gracious host, possessed of great knowledge across many fields, many eras, many issues. His study spoke of his erudition, an erudition that was its own reward but which was also a tool for him—a means of persuasion and a claim to authority. Like his teacher Wilhelm Wundt, Titchener sought authority in his discipline by placing himself in a commanding position, commenting on a huge variety of issues, judging the state of his discipline, writing prolifically to stake out the bound-aries of what was and was not fruitful in psychology. If Titchener's erudition did not reach as far as Wundt's, that is only to say how truly staggering the older man's grasp had become—no domain of human knowledge seemed impervious to Wundt's scholarship. During a long career, Wundt wrote entire books on medicine, physics, physiology, linguistics, law, and history, as well as many volumes in his own fields of philosophy and psychology. Though Titchener's scope was comparatively narrower, for both Titchener and Wundt, psychology as a science could only make sense if it was seen as part of a larger circle of sciences: One could not understand psychology except from such a broad perspective.

Figure 1 E. B. Titchener's study. (Archives of the History of American Psychology, Photographic File)

It is ironic, therefore, that Titchener is usually portrayed as the major proponent of what seems today to be a narrow, restrictive view of psychology's goals and methods. He is usually pictured only as the advocate of a discredited "soft" methodology (introspection) and as Wundt's slavish follower in the new world. In fact, the usual view is wrong. His version of introspection was intended to be a precise tool and was firmly rooted in the careful refinements of the experimental laboratory. Further, he was definitely *not* a Wundt clone. I will try to make each of my revisionist claims explicit, while arguing a third point: Titchener provided a clearly identifiable, clearly articulated touchstone against which much of early 20th-century American psychology was able to define itself. *Clarity* is the legacy of Edward Bradford Titchener, clarity about who we are, who we are not, and who we might become. We may have rejected his view of what psychology should be, but we cannot reject his view that psychology, perhaps more than other sciences, needs to know exactly what it is supposed to be doing.

Titchener's views on psychology reflected the cultural and social background of his life (for an overview of Titchener's life and work see the chapter written by Rand Evans in Watson & Evans, 1991, Evans's forthcoming biography of Titchener, and E.G. Boring's 1928 obituary of Titchener). Born in 1867 in Chichester, England, Titchener was raised by his paternal grandfather amid gentlemanly circumstances. During his teens, his grandfather's financial failure and subsequent death left the young Titchener in poor circumstances. Fortunately, he continued his education by obtaining scholarships, first to Malvern College, then to Oxford University, where he majored in philosophy and classics, receiving his AB in 1890. Distinguishing himself as an undergraduate, his first research interests were in biology: Ten papers were published by Titchener in the journal *Nature* between 1889 and 1891. Though he did not later advocate a psychology grounded in biology (unlike, say, John Watson), his systematization of the new science of psychology relied upon an analogical extension of the organization of biology, as we will see below.

Titchener, during a fifth year at Oxford University, studied under the physiologist John Scott Burdon-Sanderson (1828–1905), whose *Syllabus of Lectures on Physiology* (1880) included an account of the use of reaction time methods to study perceptual and behavioral systems, and is strikingly in

Figure 2 E. B. Titchener, 1867–1927. (From *Studies in psychology contributed by colleagues and former students of Edward Bradford Titchener*, 1917. Worcester, MA: Louis N. Wilson)

accord with some of Wundt's efforts of the time (Gieson, 1978; Tweney, 1987). By then, Titchener had already encountered the works of Wundt on physiological psychology. Even before going to study for his doctorate in Wundt's laboratory in Leipzig in 1890, Titchener had translated Wundt's *Physiological Psychology*, though he could never keep up with Wundt's frequent revisions of the text and never published the full result (a partial translation was later published; Wundt, 1904). Staying at Leipzig only two years, he received his doctorate in 1892 and went to Ithaca, New York, to take over the newly founded psychology laboratory at Cornell University. He spent his entire career there, working till his death in 1927.

At Leipzig, Titchener found himself at the center of an active group of young researchers, all drawn to Wundt's orbit. In particular, Oswald Külpe was Wundt's *Dozent* (assistant) at the time, and he and Titchener became good friends; Külpe introduced Titchener to the work of the positivists Ernst Mach and Richard Avenarius. Mach, especially, anchored Titchener's systematic thought about methodology. This is probably the major reason why Titchener's system is so different from Wundt's; Titchener was a positivist and hence sought for his system a firm grounding in physicalistic observability. Whereas Wundt was opposed to positivism and felt instead that psychology would necessarily have to incorporate methods very different from those of the natural sciences, methods akin to the ones used in the humanities. For Wundt, the range of applicability of experimental methods was narrow; in modern terms, we would say that he rejected their use whenever higher thought processes were involved. For Külpe and Titchener no such limits existed—the experimental method was the keystone for all of psychology. Külpe later modified this view, in favor of philosophical approaches (see Kurz, in press, for a full account), but Titchener carried the faith with him to Cornell and remained a staunch positivist throughout his career.

Danziger (1990) described the social context of research as consisting of three concentric circles, the innermost one representing the experimental situation itself, a surrounding circle representing the research community, and the largest, outer circle representing the professional environment. Titchener's positivism meant that his views on the best way to conduct psychological experimentation (the innermost circle) were very different from Wundt's. With respect to the outer circles, however, Titchener was perhaps more influenced by Wundt than by any other single figure. In particular, he admired Wundt's attempt to systematize his psychology, shared Wundt's concern that psychology be situated historically and philosophically among its neighboring disciplines, and accepted Wundt's belief that psychology should concern itself with conscious experience as its subject matter. Thus, his construal of the research community and the professional environment of psychology were similar to his mentor's. Like Wundt, Titchener thought that all science dealt with experience; for Wundt, the natural sciences dealt with consciousness as an immediate experience (i.e., as a given), whereas psychology dealt with it as a mediate product (i.e., as the product of an external reality and an experiencing subject). While accepting the underlying notion, Titchener modified it somewhat and made it less polarized—the distinction for him was based on point of view generally, rather than in mediate ver-

sus immediate experience (Leys & Evans, 1990, have a careful account of the difference between Wundt and Titchener on this issue, and of its importance to the formation of Titchener's views). Titchener also accepted Wundt's view on the need to develop the basic science of psychology much further before applications would be possible; thus both men remained aloof from most of the applied psychological movements of their day—testing, pedagogical applications, and clinical applications. Finally, and perhaps most importantly, Titchener accepted Wundt as a role model for how to organize a research laboratory, a model he followed at Cornell.

When Titchener arrived at Cornell in 1892, the laboratory consisted of six rooms in White Hall; later, it moved to Morrill Hall (Figure 3), where Titchener had 10 rooms to work in (and eventually 26). The lab had just been formed and was not yet furnished; Titchener had brought some equipment from Leipzig, but had to order and build much more. His first years at Cornell were busy ones; within four years he had graduated his first PhD student (Margaret Floy Washburn, in 1895) and had published his *Outline of Psychology* (1896), translations of Külpe and Wundt, and dozens of articles and book reviews (see Tweney & Yachanin, 1980, for information on Titchener's translation activity). Such productivity was not unrewarded, and Titchener was promoted to full professorship in 1896.

By the end of the century, the main lines of Titchener's systematic approach to psychology were apparent: He would be the advocate of a structural approach to psychology, using experimentation to anchor the theory, developing and refining methods to make this possible, and posing his system in direct opposition to the growing dominance of American functional psychology. The affinities of his ideas are made clear in his *Outline of Psychology*: "The general standpoint of the book is that of the traditional English psychology. The system . . . stands also in the closest relation to that presented in . . . Külpe's *Outlines of Psychology* and Wundt's *Grundzuege der physiologischen Psychologie*" (1896, p. vi). Locke's is the only "English psychology" cited in the first edition of the book. The quoted claim, made in the preface to the 1896 edition of the *Outlines*, was removed from the 1899 preface to the second edition. For the latter, Titchener made no mention of English psychology and no claim to stand in "the closest relation" to anything. Instead, Külpe's book, Wundt's book, James's *Principles* (1890), and

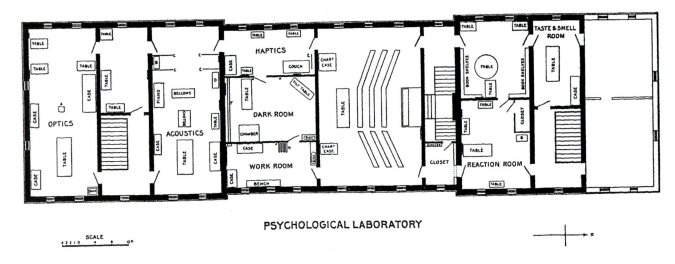

Figure 3 Titchener's laboratory in Morrill Hall, Cornell University, as of 1898. A proposed two-room addition is shown on the right. (From E. B. Titchener, 1898. A psychological laboratory. *Mind, N.S. 7,* 311–331)

Volume 1 of Ebbinghaus's *Grundzuege* (1897) were recommended by Titchener merely as "the standard books of reference" (1899, p. vii).

In his important 1898 paper "The Postulates of a Structural Psychology," which counts as a major systematic outline of his system, Titchener directly opposed functional psychology, taking issue with Dewey and James but reserving most of his fire for Brentano's act psychology. In sketching out the elements of a structural psychology, Titchener included sensations and affects; these are the elementary processes that all experimentalists agree upon. Images were also included as elementary processes, but these were problematic; eventually, he subsumed them as sensations, since the attributes of sensations and images were introspectively identical. Other processes, such as attention or will, were dismissed by Titchener as clearly functional in character and not elementary processes—because they were analyzable into simpler components. Sensations and affects were considered elementary precisely because they cannot be broken down into simpler processes; all we can do is outline their attributes. Note also that the "elements of mind" are elementary processes, Titchener's systematic psychology is not a static mental chemistry.

The approach is not so sparse as it might seem initially. Titchener's readers were often treated to a rich sensory feast when he chose to elaborate his ideas by providing a concrete example. Consider the following passage in which he shows how the complex "idea" of book can be analyzed into elementary sensations:

> My idea of a particular book is an idea derived from the cooperation of several bodily organs. It may include at any moment the look of the book (eye), the sound of its contents when read aloud (ear), its weight (skin, etc.), and the scent of its cover (nose). Now let us leave out of account all the constituents of the idea except those which come from the eye. We have remaining the red of the leather and gold of the lettering on the cover, and the black and white of the printed pages. Each of these quite simple components of the idea is a *sensation* of sight. Or let us leave out of account all the constituents except those coming through the ear. We then have the sounds of a familiar voice, which we imagine to be speaking certain successions of words. Each word uttered has a particular pitch, is a particular musical tone; while at the same time its consonants are heard as noises or auditory shocks. . . . (1896, pp. 26–27)

It is not hard to imagine the context in which Titchener is placing the reader: we are in an English gentleman's study (Figure 1!) surrounded by the fruits of erudition, a fine old leather-bound volume at hand, a British voice reading slowly as we savor the sounds, the sights, the smells. The experience is slowed by our deliberated use of attention to the purest aspects of the experience. "Introspection" Titchener called it, and it took training, and practice, and the right frame of mind. To see what he is asking of us, contrast the above quote with the rush of a famous passage from the foremost American functionalist, William James, who could have been talking, in this passage, about Titchener:

> The traditional psychology talks like one who should say a river consists of nothing but pailsful, spoonsful, quartpotsful, barrelsful, and other molded forms of water. Even were the pails and pots all actually standing in the stream, still between them the free water would continue to flow. . . . Every definite image in the mind is steeped and dyed in the free water that flows around it. With it goes the sense of its relations, near and remote, the dying echo of whence it came to us, the dawning sense of whither it is to lead. . . . (1890, p. 255)

James here is most certainly not in his study; instead, he is knee-deep in an open mountain stream, surrounded (we can imagine) by an American landscape, himself charged with Whitmanesque energy, an exuberant self-made man by contrast to Titchener's studied and nuanced "gentleman," the heir of centuries. Both James and Titchener sought the source of psychology in the experienced world but each saw that world in different ways. For the structuralist Titchener, the world demands meditative quiet and careful attention and can only really be seen objectively in the carefully controlled laboratory. For the functionalist James, the world is inherently in motion and the sensations of the structuralist are an illusion—to *really* see the world, says James, one must live in it, not contemplate it. No deep cultural analysis is necessary here to see why James inspired more American psychologists than did Titchener.

One reading of James suggests that he freed up American psychological thought from the constraints of the Lockean theory of ideas (as in the passage above), opening the way to a functional system which allowed greater emphasis on adaptive behavior, and hence paving the way for behaviorism. Titchener stands in the starkest contrast, not because he is a Lockean (he is not, and he makes the point clear), but because for him the real nature of experience could only be fathomed by a scientific approach—and "scientific" meant, for him, "positivistic." Like James, Titchener had no use for Wundt's apperceptions or psychical causalities, but his reasons differed. James did not like such notions because he disliked the systematizing that made them necessary, had no taste for the careful experimentation needed for their final justification, and perceived them as removed from the immediate world of lived experience. Titchener, on the other hand, disliked apperception and psychical causality because they were not part of his ultimate reduction of experience to the attributes of sensations and feelings; they were instead theoretical constructs for which no direct evidence could be had introspectively, and hence they did not meet his positivistic criteria for scientific acceptability. In short, while both Titchener and James were empiricists, each saw the task of psychology differently.

Experimentation was Titchener's bedrock, and it is a fair claim that he was the single most important voice in early American psychology that established the experiment as the final arbiter of truth in psychology. Titchener thus presented his own authority as resting on the ultimate authority of the laboratory. To establish that authority, he brought out his four-volume *Experimental Psychology* between 1901 and 1905, a monumental work that is perhaps the most thorough manual of experimental technique ever prepared in the English language. The title page quote from the first volume, by the English physicist Michael Faraday, makes the point (Figure 4). Two of the volumes are slim student manuals of experiments, and two are instructor's manuals, encyclopedic summaries of alternate experiments, reviews of past literature, detailed discussions of equipment, and so forth. The instructor's volumes are masterful summaries of the achievements and possibilities of experimental psychology at the beginning of the century and bespeak a new maturity for the discipline.

Methodologically, Titchener is best known for his use of controlled introspection; for him, this represented a kind of formalization of the deliberated attention noted in the example given earlier of the red leather-bound book. In the laboratory, the principal challenge to the use of the method was avoiding the "stimulus error," that is, giving a report of the sensory contents of experience that confused the actual experience with the "meaning" of that experience, describing the book as a "red book," say, rather than describing the actual sensations that compose the experience. For Titchener, introspection was "simply the common scientific method of observation, applied from the standpoint of a descriptive psychology" (1912, p. 487). He distinguished it sharply from "phenomenology," a descriptive approach to consciousness, which proceeds in terms of the meanings of the contents of experience. Such meaning must be eliminated from

EXPERIMENTAL PSYCHOLOGY

A Manual of Laboratory Practice

BY

EDWARD BRADFORD TITCHENER

VOLUME I

QUALITATIVE EXPERIMENTS:

PART I. STUDENT'S MANUAL

As an experimentalist, I feel bound to let experiment guide me into any train of thought which it may justify. — FARADAY.

New York

THE MACMILLAN COMPANY

LONDON: MACMILLAN & CO., LTD.

1924

All rights reserved

Figure 4 The title page from Titchener's *Experimental Psychology* (a later printing of the 1901 first edition). Note the quote by Michael Faraday, the 19th-century English physicist. (From E. B. Titchener, 1901. *Experimental Psychology*. New York: Macmillan)

scientific description, according to Tichener, because they presuppose the very thing they are supposed to make possible; they reflect our interpretation of what happened in experience, not the experience itself. It is a common misconception that Titchener's procedure is an "armchair" enterprise, but this is false. For him, the only way to get the appropriate scientific data from an observer was to carefully control the stimulus conditions and to vary those conditions in a systematic fashion—hence his emphasis on experimental procedures and the careful attention given to apparatus. Titchener's introspection was strictly a laboratory endeavor.

Titchener's version of introspective method was centrally challenged by the findings of the Wuerzburg school concerning "imageless thought" (Humphrey, 1951). In brief, these investigators claimed that certain mental events occurred in the absence of any sensory content. For example, Karl Bühler, in 1907, asked observers to introspect upon their thought processes in response to abstract

questions of the form "Can you get to Berlin from here in 7 hours?" or "Is this correct: 'The future is as much a condition of the present as of the past'?" (Humphrey, 1951, describes these examples and a number of others). Examination of the protocols always revealed a disjointed succession of sensations and images *and* a continuous awareness of thought itself; these "directing tendencies" were, for Bühler, a new element of thought—not sensations, not affects, and not images. If this were true, then it obviously held bleak implications for the fundamental method advocated by Titchener. In response, he devoted major effort in the years 1907 to 1915 to defending his approach; he and his students published a series of direct experimental attempts to isolate the imageless thoughts. In every case, Titchener concluded, what appeared to be imageless content could be resolved, if the introspections were carefully done, into a further series of sensory components. What Bühler called "thought elements" were simply vague sensory experiences (frequently visceral) that were hard to detect but which were observable.

Henle (1971), in a much-quoted paper, claimed that Titchener's introspections always included stimulus error, since all introspections include the presence of an awareness of the end or goal of thought. Henle failed to consider, however, the extensive work done by Titchener and his students on exactly this issue; no fewer than seven papers, none cited by Henle, were published on the topic between 1909 and 1915. Humphrey (1951) also critiqued Titchener in his review. He faulted introspective reports as being inadequate descriptions of the phenomena studied in Würzburg-style experiments; given the introspective report (for example, the list of sensations and affects generated by introspection on the book described above), one could not reconstruct what the object that elicited the report must have been. Titchener (1913) was aware of this claim too, however, and, in fact, used it to dismiss the possibility of an *experimental* test of the claims made by the Würzburgers! For Titchener, the issue was whether or not to allow meaning into our descriptive accounts of the phenomena of psychology—if we allowed them in (as the imageless thought school wanted to do) we were simply begging the question. Humphrey, like Henle, thus seems to have missed the point—Titchener was not disputing the evidence but the theoretical use made of that evidence. Unfortunately, neither Humphrey nor Henle cited Titchener's 1913 paper (see also Tweney, 1987). In later years, the imageless thought school has been assumed to have "won" the dispute with Titchener. Even Boring (1953), Titchener's student, later regarded imageless thought as a "discovery," somewhat akin to the empirical side of the unconscious mind! What remains clear, however, is that Titchener and his critics (both in his day and in our own) were simply approaching the issue on two different levels.

If the controversy with the imageless thought school pitted Titchener against European thought in psychology, it even more clearly reveals how differently his American peers must have perceived Titchener's goals. We can see this by looking at a paper by William Frederick Book, published in 1910, which frames the issues nicely. Book is best remembered for his landmark studies of typing skill (1908); his 1910 paper, however, applied some of the previously unpublished findings of the earlier study to the issue of imageless thought, inspired, so he tells us, by a reading of Titchener's *Experimental Psychology of the Thought Processes* (1909). As part of his typing skill study, Book had gathered introspections at regular intervals during the course of learning, along with the more behavioral records that were the main focus of his 1908 report. Book's "cross section" of the states of consciousness showed that at the earliest stages of skill learning, the imagery was very distinct, but that it gradually became less distinct, finally disappearing altogether as the skill was mastered, leaving only the awareness of a "conscious attitude," an imageless thought. For Book, this meant that the role of conscious awareness changed as a function of skill—Titchener was right for the earliest stages and the Würzburgers were right for the later stages. "All observed the same group of phenomena, but at different stages of its development" (Book, 1910, p. 396). The lesson, says Book, is to take seriously what Titchener called "the *genetic* method," to look closely at the time course of these developments of thought. Yet Book's approach is functionalist, not structuralist. Titchener did indeed advocate a

genetic method (see Titchener, 1909, pp. 168–170, especially), but he carefully separated out the analytic use of the method that he was advocating from its functionalist appearances. In effect, Titchener agreed with Book about the phenomena but disagreed about the interpretation. Imageless thoughts *did* appear in reports but only, as Book noted, at some stages of the process. They could not therefore be taken as elemental. Sensations were elemental because sensations were present—always present—in all reports at all stages of development. In short, for Titchener, the elements of conscious experience were those things that were constitutive of consciousness. How could an ultimate constituent be sometimes present and sometimes absent? That, in a nutshell, was the criterion of Titchener's structuralism.

It is interesting to consider the later fate of Titchener's notion of stimulus error in psychology. We have already noted the criticisms leveled against the distinction, but we have not considered an essential part of the issue, namely, the fact that what Titchener and his opponents were arguing about reduces to the attitude of the observer, to a particular point of view; that is why Titchener called for *trained* introspectors. In subsequent decades, this issue was not seen in quite such black-and-white terms. Consider, for example, the researches of Brunswik in the 1930s, which showed that the attitude of the observer in a psychophysical task could be manipulated (Kurz & Tweney, this volume). Titchener's student, E. G. Boring had suggested something similar in 1921 and had noted, following Titchener's claims, that there was a perfectly legitimate focus upon the stimulus (not the sensation) in the Fechnerian psychophysical task; if you are seek-

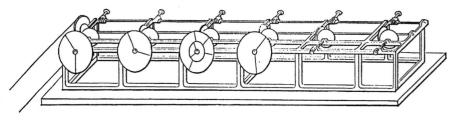

FIG. 4. Demonstrational Colour Mixer, for six sets of discs.

Figure 5 Titchener's design for a demonstration color mixer, with six sets of discs. (From E. B. Titchener, 1909. *A text-book of psychology*. New York: Macmillan, p. 69)

ing to detect a just barely detectable stimulus, then the only meaningful report is whether or not the stimulus is present. But Titchener's use of systematic introspection was not directed toward such questions; given that there is a stimulus, the observer must note the sensations that compose it—a task for which the stimulus identity is at best irrelevant and at worst a barrier to the desired sensory report. The attitude of the observer is therefore a variable, as Brunswik noted, and is itself subject to experimental investigation. Titchener chose not to make such manipulations the core of his approach since that would have led him into the realm of functional psychology—prematurely, in his view, until the structural psychology was completely worked out.

During the same period that Titchener was defending his structuralist approach against the imageless thought school, he was also forced to defend it from the uniquely American call for a new approach to psychology—behaviorism. In 1913, John Broadus Watson published his famous polemic, "Psychology as the Behaviorist Views It." If there was anything like an official response of the old order to this new upstart, it must be seen as Titchener's (1914) reply to Watson. Titchener mostly concentrated on the irrelevance of Watson's call to the science of psychology as such. For Titchener, Watson's urging of a predictive and manipulative science of behavior was in effect a call for a technology, not a science. It is not so much that Watson had urged a false path as that Watson had failed to see what psychology is really about: "Introspective psychology . . . will go quietly about its task, wishing the new movement all success, but declining—with the mild persistence natural to matters of fact—either to be eliminated or to be ignored" (Titchener, 1914, p. 17). In retrospect, the critique seems surprisingly mild. By present-day appearances, Watson's behaviorism appears as different from Titchener's mentalist structuralism as two systems could possibly be. Why then did Titchener not utterly condemn Watson's attempt?

The answer resides in Titchener's positivism, a view of science which he by and large shared with Watson. Both felt that science had to be grounded in observation, and both were suspicious of the kind of elaborate theorizing that went beyond the observable data. They differed, of course, on where such data was to be found, but they did not differ on the ultimate goal of science—reduction of the

observable to as small a number of precise, even mathematical, laws as possible. Each shared a vision of science that transcended their separate visions of the specific science of psychology. It is no surprise, then, that Titchener and Watson became friends, engaging for a number of years in an extensive correspondence about matters both psychological and nonpsychological. And when, in the wake of the scandal that drove Watson out of psychology (Buckley, 1989), Watson's name was removed from *Who's Who in America*, it was Titchener alone among American psychologists who sought to have it restored—successfully (Larson & Sullivan, 1965).

By 1915, Titchener had spent a good deal of time

ON "PSYCHOLOGY AS THE BEHAVIORIST VIEWS IT."

BY E. B. TITCHENER.

(*Read April 3, 1914.*)

When we speak of a science, we have in mind a logically organized body of knowledge that has resulted from certain methods of attacking the problems presented by a particular subject-matter. The methods of science are all, in the last resort, observational; the problems of science are all, in the last resort, analytical. The subject-matter of a given science may be indicated in two different ways: by a simple enumeration of objects, or by a characterization of the point of view from which the science in question regards the common subject-matter of all science, namely, human experience. Thus we may say that our psychology will deal with such things as perceptions, feelings, thoughts, or we may say that psychology, dealing "in some sort with the whole of experience," is to be distinguished as "individualistic" from other sciences which are "universalistic." It is clear that a characterization of this kind, though it necessarily transcends the limits of the science in order to show how those limits are drawn, is far more satisfactory than a mere list of objects; and psychology, these many years past, has therefore had recourse to it.[1]

[1] J. Ward, "Psychology," Encyc. Brit., XX., 1886, 38 (and later); R. Avenarius, "Bemerkungen zum Begriff des Gegenstandes der Psychologie," *Vjs. f. wiss. Phil.*, XVIII., 1894, 418; H. Ebbinghaus, "Grundzüge der Psych.," I., 1897, 8 (and later editions). On the general subject, cf. E. B. Titchener, "Psychology: Science or Technology?", in *Pop. Sci. Mo.*, LXXXIV., 1914, 39 ff.

Reprinted from Proceedings American Philosophical Society, Vol. liii., 1914.

Figure 6 The "official" reply to Watson. (From E. B. Titchener, 1914. On "Psychology as the behaviorist views it." *Proceedings American Philosophical Society, 53*, 1–17, p. 1)

in a defensive posture. For the next ten years, he focused upon the positive side of his enterprise. His publication rate declined during this period, though the number of publications by his students increased dramatically (Tweney, 1987). He himself was supposedly working on a "big book," a systematic exposition of his ideas (Evans, 1972), and the many reports of his aloofness, isolation, and imperious personal manner generally date from this era, from 1915 on (see, for example, the article by his former student, Grace Adams, 1931). His premature death in 1927 meant that the system itself was never published; only a kind of prolegomena appeared, slightly edited by H. P. Weld (Titchener, 1929). After his death, the laboratory at Cornell came under Madison Bentley's chairmanship. Bentley reorganized it completely, dramatically altering its direction (Ryan, 1982). Though Bentley was himself a student of Titchener, his conception of the nature and direction of psychology was very different. Structuralism without Titchener quickly vanished from the American scene.

To claim that Titchener's legacy was clarity, as I did at the beginning of this article, is then a claim that must be qualified—the clarity is of a special sort. American psychology rejected his view of the necessity for a psychology based upon conscious experience, his view of the need to establish a structural account of mind prior to any functional account, and the introspective methodologies that were a consequence of his view. For a time, some even rejected the view that psychology should have anything at all to do with mind. But American psychology did accept his positivist rigor and the privileged role he gave to experimentation, and the tangible results of much of his empirical research have quietly found their way into our textbooks. We should appreciate him for this; without his work, we would be less sure of our stance than we are.

Bibliography

Adams, G. (1931). Titchener at Cornell. *American Mercury, 24,* 440–446.

Book, W. F. (1908). *The psychology of skill. With special reference to its acquisition in typewriting.* Missoula, MT: University of Montana Press.

Book, W. F. (1910). On the genesis and development of conscious attitudes (Bewustseinslagen). *Psychological Review, 17,* 381–398.

Boring, E. G. (1921). The stimulus-error. *American Journal of Psychology, 32,* 449–471.

Boring, E. G. (1927). Edward Bradford Titchener, 1867–1927. *American Journal of Psychology, 38,* 489–506.

Boring, E. G. (1953). A history of introspection. *Psychological Bulletin, 50,* 169–189.

Buckley, K. W. (1989). *Mechanical man: John Broadus Watson and the beginnings of behaviorism.* New York: Guilford Press.

Burdon-Sanderson, J. (1880). *Syllabus of a course of lectures on physiology* (2nd ed.). Philadelphia: Lindsay & Blakiston.

Danziger, K. (1990). *Constructing the subject: Historical origins of psychological research.* Cambridge: Cambridge University Press.

Ebbinghaus, H. (1897). *Grundzuege der Psychologie.* (1. Halbband). Leipzig: Veit & Comp.

Evans, R. B. (1972). E. B. Titchener and his lost system. *Journal of the History of the Behavioral Sciences, 8,* 168–180.

Gieson, G. L. (1978). *Michael Foster and the Cambridge School of Physiology.* Princeton: Princeton University Press.

Henle, M. (1971). Did Titchener commit the stimulus error? The problem of meaning in structural psychology. *Journal of the History of the Behavioral Sciences, 7,* 279–282.

Humphrey, G. (1951). *Thinking: An introduction to its experimental psychology.* London: Methuen & Co.

James, W. (1890). *Principles of psychology.* New York: Henry Holt.

Kurz, E. M. (in press). Marginalizing discovery: Karl Popper's intellectual roots in psychology, Or, How the study of discovery was banned from science studies. *Creativity Research Journal.*

Larson, C., & Sullivan, J. J. (1965). Watson's relation to Titchener. *Journal of the History of the Behavioral Sciences, 1,* 338–354.

Leys, R., & Evans, R. B. (Eds.). (1990). *Defining American psychology: The correspondence between Adolf Meyer and Edward Bradford Titchener.* Baltimore, MD: Johns Hopkins University Press.

Ryan, T. A. (1982). Psychology at Cornell after Titchener: Madison Bentley to Robert MacLeod, 1928–1948. *Journal of the History of the Behavioral Sciences, 18,* 347–369.

Titchener, E. B. (1896). *An outline of psychology.* New York: Macmillan.

Titchener, E. B. (1898). The postulates of a structural psychology. *Philosophical Review, 7,* 449–465.

Titchener, E. B. (1899). *An outline of psychology* (New edition with additions). New York: Macmillan.

Titchener, E. B. (1901–1905). *Experimental psychology: A manual of laboratory practice. Vol. I. Qualitative experiments; Part I. Student's manual; Part II. Instructor's manual. Vol. II. Quantitative experiments; Part I. Student's manual; Part II. Instructor's manual.* New York: Macmillan.

Titchener, E. B. (1909). *Lectures on the experimental psychology of the thought-processes.* New York: Macmillan.

Titchener, E. B. (1912). The schema of introspection. *American Journal of Psychology, 22,* 485–508.

Titchener, E. B. (1913). The method of examination. *American Journal of Psychology, 24,* 429–440.

Titchener, E. B. (1914). On "Psychology as the behaviorist views it." *Proceedings of the American Philosophical Society, 53,* 1–17.

Titchener, E. B. (1929). *Systematic psychology: Prolegomena.* New York: Macmillan.

Tweney, R. D. (1987). Programmatic research in experimental psychology: E. B. Titchener's laboratory investigations, 1891–1927. In M. G. Ash & W. R. Woodward (Eds.), *Psychology in twentieth-century psychology* (pp. 35–57). Cambridge: Cambridge University Press.

Tweney, R. D., & Yachanin, S. (1980). Titchener's Wundt. In W. B. Bringmann & R. D. Tweney (Eds.), *Wundt studies: A centennial collection* (pp. 380–395). Toronto: C. J. Hogrefe.

Watson, J. B. (1913). Psychology as the behaviorist views it. *Psychological Review, 20,* 158–177.

Watson, R. I., & Evans, R. B. (1991). *The great psychologists: A history of psychological thought* (5th ed.). New York: Harper Collins.

Wundt, W. (1904). *Principles of physiological psychology. Vol. 1, Part 1. The bodily substrate of the mental life.* (Trans. by E. B. Titchener from the 5th German edition). London: Swan Sonnenschein & Co.

Wilhelm Wirth and the Psychophysical Seminar of Leipzig

Christina Schröder

On June 10, 1917, the psychophysics branch of the Psychological Institute of Leipzig University was given the official status of an independent university facility at the recommendation of the Royal Saxon Ministry for Religion and Public Education. The new institution was given the name Psychophysical Seminar, and Wilhelm Wirth (1876–1952), the long-time co-director of Wundt's Leipzig laboratory was appointed as its director. On the same day, Felix Krueger (1874–1948) became the official successor to Wilhelm Wundt (1832–1920), who had just decided to retire at the age of 85. The division of Wundt's original institute resulted in a redefinition of Wirth's academic responsibilities. From then on he was exclusively responsible for the teaching of "Philosophy, including Psychophysics." The new Psychophysical Seminar of Leipzig University was to assume a central place in the history of German psychology through its rich resources in equipment and the high quality of its applied research and instruction.

Wilhelm Wirth was born on July 27, 1876, in the idyllic town of Wunsiedel in the Pine Mountain region of the German Kingdom of Bavaria. Wirth's father, a teacher at the local classical high school, was familiar with Wundt's early writings and introduced his son to key philosophical and psychological questions. In 1894, the 18-year-old Wirth began to study law at Munich University. He generally disdained the philosophy of his time and was convinced that religious faith always involved a personal decision. Throughout his life Wirth worked on the ethical and logical foundation of his own belief system, which he expressed in his philosophical lectures and publications.

At the suggestion of the philosopher and Wundt student Theodor Lipps (1851–1917), Wirth switched

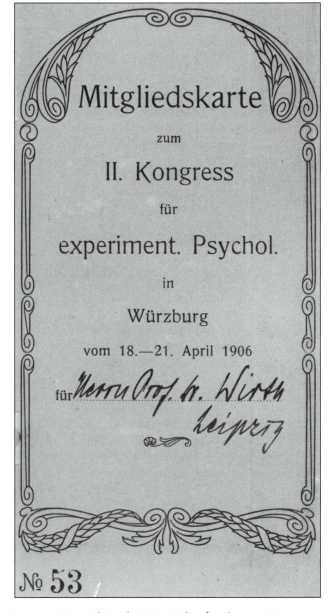

Figure 1 Wirth's admission ticket for the 1906 German Congress of Experimental Psychology.

Figure 2 Wirth (standing) and his guest and fellow Wundt student, Charles Spearman (1863–1945), in 1923.

from law to the study of philosophy, after less than three semesters. In addition, he studied mathematics and physics to qualify eventually as a high school teacher. After attending the Munich International Congress of Psychology with its heavy emphasis on experimental research, Wirth decided to become an experimental psychologist. After receiving his PhD in 1897, he spent some time in Wundt's Leipzig laboratory. Wirth accepted a formal appointment as Wundt's second assistant in 1900.

Wundt also offered to help advance Wirth's academic career by sponsoring his second dissertation (i.e., his research dissertation), which would qualify him to become an instructor at Leipzig. Beginning in 1901, Wirth assumed responsibility for the mathematical and methodological training of Wundt's psychology students. Only a year later, he began the lifelong editorship of the German *Archive of General Psychology*, which gave him access to a broad range of research in the growing field of psychology. In

1904, Wirth became one of the founders of the German Society for Experimental Psychology.

Only four years after Wirth's Leipzig appointment, Wundt recommended him for the position of

Figure 3 Wirth's university ID card during the 1930s.

co-director of Wundt's own institute, and he also recommended him for promotion to the next higher academic rank of untenured professor. In this context, Wundt (unpublished letter, 1905) described the work of his young associate as follows: "All of [Dr. Wirth's] publications are characterized by brilliance, a rich knowledge of the subject matter and great originality in the choice of experimental methods." Wundt's request was not answered until the summer of 1908 because his colleagues in the philosophical faculty could not agree on what subjects Wirth would teach. At long last, Wirth was approved as co-director of the Psychological Institute until Wundt's eventual retirement.

During the next few years, Wirth produced his major scientific works (1908, 1912). The chief aim of his psychophysical work was: "the discovery [of relationships between] well-defined stimuli and specific behavior patterns" (Wirth, 1908, p. 21). According to Wirth, the field of psychophysics focused on

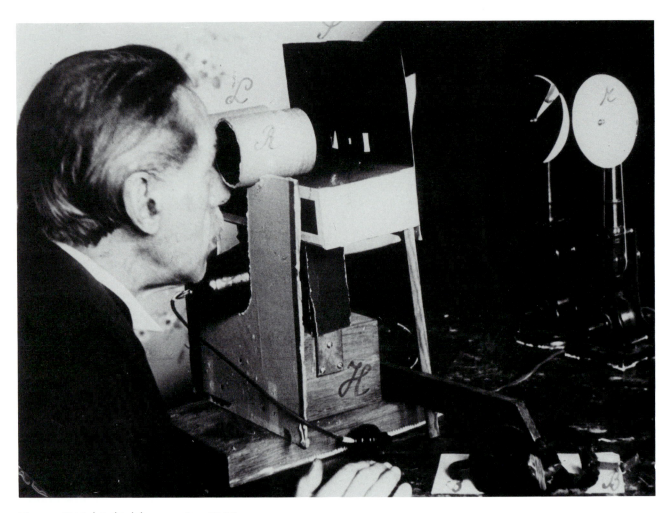

Figure 4 Wirth in his laboratory (ca. 1943).

the study of the relationship between a temporary, spatial event and its conversion into conscious, mental achievements. Wirth believed that the methods and results of his psychophysical research were directly applicable to the field of psychotechnology, so he began working in this area during World War I.

The harmonious relationship that existed between Wundt and Wirth deteriorated after Wundt decided to change the institute's organization in 1908. When both men sought redress from the university administration, Wirth's responsibilities were reduced to the directorship of the psychophysics branch. He was also enjoined not to interfere with the administration of the institute's four other branches.

In 1917 Wirth's new Psychophysical Seminar was assigned a few rooms under the eaves of the Paulinum. The Paulinum was the main classroom building at Leipzig University, which also housed Wundt's institute. In addition, Wirth and his students were permitted to make use of the seminar room, the library, and the classrooms of the original Psychological Institute. The new university seminar was given its own equipment budget of 600 marks and a share of the existing research equipment. Wirth's salary was raised to 4,800 marks, and funds were provided for the employment of student assistants.

The autonomous Psychophysical Seminar focused on the same teaching and research topics that Wirth covered in his lectures and practicum courses (i.e., general psychophysical methods, psychophysics of time perception, voluntary reactions, apperception, and content of consciousness, to name a few). Generous financial gifts of more than 750,000 marks permitted the purchase of a great deal of new equipment. When Wirth's seminar acquired new offices and classrooms at 7 Schiller Street in 1933, the last remaining ties to Wundt's original institute were cut.

Apart from the continuing laboratory courses, Wirth's department provided three to six students per semester with opportunities to conduct their own statistical and experimental studies. The 18 to 20 members of Wirth's seminar paid a membership fee and laboratory costs. Wirth tried to put his psychophysical ideas into practice with the assistance of more than 50 students, whose dissertations he supervised between 1917 and 1942. As early as 1926, Wirth's research interests were focused on the improvement of target shooting and marksmanship.

With the support of the German military, he developed special equipment that made it possible to practice aiming and shooting without actually using ammunition. In 1938 Wirth was honored for his military research by being elected to the prestigious Leopoldina, the Halle Academy of Natural Sciences. The 25th anniversary of his Psychophysical Seminar was celebrated by Leipzig University in 1942. After the facilities and all of the equipment of the Psychophysical Seminar were destroyed in 1943, Wirth retired from his academic responsibilities at the age of 68 and moved with his family to Amberg in Bavaria. He died on July 7, 1952. Plans developed for the re-opening of the Psychophysical Seminar at the university were never realized.

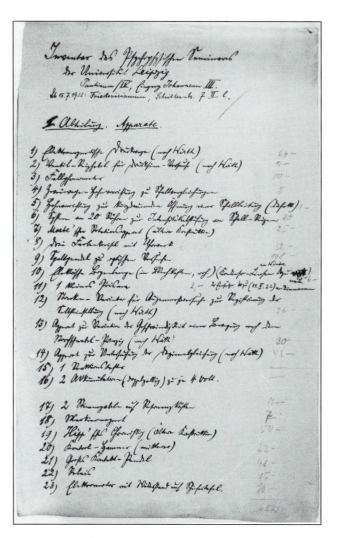

Figure 5 Handwritten equipment list from Wirth's seminar.

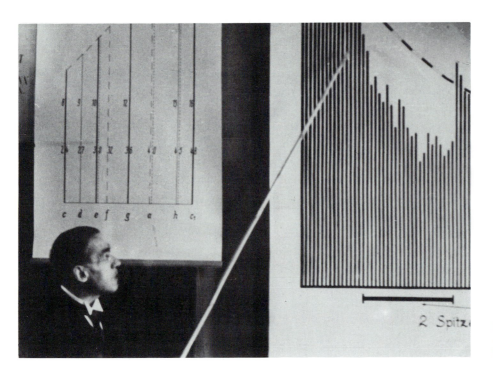

Figure 6 Wirth during the 25th anniversary of his laboratory (December 9, 1942).

Bibliography

Fritsche, C. (1976). *Zur Geschichte des Leipziger Psychologischen Instituts—Wilhelm Wirth*. Unpublished thesis, Leipzig University.

Wirth, W. (1908). *Die experimentelle Analyse der Bewußtseinsphänomene*. Braunschweig, Germany: Vieweg & Sohn.

Wirth, W. (1912). Psychophysik: Darstellung der Methoden der experimentellen Psychologie. In R. Rigerstedt (Ed.), *Handbuch der physiologischen Methodik*. Leipzig: Hirzel.

Wirth, W. (1920). Unserem großen Lehrer Wilhelm Wundt in unauslöslicher Dankbarkeit zum Gedächtnis (mit zwei Bildtafeln). *Archiv für die gesamte Psychologie, 40*, I–XVI.

Wirth, W. (1931). Wie ich zur Philosophie kam. Eine entwicklungspsychologische Studie. *Archiv für die gesamte Psychologie 80*, 452–510.

Wirth, W. (1936). Autobiographischer Beitrag zu "A History of Psychology in Autobiography." In C. Murchison (Ed.), *The International University Series in Psychology* (Vol. III, pp. 283–327). Worcester, MA: Clark University Press.

Wirth, W. (1938). Die Bedingungen der Genauigkeit psychophysischer Leistungen. Vortrag bei der Kaiserlichen Akademie der Naturforscher in Halle a S. am 20.05.1939. In E. Abderhalden (Ed.), *Nova acta Leopoldina* (NF Bd. 6, Nr. 35, pp. 41–80).

Wissenschaftliche Veröffentlichungen und Vorträge W. Wirths (1976). Zusammengestellt von A. Wirth. *Archiv für die Geschichte von Oberfranken, 56*, pp. 419–430.

Hermann Ebbinghaus

ermann Ebbinghaus (1850–1909) was born on January 24 in the city of Barmen in the Rhine Province of the German Kingdom of Prussia. After 1867, he studied philology and then philosophy at the universities of Bonn, Halle, Berlin, and, after 1871, Bonn again. In 1873 he received his PhD summa cum laude for a dissertation about *Hartmann's Philosophy of the Unconscious*. After additional postdoctoral studies in Germany, Ebbinghaus spent time from the spring of 1875 until the fall of

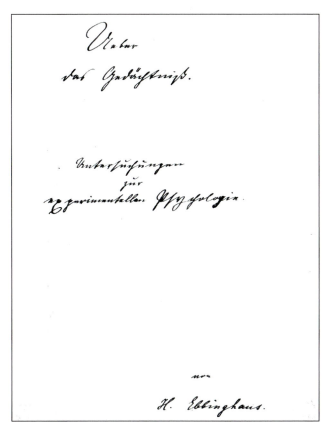

Figure 2 Handwritten title page of Ebbinghaus's second dissertation "On Memory" (1880).

1878 in England and France as a teacher and private language tutor (Bringmann & Bringmann, 1986).

Beginning in the fall of 1878, Ebbinghaus was employed as a French teacher to Prince Waldemar of Prussia (1868–1879), the youngest son of the Prussian and German Crown Prince. During this same period of time, Ebbinghaus carried out his painstaking memory research with "meaningless" syllables. The results of these time-consuming stud-

Figure 1 Ebbinghaus as a second lieutenant in 1874.

ies were submitted to the Philosophical Faculty of Berlin University as a second research dissertation. Ebbinghaus's work was favorably evaluated by the Berlin philosopher Eduard Zeller (1814–1908) and the famous physicist and psychologist Hermann von Helmholtz (1821–1894). The work has only been preserved in the form of a handwritten manuscript by Ebbinghaus, which was published in 1983 by the Institute for the History of Modern Psychology at Passau University in Germany. This facility also houses Ebbinghaus's private and scientific papers.

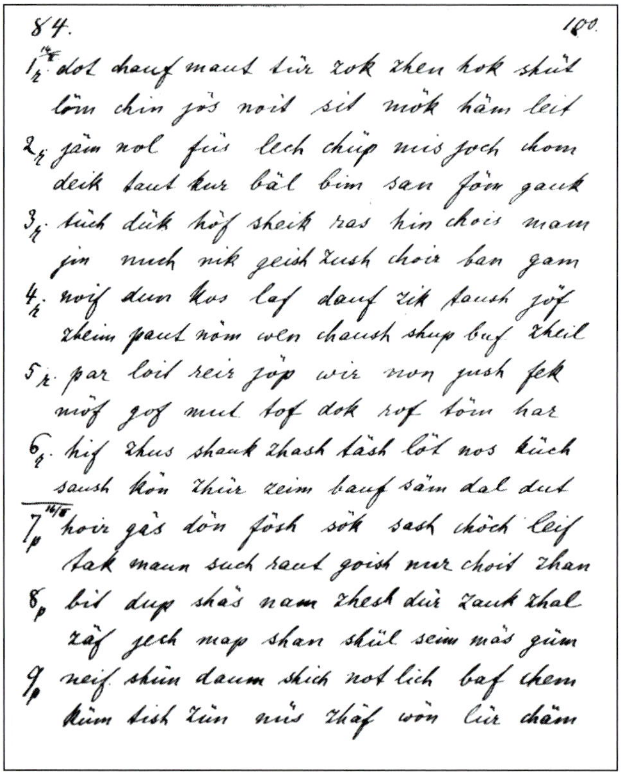

84. 100.
1 dol dauf maut lir zok zhen kok shül
löm chin jös noit sit mök häm leif
2 jäm nol füs lech chüp nis joch chom
deik baut kur bäl bim san föm gauk
3 tuch dük höf sheik ras hin chois maum
jin nuch nik geish zush choir ban gam
4 noif dun kos laf dauf zik faush jöf
zheim paul nöm wen chaush shup buf zheil
5 par loit reis jöp wir non jush fek
nöf gof mul tof dok rof töm har
6 hif zhus shauk zhash täsh löl nos küch
sauch kön zhür zeim bauf säm dal dut
7 hoir gäs dön fösh sök sash chöch leif
tak maun such raul goish nur choit zhan
8 bit dup shäs nam zhesh dür zauk zhal
zäf jech map shan shül seim mäs güm
9 neif shün daum shich not lich baf chem
küm tish zün nüs zhäf wön lür chäm

Figure 3 Sample of "meaningless" (nonsense) syllables in Ebbinghaus's handwriting.

Ebbinghaus began his academic career on October 25, 1880, as an untenured instructor at Berlin University. In June of 1886, he was promoted to an untenured professorship at that same institution on the recommendation of Zeller and the philosopher Wilhelm Dilthey (1833–1911). The 14 years he spent in Berlin was a productive period for Ebbinghaus. It was during this time that Ebbinghaus published his monograph *On Memory* (1885), which made him famous as one of the founders of experimental psychology. The importance of his early memory research lies in its programmatic content, which formed the scientific basis of his brand of experimental psychology. The much-quoted "memory curve" is only a small part of his contribution to the development of modern psychology as an empirical science. Ebbinghaus also invented a sophisticated research design to confirm the laws of association and to demonstrate how "experiment and measurement" can be applied successfully to the study of complex cognitive events. In 1890, along with the physiologist Arthur König (1856–1901), he founded the German *Journal for Psychology and the Physiology of Sensory Organs*, which helped promote psychology as a natural science.

ÜBER DAS

GEDÄCHTNIS.

UNTERSUCHUNGEN

ZUR

EXPERIMENTELLEN PSYCHOLOGIE

VON

HERM. EBBINGHAUS,

PRIVATDOCENTEN DER PHILOSOPHIE AN DER UNIVERSITÄT BERLIN.

„De subjecto vetustissimo novissimam promovemus scientiam."

Bibliotheca Universitatis Lipsiensis 1885.

179

LEIPZIG,

VERLAG VON DUNCKER & HUMBLOT.

1885.

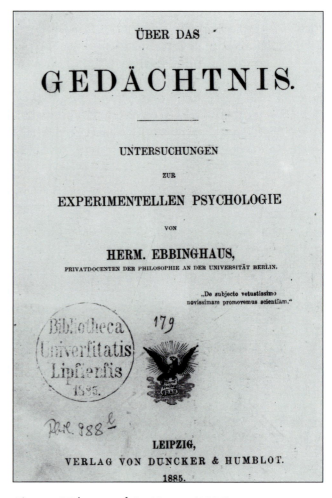

Figure 4 Title page of *On Memory* (1885).

In 1894, Ebbinghaus accepted a call to the Prussian University of Breslau, where he taught for nine years. At least two reasons for this change in employment are known. The appointment of Carl

Stumpf (1848–1936), instead of Ebbinghaus, to the University of Berlin was a bitter disappointment. More importantly, both Helmholtz and the influential philosopher Dilthey opposed the development of experimental psychology at Berlin. The scientific conflict between Dilthey and Ebbinghaus is reflected in their heated written exchange about the nature of psychology (Dilthey, 1894; Ebbinghaus, 1896). This debate is of considerable importance to the history of psychology because it resulted in a major divergence of views over what constitutes the legitimate subject matter of psychology—a rift which still exists today. During his Breslau years, Ebbinghaus developed an early intelligence test, the *Ebbinghaus Completion Test*, and published the first part of his *Principles of Psychology* (1897), which became a major source of information in the field of general psychology.

Figure 6 Ebbinghaus at the age of 57.

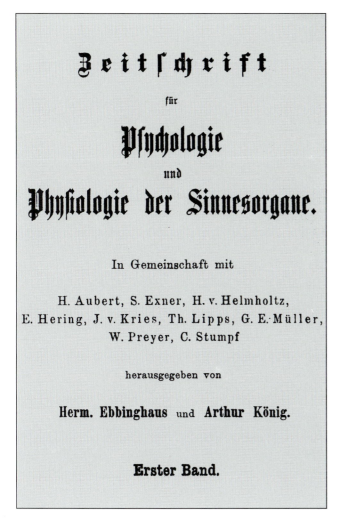

Figure 5 Title page of Ebbinghaus's *Journal for Psychology and A Sensory Physiology*.

In 1905, Ebbinghaus accepted an appointment as full professor at the University of Halle near Leipzig. During the remaining four years of his life, he worked on the completion of his introductory textbook and wrote the short *Survey of Psychology* (1908), which included a statement regarding his views on the history of psychology. Ebbinghaus died on February 26, 1909, from pneumonia when he was only 59 years old. He is buried in the St. Laurentius Cemetery in Halle.

Bibliography

Bringmann, W., & Bringmann, N. (1986). Hermann Ebbinghaus 1875–1879: The missing years. In W. Traxel & H. Gundlach (Eds.). *Ebbinghaus Studien 1* (pp. 101–115). Passau: Passavia.

Dilthey, W. (1894). Ideen über eine beschreibende und zergliedernde Psychologie. *Sitzungsberichte der Königlich Preußischen-Akademie der Wissenschaften zu Berlin, 2.* Halbband: Berlin.

Ebbinghaus, H. (1885). *Über das Gedächtnis.* Leipzig: Duncker & Humblot.

Ebbinghaus, H. (1896). Über erklärende und beschreibende Psychologie. *Zeitschrift für Psychologie, 9,* 161–205.

Ebbinghaus, H. (1897a). Über eine neue Methode zur Prüfung geistiger Fähigkeiten und ihre Anwendung bei Schulkindern. *Zeitschrift für Psychologie, 13,* 401–459.

Ebbinghaus, H. (1897b). *Grundzüge der Psychologie* (Vols. 1 & 2). Leipzig: Feit.

Ebbinghaus, H. (1908). *Abriß der Psychologie.* Leipzig: Feit.

Ebbinghaus, H. (1983). *Urmanuskript "Über das Gedächtnis," 1880*. Passau: Passavia.

Jaensch, E. (1908). Hermann Ebbinghaus. *Zeitschrift für Psychologie, 51*, 1–8.

Klix, F. (1979). Hermann Ebbinghaus, Ursprünge und Anfang psychologischer Forschungen an der Berliner Universität. In G. Eckardt (Ed.), *Zur Geschichte der Psychologie* (pp. 85–109). Berlin: Verlag der Wissenschaften.

Lander, H. J. (1985). Hermann Ebbinghaus: ein problematischer Beitrag zur Entwicklung der Gedächnispsychologie. *Zeitschrift für Psychologie, 193*, 9–25.

Mühle, G. W. (1959). Ebbinghaus. In Historische kommission bei der bayrischen Academie der Wissenschaften (Ed.), *Neue Deutsche Biographie* (Vol. 4, pp. 216–217). Berlin: Duncker & Hümblot.

Shakow, H. (1930). Hermann Ebbinghaus. *American Journal of Psychology, 17*, 505–518.

Sprung, L., & Sprung, H. (1985a). Zur Geschichte der Psychologie an der Berliner Universität (1850–1922). *Psychologie für die Praxis, 1*, 5–21.

Sprung, L., & Sprung, H. (1985b). Hermann Ebbinghaus zum Gedenken-Leben, Werk und Wirken für eine wissenschaftliche Psychologie. *Zeitschrift für Psychologie, 193*, 2–7.

Sprung, L., & Sprung, H. (1985c). Hermann Ebbinghaus (1850–1909). Marginalien zu einem Zentenarium. *Zeitschrift für Psychologie, 193*, 313–323.

Traxel, W. (Ed.). (1986). *Ebbinghaus-Studien 1*. Passau: Passavia.

Traxel, W. (Ed.). (1986). *Ebbinghaus-Studien 2*. Passau: Passavia.

G. E. Müller: The Third Pillar of Experimental Psychology

Peter J. Behrens

The year is 1905. Scientific psychology is in its formative years, yet considerable research is available in both journal and textbook form, particularly on the psychology of the senses, visual perception, and memory. You are going to write a textbook on the experimental psychology of your day. You know the two most important contributors who must be referenced in your book. These are, of course, Wilhelm Wundt (1832–1920), the founder of the first laboratory of experimental psychology at Leipzig University, and his elder, Gustav Fechner (1801–1887), the founder of psychophysics, who also held a position at Leipzig. But who is the next most important figure? Who takes the place as the third most significant contributor to experimental psychology at the turn of the 20th century? Is it Hermann Ebbinghaus (1850–1909), the founder of research on verbal memory; William James (1842–1910), the philosopher-psychologist; G. Stanley Hall (1844–1924), who established psychology at The Johns Hopkins University; Hugo Münsterberg (1863–1916), who brought experimental methods to America; or, perhaps, John Watson (1878–1958), the founder of behaviorism?

Figure 1 Panoramic view of the old, inner city of Göttingen (ca. 1930).

Figure 2 An old engraving of the location of the Psychological Institute of Göttingen University at Paulinerstraße.

When this question was posed in an informal poll at a gathering of colleagues of the psychology department of a large university (whose identity shall not be revealed), there was general agreement (70%) that Wilhelm Wundt held considerable prominence within the history of experimental psychology; and a few identified Fechner (20%). But no one identified Georg Elias Müller (1850–1934), a contemporary of Wundt, Fechner, and Ebbinghaus. But for his time, Müller was, with the possible exception of Wundt, the most influential and prolific contributor to experimental psychology.

The hypothetical textbook in this discussion was, in fact, an important work written by E. B. Titchener (1867–1927), titled *Experimental Psychology* (1905). Titchener referenced Müller 88 times, the third largest number of entries, superseded only by references to Wundt and Fechner in total number. Further, Titchener had to delay the publication of his text to take into account a major work by Müller which had appeared in print one year earlier (Boring, 1957; Müller, 1904).

Today, the name of G. E. Müller no longer carries with it the recognition it had in earlier years. Introductory textbooks in psychology (e.g., Atkinson, Atkinson, Smith, & Bem, 1990; Lahey, 1995; Zimbardo & Weber, 1994) and even some texts in the history of psychology (e.g., Fancher, 1990; Sahakian, 1968; Wertheimer, 1970) fail to mention Müller. Ironi-

cally, Müller himself may have contributed to his own fading recognition.

Müller's legacy is obscured partly because of his own penchant for contribution without notoriety (Katz, 1935), and partly because many of his ideas about memory, perception, and vision have been so completely absorbed into the fabric of modern psychology (Boring, 1957). But a third reason for Müller's lack of recognition today is that none of his major works is accessible in English translation (Behrens, 1978). Indeed, at the turn of the century, when European experimental psychology began to embrace the contributions of research conducted at the prominent American university laboratories, Müller doggedly remained relatively isolated at Göttingen University in Germany among like-minded colleagues and students. He also relied exclusively on the prominent German-language journals of his day, forgoing English-language journals, to disseminate his work. Although his original ideas about visual perception, memory, imagery, localization, psychophysical theory, sensory processes, and color vision significantly influenced experimental psychology during the years between his doctoral dissertation from Leipzig University (Müller, 1873) and his posthumous *Contribution to Eidetics* (Müller, 1935), this author of 40 articles and books is today an anomaly, distanced by the formidable barriers of time, culture, and language from the psychology he

Table 1 A Catalog of G. E. Müller's Forty Publications

Topic	Date(s) of Publication
The Aubert Phenomenon	1915
Eidetics	1935
The Elberfelder Horses	1915
C. Ladd Franklin's Theory of Color Sensations	1928
E. R. Jaensch's View of Visual Perception	1923
Remarks to W. Koehler	1926
The Liebmann Effect	1934
Memory and Imagery	1893, 1900, 1904, 1911, 1912 (2), 1913 (2), 1917
Correction to Muensterberg	1893
Outline of Psychology	1924
Psychophysics	1878, 1879, 1889, 1896, 1899, 1900, 1903
Sensation and Physiology	1873, 1889, 1894, 1924, 1925
Visual Perception	1897 (2), 1904, 1922, 1923, 1924, 1930, 1931, 1934 (2)

helped to shape. Table 1 presents a catalog of Müller's publications.

Müller's School of Psychology

At least one visitor to Müller's laboratory at Göttingen University observed that it was the best research facility in all of Germany (Krohn, 1893). In concert with this commendation, more than 40 years later in his obituary of Müller, E. G. Boring remarked that Müller had operated the finest laboratory for psychological research in Prussia (Boring, 1935). These observations do more than document a research facility of consistently high quality. They are typical of the general high regard in which Müller and his laboratory were held in experimental psychology over an impressive span of 40 years between 1881 and 1921.

G. E. Müller was born in Saxony, Germany, and studied philosophy and history at Leipzig University. There he was influenced by the philosophy of Johannes Herbart (1776–1841), which proposed that psychology is a science, grounded in experience, metaphysics, and mathematics (Boring, 1957). After a period of enlistment in the army during the Franco-Prussian War, Müller returned to Leipzig for a year and then went to Göttingen, where he met Hermann Lotze (1817–1881). Müller became a student of Lotze, and Lotze's influence on Müller was lasting, showing him the importance of physiology for perception and the associationistic qualities of perception. Müller dedicated his 1878 work, *Fundamentals of Psychophysics*, to Lotze (Müller, 1878).

But Müller was never the philosopher that Lotze, or Lotze's predecessor at Göttingen, Herbart, had been. Müller never wrote a philosophical treatise, and he only adopted a philosophical perspective in order to pursue his real interest, which was laboratory experimentation on vision, psychophysics, and memory. To this end he devoted his Göttingen laboratory. He attracted a large number of students in the process and trained many prominent psychologists of the late 19th and early 20th centuries. These included Hans Rupp, Adolf Jost, Eleanor Gramble, David Katz, E. R. Jaensch, Edgar Rubin, and Harry Helson (Boring, 1957).

To his contemporaries, Müller was the master experimentalist and methodologist in three areas of experimental psychology: the study of memory, visual perception (including color vision), and psychophysics. Influenced by Ebbinghaus's experimental study of human memory, Müller derived his initial work from this tradition but added an introspective component to Ebblinghaus's associationistic account of learning and recall. He found that learning and recall for his subjects involved active processes such as grouping, rhythms, and generally conscious organizational strategies for the verbal tasks (Watson, 1978). Müller also, with his student Schumann, invented the memory drum for the study of verbal learning (Müller & Schumann, 1893). With Pilzecker, he devised the interference theory of forgetting, particularly the concept of retroactive inhibition, which stated that new learnings can interfere with old ones (Müller & Pilzecker, 1900).

For visual perception, Müller contributed to the psychology and physiology of the sense organs (Müller, 1894; 1896), visual imagery (e.g., Müller, 1911, 1912), and color theory (e.g., Müller, 1922, 1930). Müller followed Ewald Hering's (1834–1918) three-process theory of color vision (black-white, red-green, blue-yellow) but considered it to be a chemical, not a metabolic, process, as Hering had proposed. Müller also added to color theory the concept of "cortical gray," the zero point from which color sensations derive (Boring, 1942: Müller, 1897). As with memory, Müller's observations led him to propose that perceptions are not only influenced by expectations, images, and feelings, but also by mental events that cannot be so clearly categorized: readiness, hesitation, doubt, and other "attitudes."

Müller's third field of research was his most ambitious. After Fechner, Müller's work in psychophysics stands out as the most significant in the history of experimental psychology. His research program at Göttingen was a thorough refinement of Fechner's methods. For example, although Fechner had developed the method of right and wrong cases, Müller expanded the stimulus values, applied the statistical method of least squares, and used probability theory for judgments (Boring, 1942; Müller, 1879). Lillien Martin, a student with Müller from 1894 to 1898, collaborated with him on the definitive study of the psychophysics of lifted weights (Müller & Martin, 1899). This followed an earlier study by Müller and Schumann on the mechanism of discrimination of lifted weights, in which they contended that a second weight is judged heavier or lighter than a preceding one because the subject exerts the same effort ("Einstellung"), or set, for the second weight as the first. This Einstellung, they concluded, is unconscious until its effect is noticed (Müller & Schumann, 1889).

Müller's views of the importance of mental activity, organization, set, and strategies appear remarkably similar to the propositions for psychological judgment developed by the Gestalt psychology of Koehler, Koffka, and Wertheimer. In fact, Müller was less than enthusiastic (some would say hostile) about Gestaltpsychologie and placed his own Komplextheorie (structure theory) in opposition to it (Müller, 1923). He held fast to the physiological and sensory elements of perception and outright rejected such phenomenological constructs as figure, ground, and contour, even though his students Jaensch, Katz, and Rubin did not (Boring, 1957).

Müller further proposed that there was nothing new in the Gestalt approach to perceptual theory that could not be explained by his research from the Göttingen laboratory (Marx & Hillix, 1963).

Figure 3 Georg Elias Müller (ca. 1935).

The Legacy of G. E. Müller

The immediate influence—and decline in influence—of Müller on psychology can be measured in various ways. Mention has already been made of his importance for American psychology as perceived and documented by E. B. Titchener at the turn of the century. On the occasion of his death in 1934 at the age of 84, journal obituaries on Müller appeared in four languages: English, Dutch, French, and German. Müller's most famous student, David Katz (1884–1953), was responsible for two of them, and E. G. Boring (1886–1968) for one.

Katz's accounts, one in English (Katz, 1935a) and one in German (Katz, 1935b), are highly personal and reflect the respect and admiration of a student for his professor and mentor. The obituary by Boring (1935), while more objective and typical of his penchant for factual detail, also provides the only autobiographical material by Müller (which nevertheless still required translation from German to English by D. W. Chapman). By his own account in these letters written to Boring in 1931, Müller identified psychophysics, memory, and visual perception as the three research interests for which he wished to be remembered. In addition, he revealed his penchant for defining psychology in the language of the laboratory:

> As for psychology, I was of the opinion that a student could get a true mastery of psychology only if there was given him besides the lectures in general psychology a series of special lectures and recitation courses, in which he might be made more familiar with psychological thinking and experiment. (Boring, 1935, p. 346)

Not surprising is the fact that in the decades following his death, references to Müller first increased dramatically, and then, just as dramatically, decreased. Figure 4 presents the results of a citation analysis of 57 English-language texts of experimental psychology published between 1930 and 1989. Citations of Müller peaked in the decade 1950–1959 and diminished thereafter, even though the number of texts published rose markedly between 1950 and 1989. If the frequency of citations to Müller had remained constant, then the two lines in Figure 4 would be nearly parallel over the decades. Since the lines diverge after the decade of the 1950s, the interpretation can be made that Müller's direct influence on experimental psychology has essentially vanished. A similar "decay" in citation frequency has been noted with regard to Wundt's experimental papers in the *American Journal of Psychology* between 1887 and 1977 (Brožek, 1980).

Much of the trend in the decline of Müller's influence can, of course, be attributed to the changes in the subject matter of experimental psychology, which has moved away from the traditional study of psychophysics, sensory processes, and narrowly defined human memory. This is especially important in Müller's case because of his emphasis on contributions to methodology, rather than psychological theory. In addition, note needs to be taken again that whatever recognition Müller has among English-speaking psychologists today is achieved

without the benefit of a complete translation of any of his major works. Indeed, until recently, even an accounting of his publication record was inconsistently documented (Behrens, 1978). At the same time, however, Müller's focus on exactness, objective science, and the importance of physiology for psychology formed the bases for his criticisms of other research programs. These are highly significant qualities and should not be overlooked as lasting contributions to experimental psychology.

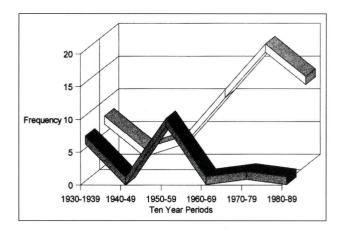

Figure 4 References to G. E. Müller's writings in American textbooks of experimental psychology (1930–1989). Bar in foreground represents the number of citations; in background, the number of textbooks published.

Bibliography

Atkinson, R. L., Atkinson, R. C., Smith, E. E., & Bem, D. J. (1990). *Introduction to psychology* (10th ed.). San Diego, CA: Harcourt Brace Jovanovich.

Behrens, P. J. (1978). Bibliography of the works of G. E. Müller. *JSAS Catalog of Selected Documents in Psychology, 8* (28), (Ms. No. 1669).

Boring, E. G. (1935). Georg Elias Müller: 1850–1934. *American Journal of Psychology, 25,* 110–114.

Boring, E. G. (1942). *Sensation and perception in the history of experimental psychology.* New York: Appleton-Century-Crofts.

Boring, E. G. (1957). *History of experimental psychology.* New York: Appleton-Century-Crofts.

Brožek, J. (1980). The echoes of Wundt's work in the United States, 1887–1977: A quantitative citation analysis. *Psychological Research, 42,* 103–107.

Fancher, R. E. (1990). *Pioneers of psychology.* New York: W. W. Norton.

Katz, D. (1935a). Georg Elias Müller. *Acta Psychologia, 1,* 234–240.

Katz, D. (1935b). Georg Elias Müller. *Psychological Bulletin, 32,* 377–380.

Krohn, W. O. (1893). The laboratory of the Psychological Institute at the University of Göttingen. *American Journal of Psychology, 5,* 282–284.

Lahey, B. B. (1995). *Psychology: An introduction.* Madison, WI: Brown & Benchmark.

Marx, M. H., & Hillix, W. A. (1963). *Systems and theories in psychology.* New York: McGraw-Hill.

Müller, G. E. (1873). *Zur Theorie der sinnlichen Aufmerksamkeit* [On the theory of sensory attention]. Unpublished doctoral dissertation, Leipzig University.

Müller, G. E. (1878). *Zur Grundlegung der Psychophysik* [Fundamentals of psychophysics]. Berlin: T. Grieben.

Müller, G. E. (1879). Über die Maasbestimmungen des Ortsinnes der Haut [Measurements of sensitivity of areas of the skin]. *Archiv für die gesamte Physiologie, 19*, 191–235.

Müller, G. E. (1894). *Beiträge zur Psychologie und Physiologie der Sinnesorgane* [Contributions to the psychology and physiology of the sense organs]. Göttingen.

Müller, G. E. (1896). Zur Psychophysik der Gesichtsempfindungen I–III [The psychophysics of visual sensations I–III]. *Zeitschrift für Psychologie und Physiologie der Sinnesorgane, 10*, 1–82, 321–413.

Müller, G. E. (1897). Zur Psychophysik der Gesichtsempfindungen IV–VI [The psychophysics of visual sensations IV–VI]. *Zeitschrift für Psychologie und Physiologie der Sinnesorgane, 14*, 1–76, 161–193.

Müller, G. E. (1904). Die Theorie der Gegenfarben und die Farbenblindheit [The theory of complementary colors and color blindness]. *Bericht I. Kongress der experimentellen Psychologie*, 6–10.

Müller, G. E. (1911). Zur Analyse der Gedaechtnistaetigkeit und der Vorstellungsverlaufes I [An analysis of memorial activity and the process of imagery I]. *Zeitschrift für Psychologie, 5.* Supplement

Müller, G. E. (1912). Über die Lokalization der visuellen Vorstellungsbilder [On the localization of visual images]. *Bericht V. Kongress der experimentellen Psychologie*, 216–222.

Müller, G. E. (1922). Zur Theorie des Staebchenapparates und der Zapfenblindheit [A theory of the rod mechanism and cone blindness]. *Zeitschrift für Sinnesphysiologie, 54*, 9–48, 102–145.

Müller, G. E. (1923). *Komplextheorie und Gestalttheorie. Ein Beitrag für Wahrnehmungspsychologie* [Structure theory and Gestalt theory: A contribution to the psychology of perception]. Göttingen.

Müller, G. E. (1930). Über die Farbenempfindungen. Psychologische Untersuchungen [On color sensations: Psychological investigations]. *Zeitschrift für Psychologie,* Supplement *17, 18.*

Müller, G. E. (1935). Ein Beitrag zur Eidetik [A contribution to eidetics]. *Zeitschrift für Psychologie, 134*, 1–24.

Müller, G. E., & Martin, L. J. (1899). *Zur Analyse der Unterschiedsempfindlichkeit* [An analysis of sensitivity to difference]. Leipzig: Barth.

Müller, G. E., & Pilzecker, A. (1900). Experimentelle Beiträge zur Lehre vom Gedächtniss [Experimental contributions to the theory of memory]. *Zeitschrift für Psychologie, 1.* Supplement

Müller, G. E., & Schumann, F. (1889). Ueber die psychologischen Grundlagen der Vergleichung gehobener Gewichte [On the psychological bases of lifted weight comparisons]. *Archiv fuer die gesamte Physiologie, 45*, 37–112.

Müller, G. E., & Schumann, F. (1893). Experimentelle Beiträge zur Untersuchungen des Gedächtnisses [Experimental contributions to the investigation of memory]. *Zeitschrift für Psychologie und Physiologie der Sinnesorgane, 6*, 81–190, 257–339.

Sahakian, W. S. (Ed.). (1968). *History of psychology: A sourcebook in systematic psychology*. Itasca, IL: F. E. Peacock.

Titchener, E. B. (1905). *Experimental psychology*. New York: Macmillan.

Watson, R. I. (Ed.). (1978). *Eminent contributors to psychology*. New York: Springer.

Wertheimer, M. (1970). *A brief history of psychology*. New York: Holt, Rinehart & Winston.

Zimbardo, P. G., & Weber, A. L. (1994). *Psychology*. New York: Harper Collins.

The Würzburg School of Psychology

Wolfgang G. Mack

The name "Würzburg School" refers to a group of scholars at Würzburg University in Germany who were led by the experimental psychologist and philosopher Oswald Külpe (1862–1915). During the first decade of the 20th century, the "Würzburgers" initiated the experimental study of "higher mental" functions by studying the psychological processes of thought and volition in the psychological laboratory. As a result, their work contributed significantly to the development of modern cognitive and motivational psychology.

Leading Representatives of the Würzburg School

In 1894, Oswald Külpe was appointed to a full professorship of philosophy at Würzburg. Previously, he had worked from 1887 to 1894, first as an assistant in Wilhelm Wundt's (1832–1920) laboratory, and then as an instructor and untenured professor at Leipzig University. In 1896, Külpe established his own psychological laboratory at Würzburg, which made it one of the earliest and later, among the most important, experimental facilities in Germany.

Külpe's students and associates included the following eminent psychologists: Narziß Ach (1871–1946), Karl Bühler (1879–1963), Karl Marbe (1869–1953), August Mayer (1874–1951), August Messer (1867–1937), Johannes Orth (1872–1949), Otto Selz (1881–1943), and Henry J. Watts (1879–1925). There were also a few psychologists, who later became well known, who completed their degrees under Külpe or worked in his Würzburg laboratory. These included Max Wertheimer (1880–1943), Kurt Koffka (1886–1941), Richard Pauli (1886–1951), and Charles Spearman (1863–1945). Other, lesser-known associates of Külpe included

Johannes Lindworsky (1875–1939), Anton Grünbaum (1885–1932), Ernst Dürr (1878–1913), and Friedrich Schulze (1872–1950).

Figure 1 Oswald Külpe.

Research Methods at Würzburg

Systematic experimental introspection or self-observation was the chief research method at Würzburg. This method employed carefully trained experimental subjects who often were university professors. All subjects were asked to report in full detail what sensations and images they experienced during their participation in an experimental task. The results were recorded in the form of an "experiential protocol." Reaction times were usually recorded

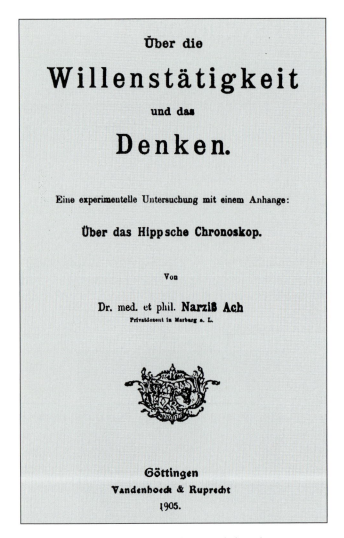

Figure 2 Title page of Ach's *Volition and Thought* (1905).

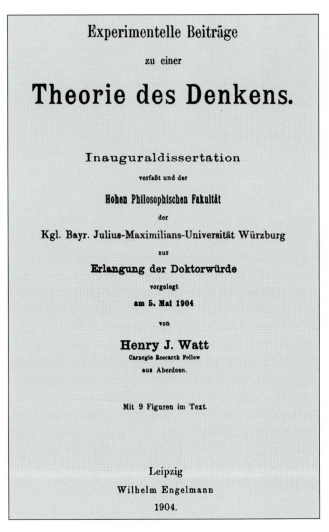

Figure 3 Title page of Watt's dissertation "Experimental Contributions to a Theory of Thought" (1904).

but, as a rule, not subjected to the same sort of introspective, psychological analysis. The research techniques that were used to collect data included free and controlled word association techniques (i.e., naming of superordinate or generic terms involving verbal as well as nonverbal materials), reaction time and choice reaction time experiments, psychophysical tasks (i.e., weight judgments), puzzles, and word problems.

Research on Imageless Thoughts

The most important studies of the Würzburg school were carried out from 1901 to 1908. Of all the research conducted, only the most important experimental findings of the Würzburg School can be summarized in this article; however, a full account can be found in Humphrey's excellent and comprehensive monograph (1951) about the history of cognitive psychology and, especially, the Würzburg school.

In one of the most significant early studies, Mayer and Orth (1901) classified their subjects' associations logically as well as psychologically (i.e., experience of sensations and images). In this context, they discovered cognitive experiences, which did not fit into the customary schema of psychological categories because they totally lacked any sensory and imaginary characteristics. Following William James (1842–1910), Mayer and Orth labeled the above experiences as "state of consciousness" (Humphrey, 1951). Marbe (1901) confirmed the existence of the "state of consciousness." He also noted that the process of judgment is frequently "imageless" and that logical judg-

Table 1 Würzburg Research Paradigm

Controlled Introspection		Introspective Protocol		
Stages of Problem Solving	Preparation for Task	Posing of Task	Thinking about Task	Solution of Task (Reaction)
Mechanism: Setting Up of Task		Determining Tendency	Unconscious Facilitation of Solution	

ments cannot always be reduced to psychological experiences.

In 1904, Külpe demonstrated the selective function of a "task" for producing a specific reaction. He used the term "positive abstraction" as a label for the subject's attention to task-relevant stimuli. The process of disregarding task-irrelevant stimuli was called "negative abstraction" (Watt, 1904). By identifying a task as a motive (or "determining tendency") with the reproductive tendency, both Watt (1904) and Ach (1905) tried to refute traditional associationistic explanations of cognition. Specifically, these researchers demonstrated that a task can serve as an abstract goal, which ultimately can alter resulting ideas, reaction times, and thought processes. Shortly thereafter, in 1906, Messer equated the concept "state of consciousness" with thought. However, he distinguished between developed and undeveloped thoughts and stressed that thoughts were for the most part unconscious.

Bühler (1907, 1908a) defined thoughts as basic units of cognition, which could not be analyzed further and which were largely independent of words and perceptual experience. He argued that the recall of thoughts and the comprehension of aphorisms could not be explained through simple association (the contiguity principle), but rather depended on a knowledge of rules and relationships. Human understanding or comprehension is typically expressed by the proverbial "aha experience" of insight, which gives little conscious awareness of the processes leading up

to it. Furthermore, Bühler believed that human thought is characterized by three components: rule consciousness, awareness of relationships, and intentions.

The Würzburg school did indeed succeed in refuting naive associationism. However, it was Selz who developed a complete nonassociationistic theory of cognition. In 1909, Külpe accepted a professorial appointment at Bonn, where Bühler became his assistant and Selz carried out his important research into cognitive psychology. It was at Bonn University that Selz and Bühler formulated their dynamic approach to thought by regarding it as a special form of problem solving. Selz conceptualized thinking as a continuum of productive and reproductive intellectual operations. Knowledge, in turn, was defined as a structure of varying degrees of complexity. A problem was defined as an incomplete structure of knowledge. Gaps or blanks in the structure could be completed or filled by "determined" mediating abstractions. Finally, Selz's view

Figure 4 Watt's experimental setup.

Figure 5 Otto Selz.

Figure 6 August Messer.

of the "total task as a schematic anticipation of goal awareness" anticipated future concepts such as problem space and means-ends analysis.

Evaluation of the Würzburg School

The members of the Würzburg school initiated the experimental psychology of cognition and volition. Although their methods, especially the use of introspection, are quite incomplete from our modern perspective, they demonstrated, nonetheless, that "higher mental functions" could be studied experimentally. A rather polemic controversy that developed between Bühler and Wundt about the basic methodology of cognitive research, specifically about the role of introspection (Wundt, 1907; Bühler, 1908b), is still an open question (Ericsson & Crutcher, 1991). Nevertheless, one must agree with Bühler that introspection should have the same status as any other "normal" observation, since both must eventually be interpreted (Bühler, 1907).

It is quite possible that the really significant contribution of the Würzburg school stems from its introduction of phenomenological problems and perspectives into the field of cognitive psychology

Figure 7 Karl Marbe (1909).

(Reusser, 1983). Of course, other philosophical roots of cognitive psychology should not be overlooked, such as the influence of Franz Brentano (1838–1917) and Edmund Husserl (1859–1938). Lindenfeld (1978) and Hammer (1990) have recently documented that Külpe's philosophical outlook remained an essential source of his psychological work. The aggregate writings of Külpe, Bühler, and Selz make it very clear that the leaders of the Würzburg school always viewed themselves as philosophical psychologists.

Bibliography

Ach, N. (1905). *Über die Willenstätigkeit und das Denken*. Göttingen: Vandenhoeck & Ruprecht.

Bühler, K. (1907). Tatsachen und Probleme zu einer Psychologie der Denkvorgänge. I. Über Gedanken. *Archiv für die gesamte Psychologie, 9*, 297–365.

Bühler, K. (1908a). Tatsachen und Probleme zu einer Psychologie der Denkvorgänge. II. Über Gedankenzusammenhänge. III. Gedankenerinnerungen. *Archiv für die gesamte Psychologie, 12*, 1–23; 24–92.

Bühler, K. (1908b). Antwort auf die von W. Wundt erhobenen Einwände gegen die Methode der Selbstbeobachtung an experimentell erzeugten Erlebnissen. *Archiv für die gesamte Psychologie, 12*, 93–122.

Ericsson, K. A., & Crutcher, R. J. (1991). Introspection and verbal reports on cognitive processes—Two approaches to the study of thinking: A response to Howe. *New Ideas in Psychology, 9*, 57–71.

Hammer, S. (1990). *Denkpsychologie-Kritischer Realismus. Eine wissenschaftshistorische Studie zum Werk Oswald Külpes (1862–1915) unter Beachtung wissenschaftstheoretischer Aspekte*. Dissertation, Martin-Luther-Universität Halle-Wittenberg.

Humphrey, G. (1951). *Thinking*. London: Methuen.

Külpe, O. (1904). Versuche über Abstraktion. In *Bericht über den I. Kongreß für experimentelle Psychologie in Gießen 1904*. Leipzig: Barth.

Lindenfeld, D. (1978). Oswald Külpe and the Würzburg School. *Journal of the History of the Behavioral Sciences, 14*, 132–141.

Marbe, K. (1901). *Experimentell-psychologische Untersuchungen über das Urteil*. Leipzig: Engelmann.

Mayer, A., & Orth, J. (1901). Zur qualitativen Untersuchung der Assoziationen. *Zeitschrift für Psychologie, 26*, 1–13.

Messer, A. (1906). Experimentell-psychologische Untersuchungen über das Denken. *Archiv für die gesamte Psychologie, 8*, 1–224.

Reusser, K. (1983). Die kognitive Wende in der Psychologie: Eine Annäherung an phänomenologische und geisteswissenschaftliche Problemstellungen. In L. Montada, K. Reusser, & G. Steiner (Eds.), *Kognition und Handeln*. Stuttgart: Klett-Cotta.

Selz, O. (1913). *Über die Gesetze des geordneten Denkverlaufes. Eine experimentelle Untersuchung*. Stuttgart: Speemann.

Selz, O. (1922). *Zur Psychologie des produktiven Denkens und des Irrtums*. Bonn: Cohen.

Watt, H. J. (1904). *Experimentelle Beiträge zu einer Psychologie des Denkens*. Leipzig: Engelmann.

Wundt, W. (1907). Über Ausfrageexperimente und über die Methoden zur Psychologie des Denkens. *Psychologische Studien, 3*, 301–360.

The Experimental Analysis of Volition

Heinz-Dieter Schmalt

The experimental analysis of volition was initiated by Narziss Kaspar Ach (1871–1946), an eminent German experimental psychologist, at the beginning of the 20th century. Ach (1913) was primarily interested in learning more about the phenomenological aspects of the process of volition.

Ach was born on October 29, 1871, in the village of Ermershausen in the Kingdom of Bavaria. He received his medical doctorate from Würzburg University in 1895 and afterwards worked temporarily as a ship's physician. He completed a psychiatric residency at Heidelberg University under Emil Kraepelin (1856–1926) and worked in the Pharmacological Institute of Straßburg from 1896 to 1899. Afterwards, Ach returned to Würzburg to study psychology under the Wundt student Oswald Külpe (1862–1915). Ach received his first PhD in 1899 at Würzburg and his second in 1902 at Göttingen University under the famous experimentalist Georg Elias Müller (1850–1934).

During the next six years, Ach held low-paying instructorships at Göttingen (1902–1904), Marburg (1904–1906), and Berlin University (1906–1907). Finally, in 1907, he received an appointment as Professor of Philosophy and Director of the Philosophical Seminar at Königsberg University in East Prussia. In 1922, at the age of 51, he was called to Göttingen University to succeed G. E. Müller. He retired in 1937 and died on January 4, 1946, in Munich. Apart from his books and publications, Ach received more than 50 patents for his inventions of technical instruments, including a gyrocompass. In fact, it has been suggested that technical ingenuity was one of Ach's chief personality traits (Düker, 1966).

According to Ach, the act of volition or will has

Figure 1 Portrait of Narziss Ach.

four phenomenological attributes, which he called aspects or moments. The two most important of these parameters are the objective aspect and the ego-related aspect. The objective aspect specifies both the goal, which a person wants to reach, and the conditions under which adequate goal-directed behavior can take place. On the other hand, the ego-related aspect indicates that an individual is strongly committed to actually reaching a goal. Thus, according to Ach, each volitional act involves conscious awareness of a goal, an opportunity to take proper goal-directed action, and a personal commitment to be successful.

It was Ach's unique contribution to endow the mental representations of these aspects with dynamic properties, which he called the determining tendency. This tendency can best be thought of as an automatic process which controls subjective experience and ongoing behavior to ensure that an intended goal will be reached. The strength of a determining tendency is a positive linear function of the difficulty of the anticipated goal. Hence, the more difficult the goal is to reach, the stronger the determining tendency and the higher the actual expenditure of energy. This relationship has been called the *motivation law of difficulty*. The basic assumptions Ach made about the dynamic interplay between the determining tendency and the difficulty of goal achievement encouraged the development of special experimental methods for studying the volitional processes. Specifically, systematic variations in goal difficulty served as the independent variable. In turn, changes of the individual's success level were chosen as the dependent variable.

During his brief association with Marburg University (1904–1906) as an untenured instructor, Ach discovered that changes in task difficulty could be produced by creating a type of inner resistance against the determining tendency. The actual experimental procedure went as follows: First, subjects were asked to memorize pairs of nonsense syllables, and the number of acquisition trials necessary was used as a measure of the strength of association between the syllables. Next, subjects with different levels of acquisition trials were shown the first of the two syllables again but under somewhat different conditions. During this second phase of the experiment, subjects were told not to retrieve the second syllable but to unscramble the letters of the second syllable. In this manner, the intention to unscramble the second syllable was counteracted by the tendency to merely reproduce it. Thus conflict between the determining and reproductive tendencies was produced. The strength of the conflict could be veri-

fied experimentally by changing the number of acquisition trials. After a certain level of conflict had been reached, increases in the number of errors and reaction times confirmed that the determining tendency was no longer effective.

During the first phase of the experiment, all syllables were presented by means of a memory drum. In the second stage of the experiment, the first syllable was presented alone. The interval between the presentation of the first syllable and the subject's response with the decoded second syllable was recorded by a Hipp chronoscope (Ach, 1905). This apparatus allowed for measurements as precise as ±1/1000 sec.

During his early Königsberg years, Ach improved his research methodology by employing and inventing equipment for the continuous presentation of stimulus materials and the simultaneous recording of responses. This novel approach, which Ach called the "serial method" (Ach, 1912), made it possible to force the subject to work faster by systematically reducing the interstimulus intervals. It was assumed that the reduction of the interstimulus intervals would in turn increase the strength of the determining tendency to reach the intended performance level. While Ach's serial method made the creation of internal resistances unnecessary, it unfortunately also prevented the observation and recording of the phenomenological aspects of volition (Ach & Düker, 1934).

Three types of apparatus were required to run the new volition experiments (Ach, 1912, p. 4): (1) a serial apparatus for presenting the stimulus materials, (2) a reaction time apparatus for continuous registration of the responses, and (3) a chronometer. Figure 2 (above) shows an instrument for the registration of verbal productions with a kind of megaphone. The stimuli were printed on a paper tape and exposed at prearranged interstimulus intervals. The responses were recorded by the chronograph. This instrument was driven by a clockwork mechanism that moved and controlled the big recording drum (Figure 3). Later, Ach built an even larger apparatus which could run up to 15 minutes and during that time draw a curve of 900 meters on the paper tape that was attached to the drum.

After moving to Göttingen University, Ach and his assistant Heinrich Düker (1898–1987) modified the serial method equipment to permit the study of the

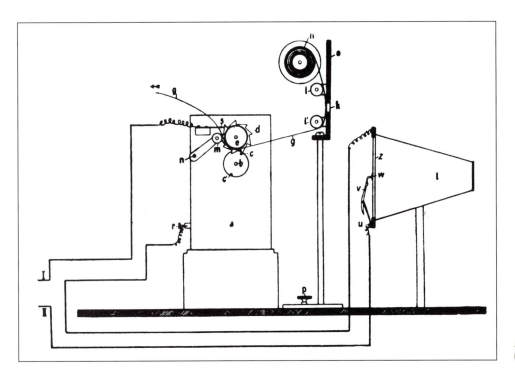

Figure 2 Serial apparatus (Ach, 1912).

determining tendency in voluntary and "assembly-line" work (Düker, 1931; Ach & Düker, 1934). In his autobiography, Düker recalled that some of the Göttingen equipment was primitive and that Ach's chronotyper (Figure 4) was clumsy and "noisy like a machine gun" (1972, p. 48). A few years later, this instrument was presented in a handsome casing. The chronotyper measured diverse, consecutive responses and printed the related response times on a paper tape. Since it could be used to record multi-

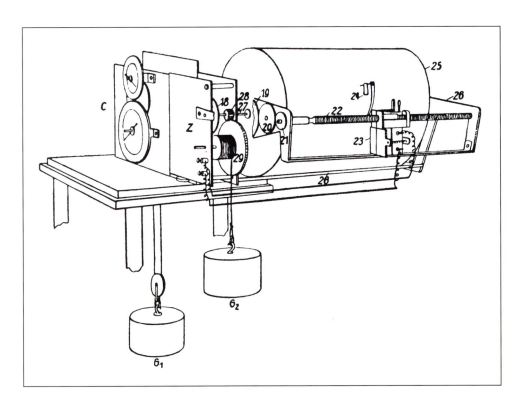

Figure 3 Chronoscope-chronograph (Ach, 1912).

Figure 4 Chronotyper (Ach & Düker, 1934).

Figure 5 Portrait of Düker.

ple parallel responses, its invention constituted a remarkable technical advance for the period.

Düker did not carry on his teacher's pure research, but concentrated instead on the investigation of motivational factors in assembly-line work (1931). Specifically, he was interested in strategies that individuals used to reach self-initiated goals. Düker was unable to complete this interesting research, however, because in 1936, he lost his academic appointment as Ach's assistant at Göttingen for political reasons. As an active member of the opposition Social Democratic Party, Düker was imprisoned by the Nazis from 1936 to 1939 and from 1944 to 1945. Düker received his first appointment as a full professor in the fall of 1946, at Marburg University, where he remained until his retirement in 1967. The bulk of Düker's work on volition was not published until 1975.

In conclusion, the psychology of volition, which began with the original and important work of

Narziss Ach and Heinrich Düker during the early decades of our century, has long been neglected by experimental psychologists in Germany and elsewhere (Kornadt, 1988; Tent, 1988). It is our hope that this important research tradition will eventually be recognized once again by modern researchers and integrated into contemporary motivational research.

Bibliography

Ach, N. (1905). *Über die Willenstätigkeit und das Denken.* Göttingen: Vandenhoeck & Ruprecht.

Ach, N. (1912). Eine Serienmethode für Reaktionsversuche. Bemerkungen zur Untersuchung des Willens. In *Untersuchungen zur Psychologie und Philosophie* (Vol. 1, No. 5). Leipzig: Quelle & Meyer.

Ach, N. (1913). Wille. In E. Korschelt, G. Linck, F. Oltmanns, K. Schaum, H. T. Simon, M. Verworn, & E. Teichmann (Ed.), *Handwörterbuch der Naturwissenscchaften* (Vol. 10, pp. 619–628). Jena: Fischer.

Ach, N., & Düker, H. (1934). Über Methoden und Apparaturen zur Untersuchung fortlaufender Arbeitsprozesse. *Zeitschrift für Psychologie, 133*(4–6), 209–221.

Düker, H. (1925). Über das Gesetz der speziellen Determination. Ein experimenteller Beitrag zur Lehre vom Willen. Untersuchungen zur Psychologie. *Philosophie und Pädagogik, 5,* 97–174.

Düker, H. (1931). Psychologische Untersuchungen über freie und zwangsläufige Arbeit. Experimentelle Beiträge zur Willens- und Arbeitspsychologie. *Zeitschrift für Psychologie,* Erg.-Bd. 20.

Düker, H. (1966). Narziss Ach (1871–1946) zum Gedenken. *Archiv für die gesamte Psychologie, 118,* 189–194.

Düker, H. (1972). Heinrich Düker. In L. J. Pongratz, W. Traxel, & E. G. Wehner (Ed.), *Psychologie in Selbstdarstellungen* (pp. 43–86). Bern: Huber.

Düker, H. (1975). *Untersuchungen über die Ausbildung des Wollens.* Bern: Huber.

Kornadt, H.-J. (1988). Motivation und Volition. Anmerkungen und Fragen zur wiederbelebten Willenspsychologie. *Archiv für Psychologie, 140,* 209–222.

Tent, L. (1988). Heinrich Düker: dem Wegbereiter und Bewahrer zum Gedenken. *Archiv für Psychologie, 140,* 143–148.

Margaret Floy Washburn

Ronda J. Carpenter

Margaret Floy Washburn, the first American woman to receive a PhD in psychology, is best remembered as the author of *The Animal Mind* (1908). First published when she was 37 years old, this textbook of comparative psychology went through four editions, the last in 1936, and was regarded by Boring (1950) as the classical text in the field. She is also remembered for her work with

Figure 1 Margaret Floy Washburn.

undergraduate students at Vassar College, where she established a laboratory and taught from 1903 to 1937 (Scarborough & Furumoto, 1987; Stevens & Gardner, 1982).

Born in New York City, July 25, 1871, Washburn was the only child of affluent parents. By her own account, she was a prodigious reader whose intellectual life began on her fifth birthday (Washburn, 1932/1961). She began high school at the age of 12 and started her studies at Vassar College at the age of 15. At the end of her senior year at Vassar, Washburn became excited about the "wonderful new science of experimental psychology," which she believed combined science and philosophy, her "two dominant intellectual interests" (Washburn, 1932/1961, p. 338). She applied to become a student of James McKeen Cattell (1860–1944) at Columbia University but was admitted only as a "hearer," because Columbia did not admit women as graduate students. She was, however, well-received by Cattell, who she reported "treated me as a regular student and required of me all that he required of the men" (p. 339).

In 1892, Washburn went to Cornell University where she became E. B. Titchener's first doctoral student. While at Cornell, Washburn conducted research on perception. Her doctoral thesis on the influence of visual imagery on judgments of tactual distance and direction was published by Wundt in *Philosophische Studien*, and she was granted the PhD by Cornell in 1894.

Washburn did not identify herself as a structuralist. Though she "accepted the general point of view of what Titchener called structural psychology" (Washburn, 1932/1961, p. 343), she had doubts about Titchener's elaborate introspective method and how it turned conscious states into "something

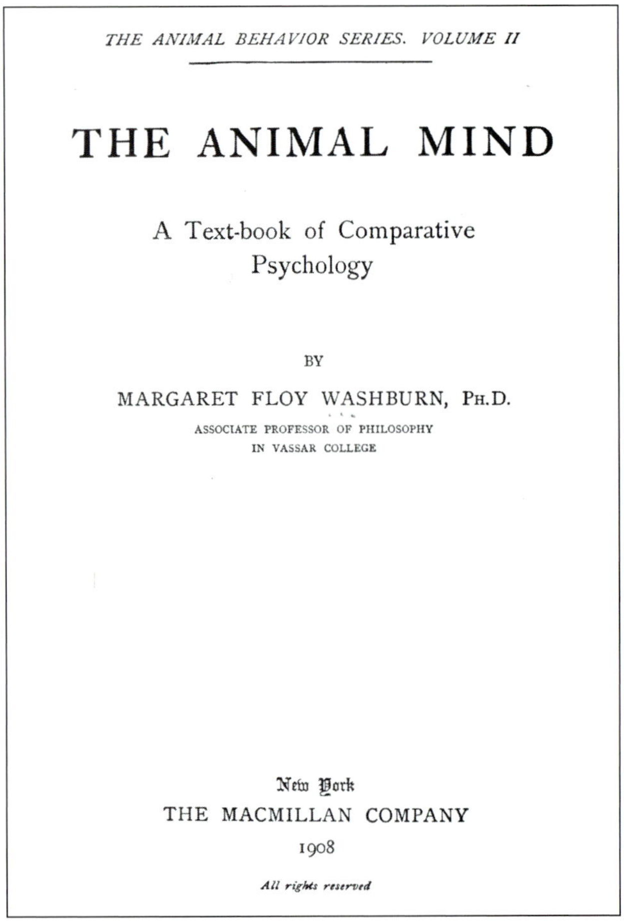

THE ANIMAL BEHAVIOR SERIES. VOLUME II

THE ANIMAL MIND

A Text-book of Comparative
Psychology

BY

MARGARET FLOY WASHBURN, Ph.D.

ASSOCIATE PROFESSOR OF PHILOSOPHY
IN VASSAR COLLEGE

New York
THE MACMILLAN COMPANY
1908

Figure 2 Frontispiece from *The Animal Mind* (1908).

unrecognizable." Washburn expressed her doubts as follows:

> To a person with a liking for chemistry the idea of introspectively analyzing mental states into irreducible elements had attraction, yet one could not forget James's conception of consciousness as a stream and the impossibility that it should be at once a stream and a mosaic. (p. 343)

Between 1894 and 1900, Washburn taught psychology and ethics at Wells College. In 1900 she returned to Cornell as the Warden of Sage College. In her second year at Cornell, she taught a course in animal psychology which stimulated the interest that would lead to her writing *The Animal Mind.*

Washburn taught one year (1902–1903) at the University of Cincinnati and then accepted an associate professorship at Vassar in 1903. It was from this base of operation that she continued to conduct her own research, supervise student research, and write two books. Many studies that she designed were conducted by senior students who then served as coauthors in publication. Over 70 articles were published in the *American Journal of Psychology* as "Minor Studies from the Psychological Laboratory at Vassar College" (Scarborough & Furumoto, 1987; Stevens & Gardner, 1982).

The Animal Mind (1908) was begun after Washburn spent six weeks in the summer of 1905 at Cornell, where she collaborated with I. M. Bentley on experiments in the color vision of fish (Washburn, 1932/1961). Intended as a collection of facts produced by the experimental method, *The Animal Mind* was a summary of the research literature on sensation, perception, learning, and memory in a variety of species. Washburn advocated the "Method of Experiment," rather than the "Method of Anecdote," but criticized the use of "abnormal conditions" which might distort the usual reactions of the animal. For Washburn (1908),

> The ideal method for the study of a higher animal involves patient observation upon a specimen known from birth, watched in its ordinary behavior and environment, and occasionally experimented upon with proper control of the conditions and without frightening it or otherwise rendering it abnormal (p. 12).

Washburn's interest was in inference of mental processes from observations of behavior, from the highest to the lowest of organisms (Washburn, 1908). Even in the third edition (Washburn, 1926), she continued to advocate studying the "inner experience" of animals and interpretation by analogy to human experience. By 1926, Washburn's views were clearly counter to those of the increasingly influential behaviorists, who rejected the study of mental processes even in human beings (Watson, 1913). However, she would no doubt find a place today in the field of cognitive ethology, the goal of which is to investigate animal consciousness (Blumberg & Wasserman, 1995).

After publication of *The Animal Mind*, Washburn continued to pursue her interest in human higher mental processes. As early as 1903, she had begun to develop a theory about the involvement of kinesthetic processes in perception and thinking. She summarized these ideas in her second book, *Movement and Mental Imagery: Outline of a Motor Theory of Consciousness* (1916). Published by Vassar College as part of a commemorative series, this book did not receive widespread attention (Washburn, 1932/1961).

Washburn's interest in consciousness became increasingly out of vogue in American psychology in the 1920s, as behaviorism gradually replaced structuralism and functionalism in mainstream experimental psychology. Washburn publicly opposed Watson's views in her 1921 Presidential Address to the American Psychological Association, "Introspection as an Objective Method" (Washburn, 1922); and she praised the Gestalt psychologists Koffka and Köhler who were continuing to study consciousness. In 1926, she became coeditor (with Karl Dallenbach) of the *American Journal of Psychology*. She continued to conduct research, teach at Vassar College, and participate in numerous professional organizations until she suffered an incapacitating stroke in 1937. She died on October 29, 1939 (Scarborough & Furumoto, 1987; Stevens & Gardner, 1982).

Figure 3 Frontispiece from *Movement and Mental Imagery* (1916).

Throughout her career, Washburn was respected by her colleagues. In recognition of her accomplishments, she was elected President of the American Psychological Association, the second woman to head that organization. In 1929, she and June Etta

Downey became the first female members of the Society of Experimental Psychologists, the organization founded by E. B. Titchener and from which he had excluded women. In 1931, Washburn became the second American woman to be elected to the National Academy of Sciences (Scarborough & Furumoto, 1987; Stevens & Gardner, 1982).

Figure 4 Washburn in her later years.

Washburn aligned herself with none of the dominant schools of psychology, thus it is difficult to place her in traditional history of psychology textbooks. Though she is typically cited as an influential comparative psychologist (e.g., Hilgard, 1987), that subject was only one of her interests. Because women were not considered for faculty positions in major universities in those days (Scarborough & Furumoto, 1987), she had no PhD students to carry on her work. Her legacy to American psychology is to stand as a model of one who, despite sex discrimination in admission to graduate school and employment, produced a major work and achieved high professional recognition in her time.

Bibliography

Blumberg, M. S., & Wasserman, E. A. (1995). Animal mind and the argument from design. *American Psychologist, 50*, 133–144.

Boring, E. G. (1950). *A history of experimental psychology* (2nd ed.). New York: Appleton-Century-Crofts.

Hilgard, E. R. (1987). *Psychology in America: A historical survey*. San Diego: Harcourt Brace Jovanovich.

Scarborough, E., & Furumoto, L. (1987). *Untold lives*. New York: Columbia University Press.

Stevens, G., & Gardner, S. (1982). *The women of psychology: Vol. 1. Pioneers and innovators*. Cambridge, MA: Schenkman.

Washburn, M. F. (1908). *The animal mind: A text-book of comparative psychology*. New York: Macmillan.

Washburn, M. F. (1916). *Movement and Mental Imagery: Outline of a Motor Theory of Consciousness*. Boston: Houghton Mifflin.

Washburn, M. F. (1922). Introspection as an objective method (Presidential Address, American Psychological Association, Princeton, NJ, 1921). *Psychological Review, 29*, 89–112.

Washburn, M. F. (1926). *The animal mind: A text-book of comparative psychology* (3rd ed.). New York: Macmillan.

Washburn, M. F. (1961). Some recollections. In C. Murchison (Ed.), *History of psychology in autobiography: Vol. 2* (pp. 333–358). New York: Russell & Russell. (Original work published 1932, Clark University Press)

Watson, J. B. (1913). Psychology as the behaviorist views it. *Psychological Review, 20*, 158–177.

Can Apes Learn a Human Language?

B. Michael Thorne

Charles Darwin's *The Descent of Man* (1871) placed humans firmly in the animal kingdom. In this work Darwin offered numerous examples of animal behavior—including language—that he felt illustrated the essential continuity in abilities between humans and other animals. Darwin concluded that "the difference in mind between man and the higher animals, great as it is, certainly is one of degree and not of kind" (Darwin, 1874, p. 143).

Given the obvious similarities between humans and the Great Apes, a number of people have speculated about whether it might be possible to teach our closest living relatives some version of human language. For example, in *Man a Machine*, Julien de La Mettrie (1748/1912, p. 100) posed the question: "Would it be absolutely impossible to teach the ape a language?" Answering his own question affirmatively, La Mettrie outlined a plan for the ape's education that he thought would produce "a perfect man, a little gentleman, with as much matter or muscle as we have, for thinking and profiting by his education" (p. 103).

In one of the first efforts to teach an ape to talk, Lightner Witmer (1909) described a chimpanzee that had been trained to approximate the word "mama." William Furness (1916) had slightly more success with an orangutan, teaching it to say "papa" and "cup." Unfortunately, the death of the orangutan "four or five months after this first tiny inkling of language" (p. 285) brought his efforts to an end. Comparing the chimpanzee and the orangutan, Furness concluded that the orangutan was better suited to learn human language.

In the 1970s, British zoology graduate student Keith Laidler (1980) devoted more than a year to an attempt to teach an infant orangutan named Cody to communicate vocally. By the end of the effort, Cody was using four sounds—"fuh," "kuh," "puh," and "thuh"—to express his desires for rewards such as food, drink, and contact comfort. Laidler concluded that only the surface of the orangutan's language potential had been touched.

Gua

In 1909, Witmer had speculated that soon chimpanzees might be reared in a manner approximating that of a human child. This approach was taken by Winthrop and Luella Kellogg (1933) with a 7½-month-old female chimp that they named Gua. Although the Kelloggs would have preferred an orangutan, they settled for Robert Yerkes's loan of an animal that had been forcibly separated from its mother. Gua lived with the Kellogg family, which included their 9½-month-old son Donald, for 9 months before they returned the animal to Yale's Anthropoid Experiment Station at Orange Park, Florida. Gua and Donald are shown in Figure 1.

The experiment with Gua was not specifically designed to teach the ape language, and, in fact, Gua did not learn to say a single word in her time with the human family. The Kelloggs concluded that,

> Although the possibility may still remain, we feel safe in predicting, as a result of our intimate association with Gua, that it is unlikely any anthropoid ape will ever be taught to say more than half a dozen words, if indeed it should accomplish this remarkable feat. (Kellogg & Kellogg, 1933, pp. 288–289)

However, language comprehension was another matter, and Gua at first progressed more rapidly than Donald. By the end of the study, Donald's "comprehension vocabulary" was 107, whereas Gua's was 95.

Viki

Ending on a note of self-criticism, the Kelloggs suggested that if the study were to be repeated, the ape should be younger at the time it joined the human household, it should be raised with more children, and the study should be conducted over a longer period. In the early 1950s, Keith and Catherine Hayes (e.g., Hayes & Hayes, 1951) reported the results of an experiment that satisfied two of the Kelloggs' suggestions: The ape was only a few days old at the time of her "adoption," and the work took place over a longer time period (Viki lived with the Hayeses until her death at 7 from viral encephalitis). In addition, the Hayeses specifically tried to teach Viki to talk.

As could have been predicted from the earlier studies, the Hayeses found it almost impossible to teach Viki human language. For one thing, although she was socially extraverted, Viki was also silent, exhibiting almost none of the chatter associated with human infants her age. Beginning her language instruction at 5 months, Viki eventually learned to say "mama," "papa," and "cup." Although the words were not used appropriately at first, Viki soon learned to call Cathy "mama" and Keith "papa" and to say "cup" if she wanted something to drink. When pressured by her "parents" or when highly motivated, Viki sometimes confused the terms, however.

If anything, Viki may have been more successful at teaching Cathy Hayes chimp language than vice versa. On one occasion, Florida State University graduate student Robert Thompson, who often babysat Viki in the Hayeses absence, caught Cathy Hayes using a chimp-like vocalization to warn Viki of danger. Thompson concluded that the chimp had taught its human "mother" language rather than the other way around (F. M. Crinella, personal communication, May 1994).

The Hayeses' experiment rather conclusively demonstrated that chimpanzees cannot learn to speak. Although the animals' vocal apparatus is different from that of humans and probably cannot support human speech, a greater impediment is that chimpanzee vocalization is almost exclusively under the emotional control of the limbic system, and the animals are usually silent unless disturbed (Gardner & Gardner, 1969). By contrast, human language is primarily controlled by the neocortex, with some limbic involvement (Wallman, 1992).

However, the lack of speaking ability does not mean that apes cannot be taught a language, only that some other form of discourse must be found. In fact, another approach to language that might work with chimpanzees has long been recognized: signing with the fingers and hands. The apes' natural tendency to gesture and ability to imitate prompted

Figure 1 Gua and Donald Kellogg ready for bed.

Robert Yerkes to speculate in 1925 that apes might be trained to use a simple sign language. In 1969, Allen and Beatrice Gardner reported their efforts to teach an infant female chimpanzee they named

Washoe to use a simplified version of American Sign Language (ASL), which is one of the gestural languages used by the deaf.

Washoe

Washoe was a wild-born chimpanzee whose estimated age at the beginning of the project was between 8 and 14 months. For slightly more than 4 years, Washoe lived in a trailer in the Gardners' backyard and was accompanied by a human companion during every waking hour. Her human companions were required to use ASL exclusively in Washoe's presence.

Washoe produced her first sign 3 months into the project and her first multisign "speech" by 1 year. Her vocabulary consisted of 4 signs by the 7th month, 30 signs at 22 months, and 132 signs at 51 months, when the project ended. Comparing the various techniques they used to teach Washoe to sign, the Gardners found imitation and shaping (rewarding successive approximations of the desired behavior) to be relatively ineffective, whereas molding (guiding her hands into the desired positions) became the method of choice.

In addition to reporting the results of tests of Washoe's vocabulary, the Gardners also presented anecdotal illustrations designed to show that Washoe's language performance was similar to that of a young child. Like a human child, Washoe was reported to have transferred signs from their original referents to new ones on the basis of some perceived similarity. For example, the sign for "open" was extended from its original use with a closed door to closed containers and eventually to faucets. It was also claimed that Washoe was able to create new sign combinations to name things for which she had not learned a single sign. The most commonly cited example of this behavior was the signing of "water bird" when Washoe was confronted by a swan. In late 1970, Washoe was moved from Nevada (the University of Nevada is in Washoe County, hence the name Washoe) to the University of Oklahoma, where she became

involved in studies by Roger Fouts (e.g., Fouts, 1973) of signing in chimpanzees. An example of a chimpanzee using sign language is shown in Figure 2.

Sarah

In the 1970s, David Premack (e.g., Premack, 1976) created an approach to teaching apes language that involved an artificial language of Premack's construction. The medium for Premack's language was a set of metal-backed plastic chips stuck on a magnetized board. Used to represent words, the chips varied in size, shape, color, and texture. Sentences were constructed by arranging the pieces vertically on the board. Premack's "language" avoided two difficulties of earlier studies: the articulatory problem found by the Kelloggs and the Hayeses and the recent memory constraints imposed by a spoken (or signed) language. That is, because Premack's language was written, learners did not have to hold the early parts of sentences in memory until the last elements were presented; all parts of the utterance were always present.

Premack's star pupil was a 5-year-old African-born chimp named Sarah. When observational learning proved ineffective, Premack developed a shaping procedure in which Sarah was rewarded for gradual increases in the complexity of her performance. For example, to teach her to write "Mary

Figure 2 Chimp using American Sign Language (ASL).

give apple Sarah," Sarah was first rewarded with a piece of apple for handing Mary (her trainer) the chip representing apple (a blue triangle). Next, Sarah was rewarded with an apple slice for sticking the apple chip on the magnetized board. At this point, a chip for "give" was introduced, and Sarah would earn some apple by placing the "give" chip above the "apple" chip; putting it below "apple" ("apple give") would not result in the reward. Next, Sarah would be given a "Mary" chip, and its appropriate position in the three-chip sequence "Mary give apple" taught by the shaping procedure. Finally, the ape would be trained to add the "Sarah" chip at the end of the statement to produce the desired result: "Mary give apple Sarah."

With this basic procedure, Premack was able to teach Sarah more abstract concepts, such as "same" and "different," "color of," "name of," "size of," "shape of," and so on. In addition, Sarah was taught to "read" chip sequences and to follow the instructions given by a sequence. For example, she might be supplied with a box, a cup, a banana, and an apple and the chip sequence "Sarah insert apple box." Sarah would be rewarded for placing the apple in the box but not for such actions as inserting the apple in the cup or the banana in the box. At some point, Premack shifted the focus of his research with Sarah and his other apes from language training to the study of cognition in general.

Lana

At about the same time that Premack was working with Sarah, Duane Rumbaugh (e.g., Rumbaugh, 1977) began an ape-language project using a set of abstract symbols, called lexigrams, arrayed on a computer keyboard inside a chimp's cage. Because the project used a "LANguage Analog" approach, the 2-year-old chimpanzee subject was called Lana. The language that Rumbaugh and his associates taught Lana was dubbed "Yerkish" because of the study's location at the Yerkes Regional Primate Center in Atlanta, Georgia.

Like Premack's approach, Yerkish avoids the apes' articulatory deficiencies and any short-term memory problem. In addition, inadvertent cueing of the animal by her trainers was bypassed by the imposition of a computer between the ape and humans. Finally, the presence of the computer made it possible for the experimenters to keep a permanent record of all of Lana's interactions.

Using a shaping procedure similar to Premack's, Lana was trained to type commands such as "please

machine give apple" for a piece of apple, or "please machine show slides" for a slide presentation. Sequences such as "please show machine slides" were not rewarded. Also, like Sarah, Lana learned to "read" and complete sequences in order to obtain a reward and to reject partial sequences that did not correspond to the rules of Yerkish. Generally speaking, Lana was able to initiate and sustain conversations with her trainers, although the topics were necessarily limited primarily to the ape's efforts to obtain some desired item.

But Is It Really Language?

In late 1973, Herbert Terrace began an ape-language project with a 2-week-old chimpanzee that he named Nim Chimpsky, a whimsical allusion to the well-known psycholinguist Noam Chomsky, who believes that only humans have the capacity for language acquisition. As a student of B. F. Skinner, Terrace thought it would be possible for an ape to learn human language and that "it would be ironic if Nim were to ultimately prove Chomsky wrong" (Marx, 1980, p. 1330).

Employing essentially the same training technique that the Gardners had used with Washoe, Terrace and his colleagues (e.g., Terrace, Petitto, Sanders, & Bever, 1979) initially believed that they had succeeded in teaching Nim to create sentences and that his language performance was similar to that of young children. However, more careful analysis of Nim's output, including the study of videotaped "conversations" between Nim and his trainers, convinced Terrace that most of the ape's utterances were merely imitations of a trainer's prior signing. In addition, Nim rarely signed spontaneously and interrupted his teachers much more often than a child interrupts an adult's speech. Terrace found no evidence of Nim's ability to use grammar in constructing his "speech," and in the infrequent instances in which the ape expanded on a trainer's utterances, he tended to use signs that provided no new information. A good example of this tendency is Nim's famous 16-sign "sentence": "give orange me give eat orange me eat orange give me eat orange give me you."

Not content with their critical analysis of Nim's failures, Terrace et al. (1979) looked for similar problems in the filmed utterances of other signing apes. They concluded that films of Washoe and Koko (a signing gorilla studied by Francine Patterson (e.g., Patterson, 1987) consistently revealed that the trainer initiated signing and that the utterances of the apes tended to mimic the teachers' signing.

In addition, Terrace and his colleagues (1979) were highly critical of ape-language projects in which the apes communicated by manipulating artificial symbols—the Sarah and Lana projects, for example. Terrace et al. pointed out that there was virtually no evidence to suggest that Lana and Sarah understood the human meanings of the individual words in the sequences they produced. The authors concluded reasonably that "it seems more prudent to regard the sequences of symbols glossed as *please*, *machine*, *Mary*, *Sarah*, and *give* as sequences of nonsense symbols" (p. 899).

Anecdotal evidence has often been used to illustrate the language-taught apes' ability to create new meanings through the novel combination of signs or symbols, and Terrace and others have criticized this evidence, as well. For example, as indicated above, a frequently cited example of Washoe's creative ability was her signing of "water bird" for a swan. Terrace et al. (1979) suggested that Washoe may have been identifying two separate things, a bird and a body of water, rather than characterizing the swan as a "bird that lives in water."

Another oft-cited example of this so-called creative ability is Lana's use of "apple which-is orange" to request an orange for which, at the time, she had no symbol. An examination of the actual exchange between Lana and a trainer that produced the "creative" sequence reveals that it was "preceded by several senseless and apparently random variations on it" (Wallman, 1992, p. 35). Thus, when viewed in context, the "apple which-is orange" sequence loses much of its apparent creativity.

According to Gibbons (1991), Terrace's criticisms "devastated the budding field. Funds dried up and researchers were discouraged from studying language in apes" (p. 1561). However, the study of apes learning language has been rehabilitated in the last decade, primarily on the strength of research conducted by Sue Savage-Rumbaugh and her colleagues at Georgia State University. Savage-Rumbaugh has claimed exceptional language abilities for her pigmy chimpanzee Kanzi.

Kanzi

Shortly before Terrace's critique, Savage-Rumbaugh began language research with the co-reared apes Sherman and Austin, which provided the background for her later work with Kanzi. Unlike previous ape-language work, Sherman and Austin were socially housed for much of the day, and the emphasis was on peer communication rather than on communication with a trainer or with a machine. Additionally, the apes were taught single words in Yerkish rather than the "stock phrases" Lana learned.

In order for Sherman and Austin to demonstrate comprehension, they were often required to perform a sequence of actions appropriate to the utterance of their partner, not to receive a reward for themselves, but to get it for the other. This required both the ability to comprehend the request and the ability to cooperate. Savage-Rumbaugh et al. (1993) concluded that the work with Sherman and Austin established chimps' ability to use symbols in a representational fashion and for intraspecies communication. Although the Sherman-Austin studies were not as severely criticized as their predecessors with Lana, they were often viewed as merely replications of the Lana work.

According to Savage-Rumbaugh et al. (1993), the next major advance in ape-language research came with the exposure of a new species of ape to language. Except for the study of the gorilla Koko by Patterson, all of the key studies of ape language before Kanzi used the common chimpanzee, *Pan troglodytes*. Kanzi is a pigmy chimpanzee or bonobo of the species *Pan paniscus*. Unfortunately, bonobos are rare and are vanishing rapidly in their native Zaire.

The first bonobo Savage-Rumbaugh and her group exposed to language was Matata, a wild-caught adult female. Matata proved to be untrainable, but her son Kanzi began to acquire knowledge of symbols through observing the efforts to teach his mother. Not only did Kanzi learn the symbols without being specifically taught and without being reinforced for doing so, he also began to show that he understood spoken language. This understanding has been exploited in studies of Kanzi's language comprehension. Figure 3 shows Kanzi using the lexigram keyboard with Dr. Sue Savage-Rumbaugh.

For example, in a study conducted in 1988 (Savage-Rumbaugh et al., 1993), 8-year-old Kanzi and a 2-year-old child named Alia were compared in their ability to respond appropriately to several different sentence types presented verbally. Kanzi performed correctly almost three-quarters of the time compared to Alia's correctness on approximately two-thirds of the trials. Savage-Rumbaugh et al. concluded that the ape and the child "could comprehend both the semantics and the syntactic structure of quite unusual sentences" (p. 98). Figure

Figure 3 Kanzi using lexigram keyboard with Dr. Sue Savage-Rumbaugh.

4 shows Kanzi correctly responding to the request to "Take the snake outdoors."

But does Kanzi actually understand the syntax, the grammar, of human sentences, as Savage-Rumbaugh has claimed? When Kanzi was 6, his sentence comprehension was tested informally by noting his responses to 310 sentences (Savage-Rumbaugh, 1988). Savage-Rumbaugh reported that the ape responded correctly 96% of the time. However, after an extended critical analysis of Kanzi's performance, Wallman (1992) concluded that in the vast majority of cases, Kanzi could have performed equally well if the words of each sentence had been presented in random order. In other words, on this and similar tests, there is no evidence that the animal was responding to syntactic features of the test stimuli. "What is new in the Kanzi project," Wallman wrote, "is subjects who learn the use—and arguably the meaning—of language tokens without undergoing operant conditioning. What is not new is the penchant of the experimenters for overinterpreting the achievements of their subjects, according them a linguistic competence that is simply not warranted by the data" (p. 104).

Conclusions

People have long wondered if it might be possible to communicate with the creatures with which we share the planet, and the Great Apes, as our closest living relatives, seem to offer the best hope for meaningful interaction. Early attempts to teach apes language focused on actual speech, and it soon became apparent that physiological differences between apes and humans render this approach untenable.

Because of chimpanzees' facility with gestures, ape-language researchers next tried to teach their subjects to use human sign language, apparently with success. However, a failed project by Terrace and his associates and Terrace's subsequent analysis of previous ape-language research strongly questioned the validity of the earlier efforts.

Using a different species than previous ape-language projects and employing better experimental controls, Sue Savage-Rumbaugh and her associates are convinced that Kanzi has developed at least proto-human language skills. However, throughout a comparison study with a human child, Kanzi's mean length of utterance (MLU) remained fixed at only 1.15 words, whereas the child's increased from 1.91 to 3.19. Kanzi's performance on a comprehension test of spoken English seems remarkable until you realize that the ape could have responded correctly on most items with limited word recognition and little or no appreciation of syntax.

Earlier critics of ape language (e.g., Herbert Terrace and Noam Chomsky) are not interested in the

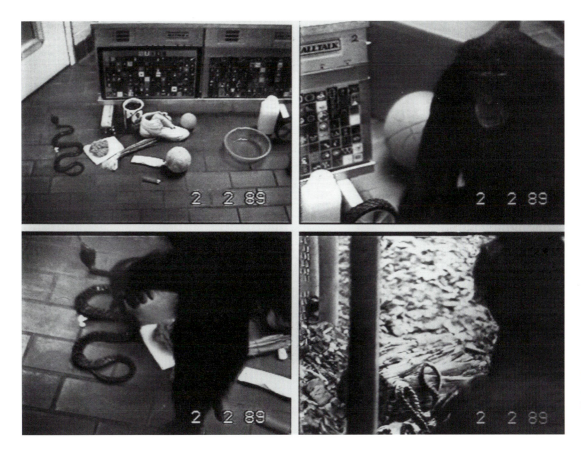

Figure 4 Kanzi responds correctly to the request to "Take the snake outdoors."

latest research on communication with apes. In fact, Chomsky "ridicules the notion that any species would have a capacity highly advantageous to survival but not use it until a researcher taught them to" (Gibbons, 1991, p. 1562). To La Mettrie's question of whether it might be possible to teach language to an ape, we still do not have a definitive answer in spite of the best efforts of a couple of generations of dedicated researchers. However, based on the evidence collected so far, it does appear to be unlikely.

Bibliography

Darwin, C. (1871). *The descent of man.* New York: Appleton.

Darwin, C. (1874). *The descent of man, and selection in relation to sex* (2nd ed.). New York: A. L. Burt, Publisher.

Fouts, R. S. (1973). Acquisition and testing of gestural signs in four young chimpanzees. *Science, 180,* 978–980.

Furness, W. (1916). Observations on the mentality of chimpanzees and orangutans. *Proceedings of the American Philosophical Society, 55,* 281–290.

Gardner, R. A., & Gardner, B. T. (1969). Teaching sign language to a chimpanzee. *Science, 165,* 664–672.

Gibbons, A. (1991). Deja vu all over again: Chimp-language wars. *Science, 251,* 1561–1562.

Hayes, K. J., & Hayes, C. (1951). The intellectual development of a home-raised chimpanzee. *Proceedings of the American Philosophical Society, 95,* 105–109.

Kellogg, W. N., & Kellogg, L. A. (1933). *The ape and the child.* New York: Whittlesey House.

Laidler, K. (1980). *The talking ape.* New York: Stein and Day.

La Mettrie, J. O. de (1912). *Man a machine.* La Salle, IL: Open Court. (Original work published 1748)

Marx, J. L. (1980). Ape-language controversy flares up. *Science, 207,* 1330–1333.

Patterson, F. (1987). *Koko's story.* New York: Scholastic.

Premack, D. (1976). *Intelligence in ape and man.* Hillsdale, NJ: Erlbaum.

Rumbaugh, D. M. (Ed.). (1977). *Language learning by a chimpanzee: The LANA Project.* New York: Academic Press.

Savage-Rumbaugh, E. S. (1988). A new look at ape language: Comprehension of vocal speech and syntax. In D. W. Leger (Ed.), *Comparative perspectives in modern psychology (Nebraska symposium on motivation 1987)* (pp. 201–255). Lincoln, NE: University of Nebraska Press.

Savage-Rumbaugh, E. S., Murphy, J., Sevcik, R. A., Brakke, K. E., Williams, S. L., & Rumbaugh, D. M. (1993). Language comprehension in ape and child. *Monographs of the Society for Research in Child Development, 58* (3–4, Serial No. 233).

Terrace, H. S., Petitto, L. A., Sanders, R. J., & Bever, T. G. (1979). Can an ape create a sentence? *Science, 206,* 891–902.

Wallman, J. (1992). *Aping language.* Cambridge, England: Cambridge University Press.

Witmer, L. (1909). A monkey with a mind. *The Psychological Clinic, 3,* 179–205.

Yerkes, R. M. (1925). *Almost human.* New York: Century.

Behaviorism

Robert H. Wozniak

In 1913, at Columbia University, John Broadus Watson (1878–1958) delivered a lecture entitled "Psychology as the Behaviorist Views It" (1913). To later generations of psychologists, reared in a discipline defining itself as the "science of behavior," this lecture would become known as the "behaviorist manifesto" and Watson would become known as the "father of behaviorism."

There is, of course, some justification for this. In this lecture, Watson mounted a scathing attack on the mainstream definition of psychology as the science of mind or consciousness. Arguing in no uncertain terms that psychology should be viewed as "a purely objective experimental branch of natural science" whose theoretical goal is not the understanding of mind but the prediction and control of behavior, Watson blamed psychology's failure to "make its place in the world as an undisputed natural science" on the "esoteric" nature of its introspective method. Rejecting both introspection and the use of consciousness as an interpretive standard, he urged psychologists to adopt behavior as their unit of analysis.

In the years that followed, Watson used positions as Professor of Psychology at Hopkins, editor of the *Journal of Experimental Psychology*, and contributor to the popular press to proselytize for behaviorism. Even after his academic career came to an abrupt and involuntary end in 1920 (Watson, 1936), Watson continued to press his case; and by the time he made his final contribution to the debate in the early 1930s, methodological behaviorism and animal behavior research had become dominant features of the psychological landscape.

Like many origin myths, however, the story of Watson's founding of behaviorism is oversimplified and misleading. Watson was not the first to use

Figure 1 John Broadus Watson (1878–1958).

objective, experimental methods in the study of behavior or to criticize psychology's use of the concept of "consciousness" or the method of introspection (Wozniak, 1993). Nor did psychologists flock suddenly to Watson's point of view (Samelson, 1981). It was more than 10 years before behaviorism began to gain any real ground within American psychology, and when it did, it did so not by converting the old guard to Watson's vision but by attracting the young to a set of intellectual commitments that had already become broader, more varied, and philosophically more sophisticated than those of Watson.

Roots of Behaviorism

The rise of behaviorism is often portrayed as a revolution in method, and in many ways it was. In 1913, psychology was the science of mind, the core phenomena of mind were those of consciousness, and the method of choice for the analysis of consciousness was introspection by a trained observer under controlled conditions. A scant 25 years later, mainstream psychology was the science not of mind but of behavior. The core phenomena of behavior were those of learning and memory, and the methods of choice for the analysis of learning and memory involved purely objective observations of behavioral data varying as a function of the experimental manipulation of stimulus conditions (Woodworth, 1938).

There is little doubt that Watson's call for an objective science of behavior played an influential role in triggering the change that ensued; but the paper of 1913 was not itself the revolutionary moment that it is sometimes thought to be. By 1913, the study of human and animal behavior by means of purely objective methods under conditions of experimental manipulation and control of stimulus conditions had a 40-year history. Indeed, Watson himself was a "behavior man" long before he was a "behaviorist," and his manifesto was prompted at least in part by the striking contrast that he perceived between the objective nature of available behavioral methods and the then prevalent ideology of an introspective psychology defined as the science of consciousness. Watson's primary goal at Columbia was to provide a rationale for the legitimation of behavior methods that had long been in use.

The first purely objective studies of behavior were probably those of Douglas Alexander Spalding and Charles Darwin. To distinguish instinctive from learned behavior, Spalding (1872, 1873) designed an extraordinary series of experiments in which he systematically manipulated an animal's experience (e.g., by placing hoods over the eyes of chicks still in the shell and only unhooding them several days after hatching) and carefully recorded relevant behaviors (e.g., the chick's first visually guided pecking movements), thereby providing a model for

use of the experimental method in the study of behavior (see Gray, 1962, for an excellent discussion of Spalding's contributions).

Darwin's (1877) "Biographical Sketch of an Infant" exhibits the same attention to the detail of infant behavior that Spalding gave to that of young animals. As did Spalding, Darwin went beyond simple observation to vary the conditions of stimulation and observe concomitant variation in behavior. To identify the effective stimulus for the infant's startle reaction, for example, Darwin compared the effect of shaking a paste-board box containing comfits near the child's face to those elicited by the same box when empty and by other noiseless objects shaken as near or much nearer the face.

PSYCHOLOGY AS THE BEHAVIORIST VIEWS IT

BY JOHN B. WATSON

The Johns Hopkins University

Psychology as the behaviorist views it is a purely objective experimental branch of natural science. Its theoretical goal is the prediction and control of behavior. Introspection forms no essential part of its methods, nor is the scientific value of its data dependent upon the readiness with which they lend themselves to interpretation in terms of consciousness. The behaviorist, in his efforts to get a unitary scheme of animal response, recognizes no dividing line between man and brute. The behavior of man, with all of its refinement and complexity, forms only a part of the behaviorist's total scheme of investigation.

It has been maintained by its followers generally that psychology is a study of the science of the phenomena of consciousness. It has taken as its problem, on the one hand, the analysis of complex mental states (or processes) into simple elementary constituents, and on the other the construction of complex states when the elementary constituents are given. The world of physical objects (stimuli, including here anything which may excite activity in a receptor), which forms the total phenomena of the natural scientist, is looked upon merely as means to an end. That end is the production of mental states that may be 'inspected' or 'observed.' The psychological object of observation in the case of an emotion, for example, is the mental state itself. The problem in emotion is the determination of the number and kind of elementary constituents present, their loci, intensity, order of appearance, etc. It is agreed that introspection is the method *par excellence* by means of which mental states may be manipulated for purposes of psychology. On this assumption, behavior data (including under this term everything which goes under the name of comparative psychology) have no value *per se*. They possess

Figure 2 Watson's "behaviorist manifesto" (1913).

Although objective in their observations and experimental in their variation of the conditions of behavior, neither Spalding nor Darwin was much inclined toward either the design of apparatus to control the scope of an animal's reaction or the quantification of response. One of the first to introduce apparatus and quantification into the study of animal behavior was Sir John Lubbock.[1] In *Ants, Bees, and Wasps. A Record of Observations on the Habits of the Social Hymenoptera*, Lubbock (1882) provided precise, detailed, quantitative descriptions of the conditions of observation that were not much different from those to be found in the methods sections of modern journal articles. In addition, he reported actual data in the body of his text and used this data to compute simple summary statistics (e.g., pace of movement in ants learning to take an experimentally contrived route between food and nest).

These advances in methodology would alone have earned Lubbock a place in the history of objective research methods, but Lubbock employed two additional techniques of even greater importance for future research. Following his ants with a pencil as they pursued their way, Lubbock made detailed tracings of the ants' paths, possibly the first attempt to make an analog record of behavior for later coding. Second, and more importantly, to observe the progress made by his ants in learning to follow a new path from food to nest, Lubbock designed,

Figure 3 Analog ant behavior records of John Lubbock.

built, and employed a number of simple pieces of apparatus that constrained the ants' movements. These pieces of apparatus were, in effect, the first animal mazes.

Between 1882 and 1894, the canons of adequate behavioral methodology continued to evolve. By the time James Mark Baldwin (1894) published his classic study of infant behavioral development, "The Origin of Right-Handedness," the use of apparatus for the measurement of behavior and registration of behavioral data was commonplace. Issues of experimental control, research design, and quantification had become paramount.

Baldwin's research consisted of a long series of controlled experiments carried out at home with his daughter. Placing different objects and cards of different colors in front of the child, he systematically varied distances and directions from her body and observed variations in her reaching. To guarantee accurate placement of the objects on each trial, Baldwin employed a set of specially designed measuring rods; and to minimize unwanted variability in the infant's behavior, he carried out his experiments under strictly controlled conditions, in the same location and at the same hour each day. To avoid biasing his daughter's hand preference, her position at the table was reversed midway through each series of experiments and, lest bias take place inadvertently, her parents even refrained from carrying her around in their arms until the experiments had been concluded. Finally, when Baldwin presented his data, he did so in quantitative, tabular form.

While Lubbock and Baldwin used laboratory-like procedures in the objective study of behavior, neither did so within the laboratory. Lubbock worked largely out of doors, making use of natural populations of insects; Baldwin worked with his daughter in the living room. The first psychologist to take intelligent animal behavior into the laboratory, to provide a clear quantitative account of the course of instrumental learning, and thereby to establish the study of animal learning as a laboratory science was Edward Lee Thorndike.

Thorndike's (1898) dissertation, *Animal Intelligence*, was one of the most influential publications of the first half-century of psychological science. Besides offering a theory of instrumental learning later termed the "law of effect" and a conception of animal intelligence couched solely in terms of the organism's ability to form new connections, Thorndike developed ingenious apparatus for the observation of animal learning and employed it in systematic laboratory research. Bitterman (1969) has nicely described the appeal that Thorndike's general experimental technique had for generations of researchers:

> It was objective: it minimized the influence of the observer. . . . It was quantitative: the course of learning could be measured accurately in terms of the time taken for the appearance of the correct response on each trial. It was reproducible: the work of one investigator could be repeated and verified by others. It was flexible: the responses required could be varied in kind and complexity. It was natural: . . . not too remote from the animal's ordinary course of life . . . [and] it was convenient: a large enough sample of animals could be studied to provide a representative picture of each of a variety of species. (p. 446)

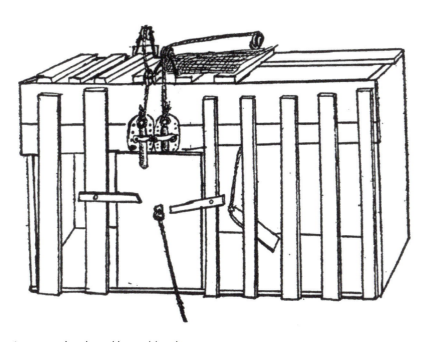

Figure 4 The Thorndike problem box.

Supplemented by additional laboratory approaches to measuring way finding, escape, and problem solving (e.g., Kline, 1899; Small, 1900–1901; Hobhouse, 1901) and advances in stimulus control and quantification of response (e.g., Yerkes, 1907; Yerkes & Watson, 1911), objective methods developed rapidly after 1900. Issues of experimental control, quantification and registration of behavior, measurement, and research design were raised and addressed. By 1913, the tools for a psychology

focused on what Watson would describe to Yerkes as "the scientific determination of modes of behavior . . . [using] an objective standard of interpretation . . . without mentioning consciousness or deviating from a [wide] biological point of view"[2] were in place. The field of psychology, if not quite ready to embrace behaviorism, was at least ready to let Watson speak. And some sort of pronouncement was needed rather badly.

When Watson ascended the speaker's platform at Columbia, psychology was a discipline in serious disarray. The root source of the problem was an almost total lack of agreement among psychologists as to the nature of consciousness. William James (1904) had triggered the debate with his famous attack on the concept of consciousness, "Does Consciousness Exist?" Was consciousness a metaphysical entity or simply a particular sort of relationship toward objects into which portions of pure experience enter? Was consciousness a stream of experience, a kind of awareness, or thought? Was it an adaptive function or a composite of states; an energetic by-product of neurophysiological process, another name for associative learning, a form of arrested movement, a regulator of future adaptation, or simply another way of describing "self"? Truly, as Ralph Barton Perry (1904) put it, there was "no philosophical term at once so popular and so devoid of standard meaning" (p. 282).

In this state of affairs psychologists found themselves faced with a significant dilemma. On the one hand, even in the midst of conceptual chaos with respect to "consciousness," there was something on which almost all psychologists could agree: The right of psychology to exist as a science independent of biology and physiology was grounded in psychology's claim to being the science of consciousness. No matter how closely related psychology might become to its sister sciences, psychologists could always carve out their own academic and intellectual niche by emphasizing the study of consciousness as theirs and theirs alone.

On the other hand, psychologists realized that their claim to autonomy as a science was founded on quicksand. How could a science of consciousness function as an independent science in the face of almost total disagreement over the nature of its most basic subject matter? Psychology found itself in the unenviable position of being the science of "who knew what." The contradiction inherent in this state of affairs was all too painfully and embarrassingly evident. By itself this would have been bad enough, but matters were actually much worse.

In principle at least, psychologists might have been able to extract themselves from the horns of their dilemma by acting as scientists are supposed to act in the face of divergent opinion; they might have let the data decide. Unfortunately, however, disagreement over the nature of consciousness was not only disagreement over content, it was also conflict over method. To many it seemed that the only adequate method for the study of consciousness, whatever consciousness might be, was introspection. Yet introspection was the use of consciousness to study consciousness; problems of interpretation were multiplied geometrically. One could hardly expect reliability from a method erected on a foundation that shifted from experimenter to experimenter and theorist to theorist.

During the first decade of the new century, it would have been difficult to pick up a theoretical journal in psychology without being confronted with this controversy. In article after article, psychologists and philosophers of all persuasions attempted to address a series of critical questions: What is the nature of psychology as a science and how is it related to biology and physiology (Angell, 1907; Calkins, 1907; Cattell, 1906; Kirkpatrick, 1907)? What is consciousness, and how should the term "consciousness" be employed (Bode, 1908; Dewey, 1906; James, 1904; Judd, 1910; Perry, 1904)? By what criteria can consciousness be attributed to animals (Yerkes, 1905), and how is consciousness related to behavior on the one hand and nervous activity on the other (Bawden, 1910; Frost, 1912; Meyer, 1912; Yerkes, 1910)? What is the nature of introspection, what are its limits, and how are the data of introspection related to those provided by the observation of behavior (Pillsbury, 1904; Dodge, 1912; Dunlap, 1912)?

This was the context for Watson's lecture of 1913. Psychology was badly in need of someone who could cut a simple path through the chaotic web of controversy in which it found itself enmeshed. Watson did just that. None of his ideas was new. None of his ideas was complex. He simply pulled the strands of controversy together and severed them with a single, radical stroke. Watson threw out consciousness. By throwing out consciousness, he rid psychology of introspection. What remained—an objective psychology of behavior—he termed "behaviorism," described as a revolution, and claimed for his own.

The Spread of Behaviorism

Between 1913 and the emergence of neobehaviorism in the early 1930s (Hull, 1930, 1934, 1937; Skinner, 1931, 1932, 1938; Tolman, 1932), behaviorism moved from the margin to the mainstream of American scientific psychology. For the vast majority of American researchers, theoretical behaviorism had come to delimit psychology's questions and methodological behaviorism to define its practice as science.

The growth of behaviorism reflected many factors. These included Watson's skill as a popularizer and publicist (Watson & McDougall, 1928; Watson, 1925, 1928), and the success of psychologists such as Floyd H. Allport (1919, 1924), Knight Dunlap (1926), Gilbert V. Hamilton (1925), Edwin B. Holt (1915a, 1915b), Karl S. Lashley (1923), George Herbert Mead (1922), Edward C. Tolman (1918, 1922), Robert S. Woodworth (1924), and Robert M. Yerkes (1917) in broadening the concept of behaviorism and extending behavioristic analysis to new psychological domains. In addition, philosophically oriented psychologists such as Albert P. Weiss (1919, 1925a, 1925b) and philosophers such as Edgar A. Singer (1924) provided a persuasive theoretical foundation for behaviorist method; and a number of widely used introductory texts written from a behavioristic point of view, most notably those of Watson (1919), Stevenson Smith and Edwin R. Guthrie (1921), and John Frederick Dashiell (1928), exerted a significant impact on students.

By the 1930s, behaviorism had become a complex affair. On the one hand, much of the program for which it stood was not exclusively its own. This was noted as early as 1924 by no less a figure than Woodworth. Identifying a small set of intellectual commitments presumed by some to define behaviorism—objectivism, reliance on an animal behavior research program, neuromechanical reductionism, an emphasis on social process—Woodworth correctly pointed out that such commitments were common to psychologists of varying persuasions. Indeed, many who referred to themselves as functionalists, pragmatists, and objectivists would have and did find much in the behaviorist program with which they could still agree.

On the other hand, even among those who identified themselves as "behaviorists," agreement on the program was by no means unanimous. Early behaviorism took a variety of forms (Lashley, 1923; Woodworth, 1924).[3] There was, of course, the *radical behaviorism* of Watson, a view notable for its extreme anti-mentalism, its radical reduction of thinking to implicit response, and, especially after 1916, its heavy and somewhat simplistic reliance on conditioned reactions (Watson, 1916, 1919; Watson & Raynor, 1920).

There was the *relational behaviorism* of the Harvard group, developed by Holt (1915a, 1915b; see also Wozniak, 1994b) under the influence of William James and transmitted, at least in part, to students such as Allport (1919) and Tolman (1918, 1922). Construing behavior as "a course of action which the living body executes or is prepared to execute with regard to some object or fact of its environment" (Holt, 1915a, p. 56), relational behaviorism was molar, purposive, and focused on the relationship between high-level behavioral mechanisms in the organism and the concrete realities of the social and physical environment. Closely related to this view was a kind of *philosophical behaviorism*, espoused primarily by philosophers and tied to pragmatism, in which "consciousness" was defined as a form of behavior guided by future results (Bawden, 1918; Bode, 1917, 1918).

At Ohio State, Albert Paul Weiss (1879–1931) was developing a *biosocial behaviorism* (1919, 1925a, 1925b) based on a radical distinction between the level of theoretical discourse appropriate to behavior analyzed as social cause (i.e., "biosocially") and that appropriate to behavior analyzed as sensorimotor effect (i.e., "biophysically"). In Baltimore, Dunlap (1926, 1930), who had been both a Harvard graduate student with Holt and Watson's former departmental colleague at Johns Hopkins, was articulating a *reaction psychology* that blended attacks on introspection, instinct, and images, with an "insistence on response or reaction as the basis of mental processes, including thought processes [and consciousness]" (Dunlap, 1930, p. 59).

At Minnesota, Lashley (1923) was arguing a

Figure 5 Albert Paul Weiss (1879–1931).

physiological behaviorism in which physiological analysis of behavior could be considered to provide a complete and adequate account of all conscious phenomena. At Chicago, Mead (1922) was elaborating a *social behaviorism* of mind, meaning, self, language, and thinking that emphasized the social character of behavior and the behavioral character of mind. Finally, in a number of institutions, a sort of *eclectic behaviorism* was emerging— a behaviorism that assimilated whatever seemed strongest and most reliable in the views of others. This was the sort of behaviorism to be found in texts such as Dashiell's (1928) *Fundamentals of Objective Psychology*.

As it existed during this period, behaviorism clearly resisted simple definition. It was complex, varied, and changing. There was, however, a common core within this variability—psychology was defined as the natural science of behavior; method and theory were objectivist; behavior, animal or human, was conceived as a pattern of adjustment (innate and acquired, skeletal and visceral, explicit and implicit) functionally dependent upon stimulus

Figure 6 John Frederick Dashiell (1888–1975).

conditions in the environment and factors of habit and drive in the organism; and finally, animal behavior, ontogenesis, drive reduction, habit formation, social behavior, and language were emphasized in theory and research (cf., Wozniak, 1994a, for a more in-depth discussion). It was this core that captured the imagination of young psychologists, spread behaviorism within American psychology, and prepared the way for the theoretically more sophisticated neobehaviorisms of the 1930s.

Bibliography

Allport, F. H. (1919). Behavior and experiment in social psychology. *Journal of Abnormal Psychology, 14*, 297–307.

Allport, F. H. (1924). *Social psychology*. Boston: Houghton Mifflin.

Angell, J. R. (1907). The province of functional psychology. *Psychological Review, 14*, 61–91.

Baldwin, J. M. (1894). The origin of right-handedness. *Popular Science Monthly, 44*, 606–615.

Bawden, H. H. (1910). Mind as a category of science. *Psychological Bulletin, 7*, 221–225.

Bawden, H. H. (1918). The presuppositions of a behaviorist psychology. *Psychological Review, 25*, 171–190.

Bitterman, M. E. (1969). Thorndike and the problem of animal intelligence. *American Psychologist, 24*, 444–453.

Bode, B. H. (1908). Some recent definitions of consciousness. *Psychological Review, 15*, 255–264.

Bode, B. H. (1917). The nature of the psychical. *Journal of Philosophy, Psychology, and Scientific Methods, 14*, 288–294.

Bode, B. H. (1918). Consciousness as behavior. *Journal of Philosophy, Psychology, and Scientific Methods, 15*, 449–453.

Buckley, K. W. (1989). *Mechanical man: John Broadus Watson and the beginnings of behaviorism*. New York: Guilford.

Calkins, M. W. (1907). Psychology: What is it about? *Journal of Philosophy, Psychology, and Scientific Methods, 4*, 673–683.

Cattell, J. McK. (1906). Conceptions and methods of psychology. In H. J. Rogers (Ed.), *Congress of Arts and Science, Universal Exposition, St. Louis, 1904* (Vol. 5, pp. 593–604). Boston: Houghton Mifflin.

Darwin, C. (1877). A biographical sketch of an infant. *Mind, 2*, 285–294.

Dashiell, J. F. (1928). *Fundamentals of objective psychology*. Boston: Houghton Mifflin.

Dewey, J. (1906). The terms 'conscious' and 'consciousness.' *Journal of Philosophy, Psychology, and Scientific Methods, 3*, 39–41.

Dodge, R. (1912). The theory and limitations of introspection. *American Journal of Psychology, 23*, 214–229.

Dunlap, K. (1912). The case against introspection. *Psychological Review, 19*, 404–413.

Dunlap, K. (1926). The theoretical aspect of psychology. In C. Murchison (Ed.), *Psychologies of 1925* (pp. 309–329). Worcester, MA: Clark University Press.

Dunlap. K. (1930). Knight Dunlap. In C. Murchison (Ed.), *History of psychology in autobiography* (Vol. 2, pp. 35–61). Worcester, MA: Clark University Press.

Frost, E. P. (1912). Can biology and physiology dispense with consciousness? *Psychological Review, 19*, 246–252.

Galton, F. (1883). *Inquiries into human faculty and its development*. London: Macmillan.

Gray, P. H. (1962). Douglas Alexander Spalding: The first experimental behaviorist. *Journal of General Psychology, 67*, 299–307.

Hamilton, G. V. (1925). *An introduction to objective psychopathology*. St. Louis: Mosby.

Hobhouse, L. T. (1901). *Mind in evolution*. London: Macmillan.

Holt, E. B. (1915a). *The Freudian wish and its place in ethics*. New York: Holt.

Holt, E. B. (1915b). Response and cognition. *Journal of Philosophy, Psychology, and Scientific Methods, 12*, 365–373, 393–409.

Hull, C. L. (1930). Simple trial-and-error learning: A study in psychological theory. *Psychological Review, 37*, 241–256.

Hull, C. L. (1934). The concept of the habit-family hierarchy and maze learning. *Psychological Review, 41*, 33–54, 134–152.

Hull, C. L. (1937). Mind, mechanism, and adaptive behavior. *Psychological Review, 44*, 1–32.

James, W. (1904). Does 'consciousness' exist? *Journal of Philosophy, Psychology, and Scientific Methods, 1*, 477–491.

Judd, C. H. (1910). Evolution and consciousness. *Psychological Review, 17*, 77–97.

Kirkpatrick, E. A. (1907). A broader basis for psychology necessary. *Journal of Philosophy, Psychology, and Scientific Methods, 4*, 542–546.

Kline, L. W. (1899). Methods in animal psychology. *American Journal of Psychology, 10*, 256–279.

Lashley, K. S. (1923). The behavioristic interpretation of consciousness. *Psychological Review, 30*, 237–272, 329–353.

Lubbock, J. (1882). *Ants, bees, and wasps. A record of observations on the habits of the social hymenoptera*. London: Kegan Paul, Trench.

Mead, G. H. (1922). A behavioristic account of the significant symbol. *Journal of Philosophy, 19*, 157–163.

Meyer, M. F. (1912). The present status of the problem of the relation between mind and body. *Journal of Philosophy, Psychology, and Scientific Methods, 9*, 365–371.

Perry, R. B. (1904). Conceptions and misconceptions of consciousness. *Psychological Review, 11*, 282–296.

Pillsbury, W. R. (1904). A suggestion toward a reinterpretation of introspection. *Journal of Philosophy, Psychology, and Scientific Methods, 1*, 225–228.

Samelson, F. (1981). Struggle for scientific authority: The reception of Watson's behaviorism, 1913–1920. *Journal of the History of the Behavioral Sciences, 17*, 399–425.

Singer, E. A. (1924). *Mind as behavior; and studies in empirical idealism.* Columbus, OH: Adams.

Skinner, B. F. (1931). The concept of the reflex in the description of behavior. *Journal of General Psychology, 5*, 427–458.

Skinner, B. F. (1932). On the rate of formation of a conditioned reflex. *Journal of General Psychology, 7*, 274–286.

Skinner, B. F. (1938). *The behavior of organisms: An experimental analysis.* New York: Appleton-Century.

Small, W. S. (1900–1901). Experimental study of the mental processes of the rat. *American Journal of Psychology, 11*, 133–165; *12*, 206–239.

Smith, S., & Guthrie, E. R. (1921). *General psychology in terms of behavior.* New York: Appleton.

Spalding, D. A. (1872). On instinct. *Nature, 6*, 485–486.

Spalding, D. A. (1873). Instinct. With original observations on young animals. *Macmillan's Magazine, 27*, 282–293.

Thorndike, E. L. (1898). Animal intelligence. An experimental study of the associative process in animals. *Psychological Review, Monograph Supplements, 2*(4), 109p.

Tolman, E. C. (1918). Nerve process and cognition. *Psychological Review, 25*, 423–442.

Tolman, E. C. (1922). A new formula for behaviorism. *Psychological Review, 29*, 44–53.

Tolman, E. C. (1932). *Purposive behavior in animals and men.* New York: Century.

Watson, J. B. (1913). Psychology as the behaviorist views it. *Psychological Review, 20*, 158–177.

Watson, J. B. (1916). The place of the conditioned-reflex in psychology. *Psychological Review, 23*, 89–116.

Watson, J. B. (1919). *Psychology from the standpoint of a behaviorist.* Philadelphia: Lippincott.

Watson, J. B. (1925). *Behaviorism.* New York: People's Institute.

Watson, J. B. (1928). *The ways of behaviorism.* New York: Harper.

Watson, J. B. (1936). John Broadus Watson. In C. Murchison (Ed.), *A history of psychology in autobiography* (Vol. 3, pp. 271–281). Worcester, MA: Clark University Press.

Watson, J. B., & McDougall, W. (1928). *The battle of behaviorism. An exposition and an exposure.* London: Kegan Paul, Trench, Trubner.

Watson, J. B., & Raynor, R. (1920). Conditioned emotional reactions. *Journal of Experimental Psychology, 3*, 1–14

Weiss, A. P. (1919). The mind and the man-within. *Psychological Review, 26*, 327–334.

Weiss, A. P. (1925a). One set of postulates for a behavioristic psychology. *Psychological Review, 32*, 83–87.

Weiss, A. P. (1925b). *A theoretical basis of human behavior.* Columbus, OH: Adams.

Woodworth, R. S. (1924). Four varieties of behaviorism. *Psychological Review, 31*, 257–264.

Woodworth, R. S. (1938). *Experimental psychology.* New York: Holt.

Wozniak, R. H. (1993). Theoretical roots of early behaviourism: Functionalism, the critique of introspection, and the nature and evolution of consciousness. In R. H. Wozniak (Ed.), *Theoretical roots of early behaviourism: Functionalism, the critique of introspection, and the nature and evolution of consciousness* (pp. ix–liii). London: Routledge/Thoemmes.

Wozniak, R. H. (1994a). Behaviourism: The early years. In R. H. Wozniak (Ed.), *Reflex, habit and implicit response: The early elaboration of theoretical and methodological behaviourism* (pp. ix–xxxii). London: Routledge/Thoemmes.

Wozniak, R. H. (1994b). Floyd Henry Allport and the Social Psychology. In F. H. Allport, *Social psychology* (pp. v–xxix). London: Routledge/Thoemmes.

Yerkes, R. M. (1905). Animal psychology and criteria of the psychic. *Journal of Philosophy, Psychology, and Scientific Methods, 2*, 141–149.

Yerkes, R. M. (1907). *The dancing mouse.* New York: Macmillan.

Yerkes, R. M. (1910). Psychology in its relations to biology. *Journal of Philosophy, Psychology, and Scientific Methods, 7*, 113–124.

Yerkes, R. M. (1917). Behaviorism and genetic psychology. *Journal of Philosophy, Psychology, and Scientific Methods, 14*, 154–160.

Yerkes, R. M., & Watson, J. B. (1911). Methods of studying vision in animals. *Behavior Monographs, 1*(2), 90 p.

Notes

1. Another exceptionally important individual in this regard was Francis Galton (see especially Galton, 1883). It will come as no surprise to anyone familiar with the work of Francis Galton that some of Lubbock's apparatus development took place in collaboration with Galton. See, for example, Lubbock (1882), p. 263.

2. Letter from Watson to Yerkes, October 29, 1909, quoted in Buckley (1989), p. 71.

3. Terms adopted here to distinguish among the varieties of early behaviorism are, for the most part, those of the author. Although detailed discussion of the variability existing within behaviorism in the 1920s is beyond the scope of this article, it is worth pointing out that disagreements typically revolved around four issues: (a) the possibility of achieving a complete explanation of behavior in terms of the principles of nervous function (the neuromechanical program); (b) rejection of any special role for the central nervous system in the organization of behavior (peripheralism); (c) the relation of acquired to hereditary mechanisms (the nature of instinct); and (d) the role of mental facts and mental terms, if any, in behavioral theory.

B. F. Skinner: Maverick, Inventor, Behaviorist, Critic

Steven R. Coleman

Burrhus Frederic Skinner was born on March 20, 1904, in a small northeastern Pennsylvania town originally named Susquehanna Depot. The town's name dates back to the third quarter of the 19th century when it served as a centrally located, locomotive construction-and-repair facility on what was the Erie Railroad's original trunk line. Figure 1 shows a view of Susquehanna taken in the early 1980s from across the Susquehanna River. The long building in the foreground was erected after the Civil War as a luxury hotel. Beyond the left edge of the picture frame are the dilapidated remnants of the Erie Railroad (now Conrail) facility, which was built on the river's flood plain. Figure 2 presents a layout of Susquehanna and its surroundings and the location of Skinner's boyhood home on Grand Street. Figure 3, which was also taken in the 1980s, displays a view of the Skinner family home, which adjoined one of the city's two cemeteries.

Early Life and Education

Skinner was the eldest son of William A. Skinner, an attorney for the railroad; his mother was Grace Burrhus. The small size of Susquehanna and the proximity of grandparents and relatives on both sides of the family created a small-town, extended-family environment. When Skinner was 19, his younger brother, Ebbe, died suddenly from what was probably a cerebral hemorrhage (Skinner, 1976).

From 1922 to 1926, Skinner majored in English at Hamilton College in Clinton, New York. After gradu-

ation, he spent a period—which he later characterized as the Dark Year of his life—fruitlessly trying to start a career as a short-story writer while living at home with his parents. Although he failed to establish such a career, his discursive reading acquainted him with John B. Watson's behaviorism. In the absence of more sensible career plans, but with little knowledge of psychology, Skinner decided that he was really a behaviorist and would pursue postgraduate education in psychology (Skinner, 1983). On the advice of the family's physician, who had taken his MD at Harvard's medical school, Skinner applied for graduate study at Harvard University in the spring of 1928. He was accepted for work toward a Master of Arts degree and enrolled in September 1928.

Figure 1 Photograph of Susquehanna from the north side of the Susquehanna River (March 1982).

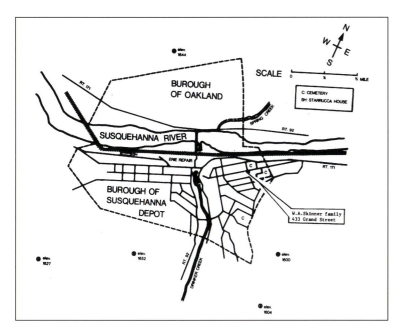

Figure 2 Line drawing of the street layout of Susquehanna, Oakland, and other landmarks, with orientation indicated.

Psychology at Harvard in the late 1920s was an odd choice for a convert to behaviorism: In the late twenties, Harvard was one of the few major American universities that had not yet separated psychology from philosophy and given psychology a department status. Instead, both were housed in Emerson Hall (Figure 4) as the Department of Philosophy and Psychology, with psychology's laboratory space on the top floor. In many ways, Harvard philosophy was very old-fashioned (Kuklick, 1977), and professors were averse to such a radical philosophical psychology as the behaviorism of the 1920s. This circumstance enabled Skinner to slip easily into the role of defender of behaviorism at Harvard. It also encouraged him to adopt a generalized attitude of contrariness to academic psychology as a whole and a contentious style in dealing with those who would not recognize the truth of behaviorism. His undergraduate background in English had equipped him with the rhetorical skills for the role of polemicist; he had already been attracted to writers who were critical of traditional cultural arrangements (e.g., Sinclair Lewis, Bertrand Russell, H. G. Wells). Acci-

dents of time and place such as these may be remotely responsible for Skinner's position as a "village scoffer" (Lasch, 1979) at conventionally accepted beliefs in academic psychology and common-sense (folk) psychology. Nevertheless, such a style may have diminished his impact upon psychology by provoking strong resistance to his ideas (Place, 1988) and a readiness to marginalize the research-and-application enterprise that he developed (Leahey, 1992). In the third volume of his autobiography (*A Matter of Consequences*, 1983), which covers the period from 1948 to 1981, several anecdotes demonstrate that vehement rejection of Skinner's ideas was seldom accompanied by a thorough grasp of them; and problems in communicating his views or being understood bedeviled Skinner as his fame (and infamy) increased. (See Skinner's late-life assessment in Catania & Harnad, 1988, pp. 487–488.)

As a graduate student at Harvard in the late twenties, Skinner took courses in psychology, philosophy, and physiology. Graduate education ordinarily socializes a student into the values and attitudes of the professional community of the student's field of specialization; however, during Skinner's graduate-school years, he did not work

Figure 3 Photograph of the home in which Skinner lived between 1904 and 1922 (March 1982).

Figure 4 Photograph of Emerson Hall on the Harvard College campus.

out a conventional relationship between his own values, interests, and ambitions to the mainstream of theory and research in psychology (Skinner, 1979). His graduate research was prompted not by published investigations in animal psychology—which would otherwise have been a sensible reference point—but rather by the writings of reflex physiologists such as Ivan Pavlov and Charles Sherrington. His first laboratory research (a study of ant locomotion on slanted surfaces) was conducted in the physiology laboratory of William J. Crozier, a student of the influential Jacques Loeb (Pauly, 1987). The results of this research were published in 1930 as Skinner's first scientific paper. His first independent research project was on a physiological topic, the measurement of reflexes in freely moving animals. Eventually, through accident and by following his own curiosity and hunches (Skinner, 1956; Coleman, 1987), he latched onto an established psychological topic, the topic of learning (conditioning), but his research and opinions continued to reflect the roundabout path by which he had linked his work to American behavioral psychology.

Origins of Operant Conditioning

Perhaps as a result of growing up in a railroad town, Skinner came to graduate school with a knack for mechanical invention. His skill enabled him to develop an influential and original piece of equipment while he was a student: a fully automated chamber in which a laboratory animal is able to perform a designated operant behavior at any time (e.g., pressing a small lever that projects into the chamber), with rewards (reinforcers) delivered automatically and according to a pre-established plan (a reinforcement schedule). This apparatus, which others identified as a "Skinner box," was the ancestor of subsequent operant-conditioning equipment. An illustration of this apparatus is seen in Figure 5.

It is widely recognized that seemingly trivial differences can produce unexpected, lasting rifts, and that is clearly so in the case of Skinner's research methods. For instance, because he did not employ separate training trials, he was unable to use the standard learning curve of the animal psychology laboratory, which displays change in some behavioral measure over practice trials, as the left panel of Figure 6 shows. Instead, Skinner made use of available physiological laboratory equipment (the kymograph) and plotted a cumulative record, that is, the cumulative number of response occurrences against time, as the right panel of Figure 6 reveals. Thus, in the course of Skinner's research, he developed a distinctive set of laboratory procedures and apparatus, and distinctive investigative interests followed these beginnings. The operant-conditioning enterprise of the "Skinnerians" (Sidman, 1960) who grew from these beginnings did so independently of

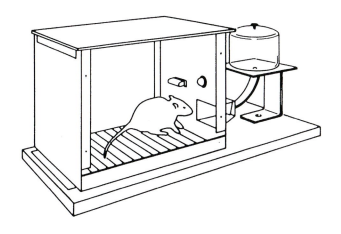

Figure 5 Line drawing of a rat in an operant chamber.

five more years at Harvard on postdoctoral support for his operant-conditioning research. He was a careful investigator and kept detailed records, many of which survived years of storage and are currently archived at the Harvard University Library. Figure 7 displays a record of his rats from the early 1930s and the experiments in which they were used.

Skinner accepted a position in the Psychology Department at the University of Minnesota in 1936. In the same year he married Yvonne Blue of Flossmoor, Illinois, and daughters Julie and Deborah were born in the ensuing years. He chaired the Psychology Department at Indiana University in Bloomington, Indiana, from 1945 to 1948. A grass-roots Skinnerian psychology developed at Indiana and the instrumental-conditioning enterprise (see Krantz, 1971) of Edward Tolman, Clark Hull, and others, which formed the mainstream of animal-psychology laboratory research and theory. Table 1 summarizes resulting differences. Such divisions underscored Skinner's maverick status in the spectrum of behaviorist laboratory research.

Professional Career

On the basis of a dissertation on the behavior of rats given reward training in an apparatus like that described above, Skinner was awarded a doctorate by Harvard University in 1931. He remained for

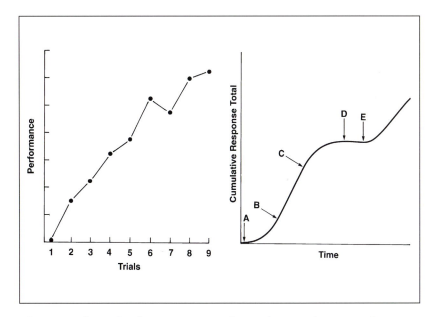

Figure 6 Left panel: A learning curve. Right panel: A cumulative record.

Table 1 Differences Between Arrangements for Instrumental Conditioning and for Operant Conditioning

Characteristic	Instrumental	Operant
Location of behavior	Maze, runway, puzzle-box	Operant chamber
Methodology	Discrete trials	Free responding
Procedure	Subject is re-placed in apparatus to begin each trial in a session	Subject is placed in the apparatus only to begin a session
Display	Learning curve	Cumulative record
Data display	On-trial performance against trials	Cumulative frequency against time
Data source	Average of performance of group of subjects	Individual-subject performance
Statistics?	Yes: significance test	No
Is a control used?	Yes: not administered the treatment variable or factor	Subject's pretreatment baseline serves as a comparison value

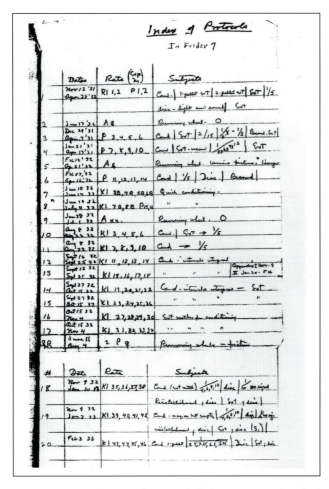

Figure 7 Reproduction of a record of Skinner's rats (identified by letter-number combinations).

was promoted elsewhere by his students, as well as by converts to his ideas, his research, his criticism of competing expositions of behaviorism, and his postwar vision of psychology. In 1948, at the age of 44, he became a professor in the Department of Psychology at Harvard. During his years at Harvard (1948–1974), a distinctive Skinnerian psychology completed the development of its own experimental methods, apparatus, vocabulary, journals, professional organization (called Behavior Analysis), and guiding philosophy (called radical behaviorism). A strong interest also grew in applying Skinner's ideas to behavior therapy and other settings (prisons, hospitals, schools, etc.) that manage or modify the behavior of human beings through reward for institutionally acceptable behavior.

In 1964, a Career Development Award from the U.S. government enabled him to disengage, at the age of 60, from frustrating events in the Psychology

Department, but he maintained a busy schedule of writing and lecturing. Though he officially retired at the age of 70 in 1974, he continued to lecture and write. In the process, he completed a three-volume autobiography (Skinner, 1976, 1979, 1983) and, with increasing frequency and pessimism, tackled questions of cultural survival (e.g., Skinner, 1987, 1989). He was at work right up to his death on August 18, 1990, at the age of 86, from complications of leukemia.

The Control of Behavior

Skinner's achievements depended upon his readiness to break with convention in psychology and to boldly extend the explanatory model of rat (and pigeon, monkey, gerbil, etc.) research in the operant-conditioning laboratory to human problems in daily life, as well as in education (programmed instruction), in rehabilitative and incarcerative institutions (token economy), and in industry (contingency management). Among his many inventions were: an air-conditioned crib for his second daughter; a "teaching machine" that a child could operate to practice (learn) arithmetic or other rote-learned facts more effectively than in the typical classroom; a procedure for teaching handwriting that used reward for letters made correctly by a student using a special pen on chemically treated paper.

His inventive skill enabled him to create instruments for applied projects; but how did he develop such readiness and confidence for tackling practical problems? His behaviorist peers accepted the positivist creed that scientific progress is necessarily gradual and incremental, and they were certain that creating an effective behavioral technology at some time in the future would require a lengthy period of basic (not applied) research in which behavioral psychologists would patiently uncover the fundamental laws of behavior (Spence, 1956). Skinner's own writing about his life provides some clues to his applied interests.

The second and third volumes of Skinner's autobiography show that his own family was often the source of puzzles that roused his inventive genius, but his research during World War II was the primary professional source of this distinctive feature of his psychology. While he was at the University of Minnesota, he initiated a wartime project (hosted at a General Mills facility) to develop training procedures for a missile-guidance system that was to employ a pigeon housed in the missile's nose cone and trained to keep the missile on target (Skinner, 1979). The pigeon was to accomplish this by pecking at a screen on which the target was displayed; the orientation of the missile to the target could be altered by the location of pecks on the screen. The proficiency of his pigeons in the training apparatus, despite severe distractions, made a very strong impression on Skinner and convinced him that it was possible to attain a much more extensive control of both animal and human behavior than psychologists had hitherto regarded as possible. These convictions about the control of behavior through operant-conditioning techniques dominated his subsequent work.

The vigorous creation of a behavioral technology was the ultimate consequence of Skinner's disenchantment with the time-honored scholarly objectives of patiently discovering the laws of learning (through laboratory research) and creating theories to explain them—objectives which his peers continued to pursue. In several papers during the 1950s, Skinner alienated his peers by demeaning the worth of current behaviorist theory (e.g., Skinner, 1950, 1956). Instead, Skinner was convinced by his experiences that techniques to control behavior could already be applied to problems beyond the laboratory without requiring the assistance of elaborate theorizing.

Moreover, Skinner's attitude toward public visibility departed from the genteel tradition of scholarly disengagement from worldly fame and fortune. He welcomed public notice. Popular magazines (e.g., *Look* and *Life*) provided photo coverage of his animal-training accomplishments, and he wrote for *Scientific American* (Skinner, 1951). He published a novel (*Walden Two*, 1948) that described a fictional utopia based on behavioral engineering. *Beyond Freedom and Dignity* (1971) provoked a storm of criticism—including a rebuke by then Vice President Spiro T. Agnew—by claiming that Western cultural practices inappropriately aggrandize the individual at the expense of society. Finally, visibility resulted from applications that he and his students developed.

B. F. Skinner as Public Philosopher

As a public figure, and in the process of attaining public visibility, Skinner developed opinions on a large range of subjects, mostly on issues germane to the United States rather than the international situation. Skinner's many opinions stem from the claim that the individual (human or otherwise) makes no self-originated contribution to the determination of its own behavior. Skinner was an environmentalist, arguing that the circumstances under which the individual behaves typically select a more effective repertoire of behaviors during the individual's lifetime (ontogenetically). For example, in *Beyond Freedom and Dignity* (1971) and *About Behaviorism* (1974), Skinner was sharply critical of Romantic philosophical psychologies that assume that individuals are creative agents who are causally responsible for their own behavior and deserve greater freedom from societal controls. (For a full account of the reception of *Beyond Freedom and Dignity*, see Bjork, 1993, chapter 9.)

Similarly, the environmental niche that a present-day species inhabited through evolutionary time (phylogenetically) shaped the anatomical and behavioral features that provided advantages for the reproductive success and survival of that species in that niche. Thus the environment has the primary causal responsibility in a process that selects more effective behavior and more effective forms of plant and animal life (e.g., see Skinner, 1953, p. 90; 1966; 1971, chapter 7). Skinner's ideas presuppose a similarity of learning and evolution, a notion that other writers have noticed (Dennett, 1974).

Inner States and Skinner's Radical Behaviorism

One of the dangers for a system of ideas that emphasizes the importance of the environment is that it is likely to be seen as an empty-organism theory that denies the existence of inner states, emotions, experiences, thoughts, and so on. Behaviorism has had a history of uncomfortable dealings with inner states, whether they are called personal, private, mental, cognitive, or experiential. Naive forms of behaviorism question whether this troublesome realm exists in favor of the claim that all we can be sure about with regard to others is their behavior. Methodological behaviorists acknowledge the existence of private phenomena but affirm either that they cannot be examined scientifically or that they can be accommodated through theoretical concepts that function as conceptual substitutes for the inner (Kimble, 1989).

Skinner adopted a materialistic philosophy by asserting that both public and private phenomena have the same status: They both consist of stimuli and behaviors. He suspected that inner phenomena such as feelings and emotions are stimuli subserved by interoceptors. So-called mental acts (thinking, planning, etc.) he regarded as covert behaviors. Skinner's materialism resembled proposals set forth by the early behaviorist John B. Watson, but his other opinions about the inner world of the mind are closer to proposals that the philosopher Ludwig Wittgenstein (1953) developed while working on the question of whether a private mentalistic language could exist. Skinner proposed that self-conscious knowledge involves making discriminations in labeling correctly the source of stimulation. External discriminations can be taught easily because the teacher has access to the stimuli to be discriminated, but teaching the language of emotions and of mental acts is more difficult because the relevant stimuli are private (Skinner, 1953, chapter 17). The result is that the individual can never know (discriminate among the stimuli of) the "world within its skin" as well as it can know the external world. Skinner employed this reasoning in a program of argumentation that diminished the significance of the inner world in explaining behavior (e.g., Skinner, 1974). Whether right or wrong, he was distinctive in explicitly and fully addressing these conceptual problems while his behaviorist brethren generally avoided such philosophical issues as not appropriate for experimental psychologists. Because he did address these matters, he reached an audience of intellectuals who held views that are less deterministic and which assign more responsibility to the individual's inner states such as feelings and thoughts.

Figure 8 Photo of B. F. Skinner taken in 1987 by Jane Reed.

Impact

Skinner outlived his primary rivals (e.g., Hull, Spence, and Tolman) and, during a decline in the apparent importance of behaviorism during the 1970s, stayed behind as the primary spokesman for behaviorist ideas in psychology. His writings on social practices (e.g., *Walden Two*) even prompted some to try out these ideas in small, experimental communities, some of which have endured (e.g., Comunidad Los Horcones, 1991; Kinkade, 1972). Figure 8 is a photograph of him in 1987.

There is a very large literature of commentary on B. F. Skinner's philosophy, research, speculations, cultural criticism, and impact on psychology, education, psychotherapy, the social sciences, and American thought. Daniel Bjork's (1993) solid biography is a good place to start. A special issue of *American Psychologist* in 1992 was devoted to an appraisal of Skinner's work. *Notebooks, B. F. Skinner* (Epstein, 1980) is an intriguing diary of observations and ideas. On the basis of a variety of accomplishments over a long career (1930–1990), one can confidently assert that B. F. Skinner was the most visible and influential American psychologist in the second half of the 20th century.

Bibliography

Bjork, D. W. (1993). *B. F. Skinner: A life*. New York: Basic.

Catania, A. C., & Harnad, S. (Eds.). (1988). *The selection of behavior. The operant behaviorism of B. F. Skinner: Comments and consequences*. Cambridge, England: Cambridge University Press.

Coleman, S. R. (1987). Quantitative order in B. F. Skinner's early research program. *The Behavior Analyst, 10*, 47–65.

Comunidad Los Horcones. (1991). Walden Two in real life: Behavior analysis in the design of a culture. In I. Waris (Ed.), *Human behavior in today's world* (pp. 249–256). New York: Praeger.

Dennett, D. (1974). Why the law of effect will not go away. *Journal for the Theory of Social Behaviour, 5*, 169–187.

Epstein, R. (Ed.). (1980). *Notebooks, B. F. Skinner*. Englewood Cliffs, NJ: Prentice-Hall.

Kimble, G. A. (1989). Psychology from the standpoint of a generalist. *American Psychologist, 44*, 491–499.

Kinkade, K. (1972). *A Walden Two experiment: The first five years of Twin Oaks community*. New York: Morrow.

Krantz, D. L. (1971). The separate worlds of operant and nonoperant psychology. *Journal of Applied Behavior Analysis, 4*, 61–70.

Kuklick, B. (1977). *The rise of American philosophy*. New Haven, CT: Yale University Press.

Lasch, C. (1979, August 4 & 11). [Review of *The shaping of a behaviorist* by B. F. Skinner]. *New Republic, 181* (5 & 6), 36–38.

Leahey, T. H. (1992). *A history of psychology* (3rd ed.). Englewood Cliffs, NJ: Prentice-Hall.

Pauly, P. (1987). *Controlling life: Jacques Loeb and the engineering ideal in biology*. New York: Oxford University Press.

Place, U. T. (1988). What went wrong? *Counseling Psychology Quarterly, 1*, 307–309.

Sidman, M. (1960). *Tactics of scientific research*. New York: Basic.

Skinner, B. F. (1948). *Walden Two*. New York: Macmillan.

Skinner, B. F. (1950). Are theories of learning necessary? *Psychological Review, 57*, 193–216.

Skinner, B. F. (1951). How to teach animals. *Scientific American, 185*, 26–29.

Skinner, B. F. (1953). *Science and human behavior*. New York: Macmillan.

Skinner, B. F. (1956). A case history in scientific method. *American Psychologist, 11*, 221–233.

Skinner, B. F. (1966). The phylogeny and ontogeny of behavior. *Science, 153*, 1205–1213.

Skinner, B. F. (1971). *Beyond freedom and dignity*. New York: Knopf.

Skinner, B. F. (1974). *About behaviorism*. New York: Random.

Skinner, B. F. (1976). *Particulars of my life*. New York: Knopf.

Skinner, B. F. (1979). *The shaping of a behaviorist*. New York: Knopf.

Skinner, B. F. (1983). *A matter of consequences*. New York: Knopf.

Skinner, B. F. (1987). Why we are not acting to save the world. In B. F. Skinner (Ed.), *Upon further reflection* (pp. 1–14). Englewood Cliffs, NJ: Prentice-Hall.

Skinner, B. F. (1989). The school of the future. In B. F. Skinner (Ed.), *Recent issues in the analysis of behavior* (pp. 85–96). Columbus, OH: Merrill.

Spence, K. W. (1956). *Behavior theory and conditioning*. New Haven, CT: Yale University Press.

Wittgenstein, L. (1953). *Philosophical investigations* (G. E. M. Anscombe, Trans.). New York: Macmillan.

A Purposive Behaviorist:
Edward C. Tolman

Nancy K. Innis

On March 13, 1963, a new building was dedicated on the Berkeley campus of the University of California. Tolman Hall, shown in Figure 1, was named in honor of Edward Chace Tolman (1886–1959), long-time professor in the Department of Psychology. It was in September 1918, after a tedious train trip across the continent, that Edward Tolman, accompanied by his wife and baby daughter, arrived in Berkeley. Edward assumed an appointment as Lecturer in Psychology in the Department of Philosophy and Psychology housed in the building shown in Figure 2. For Edward, the move to California entailed much more than taking up a new position; it resulted in a personal transformation and, of more importance for psychology, a new theoretical perspective. When he arrived in Berkeley, Edward was a self-conscious, rather retiring young man whose research had been directed at "classical introspectionist and associationistic problems" (Tolman, 1952, p. 329). But living on the West Coast resulted in a newfound freedom—Edward soon lost his East Coast inhibitions and became confident and self-assured. It also produced an intellectual liberation—Edward gave up his traditional theoretical approach and became a behaviorist.

Edward Chace Tolman, the younger son of James

Figure 1 Tolman Hall, University of California, Berkeley.

214

Figure 2 The old Philosophy Building, University of California, Berkeley.

and Mary Chace Tolman, was born in West Newton, Massachusetts, a quiet suburb of Boston, on April 14, 1886. His father was a successful manufacturer and inventor, his mother an accomplished amateur painter. Both Edward and his elder brother, Richard Chace Tolman (1881–1948), attended the Newton public schools before enrolling at the Massachusetts Institute of Technology. Richard, who completed his doctorate at M.I.T. in 1910, would become a renowned physical chemist, spending most of his career at the California Institute of Technology. Edward, after receiving his BS in electrochemistry in 1911, decided to defy family tradition (his father had been in the first graduating class of M.I.T. and was a trustee) and leave M.I.T. to study at Harvard. Edward chose psychology because it would allow him to pursue a career in science while at the same time do something to help mankind. Richard, who was both rival and role model, was already beginning to achieve success as a scientist; Edward was determined to do so as well (Tolman, 1952). However, he also had a strong desire to follow the example of an earlier generation of radical relatives, the most prominent of whom was his grandmother, Elizabeth Buffum Chace, a long-time social activist (Stevens, 1993; Wyman & Wyman, 1914).

Edward's doctoral research at Harvard, under the supervision of Hugo Münsterberg, Director of the Psychological Laboratory, examined the role of pleasant and unpleasant stimuli on human memory (Tolman, 1915). Experimentation, and the possibility of theorizing about his findings, soon drew Edward away from applied ambitions. However, he never abandoned the notion that his theoretical ideas could have some practical benefits. His most ambitious, albeit unsuccessful, attempt in this regard was a little book, *Drives Toward War*, published just after the United States entered World War II. Here Tolman's aim was to "adapt concepts derived from the behavior of rats and chimpanzees, combine them with certain Freudian notions, and then attempt to apply them to the most central and the most grievous problems of society" (1942, p. xii). In so doing, he presented an idealistic, but unrealistic, prescription for peace, and the book went largely unnoticed.

After receiving his PhD from Harvard in 1915, Tolman spent the next three years as an instructor at Northwestern University, where he continued to conduct research on problems of human learning and memory. However, soon after the move to California he started to study the inheritance of learning ability in rats (Tolman, 1924; see also Innis, 1992a). At first he didn't like the little creatures; they made him "feel creepy." But, as he expanded his rat research to explore broader issues, his relationship with his subjects improved steadily. So much so that when he penned the preface to *Purposive*

Behavior in Animals and Men, Tolman dedicated his book to them. And a few years later, in his Presidential Address to the American Psychological Association, he would claim: "I believe that everything important in psychology . . . can be investigated in essence through the continued experimental and theoretical analysis of the determiners of rat behavior at a choice-point in a maze" (Tolman, 1938, p. 34).

Edward Tolman first encountered the behaviorism of John B. Watson when, as a graduate student at Harvard, he sat in on Robert Yerkes's comparative psychology course (Tolman, 1952). He agreed with Watson (1914/1967) that psychology was the study of behavior, not consciousness, and so maintained that psychological questions could most readily be addressed through research with animal subjects. However, for Tolman, behavior was much more than Watson's "muscle-twitches" and "gland

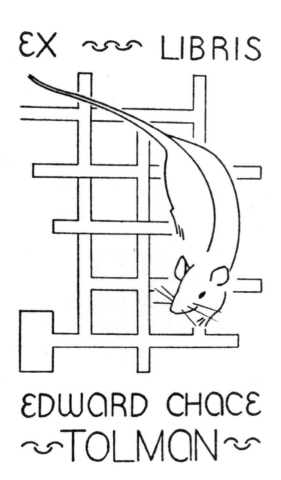

Figure 4 Edward Tolman's book plate exemplifying his fondness for his experimental subject, the rat.

Figure 3 Edward Chace Tolman, at about the time he received his PhD from Harvard.

secretions"—it involved the goal-directed activity of the entire organism. Behavior, then, was purposive, and it was molar. Beginning with "A New Formula for Behaviorism," Tolman (1922a) developed his position, which became known as "purposive behaviorism," in a series of theoretical articles, published mainly in the *Psychological Review*. Unwilling to give up the traditional constructs of his field, he set about providing objective, behavioristic accounts of sensation (Tolman, 1922b), the emotions (Tolman, 1923), ideas (Tolman, 1926), and consciousness (Tolman, 1927), as well as presenting his views on purpose and cognition (Tolman, 1925a, 1925b, 1928). The book, *Purposive Behavior in Animals and Men*, published in 1932, summarized his final doctrine or system of psychology.

So what did this system—purposive behaviorism—involve? Tolman (1932) declared that the molar behavior of both humans and other animals, including the lowly rat, simply "reeks of purpose and of cognition" (p. 12). By purposive, he meant that behavior was goal-directed and persisted until the goal in demand (e.g., food for a hungry rat) was reached. By cognitive, he meant that behavior was determined by expectations about where and when, for example, the rat would find food. Later these expectations, or representations, about the routes to goals were called "cognitive maps" (see Tolman, 1948). Put more formally, the theory claimed that

> mental processes [purposes and cognitions] are most usefully to be conceived as but dynamic aspects, or determinants, of behavior. . . . functional variables which intermediate in the causal equation between environmental stimuli and initiating physiological states or excitements, on the one side, and final overt behavior, on the other. (Tolman, 1932, p. 2)

Such constructs later became known as "intervening variables," perhaps the most important contribution Tolman made to psychology (Tolman, 1936).

The ideas presented in Tolman's book were considered brilliant, although difficult, and it was well-received by scholars at the time (e.g., Elliott, 1932; Young, 1933). One of the difficulties was Tolman's tendency to invent convoluted terms (neologisms). A brief anonymous review of the book, in England's *New Statesman and Nation*, remarked on his "Pickwickian" use of language (e.g., "means-end-readiness" and "sign-Gestalt expectation" were used to represent what could have simply been termed "expectations"). Moreover, in contrast to the more systematic formulations of contemporary theorists such as Clark Hull, Tolman's ideas often seemed vague or ill-defined. In part, this was deliberate. Tolman believed he had presented a useful and valid approach, but concluded his book with a final caveat, pointing out the ephemeral quality of systems—"each system is so obviously bound to be wrong." He cautioned the reader and chided himself: "May neither you nor we ever seek to hold up these propositions, save in a somewhat amused, a somewhat skeptical, and a wholly adventure-seeking and programmatic behavior-attitude" (Tolman, 1932, p. 394). That sentence reflects the perspective that Tolman would always maintain regarding theoretical systems—ideas were to be played with, science involved having fun (see Tolman, 1959).

Following the publication of *Purposive Behavior*, Tolman spent a year (1933–1934) in Europe on sabbatical leave. Initially, he had planned to spend most

of his time in Berlin with Kurt Lewin, who had been a visitor at Stanford at the time Tolman was planning his sabbatical. Tolman was impressed by Gestalt psychology, in general, but particularly with Lewin's work. However, the political situation in Germany prevented Lewin from returning to Berlin and so Tolman went instead to Vienna (Figure 5). Here he spent time at the Institute of Psychology (headed by Karl Bühler) where he met Egon Brunswik. Brunswik was an active member of the Vienna Circle, a group of positivist philosophers whose ideas were becoming influential at the time, and Tolman occasionally took part in their meetings. Tolman and Brunswik also met frequently in Viennese cafes to discuss psychology, and they soon began to collaborate on a paper (Tolman & Brunswik, 1935). "The organism and the causal texture of the environment" identified the common features of their ideas; Brunswik's views developed as a result of his work

Figure 5 Edward Chace Tolman, on sabbatical leave in Vienna, 1932–1933.

in perception, while Tolman's position grew from his research in animal learning. Their suggestion that the relationship between cues and objects (or signs and goals) was probabilistic rather than one-to-one led to major changes in animal learning research. When Brunswik too was forced to escape from Europe, Tolman made it possible for him to obtain a position at the University of California.

On March 17, 1947, Edward Tolman delivered the 34th Annual Faculty Research Lecture at the University of California. The occasion, celebrating his long and distinguished career at Berkeley, provided an opportunity for him to summarize the research he and his students had carried out over the years and to differentiate his own "field" theory of learning from the generally more popular S-R approach. Tolman then concluded his lecture by turning to a topic with which he had become increasingly absorbed over the preceding decade—the role of psychology in changing the human condition.

The title of the talk, "Cognitive Maps in Rats and Men" (which soon appeared in print in the *Psychological Review*), in itself gives us the key elements of Tolman's psychology: a spatial metaphor for memory representation; the rat as a prototypical research subject; and mankind as the true and proper object of his concern. Most of the paper is devoted to a discussion of experiments with rats in mazes and the theoretical implications of his findings. Tolman indicated how his theory of animal learning differed from S-R theories which he called the "telephone-switchboard school." He employed a different metaphor, more in line with what he believed was really going on, suggesting that "in the course of learning something like a field map of the environment gets established in the rat's brain" (Tolman, 1948, p. 192). The use of a map metaphor and spatial analogies, in fact, was a salient feature of all of Tolman's theorizing about animal learning (see Smith, 1990). Data from experiments with rats were then reported to support his theoretical claims. He described (a) the studies on latent learning that led to the protracted controversy concerning the distinction between learning and performance, (b) the role of vicarious trial and error in visual discrimination learning, (c) the

idea of "hypotheses" in rats that had been developed in studies with his star student David Krech (then Krechevsky), and (d) findings from the series of spatial orientation studies carried out by Benbow Ritchie and Donald Kalish that had been completed only a year or two earlier. These experiments indicated that rats learn something very general about the location of important stimuli and events in their environment.

Tolman then turned his attention to human behavior. The three decades following his arrival in Berkeley, spanning two world wars and a devastating economic depression, were a time of great social change in America. These events caused Tolman to turn his attention to applying the knowledge of psychology to the problems facing the society in which he lived. For example, Tolman was a founding member of SPSSI, the Society for the Psychological Study of Social Issues, and the fourth president of that society (Capshew, 1986). By the 1940s, personality and social psychology had emerged as a vibrant field, and, on more than one occasion, Tolman had been heard to declare that if he were a young man just starting his career this would be his area of study. Indeed, when Edward was starting out in psy-

Figure 6 Edward Tolman during a lecture.

chology at Harvard, he was looking for a career in which he could help mankind.

Although Edward Tolman is best remembered for his theoretical contributions, his role as a university teacher should not be overlooked. Students in his undergraduate courses were either baffled or enthralled. Tolman's lectures often comprised a series of equations covering the blackboard as he thought through his latest theoretical inspiration in front of the class. And it was not unusual for him to come in the next day and tell the students to forget what they had heard the day before. For most undergraduates this was frustrating, but the budding psychologists in the class recognized that they had the good fortune to be participants in the scientific process at work. Tolman was at his best in his graduate seminar, where the students were respected, listened to, and challenged, but never put down. He was the perfect mentor, never trying to impose his views, and open to the opinions and criticisms of his students (although he usually retained his own position in the end). The result was that Tolman produced no intellectual disciples; but his graduate students adored him, and many of them became eminent in their own right.

Edward Tolman received considerable recognition during his long career. He was honored by his colleagues when he was named President of the American Psychological Association for 1937. That year, he was also inducted into the prestigious National Academy of Sciences, where he joined his brother Richard, with whom he is shown relaxing in Figure 7, to become one of only a few pairs of brothers so honored. In 1959, some 40 years after he arrived in Berkeley, Edward Tolman received an honorary doctor of laws degree from the university to which he had dedicated much of his life. A portrait showing Tolman in the robes of his honorary degree (Figure 8) hangs in the foyer of Tolman Hall. There is some irony in the recognition that Tolman received from the University of California. Ten years earlier he had stood up in strong opposition to the university regents over an oath of loyalty that was imposed on the faculty. Always concerned with the protection of individual rights, Tolman was the leader of the Group for Academic Freedom (GAF), men and women who refused to sign the loyalty oath and were fired from the university. The non-signers were loyal Americans who believed that employment at the university should not depend on

Figure 7 The Tolman brothers, Richard (left) and Edward, relaxing (ca. 1940).

Figure 8 Edward Chace Tolman in the robes of the honorary degree he received from the University of California, Berkeley (October 1959).

a political test (see Innis, 1992b). The GAF took the regents to court and eventually, after a long battle, won reinstatement. Although the GAF was portrayed by the media as disgracing the University of California, Tolman's principled stand was applauded by his colleagues. Their high regard for him is exemplified by the fact that his memory lives on in the building that bears his name.

Acknowledgment

The author wishes to thank the Canadian Social Sciences and Humanities Research Council for its support.

Bibliography

Anonymous. (1932). Shorter notices. *The Statesman and Nation, 64,* 625.

Capshew, J. H. (1986). Network of leadership: A quantitative study of SPSSI Presidents, 1936–1986. *Journal of Social Issues, 42,* 75–106.

Elliott, R. M. (1932). Editor's introduction. In E. C. Tolman, *Purposive behavior in animals and men* (pp. vii–ix). New York: Century.

Innis, N. K. (1992a). Early studies in behavior genetics: The inheritance of the ability to learn. *American Psychologist, 47,* 190–197.

Innis, N. K. (1992b). Lessons from the controversy over the loyalty oath at the University of California. *Minerva, 30,* 337–365.

Smith, L. D. (1990). Metaphors of knowledge and behavior in the behaviorist tradition. In D. E. Leary (Ed.), *Metaphors in the history of psychology* (pp. 239–266). New York: Cambridge University Press.

Stevens, E. C. (1993). *"From generation to generation": The mother and daughter activism of Elizabeth Buffum Chace and Lillie Chace Wyman.* Unpublished Doctoral dissertation, Brown University.

Tolman, E. C. (1915). *Studies in memory.* Doctoral thesis, Harvard University.

Tolman, E. C. (1922a). A new formula for behaviorism. *Psychological Review, 29,* 44–53.

Tolman, E. C. (1922b). Concerning the sensation quality: A behavioristic account. *Psychological Review, 29,* 140–145.

Tolman, E. C. (1923). A behavioristic account of the emotions. *Psychological Review, 30,* 217–227.

Tolman, E. C. (1924). The inheritance of maze-learning ability in rats. *Journal of Comparative Psychology, 4,* 1–18.

Tolman, E. C. (1925a). Behaviorism and purpose. *Journal of Philosophy, 22,* 36–41.

Tolman, E. C. (1925b). Purpose and cognition: the determiners of animal learning. *Psychological Review, 32,* 285–297.

Tolman, E. C. (1926). A behavioristic theory of ideas. *Psychological Review, 33,* 352–369.

Tolman, E. C. (1927). A behaviorist's definition of consciousness. *Psychological Review, 34,* 433–439.

Tolman, E. C. (1928). Purposive behaviorism. *Psychological Review, 35,* 524–530.

Tolman, E. C. (1932). *Purposive behavior in animals and men.* New York: Century.

Tolman, E. C. (1936). Operational behaviorism and current trends in psychology. *Proceedings of the 25th anniversary celebration of the inauguration of graduate studies.* Los Angeles: University of Southern California.

Tolman, E. C. (1938). The determiners of behavior at a choice point. *Psychological Review, 45,* 1–41.

Tolman, E. C. (1942). *Drives toward war.* New York: Appleton-Century.

Tolman, E. C. (1948). Cognitive maps in rats and men. *Psychological Review, 55,* 189–210.

Tolman, E. C. (1952). Edward Chace Tolman. In E. G. Boring, H. S. Langfeld, H. Werner, & R. M. Yerkes (Eds.), *History of psychology in autobiography* (Vol. 4, pp. 323–339). New York: Russell and Russell.

Tolman, E. C. (1959). Principles of purposive behavior. In S. Koch (Ed.), *Psychology: A study of a science* (Vol. 2, pp. 92–157). New York: McGraw-Hill.

Tolman, E. C., & Brunswik, E. (1935). The organism and the causal texture of the environment. *Psychological Review, 42,* 43–77.

Watson, J. B. (1967). *Behavior: An introduction to comparative psychology.* New York: Holt, Rinehart and Winston. (Original work published 1914 by Henry Holt)

Wyman, L. C., & Wyman, A. C. (1914). *Elizabeth Buffum Chace: Her life and its environment* (Vols. 1–2). Boston: W. B. Clark.

Young, P. T. (1933). Book reviews. *American Journal of Psychology, 3,* 177–178.

The Heretical Psychology of Egon Brunswik

Elke M. Kurz
Ryan D. Tweney

The history of psychology is interwoven with the development of other scientific disciplines, the humanities, and, of course, history at large. As a unitary subject of study, the history of psychology is thus to some extent a construction for our scholarly convenience. It is therefore not surprising that we can often identify certain aims behind historical accounts in psychology. For instance, history can be studied and written to achieve a better understanding of the present, or to establish a discipline's identity, or to identify trends that will tell about the future. Further, each of these aims is often best achieved by a close look at those who found themselves in disagreement with the prevailing views of their time. Heretics sometimes tell us more about the orthodox than the orthodox do themselves!

The present chapter is centered around Egon Brunswik (1903–1955), a psychologist who espoused a highly critical position regarding established practice in psychology (see Postman & Tolman, 1959, and Hammond, 1966, for overviews; Leary, 1987, for an historical account; and Gigerenzer & Murray, 1987, for an account focused upon Brunswik's relevance for current scientific practice in psychology). Our account of the development of his ideas will focus on his earliest research, and we will try to show how his theoretical ideas about perception and cognition and his critical stance are related. Brunswik's own view of the history of psychology showed psychology as the "crossroads" of a diversity of trends (Brunswik, 1956a, p. 151; see Figure 1), some of which originated in other sciences, and all of which were structured by methodological considerations. For instance, Darwin was placed under "systematic theorizing" rather than under "statistical approach" because, even though

the statistical concept of variation was an integral part of Darwin's evolutionary theory, Darwin did not make use of the statistical tools of the "Anglo-American statistical tradition" (Brunswik, 1956a, p. 158). Brunswik's own position is represented by the term "Representative design" in the lower right corner of Figure 1: This refers to what he (and most psychologists today) would argue is his greatest contribution. In essence, it is a concern that the validity of psychological research is established not only by the representative sampling of individuals from well-defined populations but also by the representative sampling of stimulus situations from well-defined natural-cultural "ecologies"; when experimentalists argue about the "ecological validity" of experiments, they are harking back to issues first raised by Brunswik—though not always in terms that are faithful to the original meaning (Hammond, in press). This may seem a rather dry methodological point by which to characterize one's own position in psychology (much less one's place in history), but it is at the heart of Brunswik's truly radical reconceptualization of the task of scientific psychology.

Egon Brunswik was born in Budapest on March 18, 1903, during the days of the Austrian-Hungarian Dual Monarchy (for biographical details about Brunswik, see Leary, 1987, and Tolman, 1956). Brunswik's father was a Hungarian engineer working for the Austro-Hungarian government; his mother was of Austrian descent. At only 8 years of age Egon was sent to Vienna to attend the famous Gymnasium at the Theresischen Akademie. The political situation of the Dual Monarchy entailed that at least to a certain extent pupils were taught in their respective provincial languages—in Brunswik's case Hungarian. As his later collaborator, the well-known American neobehaviorist, Edward Chace Tolman (1956, p.

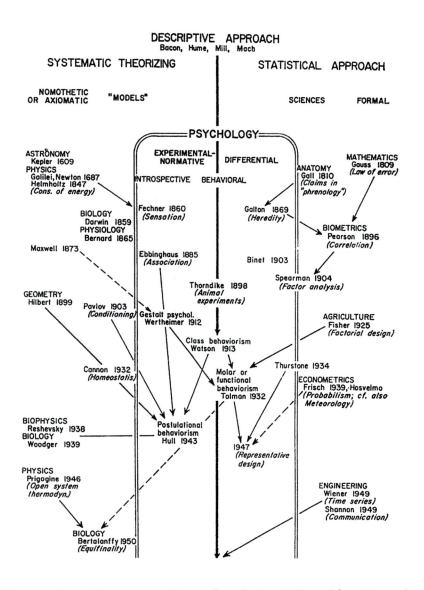

DESCRIPTIVE APPROACH
Bacon, Hume, Mill, Mach

SYSTEMATIC THEORIZING   STATISTICAL APPROACH

NOMOTHETIC
OR AXIOMATIC   "MODELS"   SCIENCES   FORMAL

PSYCHOLOGY

EXPERIMENTAL-   DIFFERENTIAL
NORMATIVE

ASTRONOMY
Kepler 1609
PHYSICS
Galilei, Newton 1687
Helmholtz 1847
(Cons. of energy)

INTROSPECTIVE   BEHAVIORAL

ANATOMY   MATHEMATICS
Gall 1810   Gauss 1809
(Claims in   (Law of error)
"phrenology")

Fechner 1860   Galton 1869
(Sensation)   (Heredity)

BIOLOGY
Darwin 1859
PHYSIOLOGY
Bernard 1865

BIOMETRICS
Pearson 1896
(Correlation)

Maxwell 1873

Ebbinghaus 1885   Binet 1903
(Association)

Spearman 1904
(Factor analysis)

Thorndike 1898
(Animal
experiments)

GEOMETRY
Hilbert 1899

Pavlov 1903
(Conditioning)

AGRICULTURE
Fisher 1925
(Factorial design)

Gestalt psychol.
Wertheimer 1912

Class behaviorism
Watson 1913

Thurstone 1934

Cannon 1932
(Homeostasis)

Molar or
functional
behaviorism
Tolman 1932

ECONOMETRICS
Frisch 1939, Hosvelmo
(Probabilism; cf. also
Meteorology)

BIOPHYSICS
Reshevsky 1938
BIOLOGY
Woodger 1939

Postulational
behaviorism
Hull 1943

1947
(Representative
design)

PHYSICS
Prigogine 1946
(Open system
thermodyn.)

ENGINEERING
Wiener 1949
(Time series)
Shannon 1949
(Communication)

BIOLOGY
Bertalanffy 1950
(Equifinality)

Figure 1 Brunswik's systematic history of psychology. (Adapted from Brunswik, 1956a, p. 158. Copyright 1956 American Association for the Advancement of Science. Reprinted with permission)

315), noted: "This meant, for example, that he studied the history of the Empire both in Hungarian and in German and early noticed the discrepancies between the two accounts. Perhaps it was this early experience which gave him his initial insight into the merely probabilistic character of one's knowledge of one's environment."

World War I cast a shadow over Brunswik's school days in Vienna. After the war ended in 1918, Brunswik and his sister were sent for a few months to Sweden to recover from the malnutrition of the war years. Brunswik graduated from the Gymnasium at the Theresisische Akademie in 1921 and from there went on to study engineering at the Vienna

Technische Hochschule. However, having passed the first state examination in 1923, he switched to a new domain of study—psychology.

The institute that Brunswik entered as a psychology student had been founded only recently under Karl Bühler and his wife, Charlotte Bühler, who established a flourishing psychological center that attracted students and visitors from around the world to Vienna (Benetka, 1995). Brunswik, like many other students in the Vienna Psychological Institute (Kurz, in press), graduated with a joint degree as a schoolteacher—of mathematics and physics—and a PhD under the auspices of Karl Bühler. Brunswik's doctoral committee also included the philosopher Moritz Schlick, initiator of the discussion group later known as the Vienna Circle. The impetus of the new philosophy of science which emerged around Moritz Schlick had a lasting influence on Brunswik, an influence especially evident in his later affiliation with the Unity of Science movement (e.g., Brunswik, 1952; see Leary, 1987). This diverse intellectual background is readily evident in his dissertation, titled "Strukturmonismus und Physik."

Immediately after receiving his doctoral degree in 1927, Brunswik became an assistant in the Bühlers' institute. The social psychologist Paul F. Lazarsfeld (1959) later described the organization of the Vienna Psychological Institute as consisting of subdivisions, each focusing on a different area of psychology but all inspired and tied together by Karl Bühler. Brunswik was his "first assistant" (C. Bühler, 1972, p. 29) and was responsible for the experimental work, especially in the area of perception. In addition, Brunswik taught for many years the "Einführungskurs in die experimentelle Psychologie," a course that offered demonstrations and practical training as an accompaniment to Karl Bühler's lectures on general psychology. The exercises and demonstrations for this course are described for both teacher and student in Brunswik's little volume "Experimentelle Psychologie in Demonstrationen" (1935). As a historical document, this volume reflects the change in psychology from the restricted focus, characteristic of Wundt, that limited experimentation to only a few domains (Danziger, 1990), to a broad range of topics that were now subsumed under the heading of "experimental psychology."

Figure 2 Egon Brunswik, 1903–1955. (Courtesy of the Department of Psychology, University of California, Berkeley)

Brunswik's research at the Vienna Psychological Institute was devoted mostly to the investigation of perceptual constancy, i.e., the tendency of our perceptual apparatus to perceive size, color, shape, and other features of our surroundings as relatively constant despite changing projections on perceptual surfaces. Size constancy, for example, means

that "for a somewhat developed human being, an approaching visitor will not grow from a tiny fingerlike dwarf up to an immense giant, but will, within certain limits, quite fairly retain a constant apparent size" (Brunswik, 1937, pp. 228). Earlier Bühler had also been interested in the phenomenon of color constancy and had proposed a principle—"das Dupliztätsprinzip" (duplicity principle; see Brunswik & Kardos, 1929)—which asserted that perceptual constancy is based on a twofold stimulus basis, the projection on a perceptual surface (for example, the retina) of the object or feature of interest and of context criteria. In the case of color perception the feature of interest is the reflectance of a surface (also called albedo), the empirical context is the ambient illumination, and the projection on a perceptual surface is the light falling on the retina (also called luminance). More specifically, the duplicity principle challenged the view that context, like illumination in color perception or distance in size perception, would come into play only after the fact as a modifier warranting a certain interpretation of the respective sensory stimulation. In contrast to this view Bühler and his students held that context in perception is part of the total stimulus pattern and as such not super- or subordinate in any cognitive sense.

One of Brunswik's (1929) early studies, conducted in collaboration with several students at the institute, investigated the development of "Albedowahrnehmung" (albedo perception) from kindergarten age to young adulthood. A methodological objective in this research, as in all subsequent studies, was to keep the level of introspection required of the subjects to a minimum, whenever possible, to so-called judgments of equality ("Gleichheitsurteile," Brunswik, 1932, p. 387), i.e., the subjects' task was to match an item from a comparison series to a designated test item. To compare the levels of approximate brightness constancy attained by the different age groups under different experimental conditions, Brunswik developed a measure which later came to be known as the "Brunswik Ratio" (Brunswik, 1929, p. 68). This measure related judged brightness, luminance (the amount of light projected into the eye), and albedo (reflectance of the respective surface) in one value. Since both luminance and albedo are "objectively" given, individual judgments can lean more toward one or the other, and, as Brunswik stressed, it does not really matter whether we label the attained brightness judgments subjective or objective (p. 96); either way, the perceptual system is achieving a compromise. As we will see, Brunswik developed a new vocabulary and his own theoretical system to characterize such "perceptual compromises" (Brunswik, 1934). The implications of this system went far beyond perceptual issues.

In 1931–1932 Brunswik spent a year in Ankara, Turkey, as a visiting lecturer in the School of Education. There he established Turkey's first psychological laboratory. By 1932 Brunswik had greatly extended his investigations and his theoretical account of perceptual constancy. Size constancy became the major ground for further investigations. In size perception, the perceptual judgment of the observer (*s* in Figure 3) was assumed to amount to a compromise between two "poles" (Brunswik, 1932, p. 382), "real size" of the distant object (*w* in Figure 3) and size of the projected image on a reference plane (*p* in Figure 3). Furthermore size constancy also revealed the importance of the "innere Einstellung" (attitude) of the observer. For example, subjects can be instructed to match objects either by their "real" size as measured by a ruler or by their "photographic" or projected size on the retina. This was actually one of the experimental demonstrations he used in Vienna (Brunswik, 1935, p. 89). While the induced match in terms of projected size seems somewhat artificial, it is a match that artists, for example, might strive to achieve (Brunswik, 1932, p. 380). Subsequently, the investigation of perceptual compromise was extended to tasks in which the poles spanning the range of possible compromise seemed more natural in that they reflected features of the observed objects.

One such "extended" constancy problem was used by Mr. Fasil, a Turkish colleague (Brunswik, 1934). In this study subjects were asked to match groups of coins. The stimulus field was spanned by three "poles" or features: number of coins in the presented group, the surface area covered by the coins, and the value of the coins. The results confirmed that under no conditions were the selected matches based on just one of the features. Instead, the subjects actually attained so-called "Zwischengegenstände" (in-between-objects), perceptual

compromises between "intended poles." Similarly, comparisons of rectangles can be based on area, height, and "Gestalt" (shape) (p. 151). In addition it was shown that the kind of match—and consequently the attained degree of perceptual constancy—was partially manipulable through the instructions given to the observers. This concern for the importance of the task under which the perceptual system operates shows Brunswik to be in the tradition of his teacher Bühler and the "Würzburger Schule" (see Mack, this volume).

In 1934 Brunswik was promoted to "Privatdozent" at Vienna. In the same year his monograph "Wahrnehmung und Gegenstandswelt: Grundlegung einer Psychologie vom Gegenstand her" was published, a comprehensive and theoretically refined account of his research on perceptual constancy (Brunswik himself, 1937, p. 235, translated the phrase "Psychologie vom Gegenstand her" as "psychology in terms of objects"). Central to the volume

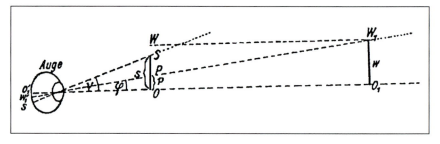

Figure 3 The two poles of size constancy. (Adapted from Brunswik, 1932, p. 391)

was a discussion of the difference between perception and measurement. According to Brunswik (1934, pp. 8–9) "measurement is perception under the most favorable conditions," conditions that are as stable and as independent of context as possible, thus locating both perception and measurement on a continuum warranting varying degrees of reliability. But while measurement results in "Gegenstände" (objects), perception results in "Gegebenheiten" (givens). Note also that the term *object* need not mean physical object alone; it can equally well refer to feature(s) of some distant object, where the distant object can even be another person and the feature, for instance, the person's intelligence. However, a person's intelligence might also be a given, in the sense that this person might appear to be more or less intelligent.

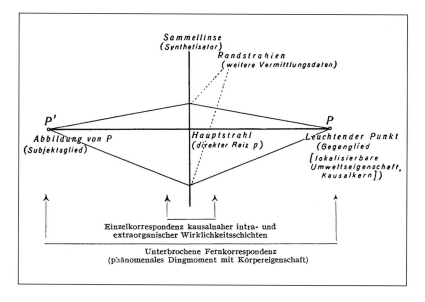

Figure 4 Visual perception as synthesis (Brunswik, 1934, p. 97).

In line with Bühler's duplicity principle (see above), Brunswik conceptualized the perceptually given as a "synthesis of effects emanating from the situation." The perceptual apparatus was accordingly conceived of as "synthesizer." Figure 4 depicts this conceptualization which first referred to visual perception, but "by analogy" was meant to refer to all of perception (Brunswik, 1934, pp. 97–99). Notably, however, this was not the only approach to perception that Brunswik offered in "Wahrnehmung und Gegenstandswelt" (1934). A cue-based approach to perception was interspersed that evolved from Karl Bühler's notion of sign (Bühler, 1927; see Doherty & Kurz, in press). Brunswik did not explicitly distinguish between the two approaches; nevertheless, they are conceptually quite different and can lead to conflicting predictions of perceptual judgment (see Gigerenzer & Murray, 1987, p. 72). However, Brunswik's subsequent work gravitated more and more toward a cue-based approach.

Philosophically "Wahrnehmung und Gegenstandswelt" (1934) was tied to the philosophical-psychological tradition represented by the Austrian philosopher Franz Brentano and places Brunswik in the heritage of act psychology (Leary, 1987). Intentionality, a concept central to Brentano's philosophy (see Baumgartner, this volume), acquired an "objective redefinition" with Brunswik (1937, p. 243), denoting the orientation towards the "distant object." In this respect, his approach was also very different from classical psychophysics (see Brunswik, 1934; 1937; 1939/1951), since his

goal was to understand perception in terms of the "practical achievements of living beings" (Brunswik, 1937, p. 246). Furthermore, his emphasis on objectivity via measurement allied him with the neopositivism of the Vienna Circle and the Unity of Science movement (Brunswik, 1937; 1939/1951; 1952). Most importantly, the focus on organismic achievement allied him with functionalism, especially the functionalist or molar behaviorism of Edward Tolman (see Tolman & Brunswik, 1935).

The liveliness and productivity of the Vienna Psychological Institute in the early '30s attracted visitors from all over the world (C. Bühler, 1965). In 1933–1934 Edward Tolman spent a few months in Vienna and became acquainted with Brunswik (Tolman 1955; see also Innis, this volume). This acquaintance turned out to be a decisive one for Brunswik and his future wife, Else Frenkel, then also an assistant at the institute. Brunswik and Tolman immediately discovered their common interests and coauthored a renowned article in the *Psychological Review*, "The organism and the causal texture of the environment" (Tolman & Brunswik, 1935).

For Brunswik distant objects are intentionally attained in perception; for Tolman distant goals are what is "of final importance to the organism" (Tolman & Brunswik, 1935, p. 45). In the collaborative article, they further held that the distant is mediated by "local representation" through "stimulus cues" and/or "means-objects" (p. 44). Moreover, this local representation was conceived as "equivocal," neither cues nor means are tied one-to-one to

225

objects or goals. This is why our perceptual apparatus can be fooled, as in illusions, and why rats (and humans) can be led astray. Still, the environment was conceptualized as having a "causal texture (Kausalgefüge) in which different events are regularly dependent upon each other" (p. 43). The major task for psychology was thus to explore the "organism's abilities and tendencies for adjusting to these actual causal textures—these actual probabilities as to causal couplings" (p. 73). And in their respective " 'normal' average environments," Tolman and Brunswik thought that organisms perform this task quite well (p. 71).

The collaboration with Tolman highlighted the differential value of cues. While Brunswik already had a clear sense of the importance of cue substitutability in perception, the joint paper emphasized that some cues are reliable, some are ambiguous, some are simply insignificant, and some are actually misleading (Tolman & Brunswik, 1935, p. 75). For Brunswik, this implied that psychology had to understand the environment as it presented itself to the organism before the behavior of that organism could be understood. There could be no reductionistic understanding, whether toward physiological principles or autonomous inner processes (such as those Brunswik felt the Gestalt psychologists were pursuing; Brunswick & Kamiya, 1953). For all their common ground, however, some of the terminology used in their joint work is rather atypical for Brunswik. For Brunswik, perception, indeed, all organismic achievement, was more akin to measurement than to logic. The statement that organisms hold "hypotheses" about the causal texture of the environment (p. 71) is atypical of Brunswik, with cognitive overtones more like those in Tolman's work. Rather than a strict separation between the outer events of the environment and the inner events of the mind, Brunswik's approach demands a continuous gradation from inner to outer, an intentionality which is only coherent when both the organism and the environment are included in the account (Brunswik, 1952).

Shortly after Tolman's stay in Vienna, Brunswik reciprocated the visit, spending a year as a visiting lecturer and research fellow in psychology at the University of California, Berkeley, on a Rockefeller Fellowship in 1935–1936. This visit was the prelude to a transition in Brunswik's life and work. In Austria the political situation had become very tense in the years just prior to the 1938 annexation of Austria by the Nazi regime. Just in time, in 1937 Brunswik returned to Berkeley as Assistant Professor, staying there for the rest of his life. The adverse situation in Austria had not left the Vienna Psychological Institute unaffected (Ash, 1987). Brunswik was informed by Charlotte Bühler "that Professor Karl Bühler has been imprisoned 'because of the preference of Jewish assistants'" (Brunswik in a letter of April 22, 1938, to W. Miles; Archives of the History of American Psychology, Ms.#1134; but see Ash, 1987). Fortunately, soon thereafter, Karl Bühler was able to leave Austria to follow his wife to Norway. Forced into exile, the Bühlers were desperately looking for suitable positions in the United States (C. Bühler, 1972). Since Berkeley had already hired Brunswik, they could not find positions there. Brunswik sent letters to various psychology departments in the United States, trying to assist the Bühlers. Eventually, they found positions at colleges in Minnesota. Else Frenkel fled Austria in 1938 and shortly after her arrival in New York married Brunswik. They had known each other for years at the Vienna Psychological Institute where Frenkel had been involved in research on developmental psychology under Charlotte Bühler (see Heiman & Grant, 1974, for an overview of Frenkel-Brunswik's work).

After Brunswik's move to the United States, new influences on his work became apparent, most notably "the Anglo-American statistical tradition." In an early exposition of his ideas for American readers, Brunswik described his Vienna program as "generalized 'multipolar,' or 'multidimensional,' psychophysics" and expressed the hope that "precise statements as to the minimum number of abstract physical factors ('objects') which have to be considered to participate in the in-between object attained in any particular type of perception will . . . be available by some application of the mathematical methods used in factor-analysis" (Brunswik, 1937, p. 251). Soon thereafter Brunswik spelled out the application of correlational statistics in the investigation of perceptual constancy (Brunswik, 1940). But before this consequential innovation by the "Berkeley Brunswik" (Gigerenzer, 1987b) can be understood, we must consider his psychophysics of probability (Brunswik, 1939, p. 194), the domain of Brunswik's first research projects in the United States.

"Psychophysics of probability" referred to the investigation of the ability of organisms to adjust to "environmental probabilities" (Brunswik, 1943). In an experiment conducted with rats, the relative number of times for which turning left versus right in a T-maze led to food was manipulated (Brunswik, 1939). This research was obviously inspired by Tolman, though corresponding experiments investigating the probability learning of perceptual cues in humans (Brunswik & Herma, 1951) were also carried out (in later years, Smedslund in Oslo, Björkman and Brehmer in Stockholm, and Hammond in the United States continued this line of research known as "multiple cue probability learning"). Brunswik's studies confirmed his thinking about the artificiality and lack of representativeness of the psychological experiment: "Situations in which food can be found always to the right and never to the left, or always behind a black door and never behind a white one, are not representative of the structure of the environment, but are based on an idealized black-white dramatization of the world, somewhat in a Hollywood style" (1943, p. 261).

To capture the uncertainty of cues, from the 1940s on, correlation statistics figured prominently in Brunswik's work (Brunswik, 1940) and mostly replaced the Brunswik Ratio. While he had some reservations about the use of correlations (p. 73), they found their way into a new model of perception developed by the Berkeley Brunswik—the lens model. At the same time he adopted the term *distal* which had then only recently been coined by the Austrian-American psychologist Fritz Heider (Brunswik, 1940, p. 69).

Whereas the Brunswik Ratio expressed in one measure the relationship between a distant object, its projection or mediation through a perceptual surface, and the corresponding perceptual judgment, the new tool led to three values (see Figure 5), the correlation between distal stimulus and proximal stimulus r_{bp}), the correlation between proximal stimulus and perceptual response (r_{ep}), and the correlation between distal stimulus and perceptual response (r_{eb}).

The reported correlation coefficients shown in Figure 5 were determined in a study on size perception. The "paradoxical" result, that "the distal correlation *eb*, directly expressing far-reaching perceptual achievement, is high, whereas the two correlations containing the mediating proximal link *p* are low," indicating for Brunswik, "that something has been left out of the picture" (p. 72). This something, he argued, is due to the context and signals the presence of multiple mediation. A similar notion was expressed earlier in Brunswik's lens analogy (see Figure 4) as "Randstrahlen (weitere Vermittlungsdaten)," literally, "marginal rays (additional mediating data)" (Brunswik, 1937, p. 233). The lens analogy of the Vienna Brunswik in Figure 4 and the correlational statistics of the Berkeley Brunswik in Figure 5 thus combined in Brunswik's lens model, a model of organismic achievement, described at various places throughout his later work (e.g., Brunswik, 1943, p. 258); Figure 6 shows a pictorial representation.

Brunswik's lens model thus represented a new integration of his ideas. With this integration Brunswik created a theoretical basis that transcended his Vienna program of "multidimensional psychophysics" and led to a new research program called "probabilistic functionalism." Functionalism was at the core of this new program because of its focus on organismic achievement (represented by

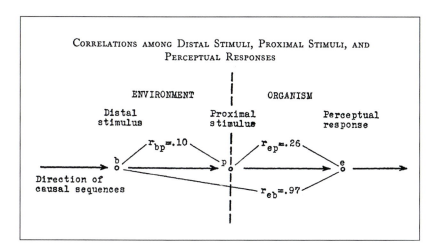

Figure 5 Correlations among distal stimuli, proximal stimuli, and perceptual responses (Brunswik, 1940, p. 72).

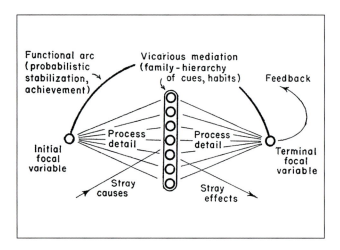

Figure 6 The lens model. (Brunswik, 1952, p. 20. Copyright 1952 by The University of Chicago. Reprinted with permission)

the "functional arc" in Figure 6); it was decidedly probabilistic since cues were conceptualized as intrinsically equivocal and to some extent substitutable for one another. In Figure 6, the "family hierarchy of cues," a phrase intended to resemble Hull's "habit family hierarchy" (Brunswik, 1943, p. 257), expressed the new emphasis on vicarious mediation.

Brunswik's new program called for a new methodology. The methodological principle of holding all the conditions constant except for one, the classical ideal of experimentation, had long appeared to Brunswik as a misguided practice. With his new program this critique became even more salient. American psychology, however, proclaimed the classical ideals of "isolation and control," as, for example, spelled out in a standard text on experimental methodology in psychology, Woodworth's *Experimental Psychology* of 1938. Figure 7 shows page 2 of this title reproduced from Brunswik's personal copy with his underlinings and careful annotations. Note that Brunswik commented, next to the "rule of one variable," "imposs" (impossible)—underlined and with an exclamation mark. What Woodworth saw as essential to rigorous scientific psychology, Brunswik felt was false to the ideal of representativeness and, in fact, an impossible goal anyway.

Extending the case of one independent variable to the simultaneous variation of several independent variables, Brunswik regarded as a step in the right direction (Brunswik, 1956b). But it was still inherently unsatisfactory because the systematic variation of factor levels meant that such research

remained "confined to self-created ivory-tower ecology" (p. 110). Though at first glance the analysis of variance (ANOVA) might appear to be compatible with Brunswik's earlier program of multidimensional psychophysics, its logic of so-called "main effects" and "interactions" never fit Brunswik's psychology (see Brunswik, 1956b, p. 41; and Figure 7, where "interaction" is doubly underlined). Brunswik's methodological critique was, alas, out of step with the direction of American psychology. Ironically, ANOVA was, at this time, just becoming firmly institutionalized in the United States (Rucci & Tweney, 1980).

As an alternative to "systematic design," Brunswik proposed "representative design" (Brunswik, 1944; 1956b) for psychological research.

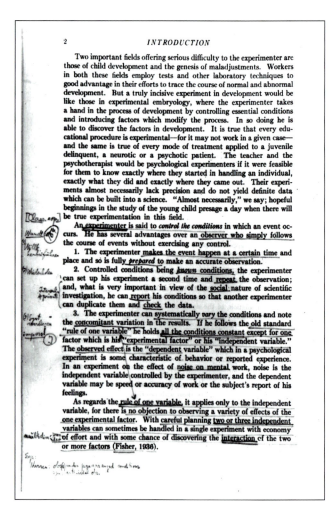

Figure 7 Brunswik's annotations on p. 2 of Robert S. Woodworth's *Experimental Psychology* (1938). (Copyright 1921, 1929, 1934, 1940 by Henry Holt and Co., Inc. Reprinted with permission)

By sampling situations from the natural (and cultural) ecologies of organisms, representative design "grafts the controlled uncontrol of statistical sampling upon the hitherto rigidly controlled content of experimental psychology" (Brunswik, 1956b, p. 99). Brunswik was well aware of the demanding character of the approach: "Representative design in its full scope requires not only a basic theoretical and methodological restructuring but is a formidable task in practice as well" (p. viii). Brunswik himself claimed to have conducted (with collaborating students) only two "fully representative studies" (p. 119), one investigating size constancy (Brunswik, 1944), the other social perception (1956b, p. 26), each a culmination of a series of investigations using hybrid designs that exhibited features of systematic as well as representative design (p. viii; see Gigerenzer, Hoffrage, & Kleinbölting, 1991, and Juslin, 1994, for recently conducted studies employing representative sampling). Representative design is more than just hard work, however: It also requires rethinking of the traditional role of the experimenter (see Brunswik, 1944). Instead of the God-like controller of environments, Brunswik's experimenter is a more humble sampler of environments that already exist.

The new program, probabilistic functionalism, eventually led Brunswik to coin a new metaphor of perception. We have seen that for the Vienna Brunswik, the perceptual apparatus was a synthesizer (as in Figure 4, above). But for the Berkeley Brunswik, it became an "intuitive statistician" (Brunswik, 1956b, p. 80). The probabilistic nature of the relationship between organism and environment was conceptualized using two kinds of probabilistic interplay (Brunswik, 1964, p. 9): "ecological validity" to capture the uncertainty due to the proximal-distal relationship (left-hand side of "process detail" in Figure 6), and "cue utilization" to capture the uncertainty due to the central-distal relationship (right-hand side of "process detail" in Figure 6).

In 1943 Brunswik became an American citizen, thus making a final decision to live and work in the United States. At about the same time, a serious health problem emerged, and he underwent sympathectomy for hypertension. As Tolman later (1956) reported, this health condition would eventually restrain his activity quite considerably. In 1947 Brunswik was promoted to Professor at the University of California, Berkeley. Else Frenkel-Brunswik held a position as research psychologist in the university's Institute of Child Welfare (Heiman & Grant, 1974), but apparently was never on the university's payroll. She had also developed a very active and successful career, and Brunswik "was always intensely informed of, interested in, and sympathetic to the wider psychoanalytical and sociological studies of his wife, Else Frenkel-Brunswik, and he took enormous pride in her achievements" (Tolman, 1956, p. 316). For instance, when asked what he would consider important entries for a new dictionary of psychology, he singled out the following (letter of May 20, 1955, to H. B. English, Archives of the History of American Psychology, #M519): "If not all the items can be included, I would tend to think of 'distal,' 'ecological validity,' 'intolerance of ambiguity,' and 'representative design' as especially important." The term "intolerance of ambiguity" was coined by Frenkel-Brunswik and is a basic concept in her work.

How was Brunswik's probabilistic functionalism accepted by his academic peers? Brunswik himself put it in rather personal terms:

> The difficulties [the present writer] encountered in explaining his point, after he had succeeded in at least establishing a bridgehead for himself in abstract terms and in a few concrete examples, have given him the impression of resistance approaching in intensity those encountered in the opening up of emotionally highly loaded topics, such as those dealt with in psychoanalysis. Indeed, the deliberate abandonment of 'systematic' policies, especially where such policies are technically feasible, in favor of statistical practices which by comparison seem slovenly, must on the surface seem to violate one of the most fundamental taboos developed in the traditional ideology of the 'exact' sciences. (1956b, p. 39)

And indeed, while the intellectual achievement of Brunswik's work was not doubted, his ideas were met with resistance. This is evident from two symposia, both held at Conferences for the Unity of Science, both perhaps arranged by Brunswik himself (Hammond, 1966, p. vi). At the first, in 1941, Clark Hull (1943) and Kurt Lewin (1943) took (and mistook) Brunswik's position to enhance the contours of their own positions. At the second, in 1953 (published as "Symposium on the Probability Approach in Psychology" in the 1955 *Psychological Review*), Brunswik's position had become sharpened—especially with respect to the built-in probabilism (Brunswik, 1955a; Gigerenzer, 1987b, p. 66)—and elicited strong adverse reactions. It is tempting to describe these reactions, using Frenkel-Brunswik's characterization, as intolerance for ambiguity.

In one form or another, the discussion papers at the 1953 symposium given by Leo Postman, Ernest Hilgard, David Krech, and Herbert Feige, "put in a plea for the *status quo*" (Postman, 1955, p. 224), i.e., a nomological orientation in theory and practice. The emphatic manner by which some of the arguments were brought forward shows that Brunswik had touched what was considered to be a vital nerve of psychology, the very status of psychology as science. Brunswik challenged "law-finding" as the aim of scientific psychology and thereby alienated his peers who felt psychology's place among the sciences was in jeopardy (Gigerenzer, 1987a). Moreover, his peers interpreted the probabilism built into probabilistic functionalism in ways other than intended by Brunswik. Hilgard appealed to an epistemic interpretation of probabilism, implying that Brunswik's psychology would lead towards *less* certain knowledge. Krech (1955) on the other hand, took Brunswik to hold (contrary to Einstein's dictum) that "God does gamble." In his reply Brunswik clarified that he was not adhering to this ontological interpretation. His position in fact was "that while God may not gamble, animals and humans do, and they cannot help but to gamble in an ecology that is of essence only partly accessible to their foresight" (Brunswik, 1955b, p. 236). Last but not least, the historically developed partition of psychology into two subdisciplines, an "experimental" and a "correlational" (differential) psychology, worked against him, for he had adopted the statistical tool of the "other discipline" (Gigerenzer, 1987b; Cronbach, 1947). There seemed to be little specific in their criticisms of his use of correlational statistics. For example, Hilgard (1955, p. 228) simply dismissed correlation without explanation as "an instrument of the devil."

Tolman (1955) observed that Brunswik's participation as an organizer of the Berkeley Conference for the Unity of Science in the summer of 1953 had taken "a heavy toll from his health." Still, Brunswik's academic activities scarcely slowed in the months that followed. He himself noted, in a letter to the dean of the university in 1955, that he regarded the previous months as "an especially fruitful period in my work" (Brunswik, March 14, 1955, to A. R. Davis; Psychology Department, University of California, Berkeley).

One of the issues that occupied his attention during this period concerned the relation between perception and thinking, and thereby the question of the nature of thinking itself. Brunswik's account of cognition can be traced back to his early research on size constancy, where the attitude of the observers was manipulated to focus on one or the other pole (see above). With a critical or analytical attitude (in contrast to a naive-realistic one), perceptual constancy can be undermined (e.g., the perceptual judgment can be shifted toward photographic—projected—size), and perceptual illusions can be attenuated (Brunswik, 1956b, p. 94). In the final stages of his research, Brunswik began to investigate perception and thinking as two different modes of cognition, thus attempting to separate them empirically.

Thinking, i.e., reasoning, was characterized as "certainty-geared," and intuitive perception as "uncertainty-geared" (Brunswik, 1956b, p. 89). These two modes of cognition were investigated in a classroom study involving two versions of a size constancy task (p. 91): "In the perception version a stimulus situation was actually presented in the laboratory, with the normal array of distance cues left intact. In the intellectual or 'thinking' version, the question was made part of a subsequent examination, giving such numerical indications about the situation that the correct answer could be univocally ascertained." Brunswik found that the distributions of correct and erroneous responses were very different for the two tasks: The number of undergraduates giving the exactly correct size as an answer was much larger in the intellectual than in the perceptual version. However, the standard deviation was also considerably higher for the error distribution created by the intellectual version. Thus, more people were markedly off in their calculated results than in their perceptual judgments. Overall then, reasoning potentially meets "the needs for supreme accuracy" but pays the price of sometimes being wildly wrong. Intuitive perception, on the other hand, affords approximate closeness to the "true" value but with less likelihood of being precisely correct. Apart from differences in error distributions, perception and thinking show differences in speed: Thinking lacks the "flash-like speed of perceptual responses" (p. 92). But in the end, Brunswik thought that "considering all the pros and cons of achievement, the balance sheet of perception versus thinking may thus seem seriously upset against thinking, unquestioned favorite of a culture of rational enlightenment as the latter has been. . . . The constantly looming catastrophes of the intellect would be found more often to develop into catastrophes of action were it not for the mellowing effects of the darker, more feeling-like and thus more dramatically convincing primordial layers of cognitive adjustment" (p. 93).

As Brunswik (1956b, p. 96; 1966, p. 491) argued, these modes of cognition show many important differences at the level of achievement, but they are still subsystems of a unified system of cognition. As such they work together, most notably in the domains of creative thinking and decision making (Brunswik, 1966, p. 490). That thinking and perception can work so smoothly together reveals the common nature of all cognition, for which he coined the term *ratiomorphism* (Brunswik, 1966, p. 491; 1964, p. 23). At the heart of this conceptualization was a cue-based model, locating cognition at the interface of organism and environment. Ratiomorphism also connected Brunswik's psychology with the newly developed fields of cybernetics and communication theory, precursors of the so-called cognitive revolution in psychology (Brunswik, 1952, p. 743; 1966, p. 491; see also above, Figure 1). Brunswik thereby left us some, albeit sparing, indication of how he would have integrated his probabilistic functionalism with the new ideas and tools beginning to attract the fancy of psychologists in the information processing age.

Given the richness of Brunswik's work, there should have been much opportunity for students to take up his ideas and to collaborate, but this actually happened only to a very limited degree. In fact, the prevailing impression among the students at Berkeley was that, not only the ideas, but also the person were very demanding (see Hammond, in press). Brunswik himself was apparently only aware of two young psychologists carrying out "Brunswikian research," namely Kenneth R. Hammond in Berkeley and Jan Smedslund in Oslo (see Hammond, 1966; p. 9). Hammond had attended Brunswik's classes at Berkeley and, inspired by Brunswik's ideas, used the lens model to investigate clinical judgment. Hammond became (and is) one of the foremost disseminators of Brunswik's ideas (e.g., Hammond, 1966, see also Leary, 1987). Since Hammond's early work on clinical judgment,

Brunswikian psychology has been largely concentrated on human judgment and decision making, thus making Brunswik's psychology today most visible in this context. Still, the overall picture of Brunswik's legacy in psychology is rather modest in the face of the scope of his ideas. Many have taken bits and pieces, but few have followed Brunswik in the far-reaching implications of his ideas.

In 1955, Brunswik decided to end his life. We cannot help but speculate that the difficulties he encountered in making his "heretical" psychology understood contributed to an ultimate feeling of hopelessness.

Acknowledgement

The authors are grateful to Michael Doherty for a careful reading of the manuscript; to John Popplestone, Director of the Archives of the History of American Psychology for his assistance; to Kenneth Hammond for his permission to use the unique source shown in Fig. 7, and to Gerd Gigerenzer and Peter Juslin for their help in making this source available to us; and to Carolyn Scott for her assistance in locating materials in the archival files of the Department of Psychology, University of California, Berkeley.

Bibliography

Ash, M. G. (1987). Psychology and politics in interwar Vienna; The Vienna Psychological Institute, 1922–1942. In M. G. Ash & W. R. Woodward (Eds.), *Psychology in twentieth-century thought and society* (pp. 143–164). Cambridge, England: Cambridge University Press.

Benetka, G. (1995). *Psychologie in Wien: Sozial- und Theoriegeschichte des Wiener Psychologischen Instituts, 1922–1938.* Vienna: Wuv.

Brehmer, B., & Joyce, C. R. (Eds.). (1988). *Human judgment: The SJT view.* Amsterdam; Elsevier.

Brunswik, E. (1929). Zur Entwicklung der Albedowahrnehmung. *Zeitschrift für Psychologie, 109*, 40–115.

Brunswik, E. (1932). Untersuchungen über Wahrnehmungsgegenstände. *Archiv für die gesamte Psychologie, 88*, 377–418.

Brunswik, E. (1934) *Wahrnehmung und Gegenstandswelt: Grundlegung einer Psychologie vom Gegenstand her.* Leipzig: Franz Deuticke.

Brunswik, E. (1935). *Experimentelle Psychologie in Demonstrationen.* Vienna: Julius Springer.

Brunswik, E. (1937). Psychology as a science of objective relations. *Philosophy of Science, 4*, 227–260.

Brunswik, E. (1939). Probability as determiner of rat behavior. *Journal of Experimental Psychology, 25*, 175–197.

Brunswik, E. (1940). Thing constancy as measured by correlation coefficients. *Psychological Review, 47*, 69–78.

Brunswik, E. (1943). Organismic achievement and environmental probability. *Psychological Review, 50*, 255–272.

Brunswik, E. (1944). Distal focussing of perception: Size-constancy in a representative sample of situations. *Psychological Monographs, 56*, 1–49.

Brunswik, E. (1951). The conceptual focus of systems. In M. H. Marx (Ed.), *Psychological theory: Contemporary readings* (pp. 131–143). New York: Macmillan. (Original work published 1939)

Brunswik, E. (1952). The conceptual framework of psychology. In O. Neurath, R. Carnap, & C. Morris (Eds.), *International encyclopedia of unified science: Vol. 1, No. 10*, (pp. 675–760). Chicago: University of Chicago Press.

Brunswik, E. (1955a). Representative design and probabilistic theory in a functional psychology. *Psychological Review, 62*, 193–217.

Brunswik, E. (1955b). In defense of probabilistic functionalism: A reply. *Psychological Review, 62*, 236–242.

Brunswik, E. (1956a). Historical and thematic relations of psychology to other sciences. *The Scientific Monthly, 83*, 151–161. (Reprinted in Hammond, K. R., 1966.)

Brunswik, E. (1956b). *Perception and the representative design of psychological experiments*. Berkeley: University of California Press.

Brunswik, E. (1964). Scope and aspects of the cognitive problem. In H. Gruber, R. Jessor, & K. R. Hammond (Eds.), *Contemporary approaches to cognition: A symposium held at the University of Colorado* (pp. 5–40). Cambridge, MA: Harvard University Press.

Brunswik, E. (1966). Reasoning as a universal behavior model and a functional differentiation between "perception" and "thinking." In K. R. Hammond (Ed.), *The psychology of Egon Brunswik* (pp. 487–494). New York: Holt, Rinehart and Winston.

Brunswik, E., & Herma, H. (1951). Probability learning of perceptual cues in the establishment of a weight illusion. *Journal of Experimental Psychology, 41*, 281–297.

Brunswik, E., & Kamiya, J. (1953). Ecological cue-validity of "proximity" and of other Gestalt factors. *American Journal of Psychology, 66*, 20–32.

Brunswik, E., & Kardos, L. (1929). Das Duplizitätsprinzip in der Theorie der Farbenwahrnehmung. *Zeitschrift für Psychologie, 111*, 307–320.

Bühler, K. (1927). *Die Krise der Psychologie*. Jena: Fischer.

Bühler, C. (1965). Die Wiener Psychologische Schule in der Emigration. *Psychologische Rundschau, 16*, 187–196.

Bühler, C. (1972). Charlotte Bühler. In J. Pongratz, W. Traxel, & E. G. Wehner (Eds.), *Psychologie in Selbstdarstellungen* (pp. 9–42). Bern: Huber.

Cronbach, L. (1947). The two disciplines of scientific psychology. *American Psychologist, 12*, 671–684.

Danziger, K. (1990). *Constructing the subject: Historical origins of psychological research*. Cambridge, England: Cambridge University Press.

Doherty, M. E., & Kurz, E. M. (in press). Social judgment theory. *Thinking & Reasoning*.

Feigl, H. (1955). Functionalism, psychological theory, and the uniting science: Some discussion remarks. *Psychological Review, 62*, 232–235.

Gigenrenzer, G. (1987a). Probabilistic thinking and the fight against subjectivity. In L. Krüger, G. Gigerenzer, & M. S. Morgan (Eds.), *The probabilistic revolution. Vol. 2: Ideas in the sciences* (pp. 11–33). Cambridge, MA: MIT Press.

Gigerenzer, G. (1987b). Survival of the fittest probabilist: Brunswik, Thurstone, and the two disciplines of psychology. In L. Krüger, G. Gigerenzer, & M. S. Morgan (Eds.), *The probabilistic revolution, Vol. 2: Ideas in the sciences* (pp. 49–72). Cambridge, MA: MIT Press.

Gigerenzer, G., Hoffrage, U., & Kleinbölting, H. (1991). Probabilistic mental models: A Brunswikian theory of confidence. *Psychological Review, 98*, 506–528.

Gigerenzer, G., & Murray, D. J. (1987). *Cognition as intuitive statistics*. Hillsdale, NJ: Erbaum.

Hammond, K. R. (Ed.). (1966). *The psychology of Egon Brunswik*. New York: Holt, Rinehart and Winston.

Hammond, K. R. (in press). Expansion of Egon Brunswik's psychology, 1955–1995. *Vienna Circle Institute Yearbook, No. 3*. Dordrecht: Kluwer Publishers.

Hammond, K. R., & Wascoe, N. E. (Eds.) (1980). Realization of Brunswik's representative design. *New Directions for Methodology of Social and Behavioral Science, 3*.

Heiman, N., & Grant, J. (Eds.). (1974). *Else Frenkel-Brunswik: Selected papers*. New York: International University Press.

Hilgard, E. R. (1955). Discussion of probabilistic functionalism. *Psychological Review, 62*, 226–228.

Hull, C. L. (1943). The problem of intervening variables in molar behavior theory. *Psychological Review, 50*, 273–291.

Juslin, P. (1994). The overconfidence phenomenon as a consequence of informal experimenter-guided selection of almanac items. *Organizational Behavior and Human Decision Processes, 57*, 226–246.

Krech, D. (1955). Discussion: theory and reductionism. *Psychological Review, 62*, 229–231.

Kurz, E. M. (in press). Marginalizing discovery: Karl R. Popper's intellectual roots in early psychology of thinking, or how the study of discovery was banned from science studies. *Creativity Research Journal*.

Lazarsfeld, P. F. (1959). Amerikanische Beobachtungen eines Bühler-Schülers. *Zeitschrift für Experimentelle und Angewandte Psychologie, 6*, 69–76.

Leary, D. E. (1987). From act psychology to probabilistic functionalism: The place of Egon Brunswik in the history of psychology. In M. G. Ash & W. R. Woodward (Eds.), *Psychology in twentieth-century thought and society* (pp. 115–142). Cambridge, England: Cambridge University Press.

Lewin, K. (1943). Defining the "field at a given time." *Psychological Review, 50*, 292–310.

Postman, L. (1955). The probability approach and nomothetic theory. *Psychological Review, 62*, 218–225.

Postman, L., & Tolman, E. C. (1959). Brunswik's probabilistic functionalism. In S. Koch (Ed.), *Psychology: A study of a science, Vol. 1: Sensory, perceptual, and physiological formulations*. New York: McGraw Hill.

Rucci, A., & Tweney, R. D. (1980). Analysis of variance and the "Second Discipline" of scientific psychology: An historical account. *Psychological Bulletin, 87*, 166–184.

Tolman, E. C. (1955). Egon Brunswik, psychologist and philosopher of science. *Science, 122*, 910.

Tolman, E. C. (1956). Egon Brunswik: 1903–1955. *American Journal of Psychology, 69*, 315–324.

Tolman, E. C., & Brunswik, E. (1935). The organism and the causal texture of the environment. *Psychological Review, 42*, 43–77.

Woodworth, R. (1938). *Experimental Psychology*. New York: Holt.

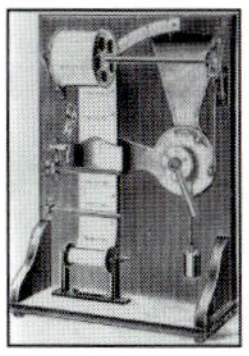

Psychological Experiments

Kurt Danziger
Paul Ballantyne

What is a psychological experiment? Do we engage in psychological experimentation when we construct an attitude or personality scale, or when we recalibrate an intelligence test? Was it a psychological experiment when Freud and others began systematically recording their own free associations on particular occasions? Towards the end of the 19th century, when French psychiatrists used hypnosis to elicit hysterical symptoms, were they conducting psychological experiments?

Throughout the history of modern psychology different authorities would have given different answers to these and similar questions. Some would have defined psychological experiments broadly, others quite narrowly, and their criteria for defining the nature of an experiment would have varied widely. These changes in the definition of experimentation are related to changes in the material, social, and symbolic technology used in our science.

The first group of investigators whose members explicitly defined their research practice as psychological experimentation was formed at the University of Leipzig in Germany during the 1880s. Under the direction of Wilhelm Wundt, their work quickly attracted students from other countries who then set up psychological laboratories elsewhere in imitation of what they had seen at Leipzig. Wundt's laboratory thus became an early model for the first generation of experimental psychologists.

What were the major features of this model? Above all, the practice of psychological experimentation was explicitly derived from physiological experimentation. In fact, Wundt generally spoke of "physiological psychology" when referring to experimental psychology. He had qualified in medicine and was well versed in physiological research. His psychological experiments relied heavily on the *material technology* associated with the physiology of his time. This technology involved two categories of hardware: first, apparatus for exposing experimental subjects to controlled and precisely known forms of stimulation; second, apparatus for recording and measuring responses. Figure 1 shows how some of this

![The Psychological Laboratory]

THE PSYCHOLOGICAL LABORATORY.

Figure 1 Chicago World Fair, 1893. (Archives of the History of American Psychology)

Figure 2 Experiment with just noticeable differences (jnds) of weights (Givler, 1920).

means of psychophysical methods, constituted by far its largest research area, though perceptual processes claimed an increasing share of the experimenters' attention. Research on reaction times, though receiving much less interest, was theoretically significant from the beginning because Wundt thought that it could be used to explore central processes like attention and volition. But most of the topics that came to define 20th-century psychology were not accessible by means of these early, quasi-physiological methods.

hardware was displayed at the Chicago World Fair in 1893. This glass case display of brass instruments was the first of many public relations exercises designed to acquaint a wider American public with the scientific aspirations of the "New Psychology." Joseph Jastrow, the first American psychology PhD, organized the display for the fair.

The goal of this early variant of psychological experimentation was quite analogous to the goal of physiological experimentation. Where the physiologists aimed at exploring the material processes underlying the functioning of the normal biological organism, the psychologists sought to illuminate the mental processes characteristic of the normal individual consciousness. "Normal" here excluded not only pathological processes, but also immature or idiosyncratic ways of functioning. "Physiological psychology" therefore did not experiment on children or on cases from the clinic, and it regarded individual and social differences among experimental subjects as a nuisance to be avoided by the appropriate selection of subjects and of research topics.

This imposed severe restrictions on the scope of the early experimental psychology. Sensory processes, usually investigated by

Figures 2 and 3 illustrate the investigation of sensory processes in the classical, Wundtian tradition. In Figure 2 the experimenter (sometimes called the "manipulator" in early studies) presents the subject (often called the "observer") with a series of different weights shielded from sight by a wooden screen. The

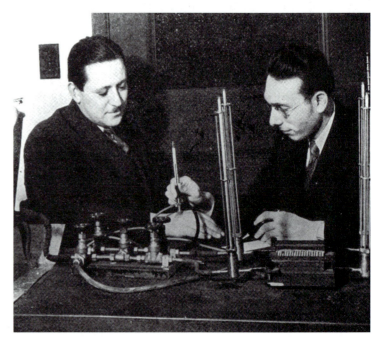

Figure 3 Touch sensation experiment (Murphy, 1935).

Figure 4 Simple reaction time experiment (Givler, 1920).

observer has to compare the weights but is limited to a choice between the responses "heavier than," "lighter than," or "equal."

In Figure 3 a metal instrument is heated by passing warm water through it. It is then brought down lightly on the squares of a grid previously inscribed on the observer's hand. The observer reports sensations of warmth and touch when they occur. For many spots on the skin there may be no discrimination of temperature and touch sensations. The two upright pieces of apparatus in the foreground allow both warm and cold water to be passed through different tubes. Karl Dallenbach, a product of the Cornell laboratory established by Wundt's student Titchener, was carrying out such experiments between 1927 and 1937.

Several years before the founding of his Leipzig laboratory, Wilhelm Wundt had become interested in the study of reaction times. He regarded these as making possible a "mental chronometry"; that is, the timing of mental processes, especially decisions or acts of volition. He utilized methods pioneered by F. C. Donders, a Dutch physiologist. Figure 4 illustrates a simple reaction time situation. One person controls the presentation of stimuli while the other "reacts" by depressing a telegraph key. In this case, the duration of each reaction is recorded by a Hipp chrononoscope.

But Wundt accorded much greater significance to choice reaction times, where the experimental

subject must choose the proper reaction to different stimuli. This is illustrated in Figure 5. The subject (top) must discriminate between two lights which are presented by the experimenter (bottom) who, in

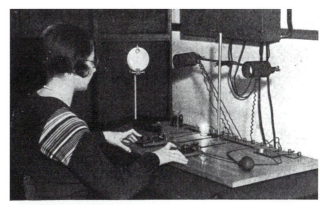

Figure 5 Complex reaction time experiment (Murphy, 1935).

235

Figure 6 Charcot lecturing on Blanche Wittmann. (National Library of Medicine)

this case, is located in another room of the building. The subject must then react by pushing one of two telegraph keys according to prior instructions. In this case, the duration of each reaction is recorded by a Dunlap chrononoscope (bottom right). Such choice reaction times were found to be longer than simple reaction times. As the assigned task becomes more complex, the reaction time also increases. Wundt argued that incremental increases in reaction time indicated the operation of deeper mental processes.

Even as the fame of the Leipzig style of experimentation spread, others elsewhere were laying the foundations for different kinds of experimentation. Some medically oriented investigators, especially in France, began using hypnosis for a systematic study of human reactions under abnormal conditions. These were "clinical experiments" directed at the illumination of psychopathology rather than the exploration of normal adult consciousness.

The painting reproduced in Figure 6 shows Jean-Martin Charcot, the most famous of the French investigators, demonstrating a case of "la grande hysterie" to a medical audience. Charcot was something of a showman, but others, including the young Alfred Binet, were subjecting hysterics to experimental procedures under laboratory conditions.

When we compare these French studies to what was happening in Wundt's Leipzig laboratory, we become aware of the fact that, in addition to their material technology, psychological experiments also involve a *social technology*. Figure 7 shows Wundt and some of his collaborators in the Leipzig laboratory. These men were Wundt's students and graduate assistants, and they alternated in the roles of experimenter and experimental subject. Whatever role they took, they were well informed about the general purpose of the experiments in which they participated. That was very different from clinical experiments in which there was typically a vast gulf, both socially and intellectually, between experimenters and subjects. A juxtaposition of the social situation in Figures 6 and 7 illustrates this very well.

More generally, the social technology of psychological experimentation with human subjects involves an elaborate set of rules and relationships which provides a social framework for the collection of psychological data. Within this framework, the roles of all participants in the experimental situation are strictly defined.

Historically, the social technology of experimentation has changed as much as the material technology. In some of the earliest experiments that gave rise to long research traditions, the investigator simply experimented on himself. This was true of Fechner's psychophysical studies and of Ebbinghaus's work on memory. But as the material and symbolic technology of experiments became more complicated, a division of labor was introduced, so that one participant supervised the application of the

Figure 7 Wundt in his laboratory (ca. 1910). From left to right: M. Dittrich, W. Wirth, W. Wundt, O. Klemm, and F. Sander (Bringmann & Tweney, 1980).

technology, while the other was the source of the psychological data which the experiment was designed to obtain. Thus, a role division between experimenters and subjects came into being—though in the Leipzig model of experimentation these roles were frequently exchanged among the same set of investigators, who generally used each other as subjects.

That exchange could not happen in clinical experiments, where medical experimenters studied pathological phenomena. Here, there was a permanent division between experimenters, who controlled the experimental situation as well as the knowledge it produced, and the subjects, who were required to carry out instructions. As psychologists extended the scope of their experimental investigations to include psychologically naive individuals, the social technology of their experiments came to resemble that of the clinical experiment rather than that of the Wundtian experiment.

While the social and material technology of psychological experimentation was being established in France and Germany, another important development was taking place in England. In London, Francis Galton launched a large-scale project of "anthropometric measurement" which had far-reaching consequences for the way in which psychological experimentation evolved in the 20th century. Where Wundtian experimentation regarded individual differences as a nuisance, Galton made them the main focus of his research. In his anthropometric labora-

tory, large numbers of people had themselves investigated to find out how their visual acuity or strength of grip, for example, compared with that of others. This required quantitative measures of individual performance and statistical techniques for comparing individuals.

In pioneering the practical use of such techniques, Galton initiated a line of research which resulted in the transformation of psychological experimentation during the first half of the 20th century. Instead of limiting themselves to experimenting on a few subjects representing either normal or specific abnormal states of mind, psychologists could now focus on the common effects of experimental interventions on groups of individuals. This they accomplished by the statistical segregation of individual differences. As a consequence, the range of psychological topics to which the method of experimentation could be applied was enormously extended.

Eventually statistical considerations came to dominate not only the analysis of experimental data but the very design of psychological experiments. This is an example of historical change in the *symbolic technology* of experiments. All experiments depend on some sort of symbolic technology as much as they depend on material and social technology.

For many experimentalists the statistics of individual differences were a tool that could make the traditional search for general effects more effective. But others lost interest in this traditional goal and followed Galton in making quantified individual differences the primary object of study. First among this latter group was J. McKeen Cattell, one of many Americans to have studied under Wundt at Leipzig. There, he had participated in reaction time studies and even become Wundt's first assistant.

However, once Cattell became acquainted with Galton and Galton's methods, his interest in individual differences burgeoned. Back in America, he lost no time setting up a program for the study of such

Figure 8 Group testing of complex reaction times (U.S. Air Force).

became an interaction among anonymous strangers.

But it was precisely this feature which opened up new horizons for psychology, for it made possible the large-scale institutional usage of psychological methods. There is considerable irony in the fact that Cattell himself was dismissed from Columbia University for his pacifist views during World War I, for it was at this juncture that the U.S. Army provided the institutional setting for the first really large-scale application of the approach that Galton and Cattell had pioneered. Well over 1.7 million recruits were subjected to mental testing.

Although this testing movement employed mostly paper and pencil methods, some aspects of the traditional experimental technology did survive within the new framework. By World War II, for instance, reaction time tasks had been incorporated into the process of selecting military personnel. Figure 8 shows complex discrimination reaction time tasks being performed by U.S. Army Air Force

differences among college students. For Galton's awkward term "anthropometry" he substituted "mental tests." The material of his tests was not new, but the symbolic and social technology owed its inspiration to the pioneering efforts of Galton. The goal was no longer the investigation of the generalized human mind but, as historian E. G. Boring put it, "a description of human nature in respect of its range and variability" (Boring, 1950, p. 539).

With such a goal, the social technology of experimentation had to change too. It was no longer appropriate to limit oneself to a small number of sophisticated experimental observers as a source of psychological data. Large numbers of psychologically naive subjects—even children—had to be studied if one wanted to explore the range and variability of human nature. That meant that psychological experimentation

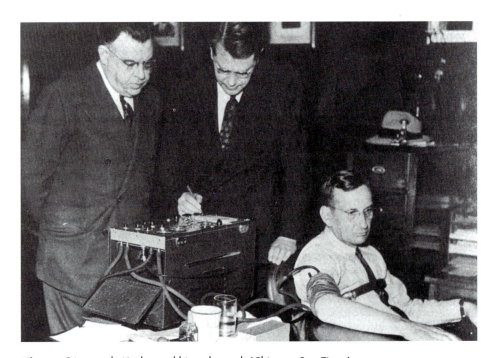

Figure 9 Leonarde Keeler and his polygraph (Chicago *Sun-Times*).

cadets. This was one of a standard battery of aptitude tests aimed at determining relative skill or ability rather than at gaining insight into what all human minds have in common.

The practical applications of psychological experimentation had first been energetically promoted by Hugo Münsterberg, who had spent some time in Wundt's laboratory in its early days and then was invited to run Harvard's psychology laboratory. He remained there until his death in 1916, increasingly active in suggesting new ways in which psychological experimentation might be applied to business, industry, and the law.

One particularly successful example of such application was the lie detector. An early version, developed by William Marston, was designed to indicate changes of blood pressure that accompanied changes in emotional states.

Leonarde Keeler built a commercially viable model of the lie detector in 1926. This "polygraph" apparatus measures changes in a suspect's heartbeat, blood pressure, respiration, and electrical skin conductance. The pens of the polygraph produce a permanent record of these measurements onto a moving strip of graph paper. The record of "relevant" questions is then compared with that of interspersed "neutral" questions. Figure 9 shows Keeler, standing in the middle as he questions a prison guard about a prison break in 1942.

By then, psychological experiments had acquired a certain mystique for the lay public, and excessive claims for what they could accomplish were not uncommon. This eventually led to greater awareness of the social and ethical responsibilities of experimenters.

Bibliography

Boring, E. (1950). *A History of Experimental Psychology* (2nd ed.). New York: Appleton-Century-Crofts.

Bringmann, W., & Tweney, R. (Eds.). (1980). *Wundt Studies: A Centennial Collection*. Toronto: C. J. Hogrefe.

Danziger, K. (1990). *Constructing the Subject: Historical Origins of Psychological Research*. New York: Cambridge University Press.

Givler, C. G. (1920/1922). *Psychology: The Science of Human Behavior*. New York: Harper.

Keeler, E. (1984). *The Lie Detector Man: The Career and Cases of Leonarde Keeler*. New York: Telshare Publishers.

Murphy, G. (1935). *A Briefer General Psychology*. New York: Harper.

Pearson, K. (1914/1930). *The Life, Letters and Labours of Francis Galton*. Cambridge, England: Cambridge University Press.

GESTALT PSYCHOLOGY

Ernst Mach and the Perception of Movement

Michael Ley

T he Austrian physicist and philosopher Ernst Mach (1838–1916) is often counted by historians of psychology to be among the forerunners of Gestalt psychology. This claim is usually documented by references to Mach's famous book, *Contributions to the Analysis of Sensations* (1886, 1897), which Christian von Ehrenfels (1859–1932) acknowledged as an early version of his own Gestalt thinking. The *Contributions*, which scandalized late 19th-century Vienna due to its sharp criticism of traditional methodology, is not the only example of Mach's interest in psychological questions. Mach's first experimental studies of sensory psychology were carried out as early as the 1860s and 1870s and characterize him as a classical representative of the scientific psychology of the period.

According to Mach, financial problems forced him to switch his research activities from his specialty of physics to the less expensive field of sensory physiology. Specifically, he noted that basic research in physiology could be carried out without the expensive equipment required for experiments in physics (Blackmore, 1978, p. 415). In addition, as Swoboda (1988, p. 362) pointed out, during the 1860s it was quite logical for a young and ambitious university instructor to choose the growing field of physiology as his career. After all, around the middle of the 19th century, physiology seemed to promise a new level of unification which was likely to lead to a redefinition of the entire field of science.

Among Mach's early physiological writings, two studies in particular have assured him a secure place in the physiology textbooks, and these studies also play a major role in our assessment of him as a psychologist. These are his studies on brightness perception and his analyses of the "perception of movement."

Mach Bands

During his work on contrast perception, Mach studied the "light effect" of black-and-white colored disks, which appear as a series of gray tones as soon as the disks are put in rotation. This phenomenon was known before Mach as the Talbot-Plateau law. However, Mach discovered an unexpected ring-shaped intensification of the bright and dark values at the transition between the black and white areas. These ring-shaped intensifications are known today as "Mach bands." Although the brightness of the

Figure 1 Portrait of Ernst Mach (ca. 1864–1865).

upper left disk and the central disk should steadily increase towards the center, the transitions to the zones Beta and Gamma are interrupted by a bright ring. This can be seen clearly in the top right circle of Figure 3.

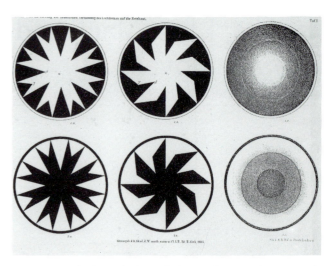

Figure 3 Black-and-white disks used to produce "Mach Bands."

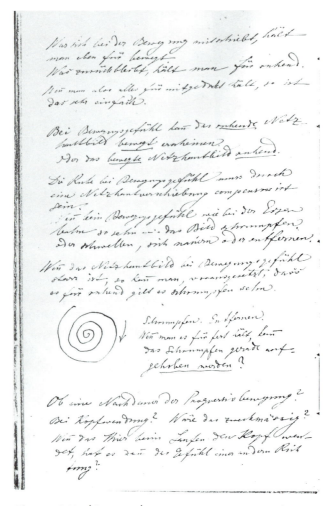

Figure 2 Mach's research notes on movement perception.

Mach's explanation of these phenomena, which he offered between 1866 and 1868 in four publications for the Vienna Academy of Sciences, are model examples of psychological theorizing from the middle of the 19th century. Specifically, Mach tried to use "firm" mathematical laws to explain "transient" sensory phenomena which disagreed with known physical facts. He computed special "light curves" for the perception of the rotating disks. In turn, Mach used these curves to indicate exactly where

and when perception would be "enlarged, reduced, schematized," or "caricatured" (Mach, 1868).

The theory which Mach proposed was later elaborated and refined by neurologists into what became known as the hypothesis of neural inhibitions. Most importantly, Mach's research on brightness perception reveals his remarkable skill in applying the entire armamentarium of mathematical and physical methods, as well as the instruments of his time.

Movement Perception

Between 1867 and 1875, Mach performed a second series of elegant experiments in the field of sensory physiology, and these carry important psychological implications. The new research project was concerned with the perception of movement, which at that time was the focus of international attention among sensory physiologists and psychologists. Mach's competitors included Freud's mentor, the Austrian otolaryngologist Josef Breuer (1842–1925) and the English chemist Alexander Crum Brown (1838–1922).

Mach, who, meanwhile, had been appointed to a professorship at Prague University, constructed a special rotation apparatus, a swing, a centrifuge for use with animal subjects, and equipment for the production of low pressure. These were used to determine the role of physical stimuli and sensory organs in the perception of movement. The wooden frame "R" (see Figure 4) was 4 × 2 meters in size. It

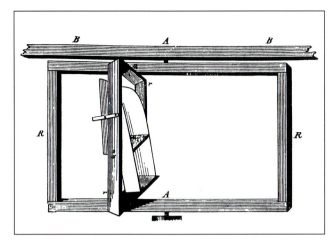

Figure 4 Rotation apparatus for study of movement perception.

experience were primarily mediated by the actual, physical nature of the rotating disks and chairs, which Mach employed in his experiments.

Figure 5 Drawing of Mach by Felix Mach.

and the smaller frame "r" could be rotated vertically. The experimental subject (Mach) sat down in the chair, which could be inclined horizontally. In addition, the visual field of the subject was covered with a pasteboard box.

As was the case in his studies of contrast perception, Mach's new results were fairly obvious. He discovered that the "progressive or angle speed" rather than the speed of movement was the stimulus for the perception of movement. In turn, he found out that it was the inner ear that serves as the sense organ for movement perception, and not—as contemporary scientists of Mach's time had assumed—the skin, the eyes, or the brain.

To evaluate properly Mach's physiological research achievements, one must realize that the perception of movement was a topic far removed from the subject matter of mathematics and physics. The experience of turning, whirling, falling, climbing, and vertigo presented a sharp contrast to the orderly world of mathematics. Still, Mach continued his experiments until even this field yielded regular and predictable results.

Mach fully deserves his place in the history of science on the basis of his original, empirical researches and their results. More importantly, however, his work created a "rotating reality," which required the use of such complex research methods that his very methods themselves appear to be in rotation. While contemporary mathematics and physics helped Mach to explain the experience of rotation and movement, the specific qualities of this

Mach's work on the perception of movement can be regarded as an important contribution to this field of research. In addition, his research revealed a paradoxical relationship between scientific theory and methodology. In a manner of speaking, Mach's research produced a high degree of versatility through his efforts to establish total stability in an environment of complete mobility.

When Mach published his book, *Principles of a Theory of Movement Perception* (1875/1967), contemporary science had already turned away from concepts of such extreme contrasts and, consequently,

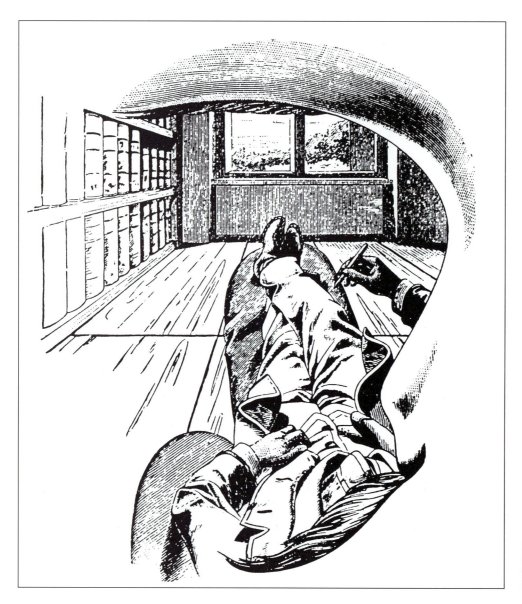

Figure 6 Drawing by Mach illustrating "The view out of the left eye" or "The transition from physics to psychology."

the empirical study of movement perception had ceased to be of interest to the scientific community. It was not until the beginning of the 20th century, at another turning point in the history of psychology, that advocates of Gestalt psychology resumed research on the important topic of movement perception.

Bibliography

Blackmore, J. T. (1978). Three autobiographical manuscripts by Ernst Mach. *Annals of Science, 35,* 401–418.

Mach, E. (1865). Über die Wirkung der räumlichen Vertheilung des Lichtreizes auf die Netzhaut (Treatise 1). Sitzungsberichte der Kaiserlichen Akademie der Wissenschaften. *Mathematisch-natur-wissenschaftliche Classe, 52*(2), 303–322.

Mach, E. (1866a). Über den physiologischen Effect räumlich vertheil-ter Lichtreize (Treatise 2). Sitzungsberichte der Kaiserlichen Akademie der Wissenschaften. *Mathematisch-naturwis-senschaftliche Classe, 54*(2), 131–144.

Mach, E. (1866b). Über die physiologische Wirkung räumlich vertheil-ter Lichtreize (Treatise 3). Sitzungsberichte der Kaiserlichen Akademie der Wissenschaften. *Mathematisch-naturwis-senschaftliche Classe, 54*(2), 393–408.

Mach, E. (1868). Über die physiologische Wirkung räumlich vertheil-ter Lichtreize (Treatise 4). Sitzungsberichte der Kaiserlichen Akademie der Wissenschaften. *Mathematisch-naturwis-senschaftliche Classe, 57*(2), 11–19.

Mach, E. (1967). *Grundlinien der Lehre von den Bewegungsempfindun-gen.* Amsterdam: E. J. Bonset. (Original work published 1875)

Mach, E. (1886). *Beiträge zur Analyse der Empfindungen.* Jena: G. Fi-scher. (1900 Edition: Die Analyse der Empfindungen und das Ver-hältnis des Physischen zum Psychischen.)

Swoboda, W. W. (1988). Physik, Physiologie und Psychophysik—Die Wurzeln von Ernst Machs Empiriokritizismus. In R. Haller & F. Stadler (Ed.), *Ernst Mach, Werk und Wirkung* (pp. 356–403). Vienna: Hölder-Pichler-Tempsky.

Carl Stumpf

Helga Sprung

The psychologist, philosopher, and musicologist Carl Stumpf (1848–1936) was an important scientist during the late 19th and early 20th centuries. He was born on April 21, 1848, the son of the court physician Eugen Stumpf (1810–1889) in the Franconian village of Wiesentheid in the German Kingdom of Bavaria. Stumpf received a classical high school education, first in nearby Bamberg and then in Aschaffenburg, between 1859 and 1865. He began his university studies at Würzburg in 1865. His major professor was the philosopher Franz Brentano (1838–1917), whose ideas and work exerted a lasting influence on Stumpf's scientific life and career. At the suggestion of Brentano, Stumpf transferred to Göttingen University in 1867, where he studied philosophy and psychology with Hermann Lotze (1817–1881) and the natural sciences with the physiologist Georg Meissner (1829–1905) and the physicist Wilhelm Weber (1804–1891). His studies under the experimental physicist Friedrich Kohlrausch (1840–1910) provided Stumpf with valuable experience in the techniques of experimental research. Stumpf received his doctorate at Göttingen for a philosophical dissertation on "The Relationship between Plato's God and his Idea of Goodness." Two years later, Stumpf qualified as an academic teacher at the same university with a mathematical research dissertation. From 1870 to 1873, he held an untenured instructorship at Göttingen, lecturing on classical philosophy. He accepted a call to Würzburg in 1873 to succeed his former teacher Brentano.

In 1878, Stumpf married Hermine Biedermann (1849–1930), whom he had met through their common love of music. The Stumpfs had one daughter and two sons. Stumpf played the violin from the

Figure 1 Hermine and Carl Stumpf (ca. 1882).

time he was 7 years old, and eventually learned to play five other instruments!

His fascination with music provides a key to understanding his research in the psychology of music, which he began in 1875 and continued throughout much of his life. In 1879 Stumpf was appointed to a full professorship at the German University in Prague in the Austrian Empire. Five years later, he accepted a call to Halle, and in 1889 he moved to the University of Munich. He was called to Berlin in 1894.

Stumpf had some initial reservations about exchanging the "Bavarian Metropolis" for the "capital of Prussia." In Berlin, Stumpf, along with Hermann Ebbinghaus (1850–1909), became the cofounder of the Psychological Institute of Berlin University (Sprung & Sprung, 1986). The senior faculty at Berlin and the Royal Prussian Ministry of Education chose Stumpf rather than Ebbinghaus because Stumpf was a philosopher with solid qualifications in the nascent field of experimental psychology. Ebbinghaus, who had taught at Berlin since 1880, was turned down because of his limited background in philosophy. In addition, Stumpf served as a member of the prestigious Royal Prussian Academy of Sciences from 1894 until his death. Eventually, his attitude toward living in Berlin changed. Thus, he wrote in his autobiography: "Berlin's local genius, the all-pervasive spirit of work, has won me over" (Stumpf, 1924, p. 15). He worked in Berlin for a total of 28 years, until his retirement in 1921 at the age of 73. Stumpf died on December 25, 1936, at the age of 88 in the Berlin suburb of Lichterfelde.

Stumpf began his academic career with the question of space perception. His subsequent study of acoustical perception resulted in major publications in the psychology of music (Stumpf, 1883, 1890). Within the context of this research, Stumpf was primarily interested in the problems of attention and judgment. He conceptualized the field of experimental psychophysics as a theory of metric judgment. His research on tonal perception may have encouraged his later studies of emotions (Stumpf, 1899b, 1907b, 1916, 1928).

Stumpf defined psychology as the study of "psychic functions," which involved intellectual as well as emotional parameters. Intellectual functions included observation or discrimination, concept formation, and judgment. "Passive" emotions and the "active" will are emotional functions. According to Stumpf, all psychic functions are correlated with associated phenomena (i.e., psychological experiences), which provide them with content. Since other sciences, like physics or physiology, also deal with phenomena, Stumpf regarded "phenomenology" as a "propaedeutic" adjunct to science. Phenomenology involves a detailed analysis which goes back to the basic elements of sensory experiences and memory images. In this context, Stumpf became

Figure 2 Stumpf as elected president of Berlin University (1907).

involved in a sharp scientific controversy with Wilhelm Wundt (1832–1920). Wundt regarded the musicological research of Stumpf at best as a pilot project and expressed his views publicly in a critical review of Stumpf's magnum opus. Stumpf, however regarded the psychology of music as a core topic of experimental psychology in the tradition of Gustav Fechner (1801–1887). Carl Stumpf's scientific work included interests in questions of basic scientific research methodologies, theories, and policy. Within this context, he often commented about basic problems facing the psychology of his time, including his incisive essays on "Developmental Theory" (Stumpf, 1899a), the "Mind-Body Problem" (1897), "Psychic Phenomena and Functions" (1906a), and "Directions and Contradictions in Psychology" (1907a). The relationship between psychology and philosophy was the focus of his writings on "Psychology and Epistemology" (1891), "The Classification of the Sciences" (1906b), "The Renaissance of Philosophy" (1907c), and his elegant essays (Stumpf, 1928b) about his friend William James (1842–1910). In 1917, Stumpf characterized the relationship between philosophy and psychology as follows:

> [Psychology] . . . is the youngest branch [of philosophy], which some worried gardeners would like to clip. We have not been pruned as yet, and can still share our youthful strength with philosophy. If it should [ever] come to an external separation [between our fields], the internal attitude . . . must remain. Otherwise, philosophy will become totally abstracted from the world and life, and psychology will be transformed into merely an applied discipline. (p. 25)

Personally, Stumpf regarded the field of applied psychology rather positively. He made efforts to apply his work in the psychology of music to the field of medicine. In addition, he was involved in the application of psychological research to military problems during World War I. After the war, he approved the establishment of a department for applied psychology in his Berlin institute, headed by Hans Rupp (1880–1954).

Stumpf's final thoughts about basic scientific theory and psychology are contained in the two volumes of his posthumous publication, *Epistemology* (1939–1940). Stumpf also influenced the field of musicology through a wealth of empirical and theoretical studies. He edited the journal *Contributions to Acoustics and Musicology* from 1898 on, and wrote many of its articles himself.

Stumpf played an important methodological and political role in the development of modern psychology as an independent, institutionalized specialty (Ash, 1980; Lück, 1991). As a student of Brentano and Lotze, and especially through his work in the psychology of music, Stumpf became a mediator of early Gestalt psychological ideas (Sprung & Sprung, 1995). His students and colleagues included most of the impor-

tant Gestalt psychologists, such as Wolfgang Köhler (1887–1967), Max Wertheimer (1880–1943), and Kurt Koffka (1886–1941); as well as Kurt Lewin (1890–1947), Erich Moritz von Hornbostel (1877–1935), Hans Rupp (1880–1954), and Friedrich Schumann (1863–1940).

Early in the 20th century, Stumpf played a major role in the nascent field of experimental, comparative psychology. During the heated controversy about the horse "Clever Hans," which reportedly was able to think, solve mathematical problems, and answer a variety of questions, Stumpf and his student Oskar Pfungst (1874–1932) designed an ambitious plan to determine the nature of the horse's alleged intelligence. They concluded from their empirical observations and experiments that Clever Hans was unable to think but had learned to be guided in his answers by unconscious clues from his trainer. Stumpf's famous work with animals was followed shortly afterwards by the cognitive work of his doctoral student, Wolfgang Köhler, with primates and anticipated the so-called "experimenter expectation (Rosenthal) effect."

Figure 3 Stumpf (right) and the botanist Gottlieb Haberlandt (1854–1945) in the Austrian mountains (1929).

Finally, Stumpf's work as a promoter and "statesman" of science must be mentioned. His specific accomplishments include the dramatic expansion of

Figure 4 Bust of Stumpf by Kolbe.

the Berlin Psychological Institute, the expansion of the Berlin Sound and Record Archive into a full-fledged center of ethnological musicology, and the planning and establishment of Köhler's famous Primate Research Center on the Spanish island of Tenerife (Sprung, Sprung, & Kernchen, 1984; Sprung & Schönpflug, 1992).

Bibliography

Ash, M. G. (1980). Academic politics in the history of science: Experimental psychology in Germany, 1879–1941. *Central European History, 13,* 255–286.

Lück, H. E. (1991). *Geschichte der Psychologie. Strömungen, Schulen. Entwicklungen.* Stuttgart: Kohlhammer.

Sprung, H. & Sprung, L. (1995). Carl Stumpf (1848–1936) und die Anfänge der Gestaltpsychologie an der Berliner Universität. In S. Jaeger, I. Staeuble, L. Sprung, & H.-P. Brauns (Eds.), *Psychologie im soziokulturellen Wandel - Kontinuitäten und Diskontinuitäten.* Frankfurt: Lang.

Sprung, L., & Schönpflug, W. (Eds.). (1992). *Zur Geschichte der Psychologie in Berlin.* Frankfurt: Lang.

Sprung, L., & Sprung, H. (1986). Hermann Ebbinghaus—Life, Work and Impact in the History of Psychology. In F. Klix & H. Hagendorf (Eds.), *Human memory and cognitive capabilities. Mechanismus and performances. Symposium in memoriam Hermann Ebbinghaus. Berlin Humboldt University* (Vol. 1, pp. 23–34). Amsterdam: Elsevier (North-Holland).

Sprung, L., Sprung, H., & Kernchen, S. (1984). Carl Stumpf and the origin and development of psychology as a new science at the university of Berlin. In H. Carpintero & J. M. Peiro (Eds.), *Psychology in its historical context. Monografias de la Revista de Historia de la Psicologia* (pp. 349–355). Valencia, Spain.

Stumpf, C. (1883). *Tonpsychologie* (Vol. 1). Leipzig: Hirzel.

Stumpf, C. (1890). *Tonpsychologie* (Vol. 2). Leipzig: Hirzel.

Stumpf, C. (1891). Psychologie und Erkenntnistheorie. In *Abhandlungen der philosophisch-philologischen Classe der Königlich Bayerischen Akademie der Wissenschaften* (Vol. 19 [2], pp. 465–516). Munich: Verlag der K. Akademie.

Stumpf, C. (1897). Eröffnungsrede des Präsidenten, Prof. Dr. Carl Stumpf (Berlin). In *Dritter Internationaler Congress für Psychologie in München vom 4 bis 7* August 1896 (pp. 3–16). Munich: Lehmann.

Stumpf, C. (1899a). Der Entwicklungsgedanke in der gegenwärtigen Philosophie. Festrede, gehalten am Stiftungstage der Kaiser Wilhelms-Akademie für das militärische Bildungswesen am 2. Dezember 1899 (pp. 5–32). Berlin: Lange.

Stumpf, C. (1899b). Ueber den Begriff der Gemüthsbewegung. *Zeitschrift für Psychologie und Physiologie der Sinnesorgane, 21,* 47–99.

Stumpf, C. (1906a). Erscheinungen und psychische Funktionen. In *Abhandlungen der Königlich Preussischen Akademie der Wissenschaften aus dem Jahre 1906. Philosophisch-historische Abhandlungen* (Vol. 4, pp. 1–40). Berlin: Reimer.

Stumpf, C. (1906b). Zur Einteilung der Wissenschaften. In *Abhandlungen der Königlich Preussischen Akademie der Wissenschaften aus dem Jahre 1906. Philosophisch-historische Abhandlungen* (Vol. 5, pp. 1–94). Berlin: Reimer.

Stumpf, C. (1907a). Richtungen und Gegensätze in der heutigen Psychologie. Internationale Wochenschrift für Wissenschaft Kunst und Technik. Sonnabendbeilage der "Münchener Allgemeinen Zeitung" vom 19. Oktober 1907 (pp. 903–914). Berlin: August Scherl GmbH.

Stumpf, C. (1907b). Über Gefühlsempfindungen. *Zeitschrift für Psychologie und Physiologie der Sinnesorgane 44,* pp. 1–49.

Stumpf, C. (1907c). *Die Wiedergeburt der Philosophie. Rede zum Antritt des Rektorates der Königlichen Friedrich-Wilhelms-Universität in Berlin.* Berlin: Universitäts-Buchdruckerei von Gustav Schade (Otto Francke).

Stumpf, C. (1916). Apologie der Gefühlsempfindung. *Zeitschrift für Psychologie und Physiologie der Sinnesorgane, 75,* 1–38.

Stumpf, C. (1917). Zum Gedächtnis Lotzes. *Kantstudien, XXII,* 1–26.

Stumpf, C. (1924). Carl Stumpf. In R. Schmidt (Ed.), *Die Philosophie der Gegenwart in Selbstdarstellungen* (Vol. 5, pp. 205–265). Leipzig: Meiner.

Stumpf, C. (1928a). *Gefühl und Gefühlsempfindung.* Leipzig: Barth.

Stumpf, C. (1928b). *William James.* Charlottenburg: Pan.

Stumpf, C. (1939). *Erkenntnislehre* (Vol. 1). Leipzig: Barth.

Stumpf, C. (1940). *Erkenntnislehre* (Vol. 2). Leipzig: Barth.

Wertheimer, M. (1971). *Kurze Geschichte der Psychologie.* Munich: Pieper.

The Graz School of Gestalt Psychology

Reinhard Fabian

During the second half of the 19th century, Alexius Meinong (1853–1920) contributed decisively to the development of an autonomous Austrian philosophy through his writings on epistemological theory, the psychology of values, and object theory. Meinong, who had received his philosophical education under Franz Brentano (1838–1917) at the University of Vienna, initially followed Brentano's program of descriptive psychology. In his later years, however, he pursued his own very different interests in experimental psychology and philosophy.

In 1894, Meinong was able to establish his own psychological laboratory at Graz University in the Province of Styria of the Austro-Hungarian Empire. Meinong's Institute of Psychology, along with the Philosophical Seminar (which was opened at Graz in 1897), played a central role in the origin of the Graz School of Gestalt Psychology. Among Meinong's many students during the almost 40 years of his academic association with the University of Graz, the following individuals deserve special mention: Stephan Witasek (1870–1915), Vittorio Benussi (1878–1927), Rudolf Ameseder (1877–1937), Wilhelm M. Frankl (1878–1933), Eduard Martinak (1859–1943), Ernst Mally (1879–1944), and Franz Weber (1890–1975). In addition, Meinong maintained close contact with two fellow students from Vienna, Alois Höfler (1853–1922) and Christian von Ehrenfels (1859–1932). Meinong's autobiography (1921) contains the names of no less than 19 students and associates. More detailed information about the "Graz School" and its members is readily available through other sources such as Haller & Fabian (1985) and Stock & Stock (1990), but a few of the key figures are highlighted below.

The term "Graz School" (or "Austrian School")

Figure 1 Alexius Meinong (1853–1920).

pertains primarily to the purely psychological writings of Meinong and his students. Details about the experimental work of the Graz School can be found in several studies (e.g., Höfler, 1930; Herrmann, 1976; Heider, 1970; Lindenfeld, 1980); a brief conceptual overview will give the reader a sense of what the school was about.

Figure 2 Christian von Ehrenfels (1859–1932).

Christian von Ehrenfels and "Gestalt Qualities"

The impetus which encouraged Meinong and his associates at Graz to concentrate on the psychological study of Gestalt concepts was provided by Christian von Ehrenfels' famous treatise "On Gestalt Qualities" (1890). (The scientific career of Ehrenfels has been described in rich detail by Fabian [1986]). Following a suggestion by Ernst Mach (1838–1916), Ehrenfels illustrated the concept of a "Gestalt quality" through the example of a melody.

A simple melody consists basically of a series of individual tones. The sum of these successively perceived tones forms a complex idea which cannot exist without those individual component tones. At the same time, however, a mere series of discrete individual tones does not necessarily produce a melody. Furthermore, if one transposes the same melody into another key, it will now consist of very

different tonal elements. Thus, the special character of a melody is its Gestalt quality, which satisfies the criteria of "supersummativity and transposability." Whereas Ehrenfels was mainly concerned with documenting a wide range of Gestalt phenomena through his description and classification of configurations, Meinong's work was primarily concerned with providing more precise definitions of the Gestalt concept.

As early as 1891, Meinong discussed Ehrenfels's essay in a thorough review. Specifically, he viewed Gestalt ideas and their content as configurations which are derived from "basic contents." He also proposed replacing the term "Gestalt quality" first with the term "basic content" and later with "object of higher order." Apart from their terminological differences, Meinong viewed Gestalt phenomena not as something static but as a matter of special psychological acts, which create the configuration of a Gestalt from existing elements. Therefore, a Gestalt idea is the result of a psychic event, which has been defined as one of "perceptual production" (Witasek,

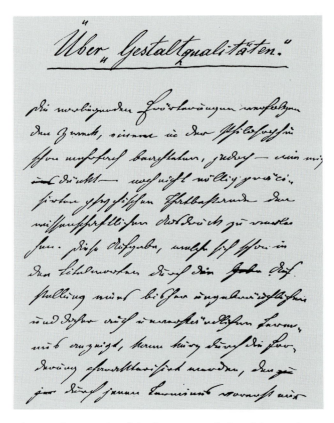

Figure 3 Facsimile of the beginning of Ehrenfels' article on "Gestalt Quality."

252

1908, p. 222–246). Witasek not only provided the clearest description of the "production theory" of the Graz School, he also showed how artists often create Gestalt patterns spontaneously, even when the basic preconditions are missing.

Stephan Witasek

According to his handwritten curriculum vitae (see Figure 5), Stephan Witasek was born into a German-speaking Catholic family on May 17, 1870, in Vienna. His father held an appointment as chief inspector of the Austrian Railroads. Witasek graduated from the Empress Elizabeth Classical High School in Vienna and attended the University of Graz, where he majored in philosophy and the history of art. His minor subjects were mathematics and physics. In

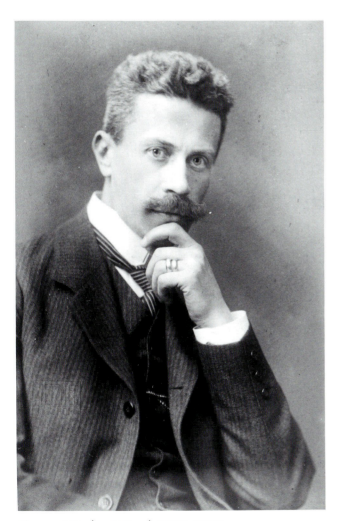

Figure 4 Stephan Witasek (1870–1915).

Stephan Witasek,
geboren am 17. Mai 1870, in Wien.
Katholisch, deutsch.
Vater Eisenbahn-Oberinspektor, †1902.

Kaiserin Elisabeth-Staatsgymnasium in Wien,
Universität in Graz, (Philosophie als Hauptfach, zuerst Philologie und Kunstgeschichte, dann Mathematik und Physik als Nebenfächer).
1894 Wartingerpreis,
1895 März Rigorosen u. Promotion.

Eintritt in den Bibliotheksdienst Oktober 1895. Zum Amanuensis ernannt Mai 1901.

1895–1902 Assistent am psycholog. Laboratorium.

Habilitation März 1899, Titel Extraordinarius November 1905, Lehrauftrag Mai 1909.

Arbeitsurlaub 1902/03, Studienreise 1908 nach Leipzig, Berlin, Göttingen etc.
Kongressberichte 1896 München, 1905 Rom, 1906 Würzburg und Basel.

Verheiratet seit Juli 1908.

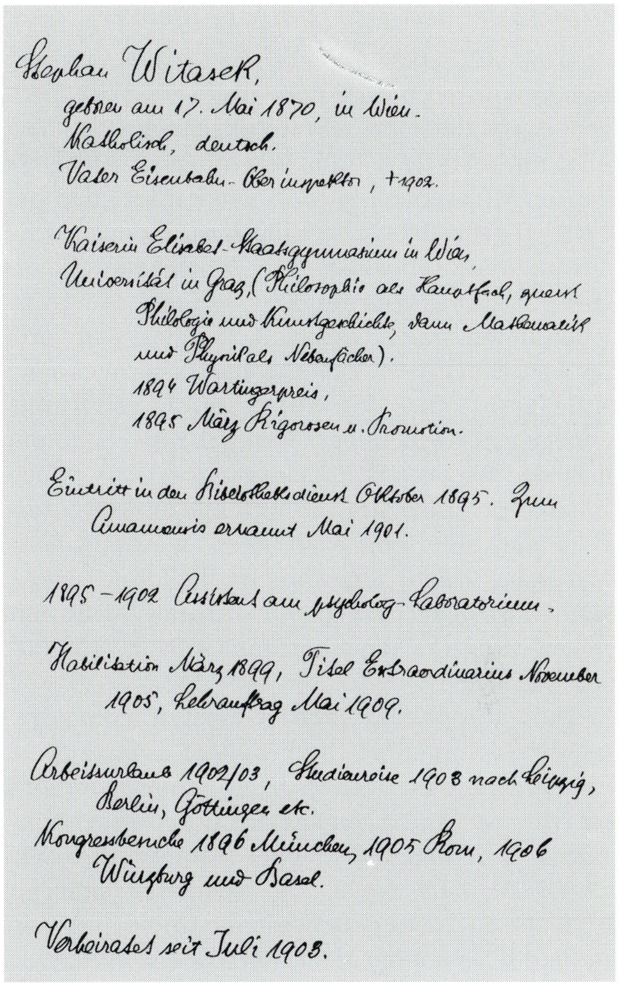

Figure 5 Facsimile of Witasek's curriculum vitae.

1894, he received the "Warting" award and in 1895 completed the oral examination for his PhD. In October of 1895, Witasek was employed first as a librarian and later promoted to the rank of "Amanuensis" in 1901. He also served from 1895 to 1902 as assistant at the psychological laboratory at Graz University. While there he became an untenured instructor in 1899, was married in July 1903, and in November of 1905 was awarded the rank of untenured professor. In 1909 he received a teaching position in psychology. Other important events in his career included a sabbatical leave from 1902 to 1903; a research trip to the universities of Leipzig, Berlin, and Göttingen in 1908; and his participation in scientific congresses held in Munich (1896), Rome (1905), and Würzburg and Basel (1906). Witasek died in 1915.

Vittorio Benussi and Optical Illusions

After the basic principles of Gestalt psychology had been formulated, a very productive period of experimental psychological research began at Graz. The chief interests of Meinong's younger colleagues Stephan Witasek and Vittorio Benussi included the so-called geometric-optical illusions. Through their research with the well-known Zöllner and Müller-Lyer illusions, Witasek and Benussi hoped to underpin their ideas (especially the idea of the production theory) with experimental data. According to Benussi (1914), different types of Gestalt phenomena can be identified during the perception of illusions: "Between the sensory impressions, which remain constant, and the perception of figures, which may differ from each other, an event X must take place, which, depending on the form it takes, will lead to the perception of totally different objects from the same constant sensory stimulation" (p. 400).

Thus, the phenomenon of "Gestalt ambiguity" can be explained as the result of a perceptual process. The basic idea that Gestalt configurations are the result of synthetic and nonsensory processes became a distinctive feature of the Graz School. The same explanatory model was the major focus of a controversy between the Graz School and the Berlin School of Gestalt Psychology. The Berlin School had offered a negative critique of the Graz model (Koffka, 1915), but Benussi adhered to his basic position. However, he did alter his views about the production of ideas by replacing his concept of "produced idea" with the concept of "idea of extrasensory origin" (Benussi, 1914, p. 104). Similarly, Alois Höfler (1930, pp. 428, 432f) suggested that the term "co-induction" should be used as a replacement for the earlier term "production."

The End of the Graz School

In addition to his studies of geometric-optical illusions, Witasek was interested in the problems of space perception and the principles of aesthetics. Benussi eventually turned to the psychology of time perception and the sense of touch. When Meinong died in 1920, the Graz psychological laboratory had existed for almost 30 years. Nonetheless, the work of the Graz School came to an end as a result of dramatic reductions in personnel. Witasek died unexpectedly in 1915, and Benussi, shortly before the end of World War I, moved to Italy, where he was appointed to the chair of psychology at the University of Padua. At Padua, he was able to continue the traditions of Graz psychology to a limited extent. In addition, he influenced the work of Italian psychologists like Cesare Musatti, Fabio Metelli, and Gaetano Kanizsa (Smith, 1988, p. 26–31) on illusions and perceptual phenomenology.

Figure 6 Vittorio Benussi (1878–1927).

Meinong's immediate successor was Ernst Mally (1879–1944), whose teaching and research concentrated primarily on the field of philosophy. Ferdinand Weinhandl (1896–1973) and Fritz Heider (1896–1988) were the last members of the original Graz School.

After receiving their doctorates, both left Graz to continue their psychological education in Germany. Weinhandl, who returned to Graz in 1944, developed his own method of Gestalt analysis. Heider worked after 1930 in the United States and became famous through his writings on the psychology of interpersonal relations.

Detailed bibliographies of publications by the members of the Graz School were recently published by Smith (1988) and Stock and Stock (1990).

Bibliography

Antonelli, M. (1994). *Die experimentelle Analyse des Bewußtseins bei Vittorio Benussi.* Amsterdam/Atlanta: Rodopi.

Benussi, V. (1904). Zur Psychologie des Gestalterfassens. (Die Müller-Lyersche Figur). In A. Meinong (Ed.), *Untersuchungen zur Gegenstandstheorie und Psychologie* (Zum zehnjährigen Bestande des Psychologischen Laboratoriums der Universität Graz) (pp. 303–448). Leipzig: Barth.

Benussi, V. (1914). Gesetze der inadäquaten Gestaltauffassung (Die Ergebnisse meiner bisherigen experimentellen Arbeiten zur Analyse der sogen. Geometrisch-optischen Täuschungen [Vorstellungen außersinnlicher Provenienz]). *Archiv für die gesamte Psychologie, 32,* 396–419.

Ehrenfels, C. von. (1890). Über 'Gestaltqualitäten'. *Vierteljahresschrift für wissenschaftliche Philosophie 14,* 242–292. In C. von Ehrenfels, *Psychologie-Ethik-Erkenntnistheorie (Philosophische Schriften III,* pp. 128–167) edited by R. Fabian. Munich: Philosophia, 1988.

Fabian, R. (Ed.) (1986). *Christian von Ehrenfels—Leben und Werk.* Amsterdam: Rodopi.

Haller, R., & Fabian, R. (1985). Alexius Meinong und die Grazer Schule der Gegenstandstheorie. In K. Freisitzer et al. (Eds.), *Tradition und Herausforderung. 400 Jahre Universität Graz* (pp. 277–291). Graz: Akademische Druck- und Verlagsanstalt.

Heider, F. (1970). Gestalt theory: Early history and reminiscences. *Journal of the History of the Behavioral Sciences, 6,* 131–139.

Heider, F. (1983). *The life of a psychologist. An autobiography.* Lawrence: University of Kansas Press.

Herrmann, T. (1976). Ganzheitspsychologie und Gestalttheorie. In H. Balmer (Ed.), *Die Psychologie des 20. Jahrhunderts, I: Die europäische Tradition* (Vol. 574–658). Zürich: Kindler.

Höfler, A. (1930). *Psychologie* (2. sehr vermehrte Auflage, mit Beiträgen von A. Wenzl und O. Sterzinger), edited by A. Wenzl. Vienna/Leipzig: Hölder-Pichler-Tempsky.

Koffka, K. (1915). Zur Grundlegung der Wahrnehmungspsychologie. Eine Auseinandersetzung mit V. Benussi. (Beiträge zur Psychologie der Gestalt III). *Zeitschrift für Psychologie, 73,* 11–90.

Lindenfeld, D. F. (1980). *The Transformation of Positivism: Alexius Meinong and European Thought 1880–1920.* Berkeley/Los Angeles: University of California Press.

Lück, H. E. (1990). Ein Briefwechsel zwischen William Stern und Alexius Meinong. *Psychologie und Geschichte, 1*(4), 38–54.

Meinong, A. (1969). Zur Psychologie der Komplexionen und Relationen. In R. Kindlinger & R. Haller (Eds.). *Abhandlungen zur Psychologie (Meinong Gesamtausgaben* [Complete Edition] I, pp. 279–300). Graz: Akademische Druck- und Verlagsanstalt. (Originally published 1891 in *Zeitschtrift für Psychologie, 2,* 245–265)

Meinong, A. (1978) A. Meinong. In R. Haller (Ed.). *Selbstdarstellung - Vermischte Schriften (Meinong Gesamtausgaben* [Complete Edition] VII, pp. 7–62). Graz: Akademische Druck- und Verlagsanstalt. (Originally published 1921 in R. Schmidt [Ed.], *Die Deutsche Philosophie der Gegenwart in Selbstdarstellungen* [Vol. I, pp. 91–150]. Leipzig: Meiner).

Meinong, A. (Ed.). (1904). *Untersuchungen zur Gegenstandstheorie und Psychologie* (Zum zehnjährigen Bestande des Psychologischen Laboratoriums der Universität Graz). Leipzig: Barth.

Smith, B. (Ed.). (1988). *Foundations of Gestalt theory.* Munich/Vienna: Philosophia Verlag. (Annotated Bibliography, pp. 227–478).

Stock, M., & Stock, W. (1990). *Psychologie und Philosophie der Grazer Schule. Eine Dokumentation zu Werk und Wirkungsgeschichte* (Vols. 1–2) (Supplement to Internationalen Bibliographie zur Österreichischen Philosophie, edited by W. L. Gombocz et al.). Amsterdam: Rodopi.

Witasek, S. (1899). Über die Natur der geometrisch-optischen Täuschungen. *Zeitschrift für Psychologie, 19,* 81–174.

Weinhandl, F. (1927). *Die Gestaltanalyse.* Erfurt: Stenger.

Weinhandl, F. (1960). Der Gestaltlegetest, seine Interpretation und Auswertung. In F. Weinhandl (Ed.), *Gestalthaftes Sehen* (pp. 365–383). Darmstadt: Wissenschaftliche Buchgesellschaft.

Witasek, S. (1899). Über die Natur der geometrisch-optischen Täuschungen. *Zeitschrift für Psychologie, 19,* 81–174.

Witasek, S. (1908). *Grundlinien der Psychologie.* Leipzig: Dürr (Ed. 2, Leipzig: Meiner, 1923).

Gertrude Stein, William James, and Pablo Picasso's Cubism

Marianne L. Teuber

In *The Autobiography of Alice B. Toklas* (1933), Gertrude Stein (1874–1946) wrote: "In the long struggle with the portrait of Gertrude Stein, Picasso passed from the charming Harlequin period to the intensive struggle which was to end in cubism" (p. 66). During her Radcliffe years (1893–1897), and before moving to Paris, Stein was an admiring, knowledgeable student of William James (1842–1910). With youthful enthusiasm she wrote in 1895: "Is life worth living? Yes, a thousand times yes, when the world still holds such spirits as Professor James" (Hoffman, 1966, p. 226). Did she single out the ambitious, gifted Picasso (1881–1973) to share with him her former teacher's ideas on form and space and possibly contribute to the beginnings of Cubism (1907–1914)?

The Early Years

The youngest of five children, Gertrude Stein was born into a family of textile merchants who had emigrated from Bavaria and settled in Baltimore, Maryland. After a family feud the textile business was dissolved; her father took his family to Europe, then moved to California. Gertrude's education was interrupted by frequent trips to Europe, but she was an avid reader. At the Oakland Public Library she found reading matter which ranged from the Elizabethan authors to 18th- and 19th- century novels and poetry. At 19, she entered "The Annex"—called Radcliffe by 1894—without a high school diploma. Her favorite brother, Leo, who was two years older, had already begun taking courses at Harvard College but had no plans to graduate. Gertrude, however, was more determined. She excelled in the sciences and William James admitted her to graduate courses and seminars. She became secretary of the Philosophy Club, and in addition, enjoyed Boston's theater and

opera. She and a graduate student, Leon Solomons (whom she had known in California), took turns as experimenter and subject in experiments on automatic writing at the Harvard Psychological Laboratory. The lab had been started by James about 1875 and was later directed by Hugo Münsterberg (1863–1916) beginning in 1892. Münsterberg found her the model of a young scholar. In "Normal Motor Automatism," by Solomons and Stein (1896), she argued against the idea that automatic writing consisted of bringing the subconscious to the surface. She insisted that *diversion of attention*, not the subconscious, was at work when reading from a captivating novel, so that words from the novel intruded on the writing. "Miss Stein found it sufficient distraction to simply read what her arm wrote, but following three or four words behind her pencil" resulting in "a tendency toward marked repetition" (p. 506).

In *The Autobiography of Alice B. Toklas* (1933), Stein admitted that she had made her method of repetitive automatic writing an ingredient of her later style. An excerpt from her "word portrait" entitled "Picasso" is a good example:

> One whom some were certainly following was one who was completely charming. . . . Some were certainly following and were certain that the one they were then following was one working and was one bringing out of himself then something that was coming to be a heavy thing, a solid thing and a complete thing. . . . This one was one whom some were following. This one was one who was working. (Stein, 1912, pp. 29–30)

In addition, by using the present participle, a Stein landmark, she maintains a "continuous permanent present," a Jamesian notion of time (James, 1890, "Perception of Time"). In his "Has Gertrude Stein a Secret?" Fred Skinner (1934) had a point when he claimed—like Stein herself—that her automatic writing experiments helped shape her later style; she intentionally constructed rhythmic, repetitive prose that would let events and personalities *emerge*, as in "Picasso." In an article of her own, Stein (1898) arrived at two types of personality with different reactions to automatized movement. Again she argued for diversion of attention and against sub-conscious reactions—which she "never had" (Stein, 1933, p. 97).

James counseled her to attend Johns Hopkins Medical School if she wanted to become a psychologist. Harvard Medical School did not admit women. He recognized her clear-headed brilliance and sympathized with her interrupted schooling. Had he not had the same experience when his father, Henry James, Sr., took his family to Europe for months and years? Striving for "gloire" even as an undergraduate, she received her Radcliffe BA in 1898 and entered Johns Hopkins Medical School after having passed her Radcliffe entrance exams, which included Latin. Her first novel, *Q.E.D.* (Quod erat demonstrandum) written in 1903, had a Latin title and was published posthumously (1971). It deals with an unhappy lesbian relationship that may have contributed to her not completing her final medical school exams. She had done well in the science-oriented first two years of medical school, but became disaffected during the next two years of practical medicine.

Paris

With medicine relinquished—though she enjoyed giving medical advice all her life—Stein followed her brother Leo to Florence and then to Paris. From 1904 to 1914, Leo and Gertrude built up the first private collection of modern art, starting with Cézanne in 1904, followed by Matisse in the fall of 1905, and then Picasso late in 1905 and through the Cubist period of 1907–1914. Why did the Stein Collection contain so many Cubist Picassos, when Leo turned his back on Cubism soon after it

came onto the scene? We shall see that Gertrude shared her love of James's psychology with Picasso. Her friends have testified that she often talked about James. But it was to the bright and ambitious Picasso that she chose to relate the experiments and ideas from James's *The Principles of Psychology* (1890) and *Psychology, Briefer Course* (1892), her textbooks as a student at Harvard. She had these books on her bookshelf at 27 Rue de Fleurus, Paris. She also owned James's *Varieties of Religious Experience* (1902) and his 1907 *Pragmatism*. But discussions with Picasso centered on what she knew best, and almost by heart from her student days. Besides, it was in *Principles* and the *Briefer Course* that James dealt with form and space.

There were many occasions for discussion between Gertrude and Pablo, starting with the approximately 90 sittings for her portrait (Figure 1)

Figure 1 Pablo Picasso, "Portrait of Gertrude Stein" (1906). Oil on canvas.

Figure 3 Pablo Picasso, "House and Trees" (1908). Oil on canvas.

Figure 2 Photo of Picasso, age 27, in his studio with sculptures from New Caledonia (1908).

at Picasso's studio (Figure 2); after luncheons and dinners at the Steins' and walks together from his studio to join the Saturday soirées at the Steins'. Matisse complained in 1907 that Miss Stein devoted all her attention to Picasso. There was an electricity between them, even if Picasso was not particularly fond of her. It has been contended that Gertrude Stein adopted a Cubist style from Picasso. In the following sections I intend to show that both drew on the same source: the teachings of William James. With Stein, Jamesian ideas prevailed up to 1914. Picasso incorporated into his Cubist works both visual experiments and theories from William James

that would shape Cubism's new picture space and philosophy.

Visual Evidence: Picasso's Cubism and Jamesian Space Perception

A main criterion of Cubist painting is its new relief-like picture space. No longer is an illusion of depth created *behind* the picture plane by means of perspective and objects shrinking in size. Instead, objects, landscapes, figures *protrude* from the surface like a relief, as in Picasso's "House and Trees" (Figure 3) or his overwhelming, huge "Three Women" (not shown) which Gertrude Stein owned. Light no longer casts a shadow in the opposite direction, as in traditional painting. In Cubist works, light and shade are arbitrary. Art critics of the Cubist period (1907–1914) stress protruding relief and ambiguous light and shade in Picasso's works (Fry, 1966, p. 82; Kahnweiler, 1920/1949, pp. 8, 11).

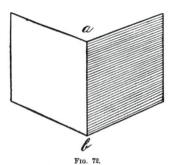

THE PERCEPTION OF SPACE.   **255**

sion, after long fixation, that a friend who painted such a mask for me told me it soon became difficult to see how to apply the brush. Bend a visiting-card across the middle, so that its halves form an angle of 90° more or less; set it upright on the table, as in Fig. 72, and view it with one eye.

FIG. 72.

You can make it appear either as if it opened towards you or away from you. In the former case, the angle *ab* lies

upon the table, *b* being nearer to you than *a*; in the latter case *ab* seems vertical to the table—as indeed it really is— with *a* nearer to you than *b*.* Again, look, with either one or

* Cf. E. Mach, Beiträge zur Analyse der Empfindungen, p. 87.

Figure 4 William James, "folded visiting card" experiment, from "The Perception of Space" in *The Principles of Psychology* (Vol. 2, 1890, p. 255).

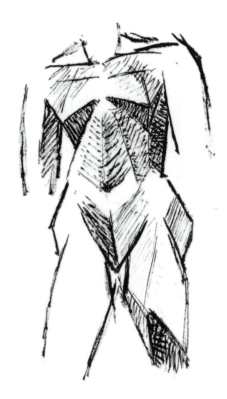

Figure 5 Pablo Picasso, "Standing Figure" (1908). Pen and ink.

They appeal to philosophy and science. But which science and philosophy inspired the Cubists?

Consider first the "folded visiting card" experiment (Figure 4) from Chapter 20 of *Principles of Psychology*. Compare it with Picasso's "House and Trees" (Figure 3): The garden wall resembles the "folded card," both in proportion and in the way the shadow falls on the right side. No one has paid attention to this peculiar wall (Teuber, 1982, pp. 26–29). The observer will notice that the folded card flips forward and back, so that the vertical in the center fluctuates between groove and ridge. As James explained—referring to Ernst Mach's *Analysis of Sensations* (1886/1959) in his footnote—the mind selects between two objects, each possible: one with a groove and receding; the other with a ridge and coming forward. According to James, the latter position with its protruding volume prevails. The reversible card flips forward and back only when we look at it; on the page it lies perfectly still. The movement occurs cognitively in our brain (in the temporal lobes). When the card reverses, light and shade do not change; in a real card bent in the opposite direction, the shadow would be on the other side. Hence, light and shade become arbitrary.

Since 1907, Picasso constructed human figures, heads, still lifes, architecture, drapery, and surfaces from the ambiguous flip-flop card with the prominent ridge coming forward. To give but a few of a multitude of examples: you see the folded card with ambiguous light and shade applied to the breasts and belly of Picasso's "Standing Figure" (Figure 5). Such striated areas were said to reflect Picasso's interest in African sculpture with its scarification marks. But in this and the majority of his drawings of 1907–1908 the striated forms derive from Jamesian diagrams (Teuber, 1982, pp. 28, 36, 41). From now on, we have to differentiate between what comes from African art and what in Picasso's early Cubism comes from Jamesian illustrations in the *Principles*.

In the course of 1908, Picasso changed his striated shadows to solid dark areas (see the wall in Figure 3). Kahnweiler (1920/1949, p. 8) remarked on this change. By the summer of 1909, all striations are gone. That summer, while painting at Horta de Ebro in the Basque Pyrenees, Picasso indulged in an orgy of protruding and receding form with ridges and arbitrary light and shade, as found in two landscapes, "Reservoir," and his magnificent "Houses on a Hill," both in the Collection of Gertrude Stein (not

Figure 6 Pablo Picasso, "Woman with Mantilla" (1909). Oil on canvas.

its new relief-like picture space is related to Jamesian protruding and receding relief, not to African art. One can hardly distinguish the "Nude" from the striated ups and downs of the drapery. She reveals an important feature of Cubism: the *emergence* of form or figure from a ground, instead of the traditional contrast between figure and ground. In Analytic Cubism (1910–1912), emerging objects and figures become a major topic, similar to Stein's word portrait of "Picasso."

William James visited the Stein Collection, probably in September of 1908. He saw "Nude with Drapery" and Picassos of the Blue and Rose periods, works by Matisse, and others. Stein met him at his hotel. "He went with her to her house to see the pictures. He looked and gasped. I told you, he said. I always told you that you should keep your mind open" (Stein, 1933, p. 98). In 1910 he planned to see Gertrude and Leo again, but his final illness prevented him from stopping in Paris on his way home.

Analytic Cubism: The Cooperation between Picasso and Georges Braque

In 1909, but especially during the period of Analytic Cubism (1910–1912), Georges Braque (1882–1963) and Picasso formed a close friendship. They saw each other almost daily. In "Violin and Pitcher" (Figure 8) Braque adopted ambiguously lit folded card motifs with ridges; they inhabit the entire surface and protrude from a closed-off background. Toward the center they join to form a pitcher and a violin. Picasso's portrait of Kahnweiler, the young dealer for the Cubists, shows similar folded card motifs that coalesce (Figure 9). Form elements are in a process of becoming objects or figures, though they never quite reach the full state of objecthood. Throughout, protruding and receding forms, arbitrarily lit, contribute to the shallow relief. At the top of Braque's work there is even a huge French visiting card with a bent corner (meaning "I left my card while you were out") and a private joke: a much-discussed nail with a cast shadow (Rudenstein, 1976). The nail belongs to the real world where objects cast shadows in only one

shown). "Woman with Mantilla" (Figure 6) has the folded card on her forehead, over the eyebrows, and on her cheeks. So do the other approximately 15 female heads Picasso painted that summer, including the bronze head (not shown) he sculpted in Paris in the fall of 1905. Ambiguous light plays over all these works, as grooves and ridges interchange.

Gertrude Stein owned an important early Cubist work by Picasso, his "Nude with Drapery" (Figure 7), a painting completed in the late summer of 1907. The vertical relief of protruding striated forms with arbitrary light and shade displays a sleeping nude. She reposes like a Giorgione or Titian Venus. But she is formed from a welter of lines that produce the hills and valleys of her body and the drapery. Is the drapery outfitted with scarification marks? Do the hatch marks along the nose derive from Gabon Reliquary figures? African art did play a role in Picasso's œuvre, as Rubin (1984) has shown. But Cubism and

Figure 7 Pablo Picasso, "Nude with Drapery" (1907). Oil on canvas.

Caledonia; it was owned by Picasso (see Figure 2; better photos appear in Rubin, 1984, pp. 299, 310). Picasso treated it in the high Cubist manner as a figure in the making; it is subject matter, like the bottle, and not a source for the form-analytic method of Cubism's protruding space. Nor is African sculpture a source for the ambiguous relief of Cubism.

Theoretical Evidence: Jamesian Form and Space Theory in Picasso's Cubism

James spoke of preperceptions not only in visual, but also in linguistic, terms. He presented his students with a string of unrelated French words: "pas de lieu Rhône que nous." If spoken rapidly it becomes "paddle your own canoe" in English (James, 1890, Vol. 1, p. 442). In 1913, Stein tried the

Figure 8 Georges Braque, "Violin and Pitcher" (1910). Oil on canvas.

direction; the nail nails the painting to the wall. But a painting consists of signs that the painter makes. Such signs are ambiguous, as long as they do not yet belong to objects. James called this state "preperceptions," a term he said he had borrowed from G. H. Lewes (1817–1878), the English philosopher and critic (Lewes, 1879, pp. 106–108; James, 1890, Vol. 1, p. 439). Kahnweiler (1920/1949, p. 13), surprisingly, speaks of preperceptions in conjunction with Analytic Cubism. He refers to G. H. Lewes and uses the English term in his German text. Gertrude Stein was puckish enough to give away half of the secret, perhaps on a visit to the art dealer who prided himself on having studied philosophy. Note in the lower left corner of Picasso's "Kahnweiler" a Cubist still life with a liquor bottle, protruding and incomplete, as Analytic Cubism demands. In the upper left corner there appears the domed headgear of an Oceanic sculpture from New

Figure 9 Pablo Picasso, "Portrait of Daniel Henry Kahnweiler" (1910). Oil on canvas.

vard University Archives). No doubt these ideas were familiar to Gertrude Stein since her earliest days of study with James. Analytic Cubist works by Picasso and Braque deal with the gradual becoming of objects and figures from a "Confusion" that is never quite resolved.

Abolishing Perspective

Cubism is best known for denying perspective. William James despised perspective as a deformation. In his "Stream of Thought" chapter in *Principles*, James calls on our ability to select from the flux of accidental views in perspective, the true view of a table or glass:

> My table-top is named square, after but one view of an infinite number. All the other views show two acute and two obtuse angles; but I call the latter perspective views, and the four right angles the true form of the table, and I erect the attribute squareness into the table's essence, for aesthetic reasons of my own. In like manner, the real circular form (of the opening of a glass) when seen perpendicularly from above is the true form, all others [e.g., ovals in perspective] are only signs [of the true form]. (1890, Vol. 1, p. 285)

James had many examples: a table set with dinner plates that *look* oval *are* to us circular, as if seen from above. A ring waved through the air "will pass through every conceivable angular and elliptical form. All the while, however, we hold fast to the real shape" (James, 1890, Vol. 2, p. 259). The glass or ring in the mind is truer to the real form than the seen glass or ring.

Amazingly, the following statement by Maurice Princet closely reflects the Jamesian praise of the true form projected onto the picture plane, while perspective distorts.

> You represent, by means of a trapezoid, a table, just as you see it, *distorted* [italics added] by perspective; but what would happen if you decided to express the universal table (la table type)? You would have to straighten it up into the picture plane, and from the trapezoid, return to the *true rectangle* [italics added]. If that table is covered with objects equally *distorted* [italics added] by perspective, the same straightening up

idea the other way around, from English to French, in a brief word portrait honoring the poet and art critic Apollinaire who had published his *Cubist Painters* that year (1913/1949). Here only the title "Give known or pin ware" becomes "Guillaume Apollinaire" (see also Dydo, 1993, pp. 278–279). Closely related to preperceptions is James' famous description of the infant's vision as a "big blooming buzzing Confusion. That Confusion is the baby's universe; and the universe of all of us is still to a great extent such a Confusion, potentially resolvable" (James, 1892/1984, p. 21). Unpublished Harvard student notes of the 1890s after James's Philosophy I lectures show that he always included the "big blooming buzzing Confusion" and preperceptions (Har-

process would have to take place with each of them. Thus, the oval of a glass would become a perfect circle. But this is not all: this glass and this table, seen from another angle are nothing more than . . . a horizontal bar a few centimeters thick, the glass a profile whose base and rim are horizontal. (Golding, 1968, p. 102)

Picasso knew Princet well, as did Gertrude Stein; she may have asked him to introduce Picasso to James's ideas of the true form appearing in the flux of things in but *one* position (all others being in perspective). According to Picasso, Princet was an actuary who did *not* teach him mathematics or geometry. In May or June of 1907, Picasso wrote Princet's name three times on the back cover of a sketch book, like an incantation (MP 1860, Musée Picasso). Among the sketches are two of a bowl seen from above and in profile (Figure 10), as Princet had advised.

Figure 10 Pablo Picasso, "Bowl seen from Above and in Profile" (1907). Black ink.

The poet and art critic Guillame Apollinaire (1880–1918) also goes back to James. In his *Cubist Painters* (1913/1949), Apollinaire, Picasso's close friend, decried perspective; he stressed essential conceptual form and science. In *Principles* and *Briefer Course*, James had defended a scientific psychology. As Apollinaire put it:

Scientific Cubism is one of the pure tendencies. It is the art of painting new structures out of ele-

ments borrowed not from the reality of sight (réalité de vision) but from the reality of insight (réalité de connaissance). All human beings have a sense of this interior reality. One does not have to be educated to conceive, for example, of a round form. The geometrical aspect that made such an impression on those who saw the first canvases of the scientific Cubists, came from the fact that essential reality was rendered with great purity, while visual accident and anecdotes had been eliminated. (1913/1949, p. 17)

Gertrude Stein (1933, p. 72) wrote that Apollinaire was brilliant; that, whatever the topic, he immediately saw the meaning, whether he knew anything about it or not. In line with James, Apollinaire (1913/1970) derided perspective: "That miserable, tricky perspective . . . that infallible device of making all things shrink" (p. 45). One of Picasso's witty remarks refers to the true extent of form: "In an (illusionistic) painting by Raphael, it is not possible to determine the distance from the tip of the nose to the mouth. I want to paint pictures where this is possible" (cited in Kahnweiler, 1920/1949, p. 8).

Cubism, a Psychology of Form

There are few early interviews with Picasso. But one from the Cubist period, conducted in Spanish by Marius de Zayas, is most revealing. Zayas interviewed Picasso in Paris, in advance of the painter's first U.S. exhibition in 1911 at the Stieglitz "Gallery 291" (Fifth Avenue), New York City. In the rather confusing English version (see *Camera Work*, 1911, pp. 65–67), Zayas elicits references to many of the Jamesian ideas we have discussed. Picasso speaks of his "present sensations," twice calls his new art a "psychology of form," and says that he represents the essence of form.

We have considered several important links between Picasso's Cubism and the space perception theories of William James, as mediated by Gertrude Stein. Jamesian ideas circulated in the group around Picasso, including Braque, Apollinaire, and Juan Gris (1887–1927). Fernand Leger (1881–1955) also benefited from Picasso's Jamesian Cubism (Teuber, 1982). Yet, Cubists on the periphery interpreted the new art from what they saw and heard. For instance, they referred to Henri Bergson, who in *L'Évolution Créatrice* (1907) had borrowed several ideas from his friend William James.

Not all Jamesian ideas of form and space relevant to the beginnings of Cubism have been discussed here. Nor does space permit further comment about the interactions between Picasso and Braque. Yet it should be evident that Jamesian space perception experiments and theories contributed to the original formative feature of Cubism: Protruding relief, arbitrary light and shade, preperceptions and the "big, blooming buzzing Confusion," the rejection of perspective, and the selection of the true extent of form in contrast to illusionism—these Jamesian ideas are as important for Cubism as the invention of perspective and Neoplatonic thought had been for Renaissance painting in Italy. Via Gertrude Stein and William James, the United States apparently participated in the origins of Cubism in France.

Acknowledgment

This article is a condensed, partial version of a longer chapter on Cubist painting in France (1907–1914) which will appear in a forthcoming book by the author.

Bibliography

Apollinaire, G. (1949). *The Cubist painters.* (L. Abel, Trans.). New York: Wittenborn. (Original work published 1913)

Dydo, U. (1993). *A Stein reader.* Evanston, IL: Northwestern University Press.

Fry, E. (1966). *Cubism.* New York, Toronto: McGraw-Hill.

Golding, J. (1968). *Cubism 1907–1916.* Boston: Boston Book & Art Shop.

Hoffman, M. J. (1966). Gertrude Stein and William James. *The Personalist, 47*(2), 226–233.

James, W. (1890). *The principles of psychology* (Vols. 1 & 2). New York: Henry Holt & Co.

James, W. (1984). *Psychology: Briefer Course.* Cambridge, MA: Harvard University Press. (Original work published 1892)

Kahnweiler, D. H. (1949). *The rise of Cubism* (H. Aronson, Trans.). New York: Wittenborn. (Original work published 1920, *Der Weg zum Kubismus,* Munich: Delphin)

Lewes, G. H. (1879). *Problems of life and mind.* London: Trübner.

Mach, E. (1959). *The analysis of sensations.* (C. M. Williams, Trans.). New York: Dover. (Original work published 1886)

Rubin, W. (1984). Picasso. In W. Rubin (Ed.), *Primitivism in 20th century art* (pp. 240–343). New York: The Museum of Modern Art.

Rudenstein, A. (1976). Georges Braque. In *The Guggenheim Museum Collection: Paintings 1880–1945* (Vol. 1, pp. 42–45). New York: The Solomon R. Guggenheim Museum.

Skinner, B. F. (1934). Has Gertrude Stein a secret? *Atlantic Monthly, 153,* 50–57.

Solomons, L., & Stein, G. (1896). Normal motor automatism. *Psychological Review, 3,* 492–512.

Stein, G. (1898). Cultivated motor automatism: A study of character in its relation to attention. *Psychological Review, 5,* 295–306.

Stein, G. (1912, August). Picasso. *Camera Work.* A. Stieglitz (Ed.), 29–30.

Stein, G. (1933). *The Autobiography of Alice B. Toklas.* New York: Harcourt, Brace.

Stein, G. (1971). *Fernhurst, Q.E.D., and other early writings.* New York: Liveright.

Teuber, M. L. (1982). Conceptualization of form and Cubism or Pablo Picasso and William James. In S. Gohr (Ed.), *Cubism* (pp. 9–57). Cologne: Josef-Haubrich-Kunsthalle.

Zayas, M. de. (1911, April). Pablo Picasso. *Camera Work.* A. Stieglitz (Ed.), 65–67.

The Psychologist Robert Musil

Annette Daigger

The novelist and essayist Robert Musil (1880–1942) was born on November 6 in Klagenfurt, the capital of the Province of Carinthia of the Austro-Hungarian Empire. His most important contribution to world literature is the psychological novel, *The Man Without Qualities* (1930–1943), which overshadows his other writings. In 1906, the 26-year-old Musil suddenly became famous with the publication of his highly praised novel, *Young Törleß*. This autobiographical novel chronicled the confusing story of an adolescent cadet at an Austrian military school who discovered that: "Things are things and will always remain so and I shall always look at them like that, sometimes with the eyes of the mind, sometimes with the others" (Musil, 1906, p. 138).

For Musil, everything in life depended on one's particular viewpoint. There is not just one truth, there are many truths; and reality is composed of a thousand possibilities. People must critically examine reality and change it through their dynamic ethics.

Musil's attitude towards life cannot be fully appreciated without a basic knowledge of his early career. Musil, whose noble ancestors included many military officers and high-ranking civil servants, initially wanted to become an officer himself. Consequently, he spent his formative years as a military cadet at the junior service academies in Eisenstadt and Mährisch-Weißkirchen. However, later he dropped out of the prestigious Technical Military Academy in Vienna after only three months to study mechanical engineering at Brünn Polytechnical Institute. Musil spent the years 1898–1901 at Brünn, and after receiving his degree in 1901, he accepted a position as an unpaid "voluntary assistant" at the Stuttgart Polytechnical Institut in Germany. During

Figure 1 Lieutenant Robert Musil (1903).

his first stay in Germany, Musil began writing his novel *Törleß*.

In 1903, Musil changed his vocational goals once more by enrolling at Berlin University as a full-time student. He majored in philosophy and psychology

Figure 2 Musil's "color mixer" (1906/1907).

and chose physics and mathematics as his minor subjects. His teachers in Berlin included the philosophers Wilhelm Dilthey (1833–1911), Ernst Simmel (1858–1918), and Ernst Cassirer (1874–1945). The philosopher and experimental psychologist Carl Stumpf (1848–1936) became Musil's chief professor and supervisor of his dissertation, which was titled *Contributions to an Evaluation of [Ernst] Mach's Theories* (1908). During his early Berlin years, Musil and his fellow student Johannes von Allesch (1882–1967) (a future psychology professor at the universities of Greifswald, Halle, and Göttingen) invented the "Musil color mixer." This instrument for the study of color perception was built and distributed by the Göttingen Company of Spindler and Hoyer. The design of psychological research equipment allowed Musil to utilize fully his technical expertise and his training in psychology. In Berlin Musil was closely associated with the local Gestalt psychologists, including Kurt Koffka (1886–1941), Erich von Hornbostel (1837–1935), Wolfgang Köhler (1887–1967), and Max Wertheimer (1880–1943). However, when Alexius Meinong (1853–1920), the Austrian philosopher and Gestalt psychologist, offered him an assistantship at Graz University, Musil decided to become a professional writer instead.

Musil, who recorded his original approach to life in his first novel, pursued and expanded his ideas in his later literary works. Again and again, he tried to reconcile mind and soul, reason and unreason. His university background in the natural sciences appears to have encouraged his abstract-theoretical approach to literature. Although Musil was quite critical of psychoanalysis, his 1911 short stories "The Perfection of a Love" and "The Temptation of Quiet Veronica" follow an analytic theme.

During World War I, Musil served initially with an infantry reserve unit at the Italian border. Beginning in 1916, he took on the editorship of a newspaper for enlisted men in the same region. After the war, he was responsible for the democratic re-education of Austrian officers, including the application of psychological tests and methods of personnel selection.

World War I and its aftermath disturbed Musil deeply and strengthened his conviction that mankind could only be saved by radically changing its thinking about the world. He believed that writers had to become the pointmen of a new world. Thus, the character of Ulrich in Musil's three-volume novel, *The Man Without Qualities*, shows how a just life can and should be lived. The protagonist and his sister Agatha are not restricted by the rigid code imposed by traditional values, but rather

Figure 3 Musil (ca. 1926).

266

pursue a situation ethics of possibilities. The background of Musil's famous, yet incomplete novel, is provided by the final years of the declining Austro-Hungarian Empire, which Musil called "Kakania," after the German initials of its official title, the "Imperial and Royal" monarchy. Musil hoped that his novel, which presents a rich spectrum of human life, would eventually make a "contribution to the mental conquest of the world" (Musil, 1930–1943, p. 942).

Bibliography

Berghahn, W. (1973). *Robert Musil.* Reinbeck: Rowohlt.

Luft, D. S. (1980). *Robert Musil and the crisis of European culture.* Berkeley: University of California Press.

Musil, R. (1906). *Die Verwirrungen des Zöglings Törleß.* Vienna/Leipzig: Wiener Verlag.

Musil, R. (1911). *Vereinigungen.* Munich: G. Müller.

Musil, R. (1921). *Die Schwärmer.* Dresden: Sibyllen-Verlag.

Musil, R. (1923). *Grigia.* Potsdam: Müller.

Musil, R. (1923). *Die Portugiesin.* Berlin: Rowohlt.

Musil, R. (1924). *Vinzenz und die Freundin bedeutender Männer.* Berlin: Rowohlt.

Musil, R. (1924). *Drei Frauen.* Berlin: Rowohlt.

Musil, R. (1927). *Rede zur Rilke-Feier.* Berlin: Rowohlt.

Musil, R. (1930–1943). *Der Mann ohne Eigenschaften* (Vols. 1–3). Berlin: Rowohlt.

Musil, R. (1936). *Nachlaß zu Lebzeiten.* Prosastücke. Zürich: Humanitas.

Musil, R. (1937). *Über die Dummheit,* Rede. Vienna: Bermann-Fischer.

Musil, R. (1953, 1954, 1960). *The man without qualities.* New York: Putnam.

Musil, R. (1964). *Young Törleß.* New York: Putnam.

The Berlin School of Gestalt Psychology

Lothar Sprung
Helga Sprung

The roots of Gestalt psychology can be traced to Frankfurt University and Berlin University around the beginning of the 20th century (Ash, 1982; Ash & Woodward, 1987; Zimmer, 1987; Sprung, 1991). Of course, Gestalt psychology can also be traced to other and considerably earlier traditions. For example, within the context of philosophical psychology, holistic thinking has been described systematically in the ancient Chinese theory of the "yin and yang." Attributed to Chinese emperors around 3000 B.C., this doctrine was first recorded by Confucius (552–479 B.C.) in his *I Ching* or *Book of Changes*. Holistic thinking can also be found in the works of Aristotle (384–322 B.C.), who first formulated one of the best-known tenets of Gestalt psychology: "The whole is more than the sum of its parts." Aristotle also pointed out that "the whole is earlier than its parts." Another example of holism from the Age of Enlightenment can be found in the "monodology" of Gottfried Wilhelm Leibniz (1646–1716).

More recent influences on Gestalt psychology's origins can be found primarily in the anti-elementarism of 19th-century "act psychology" and the "holistic psychology" of the early 20th century. Key personalities associated with these movements include Franz Brentano (1838–1917), Alexius Meinong (1853–1920), Christian von Ehrenfels (1859–1932), and Ernst Mach (1838–1916) of the universities of Vienna, Graz, Würzburg, and Prague, respectively (Lück, 1991). These scholars generally opposed the elementarism which dominated late 19th-century experimental psychology and found expression in the psychophysical models of Ernst Heinrich Weber (1795–1878) and Gustav Theodor Fechner (1801–1887), and in the psychology of Wilhelm Wundt (1832–1920). This elementarist view of psychology rested on the assumption that mental phenomena, like chemical substances, are com-

Figure 1 Imperial Palace in Berlin where the Psychological Institute of Berlin University and its Gestalt laboratories were located (after 1922).

268

Figure 2 Max Wertheimer.

Figure 3 Kurt Koffka.

Figure 4 Wolfgang Köhler.

Figure 5 Erich Moritz von Hornbostel.

Figure 6 Karl Duncker.

posed of different elementary units (e.g., sensations, ideas, etc.) which can identified by the research method of introspection. In turn, psychic elements, again like chemical substances, could be combined according to the principles of "associationism," which can also be traced to Aristotle's writings.

In sharp contrast, the theoreticians of holism and Gestalt psychology stressed the importance of a "phenomenological analysis" of mental phenomena as the initial stage of scientific research in psychology. In addition, they preferred "biotic" experiments under life-like conditions over the "artificial" laboratory studies of Wundt and his disciples. For Gestalt psychologists and their immediate forerunners, a scientific investigation begins with the phenomenon itself rather than the stimulus conditions of traditional experimental psychology. The study of psychic phenomena is thus seen as the exclusive road toward the discovery of psychic structures and processes (e.g., Brentano's "acts" and Stumpf's "functions").

Holistic and Gestaltist ideas were introduced to Berlin University mainly by Carl Stumpf (1848–1936), who was a student of Brentano and Rudolph Hermann Lotze (1817–1881). Stumpf's students and collaborators at Berlin—people like Wolfgang Köhler (1887–1967), Kurt Koffka (1886–1941), Kurt Lewin (1890–1947), and Max Wertheimer (1880–1943)—developed this scientific brand of psychology, which is now known in the history of the field as the "Berlin School of Gestalt Psychology" or the "Berlin-Frankfurt School of Gestalt Psychology."

The integration of the psychological theories and methods of Brentano, Lotze, and Stumpf with those of Wertheimer yielded the following four principles of Gestalt theory and research:

1. *Holistic thinking:* "The whole is always more than the sum of its parts." This was its central tenet—the concept of "supersummativity."

2. *Phenomenological basis:* "Phenomena" form the basis of all empirical analyses. Psychological analysis must proceed from phenomena to their essence, because while the essence is reflected in the phenomena, it is not identical to them.

3. *Experimental methodology:* "Biotic" or life-like experiments and mathematics are the key for an empirical analysis of psychic phenomena.

4. *Psychophysical isomorphism:* All psychic events can clearly and directly be related to physical processes. Therefore, all psychological research must ultimately seek the organic foundation of psychic processes.

A typical example of Gestalt theorizing and research can be found in a 1912 study by Wertheimer. He had discovered experimentally that certain continuous and discontinuous stimulation of the optical sense yield a similar continuous perception of movement. He concluded that the perception of pseudo-movement was configurational and not elementaristic or stimulus-bound. Wertheimer's informal mini-experiment led to his later systematic

study of the "stroboscopic effect" or "phi phenomenon" (Wertheimer, 1912; Brett King, & Wertheimer, 1995). Similar model experiments were later carried out in comparative psychology (Köhler, 1917), the experimental psychology of thinking (Duncker, 1935; Wertheimer, 1982), and the psychology of memory (Köhler & von Restorff, 1933, 1937).

By the end of the 1920s and the beginning of the 1930s, the theory and methodology of Berlin Gestalt psychology had expanded into several diverse research specialties. From its beginnings in the fields of perception and the psychology of thinking, for example, important contributions soon came from people like Kurt Lewin (1890–1947) in developmental and social psychology. Lewin's "field theory" also included the psychology of action and effect (Schönpflug, 1992). The ethnological and comparative musicological studies of Erich Moritz von Hornbostel (1877–1935) and the problem-solving studies of Karl Duncker (1903–1940) serve as additional examples.

The work of Kurt Gottschaldt (1902–1991) extended Gestalt psychological thought in Berlin to developmental psychology and the psychology of personality after the majority of Berlin psychologists had emigrated to the United States. Gottschaldt was a student of Köhler and Wertheimer, and he was also strongly influenced by Lewin's field theory and the "layer theories" of personality by Erich Rothacker (1888–1965). He taught at Berlin from 1935 to 1962 (Gottschaldt, 1960) and exerted a formative influence on generations of psychologists who completed their studies at Humboldt University in East Berlin during the late 1940s and 1950s (Sprung & Schönpflug, 1992).

Looking back from the present, it is clear that the Berlin School of Gestalt Psychology represented an important transitional stage between the classical experimental psychology of Wundt, Fechner, and Ebbinghaus, and modern experimental psychology. Specifically, the Berlin School provided a balance against the elementarism and associationism of classical experimentalism. Today, the essential ideas of Gestalt psychology are an intrinsic part of contemporary experimental psychology. The holistic perspective of the field is also reflected in modern systems theory and ecological psychology. The objections raised by Gestalt psychologists to the oversimplified and mechanistic stimulus-response models of behavior have now become fully incorporated into modern information theory and cognitive

Figure 7 Gestalt experiment in the lecture hall of the Berlin Psychological Institute (ca. 1930).

psychology. Furthermore, concepts such as isomorphism, which have an important heuristic function, are directly relevant to the current search for the organic basis of psychic events.

A serious shortcoming of the Berlin School was the monopolistic perspective of its leaders, who were convinced that their theories and methods were applicable to all psychological problems. Moreover, German Gestalt psychologists wasted a great deal of time combating or ignoring plausible alternative theoretical positions (Stumpf, 1939; Sprung, Sprung, & Kernchen, 1984). Given these latter characteristics, it is clear that the Berlin School of Gestalt Psychology was a rather typical representative of the "Age of Schools and Systems" within the history of psychology, which influenced the discipline between 1890 and 1940 (Sprung, Sprung, & Müller, 1991).

The Berlin School of Gestalt Psychology ceased to exist after its leading experts were forced into exile during the initial years of the Nazi dictatorship. Some of the ideas of Gestalt psychology, however, survived by being integrated with other psychological theories. In this context, Kurt Gottschaldt (1902–1991) who taught at Berlin University from 1935–1962, needs to be mentioned. His departure for Göttingen University in the Federal Republic of Germany marks the final end of the Berlin tradition of Gestalt thought and research.

Bibliography

Ash, M. G. (1982). The emergence of Gestalt theory: Experimental psychology in Germany 1890–1920. *Dissertation Abstracts International 43.*

Ash, M. G. (1995). Gestalt psychology in German culture, 1890–1967. Holism and the quest for objectivity. (Cambridge Studies History of Psychology). Cambridge, England: Cambridge University Press.

Ash, M. G., & Woodward, W. R. (Eds.). (1987). *Psychology in twentieth-century thought and society.* Cambridge: Cambridge University Press.

Brett King, D., & Wertheimer, M. (1995). Max Wertheimer at the University of Berlin. In S. Jaeger, I. Staeuble, L. Sprung, & H.-P. Brauns, (Eds.), *Psychologie im sozial-kulturellen Wandel—Kontinuitäten und Diskontinuitäten* (pp. 276–280). Frankfurt/Main: Lang.

Duncker, K. (1935). *Zur Psychologie des produktiven Denkens.* Berlin: Springer.

Gottschaldt, K. (1960). Das Problem der Phänogenetik in der Persönlichkeit. In P. Lersch & H. Thomae (Eds.), *Persönlichkeitsforschung und Persönlichkeitstheorie* (pp. 222–280). Göttingen: Hogrefe.

Jaeger, S. (Ed.). (1988). *Briefe von Wolfgang Köhler an Hans Geitel 1907–1920.* Passau: Passavia.

Köhler, W. (1917). Intelligenzprüfungen an Anthropoiden. In *Abhandlungen der Königl. Preuss. Akademie der Wissenschaften. Physikalisch Mathematische Klasse 1.* Berlin: Reimer.

Köhler, W., & von Restorff, H. (1933, 1937). Analyse von Vorgängen im Spurenfeld I. Über die Wirkung von Bereichsbildung im Spurenfeld II. Zur Theorie der Reproduktion. In *Psychologische Forschung, 18 & 21.*

Lück, H. E. (1991). *Geschichte der Psychologie. Strömungen, Schulen, Entwicklungen.* Stuttgart: Kohlhammer.

Schönpflug, W. (Ed.). (1992). *Kurt Lewin-Person, Werk, Umfeld.* Frankfurt/Main: Lang.

Sprung, L. (1991). The Berlin psychological tradition: Between experiment and quasi-experimental design, 1850–1990. In W. R. Woodward & R. S. Cohen (Eds.), *World views and scientific discipline formation* (pp. 107–116). Dordrecht: Kluwer.

Sprung, L., & Schönpflug, W. (Eds.). (1992). *Zur Geschichte der Psychologie in Berlin.* Frankfurt/Main: Lang.

Sprung, L., Sprung, H., & Kernchen, S. (1984). Carl Stumpf and the origin and development of psychology as a new science at the university of Berlin. In H. Carpintero & J. M. Peiro (Eds.), *Psychology in its historical context. Monografias de la Revista de Historia de la Psicologia* (pp. 349–355). Valencia: University Press.

Sprung, L., Sprung, H., & Müller, M. (1991). Psychologische Methodentheorie und Psychologiegeschichte. In H. E. Lück & R. Miller (Eds.), *Theorien und Methoden psychologiegeschichtlicher Forschung* (pp. 43–53). Göttingen: Hogrefe.

Stumpf, C. (1907). Erscheinungen und psychische Funktionen. In *Abhandlungen der Königl. Preuss Academie der Wissenschaften vom Jahre, 1906.* Berlin: Reimer.

Stumpf, C. (1939). *Erkenntnislehre. Vol. I.* Leipzig: Barth.

Wertheimer, M. (1912). Experimentelle Studien über das Sehen von Bewegung. *Zeitschrift für Psychologie, 61,* 161–265.

Wertheimer, M. (1982). *Productive thinking* (Enlarged edition). (M. Wertheimer, Ed.). Chicago: University of Chicago Press.

Zimmer, A. (Ed.). (1987). Wolfgang Köhler Sonderheft zu seinem 100. Geburtstag. *Gestalt Theory, 9,* 3–4.

Gestalt Psychology at Frankfurt University

Viktor Sarris

The origin and development of Gestalt psychology at Frankfurt University in Germany is closely associated with the name of Max Wertheimer (1880–1943). Wertheimer worked in Frankfurt from 1910 to 1914 and from 1929 to 1933, respectively (Ash, 1989, 1995; Sarris & Wertheimer, 1987; Wertheimer, 1980).

Frankfurt Years I: 1910–1914

Wertheimer's experimental studies of the so-called phi phenomenon go all the way back to the year 1910 (Sarris, 1987a, 1987b). According to an anecdote, which Wertheimer later liked to share with his students, the basic idea for his experiments occurred to him almost playfully while riding in a train. Consequently, he interrupted his trip in Frankfurt to study the "movie effect" in his hotel room by means of a play tachistoscope (Luchins & Luchins, 1972; quoted after Sarris, 1987a):

> I noticed certain movements of the toy. . . . One turns the inner disk and sees moving film through the openings on the outer disk. . . . I made a few of them and then called the laboratory in Frankfurt. . . . They sent me Dr. Köhler, who was still a lecturer [assistant] at that time. . . . Later we also gained the support of Koffka. (p. 298f)

At the well-equipped laboratory of Frankfurt University, Wertheimer employed Schumann's wheel tachistoscope to study the typical, individual variations of the phi phenomenon. His 1912 research "Habilitation" on the same topic contains the first multifactorial analysis of the configuration of perceived movements. In addition, this work helped Wertheimer qualify as an untenured university instructor (Ash, 1995; Sarris, 1995).

Figure 1 Drawing of the administration building of Frankfurt University, which contained the laboratory of the Psychological Institute (ca. 1913).

Wertheimer investigated the phi phenomenon with subjects of normal vision, like his friends Wolfgang Köhler (1887–1967) and Kurt Koffka (1886–1941), and with neurological patients suffering from impairments of the occipital lobes in the cortex (Wertheimer, 1912):

> I also mention that recently a *pathological case* suffering (with an impairment of occipital lobes) speaks for a central location of the perception of movement. Specifically, Dr. Pötzl [the author] reports: '. . . *if one directs a strong light source slowly and quickly [towards the female patient], she does not appear to perceive a [continuous] movement of the object but only several (isolated) lights.*' In May of 1911, I contacted Dr. P., the author, and had the opportunity to test the patient using real [as well as apparent] motion. (p. 246f)

In passing, it should be mentioned that Max Wertheimer formulated the Gestalt laws (which he

Figure 2 Max Wertheimer with Schumann´s wheel tachistoscope (ca. 1913).

Figure 3 Max Wertheimer portrait in Frankfurt (ca. 1930).

Table I *Extensions of Wertheimer's 1912 Phi Phenomenon Research (Adapted from Sarris, 1989)*

Subject	Time	Place	Related Works[a]
Experiments on apparent motion ("phi") Gestalt principles	1910–1914	Frankfurt	K. Koffka, 1915, 1922; A. Gelb, 1914 ff; Korte, 1915; W. Köhler, 1920
Neurophysiological & clinical psychological studies	1911–1913 1920	Vienna, Frankfurt Bad Nauheim (Berlin)	O. Plötzl & E. Redlich, 1911; M. Wertheimer, 1912a, 1913, 1920; A. Gelb & K. Goldstein, 1918; W. Fuchs, 1920
Sound-detection device & acoustic "phi"; opticohaptical apparatus for the blind (TV principle)	1915	Berlin	E. M. von Hornbostel & M. Wertheimer, 1920; M. Wertheimer, 1916/1920
Wertheimer-Koffka ring: brightness contrast & Gestalt effects, with later quantification	1912–1916	Frankfurt	K. Koffka, 1915; M. Wertheimer & W. Benary, 1924

[a] References in Sarris, 1987a, 1987b, 1988.

did not publish until later) during his first Frankfurt period (Wertheimer, 1923). During this period, he and several friends and colleagues were able to expand the experimental foundation of Gestalt psychology (Table 1) significantly. Wertheimer also covered the following pertinent topics as an instructor at Frankfurt University between 1910 and 1912: "Seminar on the Psychology of Mental Abilities," "Selected Chapters of Psychology for Medical Students," and "The Psychological Analysis of Patients with Brain Injuries."

Frankfurt II: 1929–1933

During his second Frankfurt period, Wertheimer, who now held an appointment as full professor of psychology and philosophy and was department chair, continued his experimental research with his assistants E. Levy and W. Metzger, and his doctoral students J. Becker, E. Goldmeier, H. Koppermann, W. Krolik, E. Oppenheimer, G. Siemsen, and M. Turhan. In contrast to most contemporary psychologists who

investigated the motion phenomena with only qualitative methods, Wertheimer's research included both qualitative and quantitative analyses. Moreover, experimental researches on Wertheimer's phi phenomenon attracted considerable research interest during those years. Wertheimer, who had loved music since his childhood, often enlivened his courses by providing illustrations of Gestalt phenomena with examples from music psychology. His Frankfurt lectures during the second period again included a number of topics from Gestalt psychology, including "Perception and Cognition," "Productive Thinking," and "Gestalt Theory in Philosophy and Psychology."

Farewell to Frankfurt

Wertheimer's second stay at Frankfurt University ended suddenly when early in 1933 Hitler and his National Socialist Party assumed political power in Germany. Wertheimer's eldest son, Valentin, described his father's situation as follows (Sarris & Michael Wertheimer, 1987):

Figure 4 Wertheimer with his violin, perhaps demonstrating Gestalt principles in a Frankfurt lecture hall.

Figure 5 Caricature of Wertheimer playing the piano before his students at the "New School" in New York (ca. 1937).

We had gone to Czechoslovakia in March 1933, the day before the March elections [in Germany]. My father and my mother had heard Hitler's radio speech two evenings before the elections, and he decided to leave the next day because, as he told us, he didn't want his children to be in a country where a man like Hitler could run for the highest post of the land expecting to succeed. By June 1933, he felt that Hitler was not a passing phenomenon, and searched for a place to go. He had invitations to London, Jerusalem, and to New York, and chose the latter. (p. 485)

Although he worked at Frankfurt/Main less than eight years altogether, Max Wertheimer was clearly

the most talented and successful representative of psychology at this university. Among his many other accomplishments during those years were his famous lectures there on "Truth," a brief summary of which was later published in New York (Wertheimer, 1934):

> Science is rooted in the will to truth. With the will to truth it stands or falls. Lower the standard even slightly and science becomes diseased at the core. Not only science, but man. The will to truth, pure and unadulterated, is among the essential conditions of his existence; if the standard is compromised he easily becomes a kind of tragic caricature of himself. (Wertheimer, 1934, p. 135)

Bibliography

Ash, M. G. (1989). Max Wertheimer's university career in Germany. *Psychological Research, 51,* 52–57.

Ash, M. G. (1995). *Gestalt psychology in German culture 1890–1967: Holism and the quest for objectivity.* Cambridge, MA: Cambridge University Press.

Luchins, A., & Luchins, E. (1972). *Wertheimer's seminars revisited: Perception* (Vol. I). Albany, NY: State University of New York.

Sarris, V. (1987a; 1988). Max Wertheimer in Frankfurt—über Beginn und Aufbaukrise der Gestaltpsychologie (I–III). *Zeitschrift für Psychologie, 195,* pp. 283–310, 403–431; *196,* 27–61.

Sarris, V. (1989). Max Wertheimer on seen motion: Theory and evidence. *Psychological Research, 51,* 58–68.

Sarris, V. (1995). *Max Wertheimer in Frankfurt: Beginn und Aufbaukrise der Gestaltpsychologie.* Lengerich: Pabst Science Publishers.

Sarris, V. (1995, in press). Relexionen über den Gestaltpsychologen Max Wertheimer und sein Werk: Vergessenes und wieder Erinnertes. In O. Hassler & J. Wertheimer (Eds.), *Exodus aus Nazideutschland und die Folgen.* Attempo-Verlag.

Sarris, V., & Wertheimer, M. (1987). Max Wertheimer (1880–1943) im Bilddokument—ein historiographischer Beitrag. *Psychologische Beiträge, 29,* 469–493.

Wertheimer, M. (1912). Experimentelle Studien über das Sehen von Bewegung. *Zeitschrift für Psychologie, 61,* 161–265.

Wertheimer, M. (1934). On truth. *Social Research, 1,* 135–146.

Wertheimer, M. (1923). Untersuchungen zur Lehre von der Gestalt. *Psychologische Forschung, 4,* 301–350.

Wertheimer, M. (1980). Max Wertheimer: Gestalt prophet. *Gestalt Theory, 2,* 3–17.

Wolfgang Köhler

Siegfried Jaeger

Wolfgang Köhler was a scholar who may be rightfully claimed by several disciplines. Not only was he an eminent psychologist, his varied interests led him to make important contributions to physics, biology, philosophy, and art, as well. Köhler also deserves recognition as a member of a very small group of German scientists who publicly expressed their opposition to the persecution carried out by the National Socialist Party. He always believed that scientific research itself was so important that the individuals involved had to rise above any personal differences. Accordingly, Köhler was able to work harmoniously with colleagues and students who had different research interests and values, and who came from many different countries. He also shared his strong interest in music with them.

Wolfgang Felix Ulrich Köhler (1887–1967) was born to a German high school teacher and his wife on January 21, 1887, in Reval (today: Tallinn), Estonia, at that time a part of the Russian Empire. In 1905, he began his study of philosophy and the natural sciences upon the advice of one of his high school teachers. After two semesters at Bonn and Tübingen, respectively, he studied for five semesters at Berlin University, where he received his PhD in 1909 under his mentor, Carl Stumpf (1848–1936), for a dissertation in the field of music psychology. Working as a junior academic at Frankfurt University from 1910 to 1913, Köhler developed his revolutionary Gestalt perspective, together with his somewhat older colleagues Max Wertheimer (1880–1943) and Kurt Koffka (1886–1941). He expanded his ideas in his chief theoretical work, *Physical Configuration in Rest and Stationary Condition* (1920), in which he sought to unite philosophy and the natural sciences through Gestalt theory.

As director of the Anthropoid Research Center of the Prussian Academy of Sciences on the Spanish island of Tenerife from 1914 to 1920, Köhler demonstrated through his work with chimpanzees and orangutans (Jaeger, 1988; Köhler, 1993) that our views concerning the cognition of primates were severely limited and in need of revision. He also identified the limits of associationism for the expla-

Figure 1 Portrait of Köhler (1920).

Figure 2 Two chimps in an experimental cage at La Costa, on Tenerife (ca. 1913).

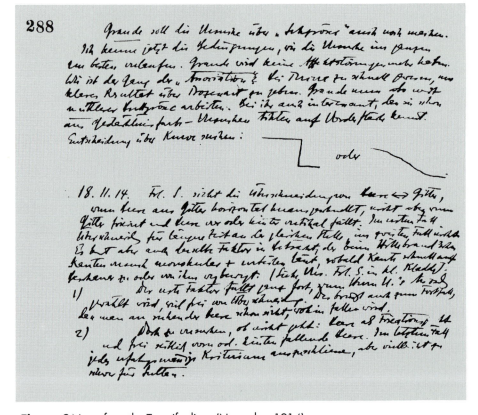

Figure 3 Notes from the Tenerife diary (November 1914).

Figure 4 Köhler in his office in the Royal Palace in Berlin.

nation of human behavior. His 1921 book, *The Mentality of Apes,* which was translated into several languages (first English edition was in 1925), made him famous.

During his tenure as chairman of the Psychological Institute of Berlin University (1922–1935), Köhler contributed greatly to the international fame of the Berlin School of Gestalt Psychology. Together with Wertheimer and Kurt Lewin (1890–1947), he concentrated on problems of cognition, learning, and motivation. His new Gestalt psychology was a branch of modern psychology, which took an intermediate position towards the old nativism-empiricism question (Köhler, 1929, 1940, 1969; Henle, 1971). Beginning with a nonmechanistic perspective from the natural sciences (i.e., field theory), Köhler tried to establish a direct connection with philosophy through modern psychology. Specifically, he argued that psychology must leave its epistemological ghetto and actively engage itself with the basic questions of modern natural science and the practical problems of human life (Köhler, 1938). Köhler's interdisciplinary outlook made him a popular topic of discussion among philosophers and natural scientists, as well as social scientists in Europe, the Soviet Union, the United States, and even South America. Consequently, he held visiting appointments at Clark University (1925–1926) and Harvard

University (1934–1935). He also gave lectures at Yale (1929) and in France, Spain, Uruguay (1930), Brazil, and Argentina (1932).

Although he was not directly affected by the racial legislation of Nazi Germany, Köhler was the only German scholar who, in his lectures and in a much-read newspaper column, had the courage to protest against the politically and racially motivated discharge of academic scholars. An article he wrote on April 28, 1933, about the resignation of the eminent German physicist and Nobel Prize winner James Franck (1888–1964), received international attention and evoked support from colleagues and the public at large (Henle, 1978; Jaeger, 1993). Köhler similarly opposed the efforts of the Nazi government to subject all universities and scientific organizations to party control. When his assistants were discharged in 1935, Köhler followed his friends to exile in the United States.

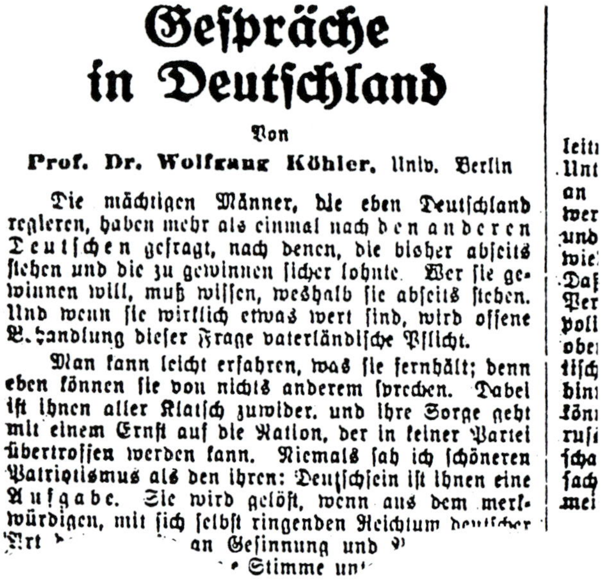

Figure 6 Main building at Swarthmore College.

Figure 5 Newspaper column by Köhler opposing Nazi racial discrimination.

At Swarthmore College, a small American undergraduate institution near Philadelphia where he taught from 1935 to 1958, Köhler had reasonably good research facilities. Nevertheless, the continuation and expansion of Gestalt psychology as a theory or "school" of psychology became impossible because of the absence of a graduate program at

Swarthmore and the dispersion of other leaders in the movement.

Gestalt psychology nevertheless influenced American psychologists as an important alternative to behaviorism. After his retirement, Köhler was able to continue his neuropsychological perceptual studies at the Institute for Advanced Study in Princeton (1954–1956), at Dartmouth College in New Hampshire, and at the Massachusetts Institute of Technology (MIT), where he inaugurated its graduate program during the years between 1960 and 1967. Unfortunately, his ambitious research on "psychoisomorphism" (the structural similarities

Figure 7 Piéron (1881–1964), Piaget (1896–1980), and Köhler at the 1957 IUPS Congress in Brussels.

Figure 8 Köhler and his second wife, Lilli Hårleman (1899–1985) (ca. 1960).

Figure 9 Köhler on his farm.

between mental phenomena and neural processes) proved inconclusive.

After World War II, Köhler resumed his teaching in Europe on an intermittent basis. In 1950, he lectured at the newly established Free University in West Berlin and advised its president during the establishment of its new Psychological Institute. Kripal Sing Sodhi (1911–1961) and Hans Hörmann (1924–1983) were able to secure Köhler's expertise through continued appointments, first as a visiting lecturer and later through an "honorary" professorship, which enabled him to continue some of his research and to be involved in the supervision of doctoral students. In honor of his 75th birthday, Köhler received "honorary citizenship" of the Free University in Berlin. International recognition included seven honorary doctorates from European and American universities, the presidency of the American Psychological Association for the 1958–1959 term, and honorary memberships in the psychological organizations and scientific academies of several countries. Wolfgang Köhler died on June 11, 1967, at the age of 80 on his farm in Enfield, New Hampshire, where he is buried.

Bibliography

Henle, M. (Ed.). (1971). *The selected papers of Wolfgang Köhler.* New York: Liveright.

Henle, M. (1978). One man against the Nazis—Wolfgang Köhler. *American Psychologist, 33,* 935–944.

Jaeger, S. (Ed.). (1988). *Briefe von Wolfgang Köhler an Hans Geitel 1907–1920. Mit zwei Arbeiten Köhlers "Über elektromagnetische Erregung des Trommelfelles" und "Intelligenzprüfungen am Orang im Anhang."* Passau: Passavia.

Jaeger, S. (1993). Zur Widerständigkeit der Hochschullehrer zu Beginn der nationalsozialistischen Herrschaft. *Psychologie und Geschichte, 4,* 219–228.

Köhler, W. (1920). *Die physischen Gestalten in Ruhe und im stationären Zustand. Eine naturphilosophische Untersuchung.* Braunschweig, Germany: Vieweg.

Köhler, W. (1921). *Intelligenzprüfungen an Menschenaffen.* Berlin: Springer

Köhler, W. (1925). *The mentality of apes* (E. Winter, Trans.). New York: Harcourt, Brace & World.

Köhler, W. (1929). *Gestalt psychology.* New York: Liveright.

Köhler, W. (1933). Gespräche in Deutschland. *Deutsche Allgemeine Zeitung, 197,* 2 (28.4.1933).

Köhler, W. (1938). *The place of value in a world of facts.* New York: Liveright.

Köhler, W. (1940). *Dynamics in psychology.* New York: Liveright.

Köhler, W. (1969). *The tasks of Gestalt psychology.* Princeton, NJ: Princeton University Press.

Köhler, W. (1993). The mentality of orangs. *International Journal of Comparative Psychology, 6*(4), 189–229.

Kurt Lewin—Filmmaker

Helmut E. Lück

On February 12, 1932, one of the first sound pictures about the "everyday life of children" was shown in the auditorium of the Urania Science Club in Hamburg. The new film was introduced with the following words (Stern, 1987):

> Some of you may ask whether it makes sense to repeat something in a film which everyone knows. . . . The answer must be a clear "Yes, it really does make sense!" . . . With this film we wish to show to mature . . . adults that children are totally different from us, and that their world is a completely different world, even though they share the same space and its objects. . . . All understanding and caring adults, upon whom children depend during their early lives, must know this. (p. 17)

The man who gave this prefatory speech and who praised the film so highly was none other than William Stern (1871–1938), the eminent German pioneer of developmental and applied psychology. The author and director of the film was Kurt Lewin (1890–1947). According to Stern, there are two reasons why Lewin was able to attract the attention of his audience to the problems of children: The children did not know that they were being filmed; and the natural soundtrack gave a very realistic impression of the children's lives. In addition, Lewin's film focused on the expanding life space of babies, toddlers, and adolescents. From a modern perspective, Lewin's 1932 film has value in its own right for the history of the social sciences (van Elteren & Lück, 1990).

Alongside other towering figures in the field of psychology such as Sigmund Freud (1856–1939) and Jean Piaget (1896–1980), Kurt Lewin is one of the most important psychologists of the 20th century. This assessment may come as a surprise because

Figure 1 Portrait of Kurt Lewin.

Lewin established no system or school of his own. His name is hardly known among nonpsychologists. In sharp contrast to the many of books and articles about Freud's life and work, only a handful of biographies have been written about Lewin (Marrow, 1969; Lewin, 1992). Nevertheless, Lewin's accomplishments are impressive. He published basic theoretical essays and important research articles in developmental and educational psychology, including his famous experiments about the differential effects of leadership styles. He was a cofounder of experimental social psychology and coined the term "group dynamics." Lewin established the field of action research and encouraged the use of group dynamics in sensitivity and T-groups. In turn, some of his students founded the National Training Laboratory (NTL), one of the most important organizations for the promotion of group dynamics. Finally, Lewin encouraged the development of ecological psychology through his student, Roger Barker (1903–1990). Lewin's experimental methods, his concepts (i.e., "level of aspiration"), his theories, and his dynamic perspectives have all become an intrinsic part of modern academic psychology, but we often forget their originator.

The Man

Kurt Lewin was born on September 9, 1890, in the rural town of Mogilno, in the Polish territory of the German Kingdom of Prussia. He died on February 11, 1947, at the age of 56 in Newtonville, Massachusetts. He had an older sister and two younger brothers. Lewin identified his father as a "land owner and merchant" (Lewin, 1916, p. 37). His parents and all four grandparents were Jews, and throughout his life Lewin identified himself with Judaism. In 1905, Lewin's family moved to Berlin. Although Lewin initially wanted to become a "country doctor," he attended lectures in biology and philosophy, as well as those in medicine, at the universities of Freiburg, Munich, and Berlin.

Like many young men of his generation, Lewin volunteered for military service at the beginning of World War I and served from 1914 to 1918 with an artillery unit. He was decorated with the Iron Cross and held the rank of first lieutenant at the time of his discharge. During a brief leave from active duty, Lewin received his PhD on September 11, 1914, from Berlin University. His work there had been conducted under the direction of Carl Stumpf (1848–1936).

Under the influence of Ernst Cassirer (1874–1945), the German philosopher, and the German Gestalt psychologists Wolfgang Köhler (1887–1967), Max Wertheimer (1880–1943), and Kurt Koffka (1886–1941), Lewin became involved in Gestalt psychological research. With this background he later developed his ideas on field theory and how it applied to psychology. Today, field psychology provides the matrix for understanding a variety of phenomena, ranging from conflict resolution to group processes—and even the study of how psychological regressions can be conceptualized and explained. Throughout his life, Lewin renamed his research approach, including his work on the now-famous terms "dynamic theory," "topological psychology," "vector psychology," and finally "field

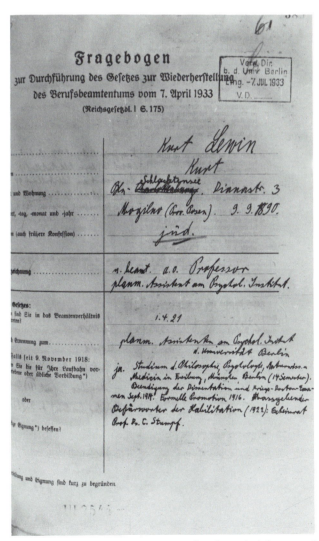

Figure 2 German "Questionnaire for the Rehabilitation of Civil Servants" with Lewin's handwritten information entries about his religious and occupational background.

theory." It was the latter concept he favored toward the end of his life, and he also tried to re-interpret his earlier research within this context.

Lewin quickly recognized the danger of Nazi control of Germany's government, so he left the country early on in August of 1933. He found temporary employment in the United States at Cornell University in Ithaca, New York, and was able to continue his research with the support of American foundations. Lewin's time-limited appointment was in the home economics department, which was responsible for the training of nursery school teachers.

Figure 3 Lewin's Berlin villa.

After his exile from Germany, Lewin was offered positions not only in the United States and the Soviet Union, but also at Hebrew University in Jerusalem (Lück & Rechtien, 1989). His appointment to a full professorship in psychology in Palestine was strongly opposed by Sigmund Freud, apparently because Freud believed that Lewin "was not the right man to accomplish a synthesis between psychoanalysis and [academic] psychology" (1989, p. 411).

In the United States Lewin leaned increasingly toward research problems in developmental and educational psychology. He also developed his new system of group dynamics and influenced the field of social psychology through students like Tamara Dembo (1902–1993), Leon Festinger (1919–1989), Roger Barker (1903–1990), and others.

Many of Lewin's students have commented on his vivacity, a certain lack of organizational abilities, his strong social skills, and his willingness to dedicate his life to a new undertaking. Lewin had many interests. He was a sailing enthusiast and a friend of artists. In Berlin, he had Peter Behrens (1886–1940), the famous architect, design and build a modern country villa for him. The furniture for the new house was designed by the young Marcel Breuer (1902–1981), with whom Lewin continued to be associated in the United States.

Upon becoming more familiar with the life and work of Lewin, one quickly discovers his intense involvement with Judaism—a commitment which increased after his exile. Thus, he cooperated with a number of Jewish-American organizations in publishing a surprising number of articles about Jewish culture and education (Lück, 1993).

The Filmmaker

From about 1923 until his death, Lewin was involved in the making of motion and later sound pictures. He may have been encouraged to make films by Köhler, who had made a number of films at his primate research center on the Spanish island of Tenerife. Lewin's filmmaking probably began as a private hobby. He began making home movies of his own children, as well as those of relatives and friends. During the filming of his children, Lewin seems to have realized that emotions and conflicts could easily be captured on film. In addition, he used his films to supplement and illustrate academic lectures and speeches.

Lewin discussed his film work in several of his publications on developmental psychology. He reported that he initially used his own spring-controlled "Kinamo" camera, but he also had access to a 35-mm camera owned by the Psychological Institute of Berlin University which allowed him to record up to six minutes of film at one time. According to Lewin (1926): "We did not use a hedge or other cover to detract attention from the motion picture camera but employed a small tent, as a rule, and showed only the objective of the camera through a small opening" (p. 7).

Clips from the 1931 film *The Child and the World* illustrate Lewin's approach (Figure 6): An object on a table arouses the child's interest; building material, old equipment, and tools are used by children to create their play world; three boys play rowboat in an old horse wagon; children have a "hideout" under an old lumber cart; a railroad set provides an introduction to the world of adults; an organized youth group marches and sings together.

Figure 5 One of Lewin's films with mailing wrapper from his association with Stanford University as a visiting professor (1932–1933).

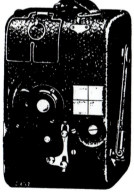

Figure 4 Advertisement describing Lewin's private "Ica Kinamo" film camera with special spring-operated mechanism.

Lewin's work as a film director and producer brought him a good deal of recognition in Germany and abroad. William Stern, for example, asked Lewin to contribute an illustrated chapter about his film work to the fourth edition of his book, *Psychology of Early Childhood* (Stern, 1927). A 1937 lecture manuscript by Lewin, with illustrations from his films, was published in 1987. It shows that Lewin could always make himself understood through his films, if his theoretical ideas were otherwise too abstract or difficult. This was especially true for his presentation at the Ninth International Congress of Psychology at Yale University in 1929. According to Graumann (1981): "The Soviet psychologist Luria was so impressed with Lewin's films that he arranged for him to meet with the [Russian] director, Sergei Eisenstein. Luria also made plans to establish a psychological laboratory [for Lewin] in Moscow in cooperation with the local state film academy" (p. 9).

Except for his well-known film about the impact of leadership style on youth groups, the rest of

Figures 6 Sample scenes from Lewin's 1935 sound movie *The Child and the World.*

Lewin's films were lost for a long time. Some of them were rediscovered during the 1970s at the University of Kansas. In 1984, the German Distance University produced the instructional film "Kurt Lewin," which made Lewin's forgotten documentary films available once again. In the fall of 1987, the sound film *The Child and the World* was discovered by Mel van Elteren, a Dutch historian of psychology. This film had not been shown publicly for almost 50 years.

Bibliography

Elteren, Mel van, & Lück, H. (1990). Lewin's films and their role in field theory. In S. A. Wheelan, E. A. Pepitone, & V. Abt (Eds.), *Advances in field theory*. New York: Sage.

Graumann, C. (1981). Zur Kurt Lewin-Werkausgabe. In K. Lewin, *Werkausgabe* (Vol. 1, pp. 7–15). Bern: Huber.

Lewin, K. (1916). Die Psychische Tätigkeit bei der Hemmung von Willensvorgängen und das Grundgesetz der Assoziation. Dissertation. Leipzig: Barth.

Lewin, K. (1926). Filmaufnahmen über Trieb- und Affektäußerungen psychopathischer Kinder (verglichen mit Normalen und Schwachsinnigen). *Zeitschrift für Kinderforschung 32,* 414–447.

Lewin, M. (1992). The impact of Kurt Lewin's life on the place of social issues in his work. *Journal of Social Issues, 48,* 15–29.

Lück, H. E. (1993). Kurt Lewin: A German-Jewish psychologist. *Journal of Psychology and Judaism, 17,* 153–168.

Lück, H. E., & Rechtien, W. (1989). Freud und Lewin. Historische Methode und "Hier und Jetzt." In B. Nitzschke (Ed.), *Freud und die akademische Psychologie* (pp.137–159). Munich: Psychologie Verlags Union.

Marrow, A. J. (1969). *The practical theorist.* New York: Basic Books.

Stern, W. (1927). *Psychologie der frühen Kindheit* (4th ed.). Leipzig: Quelle & Meyer.

Stern, W. (1987). Das Kind und die Welt. *Geschichte der Psychologie, 4,* 17–22.

Roger Barker's Ecological Psychology

The aerial photograph shown in Figure 1 provides an overview of the Midwestern town of Oskaloosa, Kansas. The photograph also can be viewed as a visual expression of Roger G. Barker's (1903–1990) life and work.

This noted American psychologist and pioneer of modern ecological psychology originally moved to Oskaloosa in 1947 after accepting the chairmanship of the Department of Psychology at the University of Kansas in nearby Lawrence. Barker lived and

Figure 1 Aerial view of Oskaloosa, Kansas. The Field Station was located at the southeast corner of the large square in the center of the small town.

288

Figure 2 Downtown corner building, which contained the offices of the Field Station from about 1947–1970. The tall structure in the background is the water tower of Oskaloosa.

worked in this almost prototypical Midwestern American community of about 715 people for more than 40 years. He even died there in 1990 at the age of 87.

Following the lead of ecological researchers in biology, who locate, observe, and systematically study plants and animals in their natural surroundings, Roger Barker wanted to study, describe, and analyze the psychological behavior of humans, especially children, in everyday life situations. For this purpose, he and his colleague Herbert F. Wright (1907–1990) established the "Midwest Psychological Field Station" in Oskaloosa in 1947. This community was identified by the code name "Midwest" in the scientific publications of Barker and his associates. The research center existed until 1972.

Barker and his team were interested in finding out to what extent everyday human life could and should be assessed representationally. Specifically, they decided to describe the entire publicly accessible daily life of "Midwest" during the 1951/1952 year. The sheer size of Barker's psychological project must have caused considerable headshaking among fellow researchers in the early 1950s and continues to do so even today. A similar study was carried out in 1954 in Leyburn, England (cover name "Yordale"). Both studies were replicated in 1963/1964 to provide a longitudinal comparison. Barker was not satisfied with the mere collection and analysis of his empirical data, however. In addition, he worked on the development of a conceptual framework for interpreting the functional organization of everyday life and its impact on the development of children and teenagers.

How did Barker become involved in such an unprecedented, ambitious, and complex psychological-ecological research project? What did he and his colleagues expect to discover and how is their work related to traditional psychology? Barker and his associates repeatedly provided answers to these and similar questions (Barker, 1987, 1989; Bechtel, 1990; Schoggen, 1992; Wicker, 1991).

After receiving his PhD from Stanford in 1934, Barker accepted a series of time-limited research appointments at major American universities (Stanford, Iowa, Harvard, Illinois, Chicago, and Clark). During this period, most of Barker's research and teaching followed a fairly traditional academic pattern. However, experiences that impressed him as almost incompatible with the conventional psychology of the period inspired him to develop his innovative ecological perspectives on everyday life. He eventually implemented upon his appointment at Kansas.

His wife, Louise, who he had met in 1927 at Stanford University, was a biologist. She and an "agronomist" introduced Barker to the descriptive-ecological approaches and research methods of modern biology. Next, Barker worked two years with Kurt Lewin (1890–1947) at the University of Iowa. Through their association with Lewin, Barker and his friend Herbert Wright learned how to investigate the molar actions of children and describe its full complexity in everyday English. Lewin also introduced Barker to a type of theorizing, quite new among American

Figure 3 This old wooden building was the home of "Raymond Birch," a 7-year-old boy, whom Barker and his associates observed for an entire day on April 26, 1949.

Figure 4 Weekly staff meeting of the field station project teams. Barker is shown with his back to the camera on the left.

cifically, this included the study of the "behavior stream" of individual children throughout the day by a team of successive observers and the descriptions of the numerous "episodes" in nontechnical English. The project team soon discovered that the daily behavior of children was strongly determined by the social and material context in which they spent their time—for example, a class, a playground, a party, a grocery store, a church service, and so on. Barker and his associates named them "behavior settings," defined them as a special type of supraindividual social system, and developed a method for the identification and the coarse-grained descrip-

psychologists, that addressed everyday phenomena and took into account the individual's actions and psychological environments. He also acquired an in-depth knowledge of laboratory research and developmental psychology. In addition, Barker gained first-hand information about the daily life of school children from his teaching of developmental psychology courses to teachers in the extension program of the University of Illinois. In this context, his visits to small teachers' colleges and public schools impressed Barker with the attractions of rural life and the scenery of small-town America. All these influences helped Barker formulate his chief research question, "What kind of daily life do children experience in small American communities, and how does their life differ from what we know about them from the laboratories of developmental psychology?"

Barker's "Midwest Project," was explicitly welcomed and supported by Lewin. Initially, Barker and Wright experimented with a variety of methods, which they hoped would help them answer their basic and still very general research questions. Thus, they developed a type of case study methodology involving the use of "specimen records." Spe-

Figure 5 Louise Mason, a project worker, observes the "behavior stream" of a child playing with a turtle at the local Presbyterian Daily Vocation Bible School.

Figure 6 Market Booth behavior setting at weekly market in Leyburn, England.

Figure 7 Roger Barker at his desk.

Figure 8 Barker in wheel chair and his wife Louise in the garden of their home in Oskaloosa.

tion of such systems ("Behavior Setting Survey"), which they used extensively for describing and comparing "Midwest" and "Yordale."

Behavior settings, as conceptualized by Barker, are concrete, spatio-temporally localized, quasi-stationary, self-maintaining social event systems. Their action patterns are closely coordinated ("synomorphic") to the immediate surroundings (the "milieu" and "behavioral objects"). Barker also tried to describe the systematic dynamics of the behavior settings through the TOTE Model and through models first proposed by Egon Brunswilk (1903–1955) and Fritz Heider (Barker, 1968; Schoggen, 1989). Behavior settings can be differentiated with respect to their "staffing," with moderate understaffing (e.g., in schools) expected to have favorable effects on the participants and their performance.

The generations of researchers at the Midwest Psychological Field Station in Oskaloosa included many eminent psychologists who co-authored with

Barker (among them Gump and Schoggen), or who further developed his theoretical framework and/or his empirical approach (Bechtel, Gump, Wicker, Willems). The reception of Barker's work in Germany was promoted by Kaminski (1989) and Fuhrer (1990). Barker's wife, Louise, was his closest collaborator during his demanding and lengthy research activities. She supported him actively and courageously from the beginning of his career, especially after his serious osteomyelitis recurred. This debilitating illness first affected Barker in childhood and restricted his daily activities significantly for most of his long life. So he drew on personal experience, as well as Lewinian concepts, in his work "surveying the current knowledge of the psychological aspects of physical disability" (Barker, 1989, p. 24), which aimed at assisting the rehabilitation of those with war injuries.

Barker received many honors for his innovative research. His appointment to a research professorship with minimal teaching responsibilities permitted him to devote most of his time to research and publication.

Bibliography

Barker. R. G. (1987). Prospecting in environmental psychology, Oskaloosa revisited. In D. Stokols & I. Altman (Eds.), *Handbook of environmental psychology* (Vol. 2, pp. 1413–1432). New York: Wiley.

Barker, R. G. (1989). Roger G. Barker. In Gardner Lindzey (Ed.), *A history of psychology in autobiography* (Vol. VIII, pp. 3–35). Stanford, CA: Stanford University Press.

Barker, R. G., et al. (1978). *Habitats, environments, and human behavior. Studies in ecological psychology and ecobehavioral science from the Midwest Psychological Field Station, 1947–1972.* San Francisco: Jossey-Bass.

Barker, R. G., & Wright, H. F. (1951). *One boy's day.* New York: Harper & Row.

Bechtel, R. (1990). Editor's preface (Introduction to special issue on the Midwest Psychological Field Station). *Environment and Behavior, 22*(4), 435.

Fuhrer, U. (1990). Bridging the ecological-psychological gap. Behavior settings as interfaces. *Environment and Behavior, 22*(4), 518–537.

Kaminski, G. (1989). The relevance of ecologically oriented theory building in environment and behavior research. In: E. H. Zube & G. T. Moore (Eds.), *Advances in environment, behavior, and design* (Vol. 2, pp. 3–36). New York: Plenum.

Schoggen, P. (1989). *Behavior settings: A revision and extension of Roger G. Barker's ecological psychology.* Stanford, CA: Stanford University Press.

Schoggen, P. (1991). Roger Garlock Barker (1903–1990). *American Psychologist, 47*(1), 77–78.

Wicker, A. W. (1991). A Tribute to Roger G. Barker (1903–1990). *Journal of Environmental Psychology, 11,* 287–290.

HUMAN DEVELOPMENT AND PERSONALITY

The Mental Life of Newborn Children

Wolfgang G. Bringmann
William D. G. Balance
Norma J. Bringmann

The 1882 publication of the first volume of *The Mind of the Child* (1882, 1888–1889) by William T. Preyer (1841–1878) of Jena University in Germany is widely regarded as the first milestone in the scientific development of child psychology (Stern, 1914; Cairns, 1983; Munn, 1965). However, during ongoing research for a documentary biography of Wilhelm Wundt (1832–1920), we discovered an even

Figure 1 Drawing of William T. Preyer after an old photograph.

DIE SEELE DES KINDES.

BEOBACHTUNGEN

ÜBER DIE

GEISTIGE ENTWICKELUNG DES MENSCHEN

IN DEN ERSTEN LEBENSJAHREN

VON

W. PREYER,

ORDENTLICHEM PROFESSOR DER PHYSIOLOGIE AN DER UNIVERSITÄT
UND DIRECTOR DES PHYSIOLOGISCHEN INSTITUTS ZU JENA.
DOCTOR DER MEDICIN UND PHILOSOPHIE.

LEIPZIG.
TH. GRIEBEN'S VERLAG (L. FERNAU).
1882.

Figure 2 German title page of *The Mind of the Child* (1882) by Preyer.

earlier sophisticated study of child development. This newly found work was first published 23 years before Preyer's *magnum opus* was completed and was used by Preyer as a major source of empirical information about early childhood (Preyer, 1882, 1888–1889). The original research was carried out by the eminent German internist, Adolf Kußmaul

(1822–1902), and was published under the title *Investigations of the Mental Life of Newborn Human Children* (1859).

One can, of course, discover antecedents to almost any modern discovery in psychology if one only searches long and hard enough. Kußmaul's series of mini-experiments merits our full attention because it is a far more sophisticated example of child research than the more popular writings by his famous successors (e.g., Darwin, 1877; Preyer, 1882; Hall, 1883).

Elaborate details about Kußmaul's life and intellectual career are richly available in the two volumes of his autobiography, which may be rightly counted as among the very best medical autobiographies available (Kußmaul 1899, 1903). He was born on February 22, 1822, in the village of Graben in the German Grand Duchy of Baden. His father, the son of peasants, was a "self-made man," who became a military surgeon and later a public health physician.

Kußmaul graduated from the Heidelberg Lyceum—as did Wundt—and began to study medicine at Heidelberg University in 1840. Both he and Wundt were awarded the coveted "Charles-Frederic" research medal by the Medical Faculty at Heidelberg. After passing his state medical boards in 1846, Kußmaul spent the next seven years as a postgraduate student of medicine at the universities of Vienna and Prague (1847–1848), as a military physician in the Baden army (1848–1849), and as a country physician in the Black Forest mountains (1850–1853). At long last, in 1853, he obtained his medical doctorate from Würzburg University at the age of 33.

Between 1853 and 1856, Kußmaul lived a very active professional life, first as a physician at two mental institutions, and later as an assistant physician at a major hospital in Heidelberg (1856–1859). During this period, he also taught a variety of medical courses, including forensic psychiatry, as a tenured instructor at Heidelberg. Between 1859 and 1887, he held full professorships in internal medicine at the Universities of Erlangen (1859–1863), Freiburg (1863–1876), and Straßburg (1876–1887). During his long academic career, he published 54 scientific books and articles and supervised more than 90 medical dissertations. He spent his retirement years in Heidelberg and died in 1902 at the age of 80, after publishing the first volume of his popular autobiography (1899).

Figure 3 Portrait of Adolf Kußmaul as a college student.

Kußmaul's Study of Neonates

Kußmaul collected the information about the mental life of newborn children while working as a public health physician for the poor in Heidelberg. He published his results in 1859 and presented his findings as his inaugural lecture at Erlangen University (Kußmaul, 1899):

> . . . during my psychological studies [at Heidelberg University], I became interested in the mental activities of newborn children. Neither philosophers, nor scientists and physicians had previously addressed this question through exact observation and experiment. The results of my investigation were well received and . . . published in a third edition. (p. 7)

Like any good scholar, Kußmaul began his monograph by defining his subject matter as the psychological processes (i.e., "sensation, imagination, thought, and motivation") in the newborn child (1859, p. 3). About one-fourth of his book is devoted to a scholarly review of classical and recent literature concerning the behavioral reper-

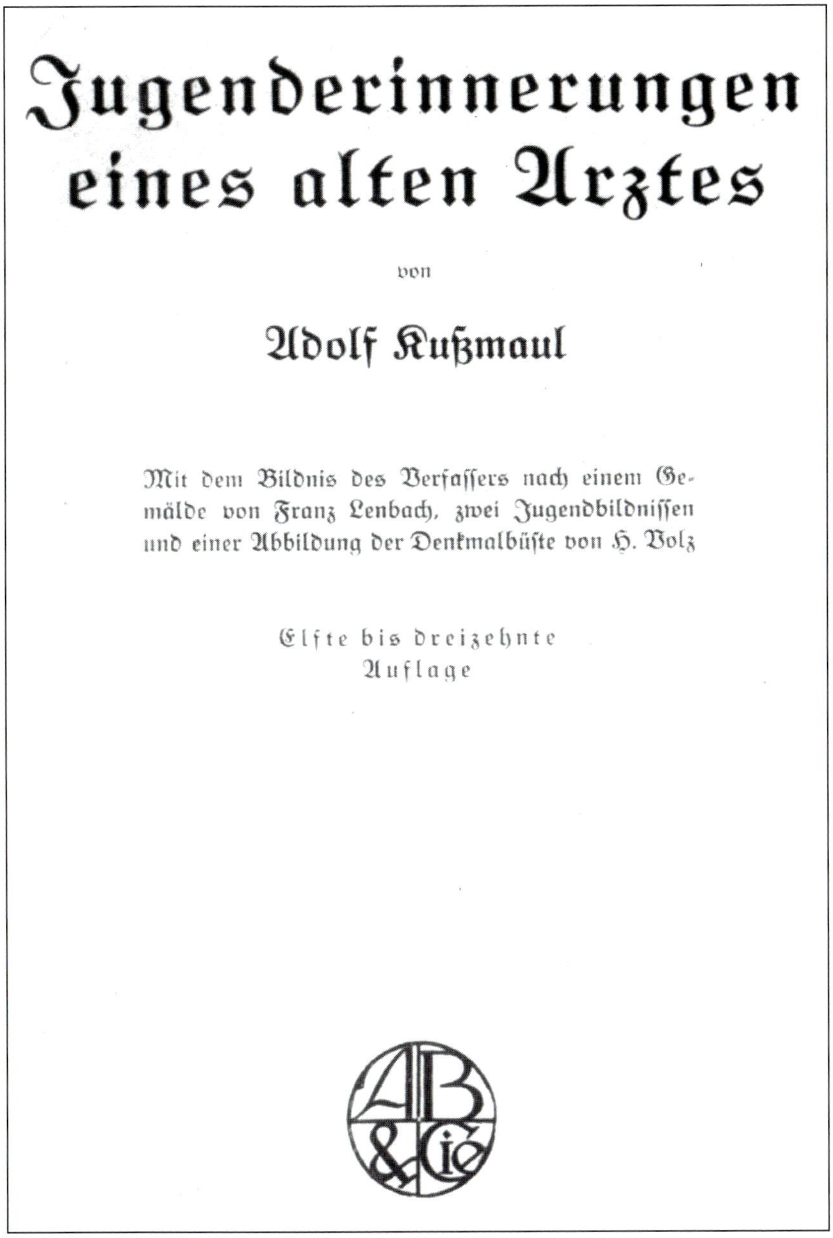

Jugenderinnerungen eines alten Arztes

von

Adolf Kußmaul

Mit dem Bildnis des Verfassers nach einem Gemälde von Franz Lenbach, zwei Jugendbildnissen und einer Abbildung der Denkmalbüste von H. Volz

Elfte bis dreizehnte
Auflage

Figure 4 Title page of Kußmaul's autobiography.

He addressed himself to the investigation of hunger and thirst, and he closed the book with a discussion of responses which were to him indicative of intelligence. Kußmaul described each set of experiments with the traditional information about the subjects of the investigation, the experimental equipment and materials, the testing procedures employed, and, finally, the results.

Kußmaul also critically evaluated the results of each experiment and attempted to integrate his findings with the existing information in the field. Whenever his own results were unsatisfactory or incomplete, he made use of other data which he thought were pertinent. We have provided the following examples to illustrate Kußmaul's research from his mini-experiments on the sensations of taste, touch, hunger, and thirst in newborn children.

Taste

The subjects from Kußmaul's study of the sense of taste consisted of slightly more than 20 newborn children. Although we do not know the exact composition of the sample, the author informs us that they included children "who had barely left the womb and who had not yet taken any milk . . . full-term and strong babies of both sexes, as well as some children who were born prematurely in the seventh or eighth months" (1859, pp. 22–23).

"Sweet" and "bitter" liquids were used as experimental stimuli for the experiments on taste. These substances were first warmed to body temperature and applied to the mouths of the children with a "fine camel hair brush." Kußmaul's rigorous concern with experimental control is illustrated by his description of the sweet and bitter stimuli (1859): "The liquids consisted of a saturated sugar solution and a solution of 10 grains of sulphate quinine in

toire of the human neonate. Interestingly, he found the developmental views of Aristotle (384–322 B.C.) more compatible with his experimental findings than those of John Locke (1632–1704). With rare exceptions, Kußmaul saw little of value in the existing literature (1859).

In the remaining half of the book Kußmaul described his experiments and collected baseline information on the sensory repertoire of newborn children. He studied taste, touch, temperature sense, smell, vision, hearing, and the muscle sense.

half an ounce of water. This substance had a very bitter taste and was used in this concentration in all experiments without exception" (p. 22). His major findings were (1859): "The sugar and quinine solutions produced the same muscular movements in the neonate, which are designated in adults as the facial expressions of sweet and bitter taste" (p. 22).

Kußmaul's graphic description of the children's behavior clearly demonstrated the presence of differential taste response patterns (1859):

Figure 5 Kußmaul at the time of his research with newborn children.

When sugar was brought into the mouth, the children shaped their lips like the snout of an animal, pressed their tongues between the lips and began to suck with pleasure. . . . When small amounts of quinine were applied, only the muscles controlling the nostrils and the upper lip contracted. Larger amounts of quinine caused the muscles which control the wrinkling of eyebrows and eyelids to be activated. . . . The throat contracted spasmodically, the children choked, the mouth was opened wide and the tongue pro-

truded as much as an inch, and the applied liquids were often partially expelled together with a great amount of saliva. At times the children shook their heads like an adult who is overcome by nausea. (p. 26)

On the basis of the above observations, Kußmaul drew the following conservative conclusion (1859): "The sense of taste already functions among newborn children in its major forms. . . . They do not merely experience taste in a vague manner, as Bichat thought" (p. 26).

Touch

Kußmaul's experiments on the sense of touch in newborn children were extensive, although they concentrated primarily on the facial area. Specifically, he explored the touch sensitivity of the tongue, the lips, the nasal membranes, and the eyelashes. The following experiments on the sensory function of the eyelashes serve to illustrate his innovative and painstaking methodology:

The eyelashes are extremely sensitive to the lightest touch. If the waking child has opened his eyes, one can proceed with a thin glass rod almost to the cornea of the eye before the eye will be closed. However, as soon as a single eyelash is touched, the eye closes at once. The touching of the eyelids is by no means as effective in producing a closure of the eye. . . . The extreme sensitivity of the eyelashes can be beautifully demonstrated by the following experiment: If one blows on the cheeks or the forehead of a newborn, it blinks with his eyes. At first, I had incorrectly explained this behavior as a response to changes in temperature. If one, however, directs air through a narrow paper tube alternatively to different parts of the face, one can observe that the child will blink only if the airstream touches one of the eyelashes. The eye on the stimulated side responds more intensively and quickly. (1859, pp. 32–33).

Kußmaul concluded that this reflexive response served to guard the eye against injury at a time when conscious experience cannot as yet control the closure of the eyelids.

Hunger and Thirst

Kußmaul's research on hunger and thirst in the newborn is also quite valuable. He suggested that neonates experience a combination of hunger and thirst during the first 6 to 24 hours of their lives. An experiment, which he performed with a "lively, pretty newborn girl" provides additional information on his experimental approach (1859):

> She was born around 7 a.m. and soon gave repeated signs of hunger but was not fed until noon. By that time, she had become very restless, moved her head back and forth as if searching for something and cried a lot. I stroked her left cheek softly with my index finger without touching the lip when she did not cry. Quickly she turned her head to the left side, grabbed my finger and began to suck. Next, I removed my finger and began stroking the right cheek. Just as quickly she turned to that side and once again took hold of my finger. Again I removed my finger and stroked the left cheek. It was quite a surprise how deftly the child turned back on the left side and again grasped the finger. (pp. 45–46)

Kußmaul continued the stimulation of the baby's cheeks until the child began to scream loudly and became quite upset. He then had the baby placed at her mother's breast without placing the nipple directly into her mouth (1859):

> She again calmed down and moved her head back and forth in a searching manner but was unable to find and take hold of the nipple. The nipple had to be placed between her lips and jaws and then she began to suck. Thus, it is clear that the child was able to grasp the firm, long index finger at once but not the soft, small nipple. (p. 46)

He concluded that newborn children are able to make sucking movements but cannot nurse well without assistance. There are significant individual differences among children in acquiring this important skill, and some very clumsy children may never successfully learn to nurse.

A Modern Successor to Kußmaul

In recent years test procedures which are strikingly similar to those applied by Kußmaul (1859) have been standardized to provide objective information about the behavioral repertoire and developmental potential of newborn children. The original research was conducted by T. Berry Brazelton, MD, the Director of the Child Development Unit of the Children's Hospital Medical Center in Boston (Brazelton, 1973). The Brazelton Neonatal Behavior Assessment Scale (BNBAS) consists of 20 neurological items (e.g., 1. Plantar grasp, 2. Hand grasp . . . 17–20, Passive movements of arms and legs), which are rated on a four-point scale for intensity of response. In addi-

tion, 11 specific behaviors are observed or elicited with simple instruments like: "a red spice box with popcorn kernels, a small bell, a flashlight, an orange rubber ball one inch in diameter, a paper clip" (p. 25). The following items on the behavior scale are reminiscent of Kußmaul's techniques:

Figure 6 Commemorative bust of Kußmaul.

1. Response decrement to light
2. Response decrement to rattle
3. Response decrement to bell
4. Response decrement to pinprick
5. Focusing and following an object
6. Reaction to an auditory stimulus

The 11 behavioral items are each rated on a nine-point scale. The midpoint of the scale denotes the expected performance of a normal, 3-day-old infant.

The BNBAS has been found useful in the assessment of crosscultural differences in newborn children (Freedman & Freedman, 1969) and can detect the developmental impact of socioeconomic differences in infant behavior (Justice, Self, & Gutrecht, 1976). The Brazelton scale has also been used on neonates to detect the effects of maternal drug use (Aleksandrowicz & Aleksandrowicz, 1974). The scale also has promise for predicting physical and mental development during a child's first year of life (Scarr, Salapatek, & Williams, 1973).

Kußmaul and Psychology

An English summary of Kußmaul's results was published in the *Cornhill Magazine* in 1863. Preyer (1882) appears to have regarded Kußmaul chiefly as a reliable source of normative information but also seems to have disregarded the experimental source of his data. Among standard histories of psychology and developmental psychology (Watson, 1978), we found only a single source that included relevant information about Kußmaul's infant research. This was a German book by Hehlmann titled *History of Psychology* (1963, 1967). The book briefly mentioned Kußmaul in the text and correctly placed his name at the very beginning of a "Chronology of Child and Adolescent Psychology" (1967, p. 435).

English-speaking historians of psychology have long subscribed to the presentist position that no significant research in child and developmental psychology occurred before the publication of Preyer's epochal book (1882, 1888–1889). This claim was refuted by presenting in some detail Kußmaul's (1859) experimental study of the sensory functioning of newborn children, which was carried out and published more than 30 years before Preyer. The Brazelton Neonatal Behavior Assessment Scale was used as a modern analog to Kußmaul's basic approach to child study.

Bibliography

Aleksandrowicz, M., & Aleksandrowicz, D. (1974). Obstetrical pain-relieving drugs as predictors of infant behavior variability. *Child Development, 45,* 935–945.

Brazelton, T. (1973). *Neonatal behavioral assessment scale.* Philadelphia: Lippincott.

Brazelton, T., Tronick, E., Lechtig, A., & Lasky, R. (1977). The behavior of nutritionally deprived Guatemalan infants. *Developmental Medicine and Child Neurology, 19,* 364.

Cairns, R. C. (1983). The emergence of developmental psychology. In P. H. Mussen (Ed.), *Handbook of Child Psychology* (Vol. 1, pp. 41–102). New York: Wiley.

Darwin, C. (1877). A biographical sketch of an infant. *Mind, 2,* 285–294.

Freedman, D., & Freedman, N. (1969). Behavioral differences between Chinese American and European American newborns. *Nature, 24,* 1227.

Hall, G. S. (1883). The contents of children's minds. *Princeton Review, 11,* 249–272.

Hehlmann, K. (1963, 1967). *Geschichte der Psychologie.* Stuttgart: Kröner.

Justice, L., Self, P., & Gutecht, N. (1976). *Socioeconomic status and scores on the Brazelton Neonatal Behavioral Assessment Scale.* Paper presented at the Southeastern Conference on Human Development, Nashville, TN.

Kessen, W., Haith, M., & Salapatek, P. (1970). Infancy. In P. H. Mussen (Ed.), *Carmichael's manual of child psychology* (3rd ed.). New York: Wiley.

Kußmaul, A. (1859) *Untersuchungen über die Sinneswahrnehmungen des neugeborenen Menschen.* Heidelberg: Winter.

Kußmaul, A. (1899). *Jugenderinnerungen eines alten Arztes.* Stuttgart: Bonz.

Kußmaul, A. (1903). *Aus meiner Dozentenzeit.* Stuttgart: Bonz.

Munn, N. L. (1965). *The evolution and growth of human behavior.* Boston: Houghton-Mifflin.

Preyer, W. (1882). *Die Seele des Kindes.* Leipzig: Grieben.

Preyer, W. (1888–1889). *The mind of the child* (Vols. 1 & 2). New York: Appleton.

Scarr, M., Salapatek, S., & Williams, M. (1973). The effects of early stimulation of low birth weight infants. *Child Development, 44,* 94–101.

Stern, W. (1914). *Die differentielle Psychologie in ihren methodischen Grundlagen.* Leipzig: Barth.

Watson, R. (1978). *The history of psychology and the behavioral sciences.* New York: Springer.

G. Stanley Hall and American Psychology

Charles E. Early
Wolfgang G. Bringmann
Michael W. Bringmann

Granville Stanley Hall stands as one of the towering figures in the history of American psychology. As a result of his many contributions, Hall is widely recognized as one of psychology's foremost organizers and promoters. A. A. Roback (1964) summarized Hall's initiatives and achievements in the following account:

> [Hall] was the *first* to receive a Ph.D. in the philosophy department at Harvard. He was the *first* American student, during the *first* year of its existence, at the *first* officially accepted psychological laboratory in the world—at Leipzig under Wundt. He founded the *first* psychological laboratory in America at Johns Hopkins in 1883. . . . Hall, furthermore, launched the *first* psychological journal in English, the *American Journal of Psychology* in 1887. . . . He was the *first* president of Clark University (1888), where he established a psychological laboratory for advanced research. . . . he was the *first* president of the American Psychological Association, virtually its organizer, in 1892. (p. 171)

How does one briefly characterize a man like Hall? The task is not an easy one, for even a cursory examination of his life and interests reveals a complex and often paradoxical figure. Some descriptive terms one finds in the historical sources include: aggressive, timid, romantic, eclectic, pioneer, promoter, founder, imperious, ambitious, dynamic, standoffish, dabbler, popularizer, inspirational, and mercurial. As Hothersall put it, Hall was "an eclectic with his feet firmly anchored in midair" (1990, p. 294).

Hall's own assessment of his life included the observation that it was a "series of fads or crazes, some strong, some weak; some lasting long and recurring over and over again at different periods of life and in different forms, and others ephemeral" (Hall, 1923, pp. 367–368). He enjoyed exploring new fields of interest but often then just moved on and left it up to others to follow through. He had a lifelong interest in novel ideas—for example, the concept of evolution was a pervasive theme for him—and as a result he was beset with the kinds of conflicts that occur when novelty meets tradition. Ironically, the very nature of this conflict mirrored the very process of evolution he embraced, and perhaps that's why he embraced it. Hall was himself

Figure 1 G. Stanley Hall in his later years.

dynamically adjusting to his environment, constantly trying to integrate the old with the new. After reading about Hall's life, one begins to see why education and the process of human development were so important to him, since these are central to the idea of adjustment.

Figure 2 Hall in 1850 at the age of 6.

In the history of psychology textbooks, Hall gets varying amounts of attention, ranging from very little coverage (or even none at all!) in one or two of the better-known books, to longer treatments in Boring (1950), Hothersall (1990), and Watson and Evans (1991). Dorothy Ross's biography of Hall (1972) provides an excellent source for those interested in many of the fascinating details of his life, and, of course, Hall's own autobiography (1923) is a key reference. In these sources examples may be found that provide evidence for all of the descriptive terms mentioned above. One is especially struck with the ambition and energy he invested in new ideas. This enthusiasm figured prominently in the leadership role he assumed for advancing the relatively new discipline of scientific psychology.

Early Life and Education

Hall was born in Ashfield, Massachusetts, on February 1, 1844. Ashfield was a rural, farming community which reflected the traditional religious and family values characteristic of New England at that time. He was descended from English immigrants who had been among the signers of the Mayflower Compact of 1620. Hall proudly described his family history in the second chapter of his autobiography (1923):

> On the whole my blood is more Saxon than Norman. Most of my ancestry was English with a slight admixture of Scotch and Irish. My parents, who cherished these traditions, made some effort, when we were small, to interest us in some of our forebears in the many volumed Plymouth records which came into our possession about 1855. (p. 27)

His mother was particularly religious and both parents were fairly well educated. According to Ross (1972), Hall's father gave Stanley six rules when he was 9 years old to "help him 'to be a good man if God lets you grow up' ":

> In the first place then, ask the advice of your parents. . . . 2nd—Hear all they have to say and remember it all. 3rd—Never reject their advice because *you cannot see* it to be wise. . . . 4th—Never allow yourself to lean to your own understanding when it conflicts with the experience of your elders. . . . 5th—Shun the person who would have you do anything that your parents disapprove. . . . 6th and last, Do not manifest a spirit of disobedience by making words before you obey. (cited in Ross, p. 5)

It is not too difficult to imagine how Hall could easily develop into the complex and seemingly paradoxical figure he became when one considers the nature of these kinds of formative constraints. During his entire life Hall walked a careful balance between his ambitions and interests on the one hand, and a sense of propriety on the other. For example, as a respected intellectual and university president he also admitted to an interest in "a love for glimpsing at first hand the raw side of human life" (Hall, 1923, p. 578). These interests took him to boxing matches, circus sideshows, morgues, and revivalist meetings.

After completing his basic schooling at the age of 16, Hall taught basic academic subjects, as well as Latin, algebra, music, and elocution, in a small private school (Hall, 1923). This period in his life lasted about a year, from the winter of 1860 to the late spring of 1861.

As he was approaching the end of his initial teaching experience, Hall missed the opportunity to participate in a major historical event, the American Civil War, which began on April 12, 1861. Although Hall was able-bodied, his father, unbeknownst to Hall at the time, bribed a "government physician" to provide his son with a "certificate of exemption from military service" and "hired a 'substitute' for me for three hundred dollars in case I should be drafted [anyway]" (1923, p. 148).

In the fall of 1862, Hall was "packed off to Williston Seminary at Easthampton, Massachusetts, only some twenty-four miles away. . . . [He] entered the senior class of 1863 in the classical department, which numbered forty-one students, three of whom were girls" (1923, p. 151). After overcoming an initial sense of social and academic inadequacy, Hall clearly liked his new school. Williston helped him improve his skills in reading and writing Latin and classical Greek—skills which were to prove helpful in his subsequent studies in theology, philosophy, and history (Sawyer, 1917).

After studying a year at Williston Seminary, Hall seems to have felt that he was sufficiently prepared for admission to a regular college:

> One day in July, 1863, I left the hayfield, where I was working with my uncle for a dollar a day, and went to Williamstown, walking eighteen miles of the way, to take private entrance examinations. I visited the three professors in mathematics, Greek, and Latin, and came home late at night, entered as a freshman in the [Williams College] class of 1867. (1923, pp. 155–156)

Williams College was regarded as a "symbol of what Americans have . . . meant by a college education" in the 1860s (Rudolph, 1956). Founded in 1793, the small liberal arts college had a faculty of 10 professors and 3 instructors, the majority of whom held doctoral degrees in theology, medicine, or philosophy (Spring, 1917). In addition, three of Hall's teachers at Williams had also studied at universities in Europe (Rudolph, 1956). Nevertheless, Hall concluded in his autobiography that "the intellectual caliber of the faculty as a whole . . . was in my period [at Williams] pretty low, probably a little lower than it had been before and certainly far more so than it later became" (1923, p. 158). Hall did well academically at Williams "with little work" and spent most of his free time reading the works of recent "poets, novelists, essayists and . . . historians" (1923, p. 160).

Figure 3 Hall shortly after his first trip to Germany.

Near the end of his freshman year in the early spring of 1864, Hall told his parents in a lengthy letter that he had experienced a religious conversion during a college revival (Ross, 1972). According to his autobiography, he was convinced at the time that "I was suffering from a conviction of sin, and accordingly, by various stages which I do not recall in detail, I was led to believe that I had been converted" (Hall, 1923, p. 163). While at Williams Hall also read romantic literature and developed an interest in philosophy.

Hall graduated from Williams College on July 31, 1867. Although he was "very uncertain as to what I would be and do in the world" (Hall, 1923, p. 177), he became a student at Union Theological Seminary in New York in September of 1867.

Hall initially studied at Union for two years from 1867 to 1869. Many of his teachers there had studied in Germany and held advanced degrees from major German universities (Prentiss, 1889). Although the facilities of the seminary were quite cramped, it had an excellent library, including many rare books. During his five terms at the seminary, Hall was subjected to a strict regimen of courses in Hebrew, Biblical exegesis, "higher" and "lower" textual criticism, church history, music, and homiletics. His favorite subject at Union was church history, which he judged to be "perhaps the strongest course" (Hall, 1923, p. 178) in his program. During this time Hall also developed a desire "to pursue advanced studies abroad" (p. 183) and an interest in the "possibility of some time becoming a professor" (p. 184).

Figure 4 Main building of Berlin University in downtown Berlin.

Germany, Antioch College, Harvard, and Germany Again

Hall arrived in Europe in July of 1869 (Ross, 1972). He worked on his German language skills in Bonn until the beginning of the school year in the autumn (Hall, 1923). Hall became a student at the University of Bonn at the beginning of the winter semester. His major professors were two conservative theologians, Johann Peter Lange (1802–1884) and Theodor Christlieb (1833–1889), and the philosopher Juergen Bona Meyer (1829–1897). Meyer was a follower of Kant with strong interests in psychology and university reform. In addition, Hall "dropped into many other [lectures]" (1923, p. 188) to further improve his skills in understanding and speaking German. He left Bonn around Christmas 1869, without completing the winter term (Eulenburg, 1904; Hall, 1923; Schaff, 1857).

In January of 1870, Hall resumed his academic studies at Berlin University, where he was formally

registered as a student of philosophy for the winter semester of 1869–1870 and the summer semester of 1870 (L. Sprung, personal communication, August 28, 1989). Hall reported that he was a very busy student during his first two terms at Berlin University, with courses in theology, church history, physiology, surgery, philosophy, physics, anthropology, and even Egyptology (Hall, 1912, 1923). He also confessed that there were some problems: "I think I must have attended lectures seven or eight hours a day, but I had too little experience in note-taking at first to get much benefit from most of them, and some, even those I had paid for, were sooner or later abandoned" (1923, p. 190).

The document from the student register lists Hall at the very bottom. It identifies him as a native of "Ashville, Massachusetts, USA" and a student of "philosophy." The occupation of his father is listed as "farming." His native country is listed as "America." The last notation indicates that he was "dropped" as a student on July 17, 1870, "due to insufficient industry in his studies." Elsewhere, he is listed as having begun his studies at Berlin University with the winter semester of 1869–1870.

In the late fall of 1870, Hall returned to New York to resume his theological studies (Ross, 1972). It was probably at this time that the famous incident occurred in which the president of the seminary prayed that Hall would be "shown the true light" (Hall, 1923, p. 178) after he had given his trial sermon. He received his degree from Union Theological Seminary in the summer of 1871 but was not ordained (Gillett, 1926).

In the fall of 1872, Hall obtained his first academic appointment at Antioch College in Yellow Springs, Ohio (Hall, 1923). He remained at this struggling Unitarian institution until 1876. When the college president retired after Hall's first year at Antioch, Hall took over his philosophy course for seniors. Hall's new course focused almost exclusively on the history of philosophy (Ross, 1972). Hall also included discussions of psychological topics in his philosophy course. After becoming acquainted with the first volume of Wundt's *Principles*, he decided to eventually return to Europe and study "experimental or physiological psychology" in Leipzig (Hall, 1923, p. 204).

After four years at Antioch, Hall decided to leave, and in September of 1876 he began two years at Harvard as an instructor of sophomore English. He also enrolled as a student of philosophy in the new graduate school at Harvard, taking most of his graduate work in psychology under William James (1844–1910). Hall also made use of a small laboratory which James had organized "under the stairways of the Aggasiz Museum" (1923, p. 218). In 1878 Hall received the first PhD ever awarded by Harvard's philosophy department. His degree was also the first American PhD on a psychological topic with a theoretical dissertation on "The Perception of Space" (Ross, 1972). This work was primarily based on library research, but he also tried to confirm his findings through experimental research in the physiological laboratory of Henry Pickering Bowditch (1840–1911).

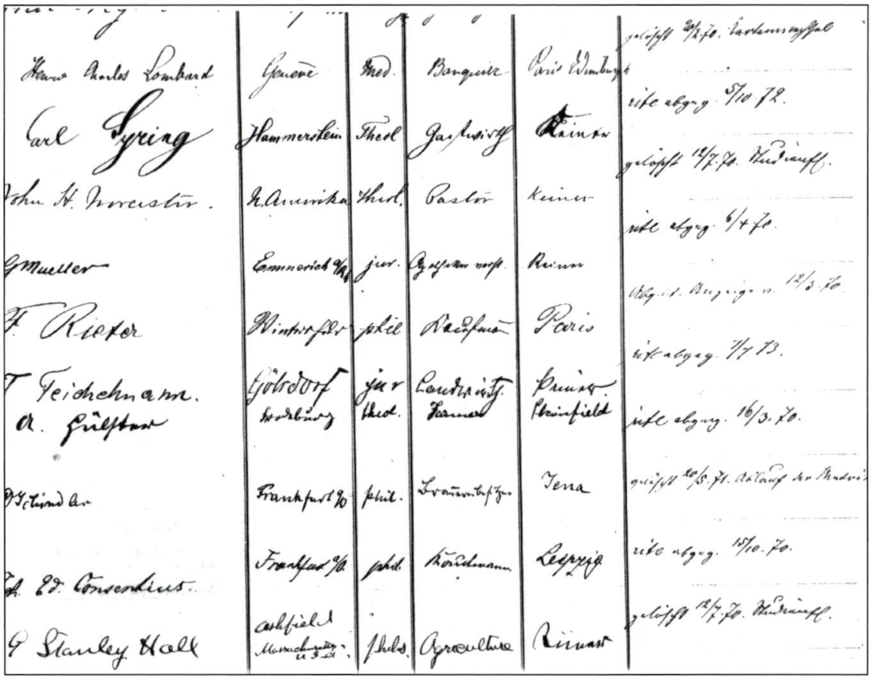

Shortly after receiving his degree, Hall returned to Germany and Berlin University in the fall of 1878. At Berlin Hall busied himself primarily with physiological studies under Hugo Kronecker for almost a year (Ross, 1972). He attended at least one course in psychology, which was offered by Friedrich Harms (1816–1880). In Berlin, Hall also became personally acquainted with the historian of early Greek philosophy, Eduard Zeller (1819–1908), whom he later included among his six "founders" of psychology (Hall, 1912).

Hall was a postgraduate student at Leipzig University during the winter term of 1879 through the following summer term (Bringmann & Bringmann, 1980). During this time, Hall "participated . . . [in

the] psychophysical laboratory" of Wilhelm Wundt (1832–1920) with "great industry and success" (Bringmann, Bringmann, & La Guardia, 1991). However, Hall was more impressed by Wundt's lectures on folk psychology with their strong historical orientation (Baldwin, 1921) than with his laboratory

Figure 5 Page from Berlin University record with information about Hall.

skills (Hall, 1923). While in Germany Hall was also married to Cornelia Fisher, a young woman he first met at Antioch.

Johns Hopkins University and Clark University

It was during the 1880s that Hall became a well-known figure in American intellectual circles. After returning to America in the fall of 1880, Hall supported himself with difficulty through lectures on educational topics for the Harvard extension program (Ross, 1972). The following spring he "was surprised and delighted to receive an invitation from the Johns Hopkins University, then the cynosure of all aspiring young professors throughout the country, to deliver a course of twelve semipublic lectures on psychology" (1923, p. 225). Hall was fully aware that any appointment at Johns Hopkins University

G. STANLEY HALL
1844-1924

Figure 6 Hall as Clark University President (ca. 1888).

opened the ultimate possibility of a chair and [I] spent the entire summer in the work of preparation. At the close of these lectures I was asked to teach a half year, after which, to my great delight, I was appointed full professor for five years with the salary of four thousand dollars, then very generous. (pp. 225–226)

Interestingly, Hall had previously applied to lecture at Johns Hopkins and was turned down three times! At this new and revolutionary American university (Hawkins, 1960), Hall taught psychology, pedagogy, and history of education until 1887. In addition, he was also responsible for a three-year course in the history of philosophy from the beginnings of Greek philosophy to Hegel (Ross, 1972).

According to his inaugural lecture as professor of psychology on October 6, 1884, the subject matter of the "New Psychology" included not only the study of "instincts" and "experimental psychology," but also "historical psychology." He clearly regarded experimental psychology as the "more central" (Hall, 1885, p. 123) of the three specialties, but he viewed historical psychology as more appropriate for students with a background in the humanities (p. 128).

In addition to his lectures and seminars at Johns Hopkins, Hall opened a small research and teaching laboratory less than a year after his initial appointment (Ross, 1972). This laboratory has arguably been described as the first psychological laboratory in the United States. He also began to publish his own journal, *The American Journal of Psychology* in the fall of 1887.

In early April of 1888, Hall was offered the presidency of Clark University in Worcester, Massachusetts, by the university's founder, Jonas Gilman Clark (1815–1900). The new university had been chartered in 1887 and possessed neither a faculty nor a campus (Koelsch, 1987). Hall accepted the appointment on the condition that the graduate school would be the "central core" of the new university and that "an undergraduate division, if it existed at all, was [to be] subordinate in importance" (Ross, 1972, p. 193). The first graduate pro-

---

2   *Proceedings of the American Psychological Association.*

ciation in Philadelphia, at the University of Pennsylvania, on Tuesday, December 27, 1892, at 10 A.M.

Professor Jastrow was appointed secretary to provide a programme for that meeting. He invites all members to submit to him at Madison, Wisconsin, titles of papers with brief abstracts and estimates of time required for presentation.

The original members who were either present at this meeting or sent letters of approval and accepted membership are the following:

Angell, Frank, Leland Stanford, Jr., University,
Baldwin, J. Mark, Toronto University,
Bryan, W. L., Indiana University,
Burnham, W. H., Clark University,
Cattell, J. McK., Columbia College,
Cowles, Edward, McLean Asylum,
Delabarre, E. B., Brown University,
Dewey, John, University of Michigan,
Fullerton, G. S., University of Pennsylvania,
Gilman, B. I., Clark University,
Griffin, E. H., Johns Hopkins University,
Hall, G. Stanley, Clark University,
Hume, J. G., Toronto University,
Hyslop, J. H., Columbia College,
James, William, Harvard University,
Jastrow, Joseph, University of Wisconsin,
Krohn, W. O., Clark University,
Ladd, G. T., Yale University,
Nichols, Herbert, Harvard University,
Noyes, William, McLean Asylum,
Patrick, G. T. W., University of Iowa,
Royce, Josiah, Harvard University,
Sanford, E. C., Clark University,
Scripture, E. W., Yale University,
Witmer, Lightner, University of Pennsylvania,
Wolfe, H. K., University of Nebraska.

The following additional members were elected:

Mills, T. Wesley, McGill College, Montreal,
Münsterberg, Hugo, Harvard University,
Ormond, A. T., Princeton College,
Pace, Edward, Catholic University, Washington,
Titchener, E. B., Cornell University.

Professor Jastrow asked the co-operation of all members for the Section of Psychology at the World's Fair, and invited correspondence upon the matter.

Figure 7 List of 1892 founding members of the American Psychological Association (APA).

II. FIRST ANNUAL MEETING:

UNIVERSITY OF PENNSYLVANIA, PHILADELPHIA, PA., 1892.

ABSTRACTS OF PAPERS.

(1) *History and Prospects of Experimental Psychology in America.* By President G. STANLEY HALL, Clark University.

This paper consisted of an abstract of an extensive History of Psychology in this country beginning with Jonathan Edwards, and coming up to the present time. The history is intended to include an account of all the important investigations, and in anticipation of the final paper any more detailed account is omitted.

Discussion by Professors Ladd and Baldwin.

Figure 8 Summary of Hall's 1893 presidential address on history and prospects of experimental psychology in America given at the first annual APA meeting in Philadelphia (1893).

grams were to include the fields of "mathematics, chemistry, physics, biology and history and social science" (Hall, 1888).

Hall moved to Worcester during that same spring and stayed as a guest in Jonas Clark's home. The university opened in the fall of 1889 with 18 faculty and 34 students. The following summer tragedy struck, and Hall's wife and 8-year-old daughter accidentally died of asphyxiation while he was away. In the aftermath of this terrible loss, it wasn't long before problems developed at the university. In fact, two years later, the faculty was in revolt, and on top of it all, President William Harper of the University of Chicago raided the campus so that by the spring of 1892 two-thirds of the faculty and 70 percent of the students had left. Hall managed to get through these difficulties, but they left their imprint on him. One effect seems to have been the development of a greater interest in religion.

Throughout the 35 years from his appointment as president to his retirement in 1923, Hall was actively involved in the teaching of psychology, philosophy, education, and related subject matters. For example, as Hall wrote (1923): "At Clark, for nearly thirty years, I have met my students at my house every Monday night from seven, often to eleven, occasionally till twelve or even later" (1923, p. 327).

In the early days at Clark, Hall and his students jointly read the works of historically important philosophers, psychologists, and scientists (viz., Plato, Descartes, Spinoza, Locke,

Hume, Kant, Schopenhauer, Hegel, etc.). As his student enrollment grew, however, Hall wrote that "nearly all our time was devoted to the reading of generally two papers an evening . . . with distinguished men brought in from outside several times a year for our edification" (p. 327).

It was also during the early years at Clark that Hall founded the American Psychological Association (APA) with a meeting in his study in July of 1892. The first formal APA meeting was held at the University of Pennsylvania on December 27 of the same year. Hall became the first APA president, and his presidential address focused on "the history and prospects of experimental psychology in America" (Hilgard, 1978).

During the remaining years of his life, Hall was active in a number of professional activities. He had already founded the *American Journal of Psychology* in 1887 and the *Journal of Genetic Psychology* (then called *Pedagogical Seminary*) in 1891; his famous two-volume work on *Adolescence* was published in 1904; he brought Freud and Jung to Clark in the fall of 1909; and in 1917 he started the *Journal of Applied Psychology*. Hall retired from Clark University after 31 years of service in June of 1920 and during the next three years published *Recreations of a Psychologist* (1920), *Senescence* (1922), and his autobiography, *Life and Confessions of a Psychologist* (1923). He died on April 24, 1924, in Worcester.

Figure 9 Cartoon of Hall and other eminent early psychologists on Mount Rushmore (1992).

Acknowledgment

Portions of this article were adapted from an earlier article which appeared in *American Psychologist, 47*(2), 281–289, copyright 1992, by the American Psychological Association. Adapted by permission of the publisher.

Bibliography

Baldwin, B. J. (1921). In memory of Wilhelm Wundt. *Psychological Review, 28,* 153–188.

Boring, E. G. (1950). *A history of experimental psychology* (2nd ed.). New York: Appleton-Century-Crofts.

Bringmann N., & Bringmann, W. (1980). Wilhelm Wundt and his first American student. In W. G. Bringmann & R. D. Tweney (Eds.), *Wundt studies* (pp. 176–192). Toronto: Hogrefe.

Bringmann, W., Bringmann, M., & La Guardia, R. (1991, March). *Hall and Wundt: A reassessment.* Paper presented at the meeting of the Southern Society for Philosophy and Psychology, Atlanta, GA.

Eulenburg, F. (1904). *Die Frequenz der Deutschen Universitaeten.* Leipzig: Teubner.

Gillett, C. R. (1926). *Alumni catalogue of the Union Theological Seminary in the city of New York 1836–1926.* New York: Union Alumni Association.

Goetzmann, W. H. (1973). *The American Hegelians.* New York: Knopf.

Hall, G. S. (1885). The new psychology. *Andover Review, 3,* 120–135, 239–248.

Hall, G. S. (1888). Letter to J. G. Clark, November 14. Worcester, MA: Clark University Archive.

Hall, G. S. (1904). *Adolescence: Its psychology and its relations to physiology, anthropology, sociology, sex, crime, religion, and education* (Vols. 1–2). New York: Appleton.

Hall, G. S. (1912). *Founders of modern psychology.* New York: Appleton.

Hall, G. S. (1920). *Recreations of a psychologist.* New York: Appleton.

Hall, G. S. (1922). *Senescence.* New York: Appleton.

Hall, G. S. (1923). *Life and confessions of a psychologist.* New York: Appleton.

Hawkins, H. (1960). *A history of the Johns Hopkins University 1874–1889.* Ithaca, NY: Cornell University Press.

Hilgard, E. (Ed.). (1978). *American psychology in historical perspective.* Washington, DC: American Psychological Association.

Hothersall, D. (1990). *History of psychology* (2nd ed.). New York: McGraw-Hill.

Koelsch, W. A. (1987). *Clark University 1887–1987.* Worcester, MA: Clark University Press.

Prentiss, G. L. (1889). *The Union Theological Seminary in the city of New York.* New York: Anson D. F. Randolph.

Pruette, L. G. (1926). *G. Stanley Hall: Biography of a mind.* New York: Appleton.

Roback, A. A. (1964). *A history of American psychology* (Rev. ed.). New York: Collier Books.

Ross, D. (1972). *G. Stanley Hall.* Chicago: University of Chicago Press.

Rudolph, F. (1956). *Mark Hopkins and the log.* London: Oxford University Press.

Sawyer, J. H. (1917). *A history of Williston Seminary.* Norwood, MA: Plimpton Press.

Schaff, P. (1857). *Germany: Its universities, theology and religion.* Philadelphia: Lindsay and Blakiston.

Spring, L. (1917). *A history of Williams College.* Boston: Houghton Mifflin.

Watson, R. I., & Evans, R. B. (1991). *The great psychologists* (5th ed.). New York: Harper & Collins.

Wilson, L. (1914). *G. Stanley Hall: A sketch.* New York: Stechert.

Alfred Binet and the Quest for Testing Higher Mental Functioning

Jacqueline L. Cunningham

The quest for testing higher mental functioning began in antiquity. It culminated at a point in time when psychology had acquired scientific methods for measuring human thought reliably while recognizing that what was replicable experimentally was less than human thought (cf. Koch, 1985). If Alfred Binet (1857–1911) is most closely associated with bringing the quest for mental testing to fruition, it is because he, better than anyone else, was able to draw from this dilemma a motive for his daily labors and inspiration for good enough solutions to a quintessential paradox.

Binet was born on July 11, 1857, in Nice, of an artist-mother and a physician-father. His mother took him to Paris to live as a boy, and he completed his secondary studies at the Lycée Saint Louis. Later, he was educated in Paris in law, a subject in which he received his first degree in 1878, but he abandoned law when he developed stronger interests in the sciences and in medicine. He took a doctorate in natural science in 1894 with a thesis on the nervous system of insects. While still a law student, Binet worked under the charismatic Jean Martin Charcot (1825–1893) at the famed Salpêtrière where he developed an interest in experiments on hypnosis. In 1886, a book he coauthored on this subject was criticized acrimoniously by a group of scholars at Nancy who were opposed to Charcot's view on the nature of suggestibility in hysterics. Criticism surrounded the authors' report that the behavior of patients observed under hypnotism was caused by energy flowing from giant magnets placed near them, rather than obviously caused by the power of suggestion. The embarrassment the criticism created for Binet formed a powerful motive for devoting his life to the study of mental processes (Wolf, 1973). Eventually, the sting of the criticism appears to have been pal-

Figure 1 The Binet family. From left to right: daughter Alice, Madame Binet (née Laure Balbiani), Alfred Binet, daughter Madeleine. (Photograph graciously contributed by Binet's granddaughters, Mlles Géraldine and Georgette Binet.)

Figure 2 Madeleine and Alice, who served sometimes as their father's research subjects, in early adolescence.

unsuccessful in obtaining the chair in experimental psychology at the Sorbonne when it was awarded to George Dumas (1866–1946) in 1905. Nonetheless, as the proper director of the laboratory in physiological psychology at the Sorbonne from 1894 until his death, and as publisher of *L'Année Psychologique*, he held a foremost position within early French psychology (Boring, 1926; Wolf, 1973).

Binet always held the experimental approach to studying psychological events in high regard, and he is best remembered as an experimental psychologist. However, he was ever mindful of the limits of this approach for studying complex human phenomena (Fancher, 1985; Varon, 1935, Wolf, 1973). His tolerance and independence of spirit made lasting impressions upon those who worked with him. This is poignantly noted in the eulogy to him by J. Larguier des Bancels (1912), which was published in *L'Année Psychologique* shortly after Binet's brutal death from a brain tumor in 1911.

The photograph in Figure 4 depicts Binet seemingly reflecting on the limited value of a laboratory apparatus for yielding significant information about the boy who appears by its side. The inscription below the picture reads: "One only needs to experi-

liated by his adoption of a disciplined but open-minded outlook regarding the means of seeking psychological knowledge.

Binet was highly productive as a psychologist. He founded with Henri Beaunis (1830–1921) the first French psychological laboratory, at the Sorbonne in 1889, and the first French journal of psychology, *L'Année Psychologique*, in 1894. Although he was unquestionably influential, his career was beleaguered by his having to bear the disappointment of losing the competition with Pierre Janet (1859–1947) for the chair of Théodule Ribot (1839–1916) in experimental and comparative psychology at the Collège de France in 1896. He was also

Figure 3 Binet and some of his collaborators in the Laboratory of Physiological Psychology at the Sorbonne (ca. 1894), the year in which Binet became director of the laboratory. From left to right: J. Courtier, Binet, J. Philippe, and V. Henri.

ment and observe, this is true; but how difficult it is to find the true formula of an experiment" (p. 15).

Interest in testing higher mental functioning required a willingness to abandon conventional ideas about the appropriateness of data, the use of subjects, and the kind of subject matter needed to serve psychology's fundamental purpose of understanding human nature. To Binet, such a quest meant seeking a way to measure thought in its activity and fluidity, or as an assemblage of complex operations comprised of, among others, acts of judgment and comprehension. This signified a need to diverge from the experimentation characteristic of established traditions (Binet, 1886).

Binet's ability to depart from German structuralism was a contribution which was emphasized by his long-time associate, Théodore Simon (1873–1961), in the latter's own eulogy to Binet in the 1912 edition of *L'Année Psychologique*. The signature page reproduced at right served as the preface to Simon's memorial to Binet; as such, it left his lasting epithet. The inscription reads: "Thought evolves from a vague state toward a fixed state" (p. 1).

Binet's goal of observing the fluidity rather than content of thought was realized when he found ways to observe systematically differences among

Figure 5 Signature page which accompanied Théodore Simon's eulogy to Binet (1912).

individuals in their performance of complex cognitive tasks. Examples of this work included: naturalistic observations of his two daughters' approaches to solving novel problems; analogue studies of the eyewitness testimony of schoolchildren and group conformity; analyses of the cognitive strategies used by extraordinary chess players and mental calculators; and laboratory research of memory, including memory for prose passages. All of this research was conducted in addition to the popularly known mental scale of intelligence, which Binet first published with Simon in 1905. Several reviewers have re-evaluated Binet's lesser known work and found it surprisingly modern and of greater importance than was generally recognized in the 100 years that followed (Thieman & Brewer, 1978; Cunningham, 1988; Siegler, 1992).

Binet's success in observing complex mental functioning required a penchant for inference when interpreting psychological results and caution in

Figure 4 Signature page which accompanied J. Larguier des Bancel's 1912 eulogy to Binet.

accepting quantitative data. Indeed, to him, being scientific meant being "prudent" and "modest" regarding laboratory findings. To illustrate this point, in a 1908 article in *L'Année Psychologique*, Binet reported on one of his experiments from his educational anthropometric laboratory, a laboratory which frequently observed physical stigmata in abnormal children. In this case, the study had compared the respiration of students using either a proper or improper posture when handwriting. A "pneumograph" had been used to accurately measure their rate of respiration.

Binet reported that the results of the study had been identical for both students. He went on to say:

> Surely, we must not . . . reach from these results, [which were] very well measured, very precise and consequently *very limited* [italics added], general conclusions which they do not comport. . . . Do they mean that among young boys, it is useless to correct and prevent [poor posture]? That would be a dangerous overstatement. . . . If we conducted this observation of [experimental] control it was to reinforce, once and for all, a lesson in prudence and modesty. The questions of pedagogical physiology are extremely complicated. A phenomenon which can inscribe a clear tracing [on a measuring device] is not a phenomenon . . . which is explained. . . . The most perfected instruments . . . are not infallible. Infallibility does not exist in instruments any more than it does in *minds* [italics added]. (1908, pp. 430–431)

Figures 6 and 7 Figure 6 (top) shows the student with the proper posture having his respiration monitored by "pneumography" in Binet's educational anthropometric laboratory, while Figure 7 (bottom) shows the one with the improper posture having his respiration monitored.

Indeed, a specific focus on the "fallibility" of human minds, or on the possibilities for individual variation in the expression of a complex mental function, was characteristic of Binet's work in psychology. Whereas the Wundtian style of experimentation emphasized laboratory investigation of the normal processes of cognition—primarily at the level of the perception of simple sensory stimulations by trained adult observers—Binet himself never intended to illuminate the invariant qualities of mind (Fancher, 1985). Accordingly, his lasting contribution was to find ways of observing how

specific mental attributes are manifested within groups of individuals. This orientation is well represented in his studies of the eyewitness testimony of children.

The eyewitness testimony investigations were conducted with students in the natural environment of their school rooms using multimethod strategies which were radical at the time, but which bore the hallmark of Binet's approach to experimentation. As described in *La suggestibilité* (Binet, 1900), the procedure was to specify the age and academic aptitude of each member of a small group of male ele-

312

mentary schoolchildren between the ages of 7 through 14 years, and to study the relationships between these variables and various tests of suggestibility arranged serially for their level of cognitive and social complexity. Beginning with simple laboratory tasks, Binet, as the experimenter, took each of the students through a set of experiments which culminated in observations on eyewitness behavior and on the phenomenon of social contagion. The research questions centered on how age and aptitude are associated with resistance to conformity as attempts to influence become more compelling.

Interestingly, in the French manner of seeing the subject as a case study rather than an anonymous object (cf. Danziger, 1990), Binet published the pictures of the children who participated in the investigations. These are shown in Figures 8 and 9, with the picture on the left showing the children who were most suggestible, and the one on the right showing those most resistant to suggestion.

One of Binet's tests in the series of analogue studies of eyewitness testimony consisted of directing the students, who were tested individually, to attend carefully to a poster which would be shown for only 12 seconds. The students were to try to remember as many details on it as possible. He then showed the poster, on which was affixed a coin, a button, a stamp, a tag, a photograph, and a small magazine picture of a crowd. When asking for the students' recall of the objects, Binet used varying forms of interrogation.

Given that Binet's classification of the students into two groups consisting of the most and least suggestible had obvious implications for interpreting differences between the groups, results were probably more than expected, although unsurprising. It seems that Binet's quest since the humiliation he had suffered regarding the nature of suggestibility 14 years earlier had run a fateful course. Overall findings (Binet, 1900) on the several experimental tests indicated that, while individual characteristics

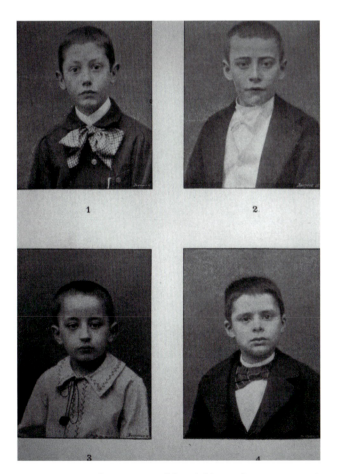
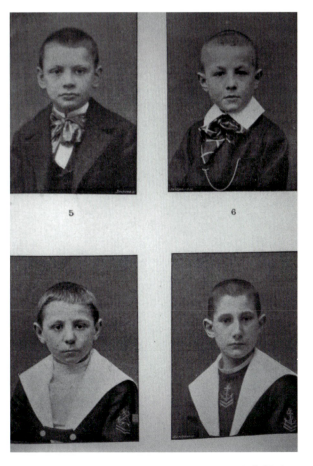

Figures 8 and 9 Pictures of the children who participated in Binet's investigations on eyewitness testimony. Figure 8 (left) shows the children who were most suggestible, and Figure 9 (right) shows those who were most resistant to suggestibility.

of the children contributed much variability, results on accuracy of recall and resistance to leading questions were mainly a function of method of obtaining information! Similar findings have been consistently reported in contemporary investigations of memory reconstruction (Loftus, 1975).

Binet's approaches to studying suggestibility are cogent examples of how his interest in the fallibility of mind, rather than its invariance, required that he depart from established notions of what was possible for psychology. In his quest to observe complex mental functioning, he contributed a tolerance and originality which broadened the parameters of psychological science. Ultimately, his interest in the fluidity of thought helped build a bridge linking the fluxional quality of human nature with the surer hubris of psychological knowledge. Because of this, as J. Larguier des Bancels (1912) said at the time of Binet's death: "His name is assured the most enduring future" (p. 2).

Bibliography

Binet, A. (1900). *La suggestibilité* [Suggestibility]. Paris: Schleicher Frères.

Binet, A. (1908). Le pédagogue doit-il être psychologue? [Should the educator be a psychologist?]. *L'Année Psychologique, 14,* 405–431.

Boring, E. G. (1926). *A history of experimental psychology.* New York: The Century Co.

Cunningham, J. L. (1988). The pioneer work of Alfred Binet on children as eyewitnesses. *Psychological Reports, 62,* 271–277.

Danziger, K. (1990). *Constructing the subject: Historical origins of psychological research.* New York: Cambridge University Press.

Fancher, R. E. (1985). *The intelligence men: Makers of the I.Q. controversy.* New York: W. W. Norton.

Koch, S. (1985). The nature and limits of psychological knowledge: Lessons of a century qua "science." In S. Koch & D. E. Leary (Eds.), *A century of psychology as science* (pp. 75–97). New York: McGraw-Hill Book Company.

Larguier des Bancels, J. (1912). L'oeuvre d'Alfred Binet [The work of Alfred Binet]. *L'Année Psychologique, 18,* 15–32.

Loftus, E. F. (1975). Leading questions and the eyewitness report. *Cognitive Psychology, 7,* 560–572.

Siegler, R. (1992). The other Alfred Binet. *Developmental Psychology, 28,* 179–190.

Simon, T. (1912). Alfred Binet. *L'Année Psychologique, 18,* 1–14.

Thieman, T. J., & Brewer, W. F. (1978). Alfred Binet on memory for ideas. *Genetic Psychology Monographs, 97,* 243–264.

Varon, E. J. (1935). The development of Alfred Binet's psychology. *Psychological Monographs, 46*(3) (Whole No. 207).

Wolf, T. H. (1973). *Alfred Binet.* Chicago: University of Chicago Press.

The Beginnings of Educational Psychology in Germany

Paul Probst

Ernst Friedrich Wilhelm Meumann (1862–1915) is recognized for his contributions to the establishment of educational psychology in Germany. He did this by applying and adapting the ideas and methods of experimental psychology to pedagogical issues and problems. While the following overview of Meumann's life focuses primarily on his scientific achievements, his personal qualities and the cultural context in which he lived and worked will also be addressed.

The son of a Protestant minister, Ernst Meumann was born in 1862, in the small community of Uerdingen in the Rhine Province of the German Kingdom of Prussia. In 1915, Meumann died in Hamburg, where he had held a tenured professorship in philosophy and psychology since 1911. Meumann's life was largely influenced by the political situation of the Second German Empire (1871–1914). This period was characterized by far-reaching cultural change, the dissolution of intellectual traditions, and pronounced societal tensions. These were caused by the clash between the authoritarian government of Germany and a wealth of social, cultural, and intellectual reform organizations and movements.

Meumann studied Protestant theology and philosophy from 1883 to 1891, at the universities of Tübingen, Berlin, Halle, and Bonn. After completing all of the required examinations, he decided not to become a minister after all. Meumann's decision not to follow in his father's footsteps was caused by a serious religious crisis which caused him to lose his faith and sever all ties with organized Christianity.

After leaving theology, Meumann decided to pursue a career in philosophy and psychology. He studied philosophy under the philosophers Christoph Sigward (1830–1904) and Edmund Pfleiderer (1842–1902) at Tübingen University. He completed

Figure 1 Ernst Meumann (ca. 1912).

his first dissertation on "Principles of Association and Reproduction" in 1891. After Tübingen, Meumann became associated with Wilhelm Wundt (1832–1920), first as a student and then as Wundt's assistant. While he was with Wundt, he conducted research on the "Psychology of the Time Sense"

Figure 2 Celebration of Wundt's 70th birthday in 1902. Meumann is in the back row, second on the right.

tion of the knowledge that was accumulating from the empirical research in psychology. Meumann's interest in these issues may well go back to his unhappy experiences as a high school and boarding school student in Elberfeld and Gütersloh (according to his brother, Friedrich Meumann, 1915).

Meumann named his new field of expertise "experimental pedagogy," which included the modern fields of educational psychology and applied education. His first program for experimental pedagogy, which was based on a lecture before a convention of Swiss teachers, appeared in 1900.

It is obvious that Meumann's view of educational psychology was strongly influenced by the international reform movements in education, which at this time were popular in Europe and North America. These intellectual movements are associated with the names of John Dewey (1859–1952) and his progressive education movement, of G. Stanley Hall (1844–1924) and his child study movement (Misawa, 1908), and of Ellen Key (1849–1926) and her child-centered education group. Ellen Key, a Swedish educational reformer and advocate of women's rights, argued in her most popular book, *The Century of the Child* (1900), that during the 20th century an understanding of the nature of the child had to play a greater role in the field of education. The only educational authorities Key accepted were "Montaigne, Rousseau . . . Spencer and the new writings in child psychology" (Key, 1921, p. 283). Meumann had a special interest in developing Key's "psychology of children and youths" on a scientific basis. Specifically, he viewed experimental pedagogy as a branch of the contemporary German School Reform Movement.

To Meumann, experimental psychology was to be the "intellectual mother" of empirical and experimental research in the field of education (Meumann, 1911b, p. 2). It was his goal to utilize these fields to change radically the traditional "schools with their exclusive emphasis on academic learning" and their "oppression of the children's natural inclinations" (Meumann, 1911a, p. 6). Meumann also believed that

(Meumann, 1893, 1894a, 1896). His second dissertation (his "research dissertation") focused on "The Psychology and Esthetics of Rhythm" (1894b). This work, which was published in Wundt's *Philosophical Studies*, was evaluated by Wundt as "the most outstanding achievement in experimental psychology" of the period (Wundt, 1915, p. 212). In later years, Meumann was involved in a number of scientific controversies with his former teacher, yet they managed to remain friends (Bringmann & Ungerer, 1980).

In 1897, the 35-year-old Meumann accepted a tenured appointment as Professor of Philosophy and Theory of Education at Zürich University in Switzerland. At this small but excellent university, Meumann began to reform the science of education and the German public school systems through the applica-

his own views of education were an improvement on the educational traditions of Jean-Jacques Rousseau (1712–1778) and Johann Heinrich Pestalozzi (1746–1827): "Due to the inadequate psychology of his time, Rousseau could only sense but not formulate clearly how the child differs from adults. Modern school reformers possess [precise] norms for the field and can reorganize the curriculum and the activities of the classroom accordingly" (1911a, p. 6).

In the same article he made the following comments about Pestalozzi: "What Pestalozzi and his incomplete psychology could only speculate about and not prove, our experimental analysis of the intellectual work of the school child will directly affect the teaching of basic subjects [like] reading and writing" (1911a, p. 11).

Beginning with his first academic position in Zürich, Meumann actively followed the research in psychology as it was developing internationally. According to Fraser, who knew him well (1915): "[Meumann] actually attempted to read all the articles first hand in four or five languages" (p. 428).

Meumann's laboratory was a frequent stop for visitors from Germany and abroad who wanted to learn more about his methods of experimental pedagogy. Henry H. Goddard (1886–1957), the scientific director of a large residential center for the mentally retarded, was one of the early visitors. In this communication, Meumann agreed to make his own "very small" Zürich laboratory available to Goddard during the summer of 1904 to conduct a series of studies on "fatigue." He suggested some research questions for his American guest but regretfully would not be able to meet Goddard due to other, earlier plans.

Meumann also maintained close contact with teachers, especially those at the elementary levels throughout his university career.

After Zürich, Meumann held prestigious appointments at the universities of Königsberg, Münster, Halle, Leipzig, and finally at the Hamburg Colonial Institute. His feelings about the call from Albertus University in Königsberg were rather mixed, as he expressed them in a letter to a friend in Zürich (Meumann, 1905):

> I would not exactly like to leave Zürich. Königsberg frightens me—the Russian border, the long snow-filled winters, the lack of mountains and only the ocean as consolation. The appointment in Prussia has many advantages. One gradually rises in salary to 7,500 Swiss Franks. In addition, there is a housing allowance of 740. Thus, one does not have to worry about old age, because the full salary continues after retirement. (pp. 5–6)

Between 1907 and 1908, Meumann published four major works. The first was his monograph, *Intelligence and Will* (1908a), which focused on the interplay of cognitive and motivational processes. In this work, Meumann introduced ideas and models which are still relevant for modern research in the field (Schmalt & Heckhausen, 1990).

Meumann's most important work, his *Introductory Lectures on Experimental Pedagogy and its Psychological Basis* (1907), came out in two heavy volumes. This book, which was dedicated to the professional organizations of teachers in Germany, was a required textbook for several generations of education students. A second and much larger printing was produced from 1911 to 1914 (1911b, 1913a, 1914). The content of the work included information and discussions of developmental psychology, differential psy-

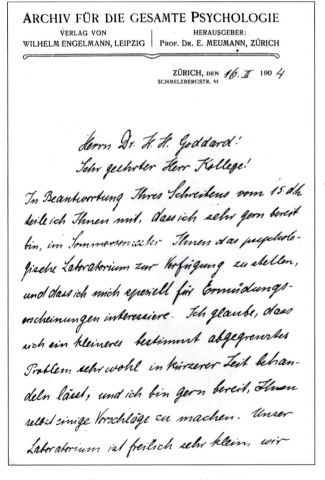

Figure 3 Letter from Meumann to Goddard (1904).

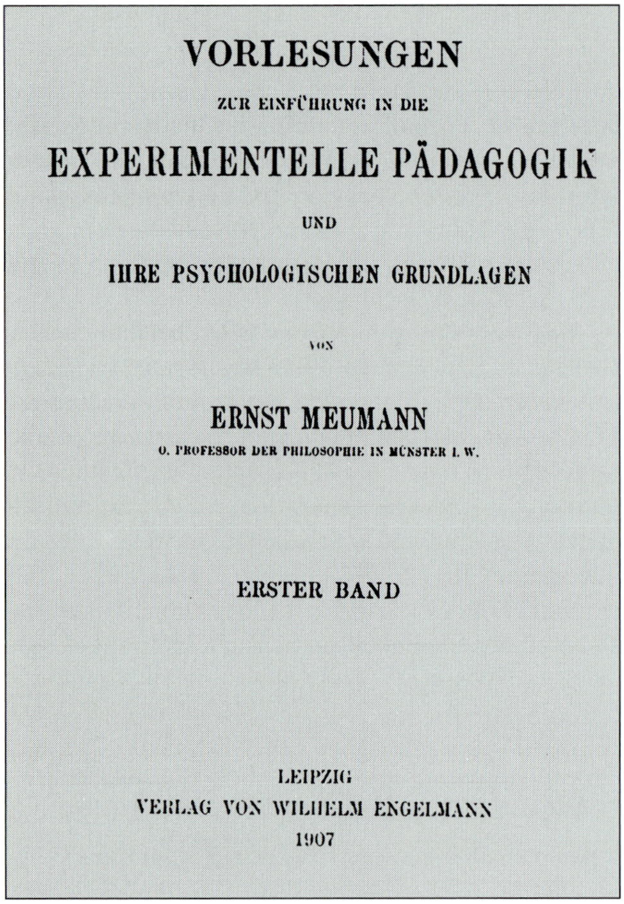

VORLESUNGEN

ZUR EINFÜHRUNG IN DIE

EXPERIMENTELLE PÄDAGOGIK

UND

IHRE PSYCHOLOGISCHEN GRUNDLAGEN

VON

ERNST MEUMANN

O. PROFESSOR DER PHILOSOPHIE IN MÜNSTER I. W.

ERSTER BAND

LEIPZIG
VERLAG VON WILHELM ENGELMANN
1907

Figure 4 Title page of *Lectures* (1907).

schools that sound rather modern. His lengthy discussion of "Mental Hygiene in the Schools," focused on the adjustment of students and teachers.

Meumann's magnum opus was well received by educational specialists around the world. Terman (1914/1915) regarded the publication of Meumann's *Lectures* as "one of the most important events in the history of applied psychology" (p. 75). An even more laudatory book review was published in the *Psychological Bulletin* by Bell (1915): "It is monumental in its size, in its scope, in its penetrating analysis, and in the fact that it comes as the crowning effort of a life of untiring industry and enthusiastic investigation. . . . Almost every page of the book reveals the catholicity of the author's reading" (p. 400).

Meumann's compendium of memory research, *Economy and Technique of Memory*, appeared in 1908b. This volume concentrated on the practical needs of school life. Its third, expanded edition (1912a), was translated into English by Baird. Meumann's introduction to the English edition stressed the close relationships between American and German psychologists and educators (Meumann, 1913b):

> Experimental psychology and . . . experimental pedagogy are based on the joint effort of students of psychology in the United States and Germany; it may indeed be said that these sciences have been created by the two nations . . . . In both

chology, intelligence testing, and a psychology-based presentation of teaching methods.

In his books Meumann covered many problems and issues which are still relevant even today. For example, he discussed the "ecological validity" of laboratory research. Specifically, he stressed that traditional memory experiments with nonsense syllables must be expanded to include meaningful materials, like vocabulary lists and prose texts. To maximize the transfer of research results to actual educational practice, Meumann (1911b) urged researchers to concentrate their work on school-related learning. He also offered comments about the preventive and mental health functions of

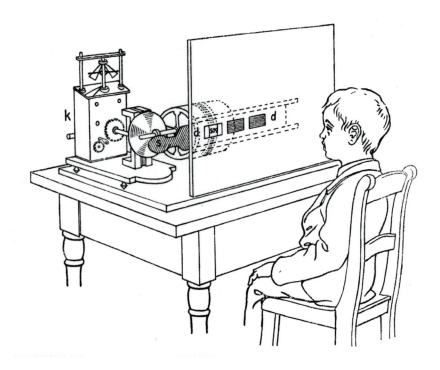

Figure 5 Typical memory experiment after Meumann (1911).

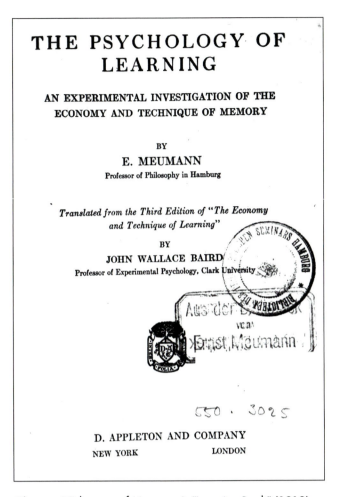

Figure 6 Title page of Meumann's "Learning Book" (1913).

countries there is a deep-rooted conviction that the most important problems of . . . education can only be solved by an appeal to experimental psychology and by the application of psychological methods to the problems of pedagogy. (p. V)

In 1908c, Meumann also published his *Introduction to Modern Esthetics*. The field of psychological aesthetics enabled Meumann, who also maintained close contacts with representatives of art history and related specialties, to establish another research specialty. His chief interest remained the aesthetic aspects of modern life as expressed in furniture and interior decoration.

Meumann's work was well received outside Germany. Translations of his books appeared primarily in Russia and later in the newly formed Soviet Union. Latvia and Estonia should also be singled out in this context, as well as Spain, Portugal, and Argentina.

In 1909, Meumann was appointed to succeed Hermann Ebbinghaus (1850–1909) at the University of Halle-Wittenberg. He moved to a Professorship of

Philosophy and Education at Leipzig in 1910, and in 1911, he was called to a full professorship of "philosophy with a concentration in psychology" at the Colonial Institute in Hamburg. This institute and the so-called "Hamburg Lecture Program" were the antecedents of the present-day University of Hamburg, which was officially established in 1919. The Colonial Institute was organized to prepare civil servants and merchants who planned to pursue careers in the German colonies, by providing scientific and praxis-oriented training programs. The Lecture Program, on the other hand, was designed to provide a variety of continuing education courses for various academic careers. Primarily, however, it served the educational needs of male and female elementary school teachers. Although it was originally anticipated that psychology would be included in the training program of the Colonial Institute, this did not materialize due to Meumann's limited interest in this particular program. At Hamburg, Meumann offered some courses in philosophy proper, but his chief responsibility was teaching experimental psychology.

Meumann's call to Hamburg and the definition of his academic responsibilities were strongly influenced by the organizations of public school teachers in Hamburg. These teachers were often members of the organization designated The Friends of Patriotic Schools and Education and they hoped that Meumann and modern psychology would help improve their status and working conditions. In general, the teachers supported the powerful, local School Reform Movement, which is still known today as the Hamburg School Movement. This group was particularly interested in the artistic, ethical, and emotional education of children.

Meumann accepted the call to Hamburg in 1911. Thus, his appointment to the directorship of the Philosophical Seminar and Psychological Laboratory can be viewed as the beginning of academic psychology in Hamburg (Probst, 1989, 1990a,b, 1991, 1995). Meumann himself viewed this appointment as the culmination of his scientific and professional life because his working conditions in Hamburg were the best he had ever known. Meumann's work was especially popular among Hamburg's elementary school teachers. For example, his lecture course titled "Introduction to Experimental Psychology and Applied Pedagogy" had to be moved to the largest auditorium because it attracted almost 200 students.

Meumann was the founder and editor of several internationally respected journals in psychology.

These included *The Archives of Psychology* (1903–1914/1915) and *The Journal for Educational Psychology* (1911–1915)—formerly called *The Journal of Experimental Education.*

Meumann became involved in political and social questions as a university student (Petersdorff, 1900). In Hamburg he continued active political involvement with scientific and educational questions. As a member of the executive committee of the German Federation for School Reform, Meumann was regarded as one of the "most progressive" reformers in Germany. He advocated a fully unified school system and the organization of academic rather than normal school training programs for teachers.

Between 1912 and 1914, Meumann designed and organized the Institute for Youth Research in Hamburg which was financed by the various teachers' organizations. This facility focused chiefly on the regional and international coordination of research with children and adolescents. In addition, it maintained a resource library for the school reform movements, including collections of children's drawings and essays. According to Meumann, the new institute (1912b) was to serve as a "a center for . . . practical efforts associated with . . . research on the problems of the young. Such an institute was to form the core of work with young people in psychology, anthropology, ethics, education, mental hygiene and social work" (p. 1).

As far as his character and personality were concerned, Meumann was not a quiet and stable individual. His extended correspondence with Wundt depicts Meumann as a person who went through phases of enthusiastic optimism and energy alternated with periods of sickness and depression (Probst, in press). Some of his contemporaries noted his "untiring industry and enthusiastic investigation" (Bell, 1915, p. 400) and regarded him as an "indefatigable worker" (Fraser, 1915, p. 428).

Meumann was generally known as an exciting and "stimulating" teacher (Fraser, 1915, p. 428). Others noted his "enthusiasm for social ideas . . . his strictly ethical view of life and a truly Kantian conscientiousness" (Störring, 1915, p. 271).

Fraser described Meumann as shy and humble in personal contact (1915): "he was always modest and unassuming. . . . As a man Meumann was the essence of courtesy. It was next to impossible to get the better of him in a bout of compliments. When all resources failed, he would come out victorious with the remark 'I feel just the same about you' " (p. 429).

In 1915, shortly after the beginning of World War I, Meumann was invited to give a series of lectures on "Applied Psychology" and "Business Ethics" at the Business School of New York University. Meumann was to receive an honorary doctorate from NYU on that occasion; however, he died from pneumonia shortly before the planned trip to New York.

Meumann remained an agnostic (or, more likely, an atheist) until the end of his life. His last will and testament reflect this outlook on life (Meumann, 1912c): "I wish to be cremated without any religious ceremony. . . . I have lived without religion and wish to die and be buried without religion. My life was a hard struggle for wisdom, personal nobility and inner peace" (p. 6). A clause in Meumann's will donated his extensive scientific library to the Philosophical Seminar in Hamburg. The approximately 2,000 volumes are preserved today in the libraries of the academic institutes for psychology, education, and philosophy. Meumann's books can be identified by the special stamp on them which reads "Gift from Professor Ernst Meumann" (Probst, 1988).

Meumann's ideas and published research were not accepted by

Figure 7 Major lecture hall in Hamburg (1911).

Figure 8 Meumann's personal bookmark ("Ex Libris").

everyone. He was accused of overestimating the importance and relevance of empirical psychology for everyday life and professional practice. Leaders in education and philosophy opposed Meumann's inclination towards "psychologism," the view that psychology should hold a dominant position in the human sciences. These opponents feared that empirical psychology and its mountain of facts would eventually destroy the normative branch of education and ethics in general. Criticisms of Meumann's somewhat naive art psychology did result in a significant revision of his views.

Although no comprehensive history of Meumann's work exists as yet, a preliminary assessment of his contributions to psychology is possible. Meumann deserves full credit for making the empirical and experimental psychology of his time accessible to the field of education. This achievement provided an important foundation for the future expansion of applied psychology.

Bibliography

Bell, J. C. (1915). Special Review: Vorlesungen sur Einführung in die experimentelle Pädagogik und ihre psychologischen Grundlagen (E. Meumann, 2nd ed, Vol. 3, 1914). *Psychological Bulletin, 12*, 400–402.

Bringmann, W. B. & Ungerer, G. A. (1980). Experimental vs. educational psychology: Wilhelm Wundt's letters to Ernst Meumann. *Psychological Research, 42*, 57–73.

Key, E. (1921). *Das Jahrhundert des Kindes: Studien.* Berlin: Fischer. (Originally published in 1900 in Swedish, 1902 in German.)

Meumann, E. (1894a). Beiträge zur Psychologie des Zeitsinns (Fortsetzung). *Philosophische Studien, 9*, 264–306.

Meumann, E. (1894b). Untersuchungen sur Psychologie und Ästhetik des Phythmus. *Philosophische Studien, 10*, 249–322, 393–430.

Meumann, E. (1896). Beiträge zur Psychologie des Zeitbewußtsein. *Philosophische Studien, 12*, 127–254.

Meumann, E. (1900). Entsehung und Ziele der Experimentellen Pädagogik. *Bericht über die Verhandlungen der Zürcherishen Schulsynode,* p. 70–105.

Meumann, E. (1905). *Brief Ernst Meumanns an Frl. Keller* (Zürich, June 29, 1905) Hamburg: Privatsammlung P. Probst.

Meumann, E. (1907). *Vorlesungen zur Einführung in die experimentelle Pädagogik und ihre psychologischen Grundlagen* (2 vols.) Leipzig:Engelmann.

Meumann, E. (1908a). *Intelligenz und Wille.* Leipzig: Quelle & Meyer.

Meumann, E. (1908b). *Ökonomie und Technik des Gedächtnisses. Experimentelle Untersuchungen über das Merken und Behalten* (2nd ed. of *Über Ökonomie und Technik des Lernens*). Leipzig: Klinkhardt.

Meumann, E. (1908c). *Einführung in die Ästhetik der Gegenwart* (Wissenschaft und Bildung, 30). Leipzig: Quelle & Meyer.

Meumann, E. (1911a). Experimentelle Pädagogik und Schulreform. *Zeitschrift für pädagogische Psychologie, 12*, 1–13.

Meumann, E. (1911b). *Vorlesungen zur Einführung in die experimentelle Pädagogik und ihre psychologischen Grundlagen* (2nd ed., Vol. 1). Leipzig: Engelmann.

Meumann. E. (1912a). *Ökonomie und Technik des Gedächtnisses. Experimentelle Untersuchungen über das Merken und Behalten* (3rd ed.). Leipzig: Klinkhardt.

Meumann, E. (1912b). *Über Institute der Jugendkunde.* Leipzig: Teubner.

Meumann, E. (1912c). *Mein Testament: Ernst Friedrich Wilhelm Meumann.* County Court, Hamburg, Division II for Wills and Probate (T. 700-15), File on the will of Dr. E. F. W. Meumann, deceased April 26, 1915, Hamburg.

Meumann, E. (1913a). *Vorlesungen zur Einführung in die experimentelle Pädagogik und ihre psychologischen Grundlagen* (2nd ed., Vol. 2). Leipzig: Engelmann.

Meumann, E. (1913b). *The psychology of learning: An experimental investigation of the economy and technique of memory* (J. W. Baird, Trans.). New York: Appleton. (Original work published in 1912, *Ökonomie und Technik des Gedächtnisses. Experimentelle Untersuchungen über das Merken und Behalten* [3rd ed.])

Meumann, E. (1914). *Vorlesungen sur Einführung in die experimentelle Pädagogik und ihre psychologischen Grundlagen.* (2nd ed., Vol. 3). Leipzig: Engelmann.

Meumann, F. (1915). Im Gedenken an Ernst Meumanns Jugend und Studienzeit. *Zeitschrift für Pädagogische Psychologie, 16*, 257–262.

Misawa, T. (1908). Psychological Literature: Vorlesungen sur Einführung in die experimentelle Pädagogik und ihre psychologischen Grundlagen von Ernst Meumann, 2 Vols., Leipzig, 1907. *American Journal of Psychology, 19*, 568–569.

Probst, P. (1988). Das Schicksal der Bibliotek Ernst Meumanns (Historische Seite), *Psychologie Rundschau, 39*, 212.

Probst, P. (1989). ernst Meumann als Begründeder empirischen Psychologie in Hamburg. *Psychologie und Geschichte, 1*(2), 6–16.

Probst, P. (1990b). "Den Lehrplan tunlichst noch durch eine Vorlesung über Negerpsychologie ergänzen"—Bedeutung des Kolonialinstituts für die Institutionalisierung der akademisch-empirischen Psychologie in Hamburg. *Psychologie und Geschichte, 2*(1), 25–36.

Probst, P. (1995). Das Hamburger Psychologische Institut (1911-1994): Vom Psychologischen Laboratorium sum Fachbereich Psychologie: Ein geschichtlicher Überblick. In K. Pawlik (Ed.). *Bericht über den 39. Kongreß der Deutschen Gesellschaft für Psychologie in Hamburg 1994: Schwerpunktthema Persönlichkeit und Verhalten.* Göttingen: Hogrefe.

Probst, P. (in press). *Briefwechsel Ernst Meumann—Wilhelm Wundt 1895–1915.*

Schmalt, H.-D. & Heckhausen, H. (1990). Motivation. In H. Spada (Ed.) *Allgemeine Psychologie* (pp. 451–494). Bern: Huber.

Störring, G. (1915). Ernst Meumann, 1869–1915. *American Journal of Psychology, 34*, 271–274.

Terman, L. M. (1914/15). Review of Meumann on the Test of Endowment. *Journal of Psycho-Asthenics, 19,* 75–94, 123–134, 187–192.

Wundt, W. (1915). Zur Erinnerung an Ernst Meumann. *Zeitschrift für Pädagogische Psychologie, 16*, 211–214.

William Stern

Wilfred Schmidt

On May 7, 1885, William Stern, who was then 14 years old, wrote in his diary: "I was reading old letters written by my grandfather; what a great man that must have been! To emulate him is my most ardent desire" (Stern, 1926, p. 58).

The grandfather to whom he referred was Sigismund Stern (1812–1867), historian, educator, and one of the leading men in the Jewish religious reform movement in Germany. The admiration of the 14-year-old Stern was no passing infatuation; it determined not only his choice of an academic career, but also his self-understanding as a German of Jewish faith, no less German than Catholic or Protestant Germans.

Although his parents were always financially troubled, he attended the classical Gymnasium (high school) and studied at the University of Berlin. At Berlin he obtained his PhD as a student of Moritz Lazarus (1824–1903), the noted linguist, and of Hermann Ebbinghaus (1850–1909), the experimental psychologist, known best for his classical experiments on memory. Under the sponsorship of Ebbinghaus, who in the meantime had moved to Breslau in Silesia (today Wroclaw in Poland), Stern submitted his second dissertation for the Dr. habil., which secured for him the right to teach at Breslau University. He spent the next 19 years at the University of Breslau, first as an unsalaried lecturer until 1909, and then as associate professor. In 1916 he moved to Hamburg as successor to Ernst Meumann at the Colonial Institute and in 1919 became professor and director of the psychological institute at the University of Hamburg, which he had helped found. In 1931, on the occasion of the congress of the Deutsche Gesellschaft für Psychologie and as its newly elected president, he was able to point with pride to the spacious accommodations of the Insti-

tute of Psychology and to the numerous research projects carried out or still in progress since 1919 and to a long list of publications. In the same year, on the occasion of his 60th birthday, a *Festschrift* honored him, and in 1932 a large contingent of American psychologists attending the International Psychology Congress in Copenhagen visited Stern's institute. Only one year later, when Hitler came to power, Stern was dismissed from his position as professor and director of the institute. Eventually he emigrated via Holland to the United States, where until his sudden death on May 28, 1938, he taught at Duke University in North Carolina as a guest professor.

According to his son Günther (Anders, 1950), William Stern, while still a student at the University of Berlin, listed all the themes that he wanted to work on during his lifetime, and he did, in fact, remain remarkably close to those early plans. But even more remarkable is the record of creative and innovative research that he had carried out between 1897 and 1909. International recognition followed. In 1909, at the age of 38, he was invited, together with Sigmund Freud and Carl Jung, by Stanley Hall, the president of Clark University, to participate in the celebrations of the 20th anniversary of the founding of Clark University. At Clark, Stern had an honorary doctorate bestowed on him; but for exactly what was he being honored?

One look at Stern's own monographs and books (9) and papers in scientific journals (59) is sufficient to make us realize that here a kind of psychology was in the process of emerging that differed fundamentally from the traditional mainstream psychology. His programmatic work on the psychology of individual differences (1900), in which he introduced the term "differential psychology," indicated

Figure 1 William and Clara Stern in Hamburg (1916).

the new direction in which psychology was to move: towards understanding individuality, the person, the total personality, and closely related to this, the applications of psychology in all domains of public life. In order to promote research in one of the areas of applied research, he founded the *Contributions to the Psychology of Testimony* which appeared from 1903 to 1906. The lectures he gave at the Clark Uni-

versity celebrations were on the study of individuality and on the psychology of testimony. In the very first issue of the *Contributions* in 1903, he published a lengthy paper in which he dealt with theoretical and methodological issues in all domains of applied psychology, specifically in education and schools, and in commerce and industry. This venture was followed in 1908 by the founding of the *Journal of*

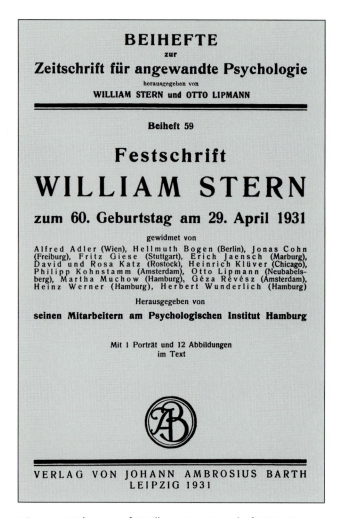

BEIHEFTE
zur
Zeitschrift für angewandte Psychologie
herausgegeben von
WILLIAM STERN und OTTO LIPMANN

Beiheft 59

Festschrift
WILLIAM STERN
zum 60. Geburtstag am 29. April 1931

gewidmet von

Alfred Adler (Wien), Hellmuth Bogen (Berlin), Jonas Cohn (Freiburg), Fritz Giese (Stuttgart), Erich Jaensch (Marburg), David und Rosa Katz (Rostock), Heinrich Klüver (Chicago), Philipp Kohnstamm (Amsterdam), Otto Lipmann (Neubabelsberg), Martha Muchow (Hamburg), Géza Révész (Amsterdam), Heinz Werner (Hamburg), Herbert Wunderlich (Hamburg)

Herausgegeben von

seinen Mitarbeitern am Psychologischen Institut Hamburg

Mit 1 Porträt und 12 Abbildungen
im Text

VERLAG VON JOHANN AMBROSIUS BARTH
LEIPZIG 1931

Figure 2 Title page of "William Stern Festschrift" (1931).

Applied Psychology, with Stern and Otto Lipmann as cofounders and coeditors from 1908 to 1933. For Stern the most important public domain for applying psychology was education and the schools. He played a leading role in the German Association for School Reform and his Hamburg Institute became known for its contributions to selection procedures for different types of schools as well as for its research on giftedness.

By 1909 two monographs, both coauthored with his wife Clara, had also been published: *Child Language* (1907) and *Memory, Testimony, and Fabrication in Early Childhood* (1909). Both of these were based on diaries (kept by the Sterns on the development of their three children (Hilde, b. 1900; Günther, b. 1902; Eva, b. 1904). These diaries differed from other child development diaries published up to that time in two important respects: They were recorded in close cooperation between the parents,

with most entries made by the mother; and they covered the development of the children far beyond the third year of age, which up to then had been the upper limit. Material from the diaries figured prominently also in the book *Psychology of Early Childhood up to the Age of Six Years* which was published in 1914. This became his best-known work, with five revised and expanded editions appearing during his lifetime (as late as 1967 there was a reprint with a preface written by his son Günther). There were also two English translations (Stern, 1924, 1930).

In 1912, a year after the death of Alfred Binet, Stern published a comprehensive review of the methods of testing intelligence, in which he introduced the concept of "intelligence quotient." The monograph was translated by Guy Whipple in 1914, but he translated the term as "mental ratio." Lewis Terman, who read Stern's work in the original German, correctly credited Stern with the IQ concept.

Stern's research covered so many different specialized fields that he has been called a multi-specialist. But he saw no contradiction between specialization and maintaining psychology's unity as a distinct discipline. He saw the concept of "person" as the unifying principle for not only psychology, but for all sciences—such as biology, social anthropology, history, sociology, psychiatry—that contribute to the understanding of man. While carrying out his empirical and applied research, he was also articulating his philosophy of personhood and the science of personalistics. His interpretation of empirical data, whether from experiments, tests, or observations of spontaneous behavior in ordinary life situations was made "from the personalistic standpoint." This was also true for his views on the interpretation of intelligence test results. According to Gordon Allport, when Stern came to Duke University in 1934, his "chief desire was to introduce personalistic psychology into America, to counteract, as he said, the 'pernicious' influence of his earlier invention, the I.Q." (Allport, 1968). He was delighted when his *General Psychology From the Standpoint of Personalistics* appeared in February 1938, a month before his sudden death.

The American psychologist whose ideas were most influenced by William Stern was Gordon Allport (1897–1967). The influence is particularly marked in Allport's personality theory, first published in 1937. As a postdoctoral fellow in the early 1920s, he had spent six months in Hamburg, renting a room in the Sterns' apartment. He became a friend

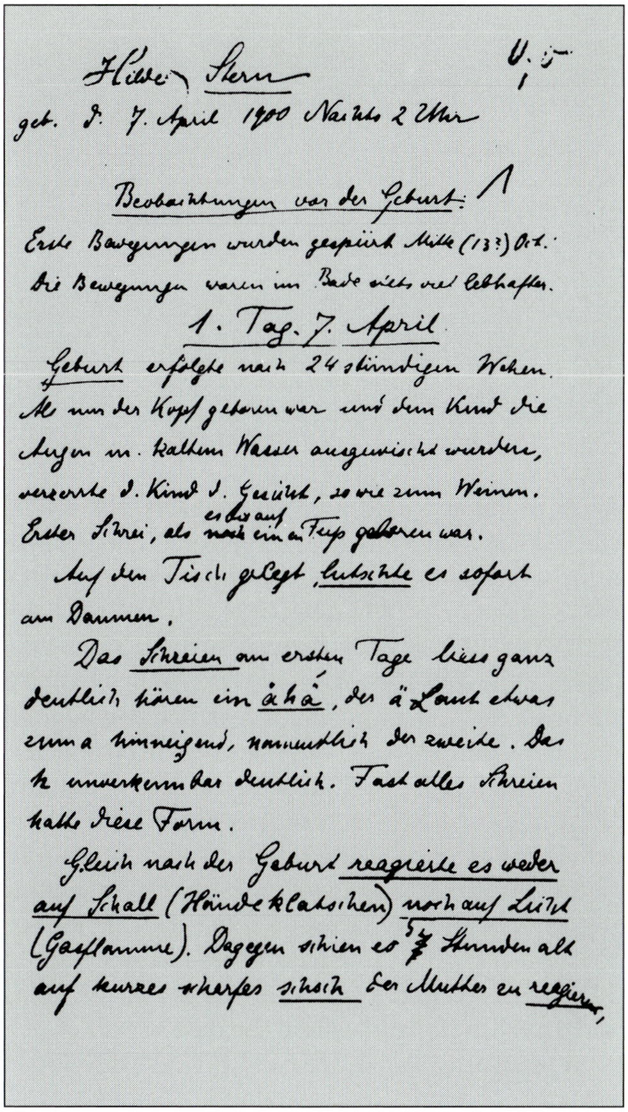

Figure 3 Facsimile page of developmental diary for daughter Hilde (1900).

of the Stern family, and he played a very active role in finding a suitable position in America for Stern. Sadly, until very recently, most textbooks in North America referred to Stern (if at all) only as the inventor of the IQ. In Germany today there is a revival of interest in the work of William Stern (Deutsch, 1991; Schmidt, 1991, 1994). This can hardly be said yet of North America, though Stern was the subject of a symposium at APA in 1988, and several papers have been presented at various conferences.

Bibliography

Allport, G. W. (1937). *Personality, a psychological interpretation.* New York: Holt.

Allport, G. W. (1968). The personalistic psychology of William Stern. In Benjamin B. Wolman (Ed.), *Historical roots of contemporary psychology* (pp. 321–337). New York: Harper & Row.

Anders, G. (1950). Bild meines Vaters [Profile of my father]. Preface to William Stern: *Allgemeine Psychologie auf personalistischer Grundlage* (2nd ed.). The Hague: Martinus Nijhoff.

Deutsch, W. (Ed.). (1991). *Über die verborgene Aktualität von William Stern* [On the hidden relevance of William Stern]. Frankfurt: Peter Lang.

Schmidt, W. (1991). "Sehnsucht nach Weltanschauung." William Stern um die Jahrhundertwende. ["Yearning for a world view." William Stern around the turn of the century]. *Psychologie und Geschichte, 3* (1/2), 1–8.

Schmidt, W. (1994). William Stern und Lewis Terman, *Psychologie und Geschichte, 6*(1/2), 3–26.

Stern, W. (1911). The supernormal child. *Journal of Educational Psychology, 2,* 143–148, 181–190.

Stern, W. (1914a). *The psychological methods of testing intelligence.* Baltimore: Warwick & York.

Stern, W. (1914b). Psychologists' song. *Journal of Educational Psychology, 5,* 413–416.

Stern, W. (1924). *Psychology of early childhood up to the sixth year of life. Supplemented by extracts from the unpublished diaries of Clara Stern* (A. Barwell, Trans.). New York: Holt. [Translated from the 3rd German edition. A translation by Anne Barwell of the 6th German edition also exists, with the same title and publisher, 1930]

Stern, W. (1925). Theory of constancy of I.Q. *Psychological Clinic, 16,* 110–116.

Stern, W. (1930). Autobiography. In C. Murchison (Ed.), *A history of psychology in autobiography* (Vol. 1, pp. 355–388). Worcester, MA: Clark University Press.

Stern, W. (1935). On the nature and structure of character. *Character and Personality, 3,* 270–289.

Stern, W. (1937a). A new method for testing imagination. *Character and Personality, 6,* 132–146.

Stern, W. (1937b). The personalistic shift in psychology. *The Personalist, 18,* 49–50.

Stern, W. (1938). *General psychology from the personalistic standpoint* (H. D. Spoerl, Trans.). New York: MacMillan.

Stern, W. (1939). The psychology of testimony. *The Journal of Abnormal and Social Psychology, 34,* 3–20.

Maria Montessori

Elena Liotta

Maria Montessori has long been considered to be one of the most popular and effective educators of our century. Born near Ancona, Italy, in 1870, her achievements include being the first woman in Italy to receive a medical degree. In 1894, she became an assistant in the psychiatric clinic at the University of Rome and gradually became interested in the education of abnormal children. After 1902, her interests broadened to include philosophy, anthropology, experimental psychology, and education. In addition, while in London and Paris, she familiarized herself with the works of E. Seguin, the famous French educator and creator of the physiological method for the treatment of the mentally retarded. She was also influenced by the works of J. M. Itard, a teacher of the deaf, who was noted for his work with the famous "Wild Boy of Aveyron." Itard was the first educator to emphasize systematic observation and is considered by some to be the founder of true scientific pedagogy.

> "It is not the teacher who applies psychology but the children themselves who reveal their psychology to the teacher."
> —*Maria Montessori*

In 1898 the Italian Minister of Public Education put Montessori in charge of a course in psychiatry that was offered to elementary school teachers in Rome. It was from this experience that a special school for teachers emerged. Gradually Montessori extended her approach to the education of the subnormal child to include normal children as well.

With the founding of the Casa dei Bambini (Children's House) in Rome in 1907, her system began to receive recognition. The publication of *The Method of Scientific Pedagogy Applied to Child Education* (1909) gave wide exposure to Montessori's ideas. The first congress of Montessori studies was held in Rome in 1931.

Opposition to Montessori's ideas was initially widespread—religious leaders rejected her positive approach, while positivists condemned her for using religious terminology. Scientists complained about her allegedly "demagogic" writing style. Educators criticized her for rejecting other educational theories and for imposing a learning regimen on children before they were sufficiently mature. Authoritarian governments refused to accept her novel approach to education and closed her schools. In fact, as a result of her distaste for fascism, Montessori left Italy in 1934 and lived abroad in Spain, Great Britain, India, and finally, in Holland, where she died in 1952.

After World War II, renewed interest developed around programs for preschoolers, and Montessori's concepts provided a psychological foundation for this movement because of her emphasis on serving the unique potential of the child rather than the demands of a social system. Evidence shows that Montessori schools facilitate the development of individual potential (e.g., Kohlberg, 1968), and, consequently, they have become very popular, particularly in the United States (Rambusch, 1962), Canada, Japan, and even in the Third World. Maria Montessori regarded school as a place *of* children and not *for* children. She believed that schools should encourage free expression through the use of stimulating materials and provide an atmosphere where the teacher assists children rather than merely "teaching" them.

Considerable emphasis is placed on developing the individual potential of children by encouraging their spontaneity. Montessori believed that any ability could be fostered through the use of "controlled

Figure 1 Portrait drawing of Maria Montessori as a young physician after an old photograph.

freedom." For example, in her textbook, *Psychoarithmetics* (1934), Montessori outlined a method for encouraging the development of mathematical skills by describing in detail the child's understanding of arithmetical structures. This work appears particularly relevant today when our educational institutions are confronted with the growing technological needs of modern society.

The interdisciplinary nature of Montessori's work makes it somewhat difficult to isolate her specific contributions to psychology. Educational, sociological, and neurophysiological factors are as important to the child's development as are psychological factors. Moreover, the psychological components are not only grounded in biology and pediatrics but are also infused with a spiritual element. Montessori's rigorous and systematic study of early childhood provided strong support for her position. For her, "the good and evil found in the adult are directly linked to the child's early life" (1909). Along with DeVries, Freud, Stern, and Gesell, Montessori believed that human development followed specific stages and "sensitive periods," and

she, too, was convinced that child psychology was a distinct area of study and not merely a derivative of adult psychology.

According to Montessori, both the prenatal and postnatal periods are particularly important stages of development because they are infused with a creative potential or "spiritual embryo," which is later manifested in the child's relationship with the environment. This creative aspect of development she named "horme," and the resulting psychological structure she called the "absorbent mind." The unconscious mind of the child was considered to be even more important than the conscious mind of the adult because it contains the essence of life itself—a kind of "mental flesh" or "mneme" or "natural memory." Montessori also believed in universal principles of growth, including those of differentiation. The child's development, however, is not solely determined by inherited behavior patterns. In addition, forces in the external environment influence and provide direction for his or her creative energies. These innate energies, or "nebular" drives, Montessori likened to the celestial nebulae that form the stars. These drives are thus raw materials from which the person emerges. For example, the child does not inherit language but rather inherits the possibility of creating language through experience with the environment. Likewise, in a very real sense the individual creates himself through dynamic interaction with the environment in a process of continuous transformation under the guidance of the "horme" and the degree of specialization determined by the nebulae.

The above are some of the ideas that represent Montessori's thought on the spiritual basis of human development. At other times her writing reflects a behaviorist orientation. After exploring infantile behaviors in her studies of sleep, crying, and grasping, she concluded that: "Behavior is established in every individual through his experiences with the environment" (1909). Interestingly, it was the consequences of behavior that were seen as fundamental for learning. For Montessori, the mother was a crucial aspect of the child's environment, and closer, more prolonged contact between mother and child for at least the first three years was emphasized.

The foundation of a child's education, whether at home or at school, was the imagination. Montessori defined imagination as "the intelligence which sees beyond things" and as "an effort to search for the truth" (1909). Both the scientific and artistic creative imaginations are derived from truth, but they were not considered *only* a means to the truth but also an end in themselves. Creativity is a product of the mind, which is constructed from the raw information collected through the senses. Accordingly, Montessori opposed the use of fairy tales and similar fantasy material in education because she feared it would alienate the child from reality. She stated that education should not engender gullibility but intelligence.

Montessori's strong interest in realistic and practice-oriented education may well be the reason for the lack of a comprehensive theoretical perspective in her psychological writings. Maria Montessori was primarily an applied rather than an experimental psychologist, and throughout her lifetime she developed a highly individualized style as a clinician. Although she began with a naturalistic perspective, she eventually moved toward an intuitive and ana-

logical methodology, which resulted in a "spiritual" or metaphysical view of the world.

In summary, one could say that Maria Montessori was indeed a spiritualist, an organicist, and a psychologist, but only to the extent that these perspectives served the practical needs of her approach to education.

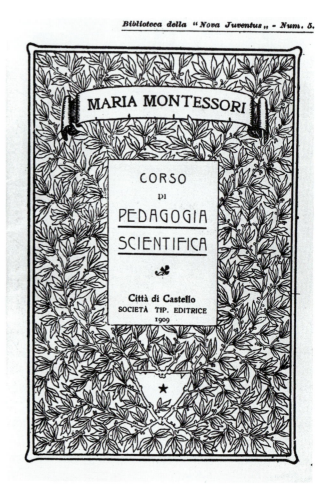

Figure 2 Teacher's version of Montessori's magnum opus.

Bibliography

Kohlberg, L. (1968). Montessori and the culturally disadvantaged: A cognitive-developmental interpretation and some research findings. In R. D. Hess & R. N. Baer (Eds.), *Early education: Current theory, research and action.* Chicago: Aldine.

Montessori, M. (1909). *Corso di pedagogia scientifica.* Cita di Castello: Societa Tip Editrice.

Montessori, M. (1934). *Psica Aritmetica.* Barcelona: Analuce.

Rambusch, N. N. (1962). *Learning how to learn: An American approach to Montessori.* Baltimore: Helicon.

Lewis M. Terman: Architect for a Psychologically Stratified Society

Henry L. Minton

Lewis M. Terman (1877–1956) was committed to applying psychological research to the needs of society. In his own specialty of measuring individual and group differences, his objective was to foster the use of psychological assessment tools to meet the demands of an industrialized society which required an increasingly specialized division of labor. In particular, he sought to demonstrate that measures of intellectual and personality differences could be used to sort individuals into the social roles they were most qualified to fulfill. The most intellectually and emotionally competent individuals would occupy the highest positions of responsibility and leadership. As a result of such a meritocratic structure, both individual and social efficiency would be maximized.

Terman was born and raised on a farm in central Indiana, the 12th of 14 children (Minton, 1988; Terman, 1932). He went to a one-room school, completing the 8th grade when he was 12. Determined to further his education and with his parents' financial support, Terman left the farm at age 15 to attend Central Normal College in Danville, Indiana. Over the course of the next six years, he completed three undergraduate degrees at the normal college. At 17, he obtained his first teaching position and two years later moved on to become a high school principal. While attending normal college, he met Anna Belle Minton (no relation to the author) whom he married in 1899.

With aspirations beyond school teaching, Terman entered Indiana University in 1901 and two years later earned a master's degree in psychology. With the encouragement of Ernest H. Lindley, his mentor at Indiana, he went on to Clark University in 1903 to do his doctoral work in psychology with G. Stanley Hall. For his dissertation, Terman carried out an experimental study of mental tests in which he compared a "bright" and a "dull" group of boys. Since Hall did not approve of mental tests, Edmund C. Sanford became his dissertation advisor, and he completed his doctoral studies in 1905 (Figure 1).

During his stay at Clark, Terman became ill with

Figure 1 Lewis M. Terman in 1905, the year he received his PhD in psychology at Clark University.

Figure 2 The Terman garden around 1909 in Glendale, California.

were several competitive versions, Terman's revision of the Binet scale utilized the largest standardized sample and by the 1920s became the most widely used individually administered intelligence test.

With the publication of his 1916 test, Terman had become a highly visible figure in the mental testing movement. It was therefore not surprising that in 1917 he was called to serve on a committee that had been assembled at Vineland, New Jersey, to devise mental tests for the army. The United States had entered World War I, and Robert M. Yerkes (1918),

tuberculosis. While he made a successful recovery, he decided that upon completing his studies it would be best to accept a position in a warm climate. He therefore accepted a high school principalship in San Bernardino, California. A year later, he was happy to obtain a college position, teaching child study and pedagogy at the Los Angeles State Normal School (see Figure 2). He remained at the normal school until 1910, when he received an appointment in the education department at Stanford University. He spent the rest of his career at Stanford, becoming head of the psychology department in 1922, a position he held until his retirement in 1942.

The move to Stanford in 1910 coincided with Terman's physical ability to pursue a more active academic schedule. He therefore was able to return to his research interests in mental testing and began to work with Alfred Binet's 1908 scale. Henry H. Goddard (1908, 1910) had published translations of Binet's original 1905 scale and the subsequent 1908 revision. Terman's first tentative revision of the Binet appeared in 1912 (Terman & Childs, 1912), and the finished product—the "Stanford-Binet"—was published in 1916 (Terman, 1916) (see Figure 3). An innovative feature of the Stanford-Binet was the inclusion of the "intelligence quotient" or IQ—that is, the ratio between mental and chronological ages—a concept first introduced by William Stern but not previously used in mental tests. While there

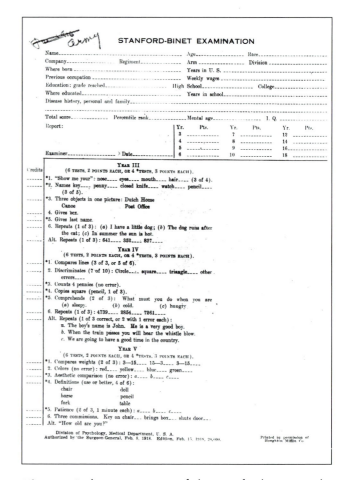

Figure 3 The cover page of the Stanford-Binet scale published in 1916. This version was used in the army during World War I.

Figure 4 The psychologists who constructed the army tests at Vineland in 1917. Top, left to right: F. L. Wells, Guy M. Whipple, Robert M. Yerkes, Walter V. Bingham, Lewis M. Terman. Bottom, left to right: Edgar A. Doll, H. H. Goddard, Thomas M. Haines.

the president of the American Psychological Association, organized the psychologists' contribution to the war effort. Yerkes chaired the test committee, and the membership was made up of the leading psychologists in the mental testing field (see Figures 4 and 5). Terman brought with him a new group-administered test of intelligence that had been developed by his doctoral student, Arthur S. Otis. The Otis test served as the basis for the development of the army group tests (the Alpha and Beta examinations). While serious questions have been raised about the significance of the psychologists' contributions to the war, there is no doubt that the war provided an enormous boost for the mental testing movement (Kevles, 1968; Samelson, 1979). Approximately 1.75 million men were tested, and on this basis recommendations were made with respect to job placements or immediate discharge from the army.

After the war, Terman (1919) seized upon the contribution of the army tests to military efficiency and predicted that they would soon be universally used in the schools. To this end, Terman and the other psychologists who constructed the army tests adapted them for school-age children. The resulting "National Intelligence Tests" for grades three to eight were published in 1920. Terman became an advocate for the use of intelligence tests as a means of reorganizing schools so that students could be classified into homogeneous ability groups (Terman et al., 1922). During the 1920s intelligence testing and the tracking system of ability grouping became common practices in schools (Chapman, 1988). Terman played a notable role in fostering this development. Not only was he instrumental in establishing the widespread use of intelligence testing, he was also a leader in the development of group achievement tests which assessed school learning. He col-

Figure 5 Terman in 1918, the year he was commissioned as a major in the army. He was on the surgeon general's staff and collaborated on the report of the army testing program.

laborated on the construction of the Stanford Achievement Test, the first test battery of its kind (Kelley, Ruch, & Terman, 1923).

Terman viewed the widespread adoption of tests in the schools as a reflection of how testing could be of use to American society. It was to be the major means of achieving his vision of a meritocracy within the American democratic ideal—a social order based on ranked levels of native ability. Consistent with the views of other leading mental testers such as Yerkes and Goddard, Terman subscribed to the Galtonian theory that mental abilities were primarily a product of heredity. The highest purpose that testing could serve was the identification of children who were intellectually gifted and therefore had the potential to become the leaders of society. It was the responsibility of the schools, once these children were identified, to devote the necessary time and effort to cultivate their potential. This goal was consistent with his support of a differentiated curriculum, and the notion of group-

ing pupils on the basis of innate ability was in keeping with the ideals of democracy. Every child would have the same opportunity "to make the most of whatever abilities nature has given him [sic]" (Terman, 1923, p. xv).

To accomplish his meritocratic objectives and with the support of a research grant from the Commonwealth Fund of New York, Terman launched a longitudinal study of gifted children in 1921. This was the first follow-up study to use a large sample of subjects. The criterion for categorizing gifted children was an IQ of at least 135. Canvassing elementary and secondary schools in urban areas of California, Terman and his research team came up with a sample of close to 1,500 gifted children. In an attempt to dispel the popular notion that gifted children were underdeveloped in nonintellectual areas, Terman included medical and physical assessments, as well as measures of personality, character, and interests. The gifted sample was compared with a control group of California schoolchildren of comparable age.

In the first of a series of monographs on the gifted study, the major finding was that gifted children excelled in measures of academic achievement when matched for age with control children (Terman, 1925). Based on their grade placement, Terman concluded that gifted pupils were kept at school tasks two or three grades below their actual level of achievement. The composite portrait of the gifted children also revealed that they were emotionally as well as intellectually mature. Based on these initial findings, Terman strongly advocated a differentiated school curriculum that would place gifted children in special classrooms where they could accelerate educationally according to their ability rather then their age (as in the traditional curriculum). With additional research grants, Terman was able to follow up his gifted sample after intervals of 6, 25, and 35 years (Burks, Jensen, & Terman, 1930; Terman & Oden, 1947, 1959). When the gifted sample had reached midlife, their intellectual level continued to be within the upper one percent of the general population. Their vocational achievement was well above the average of college graduates. Furthermore, as earlier reports had indicated, they showed few signs of such "serious maladjustments" as insanity, delinquency, or alcoholism. The midlife report also included some striking gender differences (Terman & Oden, 1959). While the men as a group had attained a high level of career success, few women had comparable levels of career achievement. As the coauthors noted, career opportunities for women were restricted by gender-role conformity and job discrimination.

Terman's involvement with the gifted included more than data collection and research reports. Particularly after he retired from teaching in 1942 (see Figures 6 and 7), he devoted himself to the interests of gifted children by promoting gifted education and, through contacts with journalists, disseminating the results of the gifted study in newspapers and magazines. He also popularized his work by making a guest appearance on the radio show "The Quiz Kids." His appearance in 1947 coincided with the publication of the 25-year follow-up. These forays into the popular media also served as a vehicle for Terman to change the public's negative myths about

gifted children. An aspect of the work with the gifted that Terman found especially satisfying was the opportunity for personal contact with the participants under study. He kept up a correspondence with many of them over the years and in some instances received them as guests in his home. For a number of the gifted children who "grew up" (and came to be identified as "Termites"), he was a benevolent father figure and psychological counselor. By the early 1950s, with plans developing for the continuation of the gifted follow-up, Terman appointed Stanford colleague Robert Sears (who also happened to be a member of the gifted sample) to take over as research director. Follow-up reports of the gifted sample thus continued (Terman, Sears, Cronbach, & Sears, 1983).

As one of the leading advocates of intelligence

Figure 6 Terman at the time of his retirement from Stanford in 1942. During his retirement years, he devoted himself to the follow-up study of the gifted.

Figure 7 Terman and his son Fred's family around 1955. Terman's wife Anna is standing second from the left. Fred is standing on the right.

as in previous exchanges, the issue was not resolved. In 1940, Terman was once again drawn into the nature-nurture debate, this time challenged by a team of environmentalist advocates at the University of Iowa led by George D. Stoddard (Minton, 1984). Stoddard campaigned for the limited use of intelligence tests because they were subject to environmental influences and could therefore not be used to make long-term predictions. Terman was concerned that Stoddard's position against mass testing would threaten his career goal of establishing a meritocracy based on IQ differences. The 1940 debate, as in the past, led to an impasse. No changes took place in the widespread use of IQ tests in the schools. It was not until the 1960s, as a result of the Civil Rights movement, that mass testing was seriously challenged. Terman did modify his position somewhat after World War II. He still held to his democratic ideal of a meritocracy, but he no longer endorsed a hereditarian explanation of race differences, and he acknowledged that among the gifted, home environment was related to degree of success.

testing, Terman was often challenged by testing critics. The first instance of this occurred in the early 1920s when the results of the army testing became widely disseminated. The influential journalist Walter Lippmann wrote a series of highly critical articles about the army tests in the *New Republic* (Minton, 1988). Lippmann singled out Terman because of his development of the Stanford-Binet and asserted that there was no scientific foundation to support the claim made by Terman and the other army psychologists that the tests measured innate ability. In response to these attacks, Terman wrote an article in the *New Republic* in which he indicated that Lippmann as a nonexpert in testing should stay out of issues he was not informed about. Lippmann, in fact, was quite technically sophisticated in many of his criticisms, yet Terman chose to be evasive in responding to the points Lippmann raised, such as an environmental interpretation of the correlation between IQ and social class.

During the 1920s, Terman also engaged in a series of published debates about testing with psychologist William C. Bagley, another critic of the hereditarian view of intelligence (Bagley, 1922; Terman, 1922). In an effort to resolve matters, Terman took on the task of chairing a committee which organized an edited book on the nature-nurture issue (Whipple, 1928). The contributors represented the leading advocates on each side of the issue, but,

Terman's interest in the measurement of individual and group differences extended beyond mental abilities and achievement. As a result of his research on the gifted, he became interested in nonintellectual traits. By assessing emotional and motivational characteristics, he hoped to demonstrate that the gifted had well-adjusted and well-rounded personalities. The approach he pursued in this area was to measure appropriate gender identification. Masculine and feminine interests were derived from questionnaire preferences about play activities, games, and amusements. The initial survey in 1922 showed that the gifted sample was similar in gender orientation to the control sample. In 1925, Terman secured a National Research Council grant to study sex differences, and, with Catharine Cox Miles, constructed a masculinity-femininity (M-F) test. The final version, published in 1936 and labeled the "Attitude-Interest Analysis Test" to disguise its purpose (see Figure 8), was based on normative samples of male and female groups ranging in age from early adolescence to late adulthood (Terman & Miles, 1936). The test was made up of about 450 multiple-choice items which assessed preferences for a variety of activities and interests, as well as responses to situations that might arouse emotions of anger or fear.

In an attempt to validate the M-F test, Terman was able to collect test protocols from a group of male homosexuals in San Francisco. As he expected, the results revealed that male homosexuals had high feminine scores. He thus concluded that marked deviations from gender-appropriate behaviors and norms were psychologically unhealthy because such deviations could very likely lead to homosexuality. Even if this "maladjustment" did not develop, other problems could arise. Referring to those with cross-gender identities, Terman and Miles (1936) commented: "One would like to know whether fewer of them marry, and whether a larger proportion of these marriages are unhappy" (p. 468). Extending this point, they observed that "aggressive and independent females" could very well be at a disadvantage in the "marriage market" (Terman & Miles, 1936, p. 452). They also expressed the fear that too much competition between the sexes would not be socially desirable. In essence, they supported the conventional patriarchal relationship between the sexes. (It is not clear the extent to which Catharine Cox Miles concurred with this position since Terman acknowledged prime responsibility for the conclusions in their book.)

Terman's interest in gender expanded to research on marital adjustment (Terman, 1938). He conducted a large-scale survey investigation of several hundred married and divorced couples in the San Francisco area. According to Terman, the major finding of the study was that the combination of personality and background factors was more influential than sexual compatibility in predicting marital happiness. This conclusion was contrary to previous marriage studies which argued that sexual compatibility was the key to marital happiness. Terman pointed out that this discrepancy was due to the fact that previous studies had neglected to consider psychological factors because they had been carried out by physicians and social workers. He thus indicated the importance of psychologists becoming involved in the study of marital relations and human sexuality. In his study, Terman stressed that the key to marital adjustment was the extent to which each spouse accepted the other's needs and feelings and did not fight to get their own way. Happily married women were thus characterized as being cooperative and not objecting to their subordinate roles. Terman's conventional views on gender carried over from his masculinity-femininity study to his marital research.

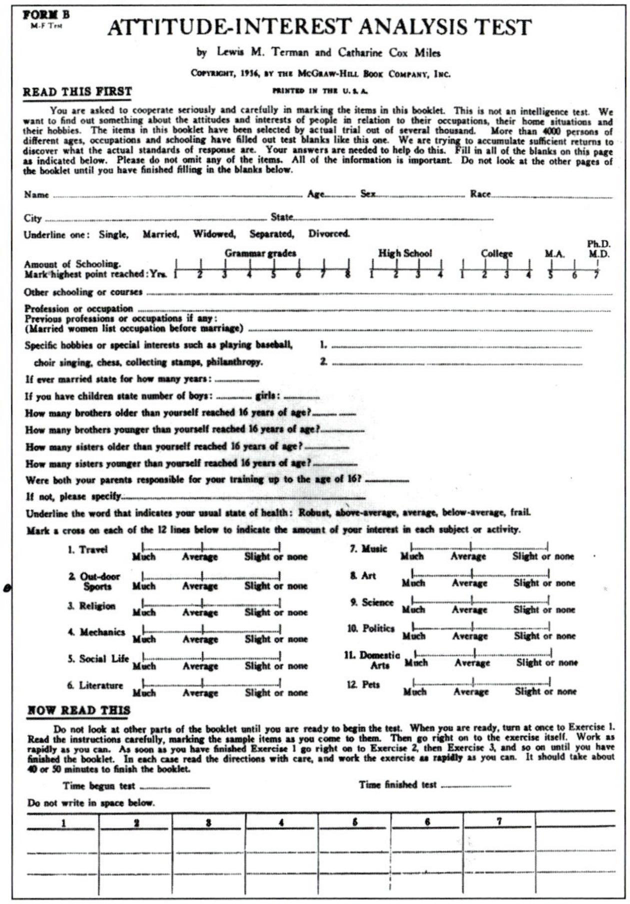

FORM B
M-F Test

ATTITUDE-INTEREST ANALYSIS TEST

by Lewis M. Terman and Catharine Cox Miles

COPYRIGHT, 1936, BY THE McGRAW-HILL BOOK COMPANY, INC.

PRINTED IN THE U.S.A.

READ THIS FIRST

You are asked to cooperate seriously and carefully in marking the items in this booklet. This is not an intelligence test. We want to find out something about the attitudes and interests of people in relation to their occupations, their home situations and their hobbies. The items in this booklet have been selected by actual trial out of several thousand. More than 4000 persons of different ages, occupations and schooling have filled out test blanks like this one. We are trying to accumulate sufficient returns to discover what the actual standards of response are. Your answers are needed to help do this. Fill in all of the blanks on this page as indicated below. Please do not omit any of the items. All of the information is important. Do not look at the other pages of the booklet until you have finished filling in the blanks below.

Name .... Age.......... Sex.......... Race..........

City .... State..........

Underline one: Single, Married, Widowed, Separated, Divorced.

Amount of Schooling. Mark highest point reached: Yrs. Grammar grades 1 2 3 4 5 6 7 8; High School 1 2 3 4; College 1 2 3 4; M.A. 5 6; Ph.D. M.D. 7

Other schooling or courses ....

Profession or occupation ....

Previous professions or occupations if any: (Married women list occupation before marriage) ....

Specific hobbies or special interests such as playing baseball, choir singing, chess, collecting stamps, philanthropy. 1. .... 2. ....

If ever married state for how many years: ....

If you have children state number of boys: .... girls: ....

How many brothers older than yourself reached 16 years of age? ....

How many brothers younger than yourself reached 16 years of age? ....

How many sisters older than yourself reached 16 years of age? ....

How many sisters younger than yourself reached 16 years of age? ....

Were both your parents responsible for your training up to the age of 16? ....

If not, please specify..........

Underline the word that indicates your usual state of health: Robust, above-average, average, below-average, frail.

Mark a cross on each of the 12 lines below to indicate the amount of your interest in each subject or activity.

1. Travel — Much, Average, Slight or none
2. Out-door Sports — Much, Average, Slight or none
3. Religion — Much, Average, Slight or none
4. Mechanics — Much, Average, Slight or none
5. Social Life — Much, Average, Slight or none
6. Literature — Much, Average, Slight or none
7. Music — Much, Average, Slight or none
8. Art — Much, Average, Slight or none
9. Science — Much, Average, Slight or none
10. Politics — Much, Average, Slight or none
11. Domestic Arts — Much, Average, Slight or none
12. Pets — Much, Average, Slight or none

NOW READ THIS

Do not look at other parts of the booklet until you are ready to begin the test. When you are ready, turn at once to Exercise 1. Read the instructions carefully, marking the sample items as you come to them. Then go right on to the exercise itself. Work as rapidly as you can. As soon as you have finished Exercise 1 go right on to Exercise 2, then Exercise 3, and so on until you have finished the booklet. In each case read the directions with care, and work the exercise as rapidly as you can. It should take about 40 or 50 minutes to finish the booklet.

Time begun test .... Time finished test ....

Do not write in space below.

1	2	3	4	5	6	7	

Figure 8 The cover page of the masculinity-femininity test published in 1936. The test's purpose was disguised by the title "Attitude-Interest Analysis Test."

Terman's seminal contributions to the development of psychological testing and the study of the intellectually gifted ensure his position as one of the pioneers of American psychology. Perhaps more than any of the other advocates of the testing movement, he was successful in devising a wide variety of methods assessing individual differences. His interest in the gifted led him to go far beyond the measurement of ability. As a result, he was in the forefront of developing indices of school achievement, gender identity, interests, marital adjustment, and sexual behavior. Aside from these personal accomplishments, Terman has left us with an unfulfilled legacy. What he wanted to accomplish with his psychological tests and identification of the intellectually gifted was a more socially just and democratic society. A considerable part of Terman's project, however, has had an unintended dehumanizing effect. For racial and ethnic minorities and lower-class individuals, his differential educational system based on IQ scores served as an obstacle for personal growth and equal opportunity. His views on gender and homosexuality worked against the creation of a more pluralistic society. What Terman failed to understand was the intricate way in which scientific knowledge reflects social power. By uncritically accepting the given power inequities of American society, he produced scientific knowledge and technology which served to perpetuate the status quo.

Bibliography

Bagley, W. C. (1922). Educational determinism; or democracy and the I.Q. *School and Society, 15,* 373–384.

Burks, B. S., Jensen, D. W., & Terman, L. M. (1930). *Genetic studies of genius. Vol. 3, The promise of youth: Follow-up studies of a thousand gifted children.* Stanford, CA: Stanford University Press.

Chapman, P. D. (1988). *Schools as sorters: Lewis M. Terman, applied psychology, and the intelligence testing movement, 1890–1930.* New York: New York University Press.

Goddard, H. H. (1908). The Binet and Simon scales of intellectual capacity. *The Training School, 5,* 3–9.

Goddard, H. H. (1910). A measuring scale for intelligence. *The Training School, 6,* 146–155.

Kelley, T. L., Ruch, G. M., & Terman, L. M. (1923). *Stanford Achievement Test.* Yonkers, NY: World.

Kevles, D. (1968). Testing the army's intelligence: Psychologists and the military in World War I. *Journal of American History, 55,* 565–581.

Minton, H. L. (1984). The Iowa Child Welfare Research Station and the 1940 debate on intelligence: Carrying on the legacy of a concerned mother. *Journal of the History of the Behavioral Sciences, 20,* 160–176.

Minton, H. L. (1988). *Lewis M. Terman: Pioneer in psychological testing.* New York: New York University Press.

Samelson, F. (1979). Putting psychology on the map: Ideology and intelligence testing. In A. R. Buss (Ed.), *Psychology in social context* (pp. 103–168). New York: Irvington.

Terman, L. M. (1916). *The Stanford revision of the Binet-Simon tests.* Boston: Houghton Mifflin.

Terman, L. M. (1919). *The intelligence of school children.* Boston: Houghton Mifflin.

Terman, L. M. (1922). The psychological determinist; or democracy and the I.Q. *Journal of Educational Research, 6,* 57–62.

Terman, L. M. (1923). Editor's introduction. In V. E. Dickson, *Mental tests and the classroom teacher* (pp. xiv–xv). Yonkers, NY: World.

Terman, L. M. (1925). *Genetic studies of genius. Vol. 1, Mental and physical traits of a thousand gifted children.* Stanford, CA: Stanford University Press.

Terman, L. M. (1932). Trails to psychology. In C. A. Murchison (Ed.), *A history of psychology in autobiography* (pp. 279–332). Worcester, MA: Clark University Press.

Terman, L. M. (1938). *Psychological factors in marital happiness.* New York: McGraw-Hill.

Terman, L. M., & Childs, H. G. (1912). A tentative revision and extension of the Binet-Simon measuring scale of intelligence. *Journal of Educational Psychology, 3,* 61–74, 133–143, 198–208, 277–289.

Terman, L. M., Dickson, V. E., Sutherland, A. H., Franzen, R. H., Tupper, C. R., & Fernald, G. (1922). *Intelligence testing and school reorganization.* Yonkers, NY: World.

Terman, L. M., & Miles, C. C. (1936). *Sex and personality: Studies in masculinity and femininity.* New York: McGraw-Hill.

Terman, L. M., & Oden, M. H. (1947). *Genetic studies of genius. Vol. 4, The gifted child grows up: Twenty-five years follow-up of a superior group.* Stanford, CA: Stanford University Press.

Terman, L. M., & Oden, M. H. (1959). *Genetic studies of genius. Vol. 5, The gifted child at mid-life: Thirty-five years follow-up of the superior child.* Stanford, CA: Stanford University Press.

Terman, L. M., Sears, R. R., Cronbach, L. J., & Sears, P. S. (1983). *Terman life cycle study of children of high ability, 1922–1982.* Ann Arbor, MI: Inter-University Consortium for Political and Social Research.

Whipple, G. M. (Ed.). (1928). *The twenty-seventh yearbook of the National Society for the Study of Education—Nature and nurture* (Parts 1 & 2). Bloomington, IL: Public School Publishing.

Yerkes, R. M. (1918). Psychology in relation to the war. *Psychological Review, 25,* 85–115.

Martha Muchow's Concept of Lifespace

Rudolf Miller

Among psychologists, Martha Muchow (1892–1933) is, at best, known only as a member of William Stern's Hamburg Psychological Institute (Moser, 1991; Probst, 1995). Nonetheless, this highly dedicated and accomplished woman earned a significant place in the history of psychology and thus merits our special attention. This essay will focus primarily on Muchow's scientific work and will deal with her political views and social concerns only in passing (Schubeius, 1990; Fries, 1995).

Martha Muchow was born on September 25, 1892, in Hamburg, Germany. In 1913, only a year after graduating from high school, she qualified as a schoolteacher and received her first practical experience in a high school for girls. Later, from 1916 to 1919, she worked in Hamburg as an elementary school teacher. According to Strnad (1949), Muchow had apparently chosen Hamburg as her residence and place of work because she wanted to prepare herself for a university career. The young teacher began her formal university studies in 1916 by enrolling part-time in psychology courses taught by William Stern (1875–1939) at the Colonial Institute in Hamburg—the forerunner of today's Hamburg University. There she soon participated as a volunteer in Stern's laboratory, working first on the development of an observation guide for the selection of gifted students.

It is likely that the accepting atmosphere of Stern's institute made it easier for Muchow to become an accepted collaborator in Stern's research group. Stern's personality and his interest in "research with talented and intellectually-gifted youths" (Moser, 1991, p. 488) offered the young woman a special opportunity to integrate her practical experience as a public school teacher with her psychological research in Stern's institute.

Figure 1 Martha Muchow (1930).

Muchow's view of science was strengthened by Stern's conviction that "scientific work must always be related to current concerns" held by the society (Moser, 1991, p. 488).

During the summer term of 1919, Muchow formally began her full-time university studies in psychology, philosophy, German philology, and history of literature at the newly organized University of Hamburg. Her chief teachers were Stern and the philosopher Ernst Cassirer (1874–1945). From the fall of 1920 until her forced resignation in 1933, Muchow was on official leave from her teaching position to assist Stern with his research and the teaching of his laboratory courses. Stern clearly valued his "scientific aid" highly, and she received her first PhD in 1923 from Hamburg University with the accolade summa cum laude for a dissertation on the "Psychology of the Educator."

Figure 2 Study group at the Hamburg Psychological Laboratory (ca. 1927). Participants from left to right: A. Mourgues, M. Scheerer, M. Muchow, M. Meumann, L. Brandes, F. Heider, G. Anschütz, O. Stender.

According to Probst (1995, p. 2), Muchow concentrated on three content areas in educational psychology during her scientific career. These included research for a psychological justification of preschool education, the mental hygiene of school children, and monographic studies about a variety of social-environmental and cultural questions. Muchow's research primarily focused on applied questions. Her responsibilities increased even more after Stern's institute became officially involved in the education of future elementary school teachers. Muchow's close association with Hamburg's principal teacher organization, "The Friends of a Patriotic School . . . System," provided her with the opportunity for realizing her practical and scientific inter-

ests. In addition, she became actively involved with respected preschool publications like *The Journal of the Fröbel Association* and *The Journal of the German Association for Child Care* (Fries, 1995). According to an early Muchow biographer (Strnad, 1949): "It is hard to imagine how [Muchow] carried out all these responsibilities, especially, since she does all her work so well. She is not one of those people who will improvise" (p. 16).

Muchow's practical work with Hamburg youth clubs, her long-term membership in prominent German youth organizations, and her preventive program for tuberculosis-prone working-class children all helped shape her social and educational views. During a stay at a children's spa on the island of Wyk, Muchow collected the data for her 1926 book, *Sea Climate and School Children.*

Muchow visited the United States in 1931. She spent the four months of her trip making contacts with American psychologists and specialists in child development and education in 12 cities. According to Wohlwill (1985), Muchow "was quite tempted to remain in the USA" and had "several offers of employment" (p. 369). She returned to Germany, however, because she could not "readily move her work and her life to this country" (p. 369).

Muchow's book-length study, *The Lifespace of the Urban Child* (1935), was not published until two years after her tragic death. The book came out in an edition of 1,000 copies published by the liberal Hamburg Education Movement. Muchow's brother, Hans Heinrich Muchow (1900–1992), who is listed as second author, made the following moving comments in the preface to the original edition:

> This account . . . was to be published by my sister in 1934. The political events of the year 1933 slowed down work on the project until death removed the pen from my sister's hand. I honor an obligation and a debt of gratitude by trying to

complete a work for publication, in which I was involved from the beginning . . . I doubt whether I will be able to fulfill the last wishes of my sister. It hurts me that I may transmit only a fragment. (1935, p. 8)

According to Zinnecker (1978), Muchow's most important contribution was to call our attention to the significance of the child's efforts to take control of his or her world. She also believed that the researcher's responsibilities included serving as a mediator of sorts between the life of the child and the world of adults. To be fully appreciated, Muchow's ideas must be understood within the context of Stern's "personalistic psychology" and his novel definition of man and his world as a dialectical relationship. In addition, Muchow tried to relate Stern's concepts of differential psychology to Uexküll's lifespace concept.

Jakob Johann von Uexküll (1864–1944) joined the faculty of Hamburg University in 1926 where he established his Institute for Environmental Research. Muchow was very likely familiar with Uexküll's ideas through her personal contacts at Hamburg University (Wohlwill, 1985). His 1909 work on the interaction between animals and their environment is generally credited with introducing the lifespace concept to biology, psychology, and related areas. According to Uexküll, it is necessary to analyze the life space in order to fully understand the behavior of animals in their physical environment. However, the physical environment of an organism is less important than the organism's perception of that environment. It is the perception that actually determines the reaction of the organism to its environment. Specifically, Uexküll's subjectivistic "environmental theory" defines an animal's environment as the segment to which it responds with its sensory organs and to which it can respond behaviorally. Both sensory and motor organs form a closed, functional unity. Unfortunately, Uexküll's ecological model of behavior has only a limited application to psychology due to its exclusive emphasis on species-specific and innate perceptual and behavioral processes. The importance of culturally defined socialization processes in the case of humans are somewhat neglected.

Martha Muchow's effort to integrate ideas and concepts from developmental psychology with those of social psychology helped her to see the significance of the child's "autonomous activity and subjectivity" for "the acquisition of his lifespace"

(Fries, 1995, p. 112). Her practical and theoretical experience with ability testing after 1918 encouraged Muchow to pay special attention to the child's uniqueness—a quality which was often overlooked in the norm-oriented developmental psychology of her time (1926): "Psychology should not only study the [child's] achievement scores, as important as they are for child study, but [should include] the subjective conditions under which the objective . . . [scores] were achieved" (p. 11). Throughout her later research Muchow stressed that the child is a totality and can only be accurately studied if regarded as an integral unit with his or her world. According to Muchow (1932):

> Anyone who is familiar with all the results of developmental psychology but does not understand the special world of children and adolescents, will make serious errors in his contact [with children]. To communicate with a child, one must not only know how the child lives in the world but in what type world the child exists. (p. 391)

In her "lifespace" book (1935), Muchow distinguished between the space in which the child lives from the space which the child experiences. To learn more about the child's world Muchow employed the sample survey, which "has long been recognized as a valuable psychological method" (1935, p. 11). First a total of 109 children, ages 9 to 14, were asked to mark their apartment, school, and other places that were important to them on a city map of Hamburg. Next, the children were asked (Muchow, 1935): "to color all streets and places in blue which you know well, in which you play often, which you often have to go through, and which you can imagine when you close your eyes" (p. 110).

Streets which the children did not know well were to be marked in red. In addition, the children were asked to record their answers on a special questionnaire. For the balance of the study, areas marked with blue were regarded as "play space" or "lifespace proper," while the red areas were viewed as the children's "extended lifespace."

The second part of Muchow's research was concerned with the "experience of space" (1935):

> Specifically, a structured interview guide was used to question the children about the location and nature of their chief playgrounds and the type of games which they played there. Information from the written survey about the homes of their relatives, their swimming places, gymnasiums and sport fields were utilized as well. The

Figures 3 and 4 Transmutations of a playground: The landing pier at the Osterbeck Canal in Hamburg 1912 (top) and 1978 (bottom).

final result was a wealth of written and pictorial information about how children spend their Sundays, their actual free times. (p. 29)

The third stage of Muchow's ground-breaking research investigated the lifespace in which the children lived. The following three observational procedures were employed (Muchow, 1935):

> ... the "flash-light-method" was used by walking through a specific territory ... while recording and describing the behavior of all children who were present at that time. ... [Alternatively], the "time sample method" was applied where the observers remained at a fixed place and recorded within a limited period of time all the behaviors of the children that took place at this location. Thirdly, the method of "constant observations" was employed. ... Specific children or groups of children were observed while they displayed a given behavior. Others were observed while they took part in a variety of activities dur-

ing a set time. These three methods yielded in the course of a year a vast number of "behavior patterns." (p. 40)

Figures 3 and 4 show a map of the "Landing Place at the Easterbeck Canal" in Hamburg, which was a favorite playground of the children in Muchow's project. The various uses of this area as a place for adults and as a playground for children can be clearly distinguished. As part of her general research Muchow also studied the behavior and the experiences of children on playgrounds and vacant lots; on streets with little or a lot of traffic; and in department stores.

At the end of her book, Muchow summed up her research on the world of urban children (1935):

> Before we investigated the lifespace of the urban child in greater detail ... it was already clear that the space in which we were interested was not the three-dimensional, mathematical space

which epistemologically provides the basic conditions of all experience. For us "space" was . . . the concrete space, "in" which we urban people live—the urban space of a metropolis. (p. 92)

In the late spring of 1933, William Stern and Heinz Werner (1890–1964) lost their academic appointments as a consequence of anti-Semitic legislation in Nazi Germany. The last report from Stern's Hamburg Institute (1933) makes reference to a variety of projects that Muchow had not completed. As the only non-Jewish member of Stern's group, Muchow was forced to transfer Stern's program to Gustav Deuchler (1883–1955), the Director of the Educational Seminar of Hamburg University, who was also a member of the Nazi party. According to her brother, Muchow suffered significant discrimination because of her previous affiliation with Stern's "Jewish Institute" (Zinnecker, 1978, p. 23). An official letter from the period—at which time all remaining members of the institute were denounced as "Jews" or "Jew lovers," contains the following denigrating comments about Muchow (Moser, 1991):

> Dr. Muchow, who was the closest intimate of Professor Stern [and who] visits him daily and discusses all plans with him, is the most dangerous. . . . She was an active member of the Marxist "World Association for Educational Reform." . . . Her educational-psychological influence is harmful and contrary to a German view of the state. (pp. 496–497)

On her 41st birthday on September 25, 1933, Muchow was informed that her appointment at the university was terminated and that she would be reassigned to a full-time public school teaching position. Two days later she committed suicide. The Nazi authorities prevented William Stern from attending her funeral and forced Muchow's brother to fly a swastika flag while she was buried (Wohlwill, 1985). Zinnecker (1978) indeed spoke the truth when he referred to Martha Muchow's work as a "lost research tradition" in modern educational and developmental psychology.

Bibliography

Fries, M. (1995). *Mütterlichkeit und Kinderseele. Zum Zusammenhang von Sozialpädagogik, bürgerlicher Frauenbewegung und Kindrpsychologie zwischen 1899 und 1933. Ein Beitrag zur Würdigung Martha Muchows.* Frankfurt: Lang.

Moser, H. (1991). Zur Entwicklung der akademischen Psychologie in Hamburg bis 1945. Eine Kontrast-Skizze als Würdigung des vergessenen Erbes von William Stern. In E. Krause, G. Otto, & W. Walter (Eds.), *Hamburger Beiträge zur Wissenschaftsgeschichte* Vol. 3, Part II (pp. 483–518). Berlin: Reimer.

Muchow, M. (1926). Psychologische Untersuchungen über die Wirkung des Seeklimas auf Schulkinder. *Zeitschrift für Pädagogische Psychologie, 27,* 18–31.

Muchow, M., & Muchow, H. H. (1935). *Der Lebensraum des Großstadtkindes.* Hamburg: Martin Riegel.

Probst, P. (1995). Martha Marie Muchow. In Historischen Kommission bei der Bayerischen Akademie der Wissenschaften (Ed.), *Neue Deutsche Biographie* (Vol. 18, p. 341). Berlin: Duncker & Humblot.

Schubeius, M. (1990). *Und das psychologische Laboratorium muß der Ausgangspunkt pädagogischer Arbeiten werden!* Frankfurt: Lang.

Stern, W. (1933). Aus den letzten Arbeiten des Psychologischen Instituts der Hamburgischen Universität 1931–1933. *Zeitschrift für angewandte Psychologie, 45,* 397–417.

Strnad, E. (1949). Martha Muchow in ihrer Bedeutung für die sozialpädagogische Arbeit. In M. Muchow, *Aus der Welt des Kindes. Beiträge zum Verständnis des Kindergarten- und Grundschulalters* (pp. 7–20). Hans Heinrich Muchow. Ravensburg: O. Maier.

Wohlwill, J. F. (Ed.). (1985) *Habitats for children: The impacts of density.* Hillsdale, NY: Lawrence Erlbaum.

Zinnecker, J. (1978). Recherchen zum Lebensraum des Großstadtkindes. Eine Reise in verschüttete Lebenswelten undWissenschaftstraditionen. In M. Muchow & H. H. Muchow, *Der Lebensraum des Großstadtkindes* (pp. 10–52). Reprint, Bensheim: päd. (Original work published, 1935. Hamburg: Martin Riegel).

Jean Piaget

Horst Heidbrink

Jean Piaget (1896–1980) is one of those scholars whose name is far better known than his
work. Most psychologists are likely to remember
more details about Freud's psychoanalysis than
about Piaget's genetic epistemology. Nonetheless,
both authors appear to share a similar fate. Their
theories and discoveries are often viewed as scientifically refuted or at least somewhat outdated. It is
likely that one of the reasons for this evaluation is
that Piaget (as well as Freud) did not adhere to the
accepted empirical research paradigm that is characteristic of modern psychology.

However, despite such reservations—and even
Piaget himself characterized himself in his autobiography as one of those 20th-century psychologists
who had to suffer a maximum of scientific criticism
(1976, p. 47)—he has long been accepted as a pioneer of developmental psychology and as the multitalented source of inspiration for countless research
studies. Piaget's fame is well established today, but
his work is at best only superficially known. According to Gardner (1989), Piaget's long-range goal,
which was the development of his genetic theory of
knowledge, is a task "which most modern scholars
find so intimidating that they dare not proceed with
Piaget's work" (p. 131).

When Piaget was asked at one time about his
reaction to the lack of understanding of his work
among philosophers and psychologists, he replied
laconically: "I wait" (Evans, 1979, p. 58). He was fully
aware that he was regarded as a "difficult" author.
Moreover, Piaget was a very prolific writer and the
mere scope of his published work presented a
rather daunting barrier before even his most industrious readers. J. A. McLaughlin's bibliography of
Piaget's works (1988) contains about 540 titles—not

Figure 1 Piaget at his desk.

including translations and his writings on biological topics.

Piaget was born on August 9, 1896, in the small University city of Neuchâtel in the French part of Switzerland. His father was an historian who specialized in medieval history and was characterized by his son as a conscientious and critical scholar. Piaget gave his father credit for having taught him to value systematic research skills. Piaget described his mother as an intelligent, energetic, and religious woman, who was a "really kind" person. Her "neurotic temperament" appears at times to have been a burden to her family. Piaget believed that his mother's outlook on life caused him to neglect games for "serious work" in childhood, not unlike his father who took refuge in his historical studies.

hometown after hours two days of each week. From about 1906 to 1910, young Piaget assisted the local museum's director with the organization of the collections and devoted much of his free time to the mollusk collection. By the end of this early scientific apprenticeship, Piaget, who had published 22 articles before 1915, had become an expert on mollusks. Consequently, the Director of the Natural Science Museum in Geneva offered Piaget a position as custodian of the Museum's Mollusk collection. Piaget had to turn the appointment down because he was only a high school student. Similarly, he refused to accept speaking invitations from foreign researchers because he did not want to reveal that he was still a minor.

Piaget's godfather, Samuel Cornut, a Swiss scholar, was concerned about the premature "specialization" of his godson. He tried to awaken Piaget's interest in philosophy by introducing him to the work of Henri Bergson (1859–1941). Bergson's fascinating union of biology and epistemology were to provide the motivational foundation for Piaget's lifelong research. Piaget was fascinated by basic questions about the development of knowledge, understanding, and especially man's ability to understand reality. He believed that these questions could only be solved through a connection between philosophy and the sciences. To Piaget (1965), philosophy alone was too "speculative" and the various individual sciences were too focused on specific facts. In his autobiography Piaget made the following comments about his early studies (1976):

Figure 2 Piaget at the age of 10 with his parents and sisters.

Piaget's scientific career reached its first peak in 1907. At the age of 11, he noticed a sparrow in a public park which seemed to be a partial albino. His one-page description of this discovery was published in the *Rameau de Sapin*, a local natural history publication.

During the same year, Piaget received official permission to study the collections of birds, fossils, and mussels in the Natural Science Museum of his

> These studies, premature as they were, were nonetheless of great value for my scientific development; moreover, they functioned, if I may say so, as protection against the demon of philosophy. Thanks to them, I had the rare privilege

Figure 3 Facsimile of Piaget's second publication.

of getting a glimpse of science and what it stands for before undergoing the philosophical crises of adolescence. To have had early experience with these two kinds of problematic approaches constituted, I am certain, the hidden strength of my later psychological activity. (p. 18)

Preparation for the Swiss school exit examination in 1915, along with his research on mollusks, his intensive philosophical readings, and his attempt to record his own thoughts in writing, affected Piaget's health to such a degree that he was sent to the quiet of the Swiss mountains for a year to recover. Even there he was plagued with the idea of having to create something. He surrendered to this temptation and wrote a philosophical book, *Research* (1917), which he constructed in the form of a novel, to "avoid compromising himself scientifically." Piaget's autobiography contains the dry comment that nobody paid attention to the work, "except for one or two indignant philosophers" (Piaget, 1976, p. 23).

After graduating from high school, Piaget enrolled at the University of Neuchâtel as a student of the natural sciences. He did not begin his actual studies until his return from the mountains. He completed his scientific studies in 1918 with a dissertation about the mollusks of the Swiss Canton of Valais. At the university he had become so strongly interested in philosophy and psychology that he moved to Zürich to work in the psychological laboratory of G. F. Lipps (1865–1931) and Arthur Wreschner (1866–1932) and at the psychiatric clinic under Eugen Bleuler (1857–1939). At the Burghölzli, Piaget became acquainted with psychoanalysis by reading Freud and the journal *Imago*, and by attending lectures given by Pfister and Jung.

Psychoanalysis appears to have had a stronger impact on Piaget than one would assume from his autobiographical comments. He admitted in a much later interview that he was analyzed in 1921. The woman who analyzed him reportedly terminated treatment after about eight months because he had been reluctant to accept Freud's theories. Vidal (1989) indicated that Piaget's analyst was Sabina Spielrein (1885–1941), a student of Jung's. Piaget also appears to have tried practicing analysis, but without much success. According to Vidal, one of Piaget's analytic "patients" reported that Piaget was obviously not cut out to be a psychoanalyst and that he appeared to go through the motions without a lot of commitment. It is possible that Piaget used these psychoanalytic activities to gain preliminary practice for his later attempt at analyzing his own mother. This effort clearly did not work out because the mother rebelled against her son's analytic interpretations (Vidal, 1989, p. 176).

At about the same time, Piaget worked with Théodore Simon (1873–1961) in Paris on the development of an adaptation of Binet's intelligence tests. In this work, he became primarily interested in the errors which children made in their answers. Piaget had now found his very own field of research—the development of children's thought. As the result of his first publications in the field, Edouard Claparede offered Piaget an academic appointment at the Jean-Jacques Rousseau Institute in Geneva. In Geneva Piaget found ideal research conditions and consequently published his findings about the cognitive development of children in five books. Piaget reported that he expected these works would be read by only a very small audience. He published them anyway, however, because he wished to use them "mainly as documentation for a later synthesis, to be addressed to a wider audience" (Piaget, 1976, p. 29). Ironically, the unexpectedly solid response to these early works did not exactly please Piaget because these books were often read and discussed as if they contained his "final word" on these issues (1976): "Besides, when one is young he does not suspect that, for a long time, he will be judged by his first works, and that only very conscientious people will read the later ones" (p. 29). Piaget noted further that the methodological weaknesses of his early books were caused by his excessive dependence on his "clinical method" dealing with the verbal expressions of children, and not on the concrete manipulation and experimentation of objects. This problem was almost automatically overcome when he began to expand his studies downward to less verbal infants who were younger than two years of age.

Piaget was also dissatisfied with the strong social and practical emphasis placed on his early work—which was viewed by many of his readers as a special strength and not a weakness. For example, his early books focused on general topics like language use in children, the development of moral

judgment, and a variety of narrowly defined questions (i.e., children's explanations of dreams and meteorological phenomena, the origin of the sun and the moon, etc.). Interestingly, the weaknesses of some of Piaget's early studies seem to have encouraged other researchers to successfully explore the same topics further (i.e., Kohlberg's studies of moral development, [1869]).

In 1924, Piaget married Valentine Chatenay. He became the father of three children, and his son became familiar to his readers. He carefully observed and recorded his children's behavior as babies and infants and used them repeatedly to illustrate his theories.

Today, almost every introductory textbook of psychology contains Piaget's famous four stages of cognitive development from infancy to adulthood: (1) The Stage of Sensory-motor Intelligence (0–2 years); (2) The Stage of Preoperational Thinking (2–7 years); (3) The Stage of Concrete Operations (7–11 years); and (4) The Stage of Formal Operations (after 11 years). Of course, the mere recollection and enumeration of the four developmental stages does not constitute an inclusive summary of Piaget's work. They do illustrate, however, the dangers facing all psychological stage theorists. Piaget regarded the age ranges associated with the cogni-

Figure 4 Piaget and his long-time collaborator Bärbel Innhelder.

logical thinking encountered little understanding. When his critics opposed his use of logic and epistemology in psychology and accused him of exceeding the limits of psychology, Piaget noted angrily:

> I am afraid that this is a new sign of almost incurable conservatism among psychologists; they show no distrust toward numbers or mathematics because they have been told of these for more than twenty-five years on a daily basis. However, they use the defense of repression as soon as one mentions the concepts of modern logic or epistemology. (1976, p. 53)

Piaget is one of the few psychologists, who was actively involved in interdisciplinary research. In 1955, he established the International Center for Genetic Epistemology in Geneva, which concentrated on the study of the increase of knowledge in children and in the history of scientific thought. Piaget worked at this facility with logicians, mathematicians, physicists, biologists, linguists, and psychologists on joint research projects. He was greatly interested in having these experts work together over an extended period of time in the hope of encouraging "sufficient reciprocity" and a perma-

Figure 5 Piaget and his family in the 1930s.

tive stages as only crude guidelines. They have often been misperceived by others as clearly distinct time periods. For example, the book *The Psychology of the Child: Problems of Genetic Psychology* (1969), by Piaget and Inhelder, contains the following blunt explanation in a footnote to the chapter on the sensory-motor stage: "It should be noted once and for all that age information in this book refers only to an average and still-approximate age" (p. 119).

Piaget's later works focused on relatively abstract topics like the development of number concepts and classification skills. In addition, his theoretical explanations became more mathematical and scientific. For example, he tried to describe thought on the basis of logical structures like his "16 binary operations" and the so-called "INCR" group of concepts (identity, negation, correlativity, and reciprocity). In psychology, Piaget's "logical" explanations of

Figure 6 Piaget the philosopher in his garden.

346

nent scientific discourse among all participants. The success of this scientific venture is illustrated in McLaughlin's (1988) Piaget bibliography, which lists almost 300 male and female coauthors during Piaget's association with his international research center.

Piaget never regarded his work as completed. This is clear from the section covering the 1950–1965 period in his autobiography (1976):

> If one systematically resumes the study of causality, it means that one begins once more with the analysis of cognitive development. Now, however, one adopts the perspective of the object and no longer that of the subject. This is a terribly vast field, which still contains many surprises. But at the end of a scientific life, it is better to be ready to change one's perspectives than to be doomed to repeat them forever. (p. 59)

Bibliography

Evans, R. I. (1979). *Psychologie im Gespräch.* Berlin: Springer.

Gardner, H. (1989). *Dem Denken auf der Spur. Der Weg der Kognitionswissenschaft.* Stuttgart: Klett-Cotta.

Kohlberg, L. (1969). Stage and sequence. The cognitive-developmental approach to socialization. In D. Goslin (Ed.), *Handbook of socialization theory and research* (pp. 347–480). Chicago: Rand McNally.

McLaughlin, J. A. (1988). *Bibliography of the works of Jean Piaget in the social sciences.* Lanham: University Press of America.

Piaget, J. (1907). Un moineau albinos. *Rameau de Sapin, 41,* 36.

Piaget, J. (1965). *Sagesse et Illusions de la Philosophie.* Paris: Presses Universitaires de France (Deutsch: Weisheit und Illusionen der Philosophie. Frankfurt/Main: Suhrkamp, 1974).

Piaget, J. (1976). Autobiographie. In J. Piaget, *Werk und Wirkung. Mit autobiographischen Aufzeichnungen von Jean Piaget* (pp. 15–59). Munich: Kindler.

Piaget, J., & Inhelder, B. (1969). *The psychology of the child: Problems of genetic psychology.* London: Routledge & Kegan Paul. (Original work published 1966: *La psychologie de l'enfant*)

Vidal, F. (1989). Freud und Piaget. Jean, "Enkel" von Sigmund. In B. Nitzschke (Ed.), *Freud und die akademische Psychologie* (pp. 162–180). Munich: PVU.

The Vienna School of Developmental Psychology

Brigitte A. Rollett

T he Psychological Institute of the University of Vienna (also referred to as the Vienna School of Psychology) was established in 1922 by Karl Bühler (1879–1963) as an independent research center. His wife Charlotte Bühler (1883–1974) joined him a

Figure 1 Charlotte Bühler ca. 1930.

year later in 1923 as his academic assistant. Previously, Charlotte Bühler had achieved distinction in her own right at the Dresden Technical University as the first female instructor in Germany. Her second dissertation (i.e., her research dissertation) was titled "Discovery and Invention in Literature and Art" (1920). In Vienna, her academic rank from Dresden was accepted by the Philosophy Faculty, and she was approved to teach courses in developmental psychology and aesthetics. The conservative faculty did not, however, appoint Frau Bühler to an associate professorship until 1929, and even then only 38 of her 56 colleagues voted for her promotion to that rank.

From the beginning, developmental psychology held a central position in the research program of the Vienna Psychological Institute (Glöckel, 1927, p. 127f). Before receiving his Vienna appointment, Karl Bühler had published a book titled *The Mental Development of the Child* (1918, 1930). Charlotte Bühler was well known for her original research, which was published in *The Mental Life of Teenagers* (1918), in which she analyzed the diaries of young adults.

Karl Bühler received his appointment at the University of Vienna only after lengthy negotiations. The Vienna chair had previously been turned down by two experimental psychologists, Erich Becher (1882–1929) and Erich Rudolf Jaensch (1883–1940), because they were dissatisfied with the available research equipment in Vienna. After arriving, Bühler solved the problem by promoting a cooperative arrangement with the new Institute of Education, which was organized and supported by the City of Vienna (Benetka, 1989, p. 178ff).

The close cooperation between the Institute of Psychology and the more practice-oriented field of teacher training played a major role in the future research and personal life of the Bühlers. Their work became closely associated with the efforts of Otto Glöckel (1874–1935), the social-democratic reformer of the Vienna school system. Charlotte Bühler believed that the political difficulties which her husband suffered after the 1938 annexation of Austria by Nazi Germany (i.e., academic demotion, discharge, and lengthy imprisonment) were related to their involvement with socialist politics in Vienna (1972, p. 24f).

Whatever the case may be, it is true that the choice of research problems by the Bühler institute was strongly influenced by their contact with educational practice. In fact, the integration of strict experimental research with controlled, empirical application became a hallmark of the Vienna School of Developmental Psychology. The culmination of Charlotte Bühler's achievement during her Vienna period was the establishment of an Institute for Child Psychology, which provided diagnosis and treatment services for children and adolescents.

Another novel research approach used by the Bühlers was the adaptation of the observational-experimental approach to the study of children which Wolfgang Köhler (1887–1967), Thorleif Schjelderup-Ebbe (1894–1977), and David Katz (1884–1953) developed for use with animals (Fadrus, 1924). This type of research, which required 24-hour "continuous observations [of children] under natural conditions," was made possible by the Reception Center for Children, the Central Children's Shelter (now called the Charlotte Bühler Home), and other child care institutions of the Vienna municipality.

Although the University of Vienna had only a single assistantship position in psychology, which was at one time filled by Egon Brunswick (1903–1955), the Bühlers and their associates carried out an exceptionally productive research program. Charlotte Bühler spent the year 1924–1925 in America as a Fellow of the Rockefeller Foundation in America. While in the United States, she visited the research institutes of Arnold Gesell (1880–1961) and Edward Lee Thorndike (1874–1949). More importantly, she succeeded in winning the generous support of the Rockefeller Foundation for her husband's institute in Vienna. The generous 10-year funding was primarily used to employ additional researchers.

Among the outstanding scholars of the Vienna group, Paul Lazarsfeld (1901–1976), the methodolo-

Figure 2 Entrance of Vienna Reception Center for Children.

gist and statistician, deserves special attention. His studies of working class teenagers complemented existing knowledge about the life of middle- and upper middle-class high school students. In addition, Else Frenkel (1908–1958), the future wife of Egon Brunswik, became well known after World War II for her coauthorship of *The Authoritarian Personality* (1950) with Theodor Adorno (1903–1969). Still another prominent figure was Hildegard Hetzer (b. 1899), who worked as Charlotte Bühler's assistant until 1931. During this period Hetzer produced important monographs on various topics in developmental psychology, most notably the development of empirical research on children's games (Hetzer, 1986).

Charlotte Bühler's 1928 book, *Childhood and Youth*, provides a summary of the work of Viennese developmental psychology during its initial phase. Apart from her interest in basic questions of infant development, Bühler was strongly interested in pro-

Figure 3 Hildegard Hetzer ca. 1935.

ducing a test of child development as a practical alternative to the existing intelligence tests. Utilizing pilot studies by Hetzer, Käthe Wolf (1907–1967) and Liselotte Frankl (b. 1910) published the "Vienna Test [of Child] Development" in 1932. Rene Spitz (1887–1974), who had become acquainted with this test procedure during a one-year stay in Vienna, adopted this instrument later for his studies of depression in institutionalized children (Schenck-Danziger, 1981, p. 67).

Among Karl Bühler's many eminent PhD students, Karl Popper (1902–1994), the philosopher and logician, merits special attention. Although Popper had initially planned only to carry out an empirical research project in cognitive psychology, he later submitted the theoretical part of his study as a dissertation to Bühler and the philosopher Moritz Schlick (1882–1936) (Popper, 1982, p. 193ff). In this work, Popper advanced his genetic theory of intelligence on the basis of Bühler's theory about the

three aspects of psychology (i.e., behavior, experience, and objective mental products). Similarities between Bühler's "aspects" and Popper's well-known three world theory are quite obvious.

In 1929 the Vienna Psychological Institute hosted the Eleventh Congress of the Society for Experimental Psychology, which changed its name to the German Society for Psychology at the same conference. The 268 members of this organization included 32 female psychologists—an impressive achievement for the time. The 1929 Congress offered many opportunities to present the broad research program of the Vienna Institute to other psychologists and the public. A special attraction of the meeting was the performance of a comedy sketch about Karl Bühler's three aspects of psychology and Charlotte Bühler's five developmental stages.

During the 1930s, Charlotte Bühler began her research on the lives of eminent personalities—research which qualifies her as the founder of modern life span developmental psychology. Later, after World War II, she began to stress the importance of a "meaningful" and "fulfilled life" for the individual, becoming one of the cofounders of humanistic psychology together with Abraham Maslow (1908–1970) and Kurt Goldstein (1878–1965) (1972, p. 39).

A special strength of academic psychology in Vienna was the persistent encouragement of junior staff and senior students to carry out their own research projects. Every Wednesday at 6 P.M. a colloquium was held during which new members of the institute were introduced (Rohracher, 1972, p. 2). The usual "post-colloquium" party and dance took place in the Hotel Regina. It was this creative and socially stimulating atmosphere which encouraged Karl Bühler to refuse a call to Harvard University in 1930—a decision he was to regret after the Nazi invasion of Austria in 1938.

There appears to have been no official contact between the Bühler institute and psychoanalysis (Bühler, 1972, p. 29). However, some personal contacts did exist among the students of both groups. Like Spitz, Heinz Hartmann (1894–1970), Rudolf Allers (1883–1963), Oswald Schwarz (1883–1949) and Erik H. Erikson (1902–1994) studied with both Freud and the Bühlers. Erikson's stage theory of life span development, for example, actually can be viewed as an integration of Freud's psycho-sexual stages and Charlotte Bühler's biographical theories. Further evidence of informal contact with psychoanalysis is suggested by the student days of Hans L.

Kreitler, the future professor of psychology at Tel Aviv University. Kreitler attended lectures by both Freud and the Bühlers.

The involuntary emigration of both Karl and Charlotte Bühler in 1939 resulted in the end of the Vienna School of Developmental Psychology. A comparison of the Vienna University catalogues for 1934–1935 with those for 1939 shows that the number of academic employees decreased significantly. More importantly, the new acting director of the department, Gunther Ipsen (1889–1984) added "racial psychology" as a new research specialty.

The Bühlers were belatedly rehabilitated at the 1960 Congress of the German Society for Psychol-

ogy, where they were enthusiastically received. Karl Bühler was honored with the Wundt Medal by Hubert Rohracher (1903–1972), who was Bühler's postwar successor at Vienna. This was a special honor because it was Bühler's 1926 critique of Wundt's "elementaristic" psychology that had first brought him to the attention of his colleagues and eventually helped him create the theoretical basis of a more life-like psychology (Lück, 1991, p. 66ff).

Figure 4 Karl Bühler, Charlotte Bühler, and Rosa Katz at the IUPS Congress in Bonn (1960).

Bibliography

Ash, M. (1987). Psychology and politics in interwar Vienna: The Vienna Psychological Institute, 1922–1942. In M. Ash & W. Woodward (Eds.), *Psychology in twentieth century thought and society* (pp. 143–146). London: Cambridge University Press.

Benetka, G. (1989). Zur Geschichte der Institutionalisierung der Psychologie in Österreich: Die Errichtung des Wiener Psychologischen Instituts. Diplomarbeit Universität Wien.

Bühler, C. (1972). Charlotte Bühler. In L. Pongratz, W. Traxel, & E. Wehner (Ed.), *Psychologie in Selbstdarstellungen* (pp. 9–42). Bern: Huber.

Bühler, C., & Hetzer, H. (1932). *Kleinkindertests.* Leipzig: Barth.

Bühler, K. (1930). *Die geistige Entwicklung des Kindes* (6th ed.). Jena: Fischer. (Original work published 1918)

Eschbach, A. (1988). Karl und Charlotte Bühler—Leben und Werk. *Zeitschrift für Sozialpsychologie und Gruppendynamik, 13*(2), 8–21.

Fadrus, V. (1924). Pädagogische Rundschau. Pädagogisches Institut der Stadt Wien. Das Forschungsprogramm des Psychologischen Institutes. Nach einem Vortrage von Universitätsprofessor K. Bühler. *Schulreform.* Vienna: Schulwissenschaftlicher Verlag, 127–129.

Glöckel, O. (1927). Die Lehrerbildung. In G. Wien (Ed.), *Das Neue Wien* (pp. 201–336). Vienna: Städtewerk .

Hetzer, H. (1986). Anfänge der empirischen Spielforschung. *Spielmittel,* Nr. 1, 4–22.

Lück, H. E. (1991). *Geschichte der Psychologie.* Stuttgart: Kohlhammer.

Popper, K. R. (1928). Zur Methodenfrage der Denkpsychologie. Phil. Diss., Universität Wien.

Popper, K. R. (1982). *Ausgangspunkte. Meine intellektuelle Entwicklung.* (2nd ed.). Hamburg: Hoffmann & Campe.

Rohracher, H. (1972). Hubert Rohracher. In L. Pongratz, W. Traxel, & E. Wehner (Eds.), *Psychologie in Selbstdarstellungen* (pp. 256–287). Bern: Huber.

Schenk-Danzinger, L. (1981). *Entwicklungspsychologie* (15th ed.). Vienna: Österreichischer Bundesverlag.

Schenk-Danzinger, L. (1984). Zur Geschichte der Kinderpsychologie: Das Wiener Institut. *Zeitschrift für Entwicklungspsychologie und Pädagogische Psychologie, 16*(2), 85–101.

Volkelt, H. (1930). *Bericht über den XI. Kongreß für experimentelle Psychologie in Wien vom 09. bis 13.04.1929.* Jena: Fischer.

Leo Semyonovitch Vygotsky

René van der Veer

Leo Semyonovitch Vygotsky (1896–1934) was born on November 5, 1896, in the small town of Orsha in Byelorussia. He began his professional career as a literary critic and public school teacher at several schools in the provincial city of Gomel near Chernobyl in the Ukraine. Later, his interests gradually changed from art to the psychology of art and eventually to psychology proper. In the early 1920s, Vygotsky established his first small labora-

Figure 1 Portrait of Vygotsky as a young man.

tory in Gomel. A series of lectures at the Second Neuropsychological Congress in Leningrad in January of 1924 led to an invitation to become a research assistant at the Institute of Experimental Psychology of Moscow State University. Thus began his brilliant but brief academic career, during which he held several professorships, wrote numerous articles and books, and advanced original theories in various subdisciplines of psychology. His writings covered many areas of psychology and related fields of science. For reasons of clarity, Vygotsky's contributions to each major subject area are described separately in the following sections; it should be realized, however, that Vygotsky himself did not make such distinctions between his different interests.

Philosophy of Science and Methodology

From the beginning of his academic career, Vygotsky was fascinated by the philosophical and methodological problems of scientific psychology. His search for answers to these persistent questions was to continue throughout his life. In 1926, he prepared a long article on "The Historical Meaning of the Crisis in Psychology," which was only published posthumously (Vygotsky, 1982). Like other important psychologists and philosophers (e.g., Binswanger, Münsterberg, Koffka, and Spranger), he devoted a great deal of attention to the respective advantages and disadvantages of introspective psychology and behaviorism. Following the German philosopher Eduard Spranger (1882–1963), Vygotsky emphasized psychology as a dichotomy which included natural, and social or "human" science branches. He was convinced that Spranger's division of psychology could be traced back to the dualistic philosophy of René Descartes (1596–1650) and that the unity of psychology could be re-established through the ideas of Baruch Spinoza (1632–1677). Vygotsky tried to apply his Spinozistic analysis of the nature of psychology in his essay, "The Theory of Emotions: A Historical-Psychological Investigation." This important work also remained unpublished until 1984 (Vygotsky, 1984).

Educational Psychology

As the result of his teaching experience, Vygotsky developed a strong interest in educational questions. Initially his ideas were influenced by the theories of Ivan Pavlov (1849–1936) and Konstantin Nikolaevich Kornilov (1879–1957) (Vygotsky, 1926). Gradually, however, Vygotsky developed his own views, in particular, about the relationship between education and child development (Vygotsky, 1935a). In this context, he originated the concept of the "zone of proximal development," which is still popular today. According to this concept, mental development results from a close, social interaction between the child and an intellectually more advanced individual. All mental functions are first shared by the child and another person, and only later become the private property of the child. This view, which can be traced back to the ideas of Josiah Royce (1855–1916), James Mark Baldwin (1861–1934), George Herbert Mead (1863–1931), and Pierre Janet (1859–1947), suggests that intellectual diagnosis should always include a determination of the degree to which children can benefit from interactions with experienced, adult members of their culture. Consequently, Vygotsky proposed that each child should routinely be given tests of intelligence on at least two occasions. During the first test session, the child would be expected to solve problems independently, and the results would yield a cross-sectional estimate of the child's abilities. During a later evaluation, the child would be given opportunities for asking help from an adult associate. The second evaluation would yield a measure of the child's developmental potential. Recent American studies have shown that such dynamic assessments provide more predictive information than standard IQ scores (Campione, Brown, Ferrara, & Bryant, 1984).

Defectology

Vygotsky's first scientific publications dealt with the field of *defectology* or child psychopathology, which focused on the diagnosis and treatment of mentally

and physically handicapped children. According to his contemporaries, Vygotsky was an experienced clinician who possessed exceptional tact and a great deal of sensitivity in his interactions with his young patients. He was particularly interested in the problems of blind and deaf children and wrote about them at length. His central argument was that many of the problems that handicapped children face are the result of their social isolation, and that these could be overcome by successful social integration. He strongly supported the mainstreaming of handicapped children and adolescents into regular classrooms and into a normal work environment. According to Vygotsky, the loss of hearing or sight is not the most serious handicap for children. Eyes and ears are "instruments of the mind" and can be replaced by artificial instruments or other sensory systems. For example, fingers can replace the eyes when blind children learn to read Braille.

Figure 2 Title page of Vygotsky's *Principles of Pedology* (1935).

Pedology

Although Vygotsky nowadays is known as a "developmental psychologist," in his own time he was seen as a pedologist and the professorships he held were mainly in pedology. He published several books and many articles in this field and served as coeditor of the *Soviet Journal of Pedology*. For Vygotsky pedology was the science that integrates disciplines, like medicine, psychology, education, and defectology, and applies knowledge from these fields to specific age ranges or developmental periods. He tried to analyze the unique nature of each developmental period and its specific problems (Vygotsky, 1929).

Unfortunately, the majority of Russian pedologists relied so much and so uncritically on the massive use of IQ tests that one can sympathize to some degree with the growing dissatisfaction of the Soviet government. Be that as it may, pedology was officially outlawed in 1936 as a science, and two years after his death, Vygotsky's writings suffered the same fate. It was decades before his articles and books were republished, and even today much of Vygotsky's work is virtually unknown (Van der Veer & Valsiner, 1991).

Figure 4 Vygotsky, his wife Rosa, and his daughter Gita, during a filmed psychological experiment.

Psychology

Vygotsky is best known through a posthumous collection of his articles, which were published under the title *Thought and Language* (1934). The central topic of this book is the relationship between thinking and speaking during child development. According to Vygotsky, speech and verbal concepts are tools or instruments which the developing personality needs in order to direct and control his or her own thinking.

Although these writings were significantly stimulated by the original work of Jean Piaget (1896–1980), Vygotsky reached very different conclusions. For him existing mental functions, like early memory and attention, are transformed as soon as a child begins to speak and acquires so-called scientific concepts (e.g., the concept of a mammal). Scientific concepts form a system and permit the child to draw various conclusions (e.g., "some animals have lungs or do not lay eggs"). According to Vygotsky, these scientific concepts are only fully acquired in early adolescence and result in a fundamental reorganization of the child's mind. For example, a child can now utilize concepts when

Figure 3 Portrait of Vygotsky shortly before his death (1934).

recalling events, and these concepts reorganize the material to be memorized and allow the child to reproduce it in a logical sequence. During the final years of his life, Vygotsky concentrated on the acquisition of scientific concepts during child development. Specifically, he explained certain mental disorders as the result of an impairment or deficiency of the conceptual system. For example, Vygotsky believed schizophrenia involved a total collapse of conceptual thought.

Vygotsky was a multitalented scientist whose ideas influenced important subspecialties of psychology and related scientific disciplines. His extensive familiarity with European psychology and philosophy shaped his thinking about important psychological problems. Only history will show which of Vygotsky's discoveries will be remembered. However, it is likely that, if nothing else, Vygotsky's profound analysis of major themes in psychology, such as the merits and shortcomings of introspection and his theory of instrumental thinking, will be mentioned in future histories of psychology.

Bibliography

Campione, J. C., Brown, A. L., Ferrara, R. A., & Bryant, N. R. (1984). The zone of proximal development: Implications for individual differences and learning. In B. Rogoff & J. V. Wertsch (Eds.), *Children's learning in the "Zone of Proximal Development"* (pp. 77–91). San Francisco, CA: Jossey-Bass.

Van der Veer, R., & Valsiner, J. (1991). *Understanding Vygotsky. The quest for synthesis.* Oxford: Blackwell.

Vygotsky, L. S. (1926). *Pedagogicheskaja psikhologija.* Moscow: Rabotnik Prosveshchenija.

Vygotsky, L. S. (1929). *Pedologija podrostka* (Vol. I). Moscow: Izdanie Bjuro Zaochnogo Obuchenija pri Pedfake 2 MGU.

Vygotsky, L. S. (1934). *Myshlenie i rech. Psikkologicheskie issledovanija.* Moscow-Leningrad: Gosudarstvennoe Socialno-Ekonomicheskoe Izdanie.

Vygotsky, L. S. (1935a) *Umstvennoe razvitie detej v processe obuchenija.* Moscow-Leningrad: Uchpedgiz.

Vygotsky, L. S. (1935b). *Osnovy pedologii.* Leningrad: Gosudarstvennyj Pedagogicheskyj Institut Imeni A. I. Gercena.

Vygotsky, L. S. (1982). Istoricheskij smysl psikhologicheskogo krizisa. In L. S. Vygotsky, *Sobranie Sochinenij. Tom I. Voprosy teorii i istorii psikhologii* (pp. 291–346). Moscow: Pedagogika.

Vygotsky, L. S. (1984). Uchenie ob emotsijakh. In L. S. Vygotsky, *Sobranie Sochinenij. Tom VI. Nauchnoe Nasledstvo* (pp. 92–318). Moscow: Pedagogika.

Vygotsky, L. S., & Luria, A. R. (1930). *Etjudy po istorii povedenija. Obez'jana. Primitiv. Rebenok.* Moscow-Leningrad: Gosudarstvennoe Izdatel'stvo.

Gordon W. Allport: A Becoming Personality

Alvin H. Smith

Gordon Allport was born on November 11, 1887, in Montezuma, Indiana. His father was a country doctor who had pursued a career in business before entering medical practice, and his mother was a schoolteacher. At the time of his birth Allport's parents already had three other sons: Harold, who was 9 years old; Floyd, who was 7; and Fayette, who was 5. The family moved from Indiana and finally settled in Glenville, Ohio, a suburb of Cleveland. There Allport entered school and graduated from Glenville High School in 1915.

Since the hospital facilities at the time were limited, Allport's father saw patients in his own home; consequently, during his early years Allport learned to tend his father's office, which required that he wash bottles and help out with patients. After his graduation from high school, Gordon's older brother Floyd, who had graduated from Harvard, suggested that he apply to Harvard also. Gordon did apply and was accepted after passing the entrance exams. For the first time in his life new intellectual horizons were opened before him, but in his first grading period he made Ds and Cs. After this experience he applied himself with considerably more effort and finally ended the first year with As.

After graduating from Harvard with a degree in psychology, Allport was offered a position teaching English and sociology at Robert College (1919–1920), which was located in Constantinople (Istanbul), Turkey. While returning home, he had an invitation to visit his brother Fayette, who was then working in Vienna with the

Figure 1 G. W. Allport on a Lake Erie trip at age 17.

United States Trade Commission during the period of the Hoover relief activities. While in Vienna, Allport wrote to Sigmund Freud and requested an interview. As Allport himself relates, Freud wrote a

Figure 2 G. W. Allport's college graduation picture.

reply in his own handwriting indicating that he would be glad to meet with Allport and gave him a time for the visit. This interview with Freud has received a great deal of attention and consequently merits further comment. The major account of the visit appeared in *The Journal of Orthopsychiatry* (Allport, 1953) under the title of "The trend in motivational theory."

As Allport later related the incident:

> Soon after I had entered the famous red burlap room with pictures of dreams on the wall, he summoned me into his inner office. He did not speak to me but sat in expectant silence, for me to state my mission. I was not prepared for silence and had to think fast to find a suitable way to his office. A small boy about four years of age had displayed a conspicuous dirt phobia. He kept saying to his mother, 'I don't want to sit there. . . . don't let that dirty man sit next to me.' To him everything was *schmutzig*. His mother was a well starched *Hausfrau*, so dominant and purposive looking that I thought the cause and effect apparent. When I finished my story Freud fixed his kindly therapeutic eyes upon me and said, 'And was that little boy you?' Flabbergasted

and feeling a bit guilty, I contrived to change the subject. While Freud's misunderstanding of my motivations was amusing, it also started a deep train of thought. I realized that he was accustomed to neurotic defenses and that my manifest motivation (a sort of rude curiosity and youthful ambition) escaped him. For therapeutic progress he would have to cut through my defenses, but it so happened that therapeutic progress was not here an issue.

> This experience taught me that depth psychology, for all its merits, may plunge too deep, and that psychologists would do well to give full recognition to manifest motives before probing the unconscious.

> Although I never regarded myself as anti-Freudian, I have been critical of psychoanalytic excesses. (Allport, 1967, pp. 7–8)

Alan C. Elms (1994) makes the claim that in fact Allport did have a dirt phobia. In his book, *Uncovering Lives* in chapter 5 entitled "Allport meets Freud and The Clean Little Boy," Elms provides several reasons supporting this claim, but one in particular is perhaps the most critical for understanding his contention:

> "I am not that little boy with the dirt phobia," we are left with its beginning: "I am not." Erikson, in his psychobiography of Martin Luther, makes much of Luther's so-called "fit in the choir," when Luther is said to have shouted out, "It isn't me!" or "I am not!" Declaring what you are not, according to Erikson, is often a way to establish who you are, what your identity is. Gordon Allport, by his testimony was not a neurotic, not a little boy, not a generic personality interchangeable with other personalities. So what was he? (p. 82)

In this context Erikson's statement about denial raises a very important question, that of the separation of denial from fact. Obviously Allport made much of this episode, but do we know that the dirt phobia is one of the constructions of his own personality, or is it a statement of fact, and what can be made of his feelings of guilt? If I deny that I am something, does that mean that I am actually what I am denying?

A more complete view might be that Freud's probing analysis as to the unconscious left Allport with a feeling that it is more important to discover the overt motives before ever looking to the unconscious ones. Since we do not have Freud's record of that conversation or writings that might have led us to a commentary on Allport's work, it still leaves the question of his encounter with Freud essentially unanswered.

Upon his return to the United States, Allport continued his education by working toward his doctorate in psychology with McDougall, Langfield, and James Ford. He also assisted his brother Floyd, who was editing the *Journal of Abnormal and Social Psychology*, a journal that Allport himself was later to edit. In somewhat of a quandary over his own career direction, Allport consulted with Langfield, who reminded him that psychology had many areas and he did not have to follow any particular path. He completed the doctorate in 1922 and began work on social problems.

In his autobiography Allport (1967) reported the following:

> I had been invited to attend the select gathering of his [Titchener's] group of experimental psychologists, which met at Clark University in May, 1922, just as I was finishing my thesis. After two days of discussing problems in sensory psychology Titchener allotted three minutes to each visiting graduate to describe his own investigations. I reported on traits of personality and was punished by the rebuke of total silence from the group, punctuated by a glare of disapproval from Titchener. Later Titchener demanded of Langfield, "Why did you let him work on that problem?" Back in Cambridge Langfield again consoled me with the laconic remark, "You don't care what Titchener thinks." And I found I did not. (p. 9)

After his graduation Allport accepted a Sheldon Traveling Fellowship which permitted him to travel in Germany for study. While in Germany he spent a considerable amount of time with William and Clara Stern, which marked the beginning of an important lifelong friendship. Later, during the era leading to World War II, Clara wrote to Allport about the troubling conditions in Germany and how Jews were being treated. The Sterns had already flown to Amsterdam, and it was from there that she had written to Allport requesting that he invite them for a visit to the United States. The letter was a plea for help so that they might leave Europe. Allport tried to get Stern appointed to Harvard, but the President of Harvard was adamantly opposed on the grounds that there were already too many faculty unemployed, and there was no room for any additional scholars. Stern did arrive in the United States and obtained a position at Duke University under the Displaced Scholars Awards, which were made possible through the Rockefeller Foundation headed by Edward R. Morrow. Allport did not like McDougall,

who was the Chair of the Psychology Department at Duke, but he did give him credit for accepting Stern as part of his faculty. Later Clara wrote to Allport describing her husband's death.

From *Vergilius, Opera* (ed. by Sebastian Brant).
Strasbourg: Grüninger, 1502.

"Swift through the Libyan cities Rumor sped.
Rumor! What evil can surpass her speed?
In movement she grows mighty, and achieves
Strength and dominion as she swifter flies.
Small first, because afraid, she soon exalts
Her stature skyward, stalking through the lands
And mantling in the clouds her baleful brow . . .
Feet swift to run and pinions like the wind
The dreadful monster wears; her carcase huge
Is feathered, and at the root of every plume
A peering eye abides; and, strange to tell,
An equal number of vociferous tongues,
Foul, whispering lips, and ears, that catch at all . . .
. . . She can cling
To vile invention and malignant wrong,
Or mingle with her word some tidings true."

(*Aeneid*, Book IV. From the translation by Theodore C. Williams, by permission of the publishers, Houghton Mifflin Company.)

Figure 3 Illustration from Renaissance edition of *Vergilius Opera* and poem by Virgil depicting "Rumor."

While in Germany Allport studied with Max Wertheimer, Wolfgang Kohler, and Eduard Spranger in Berlin and then with Stern and Heinz Werner in Hamburg. He later moved on to England and spent some time there with Frederick Bartlett and Karl Herman Breul with whom he studied Faust. A cable from Professor Ford at Harvard offered him an instructorship in social ethics, and he was also invited to offer a new course in the psychology of personality. Allport remained at Harvard for the next two years and then went to Dartmouth for the next four years; however, during the summer sessions he returned to teach at Harvard.

In 1930 Allport accepted a permanent appointment to Harvard, and there he remained for the rest of his life. At Harvard Allport became a personality theorist and a social psychologist when neither of these specialties was popular as an area of study. One of his most important works was a scientific study of rumor, which was completed with Leo Postman shortly after the Second World War. A number of illustrations were used in this study which are reproduced here. The first illustration (see Figure 3) is from the *Vergillius* Opera (edited by Sebastian Bront in 1502). The second is a long section of a poem from Virgil's *Aeneid*, Book IV (from the translation by Theodore Williams) (Allport and Postman, 1947). The study was mainly concerned with how rumor starts and how it affects behavior. The United States had just been through a period of censorship when it did not want any of the possible secrets about troop movements revealed. To help contain

Figure 5 A test for ability to report (from Freyd, 1921).

Figure 6 Battle scene used in rumor experiments.

Figure 4 Typical security of information posters (Office of War Information) used in World War II.

rumors which might reveal important information, a number of posters, such as that illustrated by Figure 4, were produced by the Office of War Information and placed in public areas.

Freyd (1921) had earlier proposed a procedure for determining how people convey information. The standard procedure which Allport adopted for the scientific study of rumor was a modification of Freyd's approach and is described as follows (Allport & Postman, 1947):

> Out of a college class or forum audience a group of people—usually six or seven—are selected (ordinarily volunteers are used). They

are asked to leave the room. It is customary not to tell that the experiment pertains to rumor, though if such suspicion exists no harm is done, for studies show that the distortions that occur are but slightly affected by such knowledge. They are told only that they must listen carefully to what they will hear when they return to the room and repeat what they have heard "as exactly as possible."

When the subjects have left the room, a slide depicting some detailed situation is thrown on the screen and some member of the audience is assigned the task of describing it (while looking at it) to the first subject. He is requested to include approximately 20 details in his description.

After the initial description of the picture a member of the group of subjects is called back into the room and is placed in a position where he cannot see the picture on the projection screen although everyone else in the room can see it. (If no alcove or other architectural feature of the room provides a shielded location near the door where the subjects enter, some movable screen should be placed in an appropriate place before the experiment commences.) The first subject listens to the "eyewitness" account given him by the selected member of the audience or by the experimenter. A second subject is called into the room, taking his position beside the first subject. Both are unable to see the screen. The first subject then repeats as accurately as he can what he has heard about the scene (still visible to the audience on the screen).

A third subject then takes his position next to the second and listens to the report.

The procedure continues in the same manner until the last subject has repeated the story he has heard, and taken his seat (usually amid laughter) to compare his final version with the original on the screen. (pp. 65–67)

The following are examples of comments reported by subjects in the 1947 study:

[Figure 6] "A church is on fire, there is a cross. I don't remember the next part. There is a church steeple. There are four Negroes working. The church has a clock. It is ten minutes past two." These are typical reports collected in these experiments.

"This is a street scene [Figure 7] on the low side of town. A couple of boys, a Negro boy and a white boy, are playing ball. There is a policeman. Across the street is a movie theater playing a Gene Autry picture. Upstairs is a bowling alley. Near the bowling alley is a blank wall with a sign, 'No ball playing.' There is a window with three flower pots, one falling out. At another window a man is smoking something, and whatever it is is falling out of his mouth."

"This takes place on a street corner [Figure 8]. Something is happening. There is a Negro with a razor, a man with a beard, two women reading newspapers, not particularly interested in what is happening."

"This is a gathering of people [Figure 9]. A group of people are interested in some incident. The center of interest is a Negro youth with clothes disarranged, shoes off, and other evidence of having been maltreated. Close to him is a police officer trying to handle the situation. It is not clear whether the police officer has arrested the Negro or is trying to protect him. In the inner circle is another Negro apparently attempting to get away from the gathering." (pp. 68–72)

Figure 7 Street scene used in rumor experiments.

Figure 8 Subway scene used in rumor experiments.

Figure 9 Riot scene used in rumor experiment.

All of these reports came from the audience part of the study, and as Allport notes, there is a social effect, but reports from places where no audience was present are somewhat the same, although with more detail. Somewhat longer reports resulted when the experiment was done only with an experimenter present.

Allport's contributions range over a variety of subjects including personality theory, the nature of prejudice, and, with Lindzey and Vernon, research on values. This latter work appeared first as a journal article (1931) followed by three editions of a book entitled *The Study of Values* (1931, 1951, 1960). This work was based on Eduard Spranger's *Types of Men* (1922/1928). As mentioned earlier, Allport had studied with Spranger while he was in Berlin. The six values Allport identified in his writing were: theoretical, economic, aesthetic, social, political, and religious.

Allport is also noted for the *A-S Reaction Study* (1928) which he published with his brother Floyd. The A-S reaction study is a study of ascendance-submission. This was a scale to measure dominant-submissive tendencies and was one of the earliest paper-and-pencil personality tests.

One of Allport's most interesting studies (1929)

Figure 10 Allport as a faculty member at Harvard in his later years.

was entitled: "The study of personality by the intuitive method: An experiment in teaching from *The Locomotive God*." *The Locomotive God* (Leonard, 1927) was an autobiographical account of a professor of English at the University of Wisconsin who had a phobia of railroads, even to the point where he would not cross railroad tracks or move but a few feet from his home. Allport's interest in this particular case stemmed from a significant controversy which existed in Europe at the time—the so-called *verstehen method*, which attracted very little attention in America.

> Verstehen, according to the definition of Eduard Spranger, is the mental process of "grasping events as fraught with meaning in relation to a totality." . . . His [Spranger's] view is that there must be two psychologies, one in the method of natural science and one based upon verstehen. This dualism is characteristic of the thought of the school. (Allport, 1928, pp. 16–17)

Allport went on to argue that intuition does have an important place in psychology—especially in personality theory. He then proceeded to use this as a teaching tool to determine if students in his class could in fact take an original case study of this kind and develop an understanding of personality that they would not have otherwise. In its final outcome, it enhanced the interest in psychology, and the students, without exception, testified that the time and labor required were well spent. "Here is an exercise in the creation of psychological truth, by combining the causal and intuitive attitudes and it is an admirable instance of the project method in psychology" (Allport 1929, p. 25). His first concluding comment from this article is: "If psychology is to remain faithful to its natural subject matter (human nature) it must consider the individual manifestations of that subject matter (the single personality) as well as general manifestations (laws of human behavior)" (Allport, 1929, p. 25). His closing comment from this paper is: "Any satisfactory theory as to 'how we know people' must recognize that inference and context are always in the service of the inherent tendency of mind to structure its content into wholes, and therefore, in a sense, to perceive intuitively" (Allport, 1929, p. 27). This is Allport's constant theme in his writings about personality, and although he wrote extensively on other matters, this is perhaps his greatest contribution, that of the individual theory of personality, and the idea that personality is not static but is dynamic and chang-

ing. This was his sharpest disagreement with Freud—his belief that personality is not fixed but constantly changing as the individual grows. This concept is central to his volume *Becoming: Basic Considerations for a Psychology of Personality* (Allport, 1955).

Allport's contributions to personality theory are many, but perhaps his most important contributions may be summarized in his insistence (a) on the uniqueness of each individual, (b) that conscious determinants of behavior are of overwhelming significance, (c) that the individual is more a creature of the present than the past, and (d) that dwelling on the history of the organism is unprofitable. His concept of functional autonomy was a deliberate attempt to free the theorist or investigator from an unnecessary preoccupation with the history of the organism. His view of humanity is positive, with the conscious elements of motivation emphasized, and behavior is seen as internally consistent and determined by contemporary factors. Functional autonomy is a concept which indicates that behavior can continue after the original stimulus has disappeared without any further stimulus to provoke it.

Allport's record of awards and distinctions is legion. He served as president of the American Psychological Association in 1939; during World War II he served on the Emergency Committee in Psychology and specialized in problems of civilian morale and rumor; he was an Honorary Fellow of the British Psychological Society; and Honorary Member of Deutsch Gesselleshaft für Psychologie, as well as other foreign societies. He was awarded the Gold Medal of the Psychological Foundation in 1963 and the Distinguished Scientific Contribution Award in 1964. Part of the latter citation reads as follows:

> For reminding us that man is neither beast or statistic, except as we choose to regard him so, and that the human personality finds its greatest measure in the reaches of time. This is to say that, while life may have its crude beginnings, it has its noble endings too, and there is a line that leads from one to the other—a line that graphically portrays the character of the individual, and of mankind as well. This is what he taught his students. (1964, p. 942)

Allport died on October 9, 1967, just short of his 70th birthday.

Bibliography

Allport, G. W. (1928). A test for ascendance-submission. *Journal of Abnormal and Social Psychology, 23,* 118–136.

Allport, G. W. (1929). The study of personality by the intuitive method: An experiment in teaching from *The Locomotive God. Journal of Abnormal and Social Psychology, 24,* 14–27.

Allport, G. W. (1931). A test for personal values. *Journal of Abnormal and Social Psychology, 26,* 231–248.

Allport, G. W. (1937a). *Personality: A psychological interpretation.* New York: Holt, Rinehart, and Winston.

Allport, G. W. (1937b). The functional autonomy of motives. *American Journal of Psychology, 50,* 141–156.

Allport, G. W. (1942). *The use of personal documents in science.* New York: Social Science Research Council Bull., 49.

Allport, G. W. (1950). *The individual and his religion.* New York: Macmillan Company.

Allport, G. W. (1953). The trend in motivational theory. *American Journal of Orthopsychiatry, 25,* 107–119.

Allport. G. W. (1955). *Becoming: Basic considerations for a psychology of personality.* New Haven: Yale University Press.

Allport, G. W. (1961). *Pattern and growth in personality.* New York: Holt, Rienhart, & Winston.

Allport, G. W. (1965). *Letters from Jenny.* New York: Harcourt, Brace, and World.

Allport, G. W. (1967). Autobiography. In E. G. Boring & G. Lindzey (Eds.), *A history of psychology in autobiography* (Vol. 5, pp. 3–25). New York: Appleton-Century-Crofts.

Allport, G. W., & Postman, L. (1947). *The psychology of rumor.* New York: Henry Holt and Company.

Allport, G. W., & Vernon, P. (1931). A test for personal values. *Journal of Abnormal and Social Psychology, 26,* 231–248. (Reprinted by Houghton-Mifflin, 1931)

Allport, G. W., Vernon, P., & Lindzey, G. (1960). *The study of values* (3rd ed.). Boston: Houghton-Mifflin Company. (2nd edition published 1951)

Distinguished scientific contribution award. (1964). *American Psychologist, 19,* 942.

Elms, A. (1994). *Uncovering lives.* New York: Oxford University Press.

Freyd, M. (1921). A test series for journalistic aptitude. *Journal of Applied Psychology, 5,* 46–56.

Leonard, W. E. (1927). *The locomotive god.* New York: The Century Company.

Spranger, E. (1928). *Types of men* (P. Pigors, Trans.). Halle: Neimeyer. (Original work published 1922)

George A. Kelly and the Development of Personal Construct Theory

Robert A. Neimeyer
Thomas T. Jackson

In one sense, the informal historical impressions of personal construct theory held by a contemporary psychologist say more about the history of the historian than they do about personal construct theory per se. Those psychologists who came of age in the late 1950s are likely to remember George A. Kelly's work (1955) as a bold and iconoclastic, if frustratingly complex, approach to personality and clinical work that brashly demanded attention in a field marked by the hegemony of behavioral theories on the one hand and the psychoanalytic tradition on the other. In contrast, those who encountered the theory a decade later would be more apt to associate it with a growing social psychological literature in cognitive complexity, a literature heavily reliant upon a unique set of repertory grid methods. Psychologists trained in the late 1970s would have developed still a different image of construct theory, perhaps construing it as a curiously lapsed American tradition that somehow found a more favorable reception in Great Britain. Finally, psychologists discovering Kelly in the late 1980s and early 1990s were likely to be introduced to him as a kind of intellectual "founding father," an early harbinger of the now burgeoning cognitive behavioral trend. The shifting image of personal construct theory over the decades provides a clear reminder that our informal histories of events are at least as much the products of the sociology of our time as they are reflections of the historical "reality" they were constructed to represent.

In another sense, each of these historical impressions is true in-as-much as they represent a partial perspective on the field's development. Although in an ironic way, the image of construct theory's freshness and iconoclasm—characteristic of the 1950s—may turn out to have the greatest contemporary validity. In this brief chapter we will try to place the development of personal construct theory in historical perspective, especially as shaped by the particulars of Kelly's life. However, any life and any intellectual history are obviously amenable to several alternative reconstructions, even when they attempt to anchor the account in the "data" of an individual's biography or a field's development. Thus, this chapter represents our own current synopsis of Kelly's life and impact, and we encourage readers to consult other accounts for alternative or fuller treatments of the influence of Kelly's work (Fransella, 1996; Neimeyer, 1985; Zelhart & Jackson, 1983).

One Man's Life

George A. Kelly was born in 1905, the only child of strict religious parents in the tiny farming community of Perth, Kansas. The rural isolation of Kelly's childhood seemed to cultivate in him a sense of resourcefulness and self-determination that later found expression in both the style and content of his theory of personality. After visiting Perth a decade following Kelly's death, the British psychologist Don Bannister remarked that,

> stuck out there on that farm in Kansas, if you didn't imagine something, then there wouldn't be much there. Kelly got the wrong model [for his theory]. The actual model is "man-the-pioneer" [in contrast to Kelly's "man the scientist" metaphor]. And that related to Kelly's personal life, that he came up from pioneering stock. He grew up on the kind of Kansas farm where you invent everything you need. And he carried that over. (cited in Neimeyer, 1985, p. 11)

As Bannister implies, Kelly's later emphasis on the capacity of persons to invent or create the meaning of their lives reflects the premium that his early environment must have placed on imagination and inventiveness. Moreover, Kelly's pioneering background—he and his parents were literally among the last homesteaders on the American frontier—may have predisposed him to conceptualize human behavior in terms of an "exploration" or "quest"; themes that Miller Mair believes pervade much of Kelly's formal theorizing.

> The kind of venture which seems to me to assume a central place in personal construct theory is not of the "big game hunting" or "conquering Everest" variety. It is something both more homey and more audacious. What Kelly seems to be advocating is something like "life on the frontier"—living on the frontiers of your experience rather than within cozily settled conventions or as a more or less willing victim of the demands of tradition. You can almost hear the "wagons trains rolling westward," seeking new pastures and more space for living, as you read Kelly's writings. (cited in Neimeyer, 1985, p. 11)

Kelly gradually transcended the limitations of his environment through educational achievement. After three years of study at Friends University and a final year at Park College, he received his bachelor's degree in 1926, majoring in physics and mathematics. However, balancing this scientific involvement, Kelly had also become increasingly involved in intercollegiate debate and was awarded first place in the Peace Oratorial Contest held at Friends in his sophomore year. Perhaps as an outgrowth of these more social concerns, he chose to pursue graduate work in sociology at the University of Kansas, earning his master's degree in 1928 with a thesis on the leisure time activities of workers in Kansas City. After taking additional coursework in sociology at the University of Minnesota that summer semester, he found employment in a variety of educational settings, teaching classes in speech for the American Bankers Association, on Americanization for future citizens, and on labor relations at a labor college in Minneapolis. As with his boyhood experiences, the abiding concerns represented by this mosaic of interests all found expression in his formulation of personal construct theory some 25 years later.

Kelly deepened his commitment to teaching in 1929 when he accepted a position as an exchange scholar at the University of Edinburgh, earning a second bachelor's degree (this time in education) and developing a nascent interest in psychology. He then returned to the United States and enrolled in the graduate program in psychology at the University of Iowa. There Kelly earned his PhD after a single year of study, suggesting that much of the novelty of his own theorizing may have resulted from his limited acquaintance with the established psychology of his day.

When Kelly entered the job market in 1931, academic work was scarce. As part of his job search, he registered with an employment agency in Chicago and was referred to a small public college in the western half of his home state—Fort Hays Kansas State College (Zelhart, Jackson, & Markley, 1982) (see Figure 1). Clearly, this was not an auspicious time to begin an academic career, with America in the midst of the Great Depression and the Dust Bowl, which had begun to devastate the economy of Midwestern farming states. Some indication of how desperate these times were can be gleaned from the

Figure 1 As a recent graduate of the University of Iowa, Kelly assumed his first faculty position at Fort Hays Kansas State College at the outset of the Great Depression.

fact that Kelly's salary was trimmed from $2,500 per year to $2,400 between the time he signed his contract and the time he arrived on campus. Over the next five years, Kelly and other faculty of the small college would experience further salary reductions, until they were reduced to 75% of their 1931 baseline figure (Zelhart, Jackson, & Markley, 1982).

Kelly's initial research was in the area of experimental psychology, and Figure 2 shows him (at left) conducting an experiment in a vertical rat maze with H. B. Reed (Kelly, 1933). However, the pressing need for psychological services, especially in the school system, soon diverted him from his more purely academic pursuits. In his first semester at Fort Hays, a 12-year-old boy was referred to the psychology department by a teacher concerned about his peculiar appearance and his "shifty eyes." Kelly accepted a psychological evaluation of the case as a class project in his class on adolescent psychology, and the Psychological Clinic informally came into being. Although Kelly and his students remained the only service providers, the clinic grew steadily in its caseload over the next few years, until in 1935, it was directly funded by an act of the state legislature (Kelly, 1937/1982).

Perhaps the most innovative outgrowth of this consultation work was a network of extension clinics begun in 1933 at the request of the superintendent of schools in a neighboring community. In the early 1930s, psychological services in American schools were rudimentary at best, even in urban areas. Work in rural school psychology was even more germinal, with few models of service delivery available and even fewer clinicians trained to implement them. Kelly's solution to this dilemma was to develop a traveling clinic, which eventually served most of western Kansas. Staffed only by Kelly and four undergraduate and master's-level students, the clinic would offer a comprehensive psychological evaluation of as many as 31 cases in a single day, conducting a "family history, social history, educational history, physical tests, psychometrics and [an] interview designed to reveal the personality and ambitions of [each] case" (Kelly, 1937/1982, p. 3). Because the time constraints were severe, the clinics were a model of organization. The various trainees on the team would conduct an extensive psychological assessment of each child, administering several of the commonly used tests from memory (Kelly literally required that they be able to give such tests as the Stanford-Binet accurately without so much as a glance at the scoring blank!). Simultaneous interviews were conducted with parents and teachers, followed by a consultation whose objective was "to make clear-cut recommendations which are within the reach of a case, helpful to those who work with him, and which have a reasonable possibility of being followed" (Kelly, 1937/1982; p. 3).

To ensure interest in the clinics, Kelly frequently would deliver a public lecture to parents, teachers, and interested others while assessments were being conducted. Originally, these concerned topics of

Figure 2 Kelly is pictured here (at left) conducting an experiment in a vertical rat maze with H. B. Reed.

direct relevance to the work of the clinic, such as "Pioneering in Public Mental Health" and "The Problems of the Adolescent." However, as World War II broke out in Europe, Kelly accommodated his lectures to reflect the times (and his own patriotism), speaking on such issues as "The Psychological Foundations of Democracy," and "How to Be a Nazi." Some measure of the success of the clinics in reaching a large and initially skeptical rural population can be gleaned from the services provided in a representative year. Kelly estimated that in fiscal 1936, some 10,538 hours had been spent in evaluation and treatment of 375 cases in 21 counties, at a total cost of $1,029 to Kansas taxpayers—or less than 10 cents an hour (Guydish, Zelhart, Jackson, & Markley, 1982).

Figure 3 Rarick Hall, home of Kelly's pioneering efforts to provide family and school consultation in rural mental health.

The founding of the Psychological Clinic at Fort Hays represented a turning point in Kelly's career, foreshadowing a lifelong attempt to wed clinical scholarship to clinical practice. As Kelly noted in his reflections on the first five years of the clinic's operation:

> The human personality is so intricate and the forces which play upon human life are so complex that the cause and result is soon lost and the psychological clinician is left to guess at the part he has played [in therapy outcome]. That there is a psychological problem in every one of us and that it is ultimately possible to attack that problem through psychological study he is definitely persuaded. He also believes that effective tools for dealing with personal problems can only be forged in the clinic, that shop in which the theories of the psychological laboratory must meet the actual problems of every-day life. (Kelly, 1937/1982, p. 3)

Rarick Hall (Figure 3) was the home of Kelly's pioneering efforts to provide family and school consultation in rural mental health. In the space of a few short years in the early 1930s, Kelly's program of extension clinics expanded to serve most of western Kansas.

Although Kelly's preparation for this clinical role had been limited, it had not been nonexistent. As a student, he had been exposed to both stimulus-response psychology, which he had found mysterious for neglecting the hyphen in the formula, and Freudian theory, which he had read with "the

mounting incredulity that anyone could write such nonsense, much less publish it" (Kelly, 1969, p. 47). But as he immersed himself in clinical practice, he began to revisit these earlier conclusions:

> The strangest thing about this period is that I went back to Freud for a second look. My recollections of Rasmussen's *Principal Nervous Pathways* and of Thorndike's electrical condenser theory of learning applied at the synapses had not proved very helpful to people who were troubled about what was to become of them. But now that I had listened to the language of distress, Freud's writings made a new kind of sense. He too must have listened to these same cries echoing from deep down where there were no sentences, no words, no syntax. (Kelly, 1969, pp. 50–51)

As a result of this experience, Kelly initially began to offer judicious and often helpful psychoanalytic interpretations to his clients. Eventually, however, he began to grow suspicious about the change processes they triggered and contrived an audacious experiment to test their role in effecting a cure:

> I began fabricating "insights." I deliberately offered preposterous interpretations to my clients. Some of them were about as un-Freudian as I could make them—first proposed somewhat cautiously, and then, as I began to see what was happening, more boldly. My only criteria were that the explanation account for the crucial facts as the client saw them and that it carry implica-

tions for approaching the future in a different way. . . .

> What happened? Well, many of my preposterous explanations worked, some of them surprisingly well. . . . In those days psychology was regarded locally as a pretty far-out kind of thing anyway, and if I said that a nervous stomach was rebelling against nourishment of all kinds—parental, educational, and nutritional—most of my clients were willing to try to make something of it. (Kelly, 1969, p. 52)

Such experiences gradually led Kelly to formulate the concept of *constructive alternativism*, the view that all of our interpretations are provisional, to be judged more on the basis of their viability than their validity per se (Kelly, 1955/1991). In keeping with this hypothetical, "as if" philosophy (Vaihinger, 1924), he and his students at Fort Hays began experimenting with novel methods of personality assessment and psychotherapy in the late 1930s. Two additional sources of inspiration were particularly significant for Kelly in the evolution of his own iconoclastic approach to treatment (Stewart & Barry, 1991). From Alfred Korzybski (1933), the founder of general semantics, Kelly borrowed an understanding of the role of linguistic abstractions as templates for referencing objects and events in the world, while not being identical with them. At a clinical level, Kelly was also indebted to Korzybski for the insight that psychotherapeutic change could result from a cognitive or semantic relabeling or "reconstruing" of one's life and role. At the level of actual clinical procedures, however, Jacob Moreno's (1937) psychodramatic work was more influential, emphasizing the utility of spontaneous enactments relevant to the client's identity, biography, and intimate relationships.

In a fresh integration of these ideas and procedures, Kelly devised a new form of role therapy which stressed the formative power of language in shaping character as an efficient alternative to psychoanalysis and other long-term therapies. A reading of Edwards's (1943/1982) and Robinson's (1943/1982) theses (under Kelly's supervision) evaluating the procedure also suggests that it anticipated the psychotherapeutic emphasis on "modeling" and "reframing" which were popularized 35 years later.

In its initial form, role therapy consisted of first asking clients to complete global personality and intellectual assessments and to write a character sketch of themselves from the standpoint of some-

one who knew them intimately and sympathetically. Working with a consultation team, the therapist would analyze these materials, extracting from them the major themes and dimensions that captured the role the client played in relation to the family, social institutions, and the community. This was followed by the team's generating an alternative sketch of a "new role" in which "one or two factors are radically reinterpreted rather than [having] little changes attempted across the entire personality" (Robinson, 1943/1982, p. 57). Therapy consisted of "dramatizing" this alternative role sketch with the client and then revising it until it could "thoroughly satisfy the case's inner needs, not merely modify his external behavior" (Robinson, 1943/1982, p. 55). The therapist then coached the client to enact the part of the character in daily life for a period of time (typically a few weeks or months).

The primary goal of this technique was to help the client recognize that alternative approaches to problematic situations were possible, and that one could change one's outlook through "experiments" in behaving differently (Markley, Zelhart, & Jackson, 1982). It is interesting to note that the two theses completed by Kelly and his students at Fort Hays represented relatively sophisticated outcome studies of a promising psychotherapeutic technique and did so over a decade before Eysenck's (1952) classic critique of the effectiveness of psychotherapy gave impetus to the field of psychotherapy research.

Kelly often joked that it took World War II to get him out of Hays, Kansas. From 1940 to 1943, Kelly had coordinated the civil aeronautics program at Fort Hays, contracting to train over 400 men and women as pilots to ready them for service in the war. The program developed rapidly, evolving into the War Training Service and eventually the Army Air Corps College Detachment (see Figure 4). As a result of this work, he was placed in the aviation psychology branch of the U.S. Navy during the war where he tabled his earlier diagnostic and therapeutic interests and turned his attention to the study of "war weariness" (combat trauma) among pilots, instrument panel design, and other pressing problems of applied military psychology. Although the war may have interrupted the development of his earlier pursuits, it also may have given him his first experience with interdisciplinary collaboration which was later to shape his role as one of the founding fathers of clinical psychology in the United States.

Figure 4 In the early 1940s, Kelly (at far left) coordinated the civil aeronautics program at Fort Hays.

Following the war, Kelly accepted a placement briefly at the University of Maryland and in 1946 was hired as professor and director of clinical psychology at Ohio State University. His appointment at a prominent university gave Kelly a more visible platform for his organizational work, permitting him to champion the development of clinical psychology as a profession and leading to his election to consecutive presidencies of both the Division of Consulting Psychology (1954–1955) and the Division of Clinical Psychology (1956–1957) of the American Psychological Association. It was at Ohio State that Kelly's interests also began to deepen along theoretical lines. Lecture notes taken in Kelly's graduate seminars in the late 1940s demonstrate his continued indebtedness to the theories of Korzybski and Moreno and the way in which Kelly began to fashion them into a unique perspective that grounded the evolution of human construction processes firmly in the social realm (Stewart & Barry, 1991).

By 1951 the rudiments of personal construct theory were sufficiently well formed for Kelly to present a paper on the topic to a gathering of professionals in Houston, Texas. In the following four years, Kelly framed a comprehensive theory of personality around his earlier forays into enactment-based role therapies and the semantic construction of personal realities. At the heart of his theory, Kelly postulated an image of persons as *incipient scientists*, forging, testing, revising, and expanding personal theories of self and world that enabled them to anticipate the recurring themes of their lives. This basic position was further amplified through 11 corollaries detailing the process of knowing, the structure of our personal systems, and the social embeddedness of our construing efforts (Neimeyer & Niemeyer, 1987). Moreover, critical aspects of the theory were operationalized in *repertory grid technique* (Kelly, 1955; Fransella & Bannister, 1977; Sewell, Adams-Webber, Mitterer, & Cromwell, 1992), which offered a flexible but quantifiable research tool for mapping personal construct systems relevant to a broad range of content areas. The result of this monastic theorizing was Kelly's (1955/1992) 1,200-page magnum opus, *The Psychology of Personal Constructs*, which not only presented his theory with remarkable systematicity but also teased out in considerable detail its implications for clinical work. Immediate recognition followed, as Kelly was invited to present at various universities around the world and was offered visiting professorships. In addition, in 1965 he was granted the American Psychological Association's Award for Distinguished Contribution to the Science and Profession of Clinical Psychology (see Figure 5). Kelly (on the right) is pictured in 1962 at the prestigious Nebraska Symposium on Motivation, along with copresenters Jack W. Brehm (on the left) and W. Edgar Vinacke (in center).

In 1965 Kelly accepted the Riklis Chair of Behavioral Science at Brandeis University where Abraham Maslow was serving as the Chair of the Psychology Department. During his brief time at Brandeis, Kelly continued to cultivate a fascination with personal construct concepts and methods (especially repertory grid technique) while avidly reading the emerging work in cognitive psychology that exemplified constructivist themes (e.g., Neisser, 1967). Unfortu-

Figure 5 Kelly became an internationally recognized figure and was widely sought out as a visiting professor and speaker. Kelly (right) is pictured here in 1962 at the prestigious Nebraska Symposium on Motivation, along with co-presenters Jack W. Brehm (left) and W. Edgar Vinacke (center).

nately, his untimely death on March 6, 1967, ended his own lively contribution to personal construct theory which was beginning to attract a growing international network of scholars, researchers, and clinicians committed to extending, testing, and applying his theory. Through his writing, his organizational work, and his impact on students (among them Boyd McCandless, Walter Mischel, Rue Cromwell, David Hunt, James Bieri, Jack Adams-Webber, Al Landfield, Lee Sechrest, Walter Crockett, and Franz Epting), Kelly made a profound, if often unrecognized, contribution to psychology in this century, one that has continued to build momentum to the present day.

A Glance at the Post-Kellian Development of Personal Construct Theory

A consideration of Kelly's life would be seriously incomplete without some mention of the evolution of his theory following his death. In terms of the sociology of science, the appearance of *The Psychology of Personal Constructs* in 1955 provided a provocative "program statement" that catalyzed the development of an ardent theory group (Neimeyer, 1985) devoted to elaborating the implications of this novel approach to personality and clinical practice. In the context of American psychology at mid-century, construct theory was unique, focusing as it did

on the way in which individuals constructed and reconstructed their sense of self and role relationships rather than casting them as the more or less hapless victims of unconscious dynamics or environmental contingencies. Because of the provocative tenor of personal construct theory, its disdain for customary concepts such as motivation, stimulus, drive, and even cognition and emotion (both of which were wedded in the process of construing), and Kelly's untimely death at the height of his career, the scholarly output of the theory group was marginalized within mainstream American psychology for more than two decades, gaining a delayed acceptance and recognition only in the last 10 to 15 years.

However, by the early 1960s Kelly's work had already begun to attract international attention as scholars like Don Bannister from England and Han Bonarius from the Netherlands came to study and work with Kelly at Ohio State (for a detailed sociohistorical study of the theory group's development, see Neimeyer, 1985, and Neimeyer, Baker, & Neimeyer, 1990). The dissemination of personal construct work to a worldwide network of research centers gradually followed, with a steady series of intellectual and social/organizational "marker events" testifying to the theory's continued development (see Table 1 for a partial list).

The outpouring of nearly 3,000 conceptual, clinical, and empirical publications generated by this international community (the majority in the last decade) demonstrates that interest in personal construct theory continues to burgeon; there is no indication that interest in the theory has peaked or entered a period of decline across its 35-year history. Unlike many other personality theories, construct theory has had a remarkably broad application to not only the clinical realm (Button, 1985; Leitner & Dunnett, 1993; Neimeyer & Neimeyer, 1987; Winter, 1992), but also to such diverse areas as education (Beail, 1985), communication (Applegate, 1990), social and cultural studies (Kalekin-Fishman & Walker, 1995), and even artificial intelligence (Adams-Webber, 1995). However, the character of this work has differentiated across time as contemporary construct theorists have begun to integrate

Table 1 *Important dates in the history of personal construct theory (PCT).*

Date	Event
1905	George A. Kelly is born in Perth, Kansas
1931	Kelly founds Psychological Clinic at Fort Hays
1939	Kelly and students begin studies of role therapy
1946	Kelly accepts position at Ohio State
1951	Kelly presents first paper on PCT
1954	A. W. Landfield & J. Bieri publish first empirical research in PCT
1955	Kelly publishes his magnum opus, *The Psychology of Personal Constructs*
1960	D. Bannister publishes first British research in PCT
1965	P. Slater creates first widely used computer programs for analyzing repgrids; Kelly granted Distinguished Contribution Award by APA
1967	Kelly dies of heart attack in new position at Brandeis
1968	A. W. Landfield creates *Clearing House* for PCT to promote continued communication among theory group members; D. Bannister & M. Mair publish first methodological handbook for personal construct research
1969	B. Maher publishes posthumous collection of Kelly's essays
1971	D. Bannister & F. Fransella publish *Inquiring Man,* best-selling text on PCT
1975	First International Congress on PCT held in U.S.; biennial congresses follow in U.K., Netherlands, Canada, Italy, Australia, and Spain
1982	F. Fransella founds Centre for PCT in London; first regional conference on PCT held in Australia; others follow in North America, U.K., & Germany
1984	Formation of first formal regional organization in North America, followed by parallel developments in Australia and Europe
1988	Appearance of *International Journal of Personal Construct Psychology* (IJPCP)
1990	First publication of periodic series, *Advances in Personal Construct Psychology,* reviewing progressive research programs in PCT
1994	IJPCP retitled *Journal of Constructivist Psychology* to reflect broader mission to promote cross-fertilization of constructivist perspectives; first Internet mailbase in PCT established to permit more global communication among theory group members

their work with broader constructivist developments, particularly in the area of psychotherapy (Feixas, 1992; Neimeyer & Mahoney, 1995).

Conclusion

Contemporary psychologists display a distrust of history, as reflected in their tendency not to cite literature that is more than 10 years old. Perhaps for this reason, George Kelly is frequently regarded as an intellectual progenitor of the current "cognitive turn" in clinical psychology, which has melded with behavioral work to produce a hybrid cognitive-behavioral tradition (Dryden & Golden, 1987). However accurate this assessment may be, it downplays those aspects of construct theory that are not easily assimilated into a cognitive-behavioral framework, such as his adherence to a constructivist rather than objectivist epistemology (Neimeyer & Mahoney, 1995), which brings construct theory into closer alignment with narrative and postmodern perspectives in psychotherapy (e.g., McNamee & Gergen, 1992) than with traditional clinical theories emphasizing distorted or irrational information processing. Moreover, a pre-emptive focus on Kelly's contribution to clinical and personality psychology ignores the continuing generativity of personal construct theory in advancing basic research and scholarship on a broad array of psychological issues beyond the clinic, per se (c.f. Fransella & Thomas, 1988; Neimeyer & Neimeyer, 1990, 1992, 1995). Relegating Kelly to an honorific position in the history books risks ignoring the vital and growing field of scholarship his work spawned. Given Kelly's emphasis on the role of anticipation in human functioning, this living tradition may be a more suitable memorial.

Bibliography

Adams-Webber, J. R. (1995). Constructivist psychology and knowledge elicitation. *Journal of Constructivist Psychology, 8, 237–249.*

Applegate, J. L. (1990). Constructs and communication: A pragmatic integration. In G. J. Neimeyer & R. A. Neimeyer (Eds.), *Advances in personal construct psychology* (Vol. 1, pp. 203–230). Greenwich, CT: JAI.

Beail, N. (Ed.). (1985). *Repertory grid technique in psychology and education.* London: Croom Helm.

Button, E. (Ed.). (1985). *Personal construct theory and mental health.* London: Croom Helm.

Dryden, W., & Golden, W. (Eds.). (1987). *Cognitive behavioral approaches to psychotherapy.* New York: Hemisphere.

Edwards, E. D. (1982). Observations of the use and efficacy of changing a client's concept of his role—A psychotherapeutic device. *Fort Hays Studies, 82.* (Reprint of Master's Thesis, Fort Hays Kansas State College, 1943)

Eysenck, H. J. (1952). The effects of psychotherapy: An evaluation. *Journal of Consulting Psychology, 16,* 319–324.

Feixas, G. (1992). Personal construct approaches to family therapy. In R. A. Neimeyer & G. J. Neimeyer (Eds.), *Advances in personal construct psychology* (Vol. 2, pp. 217–255). Greenwich, CT: JAI.

Fransella, F. (1996). *George Kelly's contribution to psychotherapy.* London: Sage.

Fransella, F., & Bannister, D. (1977). *A manual for repertory grid technique.* London: Academic.

Fransella, F., & Thomas, L. (Eds.). (1988). *Experimenting with personal construct psychology.* London: Routledge.

Guydish, J., Zelhart, P. F., Jackson, T. T., & Markley, R. P. (1982). George A. Kelly's contribution to early rural school psychology. *Fort Hays State University Forum, 28,* 4–7.

Kalekin-Fishman, D., & Walker, B. M. (Eds.). (1995). *The construction of group realities.* Malabar, FL: Krieger.

Kelly, G. A. (1933). Some observations on the relation of cerebral dominance to the perception of symbols. *Psychological Bulletin, 30,* 583–584.

Kelly, G. A. (1969). The autobiography of a theory. In B. Maher (Ed.), *Clinical psychology and personality: The selected writings of George Kelly.* New York: Wiley, pp. 46–65.

Kelly, G. A. (1982). Stories from the psychological clinic. *Fort Hays State University Forum, 28,* 2–4. (Original work published in *The Aerend, 8*[1], 1937)

Kelly, G. A. (1991). *The psychology of personal constructs.* London: Routledge. (Original work published 1955, New York: Norton)

Korzybski, A. (1933). *Science and sanity.* Lakeville, CT: Institute of General Semantics.

Leitner, L. M., & Dunnett, N. G. M. (Eds.). (1993). *Critical issues in personal construct psychotherapy.* Malabar, FL: Krieger.

McNamee, S., & Gergen, K. J. (Eds.). (1992). *Therapy as social construction.* Newbury Park, CA: Sage.

Markley, R. P., Zelhart, P. F., & Jackson., T. T. (1982). First studies of fixed role therapy. *Fort Hays State University Forum, 28,* 7–9.

Moreno, J. L. (1937). Interpersonal therapy and the psychopathology of interpersonal relations. *Sociometry, 1,* 9–76.

Neimeyer, G. J., & Neimeyer, R. A. (1981). Personal construct perspectives on cognitive assessment. In T. Merluzzi, C. Glass, & M. Genest (Eds.), *Cognitive assessment* (pp. 188–232). New York: Guilford.

Neimeyer, R. A. (1985). *The development of personal construct theory.* Lincoln: University of Nebraska Press.

Neimeyer, R. A., Baker, K. D., & Neimeyer, G. J. (1990). The current status of personal construct theory: Some scientometric data. In G. J. Neimeyer & R. A. Neimeyer (Eds.), *Advances in personal construct psychology* (Vol. 1, pp. 3–22). Greenwich, CT: JAI.

Neimeyer, R. A., & Mahoney, M. J. (Eds.). (1995). *Constructivism in psychotherapy.* Washington, DC: American Psychological Association.

Neimeyer, R. A., & Neimeyer, G. J. (1987). *Personal construct therapy casebook.* New York: Springer.

Neimeyer, R. A., & Neimeyer, G. J. (Eds.). (1990, 1992, 1995). *Advances in personal construct psychology* (Vols. 1, 2, & 3). Greenwich, CT: JAI.

Neisser, U. (1967). *Cognitive psychology.* New York: Appleton-Century-Crofts.

Robinson, A. J. (1982). A further validation of role therapy. *Fort Hays Studies, 82.* (Reprint of Master's Thesis, Fort Hays Kansas State College, 1943)

Sewell, K. W., Adams-Webber, J., Mitterer, J., & Cromwell, R. L. (1992). Computerized repertory grids: Review of the literature. *International Journal of Personal Construct Psychology, 5,* 1–24.

Stewart, A. E., & Barry, J. R. (1991). Origins of George Kelly's constructivism in the work of Korzybski and Moreno. *International Journal of Personal Construct Psychology, 4,* 121–136.

Vaihinger, H. (1924). *The philosophy of 'as if'.* London: Routledge.

Winter, D. (1992). *Personal construct theory in clinical practice.* London: Routledge.

Zelhart, P. F., & Jackson, T. T. (1983). George A. Kelly, 1931–1943: Environmental influences on a developing theorist. In J. Adams-Webber & J. C. Mancuso (Eds.), *Applications of personal construct theory* (pp. 137–154). Toronto: Academic.

Zelhart, P. F., Jackson, T. T., & Markley, R. P. (1982). George A. Kelly at Fort Hays. *Fort Hays State University Forum, 28,* 1–2.

Projective Techniques

Peter van Drunen

P sychological testing has always carried a particular appeal to the imagination of the general public. This is especially true for a diagnostic tradition which evolved between the mid-thirties and the mid-fifties: projective techniques. The most famous among these techniques are the so-called "ink-blot test" by the Swiss psychiatrist Hermann Rorschach and the Thematic Apperception Test (TAT) by the American psychologist Henry Murray. Together, they established a pattern for a host of other techniques which were developed in the forties and early fifties. Despite heavy criticism, some of these techniques are still widely used today.

The foundation for the projective test movement was laid in 1921 when Swiss psychiatrist Hermann Rorschach (1884–1922) published his famous inkblot test. With aptitude and intelligence testing already firmly established by that time, this test was one of the first attempts to devise a method for diagnosing the personality. The test consisted of 10 plates, each depicting symmetrical inkblots. These were presented successively to the subject being tested, who in turn had to respond to each plate by telling what he thought "this blot might be."

Rorschach himself didn't conceive of his test as a projective technique. Instead, he called it an "experiment in perceptual diagnosis." According to Rorschach, a subject's perception of the inkblots could be considered indicative of underlying personality characteristics. Contrary to common belief, Rorschach wasn't especially interested in the specific semantic content of the subject's responses (e.g., "a bat," "a womb," etc.). Rather, diagnosis was based on the so-called "formal characteristics." For instance, Rorschach differentiated between "color-responses" (taking account of the color of the blots), "movement-responses," and responses which reflected the plate as a whole, as opposed to those based on specific details. A specific meaning was ascribed to each of these characteristics. So, using Jung's distinction between extroversion and introversion, Rorschach thought movement-responses reflected introversion, while extroversion manifested itself in color-responses.

At first, Rorschach's test remained virtually unnoticed. From the early thirties onwards however, interest in the test began to rise sharply, both in Europe and in the United States. Within a few years, the test became an immensely popular tool for personality diagnosis, especially among clinical psy-

Figure 1 Hermann Rorschach (1884–1922). (Archives of the History of American Psychology)

Figure 2 Rorschach examination. (Archives of the History of American Psychology)

chologists. New systems of scoring and interpretation were developed, courses were organized in which psychologists were taught how to use the test, and societies and journals which were devoted exclusively to "the Rorschach" were founded. By the end of the thirties, Rorschach's invention already outranked all other tests in the number of publications written about it (Sundberg, 1954).

The success of Rorschach's test inspired many psychologists and psychiatrists to develop similar techniques. Two early examples are the Four Picture Test, devised in 1930 by Dutch psychologist David van Lennep, and the Thematic Apperception Test, devised by American psychologist Henry Murray. Unlike the Rorschach, both of these tests consisted of figurative pictures representing clearly recognizable persons and situations. However, psychologically the pictures were ambiguous, thus leaving room for a wide variety of interpretations. In the Four Picture Test, the pictures were presented simultaneously, and the subject had to write a story incorporating all four of them. The Thematic Apperception test consisted of no less than twenty pictures which were presented successively. Here, the subject was asked to tell a story about every separate picture.

Between the late thirties and the early fifties, a host of similar techniques was published. These included a variety of materials and tasks such as: (a) a series of photographs of psychiatric patients, from which the most and the least attractive had to be chosen (Szondi-test, 1937); (b) colored blocks to be arranged into a pyramid (Farbpyramidetest, 1951); (c) cartoon-balloons to be filled up with

appropriate text (Picture-Frustration Test, 1948); and (d) the simple instruction to draw a tree (Tree-test, 1949).

Although all of these tests were generically rubricized as "projective techniques," very few of them made explicit use of the concept of projection as originally described by Freud: the process of ascribing one's own needs, emotions, and dispositions to someone else. Insofar as projection was referred to, it was in the much more general sense of perceptions, preferences, or expressions being a reflection of a subject's psychological state of mind. This loose connection to psychoanalytic thought was more or less characteristic for the projective tradition in testing. Few methods were directly related to psychoanalytic theory, but many were embedded in so-called "psychodynamic" conceptions of personality which were generally derived from classical psychoanalysis.

In the decades following the Second World War, projective techniques became commonplace among clinical psychologists. In the United States, for instance, a 1959 survey of testing practices in clinical psychology showed the Rorschach to outrank

Figure 3 One of the plates of the Thematic Apperception Test (1935). (From H. A. Murray, 1943, *Thematic Apperception Test.* Cambridge: Harvard University Press)

Figures 4a and 4b Use of projective techniques in personnel selection by KLM Airlines (ca. 1950). Left: Rorschach examination. Right: the Szondi test. (KLM Archives)

the Stanford-Binet as the test most widely used, with three other projective techniques ranking in the top 10 of tests used (Sundberg, 1961). Moreover, many of the tests found their way into other fields of psychological practice as well. Both the Rorschach and the TAT, for instance, were frequently used by industrial psychologists for purposes of personnel selection (Kinslinger, 1966; Dehue, 1995).

Projective techniques also appealed strongly to laymen. The Rorschach especially was often featured in cartoons and other popular reflections of psychological practice. A good example is a cartoon by Sidney Harris depicting a scientist behind his desk with large inkblots spilled all over the place and a colleague exclaiming "Rorschach—what's to become of you?" Public fascination with the test is even better exemplified by a game called "Person-analysis," published in 1957 by Lowell Toys. In this "Psychological Game for Adults," as it was called, two teams consisting of two or more players had to compete in trying to deduce from interpretations of Rorschach-like inkblots ("the latest psycho-scientific testing technique") which member of the other team was most likely to have provided these interpretations.

Besides fascination, however, projective techniques also provoked severe criticism. This criticism stemmed mainly from quantitatively oriented test psychologists who considered projective techniques to fall short of elementary standards of test construction. In their view, most of the tests relied too heavily on the subjective interpretations of the

psychologist. As a leading psychologist once remarked, projective techniques may well tell us more about the examining psychologist than about the person being tested (Anastasi, 1976, p. 578). This critique was borne out by research which often showed that the validity and reliability of projective techniques were below commonly accepted standards. As an alternative, personality inventories such as the Minnesota Multiphasic Personality Inventory (MMPI) were advocated.

As a result of these critical evaluations, projective techniques have lost some of their popularity during recent decades. This is especially true in the realm of industrial psychology where their use has greatly diminished. Many clinical psychologists, however, still consider projective techniques to be superior to personality inventories when it comes to gaining insight into a client's personality and psychological problems.

Bibliography

Anastasi, A. (1976). *Psychological testing*. New York: MacMillan.

Anderson, H. H., & Anderson, G. L. (Eds.). (1951). *An introduction to projective techniques & other devices for understanding the dynamics of human behavior*. New York: Prentice Hall.

Dehue, G. C. G. (1995). *Changing the rules. Psychology in the Netherlands 1900–1985*. Cambridge: Cambridge University Press.

Drunen, P. van, & Strien, P. J. van (1991). *Op de proef gesteld. Geschiedenis van de psychologische test*. Groningen: Stichting Historische Materialen Psychologie.

Kinslinger, H. J. (1966). Application of projective techniques in personnel psychology since 1940. *Psychological Bulletin, 66,* 134–149.

Sundberg, N. D. (1954). A note concerning the history of testing. *American Psychologist, 9,* 150–151.

Sundberg, N. D. (1961). The practice of psychological testing in clinical services in the United States. *American Psychologist, 16,* 79–83.

A True TAT Story

Jürgen Jahnke
Wesley G. Morgan

This is a boy—about ten years old. He has taken violin lessons since he was five years old and was an industrious and precocious student. His parents and teachers encouraged his talent. His first concerts were great successes. Now, he sits in front of the violin and he is half absent in his own world and half in the present. One day he will be a famous violinist."

Any psychologist who is familiar with projective testing will immediately recognize the above as a story about the first picture of the Thematic Apperception Test (TAT) by Henry A. Murray (1893–1988). Countless projective fantasies have been stimulated by this picture, and Murray (1943) claimed that they could provide an X-ray picture of the inner self. Some of these TAT stories have an optimistic flavor; others reveal negative or even unpleasant feelings or pressures to do one's duty and to be successful. Stories for Card 1 often reveal one's aspirations and attitudes toward duty. An expert in clinical assessment might infer that the present story reflects wishes for self-actualization and fame, and a positive outlook for the future. The unique value of this TAT story about Card 1, however, is the fact that it is actually a true story and not just someone's fantasy (Y. Menuhin, 1977, personal communication to W. G. M., October 31, 1993; Menuhin, 1984). When taking the TAT, the subject is asked to make up a story about each picture. There should be no "true" or "right" story about the pictures, because they are only material to stimulate individual projections. To accomplish this, the pictures must be somewhat ambiguous because a knowledge of the facts about their true content would restrict the fantasies of the subject—the projective test would change into a test of knowledge!

Three previous series of TAT pictures were used

between 1935 and the still-current 1943/1971 edition. The current Card 1 was identified as Card 5 in the first series (Morgan and Murray, 1935) and as Card 1 in the 1936 version (Rapaport, Gill, & Schafer, 1946; White, Sanford, Murray, & Bellak, 1941). In the earliest versions of the TAT, the pictures were only about half as big as those in the final series and consisted of photographs of the images glued onto 15.3 × 15.3 cm cardboard stock rather than being printed as they are currently (Rapaport, Gill, & Schafer, 1946). Information concerning the origins of the TAT cards given by Murray is often dated, incomplete, or inaccurate, and unfortunately, little about the origin of the cards was found in the rich TAT literature (Morgan, 1995).

The famous picture of Card 1 is identified as a "Drawing by Christiana D. Morgan" in the TAT manual (Murray, 1943, p. 18). Christiana Drummond Morgan (1897–1967) was the senior author of the first accounts of the TAT method (Morgan & Murray, 1935) and as late as 1941 the test was referred to as the "Morgan-Murray Thematic Apperception Test" (Morgan & Murray, 1935, 1938; White, Sanford, Murray, & Bellak, 1941). Morgan was chiefly responsible for the initial selection of pictures from magazines and books and for redrawing some of the original pictures to disguise their origin and to perhaps avoid copyright problems (Holt, 1949). She is also credited for drawing six of the other pictures (the "old standbys") appearing in the 1943 TAT series (Murray, 1943). Frederick Wyatt (1911–1993), one of the psychologists who participated in the development of the TAT and suggested some of the pictures, believed that Morgan was not an artist (Wyatt, personal communication to J. J., 1991), but in fact, she had studied art at the Art Students League in New York and later produced a series of drawings for

YEHUDI MENUHIN

A glimpse of the home life and training of the boy who is the foremost child musician in the world today

Photograph by Lumiere

Figure 1 Photograph of the young Menuhin (Block, 1930).

Carl G. Jung which served as the basis for *The Visions Seminars* (Douglas, 1989, 1993; Murray, 1976). Morgan's name as coauthor of the test was dropped in 1943 at her request, and Murray seemed at times to minimize her contributions—perhaps corresponding to the ups and downs of their stormy romantic relationship (Douglas, 1993; Robinson, 1992).

In the German edition of the present book the fortuitous finding of the supposed model of Card 1 by one of the authors (J. J.) was reported (Jahnke, 1993). In fact, the identity of the young boy depicted in Card 1 has been recognized by many users of the TAT for quite some time. Stein (1955) provided a clue in one of the sample stories to Card 1 that he presents in his manual. In it a female subject ends her story with the question, "Was it deliberately made to look like Yehudi Menuhin?" (p. 3) And later Holt (1978) identified the picture as a "Drawing by Christiana D. Morgan, after a photograph of Yehudi Menuhin as a child." (p. 80) This is the earliest *published* account of the identity of the young boy on Card 1 that we have discovered.

The original photograph of the young Menuhin shown in Figures 1 and 2 was made by Lumiere, a New York photographer. Reproductions of the photograph have appeared in the autobiography of Moshe Menuhin, Yehudi's father (Menuhin, 1984) and Menuhin & Davis (1979). It had also appeared previously in various news and magazine reports

377

Figure 2 Collage from *The Musician* of January 1928.

and in a videorecording that has occasionally been aired on television (Block, 1930; Brower, 1928; *The Music of Man*, 1981).

The age of Yehudi at the time the photograph was made has been a matter of some disagreement. Yehudi himself stated that he was 6 years old, and the picture index for the photograph in his book reads, "Yehudi Menuhin at Six" (Collection of Yehudi Menuhin) (Menuhin & Davis, 1979, p. 314). On the other hand, Moshe Menuhin claims that the photograph shows Yehudi with the "Prince Khevenhüller" violin. The Stradivarius violin, a gift of Mr. and Mrs. Henry Goldman, was given to Yehudi on January 22, 1929 ("Yehudi Menuhin Chooses . . . ", 1929). Since Yehudi was born on April 22, 1916, this would have made him at least 13 years old when the photograph was made.

Unfortunately, both of these accounts seem to be

in error. As mentioned above, the same photograph appears in a collage on page 13 of the January 1928 edition of *The Musician* (Brower, 1928) as shown in Figure 2. So obviously, the photograph must have been taken at least a year before the gift of the Stradivarius. It would appear that the account given in Menuhin and Davis must also be in error. Yehudi first returned from San Francisco where he had lived since about age 2, to New York, the place of his birth, in the fall of 1925. The occasion was his debut at the Manhattan Opera House on January 17, 1926, when he was 9 years old. He returned again to New York in the fall of 1927, at age 11, for concerts at Carnegie Hall in November and December of that year (Menuhin, 1984; Menuhin, 1977). Since the photograph was made in New York, it seems clear that his age must have been between 9 and 11 years when the photograph was taken.

It also seems likely that another childhood photo of Yehudi was made at this same photographic sitting. The other photograph seems to have first appeared in print in December 1927 ("The Boy Violin Wonder", 1927) and is shown with Lumiere's signature in Peyser (1929). In it, Yehudi seems to be wearing the same shirt, have the same haircut, and to be sitting in a folding chair similar to the one whose back is barely visible in the Card 1 photograph.

Morgan's redrawing of the photograph clearly shows her minor changes and touch-ups. The boy's facial features are less pronounced, the background is brighter, the major contours of the picture are weaker, and the violin looks distorted. Nevertheless, the similarity between the drawing and the photograph is clear and striking.

It is interesting to note that both of the present authors followed somewhat parallel paths in the search for information concerning Card 1. In response to our independent questions, Yehudi Menuhin indicated that he had been unaware until recently that his portrait had served as a stimulus on one of the best-known psychodiagnostic tests (Yehudi Menuhin, personal communication to J. J., October 1, 1991; Yehudi Menuhin, personal communication to W. G. M., October 31, 1993). In conclusion, it came indeed as a pleasant surprise to discover that this realistic portrait of a unique and world-famous musician has been able to stimulate so many original fantasies as part of a popular projective test.

Acknowledgment

The authors are listed alphabetically. Each made an equivalent contribution to this chapter.

Thanks is extended to Ms. Susan Stricker for calling the Menuhin videorecording to my attention (W.G.M.)

Bibliography

Block, E. B. (1930). Yehudi Menuhin. *The Parents' Magazine, 5*(1), 17, 50.

Brower, H. (1928, January). Yehudi Menuhin—the miracle. *The Musician, 33,* 13, 38.

Douglas, C. (1989). Christiana Morgan's visions reconsidered: A look behind The Visions Seminars. *The San Francisco Jung Institute Library Journal, 8*(4), 5–27.

Douglas, C. (1993). *Translate this darkness: The life of Christiana Morgan.* New York: Simon & Schuster.

Holt, R. R. (1949). The early history of the TAT. *The TAT Newsletter, 3,* 492.

Holt, R. R. (1978). A normative guide to the use of the TAT cards. In *Methods in clinical psychology: Vol. 1. Projective assessment* (pp. 77–122). New York: Plenum Press.

Jahnke, J. (1993). Eine wahre TAT-Geschichte. In H. E. Lück & R. Miller (Eds.), *Illustrierte Geschichte der Psychologie* (pp. 314–316). Munich: Quintessence.

Menuhin, M. (1984). *The Menuhin Saga: The autobiography of Moshe Menuhin.* London: Sidgwick & Jackson.

Menuhin, Y. (1977). *Unfinished journey.* New York: Knopf.

Menuhin, Y., & Davis, C. W. (1979). *The music of man.* New York: Methuen.

Morgan, C. D., & Murray, H. A. (1935). A method for investigating fantasies: The Thematic Apperception Test. *Archives of Neurology and Psychiatry, 34,* 289–306.

Morgan, C. D., & Murray, H. A. (1938). Thematic Apperception Test. In H. A. Murray (Ed.), *Explorations in personality: A clinical and experimental study of fifty men of college age* (pp. 530–545). New York: Oxford University Press.

Morgan, W. G. (1995). Origin and history of the Thematic Apperception Test (TAT) images. *Journal of Personality Assessment, 65,* 237–254.

Murray, H. A. (1943). *Thematic Apperception Test manual.* Cambridge, MA: Harvard University Press.

Murray, H. A. (1976). Postscript: Morsels of information regarding the extraordinary woman in whose psyche the foregoing visions were begot. In C. G. Jung, *The visions seminars* (Vol. 2, pp. 517–521). Zurich: Spring Publications.

Peyser, H. F. (1929, February). The evanescence of prodigies. *The Musician, 34,* 11.

Rapaport, D., Gill, M., & Schafer, R. (1946). *Diagnostic psychological testing* (Vol. 2). Chicago: The Year Book.

Robinson, F. G. (1992). *Love's story told: A life of Henry A. Murray.* Cambridge, MA: Harvard University Press.

Stein, M. I. (1955). *The Thematic Apperception Test: An introductory manual for its clinical use with adults* (Rev. ed.). Cambridge, MA: Addison-Wesley.

The boy violin wonder. (1927, December 31). *The Literary Digest, 95,* 22.

The music of man with Yehudi Menuhin, Program 7: The known and the unknown [videorecording]. (1981). New York: Time-Life Video.

White, R. W., Sanford, R. N., Murray, H. A., & Bellak, L. (1941, September). *Morgan-Murray Thematic Apperception Test: Manual of directions.* Cambridge: Harvard Psychological Clinic. [mimeograph]. (Harvard University Archives, HUGFP 97.43.2, Box 5 of 7).

Yehudi Menuhin chooses $60,000 Stradivarius for birthday present. (1929, February 7). *Musical Courier, 98,* 12.

V

PSYCHIATRY, PSYCHOANALYSIS, AND ABNORMAL PSYCHOLOGY

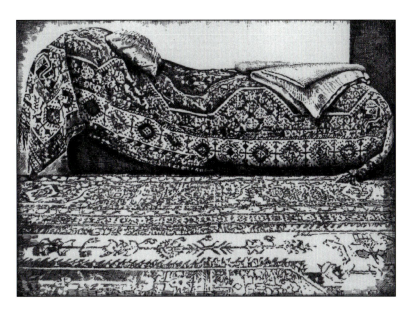

Classical Psychopathology

Giuseppe Roccatagliata

T his essay provides a historical account of the development of psychopathology and psychiatry in ancient Greece and Rome. Specifically, the long period extending from the 13th century B.C. to the late eighth century A.D. is covered.

The Pre-Christian Era

Sacred Model

At the beginning of Western thought in ancient Greece, man's mental and emotional health was controlled by the individual's fear of the gods. Anyone who did not respect the rules of the gods became mentally ill. For example, vain and proud mythological figures, like Bellerophon, Oedipus, and Orestes, were stricken by a divine curse.

Following this sacred model of insanity, the mentally ill went to a temple to pray for recovery and to implore the priests to intercede for them. The epileptic prayed to Hecate; the hysterical woman to Artemis; the melancholic, who believed that the gods detested him, delivered his gifts to the priests at the temples of Trophonius and Anphiaraus. Thus, individual psychopathological symptoms expressed the mental suffering which was caused by the wrath of the gods (Hippocrates, 1737).

Melampus

Around the 13th century B.C., Melampus of Pilus, a follower of Dionysus, was the first to practice the medical art of interpreting and treating psychiatric disorders as organic illnesses. In this context, his primary discoveries were centered around the effects of plants and other natural substances on mental illnesses. For example, hellebore root extract was used to treat severe depression in women who

Figure 1 White hellebore.

suffered from "agitated uterine melancholia." It was thought that toxic humors from the uterus poisoned the central nervous systems of these female patients. On the other hand, Melampus cured traumatic, psychogenic impotence with iron powder (Apollodorus, 1826).

Asclepius

According to a myth from the same historical period, Apollo, by impregnating a mortal woman, became the father of Asclepius and the ancestor of the Asclepiades, whose corporation monopolized the medical arts beyond the time of Hippocrates.

Exceeding even the fame of Melampus, Asclepius established a sanctuary in Epidaurus, where mental disorders were treated by a variety of physical and psychological therapies (e.g., music, massage, theater performances, the medical interpretation of dreams, therapeutic sleep, and the application of mandrake root and opium).

During this period a new explanation of the nature of mental illness was developed as well. Mental impairments were now explained as the result of traumatic experiences or a humoral imbalance which created an intoxication of the central nervous system. Consequently, such disorders were to be cured by drugs which could eliminate the excess of toxic humors from the nervous system.

Hippocrates

During the fifth century B.C., Hippocrates of Cos, a follower of Asclepius, founded psychopathology and psychiatry. He also combined methodological,

Figure 3 Cultivated poppy.

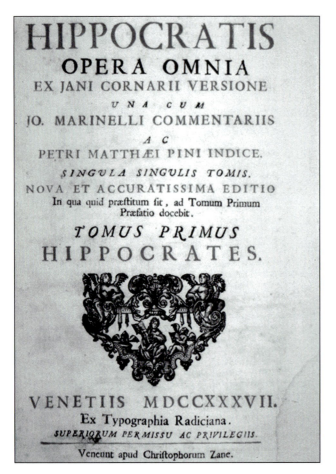

Figure 2 Title page of the *Collected Works of Hippocrates* (1737).

nosological, and clinical traditions into a novel organismic model of psychopathology. Thus, he inaugurated the biochemical approach which still provides the basis of modern psychopathology. Hippocrates is also viewed as the first physician to compose written works about medicine, surgery, and psychiatry.

According to Hippocrates, the root cause of mental disorders and of all human behavior can be traced back to the human brain. In general, psychiatric symptoms are the expression of a disharmony within the body's molecules, which normally should exist in a physiological balance. A specific symptom results from an intemperance of humors, which in turn alters the optimal homeostasis of the central nervous system (Sarton, 1952). Hippocrates emphasized that nature, which follows the order of the "logos," maintains autohomeostasis through a balanced interplay of constructive and destructive mechanisms. The central nervous system consists of a cold and humid substance which will produce mental symptoms when it undergoes physicochemical transmutations. The change of seasons, fevers, epilepsy, shock, physical injury during childbirth, and humoral irregularities—all of these change the normal physical features of the brain. For example, black bile cools the brain; yellow bile dries it up; blood heats up the brain; and the secretions of the pituitary produce a greater degree of moisture in the brain. These mechanisms were used to explain the etiology of melancholia, acute paranoid psychosis, mania, epilepsy, and hebephrenia. Fever dries out the brain and causes acute phrenitis or delirium (Hippocrates, 1737; Roccatagliata, 1991).

Figure 4 Title page of Galen's *Collected Works* (1667).

By emphasizing the etiological role of the central nervous system in mental disorders, Hippocrates strongly refuted the sacred model of insanity (Hippocrates, 1737). He also traced connections between specific psychiatric symptoms and the effects of various kinds of pathogenic organic factors. The scientific approach used by Hippocrates thus firmly established psychopathology on a biochemical basis. The humoral model of Melampus; the medical model of Asclepius; the naturalism of

Thales, Anaximenes, and Anaximander; the theories of Pythagorean physicians such as Plato's friends Timaeus, Philistion, Pausanias, Empedocles, and Philolaus; all of these contributed to the medical model of psychopathology that Hippocrates developed (Galen, 1562).

Hippocrates codified his nosology on the basis of symptomatology, the course and outcome of illness, and etiology. He identified the clinical syndromes of endogenous melancholia, reactive melancholia, manic-depressive psychosis, hypochondria, hysteria, catatonia, hebephrenia, epileptic psychoses, and others. For example, he defined endogenous melancholia (now called major depression) as follows (Hippocrates, 1737):

> Melancholia is characterized by a restriction of the soul, taciturnity and a search for solitude, which arises without a cause. On the contrary, reactive depression, which is the result of a stressful event, has a cause. In addition, the temperament of the depressive patient plays an important role. (Book III)

Hippocrates further concluded that:

> Diseases have an indivisible nature, which permits their classification by symptoms, precipitating events, the pre-morbid character of the patient and metabolic imbalances. Common causes of depressive disorders are fear, sadness, loss of a love for life and an inclination towards suicide, which coincides with the presence of dry and cold bile. (Book III)

In fact, Hippocrates thought that mental illnesses had a biochemical origin and that "derangements of the soul, like excessive sadness, unhappiness, mental brooding, fear, and dread, arise from a disturbance of the humors [of the body]" (Book III).

In general, Hippocrates' nosological descriptions are written in a lapidary style and express only the essence of the clinical picture (Hippocrates, 1737): "The melancholy patient loves death as though it were a blessing . . . and melancholia is a loss of love for life" (Book V). Elsewhere he suggests that "severe depression is caused by a humoral intoxication of the blood, which affects the heart and causes anxiety to the praecordiam and dark ideas in the mind" (Book II). Conversely, hebephrenia "stems from an increase in the cerebro-spinal liquid and the pituitary" but "mania . . . indicates the action of . . . sour and irritating bile, which causes symptoms such as hallucinations, delirium, and restlessness" (Book I). Finally, Hippocrates pointed out that "euphoric mania is accompanied by an increase of blood in the brain, which produces gaiety, euphoria, a feeling of power, verbal acceleration and so on" (Book III).

Aristotle

During the fourth century B.C. Aristotle's views of mental disorders generally followed the Hippocratic model. Thus, he maintained that psychopathology was caused by the disequilibrium of dry bile. However, if the temperature of the bile is normal, sanity will prevail. On the other hand, if the bile is excessively hot, mania (excited delirious psychosis) will be found. If an individual's bile is too cold, inhibited melancholia will be produced. According to Aristotle, an increase in the metabolism of a humor causes manic psychosis. However, a metabolic deficit of the same humor causes depressive melancholia. Psychoses with symptoms such as excitement, hallucinations, and delirium are explained by Aristotle as a pathological acceleration of the metabolism.

Figure 5 Agarico.

Aristotle also wrote about another of Hippocrates' favorite subjects—the relationship among temperament, soul, and body. According to Aristotle, the individual temperament derives from the individual's somatic characteristics. Body and soul are reciprocally connected through the individual's temperament and consequently influence each other (Aristotle, 1981).

The Hellenistic Period

From the third century B.C. to about the third century A.D., centers of scholarship moved from the Greek mainland to the Greek diaspora in Asia Minor and Egypt. During this period, the universities of Alexandria, Smyrna, Ephesus, and Pergamon flourished, thus playing a major role in the development of psychopathology for the next almost 700 years.

Although Hellenistic physicians valued the biological model of Hippocrates, Diocles, and Aristotle, they were reluctant to accept a model of illness which rested primarily on hypothetical physical causes since these could seldom be established.

The Empirical Model. As a result of their etiological scepticism, the Hellenistic physicians focused almost exclusively on the symptomatology of mental diseases. Consequently, many Greek and Roman physicians from the third century B.C. to the third century A.D. defined mental disorder in terms of syndromes or a group of symptoms which provided the clinical picture of a given disease. According to this view, only experience can teach us that sadness, fear, thoughts of death, and insomnia all belong to the clinical picture of depression. A physician can diagnose any given mental or physical illness because his own experience or that of his teachers provides him with symptomatic information about other observed cases (Galen, 1562).

The empirical physicians particularly rejected Hippocrates' treatment recommendations which utilized the purgative effects of hellebore roots and mandrake. They were convinced that only symptoms should be treated and that the body should not routinely be purged of bad humors. However, they believed that it was proper to stimulate the body with seeds of *cannabis indica* in the case of asthenia. Opium was also used to sedate agitated patients, and moderate doses of wine helped calm patients and induce restful sleep in those suffering from anxiety (Galen, 1562).

Alexandrine empiricism disdained all attempts to speculate and theorize about the etiology of mental disorders. Instead, it concentrated on descriptive studies and semiological research in its polemics with the Hippocratic school (Roccatagliata, 1986). The major representatives of the empiri-

Figure 6 Cornelius Celsus.

sceptic philosophers, Pyrrho of Elis and Sextus Empiricus. The school of the Hippocratic dogmatists came to an end during the first century A.D. (Roccatagliata, 1986; Sprengel, 1812).

Psychodynamic Approach. As a reaction to the dogmatism of the Hippocratics, a psychodynamic view of psychopathology emerged between the third century B.C. and the first century A.D. This school was strongly influenced by the philosophical thought of Socrates and Plato. In addition, the stoicism of Zenon, Posidonius, and Chrysippus made this model particularly popular in the Roman empire. According to this early psychodynamic paradigm, a strong self can help the individual overcome the passions, which are often associated with mental illnesses. Individuals become mentally ill because their personalities are too weak to deal with traumatic events (Pohlenz, 1959).

Atomistic Model. In the first century B.C. an important psychiatric movement that utilized the atomism of Democritus and Epicurus was initiated in Rome by the physician Asclepiades of Prusa. Asclepiades had been persuaded to come to Italy by Cicero, the Roman orator and philosopher. Cicero

cal model were Philinus of Cos, Eraclides of Tarentum, Antiochus of Laodicea, Menodotus of Nicomedia, and Glaucias.

Dogmatic Model. After the death of Hippocrates, a special medical guild was established which was directed by Thessalus, an important follower of Hippocrates, and Dracon and Polybus, who were Thessalus's sons. All of these physicians were staunch followers of Hippocrates, and their influence extended from the third century B.C. to the first century A.D. These physicians were called "dogmatists" because they rigidly adhered to Hippocrates' teachings and actively opposed any deviations from his tenets. The physicians who adhered to the dogmatist position were quite numerous. Diogenes of Apollonia, Siennesides of Cyprus, Diosippus of Cos, Philistion of Locri, Petron, Eudossus, Chrysippus of Cnidus, Diocles of Charystos, and Praxagoras of Cos all deserve specific mention. These physicians were convinced that mental illness was caused by an imbalance of the four humors, and consequently, they codified the humoral approach to mental diseases and its treatment regimens. The dogmatists were sharply criticized by the empirically minded

Figure 7 Galen.

hoped that Asclepiades would reform Roman medicine, which was still influenced by superstition and folk beliefs. The followers of his "atomistic" model, as it was called, included: Nico of Agrigentum, who studied bulimia; Titus Anfidius, who prescribed forced coitus as a treatment of depression; Artorius, the personal physician of the Emperor Augustus and a well-known interpreter of dreams; Niceratus, an expert on catatonia; Themison of Laodicaea, who invented treatments for bipolar disorders; Soranus of Ephesus, an expert of biological psychology; and finally, Caelius Aurelianus, who made distinctions between acute and chronic mental disorders.

The treatment approach of the atomistic school resembles modern theories on the metabolism of biogenic amino acids. The central nervous system is made up of cells (leptomeres) and of canalicula, in which the corpuscles (present-day neurotransmitters) move. Mental health lasts as long as an optimal relationship between the diameters of the canalicula and the quantity and speed of the corpuscles exists.

Methodical treatment was a hallmark of atomistic psychiatrists. Their therapeutic approach included baths, physical exercises, music therapy, travel, and small doses of opium, wine, and hellebore to repair the unsymmetrical atoms and, hence, restore mental health (Sprengel, 1812; Roccatagliata, 1986; Aurelianus, 1566a).

The following description of a depressed patient by Caelius Aurelianus (1566b) gives a good illustration of the atomistic perspective:

> The melancholic individual is always sad and angry. No joyous events can distract him from his pain. He suffers from anxiety of the soul, is sad, does not speak and hates others. He wishes to live but, at the same time, wants to die. He is suspicious and fearful of ambush. He complains of pains in the abdomen and tension at the precordium. He is sensitive to cold, perspires excessively, feels tension in the stomach after eating, and his head aches badly. He looks livid but feels somber. He feels tired and his virility is often dormant. (Book I)

Christian Era

Pneumatism

The pneumatic school, which originated during the first century A.D., was favored by the Roman emperor Nero. Some of the basic ideas of this new model of mental illness can be found in the works of Hippocrates, Diogenes of Apollonia, in Plato, and in the writings of the Stoic philosophers. According to this model, the human organism receives its primary energy from within the heart, and this energy is distributed throughout the body by the blood. This vital energy of the body or "pneuma" resembles an "invisible fiery air" (Sprengel, 1812). The pneumatists believed that the pneuma could undergo changes in temperature and viscosity. In turn, these changes would eventually be transmitted to the blood and thence to the brain. They concluded further that changes in the state of the pneuma caused mental illness and that these changes could be identified by the individual's arterial pulse.

The originators of this diagnostic method were Athenaeus of Attalia and his disciple, Magnus of Ephesus. Eminent members of the pneumatic school included Agatinus of Sparta, Archigenes of Apamea, Philippus of Caesarea, Posidonius, Philaretes, Herodotus, Andromachus, Antillus, Aretaeus of Cappadocia, Dioscorides of Apamea, Ruphus of Ephesus, and Marcellus of Sydia. Specifically, Philippus of Caesarea studied catatonia; Philaretes focused on variations of the arterial pulse in mental diseases; Herodotus was a specialist in the treatment of men-

Figure 8 Henbane.

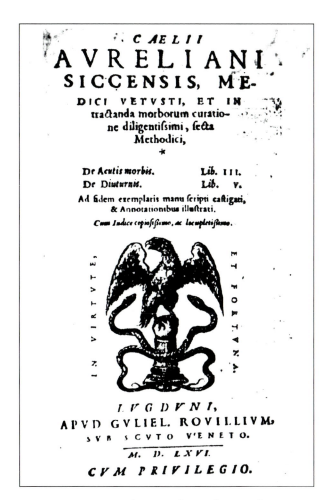

Figure 9 Cover page of writings by Caelius Aurelianus.

rologist, neuroanatomist, pharmacologist, psychiatrist, and also an outstanding philosopher. In sharp contrast to Hippocrates and his school, Galen considered hysteria to be a clear symptom of unhappiness in women who have lost their interest and enjoyment of sexuality. He also introduced the distinction between delirious and hallucinatory psychoses. Galen regarded melancholia, or depression, as a unitary disorder which is influenced by the temperament or personality of a specific patient. As an expert anatomist, Galen studied the lesions of the medullar nerve and the cranial nerves experimentally through vivisection of animals.

Galen explained hebephrenia as a mental disease of young adults who find it difficult to face reality and to grow up. Galen also regarded this disorder as a sign of mental and physical weakness. On the other hand, catatonia was explained by a deficiency in "animal spirits," which produces "lethargy, sleepiness or phrenitis" (Roccatagliata, 1991).

Galen's chief treatment of mental disorders was the cure-all theriac, which he prescribed to patients suffering from melancholia, anxiety, physical pain, hallucinations, and depression (Galen, 1567). Neurasthenia was treated by massaging the patient with an ointment of honey, elderberries, and rosemary. Impotence was treated with pills based on

tal disorders resulting from head injuries. Andromachus of Crete, a personal physician of Nero, invented the pharmaceutical compound "theriac," which was a popular curative until the late 18th century. Theriac contained 60 different ingredients, including senna, mandrake, henbane, and opium. Another early pneumatist, Antillus, was the first to describe the physical and mental symptoms deriving from heat and sunstroke. Dioscorides Pedacius wrote a famous text of pharmacology which was used as a reference text for centuries (Roccatagliata, 1986).

Galen

In the second century A.D., Galen, the personal physician of the emperor Marcus Aurelius, became as famous as Hippocrates. He was a very productive author whose original works comprised 10 volumes of 500 pages each, of which about half were preserved. Galen was an expert neurophysiologist, neu-

Figure 10 Mandrake root.

Figure 11 Belladonna plant.

beaver testicles. Wine from the vineyards of Arvisius, Lesbos, and Falernum was used to treat fatigue and sadness.

The Byzantine Period

During the fourth century A.D. Oribasius of Pergamon described the symptoms of mania, melancholia and lycanthropia. Later, Aetius of Amida classified the psychopathological symptoms resulting from the ingestion of poisonous herbs. He also studied and described hallucinations, delirium, mental confusion, and coma which are caused by excessive doses of medications derived from henbane, mandrake, hemlock, coriander, aconite, and cantharis (Galen, 1562). Alexander of Tralles, a contemporary of Aetius, published studies of mania, melancholia, hysteria, and bulimia. Finally, during the seventh century, Paulus Aegineta, the last of the ancient psychiatrists, described mental disorders which are caused by the loss of someone or something loved. Specific symptoms include anorexia, weight loss, sadness, and obsessions. Recovery from this illness of frustrated love is only possible through the god Love (Galen, 1562).

In conclusion, classical psychopathology was transmitted by Byzantine medicine during the Middle Ages and the Renaissance. It remained alive until the beginning of the 19th century. Modern psychopathology, of course, still has its roots in these ancient Greek and Roman psychiatric traditions.

Bibliography

Apollodorus. (1826). *Bibliotecca.* Milan: F. Somzogmo.

Aristotle. (1981). *De physiognomica liber.* Paris: Les Belles Lettres.

Aurelianus, C. (1566a). *De acutis morbis.* Ludguni: Rovilium.

Aurelianus, C. (1566b). *De tardis passionibus.* Ludguni: Rovilium.

Galen (1562). *Opera omnia.* Venice: V. Valgrisio.

Hippocrates. (1737). *Opera omnia.* Venice: Radiciani.

Pohlenz, M. (1959). *Die Stoa: Geschichte einer geistigen Bewegung.* Göttingen: Vandenhoeck-Ruprecht.

Roccatagliata, G. (1986). *A history of ancient psychiatry.* Westport, CT: Greenwood.

Roccatagliata, G. (1991). *Classical concepts of schizophrenia.* Washington: American Psychiatric Press.

Sarton, G. (1952). *A history of science.* Cambridge, MA: Harvard University Press.

Sprengel, C. (1812). *Storia prammatica della medicina* (Vols. 1–2). Venice: Picotti.

Sigmund Freud: A Biographical Sketch

Ernst Federn

Sigmund Freud (1856–1939) was born on May 6, 1856, in the small town of Freiburg in the Province of Moravia, which was part of the Austro-Hungarian Empire. His early family situation was somewhat complicated since he was the first child of a young mother and an older father. His father had been married twice before and had much older children from his first marriage. When Freud was 3 years old, the family moved to Vienna where they resided in humble circumstances in the Second District. There Freud was raised with three sisters and a younger brother.

Freud, who was an outstanding student, decided to study medicine after reading the poem *Nature*, which he erroneously ascribed to Johann Wolfgang von Goethe (1749–1832). It took him almost eight years, from the winter of 1873 until the spring of 1881, to complete his studies and earn his medical doctorate. It was Ernst Brücke (1819–1892), a professor and major influence, who introduced Freud to the field of neurology. Freud conducted important research in this new medical specialty, and this helped him qualify as a neurologist and as an instructor in the Medical School of Vienna University. He also spent some time in Paris as a postdoctoral student of Martin Charcot (1825–1893). August Ambroise Liebeault (1823–1904) and Hippolyte Bernheim (1840–1919), of the French University of Nancy, introduced Freud to the therapeutic use of hypnosis with psychiatric patients. Another mentor of the young Freud was Joseph Breuer (1842–1925), the noted physician. It was also during this period that the young Freud experimented with the anesthetic properties of cocaine.

In 1886, after a four-year engagement, Freud married Martha Bernays (1861–1951), a native of Hamburg and the future mother of his six children. Anna Freud (1895–1971), the youngest of his children, was the only one who became a psychoanalyst. The youngest son, Ernest Freud (1892–1970) was later instrumental in the publication of his father's correspondence. Although some biographers have attempted to dramatize his life, Freud, who changed the way we look at the human mind, actually lived a quiet life. The loss of his daughter, Sophie Halberstadt (1893–1920) and her son, Heinerle (1919–1923), caused him great grief. In 1923, he was diagnosed as

Figure 1 Freud and his father (ca. 1864).

391

suffering from cancer of the palate, for which he eventually had to undergo several painful operations.

Freud decided to study the soul of man scientifically in order to discover the etiology of hysteria. Together with Breuer, he published the initial results of his research in *Studies in Hysteria* (1895). After his father's death and the discontinuation of his relationship with Breuer, Freud began to analyze himself in his many letters to Wilhelm Fliess (1858–1928), a well-known ear and nose specialist in Berlin. At the time, Freud regarded Fliess as a friend and confidant—one with whom he could discuss all that went through his mind. This cathartic experience eventually contributed to the creation and publication of Freud's classic book, *The Interpretation of Dreams*, which he completed in 1889 and published in 1900. Freud's correspondence with Fliess has recently been published in an excellent edition by the Harvard University Press (Masson, 1985). Through a careful reading of these revealing letters, it is possible to gain significant insights into Freud's own self-analysis. One is tempted to conclude that even if Freud had died shortly after the publication of his book on dream interpretation, psychoanalysis would still exist today. Interestingly, *The Interpretation of Dreams* was no great publishing

LEHRINSTITUT DER WIENER PSYCHOANALYTISCHEN VEREINIGUNG

Das LEHRINSTITUT DER WIENER PSYCHOANALYTISCHEN VEREINIGUNG veranstaltet im Wintersemester 1926/27 folgende Kurse:

I) Fach- und Ausbildungskurse:

1. *Dr. E. Hitschmann:* Einführung in die Psychoanalyse. 10 Stunden. Beginn Samstag, den 30. Oktober, 7 Uhr abends.
2. *Dr. Paul Federn:* Seminar zur gemeinsamen Lektüre der metapsychologischen Schriften Freuds. Beginn Montag, den 18. Oktober, 8 Uhr abends.
3. *Prof. Dr. Paul Schilder:* Psychoanalytische Vorweisungen. Großer Hörsaal der Klinik Wagner-Jauregg, Samstag 7—9. Beginn Oktober.
4. *Anna Freud:* Zur Technik der Kinderanalyse und ihrer Abgrenzung gegen die Analyse der Erwachsenen. Beginn Montag, den 8. November, 8 Uhr abends.
5. *Dr. H. Nunberg:* Allgemeine Neurosenlehre. 25 Stunden. Beginn im November.
6. *Dr. Wilhelm Hoffer:* Was bietet die Psychoanalyse dem Erzieher? (Einführungskurs.) 10 Stunden. Beginn Mitte November.
7. *Dr. W. Reich:* Spezielle Neurosenlehre. 12 Stunden. Beginn Donnerstag, den 13. Januar, 7 Uhr abends.
8. *Dr. Helene Deutsch:* Schwierigkeiten des weiblichen Seelenlebens (typische Neurosen mit besonderer Berücksichtigung der Fortpflanzungsfunktionen). 8 Stunden. Beginn Dienstag, den 11. Januar, 7 Uhr abends.
9. *Dr. Theodor Reik:* Psychoanalyse der Religion. I. Das Dogma. 12 Stunden. Beginn Dienstag, den 8. Februar, 8 Uhr abends.

II) Praktische Übungen für Ausbildungskandidaten.

Am Ambulatorium der Wiener Psychoanalytischen Vereinigung: *Dr. E. Hitschmann* und *Dr. W. Reich:* Seminar für psychoanalytische Therapie.

Bei genügender Beteiligung werden im Herbst 1926 folgende englische Kurse abgehalten:

a) *Dr. Paul Federn:* Introduction into Psycho-Analysis for Physicians.
b) *Dr. Paul Federn:* Principles of Psycho-Analytic Therapy.
c) *Dozent Dr. Felix Deutsch:* What ought the Practitioner to know about Psycho-Analysis?

Ort: Vortragssaal des Lehrinstituts, Wien, IX., Pelikangasse 18.
Honorar: öst. Schilling 1·50 pro Stunde. Ermäßigungen werden fallweise gewährt.
Auskunft: Auskunft über Fragen des theoretischen Unterrichts und der praktischen Ausbildung in der Psychoanalyse bei der Vorsitzenden des Lehrinstituts, Frau Dr. Helene Deutsch, Wien, I., Wollzeile 33, jeden Mittwoch von 2—5 Uhr nachmittags.

Figure 3 Program of the Vienna Psychoanalytic Society for the winter semester of 1926–1927.

Figure 2 Freud and Fliess (ca. 1890).

success when it first came out. Only 60 copies were sold during the first six weeks after its appearance, and a second edition was not needed until 1909.

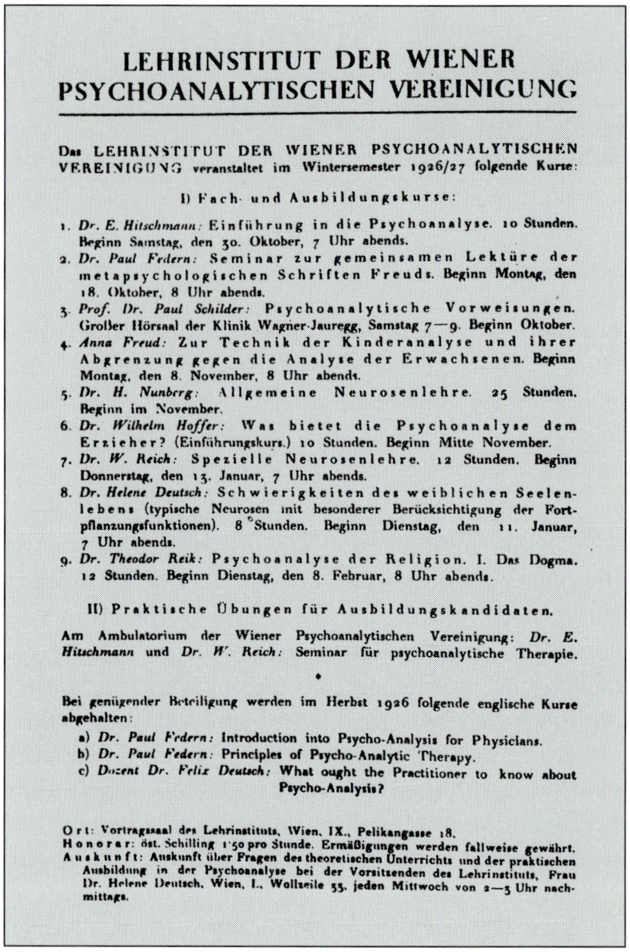

In 1902, four Viennese physicians—Adler, Stekel, Reitler, and Kahane—began to meet with Freud on a regular basis. Paul Federn (1871–1950) joined them in 1903. In 1906, Otto Rank (1884–1939) became the secretary of the small group and the editor of its newsletter. The group eventually became the famous Vienna Psychoanalytic Society. The minutes of the society are now available in a four-volume edition (Nunberg & Federn, 1962–1975). The organization also offered a range of academic courses delivered in German and English (see Figure 3) to future analysts and the interested public. During the winter semester of 1926–1927, for example, a total of nine lecture courses and two practica were offered by 11 of the organization's members. Three of these courses were offered in English for those "physicians" and "practitioners" who were not fluent in German.

Freud's promotion of the unconscious mental life of man was unquestionably his most important achievement. Specifically, Freud argued that the conscious, preconscious, and unconscious are normal functions of the human psyche, and that these are organized in different domains within the mind. According to Freud, man's search for pleasure is controlled by a type of energy which he called "libido." He identified the concept of libido with sexuality, which he felt was expressed in various forms throughout the early growth and development of the individual, beginning with infancy. It is only during puberty that human sexuality takes on its more conventional expression. According to Freud, sexuality is the dominating force of life, and sexual con-

flicts are the major causes of the classic forms of neuroses, such as hysteria and obsessive-compulsive disorder.

Freud was aware of the limitations of his discoveries as early as 1910. He realized that there had to be an additional component to the unconscious. Originally, he had equated the ego with both consciousness and preconsciousness, which, in turn, were opposed by the unconscious. However, based on his study of narcissism he came to understand that the ego can sometimes function at an unconscious level. The importance of the ego had been previously recognized by Alfred Adler (1870–1937), Paul Federn (1871–1950), and Victor Tausk (1877–1919). Between 1919 and 1923, Freud finally formulated his classic theory of psychoanalysis, which is still quite influential today. After initially

Figure 4 Group portrait of Freud's family at his silver wedding anniversary (1911).

defining aggression as an intrinsic part of the ego and, hence, consciousness, he introduced the idea of the death instinct in his book, *Beyond the Pleasure Principle* (1920). Thus there were two crucial needs—libido or eros, and the death instinct or thanatos—which control all aggression.

Freud now had his system in place. The mind was organized into the id, the ego, and the superego. It should be noted, however, that this threefold division is always dynamic and genetic, and inextricably bound to both the biological and mental life of the individual. Since a complete understanding of the mind's structure and functioning can only be gained through extensive personal analysis, it was clear to Freud that psychoanalysis needed to be taught as a distinct discipline. Accordingly, Freud founded the International Psychoanalytic Association, which focused exclusively on his approach to psychoanalysis.

In 1911 Adler and all of his followers broke with Freud. Wilhelm Stekel (1868–1940) left a year later, and Carl Gustav Jung (1875–1961) and Otto Rank broke with the master in 1913 and 1924, respectively. They all left Freud's camp and established their own schools of analysis. However, by the time

of Freud's 80th birthday in 1936, his psychoanalysis had become a broadly acclaimed success. The movement experienced a major setback only a few years later, however, when, during World War II, it was practically banished from continental Europe. Freud went into exile in 1938 and died in London on September 23 of that same year. Late in life, Freud summed up his accomplishments by saying: "I was fortunate when I discovered the unconscious." This is, of course, quite an understatement; many have argued that Freud's work stands as a vital contribution to mankind's effort to understand the human soul.

Bibliography

Freud, S. (1900). *Die Traumdeutung.* Vienna: Deuticke.

Freud, S. (1920). *Jenseits des Lustprinzips.* Vienna: Internationaler Psychoanalytischer Verlag.

Freud, S. (1940–1952). *Gesammelte Werke* (Vols. 1–17). London: Imago.

Freud, S. (1960). *Gesammelte Werke* (Vol. 18). Frankfurt: Fischer.

Masson, J. M. (Ed.). (1985). *The complete letters of Sigmund Freud to Wilhelm Fliess, 1887–1904.* Cambridge: Harvard University Press.

Nunberg, H., & Federn, E. (1962–1975). *Minutes of the Viennese Psychoanalytic Society.* New York: University Press.

Freud's Only Visit to America

Saul Rosenzweig

In 1908, G. Stanley Hall, the President of Clark University in Worcester, Massachusetts, founder and first president of the American Psychological Association, and one of America's most distinguished psychologists, began to plan for the 20th anniversary of the opening of Clark University. He was aided in his planning by the precedent of the 10th anniversary celebration in 1899, at which time he invited world leaders from several sciences, including Forel in psychiatry and S. Ramón y Cajal, father of the neurone theory. At that 10th anniversary, these and other lecturers received honorary degrees. But Hall had something larger in mind this time—not just five lecturers in a brief event, but a score or more of guests who would participate in the anniversary activities over a period of two weeks. In the field of the behavioral sciences—one of the main areas to be covered—there would be about 10 world leaders in psychology, psychiatry, anthropology, and pedagogy; and there were to be equally distinguished leaders representing the physical and the social sciences. Twenty-nine participants would eventually receive honorary degrees, among them eight representing the behavioral sciences: Franz Boas, Leo Burgerstein, Sigmund Freud, H. S. Jennings, C. G. Jung, Adolf Meyer, William Stern, and E. B. Titchener. The memory of this distinguished, multidisciplinary group would be eclipsed for most future psychologists by the legend that the Clark celebration of 1909 was a conference honoring Freud and psychoanalysis. As well-informed a historian as E. G. Boring innocently gave currency to the legend in one of his publications (Boring, 1965, p. 9). When I demonstrated the error to him, he accepted the correction but shifted the responsibility for it to his own former mentor, E. B. Titchener, one of the honored participants on that occasion.

Figure 1 Main building, with Clock Tower, at Clark University in Worcester, Massachussets, 1909.

As with most legends, a germinal element of fact is discernible. Hall, being himself a psychologist, was chiefly interested in the behavioral scientists whom he selected to participate and, even more to the point, he looked forward to the occasion as an opportunity to further his own growing interest in Freud and psychoanalysis. Hall wanted to effect a reconciliation between psychoanalysis, which was grudgingly acknowledged in Europe, with the rest of psychology—the experimental science that he had introduced to America.

A brief look at Hall's early training in psychology can help one better appreciate what he was attempting in 1909. Hall had been a student at European, especially German, universities twice. The first time was before he achieved his PhD, the second, after he had earned it at Harvard. He was the first individual to receive the PhD degree in psychology in the United States. After receiving his degree in 1878, he traveled in Europe for postdoctoral work from 1878 to 1880, at which time

Figure 2 Composite by Rosenzweig of Clark conference lecturers in the behavioral sciences: (left to right) Burgerstein, Freud, Titchener, Jung, Boas, Meyer, Stern, Jennings.

he became Wundt's first American student. But his quest for knowledge was much broader than that affiliation alone. The best description of it is found in the following words by E. B. Titchener. (It should be noted that Titchener in his remarks is referring to both of Hall's European sojourns.)

> Six years in Germany, without the haunting oppression of the doctor's thesis—such was Dr. Hall's opportunity, and he made the most of what was offered. He heard Hegel from the lips of Michelet; he sat with Paulsen in Trendelenburg's seminary; he undertook work of research in Ludwig's laboratory, with von Kries as partner; he experimented with Helmholtz; he was the first American student in Wundt's newly founded laboratory of psychology; he discussed psychophysics with Fechner, the creator of psychophysics; he was present at Heidenhain's early essays in hypnotism; he attended those lavishly experimental lectures of Czermak, where hecatombs of dogs were sacrificed on the altar of science . . . ; he followed courses in theology, metaphysics, logic, ethics, psychology, the philosophy of religion—in physics, chemistry, biology, physiology, anatomy, neurology, anthropology, psychiatry; he frequented clinic and seminary, laboratory and lecture; and he roamed afield as far as Paris on the west and Vienna on the east. (Wilson, 1914, pp. 48–49)

Returning to the 1909 celebration, we note that among the first invitations extended by Hall were

two of seemingly equal importance to him, both dated December 15, 1908. One was to Wilhelm Wundt, the creator at Leipzig University of the first laboratory of experimental psychology, and the other to Sigmund Freud, the founder of psychoanalysis. Wundt was unable to accept because of a conflict with the 500th Jubilee of Leipzig University. Freud also declined but because of a more personal conflict that was related to the time of year. Fortunately Hall was able to adjust the schedule of the conference by shifting the invitation from July to early September 1909. Hall also added two new enticements: an increase in the honorarium (to the exact figure which had originally been offered to Wundt, but not to Freud) and a contemplated honorary degree to be conferred during the celebration. This time Freud accepted. Moreover, it was eventually arranged for C. J. Jung, who was still Freud's ardent disciple in 1909, to participate along with Freud, a circumstance that Freud undoubtedly favored and may even have helped bring about.

In the event, Freud delivered five lectures "On the Origin and Development of Psychoanalysis," from September 7 to September 11—a contribution that was Freud's first and probably best summary of psychoanalytic theory in its original and classic periods.

Jung's participation in the conference was less

consonant but still relevant to the objective for psychology that Hall was pursuing. Two of Jung's three lectures (Jung, 1910) were devoted to the word-association method, a technique invented by Francis Galton in 1879 that had long interested Hall. Hall had, in fact, used this "Freud-Jung method" (as he called it) earlier in 1909 in some investigations of "psychical research" (Tanner, 1910).

There is still some enigma about Jung's invitation, a fact not made any easier by his own incorrect avowal in his autobiography (Jung, 1963, p. 120) that he was invited "simultaneously" with Freud when, in fact, the invitation was surely not extended to him in 1908, and probably not until May 1909. It may be relevant that Jung's eventual honorary degree was, unlike Freud's, in pedagogy, not in psychology. Jung's third and final lecture ("The Psychic Life of the Child") was clearly meant to fortify the most radical part of Freud's doctrine—the concept of infant sexuality—which Freud had discussed earlier the same day. As such, it provided a slim basis for his degree to be in pedagogy. It is also arresting that Jung was only 34 years old in 1909, the youngest of the 29 honored with degrees, and young indeed when compared to the other behavioral scientists invited as lecturers.

It is of interest that two of the eight behavioral scientists who lectured during the celebration represented psychoanalysis—a larger proportion than would have been expected at any similar conference

at that time. Moreover, Hall gave a special distinction to their presence by having Freud and Jung as his houseguests along with William James during the week of their participation.

We know from the published letters of William James (James, 1920, II, pp. 327–328) that he attended the Clark conference for one day in order to hear Freud. Afterward he wrote to his friend Theodore Flournoy in Switzerland to share his impressions. With characteristic gentlemanly generosity, he told his friend that he hoped Freud and his pupils would carry on their line of work so as to reveal what there was in it, but he confided that Freud impressed him as "a man obsessed with fixed ideas" (p. 328). Freud seems to have been more favorably impressed by James. In his brief autobiography (Freud, 1925), when commenting on his participation at Clark, he mentions a walk that he took with James during the conference and, with admiration, describes the courage with which his companion excused himself at one point, by asking Freud to continue while he remained behind (to recover from what was apparently an angina attack). Freud remarks that he wished he could behave with such fortitude under similar circumstances.

I have been able to reconstruct, from newspaper accounts collated against the published lectures, the actual order in which Freud treated the topics he presented at Clark. Then, using a surviving but unpublished letter from James to Hall, it became clear what topic James heard Freud discuss on the one day he was present at the conference. The day was Friday, September 10, and Freud lectured on his theory of dreams. (On that day the group picture on the steps of the Clark Library must also have been taken, with James appearing prominently in the front row.) It may then not be a mere coincidence that one of the very last papers that James wrote (on December 16–17, 1909, as his diary states) and published in 1910, the year of his death, included several of his own dreams—a unique performance for James

Figure 3 Freud, Hall, and Jung at Clark (1909).

(James, 1910). But he gave a quite different kind of interpretation of his dreams from anything recommended by Freud. To James, these dreams, which he recalled from his sojourn in San Francisco in 1906 during the great earthquake, suggested something bordering on a mystical view of the dissociated dream state. The content of one dream, with affinities to his famous brother Henry's "The Beast in the Jungle," played no part in the interpretation. Could these dreams have implicitly entered into the conversation with Freud during the walk in Worcester if, as we may reasonably suppose, that event took place after Freud's lecture (given at 11:00 A.M.)?

Of supplementary relevance to the history of psychology is the fact that at Christmas, 1909, the annual meeting of the American Psychological Association took place in Cambridge, Massachusetts, with a three-hour session devoted to Freud's theories. There were papers by Ernest Jones, Morton Prince, James J. Putnam, and Boris Sidis (among others). Jones discussed Freud's theory of dreams. Following this meeting, Sidis, an outspoken antagonist of Freud's theories and one of James's former PhD students, visited his ailing master at his Cambridge home to share the current discussion of Freud's ideas (Diary of James, December 31, 1909). As Freud's orthodox representative, Jones had been the special object of a vigorous attack by Sidis who, in the opinion of Sidis, "blew the man down." He, like Prince and James, was unable to accept Freud's emphasis on sexuality for which he sometimes preferred to substitute the pervasive influence of fear (Sidis, 1916, pp. 43–63).

From the other side, Hall shared with Freud by letter (December 30, 1909) his very different view of the APA sessions, noting particularly that Sidis "deprecated a Freud cult in this country" and predicted its quick demise; but Putnam put Sidis in his place by noting the indebtedness of Sidis to Freud's work (Rosenzweig, 1992, p. 367). In response, Freud gratefully wrote to Hall (on January 11, 1910): "I cannot suppress a certain unholy joy that you and Putnam have rejected Boris Sidis who is neither very honest nor very intelligent. I mean he deserved nothing better" (p. 370).

We may conclude that participation by Freud and Jung at the Clark conference made a strong impression on contemporary American psychologists and psychiatrists, and the event for the first time gave Freud's position a hearing in the scientific forum previously denied it in Europe. But despite this opportunity and the further momentum that this recognition gave to the psychoanalytic movement, Hall did not succeed in gaining wide acceptance for psychoanalysis as a scientific approach. For one thing, the "Boston school" led by Morton Prince, who had founded the *Journal of Abnormal Psychology* in 1906, used the event to begin crystallizing its opposition to psychoanalysis, a confrontation more evident in psychopathology than in general psychology. Freud did, however, gain an important adherent in the person of James J. Putnam, a professor at the Harvard Medical School, who for many years maintained a friendly debate about Freudian theory with Morton Prince, privately and in print (Hale, 1971).

Acknowledgment

Copyright © Saul Rosenzweig, 1992. A full account of this important event in the history of American psychology as well as in that of psychoanalysis has been published as follows: *Freud, Jung and Hall the King-Maker: The Historic Expedition to America* by Saul Rosenzweig (pp. xi, 477). St. Louis: Rana House, 1992. A second edition appeared in 1994. This book includes for the first time the complete correspondence between Sigmund Freud and G. Stanley Hall, as well as a new translation of the five lectures that Freud delivered at Clark.

Bibliography

Boring, E. G. (1965). On the subjectivity of important historical dates: Leipzig, 1879. *Journal of the History of the Behavioral Sciences, 1,* 5–9

Freud, S. (1925). An autobiographical study. *Standard edition of the complete psychological works of Sigmund Freud, 20,* 7–74. London: Hogarth, 1959. (Original work published 1925)

Hale, N. G., Jr. (Ed.). (1971). *James Jackson Putnam and psychoanalysis: Letters between Putnam and Sigmund Freud, Ernest Jones, William James, Sandor Ferenczi and Morton Prince, 1877–1917.* Cambridge, MA: Harvard University Press.

James, W. (1909). [Diary for 1909]. Unpublished ms. Harvard University, Houghton Library. Cambridge, MA.

James, W. (1910). A suggestion about mysticism. *Journal of Philosophy, Psychology, and Scientific Method, 7,* 85–92.

James, W. (1920). *The letters of William James* (Vol. II). (H. James, Ed.). Boston: Little, Brown.

Jung, C. J. (1910). The association method. (A. A. Brill, Trans.). *American Journal of Psychology, 21,* 219–269.

Jung, C. J. (1963). *Memories, dreams, reflections.* New York: Pantheon.

Rosenzweig, S. (1992). *Freud, Jung and Hall the King-Maker. The historic expedition to America (1909) with G. Stanley Hall as host and William James as guest.* St. Louis: Rana House. (2nd ed., 1994).

Sidis, B. (1898). *The psychology of suggestion.* With an Introduction by William James. New York: Appleton.

Sidis, B. (1916). *The causation and treatment of psychopathic diseases.* Boston: Richard G. Badger.

Tanner, A. E. (1910). *Studies in spiritism.* With an introduction by G. S. Hall. New York: Appleton.

Wilson, L. N. (1914). *G. Stanley Hall: A sketch.* New York: G. E. Stechert.

The Case of Little Hans

L. Dodge Fernald

oes the Professor talk to God . . . ?" Among family and close friends, Sigmund Freud was always called "the Professor." It was a sign of intimacy and respect.

Five-year-old Hans questioned his father as they left Freud's consulting rooms at 19 Bergasse and began to wind their way across the Ringstrasse, a broad circle of streets in the old section of Vienna, each segment with its historic name. Freud often strolled along the segment called Schotten Ring, two blocks from his home. Hans and his father lived across the way on Unter Viaduktgasse, facing the Hauptzollamt station (Figure 1).

The father's answer to his son's question has been lost to history, but Freud's case of Little Hans, as he called the boy, occupies an important place in the archives of psychology. It was Freud's only analysis of a child, and the interview was his only professional session with Little Hans (Freud, 1909/1955).

Hans's father, Max Graf, participated regularly in the Psychoanalytic Wednesday Society, a group of followers who met weekly in Freud's waiting room, and he thereby enjoyed a casual but precious friendship with the Professor. A mustached musician with dark, horn-rimmed glasses, Graf had achieved prominence in Viennese art, music, and journalism (Hanks & Bringmann, 1989). Freud appreciated the cultural side of the city almost as much as he despised its political life, and therefore he returned the respect which Max Graf paid to his work.

A Father's Letters and Freud's Response

Three months earlier Little Hans had developed a puzzling phobia of horses, and his father, in a series of lengthy letters, had described the problem to Sigmund Freud. It began when Hans and his nursemaid emerged from their home for a morning walk in early January. Hans inexplicably protested, became fearful, and started to cry. He asked to return to the house, and, once indoors, he immediately regained his usual good spirits—until bedtime. Then he became frightened, cried again, and asked to "coax" with

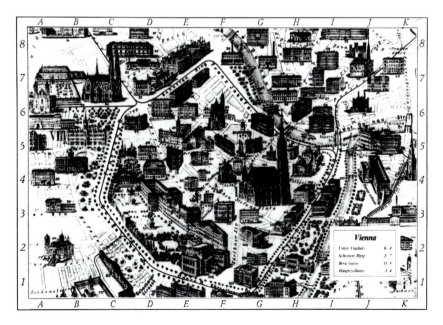

Figure 1 Freud's Vienna. The old, inner city offered magnificent public buildings and a broad sidewalk for strolling and leisure among cafes and coffeehouses.

Figure 2 A Little Hans contemporary. This picture shows a Viennese boy of approximately the same age, era, and background as Hans, depicting his development at the time of his phobia.

his mother, meaning that he wanted to exchange caresses.

The next morning he became frightened when he contemplated a trip to the zoo. Later he confessed to his mother: "I was afraid a horse would bite me." That evening he cried again and declared: "The horse'll come into the room." Still later he awoke crying and explained to his mother, "When I was asleep, I thought you were gone and I had no Mommy to coax with." His mother let him sleep with her and thereby comforted him.

Poor Hans. As the days passed, he became more and more fearful. He stayed indoors for a week after his tonsils were removed, and then he absolutely refused to go on any walk. The streets were filled with horse-drawn vehicles, especially around the Hauptzollamt station, and Little Hans would hardly venture onto the balcony, much less approach the front door. This behavior was particularly puzzling because Hans had never been bitten, kicked, or oth-

erwise injured by a horse, and typically he was a happy, friendly little boy, calm and self-assured even with strangers (Figure 2).

In response to this information, Freud instructed the father to spend more time with Hans and to explain that his fear was nonsense. They should go for walks together, discuss his nonsense, and even consider some facts about sex—providing that the boy had requested them.

One day when they were out walking, Hans said: "I'm most afraid of horses with a thing on their mouths."

"What do you mean?" the father asked. "The piece of iron they have in their mouths?"

"No," the boy replied. "They have something black on their mouth."

Hans apparently was thinking about the heavy muzzle worn by some horses. Then he declared that he was frightened by what they wore around their eyes, referring to the heavy blinders on show horses and work horses (Figure 3).

Figure 3 Horses in harness. Leather pieces attached to the bridle prevented peripheral vision, as shown in this Viennese pair trotting across the city in grand style.

With a growing interest in sex organs, Hans once asked: "Momma, have you got a widdler too?"

"Of course," she answered. "Why?"

"I was just thinking," Hans replied.

Later his mother inquired, "Do you put your hand to your widdler?" Then she warned: "It's not proper."

Hans answered, "But it's great fun."

His father explained, "You know, if you don't put your hand to your widdler any more, this nonsense of yours'll soon get better." He had decided that Hans's masturbation caused anxiety which had been displaced onto horses.

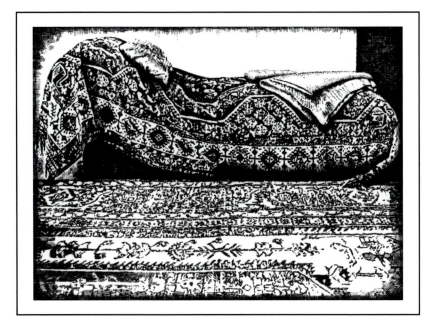

Figure 4 Freud's couch. The patient could use the blanket for warmth and the pillow to achieve a more upright position.

Freud had arrived at a very different interpretation, one which he expressed to the father and son when they came to his quarters on that Monday afternoon, March 30, 1908. They walked through the waiting room together and past the famous couch in Freud's consulting room, for Little Hans was much too young to lie still and engage in self-discovery by describing his thoughts and feelings (Figure 4). Instead, they went into the next room, at the very back of the apartment, and sat in chairs around the desk in Freud's study.

The interview was brief, partly because Freud was so familiar with the case, partly because Hans was so young. In a jocular fashion, Freud asked Little Hans if horses wore eyeglasses, which the boy denied. Then he asked if his father wore eyeglasses, and again Hans denied it, despite the presence of his bespectacled father wearing horn-rimmed glasses right next to him. Continuing in this manner, Freud jokingly inquired about the blackness around the horse's mouth and whether his father, too, had a blackness around his mouth. Eventually he suggested to the father and son that Hans's fear of horses was partly a disguised fear of his father, arising because of the boy's growing fondness for his mother. The father also was big and powerful, like a horse, and indeed he often gave Hans horsey rides.

Years ago, the Professor explained, he had known that Little Hans would experience this difficulty, loving his mother so much that he would think his father must be angry with him. Freud assured Hans that he need not be fearful; his father was fond of him anyway.

Little Hans had little to gain by displaying his fear directly, Freud wrote later. Moreover, he also loved his father, who had been kind and helpful in many ways. Wishing to disguise this feeling even from himself, Little Hans unconsciously transferred it onto a horse, a suitable substitute. Not only did it symbolize the man in several ways, it was also relatively harmless and more easily avoided. In short, this fear arose through unconscious motivation; it was a manifestation of the Oedipus complex.

Max Graf and his son were duly impressed following that visit, but Freud was less satisfied. He viewed the Oedipus complex as only a "piece of the solution" (Freud, 1909/1955). As was his custom, he sat alone at his desk many late nights pondering the case and writing his report (Figure 5).

In this report, Freud noted that he had provided treatment for Hans's mother, and modern theorists suggest that her insecurities contributed to her son's difficulties. She threatened Hans with diverse physical punishments, acted seductively toward him, gave him false information, and warned that she would leave if he misbehaved. In short, she caused him to doubt himself, as well as the support she might provide for him (Price & Calloway, 1995). For this reason, Little Hans's problem has been

Figure 5 Freud's desk. Sitting in this chair in his study, Freud met with colleagues and prospective patients, including Little Hans and his father.

viewed today in the context of family systems therapy (Wile, 1980).

Acclaim, Criticism, and New Pathways

Freud published this case under the title "Analysis of a Phobia in a Five-Year-Old Boy" (1909/1955). Of immediate interest within and outside psychoanalysis, it depicted the Oedipus complex, the clinical approach, and a child's dreams, as well as the onset of a phobic reaction. It also appeared at the time of Freud's famous voyage to America, which gave him an international reputation. Newspapers in this country declared that the story of Little Hans would ever remain a unique and exemplary study of the soul of a child (Cromer & Anderson, 1970; Hale, 1971). And indeed it was highly regarded in the immediately ensuing decades.

After the middle of the 20th century, however, the case of Little Hans came under re-examination, along with other critiques of psychoanalysis. The foremost criticism concerned the potential for bias on the part of both Max Graf and Freud. An early and determined supporter of psychoanalysis, Graf's letters provided Freud with background information, and his questioning provided Little Hans with ideas about his problem—ideas that were typically consistent with psychoanalysis. Just as Freud, perhaps unwittingly, encouraged his early patients in the false recall of childhood seduction, the father,

unwittingly or otherwise, apparently encouraged both his son and Freud in ways of thinking that were compatible with psychoanalytic theory; such as describing himself as a horse, suggesting that Hans was afraid of him, and implying that the problem lay with Hans's longing for his mother.

Freud, too, was susceptible to bias, personal and professional. Hans's mother was a former patient; his father was a personal friend; and he knew the boy socially, even bringing him a special birthday present (Figure 6).

The potential for professional bias, in particular, arises in this case, for there is no independent, direct evidence that Little Hans actually was afraid of his father. Freud made this assumption and proceeded accordingly, but nowhere in his detailed report did Little Hans ever show any outright fear of his father by word or deed (Wolpe & Rachman, 1960). The boy did want increased contact with his mother, but this behavior does not provide convincing evidence that he desired sexual relations with her or that he was experiencing the Oedipus com-

Figure 6 Rocking horse. At 50 years of age, Freud carried a rocking horse up four flights of stairs to Hans's apartment, presenting it to the boy as a gift for his third birthday (Graf, 1942).

plex. Even Hans's improvement during the period of his therapy is not conclusive, for many other events intervened. Hans grew older, lived with a new nursemaid, and moved to a new home. All of these factors could have influenced the outcome. In summary, there is no direct support for the presence of the Oedipus complex or its relief by psychoanalysis (Wolpe & Rachman, 1960). The testimony came from Freud himself.

Still further, since Freud's day the origins of phobias have been viewed from diverse psychological perspectives. Little Hans was present when a horse fell over while pulling a heavy van, a situation which created considerable anxiety among the spectators. In the context of one-trial learning, this incident could have caused a classically conditioned emotional reaction in the boy. From the viewpoints of modeling theory and direct instruction, Little Hans was present when a childhood friend was warned about horse bites. Although this caution was directed to a companion, Little Hans took it seriously, repeating it on several occasions. In short, both behaviorism and observational learning offer more parsimonious interpretations of Little Hans's phobia.

On his part, Freud was pleased with the opportunity to study Little Hans, for it gave him a chance to observe the displacement process directly, just as it occurred in the child, and psychoanalysis accounted for many details ignored in other interpretations: the significance of the muzzle and blinders, the contents of Hans's dreams, his fantasy play with dolls, and his increased interest in his mother (Freud, 1909). It was Freud's view that these fears, fantasies, and dreams were called forth by the recently awakened Oedipus complex (Figure 7).

The significance of the case, however, extends far beyond any specific interpretation, psychoanalytic or otherwise. Instead, the case contributed notably to the roots of three important developments in the field: child psychology, play therapy, and sex education.

Prior to Freud's work there was no child psychology. Childhood was regarded as an age of innocence and contentment, an idyllic period before the inevitable frustrations and demands of adult life. The case of Little Hans played a central role in dispelling this sentimental view, one which denied the child's helplessness in the face of experiences which, to the child, cannot be understood or expressed, much less controlled. It provided com-

pelling evidence about children's fantasies and fears, mistaken ideas of conception and childbirth, and misunderstandings about family members. Followed shortly by similar reports, the case of Little Hans prompted psychologists to turn to the study of childhood as a vital opportunity for understanding the human condition. Freud's youngest daughter, Anna, was among those who stimulated the early rise of child psychology.

Figure 7 Freud at 50. Shown here in the years he studied Little Hans, Freud's cigar reveals an addiction which continued throughout his adult life.

In the weeks and months after their interview with Freud, the father and son walked and talked and played together, and a form of play therapy emerged in these activities. They went to the zoo, to the park, and on other excursions; and the father regularly asked: "What did you think of . . . ?" "What do you remember?" "What did you do then?" He gave Hans horsey rides and listened carefully while Hans played with his dolls, toys, and imaginary children.

Figure 8 On the Ringstrasse. Little Hans and his father, in their therapeutic relationship, might have looked like this man and boy of the same era, strolling near the Opera House.

In their play, Freud pointed out, children repeat events which have impressed them in real life; they are trying to understand and assimilate them, making themselves the master of puzzling or difficult situations. A confusing, frightening experience often will become the theme of a subsequent game (Freud, 1920/1955). Through this guidance offered to Hans's father, Freud provided an outlook and approach for child therapy (Figure 8).

The case of Little Hans also raised the question of the sexual enlightenment of children. At a meeting of the Psychoanalytic Wednesday Society, Freud suggested that sexual enlightenment might offer a protection against childhood sexual traumata. The young child, he pointed out, does not possess the capacity for understanding or mastering strong sexual excitement; the experience makes insurmountable demands on the child's intelligence, and therefore it is repressed. Prior enlightenment might provide an inoculation against such traumata, he declared. It could limit the disruption, though not avoid it altogether (Nunberg & Federn, 1962).

Children, Freud continued, should receive whatever information they have requested in a form they can understand. The proper age depends upon the child's capacity for understanding, and the initiative should be taken by the schools in a gradual course of instruction (Freud, 1907/1959).

The earlier notion, that a child could not possibly be interested in sex, was inconceivable to Freud

and contradicted by this case, and soon other clinicians announced that Little Hans indeed had much company. Among his peers was four-year-old Little Anna, who showed astonishing similarity. She was described by Carl Gustav Jung (1910) on his trip to America with Freud.

The Little Boy in Later Days

By the end of May, Hans had made unmistakable progress in overcoming his phobia. He never resisted going for walks; he chased after horse-drawn wagons; and sometimes he even pretended to be a horse himself. He seemed to be dealing with his problem well through these activities. In any case, he eventually learned to trust himself in the streets. According to psychoanalytic theory, his phobia disappeared because he no longer needed it for a disguise against his feelings about his father, but it cannot be stated with any assurance that this therapy brought about this change. Rather, it can only be said that the improvement occurred during this period.

In his report, Freud referred to the boy as Little Hans. In fact, the child's real name was Herbert Graf, and one spring day 14 years later, Freud was surprised by a visit from a strong and healthy young man 19 years of age, announcing that he was "Little Hans." Freud was delighted to learn that he was without significant personal difficulties and decided that this outcome further corroborated his theories and therapy. Equally interesting to Freud was the fact that the young man, until reading his case history, had completely forgotten his phobia. According to Freud, this forgetting was further evidence for unconscious processes.

In still later years, Herbert Graf successfully pursued his youthful goal of becoming an opera stage director, undoubtedly influenced by his father's achievements. He attended a conservatory and later the University of Vienna, earning a doctoral degree in music. Afterwards he served as director of opera in several European cities: Vienna, Frankfurt-am-Main, Breslau, Basel; and later, Florence, Rome, Zurich, and others. Interspersed with these engagements were prominent positions in the United States, especially in Philadelphia and New York, including an extended appointment as stage director for the Metropolitan Opera (Hanks & Bringmann, 1989).

And so, as it turned out, the little boy who dared not venture into the streets made his way quite well in the world beyond, though his prime contribution to human history lay in unexpected spheres. Indeed, Herbert Graf, as Little Hans, is the most famous boy in all of child psychotherapy (Gardner, 1972). He has a place in history not for his music or his phobia but for his unintentional, highly significant role in the early growth of child psychology, play therapy, and sex education.

Bibliography

Cromer, W., & Anderson, P. (1970). Freud's visit to America: Newspaper coverage. *Journal of the History of Behavioral Science, 6,* 349–353.

Freud, S. (1955). Analysis of a phobia in a five-year-old boy. In J. Strachey (Ed. and Trans.), *The standard edition of the complete psychological works of Sigmund Freud* (Vol. 10, pp. 5–149). London: Hogarth Press. (Original work published 1909)

Freud, S. (1955). Beyond the pleasure principle. In J. Strachey (Ed. and Trans.), *The standard edition of the complete psychological works of Sigmund Freud* (Vol. 18, pp. 7–64). London: Hogarth Press. (Original work published 1920)

Freud, S. (1959). The sexual enlightenment of children. In J. Strachey (Ed. and Trans.), *The standard edition of the complete psychological works of Sigmund Freud* (Vol. 9, pp. 131–139). London: Hogarth Press. (Original work published 1907)

Gardner, R. A. (1972). Little Hans: The most famous boy in the child psychotherapy literature. *International Journal of Child Psychotherapy, 1,* 24–50.

Graf, M. (1942). Reminiscences of Professor Sigmund Freud. *Psychoanalytic Quarterly, 11,* 465–476.

Hale, N. G. (1971). *Freud and the Americans: The beginnings of psychoanalysis in the United States, 1876–1917.* New York: Oxford University Press.

Hanks, J., & Bringmann, W. G. (1989). Whatever happened to Little Hans? *History of Psychology Newsletter, 21,* 78–81.

Jung, C. G. (1910). The association method. *American Journal of Psychology, 21,* 219–269.

Nunberg, H., & Federn, E. (Eds.). (1962). *Minutes of the Vienna Psychoanalytic Society, Vol. I: 1906–1908.* New York: International Universities Press.

Price, G., & Calloway, M. J. (1995). *Little Hans to Herbert Graf.* Unpublished paper. History of Psychology 411. University of South Alabama.

Wile, J. R. (1980). Freud's treatment of Little Hans: The case of an undeveloped family therapist. *Family Therapy, 7,* 131–138.

Wolpe, J., & Rachman, S. (1960). Psychoanalytic "evidence": A critique based on Freud's case of Little Hans. *Journal of Nervous and Mental Disease, 130,* 135–148.

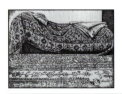

Lou Andreas-Salomé: Feminist and Psychoanalyst

Inge Weber
Ursula Welsch

The personal eminence of Lou Andreas-Salomé (1861–1937) has traditionally been defined in terms of her friendships with famous men like the philosopher Friedrich Nietzsche (1844–1900), the lyric poet Rainer Maria Rilke (1875–1926), and the founder of psychoanalysis, Sigmund Freud (1856–1939), whose work she is said to have inspired. Who was Lou Andreas-Salomé, the author and psychoanalyst, really? She does not make it easy to gain access to her life and thought. Her autobiography (Andreas-Salomé, 1951) is a reconstruction rather than a chronicle of her own life guided by the philosophy and a self-image she chose to transmit to the world.

Childhood

Louise von Salomé was born on February 12, 1861, in St. Petersburg. Her father was a general at the Imperial Russian Court, who was later promoted to the rank of Privy Councillor. Lou's mother was descended from a merchant's family in Hamburg. When his daughter was born, after 5 sons and 17 years of marriage, the reaction of her parents differed significantly. Her open-minded father, who at the age of 57 might have been her grandfather, received his only daughter with joy, but lacked the time to pay much attention to her. Her strict and God-fearing mother, however, who was only 38 years old, had hoped for another son and anticipated that her only daughter would cause difficulties in her life. The mother was proven to be correct, at least from her perspective.

Lou Andreas-Salomé told little about her childhood at home, except for a few anecdotes. On several occasions she commented, however, that her childhood had been a lonely one. For Lou this feeling remained enigmatic, although she began her autobiography with the confession that she experienced the trauma of her birth as a loss.

Lou's entire later behavior towards men permits the conclusion that she may well have experienced an emotional trauma in the sense of Sigmund Freud's primal scene early in her life. In addition,

Figure 1 Gustav von Salomé and his favorite daughter "Lou."

she describes in several of her short novels, which are concerned with young women, traumatic experiences which always end in a catastrophe. In a later short story, *The Hour Without God* (1922), she makes it clear how terrifying it was for a young girl to surprise her parents during sexual intercourse.

The child, Louise von Salomé, took refuge in a fantasy world and created a God for herself with whom she could converse about everything. She shared all her sorrows and cares with him and told stories about events of her daily life. As a child, she lost the safety of this God when she implored Him to answer her only once. With her narcissistic tendency to exaggerate, the young Louise von Salomé became convinced that all beings are destined by fate to share such deprivation. Thus, she over-generalized her sense of loneliness in order to feel no longer alone. This attitude or "basic feeling," as she called it, shaped her entire life and thinking and was—at least from her perspective—confirmed by psychoanalysis (i.e., the phyletic contents of the unconscious). Her active imagination, which had revealed itself in her association with the beloved God, was preserved. The fact that now Lou told her stories to herself was, as she pointed out, the foundation stone of her later work as an author.

Hendrik Gillot

As the time drew near to become a full-fledged member of her church, Lou questioned whether she should participate in the ritual of confirmation. It had become meaningless for her, but she did not express this opinion openly before the death of her father.

In the meantime, the 17-year-old Louise met the Dutch minister, Hendrik Gillot (1836–1916), who instructed her privately in religious and philosophical matters. Lou and her mentor became fascinated with one another. Gillot systematically helped her overcome her fantasy world by challenging her intellectually. Together, they studied Kant, Kierkegaard, and Spinoza and occupied themselves with the major world religions. In a manner of speaking, Gillot became Lou's "ideal father." From her first meeting with this "divine man," she realized that "now all loneliness had ended."

The relationship between Gillot and Lou continued to grow. Eventually, Gillot, who was married and had two children of Lou's age, filed for a divorce and proposed to Lou. Once again, the world fell apart for Lou. She had not been prepared for this action of Gillot, who did not interest her as a man. He was merely a substitute for, or even a replacement for, her father.

Lou saw no other solution to this predicament than flight from Gillot and St. Petersburg. To satisfy her awakened thirst for knowledge, she decided to study abroad. However, she needed a passport to leave Russia. The passport, in turn, depended on her confirmation. Gillot performed the ceremony, which in its solemnity, almost resembled a wedding. At that time, Lou believed that after her loving Gillot, she would never again be able to love anyone else in her life. Paul Rée (1849–1901), Friedrich Nietzsche, and later even her husband, Friedrich Carl Andreas (1846–1930), were to suffer from this tragic misperception.

Youth

Her mother decided to accompany the 19-year-old Lou to Zurich University, which at the time was one of the few educational institutions that accepted female students. Lou continued her studies with the same eagerness with which she had begun them under Gillot's guidance. After a year, however, she became seriously ill, and her physicians advised her to change climates. Lou was convinced that she did not have long to live.

During a visit with the feminist Malwida von Meysenbug (1816–1903) in Rome in 1882, Lou met the young philosopher Paul Rée. He fell in love with her and spent many a night walking through the historical center of Rome, discussing the world's problems with her. Eventually, Rée's expressed admiration for this highly intelligent, well-educated, and most attractive woman drew his friend Friedrich Nietzsche to Rome. Lou enjoyed the stimulating discussions with her friends and appears to have regarded herself as their equal. On the other hand, she was disconcerted that first Paul Rée and then Nietzsche proposed marriage to her. Lou was not interested in complicating the intellectual communication with her male friends with the intimacies of marriage. However, she was eager to expand her association with them as friends by finding a home where the three of them could live and study together. Despite the horrified warnings of her mother and Malwida von Meysenbug, Lou attempted to implement these plans.

After some complications with the hypersensi-

Figure 2 Lou Andreas-Salomé (ca. 1897).

tive Nietzsche, whose second proposal was also rejected by Lou, two weeks were spent with him in Tautenburg discussing his philosophical ideas. Nietzsche was convinced that nobody had understood his ideas as well as Lou. Still, an unpleasant break occurred between Nietzsche and Lou. After his death, his jealous and bigoted sister continued to slander Lou for the rest of her life.

Paul Rée helped Lou to forget her problems by inviting her to share an apartment with him in Berlin, where they could study and write together. Soon they made the acquaintance of a group of scholars with whom they could discuss philosophical questions. These new friends included the sociologist Ferdinand Tönnies (1855–1936), the experimental psychologist Hermann Ebbinghaus (1850–1909), and the indologist Paul Deussen (1845–1919). Rée faithfully remained by Lou's side but adhered to their mutual agreement not to become personally involved. However, when Lou met the orientalist, Friedrich Carl Andreas

(1846–1930) late in 1885 and agreed to marry him a year later, Rée was unable to tolerate the situation. He was convinced that after marriage Lou would be unable to remain loyal to him. Lou regarded the subsequent separation from Rée as the most painful loss in her life. She believed steadfastly that it had been unnecessary.

Early Marriage

Her marriage to Andreas was not always easy. She had felt compelled to accept his proposal, but was not at all willing to share his bed. After the tense early years of their marriage, an arrangement was apparently reached, which permitted them to live independent lives within a marriage that they both regarded as indissoluble.

Andreas introduced Lou to his friends in the Berlin circle of naturalistic writers, including Gerhart Hauptmann (1862–1946), Ludwig Bölsche (1861–1939), and the brothers Heinrich Hart (1855–1906) and Julius Hart (1859–1930). At that time, she began to write short stories and novels, which focused primarily on the lives of young girls and women and utilized much autobiographical information. During her extensive travels without her husband, Lou met two women, Frieda von Bülow (1857–1943) and Helene Klingenberg (1865–1943), whom she considered as her only female friends.

Rainer Maria Rilke

During a trip to Munich in 1897, Lou Andreas-Salomé first met the 21-year-old Ranier Maria Rilke. He conquered the 36-year-old author with the enthusiasm and persistence of his youth and may have been her first sexual partner. Lou wanted to help Rilke change his romantic and emotional writing style by introducing him to the values of simplicity and originality. Some of Rilke's early poems were destroyed; others were later included in his *Book of Hours* (1976). One of his most beautiful German love poems was created at that time: "Extinguish my eyes." From 1898 to 1899, Rilke lived in Berlin, not far from Lou. Although they spent much time together, Lou's husband does not appear to have been jealous.

In the spring of 1899, Lou, her husband, and Rilke traveled to Russia. This journey, especially the participation in a Russian Orthodox church service during Easter night, was to gain an outstanding but somewhat unrealistic place in Rilke's memories. During the summer of 1899, Rilke and Lou returned to Russia without her husband. In Russia, a gap (which could not be bridged) gradually developed between Lou and Rilke. Rilke showed clear symptoms of a mental disorder, which terrified both of them. Lou believed that Rilke was becoming mentally ill, because he could no longer discharge the creative energies through his literary work. Lou was convinced that her friendship interfered with his work and consequently terminated their relationship. She hoped that if Rilke worked independently, he would again realize his artistic talents.

Lou's reasoning in her attempts to help Rilke overcome his writer's block somewhat resembled Freud's new method of psychoanalysis. In fact, Lou had met Freud during the winter of 1895–1896. Their initial contact, however, did not lead further. Lou's knowledge of psychiatry and mental disorders was most likely obtained through the Viennese neurologist Friedrich Pineles (1868–1936), who for some years was her friend. Her initial acquaintance with Rilke and the resumption of her personal association with him in June of 1903 was probably responsible for her psychoanalysis.

In 1911, the 50-year-old Lou Andreas-Salomé began to discover "new sources" of meaning for her life in the new and still disreputable field of psychoanalysis. She became, in fact, one of the first female psychoanalysts, who chose to become experts in the study of human needs and childhood sexuality.

After extensive autodidactive study of the psychoanalytic literature and extensive personal contacts with the Berlin psychoanalyst Karl Abraham (1877–1925), Lou Andreas-Salomé sent the following brief letter to Sigmund Freud (1856–1939) in Vienna (Pfeiffer, 1966):

> Esteemed Professor Freud:
>
> Since I had the opportunity to attend the Weimar Congress of Psychoanalysis last fall, the study of psychoanalysis has captured all my attention, and the more I learn about this field, the stronger I am attracted. It looks now as if my wish to come to Vienna for a few months' time will soon be realized. May I ask for permission to attend your seminar and gain admission to your Wednesday night meetings? The only reason for my stay is my desire to devote myself exclusively to all aspects of psychoanalysis.
>
> Very truly yours,
>
> Lou Andreas-Salomé (p. 7)

Lou Andreas-Salomé fully kept her promise during the next six months, which she spent in Vienna. In the small group of psychoanalytically-minded physicians, lawyers, social scientists, and theologians, she quickly felt at home as among a group of brothers. Freud himself analyzed her briefly, and she used the opportunity to attend his university lectures and to become deeply involved in ongoing theoretical controversies among the local analysts. She was an astute and independent observer of the developing controversy between Freud and Alfred Adler (1870–1937) and the bitter conflict between Freud and Carl Gustav Jung (1875–1961). Sándor Ferenczi (1875–1933) was her favorite among Freud's disciples in Vienna (Andreas-Salomé, 1983): "Undoubtedly, Ferenczi's thought contains much, that is far removed from Freud's philosophical ideas . . . but they complement each other, and, therefore Ferenczi's time will eventually come" (p.147).

During her brief sojourn in Vienna, she became a close friend and confidant of Victor Tausk (1877–1919), whose unresolved inner conflicts appeared similar to her own (Andreas-Salomé, 1983, p. 189). The two could talk freely about a multitude of questions like the nature of narcissism, homosexuality, the relationship between men and women, sexuality and the Ego, the defense of sublimation, etc. Lou also accompanied her new friend on his consulting visits to the Vienna Neurological Clinic, where she became acquainted with the practice of psychoanalysis by her first personal contact with psychiatric patients.

Private Practice

In 1913, Lou Andreas-Salomé began to treat patients with psychoanalysis in the small German university town of Göttingen. Her analytic practice was and remained the first and only one in this community until her death in 1937. Despite opposition by local physicians, she treated individuals suffering from a variety of neurotic conditions. Her patients were adults as well as teenagers and children, who were accompanied by their parents. Her patients, who were referred to her by Sigmund Freud and other eminent psychoanalysts, often came from far away and had to live in Göttingen until their treatment was completed.

At that time, psychoanalysis, unlike the official psychiatry of her time, offered the only comprehensive and complex definition and treatment of the psychoneuroses. In particular, Freud's theories about the sexual etiology of neuroses were regarded as scandalous and unscientific by his medical contemporaries. Freud's pansexualistic views may well have played a role in local speculations among physicians and laymen about Lou Andreas-Salomé's psychoanalytic activities. For example, one skeptical Göttingen psychiatrist suggested to a patient that she should terminate her treatment by Lou Andreas-Salomé when the word "sexuality" was mentioned or when she experienced erotic feelings during treatment (Andreas-Salomé, 1924). Both predicted events occurred quickly and the treatment was unfortunately terminated by the unhappy patient. However, such experiences did not discourage Lou Andreas-Salomé.

As a psychoanalyst who was able to combine "deepest and most intimate empathy" with "the coldest . . . intellect" (Weber & Rempp, 1990) she applied the rules of analytic treatment far more flexibly than is customary today. Depending on the season and the weather, treatment sessions were conducted in Lou's private study, on the balcony of her house, or in the garden. Typically, Lou Andreas-Salomé sat vis-à-vis the patient, which, in addition to the couch setting, is a fairly common practice today. When she encountered major problems in her treatment, Lou Andreas-Salomé would consult Freud by mail and, later, his daughter Anna Freud (1895–1981). The two women appear to have become close personal friends after Lou Andreas-Salomé lived for an extended period of time in the Freud home in 1921. More than 400 letters testify to the exceptionally close relationship between the 26-year-old Anna Freud and her 60-year-old friend.

When she looked back at her long life, Lou Andreas-Salomé felt as if her "entire life had awaited psychoanalysis" (Weber & Rempp, 1990, p. 231). Since adolescence, she had been familiar with the philosophy of Benedict Spinoza (1632–1677), the pantheistic Dutch philosopher. As a teenager, she bought his works "secretly" by selling her jewelry. Her understanding of Spinoza's philosophy appears to have prepared her receptivity for psychoanalytic ideas. Thus, we read (Andreas-Salomé, 1983):

> It is nice that I was able to rediscover the only thinker, to whom I had an almost worshipful relationship when I was still a child, and that he is now the philosopher of psychoanalysis. Whenever one ponders a certain issue long enough, one will encounter [Spinoza]. . . . He always waits [somewhere] along the road. (p. 69)

Freud and Lou Andreas-Salomé

For Lou Andreas-Salomé, psychoanalysis became a turning point and Freud's personality, especially his "fatherly face," guided her until the end of her life. Freud, in turn, viewed her as a "highly significant woman," who possesses a "dangerous intelligence" and is "exceptionally capable of understanding." He was eager to know her ideas about women. As a "sick, old man," Freud particularly enjoyed Lou's sense of "life affirmation" and her confidence, which he discovered in her letters. When she experienced serious financial problems, Freud not only sent her patients but provided direct financial support. She remained attached to Freud until her death and remained throughout a firm but undogmatic adherent of psychoanalysis. For her, as for Freud, psychoanalysis was a science, which encourages and stimulates independent thought.

Her respect for Freud is best expressed in one of her best-known books, *My Thanks to Freud* (1931) which she published as an open letter at the age of 70. When Freud asked her afterwards why she had immersed herself so deeply in psychoanalysis, Lou Andreas-Salomé replied (1983):

> Originally, there was just a sober and neutral interest, which put me on the road to new sources. To this was added the discovery of a new science, which always seemed to start from the beginning. . . . The third and most personal reason, which was decisive, is an awareness of all the intimate enrichment I have received from psychoanalysis. (p. 89)

Feminist and Emancipatory Publications

Lou Andreas-Salomé's major analytic writings, which also reflect her views on feminism and emancipation, were republished in 1990 under the title *The "Ambiguous" Smile of Eroticism* by the Kore Publishing Company of Freiburg, Germany.

About Early Worship. This 1913 article by Lou Andreas-Salomé deals with her early religious views. Her private "childhood God" protected her from her conscience and her powerful parents. These fantasies, which psychopathologists can readily interpret as symptoms of a childhood neurosis, can also be viewed as evidence of her early creativity, which protected her against a more serious mental disorder.

Women's Types. Lou Andreas-Salomé wrote this article in 1914 at Freud's suggestion. It contains Lou Andreas-Salomé's major thoughts about feminism and psychoanalysis. Anyone acquainted with modern feminism will find much that is familiar in this article. Our summary will focus on views of psychoanalysis and feminism, bisexualism, psychosexual development, and the activity-passivity dimension in women.

Psychoanalysis and Feminism. Like science and culture in general, psychoanalysis is dominated by masculine perspectives, which assume that only men are true human beings. Lou Andreas-Salomé emphasized a feminine perspective and the positivity of female destiny. In this respect, she differed radically from the feminist movement of her time, which declaimed the inferiority of women and sought mere equality with men. Lou Andreas-Salomé was always convinced that woman can accomplish as much as men.

Bisexualism. She viewed women and men as bisexual beings, as she explained to Anna Freud (Weber & Rempp, 1990):

> . . . one does not have to become a woman, this is our native condition. In addition, women like men possess characteristics of the opposite gender. In women, these [masculine] characteristics can be expressed far more easily than femininity in men. In men, love and ambition are always in conflict with each other. Strength, courage, achievement, intellect and logic are just as much feminine characteristics as tenderness and warmth can be male traits. (p. 229)

Lou Andreas-Salomé focused on the unique features of each gender and stressed the complementarity of male and female traits. She did not wish to destroy the differences between men and women. Consequently, an androgenous perspective on life, which is prevalent in modern discussions of this issue, was truly alien to her.

Psychosexual Development. The essential differences between women and men are, of course, determined by differences in their respective psychosexual development. The young girl discovers early in life that she possesses a secret, an "internal treasure," which cannot be altered by the process of socialization. Young women reach puberty without envy but with a conviction that their passive-receptive sexuality is valuable. According to Lou Andreas-Salomé, female passivity does not represent a condition of "resignation" but an inner strength. The "passive instinct" of women represents an integration of mind and sensuality, which man can rarely achieve. Intellectual achievements in women always have a "genuine erotic" character" (Weber & Rempp, 1990, p. 46). In turn, sexuality becomes a mental event for women.

Active Passivity. Female passivity becomes an important experience through the very act of surrender. The model for this experience is, of course, the physical act of love. For Lou Andreas-Salomé, physical surrender is not an act of passive submission but an active event, through which women can discover their own worth.

Surrender can only become a formative experience for women, who are fully convinced that their lives are valuable. Neither exceptional achievements nor recognition from others can take the place of a woman's sense of value. Anxiety, shame, and unhappiness develop when women adopt masculine, rather than feminine, models of ambition and achievement. The "interplay of mind and senses," which is commonly found in women, provides emancipatory strength. (Weber, 1993, p. 179).

Old Age

After Lou Andreas-Salomé become a practicing psychoanalyst, she gradually lost her contacts with the world of literature. In financially difficult times, she still wrote for the popular press and occasionally published a novel. Lou believed that her therapeutic work utilized the same

Figure 3 Lou Andreas-Salomé (ca. 1935).

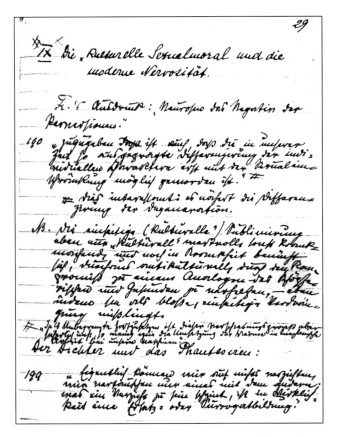

Figure 4 A facsimile page from the working diary of Lou Andreas-Salomé with notes about the relationship between "culturally conditioned sexual mores and modern nervousness."

type of unconscious energies as her literary work, and hence, her work as an author was abandoned.

In her old age, when she was no longer able to travel and after her life had quieted down, she looked back on her life. Perhaps the writing of her autobiography was a way of saying goodbye to her longtime friends.

She had suspected that Rilke was dying from leukemia two years before his actual death in 1926. Before the end, Lou briefly attempted to assist her old friend with her clinical skills. Unfortunately, Rilke, who had tried to obtain analytic help on his own, was unable to accept her help so late in life. When Lou's husband died in 1930, she once again sought to comprehend the secret of her marriage.

Although Hitler had been in power in Germany since 1933, letters between Freud and Lou Andreas-Salomé lack references to the political reality of the era. Lou died in Göttingen on February 5, 1937, of diabetes. Freud died two years later in exile in London.

Bibliography

Andreas-Salomé, L. (1913). Von Frühem Gottesdienst. *Imago, 2,* 457-467.

Andreas-Salomé, L. (1914). Zum Typus Weib. *Imago, 3,* 1–14.

Andreas-Salomé, L. (1916). "Anal" und "Sexual." *Imago, 4,* 249–273.

Andreas-Salomé, L. (1922). *Die Stunde ohne Gott und andere Kindergeschichten.* Jena: Diederichs.

Andreas-Salomé, L., to Anna Freud (letter, June 1924). Andreas-Salomé Archive, Göttingen, Germany.

Andreas-Salomé, L. (1931). *Mein Dank and Freud.* Vienna: Internationaler Psychoanalytischer Verlag.

Andreas-Salomé, L. (1951). *Lebensrückblick.* Zürich: Niehans.

Andreas-Salomé, L. (1983). *In der Schule bei Freud.* Frankfurt: Fischer.

Pfeiffer, E. (Ed.). (1966). *Sigmund Freud. Lou Andreas-Salomé. Briefwechsel.* Frankfurt: Fischer.

Rilke, R. M. (1976). *Gesammelte Werke.* Frankfurt: Fischer.

Weber, I. (1993). Lou Andreas-Salomé: Die Psychoanalytikerin. In Weber-Reich, T. (Ed.). ("Des Kennenlernens werth." Bedeutende Frauen Göttingens. Göttingen: Wallstein Verlag.).

Weber, I., & Rempp, B. (Eds.). (1990). *Das "zweideutige" Lächeln der Erotik.* Freiburg: Kore.

Welsch, U., & Wiesner, M. (1990). *Lou Andreas-Salomé* (2nd Ed.). Stuttgart: Klett-Cotta.

Psychoanalysts in Caricatures

Helmut E. Lück

For the psychoanalytic movement the year 1924 was a difficult year indeed. There were controversies over theoretical positions, issues of proper practice, and psychoanalytical associations experiencing their share of political infighting. Additionally there were quarrels within the "Secret Committee," which was the principal cadre of supporters who helped Sigmund Freud push forward his ideas of psychoanalytical theory and application. A considerable number of these controversies and problems were connected with the fact that Freud, already aged 67, had been suffering from cancer since the previous year. In 1923 he had two operations, a relatively minor one in the spring and a more serious one in the fall. His letters written during these months reveal that he expected to die in the near future. Additionally, he was dissatisfied with the quality of his publications, and he worried about personal disputes among his followers.

Freud's dissatisfaction, however, was only partly justified. His work, *The Id and the Ego* (1923/1947), revealed his new structural theory of psychoanalysis and stimulated much discussion. The psychoanalytic movement was expanding into new areas, and Freud himself was widely respected. It was also at this time that psychoanalysts from various countries were invited to take part in the Eighth Congress of the International Psycho-Analytical Association. The meeting was to be held in Salzburg, Austria, at the *Hotel de l'Europe* on April 21–23, 1924. Due to his illness, Freud himself did not participate. Neither did Anna, Freud's youngest daughter, since she was looking after her father. Still, more than 100 psychoanalysts, among them most of the leading figures in the world, took part in the congress, many coming from Austria, Germany, England, Hungary, Switzerland, the Netherlands, United States, Poland, and France.

A peculiarity of this conference was the fact that 88 of the participants had their portraits drawn by two artists from Hungary, Robert Berény (1887–1953) and Olga Székely-Kovács (1900–1971). The portraits were well-done caricatures which later were arranged in a small book that was published in 1924 by Freud's *Internationaler Psychoanalytischer Verlag* in Vienna. However, the book was a private printing and was never made available in bookstores; it had probably been given only to the participants to commemorate the congress.

The nine portraits shown in Figure 1 can be regarded as samples of the collection of 88 caricatures made by Székely-Kovács and Berény in 1924. Starting in the top right-hand corner and moving clockwise, the following individuals are depicted. Life dates and other available biographical information is provided below:

Ethilde M. B. Herford, from Reading, Great Britain, was a doctor and patient of Sándor Ferenczi. Ernest Jones described her as a "very difficult case." Herford was an active member of the British Psychoanalytical Society, and she also translated psychoanalytical texts from German into English.

Karen Horney (1885–1952) was born near Hamburg, Germany. Very early on she obtained psychoanalytical treatment from Karl Abraham, and later by Hanns Sachs. She became a medical doctor and taught psychoanalysis in Berlin. She emigrated to the United States in 1932, where she worked with Harry Stack Sullivan, Franz Alexander, and others. Her contributions to research in aggression, sexuality, and neuroticism had a lasting impact on psychoanalysis.

Dr. M. B. Herford (Reading)

Dr. Karen Horney (Berlin)

Dr. Max Eitingon (Berlin)

Dr. S. Ferenczi (Budapest)

Dr. Helene Deutsch (Wien)

Dr. Jan van Emden (Haag)

Dr. Hermine Hug-Hellmuth (Wien)

Direktor August Aichhorn (Wien)

Dr. Imre Hermann (Budapest)

Figure 1 Caricatures of nine psychoanalysts.

Max Eitingon (1881–1943) met C. G. Jung and Karl Abraham while studying medicine in Zurich. In 1907 he visited Sigmund Freud and became one of Freud's most important followers. After the Nazis came to power, Eitingon left Berlin and emigrated to Palestine, where he set up an institute and a psychoanalytical association.

Sándor Ferenczi (1873–1933) is regarded as one of the most influential Hungarian psychoanalysts. Like Eitingon, Ferenczi belonged to the "Comité," which was the inner circle of psychoanalysts around Freud.

Helene Deutsch (1884–1982) studied and practiced in Vienna and Berlin. In 1934 she emigrated to the United States.

Jan van Emden (1868–1950) was a Dutch psychiatrist who met Freud in Leiden in 1910 and became a friend of the Freud family. Van Emden translated some of Freud's works into Dutch and for many years was influential in the Dutch psychoanalytical movement.

August Aichhorn (1878–1949) was a teacher and manager of a home for young people. Aichhorn is, among those shown here, the only one without a medical degree. He belonged to the few psychoanalysts from Vienna who stayed in Austria during the Nazi years.

Hermine Hug-Hellmuth (1871–1924) can be regarded as the first child psychoanalyst. Hug-Hellmuth was murdered in September 1924 by her nephew who received psychoanalytical treatment from her.

Imre Hermann (1889–1984) was a Hungarian psychiatrist, but he worked as a researcher on the team of the psychologist Géza Révész. Hermann's interests were in the fields of logic, mathematics, and psychoanalysis. Sigmund Freud welcomed Hermann in 1922 calling him "our philosopher."

Since the first edition of the little book, some of the caricatures have been reproduced in various places over the years, occasionally with anti-semitic overtones. In at least one instance (Hermine Hug-Hellmuth) the caricature is the only portrait we have of the person, so the collection of caricatures (recently re-edited by Lück and Mühlleitner in 1993) form a valuable—if somewhat unusual—resource for the history of psychoanalysis.

It is interesting to note that both artists had close connections with psychoanalysis. Berény, who was a famous Hungarian artist, was a friend (and probably a patient) of Sándor Ferenczi. Olga Székely-Kovács was the daughter of Vilma Kovács, who has been referred to as the "mother" of the psychoanalytic movement in Hungary. Olga had a sister named Alice, who later married Michael Bálint.

Among the portraits we find a number of prominent people. We also find people who were less prominent and who belonged to the movement for only a short time. More than half of the people depicted were Jews, and many of them suffered from a dreadful fate just a decade after the congress.

Bibliography

Freud, S. (1947). *The ego and the id.* London: Hogarth Press. (Original work published 1923)

Lück, H. E., & Mühlleitner, E. (Eds.). (1993). *Psychoanalytiker in der Karikatur.* Munich: Quintessenz.

Székely-Kovács, O., & Berény, R. (1924). *Karikaturen vom achten Internationalen Psychoanalytischen Kongress, Salzburg Ostern 1924.* Privatdruck. Leipzig–Vienna–Zürich: Internationaler Psychoanalytischer Verlag.

Alfred Adler

Almuth Bruder-Bezzel
Rüdiger Schiferer

Alfred Adler (1870–1937) was the founder of Individual Psychology, which along with Freud's Psychoanalysis and Jung's Analytic Psychology form the three classical schools of depth psychology. Adler severed his relationship with Freud

Figure 1 Adler portrait by Oskar Kokoschka (ca. 1912/13).

after collaborating with him and his associates over the nine-year period from 1902–1911. In contrast to Freud, Adler focused on the individual as a goal-directed, holistic, and social being. One can readily find similarities between his views and those found in several other movements such as the German "Psychology of Understanding," Holistic Psychology, Gestalt Psychology, and the Personalistic Psychology of William Stern (1871–1938) (Ellenberger, 1970).

By 1912 Adler had the two supporting pillars of his individual psychology—"inferiority feelings" and "compensation"—in place. Later, during the 1920s, Adler modified and expanded his system with the introduction of his concept of "community feelings." During this decade individual psychology flourished in Vienna as both a school of psychology and as a therapeutic movement.

Adler was born on February 7, 1870, the second of six children. His father was a Jewish grain merchant in the Rudolfsheim suburb of Vienna. Later in his life, Adler explained his Viennese "joviality" and his practical and educational outlook as the result of his early life as a "street urchin." Adler studied medicine in Vienna from 1888–1895, and during his last years at university he was a member of the local Socialist Students' Association. His wife, Raissa Adler (née Timofejewena) (1873–1962), whom he married in 1897, was a member of the same organization. After failing to set up a practice near the main hospital of Vienna, Adler eventually opened a successful medical practice in a popular section of town not far from the Prater amusement park.

From 1911 until his emigration to the United States in 1935, Adler lived and worked in the third floor of an apartment building at "#10 Dominikaner-bastei" in Vienna. This house (see Figure 2) was con-

(1907/1917) defended the view that illnesses and neuroses are caused by the unsuccessful compensation of an inferior organ, and that, in turn, high achievement can be the result of compensation. Between 1910 and 1912, Adler elaborated on his theory of personality and neurosis, which he presented comprehensively in his magnum opus, *The Neurotic Constitution* (1912/1916). Specifically, he contended that feelings of inferiority can be compensated for by feelings of superiority, which can help protect the individual against humiliation. Inferiority feelings, which exist in a milder form in everyone and which strongly predispose people to develop neuroses, can be traced to such factors as organ inferiority, a "cold" or spoiled upbringing, and cultural devaluation—as illustrated by the prevailing attitudes toward women. Efforts to overcome inferiority feelings or low self-esteem express themselves as egotism and intensified power and achievement needs. After 1908, Adler's growing rift with Freud centered around his beliefs about the importance of aggression, the role of sexuality in neuroses, and the so-called "masculine protest."

Figure 2 Adler's house and practice in Vienna (center left).

veniently located in a middle class section of Vienna, close to the headquarters of the Austrian Postal Savings Bank, the waterfront, and the central meat market. From this location, which was just a few minutes' walk from his old office, Adler was able to stay in contact with his former patients. It was in that same year that Adler became an official resident of Vienna and a citizen of Austro-Hungary. During this period, Adler wrote and published five articles in the field of social medicine, which reflected his interest in questions of social reform. He was also one of the first four members of Freud's "Wednesday Society." Among this circle, he was one of the most important and most stimulating discussants. He sometimes served as chairman of the small group, and he and Stekel appear to have co-edited the journal of the new organization (Bruder-Bezzel, 1983).

His first major work, *Studies of Organ Inferiority*

Figure 3 Caricature of Adler, ca. 1930.

After his break with Freud (1911), Adler founded the "Association for Free Psychoanalysis," which in 1913 was given the name "Association for Individual Psychology." World War I and the subsequent revolutionary changes in Germany and Eastern Europe induced Adler to base his system on a new foundation—"the community feeling." Thus, he regarded the development of community feelings as a means for overcoming the power needs of the individual, or at least for channeling them in a more positive, social direction. He considered mental disturbances to be disorders of social relationships (Sperber, 1971).

After the end of World War I, Adler identified strongly with the republican governments of Germany and Austria. He and his followers became involved in the problems of social reform, educational reform, and adult education in "Red Vienna." As an educator, reformer, popular orator, and organizer, Adler felt confirmed, supported, and stimulated by the increasing number of his associates who primarily identified themselves with social democratic politics. In this atmosphere, individual psychology flourished in "Red Vienna" as an applied branch of clinical psychology and eventually became the leading school of psychology (Bruder-Bezzel, 1991).

Adler's chief contribution was the establishment of educational counseling centers in cooperation with schools and other educational organizations. In addition, individual psychologists worked in experimental classes and, since 1931, in experimental schools, kindergartens, residential treatment centers, day-care centers, clinics for the disabled, and in a therapeutic outpatient center. Adler's movement also strongly influenced the socialist "Friends of Children" organization. Adler himself gave a series of lectures about group psychotherapy to students, public school teachers, and to the public at large. His most important publication for that period was his book, *Understanding Human Nature* (1927). Before World War II, individual psychology spread from Vienna to Germany, then through Europe and across the world. After 1926 Adler worked primarily in the United States, where he held a visiting professorship at the Long Island Physician's College in New York.

At the beginning of the 1930s, Adler's theories increasingly focused on the metaphysical and philo-

Figure 4 Adler during a conference for teachers and educators in Scandinavia, ca. 1934.

Figure 5 Adler and his wife, Raissa, after emigrating to New York, ca. 1935.

sophical aspects of his work. This change in perspective is apparent in his book, *Social Interest: A Challenge to Mankind* (Adler, 1933/1938; Stepansky, 1983). In 1935 Adler became a permanent resident of the United States. He died two years later, on May 28, 1937, in Aberdeen, Scotland.

Bibliography

Adler, A. (1916) *The neurotic constitution: Outline of a comparitive individualistic psychology and psychotherapy*. New York: Moffat. (Original work published 1912)

Adler, A. (1917). *Study of organ inferiority and its psychical compensation: A contribution to clinical medicine*. New York: Nervous and Mental Disease Publishing Company. (Original work published 1907)

Adler, A. (1927). *Understanding human nature*. New York: Greenberg.

Adler, A. (1938). *Social interest: A challenge to mankind*. London: Faber & Faber. (Original work published 1933)

Bruder-Bezzel, A. (1983). *Alfred Adler: die entstehungsgeschichte einer theorie im historischen milieu wiens*. Göttingen: Vandenhoeck & Ruprecht.

Bruder-Bezzel, A. (1991). *Die geschichte der individualpsychologie*. Frankfurt: Fischer.

Ellenberger, H. (1970). *The discovery of the unconscious*. New York: Basic Books.

Sperber, M. (1971). *Alfred Adler oder das elend der psychologie*. Frankfurt: Fischer.

Stepansky, P. (1983) In Freud's shadow. Adler in context. Hillsdale, NJ: The Analytic Press.

Georg Groddeck

The German psychosomaticist and psychoanalyst Georg Groddeck (1866–1934) was born in Bad Kösen, Germany. He was the fifth and last child of an impecunious physician, who devoted much of his life to the medical and social needs of the poor in Berlin. During his medical studies at Berlin University, Groddeck developed a student-mentor relationship with one of his teachers, the eccentric and dominating dermatologist, Ernst Schweninger (1850–1924). Schweninger was the charismatic personal physician of the German Imperial Chancellor, Otto von Bismarck (1815–1898), whose binge eating and weight problems he had successfully treated with a dietary regimen. Groddeck's work as Schweninger's assistant turned him into a passionate opponent of the medical science of his day, as illustrated by the following outspoken letter to a medical professor in Berlin (1895):

> The entire field of medical studies is worthless. It has to be changed from the bottom up. The universities do not educate physicians but scholars, not practitioners of the medical arts but scientists. [At the university], students are plagued with formulas and hypotheses, which they need to forget to help their patients. . . . The sciences, which are taught at university, don't know any patients but only disease syndromes. They don't treat individuals, but only cases. . . . Medical science teaches knowledge but not understanding. . . . All this has to change!
>
> Only one thing can help—the total destruction [of the old system] and reconstruction. I know you don't want this. You prefer a peaceful solution, gradual changes, and compromise. You love peace. I love a good fight! (p. 104)

In 1900 (coincidentally, the same year Freud's famous book, *Interpretation of Dreams*, was published), Groddeck left academic medicine to become the medical director, and later the owner,

of a small private hospital in Baden-Baden, which originally had been established by his benefactor, Schweninger. He lived and worked in this institution until his death in 1934. Groddeck soon became a famous expert, who was consulted by patients from all over Europe. His excellent skills as a public speaker and persuasive writer led to the publication of his provocative psychoanalytic novel, *The*

Figure 1 Groddeck as German military physician (ca. 1890).

Figure 2 Dr. Groddeck's Sanitarium in Baden-Baden, Germany.

Despite its delightful humor, the book was attacked sharply. Comments ranged from "a solid meal with some obscene sections" (E. Jones) to "the most swinish book I ever read" (Anonymous Female Reader). The Swiss psychoanalysts organized a protest meeting, which only increased Groddeck's notoriety. In the meantime, *The Soul Seeker* has become a classic, which can still be enjoyed today. His lectures and essays about psychosomatic medicine, literature, and art are still popular today.

Figure 3 Illustration from Groddeck's psychoanalytic novel, *The Soul Seeker* (1921).

Soul Seeker (1921), and his classic *Book of the It* (1923). Groddeck's original novel clearly has an autobiographical basis. The protagonist, a rich eccentric, fully believes in the power of the unconscious as well as that of symbolic thinking and sexuality. After liberating himself from the restrictions of petit bourgeois convention, he travels around the world to encourage mankind to do and to enjoy what it usually only contemplates but rarely puts into action. The "soul seeker" employs his vast oratorical talent and outstanding persuasive skills everywhere—in the bowling alley, the museum, a railroad carriage, during a feminist convention, at a union meeting, during an alcoholic orgy at the Prussian court, in the zoo, and in a hospital. The publication of this work brought a good deal of attention to its author. Groddeck, actually, regarded *The Soul Seeker* as his best book. Freud called it "a delicacy" and "caviar for the people, . . . the work of a modern Rabelais." The eminent literary critic, Alfred Polgar, believed that Groddeck's book had no equal in German literature.

Groddeck is important in the history of the field because he was the first to risk applying the methods of psychoanalysis to the treatment of the physically ill. He was no abstract theoretician, no metapsychologist, but a true clinician. In direct personal contact and dialogue with his patients, Groddeck developed his original theory of psychosomatic medicine as an integral part of psychoanalysis because he wanted to encourage the unconscious of his patients to "speak out." Freud had used his self-analysis in his *Interpretation of Dreams* (1900) as the foundation of his psychoanalytic method. Groddeck, in turn, introduced his patients even more directly to his analytic views through his almost legendary 115 lectures to his patients, in which he analyzed his own psychosomatic problems through spontaneous free association. According to Groddeck, "When humans are silent, their bellies will speak," and the translation of the body's language was the chief task of the therapist. Groddeck urged his

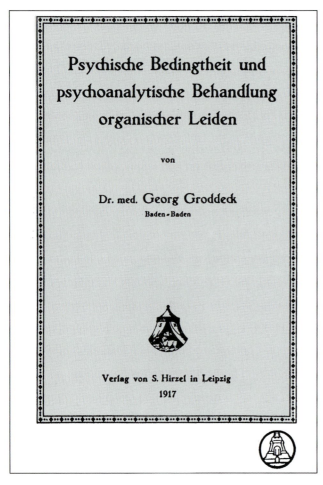

Figure 4 Title page from Groddeck's 1917 book, *Psychic Condition and Psychoanalytic Treatment of Organic Disorders.*

which seeks to remove the causes of a well-defined illness by a specific form of intervention, deludes itself. All diseases and all cures are complex events, in which the therapist facilitates healing by serving as a catalyst, not as a technician. Whenever a physician cleans and bandages an injury, it is the wound itself that does the healing, according to Groddeck.

Groddeck's views of the nature of any illness are perhaps best expressed in the following quote from *Psychic Condition* (1917):

> I believe that it is a basic and serious error to assume that only hysterical have the ability to make themselves ill for some purpose. Every human being possesses this talent and makes use of it to an unimaginable degree. . . . Anyone who delves deeper into the complicated varieties of mental life will soon discover that the physical symptoms of the hysteric are not the results of conscious decisions but the results of . . . our unknown It. I do not believe that one can know what the unconscious really is. . . . The key question is . . . , if the respective illness will disappear after one or another context of the disease is discovered. In other words, it is crucial if psychoanalysis can alleviate organic disorders. I confess that I have stressed only one aspect of the problem.
>
> It was important for me to state publicly that psychoanalytic treatment should not be limited to the neuroses. This is too narrow a perspective. (p. 32)

The Nazis included Groddeck's writings among the books they burned. After World War II, Lawrence Durrell (1912–1990), the noted English novelist, helped rediscover Groddeck for English-speaking readers. As early as 1946, he sent the following comments in a letter to the American novelist Henry Miller (1891–1980), a friend from their prewar Paris days:

> I do hope you take some afternoon off to really study the Groddeckian system. I can see what a tremendous effect it will have in the future—for the future belongs to Groddeck. Freud's part is the calculus, Groddeck's is the attitude. Ah! If only we had known about him in Paris! (letter, February 28, 1946)

Yes, Groddeck's work speaks directly to the reader. It may even irritate or anger, but one cannot remain indifferent. It is understandable that professional psychosomaticists largely overlooked this "psychoanalytic troublemaker" as long as their field had to fight for academic recognition. It is also clear that

patients to avoid abstract speculations by an unbiased and value-free curiosity toward all manifestations of the unconscious or "It."

Groddeck originated the term "It," which Freud (1923) modified for his own work as the "Id." In sharp contrast to most members of Freud's movement, Groddeck preferred his direct analytic work with his patients and, consequently, became almost a personification of the unconscious. For him, all illnesses were natural expressions of the living organism or, creations of the patient's "It," which, in a manner of speaking, makes "Itself" sick. An illness should not be regarded as an enemy who has to be attacked. Instead, one must learn to understand its meaning, as painful as this may be. Understanding the unconscious is not a quasi-philosophical ritual for the conscious mind. One must reactivate the unconscious and "make it dance." Medical science,

Figure 5 Portrait of Georg Groddeck, ca. 1925.

Groddeck's work will be increasingly important to the medical community in the future, since it is becoming increasingly aware of the limits of its rational-technical paradigm.

Bibliography

Chemouni, J. (1984). *Georg Groddeck. Psychoanalyste de l'imaginaire.* Paris: Payot.

Durrell, L., & Miller, H. (1988). *The Durell-Miller Letters, 1935–1980.* London.

Freud, S. (1923). *The ego and the id.* London: Hogarth.

Freud, S. (1953). The interpretation of dreams. In J. Strachey (Ed. & Trans.), *The standard edition of the complete psychological works of Sigmund Freud* (Vols. 4, 5). London: Hogarth Press. (Original work published 1900)

Groddeck, G. (1970). Brief an einen Professor der Medizin in Berlin (1895). In: *Der mensch und sein es (S. 103–109).* Wiesbaden: Limes.

Groddeck, G. (1917). *Psychic condition and psychoanalytic treatment of Organic Disorders.* Leipzig: Hirzel.

Groddeck, G. (1921). *The soul seeker.* A Psychoanalytic Novel. Vienna: Internationaler Psychoanalytischer Verlag.

Groddeck, G. (1923). *The book of the it. Psychoanalytic letters to a friend.* Vienna: Internationaler Psychoanalytischer Verlag.

Grossman, C., & Grossman, S. (1965). *The wild analyst: the life and work of Georg Groddeck.* New York: Braziller.

Jägersberg, O. (1984). *Groddeck, dokumente und schriften.* Bühl-Moos, Germany: Elster.

Lewinter, R. (1990). *Georg Groddeck.* Frankfurt/M: Fischer.

Will, H. (1987). *Georg Groddeck. Die geburt der psychosomatik.* Munich: Urban Schwarzenberg.

Carl Gustav Jung

Angela Graf-Nold

Carl Gustav Jung (1875–1961) was born on July 26 in Kesswil, Switzerland, on Lake Constance. Together with his sister Gertrude, who was nine years younger, he spent most of his youth in Klein-Hüningen, near Basel. His father, the Reverend Paul Jung (1842–1896) worked as a local parson and also served as the Protestant chaplain of the Friedmatt

Insane Asylum in Basel from 1879 until his early death in 1896.

In 1895 Jung began the study of medicine at Basel University, where both of his grandfathers had held academic appointments. His paternal grandfather, Carl Gustav Jung, Senior (1794–1884), had been professor of medicine (Jung, 1962) and president of Basel University. He was a refugee from Mannheim, Germany, where he had been involved in revolutionary politics, and was Grand Master of the Swiss Free Mason Lodges. A family legend made him an illegitimate son of Johann Wolfgang von Goethe. The maternal grandfather, Samuel Preiswerk (1799–1871), came from an old Basel family. He had taught theology and Hebrew at the university and served as president or "Antistes" of all reformed ministers in the Canton Basel. He wrote spiritual and mystical church hymns, some of which are still known today.

The background of these grandfathers—both fathers of 13 children—was in sharp contrast to the rather oppressive atmosphere in Jung's parental home and was to play a decisive role in his personal life and work. In his *Memories* (1962), which were written in cooperation with Aniela Jaffé, he displays the background for his inner development, his "individuation" from a day-dreaming and anxiety-torn boy into the man he ultimately became. The increasing awareness of the forces which had shaped his personal development motivated him toward a life-long study of the general, transpersonal norms, regularities, and irregularities of individual development.

Jung's specific approach to the study of mental life developed at the Burghölzli Mental Hospital in Zürich, which he joined in 1900 as assistant to its director, Eugen Bleuler (1857–1939). In his memo-

Figure 1 Portrait of Jung's paternal grandfather.

ries, Jung acknowledged: "The years at the Burghöl-zli were my apprenticeship" (Jung, 1962, p. 121). Earlier, he had confided in a letter to Bleuler's son Manfred: "The intensive form of observation, which I was taught [at the Burghölzli], has accompanied me everywhere and has helped me to understand the strange psyche objectively" (Jaffé, 1977, p. 42).

Jung had the assistance not only of his young wife Emma Jung-Rauschenbach (1882–1955), the daughter of a wealthy industrialist, but also of a highly motivated group of Swiss, German, and especially American physicians including Frederick Peterson (1859–1938), Charles Ricksher (1879–1943), and Morton Prince (1854–1929). Most of them worked at the Burghölzli as well as at the neurological laboratory of Constantin von Monakow (1853–1930), and they attended group meetings that alternated between the two. Soon enthusiasm developed for Jung's approach to association research. Jung's experience was that irregular responses to the keywords were due to the constellation of unconscious feeling-toned complexes. The records of the association's experiments were regarded as "instantaneous photographs of the soul" (Jung, 1906b) and analyzed according to Freud's principles of "repression." Interestingly, apathetic and "precocious" demented patients revealed a rich inner life and their "nonsensical" ideas and hallucinations made sense. Jung concluded we discover in the mentally ill nothing new or unknown. "We discovered only the very basis of our own mental life. This discovery was a powerful emotional experience for me at that time" (Jung, 1962, p. 133).

Bleuler, who was working on his 1911 book about "Dementia Praecox," as well as Jung and some of the residents and assistant physicians began to study Freud's work and to contact him personally. The list of Burghölzli association experimentors who were fascinated by Freud's personality and ideas reads today like a "Who's Who?" of early psychoanalysts: Max Eitingon, Karl Abraham, Ludwig Binswanger, Alphonse Maeder, Hermann Nunberg, A. A. Brill, Morton Prince, Ernest Jones. In 1908 Jung organized a first informal Psychoanalytical Congress in Salzburg which included the "Freudians" from Vienna and Zürich as well as the American psychologist Morton Prince (1854–1929) and Ernest Jones (1879–1958) from London. After this conference, a joint publication was founded, the *Yearbook for Psychoanalytic and Psychopathological Research*. Jung's

Figure 2 Jung and his wife, 1903.

support of Freud posed no problems among his immediate circle of friends and colleagues in Zürich. Bleuler's predecessor, Auguste Forel (1848–1931), had already been in contact with Freud through their common interest in the therapeutic use of hypnosis. Bleuler himself had positively reviewed Freud's early neurological research and did not mind being a scientific outsider. A greater problem, however, was the intense passion that soon characterized the relationship between Jung and Freud. Freud was convinced that he had at last found a respectable center for "his" psychoanalysis in the Burghölzli. He also believed that Jung had the potential to become his "crown prince" and worthy "successor" in the leadership of the psychoanalytic movement. Jung, in turn, seems to have believed that Freud could serve as his personal guide to the dark and mysterious regions of the soul.

Jung's ambitions and activities soon came into conflict with his duties as Bleuler's chief assistant. It is also likely that his intense relationship to Sabina

Spielrein (1885–1942), a 20-year-old Russian patient and future physician and psychoanalyst, played a role (Carotenuto, 1982; Wehr, 1989). Jung resigned from his position at the Burghölzli on March 7, 1909, because: "I want to devote myself more than previously to my scientific activities" (Jung, 1909). He also requested permission to continue his association with the hospital as an untenured and unpaid "volunteer physician."

In June of 1909, Jung, his wife, and their three young children moved from their apartment in the Burghölzli Hospital to a spacious and elegant house in Küsnacht on the shores of Lake Zürich. Jung lived in this stately house for the rest of his life and maintained his private practice there.

Shortly after his resignation from the Burghölzli staff, Jung received an important academic honor: Together with Freud and several other eminent European scholars, he was invited by the American psychologist G. Stanley Hall (1844–1924) to partici-

Figure 4 Jung's house at Lake Zürich.

pate in the celebration of the twentieth anniversary of Clark University in Worchester, Massachusetts. During the ceremonies the European guests were awarded honorary doctorates.

The intensive, six-week association of Jung with Freud and Sandor Ferenczi (1873–1933) during their joint trip to America constituted the peak as well as the turning point of the Jung-Freud relationship. Jung apparently became disturbed about some "strange reactions" from Freud, and he felt misunderstood and inhibited during their mutual dream interpretations. Freud's penchant for interpreting the imagery of dreams exclusively as the result of "repressed wishes" was diametrically opposed to Jung's understanding of the same dreams. For Jung, dreams contained messages from a greater collective unconscious. Nevertheless, Jung continued his active participation in the organizational work for the International Psychoanalytic Association, including his election to the post of president in 1910.

During this same period Jung worked intensively on the manuscript of his 1912 essay, *Transformations and Symbols of Libido*, which was to contain his "diverging" views of the unconscious. He based his analyses on an article about the young American medium, Miss Frank Miller, published by his paternal friend Théodore Flournoy (1854–1920), a professor of psychology at the University of Geneva. From this material, Jung developed the idea that Freud's conception of the sexual libido should be replaced by a conception of libido as "psychic energy." Specifically, Jung viewed the transformations and

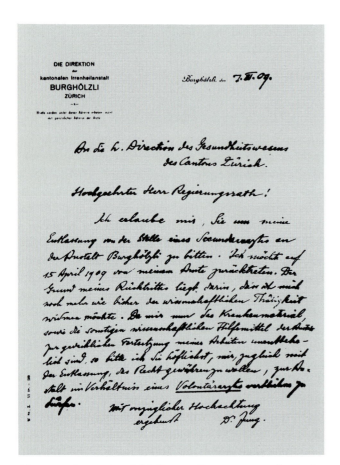

Figure 3 Jung's 1909 letter of resignation from the Burghölzli.

Figure 5 1909 Group portrait for the twentieth anniversary of Clark University. Back row, from left: A. A. Brill, E. Jones, S. Ferenczi. Front row, from left, Freud, G. S. Hall, and Jung.

symbols of the libido as an autonomous function of the unconscious in service of the wholeness of the personality and the self-development of one's own myth. The last chapters of *Transformations* (1912), which interpreted the image of mother-son incest symbolically as the immersion of consciousness in the unconscious, show how much Jung's views of sexuality were moving away from those of Freud.

Freud did not openly denounce Jung's views and those of his Swiss associates as an "illegitimate extension" of Freudian psychoanalysis until the 1913 Munich International Congress of Psychoanalysis. Soon afterwards Jung resigned from the presidency of the International Psychoanalytic Association and the editorship of the *Yearbook for Psychoanalytic and Psychopathological Researches*.

After his separation from Freud, Jung experienced a period of mental isolation and insecurity. He resigned his instructorship in psychiatry at Zürich University and devoted himself almost completely to the analysis of his own fantasies, visions, and dreams, and to his still small international practice as a psychiatrist and psychotherapist. During this period of soul-searching, he carefully wrote and illustrated the long manuscript of his "Red Book," which was never published in its entirety because of its revealing content. It was also during this time that Jung became convinced that all knowledge is intimately tied to the nature of human experience. Even our religious experience itself reveals more about the nature of the human soul than it does about God's existence. The soul itself remains

Figure 6 Portrait of Jung, ca. 1958. (Photo: A. Jaffé)

Figure 7 "Alchemist and his Mystical Sister" ca. 1702.

unknowable. We can only discover and study its symbols and their general transformations. For the field of psychotherapy, Jung developed his technique of "active imagination" as a meditative path to the unconscious. Thus, according to Jung: ". . . My life is the story of the self-actualization of the unconscious. Everything in the unconscious seeks outward manifestation, and the personality, too, desires to evolve out of its unconscious conditions and to experience itself as a whole" (1962, p. 3).

Jung's first major publication after his break with Freud was his lengthy volume *Psychological Types* (1921). In part, this book can be viewed as a retroactive and somewhat indirect discussion of his differences and disagreements with both Freud and Adler. Jung believed that their theories and treatment approaches reflected the interactions of introversion and extroversion with two rational functions (thinking and feeling) and two irrational functions (sensation and intuition) yielding eight predictably different personality types. Each person possesses all four basic functions. The predominant conscious function is compensated by the opposite function in the unconscious. Thus, Jung's typology, as well as his other scientific works, illustrate the oppositional nature of the human psyche and its tendency towards unification.

Jung's interest and study of the field of alchemy took a central place in his later work. By decoding the pictorial language of alchemistic texts from the 13th to the 17th centuries, Jung discovered how they correspond to the symbols of the individuation process. He came to see how the characteristics of alchemistic "substances" or matter were "psychological projections of the collective unconscious." Alchemistic illustrations were furthermore found

to resemble "archetypal" themes in the dreams of modern man. The alchemists' goal of transforming base substances into gold corresponded to the process of personal individuation and the reconciliation of opposites, which was often symbolized in mandalas. And the mental androgyny of the individual, which is represented by a female figure (*anima*) in the male unconscious and by a male figure (*animus*) in the female unconscious, plays a major role in this process.

A final result of Jung's interest in alchemistic thought is the concept of "synchronicity." Jung developed this view in cooperation with the German physicist, Wolfgang Pauli (1900–1958). In accordance with the alchemistic concept of a unitary universe (*unus mundus*), Jung developed his view that the psychophysical nature of the archetypes were equivalent to structural principles. In emotionally important situations, an archetype can be actualized in the form of premonitions, images, dreams, and visions. It can also become reality as a concomitant physical object or objects. The synchronicity hypothesis explains many parapsychological phenomena, which are often associated with archetypal situations like birth, marriage, disease, and death.

In 1935, Jung received an appointment as "Titular Professor of General Psychology" at the Swiss Polytechnic Institute in Zürich, and, in 1944, he accepted a Full Professorship of Medical Psychology at Zürich University for only one year. The C. G. Jung Institute in Zürich (later in Küsnacht) was established in 1948 by some of his associates and students as a training center for psychotherapists.

Figure 8 Title page of "Philosopher's Stone Treatise" (1635).

Carl Gustav Jung died on June 6, 1961, in his house in Küsnacht after completing the English manuscript version of his paper, *Approaching the Unconscious* (1964), which was to be his last and most popular work.

Bibliography

Carotenuto, A. (1982). *A secret symmetry: Sabina Spielrein between Jung and Freud* (A. Pomerans, J. Shipley, & K. Winston, Trans.). New York: Pantheon.

Freud, S., & Jung, C. G. (1974). *The Freud-Jung letters,* W. McGuire, Ed. (Bollingen Series XCIV) Princeton: Princeton University Press.

Jaffé A. (1977). *C. G. Jung: word and image.* Princeton: Princeton University Press.

Jaffé, A. (1985). *Parapsychologie, Individuation, Nationalsozialismus. Themen bei C. G. Jung.* Einsiedeln: Daimon.

Jung, C. G. (1921). *Psychological types, or the psychology of individuation.* New York: Harcourt and Brace.

Jung, C. G. (1921). *Symbols of transformation of the libido.* New York: Pantheon. (Original work published 1912)

Jung, C. G. (1953–1979). *The collected works of C. G. Jung* (Vols. 1–20, Bollingen Series XX). Princeton: Princeton University Press.

Jung, C. G. (1962). *Memories, dreams, reflections,* compiled and ed. by A. Jaffé. New York: Pantheon. (Original work published 1961: *Erinnerungen. Träume und Gedanken,* ed. by A. Jaffé. Olten: Walter.)

Jung, C. G. (1964). Approaching the unconscious. In C. G. Jung & M.-L. von Franz (Eds), Man and his symbols (pp. 18–103). Garden City, N.Y.: Doubleday.

Jung, E. (1991). *Animus and anima.* Fellbach-Oettingen: Bonz.

Meier, C A. (1984). *The psychology of C. G. Jung: with special reference to the association experiment,* E. Rolfe, Trans. Boston: Sigo Press. (Original work published 1968: *Die Empirie des Unbewußten.* Zürich: Rascher)

Wehr., G. (1987). *An illustrated biography of C. G. Jung.* Boston: Shambhala.

Erich Fromm

Rainer Funk

E rich Pinchas Fromm (1900–1980) was born in Frankfurt, Germany, on March 23, 1900, as the only child of Orthodox Jewish parents. Fromm characterized his parents as "highly neurotic" and himself as a "probably rather unbearable, neurotic child." Although he initially wanted to become a Talmudist, Fromm discontinued his study of Judaism to concentrate on other avenues of exploring the human soul. Fromm was not only interested in the souls of individuals but focused primarily on the nature of the human soul as the product of societal conditions and structures.

According to a signed document from Heidelberg University, Fromm received his doctorate from the "Philosophical Faculty" of Heidelberg University for a dissertation about "The Jewish Law: A Contribution to the Sociology of Diaspora Judaism." However, he passed his oral examination under the sociologist Alfred Weber (1868–1958) on July 20, 1922, with the grade of very good.

In 1930, after completing his analytic training in Berlin, the young sociologist became a lecturer at the Institute for Social Research of Frankfurt University. At Frankfurt, Fromm carried out his first social-psychological field study. Specifically, he employed an open-ended questionnaire to assess the political attitudes of German laborers and white-collar employees. Eventually, Fromm's studies about the authoritarian character were to make the Frankfurt Institute for Social Research famous.

During these same years, Fromm's chief theoretical achievement was the development of the concept of "social character." In addition, he created his own psychoanalytic and social-psychological method, which he employed to develop an empirical typology of the social character of a given soci-

ety. Throughout his life Fromm sought to identify the socioeconomical conditions which cause the individual to think, feel, and act in harmony with the functional needs of society.

Of course, social roles are not the only determinants of individual human behavior. Fromm was and remained a psychoanalyst who viewed human personality as the result of dynamic forces. Since he

Figure 1 Fromm and his parents near Frankfurt (ca. 1910).

431

Figure 2 Fromm (front row, third from left) among fellow students at Heidelberg University (1919).

sharply opposed Freud's libido theory, as well as Freud's concepts of life and death instincts, Fromm was forced to develop his own "drive" theory. According to this view, man is driven by psychic or existential needs such as for "relatedness, a frame of orientation, an object of devotion, a feeling of rootedness, a sense of identity," and "transcendence" (Fromm, 1955, p. 27–66). Our intrinsic psychic needs are inconveniences, which generate unpleasant states of deprivation that need to be addressed. How we deal with such needs, whether by seeking to satisfy them creatively or destructively, depends on the "social character" of the respective society in which we live.

Fromm was not satisfied with his unique contribution of psychoanalytic and sociological approach to life, conclusions resulting from his unique psychoanalytic and social-psychological perspective on life. In addition, he examined the historical and socially dominant behavior patterns of a given society to determine if and how they encouraged the productive or nonproductive character orientation of a given society. Later, during the 1960s and 1970s, Fromm formulated his theory of "normative humanism" with the distinction between "biophilia" and "necrophilia," respectively, or between the "having" and the "being" mode of existence (Fromm, 1964; Fromm, 1976).

During his researches on the social character orientations of industrial societies, Fromm (who lived in the United States from 1933–1950) discovered the so-called "marketing character," which is defined by the individual's self-identity. Somewhat later, Fromm subsumed the borderline and narcissistic traits of the marketing character under the concept of "alienation." In 1964, he made a second social-psychological discovery. Modern society, in general, unconsciously facilitates everything

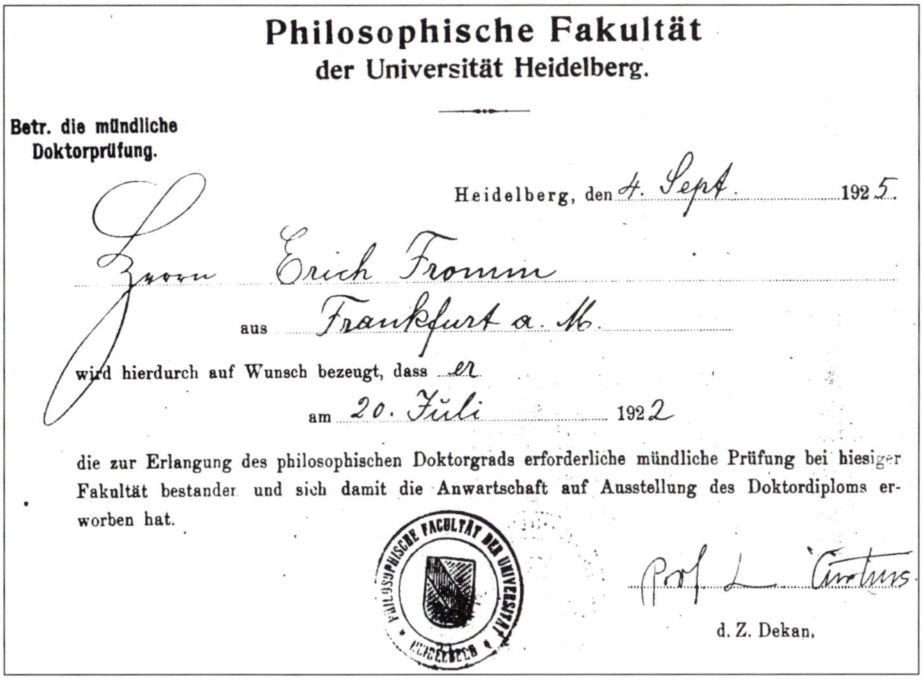

Philosophische Fakultät
der Universität Heidelberg.

Betr. die mündliche
Doktorprüfung.

Heidelberg, den 4. Sept. 1925.

Herrn Erich Fromm

aus Frankfurt a. M.

wird hierdurch auf Wunsch bezeugt, dass er

am 20. Juli 1922

die zur Erlangung des philosophischen Doktorgrads erforderliche mündliche Prüfung bei hiesiger Fakultät bestanden und sich damit die Anwartschaft auf Ausstellung des Doktordiploms erworben hat.

PHILOSOPHISCHE FACULTÄT DER UNIVERSITÄT HEIDELBERG

Prof. L. Curtius

d. Z. Dekan.

Figure 3 Heidelberg Dissertation Certificate (9–4–1925).

destructive, lifeless, mechanical, quantitative, and exclusively cerebral in life. This necrophilic social character always gives preference to anything that is diseased and dead, and this tendency becomes the greatest threat to mankind.

As much as Fromm involved himself throughout his life with the problems of society, he still remained a sort of Talmudist, who primarily lived for and through his books. During his twice yearly trips from Mexico City to New York, he and his wife always reserved two Pullman compartments. One served as their bedroom and the other became his

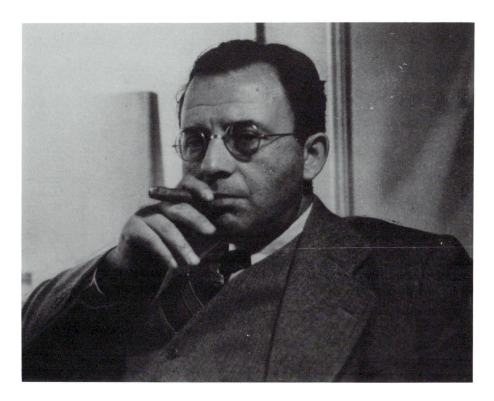

Figure 4 Erich Fromm in New York (1945).

Figure 5 Caricature by Oswaldo from the Mexican daily *Excelsior* on the occasion of Fromm's 80th birthday (1980).

traveling library. On each trip he carried along at least three suitcases with books for the regular five-day trip.

Fromm wrote nearly 20 books, which sold millions of copies and were translated in up to 40 languages. A German edition of his collected works, including an index, was published between the years 1980–1981. His major works are still available in English: *Escape from Freedom* (1941); *Psychoanalysis and Religion* (1950); *The Forgotten Language* (1951); *The Sane Society* (1955); *The Art of Loving* (1956); *Marx' Concept of Man* (1961); *Beyond the Chains of Illusion* (1962); *The Heart of Man* (1964); *You shall be Gods* (1966); *The Crisis of Psychoanalysis* (1970); *The Anatomy of Human Destructiveness* (1973); *To Have or to Be?* (1976). Of the eight volumes of posthumous writings (edited by Rainer Funk), four are available in English: *The Art of Being* (1992); *The Revision of Psychoanalysis* (1992); *On Being Human* (1993); *The Art of Listening* (1994).

The personal library of Fromm and his papers are preserved in the Erich-Fromm-Archive in Tübingen, Germany (24 Ursrainer Ring, D-72076 Tübingen, Germany). The International Erich Fromm Society can also be reached at the same address.

Bibliography

Burston, D. (1991). *The legacy of Erich Fromm.* Cambridge & London: Harvard University Press.

Claßen, J. (Ed.). (1987/1991). *Erich Fromm und die Pädagogik* (Vol. 1) and *Erich Fromm und die Kritische Pädagogik* (Vol. 2). Weinheim: Beltz.

Fromm, E. (1955). *The sane society.* New York: Rinehart.

Fromm, E. (1964). *The heart of man, its genius for good and evil.* New York: Harper & Row.

Fromm, E. (1976). *To have or to be.* New York: Harper & Row.

Fromm, E. (1980–1981). *Gesamtausgabe* (R. Funk, Ed.). Stuttgart: Deutsche Verlags-Anstalt.

Funk, R. (1978). *Mut zum Menschen. Erich Fromms Denken und Werk, seine humanistische Religion und Ethik. Mit einem Nachwort von Erich Fromm.* Stuttgart: DVA.

Funk, R. (1982). *Erich Fromm: The courage to be human.* New York: Crossroad/Continuum.

Funk, R. (1983). *Erich Fromm.* (Rowohlt Bildmonographie). Reinbek: Rowohlt.

Kessler, M., & Funk, R. (Ed.). (1922). *Erich Fromm und die Frankfurter Schule.* Tübingen: Francke.

Knapp, G. P. (1982). *Erich Fromm* (Köpfe des XX. Jahrhunderts, Vol. 97). Berlin: Colloquium.

Knapp, G. (1989). *The art of living: Erich Fromm's life and works.* New York: Lang.

Wehr, H. (1990). *Erich Fromm zur Einführung.* Hamburg: Junius.

Wissenschaft vom Menschen/Science of Man. (1990ff). *Jahrbuch der Internationalen Erich-Fromm-Gesellschaft*, Vol. 1 ff.

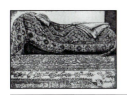

A Brief History of Child Sexual Abuse

Catalina M. Arata

Child sexual abuse is an international problem affecting a significant proportion of men and women in a number of countries. In a review of available studies in 19 different countries, Finkelhor (1994) reported histories of child sexual abuse ranging from 7% to 36% of women and 3% to 29% of men. While current awareness of child sexual abuse has increased tremendously in the last two decades, a review of the history of child sexual abuse reveals that child sexual abuse is in no way a modern phenomenon. The sexual use of children is part of our cultural heritage, and neither our awareness of it or our suppression of it is anything new.

Antiquity

The fact that historians are able to identify records about the sexual use of children that date back centuries is informative for both helping us to recognize the prevalence of child sexual abuse as well as enabling us to see the historical changes in the perception of children as sexual objects. A comparison of Greek and Roman sexual traditions highlights these differences in perceptions.

During early Greek times, pederasty, or a sexual relationship between male youths and an older male, was a common and accepted practice (Rush, 1980; Gray-fow, 1987). While there were culturally accepted rules regarding an appropriate relationship—such as fidelity and not selling one's body for sex—these relationships were looked upon with pride by the families of the young boys. The sexual use of young girls is not documented other than in the practice of very youthful marriages. Girls were to be sheltered in order to protect their virginity and then married near the age of puberty.

Sexual use of children during Roman times is better documented, with evidence of greater cultural disapproval of these practices. Roman art and literature give numerous examples of sexual abuse of young boys and girls. Writings of Catullus from around 60 B.C. suggest a condemnation of the sexual abuse of young girls, but also document its existence (Gray-fow, 1987). As in Greece, pederasty was quite common; however, it was not romanticized, and participation in it was viewed as immoral and disgraceful. Again, girls were married at puberty, and while sexual use of children appears to have been viewed negatively by the Romans, it nevertheless seems to have been a fairly common practice. Sexual use of child slaves was accepted, and slaves were sometimes raised for the sole purpose of sexual gratification. Youthful prostitutes were common and, in fact, were given a public holiday each year. Thus, while the culture appeared to disapprove of the sexual use of freeborn children, it was still common; but the sexual use of slave children went unquestioned (Kahr, 1991).

Early Judaeo-Christian Attitudes on Children and Sex

Writings found in the Old Testament of the Bible, as well as the Talmud, state that at the age of three a child could be "betrothed by sexual intercourse" (Rush, 1980, p. 17), and marriage was recommended for females between the ages of twelve and twelve and a half. Forcing a child to engage in intercourse was considered theft of property, for which payment and marriage were required. Essentially, females, adult or child, were considered property, and the laws applied to them as such. A female who prostituted herself committed theft; however, fathers were free to prostitute their daughters, although Talmudists recommended against this practice (Rush, 1980).

With the advent of Christianity the world presumably moved into a more moral atmosphere under the guidance of church law. Nevertheless, the sexual use of children continued. Marriage of young girls at the age of puberty continued to be an accepted practice even under church law, and marriages of younger girls continued, both against the wishes of the church and with the church making numerous exceptions. For instance, there are numerous references to exceptions being made for girls as young as nine, with acceptance of intercourse among children as young as seven (Rush, 1980). In fact, age was not considered relevant for the sanctity of the marriage if intercourse had occurred.

Rush's review of church history reveals indications of sex with girls as young as three. Rather than being condemned, sex with a female under the age of seven was viewed as "inconsequential" (Rush, 1980). This attitude evolved first into the belief that sex with a young child was not possible and later emerged into civil laws against the rape of young children. While forcing a young child to engage in sex became viewed as a criminal offense, a new pattern emerged in which the blame was transferred to the child who was seen as being the seducer. This is a trend which has continued into modern times. Kahr (1991) reports the emergence of the belief by parents that, "it is not I who fancies the child, but rather, it is the child who wishes to copulate with me" (p. 202).

The Middle Ages

During Medieval times, documents written about the witch hunts provide some indications of the continued sexual use of children. During this period if a child was known to have had sex with an adult, the adult could claim that the child had fornicated with the Devil and then seduced the adult. The child would then be punished (e.g., burned at the stake) for this behavior. The belief that a young child could not engage in sexual relations also contributed to the belief that evidence of sexual activity in a child was evidence of fornication with the devil. Suspicion of intercourse with the devil, regardless of the child's age, resulted in children as young as three and four at times being put to death (Rush, 1980).

The Early Modern Period

High rates of child prostitution and venereal diseases among children testify to the continued sexual abuse of children in the 17th, 18th, and 19th centuries. Cases of syphilis in children were recorded as far back as 1532, when a doctor described three children who had syphilis; and in 1540, when another doctor reported on three brothers who died of syphilis (Taylor, 1985). Reports of venereal diseases in children were regularly reported starting around 1860. While these diseases were rarely attributed to sexual abuse, current knowledge and analysis of these reports indicates that the majority—if not all—of these cases were victims of child sexual abuse (Taylor, 1985).

During the Renaissance, children continued to be blamed and killed for evidence of sexual contact. As the belief in demonic possession was buried in the late Renaissance, anecdotes of abuse and child pornography served as evidence that children were still being sexually abused. Stories regarding King Louis XIII as a small child report servants at the court playing with his genitals and sucking and fondling him. At the same time, popular literature during that time period often involved incestuous relations as a primary theme (Kahr, 1991).

Figure 1 Portrait of Jean-Jacques Rousseau as a young man.

Volume I of the *Confessions* (1781/1931) by Jean-Jacques Rousseau (1712–1788) highlights the relationship between sexual experiences in childhood and later sexual disorder and also comments on the blurring of sexual boundaries between children and adults during the Enlightenment (Cunningham, 1988). As a youth, Rousseau was sent to live with a minister and his sister, Mademoiselle Lambercier. He and his cousin would sleep in her bed, and over time, Rousseau describes sexual arousal developing towards Mademoiselle Lambercier. In particular, he found himself becoming aroused when she would spank him. He writes (1931):

> As Mademoiselle Lambercier had the affection of a mother for us, she also exercised the authority of one, and sometimes carried it so far as to inflict upon us the punishment of children when we had deserved it. . . . It needed all the strength of this devotion and all my natural docility to keep myself from doing something which would have deservedly brought upon me a repetition of it; for I had found in the pain, even in the disgrace, a mixture of sensuality which had left me less afraid than desirous of experiencing it again from the same hand. (p. 10)

Rousseau relates these incidents of spanking mingled with sexual desire to an adult obsession:

> Who would believe that this childish punishment, inflicted upon me when only eight years old by a young woman of thirty, disposed of my tastes, my desires, my passions, and my own self for the remainder of my life, and that in a manner exactly contrary to that which should have been the natural result. (Rousseau, p. 11)

He describes as an adult,

> I haunted dark alleys and hidden retreats, where I might be able to expose myself to women in the condition in which I should have liked to have been in their company. What they saw was not an obscene object, I never even thought of such a thing; it was a ridiculous object. The foolish pleasure I took in displaying it before their eyes cannot be described. There was only one step further necessary for me to take, in order to gain actual experience of the treatment I desired. (p. 78)

The 19th Century

An analysis of French psychiatry also documents the widespread prevalence of child sexual abuse during the 19th century (Cunningham, 1988). Starting in the mid-19th century, French psychiatrists began publishing reports documenting sexual abuse of children. Tardieu (1818–1879), a French psychia-trist, is especially noteworthy for his statements regarding the negative effects of sexual contact with children (Cunningham, 1988). Despite Tardieu's enlightened view, the trend to blame the child for any sexual contact continued. Garnier described pederasty as the result of heredity, thereby blaming both the child and later the adult for this behavior. At the same time, Alfred Binet's (1857–1911) writings began to suggest that childhood sexual experience could cause later sexual problems and that questioning children regarding abuse required careful consideration of suggestibility in order to maximize the accuracy of a child's testimony (Cunningham, 1988).

The end of the 19th century marks an increased awareness of child sexual abuse and the possible psychological consequences. Books available during the turn of the century documented the belief that sexual acts among children were frequent, while at the same time there were also books claiming that the majority of sexual abuse complaints were false accusations. The confusion regarding the frequency and veracity of claims of sexual assault is evident both in Freud's theories and in modern times.

Sigmund Freud's early writings report on his frequent discoveries of child sexual abuse in the histories of his patients. This became the basis for his seduction theory. Freud described sexual abuse in childhood as a causal factor in adult neuroses, particularly hysteria. Following a very negative response from the psychiatric community, as well as further analysis of his patients, Freud abandoned the seduction theory in favor of his theory of infantile sexuality. This theory included the role of fantasy in adults reporting memories of sexual experiences. While this theory has been perpetuated as the cornerstone of psychoanalysis, Freud's writing reveals that he did not believe that his new theory totally nullified the seduction theory. Rather, Freud continued to believe that child sexual abuse does occur and that some patients who report this are reporting actual events and not fantasy. Freud's own vacillation of the reality of child sexual abuse portends the 20th century conflicts regarding the acknowledgment of child sexual abuse (Masson, 1984; Eissler, 1993).

The 20th Century

During most of the 20th century evidence of child sexual abuse has been ignored and minimized, while at the same time, misinformation has been the

Figure 2 Virginia Woolf and her stepbrother George Duckworth.

(DeMause, 1991). Even when larger numbers were reported, however, the effects of child sexual abuse were minimized.

While the scientific community lagged in its acknowledgment of the existence and negative consequences of child sexual abuse, literary writings continued to document evidence of the problem. Bell (1972) chronicles Virginia Woolf's (1882–1941) descriptions of sexual abuse in her diaries. Bell reports Woolf's descriptions of her brother, George, fondling her and her sister and coming into their bedroom at night during her preadolescent years:

> There were fondlings and fumblings in public when Virginia was at her lessons and these were carried to greater lengths . . . George carried his affections from the schoolroom into the night nursery. . . . Trained as they were to preserve a condition of ignorant purity they must at first have been unaware that affection was turning to concupiscence, and were warned only by their growing sense of disgust. (p. 43)

Bell speculates about the role this sexual abuse may have played in Virginia Woolf's later mental illness and also describes the turmoil which sexual abuse by a "trusted" family member can produce.

Starting in the 1970s, researchers began focusing on sexual assault. Research on rape and child sexual abuse emerged and suggested that these events were neither rare nor harmless. Current studies estimate that one out of four women and one out of six men experience sexual abuse as children. Research on the effects of child sexual abuse has documented increased rates of mental disorders, substance abuse, sexual problems, revictimization, sex offending, and interpersonal problems.

While much of this research has been conducted on adults who were recalling memories of these events, the research has been criticized for both under-reporting and over-reporting the incidence of abuse. Recent research has begun to suggest that a significant proportion of child sexual abuse victims repress memories of abuse and therefore may not report abuse in surveys. At the same time, critics have begun arguing against the idea of repressed memory, suggesting that adults may be induced to recall memories of abuse as a result of improper therapeutic techniques. Reports of child sexual abuse made by children have been similarly discredited. Numerous articles and books have been written in the late 1980s and 1990s discussing the suggestibility of children and regarding false accusations of abuse.

norm. During the 1930s, a number of laws were enacted to deal with sexual offenders, yet the public held the perception that child sexual abuse was a rare event most often perpetrated by sexual perverts. While child sexual abuse continued to be a relatively common occurrence, it was rarely reported by its victims and when reported, rarely believed.

While scientific journals flourished in the 20th century, minimal attention was given to child sexual abuse. Articles written from the 1930s to the 1970s primarily reveal trends of victim blaming, mother blaming, and under-reporting. Theories regarding victim precipitation, repetition compulsions, and child seductiveness were common.

The incidence of child sexual abuse was greatly underestimated both in the mental health community and in government statistics. Government estimates as recent as 1985 reported less than a one percent incidence of child sexual abuse

Figure 3 David Finkelhor, University of New Hampshire, prominent American expert on sexual child abuse.

Figure 4 Title page of Finkelhor's seminal work *Sexually Victimized Children*.

As the world enters the 21st century, the future course of child sexual abuse seems fairly predictable. For the past 2000 years the sexual use of children has been a common, even normative, event. While societies have varied in their acknowledgment of child sexual abuse and their attitudes towards it, children have consistently been used as sexual objects, and society has consistently failed in its efforts to protect children. When awareness of child sexual abuse began to emerge at the turn of the century, it was followed by a backlash of victim blaming and discrediting quite similar to some of

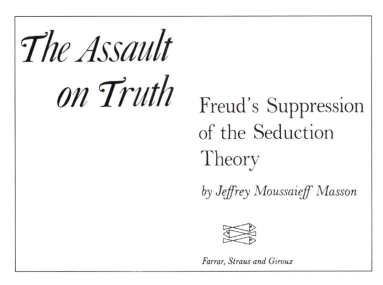

Figure 5 Pioneering critique of Freud's views of physical and sexual child abuse by Jeffrey M. Masson.

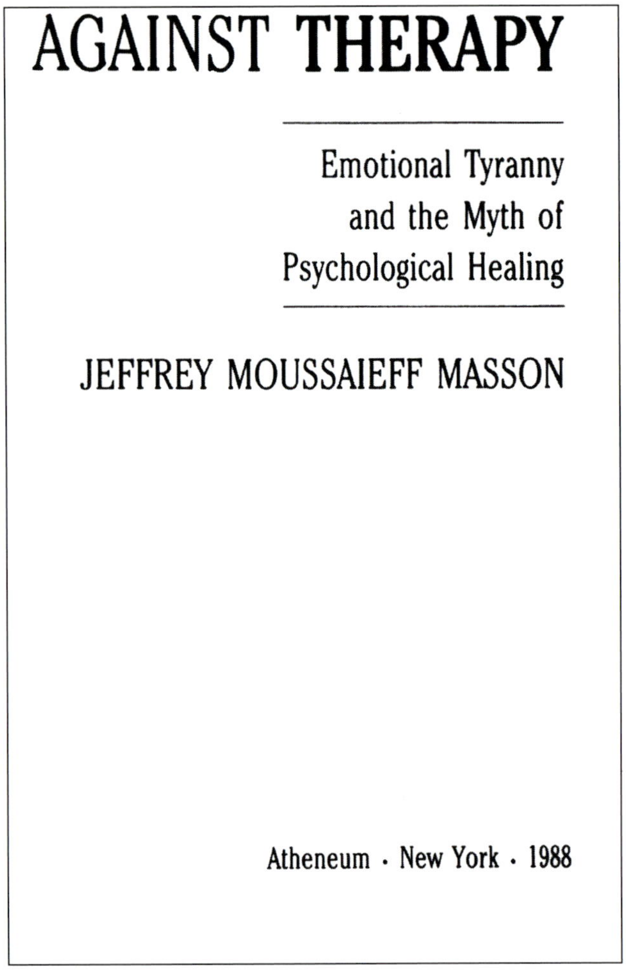

AGAINST THERAPY

Emotional Tyranny
and the Myth of
Psychological Healing

JEFFREY MOUSSAIEFF MASSON

Atheneum · New York · 1988

Figure 6 Masson's continuation of his discourse against psychoanalysis and Freud's seduction theory.

the current trends in American society. What seems apparent is that while attitudes towards sexual abuse change through time, due to the secrecy of the event and the vulnerability of children, child sexual abuse—like murder, war, and poverty—may be a permanent feature of the dark side of mankind.

Bibliography

Bell, Q. (1972). *Virginia Woolf: a biography.* New York: Harcourt, Brace, Jovanovich.

Cunningham, J. L. (1988). Contributions to the history of psychology: L. French historical views on the acceptability of evidence regarding child sexual abuse. *Psychological Reports, 63,* 343–353.

deMause, L. (1991). The universality of incest. *The Journal of Psychohistory, 19,* 123–164.

Eissler, K. R. (1993). Comments on erroneous interpretations of Freud's seduction theory. *Journal of the American Psychoanalytic Association, 41,* 571–583.

Finkelhor, D. (1994). The international epidemiology of child sexual abuse. *Child Abuse and Neglect, 18,* 409–417.

Gray-fow, M. (1987). Child abuse, historiography and ethics: The historian as moral philosopher. *The Journal of Psychohistory, 15,* 455–465.

Kahr, B. (1991). The sexual molestation of children: Historical perspectives. *The Journal of Psychohistory, 19,* 191–214.

Masson, J. M. (1984). *The assault on truth: Freud's suppression of the seduction theory.* New York: Farrar, Straus, & Giroux.

Rousseau, J. J. (1931). *Confessions* (Vol. I). London: Aldine House. (Original work published 1781)

Rush, F. (1980). *The best-kept secret: Sexual abuse of children.* Bradenton, FL: The Human Services Institute.

Taylor, K. (1985). Venereal disease in nineteenth century children. *The Journal of Psychohistory, 12,* 431–463.

Psychology and the Nuremberg Trials

Bridget O. Hannahan
Wolfgang G. Bringmann

On August 8, 1945, the governments of Great Britain, the United States, France, and the Soviet Union formally established the International Military Tribunal (IMT) (Maser, 1977). The purpose of this court was to judge war crimes committed by "German officers and members of the Nazi Party," which had resulted in the killing of millions of European civilians, including the systematic murder of six million Jews (Persico, 1994). Despite accusations that the IMT imposed *ex post facto* law on a conquered nation (Maser, 1977), it was the chief goal of the IMT to express moral outrage for Nazi atrocities and to convey the message that aggressive warfare would not be tolerated in the future (Persico, 1994).

The ancient city of Nuremberg, which had been the favorite location for Nazi party rallies and was severely damaged by allied bombing raids, was deliberately chosen as the site of the War Crimes Trials.

An American Prison Psychologist

In October of 1945, the American psychologist Gustav M. Gilbert (1910–1970) obtained an appointment, first as "Prison Commandant's Interpreter" and "Liaison Officer to the Nazi Defendants," and somewhat later as "Prison Psychologist," during the Nuremberg War Trials (Gilbert, 1975, p. XII). According to Gilbert, the idea of involving psychology in the IMT was proposed by Hadley Cantril (1906–1969), an eminent social psychologist from Princeton University. According to Gilbert (Miale & Seltzer, 1975):

> Cantril stressed the supreme importance of having a psychologist assigned to the prison in order to probe the minds of the Nazi leaders before it was too late. He realized that only an officer engaged in some aspect of military government would have any direct access to the staffing procedures of the Nuremberg Tribunal. (p. XI–XII)

American vs. German Psychology

During World War II, psychologists in the United States were enjoying increased status and employment opportunities. Specifically, they provided a variety of clinical services to the armed forces, including the development and application of psychological tests to the selection of qualified military personnel (Reisman, 1991). Psychological tests had long been employed in Germany and played an important but ancillary role in the selection of officer candidates. Most importantly, during World War II, German academic psychologists used the war situation to develop and officially approve a standard, academic curriculum for psychologists in 1942. The new specialty provided a professional degree—the "Diploma in Psychology"—which was based on a series of official examinations and the writing of a thesis. Despite the new and official status of psychology, the psychological selection programs for German officers were unexpectedly terminated in April of 1942. German Navy psychologists, however, were able to continue their human factors research and test program for the placement of enlisted men in specialized, technical positions. Apparently, the psychological prognosis of officer candidates was no longer needed since the German armed forces had lost so many young officers in combat that these positions were no longer competitive (Persico, 1994).

Gustav Gilbert

Gustav Gilbert, the Nuremberg prison psychologist, was born as the son of Austrian immigrants to America (Persico, 1994, p. 103). His father died when he was 9 years old. Shortly afterwards, his distressed mother turned him over to a Jewish welfare agency, which placed him in an orphanage.

Figure 1 Chief administrative building of Nuremberg Court House, where the original War Crimes Trials were held.

Figure 2 Gustav M. Gilbert, Nuremberg prison psychologist, on the far right in uniform.

The talented child managed to achieve a solid education at the liberal Ethical Culture School in Manhattan and at City College, "the Harvard of poor but bright students" (Persico, 1994). Gilbert spoke German fluently and took academic courses in the subject as part of his undergraduate curriculum. After receiving his PhD in psychology in 1939 from Columbia University, Gilbert accepted full-time academic employment at Connecticut College and at Bard College. During this period, he published several articles on research topics in perception, memory, and psychophysics.

During World War II, Gilbert, who was then an officer in military intelligence (G-2), interviewed German prisoners during the Battle of the Bulge and later at the G-2 Headquarters in Berlin (Gilbert, 1975).

Conflicting Roles

In Nuremberg, Gilbert served as an interpreter for the military commander of the American prison. He also assisted the prison psychiatrist, Major Douglas M. Kelley (1913–1958) and his successors in mental examinations of the German defendants (Gilbert, 1947, p. 3). In addition to his duties as personal interpreter and prison psychologist, Gilbert viewed himself as a "participant-observer," who had been given the "once-in-a-lifetime opportunity to probe the fascist mind at first hand (Gilbert, 1975, p. XII).

All of his somewhat conflicting roles required Gilbert to have unlimited access to the prisoners. He often shared their simple meals in the prison mess hall, visited them in their cells for casual conversations, and observed their interactions in the prison yard. Gilbert stressed that he never took notes in the presence of the prisoners. Instead, he recorded notes of their conversations and his observations privately at the end of each visit (Gilbert, 1947, p. 4). Finally each day, he transferred information from these contacts to his personal diary.

Gilbert (1947) reported that he made direct recommendations to the prison director about a variety of administrative and disciplinary actions involving the prisoners. For example, he recommended and helped implement seating arrangements in the mess hall, which minimized the dominant influence of Hermann Göring (1893–1946) on some of the more malleable prisoners.

Psychological Evaluations

Interestingly, despite his eagerness to take on the responsibilities of a "prison psychologist" at Nuremberg, Gilbert's books (1947, 1950, 1975) provide little and rather fragmentary information about the actual psychological evaluations he conducted with the defendants before the trial began on November 19, 1945. Before beginning the formal administration of intelligence and personality tests, Gilbert devoted three entire weeks to informal conversations with the defendants to ensure rapport with the prisoners (Gilbert, 1975, p. XII). During this period, a wealth of case history information was collected, including handwritten autobiographies of everyone. Next, Gilbert administered his own German translation of the American Wechsler-Bellevue Intelligence Scale, Form I. However, he omitted the important "Vocabulary" and "Picture Arrangement" subtests to reduce possible cultural bias. According to Gilbert, all intelligence tests were scored in the standard manner, although allowance was made for the possible reduced test performance of older prisoners.

Gilbert reported candidly that his test procedures differed significantly from standard professional practice. For example, he described his

Figure 3 Douglas Kelley—Nuremberg prison psychiatrist.

Figure 4 Gilbert, Göring, and an unknown American Military policeman.

administration of the Wechsler-Bellevue Test to Hermann Göring, the former Commander in Chief of the German Air Force, as follows (1947):

> I administered the Intelligence test in his cell. . . .
> He reacted with keen interest to the challenge of
> an intelligence test, and by the end of the first
> subtest (memory-span), he was acting like a
> bright and egotistical schoolboy, anxious to
> show off before the teacher. He chuckled with
> glee as I showed surprise at his accomplish-
> ment. . . . When he finally succeeded to my
> expressed amazement, he could hardly contain
> himself for joy, and swelled with pride. The pat-
> tern of rapport was maintained throughout the
> entire test, the examiner encouraging him with
> remarks of how few people are able to do the
> next problem. . . . Göring was given to under-
> stand that he had the highest rating so far. . . . He
> decided that American psychologists really had
> something there . . . better than the stuff our psy-
> chologists were fooling around with. (p. 15)

In addition, Major Kelley, the prison psychiatrist,

and Gilbert administered the Rorschach inkblot test to all and the Thematic Apperception Test to some of the prisoners. Kelley, who did not speak German, reportedly administered the projective tests with the aid of several interpreters. In turn, Gilbert seems to have retested most of the prisoners with the Rorschach in German while the prisoners were still in "solitary confinement." It is not clear from Gilbert's writings whether formal psychological reports were prepared for use during the court proceedings.

According to Gilbert, all Nuremberg defendants were males ranging from 40–72 years of age. As a group, they were well-educated and employed in high government and military positions. Full Scale IQ Scores on the Wechsler-Bellevue I scores ranged from a low of 106 to a high of 143. In addition, more than 86 per cent of the Nazi leaders scored within Wechsler's "superior" or "very superior" range of intelligence.

Apparently, all defendants were administered the Rorschach test at least once by either Kelley or Gilbert, but not all of these were available to Gilbert (1975, p. XIII). Gilbert's use of the Rorschach results also differed significantly from recommended clinical practice. For example, when Hermann Göring repeatedly insisted on being informed of the results of his Rorschach test, Gilbert gave him the following remarkable interpretation of Card IV—"the Card with the red spots" (1947):

> Well, morbid neurotics frequently draw back at
> the sight of this card and say there is blood on it.
> You drew back at the sight of the card but you
> did not call it blood. You tried to flick it away
> with your finger. You did the same throughout
> the trial. When proof of your guilt became so
> intolerable to you, you took off the headphone in
> the courtroom. You did just the same during the
> war when you tried to make your unconscious
> forget atrocities by drugs. . . . You are a moral
> coward. (p. 236)

Although both Gilbert and Kelley clearly placed more trust in the Rorschach results than in the Wechsler-Bellevue Test, neither Gilbert nor Kelley provided a comprehensive analysis of the Rorschach results in their publications. However, since that time, the Rorschach data from Nuremberg have been analyzed repeatedly by American clinical psychologists with a variety of theoretical and professional orientations (Harrower, 1976a, 1976b; Miale & Seltzer, 1975; Ritzler, 1978). According to a very thorough review by Borofsky and Brand (1980), all of these studies suffer to a lesser or greater extent from "serious problems" (p. 397). First, the Rorschach tests were "not administered according to standard procedures" (p. 397). Borofsky and Brand also raised questions about the suitability of the Rorschach test as an instrument for assessing the personality of war criminals or other dangerous criminals.

The brief list of diagnoses which Gilbert proposed in 1970 for the majority of the Nuremberg prisoners is rather unimpressive. After spending so much time interviewing, testing, conversing, and socializing with the prisoners, Gilbert concluded that about half of the defendants were suffering "no gross pathology." In other words, they were normal. Another 25 per cent were diagnosed as suffering from relatively minor disorders such as emotional instability, dependency, inadequacy, or aggressiveness. Finally, a mere three prisoners were given more serious labels like "schizoid personality" or "paranoid neurosis." Gilbert was candid about his reluctance to assign formal diagnostic labels to the Nuremberg group (1970): "It therefore appears that the traditional approach of clinical psychiatry, based on the diagnosis and treatment of mental disease, is really not directly applicable to the realm of antisocial or socially condemned behavior" (p. 300).

Douglas Kelley, the Nuremberg prison psychiatrist, went further in his preliminary analysis of the Nazi Rorschach records (1946):

> . . . although many of [the prisoners] were not what we call ideally normal, none of them were sufficiently deviant to require custodial care according to the laws of our country. . . . [They were] a group of individuals who were essentially sane . . . although in some instances somewhat deviated from normal. (pp. 46–47)

And Now the Rest of the Story

Gilbert and Kelley had originally planned to collaborate on a popular book about their experiences during the Nuremberg trials (Persico, 1994). However, Kelley resigned from his position with the IMT in early 1946 to return to the United States—ostensibly to write a book about "racial prejudice" (Persico, 1994). After his return to the United States, Kelley reportedly lectured for some time about the Nuremberg trials and, in 1946, published a small book, *22 Cells in Nuremberg* (1946), which was reissued in 1961 as a pocket book. Kelley later had a distinguished but somewhat eccentric career as a criminologist at the University of California in Berkeley

until his suicide in 1958 at the age of 45 (Persico, 1994). He reportedly poisoned himself with a cyanide capsule (Persico, 1994) that had been found on Hermann Göring in Nuremberg (Maser, 1977, p. 81). According to Maser (1977):

> Kelley kept all sorts of Nazi memorabilia in a secret cupboard in his study. On New Year's Eve [1957] he went up to the attic of his house while his family was downstairs. He suddenly appeared on the staircase and announced that he had swallowed the cyanide capsule found on Hermann Göring. Then he collapsed dead. (Maser, 1977, p. 304)

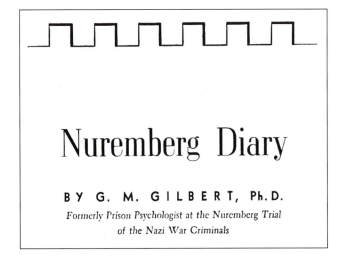

Figure 5 Title page of Kelley's book about the Nuremberg Trials.

Gilbert remained in Nuremberg until the end of the war crimes trials in September of 1946. His book about the trials, *Nuremberg Diary* (1947), was a considerable success. He provided additional information about this period of his life in his 1950 monograph, *The Psychology of Dictatorship*, and his undergraduate psychology textbook, *Personality Dynamics* (1970).

Apart from a brief interlude as a full-time Veteran's Affairs hospital psychologist, Gilbert pursued a successful academic career—first at Princeton University, then at Michigan State University, and finally as chair of the psychology department at Long Island University (LIU). At LIU, Gilbert was active in university politics, serving at one time as elected president of the faculty senate. Gilbert continued his clinical involvement as a consultant to state prison systems and served briefly as an expert witness during the 1961 Eichmann trial in

22 CELLS in NUREMBERG

A Psychiatrist Examines the Nazi Criminals

by DOUGLAS M. KELLEY, M.D.
Psychiatrist to the Nuremberg Jail

Figure 6 Gilbert's first book about the Nuremberg Trials.

Jerusalem. Gilbert died in 1976, shortly after his retirement, at the age of sixty-five.

A critical examination of historical events or personalities necessarily takes place retrospectively and thus presents the danger of a biased, presentist perspective on the past. Therefore, in the following comments we will attempt to examine the involvement of psychology in the Nuremberg trials strictly within the context of professional conditions for psychologists as they were almost fifty years ago.

Cantril's idea of having a psychologist at Nuremberg was a sound one. The individual appointed, however, would have been better chosen from recommendations by eminent psychologists or by the existing psychological services within the armed forces of the United States or the other allies. Ideally, the chosen psychologist would have become a member of a psychiatric or psychological team and part of the regular court organization. Gilbert obtained his position through connections and initiative and served throughout at the sufferance of the prison commander and later, the court psychiatrists. In such a crucial situation, a recognized expert with appropriate qualifications should have been chosen rather than an experimental psychologist with limited clinical training and a history of having been a type of policeman in the American military. A thorough knowledge of German would have been less important than broad clinical and assessment experience with normal, psychiatric, and especially, forensic populations. It would have been helpful, but not absolutely necessary, that the

chosen psychologist had a good knowledge of German. In 1945 there were many exiled psychologists and psychoanalysts from Germany in England and the United States who had far better professional qualifications than Gilbert or Kelley. Even better would have been the selection of a Swiss expert in the field with a clear anti-Nazi reputation.

A second problem area is found in the test procedures employed by Gilbert and Kelley. The Wechsler-Bellevue I was probably the best test instrument in the world at the time of the trials. A formal German translation and standardization of this test, however, was not made until the 1950s. An informal home-made translation was unacceptable and may, in part, have been responsible for the high IQ scores that Gilbert obtained. The use of existing and standardized German intelligence tests would have been more acceptable. The Rorschach test should also have been given in German—if necessary through an interpreter—and the interpretation should have been based on the German text and not on an English translation. Of course the six or seven prisoners who spoke English well could have been tested with English language tests. German norms should also have been used for the interpretation of the Rorschach test. Ideally, someone like H. A. Murray (1893–1988) of the Harvard Psychological Clinic or one of his German exile associates would have been a much better choice as the prison psychologist.

Another series of major difficulties was caused by the multiplicity of roles which Gilbert and, to a lesser extent, Kelley played in Nuremberg. There was the function as confidential interpreter of Colonel Andrus, the irascible and psychologically unsophisticated prison director. Gilbert also was pressured into serving as Andrus' "spy" (Persico, 1994) among the prisoners. Did the prisoners know of this function or did they view him as the kind American, who spoke good German and gave them interesting things to do? The subservient role of the interpreter and the commandant's liaison officer were clearly incompatible with that of a professional psychologist. Today such role confusions would be regarded as unethical; however, the first edition of the American Psychological Association's Code of Ethics was not published until 1951. Still, familiarity with the American legal system might have raised questions about such conflicts of interest in an ordinary American court room. Gilbert's private interest in writing a successful book and his open antagonism towards many of the Nuremberg defendants would have been additional difficulties in this role.

Finally, Gilbert seems to have lacked clinical experience and clinical common sense. Even beginning clinical students are taught how to handle discouraged test subjects and how to avoid giving feedback to subjects about their performance during the testing. Gilbert's interpretation of Göring's response to a marginal detail of Card IV is questionable, not only in terms of content and sensitivity, but especially if we remember that there are no "red spots" on Card IV!

As a result of the above problems with the initial appointment, the test procedures, and the multiple and contradictory roles, the books and articles by Gilbert and Kelley about the IMT are almost useless as psychological documents. As historical evidence, they are questionable as well because both authors made little or no effort to verify their case history information and their test interpretations. It is possible that some more reliable and valid information could be obtained if the original German notes, test protocols, and autobiographies could be unearthed in the US National Archives in Washington (Zillmer, Harrower, Ritzler, & Archer, 1995).

In conclusion, the Nuremberg trials presented a unique opportunity for psychology to learn more about the personalities and motivations of the military and political leaders of Nazi Germany. Ideally, a highly qualified clinical psychologist would have been appointed by the court rather than as "prison psychologist." This person would ideally have been a senior professional with a solid background in normal, abnormal, and criminal behavior. It would have been very useful to find an expert with a solid knowledge of German and experience with German-language tests and interview procedures. Military and civilian candidates for this crucial position could have been found easily and on short notice. It is noteworthy that qualified professionals did work with the allied prosecution office in Nuremberg and did an excellent job, even in the eyes of the defense.

Bibliography

Borofsky, G., & Brand, D. (1980). Personality organization and psychological functioning of the Nuremberg war criminals: The Rorschach data. In J. E. Dinsdale (Ed.), *Survivors, victims and perpetrators: Essays on the Nazi Holocaust* (pp. 359–403). Washington, DC: Hemisphere.

Gilbert, G. M. (1947). *Nuremberg diary.* New York: Signet.

Gilbert, G. M. (1950). *The psychology of dictatorship.* New York: Ronald.

Gilbert, G. M. (1970). *Personality dynamics: A biosocial approach.* New York: Harper & Row.

Gilbert, G. M. (1975). Preface. In Miale, F., & Seltzer, M., *The Nuremberg mind: The psychology of Nazi leaders.* New York: New York Times Book Company.

Harrower, M. (1976a). Rorschach records of Nazi war criminals: An experimental study after 30 years. *Journal of Personality Assessment, 40,* 341–351.

Harrower, M. (1976b, July). Were Hitler's henchmen mad? *Psychology Today,* 76–80.

Kelley, D. M. (1947). *Twenty-two cells in Nuremberg: A psychiatrist examines the Nazi war criminals.* New York: Greenberg.

Maser, W. (1977). *Nuremberg: A nation on trial.* New York: Scribner's.

Miale, F., & Seltzer, M. (1975). *The Nuremberg mind: The psychology of the Nazi leaders.* New York: New York Times Book Company.

Persico, J. (1994). *Nuremberg: Infamy on trial.* New York: Viking.

Reisman, J. (1991). *A history of clinical psychology* (2nd ed.). New York: Hemisphere.

Ritzler, B. A. (1978). The Nuremberg mind revisited : A quantitative approach to Nazi Rorschach records. *Journal of Personality Assessment, 47,* 344–353.

Zillmer, E., Harrower, M., Ritzler, B., & Archer, R. (1995). *The quest for the Nazi personality.* Hillsdale, NJ: Erlbaum.

Suicidology

Antoon A. Leenaars

In the *Oxford English Dictionary*, the arbiter of the English language, we read:

> Suicidology [f. SUICIDE sb.2 + OLOGY] The study of suicide and its prevention. Hence suicidologist. [1929 W.A. Bonger in Psychiatrisch-Juridsch Geselschap . . . De wetenschap van de zelfmoord, the suicidologie (cursivering van mij) zou men haar kunnen noemen, is ruim een eeuw oud.] 1964 E. S. Shneidman in Contemp. Psychol. IX. 371/2, I thank Louis Dublin, the Grand Old Man of suicidology, for this book because in it he . . . has given us all new clues to suicide. 1967 - Bull. Suicidology July 7/2, The 10-point program for suicide prevention here outlined is a mutual enterprise whose successful development depends on the active interest, support, and activities of 'suicidologists.' (p. 145)

Although suicidology is a new term, there is a long history on attitudes toward suicide. During classical Greek times, suicide was viewed in various ways. Pythagoras of Samos, who introduced the theory of number to our understanding of humans and the universe, proposed that suicide would upset the spiritual mathematics of all things. Plato's position (428–348 B.C.), best expressed in *Phaedo*, opposed suicide but allowed for exceptions such as that of Socrates who was condemned by the Athenian court. Socrates was found guilty of corrupting the minds of youth and believing in false deities. He then drank the poison hemlock. Aristotle (384–322 B.C.) espoused the view that suicide was against the state and therefore wrong. An individual was answerable to the state for everything and thus was to be punished for acts of wrongdoing, including suicide.

In the centuries just before the Christian era, life in classical Rome was held rather cheap, and suicide was viewed either neutrally, or, by some, positively. Zeno, the founder of Stoic philosophy, hanged himself after putting his toe out of joint in a fall at age 98. The history of Rome is filled with such incidents. Rome's civilization itself was, indeed, often inimical toward life.

The *Old Testament* does not directly forbid suicide, but in Jewish law suicide is wrong. Life had value. In the *Old Testament*, one finds only six cases of suicide: Abimelech, Samson, Saul, Saul's armor bearer, Ahithapel, and Zimni. The *New Testament*, like the *Old Testament*, does not directly forbid suicide. During the early Christian years, in fact, there was excessive martyrdom and a tendency toward suicide, resulting in considerable concern on the part of the Church Fathers. Suicide by these early martyrs was seen as redemption, and thus the Fathers began increasingly to associate suicide with sin. In the fourth century, suicide was categorically rejected by St. Augustine (354–430). Suicide was considered a sin because it violated the Sixth Commandment, "Thou shall not kill." By 693, the Church, at the Council of Toledo, proclaimed that individuals who attempted suicide were to be excommunicated. This view was elaborated by St. Thomas Aquinas (1225–1274), who emphasized that suicide was not only unnatural and antisocial, but also a mortal sin because it usurped God's power over life and death. The notion of suicide as sin took firm hold and for hundreds of years played an important part in Western culture's view of self-destruction. Only during the Renaissance and the Reformation did a different view emerge, although the Church's view of suicide remained powerful among the lower classes into this century.

The writers and philosophers from the 1500s on began to present a variety of different perspectives on suicide. Shakespeare (1564–1616), for example, has provided us with an excellent array of such views. Fourteen suicides occur in his plays.

The French philosopher Jean-Jacques Rousseau (1712–1778) emphasized the natural state of human beings. He transferred sin from the individual to society, making people generally good (and innocent) and asserting that it is society that makes them bad. The disputation as to the locus of blame —the individual or society—is a major theme that dominates the history of thought about suicide. David Hume (1711–1776) was one of the first major Western philosophers to discuss suicide apart from the concept of sin. In "On Suicide" (1777), he refuted the view that suicide is a crime by arguing that suicide is not a transgression of our duties to God, to our fellow citizens, or to ourselves.

Whereas Hume tried to decriminalize suicide and make it the individual's right, others, including Immanuel Kant (1724–1804), wrote that human life was sacred and should be preserved, in an antistoic sense, at any cost.

In more recent times, other important currents in the study of suicide have evolved. Existentialism, for example, brought suicide into sharp focus, as best exemplified in Albert Camus's *The Myth of Sisyphus* (1942/1955). In the opening lines, Camus wrote:

> There is but one truly serious philosophical problem, and that is suicide. Judging whether life is or is not worth living amounts to answering the fundamental question of philosophy. All the rest and whether or not the world has three dimensions, whether the mind has nine or twelve categories—comes afterwards. (p. 3)

The two giants in the field of suicide theory at the turn of the 20th century were Emile Durkheim (1858–1917) and Sigmund Freud (1856–1939). In *Suicide* (1897/1951), Durkheim focused on society's inimical effects on the individual. In contrast, Freud, eschewing the notions of either sin or crime, gave suicide back to the individual but put the focus of action in the unconscious. Consequently, one of the major debates in the field is whether suicide is an individual or social act. Durkheim proposed a social meaning view of suicide, proposing that the rate of suicide was affected by two social characteristics. Suicide rates are high when the degree of social integration (that is, the extent to which members of the society are bound together in social relationships) is very low (leading to *egoistic suicide*) or very high (leading to *altruistic suicide*). Suicide rates are also high when the degree of social regulation

(that is, the degree to which the desires and behaviors of the members of the society are controlled by social norms and customs) is very low (leading to *anomic suicide*) or very high (leading to *fatalistic suicide*). The social view is not without criticism. For example, Douglas (1967) stated "it is not possible to explain specific types of social events such as suicide in terms of abstract social meaning" (p. 339). Yet the social view continues to be heavily emphasized in suicidology even today. The most notable researchers have been Andrew Henry and James Short (integrative studies of suicide and homicide), David Phillips (imitation effects), Steven Stack (sociological studies of suicide, imitation effects), and David Lester (availability of methods, international comparisons).

Figure 1 Edwin Shneidman and Norman Farberow, American pioneers of suicide research in front of the famous Los Angeles Suicide Prevention Center (ca. 1951).

Before contemporary suicidology was started by Edwin Shneidman (b. 1918), Sigmund Freud was probably the best-known historical figure in psychology. In the individual-society debate, Freud placed the roots of suicide within the developmental context of the individual. His famous proposition read:

> Probably no one finds the mental energy required to kill himself unless, in the first place,

in doing so he is at the same time killing an object with whom he has identified himself or, in the second place, is turning against himself a death wish which had been directed against someone else. (Freud, 1920/1974, p. 162)

Whatever else suicide is, it is a conscious act. It is a conscious act of self-induced annihilation. However, Freud's impact on the field of suicidology is derived from his belief that although there is always an element of some awareness and conscious intentionality in suicide, the driving force is an unconscious process.

There have been numerous people since Freud espousing a psychological meaning view. The most noteworthy since the beginning of the century are: Alfred Adler, Aaron Beck, Ludwig Binswanger, C. G. Jung, Karl A. Menninger, George A. Kelly, Henry A. Murray, J. Terry Maltsberger, Edwin Shneidman, Harry Stack Sullivan, and Gregory Zilboorg (Leenaars, 1988).

The "fulcrum moment" of contemporary suici-

Figure 2 Henry Murray and Edwin Shneidman, Hollywood (1963).

dology, as Edwin Shneidman himself described it, occurred several minutes after he discovered several hundred suicide notes in a Los Angeles coroner's vault in 1949. At that moment he had a glimmering inspiration that the potential value of the notes could be immeasurably increased if he did not read them immediately, but rather compared them blindly, in a controlled experiment, with simulated suicide notes elicited from matched nonsuicidal subjects. John Stuart Mill's method of difference came to Shneidman's aid, and the seeds for the study of contemporary suicidal phenomena were sown.

As a personal aside, anyone who knows Shneidman knows that thematic windows to his ideas (and his life) are to be found in Herman Melville and literature and Henry A. Murray and psychology. Shneidman resembles both. Melville and Shneidman are certainly scholars, and Murray and Shneidman are also scientists and clinicians. These intimate relationships are central to an understanding of the development of contemporary suicidology (Leenaars, 1993).

Edwin Shneidman was joined in this early research venture by an equally important suicidologist, Norman Farberow (b. 1918–). Their collaboration resulted in suicidology's most important work—these two men literally defined the field. Most important are their publications *Clues to Suicide* (1957) and *The Cry for Help* (1961), and *The Psychology of Suicide* (1970), edited with another contemporary pioneer, Robert Litman. Shneidman's and Farberow's psychological studies—on suicide notes and psychological autopsies—continue to be the basis of current individual meaning studies.

Subsequent to their early studies, Shneidman went on to define and redefine the field. His most important work is *Definition of Suicide* (1985). In this book Shneidman defines suicide: "Currently in the Western World, suicide is a conscious act of self-induced annihilation, best understood as a multidimensional malaise in a needful individual who defines an issue for which the suicide is perceived as the best solution" (p. 203).

However, our understanding of suicide continues to evolve. One of the major advancements in suicidology in the last ten years is the biology of suicide. The research, however, has limitations; for example, small sample sizes, confounding variables, and lack of psychiatric control. The most common view today is that suicide may be a biological event in an individual and much more. Possible biological markers include urinary 17-hydroxycorticosteroids (17-OHCS), cortisol in plasma and cerebrospinal fluid, cerebrospinal fluid 5-hydroxyindoleacetic acid, tritiated impimpromine binding, 3-methoxy-4-hydroxyphenylglycol and homovanillic acid, urinary norepinephrine, epinephrine ratio, and thyroid-stimulating hormone response to thyrotiropin-releasing hormone. Andrew Slaby (1995), in his writings about the field, is optimistic—especially with regard to the relationship between suicide and affective disorders (i.e., manic-depressive disorder). If this is indeed the case, it is likely that in some suicides, specific biological correlates may be strikingly relevant to the individual level of analysis.

Ronald Maris (1993) has recently outlined the evolution of suicidology, allowing one to become aware of the considerable size of the field today. It is a multidisciplinary enterprise. It is the study of the psychological, biological, cultural, sociological, interpersonal, intrapsychic, logical, conscious, unconscious, and philosophical elements of the suicidal event. Shneidman has always insisted—and most suicidologists agree—that suicidology is not reducible to any one of its domains. It is not simply an individual nor social act. It is also not simply a biological event. Such a reductionist position would constitute a regression to the days when suicide was seen as a sin or as a crime. On this issue Shneidman's influence should not be underestimated, for like Murray, Shneidman has steadfastly opposed any reductionism.

A critical development in the advancement of suicidology in the latter half of this century has been the establishment of associations for suicide prevention. In 1968, the American Association of Suicidology (AAS) was founded by Shneidman. At the 1968 meeting of AAS, one of this century's most important dialogues on suicide occurred. Its participants were Jacques Choron, Louis I. Dublin, Paul Friedman, Robert J. Havighurst, Lawrence Kubie, Karl Menninger, Edwin S. Shneidman, and Erwin

Stengel. What is important to understand is that this meeting (see Shneidman, 1973) was seen as a "reconvening" (at least, in spirit) of the famous 1910 meeting on suicide in Freud's home in Vienna (see Friedman, 1967). The contributors at that meeting were Alfred Adler, Sigmund Freud, Josef K. Friedjung, Karl Molitor, David Ernst Oppenheim, Rudolf Reitler, J. (Isidor) Sadger, and Wilhelm Stekel. As an anecdotal aside, at this meeting Stekel was the first to remark that "No one kills himself who did not want to kill another or, at least, wish death to another" (p. 87).

Since the 1968 meeting, AAS has become the world's largest association of its kind. The organization celebrated its 25th anniversary in Chicago in 1992. That meeting too was a reconvening not only of American, but also many other international scholars in the field.

Figure 3 Participants in the 1968 inaugural Annual Conference of the American Association of Suicidology, Chicago. Left to right: Jacques Choron, Louis F. Dublin, Erwin Stengel, Edwin Shneidman.

There is also an international association, The International Association for Suicide Prevention (IASP), with Erwin Ringel as its first Past President. The first large international congress on suicide prevention was held by IASP in 1969 in London (the first IASP meeting was held in Vienna in 1960). Various countries have their own associations as well. My own experience in Canada may serve as just one example. Canada's association, the Canadian Association for Suicide Prevention (Leenaars, first Past

Figure 4 Audience shot from the international congress of the International Association for Suicide Prevention, London (1969).

Figure 5 Meeting of active suicide researchers at the 1992 Meeting of the American Association of Suicidology, Chicago.

President), became a viable group in 1988, having had its first national conference in 1990 in Vancouver, with Shneidman as the keynote speaker.

Research in the field is proliferating. The leading researchers in the field belong to an invited group, the International Academy for Suicide Research, which was founded in 1990 (Rene Diekstra, first Past President). It publishes the journal, *Archives of Suicide Research*. These people are at the leading edge

of suicidology today. A listing of these key figures (along with their respective country and specialty) includes the following: Marie Asberg (Sweden; biological); Alan Berman (USA; adolescent, assessment); Jan Beskow (Sweden; neuroscience); Unni Bille-Brahe (Denmark; epidemiology); Otmar Buyne (The Netherlands; general); David Clark (USA; third party interviews); Diego De Leo (Italy; elderly); Rene Diekstra (The Netherlands; international comparison,

Figure 6 Edwin Shneidman and Antoon A. Leenaars at Shneidman's home in Los Angeles (1991).

adolescent); Ronald Dyck (Canada; epidemiology); Werner Felber (Germany; general); Robert Goldney (Australia; depression, assessment); Walter Gulbinat (Switzerland, WHO); Keith Hawton (England; treatment evaluation); Michael Kelleher (Ireland; social epidemiology); Antoon Leenaars (Canada/ The Netherlands; suicide notes, Canada-USA comparison); David Lester (USA, availability of methods); Jouko Lonnqvist (Finland; suicide attempts, mental disorders); John Mann (USA, biological); Ronald Maris (USA; social); Forenc Moksony (Hungary; economics); Hans-Jürgen Müller (Germany; prevention and postvention evaluation); Jerome Motto (USA; risk assessment); George Murphy (USA; substance abuse); Peter Nordstrom (Sweden; biological); Cynthia Pfeffer (USA, children); Herman van Praag (The Netherlands; biological determinants); Nils Retterstol (Norway; follow-up studies, psychosis); Charles Rich (USA; general); Isaac Sakinofsky (Canada; epidemiology); Armin Schmidtke (Germany; personality); David Shaffer (USA; youth); Edwin Shneidman (USA, general); Gernot Sonneck (Austria; imitation, psychotherapy); Steven Stack (USA; social); Lil Traskman-Bendz (Sweden; biological, pharmacology); Hans Wedler (Germany; crisis intervention); Manfred Wolfersdorf (Germany; depression, schizophrenia); and Danuta Wolk-Wasserman (Sweden; psychodynamics).

There are, of course, other journals in the field besides *Archives.* The most important are *Crisis, Death Studies,* and *Suicide and Life Threatening Behavior.*

Suicidology has developed beyond Pythagoras . . . beyond Freud and Durkheim . . . and beyond Shneidman. It is my prediction that suicidology will become even more important in psychology (and beyond) by the end of the century.

Bibliography

Camus, A. (1955). *The Myth of Sisyphus.* (J. O'Brien, Trans.). New York: Vintage Books. (Original work published 1942)

Douglas, J. (1967). *The social meaning of suicide.* Princeton: Princeton University Press.

Durkheim, E. (1951). *Suicide* (J. Spaulding & G. Simpson, Trans.). Glencoe, Ill: The Free Press. (Original work published 1897)

Freud, S. (1974). A case of homosexuality in a woman. In J. Strachey (Ed. & Trans.), *The standard edition of the complete psychological works of Sigmund Freud* (Vol. 18, pp. 147–172). London: Hogarth Press. (Original work published 1920)

Friedman, P. (1967). *On suicide.* New York: International Universities Press.

Leenaars, A. (1988). *Suicide notes.* New York: Human Sciences Press.

Leenaars, A. (Ed.). (1993). *Suicidology: Essays in honor of Edwin Shneidman.* Northvale, NJ: Aronson.

Maris, R. (1993). The evolution of suicidology. In A. Leenaars (Ed.), *Suicidology: Essays in honor of Edwin Shneidman* (pp. 3–21). Northvale, NJ: Aronson.

Shneidman, E. (1973). *On the nature of suicide.* San Francisco: Jossey-Bass, Inc.

Shneidman, E. (1985). *Definition of suicide.* New York: Wiley.

Shneidman, E., & Farberow, N. (Eds.). (1957). *Clues to suicide.* New York: McGraw-Hill.

Shneidman, E., & Farberow, N. (Eds.). (1961). *The cry for help.* New York: McGraw-Hill.

Shneidman, E., Farberow, N., & Litman, R. (Eds.). (1970). *The psychology of suicide.* New York: Science House.

Slaby, A. (1995). Suicide as an indicium of biologically based brain disease. *Archives of Suicide Research, 1,* 59–73.

Antipsychiatry and Antihistory: "Nailing Jelly to the Wall"

Michael J. Kral
Karen L. Marrero
Brian R. Burke

A "new historicism" is taking hold and is now pervading virtually every discipline. It has emerged from several sources, from critical philosophy and poststructuralist literary theory to "crises" within various human sciences related to the questioning of the theoretical and methodological structures that have served as the foundations of disciplinary knowledge. Since the mid-1960s, history has been moving away from modeling itself on a science-based positivism that searches for general laws and immutable truths, seeking instead to discover how historical understanding is constructed (Roth, 1995). The idea of historical objectivity has itself been questioned, and the reference to jelly, nails, and walls in the subtitle of this chapter is from the apt phrase employed by Novick (1988), who in turn borrowed it from a political historian writing about research on intellectual history. Novick discusses the crisis of objectivity in historiography, candidly stating that in professional historical writing

> "They are playing a game. They are playing at not playing a game. If I show them I see they are, I shall break the rules and they will punish me. I must play their game, of not seeing I see the game."
>
> R. D. Laing, *Knots*

> it is considered tactless and discourteous to suggest that someone's views are a reflection of his or her background, prejudices, or psychic needs. We stick to the reasoned arguments advanced, even if privately we think those arguments are shallow rationalizations. The need to behave in this way in scholarly discussion is obvious, as are the costs of violating the rule. (p. 11)

When the given history of a discipline is criticized as being merely a highly selective, linear progression of righteous people and revolutionary events leading to the ever-improving present and moving toward a perfect future, eyebrows tend to be raised and crossed.

Danziger (1994) has made a distinction between "celebratory" and "critical" history. He refers to the former as "feel-good history," in that "whatever it discovers about the past will be implicitly a celebration of the present and of the steps by which it was achieved" (p. 469). Danziger argues that such history will, in the end, have no impact as a scientific endeavor. Many writers associated with the "antipsychiatry movement" have launched similar critiques of psychiatry, including Foucault (1965), Sedgewick (1982), and Szasz (1961, 1995). Sedgewick (1981), for example, wrote about the history of psychiatry as a "self-congratulatory account of the march of progress" (p. 237), referring to such an account as evolutionist history. He also criticized Foucault's pioneering 1965 book, *Madness and Civilization*, which proselytized one critical history of psychiatry as the battle between reason and unreason, as a decontextualized fiction amounting to antihistory. Szasz (1995) writes that the history of psychiatry as mental healing can just as easily be rewritten as a history of the coercion of undesirable people. This move from the celebratory to the critical in psychiatry, starting in the 1960s, was strongly oppositional and certainly violated the norms that ruled.

The term "antipsychiatry" has been said to have so many meanings—ranging from charlatanism to critical philosophy—as to be almost meaningless. It is, however, commonly associated with what has been termed a social movement of the 1960s. In its most basic form, antipsychiatry has been a criticism of psychiatry as a form of social control, political oppression, labeling, and inhumane treatment causing more harm than good to both individuals and society. Its impact during the 1960s was strong and took place within the context of change in mental health treatment from long-term hospitalization to community-based care, and during a time when the causes of mental illness were being increasingly attributed to social, economic, and family settings rather than primarily to individual genetic/constitutional dispositions. The loudest voices of opposition in recent years have come not from outside of psychiatry as one might expect (from competing mental health professionals in supposed lower-status roles such as social workers, nurses, clergy, or clinical/professional psychologists), but from within the discipline itself. Critical thinking has its greatest effects in producing change when its proponents come from within their own circle.

Before examining the antipsychiatry of the 1960s, it must be noted that antipsychiatry is not an idea restricted to the latter half of the 20th century (although the word "psychiatry" itself has a relatively short history of about 100 years). Tantam (1991) points out that Szasz identified Beyer as having coined the term "antipsychiatry" in 1912; Beyer had argued that the powerful psychiatrists of his time played "games" with their patients. But there have been other antipsychiatrists who preceded Beyer, especially if the term is employed to mean strong accusations of inhumane or inefficacious psychiatric treatment. There have been, arguably, many antipsychiatry movements. One of the great revolutions in mental health treatment occurred at the turn of the 19th century. Like the one of more recent times, it took place from within psychiatry/medicine when Philippe Pinel (1745–1826) ordered the chains removed from many of the insane held in the asylum of the Bicêtre in Paris, where he was physician-in-chief in 1793. Up to this time the "treatment" of the insane in asylums, which housed primarily the poor and working classes, included "emetics, purgatives, bloodletting, and various so-called harmless tortures provided by special paraphernalia" (Alexander & Selesnick, 1966,

p. 154). Chains and whips were among the paraphernalia, and beatings were common. The use of purgatives, emetics, and bleeding dated back over 2,000 years to Hippocrates. Though the living conditions in these asylums may have been abominable, the public would often include in their outings asylum visits to view the "mad." Actions taken toward those unable to adjust to society have always reflected the more general attitudes that that culture has of them (see Figure 1).

Figure 1 "The Rake's Progress" (1730–1739): Scene from an asylum in England. (National Library of Medicine)

Phlegm, yellow and black bile, passions gone awry, animalistic regressions, possession, and misshapen heads as physical manifestations of the attenuation or absence of moral and intellectual structures of the brain were among the reasons believed to be behind displays of mania, melancholia, dementia, and idiocy. The insane were relegated to asylums beginning in the medieval period after about the year 800 A.D. Prior to that, they were cared for by their relatives and were generally not integrated into the mainstream of Greek and Roman society. Some smaller-scale psychiatric reform movements also occurred, such as religious care in the asylum—without the use of chains—devoted solely to the insane in Valencia, Spain, in 1409

(Alexander & Selesnick, 1966), and the German-Dutch physician Johann Weyer's 1563 refutation of the idea that witches were harmful, which countered a pervasive fear of demonic possession during the Renaissance Period. Weyer's radical views have been referred to as psychiatry's first revolution by some historians.

The late 18th and early 19th centuries brought a major reform in the treatment of the insane. An increasing acceptance of the idea of insanity as a disease fueled the building of many mental hospitals—first privately, for the wealthy, and then publicly—across the United States and in other countries. Also, a growing belief in the possibility of rehabilitation led to the construction of many prisons for criminals and almshouses for the poor during this time, all fitting into a grand new plan for the ordering of a society experiencing an increase in crime, poverty, and general unrest (Rothman, 1990). The 18th century has been described as the "age of systems" in the applications of science and medicine,

and biological explanations of the cause of insanity readily augmented the already existing but hollow classification schemes (Alexander & Selesnick, 1966). Hope for order—and cure—was in the air.

A consequence of seeing insanity as a disease is that it will dictate methods by which such people will be treated. One of the great psychiatric reformers at the turn of the 19th century was Philippe Pinel, who became famous for championing a radical change in the institutional "care" of the insane (Figure 2). Pinel had studied classical philosophy before turning to medicine and working in Paris. Historians of psychiatry Alexander and Selesnick (1966) indicate that Pinel "himself was considered mad by his contemporaries—for he released the patients from their chains, opened their windows, fed them nourishing food, and treated them with kindness" (p. 154). Although the extent of his reforms is controversial, Pinel's work in Paris coincided with a period of major psychiatric reform in the early 19th century.

The view of insanity as disease represented a marked shift in thinking. The very public nature of this general revolution in psychiatry demonstrates the changing mood in Europe. A powerful context for the changes in the treatment of the insane during this time was the 1789 Declaration of Rights and the French Revolution. But this new spirit was in the air elsewhere, including Great Britain and North America.

A famous portrait of a patient chained in an asylum can be seen in Figure 3; this particular portrait is said to have been a major influence in the reform of the asylum of Bethleham Hospital in England, also known as Bedlam, founded in 1247 and housing the insane since 1377. The man in chains was William Norris, and he had been held in this manner in a lower gallery at Bedlam for 14 years when Edward Wakefield, a member of Parliament, found him while inspecting the asylum in 1814. Wakefield demanded that sketches be made and openly circulated. The text accompanying one of the portraits included condemnations by respected public figures of the treatment of the insane in Bedlam with statements such as "The cruel and constant coercion in which he was kept, and which, when continued unremittingly for such a length of time, I should think far better calculated to drive away the reason of a sane man than to restore a madman to his senses". Another read, "It has always appeared to me, from what I have seen at Bethlem, that *the restraint was used* THERE *more from feelings of*

Figure 2 Philippe Pinel (1745–1826), French physician and asylum reformer. (Yale University, Harvey Cushing/John Hay Whitney Medical Library)

Figure 3 William Norris enchained at Bethlehem Hospital in London (1814). (Yale University, Harvey Cushing/John Hay Whitney Medical Library)

revenge, than for purposes of medical care" (Gilman, 1982, original italics and caps).

Some would say that even progressive psychiatric reform can appear less than benevolent when viewed from the vantage point of a later period in time. Psychiatric reform in the early 19th century was also taking place in the United States. Benjamin Rush (1745–1813), considered to be the first American psychiatrist, has been described as "an ardent social reformer, a wise practical philosopher, and revolutionary patriot" (Brady, 1975) (see Figure 4). Rush obtained a bachelor's degree at age 15 and studied medicine at the College of New Jersey, which later became Princeton, and completed his medical training at the University of Edinburgh. At age 24 he was appointed to a teaching post in chemistry at the Medical School of the College of Pennsylvania, which later became part of the University of Pennsylvania, the first American medical school. At age 31, Rush was a co-signer of the Declaration of Independence. In his influential psychiatric textbook of 1812, *Medical Inquiries and Observations*

Upon the Diseases of the Mind, Rush wrote that the "times of cruelty" were passing and that humane treatment was in order. Like Pinel in France, Rush in America was as controversial a figure and helped promote the view of insanity as a medical disease. He advocated that the cause of madness was not to be found in mysterious external forces, but within the person's body.

An extremely popular lecturer on medicine at the Pennsylvania Hospital, Rush used or invented treatments that were in keeping with more "sensible" medical explanations of what he saw as congestion of the brain's blood vessels. He used the rotating bed or chair (Figure 5), one of early medicine's first "shock instruments" (Alexander & Selesnick, 1966, p. 147). The patient would be spun in a chair resulting in a loss of consciousness. Rush also had his patients strapped down on a bed and rotated so that blood would travel to the head.

Not only did he employ such devices for cure, he began to design them. His "tranquillizer chair" (Figure 6), built for him by a cabinet maker, was

Figure 4 Benjamin Rush (1745–1813), American physician. (National Library of Medicine)

457

simism settled in. By the mid-1800s the majority of asylum patients were viewed as incurable. There are a number of contexts within which this shift occurred. The asylums increasingly became custodial institutions, housing large numbers of the poor and immigrants, who were believed to be threats to the stability of the citizenry. Strongly held beliefs in biological/genetic determinism and progressivist, eugenic notions of social action based in science helped to increase negative views and fear of those now seen to have mental illness.

The early 20th century was a breeding ground in the United States and Europe for ideas that spawned such projects as immigration restriction and involuntary sterilization, and even euthanasia for "undesirables" (Kevles, 1985). At the same time, the medicalization of mental illness grew stronger in the name of "humane" treatment. One of the influential markers of this renewed undercurrent of hope was the widely publicized 1908 account of unacceptable treatment written by a former asylum patient named Clifford Beers, entitled *A Mind That Found Itself*. In America and elsewhere, optimism was replacing pessimism for a "new society."

Figure 5 Circulating swings used in treatment of insanity (ca. 1810–1819). (National Library of Medicine)

invented to replace the "evil" of the "straight waistcoat" that "never fails to increase their disease." The tranquillizer chair "lessens the force of the blood in its determination to the head" and relaxes the muscles, "weakening the force of the blood vessels in every part of the body." The treatment still included the use of "purgative medicines," bleeding, and applying ice to the head. Rush saw the device as a major improvement over previous treatments, as it prevented "subjecting the patient to the necessity of being moved from his chair or exposing him afterwards to the fector of his excretions or to their contact with his body" (Rush, 1811, pp. 170–171).

Pinel, Rush, and others, mixing morality and biology, contributed to changes in psychiatric treatment that, in the context of their times, represented major reform. They were antipsychiatrists who propagated change and caused controversy. Despite ambitious efforts toward cure, however, a pes-

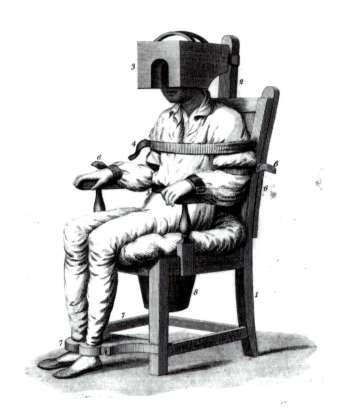

Figure 6 Rush's tranquillizer chair (1811). (Yale University, Harvey Cushing/John Hay Whitney Medical Library)

In the 1960s and 70s, individuals such as Cooper, Esterson, Laing, and Sedgewick in Britain; Althusser, Foucalt and many others in France; Goffman, Scheff, and Szasz in the United States; and Basaglia in Italy led the antipsychiatry movement of modern times. They fitted well with the rebellious 1960s and were shaped by and helped shape changes toward mental illness and its treatment. Many of them argued that the distress of the mentally ill stemmed from unbearable social contexts. Deinstitutionalization was in vogue in America, partially due to the wide-spread practice of pharmacology. In the United States, increasing concern for issues of public health and welfare in the 1950s led to the beginnings of a larger framework within which the antipsychiatry of the next decade can be placed: the community mental health movement and social psychiatry. This was a call for society's ownership of its problems, including the problems of its most distressed and disturbed members. The two most well-known and most radical (post)modern "antipsychiatric" psychiatrists have, perhaps not surprisingly, disclaimed the label of antipsychiatry for themselves. They are Ronald D. Laing of Great Britain and Thomas Szasz of the United States.

R. D. Laing (Figure 7) grew up in Glasgow, born in 1927 to parents whose Scottish roots dated back to the Vikings and Celts. He attended Hutcheson's Boys' Grammar School and Glasgow University, obtaining his medical degree from Glasgow University in 1951. He served as a lieutenant and psychiatrist in the British Army from 1951–1953 and worked at the Glasgow Royal Mental Hospital in 1955, the University of Glasgow's Department of Psychological Medicine in 1956, the Tavistock Clinic from 1957–1961, and was Director of the Langham Clinic in London from 1962–1965. Between 1961–1967 he was with the Tavistock Institute for Human Relations. He was also a Fellow of the Foundations Fund for Research in Psychiatry and chaired The Philadelphia Association in London from 1964–1982. The Philadelphia Association was a charity that offered alternatives to traditional psychiatric treatment, including the arrangement of "households as sanctuaries" for individuals. Laing died while on holiday in 1989.

Laing authored many books and papers covering not only psychiatry but philosophy and poetry, offering one of the most challenging critiques of prevailing views of psychiatry and psychotherapy in general and schizophrenia in particular in recent times (e.g., Laing, 1959/1965, 1967, 1970/1971, 1985).

Figure 7 R. D. Laing (1927–1989). (Courtesy of the Milton H. Erickson Foundation, Inc.)

A self-labeled phenomenological therapist, he argued that society should try to understand the meaning behind the schizophrenic's experience of psychosis. He emphasized the richness of the schizophrenic's fiction or tale. The seemingly convoluted and myopic orientation of schizophrenics is actually a creative act of coping within an equally convoluted and myopic society. At times he printed poems in his books written by his patients, shifting the emphasis to the creativity of the schizophrenic: one recompense for bearing the weight of an entire society's "ills."

Laing used schizophrenia as a metaphor for late 20th-century society—specifically the paranoia and hysteria informing every aspect of it. Schizophrenics are the manifest content of what lies beneath the surface of consciousness in "normal" people. Inevitably, Laing saw those of us who are "normal" as the schizophrenic ones; we are more sick than those we diagnose as schizophrenic because we are completely cut off from a large part of ourselves. In fact, we may actually make those we diagnose as schizophrenic into scapegoats for our unconscious feelings of paranoia. In this way, a small number of people are "sacrificed" for the benefit of society; schizophrenics unwittingly help us maintain our attitude of alienation. Schizophrenics, in this case, may actually be a part of the core of our psyche, which would explain why we are repelled and attracted by them and why, inevitably, we relegate them to institutions.

Laing and others of the modern antipsychiatry movement gave schizophrenics an important role in society. Indeed, they were given a place of honor. This idea is not entirely new to Western society, as there have been various points throughout history wherein the insane were viewed, albeit hesitatingly and sometimes begrudgingly, as visionaries and even prophets. Laing took the label "schizophrenic" and, when he was done theorizing, made it a corollary to 20th-century politics. In essence, he had "socialized" both the idea of schizophrenia and schizophrenics by moving it/them from the sole domain of psychiatry into the mainstream of modern thought and everyday experience. This meant a similar shift in thinking from blind allegiance to concepts of insanity and mental health, which had existed without refute for decades and even centuries (and the questioning and the moving further away from those who had originated these views, which had come to be viewed as universal and objective truth), to acceptance of the arbitrary quality which often formed a large part of a psychiatric diagnosis.

Criticisms of Laing abound, including some directed at his ideological inconsistencies across numerous books and his extreme relativism. A few critics even believe he was mentally ill himself. Vice (1992) sees Laing's central view of mental illness as a real but sensible malady of "selfhood gone wrong" (p. 108). In the end Laing adopted a position of agnosticism toward understanding mental illness, arguing that psychiatrists and other therapists must respect the patient's mystery and admit that they cannot know another person. Only then can true healing take place. In an interview one month before his death, Laing stated:

> The art of writing that is required to match simplicity is what I've got to work on. I don't think I've fully found the fulfilled, accomplished way for me to write fully to express that eternal simplicity. But I don't feel it's impossible for me to do that. (Lunt, 1990, p. 103)

Thomas Szasz (Figure 8), on the other hand, has presented a more cogent, consistent, and radical

message to psychiatry since the early 1960s: mental illness does not exist as such because illness and disease are nothing but metaphors, psychotherapy is a myth, involuntary hospitalization is a crime against humanity, and while psychiatrists think they are helping by espousing the idea of personal freedom, they are actually imposing a form of dehumanizing social control (see Szasz, 1961, 1990a, 1991). At the center of Szasz's critique of psychiatry are the notions of libertarianism and personal responsibility.

Szasz was born in 1920, in Budapest, Hungary. He describes one of his most vivid memories of childhood as the compassion he felt toward the beggars on the streets, to whom he would regularly give a portion of his allowance. At the age of 18 he moved to the United States with his family to escape the Nazis, and at 24 graduated with his MD from Cincinnati University. He entered psychiatry and psychoanalytic training in order to practice psychotherapy and at the same time "successfully" critique the field (Szasz, 1990b). Szasz questioned the

Figure 8 Thomas Szasz (1920–). (Photograph by Joel Siegel. Courtesy of Thomas Szasz)

fundamental beliefs of psychiatry well before he went to college, and during his residency at the University of Chicago, refused to work in a mental hospital because of his disdain of involuntary hospitalization. He began teaching in the Department of Psychiatry at Syracuse University in 1956 and is now Professor Emeritus of Psychiatry, State University of New York Health Science Center at Syracuse. Szasz has remained within academic psychiatry, but not without difficulty. In the 1960s he successfully fought psychiatry administrators who wanted to prevent him from lecturing (Leifer, 1990). Szasz believes that psychiatric treatment should be contractual and respectful of the individual's rights and self-determinism. In his practice, Szasz does not prescribe medications. He has maintained his critical position of psychiatry for the last three decades in over 20 books and numerous articles. A morally committed man, Szasz has not sat quietly.

Within psychiatry, more recent criticisms have become focused on the therapies offered and less on the epistemology and nomenclature of disease. Peter Breggin is a popular antagonist of all biological therapy. He relates that as an 18-year-old volunteer at Metropolitan State Hospital in 1954 he observed unkempt and poorly cared-for patients being beaten by orderlies. He believes that one-on-one counseling by volunteers with the patients resulted in their cures and discharges from the hospital, and writes that he was profoundly affected by the adverse reactions of patients to electroconvulsive therapy, leucotomies/lobotomies, and insulin coma. In his subsequent training as a psychiatrist, he eschewed all the biological therapies and has remained firmly within the camp of Thomas Szasz. In his popular books *Toxic Psychiatry* (Breggin, 1991) and *Talking Back to Prozac* (1994), he insists that medications are brain damaging, addictive, and have few redeeming qualities. He also believes that psychiatry is "the political center of a multi-billion dollar psycho-pharmaceutical complex that pushes biological and genetic theories as well as drugs on society" producing an "epidemic of brain damage" (Breggin, 1991). His solution is not just psychotherapy, but a caring, loving psychotherapy.

Conversely, Dr. E. Fuller Torrey, a long-time advocate of the biological model of schizophrenia, has been one of the leaders in the revolt against Freud, post-Freudianism, and psychoanalytic therapy. Torrey's condemnation of the Freudian world view is rigorous, and he focuses his attention on the unveri-fiable/unfalsifiable psychoanalytic claims to scientific status. Torrey links the justified backlash against the eugenics movement of the early 20th century and the horrors of the holocaust to the rapid rise of nonbiological/environmental hypotheses of the etiology of psychopathology. However, he sees this extreme environmentalism as being more political than empirically-based, and argues that the derogation of biological therapies limits treatment opportunities psychiatric patients may derive from the rapidly expanding developments in psychopharmacology (Torrey, 1992).

Recent writers have credited the antipsychiatry literature since the 1960s with directly influencing current critical theory and history within psychiatry (e.g., Ingleby, 1980, Micale & Porter, 1994; Rothman, 1990). The history of psychiatry, like that of other disciplines, is now being undone and rewritten from the vantage point of this new historicism. Even antipsychiatry has been criticized, often by those who have been labeled as antipsychiatrists (e.g., Szasz, 1988). Celebratory history is on the wane, and antipsychiatry as rude rebelliousness is becoming critical history as respected scholarship. Yet the new historians of psychiatry must remain cautious lest they succumb to the rigid dogmatism they criticize. Every time a major change has occurred in psychiatry, those leading the radical movements have all believed that they were heading in the best direction and found it easy to decry past efforts as inefficient or inhumane. We live in the present and cannot fully escape it, so presentism in historical interpretation will to some extent always be with us. Some remain optimistic, however, affirming that a "history of the future" will be one that includes subjectivity, values, commitments, and contexts (Tolman, 1995). Antipsychiatry, as critical history and theory, may become not the insistence on a narrowly defined idea of what is "right," but an effort to simply and profoundly understand.

Acknowledgment

Appreciation is extended to Maureen Beyer of the Harvey Cushing/John Hay Whitney Medical Library, Yale University.

Bibliography

Alexander, F. G., & Selesnick, S. T. (1966). *The history of psychiatry.* New York: Harper & Row.

Brady, J. P. (1975). *Classics of American psychiatry.* St. Louis: Warren H. Green.

Breggin, P. (1991). *Toxic psychiatry.* New York: St. Martin's Press.

Breggin, P. (1994). *Talking back to Prozac.* New York: St. Martin's Press.

Dain, N. (1994). Reflections on antipsychiatry and stigma in the history of American psychiatry. *Hospital and Community Psychiatry, 45,* 1010–1014.

Danziger, K. (1994). Does the history of psychology have a future? *Theory and Psychology, 4,* 467–484.

Foucault, M. (1965). *Madness and civilization: A history of insanity in the age of reason.* New York: Random House.

Gilman, S. L. (1982). *Seeing the insane.* New York: Wiley.

Ingleby, D. (Ed.). (1980). *Critical psychiatry: The politics of mental health.* New York: Pantheon.

Kevles, D. J. (1985). *In the name of eugenics: Genetics and the uses of human heredity.* New York: Knopf.

Laing, R. D. (1965). *The divided self.* New York: Penguin. (Original work published 1959)

Laing, R. D. (1967). *The politics of experience and the bird of paradise.* New York: Penguin.

Laing, R. D. (1971). *Knots.* New York: Penguin. (Original work published 1970)

Laing, R. D. (1985). *Wisdom, madness and folly: The making of a psychiatrist.* New York: McGraw-Hill.

Leifer, R. (1990). Introduction: The medical model as the ideology of the therapeutic state. *Journal of Mind and Behavior, 11,* 247–258.

Lunt, A. (1990). *Apollo versus the echomaker.* Longmead, GB: Element Books.

Micale, M. S., & Porter, R. (Eds.). (1994). *Discovering the history of psychiatry.* New York: Oxford University Press.

Novick, P. (1988). *That noble dream: The "objectivity question" and the American historical profession.* New York: Cambridge University Press.

Roth, M. S. (1995). Introduction. In R. Cohen & M. S. Roth (Eds.), *History and . . . : Histories within the human sciences* (pp. 1–22). Charlottesville, VA: University Press of Virginia.

Rothman, D. J. (1990). *The discovery of the asylum: Social order and disorder in the new republic* (rev. ed.). Boston: Little, Brown and Company.

Rush, B. (1811). Explanation of the plate of the tranquillizer. *The Philadelphia Medical Museum, 1,* 169–172.

Sedgewick, P. (1981). Michel Foucault: The anti-history of psychiatry. *Psychological Medicine, 11,* 235–248.

Sedgewick, P. (1982). *Psycho politics.* New York: Harper & Row.

Szasz, T. (1961). *The myth of mental illness.* New York: Harper & Row.

Szasz, T. (1988). *Schizophrenia: The sacred symbol of psychiatry* (2nd ed.). Syracuse, NY: Syracuse University Press.

Szasz, T. (1990a). *Ideology and insanity: Essays on the psychiatric dehumanization of man* (rev. ed.). Syracuse, NY: Syracuse University Press.

Szasz, T. (1990b). Law and psychiatry: The problems that will not go away. *Journal of Mind and Behavior, 11,* 557–564.

Szasz, T. (1991). *Ideology and insanity: Essays on the psychiatric dehumanization of man.* Syracuse, NY: Syracuse University Press.

Szasz, T. (1995). The origin of psychiatry: The alienist as nanny for troublesome adults. *History of Psychiatry, 6,* 1–19.

Tantum, D. (1991). The antipsychiatry movement. In G. E. Berrios & H. Freeman (Eds.), *150 years of British psychiatry, 1841-1991* (pp. 333–347). London: Gaskell.

Tolman, C. W. (1995). Psychology and the politics of imagination: Toward a history of the future. *History and Philosophy of Psychology Bulletin, 7* (2), 23–26.

Torrey, E. F. (1992). *Freudian fraud.* New York: Harper Collins.

Vice, J. (1992). *From patients to persons: The psychiatric critiques of Thomas Szasz, Peter Sedgewick and R. D. Laing.* New York: Peter Lang.

GROWTH OF BRANCHES

Lightner Witmer: The First Clinical Psychologist

Paul McReynolds

In the fall of 1888 Lightner Witmer (1867–1956), who was destined to become the first clinical psychologist and the father of the profession of clinical psychology (McReynolds, 1987, 1996, in press), began teaching English and history in the Rugby Academy, a college preparatory school in Philadelphia. Witmer, who was then 21 years old, had recently obtained his AB degree from the University of Pennsylvania. While teaching at Rugby he became particularly interested in one of his students who had unusual verbal difficulties in both speaking and writing, even though he otherwise seemed intelligent enough. Witmer undertook to give the lad special verbal tutoring to enable him to enter college (Witmer, 1907a). This episode was Witmer's first experience in an area somewhat similar to what he would later develop into the field of clinical psychology.

In the fall of 1889, while continuing to teach at Rugby, Witmer entered the graduate program at the University of Pennsylvania with the thought of obtaining a doctorate in political science. During the year, however, he switched to psychology. This was due in large part to the influence of James McKeen Cattell, an important pioneer in the development of mental tests and in the study of individual differences, who had just joined the Pennsylvania faculty as professor of psychology. Cattell selected Witmer as his assistant and set him to work doing research on reaction times, then a major focus in experimental psychology.

In 1891, when Cattell moved to Columbia University, Witmer transferred to the University of Leipzig to study with Wilhelm Wundt. Wundt's laboratory was the most advanced in the world, and a number of Americans, including Cattell, had journeyed to Leipzig to obtain their doctorates under his supervision. In addition to studying with Wundt, Witmer took courses in educational psychology—a fore-

Figure 1 Witmer as a young professor. (Courtesy of the Archives of the University of Pennsylvania)

taste of his later work with children. His dissertation was on the aesthetic values of different geometrical proportions. Returning to Philadelphia as Cattell's successor, Witmer plunged into a series of studies patterned after those of Cattell and Wundt, and set about building up the department.

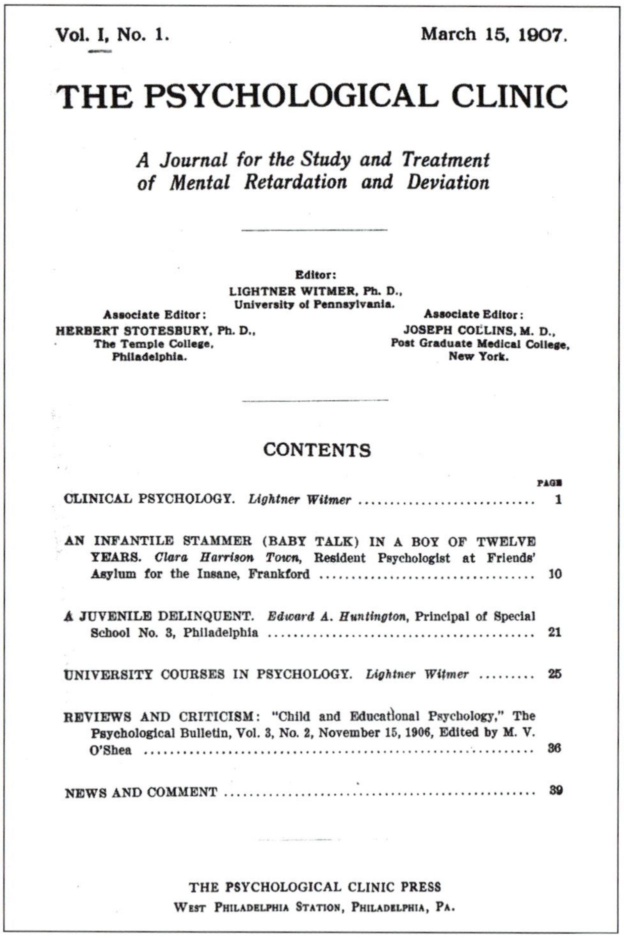

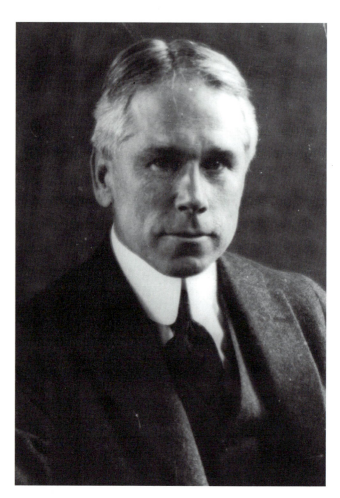

Vol. I, No. 1. March 15, 1907.

THE PSYCHOLOGICAL CLINIC

A Journal for the Study and Treatment of Mental Retardation and Deviation

Editor:
LIGHTNER WITMER, Ph. D.,
University of Pennsylvania.

Associate Editor:
HERBERT STOTESBURY, Ph. D.,
The Temple College,
Philadelphia.

Associate Editor:
JOSEPH COLLINS, M. D.,
Post Graduate Medical College,
New York.

CONTENTS

	PAGE
CLINICAL PSYCHOLOGY. *Lightner Witmer*	1
AN INFANTILE STAMMER (BABY TALK) IN A BOY OF TWELVE YEARS. *Clara Harrison Town*, Resident Psychologist at Friends' Asylum for the Insane, Frankford	10
A JUVENILE DELINQUENT. *Edward A. Huntington*, Principal of Special School No. 3, Philadelphia	21
UNIVERSITY COURSES IN PSYCHOLOGY. *Lightner Witmer*	25
REVIEWS AND CRITICISM: "Child and Educational Psychology," The Psychological Bulletin, Vol. 3, No. 2, November 15, 1906, Edited by M. V. O'Shea	36
NEWS AND COMMENT	39

THE PSYCHOLOGICAL CLINIC PRESS
WEST PHILADELPHIA STATION, PHILADELPHIA, PA.

Figure 2 Cover of first issue of *The Psychological Clinic.*

Figure 3 Witmer in mid-career.

At this point Witmer was strongly committed to basic experimental psychology, and indeed this orientation persisted for some time: for example, in 1902 he published an experimental text. Nevertheless, his interests were gradually changing as they moved toward a focus more concerned with the behaviors of whole persons, especially young persons, than with particular human capacities, such as reaction times. In 1893 the University began offering special Saturday and evening courses for public school teachers, and Witmer was intimately involved in these. In 1894 he began offering a seminar in child psychology.

The epochal year in Witmer's personal transition, and in the history of clinical psychology, was 1896. In March one of the elementary school teachers in his class for teachers brought to him the problem of one of her students, a 14-year-old boy who had unusual and unexplained difficulties in learning to spell, despite apparently having adequate intelligence. Both this boy and the youth noted in the opening paragraph were most likely instances of dyslexia, though that diagnosis was unknown at the time. The latter problem boy is considered by historians to be the first case in the history of clinical psychology. In taking on the case Witmer felt, as he wrote later, that "It appeared to me that if psychology was worth anything to me or to others it should be able to assist . . . in a retarded case of this kind" (1907a, p. 4). He worked intensively with the boy, inventing treatment methods as he went along, and brought about notable improvement. Some years later he described the case in detail (Witmer, 1907b), referring to the boy by the pseudonym of Charles Gilman.

Though Gilman was the first child seen by Witmer in 1896, this should not be thought of as an isolated event. Over 20 additional cases were examined during the year, including both boys and girls, with a variety of presenting problems. Most of the referrals were from schools, but at least one, and probably more, were from medical settings. Parents were also involved.

In November Witmer (1896) published a paper

Figure 4 The Witmer School in Devon, Pennsylvania.

titled "Practical work in psychology" in the journal *Pediatrics*, with the word "Practical" reflecting his growing view that scientific psychology should be useful. Then in December, at the fifth annual Meeting of the American Psychology Association in Boston, he gave a paper further espousing the role of practical approaches in psychology. It was in this presentation, of which we have only an abstract (Witmer, 1897), that Witmer first used the term "psychological clinic," and it is this presentation that is generally taken as announcing the beginning of clinical psychology.

During the next several years Witmer continued his clinical work, but did not immediately increase its volume. For one thing, he did not yet feel sufficiently competent in clinical work—after all, he had had no actual training in the area and was forced to learn by self-guided experience. In addition, he was occupied with directing the laboratory and organizing the departmental offerings, including the graduate program. His most prominent graduate during this period was Edwin Twitmyer, who would later pioneer the treatment of speech disorders.

By 1907, at the age of 40, Witmer felt ready to enlarge his clinic and to formally propose a new profession (McReynolds, 1987; Reisman, 1991). Acting on the basis of a sizable private

contribution, he founded a journal, *The Psychological Clinic*, and in its lead article, titled simply "Clinical Psychology" (Witmer, 1907a), he set forth the dimensions of the new discipline. "I have borrowed the word 'clinical' from medicine" he wrote, "because it is the best term I can find to indicate the character of the method I deem necessary for this work. . . . Whether the subject be a child or an adult, the examination and treatment may be conducted and their results expressed in the terms of the clinical method" (Witmer, 1907a, pp. 8, 9).

With this move Witmer's most revolutionary work was done, but it would be an error to assume that the rest of his career was routine and without drama. Believing that some cases require supervised residential treatment, in 1908 Witmer established a special school at Wallingford, Pennsylvania. This facility was a forerunner of the much larger Witmer School in Devon and represented his entry into private practice, the first clinical psychologist to fill such a role. During the ensuing years his graduate program at the University of Pennsylvania became the major center for the training of clinical psychologists, and Witmer's students carried the word to institutions around the country.

Witmer devised two psychological tests—the Witmer Formboard and the Witmer Cylinders. These instruments, which were widely utilized in the Clinic

Figure 5 Witmer Formboard test.

Figure 6 Witmer Cylinders Test.

and to some extent elsewhere, particularly the Formboard, were designed to provide opportunities to observe the child's mental processes. In general, however, Witmer cautioned against over-dependence on any tests, including his own.

Witmer was a highly principled and extremely outspoken person. He was frequently engaged in controversies defending causes that he considered important. The two most famous of these were his severe criticism, in 1909, of William James, whom he took to task for James's commitment to spiritualism and other positions that Witmer considered unscientific, and his stirring defense, in 1915, of Scott Nearing, a University of Pennsylvania faculty member who was dismissed by the trustees—a decision which Witmer considered a violation of Nearing's academic freedom. And during the latter half of his career Witmer was something of a gadfly challenging society to improve the welfare of its children.

Witmer's Psychological Clinic, in its full development, was a large facility, including PhD level psychologists, social workers, recorders, diagnostic teachers, graduate students, and medical consultants, and it dealt with thousands of cases over the years. In addition to the main clinic, there were eventually three satellite clinics: a speech disorders clinic, under Twitmyer; a vocational guidance clinic, under Morris Viteles, a Witmer graduate; and a clinic for college students and adults, under Robert Brotemarkle, another Witmer product. In running the clinic, Witmer was a demanding and sometimes brusque and difficult taskmaster. However, he was

respected, admired, and to a considerable extent, idolized by many of his clinical students and staff.

As a clinician Witmer taught his students the importance of direct observation of the subject. As already implied, he was primarily a child clinical psychologist, though he did see some adult cases, and of course many parents. Problems presented by children seen in the Clinic were as diverse as, and quite similar to, those represented in contemporary child clinics. Witmer was very cautious in coming to diagnostic judgments and strongly emphasized the importance of helping, as opposed to merely labeling, the child. His main clinical method was in the giving of direct advice, in order to

Figure 7 Three members of the Clinic staff in front of the Clinic entrance (ca. 1923) (l. to r. Helen Backus, Karl G. Miller, Alice Jones).

Figure 8 President Gates of the University of Pennsylvania presenting Witmer with commemorative book, *Clinical Psychology,* to mark the 35th anniversary of the Clinic.

the 35th anniversary of the founding of the Psychological Clinic. Many of Witmer's former students contributed chapters to a volume, *Clinical Psychology* (Brotemarkle, 1931), that was presented to him by the University's President. In 1937, on the occasion of his retirement, the University honored him with the degree of Doctor of Science. Witmer died in 1956, long after the profession that he established had become part of the modern scene.

Witmer is rightly remembered as the founder of clinical psychology. He established the first psychological

structure a child's environment. In working with children and parents he was gentle, but also firm and authoritative.

In the 1920s Witmer became very interested in gifted children. In this context he proposed that intelligence should be defined as the ability to solve new problems (Witmer, 1922). He felt strongly that IQ tests, then extremely popular, were overused and overinterpreted, and he argued vehemently against the tendency to reify the concept of IQ.

By temperament Witmer was neither a diplomat nor an organizer. Further, his interests were primarily in the role of direct service. Thus it was that during the 1920s the impetus in the movement that he had founded and nurtured was largely provided by the second generation of clinical psychologists, located in dozens of psychological clinics that by then had grown up around the country. Witmer's reputation suffered, too, because he seemed quite out of step with the two major themes that had come to the fore in clinical psychology—the strong emphasis on IQ testing and the dynamic approach as espoused by Freud. However, Witmer's positions on these issues appear, in retrospect, to have been prescient of the views that many psychologists would eventually subscribe to.

In 1931 the psychology faculty at the University of Pennsylvania arranged a special occasion to mark

Figure 9 Witmer in his later career.

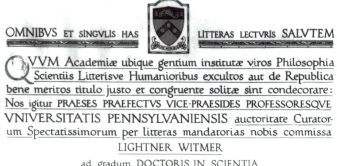

Figure 10 On his retirement in 1937, the University of Pennsylvania bestowed an honorary Doctor of Science degree on Witmer.

clinic—indeed, the very idea of such a clinic was his; he delineated, defined, and named the new profession, and trained most of its earliest members; he founded and edited the first journal in the new discipline; and he himself practiced, in both academic and private settings, as a clinical psychologist. The chief thing that he did not do that typically heralds the development of a new professional emphasis was to set up and play a leadership role in a national organization—this task, as implied above, was left to other clinical psychologists.

While it is conceivable that someone else would have founded clinical psychology if Witmer had not done so, this is by no means certain. And even if so, the new profession would probably have had a different name, possibly "consulting psychology," and might well have been less scientifically oriented.

Bibliography

Brotemarkle, R. (1931). *Clinical psychology: Essays in honor of Lightner Witmer.* Philadelphia: University of Pennsylvania Press.

McReynolds, P. (1987). Lightner Witmer: Little-known founder of clinical psychology. *American Psychologist, 42,* 849–858.

McReynolds, P. (1996). Lightner Witmer: A centennial tribute. *American Psychologist, 51,* 237–240.

McReynolds, P. (in press). Lightner Witmer: Father of clinical psychology. In G. G. Kimble, C.A. Boneau, & M. Wertheimer (Eds.), *Portraits of pioneers in psychology: Vol. II.* Washington: American Psychological Association/Hillsdale, NJ: Erlbaum.

Reisman, J. M. (1991). *A history of clinical psychology* (2nd ed.). New York: Hemisphere.

Witmer, L. (1896). Practical work in psychology. *Pediatrics, 2,* 462–471.

Witmer, L. (1897). The organization of practical work in psychology (Abstract of paper presented at the meeting of the American Psychological Association. Boston, Dec. 29–30, 1896). *Psychological Review, 4,* 116–117.

Witmer, L. (1902). *Analytical psychology: A practical manual for colleges and normal schools.* Boston: Ginn & Co.

Witmer, L. (1907a). Clinical psychology. *The Psychological Clinic, 1,* 1–9.

Witmer, L. (1907b). A case of chronic bad spelling—Amnesia visualis verbalis due to arrest of post-natal development. *The Psychological Clinic, 1,* 53–54.

Witmer, L. (1922). What is intelligence and who has it? *The Scientific Monthly, 15,* 57–67.

Hugo Münsterberg: Pioneer of Applied Psychology

Helmut E. Lück
Wolfgang G. Bringmann

Wilhelm Wundt (1832–1920) believed throughout much of his life that the application of psychological principles and methods to the solution of everyday problems was premature (Wundt, 1910). Nonetheless, a number of his best-known students made important contributions to the nascent field of applied psychology (e.g., James McKeen Cattell, Willy Hellpach, Ernst Meumann, Hugo Münsterberg, Emil Kraepelin, and Lightner Witmer). Among these pioneers, none deserves our attention more than Hugo Münsterberg, the original and controversial German-American psychologist.

Münsterberg's Life

Hugo Münsterberg (1863–1916), a native of the Prussian port city of Danzig (now Gdansk, Poland), studied psychology under Wundt at Leipzig University during the years 1882–1885. In addition, he received his MD from Heidelberg University in 1887. After Münsterberg had taught for some time at Freiburg University in Southwest Germany, William James (1842–1910) recruited the 29-year-old Münsterberg, who at that time was untenured professor (M. Münsterberg, 1922). James wrote to Münsterberg (as cited in M. Münsterberg, 1922) that he wanted Münsterberg:

> to take charge of the Psychological Laboratory and the higher instruction in that subject in Harvard University for three years [1892–1895] at a salary of say 3,000 dollars. . . . The situation is this: We are the best university in America and we must lead in psychology. I, at the age of 50, disliking laboratory work, naturally . . . am certainly not the kind of stuff to make a first-rate director. . . . We could get younger men here who would be safe enough, but we need something more than a safe man, we need a man of genius if possible. (p. 33)

After returning to the USA from an extended German sabbatical, Münsterberg was given the promised permanent professorship at Harvard. Following the model of Wundt's Leipzig Laboratory, during the next eight years Münsterberg developed an exemplary program in experimental psychology,

Figure 1 Hugo Münsterberg and family ca. 1870.

Figure 2 Münsterberg at 1894 Harvard commencement.

HARVARD PSYCHOLOGICAL LABORATORY

Figure 3 Floor plan of Harvard Laboratory ca. 1905.

founded his own journal, was elected the seventh president of the American Psychological Association—of which he had been a founding member—

Figure 4 Portrait of Münsterberg (1916).

and last but not least, opened a new Psychological Laboratory on the top floor of the newly built Emerson Hall on the Harvard Campus.

Münsterberg's goal was to use his international contacts to facilitate communication between scholars from all over the world. His first success in this area was achieved by organizing an "International Congress of the Arts and Sciences" during the 1904 World's Fair in St. Louis. In 1908, he helped with the establishment of the first "American Institute" in Berlin in hopes of strengthening cultural and economic relations between the United States and the German Empire. In an early exchange between Berlin University and professors from America, Münsterberg offered the first academic course on "Applied Psychology" during the 1910–1911 academic year.

He was an ardent German patriot and a prominent political leader of German immigrants in the United States. His extensive private papers in the Manuscript Division of the Public Library in Boston reveal extensive personal and written contacts with American political leaders, including Presidents Theodore Roosevelt (1858–1919), William Howard Taft (1857–1930), and Woodrow Wilson (1856–1924). After the beginning of World War I in 1914, Münsterberg actively opposed the entry of the United States into the war. Consequently, he was vilified as "Professor Hugo Monsterbug" or "Baron Munchausen" by many of the same newspapers which had praised and popularized his accomplishments as an applied psychologist. Disheartened by accusations that he was a secret agent for the German government, he died from a heart attack on December 16, 1916, at the beginning of his "Nine O'Clock Lecture" at Radcliffe College, the women's branch of Harvard University. He was only 59 years old. Max Dessoir (1867–1947), Münsterberg's former colleague at Berlin University, summed up the life of his friend in a belated obituary (1918): "In him was a burning life. His fire was extinguished by his death and only a glimmer remains of his work" (p. V–XVIII).

BOOKS BY HUGO MÜNSTERBERG

Psychology and Life
pp. 286, Boston, 1899
Grundzuge der Psychologie
pp. 505, Leipzig, 1900
American Traits
pp. 235, Boston, 1902
Die Amerikaner
pp. 502 and 349, Berlin, 1904 (Rev. 1912)
Principles of Art Education
pp. 118, New York, 1905
The Eternal Life
pp. 72, Boston, 1905
Science and Idealism
pp. 71, Boston, 1906
Philosophie der Werte
pp. 486, Leipzig, 1907
On the Witness Stand
pp. 269, New York, 1908
Aus Deutsch-Amerika
pp. 245, Berlin, 1909
The Eternal Values
pp. 436, Boston, 1909
Psychotherapy
pp. 401, New York, 1909
Psychology and the Teacher
pp. 330, New York, 1910
American Problems
pp. 220, New York, 1910
Psychologie und Wirtschaftsleben
pp. 192, Leipzig, 1912
Vocation and Learning
pp. 289, St Louis, 1912
Psychology and Industrial Efficiency
pp. 321, Boston, 1913
American Patriotism
pp. 262, New York, 1913
Grundzuge der Psychotechnik
pp. 767, Leipzig, 1914
Psychology and Social Sanity
pp. 320, New York, 1914
Psychology, General and Applied
pp. 488, New York, 1914
The War and America
pp. 210, New York, 1914
The Peace and America
pp. 276, New York, 1915
The Photoplay
pp. 233, New York, 1916
Tomorrow
pp. 279, New York, 1916

1868

Figure 5 List of books by Münsterberg.

Münsterberg's Psychotechnology

Münsterberg's publication record (Hildebrandt & Scheerer, 1990) contains 32 books and 61 major articles, ranging from a pseudonymous volume of lyrics (Hugo Terberg, 1897) to original books about topics in philosophy, sociology, experimental and applied psychology, and even the psychology of motion pictures (1916). Today, only his books on industrial psychology continue to be quoted.

The term "psychotechnology" (German: Psychotechnik) was popularized by Münsterberg, although it was invented by William Stern (1871–1938). Münsterberg conceptualized the field of psychotechnology as the science of the application of psychology "in the service of cultural responsibility" (1912, p. 1). Combining the methods of the classical natural sciences with the experimental traditions of Fechner, Helmholtz, and Wundt, industrial psychology became one of the first fields in which the new science could demonstrate its practical usefulness. From early on, the United States provided ample opportunities for documenting the practical value of the new psychology. Many new universities included academic courses in industrial psychology in their programs, which primarily focused on improving the efficiency of industrial workers at mass production.

The program of the American industrial engineer Frederick Winslow Taylor (1856–1915) ushered in a new era of industrial organization and productivity. Psychologists supported these reforms by the development of personnel selection techniques and by time and motion studies aimed at making workers more productive. At the request of the transportation industry, Münsterberg developed the first aptitude test for streetcar operators as early as 1910. Following the example of Walter Dill Scott (1869–1955), Münsterberg studied the effects of advertisements empirically by investigating the relationship between repetition and the recollection of ads. This research was obviously influenced by the memory research of Hermann Ebbinghaus (1850–1909) rather than the naïve drive theories favored by Scott (1908). Münsterberg's view of industrial psychology is clear. Its problems stem from everyday life, and its theories are borrowed from general psychology or, if necessary, they are tailor-made. The methodology comes from the sciences because: "[We] analyze and measure . . . mental events . . . just like physicists and . . . chemists" (Lysinski, 1923, p. 6).

Looking back on Hugo Münsterberg's research activities—especially his sensitivity to practical problems and his remarkable organizational talent—one is tempted to conclude that he developed a uniquely American form of psychology. His impact was also rather strong among businessmen and public school teachers in Germany, but less so among his German academic colleagues. Münsterberg's psychology gained independence from philosophy during the first decade of the 20th century, as is illustrated in the following fitting anecdote: According to Wilhelm Ostwald (1853–1935), the German physical chemist and Nobel Prize winner, Münsterberg, in his 1905 inaugural address for the newly-built psychological laboratory stressed

> that the lower floor [of Emerson Hall] was to be dedicated exclusively to philosophy and the upper floor to psychology, and that he regarded it as his duty to carefully separate the two disciplines. At this time, an American colleague suggested sarcastically that he hoped that the field of logic would not be restricted to the lower floor, but also [be allowed] to benefit experimental research in psychology [on the top floor of the new building]. (Ostwald, 1927, p. 306)

Bibliography

Dessoir, M. (1918). Zur Erinnerung an Hugo Münsterberg. In: H. Münsterberg: *Grundzüge der Psychologie* (2nd ed., pp. v–xviii). Leipzig: Barth.

Hildebrandt, H., & Eckardt, E. (Eds.). (1990). *Hugo Münsterberg. Frühe Schriften zur Psychologie.* Berlin: Deutscher Verlag der Wissenschaften.

Lysinski, E. (1923). *Psychologie des Betriebes. Beiträge zur Betriebsorganisation.* Berlin: Industrieverlag Spaetze & Linde.

Münsterberg, H. (1912). *Die Psychologie und das Wirtschaftsleben.* Leipzig: Barth.

Münsterberg, H. (1916). *The photoplay. A psychological study.* New York: Appleton.

Münsterberg, H. (1918a). *Grundzüge der Psychotechnik.* Leipzig: Barth.

Münsterberg, H. (1918b). *Grundzüge der Psychologie,* (2nd ed.). Leipzig: Barth.

Münsterberg, M. (1922). *Hugo Münsterberg.* New York: Appleton.

Ostwald, W. (1927). *Lebenslinien. Eine Selbstbiographie* (Part 2). Berlin: Klasing.

Scott, W. D. (1908). *The psychology of advertising.* Boston: Maynard.

Terberg, H. [Hugo Münsterberg] (1897). *Verse.* Großenhain: Baumert & Ronge.

Wundt, Wilhelm M. (1910). Über reine und angewandte Psychologie. *Psychologische Studien, 5,* 1–47.

The Origins of the Psychology of Testimony

Siegfried Ludwig Sporer

The last couple of decades have witnessed the coming of age of legal psychology as a boundary discipline at the interface of psychology and the law (see Wrightsman, Nietzel, & Fortune, 1994). Besides the numerous studies on the American jury, issues of eyewitness identification (Sporer, Malpass, & Koehnken, 1996) and the reliability and credibility of children's statements (Dent & Flin, 1992) have also received a great deal of attention. What has often been overlooked, however, is the fact that at the turn of this century a "psychology of testimony" had flourished in Europe (Sporer, 1982).

This psychology of testimony was a major area of experimental "applied" psychology that attempted to distinguish itself as an independent force within the "new psychology." This aspect of the new experimental psychology has generally been ignored in the standard literature on the history of psychology—for example, in such works as Boring (1950), Hehlmann (1967), Leahey (1980), and Murphy (1949); however, noteworthy exceptions are Ash and Geuter (1985) and Dorsch (1963). In order to close this gap in the historiography of psychology and to put the recent efforts to study the psychology of testimony into perspective, we should become more thoroughly aware of earlier attempts to struggle with these very problems. Before reviewing some of the early empirical work and its impact on the legal profession, I will briefly sketch the historical background from which the psychology of testimony grew.

Throughout the history of law, back to antiquity, one finds codified laws on who is and who is not to be considered fit to give testimony before a court of law. Generally, most of these laws excluded women and children under the age of 14, as incapable of responsibly taking an oath (e.g., the *Corpus Juris*

William Stern

Figure 1 Portrait of William Stern (1871–1938).

Canonici or the *Corpus Juris* of emperor Justinianus). Exclusionary rules of this sort are found up to the 19th century (see Bender, 1987, and Undeutsch, 1967, for further examples). Similarly, textbooks and monographs on criminal law and the law of evidence espoused rather negative views regarding the credibility of the testimony given by women and children and backed them up with psychological arguments. (Examples are found in Brauer, 1841, [as cited in Hellwig, 1910]; Henke, 1838; and Mittermaier, 1834. A more balanced view is presented by Gross, 1893, 1898; Sporer, 1982; and Undeutsch, 1967). Until the beginning of this century, many of these writings also reflected the socio-cultural biases against women and children in the belletristic, popular-psychological, and medical literature of that time (Sporer, 1982; Undeutsch, 1967). These trends made up the general legal and cultural background from which the psychology of testimony was to emerge.

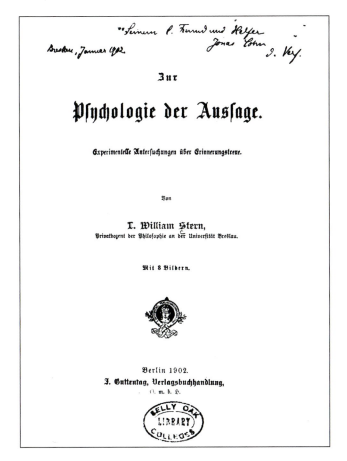

Figure 2 Title page of Stern's *Psychology of Testimony* (1902). This article, which was published in a legal journal, was dedicated by Stern to his "Friend and Helper," the German philosopher Jonas Cohn.

The beginning of the 20th century marks the advent of empirical investigations into the psychology of testimony. The idea of an experimental investigation into this area was first proposed by Alfred Binet (1857–1911) in *La suggestibilité* (1900). Binet was also the first to carry out actual experiments on the influence of various types of suggestive questioning on the error rate in school children's answers (Binet, 1900; cf. also Wolf, 1973).

Although Binet noted in passing the potential implications of this type of work for a "practical science of testimony" (1900, p. 285), it was Louis William Stern (1871–1938) in Breslau who launched the psychology of testimony [Psychologie der Aussage] as a major field of experimental investigation (Stern, 1902). Stern edited the *Contributions to the Psychology of Testimony* (1903–1906) as a publication outlet for the upsurge in research in this new area, and in 1908, he and Otto Lipmann expanded the contributions into the German *Journal for Applied Psychology*.

In these studies, quite a variety of topics were tackled and quite a variety of methodologies were employed (for a review of methods, see Lipmann, 1935). Nevertheless, at the risk of oversimplification, at least two major experimental paradigms can be distinguished: In the picture test (Stern, 1902; Lipmann, 1935), the subjects (often children) were supposed to spontaneously report on a briefly exposed picture (e.g., the famous "Farm Kitchen"—see Figure 3), or to answer a series of questions from an interrogation list. The accuracy of recall was measured as a function of personal variables such as sex, age, and intelligence. The picture test offered all the advantages of maximum laboratory control but suffered with regard to the principle of closeness to life—today, we would call this external or ecological validity.

The second paradigm, the so-called event test, reality experiment, or field experiment favored ecological validity over experimental rigor. Typically, an unsuspecting audience was confronted with a staged dramatic event, and later asked to write a report or to answer a series of questions on the incident (Jaffa, 1903). Soon, experiments of this type were quite popular with psychologists and legal scholars, and today this event methodology is still being used for scientific as well as classroom demonstration purposes (Sporer et al., 1996).

It would be impossible in the space available here to summarize the dozens of studies carried out on the psychology of testimony during the first two decades of this century (see Sporer, 1982). Many of them were published not only in psychological journals, but also in legal journals and monographs as well. Unlike research conducted in the United States, where Münsterberg's pretentious collection of essays, *On the Witness Stand* (1908), was subject

Figures 3, 4 Pictures of a "Farm Kitchen," and "Bunny Birthday Party," used in Stern's eyewitness research. After research subjects were shown the pictures for a short period of time, they were questioned about the respective content of the pictures. Both "factual" and "leading" questions were employed by the examiner.

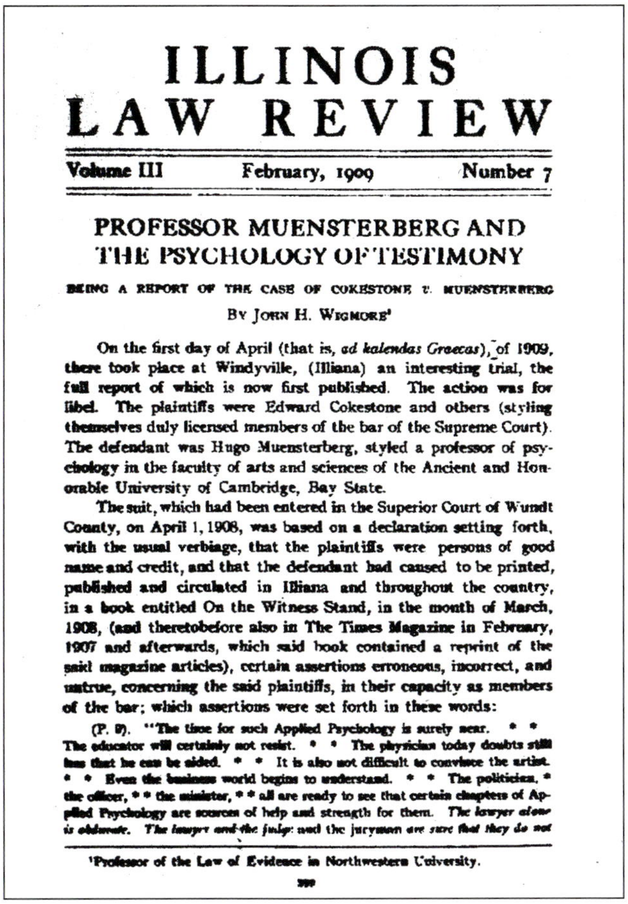

ILLINOIS LAW REVIEW

Volume III | February, 1909 | Number 7

PROFESSOR MUENSTERBERG AND THE PSYCHOLOGY OF TESTIMONY

BEING A REPORT OF THE CASE OF COKESTONE v. MUENSTERBERG

By John H. Wigmore[1]

On the first day of April (that is, *ad kalendas Graecas*), of 1909, there took place at Windyville, (Illiana) an interesting trial, the full report of which is now first published. The action was for libel. The plaintiffs were Edward Cokestone and others (styling themselves duly licensed members of the bar of the Supreme Court). The defendant was Hugo Muensterberg, styled a professor of psychology in the faculty of arts and sciences of the Ancient and Honorable University of Cambridge, Bay State.

The suit, which had been entered in the Superior Court of Wundt County, on April 1, 1908, was based on a declaration setting forth, with the usual verbiage, that the plaintiffs were persons of good name and credit, and that the defendant had caused to be printed, published and circulated in Illiana and throughout the country, in a book entitled On the Witness Stand, in the month of March, 1908, (and theretobefore also in The Times Magazine in February, 1907 and afterwards, which said book contained a reprint of the said magazine articles), certain assertions erroneous, incorrect, and untrue, concerning the said plaintiffs, in their capacity as members of the bar; which assertions were set forth in these words:

(P. 9). "The time for such Applied Psychology is surely near. * * The educator will certainly not resist. * * The physician today doubts still less that he can be aided. * * It is also not difficult to convince the artist. * * Even the business world begins to understand. * * The politician, * the officer, * * the minister, * * all are ready to see that certain chapters of Applied Psychology are sources of help and strength for them. *The lawyer alone is obdurate. The lawyer and the judge* and the juryman *are sure that they do not*

[1]Professor of the Law of Evidence in Northwestern University.

399

Figure 5 Title page of John Henry Wigmore's (Dean of the Northwestern University Law School) satirical critique of Hugo Münsterberg's *On the Witness Stand* (1908).

to scathing attacks (e.g., Wigmore, 1909; see Figure 5), the work of Stern, Lipmann, Marbe, Claparède, and many others did have some impact on the legal system (Undeutsch, 1967), although not all legal scholars accepted some of their over-generalizations uncritically. Despite the original enthusiasm over the application of psychology to the law, the gap between the contrived nature of the studies conducted and the intricate complexity of courtroom reality led to the ultimate decline of these promising beginnings. It would seem that a review of this history is particularly relevant today since many of the same issues appear to be surfacing once again.

Bibliography

Ash, M. G., & Geuter, U. (Eds.). (1985). *Geschichte der deutschen Psychologie im 20. Jahrhundert.* Opladen: Westdeutscher Verlag.

Bender, H. U. (1987). *Merkmalskombinationen in Aussagen.* Tübingen: J. C. B. Mohr.

Binet, A. (1900). *La suggestibilité.* Paris: Scheicher Frères.

Boring, E. G. (1950). *A history of experimental psychology.* New York: Appleton.

Dent, H., & Flin, R. (Eds.). (1992). *Children as witnesses.* Chichester: Wiley.

Dorsch, F. (1963). *Geschichte und Probleme der angewandten Psychologie.* Bern & Stuttgart: Huber.

Gross, H. (1893). *Handbuch für Untersuchungsrichter.* Graz: Teuschner & Lubensky.

Gross, H. (1898). *Criminalpsychologie.* Graz: Teuschner & Lubensky.

Hehlmann, W. (1967). *Geschichte der Psychologie.* Stuttgart: Kröner.

Hellwig, A. (1910). Historisches zur Aussagepsychologie. *Archiv für Kriminal-Anthropologie und Kriminalistik, 36,* 323–341.

Henke, E. (1838). *Handbuch des Criminalrechts und der Criminalpolitik.* Vierter Teil, Berlin: Nicolai.

Jaffa, S. (1903). Ein psychologisches Experiment im kriminalistischen Seminar der Universität Berlin. In W. Stern (Ed.), *Beiträge zur Psychologie der Aussage* (Vol. 2, pp. 79–99). Leipzig: Barth.

Leahey, T. H. (1980). *A history of psychology.* Englewood Cliffs, NJ: Prentice Hall.

Lipmann, O. (1935). Methoden der Aussagepsychologie. In E. Abderhalden (Ed.), *Handbuch der biologischen Arbeitsmethoden* (Section VI, Part C, II, 2, Vol. 3, pp. 967–1056). Berlin: Urban & Schwarzenberg.

Mittermaier, C. J. A. (1834). *Die Lehre vom Beweise im deutschen Strafprozesse.* Darmstadt: Heyer.

Münsterberg, H. (1908). *On the witness stand.* New York: Doubleday, Page.

Murphy, G. (1949). *Historical introduction to modern psychology.* New York: Harcourt, Brace & World.

Sporer, S. L. (1982). A brief history of the psychology of testimony. *Current Psychological Reviews, 2,* 323–340.

Sporer, S. L., Malpass, R. S., & Koehnken, G. (Eds.). (1996). *Psychological issues in eyewitness identification.* Mahwah, NJ: Lawrence Erlbaum.

Stern, W. (1902). Zur Psychologie der Aussage. *Zeitschrift für die gesamte Strafrechtswissenschaft, 22,* 315–370.

Stern, W. (1903–1906). *Beiträge zur Psychologie der Aussage* (2 Vols.). Leipzig: Barth. (1. Folge 1903–04; 2. Folge 1905–06)

Undeutsch, U. (1967). Beurteilung der Glaubhaftigkeit von Zeugenaussagen. In U. Undeutsch (Ed.), *Handbuch der Psychologie* (Vol. 11, pp. 26–181). Göttingen: Hogrefe.

Wigmore, J. (1909). Professor Münsterberg and the psychology of testimony. *Illinois Law Review, 3,* 399–445.

Wolf, T. H. (1973). *Alfred Binet.* Chicago: University of Chicago Press.

Wrightsman, L. S., Nietzel, M. T., & Fortune, W. H. (1994). *Psychology and the legal system* (3rd ed.). Pacific Grove, CA: Brooks/Cole.

Psychotechnics

Peter van Drunen

In the history of applied psychology, testing has always played an important role. In the United States and Great Britain intelligence tests provided the central "paradigm" for psychological testing. On the continent of Europe, however, a markedly different tradition emerged after the First World War. There, vocational testing by means of sophisticated apparatus and intriguing manual procedures dominated the field. The technical flavor of this tradition was reflected in the term commonly used for it in Europe: psychotechnics.

The origins of vocational testing in Europe can be traced to the first decades of this century, when psychologists in various countries started using experimental apparatus for purposes of personnel selection. Prominent among these early pioneers was Hugo Münsterberg, a German psychologist working at Harvard University. Münsterberg's work in personnel selection was part of his overall agenda for developing applied psychology or "psychotechnics," as he preferred to call it. From 1911 on, Münsterberg was engaged in devising tests for the selection of streetcar drivers, typists, and other "new" vocations—attempts which became widely known through his seminal work *Psychology and Industrial Efficiency* (1912/1913).

The First World War provided the opportunity for the large-scale application of vocational testing. New means of transportation and communication created a demand for highly trained personnel such as pilots, drivers, telephone operators, and telegraphers. In Germany, France, and other countries, psychologists began to offer their services to develop selection procedures for these new occupations. Following Münsterberg's example, they tried to apply the procedures and instruments developed in experimental psychology to the assessment of vocational aptitude. This is illustrated in Figure 1, which shows the use of the kymographion in selecting pilots for the French Air Force. This test assessed the "stability of the nervous system." The experimenter unexpectedly fired a gun, and the effects on the subject's breathing, heartbeat and trembling of the hands were registered with the apparatus (on the table).

Figure 1 Psychotechnical assessment of French pilots during the First World War. (Archives of Dutch Psychology)

Figure 2 Psychotechnical assessment of female factory workers at the Philips Psychotechnical Laboratory at Eindhoven in the Netherlands. (Philips Company Archives)

Like war-time intelligence testing in the United States, this military use of test techniques in Europe paved the way for the rapid spread of testing practices after the First World War. Beginning in 1918, a number of large companies started so-called "psychotechnical laboratories" for the selection of personnel. Although written tests were used as well, there was a heavy emphasis on the use of apparatus and intricate devices for testing manual dexterity.

This preference for apparatus tests stemmed partly from the impression of precision and scientific objectivity which they conveyed. As stated in a popular handbook of that time: "Founding psychotechnics on written tests only implies the impossibility of a further development of psychology; . . . what one can and wants to measure from the outside should be measured with apparatus" (Giese, 1925, p. 786; my translation).

Gradually, the concept of psychotechnics became associated primarily with the use of apparatus tests for the purpose of personnel selection and assessment (Figure 2). In the early twenties, various companies started selling psychotechnical testing equipment with impressive names such as "energograph" and "kinematometer." Leading psychotechnicians, however, tended to frown upon the use of such ready-made equipment. They took pride in constructing their own devices, which were based on their own ideas regarding the psychological requirements of various vocations and the most suitable instruments for measuring them. A sophisticated and internationally reputed example was the "test system for drivers," which was developed in the early thirties at the Psychotechnical Laboratory of the Dutch Postal Services by psychologist Rebecca Biegel. This system consisted of seven tests, ranging from the measurement of reaction-time to the assessment of "sensitivity to movement"

and "considered action" (Figure 3). The left illustration shows an instrument for assessing "sensitivity to movement." This device consisted of two handles connected by a belt. The candidate had to follow the movements of the experimenter as closely as possible. This test was based on the idea that a driver had to be sensitive to the movements of his car in order to react appropriately. The right picture contains a device for assessing "considered action," also known as "candle-test." Eight candles were placed at the top of the device, each of which was connected by a winding rubber hose to a squeeze-bulb (below). After the experimenter had lighted one of the candles, the candidate had to blow it out as quickly as possible, by tracing the connected squeeze-bulb and squeezing it.

Judging from articles appearing in the general press, this use of sophisticated equipment contributed significantly to the reputation of psychotechnics as a solid and scientific enterprise. Psy-

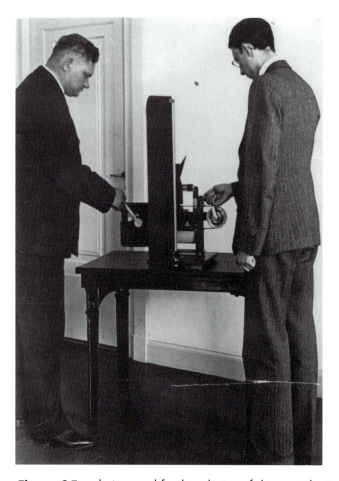 

Figure 3 Two devices used for the selection of drivers at the Psychotechnical Laboratory of the Dutch Postal Services (ca. 1933). (Archives of Dutch Psychology)

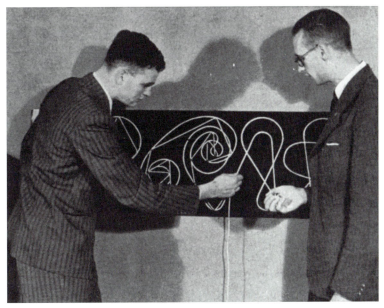

Figure 4 Top, Wiggly-Block test (KLM Airlines, ca. 1950). Above, String-board test at the Psychotechnical Laboratory of the Free University, Amsterdam (ca. 1940). (Archives of Dutch Psychology)

chologists themselves, however, gradually grew dissatisfied with what they considered to be a one-sided emphasis on exact measurement. In their view, vocational aptitude was not a matter of elementary capacities only, but also depended heavily on personality characteristics. Proper assessment of those aspects of vocational aptitude called for psychological observation and interpretation, rather than mechanical measurement. This "person-oriented" approach resulted in a gradual shift to

new kinds of tests which combined the measurement of achievement with psychological observation. Examples of these tests are the Wiggly-Block and the so-called String-board test (Figure 4). The Wiggly-Block test was an observational test, making use of a wooden block which was divided lengthwise into nine or sixteen uneven pieces. After the subject had been given the opportunity to study the block, it was disassembled by the experimenter. The subject was instructed to re-assemble the block while being closely observed by the experimenter. Points of observation included the manner in which the pieces were ordered, the sequence in block-assembly, and the reaction to mistakes or overall failure. In turn, the String-Board test required a subject to guide a string around a number of nails following a line drawn on the test board. These tests were used to assess spatial intelligence and motor skills, respectively; but in addition, close attention was paid to the personal work-style of the candidate. For example, did the candidate use a systematic approach to the problem at hand or was the work performed in a roundabout way? Did the candidate remain calm when problems occurred or were there signs of frustration?

The introduction of observational tests entailed a change in the professional role of the psychologist as well. In the early years of psychotechnics, the psychotechnicians more or less patterned themselves after engineers (in fact, many of the early psychotechnicians had a background in engineering rather than psychology). They considered their primary task to be the development of instruments which would enable them to assess vocational aptitude as exactly as possible. With the advent of observational tests, the emphasis shifted from the construction of instruments to the diagnostic qualities of the psychologist. In other words, a clinical role-model was introduced, as exemplified by the words of Dutch psychologist Van Lennep: "the psychologist is his own most important instrument" (1949, p. 14). So the personal qualities of the psychologist, as well as

those of the candidate being examined, were brought into the picture. This person-oriented approach would remain in vogue until the mid-fifties. Besides, the movement toward more observation-oriented tests led to the introduction of other diagnostic techniques, such as graphology and—after the Second World War—projective methods.

During the late forties and fifties the concept of psychotechnics gradually fell into disuse. Apparatus and observational tests lost their prominent role in testing, giving way to paper-and-pencil tests as the main tools of the trade. For some technical vocations, however, apparatus tests still play an important role—for instance in the realm of traffic psychology. Thus, current selection procedures for drivers, pilots, and railroad engineers can be said to have their roots in the psychotechnical tradition which dominated applied psychology in Europe between the two world wars.

Bibliography

Baumgarten, F. (1928). *Die Berufseignungsprüfungen.* Munich/Berlin: Oldenbourg.

Dorsch, F. (1963). *Geschichte und Probleme der angewandten Psychologie.* Bern: Huber.

Drunen, P. van, & Van Strien, P. J. (1991). *Op de proef gesteld. Geschiedenis van de psychologische test.* Groningen: Stichting Historische Materialen Psychologie.

Giese, F. (1925). *Handbuch Psychotechnischer Eignungsprüfungen* (2d ed.). Halle: Marhold.

Haas, E. (1988). The Dutch Postal Services and Psychology in the Interbellum. *Cheiron Europe Newsletter, 6*(2), 26–31.

Lennep, D. G. van. (1949). *Psychotechnick als kompas voor het beroep.* Utrecht: DeHaan.

Sports Psychology

Günther Bäumler

Among the earliest publications in the psychology of sports are two articles published in 1894 by the Frenchman Philippe Tissié (1852–1935) of Bordeaux. The first of these articles discussed the physiological and psychological aspects of bicycle racing. Tissié observed a bicycle racer who established a record for a nonstop race between Paris and Breste. The second essay is of special

Figure 2 The eminent Italian scientists Angelo and Ugolino Mosso studied the physiological and psychological effects of mountain climbing on 10 soldiers at a height of more than 13,000 feet on Monte Rosa in the Italian Alps.

interest because it contains the word "Psychologie" in its title. Specifically, this paper discussed and interpreted the more theoretical dimensions of the psychology of bicycle racing. As the result of this published research, Tissié can be counted among the forerunners or founders of modern sports psychology (Figure 1).

An interest in issues relating to sports psychology can also be found in the writings of Angelo Mosso (1846–1910), the eminent physiologist of Turin University in Italy. His works include the book *Physiology of Man in the Alps* (1897), which contains information about the physical and psychological functioning of 10 Italian mountain units during an extended stay on the heights of Monte Rosa in the Italian Alps (Figures 2, 3). Mosso described, for

Figure 1 Dr. Philippe Tissié of Bordeaux studied the physiology and psychology of bicycle racing as early as 1894.

Figure 3 Ugolino Mosso during carbon-dioxide analysis on Monte Rosa.

example, the psychological stress among the individuals who led the expedition on various occasions (the "pioneer effect") and the significantly increased achievement levels or "competition effect," which he observed during group rather than individual training. Unfortunately, chronic health problems forced Mosso to discontinue this research around 1904. He devoted the remainder of his life to archeology and became well known through his excavations on the Greek island of Crete.

One of the first laboratory experiments in sports psychology was conducted in 1898 by Norman Triplett (1861–1934) at Indiana University in Bloomington, Indiana, in the United States. Triplett was interested in the "pacemaker effect" during bicycle races—a subject which had already received some attention by Tissié in his earlier studies. Triplett was particularly interested in ways to empirically verify the much-discussed percepto-motor phenomenon of dynamogenesis. To do so, Triplett built a

special "competition machine" which permitted two people (subjects A and B) to use hand cranks to compete with each other (Figure 4). Triplett's results revealed that the act of observing the performance of another person led to increased performance by most subjects; however, in some cases, the opposite effect occurred. His research stimulated the so-called "social facilitation" studies in social psychology.

The importance of psychology for the enhancement of athletic performance was also recognized by the French Baron Pierre de Coubertin (1863–1937), the founder of the modern Olympic Games (Figure 5). He coined the term "sports psychology," which he used in the title of his 1900 article, "The Psychology of Sport." In 1913, de Coubertin's book, *Essays on Sport Psychology*, was published, and in that very same year he organized the First Congress of Sport Psychology and Physiology in the Swiss city of Lausanne (Figure 6).

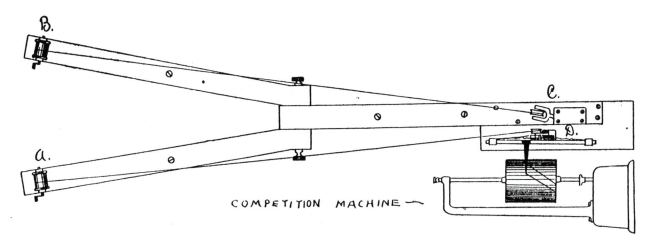

Figure 4 Diagram of Triplett's Competition Machine. Two subjects were required to roll up ropes with two different controls (a. and b.).

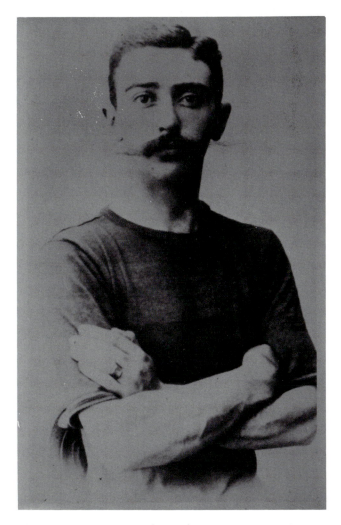

Figure 5 Baron Pierre de Coubertin (1863–1937), as a young athlete. Coubertin founded the modern Olympic Games and coined the term "sports psychology."

Figure 6 Title page of program for first Congress of Sport Psychology and Physiology in Lausanne (1913).

Figure 7 Systematic archery practice for research project by John B. Watson (1878–1958) and Karl S. Lashley (1890–1958). Try-outs on the Johns Hopkins Campus in Baltimore.

Figure 8 Coleman R. Griffith (1893–1966), Professor of Educational Psychology and Director of Athletic Research at the University of Illinois at Champaign. Griffith is regarded as the "Father of American Sports Psychology."

Under the supervision of John B. Watson (1879–1958), the famous behaviorist, Karl Lashley (1890–1958) conducted systematic practice tests of archery on the campus of Johns Hopkins University in Baltimore (Figure 7). In the resulting 1915 publication, Lashley was able to document several "practice effects," including the positive benefits of distributed rather than massed practice.

Robert Werner Schulte (1897–1933), the Berlin expert in psychotechnology, also deserves recognition as the first professional academic sports psychologist. As early as 1920, Schulte held a lectureship in psychology and education at the German and Prussian College for Physical Education in Berlin (Lück, 1994). During his tenure at this institution, he established a special laboratory for the "psycho-technical study of gymnastics, games, and sports" (Schulte, 1925). A skilled inventor and technician, Schulte developed a number of instruments for assessing athletic aptitude and achievement. He also wrote many articles and books on sports psychology. His early death was a serious loss for the development of sports psychology in Germany.

The eminent American sports psychologist, Coleman R. Griffith (1893–1966), began his professional work as a sports psychologist about the same time as Schulte (Figure 8). In 1921 he was appointed professor of educational psychology at the University of Illinois in Urbana (USA). Two years later, he lectured for the first time on the topic "Psychology and Athletics" and from 1923–1932, he directed the Athletics Research Laboratory at Illinois. Like Schulte, Griffith developed a number of special assessment procedures for measuring athletic ability. He also wrote pertinent journal articles and two books, *Psychology of Coaching* (1926) and *Psychology and Athletics* (1928). Despite their commendable achievements, Griffith and Schulte each remained "prophets without disciples" throughout their respective careers (see also Kroll & Lewis, 1978). Apparently the times were not yet ready to accept the application of psychology to sports, in spite of the research that had been conducted.

Bibliography

Comité International Olympique (Ed.). (1913). *Congrès International de Psychologie et Physiologie Sportive.* Lausanne: Toso.

Coubertin, P. de. (1900). La Psychologie du sport. *Revue des Deux Mondes, 4,* 160, 167–179.

Coubertin, P. de. (1913). *Essais de psychologie sportive.* Lausanne/Paris: Payot.

Ferretti, L. (1951). *Angelo Mosso, apostolo dello sport.* Milan: Garzanti.

Griffith, C.R. (1926). *The psychology of coaching.* New York/London: Scribner's Sons.

Griffith, C.R. (1928). *Psychology and athletics.* New York/London: Scribner's Sons.

Kroll, W., & Lewis, G. (1978). America's first sport psychologist. In Straub, W. F. (Ed.), *Sport psychology* (pp. 16–19). Ithaca, NY: Mouvement.

Lashley, K. S. (1915). The acquisition of skill in archery. *Papers from the Department of Marine Biology of the Carnegie Institution of Washington,* Vol. VII, Washington, 105–128.

Lück, H. E. (1994). ". . . und halte Lust und Leid und Leben in meiner ausgestreckten Hand." Zu Leben und Werk des psychologen Robert Werner Schulte. In H. Gundlach (Ed.) *Arbeiten zur psychologiegeschichte* (pp. 39–48). Gottingen: Hogrefe.

Mosso, A. (1897). *Fisiologia dell'uomo sulle Alpi.* Milan: Treves.

Schulte, R. W. (1921). *Leib und Seele im Sport.* Charlottenburg: Volkshochschulverlag.

Schulte, R. W. (1925). *Eignungs- und Leistungsprüfung im Sport.* Berlin: Hackebeil.

Schulte, R. W. (1926). Leistungssteigerung im Turnen, Spiel und Sport. *Zur Psycho-Biologie der körperlichen Erziehung.* Oldenburg: Stalling.

Tissié, Ph. (1894a). Observations physiologiques concernant un record velocipédique. *Archives de Physiologie, 5,* Serie 6, 823–837.

Tissié, Ph. (1894b). Psychologie de l'entraînement intensif. *Revue Scientifique, 31e Année,* 4e Série, Tome II, 481–493.

Triplett, N. (1898). The dynamogenic factors in pacemaking and competition. *American Journal of Psychology, 9*(4), 507–533.

On Telling Left from Right: The Apparatus of Handedness in Early American Psychology

Maria F. Ippolito
Ryan D. Tweney

The instruments of science possess, in addition to their function as tools, a rhetoric of their own, a "voice" that, for the historian, sometimes reveals much about their era and their makers (Heilbron, 1993). Just as diaries reveal the "microstructure" of scientific thought (as argued by, for example, Holmes, 1987; Tweney, 1989), so, too, do instruments reveal the literal hands-on practice of a discipline. In America as in Europe, the "new psychology" of the late 19th century used such instrumental voices to establish its scientific credentials, as well as to achieve the internalist goals of measurement and discovery. By the early 20th century, "brass and glass" psychology had become fashionable (Miner, 1904; Popplestone & McPherson, 1984); so much so, as we will argue in the present chapter, that genuine issues were often overlooked in the pursuit of better instrumentation. Thus, as psychology moved "from traditional rationalism to techniques of experimentation" (Popplestone & McPherson, 1984, p. 196), the laboratory instrument sometimes became an end in itself, a voice to be heard for its own sake.

Our focus will be on the apparatus employed and constructed between 1890 and World War II by American psychologists to study handedness. The beginning of the period coincides with the publication of James's *Principles of Psychology* and the end coincides roughly with the formation of the Psychological Museum in Chicago, founded by David Boder in 1936, a monument to the reverence with which instruments were by then regarded (Benjamin, 1979; Popplestone & McPherson, 1994). Handedness is an interesting domain for this inquiry because it involves so many of the central concerns of early American psychology: individual differences, the emphasis on functional relationships, the possibility

of linking behavioral and physiological processes, the issue of innate versus acquired tendencies, and—most importantly for our purpose—because it promised to be *measurable*.

As with laboratory practice in general (Danziger, 1990; Leahey, 1994), psychological studies of handedness often built upon the work of physiologists. Folklore was frequently the source of the earliest physiological theories (Bishop, 1990; Harris, 1980, 1983); usually an inherited physical asymmetry was postulated as the cause of hand preference. For example, in 1862 Andrew Buchanan, Professor of Physiology at the University of Glasgow, argued that handedness was due to asymmetrical distribution of the viscera. He maintained that the liver and a larger right than left lung altered "the mechanical relations on the two sides of the body [such] that the muscles of the right side act with superior efficacy" (Beeley, 1918, p. 65). Buchanan attempted to confirm his theory by balancing cadavers on the edge of a laboratory table. The posthumous location of the center of balance to the right or left of the center line of the body was expected to coincide with right- or left-handedness, respectively, during the individual's lifetime. While Buchanan and coworkers reported that the center of balance was a reliable indicator of handedness, attempts to replicate their findings were unsuccessful (Harris, 1980).

Alternative physiological explanations also focused on physiological asymmetries. George M. Gould, an American physician, identified Arnold (1884, cited in Parson, 1924) as an early proponent of another physiological asymmetry, differential arm length, to account for handedness. Instead of the viscera shifting the balance in favor of the right or left side, the slightly superior reach of one arm was credited with causing that hand to become dominant. Alternatively, Humphrey (1861, cited in Schiller, 1936), LeConte (1884a, 1884b), and Gould (1908) proposed an ocular-dominance theory, locating the origin of handedness in the dominance of one eye. The increased salience of right-eye images for most individuals was believed to trigger the action of the nearest or right hand; it was then the right hand or the right eye or both that affected the localization of hand preference in a dominant left hemisphere (Gould, 1908). Gould declared that his post-mortem measurement of over 20,000 eyeballs confirmed this theory. However, contradictory anatomical evidence concerning the localization of optical functioning appeared in 1890, prior to Gould's publication of his findings. By destroying selected portions of animal retinas and tracing the degenerated optical fibers to their cortical destination, Henschen found that the control of vision in the right and left eyes was by both brain hemispheres (Brodal, 1981). Gould was not the only researcher to disregard these anatomical findings. Simple portable eyedness tests using sighting tubes, such as the one devised by W. Miles (1929), or in which subjects were asked to sight objects through a small hole in a piece of paper (Scheidemann, 1931) appeared in psychological studies of handedness throughout the 1930s (e.g., Lynn & Lynn, 1938). This despite Peterson's (1934) findings—in a study "begun in Professor Lashley's laboratory at the University of Chicago and . . . continued in the animal Research Laboratory of the University of Denver" (p. 1)—that removing the left or right eyes of infant rats had no impact on their paw preference as adults.

Some 19th century physiological researchers postulated that superior development of the left cerebral hemisphere resulted in right-handedness, with adjacent brain regions in the left hemisphere controlling speech and the functioning of the dominant hand (Boyd, 1861, and Broca, 1875, cited in Schiller, 1936). Broca (L. G. Smith, 1917) maintained that the left-handed were mirror images of the right-handed with respect to the organization of brain function, although some physiological evidence contradicted Broca's contention (Hardyck & Petrovinovich, 1977).

By 1890, American psychology was a discipline beginning to cast its lot in favor of "scientificity" (Danziger, 1990, p. 89; see also Buchner, 1903; Leahey, 1994). Many psychologists chose to align themselves with the "sacred and unquestionable emblems of scientific status . . . [such as] quantifica-

tion, experimentation, and the search for universal . . . laws" (Danziger, 1990, p. 120). Physiological research had failed to find the cause of handedness despite numerous studies comparing the weight of the two sides of the body, or two halves of the brain, or the differential sizes of arms and eyeballs. Here was an opportunity for psychology to demonstrate the potential of the new quantitative science—a window of opportunity for the laboratory machine with its ability to actualize stimulus control and to quantify behavioral responses (Cleary, 1977; Grings, 1954; Popplestone & McPherson, 1984).

While physiology provided psychology with laboratory practices and suggested theories of handedness, there was, nevertheless, a difference in the goals of physiological and psychological research. The interest of psychological researchers was not merely in the singular cause of handedness; psychology's interest included the intermediate events—the "mental states" or "brain states" that moderated hand preferences (Danziger, 1990; Leahey, 1994). Thus, psychological studies of handedness that succeeded solely in quantifying behavioral responses were insufficient to advance psychological knowledge; the findings of interest to psychologists were, for example, what hand preference revealed about brain functioning. In spite of this, however, in the actual research carried out, psychological studies of handedness focused primarily on unearthing an innate (sometimes behavioral) asymmetry to explain handedness. What was really new was the use of instruments designed by psychological researchers.

Various apparatus were deployed not just to resolve whether subjects were right or left handed but to assess the *degree* of handedness. It was not uncommon for handedness researchers to employ psychological apparatus designed for other purposes. For example, the *pursuitmeter* was redesigned for use by groups of subjects. The original purpose of the pursuitmeter was to obtain a continuous measurement of eye-hand coordination; subjects had to maintain a randomly moving indicator at a zero point via compensatory movement of a slider (W. R. Miles, 1921). Figure 1a shows a side view of the pursuitmeter being utilized by a subject whose oxygen consumption is also being monitored. The letters A, F, K, L, and M designate the wattmeter, rheostat slider, platform, cabinet, and viewing screen, respectively. Plots of subjects' responses were electrically

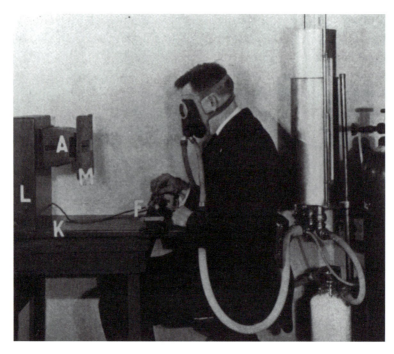

Figure 1a The pursuitmeter. (From W. R. Miles, 1921. The pursuitmeter. *Journal of Experimental Psychology, 4*, p. 86)

Figure 1b The group pursuit task. (From G. L. Freeman and J. S. Chapman, 1935. The relative importance of eye and hand dominance in a pursuit skill, *American Journal of Psychology, 47*, p. 147)

generated. The purpose of the *group pursuit task* (Figure 1b) was to evaluate "the relative importance of eye and hand dominance" (Freeman & Chapman, 1935, p. 146) and permit the simultaneous testing of the eye-hand coordination of multiple subjects. The stimulus to be followed was projected on the ceiling (rather than a screen) and subjects were positioned so that this stimulus pattern appeared in the same position on the mirror held by each subject. Subjects then attempted to trace, as exactly as possible, the pattern of the moving stimulus on a piece of cellophane placed over their mirrors—first with one eye closed and then the other (Freeman & Chapman, 1935). The *pursuit rotor*, a device similar to the pursuitmeter which required subjects to manually shadow a stimulus that followed a circular pattern, was also used in a few handedness studies (e.g., Van Riper & Bryngelson, 1936).

Tracing boards or steadiness *testers* to assess steadiness of hand movement (Whipple, 1914) and *tapping plates* to assess motor capacity (Whipple, 1914) were commonplace in psychology laboratories of the period (Popplestone & McPherson, 1984) and were utilized by handedness researchers. Thus, Beeley (1918) used tracing boards, which required subjects to trace along the inside surface of metal strips arranged in a v-shape or a rectangle with a stylus without making contact, and the steadiness tester, which required subjects to insert a metal stylus in various-sized holes drilled in an angled rectangular metal "table" without touching the sides of the holes. Both the tracing and steadiness tasks were timed; errors were electronically recorded; and performance using the right and left hands was compared. Knight Dunlap (1921) redesigned the steadiness tester, placing the holes around a rotating circular brass plate. A stationary plate with a single hole drilled in it was positioned under the rotating plate. This design ensured that the open hole in which the stylus was to be inserted by subjects was in exactly the same position for each trial.

A number of handedness studies (e.g., Downey, 1927; Ojemann, 1930) also used single, double, triple, and quadruple tapping plates, since inherited hand preference was expected to be reflected in the superior motor capacity of one hand. The use of the single tapping plate (Figure 2a) required that subjects tap the plate as many times as possible during a period of several seconds (Beeley, 1918). Beeley (1918) later added a wrist strap and thimble to the single tapping plate to reduce the contribution of

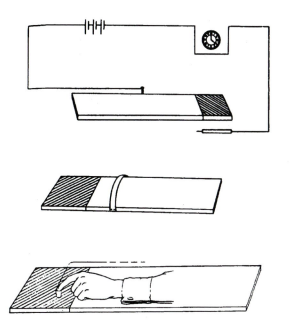

Figure 2a The single tapping plate and accessories. (From A. L. Beeley, 1918. Experimental study of left-handedness, *Supplemental Educational Monographs, 2,* (8), pp. 15, 22, and 28, respectively. Copyright 1918 by the University of Chicago Press)

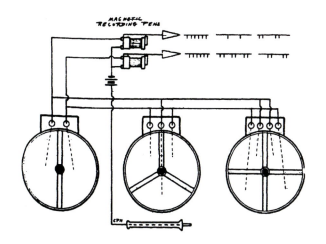

Figure 2b A line drawing of *double, triple, and quadruple tapping plates.* (From C. P. Heinlein, 1930. Multiple-plate tapping boards, *Journal of General Psychology, 3,* p. 177. Copyright by Clark University Press)

the arm muscles. In 1921, Knight Dunlap proposed the use of a double-tapping plate to increase the likelihood of an accurate electronic count. That is, the use of the pictured double, triple, and quadruple tapping plates (Figure 2b) required that subjects consecutively tap each section of the plate.

The problem with using indices of eye-hand coordination, dexterity, and motor capacity to identify native handedness was that such measurements failed to tease apart native and practiced handedness. After all, Lashley (1917) had claimed success in changing the hand preference of two monkeys by using punishment, and Kempf (1917) had successfully used practice to transfer monkeys from the initially preferred hand. Later, Milisen (1937) concluded from his training study of four rats that handedness was probably the product of the combined influence of "native qualities" and "habit formation" (p. 239). Similar experiments using human subjects were undertaken by Bowman (1928) and J. H. Heinlein (1930), who found that differential performance across hands on a pegboard task was diminished as a result of practice. Yet, the lion's share of the published pages in the intervening years between the publication of Lashley's and Kempf's studies in 1917 and Milisen's study in 1937, did not even consider whether dexterity was indicative of native handedness. Instead, most claimed merely to have reduced inconsistencies in the data, either via revisions in method or by building a better "mousetrap." Data for its own sake seemed to be the major concern. "It seems that in the early days of experimental psychology claims to scientificity rested very largely on the factor of stimulus control. This could lead to somewhat ludicrous situations, because the reliance on this factor was easily transferred to the (brass) instruments that were the means used to actualize it" (Danziger, 1990, p. 89).

In addition to Lashley, Watson's student (Buckley, 1989), and the other researchers listed above who examined the impact of experience on handedness, John Broadus Watson and Rosalie Rayner Watson also conducted research to exclude hand preference as an instinct. Watson's interest in handedness dated to at least 1913, when he and Lashley completed an unpublished study in which they were unable to demonstrate the preferential use of either hand by a young monkey (cited in Lashley, 1917). To test their contention that handedness was acquired, Watson and Watson (1921) utilized a measure of grasp strength. Specifically, after grasping a small wooden stick, infants were lifted up by one arm and the amount of time they could suspend their own weight with the right and left hands was recorded. Figure 3a depicts Watson administering the grasping task with an unknown assistant poised to catch the infant. In repeated testing of infants up to 21 days of age, the Watsons found no difference across hands in infants' ability to suspend their own weight (Figure 3b).

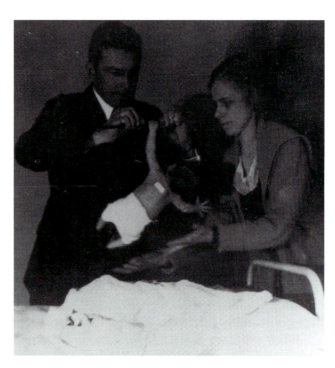

Figure 3a Watson's grasping task. (Permission by the Ferdinand Hamburger, Jr. Archives of Johns Hopkins University)

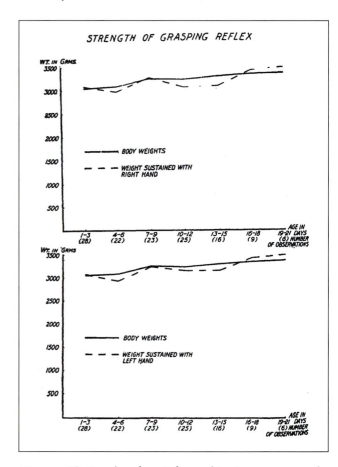

Figure 3b Graphs of an infant subject's grasp strength. (From J. B. Watson, 1919. *Psychology from the Standpoint of a Behaviorist,* p. 239. Philadelphia: J. P. Lippincott)

A specialized tool for measuring grasp strength beyond infancy was the dynamometer (Whipple, 1914) (Figure 4). The *dynamometer* was used as early as 1897 when Cattell reported on a modification of this device. Becker and Glick (1940) indicate there was concern that the oval dynamometer (Figure 4, left) provided no means of ensuring identical placement of the hand on multiple trials and that no allowance had been made for hand size or finger length. The push and pull attachment to the oval dynamometer (Figure 4, center) was "devised to increase the utility" of this device (Stoelting, 1936, p. 55). Smedley's redesign of the dynamometer (Figure 4, right) possessed "a greater degree of accuracy than any type . . . in use" (Stoelting, 1936, p. 56) and permitted the generation of kymographic records. Like the tracing board, tapping plate, and steadiness tester described earlier, the dynamometer was commonplace in psychological laboratories of the period (Popplestone & McPherson, 1984). While this device was initially designed to assess—among other things—fatigue, the dynamometer was adopted by handedness researchers in the belief that differential grasp strength would reveal native handedness (Whipple, 1914). And, like the tapping plate and steadiness tester, the dynamometer was redesigned to improve its reliability.

The first mention of the dynamometer in the handedness literature was in 1918 (Beeley). Three years later, Hugh Gordon (1921), in a widely cited article in the British journal *Brain*, stated: "It was thought that the grip dynamometer would be very useful in diagnosing left-handedness, but the results were so varying and often so inconsistent with known facts, that little value could be placed on results obtained by it" (p. 325). Other researchers of the period also expressed concern regarding the reliability of the dynamometer (Popplestone & McPherson, 1984). Nevertheless, it continued in use in handedness studies during the balance of the time period which is the focus of this chapter (e.g., Downey, 1927). In light of the Watsons' finding of no difference in infant grasp strength, how much of the superior grasp strength of the dominant hand is attributable to heredity and how much to habit? Again, however, the technology seemed to be central; whether the postulated relationship between grasp strength and native handedness was valid remained a peripheral issue. By and large, researchers tinkered with the devices rather than attending to the viability of the overriding theory.

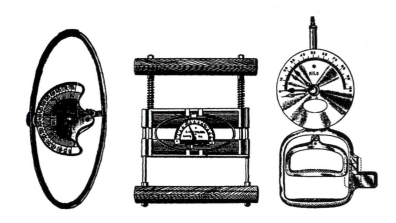

Figure 4 The dynamometer. (From C. H. Stoelting Co., 1936. *Psychological and physiological apparatus and supplies*, p. 13. Chicago: C. H. Stoelting Co. Courtesy of Stoelting Co., Wood Dale, IL)

In the tradition of Arnold's contention that hand preference resulted from differential arm length, James Mark Baldwin (1890a, 1894/1915) and a number of other researchers performed experiments using reaching. Baldwin also discussed the data gathered for his 1894/1915 study in an exchange of letters discussing handedness with William James in the October 31 (Baldwin, 1890a), November 14 (James, 1890), and November 28 (Baldwin, 1890b) issues of *Science*. Earlier, G. Stanley Hall, a left hander until age eleven when he "was made to change" (Hall, 1923/1977, p. 122) and the recipient of the first PhD in psychology awarded by an American university (Taylor, 1994), also used reaching in an 1884 study of handedness that he co-authored with Hartwell. In addition to the measurement of reaching behavior, psychologists emulated physiologists; limb length was measured using the *brachiometer* devised by W. Franklin Jones, an American Professor of Education (Gould, 1908). This device consisted of a small platform to which a ruler was affixed at a 90-degree angle. Each subject placed his or her elbow on the platform of the brachiometer and arm length was measured to the first knuckle of the middle finger (known as the ulna-plus measurement) (Beeley, 1918).

Jones measured the arms of 20,000 individuals, "ranging in age from stillborn to centigenerian, . . . [concluding that] 'born handedness is revealed by the measures of the bones of the arm . . . and this evidence is present at birth'" (J. H. Heinlein, 1930, pps. 4–5). The use of the brachiometer in psychological studies of handedness persisted for a number of years despite conflicting results (e.g., Downey, 1927; L. G. Smith, 1917). In 1930, J. H. Heinlein (see also Parson, 1924) questioned the validity of data generated by the use of the brachiometer, pointing out that this device not only misdiagnosed the handedness of a number of confirmed right- and left-handed children and classified an unusually high percentage of children as left-handed (40%), but that the difference in arm length was often slight (an average of 2.02 millimeters in Beeley's 1918 study of 123 children). Watson and Watson (1921) also measured the limbs of several hundred children using an instrument of their own design (similar to the brachiometer) and found no significant difference in length between the right and left arms of their subjects.

John B. Watson (1919; see Stevens & Ducasse, 1912 and Titchener, 1898, for similar views), the positivist "father" of behaviorism, believed that "progress in any science can be measured by the extent to which apparatus and improved methods of observation have been employed. . . . Whatever phenomenon is open to unaided observation can be more accurately studied where instrumentation and control of the subject are employed" (p. 20). In this spirit, Watson and Watson (1921) constructed a measure of differential arm activity called the *work adder*. Cords were tied to an infant's wrists and arm movements advanced the gear associated with either the right or left hand. Repeated testings were made of each infant and overall activity level was found to favor neither arm. We were unable to locate a picture or a diagram of the work adder, but Watson (1919) did include tracings for one infant subject in *Psychology from the Standpoint of a Behaviorist*. These graphs provide a kymographic record of the movement of an infant's right and left hands during free activity and in response to the sound of tearing paper, the researcher saying the word "boo," and the faint smell of ammonia. In any case, Watson and his wife (predisposed, perhaps, toward an affirmative answer) utilized several methods—the work adder as well as the measurements of arm length and grasp strength described earlier—to determine whether handedness was based upon habit.

Psychologists also explored the relation between ocular asymmetry and handedness, focusing not on the dominant eye, as Gould, a physician, had, but on the dominant hemifield. In a critical review of Gould's 1908 book on ocular-dominance theory, Stevens (1909) pointed out that Gould failed to take into account that both eyes are represented in both brain hemispheres. Eye-dominance researchers constructed a number of devices to identify the dominant visual field, since "eyedness" was believed to be an indicator of native handedness which could not be altered by experience.

Stevens's (1908a; 1908b) first device (Figure 5a) required a seated subject to place his or her head in a metal ring to stabilize subject's head position across trials. The subject's head was supported by the ring in the foreground while he or she made judgments about the sizes of the orbits of the two black dots, one on each of the white cardboard circles. The subject's task was to equalize the orbits of two black dots by repositioning the white circle on which the black dot seemed to have a larger orbit. Stevens and Ducasse (1912) felt forced to abandon this earlier "crude device" (p. 3). Figure 5b depicts the front (left) and back (right) views of this later device. In the use of the redesigned device, one of the subject's eyes was covered and the other eye was fixed on the bolt in the center of the large disk. Adjustments were made by the subject (over several trials) such that two white circles—one on the disk and one on the upper portion of the protruding stick—appeared to be equidistant from the fixation point. The reverse side of the large disk and upper portion of the protruding stick were marked off in millimeters. For both of Stevens's devices, the orbit of the black dots or the white circles, whichever appeared larger, indicated the dominant visual field; and the degree of adjustment indicated the degree of dominance. Stevens and Ducasse's belief was that the right half of the visual field would overestimate sighted objects in the native right-hander. Stevens (1908b) was able to classify only 79% of his subjects using the earlier device; of the 145 subjects he was able to characterize as distinctly right- or left-eyed, eye and hand dominance coincided for 103 (71%). It is difficult to assess whether the redesigned device (Stevens & Ducasse, 1912) was more successful since only four subjects (a professor, a graduate assistant, and the two authors) were tested. Apparently, neither Stevens, Ducasse, nor any other handedness researchers availed themselves of either of these devices in other handedness studies.

Parson (1924) also designed an instrument to

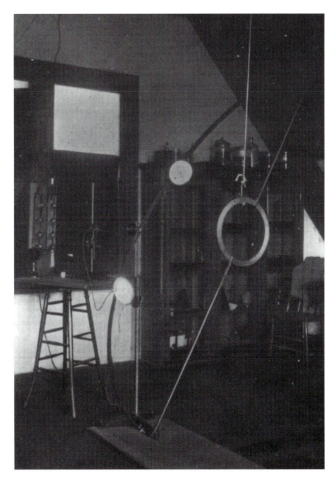

Figure 5a Stevens's 1908 device. (From H. C. Stevens, 1908. Peculiarities of peripheral vision. *Psychological Review, 15,* Plate 1)

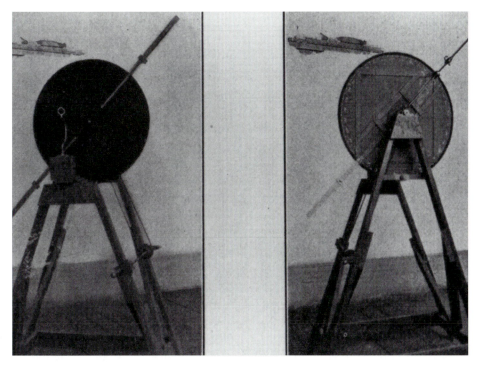

Figure 5b Stevens & Ducasse's redesigned device. (From H. C. Stevens and C. J. Ducasse, 1912. The retina and handedness. *Psychological Review, 19,* p. 3)

assess hemifield dominance which was utilized by a number of handedness researchers (e.g., Eyre & Schmeeckle, 1933; Witty & Kopel, 1936). Parson's (1924) manuscope (Figure 6) consisted of two parts: a sighting tube (right) and a slide holder (left). Using the sighting tube, subjects were first asked to fixate on the center dot of a slide, then the L on the left and R on the right were exposed by the researcher and subjects were asked what they saw. (Left-dominant subjects were expected to report seeing the L only and vice versa.) This procedure was repeated for several trials.

As is apparent from the preceding discussion of the tapping plates, steadiness tester, dynamometer, and Stevens' devices, just as industry redesigned toward greater efficiency and productivity, the psychological laboratory devised and revised the apparatus used toward greater precision of measurement. In that spirit, a series of improvements to Parson's manuscope were proposed. Cuff's (1930) *manoptometer* added a cord attaching the sighting tube to the slide holder to insure an identical distance between these two components across trials. In addition, the stationary L and R on the slides were replaced with a bird and a cat, which could be moved independently—the change in slides con-

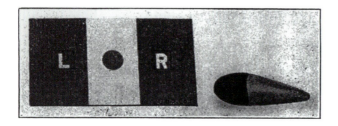

Figure 6 Parson's manuscope. (From C. H. Stoelting Co., 1936. *Psychological and physiological apparatus and supplies*, p. 55, Chicago: C. H. Stoelting Co. Courtesy of Stoelting Co., Wood Dale, IL)

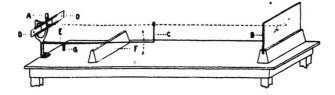

Figure 7 Lund's monoptometer. (From F. H. Lund, 1932. The monoptometer. *American Journal of Psychology, 44,* p. 180)

cealing the nature of the task and being more appropriate for the children and feeble-minded who often served as subjects. Cuff (1931) reported that the manoptometer yielded highly consistent indices of eyedness across trials. Approximately 93% of subjects were right-handed but only about 72% were right-eyed, suggesting that the manoptometer provided information about native handedness not available when hand preference alone was assessed. However, the manoptometer was normed on "right-handed" children. Thus, the norms on which decisions of eyedness were based were derived from testing children who may or may not have been right-eyed since their right-handedness could have been influenced by training. Cuff is apparently the only researcher who availed himself of this device.

Lund (1932) later proposed the *monoptometer* due to his objection to the highly artificial conditions inherent in the use of Parson's manuscope and Cuff's manoptometer. Lund's device disposed of the necessity for a sighting tube; degree of eye-hemifield dominance was determined by subjects manually repositioning a circle to line it up with a fixed disk positioned behind the circle. The monoptometer was also utilized by Freeman and Chapman (1935). Figure 7 is a line drawing of Lund's monoptometer: A is the head rest and D represents slides utilized to block the right or left visual field. The bar (E) is attached to a circle (C). The circle is adjusted by the subject to align it with the fixation disk (B) using the handle (G).

In 1935, Crider wrote of both Cuff's manoptometer and Lund's monoptometer: "Whatever quantitative results are obtained are not at all measures of the degree of ocular dominance, but merely an indication of pupillary distance, equipment failure, or subject reaction time" (p. 319). But these design flaws were overshadowed by a more substantive issue. Increasing the sophistication of the measuring equipment was insufficient to salvage eye-dominance theory. The fact that the prevalence of left-handedness was the same in the blind and the sighted (e.g., Ballard, 1912; J. M. Smith, 1933, 1934) raised serious doubts that eyedness was influential in determining hand preference.

Perhaps in the spirit of Broca's characterization of the left-handed as transposed right-handers (Harris, 1980) in combination with the observation of mirror-writing by some left-handed individuals (Blom, 1928; Judd, 1911), the ability to read and write mirror script (e.g., Downey, 1932; Kirk, 1934)

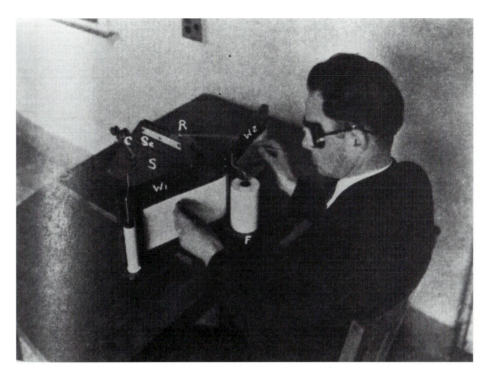

Figure 8a Van Riper's critical-angle board. (From C. Van Riper, 1935. The quantitative measurement of laterality, *Journal of Experimental Psychology, 18,* p. 373)

Figure 8b A critical-angle board sample pattern. (From C. Van Riper, 1934. A new test of laterality, *Journal of Experimental Psychology, 17,* p. 308)

or run mirror-image mazes (Herren & Lindsley, 1935) was utilized as a diagnostic tool in handedness studies. Such tasks were also subject to technical improvement. Van Riper's (1935) *critical-angle board* required blindfolded subjects to duplicate previously practiced figures simultaneously with both hands across multiple trials. Figure 8a shows this device in use by an unknown subject. W1 and W2 designate the hinged writing boards; S is the support to which the hinged writing boards were attached; R is a rider, the position of which is indicative of the angle between the writing boards; Sc is a scale which indicates the position of the rider; F is the paper feeder roll; and C is the crank which adjusts the angle between the two writing boards.

Figure 8b shows a sample pattern (left) which subjects practiced by tracing along the groove of the pattern with a stylus (center); the correct duplication of the right-hand pattern on the writing board is shown on the right of Figure 8b. The angle at which subjects correctly duplicated the practiced pattern with the preferred hand, while at the same time duplicating the pattern's mirror image with the other hand, was believed to be indicative of the degree of handedness. For the time period under consideration, Van Riper was the only researcher to utilize this device. Hecaen and Ajuriaguerra (1964) indicate that Johnson (in 1942) and Clark (in 1957) argued that the critical-angle board was not diagnostic of native handedness.

By the time World War II began, American psychology had reached near-complete consensus that psychology would benefit from a shift toward the systematic, objective laboratory methods of the more established sciences like physiology or physics. Yet historical and social context undeniably have their impact on scientific products, notwithstanding the employment of apparently objective research techniques (Brush, 1974; Bauer, 1992; Danziger, 1990). Interestingly, our review of handedness literature suggests that when techniques failed, the effort was often not to reconstruct the theories designed to explain handedness but, rather, to improve the handedness technology. This focus on apparatus is not surprising; the period under consideration was a time in which the American view of the machine was as an "improver of the world . . . and enricher of its maker" (p. 123, Leahy, 1994; see also Popplestone & McPherson, 1984). Psychology, like American culture in general, embraced a progressive view of the machine as a primary tool of the scientific method.

It is clear from the foregoing review that reliance on one kind of method and its machinery can and did hamper scientific progress. However, the interaction of researchers engaged in the gathering of experimental data who held diverging theoretical views regarding handedness eventually brought about the questioning of many features of the lore of handedness. It is not only the brachiometer, critical-angle board, and manuscope that languish in museum displays or on the pages of vintage catalogs of scientific instruments; the ideas that arm length, mirror writing ability, or eye hemifield dominance are indicative of brain organization are also curiosities.

Two disparate cultural forces—the tendency to instrumentalize scientific issues and the theoretical "baggage" of the scientists engaged in handedness studies—interacted to yield genuine scientific progress. How such interactions proceed is a fundamental issue for the history of psychology.

Note

Full bibliography available from the authors upon request.

Bibliography

Baldwin, J. M. (1894/1915). *Mental development of the child and the race.* New York: Macmillan.

Bauer, H. H. (1992). *Scientific literacy and the myth of the scientific method.* Urbana, IL: University of Illinois Press.

Beeley, A. L. (1918). Experimental study of left-handedness. *Supplemental Educational Monographs, 2,* (8).

Buchner, E. F. (1903). A quarter century of psychology in America: 1878–1903. *The American Journal of Psychology, 14,* 666–680.

Crider, B. (1935). A criticism of Lund's and Cuff's apparatus and tests of ocular dominance. *American Journal of Psychology, 47,* 317–319.

Danziger, K. (1990). *Constructing the subject: Historical origins of psychological research.* Cambridge: Cambridge University Press.

Freeman, G. L., & Chapman, J. S. (1935). Minor studies from the psychological laboratory of Northwestern University: VI. The relative importance of eye and hand dominance in a pursuit skill. *American Journal of Psychology, 47,* 146–149.

Gordon, H. (1921). Left-handedness and mirror writing, especially among defective children. *Brain, 43,* 312–368.

Grings, W. M. (1954). *Laboratory instrumentation in psychology.* Palo Alto, CA: The National Press.

Hall, G. S. (1977). *Life and confessions of a psychologist.* New York: Arno Press. (Original work published 1923)

Heilbron, J. L. (1993). Some uses for catalogues of old scientific instruments. In R. G. W. Anderson, J. A. Bennett, & W. F. Ryan (Eds.), *Making instruments count: Essays on historical scientific instruments, presented to Gerard L'Estrange Turner.* (pp. 1–16). Aldershot: Variorum.

Heinlein, C. P. (1930). Multiple-plate tapping boards. *Journal of General Psychology, 3,* 174–178.

Heinlein, J. H. (1930). Preferential manipulation in children. *Comparative Psychology Monographs, 7,* 1–121.

Leahey, T. (1994). *A history of modern psychology.* Englewood Cliffs, NJ: Prentice Hall.

Lund, F. H. (1932). The monoptometer: A new device for measuring eye-dominance. *American Journal of Psychology, 44,* 181–183.

Miles, W. R. (1921). The pursuitmeter: An apparatus for measuring the adequacy of neuromuscular coordination described together with illustrative results. *Journal of Experimental Psychology, 4,* 77–105.

Milisen, R. (1937). The effect of training upon the handedness preference of the rat in an eating activity. *Psychology Monographs, 49,* 234–243.

Miner, B. G. (1904). The changing attitude of American universities toward psychology. *Science, 20,* 299–307.

Parson, B. S. (1924). *Left-handedness.* New York: Macmillan.

Peterson, G. M. (1934). Mechanisms of handedness in the rat. *Comparative Psychology Monographs, 9,* 1–67.

Popplestone, J. A., & McPherson, M. W. (1984). Pioneer psychology laboratories in clinical settings. In J. Brozek (Ed.) *Explorations in the history of psychology in the United States,* (pp. 196–272). Cranbury, NJ: Associated University Press.

Stevens, H. C. (1908a). Peculiarities of peripheral vision. *Psychological Review, 15,* 69–93.

Stevens, H. C., & Ducasse, C. J. (1912). The retina and handedness. *Psychological Review, 19,* 1–31.

Stoelting, C. H., Co. (1936). *Psychological and physiological apparatus and supplies.* Chicago: C. H. Stoelting Co.

Van Riper, C. (1934). A new test of laterality. *Journal of Experimental Psychology, 17,* 305–313.

Van Riper, C. (1935). The quantitative measurement of laterality. *Journal of Experimental Psychology, 18,* 372–382.

Watson, J. B. (1919). *Psychology from the standpoint of a behaviorist.* Philadelphia: Lippincott.

Lillian M. Gilbreth

Philip M. Bartle

Lillian M. Gilbreth (1878–1972) was a noted industrial engineer, psychologist, household efficiency expert, teacher, lecturer, public servant, leader for women in engineering, and mother of 12 children. She conducted extensive research in home economics and designed special equipment and routines to make housework possible for handicapped individuals. As a consultant to the Institute of Rehabilitation Medicine at New York University Medical Center, she developed a model kitchen adapted to the needs of handicapped individuals. Throughout her life she actively encouraged women to become and remain engineers. Gilbreth remained active well into her eighties. She died in 1972 at the age of 93, still maintaining that "age needn't determine what one is able to do."

Lillian Moller Gilbreth was born in Oakland, California, on May 24, 1878, the first of eight surviving children. She was tutored at home by her mother until the age of nine, then attended public elementary and high schools in Oakland. In 1900 she received her Bachelor's degree in literature from the University of California at Berkeley, and it was there she was chosen to be the first female commencement speaker. She went on to earn her Master's degree in literature in 1902, and her Ph.D. in psychology from Brown University in 1915. In 1928, she received a second Master's in engineering from the University of Michigan, and in 1929, Gilbreth received a Doctorate of Engineering from Rutger's College. In 1933 she received a LL.D. from the University of California. Finally, in 1948, Gilbreth received a Doctorate in industrial psychology from Purdue University. She was an American Psychological Association (APA) Fellow and life member. In total, she accumulated more than twenty honorary degrees and special commendations from professional societies.

In the Moller home in Oakland on October 19, 1904, Lillian Moller married Frank Bunker Gilbreth, a

Figure 1 Portrait of Lillian M. Gilbreth adapted from the design of a 1984 postage stamp in her honor.

501

native of Maine. Frank Gilbreth was 35 years old and one of Boston's leading contractors when he married Lillian. At that time, Frank was gaining nationwide attention for his work on what was termed motion studies. Motion studies used various techniques which studied each part of the work process in minute detail. These techniques included the use of motion pictures to help analyze the various movements in any given task. As Lillian later wrote, motion study searched for the "one best way" to perform work. Lillian quickly became a partner with her husband in the growing motion study business. These two "efficiency experts" enjoyed better cooperation from the workers, unions, and management than did the "Father of Scientific Management," Frederick W. Taylor. Their success with these groups was no doubt largely due to Lillian's psychology background which included greater concern for the health and welfare of the workers during their studies.

Lillian and Frank Gilbreth had 12 children in the space of 17 years. The Gilbreths applied their principles of motion study and managerial theories to their homemaking and child rearing. The home life of the Gilbreths, with their 12 children, became widely known through a best-selling book written by two of their children, *Cheaper by the Dozen* (1948). The book was later made into a movie by the same name. The children claim that their father was always the "efficiency expert" and their mother was always the "psychologist."

Prior to Frank Gilbreth's sudden death in 1924, Lillian co-authored many writings with him. Upon Frank's death she took over as president of Gilbreth, Inc., an engineering (motion study) consulting firm. That same year she sailed to Europe to keep Frank's speaking engagements at the London Power Conference, the World Congress of Scientific Management, and the Masaryk Academy in Prague. During the Depression Lillian served on two presidential unemployment committees, one of which was the President's Emergency Committee for Unemployment Relief in 1930. During World War II, she was an educational advisor to the American Council of Education, the Office of War Information, and the War Manpower Commission.

The Lillian Gilbreth Collection is found in the Department of Special Collections and Archives at Purdue University Library. This collection contains a considerable number of articles, newspaper clippings, conference records, films, slides, photographs, and other material. The Frank Bunker Gilbreth collection, containing his business files, correspondence, and books, is also located at Purdue. Lillian M. Gilbreth was the first psychologist commemorated on a United States postage stamp. This stamp was issued on February 24, 1984, in Montclair, New Jersey, Lillian's last residence before her death on January 2, 1972.

Bibliography

Bales, J. (1984). Lillian Gilbreth honored on U.S. postal stamp. *American Psychological Association Monitor, 15*(2), 2.

Gilbreth, L. E. M. (1980). *Notable American women—the modern period: A biographical dictionary.* Cambridge, MA: Harvard University Press.

Gilbreth, L. M. (1973). *The psychology of management.* Easton Hive Publishing Co. (Original work published 1917)

Gilbreth, L. M. (1973). *The quest of the one best way: A sketch of the life of Frank Bunker Gilbreth.* Easton, PA: Hive Publishing Co. (Original work published 1926)

Gilbreth, L. M. (1929). Efficiency of women workers. *Annals of the Academy of Political and Social Science 143,* 61–64.

Gilbreth, L. M. (1931). Unemployment and the nation's children (editorial). *Parent's Magazine 6,* 11.

Gilbreth, L. M. (1947). Scientific management and human resources. *Occupations 26,* 45–49.

Gilbreth, L. M. (1972–1973). *Who's who of American women* (7th ed.). Chicago: Marquis.

Gilbreth, F. B., & Gilbreth, L. M. (1973). *Fatigue study.* Easton, PA: Hive Publishing Co. (Original work published 1911)

Gilbreth, F. B., & Gilbreth, L. M. (1916a). Effect of motion study upon the workers. *Annals of Political and Social Science 65,* 272–276.

Gilbreth, F. B., & Gilbreth, L. M. (1916b). Motion study for crippled soldiers. Paper presented at a meeting of the American Association for the Advancement of Science, in Columbus, Ohio, December, 27, 1915–January 1, 1916.

Gilbreth, F. B., & Gilbreth, L. M. (1917). Problem of the crippled soldier. *Scientific American Supplement 83,* 260–261.

Gilbreth, F. B., & Gilbreth, L. M. (1973). *Applied Motion Study.* Easton, PA: Hive Publishing Co. (Original work published 1917)

Gilbreth, F. B., & Gilbreth, L. M. (1920). *Motion Study for the Handicapped.* London: Rutledge.

Gilbreth, F. B., & Gilbreth, L. M. (1924). The efficiency engineer and the industrial psychologist. *Journal of the National Institute of Industrial Psychology 2,* 40–45.

Gilbreth, F. B. Jr., & Carey, E. G. (1963). *Cheaper by the Dozen.* New York: Crowell. (Original work published 1948)

Gilbreth, F. B. Jr., & Carey, E. G. (1950). *Belles on Their Toes.* New York: Crowell.

Traffic Psychology

Hartmut Häcker
Wilfried Echterhoff

From the beginning of its modern history, empirical psychology has been consulted for help with previously unsolved problems of practical life. This situation applies, in particular, to psychological research on accidents and the beginnings of traffic psychology. As early as 1910, a special aptitude test for streetcar drivers was developed by the German-American psychologist, Hugo Münsterberg (1863–1916) at the request of the American Association for Labor Legislation. This test asked potential streetcar employees to respond to changing traffic situations, which were depicted on a moving paper strip (Münsterberg, 1912, p. 44–49). Münsterberg's method was the first selection procedure for traffic participants. During World War I, his ideas were adopted by several countries for the selection of motor car operators.

After 1917, many new tests, training equipment and training centers were developed for the selection and training of engineers and drivers for railroads and streetcars. For example, the Dresden District Directorship of the German Imperial Railroad system established in 1917 an ambitious psychotechnical laboratory for the training of railroad engineers. In the same year, a similar facility was organized in Berlin for streetcar conductors. In Hamburg, William Stern (1871–1938) and his associates developed a variety of aptitude tests for female streetcar personnel (Stern, 1918). Stern's chief goal was a drastic reduction of streetcar accidents, ". . . for the employment of unqualified streetcar drivers is not only a waste of energy but presents a clear public danger." (Stern, 1918, p.3).

The German postal and railroad systems maintained such training centers until 1920 and benefited from this research for years afterwards. These

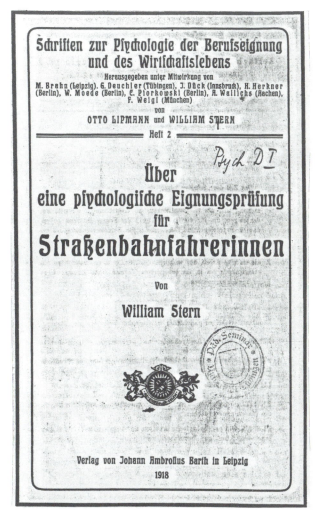

Figure 1 Title page of Stern's 1918 test for female streetcar drivers.

facilities were not expanded under the Nazi regime because many researchers in traffic psychology were forced to discontinue their work for political

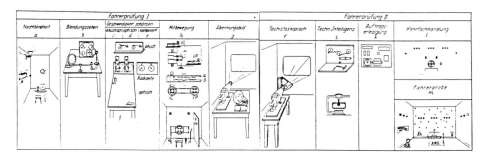

Figure 2 Performance test series for selection of military drivers.

reasons. As a result of the political situation, early German research in traffic psychology and its international impact came to a tragic halt.

During the immediate pre-war years and World War II, attention was focused once again on the same driver selection and training systems, which had been found useful during World War I.

After World War II, Germany developed a number of Medical Psychological Units (MPUs) throughout the country for the evaluation of problem drivers. During the 1960s, the first program for treating problem drivers was initiated following the model of American DUI programs. The 1980s brought public recognition and control to such programs, together with the official approval of university-educated psychologists for the identification, treatment, and re-education of individuals experiencing major problems with their driving performance.

Qualified psychologists have worked primarily in the field of driver evaluation and selection. Gaining psychological perspectives on traffic planning, including the primary prevention of road dangers, has always been a secondary concern. But preventive traffic psychology did play a significant role in the work of German industrial psychologists in the 1930s.

Recently, the field of traffic psychology has narrowed its objectives from the training and selection of competent drivers to the identification, treatment, and possible elimination of problem drivers from the traffic situation. Today, traffic psychology deals mainly with the negative consequences of modern traffic rather than the total traffic situation, including the design of safe highways and road systems.

Ideally, traffic psychology should be responsible for all traffic-related questions and not only the elimination of technical, legal, and human problems.

Figure 3 Early model electrical car by von Poppelreuter.

Much relevant research exists about the positive impact of traffic planning and design, but little of this work is ever implemented. Traffic psychologists should and can work toward the improvement and promotion of the entire national road system, as has been shown in a recent survey by Echterhoff (1991).

Within the last years, significant progress has been made, in particular after having established a legal basis for behavior modification of problem drivers in Germany, Austria, and Switzerland (Echterhoff, 1992). As a result of the privatization of some traffic systems in Australia, France, the United Kingdom, and the USA, traffic researchers were forced to utilize individual and group counseling in lieu of more generalized and preventive solutions of the problem.

Market orientation and management perspectives on transport systems, now play an important part in contemporary traffic research, especially in work sponsored by the European Union. New research topics include ecological challenges, the privatization of transportation networks, and the use of computer based information and guidance systems for road users. Some of the best known international traffic researchers include Y. Nagatsuka (Japan), T. Rothengatter (Netherlands), M. Sivak (USA), G. S. J. Wilde (Canada) W. Echterhoff, G. Kroj, and H. Häcker (Germany). Finally, in 1994, two international organizations for traffic psychology were founded: "The Division of Traffic Psychology" of the International Association of Applied Psychology and "Europsy-T", the association of European traffic psychologists.

Bibliography

Dorsch, F. (1963). *Geschichte und Probleme der angewandten Psychologie*. Bern: Huber.

Echterhoff, W. (1991). Verkehrspsychologie. In H. Häcker (Ed.), *Reihe Mensch-Fahrzeug-Umwelt.* (Vol. 26, pp. 99–118). Cologne: TÜV Rheinland.

Echterhoff, W. (1992). Erfahrungsbildung on Verkehrsteilnehmern. Aachen: Verlag Mainz.

Moede, W. (1930). *Lehrbuch der Psychotechnik.* (Vol. 1). Berlin: Springer.

Münsterberg, H. (1912). *Psychologie und Wirtschaftsleben.* Leipzig: Barth.

Stern, W. (1918). Über eine psychologische Eignungsprüfung für Straßenbahnfahrerinnen. *Zeitschrift für Angewandte Psychologie, 13*, 91–104.

The Mobile Psychologist: Psychology and the Railroads

Horst U. K. Gundlach

It was an accident which brought the railroads and scientific psychology together. In 1911, a ghastly railroad crash involving uncertain quantities of alcohol at a construction site near Müllheim, in a wine-producing region of southwestern Germany, caused many casualties. This is where Professor Karl Marbe (1869–1953) of Würzburg came in. He was an ardent apostle of temperance, touring and lecturing the country and making sundry acquaintances of a similar persuasion on the way.

One of those acquaintances designated Marbe as an authority on the influence of inebriants on human reaction time, and the board of inquiry into the crash appointed him as an expert witness. He actually simulated the fateful situation on the locomotive in his laboratory at Würzburg as well as in situ on a real engine and testified thoroughly in court. The engineer and the train conductor were found guilty, and the stoker escaped by a narrow margin due to lack of evidence. Marbe's much-acclaimed report (1912) is one of the earliest documents of forensic psychology and constitutes the first contact between the new laboratory psychology and the railroads.

It was war, however, that established a permanent connection between the two. World War I saw not only American psychologists determining the IQ scores of American GIs before bearing the expense of their transatlantic voyage; it also witnessed the Kaiser's psychologists testing potential drivers for the army's costly motorcars. The psychologists involved, mainly Walther Moede (1888–1958) and Curt Piorkowski (1888–1939), had studied at Leipzig University under Wundt and were doctoral students or assistants of Wundt's disciple Max Brahn (1873–1944), who had been in charge of a laboratory for educational psychology at Leipzig. Drawing from their experience in this field, and taking hints from Hugo Münsterberg (1863–1916) and his procedure of selecting streetcar drivers in Boston, Moede and Piorkowski built a laboratory-like environment simulating a driving situation and measured the candidates' celerity in reacting to differing automotive dilemmas.

The army was pleased with the results because the number of collisions and crashes diminished. Somehow, professor Richard Ulbricht (1849–1923), president of the Royal Saxon Railroads, learned

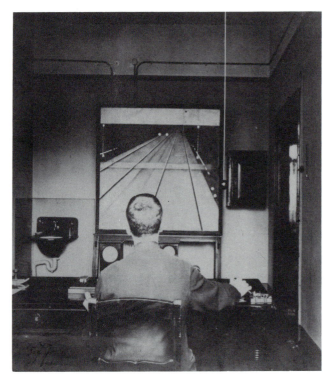

Figure 1 Applicant for engineer's test in front of stimulus canvas.

Figure 2 Examiner's seat at left of applicant.

about this innovative method for personnel selection. Since the railroads, an important means of transportation during the war, had similar safety problems, he contacted Brahn, Moede, and Piorkowski and had a testing laboratory installed in Dresden under their supervision in May 1917. This did not turn the tide of the war, but it proved to be the fruitful first step toward an enduring liaison between applied psychology and the railroads.

Various tests were devised for the task, such as sorting tests, memory tests, and "will-power" tests. The principal and most conspicuous, however, was the driving test. It resembled the army's motorcar driving test but was transformed to mimic the driving environment in a locomotive. Figures 1 and 2 show the first installation in Dresden. Figure 1 shows the optical and acoustical signals impinging on the applicant, who has to respond according to prescribed procedure. The various tasks simulate those an engineer is confronted with when driving a steam locomotive. The applicant is surrounded by levers and handles for steam, brake, whistle, injector, ejector, and various indicators. The use of the different handles and levers is explained, and the candidate practices with them until he fully understands their use. The test itself lasted 20 minutes. The applicant's reactions were evaluated for speed and precision. The setup follows the standard laboratory reaction time experiments, including the chronoscope for time measurements outside the frame to the left. The examiner was seated in the seat to the left (see Figure 2) of the applicant and controlled the optical and acoustical signals, observed the aptness of responses, and measured reaction times by operating the Hipp chronoscope to his left, next to the wall. Note that there is no discernible controlling apparatus for the chronoscope—an indispensable piece of equipment for obtaining reliable, absolute figures that was found in every research laboratory.

The management was so satisfied with the results that it was soon ruled that a man in Saxony could be admitted to the three-year training course for engineers only if he had successfully passed an examination in general knowledge, the psychological test, and a medical examination. This was obviously an important step for the spreading of the still very young field of applied psychology.

The various German railroad companies merged after the First World War and were put under foreign control in order to secure reparation payments. The new corporation, called the *Reichsbahn*, was therefore under powerful pressure to maximize profits and rationalize every conceivable segment of the enterprise, as well as to reduce staff, number of accidents, and any type of waste. The staff was told to be especially cautious about hiring and promotions, since all employees were civil servants and therefore difficult to fire, even if proven incompetent. The *Reichsbahn* therefore created a scientific committee composed of psychologists, physicians, engineers, and lawyers, who then established a network of testing laboratories and offices throughout the country, as well as new tests for most of the diverse jobs needed to run a large railroad system. Walther Moede became the leading psychologist on this committee and supervised the improvement of the test for engineers, as well as designing tests for workshop apprentices, booking-office clerks, shunters, fitters, pointsmen, brakemen, conductors, flagmen, stokers, stationmasters, and so on.

Other countries followed suit. Austria, France, (Lahy, 1933; Laugier & Weinberg, 1936), Italy (Boganelli, 1952), the Netherlands, the Soviet Union (Viteles, 1938), Sweden (Anderberg, 1939), Switzerland (Baumgarten, 1931), the United States (Sheaffer, 1924) and many others (Hondl, 1937; Lo Balbo, 1936; Nestor, 1933; Wojciechowski, 1936) established psychological services in their railroad systems. Steps to institutionalize global exchange were taken with the reunion of the Transport Commission of the International Conference of Psychotechnics in Paris in 1935 and at the 13th Conference of the International Railway Congress Association in Paris in 1937. The Second World War bluntly interrupted the international exchange, but the psychological services survived and remained an important specialty in vocational psychology. Much more could be said about the development of these services, but one aspect is of particular interest, and that is how psychological services for the railroad created one of the most unusual working environments psychologists have occupied.

By the early 1920s, the railroads' psychological services were no longer satisfied to have their laboratories installed in buildings in the major capitals. In order to get closer to the applicants for the various jobs available, they organized a mobile testing laboratory. The testing apparatus was placed in a traincar reconstructed specifically for this purpose. This enabled them to reach a larger number of

Figure 4 Interior of the last mobile testing traincar.

Figure 3 Interior of the first mobile aptitude testing laboratory.

potential recruits, even in remote villages, as long as they were connected to the railway.

Figure 3 shows the interior of the first aptitude testing traincar devised by the Dresden Laboratory. The stimulus board is the same as in the first Dresden laboratory. The surrounding apparatus, however, has been modified. Typically, more solid components were used since they needed to endure the wear and tear of traveling. Similar traincars were used, first in Berlin (Couvé, 1925), then all over Germany and in some neighboring countries. Most of them were abolished during the sixties and seventies.

The last exemplar of this rare species (Figure 4) served in the Austrian Federal Railroads. Originally built for a conspicuous individual in the Third Reich, it fell into the hands of the U.S. Army at an obscure Alpine station in 1945. The army employed it for ten years as a liaison train between their headquarters in Salzburg and Vienna. It was turned over to the Austrian Federal Railways in 1955 and transformed into a rolling testing laboratory. It was then used in that capacity from 1957 until 1993.

As the emphasis in aptitude testing shifted away from the individual's ability to manipulate heavy machinery to group paper-and-pencil procedures, the testing rooms changed in appearance. The psychologist would stand in front of the blackboard and instruct the group of applicants, seated in a class-like manner, on the tasks ahead. Motor and dexterity tests were taken at the rear end of the testing room. This traincar was a most uncommon workplace for a psychologist since it encompassed not only the testing room, but also offices, sleeping rooms, a shower, kitchenette, and other amenities for living "on the go." Psychologists traveled every rail in Austria while working and residing under one roof and on wheels but with an ever-changing panoramic view from their windows. No accident associated with this traincar was

Figure 5 Last aptitude testing traincar at Passau.

ever reported, possibly due to the increased safety standards secured by the railroad's own psychological services. Occasionally, however, a passing hobo could not resist the lure of this homey abode and made himself at home when the traincar was off duty somewhere in the country.

The Institute for the History of Modern Psychology at Passau University was able to secure this unique item which is now being transformed into a rolling museum of applied psychology in the service of the railroads (Figure 5).

Bibliography

Anderberg, R. (1939). Selecting personnel for the Swedish Railways with the aid of psychological tests. *Occupational Psychology, 13,* 211–222.

Baumgarten, F. (1931). Psychotechnische Prüfungen bei den Schweizerischen Bundesbahnen (S.B.B.). *Psychotechnische Zeitschrift, 6,* 156.

Boganelli, E. (1952). Selezione psicofisiologica dei macchinisti delle ferrovie dello stato italiano. In F. Baumgarten (Ed.), *La Psychotechnique dans le Monde Moderne. Compte rendu du IXe Congrès international de Psychotechnique. Berne, 12–17 septembre 1949* (pp. 385–387). Paris: Presses Universitaire de France.

Couvé, R. (1925). Der Prüfungswagen der Psychotechnischen Versuchsstelle bei der Reichsbahndirektion Berlin. *Industrielle Psychotechnik, 2,* 382–383.

Hondl, J. (1937). Frage XI: Auswahl, Berfsausbildung und Unterweisung der Eisenbahnbediensteten Bericht (Belgien und Kolonien, Bulgarien, Frankreich und Kolonien, Griechenland, Jugoslawien, Luxemburg, Oesterreich, Rumänien, Schweiz, Tschechoslowakei, Türkei, und Ungarn) *Monatsschrift der Internationalen Eisenbahn-Kongress-Vereinigung, 8,* 879–919.

Lahy, J. M. (1933). Le premier laboratoire psychotechnique, ferroviaire français aux Chemins de Fer du Nord. *Le Travail Humain, 1,* 409–431.

Laugier, H., & Weinberg, D. (1936). Le laboratoire du travail des Chemins de fer de l'Etat français. *Le Travail Humain, 4,* 257–268.

Lo Balbo, P. (1936). Frage XI: Auswahl, Berufsausbildung und Unterweisung der Eisenbahnbediensteten. Bericht (Amerika, Ägypten, China, Grossbritannien und Kolonien, Italien, Japan, Portugal, und Kolonien, Spanien). *Monatsschrift der Internationalen Eisenbahn-Kongress-Vereinigung, 7,* 1621–1630.

Marbe, K. (1913). Psychologisches Gutachten zum Prozess wegen des Müllheimer Eisenbahnunglücks. *Fortschritte der Psychologie und ihrer Anwendungen, 1,* 11–23, 51–58.

Nestor, J, M. (1933). Vocational tests on the European railways. *The Human Factor, 7,* 11–23; 51–58.

Sheaffer, C. M. (1924/1925). Efficiency tests of Pennsylvania railroad personnel. *Journal of Personnel Research, 3* (7), 244–251.

Viteles, M. S. (1938). Industrial psychology in Russia. *Occupational Psychology, 12,* 85–103.

Wojciechowski, J. (1936). Frage XI: Auswahl, Berufsausbildung und Unterweisung der Eisenbahnbediensteten. Bericht (Dänemark, Deutschland, Finnland, Niederlande, und Kolonien, Norwegen, Polen und Schweden. *Monatsschrift der Eisenbahn-Kongress-Vereinigung, 7,* 1607–1619.

Industrial Psychology

Gerd Wiendieck

N o one knows the exact birthdate of industrial psychology. However, the beginning of this specialty is usually associated with the name of the American engineer and inventor Frederick Winslow Taylor (1856–1915) and his system of "scientific" management. His numerous recommendations for the improvement of the workplace ushered in a new era of industrial production. Taylor regarded his approach as scientific because it seemed to avoid value judgments and stressed the use of empirical measurement procedures.

Basically, "Taylorism" consists of the systematic application of the division of labor, the introduction of time and motion studies, highly specific job descriptions, and the introduction of piece-meal systems of remuneration. Henry Ford I (1863–1947) was the first major manufacturer to systematically apply Taylor's ideas to assembly line production, creating at the same time modern mass production and a new occupation—that of the skilled industrial worker. It cannot be denied that Taylorism resulted in a previously unknown growth of productivity, which, according to Lysinski (1923), resulted primarily from an intensification rather than a rational-

Figure 2 A 1920s time study of work on an industrial drill. The observer, in suit and hat, soon became a symbol of exploitation.

ization of the work situation. Almost from the beginning of this period, the one-sided pursuit of economical benefits by factory owners produced severe health problems and a restriction of opportunities for personal development among the workers (Watts, 1922, p. 89). Although Taylorism did not result from research in industrial psychology, it soon gained strong support among the psychologists of the late 19th and early 20th centuries. The dominating position of the technological industries facilitated the development of empirical and experimental approaches to psychology. Specifically, it was hoped that the new psychology would be able to provide a scientific basis and legitimization of industry's efforts towards increased productivity.

Drawing on the applied research of Alfred Binet (1857–1911) and William Stern (1871–1939) in differential psychology, the German-American Harvard

Figure 1 Portrait of Frederick Winslow Taylor.

Figure 3 The ergograph measured the effects of fatigue.

among machine operators" (p. 57). Consequently, the psychological assessment of relevant sensory, motor, and occasional cognitive skills came into widespread use. Ergographs were employed to measure muscular function during specific activities or movements. An experimental subject was asked to repeatedly deflate a small rubber balloon. The changes in pressure over time were recorded by a kymograph. Thus, it became possible to record fatigue curves and determine the relationship between fatigue and achievement levels.

World War I sped up the development of aptitude testing because important military and industrial positions had to be filled quickly and repeatedly with qualified personnel. In this context, Giese, a pioneer in the field, called for the development of mechanized and automatic test instruments to speed and standardize employee selection.

Efforts to measure the characteristics of workers comprehensively led, at times, to the invasion of privacy. For example, Giese's (1927) "Apparatus for the Assessment of Erotic Inclinations" presented a collection of 24 "erotic postcards" during a "pseudo memory test." The postcards were hidden behind shutters. The experimental subject was typically left alone and an electrical circuit recorded which sexual pictures were chosen. Some of the pictures were stolen during the sessions, and some adolescents were observed masturbating.

The psychological design of work situations was guided by the psycho-technical or machine model,

psychologist Hugo Münsterberg (1863–1916) developed the field of psychotechnology for industrial and business applications (1912).

Eventually, industrial psychology consisted of two major branches. The field ability or aptitude testing or "subjective psycho-technology" focused on the suitability of the worker for specific work situations. In turn, the psychological design of workplaces or "objective psycho-technology" was concerned with the establishment of humane working conditions, which would at the same time optimize the worker's productivity.

Aptitude diagnosis has an almost Biblical history in civil administration and military service (Schmale, 1983, p. 66). This specialty did not expand, however, until free occupational choice became possible in the Western world by the reduction and eventual termination of the restricting influence of guilds and other professional corporations. As Jäger and Stäuble (1983) noted, the discovery of "the uniform functioning of machines revealed the absence of uniformity

Figure 4 Apparatus for measuring "erotic interest" in employees.

511

which viewed man merely as a system of joints, axes, muscles, and sensors. Personal aspects of work which might have produced personal emotions such as "joy, unhappiness, courage or weakness" were disregarded (Bravermann, 1977, p. 141) because they were thought to be inaccessible to the techniques of scientific psychology (Lysinski, 1923, p. 6). Moreover, the personality of the worker was typically equated simply with his or her industrial productivity (Jäger & Stäuble, 1983, p. 56). In general, industrial psychology disregarded the content of the work situation and, instead, concentrated on ergographic problems of fatigue, exhaustion, and recovery (Lysinski, 1923, p. 53). At the end of the 19th century, similar questions were investigated by Emil Kraepelin (1856–1926), who, in addition to Münsterberg, has been regarded as another founder of modern industrial psychology (Kraepelin, 1925).

Another important stimulus to research was the discovery that organisms will respond with different levels of fatigue when lifting a single weight of 100 pounds rather than in ten units of ten pounds each. The "difference between mechanical and physical labor equivalents" (Lysinski, 1923) is illustrated in Figure 5. Specifically, the use of a "digging fork," a "broad spade," a "pointed spade," and a "regular spade" with "soft" and "hard" soil are shown. The letters a–e at the bottom of the illustration indicate the position of "head, left shoulder, left hand, right hand," and "blade of spade" during the different tasks. Research on workplace and work station design often included training in group situations.

Looking back on the beginnings of industrial psychology today, one is surprised and even shocked about the one-sided focus of the profession on individual and differential aptitudes and, especially, the almost automatic and quite naïve adoption of capitalist objectives by early industrial psychology. This undue stress on the importance of individual differences was replaced during the 1930s by the study of workgroups by Elton May (1878–1967) and, during the 1940s, by the social psychological work of Kurt Lewin (1890–1947) at the Research Center for Group Dynamics in the USA. Figure 7 shows a group of female workers in the so-called "Mica Test Room" who participated in Mayo's famous "Hawthorne experiment."

Ethical questions about the practical application of research in industrial psychology were first raised when the exploitative elements of classical Taylorism were realized. Unfortunately, these well-founded critiques were disregarded when Hugo Münsterberg stated almost ex cathedra that the industrial psychologist's job was to be the willing servant of the economic interests of the time and, hence, had no business raising ethical questions about its use or abuse in industry.

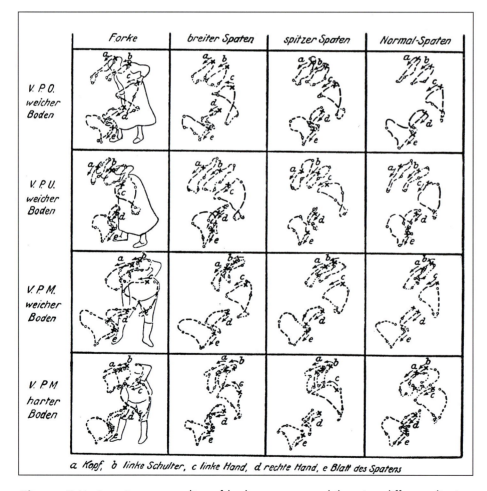

Figure 5 Motion picture recording of body movements while using different digging implements for different types of soil.

Figure 6 Group training facility for streetcar drivers in Berlin.

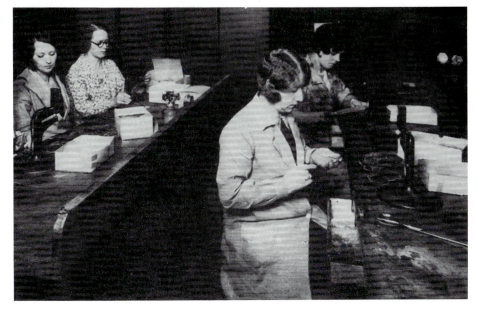

Figure 7 Participants in Mayo's Hawthorne experiments.

Bibliography

Bravermann, H. (1977). *Die Arbeit im modernen Produktionsprozeß.* Frankfurt: Campus.

Giese, F. (1927). *Methoden der Wirtschaftspsychologie.* Berlin: Urban & Schwarzenberg.

Jäger, S., & Stäuble, I. (1983). Die Psychotechnik und ihre gesellschaftlichen Emtwicklungsbedingungen. In F. Stoll. (Ed.), *Arbeit und Beruf* (Vol. 1, 2nd ed., pp. 49–91). Weinheim: Beltz.

Kräpelin, E. (1925). Arbeitspsychologische Ausblicke. *Psychologische Arbeiten, 8,* 431–451.

Lysinki, E. (1923). *Psychologie des Betriebes.* Berlin: Industrieverlag Spätze & Linde.

Münsterberg, H. (1912). *Psychologie und Wirtschaftsleben.* Leipzig: Barth.

Schmale, H. (1983). *Psychologie der Arbeit.* Stuttgart: Klett-Cotta.

Watts, F. (1922). *Die psychologischen Probleme der Industrie.* Berlin: Springer.

Weber, W. (1927). *Die praktische Psychologie im Wirtschaftsleben.* Leipzig: Barth.

Advertising Psychology

Advertising—the practice of persuading people to obtain goods or services or to adopt a point of view—has been around for ages. It always seeks to influence others and typically involves a social interaction between the advertiser and the potential customer. Today, a wealth of effective methods exist to attract the voluntary attention of the individual consumer. Without such consumer discretion and freedom of choice, advertising would become compulsion, and voluntary attention would turn into slave-like obedience. Advertising can focus on the

Figure 1 Example of an ad which appeals to fear, vanity, and eroticism at the same time (Kroppf, 1951).

Figure 2 Title page of Scott's scientific book on advertising psychology (1908).

514

Figure 3 An openly erotic advertisement.

tained almost 300 pages, was "respectfully" dedicated to "That increasing number of AMERICAN BUSINESSMEN who successfully apply science where their predecessors were confined to custom" (Scott, 1908). After stressing the benefits of experimental research, Scott discussed a broad spectrum of psychological topics like perception, attention, memory, volition, emotion, suggestion, and habits. In addition to Scott, Hugo Münsterberg (1863–1916), the German-American professor at Harvard, has to be mentioned as one of the pioneers of advertising psychology. As a visiting professor at Berlin University in 1912, he discussed his "Experiments on the Effects of Advertisements" in his lectures, which he published that same year (Münsterberg, 1912). Scott and Münsterberg were not only forerunners but also served as models for a holistic approach to advertising, which did not limit itself to the theories or methods of perceptual analysis or depth psychology.

Scientific advertising psychology in Germany

popularization of people, ideas, goods, or some combination of these. Typically, it appeals to both transitory feelings and deep emotions, as can be seen in Figure 1 which is an example of an ad appealing to fear, vanity, and eroticism at the same time (Kropf, 1951).

The use of mass media to promote advertising began in 18th-century France. According to Buchli (1966, p. 210), advertising had become such a nuisance that in 1734, Paris police were forced to outlaw the public distribution of handwritten or printed handbills. During the 19th century, the American showman Phineas T. Barnum (1810–1891) was considered the "first great advertising genius" and the world's "greatest publicity exploiter" (Presbrey, 1968). During 1886 alone, he is said to have spent the astronomical sum of more than one and one-half million dollars (Buchli, 1966) on posters, newspaper ads, and millions of gaudily colored flyers.

Academic psychology first became involved in advertising at the beginning of the 20th century. As early as 1908, Walter Dill Scott (1869–1955) published his famous book, *The Psychology of Advertising in Theory and Practice*. This book, which con-

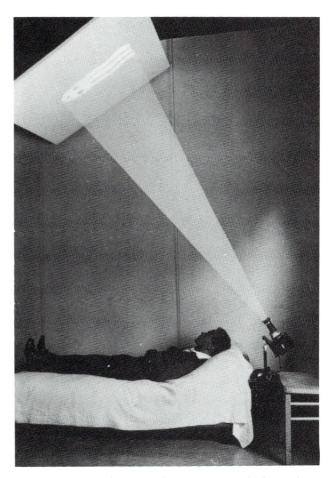

Figure 4 Spiegel's research situation, in which a subject relaxes on a couch while responding by free association to tachistoscopically presented advertising materials.

Figure 5 The white spots indicate a photographic record of a subject's eye movements while observing the advertisement (Spiegel, 1958).

developed much more slowly than in the USA, possibly due to the fear German psychologists had of losing their academic dignity (Kroppf, 1951). This overly cautious reluctance was found primarily in the field of consumer psychology. In general, German scientists seem to have been able to reconcile the industrial applications of their research with their Protestant work ethic; however, they were inclined to view the application of psychological principles to advertising as the dishonorable encouragement of idleness and waste. In this context, the virtue of honest work was often contrasted with the vice of consumption. A good example of this perspective can be found in the writings of Wal-

ter Rathenau (1838–1916), the German industrialist and politician (1918):

> Any thinking person will walk with horror through the streets and see the department stores, shops, and warehouses. . . . Most of what is stored, elegantly displayed and dearly sold is terribly ugly, serves demeaning lusts . . . and is [actually] stupid, harmful, worthless, and illegal . . . meaningless and wasteful. (p. 179)

Nonetheless, advertising continued to grow, even in Germany. Its increasing costs and the need to document its usefulness led to a closer involvement of psychologists. In 1924, the book *Advertising Psychology* was published by König. Later, in 1934, the principles of Gestalt psychology were applied to the field of advertising by Kroppf. National Socialism discouraged the development of consumer psychology but utilized its principles in the service of political propaganda.

After World War II, and with the beginning of the "Economic Miracle" period in the German economy, product advertising was rediscovered. Since academic psychology once again maintained its distance, the use of nonpsychological and even unscientific approaches expanded, including the academic specialties of economics and business management (Seyffert, 1966) and the pseudo-science of "motivational research." During the 1950s and 1960s, German translations of many speculative psychoanalytic publications by Vance Packard, Ernest Dichter, and Werner Suhr achieved great publicity. These books raised concerns over the power of manipulators and the pliability of modern man. Suhr (1963) described the ad shown in Figure 3 as follows: "No motivational researcher is needed to interpret the dream in which a . . . young lady grabs the bull by its horns, her well-formed girlishness—her 'naturally curved curves' . . . —provide her with an enormous sense of security. . . . [The slogan] 'Girl catches bull . . .' is [indeed] catching" (p. 640). This short-lived movement in advertising psychology gained a great deal of special attention by contrasting the "rationality" of the business world with the "helpless life" of the modern mass consumer. In 1976 Jacoby evaluated the popular advertising psychology of the late 1950s and 1960s in devastating terms: "In our view, more than 85 per cent of the publications in the field of consumer psychology before 1968 have a low [scientific basis] and are of questionable value" (p. 345).

Not until the 1960s did the psychologists Bernd Spiegel (1958), Reinhold Bergler (1965), and Lutz von Rosenstiel (1969), and the economist Werner Kroeber-Riel (1990) and others finally develop a broader, scientific-methodological basis for advertising psychology in German-speaking countries.

Spiegel's research situation required a subject to relax on a couch while responding by free association to tachistoscopically presented advertising materials (Figure 4). A photographic record was kept (Figure 5) of a subject's eye movements while watching posters and ads (Spiegel, 1958).

Bibliography

Bergler, R. (Ed.). (1965). *Psychologische Marktanalyse.* Bern: Huber.

Buchli, H. (1966). 6000 Jahre Werbung. Vol. III: Das Zeitalter der Revolutionen. Berlin: de Gruyter.

Dichter, E. (1961). Strategie im Reich der Wünsche. Düsseldorf: Econ.

Jacoby, J. (1976). Consumer psychology: An Octennium. *Annual Review of Psychology, 27,* 331–358.

Kroeber-Riel, W. (1990). *Konsumentenverhalten* (4th ed.) Munich: Vahlen.

König, T. (1924). *Reklame-Psychologie.* Munich/Berlin: Oldenbourg.

Kroppf, H. F. J. (1934). *Psychologie in der Reklame als Mittel zur Bestgestaltung des Entwurfs.* Stuttgart: Poeschel.

Kroppf, H. F. J. (1951). *Neue Psychologie in der neuen Werbung.* Stuttgart: Poeschel.

Münsterberg, H. (1912). *Psychologie und Wirtschaftsleben.* Leipzig: Barth.

Packard, V. (1957). *Die geheimen Verführer.* Düsseldorf: Econ.

Presbrey, F. (1968). *The history and development of advertising.* New York: Greenwood Press.

Rathenau, W. (1918). *Von kommenden Dingen.* Berlin: Fischer.

Rosenstiel, L. von (1969). *Psychologie der Werbung.* Rosenheim: Komar.

Scott, W. (1908). *The psychology of advertising.* Boston: Small, Maynard & Co.

Seyffert, R. (1966). *Werbelehre. Theorie und Praxis der Werbung.* Vols. 1 & 2. Stuttgart: Poeschel.

Spiegel, B. (1958). *Werbepsychologische Untersuchungsmethoden.* Berlin: Duncker & Humblot.

Suhr, W. (1963). *Die stärksten Appelle. Sex contra Facts.* Düsseldorf: Econ.

The History of Psychology

Charles E. Early
Wolfgang G. Bringmann

Most psychologists are painfully aware that their discipline is now composed of a variety of subspecialties co-existing in the same building under the same roof, but frequently going about their business in relatively isolated apartments. Such appears to be the fate of a science which carries extraordinary breadth. Still, there seems yet to

Figure 1 Portrait of Friedrich August Carus (1770–1807) whose *History of Psychology* was published posthumously in 1808.

be a sense of community among these various spheres of interest, and one searches for ways to enhance that feeling. Time will tell whether or not the diverse specialties within modern psychology will grow in a way that creates greater or lesser interaction with one another, but there is one thing that they will always share, and that is their history. A common history is the tie that binds, and it is likely that the growing interest in the history of psychology arises at least in part from the enhanced sense of professional identity that comes with knowing one's roots. Perhaps for this reason the history of psychology is now recommended as a capstone course for undergraduate psychology programs (see, for example, McGovern, Furumoto, Halpern, Kimble, & McKeachie, 1991) or at least appears as an integral component of the psychology curriculum at both undergraduate and graduate levels.

In the introduction to this volume we briefly presented a rationale for studying the history of psychology which echoes some of the same sentiments expressed above. One may readily find more elaborate and equally compelling arguments supporting the value of historical perspective in other sources (e.g., Wertheimer, 1984). In this article, however, we will continue under the assumption that the value of history has been sufficiently established in the reader's mind, and we will take the discussion a step further. And that is to examine the history of the history of psychology itself.

In his famous dictum, Hermann Ebbinghaus (1850–1911) told us that psychology has a long past but a short history (Ebbinghaus, 1908). This classic observation about our field seems equally appropriate as a description of the development of historical scholarship in psychology. While the interest in historical issues pertaining to psychology has been around for quite some time, it has only been in recent decades that a more professional and sophisticated study of psychology's history has become a field of interest in its own right. One result is that the new field has generated an ever-increasing quantity and quality of research. In the following pages we will examine the growth of the history of psychology—mainly as it has developed in North America—as a subspecialty of the larger discipline of modern scientific psychology. We begin with a look at the "long past," and then turn our attention to the "short history" of this new scholarly enterprise, which some say originated with Robert Watson's 1960 paper "The History of Psychology: A Neglected Area." Others, however, trace the beginning of the "short history" to the formal establishment of the American Psychological Association's Division 26 (History of Psychology) in September of 1965 (Benjamin, 1988).

The Early Stages of Psychology's Historiography

The "long past" of historical writing and research in American psychology can be conveniently organized into the following four consecutive periods or stages. As we describe each of the different periods, it must be remembered that these divisions are somewhat arbitrary and hence overlap in time and content.

The Philosophical Stage

The first or philosophical stage in the historiography of American psychology extends from the first half of the 17th century to the closing decades of the 19th century. Its beginning has been associated with the appointment of William Dunster (1609–1659) as the first president of Harvard College and, specifically, to the syllabus of instruction he proposed after the model of the older English universities (Fay, 1939; Roback, 1952; Evans, 1984). During this period, information about historically important philosophers and psychologists was included as a matter of course in books of theology and moral and intellectual philosophy which were published in America (Fay, 1939; Hall, 1895). The first American work in philosophy, the *Elementa Philosophica* (1752), by Samuel Johnson belongs to

Figure 2 Title page of the first *History of Psychology* by Carus (1808).

this type of publication, as does the first American college textbook in psychology, *Psychology; or a View of the Human Soul, Including Anthropology* (1840) by Friedrich August Rauch (1806–1841). The monumental *Principles of Psychology* (1890) by William James (1842–1910) and the pioneering *Handbook of Psychology* (1894) by James M. Baldwin (1861–1934) also belong to this genre insofar as their treatment of historical information is concerned. The authors of these early works were thoroughly familiar with the classical languages and with French and German. Sometimes they used their own translations of classical texts to make a particular point. Their work also appears to be relatively free from a presentist bias, which mars many recent publications in the history of psychology (Stocking, 1965; Woodward, 1980; Young, 1966).

The Monograph Stage

The monograph stage began during the second half of the 19th century, although this type of literature is still found today, especially in the form of dissertations. Long articles or small books which analyze a restricted topic in the history of psychology in great detail on the basis of extensive library research are typical examples. These works include the American edition of the slim monograph, *English Psychology* (1892), by Theodule Ribot (1823–1891), and *Theophrastus and the Greek Physiological Psychology before Aristotle* (1917) by George M. Stratton (1865–1957). Many of these historical analyses were published in the *American Journal of Psychology*, which G. Stanley Hall (1844–1924) founded in 1887. A cursory examination of the initial volumes of this publication yields a wealth of historical articles by eminent American psychologists.

Altogether the 30 volumes of this journal, which were edited by Hall, contain more than 200 articles of relevance to the history of psychology.

Figure 3 G. Stanley Hall (1844–1924), one of the early American pioneers of historical scholarship in psychology.

Survey Stage

The third or survey stage in the story of psychological historiography in America begins with the second decade of the 20th century. However, as indicated in Table 1, the first comprehensive German history of psychology was published more than 100 years earlier by the Leipzig philosopher Friedrich August Carus (1770–1807). According to Pongratz (1980), this work, which was published posthumously, portrays "the history of psychology . . . in a continuous . . . and . . . progressive manner." In addition, it makes extensive use of the "chronological, biographical doxographic" and "systematic" approaches to historiography which are still popular today (p. 34).

A careful examination of the items found in Table 1 reveals the following general patterns among the listed surveys of the history of psychology:

1. As mentioned, the dates indicate that this type of publication originated in Germany more than a hundred years before the first original English works in the field were published in America. The Germans preceded Americans in translations, as Schmidt's (1923) series of autobiographies predated the Murchison series (1930) which in fact borrowed some of its content in translation.

2. Most of the listed English and German histories of psychology approach their topic in a conceptual and systematic manner and provide little biographical information about eminent psychologists, with the occasional exception of their life dates.

3. Unfortunately, German as well as English-language authors rely heavily on secondary or even tertiary sources in their native languages. A notable exception is Brett's original history (1912, 1921a, 1921b) with its many notes referring to original classical sources. However, Brett's abbreviation of his comprehensive work (1928) again borrows heavily from his earlier works and provides little or no documentation.

4. While most of the German and English texts appear to have aimed at a comprehensive treatment of their subject matter, for the most part they stress the origin of psychology in Western thought and are decidedly Eurocentric in their orientation—even when they mention American contributions in psychology. The majority of texts also clearly regard modern experimental

Table 1 *Early German and American Histories of Psychology (1808–1935*

Authors	Titles	Dates
Carus	*Geschichte der Psychologie*	1808
Dessoir	*Geschichte der Neueren Deutschen Psychologie*	1894, 1910
Dessoir	*Abriss einer Geschichte der Psychologie*	1911
Klemm	*Geschichte der Psychologie*	1911
Dessoir	*Outlines of the History of Psychology*	1912
Brett	*A History of Psychology* (Vol. 1)	1912
Rand	*The Classical Psychologists*	1912
Baldwin	*History of Psychology* (Vols. 1 & 2)	1913
Klemm	*History of Psychology*	1914
Brett	*A History of Psychology* (Vol. 2)	1921
Brett	*A History of Psychology* (Vol. 3)	1921
Schmidt (Ed.)	*Die Philosophie der Gegenwart in Selbstdarstellungen* (Vol. 1)	1923
Brett	*Psychology: Ancient and Modern*	1928
Pillsbury	*The History of Psychology*	1929
Murphy	*Historical Introduction to Modern Psychology*	1929
Murchison	*A History of Psychology in Autobiography* (Vol. 1)	1930
Müller-Freienfels	*The Evolution of Modern Psychology*	1935
Spearman	*Psychology Down the Ages*	1935

psychology as superior to the psychological perspectives of earlier periods and do not hesitate to say so.

Specialty Stage

During the last or specialty stage, a number of books summarizing important information about specialized areas of psychology and various subareas of psychology appeared. They include works like Warren's *A History of Association Psychology* (1921), Peterson's *Early Conceptions and Tests of Intelligence* (1925), Fearing's *Reflex Action: A Study in the History of Physiological Psychology* (1930), or *A History of Medical Psychology* (1941) by Zilboorg and Henry. The two editions of Boring's magnum opus, *A History of Experimental Psychology* (1929, 1950), are perhaps the best known examples of this genre of historical writing. However, Boring's smaller book on *Sensation and Perception in the History of Psychology* (1942) should also be mentioned. These specialized histories differ from the early monographs by their greater scope, but they frequently rely on the same secondary sources in English and rarely question the scientific status of modern psychology. Unfortunately these works have come to be regarded as classical sources on the topics which they covered and from which many recent textbooks in the history of psychology derive their presentations and evaluations.

Evaluation

The diverse writings from the early periods of the American historiography of psychology have attracted a good deal of critical attention in recent years. Some of this criticism is summarized in the following sections.

Scissors-and-Paste History. Many works published before 1960 utilized the "scissors-and-paste" method of historiography as the chief research technique. According to Collingwood (1946) this method was the only ". . . historical method known to the later Greco-Roman world and the Middle Ages" (p. 258). It provides a so-called "patchwork history" drawn from the works of "previous historians who had already written the histories of particular societies at particular times" (Collingwood, 1946, p. 33). Today we might need to speak of "word-processor-histories" which can even more conveniently be assembled than their traditional predecessors.

Presentism. Classical works in the history of psychology often suffer from the "narrative fallacy of presentism" (Fischer, 1970), which reflects the naive belief that there is a clearcut progression in

Figure 4 Edwin G. Boring (1886–1968), eminent American historian of psychology.

the history of psychology from its "primitive" past to its current status as a respected modern behavioral science (Stocking, 1965; Woodward, 1980). Presentism is especially common in "the historical writings of men who have never been trained in the discipline of history [but] academic historians are not exempt from the same error" (Fischer, 1970, pp. 137–138). Proponents of this view, as Fischer put it so aptly, believe that the "proper way to do history is to prune away the dead branches of the past, and to preserve the green buds and twigs, which have grown into the dark forest of our contemporary world" (p. 135). Specifically, the survey stage and the specialty stage, described above, are seriously prone to the presentist bias of historiography.

The Old and the Lame. In his autobiography, the late Robert Watson (1972) suggested that historians of psychology are often those who publish only isolated and occasional works in the history of psychology and afterwards quickly return to more rewarding endeavors in their primary specialties. Other workers in the field, according to Watson are "aging psychologists who confused an interest in

their extended present with an interest in the past" (1972, p. 287). Woodward noted in the same vein that the history of science, and by implication the history of psychology, has often been viewed as an "avocation for senior colleagues, failed scientists, and others who drop out of the research mill for one reason or another" (Woodward, 1980, p. 36).

Low Standards of Scholarship. Perhaps the sharpest criticism of traditional scholarship in the history of psychology was vented in 1966 by Robert M. Young, the English historian of science. After reviewing some of the classics, including Boring's history of experimental psychology (1929, 1950), he made the following pointed observation (1966):

> If the history of psychology is to advance beyond being an avocation with very uneven standards, those professional psychologists who would contribute to scholarship must grasp that the standards of historical scholarship are no less rigorous than those of experimental science. In fact, since historians are usually dealing with softer data, the standards must in many ways be higher. (p. 54)

The Rise of the "New" History of Psychology

In this section we will briefly review a number of key events that were instrumental to the relatively recent growth and advancement of historiography in American psychology. These include (1) the development of an organization that crystallized into Division 26 (The History of Psychology) of the American Psychological Association (APA), (2) the creation of a newsletter and then a journal, (3) the creation of the Archives of the History of American Psychology, (4) the development of the first graduate program for the study of the history of psychology, and (5) the Summer Institutes set up by Brožek and Watson which led to the creation of *Cheiron*. The initial focus is placed on Robert I. Watson, who did so much to set these events in motion.

A Neglected Area

The renaissance of historical scholarship among American psychologists and the beginning of the institutional development of this field is closely associated with the late Robert I. Watson (1909–1980). In 1960 Watson published his famous manifesto, "The History of Psychology A Neglected Area" in the *American Psychologist*.

According to his autobiography, Watson first

became interested in the history of psychology in 1953, when he became Director of the Training Program in Clinical Psychology at Northwestern University in Chicago. His first historical publication, "A Brief History of Clinical Psychology," was published in the *Psychological Bulletin* and was met with an exceptionally large number of reprint requests (Watson, 1972). Watson later wrote:

> It was in about 1959 that I decided explicitly to become a historian of psychology in the sense that I resolved thereafter this would be my major area of research and publication. But there were many obstacles. For one thing, there seemed to be little in the way of company and hardly any precedent. . . . yet I knew that scattered around the country there had to be a handful of individuals with similar interests. (p. 287)

Watson's 1960 paper appears to have been an intentional attempt to "stimulate interest in the field by publishing a paper that was meant to serve as a challenge" (Watson, 1972, p. 287). Watson's "challenge" still reads like a provocation:

> In the United States psychology is provincial, both geographically and temporally. While almost any European psychologist whom we meet surprises us by his knowledge of our work, we fall far short of equivalent familiarity with psychological activities in his country. Our relative ignorance of current psychological activities outside the United States is so well known and seemingly complacently accepted as hardly to need exposition. It is not my intent to discuss our geographical provincialism except to point out that it seems to be similar to our historical provincialism. (1960, p. 251)

In that same paper Watson documented the neglect of the history of psychology as a field of specialization. Specifically, only three journals were found to sometimes publish research in the history of the field. A search of the membership directory of the American Psychological Association at the time yielded the names of "only about 60 psychologists who consider the history of psychology among their interests, irrespective of whether or not they publish [in the field]" (Watson, 1960, p. 251). Watson regarded indifference to the history of their specialty as a clear "value judgment on the part of psychologists" (Watson, 1960, p. 252). He also expressed the view that psychologists in America "as social beings share in a characteristic aberration of our times: a relative lack of curiosity about our past" (p. 252). His article concluded with a reasoned appeal to psychologists to prepare themselves for the challenges awaiting historical researchers.

History of Psychology Group

Shortly after the publication of his influential article, Watson made contact with John C. Burnham, a historian of psychoanalysis at Austin Riggs sanitarium in Stockbridge, Massachusetts, and David Bakan, the author of a well-known study of Freud's relationship with Judaism. Watson wanted to discuss plans for a special meeting of psychologists with historical interests at the 1960 meeting of the American Psychological Association in Chicago. According to the published minutes the first informal discussion session was attended by 26 people. There were an additional 15 invited who did not attend the first meeting due to other commitments. The 26 psychologists who came introduced themselves and gave short descriptions of their work and interests in the history of psychology. Information about potential publication outlets in the field were exchanged, and "the meeting resolved to send a letter to the Boards of Editors of APA . . . to make definite provision for historical articles." Before the end of the meeting, a motion was passed that all present should constitute themselves as a "special interest group within APA," and that preparations should be made to meet again and try to organize a special symposium.

Newsletter

According to Watson (1972), "a newsletter containing news and notes about meetings, publications, and courses taught was first published . . . in October of 1960" (p. 288) in the hope of maintaining contact among the members of the history interest group. The first four issues of this communication appeared in October of 1960, March 1961, November 1961, and August 1962, respectively. The *Newsletter* contained a total of 18 pages over these years. Watson apparently produced these issues before the annual APA meetings or whenever sufficient information was available. The mailing list indicated that the initial group had already more than doubled to 96. During the next APA meeting in St. Louis, the first official program was offered by the History of Psychology Interest Group on Monday, September 3, 1962, "between 1:00 and 3:00 . . . in the Khorasan of the Chase Hotel." The meeting was sponsored by Division 2 (Teaching of Psychology) of APA and the new History of Psychology Group. The title of the program was *Strategies in the Teaching of the History of Psychology*, and Robert Watson, Robert MacLeod, D. J. Harvey, and Edwin G. Boring presented original papers.

Division 26 (History of Psychology) of APA

Watson gives the impression that he was opposed to any formal organization for the history of psychology, at least initially (Watson, 1972):

> Quite deliberately the [history of psychology] group was without officers, dues or even an official name. Many of us found this state of affairs congenial. When the possibility of a formal division within APA was first broached, I demurred. The argument that convinced me that such a step was necessary was the comment of one young psychologist to the effect that a division of the history of psychology would give a stamp of authenticity to work in this area—that it would help bring recognition that the history of psychology is a form of specialization. We decided at our meeting in 1964 to proceed with a

petition for divisional status. In September 1965 the governing body of the APA approved the formation of the Division of the History of Psychology with a charter membership of 211. (p. 288)

We also read about these deliberations in *Newsletter #8* which was published in December of 1964. According to the newsletter, "Ron Mayer was asked to assume leadership in exploring the necessary procedures and extent of interest" (*Newsletter #8*, 1964, p. 2). The next newsletter (#10—January, 1965) included a special "MEMORANDUM TO THE COUNCIL OF REPRESENTATIVES OF THE AMERICAN PSYCHOLOGICAL ASSOCIATION" and contains the text of the formal application for division status.

These petitions were circulated among interested APA members to be returned to Watson at Northwestern University. At least 200 signatures had to be collected before the council would consider such a request. A few months later—in the summer of 1965—we read in the *Newsletter* "WE MAY YET . . . THIS YEAR . . . have a Division of the History of Psychology . . . over 226 petitions have been signed and continue to arrive weekly" (*Newsletter #12*, 1965, p. 1). Finally, we learn from the Fall 1965 *Newsletter*, edited by Mayer and Larson, that the petition requesting the establishment of a Division for the History of Psychology was approved unanimously by the APA Council of Representatives on September 7, 1965. The formal organizational meeting of Division 26 was scheduled for the 1966 APA Convention in New York. Although it is still one of the smaller APA divisions, Division 26 has grown to approximately 1000 members and offers a quality program of papers and symposia at the annual APA meetings.

Journal of the History of the Behavioral Sciences

Watson reports in his autobiography that initial planning for a new journal began in 1962 or 1963, and that the next year was devoted to soliciting articles and arranging for a multidisciplinary board of editors drawn from psychology, anthropology, sociology, neurophysiology, neurology, psychiatry and psychoanalysis, and history itself. In January of 1965 the first issue of the *Journal of the History of the Behavioral Sciences* appeared (1972, p. 289).

The *Journal of the History of the Behavioral Sciences* (JHBS) that resulted is today a major publication outlet for the new generation of American histo-

Figure 5 Robert I. Watson (1909–1980), clinical psychologist and leader in the rise of contemporary scholarship in the history of American psychology.

rians of psychology. Over the years the JHBS has had a profound impact on the development of the recent history of psychology, and it continues to exemplify high standards of excellence in historical scholarship.

Archives of the History of American Psychology

The creation of the Archives of the History of American Psychology in Akron, Ohio, is also clearly among the most important contributions to the growth of historical scholarship in American psychology. This facility was created on November 15, 1965, by an official act of the Board of Directors of the University of Akron. Founded by John A. Popplestone, who has also served as its long-time director, the archives are a fully funded branch of the university library system. The ever-growing collection of documents, apparatus, and visual materials has become one of our field's most precious resources.

Graduate Programs in the History of Psychology

In 1967, at the age of 59, Robert Watson accepted a position as professor of psychology at the University of New Hampshire, where a fairly classical program in General-Experimental Psychology had been initiated. Eugene Mills, the head of the department, accurately considered himself to be a historian of psychology and his eventual promotion to the presidency of the University was a boon for Watson and his history plans. At New Hampshire, Watson initiated the first graduate degree program devoted to the history of psychology. The first degree was awarded to Barbara Ross in June of 1970 for an impressive dissertation dealing with the *Genesis of Psychology within the Context of the Scientific Revolution in England, 1665–1700.* In 1981, York University in Toronto also developed a graduate program in the history and theory of psychology.

Summer Institutes and Cheiron

Another step towards strengthening the emerging history of psychology as a specialty occurred in June of 1968, when Joseph Brožek and Robert Watson organized a Summer Institute in the History of Psychology at the Durham campus of the University of New Hampshire. The six-week program attracted 25 postdoctoral, five doctoral students, and six instructors (Brožek, Jaynes, Guerlac, Mora, Krantz, and McLeod). One result of the program was the creation of a new organization, *Cheiron*, the International Society for the History of the Behavioral and Social Sciences. *Cheiron* started as a vehicle for maintaining the momentum generated by the Summer Institute, holding its first meeting in 1969. Later, in 1982, the European Cheiron Society was created.

Conclusion

In this brief review we have examined a bit of the background related to the study of psychology's history and then covered several of the key events that helped launch the field to a new level of interest and sophistication. There were, of course many other issues related to this growth that could be examined, such as the textbooks in the field, the discussion and controversies over writing history, philosophical presuppositions about the nature of psychology, and even the teaching of psychology's history; but these are beyond the scope of the present paper. The interested reader is encouraged to read the fine surveys available that examine these and other issues in depth (e.g., Furumoto, 1989; Hilgard, Leary, & McGuire, 1991; Wertheimer, 1984).

Psychology is a rapidly changing discipline with its growth fueled by an explosion of research and applications. It seems fitting that the one subject that can provide a sense of orientation within the rapid expansion taking place—the history of the discipline—should itself reflect the same dynamic process.

Bibliography

Baldwin, J. M. (1889–1891). *Handbook of psychology.* New York: Holt.

Benjamin, L. T. (1988). *A history of psychology: Original sources and contemporary research.* New York: McGraw-Hill.

Boring, E. G. (1929). *A history of experimental psychology.* New York: Appleton.

Boring, E. G. (1942). *Sensation and perception in the history of psychology.* New York: Appleton-Century-Crofts.

Boring, E. G. (1950). *A history of experimental psychology* (2nd ed.). New York: Appleton-Century-Crofts.

Brett, G. S. (1912–1921). *A history of psychology.* London: Allen.

Brett, G. S. (1928). *Psychology, ancient and modern.* New York: Longmans.

Burnham, W. (1888–1889). Memory, historically and experimentally considered. *American Journal of Psychology, 2,* 39–90, 225–270, 431–464, 566–622.

Collingwood, R. (1946). *The idea of history.* Oxford: Clarendon Press.

Ebbinghaus, H. (1908). *Abriß der Psychologie.* Leipzig: Veit.

Evans, R. (1984). The origins of American academic psychology. In J. Brožek (Ed.), *Explorations in the history of psychology in the United States* (pp. 17–80). Lewisburg: Bucknell University Press.

Fay, J. W. (1939). *American psychology before William James.* New Brunswick, NJ: Rutgers University Press.

Fearing, F. (1930). *Reflex action: A study in the history of physiological psychology.* Baltimore: Williams & Wilkins.

Fischer, D. H. (1970). *Historians' fallacies: Toward a logic of historical thought.* New York: Harper & Row.

Fraser, A. (1991). Visualization as the chief source of the psychology of Hobbes, Locke, Berkeley and Hume. *American Journal of Psychology, 2,* 230–247.

Furumoto, L. (1989). The new history of psychology. In I. S. Cohen (Ed.), *The G. Stanley Hall Lecture Series* (Vol. 9, pp. 5–34). Washington, DC: American Psychological Association.

Gilgen, A. R. (1982). *American psychology since World War II: A profile of the discipline.* Westport, CT: Greenwood Press.

Hall, G. S. (1895). The history of American college textbooks and teaching in logic, ethics, psychology and allied subjects. *Proceedings of the American Antiquarian Society* (New Series), *9,* 243–363.

Hilgard, E. R., Leary, D. E., & McGuire, G. R. (1991). The history of psychology: A survey and critical assessment. *Annual Review of Psychology, 42,* 79–107.

Hodge, C. (1891). A sketch of the history of reflex action. *American Journal of Psychology, 3,* 149–173, 243–363.

James, W. (1890). *The principles of psychology.* New York: Holt.

Johnson, S. (1752). *Elementa philosophica.* Philadelphia: Printed by B. Franklin & D. Hall.

McGovern, T. V., Furumoto, L., Halpern, D. F., Kimble, G. A., & McKeachie, W. J. (1991). Liberal education, study in depth, and the arts and sciences major—psychology. *American Psychologist, 46,* 598–605.

Murchison, C. (Ed.). (1930, 1932, 1936). *A history of psychology in autobiography* (Vols. 1–3). Worcester, MA: Clark University Press.

Nichols, H. (1890). The psychology of time. *American Journal of Psychology, 3,* 8–22.

Peterson, J. (1925). Early conceptions and tests of intelligence. Yonkers, NY: World Books.

Pongratz, L. J. (1967). *Problemgeschichte der Psychologie.* Munich: Francke.

Pongratz, L. J. (1980). German historiography of psychology. In J. Brožek & L. J. Pongratz (Eds.), *Historiography of modern psychology* (pp. 74–89). Toronto: Hogrefe.

Rauch, F. A. (1840). *Psychology: or, a view of the human soul: including anthropology.* New York: M. W. Dodd.

Ribot, T. (1892). *English psychology.* New York: Appleton.

Roback, A. A. (1952). *A history of American psychology.* New York: Philosophical Library.

Schmidt, R. (1923–1924). *Die Philosophie der Gegenwart oin Selbstdarstellungen.* Leipzig: Meinert.

Scripture, W. (1891). Arithmetical prodigies. *American Journal of Psychology, 4,* 211–218.

Stocking, G. W. (1965). On the limits of "presentism" and "historicism" in the historiography of the behavioral sciences. *Journal of the History of the Behavioral Sciences, 1,* 211–217.

Stratton, G. M. (1917). *Theophrastus and the Greek physiological psychology before Aristotle.* New York: Macmillan.

Warren, H. (1921). *A history of association psychology from Hartley to Lewes.* New York: Scribner's.

Watson, R. I. (1960). The history of psychology: A neglected area. *American Psychologist, 15,* 251–255.

Watson, R. I. (1972). Working paper. In T. S. Krawiec (Ed.), *The Psychologists* (Vol. 1, pp. 275–297). London: Oxford University Press.

Watson, R. I. (1975). The history of psychology as a specialty: A personal view of its first fifteen years. *Journal of the History of the Behavioral Sciences, 11,* 61–73.

Wertheimer, M. (1984). History of psychology: What's new about what's old. In A. M. Rogers & C. J. Scheirer (Eds.), *The G. Stanley Hall Lecture Series* (Vol. 4, pp. 159–188). Washington, DC: American Psychological Association

Woodward, W. R. (1980). Toward a critical historiography of psychology. In J. Brožek & L. J. Pongratz (Eds.), *Historiography of modern psychology* (pp. 29–67). Toronto: Hogrefe.

Young, R. M. (1966). Scholarship and the history of the behavioural sciences. *History of Science, 5,* 1–51.

Zilboorg, G., & Henry, G. W. (1941). *A history of medical psychology.* New York: Norton.

VII
INTERNATIONAL DEVELOPMENTS

Psychological Journals

Helio Carpintero

By its nature, the scientific process requires that new discoveries, before they are integrated into the current paradigm, be made available to the scientific community. New ideas must be scrutinized and tested to ensure reliable, valid knowledge. Communication is a crucial component of this process. Because of the general willingness and obligation to share its information among its members, modern science has been defined as "public knowledge" (Ziman, 1968).

Such rigid criteria for the acceptance of new knowledge, however, may only be realized if it is communicated through some channel that is appropriately designed for disseminating the information. Books, meetings, lectures, and symposia are among the best known and most important of these channels; however, today the main vehicle for presenting and discussing theoretical or factual discoveries in psychology is the journal article.

Ever since psychology emerged as a true scientific discipline in the 19th century, its character has been revealed through its journals, and these have grown in a quasi-exponential manner. In every country, little by little, new periodicals have progressively helped to enlarge the discipline by providing opportunities for publication.

At the same time, psychology has become more and more diversified and specialized with regard to not only its subject matter, but also its methodology (Carpintero & Tortosa, 1991). The proliferation of psychology journals that has taken place has been found to parallel the growth occurring in chairs and academic departments (Ben-David & Collins, 1966). While at first, psychological papers were accepted by philosophical and scientific journals, the field's rapid growth forced researchers to create new channels of their own.

The most advanced areas in science have recently developed new avenues for disseminating research results. Newsletters, technical reports, letters from laboratories, preprints, and various sorts of electronic mail are offering instant information to people working in an area. At the same time, journals are suffering from longer and longer delays in publishing the papers received, and, because of their space limitations, the volume of rejected contributions continues to grow. Competition for publication thus affects the introduction of new ideas. The constraints imposed by the publishing policies of editorial groups influence article selection and hence excercise a strong control on the development of a field or paradigm. Editors and reviewers thus serve as scientific "gatekeepers," whose active intervention is like a theoretical filter superimposed on new ideas and findings.

The scientific journals of our time accumulate the active "corpus" of ideas and thus influence research in every field. The following may be counted as their main functions:

(1) To give publicity to the results of research, and in doing so make it the property of the whole scientific community.

(2) To acknowledge the authorship of those people whose works are accepted and included in the journal's pages.

(3) To assess the published works, by reviewers, editors, and scientific peers.

(4) To offer information about a field to other researchers and general readers.

Journals may be classified according to the kinds of information they disseminate. Categories include the *research* front journal (with very recent information), the *archival* journal (with more historical and older data), and others between the two (Price, 1970). Today there are also journals dedicated to the dissemination of abstracts and reviews of the very books and articles through which the results of research are presented to readers.

The Growing Impact on Psychology

Since the 18th century, periodical publications appeared that were expressly dedicated to psychological topics. According to Wozniak (1984), psychological serials date fom 1783, when a magazine called *Gnothi Sauton* ("A Magazine of Experiential Psychology . . . for the Learned and the Unlearned") appeared in Berlin. Other such publications included the *Repertorium für Physiologie und Psychologie nach ihrem Umfange und ihrer Verbindung* (1784–1786); the *Magazin zur Erfahrungs-Seelenkunde* (1783– 1793), which was later changed into the *Psychologisches Magazin* (1796–1798); and the *Allgemeines Repertorium fuer empirische Psychologie und verwandte Wissenschaften* (1792–1801), which was followed by the *Neues Repertorium fuer empirische Psychologie* (1802–1803) (Daniel & Louttit, 1953; Osier & Wozniak, 1984).

But the true beginning of periodical literature in psychology may be traced to the foundation of *Mind* by Alexander Bain in Great Britain. The event took place in 1876, and it was soon followed by the appearance of Wilhelm Wundt's *Philosophische Studien* in Germany (1883) and of the *American Journal of Psychology*, created by G. Stanley Hall in the United States in 1887. Since then, the number of these kinds of periodicals has been growing continuously.

While many journals last a decade or less, some have survived by adapting to theoretical and social change. This can be understood largely in terms of editorial evolution. Some journals continue under the direction of people who share similar views, such as members of a particular "research group" or "invisible college" (Price & Beaver, 1966). But a change in editorship can bring with it a significant change in publishing policy as well. Attention then shifts from certain topics to others, and past priorities are relegated to a secondary status; the whole field covered by a journal may be seen in a new light. Such a change can break an existing trajectory in a revolutionary way, bringing a whole new period for a journal.

The most interesting changes result from the growing specialization of knowledge. The birth of a new specialty—for example, operant conditioning (Krantz, 1972)—has sometimes demanded the development of new information channels dedicated to that new subfield. On the other hand, social crises—including wars and economic depressions— have often produced the reduction of space available for publication with the consequence of even less attention given to specialized topics.

A periodical may therefore be viewed as an interactive member of an information network in which related journals are intertwined through mutual references. Each journal has its role within the context of its field of knowledge. The degree of development and complexity of a given field of knowledge might, in fact, be appreciated from its journal network— that is, from the number, degree of specialization, and other complementary dimensions of the journals it contains. After analyzing the input-output rate of citation, Xhignesse and Osgood (1967) suggested the existence of three subfields among psychology journals: experimental, social and personality, and clinical.

It has been argued that journals covering a certain field or area of knowledge might be distributed in various levels (the so-called Bradford's distribution) according to the concrete volume of information they provide to the researcher. In almost any scientific field—including psychology—a large percentage of the relevant articles are published by a small number of "core" journals. In a similar fashion, only a few periodicals are very frequently cited, while many others are only mentioned occasionally. The former may be considered as the highly visible group. These "core" journals in science get around 25 percent of the approximately 4 million citations included yearly in the *Science Citation Index*. Only 25 journals fall into this category (Garfield, 1977). In addition, a linguistic factor is now affecting the visibility of journals. Today, journals in English are more visible than journals in any other language—a situation that in psychology has probably held true since the great expansion of American psychology that began in the 1930s.

Some Historically Significant Journals

Mind was the first journal that devoted numerous pages to psychological research. After it was founded in 1876 by Alexander Bain, its evolution until World War II comprised three periods under different editors: the first (1876–1891) under the editorship of G. C. Robertson, Bain's pupil and friend; the second (1892–1920) under G. F. Stout; and the third (1921–1945) under G. E. Moore. From the beginning the journal was mainly focused on philosophy and psychology, and many experimental papers from

American laboratories were published in it. In its early volumes, the names of Wundt, Ward, Bain, Baldwin, James, Ribot, and Binet were not infrequently found. Among its highly productive authors, only a few may be regarded as psychologists: Alexander Bain (1818–1903), William James (1842–1910), Henry R. Marshall (1852–1927), and G. F. Stout (1866–1944). Through its pages, most of the various psychological schools offered their respective points of view to readers (Moya, Carpintero, Peiró, & Tovtosa, 1987).

Mind became more and more a philosophical magazine after the foundation of the British Psychological Society. Then, James Ward and W. H. Rivers, both professors at Cambridge, launched the *British Journal of Psychology* (1904). Many significant names in British psychology, such as Myers, McDougall, Sherrington, and Spearman, among others, collaborated with them. Both Ward and Rivers edited the journal between 1904 and 1910; then came a short period (1910–1913) with Rivers and Myers as editors, followed by a decade (1914–1924) in which Myers acted as its sole editor. Myers was followed by F. C. Bartlett from 1924–1945. The list of its most productive authors includes British names only (e.g., Thompson, Spearman, and many others). Until the end of World War II, papers on sensation, perception, and attention (n=155) nearly doubled those dedicated to general psychology (n=93), memory and learning (n=83), and intelligence (n=73) (Balaguer, Tortosa, & Carpintero, 1987).

Only a few years later (1883) in Germany, Wilhelm Wundt founded the *Philosophische Studien* to publish the results of his laboratory research. It lasted until 1903, the year in which a new publication, the *Archiv für die gesamte Psychologie*, appeared under E. Meumann's editorship. According to Wundt's words, what began as a small project with limited resources had finally became a larger and more collaborative enterprise.

Philosophische Studien published 325 articles, 53 of which were authored by Wundt. Wundt's frequency of authorship was followed by J. Merke, A. Kirschmann, and F. Kiesow, each with more than 10 articles for the whole period. The first productive non-German author appears to have been J. McKeen Cattell, Wundt's first American student. Nearly one-third of the published works (32.1%) deal with sensation and perception. This is followed by methodology (20%) and various other topics. Wundt, Fechner, Weber, and Helmholtz (all strongly oriented toward physiological psychology and psychophysics) top

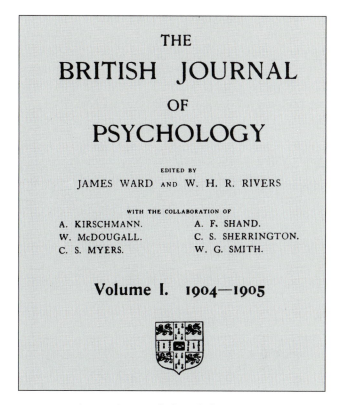

Figure 1 *The British Journal of Psychology.*

the list of authors cited. Wundt alone accounts for nearly 20% of all the citations appearing in the journal (Sáiz Roca, Sáiz Roca, Mülberger, 1990).

Wundt founded a new journal, *Psychologische Studien* (1904–1918), to substitute for the older *Philosophische Studien* in publishing the results of his laboratory research. It lasted until he retired. During its active years Wundt, W. Wirth, and O. Klemm were at the top of its list of productive authors. Its most frequently cited work was Wundt's *Grundzüge der physiologischen Psychologie* (106 citations), followed at a considerable distance by Wirth's *Die experimentelle Analyse der Bewusstseinsphänomen* (19 citations), and then by other works written by Wundt, Wirth, Ebbinghaus, and Krüger among others. No non-German author appears on the list of most frequently mentioned authors in this journal. Its main topic was sensation and perception (Bataller, 1991).

In 1921, Wolfgang Köhler, Kurt Koffka, and Max Wertheimer founded *Psychologische Forschung* to give exposure to the Gestalt viewpoint on psychological problems. The journal greatly helped the Gestalt movement appear as a definite school of thought (Ash, 1996)

In the United States, Granville Stanley Hall

(1844–1924) established the *American Journal of Psychology* in 1887 as a vehicle for publishing laboratory research. Priority was given to articles dealing with the problems of feelings, will, and thought, which were studied under the most exacting methodology (Tortosa, Carpintero, & Peiró, 1987).

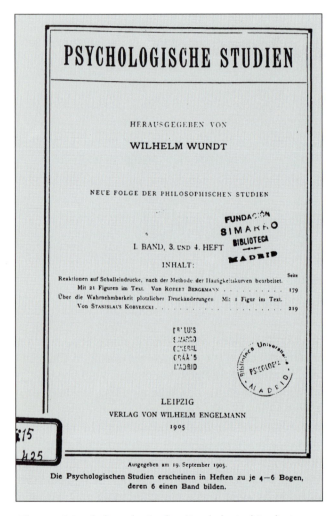

Figure 2 *Psychologische Studien* (Psychological Studies).

The history of the *American Journal of Psychology* may be divided into several periods through the end of World War II: (a) 1887–1894, when Stanley Hall was the exclusive editor; (b) 1895–1920, when E. C. Stanford and E. B. Titchener joined Hall for editorial tasks; (c) 1921–1925, when Titchener was the exclusive editor; and (d) 1926–1945, when former students of Titchener (Dallenbach, Washburn, Bentley, and Boring) were in charge. After passing through Johns Hopkins and Clark Universities during Hall's editorship, the journal became strongly connected with Cornell University, where Titchener

worked. Through its pages classic psychology and structuralism maintained a strong presence on the American scene, but its editorial policy was open-minded—Freud's well known Clark lectures also appeared in it.

A few years later, and as a result of difficulties and misunderstandings that characterized the relationship between Hall and his colleagues (Ross, 1972), James McKeen Cattell (1860–1944) and James Mark Baldwin (1861–1934) decided to establish a new journal, *The Psychological Review* (1894), to publish the results of laboratory research, review articles, and theoretical papers. The journal devoted much of its space to American functionalism, but all of the leading schools and theories found a place in it to present their key ideas.

The *Psychological Bulletin* was created in 1904 by Baldwin and Warren in order to offer critical reviews and provide information concerning bibliographic and professional questions. Closely related to both journals, *The Journal of Experimental Psychology* was established in 1916 to present the growing laboratory work and to give information on new instruments and work facilities. For decades it was the most prominent specialized channel for experimental psychology in the United States. Its first editor, J. B. Watson, was able to secure it a place among the leading research journals from its very beginning. In 1974, it was transformed into four more specific titles—*JEP: General; JEP: Animal Behavior Processes; JEP: Human Learning and Memory*; and *JEP: Human Perception and Performance*. This development clearly shows the growing level of complexity that has become more and more typical of psychological research. Experimental psychology, physiological psychology, and methodology were the main topics the original journal dealt with, and C. L. Hull, E. R. Hilgard, R. Dodge, and E. Thorndike were the most frequently cited authors (Carbonell, Burillo, Tortosa, & Carpintero, 1987). These periodicals became the core of the American Psychological Association's array of journals—a collection that has been continuously growing even to the present.

In France, Théodule Ribot (1839–1916) founded (1876) and edited the *Revue philosophique*, in which psychological work frequently appeared. After founding the laboratory (1889) at La Sorbonne, H. Beaunis and A. Binet began to publish the *Bulletin de travaux du Laboratoire* (1893–1894). This publication immediately changed into *L'Anné Psychologique* (1894), which has regularly appeared since then. The development of *L'Anné Psychologique* may be

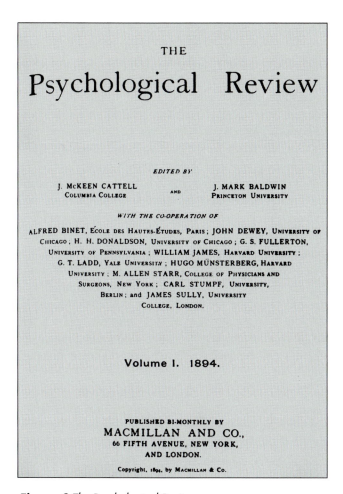

Figure 3 *The Psychological Review.*

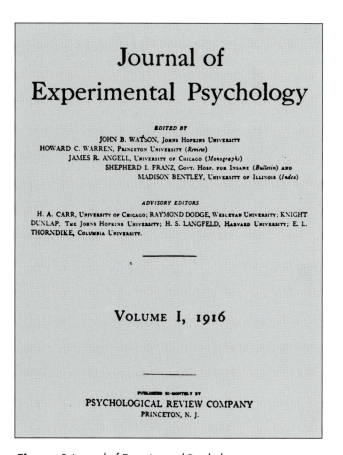

Figure 4 *Journal of Experimental Psychology.*

male et Pathologique (1904), founded by Pierre Janet (1859–1947) in collaboration with Georges Dumas (1866–1946). Janet served as the editor until 1937. The *Revue de Psychologie Appliqué* (1920), an offspring of the *Revue de L' Hypnotisme Experimentale et Therapeutique* (1886); the *Bulletin de Psychologie*, and the *Annales Médico-psychologiques* also merit our recognition.

Also published in French was the *Archives de Psychologie*. It was founded by T. Flournoy and E. Claparède in 1902 in Switzerland; both editors were professors at the University of Geneva. Child and experimental psychology were emphasized, and Claparède, Binet, Flournoy, Jung and many others were among its frequent contributors.

Italian psychology received a significant boost from the Fifth International Congress held in Rome in 1905. That same year the first specialized Italian psychological journal appeared: *Rivista di Psicologia applicata alla Pedagogia ed alla Psicopatolgia*. Its founder was the psychiatrist Giulio Cesare Ferrari (1868–1932), who was affiliated with the Instituto Psichiatrico do Reggio Emilia. He maintained close contact with European and American psychologists,

described as occurring over two principal periods until 1945: the first one, under Binet's editorship (1894–1912); and the second, when it was edited by Piéron (1913–1945). In its earlier period, significant contributions were made by people such as Bourdon, van Biervliet, Simon, Henri, Claparède, and Larguier de Bancels; while Guillaume, Fessard, Blondel, and many others are to be found in the second. The two editors appear at the top of the list of its most productive authors, and each of them had a significant group of collaborators. Among its most popular topics, sensation and perception, comparative psychology, and applied psychology are above the 10 percent level as reflected by number of articles published on these areas. It is noteworthy that the editors also appear to be the two most cited authors in the journal up to 1945—Piéron with 289 citations and Binet with 198 (Moltó & Carpintero, 1987; Carpintero & Moltó, 1994).

Other journals were also established as publication outlets for French laboratories. Among them should be counted the *Journal de Psychologie Nor-*

and he translated James's *Principles of Psychology* (1901) into Italian. Ferrari edited the journal until his death. The journal underwent many changes in its title, which clearly indicated the difficulties experienced by Italian psychology in defining its own theoretical niche. Its present name is *Rivista de Psicologia*, and it is the official publication of the Italian Psychological Society. Other significant Italian journals are the *Archivio Italiano de Psicologia* (founded by F. Kiesow and A. Gemelli in 1919–1920), and the *Archivio di Psicologia, Neurobiologia, Psichiatria e Psicoterapia* (founded by Gemelli in 1938) (Marhaba, 1981).

Russian psychological journals have suffered from the great political and social changes that have occurred in that country during our century. The first Russian periodical concerned with psychology's subject matter, *Problems of Philosophy and Psychology*, was founded in 1889 by Nikolai Grot

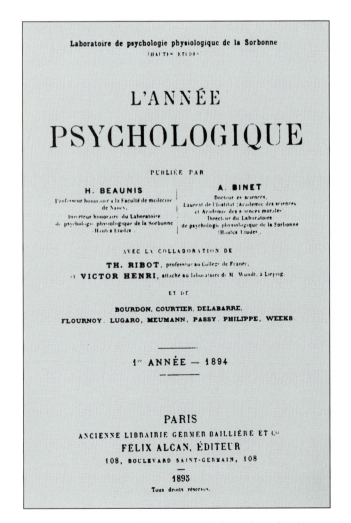

Laboratoire de psychologie physiologique de la Sorbonne
(HAUTES ÉTUDES)

L'ANNÉE
PSYCHOLOGIQUE

PUBLIÉE PAR

H. BEAUNIS
Professeur honoraire à la Faculté de médecine de Nancy,
Directeur honoraire du Laboratoire de psychologie physiologique de la Sorbonne Hautes Études.

A. BINET
Docteur ès sciences,
Lauréat de l'Institut (Académie des sciences et Académie des sciences morales.
Directeur du Laboratoire de psychologie physiologique de la Sorbonne (Hautes Études).

AVEC LA COLLABORATION DE

TH. RIBOT, professeur au Collège de France,
et **VICTOR HENRI**, attaché au laboratoire de M. Wundt, à Leipzig.

ET DE

BOURDON, COURTIER, DELABARRE,
FLOURNOY, LUGARO, MEUMANN, PASSY, PHILIPPE, WEEKS.

1ʳᵉ ANNÉE — 1894

PARIS
ANCIENNE LIBRAIRIE GERMER BAILLIÈRE ET Cⁱᵉ
FELIX ALCAN, ÉDITEUR
108, BOULEVARD SAINT-GERMAIN, 108

1895
Tous droits réservés.

Figure 5 *L'Année Psychologique* (Psychological Yearbook).

(1852–1899), and it lasted until 1917 (Kozulin, 1984). In 1904 Bekhterev (1857–1927) established the *Bulletin of Psychology, Criminal Anthropology and Hypnotism* (Brozek, 1972). After the Soviet revolution, several journals were founded in 1928: *Psychology*, edited first by K. Kornilov and then by V. Kolbanovskiy; *Pedology*, edited by A. Zalkind; and *Psychology of Work and Psychotechnics*, edited by I. Shpil'reyn (renamed *Soviet Psychotechnics* in 1934). All of them were closed in 1936, a move consistent with other repressive measures taken by the Communist Party against psychology, such as found in the well-known decree "On the Pedological Distortions in the Soviet School System" (4 July 1936). Since then, "until 1955, psychological studies could appear only if they conformed to the requirements of the physiological or educational journals" (McLeish, 1975, p. 159). Stalin died in 1953, and two years later, *Problems of Psychology* was founded and edited by K. Kornilov, A. Smirnov, and other well-known Russian psychologists.

Some similarities to the experiences of other countries may be found in the evolution of Spanish periodicals in psychology. The oldest one, *Archivos de Neurobiología, Psicología, Fisiología, Histología, Neurología, y Psiquiatría*, was founded in 1920 by the philosopher José Ortega y Gasset and the psychiatrists G. Rodriguez-Lafora and J. M. Sacristán. Among its contributing authors the names of E. Mira y López and J. Germain should not be forgotten. Other journals appeared just before the Spanish Civil War (1936–1939), but they did not last very long. After the war, *Psicotecnia* (1939) was founded and later was reorganized and changed into the *Revista de Psicología General y Aplicada* (1946). This periodical still serves as a voice for the Spanish Psychological Society. The war seriously damaged the status of Spanish psychology periodicals, and only when a degree in psychology was established in universities were new journals created to meet the publication needs of psychology departments and research groups.

A complete account of the periodicals associated with theoretical schools and specialties in psychology would never end. Psychoanalysis, research methodology, school and clinical psychology, ad infinitum, have all created their own publishing networks. Journals are a vital resource for the dissemination of psychological ideas and theories. They provide a treasure of information from which to construct a more sophisticated understanding of the history of scientific psychology.

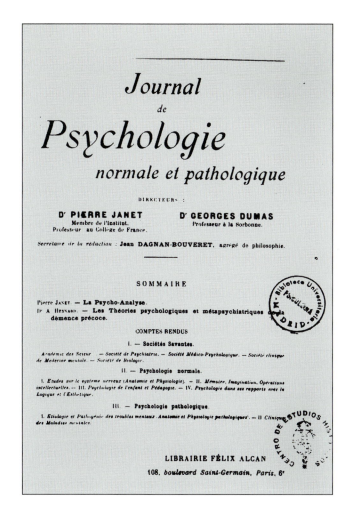

Figure 6 *Journal de Psychologie normale et pathologique* (Journal of Normal and Abnormal Psychology).

Bibliography

Ash, M. (1996). *Gestalt psychology in German culture, 1890–1967: Holism and the quest for objectivity.* New York: Cambridge University Press.

Balaguer, I., Tortosa, F., & Carpintero, H. (1987). La psicología británica a través del "British Journal of Psychology" (1904–1945). *Revista de Historia de la Psicología, 1–2,* 141–162.

Bataller, I. (1991). *Una visión de la psicología alemana: Estudio histórico de la revista "Psychologische Studien" (1904–1918).* Thesis, Universidad de Valencia, Valencia, Spain.

Ben-David, J., & Collins, R. (1966). Social factors in the origin of a new science: The case of psychology. *American Sociological Review, 31,* 451–465.

Brozek, J. (1972). Some significant historical events in the development of Soviet psychology. In J. Brozek & D. Slobin (Eds.), *Psychology in the U.S.S.R.: An historical perspective.* New York: International Arts & Sciences Press.

Calatayud, C., Carpintero, H., Peiró, J. M., & Tortosa, F. (1987). La psicología americana a través del "Psychological Review" (1894–1945). *Revista de Historia de la Psicología, 1–2,* 39–66.

Carbonell, E., Martí, C., Burillo, J. Tortosa, F., & Carpintero, H. (1987). El "Journal of Experimental Psychology" y la psicología experimental americana entre 1916 y 1945. *Revista de Historia de la Psicología, 1–2,* 87–120.

Carpintero, H., & Moltó, J. (1994). L'Annee psychologique at la naissance de la psychologie expérimentale en France (1894–1945). In P. Fraisse & J. Segui (Eds.), *Les origines de la psychologie scientifique. Centième anniversaire de "L'Année Psychologique" 1894–1994* (pp. 15–34). Paris: P. U. F.

Carpintero, H., & Tortosa, F. (1991). Die Evolution psychologischer Forschungsfelder. Eine Betrachtung anhand der "Psychological Abstracts. In H. Lück, H. & R. Miller (Eds.), *Theorien und Methoden psychologiegeschichtlicher Forschung* (pp. 91–109). Göttingen: Verlag für Psychologie Hogrefe.

Daniel, R. S., & Louttit, C. M. (1953). *Professional problems in psychology.* Englewood Cliffs, NJ: Prentice Hall.

Garfield, E. (1977). *Essays of an information scientist, I.* Philadelphia: ISI Press.

Garvey, W. D. (1977). *Communication: The essence of science.* Oxford: Pergamon.

Kozulin, A. (1984). *Psychology in Utopia: Toward a social history of Soviet psychology.* Cambridge: MIT Press.

Krantz, D. L. (1972). Schools and systems: The mutual isolation of operant and non-operant psychology as a case study. *Journal of the History of the Behavioral Sciences, 8,* 86–102.

Louttit, C. M. (1932). *Handbook of psychological literature.* Bloomington, IN: The Principia Press.

Marhaba, S. (1981). *Lineamenti della psicologia italiana, 1870–1945.* Florence: Giunti Barbera.

McLeish, J. (1975). *Soviet psychology: History, theory, content.* London: Methuen.

Moltó, J., & Carpintero, H. (1987). La psicología francesa en la revista "L'Année Psychologique" (1894–1945). *Revista de Historia de la Psicología, 1–2,* 163–182.

Montoro, L, & Carbonell, E. (1989). La comunicación de la información científica en psicología: producción y diseminación de la información. En J. Arnau & H. Carpintero (Eds.), *Historia, teoría y método* (J. Mayor & J. L. Pinillos, *Tratado de Psicología General,* Vol. I., pp. 391–416). Madrid: Alhambra.

Moya, J., Carpintero, H., Peiró, J. M., & Tortosa, F. (1987). La psicología inglesa de 1876 a 1945. Un estudio a traves de la revista "Mind." *Revista de Historia de la Psicología, 8,* 121–140.

Osier, D. V., & Wozniak, R. H. (1984). *A century of serial publications in psychology, 1850–1950. An international bibliography.* Millwood, NY: Kraus International Publications.

Peiró, J. M., & Carpintero, H. (1981). Historia de la psicología en España a través de sus revistas especializadas. *Revista de Historia de la Psicología, 2,* 143–181.

Price, D. J. (1970). Citation measures of hard science, soft science, technology and non-science. In C. E. Nelson & D. K. Pollock (Eds.), *Communication among scientists and engineers* (pp. 3–32). Lexington: Heath, Lexington Books.

Price, D. J., & Beaver, D. (1966). Collaboration in an "Invisible College." *American Psychologist, 21,* 1011–1018.

Ross, D. (1972). *G. Stanley Hall: The psychologist as prophet.* Chicago: Chicago University Press.

Sáiz Roca, M., Sáiz Roca, D., & Mülberger, A. (1990). La psicología alemana a través de la revista "Philosophische Studien." *Revista de Historia de la Psicología, 3–4,* 411–422.

Tortosa, F., Carpintero, H., & Peiró, J. M. (1987). La psicología americana a través del "American Journal of Psychology." *Revista de Historia de la Psicología, 1–2,* 5–38.

Wozniak, R. H. (1984). A brief history of serial publication in psychology. In D. V. Osier & R. H. Wozniak (Eds.), *A century of serial publications in psychology, 1850–1950. An international bibliography* (pp. xvii–xxxiii. Milwood, NY: Kraus International Publications.

Xhignesse, L. V., & Osgood, C. E. (1967). Bibliographical citation characteristics of the psychological journals network in 1950; in 1960. *American Psychologist, 22,* 778–791.

Ziman, J. (1968). *Public knowledge.* Cambridge: Cambridge University Press.

Psychological Associations and Societies

Horst U. K. Gundlach

When the various psychological associations and societies were counted in 1980, their number totaled 1107 (Jacobson & Reinert, 1980). Obviously, this figure would be higher today, even though a number of them are no longer in existence. Although the tendency among psychologists to gather together seems to be of prodigious proportions, there has been relatively little research done on this phenomenon. Any study done in this area has usually been confined to just one organization or society, rather than being comparative in nature. The following, therefore, is necessarily somewhat cursory.

The 19th century witnessed a profusion of newly founded scientific and semi-scientific, as well as pseudo-scientific societies that corresponded to the swift economic and population growth of that period. Because long distance communications and traveling were still cumbersome and expensive, scientific societies operated mainly on the local or regional level, typically located in the large capitals. They were tolerant of the amateur and usually not much engaged in professional politicking. The emerging professional class thus created their own tiny republics.

This can be seen in most fields of scientific or semi-scientific interest. Societies flourished in fields that were akin to psychology, such as Gall's phrenology and Mesmer's animal magnetism. Most of these groups fell by the wayside as they lost popularity, but some, like the British Phrenological Society (1886) in London and the *Société Magnétique de France* (1887) in Paris, were longer-lived. More popular and long lasting were groups devoted to topics such as occultism, spiritism, and so-called psychic research. Hypnotism as a modified outgrowth of animal magnetism flourished for some decades. All these fields intermingled and at times it was difficult to distinguish one from another. Societies pursuing these topics played a dual role in the developing field of psychology. On the one hand, they were frequently pioneers and precursors; on the other hand, they formed part of the pseudo-

Figure 1 President's Mansion of Clark University in Worcester, Massachusetts, where APA was founded on July 8, 1892.

Figure 2 G. Stanley Hall, the eminent American developmental psychologist and founding President of Clark University during the late 1880s.

scientific sphere against which the new psychology struggled.

Alienists formed early societies for the purpose of dealing with respected psychology-related scientific research. In London, they founded the Medico-Psychological Association (1841), which edited the *Journal of Mental Science.* In Paris, the *Société Médico-Psychologique* (1852) edited the *Annales Médico-Psychologiques.* Jean-Martin Charcot (1825–1893) presided over the *Société de Psychologie Physiologique* (1885) in Paris, which included among its members Théodule Ribot (1839–1916), Pierre Janet (1859–1947), and other pioneers of psychology in France. The focus of interest of this society was, of course, hypnosis, but it was primarily seen as a tool for research and therapy, not as an end in itself. It is to the credit of this society that it invited the first International Congress of Psychology during the Paris World's Fair in 1889. Factionalism still prevailed, however; the Nancy school of hypnotism around Hippolyte Bernheim (1840–1919) constituted a rival group—the *Société d'Hypnologie et de Psychologie* (ca. 1885).

Spiritism was the avocation of the London

Society for Psychical Research (1882). It organized the second International Congress for Psychology in London in 1892. As a counterpart to the London society, the American Society for Psychical Research (1885) was founded in Boston with Granville Stanley Hall (1844–1924) acting as vice president.

Spiritistic associations were also formed in Germany, such as the *Psychologische Gesellschaft* (1887) in Munich and the *Gesellschaft für Experimental-Psychologie* (1888) in Berlin. The two fused in 1890 to form the *Gesellschaft für Psychologische Forschung,* which organized, with Albert Freiherr von Schrenck-Notzing (1862–1929) as board member, the third International Congress for Psychology in Munich in 1896. Carl Stumpf (1848–1936), who presided over the congress, tried his best to curb spiritism and hypnotism. But the academic societies for the less sensational areas of psychology continued to have

---

2 *Proceedings of the American Psychological Association.*

ciation in Philadelphia, at the University of Pennsylvania, on Tuesday, December 27, 1892, at 10 A.M.

Professor Jastrow was appointed secretary to provide a programme for that meeting. He invites all members to submit to him at Madison, Wisconsin, titles of papers with brief abstracts and estimates of time required for presentation.

The original members who were either present at this meeting or sent letters of approval and accepted membership are the following:

Angell, Frank, Leland Stanford, Jr., University,
Baldwin, J. Mark, Toronto University,
Bryan, W. L., Indiana University,
Burnham, W. H., Clark University,
Cattell, J. McK., Columbia College,
Cowles, Edward, McLean Asylum,
Delabarre, E. B., Brown University,
Dewey, John, University of Michigan,
Fullerton, G. S., University of Pennsylvania,
Gilman, B. I., Clark University,
Griffin, E. H., Johns Hopkins University,
Hall, G. Stanley, Clark University,
Hume, J. G., Toronto University,
Hyslop, J. H., Columbia College,
James, William, Harvard University,
Jastrow, Joseph, University of Wisconsin,
Krohn, W. O., Clark University,
Ladd, G. T., Yale University,
Nichols, Herbert, Harvard University,
Noyes, William, McLean Asylum,
Patrick, G. T. W., University of Iowa,
Royce, Josiah, Harvard University,
Sanford, E. C., Clark University,
Scripture, E. W., Yale University,
Witmer, Lightner, University of Pennsylvania,
Wolfe, H. K., University of Nebraska.

The following additional members were elected:
Mills, T. Wesley, McGill College, Montreal,
Münsterberg, Hugo, Harvard University,
Ormond, A. T., Princeton College,
Pace, Edward, Catholic University, Washington,
Titchener, E. B., Cornell University.

Professor Jastrow asked the co-operation of all members for the Section of Psychology at the World's Fair, and invited correspondence upon the matter.

Figure 3 List of APA Charter members from an 1893 APA program.

Figure 4 New APA logo which was introduced at 1992–1993 Centennial Convention.

difficulties in assembling enough members to ensure enduring organizations. At the turn of the century, one still found numerous loosely knit local groups of a rather informal nature, like the *Psychologische Gesellschaft* in Breslau, linked to Hermann Ebbinghaus (1850–1909), or the "Psychologischer Verein" in Berlin. As local groups came into closer contact with each other during the occasional international gatherings, a trend toward the formation of regional and national organizations was created and strengthened by ever-improving systems of communication and transportation. The trend was also fortified by the growing number of psychologists in university positions who perceived the necessity of forming denser nets of exchange about scientific as well as academic and university matters. This led to a decline of interest in the more fantastic pursuits of spiritism and hypnotism, as well as to a more distinct segregation from those in the medical faculty or profession.

The trend setter in all this was the American Psychological Association (APA), founded in 1892 with the outspoken goal of advancing "psychology as a

Figure 5 Participants in the founding congress of the "Society for Experimental Psychology."

arranging congresses and meetings. The centennial in 1992 induced a history in book form (Evans, Sexton, & Cadwallader, 1992).

There were other associations in the United States, but they never played a comparable role. In 1904, Titchener, along with his disciples, formed a circle which called itself "The Experimentalists." When Titchener died in 1929, the group re-organized as the Society of Experimental Psychologists. Also outside the APA, the Psychometric Society and the Society for the Psychological Study of Social Issues were organized in 1935 and 1936, respectively. Both these groups later became APA affiliates, which illustrates the dominance of the APA.

This type of development has not happened everywhere. In Germany, there has never been just one society for the interests of university as well as professional psychologists. It was in 1904 that the

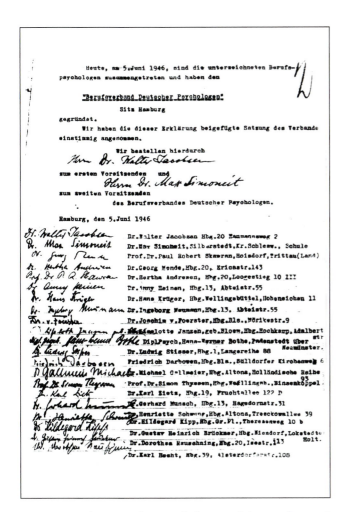

Figure 6 Title page of original charter of the "Professional Association of German Psychologists" or "BDP" (June 5, 1946).

science" (Sokal, 1992). G. Stanley Hall was its founder and first president. From the very beginning, the most renowned of American psychologists were members, including James Mark Baldwin (1861–1934), James McKeen Cattell (1860–1944), John Dewey (1859–1952), William James (1842–1910), Hugo Münsterberg (1863–1916), and Edward Bradford Titchener (1867–1927). The APA successfully integrated the fledgling field of applied psychology, although its original purpose centered around academic concerns. When Samuel Fernberger (1887–1956), long-time secretary, reviewed the first 40 years in 1932, he stated that the APA had become "big business."

Today, after many disputes and struggles (Wallin, 1960), the APA, a highly complex and multi-sectional organization, is the world's largest, most prosperous, and reasonably most influential psychological association, publishing prestigious journals and

Figure 7 Professor Curt Bondy (1894–1972), President of the BDP from 1961–1968 before a bust of William Stern (1871–1938), the premier German applied psychologist.

Gesellschaft für experimentelle Psychologie (Society for Experimental Psychology) was formed in Giessen, as Robert Sommer (1864–1937) arranged its founding congress. This society, which professed the interest of psychologists in university appointments, did not perceive itself as appertaining to any particular country, but it favored the use of German as its congress and business language, which somewhat restricted its membership. In 1929, it changed its name to *Deutsche Gesellschaft für Psychologie* (German Psychological Association), leaving out the "experimental" and introducing "German," a move that was not well received by a solid minority of its members. It concerned itself with applied psychology insofar as it championed the creation of a distinctive university degree for psychologists. But the applied psychologists formed their separate *Berufsverband Deutscher Psychologen* (BDP) in 1947. Only a loose union, *Föderation deutscher Psychologenvereinigungen* (1958/1959), was created to coordinate common interests.

There is something similar on a global level. A separate association exists for applied psychology, the International Association for Applied Psychology, founded in 1920 by the Geneva psychologist Edouard Claparède (1873–1940) as the *Association Internationale de Psychotechnique*. Since 1920, this association has organized the International Congresses for Applied Psychology.

In 1951, an international association, not of individuals, but of psychological associations was created—the International Union of Psychological Science (IUPS). The union has 53 national members and organizes the international congresses for psychology, which started under much different auspices in 1889.

Bibliography

Evans, R. B., Sexton, V. S., & Cadwallader, T. C. (Eds.). (1992). *The American Psychological Association: A historical perspective.* Washington, DC: American Psychological Association.

Fernberger, S. W. (1932). The American Psychological Association: A historical summary 1892–1932. *Psychological Bulletin, 29,* 1–29.

Jacobson, G. H., & Reinert, G. (1980). *International directory of psychologists* (3rd ed.). Amsterdam: North Holland.

Sokal, M. M. (1992). Origins and early years of the American Psychological Association, 1890–1906. *American Psychologist, 47,* 111–112.

Wallin, J. E. W. (1960). History of the struggles within the American Psychological Association to attain membership requirements, test standardization, certification of psychological practitioners, and professionalization. *Journal of General Psychology, 63,* 287–308.

Psychology in the Netherlands

Pieter J. van Strien

Anyone who looks at the practice of psychology in the Netherlands with an international perspective will note little that is unique or specific to this country. In fact, its international orientation may be just what is too typical in Dutch psychology. In general, foreign psychologists tend to be cited more frequently than fellow-countrymen writing about the same topics. Although American authors generally have a preferential status with Dutch psychologists, research from other European countries receives due attention as well.

This international perspective has encouraged Dutch psychologists to take a leading role in the foundation of European journals and scientific associations, as well as the organization of scholarly meetings in Europe. Thus, it appears that the Netherlands has assumed the same type of facilitative role in psychology as it has in trade, communications, and traffic.

Turning to the history of Dutch psychology, one discovers that it has a long tradition of taking an international perspective. Yet Dutch psychology also had its own unique character in the not-so-recent past. In particular, the religious diversity, which played such a central role in Dutch history, took a similar place in the establishment and further development of psychology in Dutch society (van Strien, 1991b).

Donders and Heymans

There was no specifically Dutch psychology before 1900. The two most important pioneers in 19th century psychology in the Netherlands were the ophthalmologist Franciscus Cornelis Donders (1818–1889) and the philosopher Gerard Heymans (1857–1930). Donders became a friend of the German physiologist and sensory psychologist Hermann von Helmholtz (1821–1894) during the 1850s. At that time, Helmholtz held a professorship at nearby Bonn University in Germany. The two scientists met regularly in the small Rhenish town of Kleve during their academic vacations. When Helmholtz was called to Heidelberg, Donders was invited to become his successor at Bonn. He refused the prestigious appointment because he felt a responsibility to continue his work at Utrecht, where he had just established a new ophthalmological clinic through public support.

Donders was involved in the teaching and research of almost the same important and extensive academic specialties as his friend Helmholtz. In addition, Donders and Helmholtz shared an interest in the velocity of nervous action. For this work, Donders invented his "noematograph" for the measurement of "central time." This was defined as either the time necessary to distinguish between different stimuli, or to choose an appropriate response from several alternatives. The subtraction method was the chief research technique that Donders used. He obtained his numerical results by subtracting the time required for a simple reaction from that needed for a complex reaction. To elicit a simple reaction, the experimenter might ask the subject to repeat immediately the sound "Ki." For a complex reaction, the subject would then be offered several syllables (Ka, Ke, Ki, or Ku) and instructed to repeat these as quickly as possible, or to repeat them only if the stimulus word given was "Ki." Donders became internationally known as a pioneer in the field of psychology when his reaction time procedures were adopted and expanded by Wilhelm Wundt (1832–1920) in his Leipzig laboratory. Actually, his work with reaction time was only one episode in a rich scientific career, since Donders

Figure 1 Portrait of Francisus Cornelis Donders with a bust of Helmholtz in the background.

of research equipment in 1892 is generally regarded as the beginning of scientific psychology in the Netherlands. In 1992, therefore, Dutch psychologists commemorated the official recognition of their field with a special centennial celebration.

Heymans's first series of studies focused on a visual illusion discovered by the German astrophysicist Johann Karl Friedrich Zöllner (1843–1882). As shown in Figure 4, a piece of pasteboard, with the stimulus for the illusion, was placed under three thin rubber bands stretched across a wooden board. Subjects were then asked to adjust the rubber bands until they perceived them to be parallel. By turning down the covering board (as shown in the picture) the degree of the deviation could be registered.

Heymans's scientific work is a good example of the mediating role of Dutch psychology between international scientific traditions. In his first book, *Laws and Elements of Scientific Thought* (1890), Heymans adopted the Anglo-Saxon inductive approach of John Stuart Mill

performed his most important work in the field of ophthalmology.

The first Dutchman who became known primarily as a psychologist was Gerard Heymans (1857–1930), who was appointed to the chair of philosophy at the University of Groningen in 1890. Following the model of German philosophers, Heymans almost immediately began a series of psychological experiments to give philosophy a solid empirical foundation. The approval of funds for the purchase

(1806–1873). His other major philosophical writings, *Introduction to Metaphysics* (1905) and *Introduction to Ethics* (1912), follow the same empirical approach. On the European continent, Heymans was the first psychologist to adopt the questionnaire method of Francis Galton (1822–1911) for the study of mental phenomena. He also employed the correlation method of Charles Edward Spearman (1863–1945) to analyze the results of his "heredity" survey and to provide a statistical basis for his typology of temperaments (Heymans & Wiersma, 1906–1918). His book on the *Psychology of Women* (Heymans, 1910) was based on the results of questionnaires as well.

The research on *telepathy*, which Heymans conducted from 1919 to 1922 together with his student, Henri J. F. Brugmans (1884–1961), remains a rare model of methodological rigor and sophistication. The research was conducted in Heymans's Psychological Laboratory at Groningen. An experimental subject worked on the lower floor of the institute, while the experimenter was located on the upper floor. Subjects were asked to identify with their index finger the one field (of 48 fields on a gameboard), on which the experimenter had been concentrating. In turn, the experimenter and his assistant were able to observe the subject's hand movements through a special sound-proofed window in the floor. The subject's number of "hits" far exceeded chance, and these results were confirmed by a modern re-evaluation of the experimental findings (Schouten & Kelley, 1978). The experimenter also employed a kymograph, a Jaquet chronograph, several Marey registration tambours, and a Hartmann-Braun mirror galvanometer to record physiological responses of each subject. In addition, some subjects were tested under the influence of various psychopharmacological substances. In general, alcohol increased the number of "hits" but the ingestion of sodium bromide yielded no significant effects.

Though Heymans drew his methodological inspiration from British thinkers, his philosophical ideas are firmly rooted in the German tradition. His epistemological and ethical writings reveal him to be an intellectual successor of the German philosopher, Immanuel Kant (1724–1804). Heymans's metaphysics ultimately even led him to the *panpsychic monism* of Gustav Theodor Fechner (1801–1887). Heymans's position at the intersection of major European intellectual traditions enabled him to unite the world of psychology—which had been drastically divided by World War I—at the Eighth International Congress of Psychology in 1926 in Groningen. Unfortunately, it became apparent during that same congress just how difficult it was to reconcile Anglo-Saxon and German psychology. The movement towards a *"geisteswissenschaftliche"* (philosophical-historical) psychology in Germany after World War I made a synthesis with Anglo-Saxon empiricism almost impossible. In the following year the 70-year old Heymans expressed his dis-

appointment about this development in his farewell address at the university. He criticized German psychologists for not having realized that empirical methods could be applied to complex psychic phenomena. In turn, he chastised English-speaking psychologists for their reliance upon sterile, association psychology, which completely neglected the normative aspects of thought. Heymans's own comprehensive theories were almost completely overlooked during the international debate of the interbellum period.

On the other hand, Heymans's empirical research—especially his typology, which has been summarized by "Heymans's Cube" (Figure 7)—attracted a good bit of popular attention. His character typology includes the dimension of activity, emotionality, and the so-called "secondary functions." The first two parameters were borrowed from Kant's theory of temperaments. The third dimension is inspired by the concept of "Secondary Cerebral Functioning" described by the German forensic psychiatrist, Otto Gross (1877–1920). From the interactions of the above, Heymans posed the following eight different personality types: sentimental, passionate, choleric, nervous, apathetic, phlegmatic, sanguine, and amorphous. Heymans's basic dimensions were empirically supported by the correlations obtained in his heredity survey. Addi-

Figure 2 Noematograph created by Donders.

Figure 3 Portrait of Gerard Heymans.

tribution to human happiness. He argued that man had increasingly learned to understand and control the laws of nature, but was still quite ignorant about the principles guiding human behavior and consciousness. It was Heymans's opinion that the insights of psychology about individual personalities would enable future generations to recognize their own limitations and learn to understand others. He also believed that similar opportunities existed for improving relations among the nations of the world. He was convinced that rational decisions about marriage would help overcome base passions and evil in man. If "better" people married with the help of psychological understanding, and if those with weaker hereditary potentials would voluntarily refrain from having children, Heymans predicted that mankind would be "ennobled" in the course of future generations. His philosophy of psychic monism was to be another means of overcoming "the limits of individual existence and to be led to a union with the higher order of the world spirit" (Heymans, 1905, p. 361). Heymans was confident that psychic monisms would take the place of religion, which had given vital support to earlier generations.

Not everyone shared Heymans's optimism about the future. This did not, however, prevent less utopian minded professionals from adopting his three-dimensional typology for the purpose of assessing individuals in vocational, legal, or educational situations. Thus, Heymans's work contributed to a "psychologization" of interpersonal relation-

tional support for Heymans's typology came from his analysis of 100 biographies of eminent individuals. His use of widely known characters as an illustration of the various types contributed substantially to the popularization of his typology.

Heymans's 1909 oration "The Future Century of Psychology," his farewell as Rector of Groningen University, contributed greatly to his fame. He regarded psychology as a basic science which was as important as physics. He also expressed the hope that psychology would ultimately make a major con-

Figure 4 Heymans's apparatus for studying the "Zöllner Illusion."

groups. Most university teachers in psychology who were appointed during the 1920s, 1930s, and 1940s applied their specialties to the social and psychological problems posed by the religious group to which they belonged. In this manner, a strong applied psychology was established which focused on questions of education, life, and vocation, and promoted the popularization of psychology.

Heymans's scientific psychology was found useless for this kind of applied activity. Like their philosophically oriented colleagues in Germany, psychologists of this new generation generally emphasized the independence of the human soul. Further, Protestant psychologists utilized concepts of Protestant theology, and their Catholic colleagues sought alliance with *Neo-Thomism*. Among university teachers, only Heymans's successor at Groningen, Henri J. F. Brugmans, and the Hungarian emigrant Géza Révész (1878–1955) of the University of

ships, which were previously regulated primarily by moral and religious norms.

Dutch Psychology in a Religious Context

Heymans was one of the leading members of a group of liberal intellectuals in Dutch society who turned to science to find the security otherwise provided by traditional religion. The majority of the population, however, adhered to the religious faith in which they had grown up. Protestantism was dominant in the western and northern parts of the country, while Roman Catholicism was typically found in the southern regions. During the 19th century, both major groups experienced a process of emancipation which enabled them to live together relatively harmoniously in three separate but equal groupings or "pillars": Protestants, Catholics, and "Neutrals." The Neutral group was composed of individuals with a liberal or socialist political outlook on life. Each "pillar" was composed of a dense net of organizations related to major aspects of community life (politics, education, youth organizations, sports, et cetera). Both the Orthodox Protestants and Roman Catholics founded their own universities, the "Free University of Amsterdam" and the "Catholic University of Nijmegen," respectively. When the field of vocational counseling began to flourish after World War I, professional activities in the Netherlands were organized by the respective

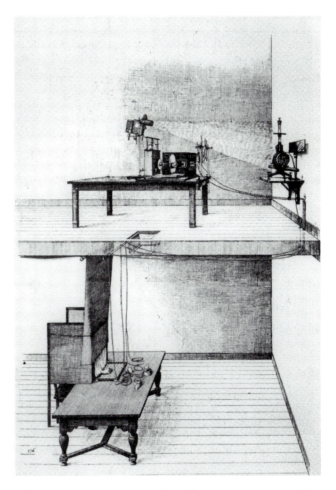

Figure 5 Heymans's telepathy experiments in his psychological laboratory at Groningen.

Figure 6 Participants of Groningen Congress in 1926—Heymans, with his white beard, stands in the center of the front row.

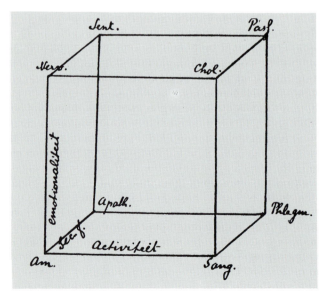

Figure 7 "Heymans's Cube."

Amsterdam were the only psychologists who continued the empirical tradition of their field.

The influence of the religious "pillars" on psychology existed until long after World War II. Although the scientific level of psychology was not too impressive, professional work in the field kept growing in the post-war period. In particular, the network of organizations which comprised each "pillar" provided unique opportunities for the permeation of Dutch society with psychological ideas and methods. Consequently, the number of psychologists in Holland is greater than that of any other European country except perhaps Sweden (van Strien, 1991a).

A distinctive strain in Dutch psychology derives from the existential phenomenology of the Utrecht School of psychology, which is associated with the name of the physiologist and animal psychologist,

Frederik J. J. Buytendijk (1887–1974). Along with German philosophical traditions and a religious world-view, French *existentialism* played a central role in this movement (viz. Dehue, 1995).

The Anglo-American Epoch

The state of Dutch psychology did not change until the 1960s. Since that time the influence of the three religious "pillars" on the practice of psychology in the Netherlands has been weakened significantly. Another remarkable fact is that, despite the negative impact of the Nazi occupation, the domination of German psychological traditions continued long after the war. The replacement of the traditional German orientation in Dutch psychology with Anglo-American perspectives can best be demonstrated by the changing citation pattern of the *Dutch*

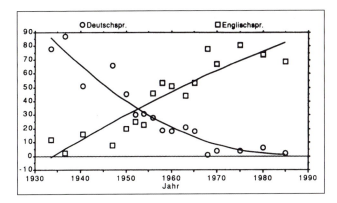

Figure 9 Distribution of German vs. English citations in the *Netherlands Journal of Psychology* after H. E. Lück (1989) and van Strien (1990).

Journal of Psychology (van Strien, 1990). Nevertheless, Dutch psychology continues to maintain its broad international perspective, despite the general Americanization of the field.

Bibliography

Bowman, W. (1891). In memoriam F. C. D. *Acta Psychologica, 30,* 389–408.

Dehue, T. (1995). *Changing the rules; psychology in the Netherlands 1900–1985.* Cambridge: Cambridge University Press.

Heymans, G. (1890). *Gesetze und Elemente des wissenschaftlichen Denkens.* Leipzig: Barth.

Heymans, G. (1905). *Einführung in die Metaphysik, auf Grundlage der Erfahrung.* Leipzig: Barth.

Heymans, G. (1908). Über einige psychische Korrelationen. *Zeitschrift für angewandte Psychologie, 1,* 303–381.

Heymans, G. (1910). *Die Psychologie der Frauen.* Heidelberg: Winter.

Heymans, G. (1912). *Einführung in die Ethik, auf Grundlage der Erfahrung.* Leipzig: Barth.

Heymans, G. (1927) *Gesammelte kleinere Schriften, III* (pp. 41–414). Haag: Martinus Nijhoff.

Heymans, G. (1932). *Einführung in die spezielle Psychologie.* Leipzig: Barth.

Heymans, G., & Wiersma, E. (1906–1918). Beiträge zur speziellen Psychologie auf Grund einer Massenuntersuchung. *Zeitschrift für Psychologie,* Vols. 42, 43, 45, 46, 49, 51, 62, & 80.

Lück, H. E. (1989). Zur Bedeutung der Gruppenprozesse für die Wissenschaftsentwicklung. *Gestalt Theory, 11,* 246– 266.

Schouten, A., & Kelley, E. (1978). On the experiments of Brugmans, Heymans, & Weinberg. *European Journal of Parapsychology, 2,* 247–290.

Strien, P. J. van (1990). Die Rezeption der deutschen Psychologie in den Niederlanden. In A. Schorr, & E. G. Wehner, (Eds.), *Psychologiegeschichte heute* (pp. 261–274). Göttingen: Hogrefe.

Strien, P. J. van (1991a). The omnipresence of the social sciences and its religious roots. *European Cheiron Newsletter,* Spring 1991, 8–16.

Strien, P. J. van (1991b). Transforming psychology in the Netherlands II: Audiences, alliances and the dynamics of change. *History of the Human Sciences, 4,* 351–369.

Strien, P. J. van, & Verster, J. (1988). The response to Fechner in the Netherlands. In J. Brozek & H. Gundlach (Eds.), *G. T. Fechner and Psychology* (pp. 169–178). Passau: Passavia Universitätsverlag.

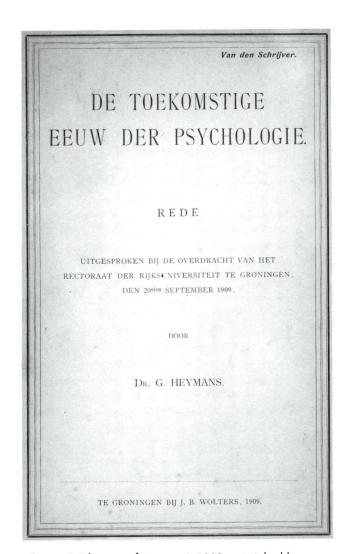

Figure 8 Title page of Heymans's 1909 rectorial address.

French Psychology

French psychology as an independent discipline developed during the last three decades of the 19th century. A group of ideologists including Destutt de Tracy and Cabanis, who were the heirs of Etienne Bonnot de Condillac (1715–1780), had paved the way for its development in the early years of that century. These men believed that the science of ideas and the way they related one to another formed the basis for all scientific knowledge. The two texts that are considered to have laid the foundation for French positive psychology both appeared in the same year—1870. They are *De L'Intelligence* (About Intelligence) by Hippolyte Taine and Théodule Ribot's *La Psychologie Anglaise Contemporaine* (Contemporary English Psychology).

Despite their differences, Taine and Ribot shared a common rejection of official spiritualist philosophy, which was chiefly represented by Victor Cousin and based upon a psychology founded on introspection. Both defined psychology as a science of well-chosen facts and, for different reasons, adopted the same approach to the study of pathological cases. Taine held the view that disease results in the magnification of events, which for the psychologist is analogous to the way the microscope or telescope magnifies events for biologists and astronomers. Ribot, a fervent admirer and translator of Spencer, was inspired by Jackson's work on aphasia. He drew from it the concept that disease, by causing regression, acts the opposite of evolution. It therefore enables us to identify and classify psychological events from the simplest at one end of the spectrum, all the way to the most complex at the other. At the same time, the evolutionary point of view, in which psychological laws are nothing more than the expression of more general laws governing life, enabled Ribot to tie psychology to biology (Carroy

Figure 1 Theodule Armand Ribot (1842–1916), early French experimental psychologist.

& Plas, 1993). In 1876 he founded the *Revue Philosophique* (Philosophical Review), which for almost 20 years was the only journal available as a publication outlet for the new psychology.

M. Courtier M. Binet M. Philippe. M. Henri.

Figure 2 Binet and his collaborators in his Paris laboratory.

Microphon enregistreur et Méthode graphique.
Cylindre enregistreur   Microphone   Piles

Figure 3 Equipment from Binet's laboratory.

cine. The neurologist Jean-Martin Charcot, of the Salpêtrière Hospital, had been using hypnosis since 1878 to experimentally reproduce the symptomatology of hysteria. The popularization of this work and the extraordinary popularity of hypnotism at the end of the 19th century led Alfred Binet and Pierre Janet, both fresh out of training, to consider using hypnosis in their experiments. This enabled them to create "at will" events which could not be seen in a subject under normal conditions. As a result, this became the experimental method par excellence of French psychology. In 1889 Binet wrote the following to English-speaking readers:

> With relatively few exceptions, the psychologists of my country have left the investigation of psychophysics to the Germans, and the study of comparative psychology to the English. They have devoted themselves almost exclusively to the study of pathological psychology, that is to say psychology affected by disease. (Binet, 1890, pp. 12–13)

Ribot, who himself was not a physician, was nevertheless the beginning of a long line of philosopher-physicians who came to characterize French psychology (e.g., Janet, Dumas, Blondel, Wallon, Lagache, etc.). This new psychology was formally consecrated by the establishment in 1887 of the first chair of experimental and comparative psychology at the

The rejection of spiritualist philosophy and the adoption of pathology as a natural experimental approach encouraged Ribot to turn towards medi-

Figure 4 Henri Piéron and Mathilde Piéron in his laboratory at the Sorbonne.

College de France. The chair was assigned to Ribot in 1888 and recognized by the first *Congrès International de Psychologie* held in Paris in 1889.

The same period saw the creation of two laboratories in which "German-style" experimental psychology of basic processes developed; the first, in 1889, at the Sorbonne, was called the *Laboratoire de Psychologie Physiologique* (Laboratory of Physiological Psychology). The physiologist Henry Beaunis was appointed its first director, but he was very shortly thereafter succeeded by Binet. In 1894, they both founded the first French psychology journal, *L'Année Psychologique* (Psychological Yearbook). The second laboratory was the *Laboratoire de Psychologie Expérimentale* (Laboratory of Experimental Psychology), created in Rennes in 1896 by Benjamin Bourdon. Despite their admiration for Germanic rigor, French psychologists—Ribot in particular—felt that the results of this precise and rigorous psychology were rather disappointing, and they were not convinced that psychological events were actually measurable. Binet himself, who achieved worldwide fame following the appearance of his intelligence test, which he completed in 1905 with Théodore Simon, had long abandoned hypnosis and stated at the end of the century that provoked introspection was the true method of psychology.

Although other models developed simultaneously, pathological psychology, along with the analysis of "collective manifestations" of behavior,

remained the dominant model in France until the First World War. In his early works, Gabriel Tarde theorized about "mass crimes" in terms of hypnotic suggestion spread by imitation. However, Tarde, who died prematurely in 1904, failed to gain popularity, and the social psychology which he engendered—the very principles of which were contested by Durkheim's powerful, sociological school—saw the light of day only much later. Gustave Le Bon, who published his famous *Psychologie des Foules* (Mass Psychology) in 1895, was very popular with the public. He was not, however, as popular with his colleagues, largely because of his conservative theoretical attitudes. For that reason, his work had little influence on the field of psychology.

Following the death of Binet in 1911, Henri Piéron was appointed to take charge of the laboratory at the Sorbonne and of *L'Année Psychologique*. (Piéron was working at the time in the laboratory of experimental psychology founded by the physician Édouard Toulouse at the Villejuif Asylum for the Mentally Ill in 1899 and attached to the *Ecole des Hautes Etudes* in 1900.) From the outset, Piéron gave *L'Anée Psychologique* a more physiological and experimental orientation, to the detriment of the individual psychology, educational psychology, and psychopathology favored by Binet. But psychopathology remained well-represented in the *Journale de Psychologie Normale et Pathologique*, founded in 1904 by Pierre Janet and Georges Dumas.

ness" as being radically different from "normal consciousness." In addition, Henri Wallon and Jean Piaget stressed the irreducibility of the infantile thought mode to the primitive thought mode. All of Wallon's subsequent work on the development of thought in the child involved reflections on the relationship between physiological conditions and historical and social conditions.

The psychology of higher mental functions, culminating with Janet's "psychology of action" and the importance of the link between the individual and society, was reported in the *Journale de Psychologie Normale et Pathologique*, which was edited by Ignace Meyerson. As editorial secretary, Meyerson was in charge of the journal from 1920 until his death in 1983. He made the journal a source of exchange and dialogue between all the human sciences (e.g., new history, anthropology, sociology, linguistics, aesthetics). Meyerson's own historical psychology and Gestalt theory (which was represented in France by Paul Guillaume), and the phenomenology of Maurice Merleau-Ponty represented a philosophical tradition in French psychology dating from Bergson, but one which attracted little institutional backing.

In contrast, the movement toward physiological psychology, like behaviorism, played a major role in the development of applied psychology. The principle figure was Piéron, surrounded by a small group of psychologists from Toulouse's laboratory. The

Figure 5 Lucien Lévy Bruhl (1857–1939) and Albert Einstein (1879–1955) in Paris (1928).

Dumas, who was professor of experimental psychology at the Sorbonne and a faithful disciple of Ribot, represented university psychology. He was the editor of the first French psychology textbook. The book was written before World War I, but its first volume was not to appear until 1923.

During the immediate post-war years, the popular psychological model based on the hypothesis of a fundamental continuity between the normal and the pathological was radically challenged by psychologists when they became aware of the anthropology studies of Lucien Lévy-Bruhl. According to Lévy-Bruhl's work on the "primitive mentality," social and cultural determinants render the primitive thought process distinct from the rational thought process. This notion soon challenged the evolutionist approach which classified primitive thought with both the thought patterns of children and with irrational consciousness. Thus the primitive, the child, and the insane were no longer considered to be adequate models capable of revealing psychological laws governing lower forms of normal thought. With regard to psychopathology, for example, Charles Blondel conceived "morbid conscious-

Figure 6 Ignace Meyerson.

Figure 7 Maurice Merleau Ponty.

Institut de Psychologie, created in 1920, formally trained the first French psychologists. The Natural Sciences section of the *Ecole des Hautes Etudes* was soon to provide a home for Wallon's child psychology laboratory, as well as Lahy's applied psychology laboratory and Laugier's applied physiology laboratory. In 1928, Piéron was responsible for the creation of the first institute for the training of vocational guidance counselors (Ohayon, Sellier, & Vermès, 1989).

It was not until the end of the Second World War that psychology acquired the status of a university discipline in its own right, with the creation in 1947 of the Bachelor of Psychology degree. Only then did psychoanalysis begin to play an important role in the history of French psychology. It is reasonable to say that a line

of separation between experimental psychology and clinical psychology was drawn during the 1950s. Paul Fraisse, who in 1952 succeeded Piéron in all his important positions, including the editorship of *L'Année Psychologique*, developed an experimental psychology in France that was founded on psychophysiology. He was also Piéron's heir in terms of his efforts to formally institutionalize the discipline.

Daniel Lagache, a philosopher, physician, and psychoanalyst who was strongly influenced by phenomenology, defined and inaugurated clinical psychology in the university and contributed to the professional establishment of psychologists in medicine. This split between an experimental psychology related to life sciences and a clinical psychology with its essential concepts grounded in psychoanalysis persists, although all the traditional sectors of psychology exist today in France.

Bibliography

Binet, A. (1890). *On double consciousness: Experimental psychological studies.* Chicago: The Open Court Publishing Co.

Carroy, J., & Plas, R. (1993). La méthode pathologique et les origines de la psychologie française au XIXe siècle. *Revue Internationale de Psychopathologie, 12,* 603–612.

Ohayon, A., Sellier, F., & Vermès, G. (1989, July). Il y a 100 ans s'institutionnalisait la psychologie française. Paper presented at the 1st European Congress of Psychology, Amsterdam.

Ribot, T. (1870). *La psychologie anglaise contemporaine.* Paris: Alcan.

Taine, H. (1870). *De L'intelligence.* Paris: Hachette.

Figure 8 Paul Fraisse (right) received an honorary doctorate in Rio de Janeiro (1967).

German Military Psychology

Ulfried Geuter

In many countries, one of the first significant uses of modern psychology was in the service of military questions and problems. For the new experimental psychology, World War I served as a sort of proving ground. In Germany, psychologists studied the aptitudes of military motor vehicle drivers, radio operators, and artillery observers. They also investigated the psychological processes involved in riflemanship and sharp shooting as well as the psychological consequences of brain injuries that occurred during war time. When the United States entered World War I in 1917, the American Psychological Association established a number of special military research and training units. Group

Figure 1 Selection interview with German Air Force psychologist. Note the photograph of Hermann Göring on the wall.

intelligence tests for the screening of recruits were used on more than one and a half million subjects within half a year, and, to that point in time, constituted the largest empirical data collection project in psychology's history.

One consequence of World War I was that academic psychology became increasingly recognized as a practical and useful discipline. After the war, industry and education in the United States became strongly interested in psychological testing. In Germany, the small army of the new German Republic concluded from its war-time experience that psychology might be beneficial in the selection of soldiers and officers. Thus, in 1925 the German army established the first regular positions for psychologists in any German civil service. Beginning in 1927, all officer candidates were examined with a large battery of psychological tests by a special committee, which included psychologists. This method of personnel selection was used by the German mili-

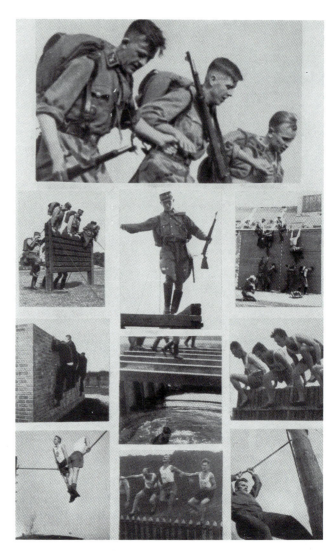

Figure 3 Series of photographs illustrating the physical skill portion of the selection process for German officer candidates.

tary until 1942, when the fatalities among young officer candidates began to far exceed the number of positions for officers. Consequently, the ambitious selection process was rendered meaningless.

When the Nazi government began to enlarge the army and expand the air force after 1935, the number of psychologists involved in selection increased dramatically. In a sense, under National Socialism, psychology became synonymous with military psychology.

The use of psychology in the army also shaped the scientific development of the discipline. The "psychology of expressions" and the field of characterology, for example, which were both widely employed during the evaluations of officer candidates, continued to play a major role in German aca-

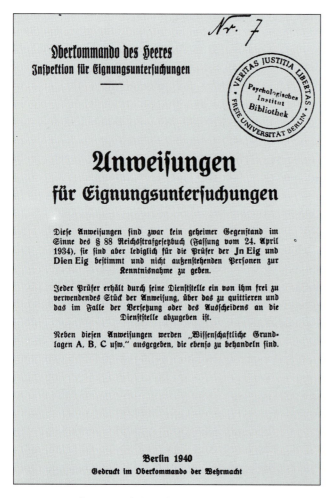

Figure 2 Title page of the selection and test manual for use by German Army psychologists.

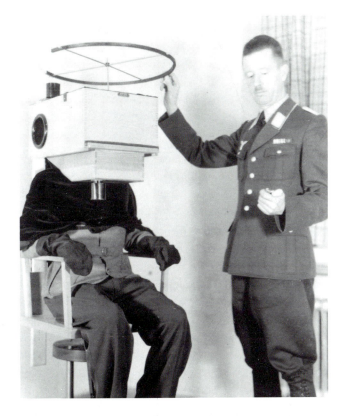

demic psychology until long after World War II. Moreover, the German military in 1937 organized the first career track for psychologists as civil servants. In 1941, growing demand by the army for trained psychologists resulted in the formal state recognition of psychology as an academic specialty. Thus, the professionalization of psychology was primarily facilitated by its close involvement with the military. This was also true for countries like England, Canada, and especially the United States, where World War II greatly facilitated the rapid development of the discipline.

The leaders of German psychology had no reservations about their work for the German army during the National Socialist period. As soon as the re-

Figure 4 Instrument for the assessment of spatial orientation for future flying personnel.

Figure 5 In the aptitude test for pilots the subject was strapped inside this wheel and asked to solve arithmetical problems while the instrument was rotating.

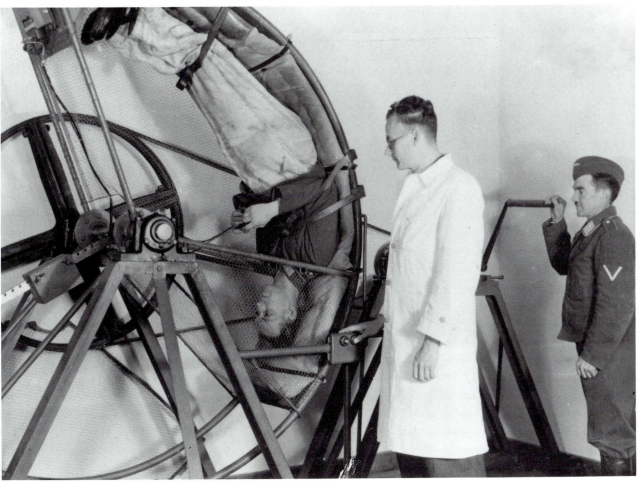

forerunners until the late 1980s. It first also took up their methods. Later, modern aptitude tests were widely used, and German military psychology became involved in ergonomics, organizational management, and the prevention and treatment of mental disorders among military personnel.

In spite of these applications, however, the relative importance of military psychology in Germany declined drastically after World War II. Sharp criticism by the student movement of the uses and abuses of psychology in the Vietnam War brought the field into discredit. Social science had dealt in Third World counterinsurgency for the United States. It was discovered that more than half of America's many civilian research projects—from the operant conditioning of pigeons to experimental studies of sensory deprivation—were financed by military and security organizations.

In recent years psychology has become increasingly involved in studies of authoritarianism, prejudices, and aggression, in order to prevent war and keep peace. But historically the relation of psychology to the military grew mainly out of the fact that psychologists offered their expertise for military objectives and tried to prove the usefulness of their methods.

Figure 6 Oswald Kroh was a member of the Board of Directors of the German Psychological Society during the Nazi period and its President from 1940–1945.

organization of a standing army was being discussed in postwar Germany, the Professional Association of German Psychologists encouraged the re-establishment of military psychology. Active work in the field began with the re-establishment of the army in West Germany in 1955. The revived German military psychology clung to the traditions of its

Bibliography

Geuter, U. (1992). The professionalization of psychology in Nazi Germany (R. J. Holmes, Trans.). New York: Cambridge University Press.

Geuter, U., & Kroner, B. (1987). Militärpsychologie. In G. Rexilius & S. Grubitzsch (Ed.), *Handbuch psychologischer Grundbegriffe* (pp. 672–689). Reinbek: Rowohlt.

Samelson, F. (1979). Putting psychology on the map: Ideology and intelligence testing. In A. R. Buss (Ed.), *Psychology in social context* (pp. 103–168). New York: Irvington.

Psychology in Spain

Enrique Lafuente

Scientific psychology was introduced in Spain at the end of the 19th century by a group of progressive intellectuals deeply influenced by German thought, specifically by the philosophy of the idealist thinker K. C. F. Krause. Led by the jurist and philosopher Julían Sanz del Río (1814–1869), Spanish Krausists aimed at a moral and intellectual regeneration of Spanish society (Lopez Morillas, 1956). The leading figure in this movement was Francisco Giner de los Ríos (1839–1915), the jurist and educator whose *Summary Lessons in Psychology* (1874) was clearly indebted to Krause's system. The second edition of this book (1877) was probably the first step taken to bring the findings of the new scientific psychology into Spain (Lafuente, 1987). Giner was also the founder of the Free Institute for Education (1876), a private teaching establishment that was to become the primary center for the reception and dissemination of modern sciences in Spain (Jiménez Landi, 1973, 1987).

Following the overthrow of Isabel II, an agitated revolutionary and republican experience during the years 1868–1874 resulted in the restoration of the Bourbon monarchy in 1875. This event opened a period of political stability as well as economic and intellectual development. This situation favored the advancement of science, which was also fostered by the reception of positivist and neo-Kantian doctrines (Nuñez, 1975). From this setting came a generation of researchers with positivist training, who, in their determination that scientific standards be raised in Spain, began to carry out rigorous experimental work. Because of his impact both in Spain and abroad, their most conspicuous representative was the histologist Santiago Ramón y Cajal (1852–1934), whose research on the structure of the nervous system won him a worldwide reputation.

Luis Simarro (1851–1921) and Ramón Turró (1854–1926) are also important as heads of two separate psychological traditions, one in Madrid and the other in Barcelona (Carpintero, 1994). Trained in psychiatry with Charcot, Simarro was deeply influenced in psychology by Wundt and Ziehen. He held the first Spanish university chair in experimental psychology at the University of Madrid (1902). Though he published little personally, he had a large group of disciples, some of whom would later play important roles in Spanish psychology (Carpintero, 1987). As for Turró, he was a biologist who was chiefly concerned with physiological, immunological, and epistemological matters. However, his work was also rich in psychological significance, as his most salient disciples, Augusto Pi y Sunyer (1879–1965) and Emilio Mira y López (1896–1964), were to show in the years to follow.

The Development of a Scientific Tradition

Throughout the first 30 years of this century, Spanish psychology showed a progressive consolidation of the scientific tradition whose foundation had been laid in the closing years of the previous century (Carpintero, 1994). During that period, a number of popular works by authors close to Giner and the Free Institute for Education appeared. In this atmosphere, many modern ideas in psychology were spread widely—especially those with a Wundtian viewpoint (Carpintero, 1981a). In addition, the ideas of other modern scholars such as Binet, Freud, James, Köhler, Koffka, Pavlov, Piaget, Ribot, and many others were incorporated into Spanish psychology through a tremendous proliferation of translations in which, again, figures linked to the Free Institute played an essential role.

Figure 1 Francisco Giner de los Ríos (1839–1915), ca. 1870.

As early as 1877, psychology had found an important organ for the dissemination of all the latest information in the *Boletín* of the Free Institute for Education, which was first published in 1877. Papers by Spanish and foreign authors (such as Binet, Dewey, Sully, and Spencer) were published in its pages, and these tended to emphasize an educational rather than a strictly psychological perspective. Since the 1920s, however, more specialized journals began to emerge in which neurological, psychiatric, and social concerns appeared together with pedagogical ones. *Archivos de Neurobiología, Psicología, Fisiología, Histología, Neurología, y Psiquiatría*, founded in 1920 by José Ortega y Gasset (1883–1955), Gonzalo Rodríguez Lafora (1886–1971), and J. M. Sacristán became exceptionally prominent. It was the first Spanish journal to be devoted in part to psychology (Peiró & Carpintero, 1981).

During that same time period, some of the most

Figure 2 First edition of *Summary Lessons in Psychology*, by Giner de los Ríos (1874).

As previously mentioned, psychology appeared for the first time in the Spanish university in 1902, when Simarro was named to the Faculty of Sciences in Madrid. Many other institutions also encouraged the development of psychology outside academia. Particularly worth mentioning are the National Organization for the Mentally Handicapped (1914) and the Institute for the Professional Re-education of Disabled Workers (1922), both in Madrid. In Barcelona, the Secretary of Learning (1914) was soon transformed into an Institute of Professional Guidance (1917). On the whole, Spanish psychology at that time had a marked applied orientation, particularly with respect to education, work, and organization.

Figure 3 The Free Institution for Education in 1915.

outstanding names in Spanish psychology gained international recognition, definitively consolidating the Europeanization of Spanish society. Ortega y Gasset and Lafora, along with Gregorio Marañón (1887–1960) are but a few notable examples of authors connected specifically with Spanish psychology. Lafora was a disciple of Cajal and Simarro in Spain, as well as Ziehen, Kraepelin, Alzheimer, and Franz. He was a solidly-trained psychiatrist who represents an essential link in the Spanish psychological tradition and therefore deserves special attention here. His institutional work includes the founding of two centers from which the development of psychology was fostered—a neuropathic sanatorium and the Medical-Pedagogical Institute (1925), both in Madrid. Besides being co-founder of *Archivos de Neurobiología*, he was a pioneer in the field of child psychopathology (Valenciano, 1977; Moya, 1986).

Thus, in addition to the reception, dissemination, institutionalization, and professionalization of psychology, we also find creation. Full incorporation of Spanish psychology into the international scene was to have had its definitive push with the organization of the 11th International Congress of Psychology in Madrid in September of 1936. The outbreak of the Civil War in July of that year, however, made its realization impossible.

The Civil War: Exile and Regression

The Spanish Civil War (1936–1939) represented the culmination of the contention between the "two Spains" which had more or less overtly pervaded the whole of Spanish life throughout the 19th and 20th centuries (Figueiredo, 1933). Its consequences could not have been more disastrous for the field of psychology (Carpintero, 1984).

The open support given to the doomed Republican cause by a great number of artists, intellectuals, and scientists forced many of them to go into exile once the war ended. Among them were figures of the utmost prestige: Ortega y Gasset, Marañón, Lorente de Nó, and Del Río Hortega. Some came back to Spain; others did not, and had to carry on their work in their adopted countries. Especially relevant to psychology are the cases of Lafora in Mexico, M. Rodrigo in Colombia, A. Garma in Argentina, and E. Mira in Brazil, where they played a prominent role.

Nevertheless, the work carried out by these and many other Spanish psychologists in exile had no repercussions whatsoever in Franco's Spain. Quite the contrary; in line with the strongly conservative regime which controlled the country, an attempt was made to take psychology back to the condition of a philosophical discipline with a rigid, neoscholastic perspective.

Figure 4 Luis Simarro (1851–1921).

Figure 5 José Ortega y Gasset (1883–1955) in August 1939.

Figure 6 Gonzalo R. Lafora (1886–1971), ca. 1923.

Scientific Tradition Restored

Beginning in the late forties, however, a few signs became apparent of what was to be the beginning of a slow and far-from-easy reconstruction of the scientific tradition that had been so sharply disrupted. The unquestionable main character in this new stage was José Germain (1897–1986), who was a physician and psychiatrist, and a disciple and co-worker of Lafora. Germain was primarily concerned with the applied aspects of psychology. His major achievements were: the founding, in 1946, of the *Revista de Psicología General y Aplicada*, the most important psychological journal in Spain; the creation, in 1948, of a Department of Experimental Psychology in the Higher Council for Scientific Research, where those responsible for many of the subsequent developments in psychology in Spain were trained; the foundation of the Spanish Psychological Society in 1952; and the creation, in 1953, of a

Graduate School of Psychology attached to the University of Madrid (Carpintero, 1981b).

Moreover, Germain gathered around him a large group of disciples who later became the leaders of the psychological work carried out in Spain. He provided them with a solid scientific and technical training, which in many cases was completed abroad. Because of their prominent academic work, several of these Spanish psychologists should be mentioned. They include: Mariano Yela (1921–1994), a professor at the University of Madrid who worked with Thurstone and Michotte, and who was the main promoter of psychometrics and factor analysis in Spain; José Luis Pinillos (1919–), who was a professor at the Universities of Valencia and Madrid whose work focused mainly on various aspects of social psychology and personality (his training was completed under Rothacker and Eysenck); and Miguel Siguán (1918–), a professor at the University of Barcelona who studied at the National Institute of Industrial Psychology in London and devoted himself mainly to topics of industrial and social psychology and psycholinguistics.

Figure 7 José Germain (1897–1986) during the opening lecture of the Third National Psychological Meeting, May 1970.

Spanish psychology gained a new momentum in the late sixties with the introduction of psychology into the university curriculum. The creation of a Degree in Psychology (first within the Faculty of Philosophy in 1968), and then the establishment of an independent Faculty of Psychology some years later (1980)—all favored by the restoration of a democratic regime in Spain—resulted in substan-

tial increases in the number of psychologists, quantity of research, and number of specialized journals. This increase has been especially sharp since the mid-1970s. In the professional domain, moreover, psychology attained definitive social and institutional status with the creation of the Official Union [College] of Psychologists in 1980.

Now, at the threshold of the 21st century, psychology in Spain has endured more than a century of striving to achieve full academic and social recognition. Today, Spanish psychology has almost 1,000 university teachers, nearly 50,000 graduates, and a professional society which is second in number only to the American Psychological Association (Prieto, 1989). Spanish psychology has, at last, reason to contemplate its future with considerable optimism.

Bibliography

Carpintero, H. (1981a). Wundt y la psicología en España. *Revista de Historia de la Psicología, 2,* 37–55.

Carpintero, H. (Ed.). (1981b). José Germain y la psicología española. Madrid: Anejos de la *Revista de Psicología General y Aplicada.*

Carpintero, H. (1984). The impact of the Spanish Civil War on Spanish scientific psychology. *Revista de Historia de la Psicología, 5,* 91–97.

Carpintero, H. (1987). El doctor Simarro y la psicología científica en España. *Investigaciones Psicológicas, 4,* 189–207.

Carpintero, H. (1994). *Historia de la psicología en España.* Madrid: Eudema.

Figueiredo, F. (1933). *Las dos Españas.* Santiago de Compostela, Spain: Universidad de Santiago de Compostela.

Jiménez Landi, A. (1973). *La Institución Libre de Enseñanza y su ambiente: Los orígenes.* Madrid: Taurus.

Jiménez Landi, A. (1987). *La Institución Libre de Enseñanza y su ambiente: Período parauniversitario.* Madrid: Taurus.

Lafuente, E. (1987). Los orígenes de la psicología científica en España: Las Lecciones Sumarias de Psicología de Francisco Giner de los Ríos. *Investigaciones Psicológicas, 4,* 165–187.

Lopez Morillas, J. (1956). *El krausismo español.* México: Fondo de Cultura Económica.

Moya, G. (1986). *Gonzalo R. Lafora. Medicina y cultura en una España en crisis.* Madrid: Universidad Autónoma.

Nuñez, D. (1975). *La mentalidad positiva en España: desarrollo y crisis.* Madrid: Túcar.

Peiró, J. M., & Carpintero, H. (1981). Historia de la psicología en España a través de sus revistas especializadas. *Revista de Historia de la Psicología, 2,* 143–181.

Prieto, J. M. (1989). La realidad universitaria en cifras: pausa para la reflexión. *Papeles del psicólogo, 36-37,* 74–78.

Valenciano, L. (1977). *El doctor Lafora y su época.* Madrid: Morata.

Academic Psychology in Prague

Josef Brožek
Jiří Hoskovec

The individuals in the following survey of early academic psychology at the University of Prague can be divided into two groups—Czech and German—based on their native languages. Jan E. Purkinje (1787–1869) was a leading personality of international rank in the smaller Czech group. A physiologist by profession, he completed his medical studies in Prague in 1818 with his excellent psychological dissertation entitled *Contributions to the Subjective Understanding of Vision*. It was published in Prague a year later. The famous "Purkinje Phe-

Figure 2 Gustav Adolf Lindner.

nomenon" was first reported in a volume which appeared in Berlin in 1825.

Gustav A. Lindner (1831–1887), who taught from 1882 to 1886 in the Czech division of the University of Prague, was the author of *Empirical Psychology According to the Genetic Method*, which, translated into English with the subtitle "A Textbook for High Schools and Colleges," was published in four editions between 1889 and 1901. His *Ideas on the Psychology of Society as the Basis for the Social Sciences*,

Figure 1 Jan Evangelista Purkinje.

562

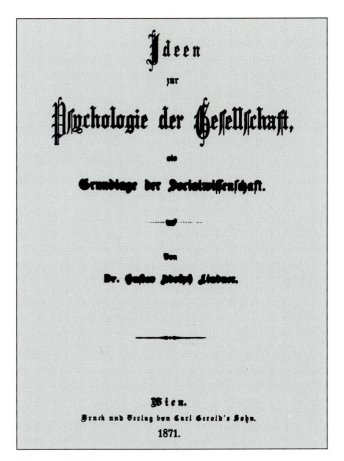

Figure 3 German title page of Lindner's *Social Psychology* (1871).

and the author of the important monograph *The Analysis of Sensations and the Relationship between Physical and Psychic Phenomena* (1885). In 1885, he received and accepted a call to a professorship at Vienna.

Anton Marty (1847–1914), a student of Brentano who taught in Prague from 1880 to 1914, was recognized as a specialist in the philosophy of language. He was also interested in the psychology of thinking. After Marty's death, J. Eisenmeier, A. Kastill, and O. Kraus published Marty's *Collected Writings* and his posthumous book, *Space and Time*.

Carl Stumpf (1848–1936) taught in Prague from 1879 to 1884. During this time, he published the first volume of his *Tone Psychology* (1883). Stumpf was a music lover and played several instruments. He also published articles in the field of musical ethnology.

Friedrich Jodel (1849–1914) was at the University from 1885–1896. His *Textbook of Psychology* was published in 1896. In this work, Jodel attempted to summarize the splintered literature of psychology and to provide an objective report on psychology's status.

Christian von Ehrenfels (1859–1932), who taught at Prague from 1896 to 1929, was famous for his article on *Gestalt Qualities* (1890). His psychology students in Prague included Max Wertheimer (1880–1943). During his Prague period, von Ehren-

which appeared in 1871, not only introduced the term *social psychology*, but offered a program for this discipline as well.

Among the senior German psychologists, several individuals were particularly noteworthy. In chronological order, they are:

Wilhelm Volkmann (1821–1877) was born in Prague and remained there throughout his life. He was the author of a widely-used *Textbook of Psychology* (1856) and held a full professorship in philosophy and related subjects from 1861 on. He believed that it was his chief responsibility to show what Herbart's realism can accomplish for the field of psychology and to give, if possible, a complete account of the basic principles of psychology.

Ewald Hering (1834–1918) was a successful sensory physiologist who wrote the book *Explanation of Color Blindness through the Theory of Complementary Colors* (1880). He taught in Prague for 25 years, and his physiological laboratory was world famous.

Ernst Mach (1838–1916) was a native of Moravia

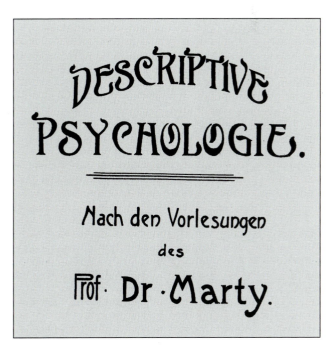

Figure 4 Anonymous and officially unpublished notes of Marty's lectures on "Descriptive Psychology."

fels was primarily interested in the philosophical theories of values and ethics.

The younger generation of Prague's academic psychologists also included several significant figures:

Josef Eisenmeier (1871–1926), a native of Bohemia, studied experimental psychology under Wundt in Berlin. He published an important book, *Psychology and its Central Position* in Philosophy, in 1914. He received an appointment as "Untenured Professor of Philosophy and Experimental Psychology" during the 1922–1923 academic year. Unfortunately, he died before realizing his plans for the establishment of a special institute for experimental psychology. However, such a facility was opened in 1926.

Johannes Lindworsky (1875–1939) was a student of Oswald Külpe (1861–1915) and an excellent experimental psychologist. He came to Prague in the winter term of 1928–1929 from Bonn University to continue Eisenmeier's work. He suffered a severe

Figure 5 Anton Marty.

Figure 6 Christian von Ehrenfels.

Figure 7 Wilhelm Volkmann.

Figure 8 Ewald Hering.

Figure 9 Ernst Mach.

years 1925–1934. He came back to Prague to become a professor and a member (together with P. Kraus and E. Otto) of the Prague "Cercle Linguistique." He survived imprisonment in a German concentration camp and returned to Prague in 1945. His book, *Psychology of Life in the Concentration Camp Theresienstadt*, was published in 1948 in Vienna.

Several German-speaking psychologists, who worked in Czechoslovakia, participated in the

stroke shortly after his arrival, but continued his work at the university until 1939 despite his health problems.

Franz Scola (1899–1945) was Lindworsky's assistant for many years and eventually became his successor. During the 1920s and 1930s, he became primarily known for his research articles in the journal *Archives of Psychology*. In tune with the times, his "Habilitationsschrift" of 1943 bore the subtitle "An attempt at a psychological foundation of racial characteristics."

Lindworsky's students included German as well as Czech psychologists—for example, Václav Příhoda (1889–1979), whose book on holistic teaching, *The Global Method* (1935), was first published in Prague in a German edition. Příhoda, an educational psychologist, became a leading figure in Czech psychology after World War II.

Emil Utitz (1883–1956) was born in Prague. He edited the *Yearbook of Characterology* in Halle from 1924–1929 and was also a professor there during the

Figure 10 Josef Eisenmeier.

Figure 11 Johannes Lindworsky.

Eighth International Conference of Psychotechnology, which was held in Prague in September of 1934 (Šeracký, 1935). A. Cibulka, who gave a paper on accident prevention in the steel industry, and E. Pechhold, who talked about employment selections, came from the Psychological Center in Vítkovice. Three other authors, O. Fanta, W. Schönfeld, and W. Simon, were interested in the application of graphology as a measure of intelligence in the selection of workers. Franz Scola spoke on "The Issue of Intelligence and Intelligence Tests."

The field of psychotechnology was successfully developed in Czechoslovakia during the 1920s and 1930s. German and Czech psychologists were able to work together. Particularly close relationships existed at that time between Prague and Dresden (Richter, 1981; Schirmer & Richter, 1989). The Czech psychologist Jan Doležal (1902–1965) worked with E. Sachsenberg in Dresden, with whom he developed a series of psychotechnological instruments.

Figure 12 The Cafe Louvre—meeting place of Brentano's followers in Prague.

Figure 13 Emil Utitz.

Figure 14 Jan Doleal.

Doležal defended his dissertation on industrial motion study at Leipzig University and published the dissertation in Munich in 1927. After his return to Czechoslovakia in the early 1930s, Doležal became one of the country's leading psychologists.

Bibliography

Brožek, J., & Hoskovec, J. (1987). *J. E. Purkyně and Psychology*. Prague: Akademie.

Brožek, J., & Hoskovec, J. (1992). Die Liste der psychologischen. Dissertationen der deutschen Universität in Prag vor dem Jahre 1939. *Geschichte der Psychologie, 9*, 48–55.

Doležal, J. (1927). Über die Bewegungsform bei der Arbeit an Drehkurbeln. *Neue Psychologische Studien, 5*, 257–316. Munich: Beck.

Ehrenfels, C. von (1890). Über Gestaltqualitäten. *Vierteljahresschrift für wissenschaftliche Philosophie, 14*, 249–292.

Geuter, U. (1987). *Daten zur Geschichte der deutschen Psychologie. Vol. 2. Psychologische Dissertationen, 1885-1967*. Göttingen: Hogrefe.

Janoušek, J., Hoskovec, J. & Štikar, J. (1993). [Psychological atlas]. Prague: Karolinum-Academia.

Linder, G. (1871). Ideen zur Psychologie der Gesellschaft als Grundlage der Sozialwissenschaft. Vienna: Geroldson.

Linder, G. (1889). *Manual of empirical psychology as inductive science*. Boston: Heath.

Otto, E. (J. Brožek, M. Rostohar, & Weiss-Nägel). (1935). Die Jugendkunde in der Tschechoslowakei. *Zeitschrift für Jugendkunde, 5*, 84–91.

Richter, P. G. (1981). *Gründung und Entwicklung des Psychotechnischen Institutes an der TU Dresden 1920-1940*. Dresden: Technische Universität.

Schirmer, F., & Richter, P. G. (1989). Zur Geschichte de Psychologie an der Technischen Hochschule Dresden von 1876 bis 1945. *Psychologie-Historische Manuskripte, Vol. 2. Kongreß/Symposium 14*. Berlin: Gesellschaft für Psychologie.

Scola, F. (1943). *Rasse und Lebensform: Versuch einer psychologischen Begründung der rassenseelischen Eigenarten*. Berlin: Junker und Dünnhaupt.

Šeracký, F. (Ed.). (1935). *Comptes rendus de la VIII conférence internationale de psychotechnique tenue à Prague du 11 au 15 septembre 1934*. Prague: Orbis.

Ühlein, H. (1986). *Johannes Lindworsky*. Universität Passau: Selbstverlag.

Ühlein, H., Hoskovec, J., & Brožek, J. (1994). Deutschsprachige Psychologie in Prag. In H. Gundlach (Ed.), *Arbeiten zur Psychologiegeschichte* (pp. 113–122). Göttingen: Hogrefe.

Ühlein, H., Brožek, J., & Hoskovec, J. (1989). Deutsche Psychologie in Prague. *Psychologische Rundschau, 40*, 226.

 # Experimental Psychology in Hungary

György Kiss

The beginnings of experimental psychology in Hungary developed concurrently with applied psychology. Hungary's first important experimental psychologist was the neurologist Pál Ranschburg (1870–1945), who opened the first Hungarian psychological laboratory in 1899. This institution became an official part of the College of Mental Hygiene in 1902 and continues to exist today as the important Psychological Institute and Research Center of the Hungarian Academy of Sciences in Budapest.

Ranschburg employed his famous "mnemometer" to conduct memory experiments with both psychiatric patients and normal control subjects. He discovered that the reading of heterogeneous number series resulted in far fewer errors than the reading of homogeneous series of numbers. When he was able to replicate and cross-validate his results, he formulated his law of "homogeneous inhibition," which is also known as "Ranschburg's Phenomenon" or "Ranschburg's Inhibition." According to this principle, successive sensory impressions influence each other more if they are heterogeneous. In turn, homogeneous impressions are prone to combine and to be perceived as a unit (Ranschburg, 1901, 1902).

Figure 2 shows the results of a typical Ranschburg experiment. The "original" numbers are printed at the left side of the table. The top column lists the subjects and the scores are recorded under each name.

The importance of Ranschburg's discovery was recognized as early as the beginning of the 20th century. It was no accident that his findings aroused the interest of Hugo Münsterberg (1863–1916), who performed the first studies of industrial labor at Harvard University. After focusing on the topic of "Monotony" in his 1913 book, *Psychology and Economic Life*, Münsterberg later conducted his own research comparing the effects of uniform and variable stimuli on work performance and achievement.

Figure 1 Portrait of Pál Ranschburg.

Objectiv szám-sorok	Dr. M. S.	Dr. H. K.	F. E.	Dr. R. N.	Dr. H. G.	Sch. E.	K. K.
119195	1194-5	119456	1194-5	119425	119465	119945	—
141993	141934	141930	141903	—	103729	141933	141393
103739	—	—	103799	—	103729	103799	107379
774886	—	774836	7748-6	774485	774865	774586	—
176468	—	176463	176408	1764--	—	—	—
710332	—	710322	710322	710392	—	710512	—
145957	145997	145597	145597	145497	145937	145-79	—
609337	—	609733	—	609937	609337	609377	—
975251	—	9--524	9725-4	975245	975261	975521	972254
147556	—	147506	147566	—	147536	147566	14756-
663732	—	663722	663752	663734	—	667732	663722
449793	449723	449703	449703	449739	449773	449793	449732
411882	—	411832	411802	411822	411832	411832	441882
654012	654902	654012	654--2	—	--	654002	—
960443	—	—	—	—	—	936--4	960043
714998	—	7149-3	719498	714089	711993	714988	714998
128786	—	128756	127876	128726	128726	—	127786
817660	—	817600	817600	—	—	817660	—
278489	278---	278196	274849	278429	278499	227849	278499
610552	—	—	—	—	—	610532	—
Hibás sorok összege	6 (6)	17 (15)	17 (16)	13 (11)	12 (12)	17 (15)	11 (11)

(Az eltévesztett számjegyeket dült szedésben adjuk.)

Figure 2 Experimental results of typical Ranschburg Experiment. The original numbers are printed at the left side of the table. The top column lists the subjects and the scores are recorded under each name.

Professor of Psychology at Amsterdam University. His research on the identification of the gifted and talented can be viewed as an extension of his Hungarian research on musical giftedness in children. This research also is the subject of his principal work, *Talent and Genius* (1952).

Révész conducted a number of studies on the early identification of giftedness. Specifically, he was interested in the variables which suggest the presence of high ability before any specific talents had fully coalesced. His 1918 discovery that intuition, spontaneity, moral behavior, strength of will, and intelligence determine the expression of a child's talent are still important for modern research in this field.

The initial identification and evaluation of a child's abilities and talents are among the most important responsibilities of elementary school teachers, who consequently require a thorough grounding in basic psychology. It was László Nagy

Apart from his role as the founder of experimental psychology in Hungary, Ranschburg also worked actively to get psychology established and recognized as an independent profession by his countrymen. Consequently, he was honored in 1928 by being elected as the first president of the Hungarian Psychological Association.

Another important figure in the history of Hungarian psychology was Géza Révész (1878–1955), who earned a law degree from the Scientific University in Budapest with a dissertation on a psychological research topic. In 1902, at the age of 30, Révész continued his studies in psychology at Göttingen University in Germany under Georg Elias Müller (1850–1934). He also occasionally attended lectures given by other well-known psychologists such as Stumpf, Brentano, and Lipps. Révész was the first Hungarian to earn a PhD in psychology, even though it was awarded by a foreign university. It was no accident that Révész was appointed in 1908 as the first instructor of experimental psychology at the Business College of the Scientific University in Budapest.

Révész became Professor and Director of the Psychological Institute of the same university in 1918. However, in 1921 he emigrated to Holland, where he was given a prestigious appointment as

Figure 3 Portrait of Géza Révész.

(1857–1931) who introduced the field of psychology to the preparation of public school teachers in Hungary. He primarily worked at a junior high school which also served as a normal school for the education of primary school teachers. Following Nagy's recommendations, teacher education was completely reformed between 1908 and 1914. As a result, the teachers were familiarized with the methods and conclusions of scientific psychology as they pertain to the identification and evaluation of psychological phenomena in the lives of children.

Figure 4 Portrait of László Nagy.

The new approach to teacher training placed heavy emphasis on a variety of psychologically-oriented courses. The classroom instruction included experiments similar to those of Ernst Meumann (1862–1915), which were designed to increase the future teachers' understanding of child behavior. To assist in the education of young teachers, the local junior high schools were richly endowed with laboratories and experimental equip-

ment. A common instrument at these schools was "Nedschajeff Tachistoscope" and the "Color Mixer of László Nagy."

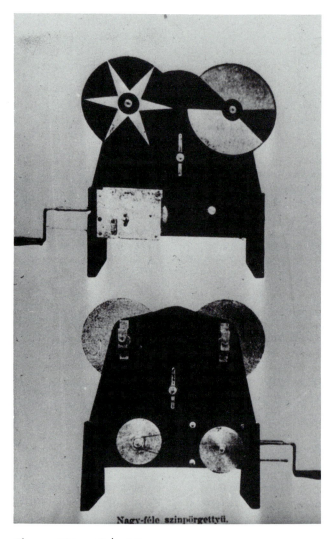

Nagy-féle szinpörgettyü.

Figure 5 Nagy Color Mixer.

Another important contributor to early Hungarian psychology was Lajos Kardos (1899–1985), who also held a professorship at the Scientific University in Budapest. Kardos had studied under Karl Bühler (1879–1963) in Vienna. His first works still show the influence of the "Vienna School." Kardos's other important writings focused on general psychology, animal psychology, and, especially, the systematic education of professional psychologists (Kardos, 1962).

Finally, Pál Harki Schiller (1908–1949), a disciple of Ranschburg, needs to be mentioned. From 1931 to 1932 he was associated with the Berlin Gesltalt

Figure 6 Portrait of Lajos Kardos.

psychology program of Köhler and Lewin. He also held a prestigious appointment as director of the Psychological Institute of the Budapest University of Sciences. Throughout his university days in Hungary, Schiller was actively involved in the field of applied psychology. Specifically, he established and directed the Hungarian Military Aptitude Institute, the National Social Security Aptitude Testing Institute, and the first Public Opinion Poll Institute in Hungary. Schiller's views about the nature and purpose of experimental psychology are best summarized in his book *The Task of Psychology* (Schiller, 1948), which presents his motivational theory in considerable detail. In 1946, Schiller was appointed to a second professorship in psychology at the Hungarian University of Cluj. Shortly afterwards he accepted an invitation from Columbia University in New York. He died tragically as a result of a car accident in May of 1949, while working as a research associate at Yerkes Laboratory of Primate Research.

Bibliography

Kardos, L. (1962). *Grundfragen der Psychologie und der Forschungen Pawlow.* Budapest.

Ranschburg, P. (1901). Apparat und Methode zur Untersuchung des optischen Gedächtnisses für medizinische und pädagogisch-psychologische Zwecke. *Monatsschrift für Psychiatrie und Neurologie, 10,* 321–333.

Ranschburg, P. (1902). Über Hemmung gleichzeitiger Reizwirkungen. Experimenteller Beitrag zur Lehre von Bedingungen der Aufmerksamkeit. *Zeitschrift für Psychologie und Physiologie der Sinnesorgane, 30,* 39–86.

Revesz, G. (1952). *Talent und Genie.* Bern: Francke.

Schiller, P. (1948). *Aufgabe der Psychologie, eine Geschichte ihrer Probleme.* Vienna: Springer.

Russian Psychology

Vladimir P. Zinchenko

After his execution had been commuted at the last possible moment, Fyodor Dostoyevsky (1821–1881) wrote to his brother Michael that dialectics were over and true life had begun. After the October Revolution of 1917, life in Russia was over and dialectics did begin. This is not just a metaphorical reflection, but rather a real description of the historical background required to understand the development of Russian science in general and psychology in particular.

Until 1917 Russian psychology developed primarily in universities—just as it did in the West. The best-known universities were located in cities like Moscow, Petersburg, Khar'kov, Kiev, and Kazan'. The first psychological laboratories in Russia were established at the end of the 19th century. Various natural scientific and philosophical trends (including theological ones) were represented in Russian psychology at that time. Russian psychologists got their education in Europe—mainly in Germany, where they worked in Wilhelm Wundt's (1832–1920) laboratory. Such areas as general, experimental, child, pedagogical, social, and medical psychology emerged, as did psychoanalysis, pedology, psychotechnology, and zoological psychology, as well as others.

In 1914 the Psychological Institute of Moscow University was established near the Kremlin under the sponsorship of the well-known patron of the arts and sciences, S. I. Shchukin (1854–1936). Professor Georgii I. Chelpanov (1862–1936) became the organizer and first director of the institute. (Today the institute is part of the Russian Academy of Education.) Both the Russian and the Moscow Psychological Societies were organized during those years, and a periodical, *News in Philosophy and Psychology*, appeared. Many translated works of European and American psychologists were also published during this period.

The first decades of the 20th century are known in Russia, justifiably, as the Silver Age of Russian Culture, and psychology was part of this age. At that time psychology was characterized by a great deal of "polyphonicity" and "dialogicality" (Bakhtin, 1972). Psychologists maintained a dialog with philosophers and poets and with Russian modernists in the arts. As early as the beginning of the 1920s, many outstanding scholars from various generations worked together in the Institute of Psychology. These included Chelpanov, who was a philosopher and psychologist, as well as author of the wonderful book, *Brain and Soul*, and a number of textbooks (on subjects such as psychology, logic, and experimental psychology); Gustav Shpet (1879–1938), the philosopher, psychologist, linguist, and connoisseur of aesthetics; Anatoly Smirnov (1894–1980) who did research on memory and understanding; Boris Teplov (1896–1965), the psychophysiologist and phenomenologist who wrote *The Psychology of Musical Abilities* and an excellent essay entitled "The Commander's Mind," and who conducted research into individual differences; Piotr Shevarev (1892–1972), the neoassociationist who authored *Generalized Associations*; Sergei Kravkov (1893–1951), the psychophysicist; Nikolai Zhinkin (1893–1979), the psychologist and linguist; and Alexei Losev (1893–1988), the philosopher, who went on to write an entire bookshelf of volumes on ancient aesthetics. The linguist Roman Jackobson (1896–1982) was also in close contact with this institute.

This older generation accepted many younger scholars into their circle, such as the physiologist and mathematician Nikolai Bernshtein (1896–1966),

572

who created a novel theory about the construction of movement and more generally outlined an activity approach to physiology that today is more often referred to as psychological physiology; Lev Vygotsky (1896–1934), the founder of the cultural-historical approach to the development of mind and consciousness; Aleksandr Luria (1902–1977), the founder of neuropsychology; and Alexei Leont'ev (1903–1979), who created the psychological theory of activity and was also a creative experimental psychologist. Few other examples can be found where such an outstanding, talented group of people worked together in the same institution. Stephen Toulmin (1980) called Vygotsky and Luria "the Mozart and Beethoven of psychology," respectively, and Jerome Bruner called Bernshtein "a genius."

There are several other figures that should be mentioned when discussing Russian psychology during the early part of the 20th century. The majority of these worked in Petersburg, including Ivan Pavlov (1849–1936) and Vladimir Bekhterev (1857–1929); Alexey A. Ukhtomsky (1875–1992), the creator of the theory of functional organs as artifacts and of the doctrine of "dominants"; Mikhail Bakhtin (1895–1975), the philosopher, psychologist, and scholar of literature who created the theory of dialogical or "polyphonic" consciousness and the theory of deed; and the animal psychologist Vladimir Vagner (1849–1934). Sergei Rubinshtein (1889–1960) was among the founders of the psychological theory of activity and wrote several very interesting philosophical-psychological treatises as well as the fundamental textbook *Foundations of Psychology*. David El'kin (1895–1983), a specialist in the psychology of time, worked in Odessa. He was the founder of set theory and the Georgian School of psychology. Another psychologist, Dmitri Uznadze (1886–1950), worked in Tbilisi.

It is very difficult to imagine what would have been the course of Russian (and world) psychology if science in Russia had continued to develop in a normal, human way after the Silver Age. Historians of world psychology often speak of a crisis that emerged in the 1920s. The history of Russian psychology, however, followed a kind of catastrophical logic under conditions of permanent repression. Philosophers and philosophically-oriented scientists were the first victims of this and were sent out of the country. Psychology stopped being the science of the mind and became instead a science of how the mind (and soul) did not exist. In 1925, dis-

cussions of psychoanalysis were curtailed, and after this the same thing occurred to inquiry into the whole sphere of the unconsciousness. Subsequently, prohibitions expanded into social psychology, and then it was time for consciousness itself to die.

The real collapse of Russian psychology occurred in the 1930s. Fields such as psychotechnology, pedology, the study of talented children and of individuality, and occupational selection all were prohibited. Psychology disappeared from universities, and professional psychological education stopped. Even pedagogical and child psychology were removed from pedagogical institutes, because of their connection to pedology (see van der Veer and Valsiner, 1991). Many psychologists were victims of repression, and others saw their approaching fate and departed Moscow and Petersburg to provincial cities to become involuntary missionaries in distant Russian locations. Contacts with Western colleagues were eliminated. Moscow and Russia in general were transformed into a "chronological provincial deep freeze" and dropped out of world civilization and culture. Fortunately, this was not wholly successful despite the efforts of the communist system to swallow up the culture of this great society.

In place of life and consciousness, "monistic dialectics" emerged. This resulted in absurd conclusions, such as the official position that consciousness was secondary to matter, and that ideology played a major and primary role in relation to science, art, and literature. In the totalitarian state with its conditions of crude censorship and constant fear, scientists worked out their own means of survival. These amounted to a form of "mental protection" that provided scientists with the opportunity to develop their ideas even under major prohibitions. This would be a topic for an extended discussion, but I shall only report one example—the one that is most familiar to me.

In the early 1930s several psychologists left Moscow and settled in Khar'kov in Ukraine, including Leont'ev, Luria, A. Zaporozhets (1905–1981), and L. Bozhovish (1908–1981). Vygotsky visited them from Moscow, and E. El'konin (1904–1984) from Petersburg. Over the course of several years, they organized a working group of psychologists that was later called the Khar'kov School of Scientific Psychology. This group was headed by Leont'ev, who had found a niche that was relatively safe, both

Figure 1 Participants in the Seventh International Conference of Psychotechnology, held in Moscow in 1931.

geographically and conceptually, for psychological research. Of central interest to the schools were problems of how mental actions, images, and conceptions developed. In this context, Zaporozhets analyzed how perceptual, mental, and sensory actions occur and develop, P. Gal'perin (1902–1988) examined tool-related action, O. Kontsevaya (1909–1960) was interested in how conceptions developed, this author focused on mnemic actions, and so forth. Meanwhile, Leont'ev was studying how sensations emerge and consciousness develops, and Luria was focusing on the disintegration and recovery of higher mental functions and on the mechanisms that govern such processes.

It was in the Khar'kov School that the major theoretical constructs of the psychological theory of activity were formulated. The notion of object-related activity was taken from German classical philosophy as interpreted by Karl Marx, and this served as a protective wall against hostile ideologists. This notion also had roots in Ivan Sechenov's (1825–1905) natural scientific psychological research. From the present perspective, we can say with confidence that the major significance of these events in Khar'kov was not that they put forward a principle of activity that would explain all areas of psychology. Such a pretension would be excessive—or premature at least. What is most important is that in *this* setting, basic research on perceptual, memory, cognitive, symbolic, practical, and object-related actions and operations was able to be carried out at all.

Thanks to Luria's participation, investigation along this line came to be connected with the activity approach to physiology developed by Ukhtomsky and Bernshtein. Mental acts came to be viewed as the functional organs in an individual similar to morphological organs in that they can experience evolution and involution and can possess the properties of responsivity and sensibility. Another major reason for the significance of activity theory consists of the fact that it served as a framework for Vygotsky and helped his colleagues maintain the basic body of his ideas. The publication of his works began in the mid-1950s and is not yet complete.

During and after World War II, psychology began little by little to revive, although it continued to experience ideological assaults. In 1946 psychology departments in universities in Moscow, Leningrad (Petersburg), Kiev, and Tbilisi were opened. After Stalin's death in 1953, contacts with Western science began to be re-established. Scientists like Jean Piaget, Paul Fraisse, K. Pribram, Jerome Bruner, Roman Jackobson, M. Holquist, Michael Cole, and J. Wertsch visited Moscow, and Russian psychologists became frequent guests in Western countries. A major contribution to establishing new contacts with Western science was made by Luria and also by Cole, the editor of the journal, *Soviet Psychology* (now the *Journal of Russian and Eastern European Psychology*).

Russian psychology began developing in a relatively normal way in the 1950s, though some ideological pressures continued to be felt. The Soviet military industry heavily supported psychology's revival and continued development. Russian scientists managed to satisfy their curiosity at the expense of military organizations—just as their Western colleagues did.

Today Russian psychology has many faces and many voices. About a dozen psychological journals covering a wide range of topics and perspectives are now published. In 1994–1995 about 30 books for higher education on various fields and areas of psychology were published under the sponsorship of G. Soros's "Cultural Initiative Foundation."

One very important outcome of this transition is that Russian psychology is no longer concerned with cognitive issues. Many approaches to consciousness, personality, individuality, and other phenomena are being developed within Russian psychology today. Both theoretical and practical dimensions of psychology, the psychology of learning/teaching, psychophysiology, psychotherapy, and ergonomics have been developed, as well as other areas within the discipline. In recent years Russian psychologists have again had the opportunity to make new discoveries—an opportunity that they did not have for decades. Barring another catastrophe, there is reason for optimism for the future of Russian psychology.

Bibliography

Bakhtin, M. M. (1972). *Problemy poetiki Dostoevskogo* [Issues of Dostoevsky's poetics]. Moscow: Sovetskaya Rossiya.

Bakhtin, M. M. (1979). *Estetica slovesnogo tvorchestva* [Aesthetics in the literary art]. Moscow: Khudozhestvennaya Literatura.

Bernshtein, N. (1967) *The coordination and regulation of movements.* Oxford: Pergamon Press.

Clark, K., & Holquist, M. (1984). *Mikhail Bakhtin.* Cambridge, MA: Harvard University Press.

Cole, M. (Ed.) (1995). The legacy of A. N. Leont'ev [Special Issue]. *Journal of Russian and East European Psychology*, 33(6).

Davydov, V. V. , & Zinchenko, V. P. (1993). Vygotsky's contribution to developmental psychology. In H. Daniels (Ed.), *Charting the agenda: Educational activity after Vygotsky* (pp. 93–106). New York: Routledge.

Toulmin, S. (1980). Mozart v psihologii [Mozart in psychology]. *Voprosy psihologii* [Problems in psychology], *10*, 129.

Van der Veer, R., & Valsiner, J. (1991). *Understanding Vygotsky*. Oxford: Blackwell.

Wertsch, J. V. (Ed.). (1979). *The concept of activity in Soviet psychology*. Armonk, NY: Sharpe.

Wertsch, J. V. (1985). *Vygotsky and the social formation of mind*. Cambridge, MA: Harvard University Press.

Zinchenko, P. (1979). Involuntary memory and goal-directed nature of activity. In Wertsch, J. V. (Ed.), *The concept of activity in Soviet psychology* (pp. 300–340). Armonk, NY: Sharpe.

Zinchenko, V. (1995a). Activity theory: Retrospect and prospect. In S. Jaeger (Ed.), *Psychologie im soziokulturellen Wandel: Kontinuitaeten und Diskontinuitaeten (Beiträge zur Geschichte der Psychologie*, Vol. 10, pp. 179–185). Berlin.

Zinchenko, V. (1995b). Cultural-historical psychology and the psychological theory of activity: Retrospect and prostpect. In J. V. Wertsch, P. del Rio, & A. Alvarez (Eds.), *Sociocultural studies of mind* (pp. 37–55). New York: Cambridge University Press.

Zinchenko, V. (1996). Developing activity theory: The zone of proximal development and beyond. In B. Nardi (Ed.), *Context and consciousness: Activity theory and human computer interaction* (pp. 283–324). Cambridge, MA:MIT Press.

Early Italian Psychology

Nino Dazzi
Luciano Mecacci

In Italy, as in other European countries in the final decades of the 19th century, positivism played an important role in the development of psychology (on the history of Italian psychology in general, see Dazzi, in press; Marhaba, 1981; Mecacci, 1992; Mucciarelli, 1982–84). Psychology was recognized as an independent science by important exponents of Italian positivism, first of all by its leader, Roberto Ardigò (1828–1920), author of *Psychology as a Positive Science* (1870). Ardigò was an emblematic figure of the positivist culture. A Catholic priest, in 1871 he "converted" to the ideals of science and freedom of thought, abandoning his cassock in a rather sensational way. From 1881 to 1909 he taught history of philosophy at the University of Padua, where he had many philosophy and psychology students. At 92 years of age, Ardigò committed suicide as the result of a serious state of depression.

In Ardigò's conception, "positive psychology" was considered a "special" science that studied "psychic acts" not from a physiological perspective but from a phenomenological one that demonstrated their genesis within the consciousness.

Another exponent of positivism was Giuseppe Sergi (1841–1878), the author of various works, including *Principles of Psychology on the Basis of Experimental Science* (1873–1874), which was widely diffused even among the non specialistic public. In 1893, Sergi founded the Rome Institute of Anthropology, where he began experimental research in psychology and anthropology. He was a patriot of the Italian Risorgimento for having taken part in the expedition of the "Thousand" led by Giuseppe Garibaldi in 1861 to free Sicily; he was also a typical positivist scientist dedicated entirely to research. In 1905, Sergi served as president of the Fifth International Congress of Psychology in Rome. He believed that a reductionist conception should be adopted in psychological research according to which "psychic phenomena are essentially physiological functions" and as such "are manifestations of physiochemical conditions" (on Sergi, see Mucciarelli, 1987).

Many works in social psychology and psychiatry were also inspired by the principles of positivism: data were gathered objectively and interpretations formulated without reference to metaphysical and spiritualistic concepts. Social psychology and crowd psychology studies were remarkably diffused also in relation to the development of new political and labor union movements and the emergence of new social classes at the end of the century. Although Gustav Le Bon's *The Crowd: A Study of the Popular Mind* (1895) is considered the first work on the psychology of the masses due to its wide circulation, actually the first book on the topic was published several years earlier by Scipio Sighele (1868–1913). A lawyer, Sighele wrote *The Delinquent Crowd* in 1891. Sighele described the evocative effects of crowds on the individual psyche and showed how criminal acts by individuals could derive from the pressures of the "delinquent crowd." Popular riots in Milan in 1898 stimulated many other publications explaining the phenomena of collective psychology from a psychological and psychiatric point of view. Pasquale Rossi (1867–1905), in his book *Collective Psychology* (1899), refocused attention on the social and political causes of the popular movements of those years, trying to avoid their condemnation as psychopathological deviation. The concept that the masses could be easily influenced and led by super-individual ideals and by a charismatic leader was widespread in nationalistic movements and in fascism (Benito Mussolini declared he had been profoundly influenced by Le Bon's book) (on Italian psychology of crowd, see van Ginneken, 1992).

Crowd psychology was inspired by Cesare Lombroso's (1836–1909) principles of "Criminal Anthropology." Lombroso was a professor at the University of Turin and the author of works such as *Delinquent Man* (1876) and *The Man of Genius* (1891) translated into many languages. For Lombroso, criminal behavior derived from hereditary inclinations which could be revealed through observation and measurement of "atavistic signs" (deviations in the shape of the head, in the eyes and ears, size of the jaws, etc.). Like many other scientists, philosophers and psychologists of his era, Lombroso was very interested in parapsychological phenomena (on Lombroso, see Bulferetti, 1975). Closely connected with Lombroso's criminal anthropology, a positivist approach to psychiatry, in which psychiatric problems could be retraced to neurological and hereditary factors, was widely diffused (Enrico Morselli, *Handbook of Semiotics of Mental Illnesses,* 1885–94; Eugenio Tanzi, *Treatise on Mental Diseases,* 1904).

Another important figure in Italian positivism was Leonardo Bianchi (1848–1927), a professor of psychiatry and neuropathology in Naples. Bianchi had a fundamental role in the development of Italian psychology. In 1905, when he was Minister of Public Education, he authorized the establishment of the first chairs of psychology in Italy. Bianchi developed an interesting concept of cerebral functions that surpassed the localization theories expressed by earlier scholars (Luigi Luciani and Tullio Seppilli, *Functional Localizations of the Brain,* 1885; Giuseppe Mingazzini, *The Brain in Relation to Psychic Phenomena,* 1895). In fact, in a series of works synthesized in the book *The Mechanism of the Brain and the Function of the Frontal Lobes* (1922), Bianchi rejected the narrow concept of localization that every psychic process could be localized in a specific cerebral area; instead, he held that psychological processes were based on an integrated organization of the functions of various cerebral areas. This theory is similar to Russian neuropsychologist A. R. Luria's theory of brain functional systems. The Russian scholar greatly esteemed Bianchi's research, particularly on the functions of the frontal lobes. Also K. S. Lashley, in *Brain Mechanisms and Intelligence* (1929), recognized an anticipation of the concepts of mass action and integrated cortical activity associated with "intelligent behavior" in Bianchi's concept.

The most interesting approach toward the foun-

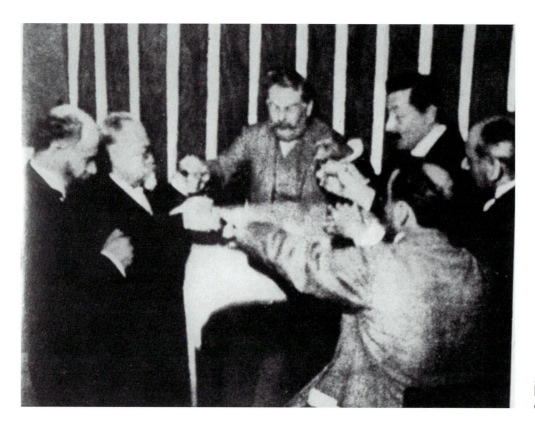

Figure 1 Cesare Lombroso (second from left) during a spiritualist séance.

578

dation of experimental psychology was developed by Gabriele Buccola (1845–85), a psychiatrist in Reggio Emilia and Turin. In a series of original studies on reaction times (presented in the book *The Law of Time in the Phenomena of Thought. Essay on Experimental Psychology* (1883), Buccola formulated the principles of a real "mental chronometry," the study of the stages of psychic processes in their temporal cadence and sequence. Buccola used the technique of reaction times and improved it by carrying out original technical improvements for stimulus presentation and response measurement. Buccola held that reaction time is a complex measure of times corresponding to the various phases of the entire process: stimulation of the peripheral sense organ, nerve conduction to cerebral centers, transformation of sensory stimulation into motor stimulation, conduction to effector muscles, and muscular contraction. Only the time taken by the central transformation is truly "psychological" and is measurable by subtracting the times of the "physiological" phases from the total time. Thus, Buccola had again taken up the subtractive method of F. C. Donders, but he greatly broadened the issue of reaction times, taking into consideration the factors that could explain individual variability in reaction times. These factors, called "modifiers" by Buccola, were of four types: biological (organic constitution, race, age, sex), psychological (attention, emotions, etc.), physiochemical (effects of pharmacological substances, alcohol, etc.), pathological (psychiatric disturbances). Buccola's premature death (at age 31) prevented his further development of a real experimental research project in psychology based on the experimental method. Thus ended Buccola's most ambitious project: the systematic foundation of psychopathology on the basis of the results of experimental research.

The first three chairs in psychology were established in 1905, one in Turin held by Friedrich Kiesow (1858–1940), one in Rome by Sante De Sanctis (1862–1935), and one in Naples by Cesare Colucci (1865–1942). Kiesow had been a student of Wundt in Leipzig and he continued his research in Turin on the senses of taste and touch using a typically structuralistic approach. Mario Ponzo (1882–1960) was a student of Kiesow; he also researched the senses and perceptions (his name has remained linked to "Ponzo's illusion"). Colucci was particularly involved in psychiatry and psychopathology. Although De Sanctis also devoted a good part of his scientific activity to neuropsychiatry (chair held at the University of Rome from 1930), several of his initial works in psychology were very interesting—*Dreams* (1899); *The Mimics of Thought* (1904)—and, translated into German, they were widely circulated (Freud often quoted De Sanctis's studies on the phenomenology of the dream and its relationships with mental diseases). De Sanctis had professional relationships with the most important European and American psychologists of his time. His autobiography was published in the series of eminent psychologists' autobiographies edited by Murchison (De Sanctis, 1936).

The year 1905 was important for Italian psychology not only because of the new university chairs, but also because of two significant events: the founding of the *Rivista di Psicologia* (Psychological Review) and the Fifth International Congress of Psy-

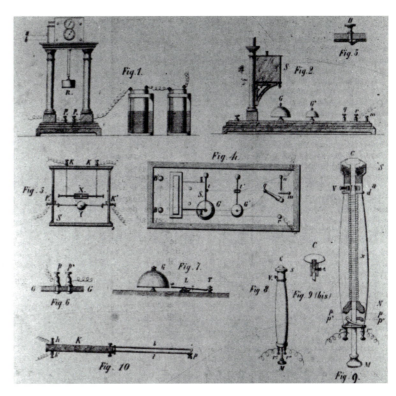

Figure 2 Equipment for experimental research in psychology recommended by Buccola (1863).

chology in Rome. By the end of the century, new journals had already been started in which articles on psychology and psychiatry appeared, but the *Rivista di Psicologia* was the first independent journal devoted entirely to psychology. It was founded by Giulio Cesare Ferrari (1868–1932), director of the mental asylum in Imola and then professor of psychology in Bologna. Ferrari's studies focused primarily on psychopathology and psychopedagogy. With his translation of James's *Principles of Psychology* in 1901, Ferrari contributed toward spreading James's thought in Italy (Ferrari was in close contact with James) and toward developing Italian pragmatism. In fact, some of the most important articles in Italian philosophy in the area of pragmatism were published in *Rivista di Psicologie* (In 1932 Ferrari wrote his autobiography for volume two of *A History of Psychology in Autobiography*; see also Mucciarelli, 1984). James was the main protagonist at the Fifth International Congress of Psychology held in Rome in 1905. During the congress, James read his very famous report on the "Notion de conscience" (which then reappeared in his Essays on radical empiricism, published posthumously in 1912).

In addition to the many Italian psychologists, physiologists, and philosophers who took part in the 1905 Congress, renowned foreign psychologists were also present. Therefore, it was the right opportunity for initiating an up-to-date discussion on the independence of psychology as a science. In the years that followed, a lively debate took place on the relationships between psychology and philosophy and on the limits of a scientific psychology.

The debate was started by Francesco De Sarlo (1864–1937), a psychiatrist in Reggio Emilia and then professor of philosophy in Florence. In 1903, his interest in psychology led De Sarlo to set up a psychology laboratory in Florence, considered the first independent Italian center for psychological research. Important research was carried out in this laboratory on the problem of measurement in psychology (Antonio Aliotta, *Measurement in Experimental Psychology*, 1905); and on introspection (Enzo Bonaventura, *Experimental Research on the Illusions of Introspection*, 1915). De Sarlo held that in psychology "every effort is understood to bring light to the 'state of consciousness,' breaking it down into its elements (analysis) and considering it in its connections (determinations of the laws)." For De Sarlo psychology was the study of the "internal psychological facts that anyone may feel in the consciousness" (*The Data of Psychological Experience*, 1903). De Sarlo proposed a sort of scientific phenomenology of the spirit in which the influence of Franz Brentano can be seen. At that time, Brentano lived in Florence and had close contacts with both De Sarlo and with Italian pragmatist philosophers.

Figure 3 Portrait of Sante De Sanctis in his laboratory.

De Sarlo's position was criticized by the idealistic philosopher, Benedetto Croce (1866–1952). According to Croce, philosophy was an independent science of the spirit to which neither the sciences of nature or the "new" scientific psychology could contribute. Idealistic philosophy's criticisms of psychology had a remarkable effect in slowing down the development of this science at the university level. In fact, idealism was not only a philosophical current; in the first half of the 19th century it had inspired the entire Italian culture, which was not very sensitive to the development of contemporary science.

Different from De Sarlo, other psychologists preferred not to involve psychology in philosophical debates and instead tried to circumscribe a field of independent experimental research. Besides De Sanctis, Agostino Gemelli (1878–1959) took this position. After working in the field of biology and the nervous system with Camillo Golgi, Gemelli dedicated himself to psychology under the influence of the school of Würzburg (among his first works in psychology, a noteworthy article was "The Experiment in Psychology" published in the *Rivista di Psicologia* in 1908. When he converted to Catholicism, Gemelli became the main exponent of the Italian Neoscholastic Movement (in 1921 he founded the Catholic University of Milan); however, he tried to keep the spiritualistic type of philosophical speculation separate from experimental research in psychology. In 1926 Gemelli founded a psychology laboratory at the University of Milan which became the most active center in Italy for psychological research. Gemelli personally conducted research in psychophysiology, the psychology of perception, thought, and language, and promoted projects for applying psychology in schools, at work, and in the armed forces. Gemelli developed a concept of psychological functions centered on the concept of personality as a biopsychological system of intrapsychological organization. Until the 1950s Gemelli was the most influential figure in Italian psychology at the institutional and academic level. Through his personal research activities and those of his students at the Catholic University of Milan, he guaranteed the survival of psychology in Italian universities during the Fascism era (Gemelli wrote in 1952 his autobiography for the vol. 4 of *A History of Psychology in Autobiography*; see also Cosmacini, 1985).

Figure 4 Agostino Gemelli—eminent Italian psychologist.

Bibliography

Ardigò, R. (1882). *Pietro Pompon azzi e la psicologia come scienza positiva.* Cremona: Tipografica Social.

Bulferetti, L. (1975). *Cesare Lombroso.* Turin: Utet.

Cosmacini, G. (1985). *Gemelli.* Milan: Rizzoli.

Dazzi, N., Ed. (in press). *Storia della psicologia italiana.* Rome: Istituto della Enciclopedia Italiana.

De Sanctis, S. (1932). [Autobiography]. In C. Murchison (Ed.), *A history of psychology in autobiography* (Vol. 3, pp. 97–121). Worcester, MA: Clark University Press.

Ferrari, G. C. (1936). [Autobiography]. In C. Murchison (Ed.), *A history of psychology in autobiography* (Vol. 2, pp. 63–88). Worcester, MA: Clark University Press.

Gemelli, A. (1952). [Autobiography]. In E. G. Boring et al. (Eds.), *A history of psychology in autobiography* (Vol. 4, pp. 83–120). Worcester, MA: Clark University Press.

Marhaba, S. (1981). *Lineamenti della psicologia italiana.* Florence: Giunti Barbèra.

Mecacci, L. (1992). *Storia della psicologia del Novecento.* Rome-Bari: Laterza.

Mucciarelli, G., Ed. (1982–1984). *La psicologia italiana.* Fonti e documenti, 2 vols. Bologna: Pitagora.

Mucciarelli, G., Ed. (1984). *Giulio Cesare Ferrari nella storia della psicologia italiana.* Bologna: Pitagora.

Mucciarelli, G., Ed. (1987). *Giuseppe Sergi nella storia della psicologia e dell'antropologia in Italia.* Bologna: Pitagora.

van Ginneken, J. (1992). *Psychology and the politics, 1871–1899.* Cambridge: Cambridge University Press.

 # Psychology in Latin America

Hannes Stubbe
Ramón León

J osef Brožek (1991), the American historian of psychology, characterized the 1980s as the "Golden Age" of Latin American historiography (Stubbe and León, 1988). An example of the work presented during this period is illustrated in the following five-stage chronology of the origins and development of Latin American psychology as it was first proposed by Stubbe (1987, 1995):

Proto-Psychology

The period of Proto-Psychology dates from about 1492 and even today some research is devoted to the ethno-psychological study of indigenous peoples and the descendants of Africans in Latin America. Pertinent research topics include the study of native myths, the soul concepts of native healers (*curanderismo*), illness models, the study of psychotropic substances, indigenous psychotherapy, the study of native languages, mourning rituals, cult initiations, et cetera. The stage of proto-psychology continues to exert influence on Latin American psychology and to enrich cultural traditions even today (Santos, 1992; Stubbe, 1987, 1990, 1992, 1995).

Missionary Psychology

The stage of Missionary Psychology, which began with the discovery of America by Europeans and ended about 1800 after the expulsion of the Jesuits (1759), reflects traditional European theologies and philosophies. The forceful conversion of native populations by Spanish and Portuguese political authorities was largely responsible for the oppression and destruction of local cultures. In general, modern research views the impact of Christian missionaries rather critically (Stubbe, 1992).

Figure 1 Portrait of Honorio Delgado.

Positivism

During the period of Positivism (ca. 1800–1900), which coincided with the political independence movements, modern science, and especially the positivism of Auguste Comte (1798–1857), exerted a strong influence on Latin American psychology. At

582

the beginning of this stage, mesmerism was brought first to the Caribbean (ca. 1785), and then to Brazil (ca. 1820), and it continues to play an important role in modern syncretistic religions and Christian sects throughout Latin America (Stubbe, 1995).

Institutional Psychology

During the period of Institutional Psychology in Latin America (ca. 1900–1960), psychological laboratories, psychological institutes or departments, and psychological organizations were started in many countries (Ardila, 1986) through the pioneering work of Latin American physicians and European philosophers and psychologists (for example, Argentina, 1898; Brazil, 1905; Chile, 1908; Mexico, 1916; Cuba, 1934; Peru, 1935).

Shortly after the establishment of Wundt's Leipzig laboratory, German and English experimental psychology (Stubbe, 1987, 1995) was first introduced to Latin America through the writings of Theodule Ribot (1839–1916) and the Brazilian philosopher Raimundo Farias Brito (1862–1917). In Chile, Wundt was more directly involved through Wilhelm Mann who equipped his laboratory in 1907 with demonstration and research equipment from Leipzig. Direct German influence was also important for the early development of Argentinian psychology. From 1906–1908, Felix Krueger (1874–1950), Wundt's eventual successor and the leader of German holistic psychology, taught psychology and philosophy in Buenos Aires. He was followed (1909–1912) by Otto Schulze (1872–1950), a student of Oswald Külpe (1862–1915) and from 1913–1935 by Krueger's former assistant, Carl Jesinghaus (1886–1948).

The beginnings of institutionalized psychology in Mexico showed the influence of German and French psychology. As early as 1907, selections from Wundt's *Principles of Physiological Psychology* (1874) were translated into Spanish for the *Sociedad Mexicana de Estudios Psicológicos*. In addition, Enrique O. Aragón established a Wundtian laboratory in Mexico in 1916, which functioned for more than thirty years.

After 1908, Freudian psychoanalysis was introduced to Latin America around the first decade of the 20th century. According to Freud (1914) an initial lecture about the analytic treatment of "anxiety states" was held as early as 1910 at the Interamerican Congress of Medicine and Hygiene in Buenos Aires. However, Freud's work was quoted even ear-

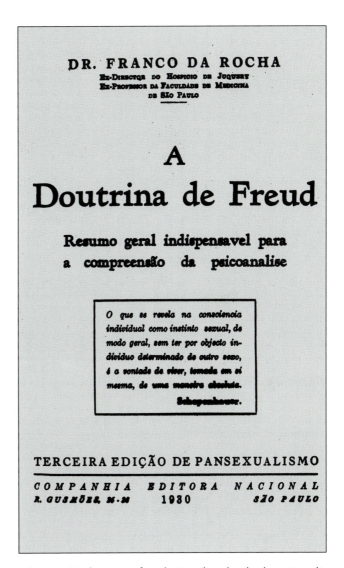

Figure 2 Title page of early Brazilian book about Freud's pansexuality.

lier in the 1908 medical dissertation of Juan A. Agrelo of Argentina. The first psychoanalytic dissertation in Latin America was written by the Peruvian psychiatrist, Honorio Delgado (1892–1969), who was the first Latin American member of Freud's International Psychoanalytic Association. Delgado's initial enthusiasm was soon replaced by pointed criticism of Freud's writings and ideas. The influence of psychoanalysis on Latin American intellectuals was strengthened further by Ballesteros's Spanish translation of Freud's works (1923). Argentina, in particular, became a center of psychoanalysis through the efforts of emigrant analysts (Stubbe, 1995) like the Spaniard Angel Garma (b. 1909) and the Austrian Maria Langer (1910–1988).

The field of "psychotechnology" was introduced to Latin America by the Cuban-Spanish psychiatrist,

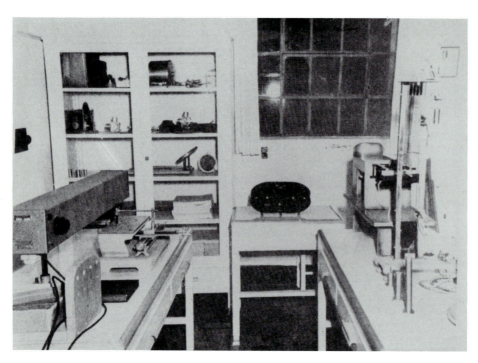

Figure 3 Psychological laboratory at Catholic Pontifical University in Sao Paulo, Brazil (ca. 1954).

Emilio Mira y López (1896–1964). His work became the foundation for the development of applied psychology, which plays an important role in modern Latin America. Apart from Mira y López, other pioneers in this field include Walter Blumenfeld (1882–1967) in Peru, Mercedes Rodrigo (1891–1982) in Colombia, Waclaw Radecki (1887–1953) in Brazil (Stubbe, 1993), and Béla Székely (1892–1955) in Argentina. The intellectual and professional influence of German-speaking psychologists, who were refugees from Nazi persecution, awaits further study (Stubbe, 1993).

Expansion

The Expansion phase of Latin American psychology began in the early 1960s and resulted in the legal establishment of professional psychology in many countries (for example, Brazil, 1962). During this period, numerous psychology programs and applied research centers were established. In addition, the number of qualified male and female psychologists grew exponentially. For example, in 1941 there were only 37 psychologists in all of Brazil. Their number increased to 1,516 in 1970 and to 22,287 in 1980 (Ardila, 1986; Marín, 1987; Stubbe, 1995; Stubbe & León, 1988)!

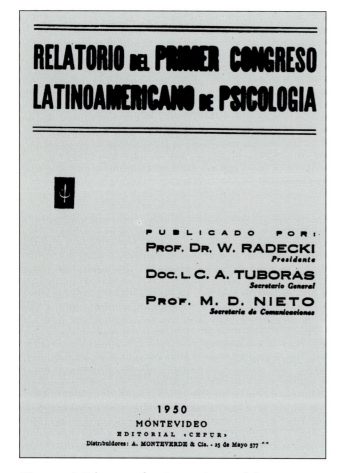

Figure 4 Title page for *Proceedings of the First Latin American Congress of Psychology* in Montevideo (1950).

Bibliography

Ardila, R. (1986). *La Psicología en América Latina.* Mexico, D. F.: Siglo XXI.

León, R., & Kagelmann, H, (Eds.). (1992). *Psychologie in Peru.* Munich: Profil.

Marín, G. (1987). *Latin American psychology: A guide to research and training.* Washington, DC: American Psychological Association.

Stubbe, H. (1987). *Geschichte de Psychologie in Brasilien.* Berlin: Reimer.

Stubbe, H. (1993). Experimentalpsychologie in den Tropen. *Psychologie und Geschichte, 4,* 278–299.

Stubbe, H. (1995). Wichtige Ereighisse in der Geschichte der Psychologie in Lateinamerika. *Kölner Beiträge zur Ethnopsychologie und Transkulturellen Psychologie, 1,* 99–149.

Stubbe, H., & León, R. (Eds.). (1988). Archivo Latinoamericano de Historia de la Psicología y Ciencias afines. Rio de Janeiro.

A History of Popular Psychology Magazines in America

Ludy T. Benjamin, Jr.
William H. M. Bryant

In the summer of 1892, a little more than a dozen psychologists met at the house of G. Stanley Hall in Worcester, Massachusetts. They were there at Hall's invitation to plan an organization of American psychologists, what would become the American Psychological Association. One of the participants was Joseph Jastrow, who had received his doctorate under Hall and gone on to found a psychology laboratory at the University of Wisconsin in 1888. Jastrow's Midwestern location gave him a special interest in the upcoming World's Columbian Exposition in Chicago. He encouraged his colleagues at the meeting to seize this opportunity to display the new scientific psychology to the public. The idea met with mixed reviews; however, Hall was particularly supportive, and with his help and aid from others, Jastrow coordinated the opening of a psychology exhibition at the world's fair in Chicago in 1893.

Modeled after Francis Galton's earlier exhibition in South Kensington, the Jastrow exhibit at the Chicago World's Fair marked the first significant public display of the "new" psychology in North America. Jastrow was among the first American psychologists to recognize the importance of educating the public about the new science of psychology. Others, such as Hall, William James, John Watson, and transplanted Europeans such as Edward Bradford Titchener and Hugo Münsterberg, were among many psychologists in the late 19th and early 20th century who attempted to translate the new psychology for the public by writing articles for the popular magazines of their day, for example, *Harpers, Colliers,* and *Atlantic Monthly.*

As the American public learned more about psychology, opportunities arose for psychologists to apply their skills outside of their university laboratories. The earliest incursions were in education and business. In the schools, psychology hoped to bring about massive changes in the nature of education: Teacher training programs would be restructured, classrooms would be redesigned, and curricula would be reorganized. Pedagogical techniques could be planned and used in such a way as to be maximally effective for all kinds of students. In the business community American psychologists focused initially on increasing product sales by investigating the psychology of advertising and selling, and then, as a result of the experiences of World War I, became increasingly interested in personnel issues of selection and training.

Less than 30 years after Jastrow had organized the public display of psychological science in Chicago, Americans were in love with psychology. The American public of the 1920s had a very favorable impression of psychology and psychologists, partly due to the extravagant claims made by pseudopsychologists and some legitimate psychologists about the validity and applicability of psychology. Historian Michael Sokal (1984) has argued that the popularity that psychology enjoyed in the 1920s was the result of a general euphoria, a wave of self-confidence embracing America after the war.

Certainly Americans in the 1920s were learning more about the new psychology. Largely this was due to the increased presence of psychology in magazines and newspapers of that time. For example, Joseph Jastrow authored a daily newspaper column entitled "Keeping Mentally Fit," which was syndicated and, at its peak, appeared in more than 150 newspapers (Jastrow, 1928).

Albert Wiggam, a nonpsychologist authored an even more popular column entitled, "Exploring Your Mind." Wiggam was among many who felt that the science of psychology held the keys to prosperity and happiness. In one of his columns he wrote: "Men and women never needed psychology so much as they need it to-day. You cannot achieve [the highest effectiveness and happiness] in the fullest measure without the new knowledge of your own mind and the personality that the psychologists have given us" (Wiggam, 1928, p. 13).

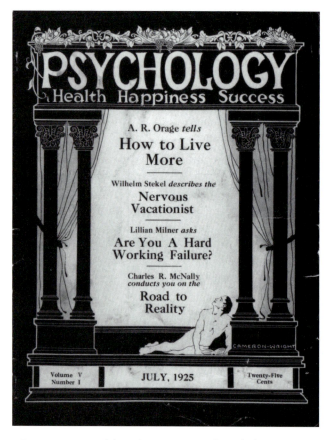

Figure 1 Cover of the July 1925 issue of *Psychology.*

Of course, not everyone subscribed to Wiggam's view that psychology was necessary to "secure the highest effectiveness and happiness." One of the doubters was Canadian humorist Stephen Leacock (1924), who proposed that America was suffering from an unfortunate outbreak of psychology. Leacock's skepticism about the applicability of psychology was not shared by most Americans who seemed bent on availing themselves of this new knowledge, if not in fact, seeking the services of a consulting psychologist. Thus, given the popularity of psychology in the 1920s, it is not surprising that the first

popular magazines devoted exclusively to psychology would appear during that time.

Consulting the reference book by Donald Osier and Robert Wozniak (1984) indicates that the first popular magazine with "psychology" in the title began publication in England in October, 1924 under the title *Practical Psychology: The Magazine of Health, Success, Happiness.* But in fact there are at least two earlier popular psychology magazines, both published in the United States in 1923. This article sketches the history of popular psychology magazines in America, focusing on those of the 1920s and 1930s.

Henry Miller's Psychology Magazine

The longest running American psychology magazine (before *Psychology Today*) began publication in April 1923 and was entitled *Psychology: Health, Happiness, Success.* (The similarity in title to the British magazine that was to appear 18 months later was no accident; the British magazine was virtually a copy of the American version in terms of design and features.) The American magazine was conceived by a Methodist minister who retired from his Brooklyn, New York, pulpit in late 1922 to pursue this publishing venture. His name was Henry Knight Miller (1891–1950), and he had been a successful minister known for his self-help sermons. A number of his sermons on achieving success and happiness had been privately published, and apparently they had been well enough received that their success made Miller believe he might be successful on a larger scale.

Miller wrote that he was fascinated with the new science of psychology and believed in its power for giving the populace the means for self determination: Psychology was the way to success, health, and happiness. Yet he was dismayed that psychologists seemed incapable of communicating the practicality of their work to the public. Miller saw his role as translator of this new science. His goal was to remove the technical terminology and strip away the theories and abstractions, providing a practical psychology for everyday living.

Miller wrote most of the first issue of *Psychology,* with contributions from several others, most notably Emil Coue, the French mental healer who promoted better health through auto-suggestion. A print run of 4,000 copies of that first issue was sold almost exclusively in the neighborhood newsstands of New York City. Not surprisingly the marketing was difficult. Distributors were not sure that a magazine with a title that no one could spell and few could pronounce would do well. But Miller eventually located a distributor. The magazine sold so well that 30,000 copies of the June issue were published and distributed in other United States cities. At that point the magazine became a monthly publication, issued in two volumes a year.

Although Miller's magazine may have enjoyed some popularity with the American public, it was likely unpopular with academic psychologists. The articles rarely drew on the research findings of the scientific literature in psychology as promised by Miller. Instead, Miller filled his magazine with home remedies and commonplace suggestions for enjoying a vacation, being more efficient, creating desire in your customers, learning to forget, and opening the gates of opportunity.

Whereas psychologists in academic settings were willing to write for popular magazines such as *Atlantic Monthly* and *Colliers*, apparently they were not willing to have their work appear in the pages of Miller's magazine. On occasion the magazine published an article by an identifiable psychologist; however, in nearly all of those cases, the articles were reprinted from some other publications.

Clearly Miller was not really interested in translating the new science of psychology for the public. His regular column rarely quoted any psychologists and almost never made reference to any scientific research. Instead, in keeping with his years as a minister, he provided his readers with a collection of homilies, built on the many pseudopsychologies of his day.

The Nature of Henry Miller's Magazine

Miller's *Psychology* was published monthly for more than a decade, yet it is a scarce find today. The magazine was not the kind of publication that libraries archived, nor did American subscribers hoard back issues in the way that they saved *National Geographic* or *Life* magazines. Plus the psychology magazine was printed on paper that was highly acidic, and thus it deteriorated rapidly. Consequently, in eight years of research on this magazine we have located only about 35 different issues. Because it is unlikely that you will ever see a copy

of this magazine, we would like to describe a typical issue for you.

The October 1924 issue, designated No. 4 of the third volume, was the eighteenth issue and coincided with the appearance of the similarly entitled British magazine. This issue of Miller's magazine was 82 pages in length. It contained 49 pages of text and the remainder in advertising.

Figure 2 Another reason for the scarcity of this magazine is that after 1928 many of its covers featured art deco paintings which decorators in recent years have used as framed art, discarding the rest of the magazine.

The text included articles on raising children without using corporal punishment, on curing yourself of depression, on doing well in a new job, on accusing others of your own shortcomings, on making yourself well with music, and on the relativity of happiness. The initial article in the magazine is Miller's regular column, this one entitled "The Strength of the Hills." It encouraged readers to leave the bustle and rush of the city and to enjoy a few days of peace vacationing in the mountains, where looking down from their vantage point, one would gain perspective that all of life's problems were small and insignificant.

There is a letters column entitled "What Can We Do for You?" It was a regular feature of the magazine and included replies written by Arthur Howland, who was the magazine's managing editor, and like Miller, also a former Methodist minister. One of the letters was from a man who lamented that he worried too much, a second from a woman who could not escape poverty, and a third from a woman seeking advice about failed love affairs. Lengthy, common-sense advice was given in reply to each, much in the same fashion of such columns in today's newspapers.

Two pages of text were devoted to the Human Progress Association, an organization founded in 1922 that professed to promote "the new science of successful living." This organization was one of sev-

Figure 3 Henry Knight Miller, editor and publisher of *Psychology*.

eral that affiliated with the magazine, and, for several years, news of its activities were published therein. Such affiliations increased subscriptions because members of these various clubs were expected to subscribe to Miller's magazine. In this particular issue there were reports from the Human Progress Association clubs in four cities in the United States.

The October 1924 issue of *Psychology* also contained a call for reports from local psychology clubs and an offer to help establish clubs where none existed. In many issues such announcements appeared, typically submitted by the club's secretary. They contained news of the club's activities, lists of officers, and testimonials of individuals lauding the value of psychology in their lives.

The advertisements, which occupied more than a third of the magazine's space, were consistent with the magazine's devotion to health, happiness, and success. Many offered programs for financial success, some targeted ways of decreasing fears, others promised to improve public speaking abilities, several offered a cure for baldness, and another promised the secrets of a happy wedded life. In terms of health there were advertisements regarding nervousness, cessation of smoking, constipation, and even bad breath. Because of the ties of the magazine to local psychology clubs and organizations such as the Human Progress Association, it was common to see advertisements for lecturers who were willing to speak to these groups.

Small advertisements, in the nature of classifieds, dealt with personal magnetism, exercise, increasing vocabulary, thought transference, astrology, and vocational testing. And several offered diplomas, including doctoral degrees, from post-office-box colleges.

In founding his magazine, Miller had acknowledged the too often pseudoscientific portrayal of psychology, and he announced his intention to bring the discoveries of this new science to his readers in a language that they could understand and apply to their everyday lives. One of his admirers expressed it this way:

> Into this clash and confusion came Dr. Henry Knight Miller, with his Psychology Magazine. He has performed the difficult task of interpreting the principles of scientific psychology in terms adapted to the understanding of the general public, setting forth a sane, sound message, inspirational in spirit, acceptable in the main to the

> orthodox psychologist, a unifying standard to the popular psychologist and a dynamic message of new hope to mankind. (McHenry, 1929, p. 82)

Of course, regarding Miller and his magazine, nothing could be farther from the truth. As noted earlier, if he had any familiarity with the science of psychology, that knowledge was rarely evident in the pages of his magazine. He could not attract legitimate psychologists to write for his magazine, and he seemed incapable of interpreting the new psychology on his own. Still, his magazine outlasted all of its American and British competitors, ceasing publication in 1938 when a prolonged economic depression brought an end to the public's interest in psychology.

The Psychological Review of Reviews

While Henry Knight Miller was promoting his new magazine on the East Coast in October of 1923, another popular psychology magazine made its appearance on the West Coast in the same month. The magazine was entitled *The Psychological Review of Reviews* and was edited chiefly by Orlando Edgar Miller (1865–1947, no apparent relation to H. K. Miller) and by Alexander Irvine and Lillian Granville White. The magazine was published in San Francisco, California, by the International Psychological Press. The magazine's masthead identified it as "The Official Organ of the International Society of Applied Psychology." Its editors described it as "a monthly magazine devoted to the varied activities of Mental Science groups throughout the world."

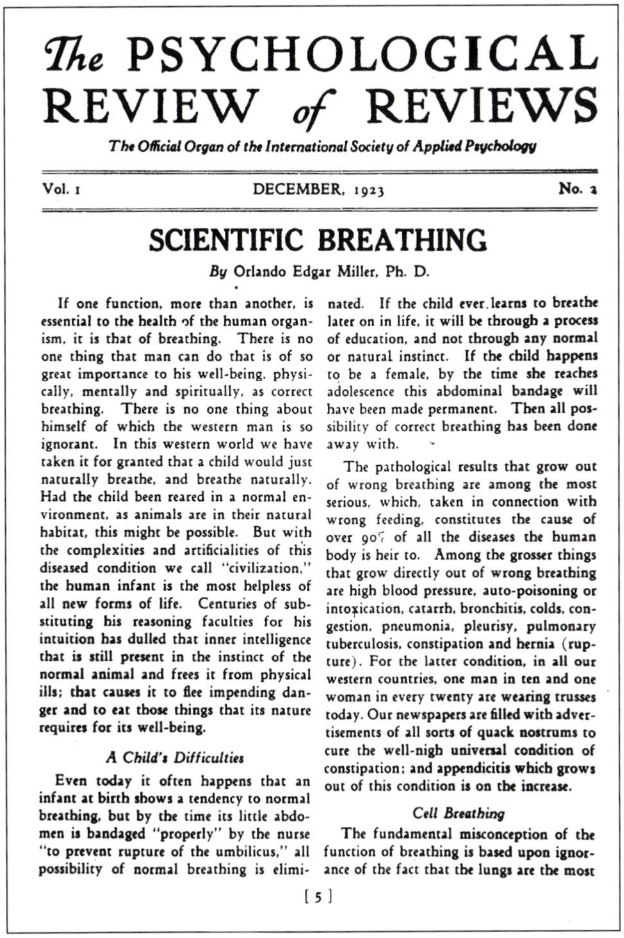
The PSYCHOLOGICAL REVIEW *of* REVIEWS

The Official Organ of the International Society of Applied Psychology

Vol. 1 DECEMBER, 1923 No. 2

SCIENTIFIC BREATHING

By Orlando Edgar Miller, Ph. D.

If one function, more than another, is essential to the health of the human organism, it is that of breathing. There is no one thing that man can do that is of so great importance to his well-being, physically, mentally and spiritually, as correct breathing. There is no one thing about himself of which the western man is so ignorant. In this western world we have taken it for granted that a child would just naturally breathe, and breathe naturally. Had the child been reared in a normal environment, as animals are in their natural habitat, this might be possible. But with the complexities and artificialities of this diseased condition we call "civilization," the human infant is the most helpless of all new forms of life. Centuries of substituting his reasoning faculties for his intuition has dulled that inner intelligence that is still present in the instinct of the normal animal and frees it from physical ills; that causes it to flee impending danger and to eat those things that its nature requires for its well-being.

A Child's Difficulties

Even today it often happens that an infant at birth shows a tendency to normal breathing, but by the time its little abdomen is bandaged "properly" by the nurse "to prevent rupture of the umbilicus," all possibility of normal breathing is eliminated. If the child ever learns to breathe later on in life, it will be through a process of education, and not through any normal or natural instinct. If the child happens to be a female, by the time she reaches adolescence this abdominal bandage will have been made permanent. Then all possibility of correct breathing has been done away with.

The pathological results that grow out of wrong breathing are among the most serious, which, taken in connection with wrong feeding, constitutes the cause of over 90% of all the diseases the human body is heir to. Among the grosser things that grow directly out of wrong breathing are high blood pressure, auto-poisoning or intoxication, catarrh, bronchitis, colds, congestion, pneumonia, pleurisy, pulmonary tuberculosis, constipation and hernia (rupture). For the latter condition, in all our western countries, one man in ten and one woman in every twenty are wearing trusses today. Our newspapers are filled with advertisements of all sorts of quack nostrums to cure the well-nigh universal condition of constipation; and appendicitis which grows out of this condition is on the increase.

Cell Breathing

The fundamental misconception of the function of breathing is based upon ignorance of the fact that the lungs are the most

[5]

Figure 4 The initial article in the December 1923 issue of *The Psychological Review of Reviews* by editor Orlando Miller.

To date we have been able to locate only a single issue of this magazine (December 1923, Vol. 1, No. 3), and we have found no mention of it in any of the reference sources on magazines published in America. However, based on this single issue, this magazine is decidedly different from its East Coast competitor. It is far more religious in nature with a strong promotion of Christianity. The magazine also has far fewer advertisements (about 20% compared to 40%); however, Henry Miller's magazine also began with a similar percentage and increased rapidly as he attracted more advertisers to his magazine. What is clearly evident, beyond the religious emphasis, is that the *Review of Reviews* focuses more on promoting physical health through its articles and its advertisements for health foods and rejuvenation lotions.

The magazine is not really a journal of reviews, although our sample of one does contain an article reprinted from another source. Rather it contained mostly original contributions, several of them written by Orlando Miller and Irvine and none by an identifiable psychologist. Articles covered such subjects as how to learn to breathe scientifically, how to teach your children the facts of life, the need to see Jesus Christ as described in the Bible and not as "reinterpreted by modern man," and why Christmas has become a vulgar celebration.

The initial issue of this magazine was used by Orlando Miller to promote his idea for a "Co-operative University and City Beautiful," a commune to be established in Mexico that would teach cooperation to its inhabitants through work in a number of agricultural and factory enterprises. Funds were initially sought via a letter sent to "a chosen list of members of the International Society of Applied Psychology" and a later plea was made to all readers of *The Psy-*

chological Review of Reviews via the December 1923 issue of the magazine. Miller (1923) wrote, "The Chapala Co-operative University will make use of scientific methods in discovering what the student can do most enthusiastically, that will be of greatest service to society and best express himself. It will then give the student a thorough training in doing that thing. If everyone were educated to do useful things well and thus to do his bit, the work of the world could be very easily done in four hours per day and thus leave to each individual 20 hours for sleep, recreation, and the development of his own individuality" (pp. 32–33). There is no evidence that this university and commune was ever begun. And the fate of this magazine is likewise unknown.

Industrial Psychology Monthly

The third of the American popular psychology magazines, which lasted only three years, began publication in January, 1926. *Industrial Psychology Monthly* was considerably different from the other two, both in terms of its focus and its portrayal of psychology. As the title implies the magazine was intended to apply psychology to business and industry. Its founding editor was Donald A. Laird, a psychologist on the faculty of Colgate University and author of more than a dozen books on applying psychology to business. The magazine is clearly more scholarly in nature, which is perhaps the reason why all of its issues have survived in various libraries.

Laird's editorial board consisted of three managers from industry and four university-based psychologists. The magazine did not contain a mission statement but did publish some testimonials in its first issue, for example, "*Industrial Psychology* will be something for which the industrial relations men and employment managers have been hoping for for sometime." Throughout its publication, Laird's balance of articles reflected the balance of his editorial board, that is, a mix of articles by psychologists and people in business. The first issue included articles on managing workers through their self interests (written by a manager in the automobile industry), industrial dissatisfaction (by Douglas Freyer, chair of the Psychology Department at New York University), tests for chauffeurs (by A. J. Snow, a consulting psychologist for the Yellow Cab Company of Chicago), and control of office output (by a management engineer in New York City).

Besides the articles, each issue contained a notes and news section announcing items of interest to the business community, drawn from both business and psychology. A section entitled "Recent Advances" included brief synopses of findings from applied psychology, drawn largely from psychology books and journals. Another section entitled "New Books to Read" alerted readers to new business psychology books and included brief descriptions of the books' contents. Advertisements were never a large part of the magazine, typically comprising less than 10% of the 80-page issues. Those ads were usually for books related to business, summer university courses in business and psychology, and tests for use in employee selection and job analysis. Occasionally the magazine published special issues, such as one on "immigration and industry" and another on "women in industry" (with women writing 7 of the 11 articles in that issue).

The magazine underwent several title changes, all involving subtitles. In July 1926 it added a subtitle: *Human Engineering for Executives*, which was replaced in January 1927 by *Edited for Executives*, and finally in June 1927 by *The Magazine of Manpower*.

The final issue of the magazine was a joint November-December issue published in 1928. The fact that the monthly magazine published the last two numbers of its third volume together suggests financial difficulties. There are no editorials calling for increased subscriptions or warning of the possible demise of the magazine. And the annual subscription price of $5.00 remained unchanged for all three years. Magazines do not survive without a substantial advertising base. Likely that situation brought an end to this magazine in a decade in which interest in psychology remained quite high.

As an editor and publisher, Laird understood the importance of both the expertise of applied psychologists as well as the expertise of individuals in business, and he brought that joint knowledge base to his readers. Laird was also interested in enlightening readers regarding some of the pseudoscientific approaches of his time—for example, character analysis via phrenological or physiognomic means—and he frequently published articles debunking such techniques. Despite its early demise, Laird's magazine was a genuine effort to produce a vehicle that would communicate scientific psychology to the business community. Its pages were not devoid of "pop" psychology, but the magazine was more research based than any of the popular psychology magazines of the 1920s and 1930s.

A Psychoanalytic Magazine

Gail Hornstein (1992) has written that by the 1920s in America ". . . psychoanalysis had so captured the public imagination that it threatened to eclipse experimental psychology entirely" (p. 254). Henry Miller's magazine published articles sympathetic to psychoanalytic theories, but they certainly were not a mainstay of the magazine. And there are none to be found in the pages of Laird's business psychology magazine. Given the popularity of psychoanalysis, it is surprising that it did not stimulate its own popular magazine in the 1920s. However, such a periodical did emerge in 1932 as *The Modern Psychologist*, a monthly magazine published and edited in New York City by Dagobert David Runes (1902–1982), who had earned his doctorate in philosophy at the University of Vienna. The fact that a magazine on psychology would start publication in the 1930s is rather unusual. In addition to the hard times of the Great Depression, psychology was experiencing its own depression in terms of public interest as mentioned earlier. Typical of the change in public attitude was a 1934 editorial in the *New York Times* that criticized psychology as a science that had ready answers in the good times of the 1920s but was now found to be lacking in any real solutions for the problems of the 1930s. The waning of psychology in popular magazines was also evidenced by a steady and marked decline of references to psychology in the *Reader's Guide to Periodical Literature* after 1929 (Benjamin, 1986).

Runes began his magazine with a board of 19 associate editors; ten of those held medical degrees, and none can be identified as a psychologist. Most of the articles were original contributions to the magazine, but each issue carried one or two pieces borrowed from other sources, including works authored by such figures as Sigmund Freud, Alfred Adler, William Stekel, and Havelock Ellis. Content included articles on neuroses, dream interpretation, repression, instincts, impotence, inferiority, sexual cruelty, introversion, hysteria, and so forth. Advertisements, which made up about 30% of an average 50-page issue, were very similar to those of Henry Miller's *Psychology*. Indeed, like Miller's ads, there were few that were psychoanalytic in content.

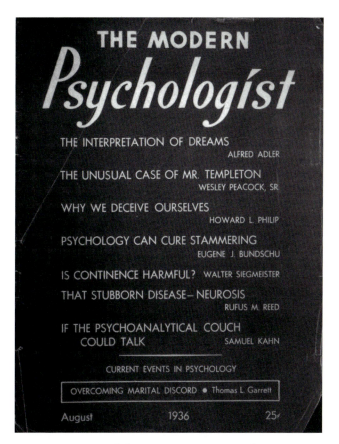

Figure 5 Cover of the August 1936 issue of *The Modern Psychologist.*

It is not clear if psychoanalysis enjoyed some immunity from the public criticism of psychology in the 1930s; it is likely that the public could not distinguish psychoanalysis from experimental psychology. And certainly by the mid-1930s there were increased attacks published in the popular press. One of the sources of criticism was a series of articles that James Thurber (1937) wrote for *The New Yorker*, carving up psychoanalysis with his rapier wit. The end for Runes's magazine came in 1938, coincidentally as Freud moved from Vienna to London to live out the last months of his life; *The Modern Psychologist* ceased publication as did Henry Miller's magazine. It would be almost 30 years before America would have another popular psychology magazine.

Popular Magazines in the 1960s and 1970s

Our emphasis in this article has been on the popular psychology magazines in America in the 1920s and 1930s; however, we will close with a brief synopsis of what might be called "the rest of the story."

The 1960s are often characterized as a decade of enormous social upheaval in the United States, marked chiefly by the civil rights movement and America's involvement in the war in Vietnam. The social sciences enjoyed considerable growth during this period of renewed public interest. Thus the appearance of *Psychology Today* in May 1967 was not surprising.

Nicholas Charney was the founding editor and publisher of *Psychology Today*, whose monthly magazine was to be a ". . . forum for the interchange of new ideas in the various disciplines of psychology" (1976, p. 5). In the beginning he attracted some distinguished psychologists as contributors, many of whom were also excellent writers. His first two issues included articles by Nathan Azrin, Stanley Milgram, Rhoda Kellogg, Philip Zimbardo, Daryl Bem, Eliot Hearst, and Hans Eysenck. But by the third volume Charney had relinquished the editorial duties to T. George Harris who favored science writers and other journalists over psychologist authors. And the nature of the magazine began to change dramatically; articles drifted farther and farther from a science base.

Psychology Today was joined in 1972 by a bimonthly magazine, *Human Behavior*, edited by Marshall Lumsden. In his inaugural editorial Lumsden echoed the words of Henry Knight Miller in calling for a magazine that would rewrite scientific psychology for a popular audience. Lumsden's magazine was better received by the scientific community in psychology, but not by the public, and it ceased publication in May, 1979. *Psychology Today* continued as the only psychology magazine on the newsstand. More and more its content mirrored the "touchy-feely psychology" that seemed so popular. And its advertisements for sleep learning tapes, biofeedback trainers that promised instant creativity and peace of mind, college degrees by mail, and so forth, only added to the embarrassment that many psychologists felt about the magazine.

In the 1970s, the American Psychological Association (APA), looking to improve public awareness of psychology, began to explore publishing its own popular psychology magazine. The APA Task Force on a Magazine was established in 1975, chaired by James Deese, a psychologist at the University of Virginia. The Task Force did an extensive analysis of the costs of such a venture for APA and even produced a sample magazine issue that was mailed to the APA membership for reaction. In the end the Association decided that the effort would be too costly, and the Task Force was disbanded. Still, there were many in the Association who longed for a popular magazine that presented psychology to the public in a way that better characterized psychological science and practice.

The 1980s represented a very different decade for the social sciences. President Ronald Reagan's administration was not a supporter of psychology as science or practice. For example, in his initial budget, Reagan's budget director, David Stockman, who had publicly referred to psychology as pseudoscience, called for a 50% reduction in funding for psychology by the National Science Foundation. The good times for psychology in the 1960s and 1970s were gone, a fact recognized by Ziff-Davis, the corporation that published *Psychology Today*.

By 1982 *Psychology Today* subscriptions were declining as were advertisers, so Ziff-Davis began looking for a buyer, ideally, a naive one. And they found it in the American Psychological Association. After considerable deliberation and some rancorous debate, the APA Board of Directors voted 5 to 5 on the question of purchasing the magazine. APA President Max Siegel then voted in favor of the purchase, thus breaking the tie, and launching APA on a financial disaster. APA published its first issue of *Psychology Today* in 1983. The Association struggled to make the venture a successful one, but after five years the Board realized that it had to sell the magazine or face bankruptcy. So having lost approximately $17 million in the five-year fiasco, APA sold the magazine in 1988 to T. George Harris and Owen J. Lipstein. The magazine continues today as a bimonthly publication and an embarrassment to many psychologists.

Conclusion

Although all three of the magazines of the 1920s purported to publish the practical findings of the new psychological research, only Laird's short-lived magazine made any real effort to do so. The others portrayed a psychology based on intuition, myth, common sense, and too often on sheer nonsense. Yet the existence of the magazines signaled a public fascination with psychology and a belief that this new science of the mind offered the keys to a life of good health, happiness, and success. With the refocusing on social issues in the 1960s, popular psychology magazines returned to America's newsstands.

Scientists in many fields have long lamented the public's disinterest in the complexity of scientific phenomena, as well as the public's penchant for answers to scientific questions that are simple and typically unscientific. Thus the history of psychologists' attempts to inform the public about their science follows the pattern seen in the older sciences. These popular psychology magazines offer the historian an opportunity to better understand the kind of information the public receives about psychology. They are also important to our understanding of the communication of scientific data; that is, how scientific psychology is portrayed in the popular media, both by scientists and nonscientists. Perhaps of greater significance, they are important as documents of social history, relevant to our understanding of the desires and motives of American culture. We hope that this brief treatment will stimulate an interest in studying these examples of popular culture and their meaning for psychology as discipline and profession.

Bibliography

Benjamin, L. T., Jr. (1986). Why don't they understand us? A history of psychology's public image. *American Psychologist, 41,* 941–946.

Charney, N. M. (1976, May). Editorial. *Psychology Today, 1*(1), 5.

Hornstein, G. A. (1992). The return of the repressed: Psychology's problematic relations with psychoanalysis, 1909–1960. *American Psychologist, 47,* 254–263.

Jastrow, J. (1928). *Keeping mentally fit.* New York: Garden City Publishing Co.

Leacock, S. (1924, March). A manual for the new mentality. *Harpers,* 471–480.

McHenry, E. S. (1929, March). The progress of psychological science: A review of principles. *Psychology, 12*(3), 32–33, 80–82.

Miller, O. E. (1923, December). Explanation of the economic basis of the Chapala Co-operative University. *The Psychological Review of Reviews, 1*(3), 32–38.

Osier, D. V., & Wozniak, R. H. (1984). *A century of serial publications in psychology, 1850–1950.* Millwood, NY: Kraus International Publications.

Sokal, M. M. (1984). James McKeen Cattell and American psychology in the 1920s. In J. Brozek (Ed.), *Explorations in the history of psychology in the United States* (pp. 273–323). Lewisburg, PA: Bucknell University Press.

Thurber, J. (1937). *Let your mind alone.* New York: Harper & Brothers.

Wiggam, A. E. (1928). *Exploring your mind with the psychologists.* New York: Bobbs-Merrill.

American Cognitive Psychology

Robert R. Hoffman

There is a very rich history to both mentalistic psychology (the works of Herbart, Wundt, Brentano, Külpe, Binet, Calkins, Bartlett, and many others) and mentalistic philosophy (Leibnitz, Descartes, J. S. Mill, Polanyi, and many others). The broad and recent histories are reviewed in detail in Baars (1986), Cofer (1978), Gardner (1985), Humphrey (1951), Mandler and Mandler (1964), Newell (1983), Posner and Shulman (1979), and Postman (1985). (A fuller bibliography is available from the author.) This essay focuses on the emergence of cognitive psychology and psycholinguistics from its roots in the late 1940s through the establishment of cognitive science as an interdiscipline in the 1980s.

During the heyday of behaviorism, topics in cognition were not neglected. For instance, throughout the 1950s a great deal of research was conducted on word list and paired-associate learning as a function of stimulus variables such as frequency, meaningfulness, and concreteness. Starting in the late 1940s there was a growing dissatisfaction with behaviorism. Karl Lashley, among others, argued that the behavioral approach could not explain the hierarchical structure of behavior (Lashley, 1951). A 1954 conference report (Estes, et al.) pronounced neobehavioral theories of learning underspecific and inconsistent—the theories predicted effects that were hard to find, and there were unresolved phenomena such as all-or-none learning, one trial learning, clustering in free recall, and verbal mediation effects (Bousfield, 1953; Cofer, 1943; Peterson & Peterson, 1959; Rock, 1957). For nearly the entire next decade, conferences on learning would involve the questioning of neobehaviorism.

Beginning in 1951 the Carnegie Institute supported interdisciplinary meetings of linguists, psy-

Figure 1 W. K. Estes.

chologists, and computer scientists (Carroll, 1953; Cofer, 1979; Osgood & Sebeok, 1954) that were seminal for the field of psycholinguistics (although the word "psycholinguistics" can be attributed to Kantor, 1936). Noam Chomsky had a profound impact beginning in the late 1950s through his work on the formalisms of generative transformational grammar, the concept of deep structure, his arguments on universal grammar and language acquisition, and his criticisms of the behaviorist approach to language. *The Journal of Verbal Learning and Verbal Behavior* was founded in 1962, its title reflecting a cautious choice of words (Cofer, 1978). (It was recently retitled *The Journal of Memory and Language*.)

Notions from the World War II–era applied

and for proving theorems in symbolic logic. Beginning in the 1960s, Edward Feigenbaum and Bruce Buchanan built inference engines based on procedural rules.

The notions of cybernetics and the digital computer had a major impact on psychology, beginning in the late 1950s. The computer metaphor allows one to go well beyond the capabilities of the telephone or telegraph switchboard metaphors that were common in the 19th century. Although some psychologists still relied on S-R associationistic terminology, flow chart models were being used to postulate stages and levels of processing (Atkinson & Shiffrin, 1968; Waugh & Norman, 1965) and stages of decision making.

Events seem to have come together at a 1956 MIT conference, at which Newell and Simon presented their seminal ideas about symbolic information processing, Noam Chomsky laid out the fundamentals of his early theories of language and syntax, and George Miller presented his research on short-

Figure 2 Charles N. Cofer.

research had a critical impact. Developments in sonar, audio recording, and signal processing technology supported a burgeoning of research on speech perception (Jenkins, Foss, & Greenberg, 1968; Liberman, Delattre, & Cooper, 1952). Information theory and signal detection theory (e.g., Shannon, 1948) led directly to a number of programs of research on perception, attention, vigilance, and related topics.

A 1956 conference at Dartmouth College involved a group of mathematicians and logicians who seemed ready to do what von Neumann (1958), Weiner (1948), and Turing (1936) had suggested—build an intelligent machine. Alan Newell and Herbert Simon reported on their project, launched in the 1950s, that led to the invention of special programming languages (Newell, Shaw, & Simon, 1958). Marvin Minsky (1963) laid out the goals and central questions of a field to be called *artificial intelligence* (AI). Throughout the 1960s, systems were created for solving geometrical problems, for playing chess,

Figure 3 Noam Chomsky.

Figure 4 Herbert Simon.

Figure 5 George Miller.

Figure 6 Roger Brown.

term memory limitations. Miller regards this meeting as the marker for the beginning of cognitive psychology as a discipline (Baars, 1986).

The year 1960 was equally dramatic. A conference supported by the Social Science Research Council brought Piaget's work to the attention of American developmental psychologists (see Flavell, 1963), at the same time that new and seminal research on language acquisition was being reported by Roger Brown (e.g., Brown & Berko, 1960).

Also in 1960 Donald Hebb called for a revolution—a return to the examination of consciousness and related topics (Hebb, 1963). As a climax to 1960, George Miller and Jerome Bruner instituted the Center for Cognitive Studies at Harvard, "using the word 'cognitive' defiantly" (Miller, 1979, p. 11).

To many psychologists, what indicated the arrival of cognitive psychology was the dovetailing of Chomsky's work (through the mid-1960s) with the publication in 1967 of *Cognitive Psychology* by Ulric Neisser. Important works of the early 1970s included Anderson and Bower's *Human Associative Memory*

(1973), Kintsch's *Representation of Meaning in Memory* (1974), Craik and Lockhart's (1972) "levels of processing" theory, and research on sensory, short-term, and episodic memory (Sternberg, 1969; Tulving & Madigan, 1970). A number of new journals

Figure 7 Jerome Bruner.

Figure 8 James Jenkins (left) and Ulric Neisser (right).

appeared, including *Cognition* (founded in 1972), and *Cognitive Psychology* (founded in 1970).

In the mid-1970s, a number of scientists called for a new discipline, to be called "cognitive science," combining philosophy, AI, and psychology (Abelson, et al., 1976). The Cognitive Science Society was founded and launched its namesake journal in 1977. The first international conference of the Cognitive Science Society was held in 1980, at which Herbert Simon declared that mainstream psychology had converged around the information processing paradigm.

The limits of cognitive psychology are continually being pushed by advances in cognitive neuroscience (such as PET scans) and advances in computer science (such as expert systems and neural network models). Cognitive psychology is a nexus for issues that are central to both psychology and philosophy—the mind/body problem, the issue of human versus machine, and so on. Debate is ongoing concerning the accomplishments and foundations of cognitive science (Estes, 1991; Mayer, 1981), the validity of the computer metaphors (Crosson, 1985; Roediger, 1993), and the ecological validity of the enterprise (Bahrick, 1987; Banaji & Crowder, 1989; Neisser, 1987). Surely cognitive science will have a long and rich history, however it may be cloaked by name or philosophy, because humankind will never give up two of its most ancient dreams—that of understanding the human mind and that of building the intelligent machine.

Bibliography

Abelson, R., et al. (1976, December). *Proposed Particular Program in Cognitive Sciences.* Report to the Sloan Foundation.

Anderson, J. R., & Bower, G. (1973). *Human associative memory.* Washington, DC: Winston.

Atkinson, R. C., & Shiffrin, R. M. (1968). Human memory: A proposed system and its control processes. In K. W. Spence & J. T. Spence (Eds.), *The psychology of learning and motivation: Advances in theory and research* (Vol. 2, pp. 89–195). New York: Academic Press.

Baars, B. (1986). *The cognitive revolution in psychology.* New York: Guilford Press.

Bahrick, H. F. (1987). Functional and cognitive memory theory: An overview of some key issues. In D. S. Gorfein & R. R. Hoffman (Eds.), *Memory and learning: The Ebbinghaus Centennial Conference* (pp. 387–395). Hillsdale, NJ: Erlbaum.

Banaji, M. R., & Crowder, R. G. (1989). The bankruptcy of everyday memory. *American Psychologist, 44,* 1185–1193.

Bousfield, W. A. (1953). The occurrence of clustering in randomly arranged associates. *Journal of General Psychology, 49,* 229–240.

Brown, R., & Berko, J. (1960). Word association and the acquisition of grammar. *Child Development, 31,* 1–14.

Carroll, J. B. (1953). *The study of language: A survey of linguistics and related disciplines in America.* Cambridge: Harvard University Press.

Cofer, C. N. (1943). An analysis of errors made during the learning of prose materials. *Journal of Experimental Psychology, 32,* 399–410.

Cofer, C. N. (1978). Origin of the *Journal of Verbal Learning and Verbal Behavior 17,* 113–126.

Cofer, C. N. (1979). Human learning and memory. In E. Hearst (Ed.), *The first century of experimental psychology* (pp. 323–370). Hillsdale, NJ: Erlbaum.

Craik, F. I. M., & Lockhart, R. S. (1972). Levels of processing: A framework for memory research. *Journal of Verbal Learning and Verbal Behavior, 11,* 671–684.

Crosson, F. J. (1985). Psyche and the computer: Integrating the shadow. In S. Koch & D. E. Leary (Eds.), *A century of psychology as a science* (pp. 437–453). Oxford: Oxford University Press.

Estes, W. K. (1991). What is cognitive science?: Introduction to a feature review. *Psychological Science, 2,* 282. (See also the articles following, up to p. 311)

Estes, W. K, Koch, S., MacCorquodale, K., Meehl, P. E., Müller, C. G., Schoenfeld, W. N., & Verplanck, W. S. (Eds.). (1954). *Modern learning theory.* New York: Appleton Century Crofts.

Flavell, J. H. (1963). *The developmental psychology of Jean Piaget.* New York: Van Nostrand.

Gardner, H. (1985). *The mind's new science: A history of the cognitive revolution.* New York: Basic Books.

Hebb, D. O. (1963). The semi-autonomous process: Its nature and nurture. *American Psychologist, 18,* 16–27.

Humphrey, G. (1951). *Thinking: An introduction to its experimental psychology.* London: Methuen.

Jenkins, J. J., Foss, D. J., & Greenberg, J. H. (1968). Phonological distinctive features as cues in learning. *Journal of Experimental Psychology, 77,* 200–205.

Kantor, J. R. (1936). *An objective psychology of grammar.* Bloomington, IN: University of Indiana Press.

Kintsch, W. (1974). *The representation of meaning in memory.* Hillsdale, NJ: Erlbaum.

Lashley, K. S. (1951). The problem of serial order in behavior. In L. A. Jeffress (Ed.), *Mechanisms in behavior* (pp. 112–146). New York: Wiley.

Liberman, A. M., Delattre, P. C., & Cooper, F. S. (1952). The role of selected stimulus variables in the perception of unvoiced stop consonants. *American Journal of Psychology, 65,* 497–516.

Mandler, J. M., & Mandler, G. (Eds.). (1964). *Thinking: From association to Gestalt.* New York: Wiley.

Mayer, R. E. (1981). *The promise of cognitive psychology.* San Francisco, CA: W. H. Freeman.

Miller, G. A. (1979, September). *A very personal history.* Occasional paper of the MIT Center for Cognitive Science.

Minsky, M. (1963). Steps toward Artificial Intelligence. In E. A. Feigenbaum & J. Feldman (Eds.), *Computers and thought* (pp. 406–450). New York: McGraw-Hill. (Originally circulated in 1957.)

Neuman, J. von (1958). *The computer and the brain.* New Haven, CT: Yale University Press.

Neisser, U. (1967). *Cognitive psychology.* New York: Appleton Century Crofts.

Neisser, U. (1987). From direct participation to conceptual structure. In U. Neisser (Ed.), *Concepts and conceptual development: Ecological and intellectual factors in development* (pp. 11–24). Cambridge: Cambridge University Press.

Newell, A. (1983). Reflections on the structure of an interdiscipline. In F. Machlup & U. Mansfield (Eds.), *The study of information: Interdisciplinary messages* (pp. 99–109). New York: Wiley & Sons.

Newell, A., Shaw, J. C., & Simon, H. A. (1958). Elements of a theory of human problem-solving. *Psychological Review, 65,* 151–166.

Osgood, C.E., & Sebeok, T. A. (Eds.). (1954). *Psycholinguistics: A survey of theory and research problems.* Bloomington, IN: University of Indiana Press.

Peterson, L. R., & Peterson, M. J. (1959). Short-term retention of individual verbal items. *Journal of Experimental Psychology, 58,* 193–198.

Posner, M. I., & Shulman, G. L. (1979). Cognitive science. In E. Hearst (Ed.), *The first century of experimental psychology* (pp. 371–406). Hillsdale, NJ: Erlbaum.

Postman, L. (1985). Human learning and memory. In G. A. Kimble & K. Schlesinger (Eds.), *Topics in the history of psychology* (Vol. 1, pp. 99–134). Hillsdale, NJ: Erlbaum.

Restle, F. (1961). *The psychology of judgment and choice.* New York: Wiley.

Rock, I. (1957). The role of repetition in associative learning. *American Journal of Psychology, 70,* 186–190.

Roediger, H. L. (1993). Learning and memory: Progress and challenge. In D. E. Meyer & S. Kornblum (Eds.), *Attention and performance XIV* (pp. 510–528). Cambridge, MA: Bradford Books.

Shannon, C. (1948). A mathematical theory of communication. *Bell System Technical Journal, 27,* 379–423, 623–656.

Simon, H. A. (1980). The social and behavioral sciences. *Science, 209,* 72–78.

Sternberg, S. (1969). The discovery of processing stages: Extensions of Donders' method. *Acta Psychologica, 30,* 276–315.

Swets, J. A., Tanner, W. P., & Birdsall, T. G. (1961). Decision processes in perception. *Psychological Review, 68,* 301–304.

Tulving, E., & Madigan, S. A. (1970). Memory and verbal learning. *Annual Review of Psychology, 21,* 437–484.

Turing, A. M. (1936). On computable numbers, with an application to the *Entscheidungsproblem. Proceedings of the London Mathematics Society,* Series 2, *42,* 230–265.

Waugh, N. C., & Norman, D. A. (1965). Primary memory. *Psychological Review, 72,* 89–104.

Weiner, N. (1948). *Cybernetics, or control and communication in the man and the machine.* Cambridge, MA: MIT Press.

The Archives of the History of American Psychology

John A. Popplestone
Marion White McPherson

The Archives of the History of American Psychology were established in 1965 at the University of Akron in Akron, Ohio, USA, to promote research in the history of psychology by collecting, cataloguing, and preserving unpublished documents and obsolete laboratory equipment. The growth of the repository exceeded projections, both in the rate at which materials were donated and in their diversity. This expansion led to the establishment in 1976 of the Child Development Film Archives, a unit that maintains both research footage and instructional films. In 1980 the decision was made to supplement numerous unsolicited gifts of books by devoting space to the published literature dealing with the substantive content of psychology as well as with its history and philosophy.

With regard to the archives, the phrase "American Psychology" refers to psychologists who were born and worked in North America or who spent part of their professional lives here and had major influences on the American scene. It does not reflect a nationalistic bias, but rather a need to impose reasonable limits on holdings. Psychology is supranational, pluralistic, extended in time, and has highly permeable boundaries.

In the language of the archival world, the Archives of the History of American Psychology is a subject-matter archive (most repositories are based on geographic, military, or political themes). Therefore, the staff is trained in archival methods but also has a comprehensive knowledge of psychology, as well as its organizational patterns and educational practices. The director is a psychologist, and a number of the members of the Board of Advisers represent subfields of psychology as well as the academic discipline of history.

Contents

The items that are preserved as the tangible resources for research in the history of psychology are varied, yet limited to those which are not in the public domain or are not preserved in other repositories. And since an archive is meant to preserve but not create history, prejudgments about value, appropriateness, or the importance of deposits are made with reluctance and great care. A question that serves as one criterion for accepting a gift is, "In 100 years would this item be helpful in understanding things as they are now?" Examples of documents that warrant preservation include laboratory notes, lecture notes (both as given and as received), and correspondence, as well as editorial papers of periodicals and books. An especially valuable acquisition is the entire collection of professional papers of an individual psychologist (not reprints but original documents). Also valued are printed, but fugitive ephemera such as standardized tests, newsletters, programs of meetings, agenda books, departmental histories, curricula, course syllabi, descriptions of graduate programs, biographical-autobiographical accounts, floor plans, and inventories of laboratories. Manufactured items that merit retention include laboratory apparatus, films, tape recordings, phonograph records, and photographs.

Current Status

The holdings of the Archives increase every day—sometimes by just a few sheets of paper, sometimes by hundreds of pounds of documents—so any statement about the status of the collection is obsolete almost as soon as it is made. However, at last count there were more than 1,200 linear feet of documents

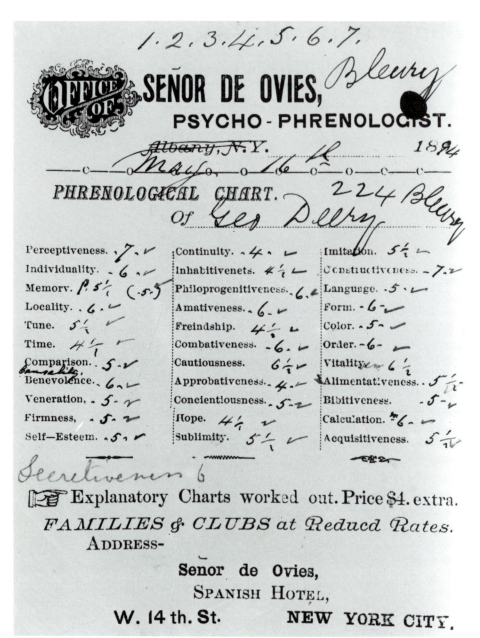

Figure 1 Phrenological chart.

immediately available to scholars. In addition, more than 800 linear feet of manuscript collections await the expiration of access restrictions or the preparation of finding aids. There are more than 3,000 photograph cards and 5,000 test cards. Child development films exceed 153 miles, and there are more than 200 demonstration or classroom films. There are more than 600 pieces of apparatus. The library of printed materials includes more than 25,000 books. The unique collection of editorial papers from journals, donated by more than 60 editors and consultants, samples almost 40 journals and consists of more than 2,000 linear feet—probably the largest collection of professional periodicals in existence. All the holdings are housed in a recently renovated (1993), high security, climate-controlled environment designed for archival storage.

Examples

Information about the history of psychology, like all other history, is usually presented as a persuasive, linguistic account, and the most important data for these accounts are primary, unpublished docu-

Figure 2 Psychological mini-laboratory (Sanford, 1893).

ments. It is the responsibility of the archivist to secure and protect these documents, as well as to make them accessible to scholars.

The following items are a very small sample of the holdings of the Archives of the History of American Psychology. The first four examples are offered as direct, unambiguous statements that evoke their era.

Experimental psychology, together with its applications, was preceded by the pseudo-science of phrenology, which relied on depressions and elevations on the surface of the skull to diagnose personality. The descriptions were intended to serve the same purpose as a modern psychological profile or psychograph.

The rare, surviving "Phrenological Chart" shown in Figure 1 is a quantitative summary of a phrenological examination. Each faculty of the mind has been measured and given a score that indicates the amount of each faculty on a scale of 1 to 7. There is also a qualitative report about each faculty. The fol-

lowing are some of the remarks about two average and two high scores:

> Continuity (4). "You can carry out to completion anything you have commenced—but you can do much better when you have the handling of several things. The wholesale business, buying and selling in large quantities would suit you best."

> Appropriateness (4). "You are not governed by public opinion—you are not insensible to praise or blame; you become suspicious when one flatters you."

> Perceptiveness (7). "You would make a first-class detective; also an architect, railroad contractor, carpenter or builder."

> Constructiveness (7). "You ought to possess a remarkable mechanical ability or I should say ingenuity—good at making excuses, getting out of difficulties and being able to manage to get a front seat at a theater or circus."

When Edmund Sanford (1859–1924) published "Some Practical Suggestions on the Equipment of A Psychological Laboratory" in 1893, he estimated

Figure 3 Memory test (1906–1907) by Goddard.

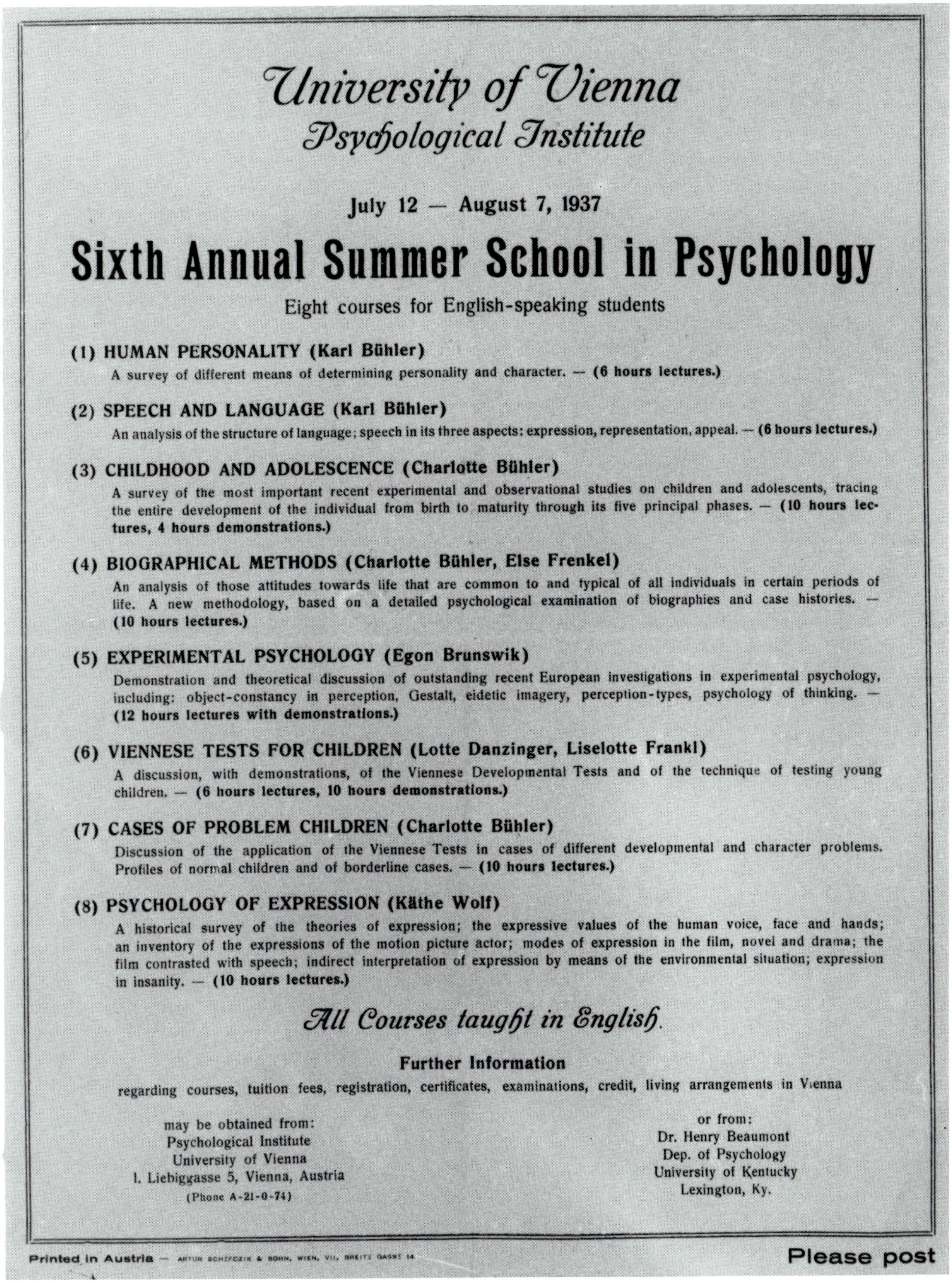

University of Vienna
Psychological Institute

July 12 — August 7, 1937

Sixth Annual Summer School in Psychology

Eight courses for English-speaking students

(1) HUMAN PERSONALITY (Karl Bühler)

A survey of different means of determining personality and character. — **(6 hours lectures.)**

(2) SPEECH AND LANGUAGE (Karl Bühler)

An analysis of the structure of language; speech in its three aspects: expression, representation, appeal. — **(6 hours lectures.)**

(3) CHILDHOOD AND ADOLESCENCE (Charlotte Bühler)

A survey of the most important recent experimental and observational studies on children and adolescents, tracing the entire development of the individual from birth to maturity through its five principal phases. — **(10 hours lectures, 4 hours demonstrations.)**

(4) BIOGRAPHICAL METHODS (Charlotte Bühler, Else Frenkel)

An analysis of those attitudes towards life that are common to and typical of all individuals in certain periods of life. A new methodology, based on a detailed psychological examination of biographies and case histories. — **(10 hours lectures.)**

(5) EXPERIMENTAL PSYCHOLOGY (Egon Brunswik)

Demonstration and theoretical discussion of outstanding recent European investigations in experimental psychology, including: object-constancy in perception, Gestalt, eidetic imagery, perception-types, psychology of thinking. — **(12 hours lectures with demonstrations.)**

(6) VIENNESE TESTS FOR CHILDREN (Lotte Danzinger, Liselotte Frankl)

A discussion, with demonstrations, of the Viennese Developmental Tests and of the technique of testing young children. — **(6 hours lectures, 10 hours demonstrations.)**

(7) CASES OF PROBLEM CHILDREN (Charlotte Bühler)

Discussion of the application of the Viennese Tests in cases of different developmental and character problems. Profiles of normal children and of borderline cases. — **(10 hours lectures.)**

(8) PSYCHOLOGY OF EXPRESSION (Käthe Wolf)

A historical survey of the theories of expression; the expressive values of the human voice, face and hands; an inventory of the expressions of the motion picture actor; modes of expression in the film, novel and drama; the film contrasted with speech; indirect interpretation of expression by means of the environmental situation; expression in insanity. — **(10 hours lectures.)**

All Courses taught in English.

Further Information

regarding courses, tuition fees, registration, certificates, examinations, credit, living arrangements in Vienna

may be obtained from:
Psychological Institute
University of Vienna
I. Liebiggasse 5, Vienna, Austria
(Phone A-21-0-74)

or from:
Dr. Henry Beaumont
Dep. of Psychology
University of Kentucky
Lexington, Ky.

Printed in Austria — ANTUN SCHIFOZIK & SOHN, WIEN, VII, BREITE GASSE 14

Please post

Figure 4 Announcement for the last English-language summer school program in psychology at the University of Vienna (1937).

KARL STUMPF

BORN 1848

that a fully equipped laboratory in an institution would cost (in 1893 currency) four to five thousand dollars. "If a starvation allowance is all that is to be had, the most satisfactory pieces would probably be a sonomometer [Figure 2, center] and a few tuning forks for audition [lower left], a color mixer [upper right] and a Wheatstone stereoscope for vision (the latter homemade) [upper left], and a stopwatch [lower left] for time measurements" (Sanford, 1893, p. 436). The minimal laboratory equipment was actually assembled (perhaps for the first time) for an exhibit in honor of the 75th anniversary meeting of the American Psychological Association in 1967.

The beginning of the measurement of "higher mental processes" is documented (Figure 3) by a collage of colored paper cut-outs pasted on a board 29 x 13 inches by Henry G. Goddard (1866–1957),

Figures 5, 6, 7 Portraits of Carl Stumpf.

Figure 8 The mysterious "Alfred Stern"—an academic joke?

the psychologist who introduced the Binet-Simon tests to the United States in 1908.

The stains came from strips of plastic mending tape. On the reverse side in Goddard's handwriting appears the following: "Memory test—one of the first tests used and made at Vineland" [The Research Laboratory at the New Jersey Training School for Feeble-Minded Girls and Boys at Vineland]. There is no evidence that the collage was used outside the Vineland laboratory.

An era, about to end, is evoked by the announcement (Figure 4) that the last summer school for English-speaking psychology students was to be held at the University of Vienna Psychological Institute from July 12–August 7, 1937. Hitler entered Austria in March of 1938, just seven months after the session. Of the seven instructors listed, five emigrated to the United States after the "Anschluß": Egon Brunswik (1903–1955), Charlotte Bühler (1893–1974), Karl Bühler (1879–1963), Else Frenkel (Brunswik) (1908–1958), and Käthe Wolf.

Figures 5, 6, and 7 contain three very dissimilar portraits of Carl Stumpf (1848–1936). In the first, he is young-looking, and handsome (perhaps idealized). In the second, we see the mature scholar looking directly at his viewer, perhaps to assess him. The signature suggests that this is "suitable for displaying in the laboratory." Lastly, we see an old man

Opening Session

B.F. Skinner, Ph.D.
Special Citation for Lifetime Contribution to Psychology

Psi Chi Edwin B. Newman Award

National Psychology Awards for
Excellence in the Media

remarks from:
Stanley R. Graham, Ph.D.
Raymond D. Fowler, Ph.D.
Mayor Raymond Flynn
Henry Tomes, Ph.D.
Commissioner for the MA Dept. of Mental Health

Friday, August 10th
5:00-6:30 p.m.
Sheraton,
Grand Ballroom

reception with cash bar to follow in the Sheraton, Constitution Room

Figure 9 Flyer with announcement of "Lifetime Award" to B. F. Skinner.

with his eyes obscured and head bent. If only one of these was to be chosen to best represent Stumpf, which one should it be and what are the criteria for the choice?

A 21 x 26 inch portrait (Figure 8) was displayed for many years in the Department of Psychology at the University of Nebraska. With its black oak frame, this sepia print makes a strong visual statement. However, there is a problem. There seems to be no "Alfred Stern" in the history of psychology—at least not in the period suggested by the clothing (late 18th century). An Albert Stern received a degree from

Leipzig in 1884, but this is Alfred Stern. One possibility is that "Alfred Stern" is a combination of Alfred Binet and William Stern, and that the portrait is actually of a clinical patient. In other words, this portrait may be merely a rather elaborate academic joke.

The flyer shown in Figure 9 was widely distributed at the 98th annual convention of the American Psychological Association (APA) in Boston, Massachusetts. It amends the events of the opening session as printed in the program with the announcement of the awarding to B. F. Skinner of a special "Citation for Lifetime Contributions to Psychology." The recipient,

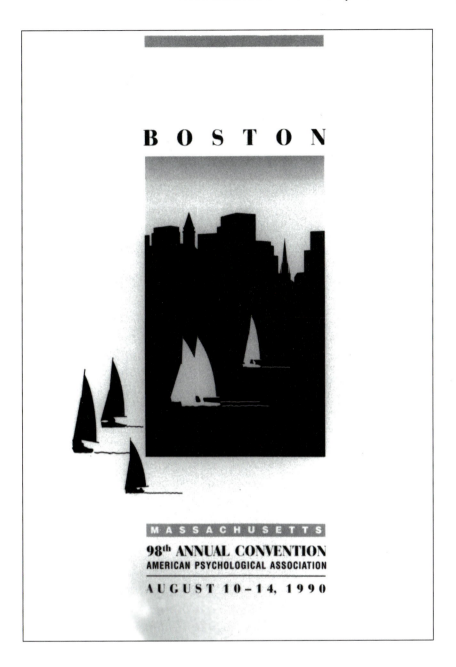

Figure 10 Cover of program for the 1990 APA convention in Boston.

then 86 years of age, informed the audience that his death was imminent, and that this presentation was a farewell between himself and the psychological community. He died just eight days later.

Although this flyer is ephemeral, it serves as an excellent documentation of the event, supplementing the convention program. However, it also contains problems. The document is ambiguous in several ways. There is no year shown (it was 1990) and no location given (it was Boston); and the three figures on the right-hand side of the page elicit questions as well. What are they? What is their statement about Skinner? Are they presentations or awards? These ambiguous visual patterns were quite recognizable to the participants at the time, since they were an element of the cover design of the program for the 98th APA convention (see Figure 10). The stylized drawings on the cover indicate quite clearly that we are seeing three sailboats on the Charles River from the Cambridge side, with the skyline of the city of Boston in the background. By their appearance on the program cover, they make a statement about the convention's location, but on the flyer, there is very little information for the viewer.

Figure 11 Motion picture still of Pavlov.

The published biographical literature contains anecdotes about the vivacity of Ivan Petrovich Pavlov (1849–1936), but formal portraits, and even informal snapshots, rarely suggest his liveliness. However, some motion picture films record and confirm his high activity level. For example, a still, which is taken from a single frame in a motion picture (Figure 11), shows Pavlov welcoming visitors (probably at the biological research station at Koltushy) in the 1930s. It manages to suggest the energy that so many have observed and described in Pavlov.

Finally, our last, poorly defined, indistinct picture in Figure 12 illustrates some problems found in using motion pictures as records. The still is an outtake from films of the classic experiments designed by Kurt Lewin (1890–1947) and completed by a graduate student at the University of Iowa in the late 1930s and early 1940s. These investigations were innovative studies of the reactions of boys to autocratic and democratic leaders, as well as to a laissez-faire atmosphere. The leader in this photograph is probably Boyd McCandless (1915–1975). Ronald Lippitt (1914–1986), one of the experimenters, described the efforts to clarify the film:

> Behind the blankets in the room, as you have seen in the motion pictures, were Jack Kounin and Joan Kalhorn, and two girls taking shorthand notes at one-minute intervals. Ralph [White] and I had a tremendous job of marking off everything at one-minute intervals for everybody, but they were all synchronized with the group observers, interaction observers, and content observers, all battered up with a buzzer set with a one-minute shift. Kurt was running around with a camera behind the burlap curtains. Kurt had a little ladder from which he could take pictures. Ralph had $400 in research money and this paid for the equipment we needed. (Bradford, 1974, p. 9)

Figure 12 Outtake from Lewin's Leadership Films

Bibliography

Bradford, L. (1974). *National Training Laboratories: Its history. 1947–1970*. Bethel, ME. Privately printed by the author.

Sanford E. (1893). Some practical suggestions on the equipment of a psychological laboratory. *American Journal of Psychology, 5,* 421–438.

Psychology in Canada

Wilfred Schmidt

The founding in 1879 of the first university-based laboratory for psychological research in Leipzig by Wilhelm Wundt is generally regarded as having ushered in the era of "modern" psychology. The impact of that event was also felt in Canadian universities in the decades that followed, and the editors of the first history of academic psychology in Canada found it appropriate to mention that the book was "being prepared in 1979, at the time when psychologists around the world were celebrating their centennial" (Wright & Myers, 1982).

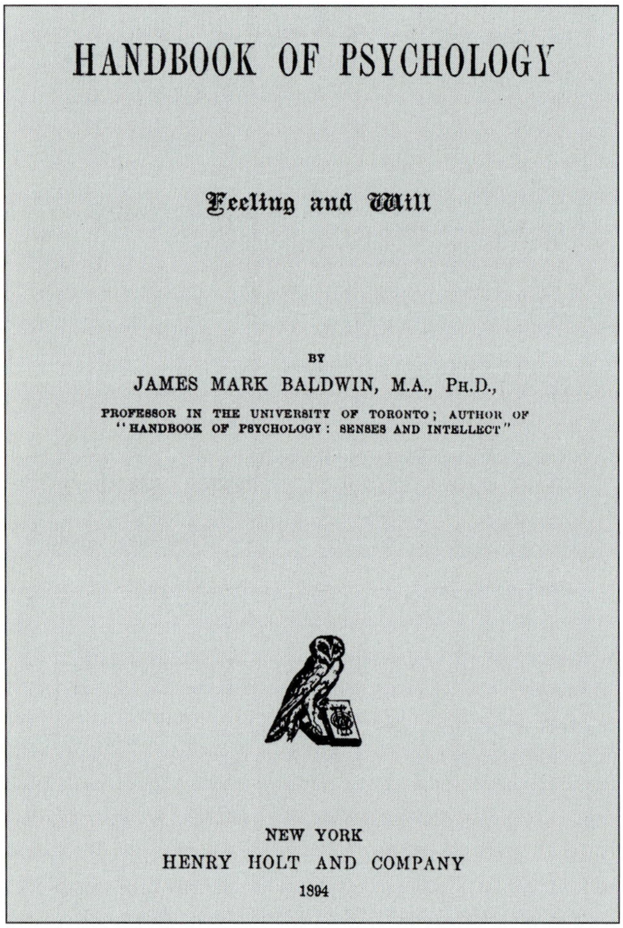

In 1879 there were six Canadian universities that had received their charters before Confederation in 1867: Dalhousie at Halifax (1790), McGill at Montreal (1821), Toronto (1827), Queen's at Kingston (1841), Laval at Quebec City (1852), Ottawa (1866). Two received their charters about a decade later: the University of Winnipeg (1877) and University of Western Ontario (1878). The University of Montreal was founded as late as 1919. At these universities psychology was taught in the context of philosophy or as part of the training in theology. For the English medium universities the teaching was usually in the tradition of the Scottish common sense philosophers (e.g., Thomas Reid) or of British idealism (e.g., T. H. Green), while at the bilingual Catholic University of Ottawa, Aristotle and Thomas Aquinas provided the model. When British Columbia joined Confederation, and Saskatchewan and Alberta were granted status as provinces, the founding of new universities followed very quickly: the Universities of Alberta and Saskatchewan received their charters in 1906 and 1907, respectively, and teaching started some two years later; while at the University of British Columbia, which had received its charter as early as 1890, classes started in 1915. These universities were secular and public from the very beginning. Compared with the situation in the USA, the creation of separate departments of psychology came very late. By 1939, when the Canadian Psychological Association was founded, there were only two departments of psychology that had achieved this official status: Toronto in 1926 (although de

HANDBOOK OF PSYCHOLOGY

Feeling and Will

BY

JAMES MARK BALDWIN, M.A., Ph.D.,

PROFESSOR IN THE UNIVERSITY OF TORONTO; AUTHOR OF "HANDBOOK OF PSYCHOLOGY: SENSES AND INTELLECT"

NEW YORK
HENRY HOLT AND COMPANY
1894

Figure 1 Title page of "Handbook of Psychology" by Baldwin.

facto since 1917) and McGill in 1924. At the other ten universities listed above, the departments of psychology became separated from philosophy between 1941 and 1960. The 1960s and 1970s saw the rapid expansion of universities and especially of psychology departments.

> Besides the acknowledgments made freely in the text, I wish to express especial thanks to my friend Dr. McCosh for the instruction and personal training I owe to him. My greatest direct indebtedness in this volume is to Prof. Wundt of Leipzig and to Prof. Rabier of Paris.
>
> J. M. B.
>
> LAKE FOREST, ILL., *July*, 1889.

Figure 2 Dedication of Baldwin's *Handbook* to Professor Wundt (Leipzig) and Rabier (Paris).

At two universities the new experimental psychology was introduced by students of Wundt: the University of Toronto in 1889 and the University of Alberta in 1909. At McGill, the psychology laboratory was founded by W. G. Tait, a student of Münsterberg, who was himself one of Wundt's students, and who had been brought to Harvard by William James.

In 1889 James Mark Baldwin (1861–1934) was appointed to the chair of Logic, Metaphysics, and Ethics at the University of Toronto. Baldwin was an American who had studied at Princeton. A scholarship enabled him to spend a full year in Wundt's Institute in Leipzig. Like a number of other Americans he saw great possibilities in a psychology based on experiments such as Wundt was performing in his laboratory. When he accepted the appointment at Toronto, he probably did not know of the fierce opposition there had been to appointing "a mere psychophysicist—little better than a materialist." He immediately founded a psychology laboratory—the first in the British Empire—and introduced a new curriculum for students of psychology. The first (1889) and the second (1891) volume of Baldwin's *Handbook of Psychology* were very influential in psychology for a while, but were eclipsed by William James's *Principles of Psychology* (1890) and its abbreviated version, *Psychology, a briefer course* (1892), as texts for psychology students.

Baldwin stayed in Toronto for only four years, but before he returned to Princeton, he saw to it that another of Wundt's students was appointed to

be in charge of the psychological laboratory: August Kirschmann (1860–1932). Kirschmann was actively involved in expanding the laboratory facilities, promoting research by students, and carrying out his own research in the psychology of vision. The Calendar of the University of Toronto for 1897/98 (p. 32) points out that the psychology laboratory had its rooms adjacent to the physics laboratory, so that psychology could make use of some of the apparatus from physics; for example, in "Psychophysics, Psychological Optics, and in the time relations between mental phenomena." It was also noted that the demand for laboratory work in psychology made it necessary to expand its space. By 1900 the laboratory already occupied 16 rooms.

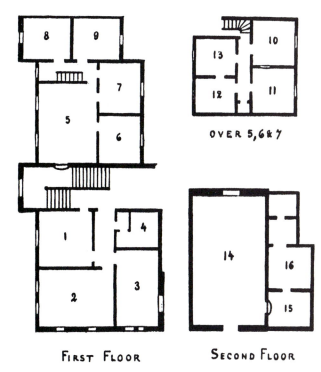

PLAN OF THE PSYCHOLOGICAL LABORATORY OF THE UNIVERSITY OF TORONTO.
SCALE 1 : 300.

Figure 3 Floor plan of Kirschmann's Toronto Laboratory (ca. 1900).

In 1909 Kirschmann returned to Germany on sick leave, but never returned. He seems to have been held in high esteem, for he was still being paid a salary by the university even for some time after the outbreak of the First World War. E. A. Bott, who was the Head of the Department of Psychology from 1926–1956, had spent a great deal of time in the psy-

Figure 4 Portrait of John MacEachran (1878–1971) of the University of Alberta, one of Wundt's last students in Canada.

Wundt, Wilhelm Wirth, and Otto Klemm in the psychological laboratory.

Although MacEachran remained primarily a philosopher, he had already taught an introductory course in general and experimental psychology in 1909; (with William James's *Psychology, a Briefer Course* prescribed), and throughout his long career he continued to teach courses in modern psychology every year. For the establishment of a laboratory his preference was to appoint a person trained under Wundt. In 1914 he started negotiations with Otto Klemm, the experimental psychologist under whom he had studied in Leipzig (personal communication from Dr. Thomas Nelson, who as member of staff since 1964 and chairman of the department of psychology for several successive terms of office, had had many conversations with MacEachran). The outbreak of the First World War put an end to these negotiations.

During the two World Wars and in the years in between, psychology in Canada was mainly "applied." More importantly, the behaviorist transformation of psychology in North America (what Hebb, in his Presidential address to the American Psychological Association in 1960, called the first phase in the American revolution in psychology) had taken place. In addition, physiological psychology had suffered a decline: a behaviorist like Skinner saw no need for physiological hypotheses, and Edward Tolman, the "purposive behaviorist," substi-

chology laboratory in the years after 1909, first as a student and then as a member of staff, when Kirschmann had already left and when the Kirschmann tradition was still very alive. Experimentation continued, but the topics of inquiry changed. In response to wartime exigencies, psychology became much more "applied" and remained so for several decades.

As indicated earlier, the other university at which experimental psychology was introduced by one of Wundt's students was the University of Alberta. The 1909 Calendar of the University lists the first six professors appointed, among them John M. MacEachran (1878–1971). He was a Canadian by birth. He had studied philosophy at Queen's University in Kingston, Ontario, where he had also taught in the department of philosophy for six years. He obtained his PhD under Wundt in Leipzig in 1910, with a dissertation on pragmatism, but he had also worked under the direction of

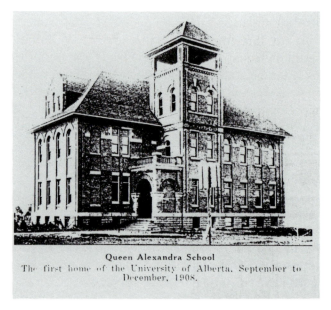

Queen Alexandra School
The first home of the University of Alberta, September to December, 1908.

Figure 5 Queen Alexandra School in Edmonton where MacEachran held his first psychology lectures.

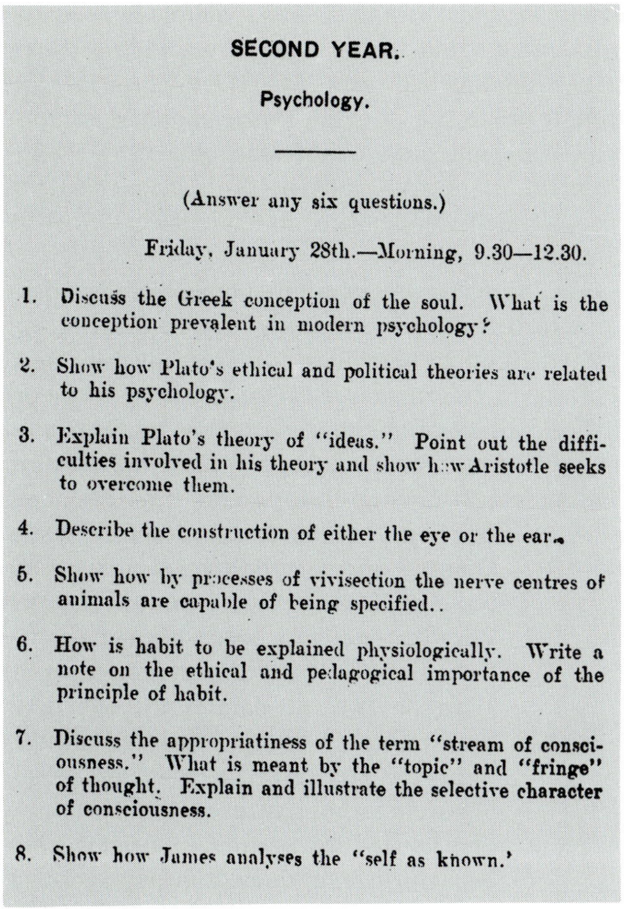

SECOND YEAR.

Psychology.

(Answer any six questions.)

Friday, January 28th.—Morning, 9.30—12.30.

1. Discuss the Greek conception of the soul. What is the conception prevalent in modern psychology?

2. Show how Plato's ethical and political theories are related to his psychology.

3. Explain Plato's theory of "ideas." Point out the difficulties involved in his theory and show how Aristotle seeks to overcome them.

4. Describe the construction of either the eye or the ear.

5. Show how by processes of vivisection the nerve centres of animals are capable of being specified.

6. How is habit to be explained physiologically. Write a note on the ethical and pedagogical importance of the principle of habit.

7. Discuss the appropriateness of the term "stream of consciousness." What is meant by the "topic" and "fringe" of thought. Explain and illustrate the selective character of consciousness.

8. Show how James analyses the "self as known."

Figure 6 Sample written test for freshman students in psychology.

tion with the work of Freud (which motivated him to seek admission to graduate studies at McGill, where he spent 1928–1932 as a part-time student and earned his MA degree), Pavlov (from whose laboratory associate Leonid Andreyev he received training in Pavlovian conditioning procedures), the Gestalt psychologist Wolfgang Köhler, and Karl Lashley (whose devastating critique of reflexology impressed him). By 1934 Hebb's mind was made up: he wanted to be a physiological psychologist, and he wanted to study under the psychoneurologist Karl Lashley. He gained admission to the University of Chicago and studied under Lashley, whom he followed to Harvard when he was appointed to a professorship there. He obtained his PhD in 1936 with a thesis on the perceptual ability of rats reared in darkness. He found—as Lashley had predicted—that rearing in the dark made no difference in size and brightness differentiation. This was a nativist position, duly confirmed and reinforced by experimental research. Then followed the challenge to that position, a challenge that ultimately led to Hebb's "organization of behavior." It came about as follows.

tuted intervening variables—between stimulus and response—when dealing with the role of thinking, purpose, and expectancies in determining behavior.

In the late forties and early fifties priorities began to change, and the psychologist most influential in bringing about this change was Donald Hebb (1904–1985). It was a change that Hebb described as the second phase of the "American Revolution," which was powerfully fueled by the publication of his book *The Organization of Behavior: a psychoneurological theory*, in 1949. Edwin G. Boring's letter to Hebb, written shortly after the book had appeared, testifies to the enthusiastic reception the book received. Hebb was an instant celebrity and much in demand as a speaker in scientific forums. The events leading up to the publication of the book, and what followed, is a fascinating part of the history of psychology in the nineteenth century in Canada, in North America, and indeed, worldwide.

Donald Hebb was born in Chester, Nova Scotia. He came to the study of psychology via confronta-

Figure 7 Portrait of D. O. Hebb of McGill University in Montreal, Canada.

613

After a postdoctoral year at Harvard, Hebb was appointed as a Fellow at the Montreal Neurological Institute for two years (1937–1939) to investigate the effects on intelligence of brain surgery, which was performed by the eminent brain surgeon Wilder Penfield. To Hebb's astonishment (and to everyone else's) even large frontal lobe lesions showed little or no effect on most tests of intellectual ability. Hebb speculated that the frontal lobes were necessary for the initial establishment of concepts and modes of thought, but perhaps not for their maintenance in adulthood. His priority now was to discover *how* concepts were formed and what the psychoneurological basis might be.

At Queen's University in Kingston, Ontario,

where he spent the next three years, Hebb developed new tools to be used in exploring these issues: intelligence tests for rats, so as to be able to determine the effects of surgery on rats more effectively; and individual tests (different in nature from the Stanford-Binet tests he had used in the research with Penfield) for human adults for use in clinical research.

When Lashley became Director of the Yerkes Laboratories of Primate Biology in Florida, he invited Hebb to participate in a research project that was to determine the effects of brain lesions on a wide variety of chimpanzee behaviors. This was an offer he could not refuse, and he spent the next five years observing chimpanzee behavior and developing tests of emotionality, while Lashley and David Nissen worked on tests of learning and problem solving suitable for chimpanzees. Though by the time Hebb left for a professorship at McGill in 1947, no data on the effects of brain surgery had yet been obtained, Hebb never regretted the time spent observing chimpanzees. He maintained that he had learned more about *human* behavior during those five years than in any other five years except the first. Moreover, during all of the five years, he had continued to think about the possible neuropsychological basis of thought, and he had already started writing the book that made him famous.

The book presented his cell assembly theory of neuropsychological functioning to account for complex psychological phenomena such as thinking, set, expectancy, and purpose. These phenomena had found no place in the work of the S-R psychologists, nor could they be explained by the old switchboard theories of psycho-motor connections and the newer field theory of the Gestaltists. The book also contained the classic distinction between Intelligence A (the innate potential for development) and Intelligence B (a hypothetical level of brain development, in which experience has played a part), and it also provided an explanation for the "puzzling" findings of his earlier research with Penfield. These ideas played a significant role in

---

HARVARD UNIVERSITY
PSYCHOLOGICAL LABORATORIES

Memorial Hall
Cambridge 38, Massachusetts

4 January 1950

Dear Hebb:

This is not going to be the letter I meant to write you because I have not even read half of your book yet. The beginning I read with such excitement and enthusiasm that I felt sure that it was likely to carry through to the end; then I was going to write you an enthusiastic letter and write something to Wiley that they could print in an advertisement if they wanted; but so many pressures are upon me that I have had little time for reading, even though I have put your book on my schedule ahead of Glenn Wever's <u>Theories of Hearing</u>.

So what can I say? The program is grand. The first chapters are magnificent. I will read the rest when I can get to them.

The book has a fresh, constructive candor, which is what is needed. Lashley and Köhler with their past commitments are not able to do this thing that you, coming freshly to the field, can do. It will make you stand out as an unusual person. I have described this thing as being illustrated by the relation of Külpe to Wundt, for Wundt was too firmly committed to habits of thought to venture what Külpe undertook, and Külpe's name continues to get greater during these many posthumous years.

I run into great enthusiasm about the book. There were eleven psychologists in conference at the Institute for Advanced Study at Thanksgiving time, and three of us brought the book along to read on the train. Your name was often mentioned. Jack Hilgard lent his copy to Jerry Bruner to read. Frank Beach was there and he already knew how good the book was. He seemed just as pleased as I did by the praise it was getting. This morning I have a note from Langfeld saying how fresh, original and effective it is going to be. Our local crowd has reacted less specifically because they are pretty much absorbed in Wever's book, about which they are not enthusiastic, but they will get around to you presently.

I send all this news along to you because I do not want to hold it up for months until I get free from some of the overwhelmingly compulsive demands on my time that prevent me from reading now. I am sure you have written an exceptionally good book, no matter what the later chapters say, and I feel confident that it is going to have considerable influence. Congratulations!

Yours,

Edwin G. Boring

Dr. D.O. Hebb
Department of Psychology
McGill University
Montreal 2, Canada

Figure 8 Facsimile of letter by E. G. Boring praising D. O. Hebb's new book *The Organization of Behavior* (1949).

the Head Start movement in the 1960s and 1970s. In the same context, a neuropsychological postulate that Hebb formulated has been widely adopted by neuroscientists and in computer models of learning. The postulate states that "when an axon of cell A is near enough to excite cell B and repeatedly or persistently takes part in firing it, some growth process or metabolic change takes place in one or both cells such that A's efficiency, as one of the cells firing B, is increased" (Milner, 1986, p. 350). The synapses that have changed in this way are commonly referred to now as "Hebb synapses."

Hebb had been appointed chairman of psychology in 1948 and for the next ten years proceeded to gather around him the staff that would share his vision of psychology. That vision was also passed on to a whole generation of undergraduate and graduate students, for Hebb chose to teach the introductory psychology course for undergraduate students as well as the theoretical seminar for graduate students himself every year until his retirement. Moreover, he wrote his own textbook for the undergraduate course (Hebb, 1958), the second edition of which was translated into French, German, Italian, Polish, Hungarian, Swedish, Danish, Finnish, Spanish, Portuguese, and Japanese in the years 1967 to 1975.

No comprehensive monograph or book on Hebb's work has yet been written. The extensive archives at McGill could be exploited for this pur-pose. In the meantime, Peter Milner, one of Hebb's former students and a colleague, summarized the essence of Hebb's contributions as follows: "After a long period when mainstream psychologists tried to expunge both the mind and the brain from theories of behavior, Hebb restored respectability to both and paved the way for the participation of the behavioral scientists in the blossoming field of neuroscience. (1986, p. 347)

Bibliography

Avidson, R. M., & Nelson, T. M. (1968). Sixty years of psychology at the University of Alberta. *Canadian Psychologist, 9,* 500–504.

Baldwin, J. M. (1889–1891). *Handbook of psychology: a psychoneurological theory. Vol. 1. Senses and intellect; Vol. 2. Feeling and will.* New York: Holt.

Hebb, D. O. (1949). *The organization of behavior.* New York: Wiley.

Hebb, D. O. (1958). *A textbook of psychology.* Philadelphia: Saunders.

Hebb, D. H. (1960). The American revolution. *American Psychologist, 15,* 735–745. [APA Presidential Address]

Hebb, D. H. (1980). Autobiography. In G. Lindzey (Ed.), *A history of psychology in autobiography* (Vol. 7, pp. 273–303). San Francisco: W. H. Freeman.

James, W. (1890). *Principles of psychology* (Vols. 1–2). New York: Holt. (Authorized scholarly edition, Vols. 1–3. Cambridge: Harvard University Press, 1981)

James, W. (1892). *Psychology, briefer course.* New York: Holt.

Milner, P. M. (1986). Obituary: Donald Olding Hebb (1904–1985). *Trends in Neurosciences, 9*(8), 347–351.

Myers, C. R. (1974). R. B. MacLeod (1907–1972) talks about psychology in Canada. *Canadian Psychologist, 15,* 105–111.

Wright, M. J., & Myers, C. R. (1982). *History of academic psychology in Canada.* Toronto: Hogrefe.

Name Index

Name Index

Hertwig, O., 104
Hester, M., 27
Hetzer, Hildegard, 349, 350
Hewett, Peggy, 37
Heyman, 73
Heymans, Gerald, 541, 542, 543, 544
Hildebrandt, H., 474
Hilgard, E. R., 140, 189, 230, 525, 532
Hilts, V. L., 54
Hipp, Matthias, 113–115
Hippocrates, 383–386, 388, 455
Hirsch, Adolph, 114
Hobhouse, L. T., 201
Hoffman, M. J., 256
Hoffman, Robert R., 594
Hoffrage, U., 229
Höfler, Alois, 251, 254
Holbein, Hans the Younger, 103–104
Hollingworth, Harry L., 146
Holmes, 490
Holt, Edwin B., 202, 203
Holt, R. R., 376, 377
Hondl, J., 507
Hörmann, Hans, 281
Horney, Karen, 413, 414f
Hornstein, Gail, 591
Horsley, Richard, 26
Hoskovec, Jiří, 94, 95
Hothersall, D., 301, 302
Howard, R., 44
Howland, Arthur, 588
Huarte, Juan, 22
Hug-Hellmuth, Hermine, 414f, 415
Hull, C. L., 202, 209, 212, 217, 228, 229, 532
Humboldt, Alexander von, 85, 86f
Humboldt, Wilhelm von, 85f, 85–89, 89f, 148
Hume, David, 449
Humphrey, G., 158, 178, 491, 594
Hunt, David, 370
Hunt, William M., 66
Husserl, Edmund, 63, 181

I

Ingleby, D., 461
Inhelder, 346
Innis, Nancy K., 214, 215
Ippolito, Maria F., 490
Irvine, Alexander, 589–590
Itard, J. M., 326

J

Jaager, J. J. de, 135
Jackobson, Roman, 572
Jackson, Thomas T., 364, 365, 366, 367, 368
Jacobson, G. H., 536
Jacoby, J., 517
Jaeger, Siegfried, 37, 278, 280
Jaensch, Erich Rudolph, 173, 174, 348
Jaffa, S., 477
Jaffé, A., 425
Jäger, 511, 512
Jahnke, Jürgen, 30, 42, 377

Jahoda, Gustav, 148, 151
James, William, 66f, 66–70, 67f, 70f, 73, 122, 126, 130, 131, 132, 143, 155, 156, 157, 171, 178, 201, 202, 249, 256–264, 305, 397, 398, 468, 471, 495, 531, 539, 580, 585, 611, 612
Janet, Pierre, 73, 310, 353, 533, 537, 549, 550
Janko, J., 95
Jastrow, Joseph, 234, 585
Jenkins, James J., 595, 597, 597f
Jennings, H. S., 395, 396f
Jensen, D. W., 332
Jesinghaus, Carl, 583
Jodel, Friedrich, 563
Johnson, 499
Johnson, Samuel, 519
Jones, Alice, 468f
Jones, Ernst, 398, 421, 425, 427f
Jones, W. Franklin, 495
Jost, A., 173
Judd, 498
Judd, Charles H., 122, 141, 202
Jung, Carl Gustav, 73, 95, 307, 344, 377, 394, 395, 396, 396f, 397, 397f, 404, 409, 424–430, 424f, 425f, 427f, 428f, 450
Jung, Paul, 424
Jung-Rauschenbach, Emma, 425
Juslin, P., 229
Justice, L., 300
Jutzler-Kindermann, Henny, 81, 82, 82f

K

Kahane, 392
Kahnweiler, D. H., 258, 259, 261, 262f, 263
Kahr, B., 436
Kalekin-Fishman, D., 370
Kalish, Donald, 218
Kaminski, Gerhard, 288, 292
Kamiya, J., 226
Kanizsa, Gaetano, 254
Kant, Immanuel, 111, 449, 543
Kantor, J. R., 594
Kardos, Lajos, 223, 570, 571f
Katz, David, 172, 173, 174, 175, 349
Keeler, Leonarde, 238f, 239
Kelleher, Michael, 453
Kelley, Douglas M., 443f, 443–447
Kelley, E., 543
Kelley, T. L., 332
Kellogg, Luella A., 191
Kellogg, Rhoda, 592
Kellogg, Winthrop N., 191
Kelly, George A., 364–372, 365f, 366f, 369f, 370f, 450
Kemp, Simon, 8, 9, 10, 11, 12
Kempf, 494
Kernchen, S., 250
Kessen, W., 40
Ketteler, Wilhelm von, 63
Kevles, D., 331, 458
Key, Ellen, 316
Kiesow, F., 531, 534, 579
Kindermann, Henny. *See* Jutzler-Kindermann, Henny.
Kinkade, K., 212

Kinslinger, H. J., 375
Kintsch, W., 596
Kirk, 498
Kirkpatrick, E. A., 202
Kirsche, W., 95
Kirschmann, August, 531, 611
Kiss, György, 568
Klaits, J., 27, 28, 29
Kleinbölting, H., 229
Klemm, Otto, 117f, 237f, 521, 531, 612
Kline, L. W., 201
Klingenberg, Hélène, 408
Koch, S., 309
Koehnken, G., 476
Koelsch, W. A., 306
Koffka, Kurt, 174, 177, 189, 249, 254, 266, 269f, 270, 273, 283, 531
Kohlberg, L., 326, 345
Köhler, Wolfgang, 80, 174, 189, 249, 266, 269f, 270, 273, 277f, 277–281, 278f, 279f, 280f, 283, 284, 349, 358, 531, 613
Kohlrausch, Friedrich, 247
Kokoschka, Oskar, 416
Kolbanovskiy, V., 534
König, Arthur, 108, 168
König, T., 516
Kontsevaya, O., 575
Kopel, 498
Koppermann, H., 275
Kornadt, H. J., 185
Kornilov, Konstantin Nikolaevich, 353, 534
Kors, A., 28
Korzybski, Alfred, 368
Kotek, V., 95
Kovács, Vilma, 415
Kozulin, A., 534
Kraepelin, Emil, 131, 134, 182, 512
Kral, Michael J., 454
Krall, Karl, 74, 80f, 80–81, 81f
Kramer, Heinrich, 11, 25
Krantz, D. L., 209, 530
Kraus, O., 63
Krause, K. C. F., 557
Kravkov, Sergei, 572
Krech, David, 218, 230
Kreitler, Hans L., 351
Kries, J. von, 135
Kristic, Kruno, 13
Kroeber-Riel, Werner, 517
Krohn, W. O., 173
Kroj, G., 505
Krolik, W., 275
Kroll, W., 489
Kronecker, Hugo, 305
Kropff, H. F. J., 515, 516
Krudrizki, 316
Krueger, Felix, 162, 583
Krüger, 85
Kruta, V., 90, 91, 92, 95
Kubie, Lawrence, 451
Kuhlmann, Frederick, 143
Kuklick, B., 207
Külpe, Oswald, 135, 154, 155, 177–181, 182, 583
Kurz, Elke M., 155, 159, 221, 222, 225
Kußmaul, Adolf, 57, 295–299, 296f
Kuthan, V., 95

Subject Index

Subject Index

N

O

P

Illustration Credits

This list is provided to give credit to the many organizations and individuals who generously provided the illustrations found in this book. Each entry consists of the page number on which an illustration is found, followed by the source. In cases where more than one illustration appears on a page, lowercase letters are used to identify the position on the page moving clockwise from the top left. We are grateful to all who have contributed illustrations and other materials for this book, and we have made every effort to provide proper recognition for their use. Should any questions be raised about the credits given, or any oversights detected, we will gladly make the appropriate changes in subsequent printings.

Cover a–e: Collection Lück; **f:** Collection Roccatagliata

1: Collection Lück

3, 5: By Permission of Art Resources, New York, NY (USA)

8–11: Collection Kemp

13, 14: Collection Bringmann-Vogtner; **15:** Universitätsarchiv Marburg (Germany); **16:** Collection Bringmann; **17:** Collection Lück; **18:** Collection Bringmann

19–21: Collection McReynolds

23–28: Lehner, E., & Lehner, J. (1971). *Picture book of devils, demons and witchcraft*. New York: Dover

30: Niedersächsische Staats-und Universitätsbibliothek Göttingen (Germany); **31–32ac:** Universitätsbibliothek, Freiburg (Germany); **32b, 33–34:** Collection Jahnke

35: Collection Bringmann (USA); **36:** Goethe-Museum, Düsseldorf (Germany)

37–38a: Collection Bringmann; **38b–39a:** Universitätsarchiv Marburg (Germany); **39b:** Collection Bringmann; **40:** Universitätsarchiv Heidelberg; **41:** Collection Bringmann

42: Photo by W. Klein, Goethe-Museum Düsseldorf (Germany); **43ab–44a:** Collection Jahnke (Germany); **44b:** Photo by E. Böhringer, Akademie der Künste Berlin (Germany)

46a: Schurian, W. (1992). *Kunst im Alltag*. Göttingen: Hogrefe; **46b:** Haberling, W. (1924). Johannes Müller. *Das Leben des rheinischen Naturforschers*. Leipzig: Akademische Verlagsgesellschaft; **47:** Sander, F. & Volkelt, H. (1962). *Ganzheitspsychologie*. Munich: Sander, p. 99; **48a:** Smythies, F. (1959). The stroboscopic patterns: II. The phenomenology of the bright phase and after images. *British Journal of Psychology*, 50, 305 ff.; **48b:** *Zwischenschritte* (1989), 8, 24; **49:** *Geography* (1984), 6, 113

51: Collection Bringmann (USA); **52ab:** Collection Lück (Germany)

53–55: Pearson, K. (1914, 1924, 1930). *The Life, Letters and Labours of Francis Galton*, (Vols. 1-3). Cambridge: Cambridge University Press

56: Descartes, R. (1637). *Discours de la méthode. La Dioptrique.* Leiden: Jean Maire; **57:** Plessen, M. L. von (Ed.). (1993). *Sehnsucht. Das Panorama als Massenunterhaltung des 19. Jahrhunderts.* Bonn: Kunsthalle; **58:** Taft R. (1942). *Photography and the American scene. A social history, 1839-1889.* New York: Macmillan; **59:** Pearson K. R. (1924). *The life, letters and labours of Francis Galton* (Vol. 2). Cambridge: Cambridge University Press; **60:** Galton, F. (1907). *Inquiries into human faculty and its developments.* London: Dent & Sons (Original work published 1883)

61–64: Archiv der Franz Brentano Forschung, Universität Würzburg (Germany)

66–70: Houghton Library, Harvard University (USA)

71–72: Institut für Grenzgebiete der Psychologie und Psychohygiene, Freiburg (Germany), *Le Compte Rendu Officiel du Premier Congrès des Recherches Psychiques, Copenhague* (1922); **73:** *Zeitschrift für Parapsychologie, 4* (1929); **74a:** Schrenck-Notzing, A. (1933). *Die Phänomene des Mediums Rudi Schneider.* Berlin/Leipzig: de Gruyter; **74b:** Rhine, J. B., & Pratt, J. G. (1962). *Parapsychologie. Grenzwissenschaft der Psyche.* Bern/Munich: Francke; **75:** Krall, K. (1927). *Denkende Tiere.* Stuttgart: Verlag der Gesellschaft für Tierpsychologie

77–81b: Krall, K. (1912). *Denkende Tiere.* Leipzig: Engelmann; **82:** Otto Jutzler, Leverkusen (Germany)

83: Collection Lück

85: Collection Robinson; **86:** Bildarchiv Preußischer Kulturbesitz (Germany); **88:** Collection Bringmann; **89:** Graphische Sammlung Albertina (Austria)

90–94: Collection Brožek-Hoskovec

97–100: Collection Brauns

101: Universitätsarchiv Leipzig (Germany); **102ab:** Collection Bringmann; **103a:** Wundt-Nachlaß, Universitätsarchiv Leipzig (Germany); **103b:** Fechnerakte Universitätsarchiv Leipzig (Germany); **104–105a:** Collection Meischner-Metge; **105b:** Lotze, R.H. (1852). *Medicinische Psychologie oder Physiologie der Seele.* Leipzig, Germany: Weidmann; **106:** Lotzer, H. *Mikrokosmus* (Vols. 1-3). Leipzig, Germany: Hirzel

107a: Koenigsberger, L. (1911). *Hermann von Helmholtz.* Braunschweig: Vieweg & Sohn; **107b–110:** Collection Brauns

112–115: Institut für Geschichte der Neueren Psychologie, Universität Passau (Germany)

117–125: Collection Bringmann

126–132: Collection Bringmann

133–134: Collection Bringmann; **135–138:** Collection Behrens

141: Collection Benjamin; **142:** Photo Courtesy of the Archives of the History of American Psychology, University of Akron (USA); **143–144:** Collection Benjamin; **146:** Photo Courtesy of the Archives of the History of American Psychology, University of Akron (USA)

148–149: Collection Lück; **150:** Collection Bringmann; **151–152:** Collection Jahoda

153: Photo Courtesy of the Archives of the History of American Psychology, University of Akron (USA); **154:** From (1917) *Studies in psychology contributed by colleagues and former students of Edward Bradford Titchener*. Worcester, MA: Louis N. Wilson; **156:** Titchener, E. B. (1898). A psychological laboratory. *Mind, N.S.7*, 311-331; **158:** Titchener, E. B. (1901). *Experimental psychology*. New York: Macmillan, title page; **159:** Titchener, E. B. (1909). *A text-book of psychology*. New York: Macmillan; **160:** Titchener, E. B. (1914). On "Psychology as the behaviorist views it." *Proceedings of the American Philosophical Society*, 53, 1-17, p. 1

162–166: Courtesy of Dr. Artur Wirth, Ansbach (Germany)

167a: Institut für die Geschichte der Neueren Psychologie, Universität Passau (Germany); **167b:** Ebbinghaus, H. (1885). *Über das Gedächtnis*. Leipzig, Germany: Duncker & Humblot; **168–169:** Institut für Geschichte der Neueren Psychologie, Universität Passau (Germany)

171–172: Psychologisches Institut, Universität Göttingen (Germany); **174–175:** Collection Behrens

177: Balmer, H. (Ed.). (1982). *Kindlers Psychologie des 20. Jahrhunderts, Vol. 1: Geistesgeschichtliche Grundlagen*. Weinheim, Germany: Beltz; **178a:** Ach, N. (1905). *Über die Willenstätigkeit und das Denken*. Göttingen: Vandenhoeck & Ruprecht; **178b:** Watt, H. J. (1904). *Experimentelle Beiträge zu einer Theorie des Denkens*. Leipzig, Germany: Engelmann, 3—Archiv der Franz Brentano Forschung, Universität Würzburg (Germany); **179:** Watt (1904); **180a:** Selz Papers, Universitätsarchiv Mannheim (Germany); **180b:** Messer, A. (1922). Selbstdarstellung. In: R. Schmidt (Ed.), *Die Philosphie der Gengenwart in Selbstdarstellungen* (p. 145 ff.), Leipzig, Germany: Meiner; **180c:** Marbe, K. (1945). *Selbstbiographie des Psychologen Geheimrat Prof. Dr. Karl Marbe zu Würzburg*. Halle, Germany: Buchdruckerei des Waisenhauses

182: Collection Schmalt; **184–185a:** From Ach, N. (1912). Eine Serienmethode für Reaktionsversuche. Bemerkungen zur Untersuchung des Willens. In: *Untersuchungen zur Psychologie und Philosophie*. Vol. 1, No. 5. Leipzig: Quelle & Meyer; **185b:** From Ach, N., & Düker, H. (1934). Über Methoden und Apparaturen zur Untersuchung fortlaufender Arbeitsprozesse. *Zeitschrift für Psychologie*, 188(4-6), 209-221

187: Photo Courtesy of the Archives of the History of American Psychology, University of Akron (USA); **188:** Washburn, M. F. (1908). *The animal mind*. New York: Macmillan; **189a:** Washburn, M. F. (1916). *Movement and mental imagery*. Boston: Houghton-Mifflin; **189b:** Photo Courtesy of the Archives of the History of American Psychology, University of Akron (USA)

192: Kellogg, W., & Kellogg, L. (1933). *The ape and the child*. New York: Whittlesey House; **193:** Collection Thorne; **196–197:** Courtesy of the Language Research Center, Georgia State University (USA)

198–203: Collection Wozniak; **204:** Photo Courtesy of the Archives of the History of American Psychology, University of Akron (USA)

206–208: Collection Coleman; **209a:** Gordon, W. C. (1989). *Learning and memory*. Pacific Grove, CA: Brooks/Cole, used with permission of the publisher; **209b:** Collection Coleman; **210:** Used by permission of the Harvard University Archives (USA); **212:** Photo by Jane Reed, used with permission of Harvard University (USA)

214–215: With permission of the Department of Psychology, University of California, Berkeley (USA); **216a:** With permission of the Tolman Family; **216b:** Photo Courtesy of the Archives of the History of American Psychology, Akron (USA); **217–219:** With permission of the Tolman Family; **220:** With permission of the Department of Psychology, University of California, Berkeley (USA)

222: Brunswik, E. (1956a). Historical and thematic relations of psychology to other sciences. *Scientific Monthly*, 83, 151-161, p. 158. Copyright 1956 American Association for the Advancement of Science; adapted with permission; **223:** Courtesy of the Department of Psychology, University of California, Berkeley (USA); **224:** Adapted from Brunswik, E. (1932). Untersuchungen über Wahrnehmungsgegenstände. *Archiv für die gesamte Psychologie*, 88, 377-418, p. 391; **225:** From Brunswik, E. (1934). *Wahrnehmung und Gegenstandswelt: Grundlegung einer Psychologie vom Gegenstand her*. Leipzig: Franz Deuticke, p. 97, with permission of F. Deuticke, Vienna (Austria); **227:** From Brunswik, E. (1940). Thing constancy as measured by coefficients. *Psychological Review*, 47, 69-78, p. 72 (Public Domain); **228a:** From Brunswik, E. (1952). The conceptual framework of psychology. In O. Neurath, R. Carnap, & C. Morris (Eds.), *International Encyclopedia of Unified Science: Vol. 1, No. 10*, p. 20, copyright 1952 by the University of Chicago. Reprinted by permission of The University of Chicago Press; **228b:** On p. 2 of Woodworth, R. S. (1938). *Experimental psychology*. Copyright 1921, 1929, 1934, 1940 by Henry Holt and Co., Inc. Reprinted by permission of Henry Holt & Company, Inc.

233: Photo Courtesy of the Archives of the History of American Psychology, Akron (USA); **234a, 235a:** From Givler, C. G. (1920). *Psychology: The Science of Human Behavior*, New York: Harper; **234b, 235b:** From Murphy, G. (1935). *A Briefer General Psychology*. New York: Harper-Collins (By permission); **236:** National Library of Medicine, Bethesda, MD (USA); **237:** Bringmann, W., & Tweney, R. (1980). *Wundt Studies*. Toronto: C. J. Hogrefe; **238a:** U. S. Air Force (Public Domain); **238b:** With permission of *Chicago Sun-Times*

243: Courtesy of Ernst-Mach-Institut, Freiburg (Germany); **244a:** From Mach's diary (B3:12, April 1873), Ernst-Mach-Institut, Freiburg (Germany); **244b:** Mach, E. (1865). Über die Wirkung der räumlichen Verteilung des Lichtreizes auf die Netzhaut (1). *Sitzungsberichte der Kaiserlichen Akademie der Wissenschaften. Mathematisch-naturwissenschaftliche Classe, Vol. 52*, Part 2, 303-322; **245a:** Mach, E. (1875). *Grundlinien der Lehre von den Bewegungsempfindungen*. Nachdruck, Amsterdam, 1967: E. J. Bonset; **245b:** Ernst-Mach-Institut, Freiburg (Germany); **246:** Mach, E. (1900). *Die Analyse der Empfindungen und das Verhältnis des physischen zum Psychischen*. Jena, Germany

247–249: Carl-Alfred and Ingeborg Stumpf, Stuttgart (Germany); **250:** Collection H. Sprung

251: Courtesy of Forschungsstelle für österreichische Philosophie, Graz (Austria); **252ab:** Courtesy Baroness M. Abeille-Ehrenfels; **253a:** Witasek Family, Salzburg (Austria); **253b–254:** Courtesy of Forschungsstelle für österreichische Philosophie, Graz (Austria)

257: (c) 1996, Artists Rights Society (ARS), New York, ADAGP, Paris; **258a:** Photo by Gelett Burgess, *Architectural Record*, New York (1910); **258b:** (c) 1996, ARS, New York, SPADEM, Paris; **259a:** James (1890); **259b–260:** (c) 1996, ARS, New York, SPADEM, Paris; **261a–263:** (c) 1996, ARS, New York, SPADEM, Paris

265–266: Annette Daigger, Saarbrücken (Germany)

268–271: Collection Lothar and Helga Sprung, Berlin (Germany)

273–274a: Historisches Museum der Stadt Frankfurt, Frankfurt/Main (Germany); **274b:** Courtesy of G. Siemsen and by permission of Michael Wertheimer, Boulder, CO (USA); **275–276:** By permission of Michael Wertheimer, Boulder, CO (USA)

277: Collection Jaeger; **278ab:** By permission of The American Philosophical Society Library, Philadelphia (USA); **279:** Psychological Institute, University of Münster (Germany); **280abc:** Collection Jaeger; **281a:** Toshio Iritani (Japan); **281b:** Karin Kohler-Green

Illustration Credits

282–286: Collection Lück, Hagen (Germany)

288: Courtesy of Barry Bunch, Kenneth Spencer Research Library, University of Kansas (USA); **289a:** Collection Kaminski; **289b–291b:** Kenneth Spencer Research Library, University of Kansas (USA); **292:** Collection Kaminski

295–300: Collection Bringmann-Ungerer

301–303: Wilson, L. (1914). *G. Stanley Hall*. New York: Stechert; **304:** Collection Bringmann; **305:** Universitätsarchiv Humboldt Universität, Berlin (Germany); **306–307:** Collection Bringmann

309: Photo was graciously contributed by Binet's granddaughters, Mlles. Géraldine and Georgette Binet; **310–311:** Binet Family Archive, Montrouge (France); **312:** Binet, A. (1908). Le pèdagogue doit-et être psychologue? *L'Année Psychologique*, 14, 405-431; **313:** Binet, A. (1900). *La suggestibilité*. Paris: Schleicher Frères

315–321: Collection Probst

323: Collection Schmidt; **324:** Stern, W. (1931). Das Psychologische Institut der Hamburgischen Universität in seiner gegenwärtigen Gestalt. *Zeitschrift für angewandte Psychologie*, 39, 1-52; **325:** Deutsch, W. (Ed.). (1991). Über die verborgene Aktualität von William Stern. Frankfurt/M.: Lang

327–328: Collection Bringmann

329: Courtesy Stanford University Archives (USA); **330a:** Courtesy of Doris Tucker; **330b:** Courtesy of Stanford University Archives (USA); **331:** Courtesy of Robert Mearns Yerkes Papers, Manuscript and Archives, Yale University Archives (USA); **332:** Courtesy of *Stanford Illustrated Review*, March 1919 (USA); **333:** Courtesy of Stanford University Archives (USA); **334:** Courtesy of Doris Tucker; **335:** Courtesy of Stanford University Archives (USA)

337: Muchow, M., & Muchow, H. D. (1978). *Der Lebensraum des Großstadtkindes*; **338:** Probst, P. (1991). *Bibliographie Ernst Meumann*. Herzberg: Traugott Bautz; **340ab:** Collection Miller

342: G. Steiner, (Ed.). (1978). *Die Psychologie des 20. Jahrhunderts, Vol. 7: Piaget und die Folgen*. Zürich: Kindler; **343–346:** Ducret, J.-J. (1990). *Jean Piaget, Biographie et parcours intellectuel*. Neuchâtel: Delachaux et Niestlé

348: Bilderarchiv der österreichischen Nationalbibliothek, Vienna, (Austria); **349:** Collection Rollett; **350:** Bilderarchiv der österreichischen Nationalbibliothek, Vienna (Austria); **351:** Collection Rollett

352: Van der Veer, R., & Valsiner, J. (1991). *Understanding Vygotsky. The quest for synthesis*. Oxford: Blackwell; **353:** Collection Van der Veer; **354a:** Van der Veer, R., & Valsiner, J. (1991). *Understanding Vygotsky. The quest for synthesis*. Oxford: Blackwell; **354b:** Collection Van der Veer

356: By permission of Harvard University Archives (USA); **357:** By permission of Harvard University Archives (USA); **358–359a:** From Allport, G., & Postman L. (1947). *The psychology of rumor*. New York: Holt, with permission of the publisher; **359b,c:** Freyd, M. (1921). A test series of journalistic aptitude. *Journal of Applied Psychology*, 5, 46-56; **360–361a:** By permission of the publisher (see 358-359 above); **361b:** By permission of Harvard University Archives (USA)

365–367, 369: Photo courtesy of Fort Hays State University, Fort Hays, Kansas (USA); **370:** Photo courtesy Hemant Desai and the University of Nebraska, Lincoln (USA)

373–374a: Photo courtesy of the Archives of the History of American Psychology, Akron (USA), **374b:** From H. A. Murray, 1943, Thematic Apperception Test. Cambridge, MA: Harvard University Press. Used with permission. **375:** KLM Archives

377: From Block, E. B. (1930). Yehudi Menuhin. *The Parents' Magazine*, 5(1), 17, 50; **378:** From Brower, H. (1928, January). Yehudi Menuhin—the miracle. *The Musician*, 33, 13, 38, Collection Morgan-Jahnke

381: Collection Fernald

383–390: Collection Roccatagliata

391–393: Freud, E., Freud, L., & Grubrich-Simitis, I. (Eds.). (1974). *Sigmund Freud. Sein Leben in Bildern und Texten*. Frankfurt: Suhrkamp

395–397: Collection Rosenzweig

399–402a: Collection Fernald; **402b:** From Graf, M. (1942). Reminiscences of Professor Sigmund Freud. *Psychoanalytic Quarterly*, 11, 465-476; **403–404:** Collection Fernald

406–412: Andreas-Salomé Archiv, Göttingen (Germany)

414: Lück, H. E., & Mühleitner, E. (Eds.). (1993). *Psychoanalytiker in der Karikatur*. Munich: Quintessence

416: Courtesy of Kurt Adler, New York, NY (USA); **417a:** Collection Schiferer; **417b:** Marion Sabish, New York (USA); **418:** Courtesy of Alexandra Adler; **419:** Photopress, Johnson's Court, Fleet Street, 1936, London, England

420: Courtesy of Kurt Adler, New York, NY (USA); **421–423:** Courtesy of Georg-Groddeck-Gesellschaft, Baden-Baden (Germany)

424: Courtesy of Zentralbibliothek Zürich (Switzerland); **425:** Courtesy of Museumarchiv Burghölzli, (Switzerland); **426a:** Staatsarchiv des Kantons Zürich (Switzerland); **426b:** Courtesy of Franz Jung, Küsnacht (Switzerland); **427:** Courtesy of Staatsarchiv des Kantons Zürich (Switzerland); **428:** Collection Graf-Nold; **429–430:** Staatsarchiv des Kantons Zürich (Switzerland)

431–434: Collection Funk, Tübingen (Germany)

436: Collection Bringmann; **438:** Collection Bringmann-Goin; **439ab:** Courtesy of David Finkelhor, **439c–440:** Collection Bringmann

442a: With permission of the United States Holocaust Museum; **442b:** National Archives, Washington, DC (USA); **443–446:** Collection Bringmann

449–453: Collection Leenaars

455: National Library of Medicine, Bethesda, MD (USA); **456–457a:** With permission of Harvey Cushing/John Hay Whitney Medical Library, Yale University (USA); **457b–458a:** National Library of Medicine, Bethesda, MD (USA); **458b:** Harvey Cushing/John Hay Whitney Medical Library, Yale University (USA); **459:** Courtesy of the Milton Erickson Foundation, Phoenix, AZ (USA); **460:** Photo by Joe Siegel, courtesy of Thomas Szasz

463: Collection Van Drunen

465: Courtesy of University of Pennsylvania Archives, Philadelphia (USA); **466–470:** Collection McReynolds

471: Collection Bringmann; **472:** Collection Lück; **473a:** Collection Bringmann; **473b:** Collection Lück; **474:** Collection Bringmann

476: Collection Bringmann; **477:** Collection Lück; **478–479:** Collection Sporer

480, 482ab, 483b: Archives of Dutch Psychology; **481;** Philips Company Archives; **483a:** KLM Archives

485–488: Collection Bäumler

492a: Miles, W. R. (1921). The pursuitmeter: An apparatus for measuring the adequacy of neuromuscular coordination described together with illustrative results. *Journal of Experimental Psychology, 12*, 86 (Public Domain); **492b:** Freeman, G. L., & Chapman, J. S. (1935). Minor studies from the psychological laboratory of Northwestern University: VI. The relative importance of eye and hand dominance in a pursuit skill. *American Journal of Psychology, 47*, 147 (Public Domain); **493a:** Beeley, A. L. (1918). Experimental study of left-handedness. *Supplemental Educational Monographs, 2*(8), 15, 22, 28 (With Permission of University of Chicago Press); **493b:** Heinlein, C. P. (1930). Multiple-plate tapping boards. *Journal of General Psychology, 3*, 177 (With Permission of Clark University Press); **494a:** Permission by the Ferdinand Hamburger, Jr., Archives of The Johns Hopkins University; **494b:** Watson, J. B. (1919). *Psychology from the standpoint of a behaviorist.* Philadelphia: Lippincott, p. 239 (Public Domain); **495:** From C. H. Stoelting Co. (1936). *Psychological apparatus and supplies*, p. 13, Chicago: C. H. Stoelting (With Permission of C. H. Stoelting Co., Wood Dale, IL); **497a:** Stevens, H. C. (1908). Peculiarities of peripheral vision. *Psychological Review, 15*, Plate 1 (Public Domain); **497b:** Stevens, H. C., & Ducasse, C. J. (1912). The retina and handedness. *Psychological Review, 19*, 3 (Public Domain); **498a:** From C. H. Stoelting Co. (1936). *Psychological apparatus and supplies*, p. 55, Chicago: C. H. Stoelting (With Permission of C. H. Stoelting Co., Wood Dale, IL); **498b:** Lund, F. H. (1932). The monoptometer: A new device for measuring eye-dominance. *American Journal of Psychology, 44*, 180 (Public Domain); **499a:** Van Riper, C. (1935). The quantitative measurement of laterality. *Journal of Experimental Psychology, 18*, 373 (Public Domain); **499b:** Van Riper, C. (1934). A new test of laterality. *Journal of Experimental Psychology, 17*, 308 (Public Domain)

501: Collection Bringmann

503–504: Collection Häcker

506–509: By permission of Institut für Geschichte der Neueren Psychologie, Universität Passau (Germany)

510a: Collection Wiendieck; **510b:** Giese, F. (1927). *Methoden der Wirtschaftspsychologie.* Berlin: Urban-Schwarzernberg; **511a:** Schulze, R. (1909). *Aus der Werkstatt der experimentellen Psychologie und Pädagogik.* Leipzig, Germany: Voigtländer; **511–513:** Giese (1927). *Methoden der Wirtschaftspsychologie.* Berlin: Urban & Schwarzenberg

514a: From Kroppf, H. F. J. (1951). *Neue Psychologie in der neuen Werbung.* Stuttgart: Poeschel; **514b:** From Scott, W. D. (1908). *The psychology of advertising in theory and practice.* Boston: Small, Maynard, & Co.; **515:** Collection Wiendieck; **516:** From Spiegel, B. (1958). *Werbepsychologische Untersuchungsmethoden.* Berlin: Duncker & Humblot

518–524: Collection Bringmann

527: Collection Lück

531–535: Collection Carpintero

536–538a: Collection Bringmann; **538b:** Institut für die Geschichte der Neueren Psychologie, Universität Passau (Germany); **539a:** Berufsverband Deutscher Psychologen e. V. (Germany); **539b:** Collection Schorr

542–543: Courtesy of Universiteitsmuseum Utrecht, Rijksuniversiteit (Netherlands); **544:** Collection Van Strien; **545a–546a:** Universiteitsmuseum Groningen, Rijksuniversiteit (Netherlands); **546b–547:** Collection Van Strien

548–552: Collection Plas

553–556: Collection Geuter

558–561: Collection Lafuente

562–567: Collection Brožek-Hoskovec

568–571: Courtesy of Tibor Horváth, National Educational Library and Museum, Budapest (Hungary)

574: Collection Lück-Meili

578–581: Collection Dazzi-Mecacci

582–584: Collection Stubbe-León

586–591: Collection Benjamin

594: Courtesy W. K. Estes; **595a:** Courtesy of C. N. Cofer; **595b:** Courtesy of N. Chomsky; **596a:** Courtesy of H. Simon; **596b:** Courtesy of G. Miller; **596c:** Courtesy of R. Brown; **597a:** Courtesy of J. Bruner, **597b:** Courtesy of James Jenkins and Ulric Neisser

600: Photo Courtesy of the Archives of the History of American Psychology (Helen Livingston Memoirs), University of Akron (USA); **601:** From Sanford, E. (1893). Some Practical Suggestions on the Equipment of a Psychological Laboratory. *American Journal of Psychology, 5*, 421-438; **602:** Photo Courtesy of the Archives of the History of American Psychology (Henry H. Goddard Papers), University of Akron (USA); **603:** Archives of the History of American Psychology, Literature Collection (Identification with the help of Mitchell Ash), University of Akron (USA); **604a:** Reprinted from *Philosophical Portrait Series*, Open Court Publishing Company (1898-99), with permission of the publisher; **604b:** Courtesy of the University of Illinois Press; **604c:** Photo Courtesy of the Archives of the History of American Psychology, University of Akron (USA); **605:** Photo Courtesy of the Archives of the History of American Psychology (University of Nebraska Collection), University of Akron (USA); **606:** Photo Courtesy of the Archives of the History of American Psychology (Literature Collection), University of Akron (USA); **607:** Courtesy of the American Psychological Association, Washington, DC (USA); **608:** Photo Courtesy of the Archives of the History of American Psychology (Marion Bunch Gift, Photograph by Morton May), University of Akron (USA); **609:** Photo Courtesy of the Archives of the History of American Psychology (Child Development Film Archives, Grace Heider Gift), University of Akron (USA)

610–611b: Collection Schmidt; **612a–613a:** Courtesy of University of Alberta Archives, Alberta (Canada); **613b:** Collection Schmidt; **614:** McGill University Archive, Montreal, Canada.